W9-CED-870

JAMES E. MILLER, JR.
Professor of English, University of Chicago. Fulbright Lecturer in Naples and Rome, 1958–59, and in Kyoto, Japan, 1968. President of the National Council of Teachers of English, 1970. Awarded a Guggenheim fellowship, 1969–70. Recent books: *Quests Surd and Absurd: Essays in American Literature; Theory of Fiction: Henry James;* and *Word, Self, Reality: The Rhetoric of Imagination.*

MYRTLE J. JONES
Assistant Professor of English, Floyd Junior College, Rome, Georgia. John Hay Fellow, Colorado College, 1964. Formerly teacher of English, East Rome High School.

HELEN McDONNELL
Chairman, English Department, Ocean Township High School, Oakhurst, New Jersey. Associate Chairman of the Committee on Comparative Literature, National Council of Teachers of English. Reviewer of books in English and English education for *Scholastic Teacher* and contributor of articles on education to magazines and books.

ENGLAND in Literature

MACBETH EDITION

SCOTT FORESMAN AND COMPANY • Glenview, Illinois
Dallas, Tex. • Oakland, N.J. • Palo Alto, Cal. • Tucker, Ga. • Brighton, England

America Reads

PROJECTION IN LITERATURE
COUNTERPOINT IN LITERATURE
OUTLOOKS THROUGH LITERATURE
EXPLORING LIFE THROUGH LITERATURE
THE UNITED STATES IN LITERATURE (All My Sons edition)
THE UNITED STATES IN LITERATURE (The Glass Menagerie edition)
ENGLAND IN LITERATURE (Macbeth edition)
ENGLAND IN LITERATURE (The Taming of the Shrew edition)

ENGLAND in Literature

MACBETH EDITION

Cover: "Racing to London," a collage by the contemporary British artist Peter Blake.

ISBN: 0-673-10214-9

Printed in the United States of America.

345678910-RRC-858483828180797877

PART ONE:
THE DEVELOPMENT OF
ENGLISH LITERATURE

CONTENTS

chapter one
ANGLO-SAXON ENGLAND
PAGE 2

chapter two
THE MEDIEVAL AGE
PAGE 62

chapter three
THE ELIZABETHAN AGE

These first three chapters are also available in a softbound book entitled THE EARLY DEVELOPMENT OF ENGLISH LITERATURE. Chapters four through eight are available under the title THREE CENTURIES OF ENGLISH LITERATURE.

chapter four

THE SEVENTEENTH CENTURY

PAGE 234

chapter five

THE EIGHTEENTH CENTURY

PAGE 276

(cont.)

chapter six

THE ROMANTICS

chapter seven

THE VICTORIANS

PAGE 386

chapter eight

ALICE IN WONDERLAND

PAGE 439

PART TWO: THE TWENTIETH CENTURY

chapter nine
MODERN SHORT STORIES
PAGE 492

chapter ten
TWENTIETH-CENTURY POETRY
PAGE 616

Part One: A Poetic Revolution

Part Two: The Age of Anxiety

chapter one

ANGLO-SAXON ENGLAND

c. 450–1066

"No man grows wise
without he have
his share of winters..."
(The Wanderer)

I. BEOWULF

Translated by
Kevin Crossley-Holland

Beowulf[1]—composed in the eighth century—is the oldest epic poem in a modern European language. The Old English dialect the poet used was a direct ancestor of the English we speak today, but it was so different from modern English that only scholars can understand it now. Most modern readers must rely on a translation.

The narrator in *Beowulf* begins the way listeners of his day expected—with a short summary of the career of the first great king of the Danes, Scyld Scefing, whose name at that time was still used to designate the Danish people. He traces the royal line down to the present king, Hrothgar, and then launches into his main story.

Listen!
The fame of Danish kings
in days gone by, the daring feats
worked by those heroes are well known to us.
Scyld Scefing[2] often deprived his enemies,
5 many tribes of men, of their mead-benches.
He terrified his foes; yet he, as a boy,
had been found a waif; fate made amends for that.
He prospered under heaven, won praise and honour,
until the men of every neighbouring tribe,
10 across the whale's way, were obliged to obey him
and pay him tribute. He was a noble king!
Then a son was born to him, a child
in the court, sent by God to comfort
the Danes; for He had seen their dire distress,
15 that once they suffered hardship for a long while,
lacking a lord; and the Lord of Life,
King of Heaven, granted this boy glory;
Beow[3] was renowned—the name of Scyld's son
became known throughout the Norse lands. . . .
20 Then Scyld departed at the destined hour.
His own close companions carried him
down to the sea, as he, lord of the Danes,
had asked while he could still speak.
That well-loved man had ruled his land for many years.
25 There in harbour stood the ring-prowed ship,
the prince's vessel, icy, eager to sail;
and then they laid their dear lord,
the giver of rings, deep within the ship
by the mast in majesty; many treasures
30 and adornments from far and wide were gathered there.
I have never heard of a ship equipped
more handsomely with weapons and war-gear,
swords and corslets; on his breast
lay countless treasures that were to travel far
35 with him into the waves' domain.
They gave him great ornaments, gifts
no less magnificent than those men had given him

1. *Beowulf* (bā′ ə wůlf)
2. *Scyld Scefing* (shild′ shāf′ ing)
3. *Beow* (bā′ ō)

who long before had sent him alone,
child as he was, across the stretch of the seas.
40 Then high above his head they placed
a golden banner and let the waves bear him,
bequeathed him to the sea; their hearts were grieving,
their minds mourning. Mighty men
beneath the heavens, rulers in the hall,
45 cannot say who received that cargo.

When his royal father had travelled from the earth,
Beow of Denmark, a beloved king,
ruled long in the stronghold, famed
amongst men; in time Healfdene[4] the brave
50 was born to him; who, so long as he lived,
grey-haired and redoubtable, ruled the noble Danes.
Beow's son Healfdene, leader of men,
was favoured by fortune with four children:
Heorogar[5] and Hrothgar and Halga the good;
55 Yrse, the fourth, was Onela's queen,
the beloved wife of that warlike Swedish king.

Hrothgar won honour in war,
glory in battle, and so ensured
his followers' support—young men
60 whose number multiplied into a mighty troop.
And he resolved to build a hall,
a large and noble feasting-hall
of whose splendours men would always speak,
and there to distribute as gifts to old and young
65 all the things that God had given him—
but not men's lives or the public land.
Then I heard that tribes without number, even
to the ends of the earth, were given orders
to decorate the hall. And in due course
70 (before very long) this greatest of halls
was completed. Hrothgar, whose very word was counted
far and wide as a command, called it Heorot.[6]
He kept his promise, gave presents of rings
and treasure at the feasting. The hall towered high,
75 lofty and wide-gabled—fierce tongues of loathsome fire
had not yet attacked it, nor was the time yet near
when a mortal feud should flare between father-
and son-in-law, sparked off by deeds of deadly enmity. . . .
So those warrior Danes lived joyful lives,
80 in complete harmony, until the hellish fiend
began to perpetrate base crimes.
This gruesome creature was called Grendel,
notorious prowler of the borderland, ranger of the moors,
the fen and the fastness; this cursed creature
85 lived in a monster's lair for a time
after the Creator had condemned him
as one of the seed of Cain[7]—the Everlasting Lord
avenged Abel's murder. . . .

Then, under cover of night, Grendel came
90 to Hrothgar's lofty hall to see how the Ring-Danes
were disposed after drinking ale all evening;
and he found there a band of brave warriors,
well-feasted, fast asleep, dead to worldly sorrow,
man's sad destiny. At once that hellish monster,
95 grim and greedy, brutally cruel,
started forward and seized thirty thanes
even as they slept; and then, gloating
over his plunder, he hurried from the hall,
made for his lair with all those slain warriors.
100 Then at dawn, as day first broke,
Grendel's power was at once revealed;
a great lament was lifted, after the feast
an anguished cry at that daylight discovery.
The famous prince, best of all men, sat apart in mourning;
105 when he saw Grendel's gruesome footprints,
that great man grieved for his retainers.
This enmity was utterly one-sided, too repulsive,
too long-lasting. Nor were the Danes allowed respite,
but the very next day Grendel committed
110 violent assault, murders more atrocious than before,
and he had no qualms about it. He was caught up in his crimes.
Then it was not difficult to find the man
who preferred a more distant resting-place,
a bed in the outbuildings, for the hatred
115 of the hall-warden was quite unmistakable.
He who had escaped the clutches of the fiend
kept further off, at a safe distance.

Thus Grendel ruled, resisted justice,
one against all, until the best of halls
120 stood deserted. And so it remained:
for twelve long winters the lord of the Danes
was sorely afflicted with sorrows and cares;
then men were reminded in mournful songs
that the monster Grendel fought with Hrothgar
125 for a long time, fought with fierce hatred

4. *Healfdene* (hā′ alf den ə)
5. *Heorogar* (hā′ ə rō gär)
6. *Heorot* (hā′ ə rot)

7. *Cain*, son of Adam and Eve. According to the Bible story (Genesis 4), he killed his brother Abel and was cursed by God.

committing crime and atrocity day after day
in continual strife. He had no wish for peace
with any of the Danes, would not desist
from his deadly malice or pay wergild[8]—
130 No! None of the counsellors could hold out hope
of handsome compensation at that slayer's hands.
But the cruel monster constantly terrified
young and old, the dark death-shadow
lurked in ambush; he prowled the misty moors
135 at the dead of night; men do not know
where such hell-whisperers shrithe[9] in their
wanderings.
Such were the many and outrageous injuries
that the fearful solitary, foe of all men,
endlessly inflicted; he occupied Heorot,
140 that hall adorned with treasures, on cloudless nights.
This caused the lord of the Danes deep,
heart-breaking grief. Strong men often sat
in consultation, trying in vain to devise
a good plan as to how best valiant men
145 could safeguard themselves against sudden
attack. . . .

Thus Healfdene's son endlessly brooded
over the afflictions of this time; that wise warrior
was altogether helpless, for the hardship upon them—
violent visitations, evil events in the night—
150 was too overwhelming, loathsome, and long-lasting.

One of Hygelac's[10] thanes, Beowulf by name,
renowned among the Geats[11] for his great bravery,
heard in his own country of Grendel's crimes;
he was the strongest man alive,
155 princely and powerful. He gave orders
that a good ship should be prepared, said he would
sail
over the sea to assist the famous leader,
the warrior king, since he needed hardy men.
Wise men admired his spirit of adventure.
160 Dear to them though he was, they encouraged
the warrior and consulted the omens.
Beowulf searched out the bravest of the Geats,
asked them to go with him; that seasoned sailor
led fourteen thanes to the ship at the shore.

165 Days went by; the boat was on the water,
moored under the cliff. The warriors, all prepared,
stepped onto the prow—the water streams eddied,
stirred up sand; the men stowed
gleaming armour, noble war-gear
170 deep within the ship; then those warriors launched
the well-built boat and so began their journey.
Foaming at the prow and most like a sea-bird,
the boat sped over the waves, urged on by the wind;
until next day, at the expected time,
175 so far had the curved prow come
that the travellers sighted land,
shining cliffs, steep hills,
broad headlands. So did they cross the sea;
their journey was at its end. Then the Geats
180 disembarked, lost no time in tying up
the boat—their corslets clanked;
the warriors gave thanks to God
for their safe passage over the sea.

Then, on the cliff-top, the Danish watchman
185 (whose duty it was to stand guard by the shore)
saw that the Geats carried flashing shields
and gleaming war-gear down the gangway,
and his mind was riddled with curiosity.
Then Hrothgar's thane leapt onto his horse
190 and, brandishing a spear, galloped
down to the shore; there, he asked at once:
"Warriors! Who are you, in your coats of mail,
who have steered your tall ship over the sea-lanes
to these shores? I've been a coastguard here
195 for many years, kept watch by the sea,
so that no enemy band should encroach
upon this Danish land and do us injury.
Never have warriors, carrying their shields,
come to this country in a more open manner.
200 Nor were you assured of my leaders' approval,
my kinsmen's consent. I've never set eyes
on a more noble man, a warrior in armour,
than one among your band; he's no mere retainer,
so ennobled by his weapons. May his looks never
belie him,
205 and his lordly bearing. But now, before you step
one foot further on Danish land
like faithless spies, I must know
your lineage. Bold seafarers,
strangers from afar, mark my words
210 carefully: you would be best advised
quickly to tell me the cause of your coming."

The man of highest standing, leader of that troop,
unlocked his hoard of words, answered him:

---

8. *wergild,* the price set upon a man according to his rank, which could be claimed from the slayer by the relatives of a man wrongfully killed. If the wergild was not paid, the death could be avenged by killing the slayer. Here Grendel's refusal to pay emphasizes that he lives outside the law.

9. *shrithe,* an Old English word meaning "glide, wander, stride" which the translator has chosen to revive.

10. *Hygelac* (hij′ ə läk)

11. *Geats* (gā′ ats), a tribe living in the southern part of Sweden.

"We are all Geats, hearth-companions of Hygelac;
215 my father was famed far and wide,
a noble lord, Ecgtheow[12] by name—
he endured many winters before he,
in great old age, went on his way; every wise man
in this world readily recalls him.

220 We have sailed across the sea to seek your lord,
Healfdene's son, protector of the people,
with most honourable intentions; give us your guidance!
We have come on an errand of importance
to the great Danish prince; nor, I imagine, will the cause
225 of our coming long remain secret. You will know

12. *Ecgtheow* (edj' thā ō)

OF HUMAN INTEREST

Translator's Note

In my first week at Oxford I came across the rather beautiful Old English riddle about a swan. I remember that I tried to translate it, and failed. I failed my Old English exams too, at the end of my second term.

On a soft evening shortly before resitting that vital exam I was in a moored punt with a friend, a pork pie, and my grammar when a swan attacked me. It was hardly a matter of "a sudden blow" or of "great wings beating,"[1] but sufficient none the less to inspire terror. I leaped for the bank and landed in hospital with a torn cartilage. To that swan, I am quite sure, which offered me ten hygienic days with so little to distract, I owed my continuing presence in the University.

In my last term I came across the riddle again, and again tried to translate it. This time there was something to show for it:

Silent is my dress when I step across the earth,
Reside in my house, or ruffle the waters.
Sometimes my adornments and this high windy air
Lift me over the livings of men,
The power of the clouds carries me far
Over all people. My white pinions
Resound very loudly, ring with a melody,
Sing out clearly, when I sleep not on
The soil or settle on grey waters . . . a travelling spirit.

These lines, the first I had translated from Old English, add up in the original to an elegant, highly-wrought little diversion (though not to much of a riddle); they curiously foreshadow a famous poem by Yeats, "The Wild Swans at Coole."

Although I had no taste for learning the mechanics of the language, the mood of much Old English poetry had attracted me immediately; and my sympathy with it has seemed to grow from day to day. Sometimes passionate, often sorrowful, occasionally wry, but always stoic, formal, and highly sophisticated, the voice of the Old English poets is absolutely distinctive. Theirs was a poetry born of a chill, unfriendly world peopled by warrior bands, where loyalty was the greatest virtue and life an endless struggle against meaningless fate. The Saxon warrior's attitude to life is nicely summed up in the Norse proverb, "One thing I know never dies nor changes, the reputation of a dead man," and it is pertinent that the last word of *Beowulf* describes that hero as *lofġeornost*, "most eager for fame."

Beowulf is by far the finest of the Old English poems that have come down to us. It is a poem of tremendous power and range, the work of a man (most probably a Christian) fully able to carry out what I take to be his purpose: the depiction of an ideal Germanic hero within the framework of a gripping, human story. Those who come to *Beowulf* for the first time, perhaps expecting it to be remote, may be surprised by the essentially English character of the poem. For if the society reflected in it now seems alien, many of its moods are wholly familiar: an out-and-out heroism, a dogged refusal to surrender, a love of the sea, an enjoyment of melancholy, nostalgia. *Beowulf* has the power to stir us to the roots of our being; through it, we can come to understand more about our origins, and thus achieve a deeper sense of perspective. It will not be enough to "taste" a page here and a page there; much of the poem's strength lies in accumulative impact.

My aim in attempting this translation was to achieve a truly accessible version of the poem, one that avoided the use of archaic terms, inverted word orders, and all "poetic" language. This translation is, I believe, by and large faithful to the letter of the original, but it is the mood that I have been after.

Finally, I must add that I believe this translation should be read out loud—an epic in the oral tradition is never going to sit very easily on the printed page.

Kevin Crossley-Holland

1. Quoted from the poem "Leda and the Swan" by William Butler Yeats.

TWO BIRD APPLIQUES FROM AN ANGLO-SAXON SHIELD, CA. 600 A.D. COURTESY OF THE TRUSTEES OF THE BRITISH MUSEUM.

whether it is true—as we have heard tell—
that here among the Danes a certain evil-doer,
a fearful solitary, on dark nights commits deeds
of unspeakable malice—damage
230 and slaughter. In all good conscience
I can counsel Hrothgar, that wise and good man,
how he shall overcome the fiend,
and how his anguish shall be assuaged—
if indeed his fate ordains that these foul deeds
235 should ever end, and be avenged;
he will suffer endless hardship otherwise,
dire distress, as long as Heorot, best of dwellings,
stands unshaken in its lofty place."
Still mounted, the coastguard,
240 a courageous thane, gave him this reply:
"The discriminating warrior—one whose mind is keen—
must perceive the difference between words and deeds.
But I see you are a company well disposed
towards the Danish prince. Proceed, and bring
245 your weapons and armour! I shall direct you.
And I will command my companions, moreover,
to guard your ship with honour
against any foe—your beached vessel,
caulked so recently—until the day that timbered craft
250 with its curved prow shall carry back
the beloved man across the sea currents
to the shores of the storm-loving Geats:
he who dares deeds with such audacity and valour
shall be granted safety in the squall of battle."
255 Then they hurried on. The ship lay still;
securely anchored, the spacious vessel
rode on its hawser. The boar crest, brightly gleaming,
stood over their helmets: superbly tempered,
plated with glowing gold, it guarded the lives
260 of those grim warriors. The thanes made haste,
marched along together until they could discern
the glorious, timbered hall, adorned with gold;
they saw there the best-known building
under heaven. The ruler lived in it;
265 its brilliance carried across countless lands.
Then the fearless watchman pointed out the path
leading to Heorot, bright home of brave men,
so that they should not miss the way;
that bold warrior turned his horse, then said:
270 "I must leave you here. May the Almighty Father,
of His grace, guard you in your enterprise.
I will go back to the sea again,
and there stand watch against marauding bands."
The road was paved; it showed those warriors
275 the way. Their corslets were gleaming,
the strong links of shining chain-mail
clinked together. When the sea-stained travellers
had reached the hall itself in their fearsome armour,
they placed their broad shields
280 (worked so skilfully) against Heorot's wall.
Then they sat on a bench; the brave men's
armour sang. The seafarers' gear
stood all together, a grey-tipped forest
of ash spears; that armed troop was well equipped
285 with weapons.
Then Wulfgar, a proud warrior,
asked the Geats about their ancestry:
"Where have you come from with these gold-plated shields,
these grey coats of mail, these visored helmets,
and this pile of spears? I am Hrothgar's
290 messenger, his herald. I have never seen
so large a band of strangers of such bold bearing.
You must have come to Hrothgar's court
not as exiles, but from audacity and high ambition."
Then he who feared no man, the proud leader
295 of the Geats, stern-faced beneath his helmet,
gave him this reply: "We are Hygelac's
companions at the bench: my name is Beowulf.
I wish to explain to Healfdene's son,
the famous prince, your lord,
300 why we have come if he, in his goodness,
will give us leave to speak with him."
Wulfgar replied—a prince of the Vandals,
his mettle, his wisdom and prowess in battle
were widely recognized: "I will ask
305 the lord of the Danes, ruler of the Scyldings,
renowned prince and ring-giver,
just as you request, regarding your journey,
and bring back to you at once whatever answer
that gracious man thinks fit to give me."
310 Then Wulfgar hurried to the place where Hrothgar sat,
grizzled and old, surrounded by his thanes;
the brave man moved forward until he stood
immediately before the Danish lord;
he well knew the customs of warriors.
315 Wulfgar addressed his friend and leader:
"Geatish men have travelled to this land,
come from far, across the stretch of the seas.
These warriors call their leader Beowulf;
they ask, my lord, that they should be allowed

320 to speak with you. Gracious Hrothgar,
do not give them *no* for an answer.
They, in their armour, seem altogether worthy
of the highest esteem. I have no doubt of their leader's
might, he who has brought these brave men to
Heorot."
325 Hrothgar, defender of the Danes, answered:
"I knew him when he was a boy;
his illustrious father was called Ecgtheow;
Hrethel the Geat gave him his only daughter
in marriage; now his son, with daring spirit,
330 has voyaged here to visit a loyal friend.
And moreover, I have heard seafarers say—
men who have carried rich gifts to the Geats
as a mark of my esteem—that in the grasp
of his hand that man renowned in battle
335 has the might of thirty men. I am convinced
that Holy God, of His great mercy,
has directed him to us West-Danes[13]
and that he means to come to grips with Grendel.
I will reward this brave man with treasures.
340 Hurry! Tell them to come in and meet
our band of kinsmen; and make it clear, too,
that they are most welcome to the Danes!"
Then Wulfgar went to the hall door with Hrothgar's
reply:
"My conquering lord, the leader of the East-Danes,[13]
345 commands me to tell you that he knows your lineage
and that you, so bold in mind, are welcome
to these shores from over the rolling sea.
You may see Hrothgar in your armour,
under your helmets, just as you are;
350 but leave your shields out here, and your deadly
ashen spears,
let them await the outcome of your words."
Then noble Beowulf rose from the bench,
flanked by his fearless followers; some stayed behind
at the brave man's bidding, to stand guard over their
armour.
355 Guided by Wulfgar, the rest hurried into Heorot
together; there went that hardy man, stern-faced
beneath his helmet, until he was standing under
Heorot's roof.
Beowulf spoke—his corslet, cunningly linked
by the smith, was shining: "Greetings, Hrothgar!
360 I am Hygelac's kinsman and retainer. In my youth
I achieved many daring exploits. Word of Grendel's
deeds
has come to me in my own country;
seafarers say that this hall Heorot,
best of all buildings, stands empty and useless
365 as soon as the evening light is hidden under the sky.
So, Lord Hrothgar, men known by my people
to be noble and wise advised me to visit you
because they knew of my great strength:

13. *West-Danes, East-Danes.* To make his lines alliterate (see "The Poetry of *Beowulf*" on page 40), the poet at various times refers to Hrothgar's people as North-, South-, East-, and West-Danes, and also as Bright-, Ring-, and Spear-Danes.

OF LITERARY INTEREST

The Epic

Beowulf is one of the world's great epics—a long narrative poem presented in an elevated style, relating the heroic deeds of noble or semidivine personages. Like other traditional or folk epics (for example, *The Iliad* and *The Odyssey*), *Beowulf* originated in traditional tales or legends dating back to a remote past and handed down orally by generations of bards or singers. At some point, a literary artist put all the materials together in written form.

Literary epics developed later and were modeled on the traditional epics. Among the first was a Latin poem, Vergil's *Aeneid.* The most famous English literary epic is Milton's *Paradise Lost.*

Certain features are associated with the epic: The central character has heroic or superhuman qualities. The action is on an immense scale and involves the fate of a whole people or even the entire human race. Gods or semidivine creatures come to the aid of one side or another.

Certain devices also recur. The author usually announces his theme at the opening and calls on the muses to help him in his task of narration. The poem usually begins *in medias res* (in the middle of things), at a critical point in the action. The style is noble and majestic; the characters speak ceremoniously in long set speeches. Literary inventories—catalogues of characters or objects—often form part of the descriptive passages.

Such features and devices became so predictable that there developed a kind of anti-epic, a literary form known as mock epic. The mock epic uses all the epic elements in wrong or bizarre ways in order to make them seem ridiculous; for example, a trivial action is presented in an inflated style and celebrated in elaborate terms. The most famous mock epic in English, and one of the funniest poems in any language, is Alexander Pope's "The Rape of the Lock." See pages 291-296.

they saw me themselves when, stained by my enemies' blood,
370 I returned from the fight when I destroyed five,
a family of giants, and by night slew monsters
on the waves; I suffered great hardship,
avenged the affliction of the Storm-Geats and crushed
their fierce foes—they were asking for trouble.
375 And now, I shall crush the giant Grendel
in single combat. Lord of the mighty Danes,
guardian of the Scyldings, I ask one favour:
protector of warriors, lord beloved of your people,
now that I have sailed here from so far,
380 do not refuse my request—that I alone, with my band
of brave retainers, may cleanse Heorot.
I have also heard men say this monster
is so reckless he spurns the use of weapons.
Therefore (so that Hygelac, my lord,
385 may rest content over my conduct) I deny myself
the use of a sword and a broad yellow shield
in battle; but I shall grapple with this fiend
hand to hand; we shall fight for our lives,
foe against foe; and he whom death takes off
390 must resign himself to the judgement of God.
I know that Grendel, should he overcome me,
will without dread devour many Geats,
matchless warriors, in the battle-hall,
as he has often devoured Danes before. If death claims me
395 you will not have to cover my head,
for he already will have done so—
with a sheet of shining blood; he will carry off
the blood-stained corpse, meaning to savour it;
the solitary one will eat without sorrow
400 and stain his lair; no longer then
will you have to worry about burying my body.
But if battle should claim me, send this most excellent
coat of mail to Hygelac, this best of corslets
that protects my breast; it once belonged to Hrethel,
405 the work of Weland.[14] Fate goes ever as it must!"

Hrothgar, protector of the Scyldings, replied:
"Beowulf, my friend! So you have come here,
because of past favours, to fight on our behalf! . . ."

(Hrothgar tells of a feud in which Beowulf's father, Ecgtheow, was involved and which Hrothgar settled by paying a wergild. He seems to suggest that Beowulf's fighting against Grendel would even the score of obligations, but he does not yet grant Beowulf's request. Instead, he invites Beowulf and his men to join him and his thanes in a feast.)

Then, in the feasting-hall,
410 a bench was cleared for the Geats all together,
and there those brave men went and sat,
delighting in their strength; a thane did his duty—
held between his hands the adorned ale-cup,
poured out gleaming liquor; now and then the poet sang,
415 raised his clear voice in Heorot; the warriors caroused,
no small company of Scyldings and Geats.
Ecglaf's[15] son, Unferth, who sat at the feet
of the lord of the Scyldings, unlocked his thoughts
with these unfriendly words—for the journey of Beowulf,
420 the brave seafarer, much displeased him
in that he was unwilling for any man
in this wide world to gain more glory than himself:
"Are you the Beowulf who competed with Breca,
vied with him at swimming in the open sea
425 when, swollen with vanity, you both braved
the waves, risked your lives on deep waters
because of a foolish boast? No one,
neither friend nor foe, could keep you
from your sad journey, when you swam out to sea,
430 clasped in your arms the water-streams,
passed over the sea-paths, swiftly moved your hands
and sped over the ocean. The sea heaved,
the winter flood; for seven nights
you both toiled in the water; but Breca outstayed you,
435 he was the stronger; and then, on the eighth morning,
the sea washed him up on the shores of the Heathoreams.[16]
From there he sought his own country,
the land of the Brondings who loved him well;
he went to his fair stronghold where he had a hall
440 and followers and treasures. In truth, Beanstan's son
fulfilled his boast that he could swim better than you.
So I am sure you will pay a heavy price—
although you have survived countless battle storms,
savage sword-play—if you dare
445 ambush Grendel in the watches of the night."
Beowulf, the son of Ecgtheow, replied:
"Truly, Unferth my friend, all this beer
has made you talkative: you have told us much

14. *Weland,* in Norse myth, the blacksmith of the gods.

15. *Ecglaf* (edj′ läf)
16. *Heathoreams* (hā′ ath ə rā′ əmz)

about Breca and his exploits. But I maintain
450 I showed the greater stamina, endured
hardship without equal in the heaving water.
Some years ago when we were young men,
still in our youth, Breca and I made a boast,
a solemn vow, to venture our lives
455 on the open sea; and we kept our word.
When we swam through the water, we each held
a naked sword with which to ward off
whales; by no means could Breca
swim faster than I, pull away from me
460 through the press of the waves—
I had no wish to be separated from him.
So for five nights we stayed together in the sea,
until the tides tore us apart,
the foaming water, the freezing cold,
465 day darkening into night—until the north wind,
that savage warrior, rounded against us.
Rough were the waves; fishes in the sea
were roused to great anger. Then my coat of mail,
hard and hand-linked, guarded me against my
enemies;
470 the woven war-garment, adorned with gold,
covered my breast. A cruel ravager
dragged me down to the sea-bed, a fierce monster
held me tightly in its grasp; but it was given to me
to bury my sword, my battle weapon,
475 in its breast; the mighty sea-beast
was slain by my blow in the storm of battle.
In this manner, and many times, loathsome monsters
harassed me fiercely; with my fine sword
I served them fittingly.
480 I did not allow those evil destroyers to enjoy
a feast, to eat me limb by limb
seated at a banquet on the sea-bottom;
but the next morning they lay in the sand
along the shore, wounded by sword strokes,
485 slain by battle-blades, and from that day on
they could not hinder seafarers from sailing
over deep waters. Light came from the east,
God's bright beacon; the swell subsided,
and I saw then great headlands,
490 cliffs swept by the wind. Fate will often spare
an undoomed man, if his courage is good.
As it was I slew nine sea-beasts
with my sword. I have never heard
of a fiercer fight by night under heaven's vault
495 nor of a man who endured more on the ocean
streams.
But I escaped with my life from the enemies' clutches,
worn out by my venture. Then the swift current,
the surging water, carried me
to the land of the Lapps. I have not heard tell
500 that you have taken part in any such contests,
in the peril of sword-play. Neither you nor Breca
have yet dared such a deed with shining sword
in battle—I do not boast because of this—
though of course it is true you slew your own
brothers,
505 your own close kinsmen. For that deed, however
clever
you may be, you will suffer damnation in hell.
I tell you truly, son of Ecglaf,
that if you were in fact as unflinching
as you claim, the fearsome monster Grendel
510 would never have committed so many crimes
against your lord, nor created such havoc in Heorot;
but he has found he need not fear unduly
your people's enmity, fearsome assault
with swords by the victorious Scyldings.
515 So he spares none but takes his toll
of the Danish people, does as he will,
kills and destroys, expects no fight
from the Spear-Danes. But soon, quite soon,
I shall show him the strength, the spirit and skill
520 of the Geats. And thereafter, when day dawns,
when the radiant sun shines from the south
over the sons of men, he who so wishes

OF CRITICAL INTEREST

Why does Unferth insult Beowulf?

"Unferth directs against the hero a speech which—to the modern reader at least—seems shockingly insulting, and utterly out of harmony with the extreme courtesy which Hrothgar has shown Beowulf. This challenge, and Beowulf's vigorous reply, seem to interrupt the main narrative; but in actuality they advance it. For Unferth's words spur Beowulf to claim for himself the right to confront Grendel, and to prove his competence to do so; and when the hero has spoken, there is no longer any question that Hrothgar will grant his request. Thus the clash between Unferth and Beowulf becomes the mechanism which triggers all the ensuing action of Part 1."

From *The Art of Beowulf* by Arthur Gilchrist Brodeur. Originally published by the University of California Press, 1959. Reprinted by permission of The Regents of the University of California.

may enter the mead-hall without terror."
Then the grizzled warrior, giver of gold,
525 was filled with joy; the lord of the Danes,
shepherd of his people, listened to Beowulf's
brave resolution and relied on his help.
The warriors laughed, there was a hum
of contentment. Wealhtheow[17] came forward,
530 mindful of ceremonial—she was Hrothgar's queen;
adorned with gold, that proud woman
greeted the men in the hall, then offered the cup
to the Danish king first of all.
She begged him, beloved of his people,
535 to enjoy the feast; the king, famed
for victory, ate and drank in happiness.
Then the lady of the Helmings walked about the hall,
offering the precious, ornamented cup
to old and young alike, until at last
540 the queen, excellent in mind, adorned with rings,
moved with the mead-cup towards Beowulf.
She welcomed the Geatish prince and with wise words
thanked God that her wish was granted
that she might depend on some warrior for help
545 against such attacks. The courageous warrior
took the cup from Wealhtheow's hands
and, eager for battle, made a speech:
Beowulf, the son of Ecgtheow, said:
"When I put to sea, sailed
550 through the breakers with my band of men,
I resolved to fulfil the desire
of your people, or suffer the pangs of death,
caught fast in Grendel's clutches.
Here, in Heorot, I shall either work a deed
555 of great daring, or lay down my life."
Beowulf's brave boast delighted Wealhtheow:
adorned with gold, the noble Danish queen
went to sit beside her lord.
Then again, as of old, fine words were spoken
560 in the hall, the company rejoiced,
a conquering people, until in due course
the son of Healfdene wanted to retire
and take his rest. He realized the monster
meant to attack Heorot after the blue hour,
565 when black night has settled over all—
when shadowy shapes come shrithing
dark beneath the clouds. All the company rose.
Then the heroes Hrothgar and Beowulf saluted
one another; Hrothgar wished him luck
570 and control of Heorot, and confessed:
"Never since I could lift hand and shield,
have I entrusted this glorious Danish hall
to any man as I do now to you.
Take and guard this greatest of halls.
575 Make known your strength, remember your might,
stand watch against your enemy. You shall have
all you desire if you survive this enterprise."
Then Hrothgar, defender of the Danes,
withdrew from the hall with his band of warriors.
580 Truly, the leader of the Geats fervently trusted
in his own great strength and in God's grace.
Then he took off his helmet and his corslet
of iron, and gave them to his servant,
with his superb, adorned sword,
585 telling him to guard them carefully.
And then, before he went to his bed,
the brave Geat, Beowulf, made his boast:
"I count myself no less active in battle,
no less brave than Grendel himself:
590 thus, I will not send him to sleep with my sword,
so deprive him of life, though certainly I could.
Despite his fame for deadly deeds,
he is ignorant of these noble arts, that he might strike
at me, and hew my shield; but we, this night,
595 shall forego the use of weapons, if he dares fight
without them; and then may wise God,
the holy Lord, give glory in battle
to whichever of us He should think fitting."
Then the brave prince leaned back, put his head
600 on the pillow while, around him,
many a proud seafarer lay back on his bed.
Not one of them believed he would see
day dawn, or ever return to his family
and friends, and the place where he was born;
605 they well knew that in recent days
far too many Danish men had come to bloody ends
in that hall. But the Lord wove the webs of destiny,
gave the Geats success in their struggle,
help and support, in such a way
610 that all were enabled to overcome their enemy
through the strength of one man. We cannot doubt
that mighty God has always ruled
over mankind.
Then the night prowler
came shrithing through the shadows. All the Geats
615 guarding Heorot had fallen asleep—
all except one. Men well knew that the evil enemy
could not drag them down into the shadows
when it was against the Creator's wishes,

17. *Wealhtheow* (wā′ al thā ō)

but Beowulf, watching grimly for his adversary
Grendel,
620 awaited the ordeal with increasing anger.
Then, under night's shroud, Grendel walked down
from the moors; he shouldered God's anger.
The evil plunderer intended to ensnare
one of the race of men in the high hall.
625 He strode under the skies, until he stood
before the feasting-hall, in front of the gift-building
gleaming with gold. And this night was not the first
on which he had so honoured Hrothgar's home.
But never in his life did he find hall-wardens
630 more greatly to his detriment. Then the joyless warrior
journeyed to Heorot. The outer door, bolted
with iron bands, burst open at a touch from his hands:
with evil in his mind, and overriding anger,
Grendel swung open the hall's mouth itself. At once,
635 seething with fury, the fiend stepped onto
the tessellated floor; a horrible light,
like a lurid flame, flickered in his eyes.
He saw many men, a group of warriors,
a knot of kinsmen, sleeping in the hall.
640 His spirits leapt, his heart laughed;
the savage monster planned to sever,
before daybreak, the life of every warrior
from his body—he fully expected to eat
his fill at the feast. But after that night
645 fate decreed that he should no longer feed off
human flesh. Hygelac's kinsman,
the mighty man, watched the wicked ravager
to see how he would make his sudden attacks.
The monster was not disposed to delay;
650 but, for a start, he hungrily seized
a sleeping warrior, greedily wrenched him,
bit into his body, drank the blood
from his veins, devoured huge pieces;
until, in no time, he had swallowed the whole man,
655 even his feet and hands. Now Grendel stepped
forward,
nearer and nearer, made to grasp the valiant Geat
stretched out on his bed—the fiend reached towards
him
with his open hand; at once Beowulf perceived
his evil plan, sat up and stayed Grendel's outstretched
arm.
660 Instantly that monster, hardened by crime,
realized that never had he met any man
in the regions of earth, in the whole world,
with so strong a grip. He was seized with terror.
But, for all that, he was unable to break away.
665 He was eager to escape to his lair, seek the company
of devils, but he was restrained as never before.
Then Hygelac's brave kinsman bore in mind
his boast: he rose from the bed and gripped
Grendel fiercely. The fiend tried to break free,
670 his fingers were bursting. Beowulf kept with him.
The evil giant was desperate to escape,
if indeed he could, and head for his lair
in the fens; he could feel his fingers cracking
in his adversary's grip; that was a bitter journey
675 that Grendel made to the ring-hall Heorot.
The great room boomed; all the proud warriors—
each and every Dane living in the stronghold—
were stricken with panic. The two hall-wardens
were enraged. The building rang with their blows.
680 It was a wonder the wine-hall withstood
two so fierce in battle, that the fair building
did not fall to earth; but it stood firm,
braced inside and out with hammered
iron bands. I have heard tell that there,
685 where they fought, many a mead-bench,
studded with gold, started from the floor.
Until that time, elders of the Scyldings
were of the opinion that no man could wreck
the great hall Heorot, adorned with horns,
690 nor by any means destroy it unless it were gutted
by greedy tongues of flame. Again and again
clang and clatter shattered the night's silence;
dread numbed the North-Danes, seized all
who heard the shrieking from the hall,
695 the enemy of God's grisly lay of terror,
his song of defeat, heard hell's captive
keening over his wound. Beowulf held him fast,
he who was the strongest of all men
ever to have seen the light of life on earth.
700 By no means did the defender of thanes
allow the murderous caller to escape with his life;
he reckoned that the rest of Grendel's days
were useless to anyone. Then, time and again,
Beowulf's band brandished their ancestral swords;
705 they longed to save the life, if they
so could, of their lord, the mighty leader.
When they did battle on Beowulf's behalf,
struck at the monster from every side,
eager for his end, those courageous warriors
710 were unaware that no war-sword,
not even the finest iron on earth,
could wound their evil enemy,
for he had woven a secret spell
against every kind of weapon, every battle blade.

OF CRITICAL INTEREST

How does the poet build up suspense?

"The several forecasts (lines 609ff, 618ff, 646ff, and 717ff) of Beowulf's victory over Grendel, which one critic regards as destructive of suspense, are so blanketed by the oppressive sense of fear that the brief release from tension which each affords only increases the hearer's responsiveness to each succeeding shock.

"Through much of the narrative that precedes Beowulf's encounter with Grendel, the bloody evidence of the ogre's power and ferocity had been piling up. All this accumulated horror was vibrant in the recollection of the poet's hearers. For them, monsters of Grendel's kind lurked ever in the night shadows, waiting to ensnare and devour. After the repeated reports of his persecutions their nerves were stretched taut; and as Beowulf lay down to await the troll, they were subjected to fresh strain by the ominous statement of the fear of the hero's men (lines 604–609a). At this point, the poet offers his first assurance that Beowulf will prevail. It does not so much allay fear as it prepares the listener to experience freshly and keenly the dreadful impact of Grendel's advance on Heorot; it must have been all but forgotten in the course of the ogre's nerve-shredding progress."

Condensed from *The Art of Beowulf* by Arthur Gilchrist Brodeur.

715 Grendel's death, his departure from this world,
was destined to be wretched, his migrating spirit
was fated to travel far into the power of fiends.
Then he who for years had committed crimes
against mankind, murderous in mind,
720 and had warred with God, discovered
that the strength of his body could not save him,
that Hygelac's brave kinsman held his hand
in a vise-like grip; each was a mortal enemy
to the other. The horrible monster
725 suffered grievous pain; a gaping wound
opened on his shoulder; the sinews sprang apart,
the muscles were bursting. Glory in battle
was given to Beowulf; fatally wounded,
Grendel was obliged to make for the marshes,
730 head for his joyless lair. He was
well aware that his life's days were done,
come to an end. After that deadly encounter
the desire of every Dane was at last accomplished.
In this way did the wise and fearless man
735 who had travelled from far cleanse Hrothgar's hall,
release it from affliction. He rejoiced in his night's
work,
his glorious achievement. The leader of the Geats
made good his boast to the East-Danes;
he had removed the cause of their distress,
740 put an end to the sorrow every Dane had shared,
the bitter grief that they had been constrained
to suffer. When Beowulf, brave in battle,
placed hand, arm and shoulder—Grendel's
entire grasp—under Heorot's spacious roof,
745 that was evidence enough of victory.
Then I have heard that next morning
many warriors gathered round the gift-hall;
leaders of men came from every region,
from remote parts, to look on the wonder,
750 the tracks of the monster. Grendel's death
seemed no grievous loss to any of the men
who set eyes on the spoor of the defeated one,
saw how he, weary in spirit, overcome in combat,
fated and put to flight, had made for the lake
755 of water-demons—leaving tracks of life-blood.
There the water boiled because of the blood;
the fearful swirling waves reared up,
mingled with hot blood, battle gore;
fated, he hid himself, then joyless
760 laid aside his life, his heathen spirit,
in the fen lair; hell received him there.
After this, the old retainers left the lake
and so did the company of young men too;
brave warriors rode back on their gleaming horses
765 from this joyful journey. Then Beowulf's exploit
was acclaimed; many a man asserted
time and again that there was no better
shield-bearer in the whole world, to north or south
between the two seas, under the sky's expanse,
770 no man more worthy of his own kingdom.
Yet they found no fault at all with their friendly lord,
gracious Hrothgar—he was a great king.
At times the brave warriors spurred their bays,
horses renowned for their speed and stamina,
775 and raced each other where the track was suitable.
And now and then one of Hrothgar's thanes
who brimmed with poetry, and remembered lays,
a man acquainted with ancient traditions
of every kind, composed a new song
780 in correct meter. Most skilfully that man
began to sing of Beowulf's feat,
to weave words together, and fluently
to tell a fitting tale. . . .

(The scop weaves in stories of the exploits of Sigemund, most renowned of Germanic heroes, who slew a dragon and claimed the treasure the dragon had been guarding. He also sings about Heremod, an early Danish king, who failed to live up to the promise of his youth. These stories—no doubt familiar to the poet's original audience—were included in order to compare and contrast Sigemund and Heremod with Beowulf. Thus the hours quickly pass.)

Stout-hearted warriors
785 without number travelled to the high hall
to inspect that wonder; the king himself, too,
glorious Hrothgar, guardian of ring-hoards,
came from his quarters with a great company, escorted
his queen and her retinue of maidens into the mead-hall.
790 Hrothgar spoke—he approached Heorot,
stood on the steps, stared at the high roof
adorned with gold, and at Grendel's hand:
"Let us give thanks at once to God Almighty
for this sight. I have undergone many afflictions,
795 grievous outrages at Grendel's hands; but God,
Guardian of heaven, can work wonder upon wonder.
Until now, I had been resigned,
had no longer believed that my afflictions
would ever end: this finest of buildings
800 stood stained with battle blood,
a source of sorrow to my counsellors;
they all despaired of regaining this hall
for many years to come, of guarding it from foes,
from devils and demons. Yet now one warrior
805 alone, through the Almighty's power, has succeeded
where we failed for all our fine plans.
Indeed, if she is still alive,
that woman (whoever she was) who gave birth
to such a son, to be one of humankind,
810 may claim that the Creator was gracious to her
in her child-bearing. Now, Beowulf,
best of men, I will love you in my heart
like a son; keep to our new kinship
from this day on. You shall lack
815 no earthly riches I can offer you. . . ."

After this, the son of Ecglaf boasted less
about his prowess in battle—when all the warriors,
through Beowulf's might, had been enabled
to examine that hand, the fiend's fingers,
820 nailed up on the gables. Seen from in front,
each nail, each claw of that warlike,
heathen monster looked like steel—
a terrifying spike. Everyone said
that no weapon whatsoever, no proven sword
825 could possibly harm it, could damage
that battle-hardened, blood-stained hand.

Then orders were quickly given for the inside of Heorot
to be decorated; many servants, both men and women,
bustled about that wine-hall, adorned that building
830 of retainers. Tapestries, worked in gold,
glittered on the walls, many a fine sight
for those who have eyes to see such things. . . .
Then it was time
for Healfdene's son to proceed to the hall,
835 the king himself was eager to attend the feast.
I have never heard of a greater band of kinsmen
gathered with such dignity around their ring-giver.
Then the glorious warriors sat on the benches,
rejoicing in the feast. Courteously
840 their kinsmen, Hrothgar and Hrothulf,
quaffed many a mead-cup, confident warriors
in the high hall. Heorot was packed
with feasters who were friends; the time was not yet come
when the Scyldings practised wrongful deeds.
845 Then Hrothgar gave Beowulf Healfdene's sword,
and a battle banner, woven with gold,
and a helmet and a corslet, as rewards for victory;
many men watched while the priceless, renowned sword
was presented to the hero. Beowulf emptied
850 the ale-cup in the hall; he had no cause
to be ashamed at those precious gifts.
There are few men, as far as I have heard,
who have given four such treasures, gleaming with gold,
to another on the mead-bench with equal generosity.
855 A jutting ridge, wound about with metal wires,
ran over the helmet's crown, protecting the skull,
so that well-ground swords, proven in battle,
could not injure the well-shielded warrior
when he advanced against his foes.
860 Then the guardian of thanes ordered
that eight horses with gold-plated bridles
be led into the courtyard; onto one was strapped
a saddle, inlaid with jewels, skilfully made.
That was the war-seat of the great king,
865 Healfdene's son, whenever he wanted
to join in the sword-play. That famous man

never lacked bravery at the front in battle,
when men about him were cut down like corn.
Then the king of the Danes, Ing's descendants,
870 presented the horses and weapons to Beowulf,
bade him use them well and enjoy them.
Thus the renowned prince, the retainers' gold-warden,
rewarded those fierce sallies in full measure,
with horses and treasure, so that no man
875 would ever find reason to reproach him fairly.
Furthermore, the guardian of warriors gave
a treasure, an heirloom at the mead-bench,
to each of those men who had crossed the sea
with Beowulf; and he ordered that gold
880 be paid for that warrior Grendel slew
so wickedly—as he would have slain many another,
had not foreseeing God and the warrior's courage
together forestalled him. The Creator ruled over
all humankind, even as He does today.
885 Wherefore a wise man will value forethought
and understanding. Whoever lives long
on earth, endures the unrest of these times,
will be involved in much good and much evil.
Then Hrothgar, leader in battle, was entertained
890 with music—harp and voice in harmony. . . .

(The scop sings a lay about Finn, king of the Frisians, his Danish wife Hildeburh, and Hildeburh's brother Hnaef. While Hnaef and his followers were visiting Finn, they were treacherously attacked by Finn's thanes, in retaliation for some earlier wrong. Hnaef and Hildeburh's son were killed in the battle. An uneasy truce ensued, but in the spring the fighting was resumed. Finn was killed and the Danes returned to Denmark, taking with them Hildeburh, who had lost her husband, son, and brother. The story seems to hint at similar treachery and tragedy that will later come to the court of Hrothgar.

This same story was told in another Old English poem, "The Fight at Finnsburg.")

Thus was the lay sung,
the song of the poet. The hall echoed with joy,
waves of noise broke out along the benches;
cup-bearers carried wine in glorious vessels.
895 Then Wealhtheow. wearing her golden collar, walked
to where Hrothgar and Hrothulf were sitting side by side,
uncle and nephew, still friends together, true to one another.
And the spokesman Unferth sat at the feet
of the Danish lord; all men admired
900 his spirit and audacity, although he had deceived
his own kinsmen in a feud. Then the lady of the Scyldings
spoke these words: "Accept this cup, my loved lord,
treasure-giver; O gold-friend of men,
learn the meaning of joy again, and speak words
905 of gratitude to the Geats, for so one ought to do.
And be generous to them too, mindful of gifts
which you have now amassed from far and wide.
I am told you intend to adopt this warrior,
take him for your son. This resplendent ring-hall,
910 Heorot, has been cleansed; give many rewards
while you may, but leave this land and the Danish people
to your own descendants when the day comes
for you to die. I am convinced
that gracious Hrothulf will guard our children
915 justly, should he outlive you, lord of the Scyldings,
in this world; I believe he will repay our sons
most generously if he remembers all we did
for his benefit and enjoyment when he was a boy."
Then Wealhtheow walked to the bench where her sons,
920 Hrethric and Hrothmund, sat with the sons of thanes,
fledgling warriors; where also that brave man,
Beowulf of the Geats, sat beside the brothers.
To him she carried the cup, and asked in gracious words
if he would care to drink; and to him she presented
925 twisted gold with courtly ceremonial—
two armlets, a corslet and many rings,
and the most handsome collar in the world. . . .

(Here follows a brief digression telling how Beowulf's uncle, Hygelac, king of the Geats, later wore this collar when he was killed in a foolhardy raid on the Frisians and Franks.)

Applause echoed in the hall.
Wealtheow spoke these words before the company:
930 "May you, Beowulf, beloved youth, enjoy
with all good fortune this necklace and corslet,
treasures of the people; may you always prosper;
win renown through courage, and be kind in your counsel
to these boys; for that, I will reward you further.

935 You have ensured that men will always sing
your praises, even to the ends of the world,
as far as oceans still surround cliffs,
home of the winds. May you thrive, O prince,
all your life. I hope you will amass
940 a shining hoard of treasure. O happy Beowulf,
be gracious in your dealing with my sons.
Here, each warrior is true to the others,
gentle of mind, loyal to his lord;
the thanes are as one, the people all alert,
945 the warriors have drunk well. They will do as I ask."
Then Wealhtheow retired to her seat
beside her lord. That was the best of banquets,
men drank their fill of wine; they had not tasted
bitter destiny, the fate that had come and claimed
950 many of the heroes at the end of dark evenings,
when Hrothgar the warrior had withdrawn
to take his rest. Countless retainers
defended Heorot as they had often done before;
benches were pushed back; the floor was padded
955 with beds and pillows. But one of the feasters
lying on his bed was doomed, and soon to die.
They set their bright battle-shields
at their heads. Placed on the bench
above each retainer, his crested helmet,
960 his linked corslet and sturdy spear-shaft
were plainly to be seen. It was their habit,
both at home and in the field,
to be prepared for battle always,
for any occasion their lord might need
965 assistance; that was a loyal band of retainers.
And so they slept. One man paid a heavy price
for his night's rest, as often happened
after Grendel first held the gold-hall
and worked his evil in it, until he met his doom,
970 death for his crimes. For afterwards it became clear,
and well known to the Scyldings, that some avenger
had survived the evil-doer, still lived after
that grievous, mortal combat.
Grendel's mother
was a monster of a woman; . . .
975 mournful and ravenous, she resolved to go
on a grievous journey to avenge her son's death.
Thus she reached Heorot; Ring-Danes, snoring,
were sprawled about the floor. The thanes suffered
a serious reverse as soon as Grendel's mother
980 entered the hall. The terror she caused,
compared to her son, equalled the terror
an Amazon inspires as opposed to a man,
when the ornamented sword, forged on the anvil,
the razor-sharp blade stained with blood,
985 shears through the boar-crested helmets of the enemy.
Then swords were snatched from benches, blades
drawn from scabbards, many a broad shield
was held firmly in the hall; none could don helmet
or spacious corslet—that horror caught them by
surprise.
990 The monster wanted to make off for the moors,
fly for her life, as soon as she was found out.
Firmly she grasped one of the thanes
and made for the fens as fast as she could.
That man whom she murdered even as he slept
995 was a brave shield-warrior, a well-known thane,
most beloved by Hrothgar of all his hall retainers
between the two seas. Beowulf was not there;
the noble Geat had been allotted another lodging
after the giving of treasure earlier that evening.
1000 Heorot was in uproar; she seized her son's
blood-crusted hand; anguish once again
had returned to the hall. What kind of bargain
was that, in which both sides forfeited
the lives of friends?
Then the old king,
1005 the grizzled warrior, was convulsed with grief
when he heard of the death of his dearest retainer.
Immediately Beowulf, that man blessed with
victory,

OF LITERARY INTEREST

What audience was the poet addressing?

"I do not believe that *Beowulf* was composed merely for people who could read, which is almost equivalent to saying, for the clergy. Though it may contain elements intended for edification, it is surely first and foremost literature of entertainment, and as such, intended mainly for laymen. I do not consider its length an insuperable obstacle to the view that it was intended for oral recital. It could easily have been delivered in three sittings. It is perhaps not by accident that the second episode, the fight with Grendel's mother, begins with a neat synopsis* of what has gone before; this may be intended to inform newcomers and remind the previous audience of what has happened in the first part. The third episode, the dragon fight, is intelligible by itself."

*Deleted in this book. It occurs at line 976.

was called to the chamber of the king. At dawn
the noble warrior and his friends, his followers,
1010 hurried to the room where the wise man was waiting,
waiting and wondering whether the Almighty
would ever allow an end to their adversity.
Then Beowulf, brave in battle, crossed
the floor with his band—the timbers thundered—
1015 and greeted the wise king, overlord of Ing's
descendants; he asked if the night had passed off
peacefully, since his summons was so urgent.
Hrothgar, guardian of the Scyldings, said:
"Do not speak of peace; grief once again
1020 afflicts the Danish people. Yrmenlaf's
elder brother, Æschere,[18] is dead,
my closest counsellor and my comrade,
my shoulder-companion when we shielded
our heads in the fight, when soldiers clashed on foot,
1025 slashed at boar-crests. Æschere was all
that a noble man, a warrior should be.
The wandering, murderous monster slew him
in Heorot; and I do not know where that ghoul,
drooling at her feast of flesh and blood,
1030 made off afterwards. She has avenged her son
whom you savaged yesterday with vise-like holds
because he had impoverished and killed my people
for many long years. He fell in mortal combat,
forfeit of his life; and now another mighty
1035 evil ravager has come to avenge her kinsman;
and many a thane, mournful in his mind
for his treasure-giver, may feel she has avenged
that feud already, indeed more than amply;
now that hand lies still which once sustained you.
1040 I have heard my people say,
men of this country, counsellors in the hall,
that they have seen *two* such beings,
equally monstrous, rangers of the fell-country,
rulers of the moors; and these men assert
1045 that so far as they can see one bears
a likeness to a woman; grotesque though he was,
the other who trod the paths of exile looked like a man,
though greater in height and build than a goliath;
he was christened *Grendel* by my people
1050 many years ago; men do not know if he
had a father, a fiend once begotten
by mysterious spirits. These two live
in a little-known country, wolf-slopes, windswept headlands,
perilous paths across the boggy moors, where a mountain stream
1055 plunges under the mist-covered cliffs,
rushes through a fissure. It is not far from here,
if measured in miles, that the lake stands
shadowed by trees stiff with hoar-frost.
A wood, firmly-rooted, frowns over the water.
1060 There, night after night, a fearful wonder may be seen—
fire on the water; no man alive
is so wise as to know the nature of its depths.
Although the moor-stalker, the stag with strong horns,
when harried by hounds will make for the wood,
1065 pursued from afar, he will succumb
to the hounds on the brink, rather than plunge in
and save his head. That is not a pleasant place.
When the wind arouses the wrath of the storm,
whipped waves rear up black from the lake,
1070 reach for the skies, until the air becomes misty,
the heavens weep. Now, once again, help may be had
from you alone. As yet, you have not seen the haunt,
the perilous place where you may meet this most evil monster
face to face. Do you dare set eyes on it?
1075 If you return unscathed, I will reward you
for your audacity, as I did before,
with ancient treasures and twisted gold."
Beowulf, the son of Ecgtheow, answered:
"Do not grieve, wise Hrothgar! Better each man
1080 should avenge his friend than deeply mourn.
The days on earth for every one of us
are numbered; he who may should win renown
before his death; that is a warrior's
best memorial when he has departed from this world.
1085 Come, O guardian of the kingdom, let us lose
no time but track down Grendel's kinswoman.
I promise you that wherever she turns—
to honeycomb caves, to mountain woods,
to the bottom of the lake she shall find no refuge.
1090 Shoulder your sorrows with patience
this day; this is what I expect of you."
Then the old king leapt up, poured out his gratitude
to God Almighty for the Geat's words.
Hrothgar's horse, his stallion with plaited mane,
1095 was saddled and bridled; the wise ruler
set out in full array; his troop of shield-bearers
fell into step. They followed the tracks
along forest paths and over open hill-country
for mile after mile; the monster had made
1100 for the dark moors directly, carrying the corpse

18. *Æschere* (ash′ her rə)

of the foremost thane of all those
who, with Hrothgar, had guarded the hall.
Then the man of noble lineage left Heorot far behind,
followed narrow tracks, string-thin paths
1105 over steep, rocky slopes—remote parts
with beetling crags and many lakes
where water-demons lived. He went ahead
with a handful of scouts to explore the place;
all at once he came upon a dismal wood,
1110 mountain trees standing on the edge
of a grey precipice; the lake lay beneath,
blood-stained and turbulent. The Danish retainers
were utterly appalled when they came upon
the severed head of their comrade Æschere
1115 on the steep slope leading down to the lake;
all the thanes were deeply distressed.

The water boiled with blood, with hot gore;
the warriors gaped at it. At times the horn sang
an eager battle-song. The brave men all sat down;
1120 then they saw many serpents in the water,
strange sea-dragons swimming in the lake,
and also water-demons, lying on cliff-ledges,
monsters and serpents of the same kind
as often, in the morning, molest ships
1125 on the sail-road. They plunged to the lake bottom,
bitter and resentful, rather than listen
to the song of the horn. The leader of the Geats
picked off one with his bow and arrow,
ended its life; the metal tip
1130 stuck in its vitals; it swam more sluggishly
after that, as the life-blood ebbed from its body;
in no time this strange sea-dragon
bristled with barbed boar-spears, was subdued
and drawn up onto the cliff; men examined
1135 that disgusting enemy.

Beowulf donned
his coat of mail, did not fear for his own life.
His massive corslet, linked by hand
and skilfully adorned, was to essay the lake—
it knew how to guard the body, the bone-chamber,
1140 so that his foe's grasp, in its malicious fury,
could not crush his chest, squeeze out his life;
and his head was guarded by the gleaming helmet
which was to explore the churning waters,
stir their very depths; gold decorated it,
1145 and it was hung with chain-mail, as the weapon smith
had wrought it long before, wondrously shaped it
and beset it with boar-images, so that
afterwards no battle-blade could do it damage.
Not least amongst his mighty aids was Hrunting,
1150 the long-hilted sword Unferth lent him in his need;
it was one of the finest of heirlooms; the iron blade
was engraved with deadly, twig-like patterning,
tempered with battle blood. It had not failed
any of those men who had held it in their hands,
1155 risked themselves on hazardous exploits,
pitted themselves against foes. That was not
the first time it had to do a hard day's work.
Truly, when Ecglaf's son, himself so strong,
lent that weapon to his better as a swordsman,
1160 he had forgotten all those taunts he flung
when tipsy with wine; he dared not chance
his own arm under the breakers, dared not
risk his life; at the lake he lost
his renown for bravery. It was not so with Beowulf
1165 once he had armed himself for battle.

The Geat, son of Ecgtheow, spoke:
"Great son of Healfdene, gracious ruler,
gold-friend of men, remember now—
for I am now ready to go—
1170 what we agreed if I, fighting on your behalf,
should fail to return: that you would always
be like a father to me after I had gone.
Guard my followers, my dear friends,
if I die in battle; and, beloved Hrothgar,
1175 send to Hygelac the treasures you gave me.
When the lord of the Geats, Hrethel's son,
sees those gifts of gold, he will know
that I found a noble giver of rings
and enjoyed his favour for as long as I lived.
1180 And, O Hrothgar, let renowned Unferth
have the ancient treasure, the razor sharp
ornamented sword; and I will make my name
with Hrunting, or death will destroy me."

After these words the leader of the Geats
1185 dived bravely from the bank, did not even
wait for an answer; the seething water
received the warrior. A full day elapsed
before he could perceive the bottom of the lake.

She who had guarded the lake's length and breadth
1190 for fifty years, vindictive, fiercely ravenous for blood,
soon realized that one of the race of men
was looking down into the monsters' lair.
Then she grasped him, clutched the Geat
in her ghastly claws; and yet she did not
1195 so much as scratch his skin; his coat of mail
protected him; she could not penetrate
the linked metal rings with her loathsome fingers.
Then the sea-wolf dived to the bottom-most depths,
swept the prince to the place where she lived,

1200 so that he, for all his courage, could not
wield a weapon; too many wondrous creatures
harassed him as he swam; many sea-serpents
with savage tusks tried to bore through his corslet,
the monsters molested him. Then the hero saw
1205 that he had entered some loathsome hall
in which there was no water to impede him,
a vaulted chamber where the floodrush
could not touch him. A light caught his eye,
a lurid flame flickering brightly.
1210 Then the brave man saw the sea-monster,
fearsome, infernal; he whirled his blade,
swung his arm with all his strength,
and the ring-hilted sword sang a greedy war-song
on the monster's head. Then that guest realized
1215 that his gleaming blade could not bite into her flesh,
break open her bone-chamber; its edge failed Beowulf
when he needed it; yet it had endured
many a combat, sheared often through the helmet,
split the corslet of a fated man; for the first time
1220 that precious sword failed to live up to its name.
Then, resolute, Hygelac's kinsman took his courage
in both hands, trusted in his own strength.
Angrily the warrior hurled Hrunting away,
the damascened sword with serpent patterns on its hilt;
1225 tempered and steel-edged, it lay useless on the earth.
Beowulf trusted in his own strength,
the might of his hand. So must any man
who hopes to gain long-lasting fame
in battle; he must risk his life, regardless.
1230 Then the prince of the Geats seized the shoulder
of Grendel's mother—he did not mourn their feud;
when they grappled, that brave man in his fury
flung his mortal foe to the ground.
Quickly she came back at him, locked him
1235 in clinches and clutched at him fearsomely.
Then the greatest of warriors stumbled and fell.
She dropped on her hall-guest, drew her dagger,
broad and gleaming; she wanted to avenge her son,
her only offspring. The woven corslet
1240 that covered his shoulders saved Beowulf's life,
denied access to both point and edge.
Then Ecgtheow's son, leader of the Geats,
would have died far under the wide earth
had not his corslet, his mighty chain-mail,
1245 guarded him, and had not holy God
granted him victory; the wise Lord,
Ruler of the Heavens, settled the issue
easily after the hero had scrambled to his feet.
Then Beowulf saw among weapons an invincible sword
1250 wrought by the giants, massive and double-edged,
the joy of many warriors; that sword was matchless,
well-tempered and adorned, forged in a finer age,
only it was so huge that no man but Beowulf
could hope to handle it in the quick of combat.
1255 Ferocious in battle, the defender of the Scyldings
grasped the ringed hilt, swung the ornamented sword
despairing of his life—he struck such a savage blow
that the sharp blade slashed through her neck,
smashed the vertebrae; it severed her head
1260 from the fated body; she fell at his feet.
The sword was bloodstained; Beowulf rejoiced.
A light gleamed; the chamber was illumined
as if the sky's bright candle were shining
from heaven. Hygelac's thane inspected
1265 the vaulted room, then walked round the walls,
fierce and resolute, holding the weapon firmly
by the hilt. The sword was not too large
for the hero's grasp, but he was eager to avenge
at once all Grendel's atrocities, . . .
1270 But the resolute warrior
had already repaid him to such a degree
that he now saw Grendel lying on his death-bed,
his life's-blood drained because of the wound
he had sustained in battle at Heorot. Then Grendel's corpse
1275 received a savage blow at the hero's hands,
his body burst open: Beowulf lopped off his head.
At once the wise men, anxiously gazing at
the lake with Hrothgar, saw that the water
had begun to chop and churn, that the waves
1280 were stained with blood. The grey-haired Scyldings
discussed that bold man's fate, agreed
there was no hope of seeing that brave thane again—
no chance that he would come, rejoicing in victory,
before their renowned king; it seemed certain
1285 to all but a few that the sea-wolf had destroyed him.
Then the ninth hour came. The noble Scyldings
left the headland; the gold-friend of men
returned to Heorot; the Geats, sick at heart,
sat down and stared at the lake.
1290 Hopeless, they yet hoped to set eyes
on their dear lord.
Then the battle-sword
began to melt like a gory icicle
because of the monster's blood. Indeed,
it was a miracle to see it thaw entirely,

1295 as does ice when the Father (He who ordains
all times and seasons) breaks the bonds of frost,
unwinds the flood fetters; He is the true Lord.
The leader of the Geats took none of the treasures
away from the chamber—though he saw many
there—
1300 except the monster's head and the gold-adorned
sword-hilt; the blade itself had melted,
the patterned sword had burnt, so hot was that blood,
so poisonous the monster who had died in the cave.
He who had survived the onslaught of his enemies
1305 was soon on his way, swimming up through the
water;
when the evil monster ended his days on earth,
left this transitory life, the troubled water
and all the lake's expanse was purged of its impurity.
Then the fearless leader of the seafarers
1310 swam to the shore, exulting in his plunder,
the heavy burdens he had brought with him.
The intrepid band of thanes hurried towards him,
giving thanks to God, rejoicing
to see their lord safe and sound of limb.
1315 The brave man was quickly relieved of his helmet
and corslet.
The angry water under the clouds,
the lake stained with battle-blood, at last became
calm.
Then they left the lake with songs on their lips,
retraced their steps along the winding paths
1320 and narrow tracks; it was no easy matter
for those courageous men, bold as kings,
to carry the head away from the cliff
overlooking the lake. With utmost difficulty
four of the thanes bore Grendel's head
1325 to the gold-hall on a battle-pole;
thus the fourteen Geats, unbroken
in spirit and eager in battle, very soon
drew near to Heorot; with them, that bravest
of brave men crossed the plain towards the mead-
hall.
1330 Then the fearless leader of the thanes,
covered with glory, matchless in battle,
once more entered Heorot to greet Hrothgar.
Grendel's head was carried by the hair
onto the floor where the warriors were drinking,
1335 a ghastly thing paraded before the heroes and the
queen.
Men stared at that wondrous spectacle. . . .

(Beowulf tells Hrothgar about the underwater fight.)

Then the golden hilt, age-old work of giants,
was given to Hrothgar, the grizzled warrior,
the warlike lord; wrought by master-smiths,
1340 it passed into the hands of the Danish prince
once the demons died; for that embittered fiend,
enemy of God, guilty of murder
had abandoned this world—and so had his mother.
Thus the hilt was possessed by the best
1345 of earthly kings between the two seas,
the best of those who bestowed gold on Norse men.
Hrothgar spoke, first examining the hilt,
the ancient heirloom. On it was engraved
the origins of strife in time immemorial,
1350 when the tide of rising water drowned
the race of giants; their end was horrible;
they were opposed to the Eternal Lord,
and their reward was the downpour and the flood.
Also, on the sword-guards of pure gold,
1355 it was recorded in runic letters, as is the custom,
for whom that sword, finest of blades,
with twisted hilt and serpentine patterning
had first been made.
Then Healfdene's wise son
lifted his voice—everyone listened:
1360 "This land's grizzled guardian, who promotes truth
and justice amongst his people, and forgets nothing
though the years pass, can say for certain that this man
is much favoured by fate! Beowulf my friend,
your name is echoed in every country
1365 to earth's end. You wear your enormous might
with wisdom and with dignity. I shall keep
my promise made when last we spoke. You will
beyond doubt be the shield of the Geats
for days without number, and a source
1370 of strength to warriors.
Heremod was hardly that
to Ecgwala's sons, the glorious Scyldings;
he grew to spread slaughter and destruction
rather than happiness amongst the Danish people.
In mad rage he murdered his table-companions,
1375 his most loyal followers; it came about
that the great prince cut himself off
from all earthly pleasures, though God had endowed
him
with strength and power above all other men,
and had sustained him. For all that, his heart
1380 was filled with savage blood-lust. He never gave
gifts to the Danes, to gain glory. He lived joyless,
agony racked him; he was long an affliction
to his people. Be warned, Beowulf,

learn the nature of nobility. I who tell you
1385 this story am many winters old.
It is a miracle
how the mighty Lord in his generosity
gives wisdom and land and high estate
to people on earth; all things are in His power.
At times he allows a noble man's mind to experience
1390 happiness, grants he should rule over a pleasant,
prosperous country, a stronghold of men,
makes subject to him regions of earth,
a wide kingdom, until in his stupidity
there is no end to his ambition.
1395 His life is unruffled—neither old age
nor illness afflict him, no unhappiness
gnaws at his heart, in his land no hatred
flares up in mortal feuds, but all the world
bends to his will. He suffers no setbacks
1400 until the seed of arrogance is sown and grows
within him, while still the watchman slumbers;
how deeply the soul's guardian sleeps
when a man is enmeshed in matters of this world;
the evil archer stands close with his drawn bow,
1405 his bristling quiver. Then the poisoned shaft
pierces his mind under his helmet
and he does not know how to resist
the devil's insidious, secret temptations.
What had long contented him now seems insufficient;
1410 he becomes embittered, begins to hoard
his treasures, never parts with gold rings
in ceremonial splendour; he soon forgets
his destiny and disregards the honours
given him of God, the Ruler of Glory.
1415 In time his transient body wizens and withers,
and dies as fate decrees; then another man
succeeds to his throne who gives treasures and heirlooms
with great generosity; *he* is not obsessed with suspicions.
Arm yourself, dear Beowulf, best of men,
1420 against such diseased thinking; always swallow pride;
remember, renowned warrior, what is more worthwhile—
gain everlasting. Today and tomorrow
you will be in your prime; but soon you will die,
in battle or in bed; either fire or water,
1425 the fearsome elements, will embrace you,
or you will succumb to the sword's flashing edge,
or to the arrow's flight, or to extreme old age;
then your eyes, once bright, will be clouded over;
all too soon, O warrior, death will destroy you.

1430 I have ruled the Ring-Danes under the skies
for fifty years, shielded them in war
from many tribes of men in this world,
from swords and from ash-spears, and the time had come
when I thought I had no enemies left on earth.
1435 All was changed utterly, gladness
became grief, after Grendel,
my deadly adversary, invaded Heorot.
His visitations caused me continual pain.
Thus I thank the Creator, the Eternal Lord,
1440 that after our afflictions I have lived to see,
to see with my own eyes this blood-stained head.
Now, Beowulf, brave in battle,
go to your seat and enjoy the feast;
tomorrow we shall share many treasures."
1445 The Geat, full of joy, straightway went
to find his seat as Hrothgar had suggested.
Then, once again, as so often before,
a great feast was prepared for the brave warriors
sitting in the hall.
The shadows of night
1450 settled over the retainers. The company arose;
the grey-haired man, the old Scylding,
wanted to retire. And the Geat, the shield-warrior,
was utterly exhausted, his bones ached for sleep.
At once the chamberlain—he who courteously
1455 saw to all such needs as a thane,
a travelling warrior, had in those days—
showed him, so limb-weary, to his lodging.
Then Beowulf rested; the building soared,
spacious and adorned with gold; the guest
1460 slept within until the black raven gaily
proclaimed sunrise. Bright light
chased away the shadows of night.
Then the warriors
hastened, the thanes were eager to return
1465 to their own people; the brave seafarer
longed to see his ship, so far from that place.
Then the bold Geat ordered that Hrunting,
that sword beyond price, be brought before Unferth;
he begged him to take it back and thanked him
for the loan of it; he spoke of it as an ally
1470 in battle, and assured Unferth he did not
underrate it: what a brave man he was!
After this the warriors, wearing their chain-mail,
were eager to be off; their leader,
so dear to the Danes, walked to the daïs
1475 where Hrothgar was sitting, and greeted him.
Beowulf, the son of Ecgtheow, spoke:

"Now we seafarers, who have sailed here from far,
beg to tell you we are eager
to return to Hygelac. We have been happy here,
1480 hospitably entertained; you have treated us kindly.
If I can in any way win more of your affection,
O ruler of men, than I have done already,
I will come at once, eager for combat.
If news reaches me over the seas
1485 that you are threatened by those around you
(just as before enemies endangered you)
I will bring thousands of thanes,
all heroes, to help you. I know that Hygelac,
lord of the Geats, guardian of his people,
1490 will advance me in word and deed
although he is young, so that I can back
these promises with spear shafts, and serve you
with all my strength where you need men.
Should Hrethric, Hrothgar's son, wish
1495 to visit the court of the Geatish king,
he will be warmly welcomed. Strong men
should seek fame in far-off lands."
Hrothgar replied: "The wise Lord put these words
into your mind; I have never heard a warrior
1500 speak more sagely while still so young.
You are very strong and very shrewd,
you speak with discerning. If your leader,
Hrethel's son, guardian of the people,
were to lose his life by illness or by iron,
1505 by spear or grim swordplay, and if you survived him,
it seems to me that the Geats could not choose
a better man for king, should you wish to rule
the land of your kinsmen. Beloved Beowulf,
the longer I know you, the more I like your spirit.
1510 Because of your exploit, your act of friendship,
there will be an end to the gross outrages,
the old enmity between Geats and Danes;
they will learn to live in peace. . . ."

(Hrothgar gives Beowulf twelve rich gifts and bids him an affectionate farewell.)

Then Beowulf the warrior,
1515 proudly adorned with gold, crossed the plain,
exulting in his treasure. The ship
rode at anchor, waiting for its owner.
Then, as they walked, they often praised
Hrothgar's generosity. He was an altogether
1520 faultless king, until old age deprived him
of his strength, as it does most men.
Then that troop of brave young retainers
came to the water's edge; they wore ring-mail,
woven corslets. And the same watchman
1525 who had seen them arrive saw them now returning.
He did not insult them, ask for explanations,
but galloped from the cliff-top to greet the guests;
he said that those warriors in gleaming armour,
so eager to embark, would be welcomed home.
1530 Then the spacious ship, with its curved prow,
standing ready on the shore, was laden with armour,
with horses and treasure. The mast towered
over Hrothgar's precious heirlooms.
Beowulf gave a sword bound round with gold
1535 to the ship's watchman—a man who thereafter
was honoured on the mead-bench that much the more
on account of this heirloom.
The ship surged forward,
butted the waves in deep waters;
it drew away from the shores of the Scyldings.
1540 Then a sail, a great sea-garment, was fastened
with guys to the mast; the timbers groaned;
the boat was not blown off its course
by the stiff sea-breezes. The ship swept
over the waves; foaming at the bows,
1545 the boat with its well-wrought prow sped
over the waters, until at last the Geats
set eyes on the cliffs of their own country,
the familiar headlands; the vessel pressed forward,
pursued by the wind—it ran up onto dry land.
1550 The harbour guardian hurried down to the shore;
for many days he had scanned the horizon,
anxious to see those dear warriors once more.
He tethered the spacious sea-steed with ropes
(it rode on its painter restlessly)
1555 so that the rolling waves could not wrench it away.
Then Beowulf commanded that the peerless treasures,
the jewels and plated gold, be carried up from the shore.
He had not to go far to find the treasure-giver,
Hygelac son of Hrethel, for his house and the hall
1560 for his companions stood quite close to the sea-wall. . . .
Then Beowulf and his warrior band walked
across the sand, tramped over
the wide foreshore; the world's candle shone,
the sun hastening from the south. The men hurried too
1565 when they were told that the guardian of thanes,
Ongentheow's slayer, the excellent young king,
held court in the hall, distributing rings.
Hygelac was informed at once of Beowulf's arrival—

that the shield of warriors, his comrade in battle,
1570 had come back alive to the fortified enclosure,
was heading for the hall unscathed after combat.
Space on the benches for Beowulf and his band
was hastily arranged, as Hygelac ordered.
The guardian of thanes formally greeted
1575 that loyal man; then they sat down—
the unfated hero opposite the king,
kinsman facing kinsman. Hæreth's daughter[19]
carried mead-cups round the hall,
spoke kindly to the warriors, handed the stoups
1580 of wine to the thanes. Hygelac began
to ask his companion courteous questions
in the high hall; he was anxious to hear
all that had happened to the seafaring Geats: . . .

(Beowulf begins to tell about his exploits in Denmark. He digresses to report some news that will interest Hygelac: that Hrothgar has betrothed his daughter Freawaru to Ingeld, prince of the Heathobards, in an effort to heal a long-standing feud. Beowulf predicts that this well-intentioned effort at peacemaking will fail.

He then picks up his story again and tells how he killed Grendel and Grendel's mother.)

Then Beowulf caused to be brought in
1585 a standard bearing the image of a boar,
together with a helmet towering in battle,
a grey corslet, and a noble sword; he said:
"Hrothgar, the wise king, gave me
these trappings and purposely asked me
1590 to tell you their history: he said that Heorogar,
lord of the Scyldings, long owned them.
Yet he has not endowed his own brave son,
Heoroweard,[20] with this armour, much
as he loves him. Make good use of everything!"
1595 I heard that four bays, apple-brown,
were brought into the hall after the armour—
swift as the wind, identical. Beowulf gave them
as he gave the treasures. So should a kinsman do,
and never weave nets with underhand subtlety
1600 to ensnare others, never have designs
on a close comrade's life. His nephew,
brave in battle, was loyal to Hygelac;
each man was mindful of the other's pleasure.
I heard that he gave Hygd the collar,
1605 the wondrous ornament with which Wealhtheow,
daughter of the prince, had presented him,
and gave her three horses also, graceful creatures
with brightly-coloured saddles; Hygd
wore that collar, her breast was adorned. . . .
1610 Then the guardian of thanes, the famous king,
ordered that Hrethel's gold-adorned heirloom
be brought in; no sword was so treasured
in all Geatland; he laid it in Beowulf's lap,
and gave him seven thousand hides of land,
1615 a hall and princely throne. Both men
had inherited land and possessions
in that country; but the more spacious kingdom
had fallen to Hygelac, who was of higher rank.

II

In later days, after much turmoil,
1620 things happened in this way: when Hygelac lay dead
and murderous battle-blades had beaten down
the shield of his son Heardred,[21]
and when the warlike Swedes, savage warriors,
had hunted him down amongst his glorious people,
1625 attacked Hereric's[22] nephew with hatred,
the great kingdom of the Geats passed
into Beowulf's hands. He had ruled it well
for fifty winters—he was a wise king,
a grizzled guardian of the land—when, on dark
nights,
1630 a dragon began to terrify the Geats:
he lived on a cliff, kept watch over a hoard
in a high stone barrow; below, there was
a secret path; a man strayed
into this barrow by chance, seized
1635 some of the pagan treasures, stole drinking
vessels. . . .
There was conflict once more after the dragon
awoke; intrepid, he slid swiftly
along by the rock, and found the footprints
of the intruder; . . .
1640 He realized at once that one of the race of men
had discovered the gold, the glorious treasure.
Restlessly the dragon waited for darkness;
the guardian of the hoard was bursting with rage,
he meant to avenge the vessel's theft
1645 with fire.

19. *Haereth's daughter,* the young queen, Hygd.
20. *Heoroweard* (hā′ə rō wā′ärd)
21. *Heardred* (hā′ärd red)
22. *Hereric* (her′rə rik)

Then daylight failed
as the dragon desired; he could no longer
confine himself to the cave but flew in a ball
of flame, burning for vengeance. The Geats
were filled with dread as he began his flight;
1650 it swiftly ended in disaster for their lord.
Then the dragon began to breathe forth fire,
to burn fine buildings; flame tongues flickered,
terrifying men; the loathsome winged creature
meant to leave the whole place lifeless.
1655 Everywhere the violence of the dragon, the venom
of that hostile one, was clearly to be seen—
how he had wrought havoc, hated and humiliated
the Geatish people. Then, before dawn he rushed
back
to his hidden lair and the treasure hoard.
1660 He had girdled the Geats with fire,
with ravening flames; he relied on his own strength,
and on the barrow and the cliff; his trust played him
false.
Then news of that terror was quickly brought
to Beowulf, that flames enveloped
1665 his own hall, best of buildings,
and the gift-throne of the Geats. That good man
was choked with intolerable grief.
Wise that he was, he imagined
he must have angered God, the Lord Eternal,
1670 by ignoring some ancient law; he was seldom
dispirited, but now his heart was like lead.
The fire dragon had destroyed the fortified hall,
the people's stronghold, and laid waste with flames
the land by the sea. The warlike king,
1675 prince of the Geats, planned to avenge this.
The protector of warriors, leader of men,
instructed the smith to forge a curious shield
made entirely of iron; he well knew
that a linden shield would not last long
1680 against the flames. The eminent prince
was doomed to reach the end of his days on earth,
his life in this world. So too was the dragon,
though he had guarded the hoard for generations.
Then the giver of gold disdained
1685 to track the dragon with a troop
of warlike men; he did not shrink
from single combat, nor did he set much store
by the fearless dragon's power, for had he not before
experienced danger, again and again
1690 survived the storm of battle, beginning with that time
when, blessed with success, he cleansed
Hrothgar's hall, and crushed in battle
the monster and his vile mother? . . .

(Beowulf continues to think back over other dangers he has survived, including the battle in Frisia in which Hygelac was killed. After avenging his uncle's death, Beowulf escaped by swimming, "bearing no fewer than thirty corslets." Hygelac's widow had then offered him the throne of the Geats, but he refused it and instead helped Hygelac's young son, Heardred, to rule. After Heardred was killed in a feud between Geats and Swedes, Beowulf became king. The feuds had continued for many years.)

Thus the son of Ecgtheow had survived
1695 these feuds, these fearful battles, these acts
of single combat, up to that day
when he was destined to fight against the dragon.
Then in fury the leader of the Geats set out

OF CRITICAL INTEREST

Why stories of monsters?

"Let me now consider why the poet chose for his central subject a story of monster-slaying, using heroic stories merely as illustration or as background. It is no longer usual for scholars to spend time regretting that he did so, or accusing him of a perverted sense of proportion. He was composing for men of his own day, and he doubtless had good reason for his choice of theme. His main story would be as real to his audience as would have been an account of the strife for the Danish throne among the members of the Scylding dynasty; and in the course of it, the poet has placed the race of monsters in relationship to a Christian universe, and has shown that they can be overcome by human beings of courage and fortitude who fight them with faith in God. He has shown that humanity is not left helpless in the hands of the evil powers. That was no trivial theme to the men of that day.

"Yet one may wonder why he was so concerned that his hearers should at the same time have present in their minds certain stories about human conflicts. . . . The poet is making a contrast, I think, not between unreal adventures and realistic stories, but one between noble, disinterested deeds for the good of the human race and actions of violence and passion, arising from divided loyalties, or, worse still, from ambition and treachery."

Abridged and adapted from *The Audience of Beowulf* by Dorothy Whitelock.

with eleven to search for the winged serpent.
1700 By then Beowulf knew the cause of the feud,
bane of men; the famous cup
had come to him through the hands of its finder.
The unfortunate slave who first brought about
such strife made the thirteenth man
1705 in that company—cowed and disconsolate,
he had to be their guide. Much against his will,
he conducted them to the entrance of the cave,
an earth-hall full of filigree work
and fine adornments close by the sea,
1710 the fretting waters. The vile guardian,
the serpent who had long lived under the earth,
watched over the gold, alert; he who hoped
to gain it bargained with his own life.
Then the brave king sat on the headland,
1715 the gold-friend of the Geats wished success
to his retainers. His mind was most mournful,
angry, eager for slaughter; fate hovered
over him, so soon to fall on that old man,
to seek out his hidden spirit, to split
1720 life and body; flesh was to confine
the soul of the king only a little longer. . . .

(Beowulf recalls his earlier life and various tragic events in the history of the Geatish royal family. He tells how he always loyally fought for Hygelac, and when Hygelac was slain, avenged his death by killing the champion of the Franks.)

"... Now the shining edge,
hand and tempered sword, shall engage in battle
for the treasure hoard. I fought many battles
1725 when I was young; yet I will fight again,
the old guardian of my people, and achieve
a mighty exploit if the evil dragon dares
confront me, dares come out of the earth-cave!"
Then he addressed each of the warriors,
1730 the brave heroes, his dear companions,
a last time: "I would not wield a sword
against the dragon if I could grasp this hideous being
with my hands (and thus make good my boast),
as once I grasped the monster Grendel;
1735 but I anticipate blistering battle-fire,
venomous breath; therefore I have with me
my shield and corslet. I will not give an inch
to the guardian of the mound, but at that barrow
it will befall us both as fate ordains,
1740 every man's master. . . ."

Then the bold warrior, stern-faced beneath his helmet,
stood up with his shield; sure of his own strength,
he walked in his corslet towards the cliff;
the way of the coward is not thus!
1745 Then that man endowed with noble qualities,
he who had braved countless battles, weathered
the thunder when warrior troops clashed together,
saw a stone arch set in the cliff
through which a stream spurted; steam rose
1750 from the boiling water; he could not stay long
in the hollow near the hoard for fear
of being scorched by the dragon's flames.
Then, such was his fury, the leader of the Geats
threw out his chest and gave a great roar,
1755 the brave man bellowed; his voice, renowned
in battle, hammered the grey rock's anvil.
The guardian of the hoard knew the voice for human;
violent hatred stirred within him. Now no time
remained to entreat for peace. At once
1760 the monster's breath, burning battle vapour,
issued from the barrow; the earth itself snarled.
The lord of the Geats, standing under the cliff,
raised his shield against the fearsome stranger;
then that sinuous creature spoiled
1765 for the fight. The brave and warlike king
had already drawn his keen-edged sword,
(it was an ancient heirloom); a terror of each other
lurked in the hearts of the two antagonists.
While the winged creature coiled himself up,
1770 the friend and lord of men stood unflinching
by his shield; Beowulf waited ready armed.
Then, fiery and twisted, the dragon swiftly
shrithed towards its fate. The shield protected
the life and body of the famous prince
1775 for far less time than he had looked for.
It was the first occasion in all his life
that fate did not decree triumph for him
in battle. The lord of the Geats raised
his arm, and struck the mottled monster
1780 with his vast ancestral sword; but the bright blade's
edge was blunted by the bone, bit
less keenly than the desperate king required.
The defender of the barrow bristled with anger
at the blow, spouted murderous fire, so that flames
1785 leapt through the air. The gold-friend of the Geats
did not boast of famous victories; his proven sword,
the blade bared in battle, had failed him
as it ought not to have done. That great Ecgtheow's
greater son had to journey on from this world

1790 was no pleasant matter; much against his will,
he was obliged to make his dwelling
elsewhere—sooner or later every man must leave
this transitory life. It was not long
before the fearsome ones closed again.
1795 The guardian of the hoard was filled with fresh hope,
his breast was heaving; he who had ruled a nation
suffered agony, surrounded by flame.
And Beowulf's companions, sons of nobles—
so far from protecting him in a troop together,
1800 unflinching in the fright—shrank back into the forest
scared for their own lives. One man alone
obeyed his conscience. The claims of kinship
can never be ignored by a right-minded man.
His name was Wiglaf, a noble warrior,
1805 Weohstan's[23] son, kinsman of Ælfhere,
a leader of the Swedes;[24] he saw that his lord,
helmeted, was tormented by the intense heat.
Then he recalled the honours Beowulf had bestowed
on him—the wealthy citadel of the Wægmundings,[25]
1810 the rights to land his father owned before him.
He could not hold back then; he grasped the round,
yellow shield; he drew his ancient sword, . . .
This was the first time
the young warrior had weathered the battle storm,

23. *Weohstan* (wā′ ō stän)
24. Wiglaf and his father Weohstan were also kinsmen of Beowulf. All were members of the Wægmunding family.
25. *Wægmundings* (wag′ mu̇n dingz)

OF CRITICAL INTEREST

How is the poem structured?

"We must dismiss from mind the notion that *Beowulf* is a 'narrative poem,' that it tells a tale or intends to tell a tale sequentially. The poem 'lacks steady advance': so one critic writes. But the poem was not meant to advance, steadily or unsteadily. It is essentially a balance, an opposition of ends and beginnings. In its simplest terms it is a contrasted description of two moments in a great life, rising and setting; an elaboration of the ancient and intensely moving contrast between youth and age, first achievement and final death."

Adapted from "*Beowulf:* The Monsters and the Critics" by J. R. R. Tolkien, which originally appeared in *Proceedings of the British Academy XXII*, 1936.

1815 standing at the shoulder of his lord.
His courage did not melt, nor did his kinsman's sword
fail him in the fight. The dragon found that out
when they met in mortal combat.

(Wiglaf tries unsuccessfully to rally his retainers to join in the fight.)

Then that man fought his way through the fumes,
1820 went helmeted to help his lord. He shouted out:
"Brave Beowulf, may success attend you—
for in the days when you were young, you swore
that so long as you lived you would never allow
your fame to decay; now, O resolute king,
1825 renowned for your exploits, you must guard your life
with all your skill. I shall assist you."
At this the seething dragon attacked a second time;
shimmering with fire the venomous visitor fell on his foes,
the men he loathed. With waves of flame, he burnt
1830 the shield right up to its boss; Wiglaf's
corslet afforded him no protection whatsoever.
But the young warrior still fought bravely, sheltered
behind his kinsman's shield after his own
was consumed by flames. Still the battle-king
1835 set his mind on deeds of glory; with prodigious strength
he struck a blow so violent that his sword stuck
in the dragon's skull. But Nægling snapped!
Beowulf's old grey-hued sword
failed him in the fight. Fate did not ordain
1840 that the iron edge should assist him
in that struggle; Beowulf's hand was too strong.
Indeed I have been told that he overtaxed
each and every weapon, hardened by blood, that he bore
into battle; his own great strength betrayed him.
1845 Then the dangerous dragon, scourge of the Geats,
was intent a third time upon attack; he rushed
at the renowned man when he saw an opening:
fiery, battle-grim, he gripped the hero's neck
between his sharp teeth; Beowulf was bathed
1850 in blood; it spurted out in streams.
Then, I have heard, the loyal thane
alongside the Geatish king displayed great courage,
strength, and daring, as was his nature.
To assist his kinsman, that man in mail
1855 aimed not for the head but lunged at the belly
of their vile enemy (in so doing his hand
was badly burnt); his sword, gleaming and adorned,

sank in up to the hilt and at once the flames
began to abate. The king still had control then
1860 over his senses; he drew the deadly knife,
keen-edged in battle, that he wore on his corslet;
then the lord of the Geats dispatched the dragon.
Thus they had killed their enemy—their courage
enabled them—the brave kinsmen together
1865 had destroyed him. Such should a man,
a thane, be in time of necessity!

That was the last
of all the king's achievements, his last
exploit in the world. Then the wound
the earth-dragon had inflicted with his teeth
1870 began to burn and swell; very soon he
was suffering intolerable pain as the poison
boiled within him. Then the wise leader
tottered forward and slumped on a seat
by the barrow; he gazed at the work of giants,
1875 saw how the ancient earthwork contained
stone arches supported by columns.
Then, with his own hands, the best of thanes
refreshed the renowned prince with water,
washed his friend and lord, blood-stained
1880 and battle-weary, and unfastened his helmet.

Beowulf began to speak, he defied
his mortal injury; he was well aware
that his life's course, with all its delights,
had come to an end; his days on earth
1885 were exhausted, death drew very close:
"It would have made me happy, at this time,
to pass on war-gear to my son, had I
been granted an heir to succeed me,
sprung of my seed. I have ruled the Geats
1890 for fifty winters; no king of any
neighbouring tribe has dared to attack me
with swords, or sought to cow and subdue me.
But in my own home I have awaited
my destiny, cared well for my dependants,
1895 and I have not sought trouble, or sworn
any oaths unjustly. Because of all these things
I can rejoice, drained now by death-wounds;
for the Ruler of Men will have no cause to blame me
after I have died on the count that I deprived
1900 other kinsmen of their lives. Now hurry,
dear Wiglaf; rummage the hoard
under the grey rock, for the dragon sleeps,
riddled with wounds, robbed of his treasure.
Be as quick as you can so that I may see
1905 the age-old golden treasure, and examine
all the priceless, shimmering stones; once I
have set eyes on such a store, it will be
more easy for me to die, to abandon
the life and land that have so long been mine." . . .

(Wiglaf hastens into the cavern, where he finds a hoard of golden vessels, wall-hangings, and adornments, "the antique work of giants." He takes as much as he can carry.)

1910 Then at last he came, carrying the treasures,
to the renowned king; his lord's life-blood
was ebbing; once more he splashed him
with water, until Beowulf revived a little,
began to frame his thoughts.

Gazing at the gold,
1915 the warrior, the sorrowing king, said:
"With these words I thank
the King of Glory, the Eternal Lord,
the Ruler, for all the treasures here before me,
that in my lifetime I have been able
1920 to gain them for the Geats.
And now that I have bartered my old life
for this treasure hoard, you must serve
and inspire our people. I will not long be with you.
Command the battle-warriors, after the funeral fire,
1925 to build a fine barrow overlooking the sea;
let it tower high on Whaleness
as a reminder to my people.

OF CRITICAL INTEREST

Why do Beowulf's men desert him?

"The desertion of the thanes is required, to give full plausibility to the representation of Beowulf's mortal peril. The hero's men had not deserted him in his fight with Grendel, nor even at the Haunted Mere, when they thought him slain. It is the panic of all but one of his bravest men which convinces us that, in the dragon, he faces a foe far more terrible than Grendel or Grendel's dam. The intervention of Wiglaf is equally necessary, both to demonstrate the extremity of the hero's peril and to supply him, in his darkest hour, with a companion as loyal as he himself had been to Hygelac. Moreover, it is the devoted gallantry of Wiglaf which justifies Beowulf's sacrifice. . . ."

From *The Art of Beowulf* by Arthur G. Brodeur.

And let it be known as Beowulf's barrow
to all seafarers, to men who steer their ships
1930 from far over the swell and the saltspray."
Then the prince, bold of mind, detached
his golden collar and gave it to Wiglaf,
the young spear-warrior, and also his helmet
adorned with gold, his ring and his corslet,
1935 and enjoined him to use them well:
"You are the last survivor of our family,
the Wægmundings; fate has swept
all my kinsmen, those courageous warriors,
to their doom. I must follow them."
1940 Those were the warrior's last words. . . .
Not long after that
the lily-livered ones slunk out of the wood;
ten cowardly oath-breakers, who had lacked
the courage to let fly with their spears
1945 as their lord so needed, came forward together;
overcome with shame, they carried their shields
and weapons to where their leader lay;
they gazed at Wiglaf. That warrior, bone-weary,
knelt beside the shoulders of his lord; he tried
1950 to rouse him with water; it was all in vain.
For all his efforts, his longing, he could not
detain the life of his leader on earth,
or alter anything the Ruler ordained.
God in His wisdom governed the deeds
1955 of all men, as He does now.
Then the young warrior was not at a loss
for well-earned, angry words for those cowards.
Wiglaf, Weohstan's son, sick at heart,
eyed those faithless men and said:
1960 "He who does not wish to disguise the truth
can indeed say that—when it was a question
not of words but war—our lord completely wasted
the treasures he gave you, the same war-gear
you stand in over there, . . ."
1965 Then Wiglaf ordered that Beowulf's great feat
be proclaimed in the stronghold, up along the cliff-edge,
where a troop of shield-warriors had waited all morning,
wondering sadly if their dear lord was dead,
or if he would return.
The man who galloped
1970 to the headland gave them the news at once;
he kept back nothing but called out:
"The lord of the Geats, he who gave joy
to all our people, lies rigid on his death-bed;
slaughtered by the dragon, he now sleeps;
1975 and his deadly enemy, slashed by the knife,
sleeps beside him; . . ."

(The messenger says that now that their king is dead, the Geats must expect the wars with their traditional enemies to be revived. He reviews events in the long-standing Geatish-Swedish feud. Then he continues:)

"Let us lose no time now
but go and gaze there upon our king
and carry him, who gave us rings,
1980 to the funeral pyre. And let us not grudge gold
to melt with that bold man, for we have a mighty hoard,
a mint of precious metal, bought with pain; . . .
Henceforth, fingers must grasp,
hands must hold, many a spear
1985 chill with the cold of morning; no sound of the harp
shall rouse the warriors but, craving for carrion,
the dark raven shall have its say
and tell the eagle how it fared at the feast
when, competing with the wolf, it laid bare the bones of corpses."
1990 Thus the brave messenger told of and foretold
harrowing times; and he was not far wrong.
Those events were fated. Every man in the troop
stood up, stained with tears, and set out
for Eagleness to see that strange spectacle.
1995 There they found him lifeless on the sand,
the soft bed where he slept, who often before
had given them rings; that good man's days
on earth were ended; the warrior-king,
lord of the Geats, had died a wondrous death.
2000 But first they saw a strange creature
there, a loathsome serpent lying
nearby; the fire-dragon, fierce
and mottled, was scorched by its own flames.
It measured fifty paces from head to tail; . . .
2005 Wiglaf, the son of Weohstan, said:
"Many thanes must often suffer
because of the will of one, as we do now.
We could not dissuade the king we loved,
or in any way restrain the lord of our land
2010 from drawing his sword against the gold-warden,
from letting him lie where he had long lain
and remain in his lair until the world's end;
but he fulfilled his high destiny. . . ."
Then the brave warrior, Weohstan's son,
2015 directed that orders be given to many men

(to all who owned houses, elders of the people)
to fetch wood from far to place beneath
their prince on the funeral pyre:
"Now flames,
the blazing fire, must devour the lord of warriors
2020 who often endured the iron-tipped arrow-shower,
when the dark cloud loosed by bow strings
broke above the shield-wall, quivering;
when the eager shaft, with its feather garb,
discharged its duty to the barb."

2025 I have heard that Weohstan's wise son
summoned from Beowulf's band his seven
best thanes, and went with those warriors
into the evil grotto; the man leading
the way grasped a brand. Then those retainers
2030 were not hesitant about rifling the hoard
as soon as they set eyes on any part of it,
lying unguarded, gradually rusting,
in that rock cavern; no man was conscience-stricken
about carrying out those priceless treasures
2035 as quickly as he could. Also, they pushed the dragon,
the serpent over the precipice; they let the waves take him,
the dark waters embrace the warden of the hoard.
Then the wagon was laden with twisted gold,
with treasures of every kind, and the king,
2040 the old battle-warrior, was borne to Whaleness.

Then, on the headland, the Geats prepared a mighty pyre
for Beowulf, hung round with helmets and shields
and shining mail, in accordance with his wishes;
and then the mourning warriors laid
2045 their dear lord, the famous prince, upon it.

And there on Whaleness, the heroes kindled
the most mighty of pyres; the dark wood-smoke
soared over the fire, the roaring flames
mingled with weeping—the winds' tumult subsided—
2050 until the body became ash, consumed even
to its core. The heart's cup overflowed;
they mourned their loss, the death of their lord.
And, likewise, a maiden of the Geats,
with her tresses swept up, intoned
2055 a dirge for Beowulf time after time,
declared she lived in dread of days to come
dark with carnage and keening, terror of the enemy,
humiliation and captivity.
Heaven swallowed the smoke.

Then the Geats built a barrow on the headland—
2060 it was high and broad, visible from far
to all seafarers; in ten days they built the beacon
for that courageous man; and they constructed
as noble an enclosure as wise men
could devise, to enshrine the ashes.
2065 They buried rings and brooches in the barrow,
all those adornments that brave men
had brought out from the hoard after Beowulf died.
They bequeathed the gleaming gold, treasure of men,
to the earth, and there it still remains
2070 as useless to men as it was before.

Then twelve brave warriors, sons of heroes,
rode round the barrow, sorrowing;
they mourned their king, chanted
an elegy, spoke about that great man:
2075 they exalted his heroic life, lauded
his daring deeds; it is fitting for a man,
when his lord and friend must leave this life,
to mouth words in his praise
and to cherish his memory.
2080 Thus the Geats, his hearth-companions,
grieved over the death of their lord;
they said that of all kings on earth
he was the kindest, the most gentle,
the most just to his people, the most eager for fame.

THE END

FULLER BROOCH, 9TH CENTURY, SILVER AND ENAMEL.
COURTESY OF THE TRUSTEES OF THE BRITISH MUSEUM.

BEOWULF AND ITS CRITICS

by Bruce Mitchell

OVER the years, *Beowulf* has been translated many times into modern verse and prose, and hundreds of books and articles have been written about it in many languages. Scholars and critics have produced a bewildering variety of theories about the *Beowulf* poet's ideas and aims.

Clearly there is something peculiar about a poem which produces such a variety of reactions. It is at least in part a failure of communication. This is not the poet's fault but the result of our ignorance of the conventions within which Anglo-Saxon poems were written. We do not know who wrote *Beowulf*, or when, where, and by whom it was first heard. What the author took for granted in his audience we can never determine with any accuracy.

Let us reverse the roles. Let us imagine the scholarly Northumbrian monk the Venerable Bede placed in front of a television set to look at a series of Perry Mason stories. We can suppose that Bede might be convinced that he was watching a religious rite designed to placate some twentieth-century god. He might even detect in them allegories of the struggle between right and wrong.

When and Where Was Beowulf *Composed?*

Beowulf survives only in a single manuscript, dating from about the year 1000 and now in the British Museum. In 1731, parts of this manuscript were damaged by fire, and in later years sections crumbled away. Fortunately, however, an Icelandic scholar by the name of Thorkelin had copied the poem in 1786, when most of it could still be made out, and this copy exists undamaged.

No exact date can be given for the composition of *Beowulf*, but scholars agree that it was composed considerably earlier than the date of the manuscript in the British Museum. The mention of the death of Hygelac—an actual person whose death date (around 521) is known from reliable histories of the time—gives us an early limit. But other historical evidence suggests that the earliest date is after 680, when Germanic alliterative verse began to be used for Christian purposes. Some have argued that, since the poem glorifies the Danes, it is unlikely to have been written after 835, when the Danish raids on Anglo-Saxon England began in grim earnest. Examination of the language of the poem can do little more than confirm the possibility that it was composed between 680 and 800 (or perhaps later).

The view perhaps most current today is that *Beowulf* was composed in its present form by one poet who may or may not have inherited the plot ready-made. Even if we accept this assumption, we are by no means out of the wood; there are still many ways of interpreting the poem. The problem of authorship is insoluble, but we need not be unduly embarrassed by this. We can simply deal with the poem as it stands and assume that its text as found in the British Museum manuscript represents approximately the form given the story by one man—whether he was the original poet, or a kind of poet-editor, or a reciter of poetry who could adapt stories that already existed in verse.

The Aims of the Beowulf *Poet*

It seems reasonable to believe that one of the aims of the author was to entertain—we have sea-monsters, man-eating giants, and a fire-spouting dragon, alongside human kings and warriors; we have fighting and treasure, blood and jewels.

There is, however, much evidence for the belief that we are dealing with a somewhat more sophisticated poet than the mere teller of tales. But what aim had he other than entertainment? Did he intend to give us a view of man and of his place in the universe? If so, what view? The particular answer we choose to adopt will depend (among other things) on our attitude to two other problems—"the nature of the monsters" and "How Christian a poem is *Beowulf?*"

The Nature of the Monsters

Are Grendel, his mother, and the dragon anything more than the traditional characters of folk tales, fairy tales, or the old romances of chivalry? Many writers have claimed that they are more. The most usual view is that they are Foes of God—a view not hard to defend for Grendel and his mother, since the poet tells us they are descendants of Cain, whom God

Abridged and adapted from *Beowulf*, translated by Kevin Crossley-Holland and introduced by Bruce Mitchell.

drove far away from men for his sin in slaying his brother Abel, and since he actually calls Grendel "God's adversary."

But what of the dragon? If he is of the same kind as Grendel, why was Beowulf unable to defeat him too? To this question the usual answer is that Beowulf has lost the favor of God. Attempts to explain why have given rise to theories that Beowulf was being criticized by the poet. To some, however, the dragon is a foe of a different kind. Can he, they ask, be death, the foe no man can overcome until death is swallowed up in victory?

Christianity in Beowulf

How Christian is *Beowulf?* Indeed, what is Christian about it?

By the time *Beowulf* was composed, missionaries from Rome had reëstablished the Christian religion throughout much of Anglo-Saxon England. But the effect of the Christian message must have varied then, as it does today, from individual to individual. To some, conversion must have been a deep and lasting experience. To others it seems to have been an easy shift for reasons of convenience from a not very vital paganism which made little real impact on the heroic outlook. To some, earthly warfare became irreconcilable with the new faith, and the chronicles record stories of Anglo-Saxon kings who died rather than fight. On the other hand, there were churchmen who fought and died to save their country.

And what of the ordinary warrior? To what extent was the heroic code he held influenced by Christian ideas? The *comitatus*[1] duty of loyalty to one's lord survived the coming of Christianity. Late in the seventh century the church put homicide at a lord's command on a level with killing in battle as an act which demanded only a slight penance. Some churchmen accepted killing for the sake of vengeance until the middle of the eleventh century.

In considering what is Christian about *Beowulf*, we also need to remember that there was then a less critical attitude toward marvels and wonders. There might be a dragon around the corner; according to the Anglo-Saxon Chronicle, a generally accurate history kept for several hundred years, dragons flew over Northumbria in 793—portents of the Danish invasions when seen with hindsight. The stories of miracles told in the Lives of the Saints also emphasize the gulf between Christians of Anglo-Saxon England and those of today in this respect.

If our question is "What is obviously and unambiguously Christian in *Beowulf?*" the answer is "Nothing." There is no clear evidence in the poem that its author had any knowledge of the New Testament. Of course, we have to admit that it was Christian missionaries who brought to Britain the story of Cain and Abel and the good news of the power of God. Yet the absence of obvious Christian references remains a problem.

To some, *Beowulf* is the work of a recently converted pagan who has assimilated the Old Testament to the Germanic code. Such an assimilation would be a natural thing—both the Anglo-Saxons and the Jews of the Old Testament were "heroic" peoples, warlike, with loyalties to comrade, tribe, and lord, and with a love of jewels and precious metals. The qualities shown by the characters in *Beowulf* whom we are supposed to admire—qualities such as courage, generosity, and loyalty—have been valued by most peoples, regardless of creed.

Other critics have given the poem a more specifically Christian interpretation. Some have seen in it an allegory of salvation in the Christian sense. The Anglo-Saxon audience, one writer argues, had a taste for obscure allegory and riddles. To such an audience, all that was necessary was a clue sufficient to suggest the identification of Beowulf and the Christian Saviour. The clue, according to this writer, is the fact that Grendel and his mother are repeatedly described as inmates of Hell, powers of darkness, and so on. Thus the fight with Grendel betokens the Salvation of Man, the fight with Grendel's mother Christ's Resurrection and the Harrowing of Hell, and the fight with the dragon Christ's death. Such an interpretation is, I believe, possible, but the fact that allegory is elsewhere made explicit in Old English poetry argues against it, as does the lack of real Christian feeling.

Some recent writers have advanced the idea that Beowulf is being criticized by the poet. According to this view, Beowulf's final failure arose from his pride, his love of treasure, and his rejection of God's help.

In my opinion, this is a misreading of the poem. I would argue that Beowulf did exactly what one

1. *comitatus*, a band of warriors attached to the king by the strongest possible bonds of loyalty. The king's followers were supposed to fight and die for him. The king in turn was obligated to protect his warriors and reward them generously.

would expect of an heroic king in the circumstances. It is true that Hrothgar's homily (lines 1360–1429) warns Beowulf against pride and greed. But it ends with the reminder that Beowulf too must die. The fact that Beowulf dies is no reason for believing that he has been deserted by God or that he has done something wrong.

There are still other theories—for example, that the poem presents a criticism of the essential weakness of the society and the code of conduct it portrays. I myself am reluctant to read the poem in any such way. The final epitaph reads to me as a climax of praise, not an anticlimax of criticism:

> they said that of all the kings on earth
> he was the kindest, the most gentle,
> the most just to his people, the most eager for fame.

When I close my copy of *Beowulf,* I find myself in sympathy with the view that the poem is a mirror of noble conduct. But this is no more than an opinion held by one twentieth-century reader at one point in time as he reacts to the poem, and in the end you too will have to adopt an interpretation which appeals to you. Whether the poem leaves you with a feeling of despair or of hope is a personal matter. Of course Beowulf's efforts were wasted in one sense: the Geats are no longer a great people. But there is another way to view the poem. In this nuclear age, with man's inhumanity to man daily more apparent on all levels and the powers of darkness in seeming ascendancy throughout the world, we may see *Beowulf* as a triumphant affirmation of the value of a good life. □

DISCUSSION

1. (a) Describe each of Beowulf's three major battles with regard to
(1) the kinds of difficulties he faces
(2) the preparations he makes
(3) the supernatural elements involved, if any
(4) the extent to which the poet forecasts what will happen
(5) the outcome of the battle

(b) What logical or artistic justification might the poet have had for varying the three battles as he did?

(c) With which monster, if any, do you feel most sympathy? Why?

2. In lines 452–499, Beowulf tells the story of his swimming match with Breca and the dangers he met and overcame. What foreshadowings of his future exploits are there in this early adventure?

3. Minor characters in this epic are important, both for what they reveal about Beowulf's character and the parts they play in the action of the poem. Discuss these points with regard to Hrothgar, Unferth, Wealhtheow, and Wiglaf.

4. The poem begins and ends with a description of the funeral of a king. What point do you think the poet was making through this device?

5. Like most epic heroes, Beowulf embodies the qualities of character that were most admired by the people of his time and place.

(a) Reconstruct the code of conduct of an ideal Anglo-Saxon warrior and king as you see it revealed in this poem. Which parts of this code are still valid today?

(b) What character traits are criticized in the poem, either directly or indirectly? Does Beowulf possess any of these traits? Explain.

6. One critic has commented: "*Beowulf* is at least in part a study of kingship—of the attributes of a good king, of the difficulties he faces and how he overcomes them, of the problems of succession that arise upon his death." Discuss the validity of this statement, making references to the text to support your view.

7. *Beowulf* contains much that is reminiscent of folklore or fairy tales—lurid and sensational events, man-eating monsters, a dragon who guards a golden hoard. Why, with all these elements, has the poem appealed to sophisticated audiences for more than twelve hundred years? Are there counterparts to *Beowulf* in modern entertainment media?

8. In the translator's note, Kevin Crossley-Holland quotes a Norse proverb: "One thing I know never dies or changes, the reputation of a dead man." Assume that Beowulf's exploits are based on those of a real-life warrior and discuss whether the proverb is true in this case.

9. The description of the place where Grendel and his mother live, beginning in line 1052, is considered one of the masterpieces of Old English poetry. Comment as to why this might be true.

10. Read the discussion of the epic on page 11. Which features and devices mentioned do you find in *Beowulf?*

11. (a) Much of the modern view of life is based on the assumption that man can control his actions and to some extent is responsible for what happens to him. How does the view of life given in *Beowulf* compare with the modern view?

(b) The critic and novelist J. R. R. Tolkien has suggested that the theme of *Beowulf* deals with "man alien in a hostile world, engaged in a struggle which he cannot win. . . ." Do you agree with this analysis? In what way does modern "alienation" differ from the alienation depicted in *Beowulf?* In what way is it similar?

READERS' THEATER

1. Kevin Crossley-Holland has said that *Beowulf* must be read aloud to be appreciated. Join with some of your classmates in preparing a part of it for oral presentation. One or more students could serve as general narrators, and others take the parts of individual characters.

2. Prepare a portion of *Beowulf* for class presentation as it was performed by the *scop* in Anglo-Saxon England. You will need a stringed instrument to strike chords when you pronounce the accented syllables.

WRITING

1. Pretend you are Grendel (or Grendel's mother). Write a diary from the monster's point of view, recording at least one week in his life.

2. Write a complete description of Grendel or his mother. Use details given in the poem, but fill them out with further appropriate details.

3. Prepare a dialogue in which a modern student discusses with an Anglo-Saxon youth both the content and philosophy of *Beowulf*. Each is to maintain the viewpoint of the age to which he belongs.

4. Prepare a character sketch of Beowulf in youth and old age. Discuss his physical attributes and his character, pointing out both positive and negative qualities.

5. Retell the events in *Beowulf* from the viewpoint of one of the following:

(a) A historian writing objectively about the age

(b) A writer of a newspaper epitaph on Beowulf's death

(c) A novelist gathering material for a historical novel

(d) A relative of Grendel's reporting Beowulf's death to other relatives

(e) A television or motion picture scenario writer preparing to turn this folk epic into a TV or film epic

6. Reread the article "*Beowulf* and Its Critics." Take as your title either "The Nature of the Monsters" or "Christianity in *Beowulf*" and write a short composition discussing the validity of Mitchell's statements. If you prefer, disregard his statements and draw on the epic itself to develop your own theories.

7. Choose an incident in *Beowulf* and turn it into a film script. Include specific camera and lighting directions, as well as dialogue if any is needed. Try to get across the atmosphere of the scene.

8. Take a familiar fairy tale, myth, or fable and develop it into a short alliterative epic. (See "The Poetry of *Beowulf*" on the next page.)

9. Use the library to do some research on dragons and various other mythical monsters; then prepare a short paper for reading in class.

DETAIL FROM MEROVINGIAN BUCKLE OF THE 7TH CENTURY, GOLD WITH POLYCHROME AND JEWELS. MUSÉE DES ANTIQUITÉS NATIONALES, SAINT GERMAINE-EN-LAYE.

The Poetry of Beowulf

BIRD BROOCH OF OSTROGOTHIC ORIGIN, 6TH CENTURY, GERMANISCHES NATIONALMUSEUM, NUREMBERG.

To celebrate Beowulf's victory over Grendel, one of Hrothgar's thanes

> "who brimmed with poetry, and remembered lays,
> a man acquainted with ancient traditions
> of every kind, composed a new song
> in correct metre. Most skilfully that man
> began to sing of Beowulf's feat, . . ."

This is the way Old English poetry originally was composed—orally, in front of an audience, by *scops* or bards who could draw on a vast store of traditional formula-phrases to express almost any idea in correct metrical form. Every scop also knew many ancient lays or poetic hero-tales which he recited to the warriors gathered in the mead-hall of an evening, to the accompaniment of harp or lyre, varying the story each time to suit the audience and the occasion. Even today there are improvisational singers who are able to compose extemporaneous verse, narrative and otherwise, before a live audience. A good singer can go on as long as an audience will listen. These singers likewise make use of a common fund of formula-phrases.

Beowulf must have been composed by a man who could read and write, but he used the traditional devices of the older oral poetry. Almost all the large body of Old English poetry which has survived is in a style which grew out of the oral tradition.

Here are a few lines from the Old English text of *Beowulf*.[1] (The symbol ð stands for the *th* sound.)

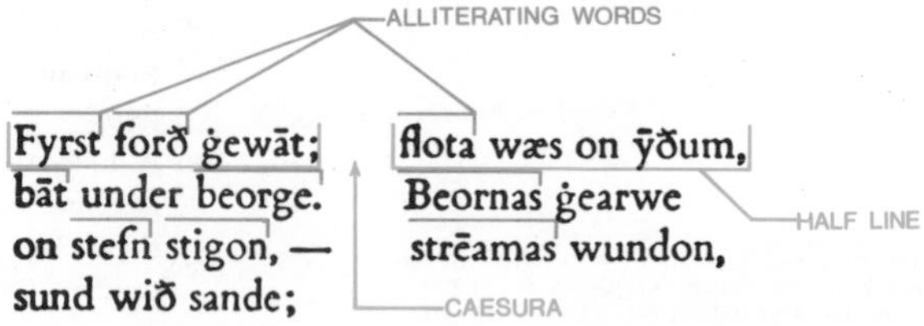

ALLITERATING WORDS

Fyrst forð ġewāt; flota wæs on ȳðum,
bāt under beorge. Beornas ġearwe
on stefn stigon, — strēamas wundon,
sund wið sande;

HALF LINE

CAESURA

Each line has a break or caesura in the middle; the metrical unit is the half-line. Each half-line contains two stressed words or syllables and an irregular number of syllables without stress. Note that there is no end rhyme to bind one line with another; rather, alliteration is used within the line to link important

---

1. The literal translation is:
Time forth went; floater was on waves,
boat under cliff. Warriors eager
on prow climbed,— streams eddied,
sea against sand;
See lines 165–168 in the Crossley-Holland translation.

words. In a normal line, either one or two stressed words or syllables in the first half-line alliterate with one stressed word or syllable in the second half-line. Alliterating words either begin with the same consonant, or begin with a vowel; any vowel was considered as alliterating with any other. Mr. Crossley-Holland's translation makes occasional use of alliteration to give the flavor of the original.

In general, Old English poetry tends to fall into verse paragraphs, with the thought running over from line to line and with frequent repetition of ideas in slightly different form. Such repetition or variation helped the singer by giving him time to compose the next line that would carry the story forward while he automatically sang a phrase that reinforced the meaning of a previous half-line.

The *Beowulf* poet, like other Old English poets, made use of the poetic conventions expected and understood by his audience. These conventions included a special poetic vocabulary, fixed expressions or formula-phrases, and poetic compounds.

The formulas are set metrical combinations that could be varied according to the needs of alliteration. For example, the phrase "on the sea" could be expressed by *on hranrāde* ("on the whale-road") or by *on seglrāde* ("on the sail-road"), depending on whether the poet needed a word beginning with *h* or one beginning with *s*. A person, place, or object was almost never referred to by a single, plain word, but almost always by a more elaborate expression. Hrothgar is "Healfdene's son," "ring-giver," "protector of warriors," "gold-friend," "ruler of the Scyldings," "grizzled warrior," and so on. Heorot is "best of dwellings," "greatest of halls," "gold-hall," or "hall adorned with treasures." Beowulf is "son of Ecgtheow," "strongest of all men," "defender of thanes," and so on. He is several times described as "stern-faced beneath his helmet." A man who speaks "unlocks his hoard of words" or "unlocks his thoughts." Thanes are "companions at the bench" or "hearth-companions."

Most of the compounds used by the *Beowulf* poet —like "helm-bearer" or "shield-bearer" for *warrior*, or "battle-blade" for *sword*—are easily understood. The more far-fetched, riddling kind of descriptive comparisons known as kennings, so popular with other Old English and Norse poets, are used only sparingly in *Beowulf*. Examples are "battle-light" (*sword*, referring to the light reflected by the sword-blade), "candle of the sky" and "gem of heaven" (*sun*), "great sea-garment" (*sail*), "bone chamber" (*body*).

The *Beowulf* poet used the conventional devices of Old English poetry, but he used them with incomparable artistry and skill to impart dignity, eloquence, and beauty to his work.

MEROVINGIAN BUCKLE OF THE 7TH CENTURY, MUSÉE DES BEAUX-ARTS, AUXERRE—GIRAUDON.

EXTENSION

Reading the Old English epic moved a contemporary American poet to write this poem which captures some of the mood and feeling of the original.

BEOWULF
by Richard Wilbur

The land was overmuch like scenery,
The flowers attentive, the grass too garrulous green;
In the lake like a dropped kerchief could be seen
The lark's reflection after the lark was gone;
5 The Roman road lay paved too shiningly
For a road so many men had traveled on.

Also the people were strange, were strangely warm.
The king recalled the father of his guest,
The queen brought mead in a studded cup, the rest
10 Were kind, but in all was a vagueness and a strain,
Because they lived in a land of daily harm.
And they said the same things again and again.

It was a childish country; and a child,
Grown monstrous, so besieged them in the night
15 That all their daytimes were a dream of fright
That it would come and own them to the bone.
The hero, to his battle reconciled,
Promised to meet that monster all alone.

So then the people wandered to their sleep
20 And left him standing in the echoed hall.
They heard the rafters rattle fit to fall,
The child departing with a broken groan,
And found their champion in a rest so deep
His head lay harder sealed than any stone.

25 The land was overmuch like scenery,
The lake gave up the lark, but now its song
Fell to no ear, the flowers too were wrong,
The day was fresh and pale and swiftly old,
The night put out no smiles upon the sea;
30 And the people were strange, the people strangely
cold.

They gave him horse and harness, helmet and mail,
A jeweled shield, an ancient battle-sword,
Such gifts as are the hero's hard reward
And bid him do again what he has done.
35 These things he stowed beneath his parting sail,
And wept that he could share them with no son.

He died in his own country a kinless king,
A name heavy with deeds, and mourned as one
Will mourn for the frozen year when it is done.
40 They buried him next the sea on a thrust of land:
Twelve men rode round his barrow all in a ring,
Singing of him what they could understand.

DISCUSSION

"Beowulf" briefly retells the story in the Old English poem, but Wilbur has had to be highly selective.

1. How does his account differ from or extend the original story?

2. What does Wilbur leave out, and why?

3. Stanzas 1 and 5 are primarily descriptive and use similar detail.

(a) Examine the two stanzas and explore their subtle differences.

(b) Why are the people "strangely warm" on Beowulf's arrival and "strangely cold" when he leaves?

4. What seems special in Wilbur's references to Grendel, and what is the effect?

5. What is the effect of not naming anyone, not even Beowulf or Grendel?

II. OTHER ANGLO-SAXON LITERATURE

The Ruin

Translated by Michael Alexander

This poem was found written on two leaves of parchment badly scarred by fire; parts of lines are missing. The translator says, ". . . my attempts to translate the defective lines, wherever it was possible, should not be taken as more than guesses."

Picture the speaker in this poem walking through the overgrown streets of an ancient Roman city, perhaps the city of Bath. The Anglo-Saxons, who did not build in stone, usually referred to Roman ruins as "the work of the Giants."

Well-wrought this wall: Wierds[1] broke it.
The stronghold burst. . . .

Snapped rooftrees, towers fallen,
the work of the Giants, the stonesmiths,
5 mouldereth.
Rime scoureth gatetowers
rime on mortar.

Shattered the showershields, roofs ruined,
age under-ate them.
And the wielders & wrights?
Earthgrip holds them—gone, long gone,
10 fast in gravesgrasp while fifty fathers
and sons have passed.
Wall stood,
grey lichen, red stone, kings fell often,
stood under storms, high arch crashed—
stands yet the wallstone, hacked by weapons,
15 by files grim-ground . . .
. . . shone the old skilled work
. . . sank to loam-crust.

Mood quickened mind, and a man of wit,
cunning in rings, bound bravely the wallbase
20 with iron, a wonder.

Bright were the buildings, halls where springs ran,
high, horngabled,[2] much throng-noise;
these many meadhalls men filled
with loud cheerfulness: Wierd changed that.

25 Came days of pestilence, on all sides men fell dead,
death fetched off the flower of the people;
where they stood to fight, waste places
and on the acropolis, ruins.
Hosts who would build again
shrank to the earth. Therefore are these courts dreary
30 and that red arch twisteth tiles.
wryeth from roof-ridge, reacheth groundwards. . . .
Broken blocks. . . .

There once many a man
mood-glad, goldbright, of gleams garnished,
flushed with wine-pride, flashing war-gear,
35 gazed on wrought gemstones, on gold, on silver,
on wealth held and hoarded, on light-filled amber,
on this bright burg of broad dominion.

Stood stone houses; wide streams welled
hot from source, and a wall all caught
40 in its bright bosom, that the baths were
hot at hall's hearth; that was fitting . . .
. . . .

Thence hot streams, loosed, ran over hoar stone
unto the ring-tank . . . .
45 . . . It is a kingly thing
. . . city . . . .

1. *Wierds,* the powers that rule man's destiny; the Fates.

2. *horngabled.* The hall-gables were often made to appear more fearsome by means of animal horns mounted as decorations.

OF LITERARY INTEREST

Anglo-Saxon Lyrics

Around the year 1070, Leofric, the first bishop of Exeter Cathedral, presented to the cathedral library an old manuscript which the library catalogue described as "a big English book about every sort of thing, wrought in songwise." Into this book, monks had copied (sometimes carelessly), a miscellaneous collection of Anglo-Saxon poems.

Because Exeter is inland, it escaped the destructions of the Danish raids on coastal areas. However, the vicissitudes of a thousand years had their effects on the ancient volume. The front was used at one time as a cutting-board and as a beer mat, and the back fourteen pages were burned through by a brand. Nevertheless, this book is the source of most of the Anglo-Saxon poetry that has survived.

Half the poems in the Exeter Book are paraphrases of Old Testament stories or lives of the saints; the others are on secular subjects out of the pagan past. Several of the most important poems are *elegies*—melancholy thoughts about loneliness, the mutability of earthly things, the terrors of the northern winter, and the immensity and cruelty of the sea. These lyrics, like *Beowulf,* first developed orally, and use the same alliterative verse form and other poetic devices.

DISCUSSION

1. Trace the order in which the poet presents the details of the ruin, and discuss the effect of the arrangement.

2. (a) Do you think the translator was right in retaining the archaic *-eth* endings in lines 5, 6, 32, and 33? Explain.

(b) What poetic devices used by the translator add to the feeling of doom and destruction?

3. Does the speaker in the poem feel that stone outlasts human life, or vice versa, or neither? Explain.

WRITING

1. If you live in a long-established community, find a run-down or collapsing structure and write a lament in which you compare its current state with its previous glory. Or write about ruins you have seen pictured, or about an imaginary building.

2. Write a descriptive composition based on the ideas in the poem.

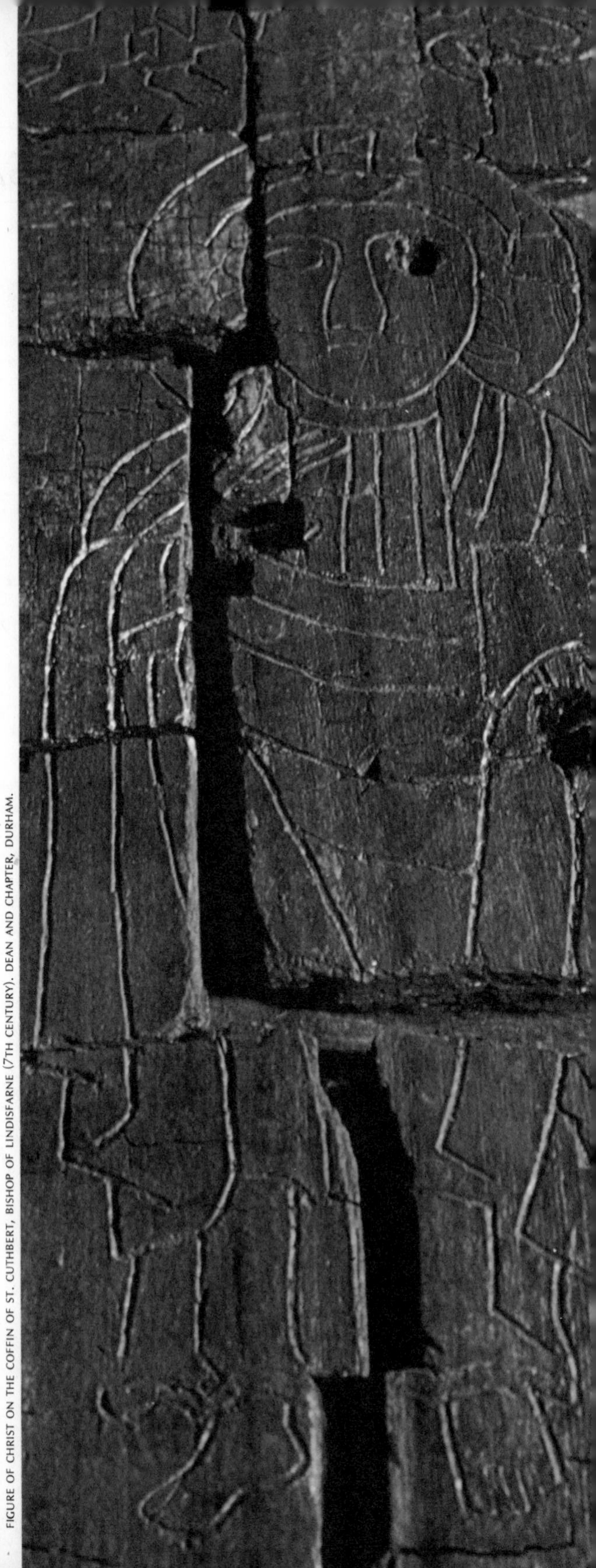

FIGURE OF CHRIST ON THE COFFIN OF ST. CUTHBERT, BISHOP OF LINDISFARNE (7TH CENTURY). DEAN AND CHAPTER, DURHAM.

THE WIFE'S COMPLAINT

Translated by
Michael Alexander

I have wrought these words together out of a wryed
existence,
the heart's tally, telling off
the griefs I have undergone from girlhood upwards,
old and new, and now more than ever;
5 for I have never not had some new sorrow,
some fresh affliction to fight against.

The first was my lord's leaving his people here:
crossed crests. To what country I knew not,
wondered where, awoke unhappy.
10 I left, fared any road, friendless, an outcast,
sought any service to staunch the lack of him.

Then his kinsmen ganged, began to think
thoughts they did not speak, of splitting the wedlock;
so—estranged, alienated—we lived each
15 alone, a long way apart; how I longed for him!

In his harshness he had me brought here;
and in these parts there were few friendly-minded,
worth trusting.
Trouble in the heart now:
I saw the bitterness, the bound mind
20 of my matched man, mourning-browed,
mirk in his mood, murder in his thoughts.

Our lips had smiled to swear hourly
that nothing should split us—save dying—
nothing else. All that has changed:
25 it is now as if it never had been,
our friendship. I feel in the wind
that the man dearest to me detests me.
I was banished to this knoll knotted by woods
to live in a den dug beneath an oak.
30 Old is this earthen room; it eats at my heart.

I see the thorns thrive up there in thick coverts
on the banks that baulk these black hollows:
not a gay dwelling. Here the grief bred
by lordlack preys on me. Some lovers in this world
35 live dear to each other, lie warm together
at day's beginning; I go by myself
about these earth caves under the oak tree.
Here I must sit the summer day through,
here weep out the woes of exile,
40 the hardships heaped upon me. My heart shall never
suddenly sail into slack water,
all the longings of a lifetime answered.

May grief and bitterness blast the mind
of that young man! May his mind ache
45 behind his smiling face! May a flock of sorrows
choke his chest! He would change his tune
if he lived alone in a land of exile
far from his folk.
Where my friend is stranded
frost crusts the cracked cliff-face
50 grey waves grind the shingle.
The mind cannot bear in such a bleak place
very much grief.
He remembers too often
less grim surroundings. Sorrow follows
this too long wait for one who is estranged.

DISCUSSION

1. Reconstruct the story told or suggested in this poem.

2. Where in the poem can you detect a sudden shift in feeling?

WRITING

Write "The Student's Complaint" or "The Rejected Lover's Complaint" or "The Misunderstood Son's Complaint."

THE WANDERER

Translated by Michael Alexander

Who liveth alone longeth for mercy,
Maker's mercy. Though he must traverse
tracts of sea, sick at heart,
—trouble with oars ice-cold waters,
5 the ways of exile—Wierd is set fast.

Thus spoke such a "grasshopper," old griefs in his mind,
cold slaughters, the death of dear kinsmen:

"Alone am I driven each day before daybreak
to give my cares utterance.
10 None are there now among the living
to whom I dare declare me throughly,
tell my heart's thought. Too truly I know
it is in a man no mean virtue
that he keep close his heart's chest,
15 hold his thought-hoard, think as he may.

No weary mind may stand against Wierd
nor may a wrecked will work new hope;
wherefore, most often, those eager for fame
bind the dark mood fast in their breasts.

20 So must I also curb my mind,
cut off from country, from kind far distant,
by cares overworn, bind it in fetters;
this since, long ago, the ground's shroud
enwrapped my gold-friend. Wretched I went thence,
25 winter-wearied, over the waves' bound;
dreary I sought hall of a gold-giver,
where far or near I might find
him who in meadhall might take heed of me,
furnish comfort to a man friendless,
30 win me with cheer.
He knows who makes trial
how harsh and bitter is care for companion
to him who hath few friends to shield him.
Track ever taketh him, never the torqued gold,
not earthly glory, but cold heart's cave.
35 He minds him of hall-men, of treasure-giving,
how in his youth his gold-friend
gave him to feast. Fallen all this joy.

He knows this who is forced to forgo his lord's,
his friend's counsels, to lack them for long:
40 oft sorrow and sleep, banded together,
come to bind the lone outcast;
he thinks in his heart then that he his lord
claspeth and kisseth, and on knee layeth
hand and head, as he had at otherwhiles
45 in days now gone, when he enjoyed the gift-stool.

Awakeneth after this friendless man,
seeth before him fallow waves,
seabirds bathing, broading out feathers,
snow and hail swirl, hoar-frost falling.
50 Then all the heavier his heart's wounds,
sore for his loved lord. Sorrow freshens.

Remembered kinsmen press through his mind;
he singeth out gladly, scanneth eagerly
men from the same hearth. They swim away.
55 Sailors' ghosts bring not many
known songs there. Care grows fresh
in him who shall send forth too often
over locked waves his weary spirit.

"The Wanderer" from *The Earliest English Poems,* translated by Michael Alexander.

OF LITERARY INTEREST

The worst thing that could happen to an Anglo-Saxon warrior was to lose his lord, the leader to whom he was bound by the strong ties of the *comitatus* relationship. Within the firelit, gold-adorned mead-hall where the men gathered round their lord at supper there was warmth and fellowship, protection and safety. Outside was cold and darkness.

"The Wanderer" seems to consist basically of two speeches linked by a moralizing passage. The first speech is that of an *eardstapa* or "earth-stepper," a word meaning "wanderer" or "grasshopper." His *wierd* is to roam the seas in search of a lord to replace his dead "gold-friend." The second speech appears to be that of the wise man described at the beginning of the link passage. These two bleak monologues, essentially pagan in spirit, are sandwiched between two expressions of pious faith in God, suggesting that the monastic scribe who wrote down the poem might have been trying to make his recalcitrant materials palatable to a Christian audience.

Therefore I may not think, throughout this world,
60 why cloud cometh not on my mind
when I think over all the life of earls,
how at a stroke they have given up hall,
mood-proud thanes. So this middle earth
each of all days ageth and falleth."
65 Wherefore no man grows wise without he have
his share of winters. A wise man holds out;
he is not too hot-hearted, nor too hasty in speech,
nor too weak a warrior, not wanting in fore-thought,
nor too greedy of goods, nor too glad, nor too mild,
70 nor ever too eager to boast, ere he knows all.

A man should forbear boastmaking
until his fierce mind fully knows
which way his spleen shall expend itself.

A wise man may grasp how ghastly it shall be
75 when all this world's wealth standeth waste,
even as now, in many places, over the earth
walls stand, wind-beaten,
hung with hoar-frost; ruined habitations.
The wine-halls crumble; their wielders lie
80 bereft of bliss, the band all fallen
proud by the wall. War took off some,
carried them on their course hence; one a bird bore
over the high sea; one the hoar wolf
dealt to death; one his drear-cheeked
85 earl stretched in an earthen trench.

The Maker of men hath so marred this dwelling
that human laughter is not heard about it
and idle stand these old giant-works.

A man who on these walls wisely looked
90 who sounded deeply this dark life
would think back to the blood spilt here,
weigh it in his wit. His word would be this:
"Where is that horse now? Where are those men:
Where is the hoard-sharer?
Where is the house of the feast? Where is the hall's uproar?

95 Alas, bright cup! Alas, burnished fighter!
Alas, proud prince! How that time has passed,
dark under night's helm, as though it never had been!

There stands in the stead of staunch thanes
a towering wall wrought with worm-shapes;
100 the earls are off-taken by the ash-spear's point,
—that thirsty weapon. Their Wierd is glorious.

Storms break on the stone hillside,
the ground bound by driving sleet,
winter's wrath. Then wanness cometh,
105 night's shade spreadeth, sendeth from north
the rough hail to harry mankind.

In the earth-realm all is crossed;
Wierd's will changeth the world.
Wealth is lent us, friends are lent us,
110 man is lent, kin is lent;
all this earth's frame shall stand empty."

So spoke the sage in his heart; he sat apart in thought.
Good is he who keeps faith: nor should care too fast
be out of a man's breast before he first know the cure:
115 a warrior fights on bravely. Well is it for him who seeks forgiveness,
the heavenly Father's solace, in whom all our fastness stands.

DISCUSSION

Like all Old English poetry, "The Wanderer" achieves its best effect when read aloud. Read the poem aloud in its entirety and respond as fully as you can to the bleakness or darkness of its tone.

1. How do the opening and closing appear, in your reading, to be related to the rest of the poem? Do they seem to conflict in tone? Or are you able to make them harmonize?

2. What shift do you detect beginning in line 65? How would you relate this latter part of the poem to the first part?

WRITING

The wanderer laments the harshness of the world in which he lives. Not only Man but Nature was cruel. Write a short essay agreeing or disagreeing with the Wanderer's world-view, and give your reasons for doing so.

EXTENSION

The enduring appeal of Anglo-Saxon poetry is revealed in its influence on later poets. All the early poetry of the modern British poet W. H. Auden, for example, reflects his appreciation of the older verse. This poem has the same title as the Anglo-Saxon lyric which inspired it.

THE WANDERER

by W. H. Auden

Doom is dark and deeper than any sea-dingle.
Upon what man it fall
In spring, day-wishing flowers appearing,
Avalanche sliding, white snow from rock-face,
5 That he should leave his house,
No-cloud-soft hand can hold him, restraint by women;
But ever that man goes
Through place-keepers, through forest trees,
A stranger to strangers over undried sea,
10 Houses for fishes, suffocating water,
Or lonely on fell[1] as chat,[2]
By pot-holed becks[3]
A bird stone-haunting, an unquiet bird.

There head falls forward, fatigued at evening,
15 And dreams of home,
Waving from window, spread of welcome,
Kissing of wife under single sheet;
But waking sees
Bird-flocks nameless to him, through doorway voices
20 Of new men making another love.

Save him from hostile capture,
From sudden tiger's spring at corner;
Protect his house,
His anxious house where days are counted
25 From thunderbolt protect,
From gradual ruin spreading like a stain;
Converting number from vague to certain,
Bring joy, bring day of his returning,
Lucky with day approaching, with leaning dawn.

1. *fell,* a barren hill.
2. *chat,* a bird, the European winchat.
3. *becks,* rocky-bottomed streams.

DISCUSSION

Like the Anglo-Saxon poem, Auden's expresses extreme loneliness and sadness. Reread lines 38–58 of the Anglo-Saxon poem and show how the Auden poem is related.

WRITING

Discuss how the "doom" of Auden's poem is as likely to fall on a man today as in Anglo-Saxon days. Or write a narrative account of a man who feels its fall.

Anglo-Saxon Riddles

Riddling is very ancient, and may originally have had some connection with magic. It was a popular pastime among the Anglo-Saxons, especially in the monasteries. The Exeter Book includes ninety-five riddles, four of which are given here. No solutions were included, but scholars have guessed answers; see the bottom of the page.

26

I am the scalp of myself, skinned by my foeman:
robbed of my strength, he steeped & soaked me,
dipped me in water, whipped me out again,
set me in the sun. I soon lost there
5 the hairs I had had.
The hard edge
of a keen-ground knife cuts me now,
fingers fold me, and a fowl's pride
drives its treasure trail across me,
bounds again over the brown rim,
10 sucks the wood-dye, steps again on me,
makes his black marks.
A man then hides me
between stout shield-boards stretched with hide,
fits me with gold. There glows on me
the jewelsmith's handiwork held with wires.

15 Let these royal enrichments and this red dye
and splendid settings spread the glory
of the Protector of peoples—and not plague the fool.
If the sons of men will make use of me
they shall. . . .

68

The wave, over the wave, a weird thing I saw,
through-wrought, and wonderfully ornate:
a wonder on the wave—water became bone.

35

The womb of the wold, wet and cold,
bore me at first, brought me forth.
I know in my mind my making was not
through skill with fells or fleeces of wool;
5 there was no winding of wefts, there is no woof in
me,
no thread thrumming under the thrash of strokes,
no whirring shuttle steered through me,
no weaver's reed rapped my sides.
The worms that braid the broidered silk
10 with Wierd cunning did not weave me;
yet anywhere over the earth's breadth
men will attest me a trustworthy garment.

Say truly, supple-minded man,
wise in words, what my name is.

47

I heard of a wonder, of words moth-eaten;
that is a strange thing, I thought, weird
that a man's song be swallowed by a worm,
his binded sentences, his bedside stand-by
5 rustled in the night—and the robber-guest
not one whit the wiser for the words he had
mumbled.

DISCUSSION

1. If No. 26 may be taken as a typical example, a riddle opens with a deliberate deception ("I am the scalp of myself") and keeps up the deception throughout. At the same time, it throws out a few clues ("fingers fold me," "a fowl's pride drives its treasure trail across me"). What are the other clues in this riddle?

2. Analyze the other riddles. Which is most similar to No. 26 in its pattern?

26. Bible or prayer-book 35. coat of mail
47. bookworm 68. ice

MANUSCRIPT ILLUMINATION DEPICTING THE VENERABLE BEDE. COURTESY OF THE TRUSTEES OF THE BRITISH MUSEUM.

BEDE'S HISTORY

The first important writer of prose in England was a Benedictine monk from Northumbria—a scholar, historian, and teacher known as the Venerable Bede (673–735). Most of his many books are no longer read, but his *Ecclesiastical History of the English People* is still a valuable source of information about the early history of Britain.

As a churchman and scholar, Bede wrote in Latin. His *History* was translated into Old English by Alfred the Great (849–901), both a great king and a great man of learning. The excerpt included here tells the story of the greatest triumph achieved by the early Christian missionaries sent from Rome.

THE CONVERSION OF KING EDWIN

THE Northumbrian people's acceptance of the Faith of Christ came about through King Edwin's alliance with the kings of Kent, and his marriage to Ethelberga, a daughter of King Ethelbert. Edwin sent an embassy of nobles to request her hand in marriage, but received the reply that it was not permissible for a Christian maiden to be given in marriage to a heathen husband, lest the Christian faith and Sacraments be profaned by her association with a king who was wholly ignorant of the worship of the true God. When Edwin's messengers returned with this reply, he gave assurance that he would place no obstacles in the way of the Christian Faith, and would afford complete freedom to Ethelberga and her attendants to live and worship in accordance with Christian belief and practice. He also stated himself willing to accept the religion of Christ if, on examination, his advisers decided that it appeared more holy and acceptable to God than their own.

On this understanding, the maiden was betrothed and sent to Edwin, and in accordance with the agreement, Paulinus, a man beloved of God, was consecrated bishop, so that he could accompany the maiden as her chaplain.

During the following year, an assassin named Eumer was sent into the province by Cuilchelm, King of the West Saxons, in order to rob Edwin both of his kingdom and his life. This vile creature employed a double-edged, poisoned dagger, to ensure that if the wound itself were not mortal, the poison would complete its work. On Easter Day Eumer arrived at the king's country-seat by the Derwent, and was admitted into his presence on the pretext of delivering a message from his master. And while he was artfully delivering his pretended message, he suddenly rose, and drawing the dagger from beneath his clothes, attacked the king. Swift to see the king's peril, Lilla, his counsellor and best friend, having no shield to protect the king, interposed his own body to receive the blow; but even so, it was delivered with such force that it wounded the king through the body of his knight.

On the same holy night of Easter Day, the queen was delivered of a daughter, and as the king thanked his gods in the presence of Bishop Paulinus for the birth of his daughter, the bishop gave thanks to Christ, and told the king that it was Christ who had given the queen a safe and painless delivery in response to his prayers. The king was greatly pleased at his words, and promised that if God would grant him life and victory over his enemy who had sent the assassin, he would renounce his idols and serve Christ.

When the king had recovered from the assassin's wound, he summoned his forces, marched against the West Saxons, and in the ensuing campaign either slew or forced to surrender all those who had plotted his murder. Returning home victorious, the king would not receive the Sacrament of Christian baptism without due consideration. He wished, firstly, to receive a full course of instruction in the Faith from the venerable Paulinus, and to discuss his proper course with his chief counsellors, on whose wisdom he placed great reliance. [*Bede then quotes a long letter written by Pope Boniface to Edwin, urging him to accept the Christian faith.*]

* * *

But the principal factor influencing the king to study and accept the truths of salvation was a heavenly vision which God in his mercy had once granted the king when he was an exile at the court of Redwald,[1] king of the Angles. For although Paulinus found it difficult to bring the king's proud mind to accept the humility of the way of salvation, he nevertheless continued to preach the word among the people, and to implore God's mercy to bring about the conversion of the king and his nation. It appears that at length the nature of the king's earlier vision was revealed to Paulinus, and he immediately urged the king to implement the promise that he had made at the time of the vision.

Now the vision was this. When his predecessor [King Ethelfrid] was persecuting him, Edwin wandered as an unknown fugitive for many years, until at length he came to Redwald, and asked him for protection. Redwald gave him a ready welcome, and promised to do everything he asked, but as soon as Ethelfrid heard that Edwin and his companions were living at the king's court as his friends, he sent messengers to offer Redwald a large sum of money to murder him. Obtaining no satisfaction, he sent a second and third time, offering even heavier bribes, and threatening war if his demand were refused. At length Redwald agreed to his demand and promised either to kill Edwin, or to surrender him to Ethelfrid's messengers. This plot was discovered by a loyal friend of Edwin, who went to his room early one night when he was about to retire, and calling him out, warned him of the king's wicked intention, adding: "If you are willing, I will take you immediately to some place where neither Redwald nor Ethelfrid can find you."

Edwin replied: "Thank you for your goodwill, but I cannot break the agreement that I have made with so great a king, who has so far done me no harm, nor showed any hostility towards me. If I must die, I would rather die by his hand than by an hand less noble." When his friend had left, Edwin remained, sitting sadly alone outside the palace, burdened with many gloomy thoughts.

He had remained a considerable time in silence, grieving and desperate, when suddenly, at dead of night, he saw a man approaching whose face and clothes were strange to him, and whose unexpected arrival caused him considerable alarm. But the stranger came up and greeted him, saying: "Don't think that I am unaware why you are sad and sleepless. I know very well who you are, what your troubles are, and what coming evils you dread. But tell me this: what reward will you give the man who can deliver you from your troubles, and persuade Redwald not to harm you or betray you?"

Edwin answered that he would give any reward in his power in return for such an outstanding service.

Then the other went on: "And what if he also promised that you should become king, defeat your enemies, and enjoy greater power than any of your predecessors who have ever ruled the English nation?"

Heartened by these enquiries, Edwin readily promised that, in return for such blessings, he would give ample proofs of his gratitude.

The stranger then asked a third question. "If the man who can truthfully foretell such good fortune can also give you better and wiser guidance for your life and salvation than anything known to your parents and kinsfolk, will you promise to obey and follow his advice?"

Edwin at once promised that he would. On this assurance, the man laid his right hand on Edwin's head, saying: "When you receive this sign, remember this occasion and our conversation, and do not delay the fulfillment of your promise." Hereupon, it is said, he vanished, and Edwin realized that it was not a man but a spirit who had appeared to him.

The young prince was still sitting there alone, greatly heartened by what he had heard, and puzzling over the identity of the being who had talked with him, when his loyal friend approached with a cheerful greeting, and said: "Get up and come inside. You can now sleep without fear, for the king has had a change of heart. For when he privately told the queen of his intention to deal with you as I warned, she dissuaded him, saying that it was unworthy in a great king to sell his best friend for gold." In brief, the king did as she advised, and not only refused to surrender the exiled prince to the envoys of his enemy, but assisted him to recover his kingdom.

* * *

While King Edwin hesitated to accept the word of God at Paulinus' preaching, he used to sit alone for hours, deliberating what religion he should

1. Some scholars believe Redwald was the king memorialized in the Sutton Hoo ship burial. See the article on page 57.

follow. On one of these occasions, the man of God came to him, and laying his right hand on his head, enquired whether he remembered this sign. The king trembled, and would have fallen at his feet, but Paulinus raised him, and said in a friendly voice: "God has helped you to escape from the hands of the enemies whom you feared, and it is through His bounty that you have received the kingdom that you desired. Remember the third promise that you made, and hesitate no longer. Accept the Faith and keep the commands of Him who has delivered you from all your earthly troubles, and raised you to the glory of an earthly kingdom. If you will henceforward obey His will, which he reveals to you through me, he will save you from the everlasting doom of the wicked, and give you a place in His eternal kingdom in heaven."

When Paulinus had spoken, the king answered that he was both willing and obliged to accept the Faith which he taught, but said that he must discuss the matter with his principal advisers and friends, so that if they were in agreement, they might all be cleansed together in Christ the Fount of Life. Paulinus agreed, and the king kept his promise. He summoned a council of the wise men, and asked each in turn his opinion of this new faith and the new God being proclaimed.

Coifi, the High Priest, replied without hesitation: "Your Majesty, let us give careful consideration to this new teaching, for I frankly admit that, in my experience, the religion that we have hitherto professed seems valueless and powerless. None of your subjects has been more devoted to the service of the gods than myself, yet there are many to whom you show greater favour, and who are more successful in all their undertakings. Now, if the gods had any power, they would surely have favoured myself, who have been more zealous in their service. Therefore, if on examination these new teachings are found to be more effectual, let us not hesitate to accept them."

Another of the king's chief men signified his agreement with this prudent argument, and went on to say: "Your Majesty, when we compare the present life of man with that time of which we have no knowledge, it seems to me like the swift flight of a lone sparrow through the banqueting-hall where you sit in the winter months to dine with your thanes and counsellors. Inside there is a comforting fire to warm the room; outside the wintry storms of snow and rain are raging. This sparrow flies swiftly in through one door of the hall, and out through another. While he is inside, he is safe from the winter storms; but after a few moments of comfort, he vanishes from sight into the darkness whence he came. Similarly, man appears on earth for a little while, but we know nothing of what went before this life, and what follows. Therefore if this new teaching can reveal any more certain knowledge, it seems only right that we should follow it." The other elders and counsellors of the king, under God's guidance, gave the same advice.

Coifi then added that he wished to hear Paulinus' teaching about God in greater detail; and when, at the king's bidding, this had been given, the High Priest said: "I have long realized that there is nothing in what we worshipped. I now publicly confess that this teaching clearly reveals truths that will afford us the blessings of life, salvation, and eternal happiness. Therefore, Your Majesty, I submit that the temples and altars that we had dedicated to no advantage be immediately desecrated and burned."

And when the king asked the High Priest who should be the first to profane the altars and shrines of the idols, Coifi replied: "I will do this myself, for now that the true God has granted me knowledge, who more suitably than I can set a public example, and destroy the idols that I worshipped in ignorance?" So he asked the king to give him arms and a stallion—for hitherto it had not been lawful for the High Priest to carry arms, or to ride anything but a mare—and, thus equipped, he set out to destroy the idols. Girded with a sword and with a spear in his hand, he mounted the king's stallion and rode up to the idols.

When the crowd saw him, they thought he had gone mad, but without hesitation, as soon as he reached the temple, he cast a spear into it and profaned it. Then, full of joy at his knowledge of the worship of the true God, he told his companions to set fire to the temple. The site where these idols once stood is still shown, not far east of York, beyond the river Derwent, and is known as Goodmanham. □

EXTENSION

Bede's story of the briefly glimpsed bird has haunted English writers ever since it was told. Here is one retelling in modern English by a contemporary British poet, Louis MacNeice. (Another is Wordsworth's sonnet "Persuasion.")

DARK AGE GLOSSES ON THE VENERABLE BEDE

by Louis MacNeice

Birds flitting in and out of the barn
Bring back an Anglo-Saxon story:
The great wooden hall with long fires down the centre,
Their feet in the rushes, their hands tearing the meat.
5 Suddenly high above them they notice a swallow enter
From the black storm and zigzag over their heads,
Then out once more into the unknown night;
And that, someone remarks, is the life of man.
But now it is time to sleep; one by one
10 They rise from the bench and their gigantic shadows
Lurch on the shuddering walls. How can the world
Or the non-world beyond harbour a bird?
They close their eyes that smart from the woodsmoke: how
Can anyone even guess his whence and whither?
15 This indoors flying makes it seem absurd,
Although it itches and nags and flutters and yearns,
To postulate any other life than now.

DISCUSSION

1. How does the story of the bird function in Bede's account?

2. In the Bede version, what are the various elements of analogy between the bird's flight and man's life?

3. In both the Bede and MacNeice versions, the time is night and the weather stormy. How would it change the effect to make the time daylight and the weather sunny?

4. Compare the two versions as to their ultimate meaning—religious affirmation or religious doubt.

WRITING

Find an analogy for life (like the bird) and write a narrative account of its effect on you or someone else. Life is like an electric light bulb . . . a book . . . a bee snatching honey from a flower . . . a moth fluttering briefly at the light . . . a jet zooming overhead. . . . Find your own analogy.

KING ARTHUR'S LAST BATTLE. THE ROYAL LIBRARY, THE HAGUE.

III. BACKGROUND

Anglo-Saxon England

(c. 450 / 1066)

AFTER the Roman conquerors left Britain in the fifth century, Anglo-Saxon invaders took over control of most of the country. Late in the sixth century there was a spiritual invasion by Christian missionaries sent by the Pope. Anglo-Saxon rule continued over a land compounded of a strange mixture of pagan and Christian culture until the invasion and conquest by the Normans from continental Europe in 1066.

In Anglo-Saxon England, life was primitive, insecure, and uncertain. There was no nation in the modern sense, but only a multitude of wealthy, independent lords and kings, frequently in armed conflict with each other. Surrounding each lord was his band of warriors and retainers who were highly valued for their support and who were in turn supported by gifts of jewelry, horses, and weapons. Courage, strength, and loyalty to the lord were the highest virtues. At the bottom of the social order were the churls or workers who tended the fields and the cattle and wove the cloth and baked the bread. Members of this class were bound in service to their lords. Sometimes a churl could gain his freedom by acquiring possessions and earning the favor of his lord, but the number of freemen was small. The role of women was not an important one in this highly masculine society, but individual women could through marriage attain positions of honor and power.

From the perspective of the twentieth century, Anglo-Saxon life appears brutal and oppressive. But some features have appeal and even a ring of familiarity. The great boisterous feasts in the mead-hall, where hearty drink and enormous quantities of food were dispensed and the bard or *scop* chanted his poetry celebrating the feats of tribal heroes, must have been memorable occasions of human communion. The spirit of comradeship (*comitatus*) which bound fellow warriors together under allegiance to their lord, and ideally transcended concern for self, had elements of nobility and mutuality often sorely missed in human relationships today. The total commitment of a retainer to his lord seems foreign to the democratic idea, but it may have some parallel in the strong institutional loyalty found, for example, among the managerial class today. Yet, however attractive some features of Anglo-Saxon life appear now, few would want to exchange centuries and go back to those simpler but more anxious and uncertain times. □

Old Irish Poetry

The Celts in Ireland were not, like those in England, overcome by successive invasions. Neither Romans nor Anglo-Saxons took over Ireland when they ruled Britain. But the country was converted to Christianity by St. Patrick during the fifth century. The Celtic language of Ireland (and of Highland Scotland) is known as Gaelic (sometimes called Erse and sometimes Irish), and is still spoken alongside English in some areas of Ireland today.

The following Irish poems were composed in Gaelic at about the time of *Beowulf* and other Anglo-Saxon poetry, but their tone and spirit are very different. As is the case with the Anglo-Saxon works, their authors are unknown.

THE VIKING TERROR

Since tonight the wind is high,
The sea's white mane a fury,
I need not fear the hordes of hell
Coursing the Irish Channel.

9TH CENTURY

SCHOLARS

Scholars, regrettably, must yell
In torment on the hob of hell
While louts that never learned their letters
Are perched in Heaven among their betters.

9TH CENTURY

INTO EXILE

What better fortune can we find
Than with the girl that pleased our mind
To leave our home and friend behind,
And sail on the first favouring wind?

10TH CENTURY?

THE SCHOLAR AND HIS CAT

Each of us pursues his trade,
I and Pangur, my comrade;
His whole fancy on the hunt
And mine for learning ardent.

5 More than fame I love to be
Among my books, and study;
Pangur does not grudge me it,
Content with his own merit.

When—a heavenly time!—we are
10 In our small room together,
Each of us has his own sport
And asks no greater comfort.

While he sets his round sharp eye
On the wall of my study,
15 I turn mine—though lost its edge—
On the great wall of knowledge.

Now a mouse sticks in his net
After some mighty onset,
Then into my store I cram
20 Some difficult, darksome problem.

When a mouse comes to the kill
Pangur exults—a marvel!
I have, when some secret's won,
My hour of exultation.

25 Though we work for days or years
Neither the other hinders;
Each is competent and hence
Enjoys his skill in silence.

Master of the death of mice,
30 He keeps in daily practice;
I, too, making dark things clear,
Am of my trade a master.

9TH CENTURY

ID AND LOCK FOR A PURSE, FOUND AT SUTTON HOO IN 1939. COURTESY OF THE TRUSTEES OF THE BRITISH MUSUEM.

The Treasure of Sutton Hoo

IN the late spring of 1939, archaeologists began excavating a large burial mound on an estate called Sutton Hoo, on the east coast of England in the area once known as East Anglia. The mound was the largest in a group of earth mounds or barrows that lay on a steep hundred-foot slope overlooking the inlet where the River Deben flows into the North Sea. As the painstaking work continued, the diggers realized they had uncovered the richest hoard of early Anglo-Saxon objects ever found. A jeweled sword, a richly decorated shield and helmet, gold coins, silver bowls, and, above all, nineteen pieces of magnificently wrought gold jewelry set with thousands of elaborately cut garnets—these objects must have been the treasure of a mighty king. The great gold buckle alone weighs over fourteen ounces. With these objects were found an iron standard-frame and a two-foot carved whetstone, the symbols of sovereignty of an East Anglian king.

The treasure, scattered and corroded by time, lay within the hull of what had once been an eighty-nine-foot wooden ship. Only the iron bolts and nails remained, but the outline of the ship was plainly visible in the sand. No trace of a body was found;

the ship was evidently a cenotaph or memorial to a king[1] whose bones lay elsewhere. From the evidence offered by the coins placed with the hoard—perhaps intended as payment for the ghostly oarsmen who were to convey the king to the next world—it is thought that the burial must have been made between the years A.D. 625 and 660. Ship burials were fairly numerous among the pagan Vikings of Europe at a later period, but rare in Anglo-Saxon England. The Sutton Hoo find was hailed as the most exciting archaeological discovery of the century in Britain.

In August 1939 a local Coroner's Jury was called upon to decide the legal status of the Sutton Hoo finds—whether they should be considered as treasure-trove and therefore the property of the Crown, or whether they belonged to Mrs. Pretty, the owner of the Sutton Hoo estate. If the artifacts had been secretly hidden, with the intent of recovering them later, they would become Crown property. But if it could be shown that they had been publicly buried with no intention of ever recovering them, they would remain the property of Mrs. Pretty.

The evidence presented to the jury consisted of the description in *Beowulf* of Scyld Scefing's ship-passing and the story of the final disposal of the dragon's hoard in the account of Beowulf's funeral. The jury easily concluded on the basis of this evidence that the Sutton Hoo treasures must have been buried at a public ceremony and been intended to remain forever undisturbed. Thus they became the property of Mrs. Pretty, who then generously presented them to the British Museum, where they are now on public display.

The opening section of *Beowulf* is said to be the earliest existing documentary evidence of a ship funeral. But the description of the rich treasures that were placed in the ship had generally been looked upon as poetic fancy. The find at Sutton Hoo confirmed the historical accuracy of the *Beowulf* description of a heroic society rich in gold and other beautifully wrought objects.

Beowulf may have been composed at a time when the spectacular Sutton Hoo ship burial was still remembered. Some scholars even think the poem may have been intended as a compliment to a king of East Anglia; there is evidence pointing to the possibility that an ancestor of the East Anglian royal line was a member of the Geatish or South Swedish tribe to which Beowulf belonged.

The articles found at Sutton Hoo indicate not only that Anglo-Saxon culture of the seventh century was far more advanced than had previously been imagined, but also that the Anglo-Saxons traded widely. The helmet and shield are Swedish. The blade of the sword was probably forged in the Rhineland. The silver bowls and spoons came from the Near East, and the gold coins from France.

But even more important, as Dr. Rupert Bruce-Mitford of the British Museum has pointed out, such relics of older times help us become aware of a continuing human dignity, to realize "that love of beauty, joy in creation, perfection in craftsmanship, are basic instincts in man, manifest even in the black days when the civilization of Rome had been overwhelmed and the Barbarians were slowly laying the foundations of the medieval and modern world amidst the ruins."[2] □

Clasp from the Sutton Hoo treasures, made of gold inlaid with glass. Courtesy of the Trustees of the British Museum.

---

1. Some scholars think the king may have been Redwald, mentioned by Bede in his story of the conversion of King Edwin (page 52). Redwald had been converted to Christianity, but lapsed into pagan practices. This would account for the combination of Christian and pagan elements in the cenotaph.

2. From Dr. Bruce-Mitford's Preface to *The Treasure of Sutton Hoo* by Bernice Grohskopf. Atheneum, 1970.

The Changing English Language

"Language is a city to the building of which every human being brought a stone."—RALPH WALDO EMERSON

As Emerson indicated, language is created by people, and because people change, language too must be in a perpetual state of flux. Some words die out; others are taken in and slowly come into common use; old words sometimes take on new meanings.

The English language has developed and continues to evolve as the people who speak it have been affected by social conditions, political events, and contacts with other cultures. This series of articles will explore the nature of the changes which our language has undergone, and the events and forces which have brought about those changes.

The first inhabitants of the British Isles whose language we know about were the Celts. Beginning in 55 B.C., the Roman general Julius Caesar led a series of unsuccessful attacks on the British Celts. About a hundred years later, in A.D. 43, Romans began settling in Britain. For the next four hundred years, Britain was part of the Roman Empire, and camps of the Latin-speaking Roman legions dotted the countryside. Their influence can still be seen in the names of such English towns as Lancaster, Manchester, and Worcester, the suffixes *-chester*, *-caster*, and *-cester* being derived from *castrum*, the Latin word for camp.

Early in the fifth century, when the Roman Empire began to disintegrate, the Romans were forced to withdraw their troops from Britain. Left without the defenses of the Roman legions, the Celts were soon attacked by Germanic tribes from across the North Sea—Jutes, Angles, and Saxons—whose homelands were along the Danish peninsula and the northwest coast of Germany. The invaders drove some of the Celts to Brittany across the sea and many others into what are now Wales and Cornwall. The Celtic language survives today as Welsh, the language of Wales, Gaelic, the second language of Ireland, and Scots, the surviving ancient tongue of Scotland.

The invading tribes of Germanic people spoke dialects of the language now called Old English or sometimes Anglo-Saxon. The largest group, the Angles, settled the lands from the Thames River to the north of England. It is from this group that the names England (Angleland) and English (Anglisc) are derived, although most of the literature written in the dialect of this northern area has been lost. The Saxons, who lived south of the Thames, spoke the variety of Old English in which most of the surviving documents of the period are written. In Kent were the Jutes; only a very few texts in the Kentish dialect have been preserved.

In 597, Augustine and other missionaries arrived from Rome, bringing Christianity and initiating the introduction of Latin words into Old English. The largest number of such words were those related to the new religion; among them were *altar*, *candle*, *hymn*, *organ*, *pope*, *priest*, and *temple*, which today differ only slightly from their Old English forms. Contact with the Roman church also led to the adoption of words describing clothing (e.g., our modern *sock*, *cap*), foods (e.g., *beet*, *pear*), plants and trees (*pine*, *lily*), and words related to education (*school*, *Latin*, *verse*, *meter*), as well as many others.

Beginning in the eighth century, Old English was further modified by contact with the Scandinavian languages. The inhabitants of the Scandinavian peninsula and Denmark, once close neighbors of the early Anglo-Saxons and similar to them both in blood and in language, began a series of raids on England which culminated in the eleventh century when Cnut, king of Denmark, conquered all of England and seized the English throne. For the next twenty-five years, Danish kings ruled England.

During the nearly three hundred years of Scandinavian attacks, a considerable number of Scandinavians also settled peacefully in England, especially in the northern and eastern sections. Evidence of the extent of such settlement survives in place names. A map today shows more than six hundred names such as Grimsby, Rugby, and Derby, formed from the Danish word *byr* meaning farm or town. There are also names like Thistlethwaite and Braithwaite from *thveit* meaning "isolated piece of land."

Since Old English and the language of the invaders were quite similar, there was a ready intermingling of forms of speech. In some cases, when the languages had different words to describe the same thing, the English word survived. In other cases, such Scandinavian words as *egg* and *systir* (sister) replaced their Old English equivalents. The Scandinavian pronouns *they, their,* and *them* were substituted for the Old English equivalents *hie, hiera,* and *him.* Occasionally, Old English words which had fallen into disuse were revived because of Scandinavian parallels.

You saw a brief passage in Old English in the article on the poetry of *Beowulf.* Another passage is quoted at the end of this chapter, followed by a variety of translations. You may recognize a few words of the Anglo-Saxon; still, we who speak modern English must constantly remind ourselves when we see Old English that this was not a truly foreign language but the not-far-removed ancestor of our own tongue.

Our difficulty in reading Old English becomes more understandable when we realize that it was quite different in grammatical structure from the English we speak and write today. Modern English depends heavily upon the arrangement of words in a sentence to give meaning; it relies only slightly on word endings to indicate number, gender, and case (e.g., whether a noun is the object of a verb or its subject). For example, when we read

1. The king greeted the foreigner.
2. The foreigner greeted the king.

we know that in the first sentence, *king* is the subject of the verb *greeted,* and in the second sentence, *king* is the object of the verb, even though there is no change in the spelling of *king* as the function of the word changes. In Old English, "the king," when used as the grammatical subject (as in sentence 1) would be written as *se cyning;* as the object (as in sentence 2), it would be *þǣm cyninge.* Old English was what linguists call a highly inflected language, which means that the meaning of a sentence depended on changes in the spelling of nouns, pronouns, adjectives, and verbs. Although modern English still makes use of inflections, there are far fewer inflected forms than there were in Anglo-Saxon times.

Old English verbs were of two types: "strong" and "weak." In strong verbs, the vowels changed in the principal part, as they do in modern *sing, sang, sung,* weak verbs indicated change of time by adding *d* or *t,* as do the majority of verbs today (*look, looked, looked*).

Apart from grammatical differences, some of the strangeness which Old English presents to a modern reader is due to differences in spelling and vocabulary. Old English used two characters, þ and ð, to represent the sound *th,* so that *wiþ* is our modern word *with,* and *ða* is the equivalent of *then.* The sound *sh* was represented in Old English by *sc,* and the sound of *k* was represented by *c.* Words like *scip, bæð, nacod,* and *þæt,* which look strange to us, were most likely pronounced in Anglo-Saxon times almost as we pronounce them today: *ship, bath, naked,* and *that.*

Fewer than a fourth of the words in modern English are derived from Old English, but among those are the most commonly used nouns, pronouns, verbs, connectives, and articles.

Why don't we still speak Anglo-Saxon? What forces made English take the form it has today? Later articles in this book will trace the political and social forces which influenced—and continue to influence—the evolution of the English language. □

Beowulf and Its Translations

Below is a passage from *Beowulf,* followed first by a literal translation and then by a number of literary translations. These different versions demonstrate some of the possibilities and limitations involved in moving literature from one language to another, even when the languages are as closely related as Old and Modern English.

Ðā cōm of mōre under misthleoþum
Grendel gongan, Godes yrre bær;
mynte se mānscaða manna cynnes
sumne besyrwan in sele þām hēan.
Wōd under wolcnum tō þæs þe hē wīnreced,
goldsele gumena gearwost wisse
fǣttum fāhne. Ne wæs þæt forma sīð,
þæt hē Hrōþgāres hām gesōhte;
nǣfre hē on aldordagum ǣr nē siþðan
heardran hǣle, healðegnas fand!

Literal translation:

Then came [out] of the marsh   under a mist-cover
Grendel stalking,   God's wrath [he] bore;
thought he, [that] man-harmer   [of] mankind
a certain one to entrap   in that high hall.
He strode under clouds   until that wine-hall,
the gold-hall of men   he most surely discerned
decorated with [gold] plates.   Nor was it the first time
that he Hrothgar's   home had sought;
[but] never [in his] life-days   before or afterwards
harder luck,   or [stronger] hall-warriors found.

J. M. Garnett (1882):

Then came from the moor 'neath the misty slopes
Grendel going, God's anger he bore.
The wicked foe thought of the race of man
Some one to entrap in that high hall:
He went 'neath the clouds whither he the wine-hall,
The gold-hall of men, most thoroughly knew,
Shining with gold-plates: that was not the first time
That he of Hrothgar the home had sought.
Ne'er in his life-time before nor after
Bolder warriors, hall-thanes, did he find!

J. R. Clark-Hall (1901):

Then came Grendel, advancing from the moor under the misty slopes; God's anger rested on him. The wicked foe thought to take by treachery one of the race of men in the high hall; he strode beneath the clouds until he came to where he could very clearly discern the wine-building, the gold-hall of men, gleaming with plated gold. Nor was that the first time that he had visited Hrothgar's home. Never in the days of his life, before or since, did he discover guardians in hall with worse fortune.

From "Beowulf and the Fight at Finnsburg" from *Beowulf,* translated by J. R. Clark Hall. Reprinted by permission of George Allen & Unwin Ltd.

Francis B. Gummere (1909):

Then from the moorland, by misty crags,
with God's wrath laden, Grendel came.
The monster was minded of mankind now
sundry to seize in the stately house.
Under welkin he walked, till the wine-palace there,
gold-hall of men, he gladly discerned,
flashing with fretwork. Not first time, this,
that he the home of Hrothgar sought,—
yet ne'er in his life-day, late or early,
such hardy heroes, such hall-thanes, found!

J. Duncan Spaeth (1921):

Now Grendel came, from his crags of mist
Across the moor; he was curst of God.
The murderous prowler meant to surprise
In the high-built hall his human prey.
He stalked 'neath the clouds, till steep before him
The house of revelry rose in his path,
The gold-hall of heroes, the gaily adorned.
Hrothgar's home he had hunted full often,
But never before had he found to receive him
So hardy a hero, such hall-guards there.

From *Old English Poetry* translated by J. Duncan Spaeth. Copyright 1921 by Princeton University Press. Reprinted by permission.

Charles W. Kennedy (1940):

From the stretching moors, from the misty hollows,
Grendel came creeping, accursed of God,
A murderous ravager minded to snare
Spoil of heroes in high-built hall.
Under clouded heavens he held his way
Till there rose before him the high-roofed house,
Wine-hall of warriors gleaming with gold.
Nor was it the first of his fierce assaults
On the home of Hrothgar; but never before
Had he found worse fate or hardier hall-thanes!

From *Beowulf: The Oldest English Epic,* translated by Charles W. Kennedy. Copyright 1940 by Oxford University Press, Inc. Renewed © 1968 by Charles W. Kennedy.

Kevin Crossley-Holland (1968):

Then, under night's shroud, Grendel walked down
from the moors; he shouldered God's anger.
The evil plunderer intended to ensnare
one of the race of men in the high hall.
He strode under the skies, until he stood
before the feasting-hall, in front of the gift-building
gleaming with gold. And this night was not the first
on which he had so honoured Hrothgar's home.
But never in his life did he find hall-wardens
more greatly to his detriment.

chapter two

THE MEDIEVAL AGE
1066–1485

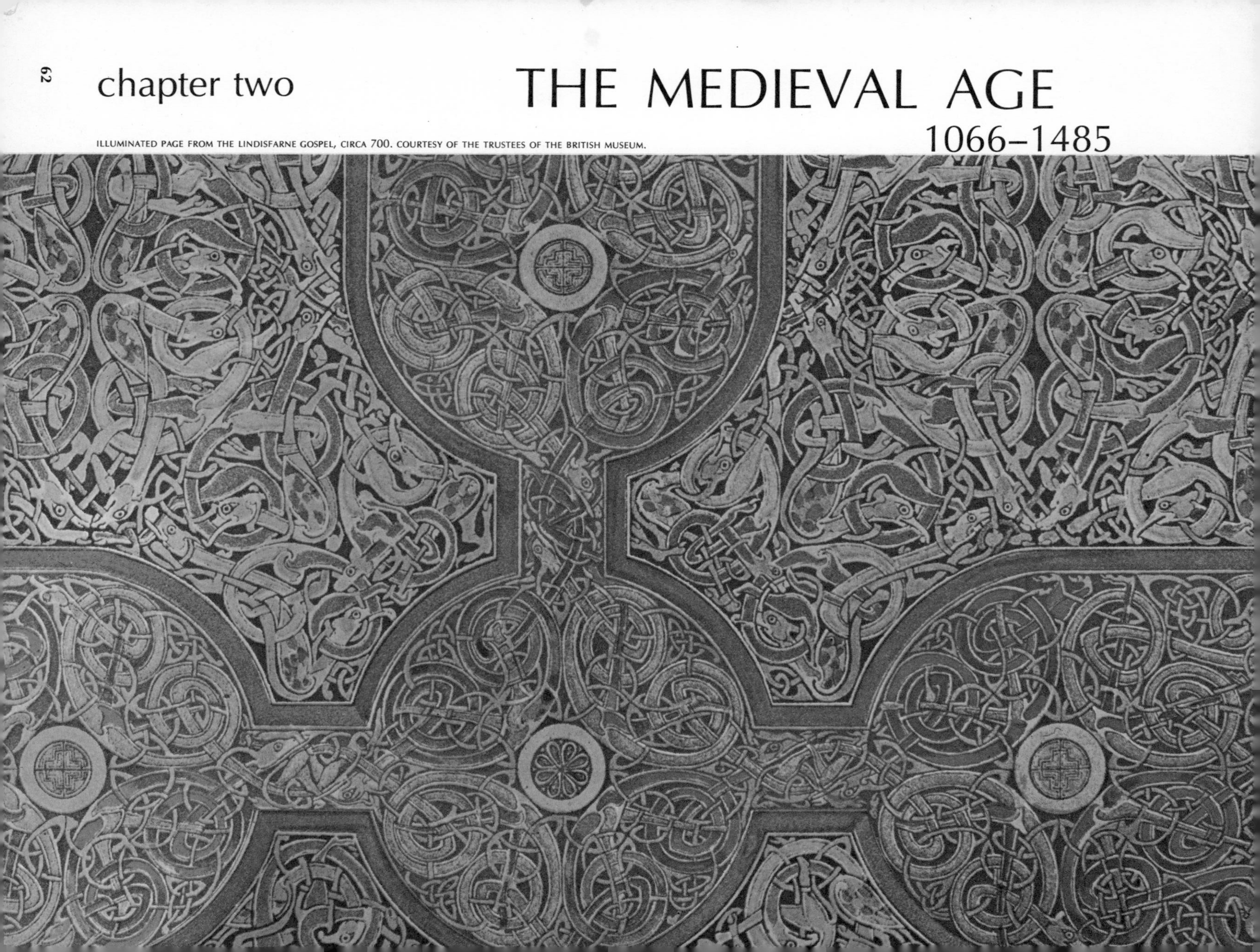

ILLUMINATED PAGE FROM THE LINDISFARNE GOSPEL, CIRCA 700. COURTESY OF THE TRUSTEES OF THE BRITISH MUSEUM.

I. THE CANTERBURY TALES

by Geoffrey Chaucer

1340? / 1400

Translated by Nevill Coghill

THE PROLOGUE

Whan that Aprill with his shoures soote
The droghte of March hath perced to the roote,
And bathed every veyne in swich licour
Of which vertu engendred is the flour;
5 Whan Zephirus eek with his sweete breeth
Inspired hath in every holt and heeth
The tendre croppes, and the yonge sonne
Hath in the Ram his halve cours yronne,
And smale foweles maken melodye,
10 That slepen al the nyght with open ye
(So priketh hem nature in hir corages);
Thanne longen folk to goon on pilgrimages,
And palmeres for to seken straunge strondes,
To ferne halwes, kowthe in sondry londes;
15 And specially from every shires ende
Of Engelond to Caunterbury they wende,
The hooly blisful martir for to seke,
That hem hath holpen whan that they were seeke.

WHEN in April the sweet showers fall
And pierce the drought of March to the root, and all
The veins are bathed in liquor of such power
As brings about the engendering of the flower,
5 When also Zephyrus with his sweet breath
Exhales an air in every grove and heath
Upon the tender shoots, and the young sun
His half-course in the sign of the *Ram* has run,[1]
And the small fowl are making melody
10 That sleep away the night with open eye
(So nature pricks them and their heart engages)
Then people long to go on pilgrimages
And palmers[2] long to seek the stranger strands
Of far-off saints, hallowed in sundry lands,
15 And specially, from every shire's end
In England, down to Canterbury they wend
To seek the holy blissful martyr,[3] quick
To give his help to them when they were sick.
It happened in that season that one day
20 In Southwark, at *The Tabard,* as I lay
Ready to go on pilgrimage and start
For Canterbury, most devout at heart,
At night there came into that hostelry
Some nine and twenty in a company
25 Of sundry folk happening then to fall
In fellowship, and they were pilgrims all
That towards Canterbury meant to ride.
The rooms and stables of the inn were wide;
They made us easy, all was of the best.
30 And shortly, when the sun had gone to rest,
By speaking to them all upon the trip
I soon was one of them in fellowship
And promised to rise early and take the way
To Canterbury, as you heard me say.
35 But none the less, while I have time and space,
Before my story takes a further pace,
It seems a reasonable thing to say
What their condition was, the full array
Of each of them, as it appeared to me
40 According to profession and degree,
And what apparel they were riding in;
And at a Knight I therefore will begin.

1. *young sun . . . has run.* Since the Ram, the first sign of the zodiac, begins its run about March 21, Chaucer dates the pilgrimage in early April.
2. *palmers,* pilgrims who had been to the Holy Land, who wore crossed palm leaves as a sign of their pilgrimage.
3. *martyr,* St. Thomas à Becket, murdered in 1170 while at prayers in the Cathedral of Canterbury. His tomb had become the favorite place of pilgrimage for Englishmen of all classes.

There was a *Knight*, a most distinguished man,
Who from the day on which he first began
45 To ride abroad had followed chivalry,
Truth, honour, generousness, and courtesy.
He had done nobly in his sovereign's war
And ridden into battle, no man more,
As well in christian as in heathen places,
50 And ever honoured for his noble graces.
When we took Alexandria,[4] he was there.
He often sat at table in the chair
Of honour, above all nations, when in Prussia.
In Lithuania he had ridden, and Russia,
55 No christian man so often, of his rank.
When, in Granada, Algeciras sank
Under assault, he had been there, and in
North Africa, raiding Benamarin;
In Anatolia he had been as well
60 And fought when Ayas and Attalia fell,
For all along the Mediterranean coast
He had embarked with many a noble host.
In fifteen mortal battles he had been
And jousted for our faith at Tramissene
65 Thrice in the lists, and always killed his man.
This same distinguished knight had led the van
Once with the Bey of Balat, doing work
For him against another heathen Turk;
He was of sovereign value in all eyes.
70 And though so much distinguished, he was wise
And in his bearing modest as a maid.
He never yet a boorish thing had said
In all his life to any, come what might;
He was a true, a perfect gentle-knight.
75 Speaking of his equipment, he possessed
Fine horses, but he was not gaily dressed.
He wore a fustian tunic stained and dark
With smudges where his armour had left mark;
Just home from service, he had joined our ranks
80 To do his pilgrimage and render thanks.
He had his son with him, a fine young *Squire,*
A lover and cadet, a lad of fire
With locks as curly as if they had been pressed.
He was some twenty years of age, I guessed.
85 In stature he was of a moderate length,
With wonderful agility and strength.
He'd seen some service with the cavalry
In Flanders and Artois and Picardy
And had done valiantly in little space
90 Of time, in hope to win his lady's grace.
He was embroidered like a meadow bright
And full of freshest flowers, red and white.
Singing he was, or fluting all the day;
He was as fresh as is the month of May.
95 Short was his gown, the sleeves were long and wide;
He knew the way to sit a horse and ride.
He could make songs and poems and recite,
Knew how to joust and dance, to draw and write.
He loved so hotly that till dawn grew pale
100 He slept as little as a nightingale.
Courteous he was, lowly and serviceable,
And carved to serve his father at the table.
There was a *Yeoman*[5] with him at his side,
No other servant; so he chose to ride.
105 This Yeoman wore a coat and hood of green,
And peacock-feathered arrows, bright and keen
And neatly sheathed, hung at his belt the while
—For he could dress his gear in yeoman style,
His arrows never drooped their feathers low—
110 And in his hand he bore a mighty bow.
His head was like a nut, his face was brown.
He knew the whole of woodcraft up and down.
A saucy brace was on his arm to ward
It from the bow-string, and a shield and sword
115 Hung at one side, and at the other slipped
A jaunty dirk, spear-sharp and well-equipped.
A medal of St Christopher[6] he wore
Of shining silver on his breast, and bore
A hunting-horn, well slung and burnished clean,
120 That dangled from a baldrick of bright green.
He was a proper forester I guess.
There also was a *Nun*, a Prioress,
Her way of smiling very simple and coy.
Her greatest oath was only "By St Loy!"[7]
125 And she was known as Madam Eglantyne.
And well she sang a service, with a fine
Intoning through her nose, as was most seemly,
And she spoke daintily in French, extremely,
After the school of Stratford-atte-Bowe;[8]
130 French in the Paris style she did not know.
At meat her manners were well-taught withal;
No morsel from her lips did she let fall,

4. *Alexandria.* Here and in the following lines Chaucer lists the Knight's campaigns, which ranged over most of the then known world.

5. *Yeoman* (yō′ mən), attendant of a noble.
6. *St Christopher,* patron saint of foresters.
7. *St Loy.* Loy, or Eligius, refused to swear upon sacred relics. To swear by St. Loy was to swear mildly or not at all.
8. *daintily . . . Stratford-atte-Bowe.* The Prioress spoke the inferior French heard in a nunnery in England, not the French of Paris.

Nor dipped her fingers in the sauce too deep;
But she could carry a morsel up and keep
135 The smallest drop from falling on her breast.
For courtliness she had a special zest,
And she would wipe her upper lip so clean
That not a trace of grease was to be seen
Upon the cup when she had drunk; to eat,
140 She reached a hand sedately for the meat.
She certainly was very entertaining,
Pleasant and friendly in her ways, and straining
To counterfeit a courtly kind of grace,
A stately bearing fitting to her place,
145 And to seem dignified in all her dealings.
As for her sympathies and tender feelings,
She was so charitably solicitous
She used to weep if she but saw a mouse
Caught in a trap, if it were dead or bleeding.
150 And she had little dogs she would be feeding
With roasted flesh, or milk, or fine white bread.
And bitterly she wept if one were dead
Or someone took a stick and made it smart;
She was all sentiment and tender heart.
155 Her veil was gathered in a seemly way,
Her nose was elegant, her eyes glass-grey;
Her mouth was very small, but soft and red,
Her forehead, certainly, was fair of spread,
Almost a span across the brows, I own;
160 She was indeed by no means undergrown.
Her cloak, I noticed, had a graceful charm.
She wore a coral trinket on her arm,
A set of beads, the gaudies tricked in green,[9]
Whence hung a golden brooch of brightest sheen
165 On which there first was graven a crowned A,
And lower, *Amor vincit omnia.*[10]
Another *Nun,* the chaplain at her cell,
Was riding with her, and *three Priests* as well.
A *Monk* there was, one of the finest sort
170 Who rode the country; hunting was his sport.
A manly man, to be an Abbot able;
Many a dainty horse he had in stable.
His bridle, when he rode, a man might hear
Jingling in a whistling wind as clear,
175 Aye, and as loud as does the chapel bell
Where my lord Monk was Prior of the cell.
The Rule of good St Benet or St Maur[11]
As old and strict he tended to ignore;
He let go by the things of yesterday
180 And took the modern world's more spacious way.
He did not rate that text at a plucked hen
Which says that hunters are not holy men
And that a monk uncloistered is a mere
Fish out of water, flapping on the pier,
185 That is to say a monk out of his cloister.
That was a text he held not worth an oyster;
And I agreed and said his views were sound;
Was he to study till his head went round
Poring over books in cloisters? Must he toil
190 As Austin[12] bade and till the very soil?
Was he to leave the world upon the shelf?
Let Austin have his labour to himself.
This Monk was therefore a good man to horse;
Greyhounds he had, as swift as birds, to course.
195 Hunting a hare or riding at a fence
Was all his fun, he spared for no expense.
I saw his sleeves were garnished at the hand
With fine grey fur, the finest in the land,
And on his hood, to fasten it at his chin
200 He had a wrought-gold cunningly fashioned pin;
Into a lover's knot it seemed to pass.

9. *A set . . . green.* The Prioress carried a coral rosary having "gaudies," or larger Paternoster beads, of green.
10. *Amor vincit omnia,* "Love overcometh all things."
11. *St Benet or St Maur,* St. Benedict, founder of the Benedictine religious order, and his disciple, St. Maur.
12. *Austin,* St. Augustine, bishop of Hippo (d. A.D. 430), who advised monks to practice manual labor.

OF LITERARY INTEREST

Chaucer's popularity

Chaucer's *Canterbury Tales* is considered the greatest piece of imaginative literature produced in medieval England. That many people of Chaucer's day and the century that followed enjoyed and valued the work is attested by the fact that eighty-four manuscript copies—partial or complete—have survived. This is a truly remarkable number, since before the invention of the printing press, each manuscript had to be painstakingly copied by hand. In 1476, when William Caxton set up the first English printing press, *The Canterbury Tales* was one of the first books he printed.

Chaucer's original plan called for approximately 120 stories, two to be told by each pilgrim during the fifty-six-mile journey from Southwark to Canterbury, and two more to be related on the return trip. Actually, Chaucer completed only twenty-four tales, of which one (the Cook's) is only a fragment.

His head was bald and shone like looking-glass;
So did his face, as if it had been greased.
He was a fat and personable priest;
205 His prominent eyeballs never seemed to settle;
They glittered like the flames beneath a kettle;
Supple his boots, his horse in fine condition.
He was a prelate fit for exhibition,
He was not pale like a tormented soul.
210 He liked a fat swan best, and roasted whole.
His palfrey was as brown as is a berry.
There was a *Friar,* a wanton one and merry,
A Limiter,[13] a very festive fellow.
In all Four Orders[14] there was none so mellow
215 So glib with gallant phrase and well-turned speech.
He'd fixed up many a marriage, giving each
Of his young women what he could afford her.
He was a noble pillar to his Order.
Highly beloved and intimate was he
220 With County folk within his boundary,
And city dames of honour and possessions;
For he was qualified to hear confessions,
Or so he said, with more than priestly scope;
He had a special license from the Pope.
225 Sweetly he heard his penitents at shrift
With pleasant absolution, for a gift.
He was an easy man in penance-giving
Where he could hope to make a decent living;
It's a sure sign whenever gifts are given
230 To a poor Order that a man's well shriven,
And should he give enough he knew in verity
The penitent repented in sincerity.
For many a fellow is so hard of heart
He cannot weep, for all his inward smart.
235 Therefore instead of weeping and of prayer
One should give silver for a poor Friar's care.
He kept his tippet stuffed with pins for curls,
And pocket-knives, to give to pretty girls.
And certainly his voice was gay and sturdy,
240 For he sang well and played the hurdy-gurdy.[15]
At sing-songs he was champion of the hour.
His neck was whiter than a lily-flower
But strong enough to butt a bruiser down.
He knew the taverns well in every town
245 And every innkeeper and barmaid too
Better than lepers, beggars and that crew,
For in so eminent a man as he
It was not fitting with the dignity
Of his position, dealing with a scum
250 Of wretched lepers; nothing good can come
Of dealings with the slum-and-gutter dwellers,
But only with the rich and victual-sellers.
But anywhere a profit might accrue
Courteous he was and lowly of service too.
255 Natural gifts like his were hard to match.
He was the finest beggar of his batch,
And, for his begging-district, payed a rent;
His brethren did no poaching where he went.
For though a widow mightn't have a shoe,
260 So pleasant was his holy how-d'ye-do
He got his farthing from her just the same
Before he left, and so his income came
To more than he laid out. And how he romped,
Just like a puppy! He was ever prompt
265 To arbitrate disputes on settling days[16]
(For a small fee) in many helpful ways,
Not then appearing as your cloistered scholar
With threadbare habit hardly worth a dollar,
But much more like a Doctor or a Pope.
270 Of double-worsted was the semi-cope
Upon his shoulders, and the swelling fold
About him, like a bell about its mould
When it is casting, rounded out his dress.
He lisped a little out of wantonness
275 To make his English sweet upon his tongue.
When he had played his harp, or having sung,
His eyes would twinkle in his head as bright
As any star upon a frosty night.
This worthy's name was Hubert, it appeared.
280 There was a *Merchant* with a forking beard
And motley[17] dress; high on his horse he sat,
Upon his head a Flemish beaver hat
And on his feet daintily buckled boots.
He told of his opinions and pursuits
285 In solemn tones, and how he never lost.
The sea should be kept free at any cost
(He thought) upon the Harwich-Holland range,[18]
He was expert at currency exchange.
This estimable Merchant so had set

13. *Limiter,* a begging friar who was granted a district to beg in, to limit his activities.
14. *Four Orders,* the four Orders of mendicant friars, the Dominicans, the Franciscans, the Carmelites, and the Austin Friars.
15. *hurdy-gurdy.* Chaucer's term in the original designated a stringed instrument resembling a lute.
16. *settling days,* days on which disputes could be settled by umpires out of court. Friars often acted as umpires and accepted "gifts" for their services.
17. *motley,* not as customarily understood, the costume of a court jester, but cloth woven with a figured design.
18. *The sea . . . Harwich-Holland range.* He wished the sea to be guarded, no matter what the cost, to permit ships to pass freely from England to Holland.

290 His wits to work, none knew he was in debt,
He was so stately in negotiation,
Loan, bargain and commercial obligation.
He was an excellent fellow all the same;
To tell the truth I do not know his name.
295 An *Oxford Cleric,* still a student though,
One who had taken logic long ago,
Was there; his horse was thinner than a rake,
And he was not too fat, I undertake,
But had a hollow look, a sober stare;
300 The thread upon his overcoat was bare.
He had found no preferment in the church
And he was too unworldly to make search
For secular employment. By his bed
He preferred having twenty books in red
305 And black, of Aristotle's philosophy,
To having fine clothes, fiddle or psaltery.
Though a philosopher, as I have told,
He had not found the stone for making gold.[19]
Whatever money from his friends he took
310 He spent on learning or another book
And prayed for them most earnestly, returning
Thanks to them thus for paying for his learning.
His only care was study, and indeed
He never spoke a word more than was need,
315 Formal at that, respectful in the extreme,
Short, to the point, and lofty in his theme.
The thought of moral virtue filled his speech
And he would gladly learn, and gladly teach.
A Serjeant at the Law[20] who paid his calls,
320 Wary and wise, for clients at St Paul's[21]
There also was, of noted excellence.
Discreet he was, a man to reverence,
Or so he seemed, his sayings were so wise.
He often had been Justice of Assize
325 By letters patent, and in full commission.
His fame and learning and his high position
Had won him many a robe and many a fee.
There was no such conveyancer as he;
All was fee-simple to his strong digestion,[22]
330 Not one conveyance could be called in question.
Nowhere there was so busy a man as he;
But was less busy than he seemed to be.
He knew of every judgement, case and crime
Recorded, ever since King William's time.[23]
335 He could dictate defences or draft deeds;
No one could pinch a comma from his screeds,
And he knew every statute off by rote.
He wore a homely parti-coloured coat
Girt with a silken belt of pin-stripe stuff;
340 Of his appearance I have said enough.
There was a *Franklin*[24] with him, it appeared;
White as a daisy-petal was his beard.
A sanguine man, high-coloured and benign,
He loved a morning sop of cake in wine.
345 He lived for pleasure and had always done,
For he was Epicurus'[25] very son,
In whose opinion sensual delight
Was the one true felicity in sight.
As noted as St Julian[26] was for bounty
350 He made his household free to all the County.
His bread, his ale were finest of the fine
And no one had a better stock of wine.
His house was never short of bake-meat pies,
Of fish and flesh, and these in such supplies
355 It positively snowed with meat and drink
And all the dainties that a man could think.
According to the seasons of the year
Changes of dish were ordered to appear.
He kept fat partridges in coops, beyond,
360 Many a bream and pike were in his pond.
Woe to the cook whose sauces had no sting
Or who was unprepared in anything!
And in his hall a table stood arrayed
And ready all day long, with places laid.
365 As Justice at the Sessions none stood higher;[27]
He often had been Member for the Shire.[28]
A dagger and a little purse of silk
Hung at his girdle, white as morning milk.
As Sheriff[29] he checked audit, every entry.
370 He was a model among landed gentry.
A *Haberdasher*, a *Dyer*, a *Carpenter*,

---

19. *Though a philosopher . . . gold.* In alchemy, the philosopher's stone was supposed to convert base metals into gold.

20. *Serjeant at the Law,* a legal officer of the King, selected from lawyers who had practiced for at least sixteen years. This was a position of considerable honor.

21. *St Paul's.* In the afternoon, when courts were closed, it was customary for lawyers to meet clients for consultation in the porch of St. Paul's Cathedral.

22. *conveyancer . . . digestion.* The Serjeant at the Law was interested in becoming a large landowner; his "strong digestion" was for property, to which he managed to obtain unrestricted possession ("fee-simple").

23. *King William's time,* the time of William the Conqueror.

24. *Franklin,* a class of landowner, a freeholder, who was also free by birth but not noble.

25. *Epicurus,* a Greek philosopher (342?–270 B.C.) who believed in the pursuit of pleasure.

26. *St Julian,* patron saint of hospitality.

27. *Justice . . . higher.* When the Justices of the Peace sat in session, he presided.

28. *Member . . . Shire,* Member of Parliament for his county.

29. *Sheriff,* the King's administrative officer for the shire or county.

A *Weaver* and a *Carpet-maker* were
Among our ranks, all in the livery
Of one impressive guild-fraternity.[30]
375 They were so trim and fresh their gear would pass
For new. Their knives were not tricked out with
brass
But wrought with purest silver, which avouches
A like display on girdles and on pouches.
Each seemed a worthy burgess, fit to grace
380 A guild-hall with a seat upon the dais.[31]
Their wisdom would have justified a plan
To make each one of them an alderman;
They had the capital and revenue,
Besides their wives declared it was their due.
385 And if they did not think so, then they ought;
To be called "*Madam*" is a glorious thought,
And so is going to church and being seen
Having your mantle carried like a queen.
They had a *Cook* with them who stood alone
390 For boiling chicken with a marrow-bone,
Sharp flavouring-powder and a spice for savour.
He could distinguish London ale by flavour,
And he could roast and seethe and broil and fry,
Make good thick soup and bake a tasty pie.
395 But what a pity—so it seemed to me,
That he should have an ulcer on his knee.
As for blancmange, he made it with the best.
There was a *Skipper* hailing from far west;
He came from Dartmouth, so I understood.
400 He rode a farmer's horse as best he could,
In a woollen gown that reached his knee.
A dagger on a lanyard falling free
Hung from his neck under his arm and down.
The summer heat had tanned his colour brown,
405 And certainly he was an excellent fellow.
Many a draught of vintage, red and yellow,
He'd drawn at Bordeaux, while the trader snored.
The nicer rules of conscience he ignored.
If, when he fought, the enemy vessel sank,
410 He sent his prisoners home; they walked the plank.
As for his skill in reckoning his tides,
Currents, and many another risk besides,
Moons, harbours, pilots, he had such dispatch
That none from Hull to Carthage[32] was his match.

30. *guild-fraternity.* Since the men belonged to different trades, their guild was not a trade guild but a social and religious guild.
31. *guild-hall . . . dais,* worthy to preside at meetings of the guild.
32. *from Hull to Carthage.* Hull is an English seaport; Carthage is probably the Spanish port of Cartagena. These and other references indicate how widely the Skipper had traveled.

OF HUMAN INTEREST

Advice for a doctor, c. 1376

"He must not be rash or boastful in speech or in deed. He had better not talk much, especially among great men. And he should answer cannily to all questions so that he may not be tripped up by his own words. . . . A doctor should also be careful not to laugh and joke too much; and, as far as he can, he should avoid the company of knaves and dishonest persons. . . . The use of books is creditable to a doctor because they both keep him occupied and teach him some thing. Above all, it is important that he be found always sober, for drunkenness spoils every good thing. . . . But most important of all is that he do not operate in any time when operation is forbidden by the astronomers."

John Arderne (from *Treatises of Fistula*).

415 Hardy he was, prudent in undertaking;
His beard in many a tempest had its shaking,
And he knew all the havens as they were
From Gottland to the Cape of Finisterre,
And every creek in Brittany and Spain;
420 The barge he owned was called *The Maudelayne.*
A *Doctor* too emerged as we proceeded;
No one alive could talk as well as he did
On points of medicine and of surgery,
For, being grounded in astronomy,[33]
425 He watched his patient's favourable star
And, by his Natural Magic, knew what are
The lucky hours and planetary degrees
For making charms and magic effigies.
The cause of every malady you'd got
430 He knew, and whether dry, cold, moist, or hot;[34]
He knew their seat, their humour, and condition.

33. *astronomy,* astrology. It was believed that the position of the planets determined the best time to treat a patient.
34. *dry . . . hot.* A man's body was conceived as being composed of the four elements, earth, water, air, and fire, in due proportion. Earth was thought to be cold and dry, water cold and moist, air hot and moist, fire hot and dry. Diseases were thought to be due to an imbalance in one or more of these qualities. A man's character could be roughly defined by reference to them, and their proportion decided his "humour"; e.g. a *sanguine* man (like the Franklin) was held to be hot and moist, which gave him the character of being a laughing, amorous, high-colored, fleshy, good-natured fellow. A *choleric* man (like the Reeve) was thought to be hot and dry. There were also *melancholy* men (cold and dry) and *phlegmatic* men, cold and moist.

He was a perfect practising physician.
These causes being known for what they were,
He gave the man his medicine then and there.
435 All his apothecaries in a tribe
Were ready with the drugs he would prescribe,
And each made money from the other's guile;
They had been friendly for a goodish while.
He was well-versed in Esculapius[35] too
440 And what Hippocrates and Rufus knew
And Dioscorides, now dead and gone,
Galen and Rhazes, Hali, Serapion,
Averroes, Avicenna, Constantine,
Scotch Bernard, John of Gaddesden, Gilbertine.
445 In his own diet he observed some measure;
There were no superfluities for pleasure,
Only digestives, nutritives, and such.
He did not read the Bible very much.
In blood-red garments, slashed with bluish-grey
450 And lined with taffeta, he rode his way;
Yet he was rather close as to expenses
And kept the gold he won in pestilences.
Gold stimulates the heart, or so we're told.
He therefore had a special love of gold.
455 A worthy *woman* from beside *Bath* city
Was with us, somewhat deaf, which was a pity.
In making cloth she showed so great a bent
She bettered those of Ypres and of Ghent.[36]
In all the parish not a dame dared stir
460 Towards the altar steps in front of her,
And if indeed they did, so wrath was she
As to be quite put out of charity.
Her kerchiefs were of finely woven ground;
I dared have sworn they weighed a good ten pound,
465 The ones she wore on Sunday, on her head.
Her hose were of the finest scarlet red
And gartered tight; her shoes were soft and new.
Bold was her face, handsome, and red in hue.
A worthy woman all her life, what's more
470 She'd had five husbands, all at the church door,[37]
Apart from other company in youth;
No need just now to speak of that, forsooth.
And she had thrice been to Jerusalem,
Seen many strange rivers and passed over them;
475 She'd been to Rome and also to Boulogne,
St James of Compostella and Cologne,[38]
And she was skilled in wandering by the way.
She had gap-teeth, set widely, truth to say.
Easily on an ambling horse she sat
480 Well wimpled up,[39] and on her head a hat
As broad as is a buckler or a shield;
She had a flowing mantle that concealed
Large hips, her heels spurred sharply under that.
In company she liked to laugh and chat
485 And knew the remedies for love's mischances,
An art in which she knew the oldest dances.
A holy-minded man of good renown
There was, and poor, the *Parson* to a town,
Yet he was rich in holy thought and work.
490 He also was a learned man, a clerk,
Who truly knew Christ's gospel and would preach it
Devoutly to parishioners, and teach it.
Benign and wonderfully diligent,
And patient when adversity was sent
495 (For so he proved in great adversity)
He much disliked extorting tithe or fee,
Nay rather he preferred beyond a doubt
Giving to poor parishioners round about
From his own goods and Easter offerings.
500 He found sufficiency in little things.
Wide was his parish, with houses far asunder,
Yet he neglected not in rain or thunder,
In sickness or in grief, to pay a call
On the remotest, whether great or small,
505 Upon his feet, and in his hand a stave.
This noble example to his sheep he gave,
First following the word before he taught it,
And it was from the gospel he had caught it.
This little proverb he would add thereto
510 That if gold rust, what then will iron do?
For if a priest be foul in whom we trust
No wonder that a common man should rust.
The true example that a priest should give
Is one of cleanness, how the sheep should live.
515 He did not set his benefice to hire
And leave his sheep encumbered in the mire
Or run to London to earn easy bread
By singing masses for the wealthy dead,

---

35. *Esculapius.* This and the names that follow belong to eminent medical authorities from ancient times to Chaucer's day. They show that the Doctor was well-read in his profession.
36. *Ypres . . . Ghent,* Flemish cities famous for the excellence of their weavers and as markets of the wool trade.
37. *five husbands . . . door.* From the 10th to the 16th century, the marriage service was celebrated at the church door, followed by a nuptial mass inside the church.
38. *Rome . . . Cologne.* The Wife had visited the most famous shrines in Italy, France, Spain, and Germany.
39. *well wimpled up,* wearing a linen garment that covered her head, neck, and the sides of her face.

"THE FOUR HUMOURS." COURTESY OF THE TRUSTEES OF THE BRITISH MUSEUM.

Or find some Brotherhood and get enrolled.[40]
520 He stayed at home and watched over his fold
So that no wolf should make the sheep miscarry.
He was a shepherd and no mercenary.
Holy and virtuous he was, but then
Never contemptuous of sinful men,
525 Never disdainful, never too proud or fine,
But was discreet in teaching and benign.
His business was to show a fair behaviour
And draw men thus to Heaven and their Saviour,
Unless indeed a man were obstinate;
530 And such, whether of high or low estate,
He put to sharp rebuke to say the least.
I think there never was a better priest.
He sought no pomp or glory in his dealings,
No scrupulosity had spiced his feelings.
535 Christ and His Twelve Apostles and their lore
He taught, but followed it himself before.

There was a *Plowman* with him there, his brother.
Many a load of dung one time or other
He must have carted through the morning dew.
540 He was an honest worker, good and true,
Living in peace and perfect charity,
And, as the gospel bade him, so did he,
Loving God best with all his heart and mind
And then his neighbour as himself, repined
545 At no misfortune, slacked for no content,
For steadily about his work he went
To thrash his corn, to dig or to manure
Or make a ditch; and he would help the poor
For love of Christ and never take a penny
550 If he could help it, and, as prompt as any,
He paid his tithes in full when they were due
On what he owned, and on his earnings too.
He wore a tabard smock and rode a mare.

There was a *Reeve*, also a *Miller*, there,
555 A College *Manciple* from the Inns of Court,
A papal *Pardoner* and, in close consort,
A Church-Court *Summoner*, riding at a trot,
And finally myself—that was the lot.

The *Miller* was a chap of sixteen stone,
560 A great stout fellow big in brawn and bone.
He did well out of them, for he could go
And win the ram at any wrestling show.
Broad, knotty, and short-shouldered, he would boast
He could heave any door off hinge and post,
565 Or take a run and break it with his head.

40. *find . . . enrolled,* become paid chaplain to a guild.

His beard, like any sow or fox, was red
And broad as well, as though it were a spade;
And, at its very tip, his nose displayed
A wart on which there stood a tuft of hair
570 Red as the bristles in an old sow's ear.
His nostrils were as black as they were wide.
He had a sword and buckler at his side,
His mighty mouth was like a furnace door.
A wrangler and buffoon, he had a store
575 Of tavern stories, filthy in the main.
His was a master-hand at stealing grain.
He felt it with his thumb and thus he knew
Its quality and took three times his due—
A thumb of gold,[41] by God, to gauge an oat!
580 He wore a hood of blue and a white coat.
He liked to play his bagpipes up and down
And that was how he brought us out of town.

The *Manciple*[42] came from the Inner Temple;[43]
All caterers might follow his example
585 In buying victuals; he was never rash
Whether he bought on credit or paid cash.
He used to watch the market most precisely
And got in first, and so he did quite nicely.
Now isn't it a marvel of God's grace
590 That an illiterate fellow can outpace
The wisdom of a heap of learned men?
His masters—he had more than thirty then—
All versed in the abstrusest legal knowledge,
Could have produced a dozen from their College
595 Fit to be stewards in land and rents and game
To any Peer in England you could name,
And show him how to live on what he had
Debt-free (unless of course the Peer were mad)
Or be as frugal as he might desire,
600 And they were fit to help about the Shire
In any legal case there was to try;
And yet this Manciple could wipe their eye.

The *Reeve*[44] was old and choleric and thin;
His beard was shaven closely to the skin,
605 His shorn hair came abruptly to a stop
Above his ears, and he was docked on top
Just like a priest in front; his legs were lean,

41. *A thumb of gold.* A miller's thumb was said to be worth its weight in gold because he used it to weight the scales, thus giving customers short measure.

42. *Manciple,* a purchasing agent.

43. *Inner Temple,* one of the four Inns of Court in London which house the four societies of lawyers. In England, these societies alone admit practitioners of the law to practice at the bar.

44. *Reeve,* a steward or minor official on an estate, generally an intermediary between a lord and his serfs.

Like sticks they were, no calf was to be seen.
He kept his bins and garners very trim;
610 No auditor could gain a point on him.
And he could judge by watching drought and rain
The yield he might expect from seed and grain.
His master's sheep, his animals and hens,
Pigs, horses, dairies, stores and cattle-pens
615 Were wholly trusted to his government.
And he was under contract to present
The accounts, right from his master's earliest years.
No one had ever caught him in arrears.
No bailiff, serf, or herdsman dared to kick,
620 He knew their dodges, knew their every trick;
Feared like the plague he was, by those beneath.
He had a lovely dwelling on a heath,
Shadowed in green by trees above the sward.
A better hand at bargains than his lord,
625 He had grown rich and had a store of treasure
Well tucked away, yet out it came to pleasure
His lord with subtle loans or gifts of goods,
To earn his thanks and even coats and hoods.
When young he'd learnt a useful trade and still
630 He was a carpenter of first-rate skill.
The stallion-cob he rode at a slow trot
Was dapple-grey and bore the name of Scot.
He wore an overcoat of bluish shade
And rather long; he had a rusty blade
635 Slung at his side. He came, as I heard tell,
From Norfolk, near a place called Baldeswell.
His coat was tucked under his belt and splayed.
He rode the hindmost of our cavalcade.
There was a *Summoner*[45] with us in the place
640 Who had a fire-red cherubinnish face,
For he had carbuncles. His eyes were narrow,
He was as hot and lecherous as a sparrow.
Black, scabby brows he had, and a thin beard.
Children were afraid when he appeared.
645 No quicksilver, lead ointments, tartar creams,
Boracic, no, nor brimstone, so it seems,
Could make a salve that had the power to bite,
Clean up or cure his whelks of knobby white
Or purge the pimples sitting on his cheeks.
650 Garlic he loved, and onions too, and leeks,
And drinking strong wine till all was hazy.
Then he would shout and jabber as if crazy,
And wouldn't speak a word except in Latin
When he was drunk, such tags as he was pat in;

45. *Summoner,* one paid to summon sinners to trial before an ecclesiastical court.

OF CRITICAL INTEREST

The physiognomists

In the Middle Ages, a "science" called physiognomy became popular. It was based on the idea that the mental and emotional characteristics of an individual could be determined from physical characteristics like physique, hair, and voice quality. Chaucer, like his readers, must have been familiar with these ideas.

The details in the description of the Pardoner, for example (lines 693–709), conveyed to Chaucer's audience information that a modern reader might miss. In medieval physiognomical lore, sparse yellow hair, soft and long, was a token of effeminacy, cunning, and deceptiveness. Hare-eyes that bulge and glitter indicated shameless effrontery, gluttony, and drunkenness. The goat-voice and beardlessness confirmed the Pardoner's lack of manhood and implied craftiness and treachery.

To a fourteenth-century audience, the fact that the Wife of Bath's teeth were set wide apart might indicate that she was envious, irreverent, bold, deceitful, and fond of luxury; or it might be interpreted as a sign that she was destined to do much traveling.

Two other significant descriptions are those of the Miller and the Reeve. According to the physiognomists, the Miller's broad, thickset physique, red beard, and large nostrils, as well as the bristly wart at the tip of his nose, indicated his bold, garrulous, quarrelsome nature. The Reeve's thin body and calfless legs were associated with the choleric humor, which denoted quick temper, sharpness of wit, and wantonness.

655 He only had a few, say two or three,
That he had mugged up out of some decree;
No wonder, for he heard them every day.
And, as you know, a man can teach a jay
To call out "Walter" better than the Pope.
660 But had you tried to test his wits and grope
For more, you'd have found nothing in the bag.
Then "*Questio quid juris*"[46] was his tag.
He was a gentle varlet and a kind one,
No better fellow if you went to find one.
665 He would allow—just for a quart of wine—
Any good lad to keep a concubine

46. *"Questio quid juris,"* "The question is, what portion of the law applies?"

A twelvemonth and dispense it altogether!
Yet he could pluck a finch to leave no feather:[47]
And if he found some rascal with a maid
670 He would instruct him not to be afraid
In such a case of the Archdeacon's curse
(Unless the rascal's soul were in his purse)
For in his purse the punishment should be.
"Purse is the good Archdeacon's Hell," said he.
675 But well I know he lied in what he said;
A curse should put a guilty man in dread,
For curses kill, as shriving brings, salvation.
We should beware of excommunication.
Thus, as he pleased, the man could bring duress
680 On any young fellow in the diocese.
He knew their secrets, they did what he said.
He wore a garland set upon his head
Large as the holly-bush upon a stake
Outside an ale-house;[48] and he had a cake,
685 A round one, which it was his joke to wield
As if it were intended for a shield.
He and a gentle *Pardoner*[49] rode together,
A bird from Charing Cross[50] of the same feather,
Just back from visiting the Court of Rome.
690 He loudly sang *"Come hither, love, come home!"*
The Summoner sang deep seconds to this song,
No trumpet ever sounded half so strong.
This Pardoner had hair as yellow as wax,
Hanging down smoothly like a hank of flax.
695 In driblets fell his locks behind his head
Down to his shoulders which they overspread;
Thinly they fell, like rat-tails, one by one.
He wore no hood upon his head, for fun;
The hood inside his wallet had been stowed,
700 He aimed at riding in the latest mode;
But for a little cap his head was bare
And he had bulging eye-balls, like a hare.
He'd sewed a holy relic on his cap;
His wallet lay before him on his lap,
705 Brimful of pardons come from Rome all hot.
He had the same small voice a goat has got.

47. *Yet . . . feather.* The Summoner indulged in the same sin which he is just said to have excused in others.
48. *Large . . . ale-house.* A tavern was customarily identified by such a bush on a stake.
49. *Pardoner,* one who has authority from the Pope to sell pardons and indulgences, though not necessarily in holy orders.
50. *Charing Cross,* district of London in which was located the hospital of the Blessed Mary of Rouncivalle. In Chaucer's time, unauthorized pardons were sold by persons claiming they were collecting money for the hospital, and Pardoners of Rouncivalle were often satirized.

His chin no beard had harboured, nor would harbour,
Smoother than ever chin was left by barber.
I judge he was a gelding, or a mare.
710 As to his trade, from Berwick down to Ware[51]
There was no pardoner of equal grace,
For in his trunk he had a pillow-case
Which he asserted was Our Lady's veil.
He said he had a gobbet of the sail
715 Saint Peter had the time when he made bold
To walk the waves, till Jesu Christ took hold.
He had a cross of metal set with stones
And, in a glass, a rubble of pigs' bones.
And with these relics, any time he found
720 Some poor up-country parson to astound,
On one short day, in money down, he drew
More than the parson in a month or two,
And by his flatteries and prevarication
Made monkeys of the priest and congregation.
725 But still to do him justice first and last
In church he was a noble ecclesiast.
How well he read a lesson or told a story!
But best of all he sang an Offertory,
For well he knew that when that song was sung
730 He'd have to preach and tune his honey-tongue
And (well he could) win silver from the crowd.
That's why he sang so merrily and loud.
Now I have told you shortly, in a clause,
The rank, the array, the number and the cause
735 Of our assembly in this company
In Southwark, at that high-class hostelry
Known as *The Tabard,* close beside *The Bell.*
And now the time has come for me to tell
How we behaved that evening; I'll begin
740 After we had alighted at the Inn,
Then I'll report our journey, stage by stage,
All the remainder of our pilgrimage.
But first I beg of you, in courtesy,
Not to condemn me as unmannerly
745 If I speak plainly and with no concealings
And give account of all their words and dealings,
Using their very phrases as they fell.
For certainly, as you all know so well,
He who repeats a tale after a man
750 Is bound to say, as nearly as he can,
Each single word, if he remembers it,
However rudely spoken or unfit,
Or else the tale he tells will be untrue,

51. *from Berwick . . . Ware,* from one end of England to the other.

The things invented and the phrases new.
755 He may not flinch although it were his brother,
If he says one word he must say the other.
And Christ Himself spoke broad in Holy Writ,
And as you know there's nothing there unfit,
And Plato says, for those with power to read,
760 "The word should be as cousin to the deed."
Further I beg you to forgive it me
If I neglect the order and degree
And what is due to rank in what I've planned.
I'm short of wit as you will understand.
765 Our *Host* gave us great welcome; everyone
Was given a place and supper was begun.
He served the finest victuals you could think,
The wine was strong and we were glad to drink.
A very striking man our Host withal,
770 And fit to be a marshal in a hall.
His eyes were bright, his girth a little wide;
There is no finer burgess in Cheapside.[52]
Bold in his speech, yet wise and full of tact,
There was no manly attribute he lacked,
775 What's more he was a merry-hearted man.
After our meal he jokingly began
To talk of sport, and, among other things
After we'd settled up our reckonings,
He said as follows: "Truly, gentlemen,
780 You're very welcome and I can't think when
—Upon my word I'm telling you no lie—
I've seen a gathering here that looked so spry,
No, not this year, as in this tavern now.
I'd think you up some fun if I knew how.
785 And, as it happens, a thought has just occurred
And it will cost you nothing, on my word.
You're off to Canterbury—well, God speed!
Blessed St Thomas answer to your need!
And I don't doubt, before the journey's done
790 You mean to while the time in tales and fun.
Indeed, there's little pleasure for your bones
Riding along and all as dumb as stones.
So let me then propose for your enjoyment,
Just as I said, a suitable employment.
795 And if my notion suits and you agree
And promise to submit yourselves to me
Playing your parts exactly as I say
Tomorrow as you ride along the way,
Then by my father's soul (and he is dead)
800 If you don't like it you can have my head!
Hold up your hands, and not another word."

52. *Cheapside,* a district of London.

Well, our consent of course was not deferred,
It seemed not worth a serious debate;
We all agreed to it at any rate
805 And bade him issue what commands he would.
"My lords," he said, "now listen for your good,
And please don't treat my notion with disdain.
This is the point. I'll make it short and plain.
Each one of you shall help to make things slip
810 By telling two stories on the outward trip
To Canterbury, that's what I intend,
And, on the homeward way to journey's end
Another two, tales from the days of old;
And then the man whose story is best told,
815 That is to say who gives the fullest measure

OF LITERARY INTEREST

Chaucer the satirist

"Chaucer was writing at a time when a poet never made his individual emotions the subject-matter of his poetry. Though the personal pronoun 'I' is used frequently in medieval narrative and lyric poetry, it is usually a dramatic 'I', that is, the 'I' is a character in the poem, bearing no different relation to the poet from that of the other characters. Chaucer's use of an 'I' character belongs to the tradition of such characters, but with an ingenious variation that the character appears naive, well-meaning, and obtuse, and the joke thus depends on the discrepancy between this figure in the poetry and the poet of wit and intelligence who wrote the whole.

"It is through this character that both the apparently vivid individuality of the pilgrims and the satiric aim are achieved. It is through the eyes of Chaucer the pilgrim, not Chaucer the poet, that the characters are chiefly presented. Obviously the choice of detail shows the sharp selectiveness of the satirist, but the friendly, enthusiastic, unsophisticated, unjudging tone is that of Chaucer the pilgrim.

"By his fiction of having been a close companion of his characters, Chaucer suggests their reality and individuality. He implies that most of the information which he gives us derives, not from a narrative-writer's omniscience but from the characters' own conversation. Chaucer makes his response that of a man who accepts and repeats with enthusiasm, and without criticism, whatever he is told."

Abridged from "Chaucer as Satirist in the *General Prologue* of *The Canterbury Tales*" from *Critical Quarterly,* Vol. 1, 1959. Reprinted by the permission of the author, Rosemary Woolf.

Of good morality and general pleasure,
He shall be given a supper, paid by all,
Here in this tavern, in this very hall,
When we come back again from Canterbury.
820 And in the hope to keep you bright and merry
I'll go along with you myself and ride
All at my own expense and serve as guide.
I'll be the judge, and those who won't obey
Shall pay for what we spend upon the way.
825 Now if you all agree to what you've heard
Tell me at once without another word,
And I will make arrangements early for it."
Of course we all agreed, in fact we swore it
Delightedly, and made entreaty too
830 That he should act as he proposed to do,
Become our Governor in short, and be
Judge of our tales and general referee,
And set the supper at a certain price.
We promised to be ruled by his advice
835 Come high, come low; unanimously thus
We set him up in judgement over us.
More wine was fetched, the business being done;
We drank it off and up went everyone
To bed without a moment of delay.
840 Early next morning at the spring of day
Up rose our Host and roused us like a cock,
Gathering us together in a flock,
And off we rode at slightly faster pace
Than walking to St Thomas' watering-place;[53]
845 And there our Host drew up, began to ease
His horse, and said, "Now, listen if you please,
My lords! Remember what you promised me.
If evensong and matins will agree[54]
Let's see who shall be first to tell a tale.
850 And as I hope to drink good wine and ale
I'll be your judge. The rebel who disobeys,
However much the journey costs, he pays.
Now draw for cut and then we can depart;
The man who draws the shortest cut shall start. . . ."

53. *St Thomas' watering-place,* a brook on the pilgrimage route to Canterbury.

54. *If evensong . . . agree,* if you feel in the morning (matins) as you did the evening before (evensong).

DISCUSSION

1. Which pilgrim does Chaucer describe most completely and thoroughly? Give evidence to support your choice.

2. If you could meet and talk with any pilgrim, whom would you select? Why?

3. (a) If you were to set out to be the Chaucer of today, what group of citizens would you assemble to represent today's society and culture?

(b) Which of the various people you bring together could you relate to counterparts in Chaucer's *Prologue*?

(c) Could some of Chaucer's descriptions of character be used without change for some of the individuals you have brought together? Discuss.

4. In lines 743–764 Chaucer disclaims responsibility for anything offensive in what he is about to present.

(a) How do you feel about his statement that an author "Is bound to say, as nearly as he can, each single word, if he remembers it, however rudely spoken or unfit"?

(b) What might have been Chaucer's reason for ending this passage with the line "I'm short of wit as you will understand"?

(c) Considered in its entirety, does the passage reflect the views of Chaucer the pilgrim, Chaucer the poet-satirist, or both?

5. Review the characters created in the *Prologue* and comment on this statement: "A zest for actual life shows itself not only in the plenty and variety of Chaucer's pilgrims, but especially in their normality. He did not exaggerate or look for freaks, he delighted in the world as he found it."

6. In one or two descriptive words (adjectives), characterize each of the major pilgrims. (Consider the Five Guildsmen as one character.) Do not use any adjective more than once.

7. Much of the effectiveness of the *Prologue* comes from Chaucer's ability to pinpoint minute but memorable details of appearance, dress, mannerisms, background, etc. Without rereading, list as many such details as you can and then attach them to the proper pilgrims.

SEE ALSO THE ARTICLE "HOW ORIGINAL WAS CHAUCER?" BEGINNING ON PAGE 123.

READERS' THEATER

Join with other class members in a dramatic reading of parts of the *Prologue*. One student might be Chaucer, introducing each pilgrim; then others in turn read Chaucer's lines describing the pilgrims. Chaucer's third-person descriptions might be converted into first-person monologues.

WRITING

Where two suggestions are given, they are intended as alternatives.

1. (a) Select two (or more) pilgrims and write an imaginary dialogue between them.

(b) Assume that in Chaucer's day there were news media of some sort and that you work for one of them. Prepare an interview with one of the pilgrims, being careful to ask questions that will reveal his character.

2. Imagine you are one of the pilgrims. Write a letter home, describing the pilgrimage and some of your fellow travelers from the point of view of the pilgrim you select.

3. (a) Imagine that you are transported to Chaucer's world—perhaps to the Tabard Inn—and write a brief impression of this older world.

(b) Pretend you are one of the pilgrims and are transposed to modern America. Write a description of the wonders and horrors of twentieth-century America as they would look to you.

4. Compare and contrast the characters of any two pilgrims.

5. Think of a character you would like to add to the pilgrimage and write a thumbnail description of him. Try to select striking details, in Chaucer's manner.

(Various pilgrims tell their stories in turn. After the Physician has finished his "pitiful" tale about an innocent girl whose father kills her rather than let her fall into the hands of a lustful judge, the Host expresses his reactions at length. Then he remarks:)

"If someone doesn't tell a cheerful tale
I'm lost in pity for that poor girl dead.
Come on, old chum and Pardoner," he said,
"Tell us a funny story, break a joke!"
5 "Right, by St Ronyan! but I'll have a soak
First at this pub. I've got a thirst to slake,"
Said he, "I'll drink and eat a bit of cake."
Outcry arose among the gentlefolk.
"No, no, don't let him tell a dirty joke!
10 Tell something with a moral, something clear
And profitable, and we'll gladly hear."
"Granted," he said, "but first I'll have to think;
I'll ponder something decent while I drink."

THE PARDONER'S TALE

The Pardoner's Prologue

My lords," he said, "in churches where I preach
I cultivate a haughty kind of speech
And ring it out as roundly as a bell;
I've got it all by heart, the tale I tell.
5 I have a text, it always is the same
And always has been, since I learnt the game,
Old as the hills and fresher than the grass,
Radix malorum est cupiditas.[1]
"But first I make pronouncement whence I come,
10 Show them my bulls[2] in detail and in sum,
And flaunt the papal seal for their inspection
As warrant for my bodily protection,
That none may have the impudence to irk
Or hinder me in Christ's most holy work.
15 Then I tell stories, as occasion calls,
Showing forth bulls from popes and cardinals,
From patriarchs and bishops; as I do,
I speak some words in Latin—just a few—
To put a saffron tinge upon my preaching
20 And stir devotion with a spice of teaching.
Then I bring all my long glass bottles out
Cram-full of bones and ragged bits of clout,
Relics they are, at least for such are known.
Then, cased in metal, I've a shoulder-bone,
25 Belonging to a sheep, a holy Jew's.
'Good men,' I say, 'take heed, for here is news.
Take but this bone and dip it in a well;
If cow or calf, if sheep or ox should swell
From eating snakes or that a snake has stung,
30 Take water from that well and wash its tongue,

1. *Radix . . . cupiditas.* "Avarice is the root of all evil."
2. *bulls,* important papal documents or letters.

MEDIEVAL BOOKSHOP, FROM THE LUTTRELL PSALTER. COURTESY OF THE TRUSTEES OF THE BRITISH MUSEUM.

And it will then recover. Furthermore,
Where there is pox or scab or other sore,
All animals that water at that well
Are cured at once. Take note of what I tell.
35 If the good man—the owner of the stock—
Goes once a week, before the crow of cock,
Fasting, and takes a draught of water too,
Why then, according to that holy Jew,
He'll find his cattle multiply and sell.
40 "'And it's a cure for jealousy as well;
For though a man be given to jealous wrath,
Use but this water when you make his broth,
And never again will he mistrust his wife,
Though he knew all about her sinful life,
45 Though two or three clergy had enjoyed her love.
"'Now look; I have a mitten here, a glove.
Whoever wears this mitten on his hand
Will multiply his grain. He sows his land
And up will come abundant wheat or oats,
50 Providing that he offers pence or groats.
"'Good men and women, here's a word of
warning;
If there is anyone in church this morning
Guilty of sin, so far beyond expression
Horrible, that he dare not make confession,
55 Or any woman, whether young or old,
That's cuckolded her husband, be she told
That such as she shall have no power or grace
To offer to my relics in this place.
But those who can acquit themselves of blame
60 Can all come up and offer in God's name,
And I will shrive them by the authority
Committed in this papal bull to me.'
"That trick's been worth a hundred marks[3] a year
Since I became a Pardoner, never fear.
65 Then, priestlike in my pulpit, with a frown,
I stand, and when the yokels have sat down,
I preach, as you have heard me say before,
And tell a hundred lying mockeries more.
I take great pains, and stretching out my neck
70 To east and west I crane about and peck
Just like a pigeon sitting on a barn.
My hands and tongue together spin the yarn
And all my antics are a joy to see.
The curse of avarice and cupidity
75 Is all my sermon, for it frees the pelf.
Out come the pence, and specially for myself,
For my exclusive purpose is to win
And not at all to castigate their sin.
Once dead what matter how their souls may fare?
80 They can go blackberrying,[4] for all I care! . . .
"But let me briefly make my purpose plain;
I preach for nothing but for greed of gain
And use the same old text, as bold as brass,

---

3. *marks,* coins worth two-thirds of a pound sterling. In Chaucer's time, the purchasing value of money was at least thirty times what it is today.

4. *They . . . blackberrying,* go wandering at large.

Radix malorum est cupiditas.
85 And thus I preach against the very vice
I make my living out of—avarice.
And yet however guilty of that sin
Myself, with others I have power to win
Them from it, I can bring them to repent;
90 But that is not my principal intent.
Covetousness is both the root and stuff
Of all I preach. That ought to be enough.
"Well, then I give examples thick and fast
From bygone times, old stories from the past;
95 A yokel mind loves stories from of old,
Being the kind it can repeat and hold.
What! Do you think, as long as I can preach
And get their silver for the things I teach,
That I will live in poverty, from choice?
100 That's not the counsel of my inner voice!
No! Let me preach and beg from kirk to kirk
And never do an honest job of work,
No, nor make baskets, like St Paul,[5] to gain
A livelihood. I do not preach in vain.
105 Why copy the apostles? Why pretend?
I must have wool, cheese, wheat, and cash to spend,
Though it were given me by the poorest lad
Or poorest village widow, though she had
A string of starving children, all agape.

5. *make baskets . . . Paul,* like St. Paul the Hermit, not St. Paul the Apostle.

OF HISTORICAL INTEREST

The profession of Pardoner

"Since no one has seen a Pardoner for close on four hundred years—their trade was swept away forever in 1562—it may be a help to know something about how Pardoners came into being, and how, in spite of every effort on the part of the Church to control them, they sank into that total but cheerful depravity which Chaucer's scoundrel shows.

"*Pardoner* is the English name for what the Church called a *Questor.* The business of a Questor was to collect money. He had no power or permission to pardon the sins of anyone. All he might do was to read out certain documents, signed and sealed by the Pope or some other Bishop, which made appeal to the charity of the congregation for some specific purpose; he was then to take up a collection, which he was to hand over intact to the authorities that had appointed him.

"How then did men like Chaucer's Pardoner come to wield their petty power, and line their own pockets with so much success? Parasites like these exist in large numbers in every age, and turn confidence-trickster, blackmailer, or charlatan according to their opportunities. But the Pardoner could go one better: he could cash in on the love of God and the fear of Hell and on all the guilt and gullibility in a simple soul.

"Not all Questors, even in Chaucer's time, were scoundrels. Their profession was founded on Catholic teaching which had evolved during the course of hundreds of years. It was rooted in the theory and practice of Penance.

"The person who wishes to avail himself of this Sacrament must fulfill three conditions. First, he must be truly repentant in his heart; second, he must confess himself fully to a consecrated priest; third, he must perform whatever penance the priest enjoins upon him after hearing his confession. The priest awards the punishment, but forgiveness comes from God. A man may be forgiven for his guilt, and still have his punishment to pay.

"In the early Church, punishments for sin were frighteningly severe. Many months, even years, of fasting on bread and water might be awarded in penance; or many hundred psalms, to be sung kneeling; or many hundred lashes on the palm of the hand."

[In the Middle Ages, the Church began to allow money payment to be substituted for temporal punishment due for sin. Such mitigation of punishment was called Indulgence or pardon. It was based on the doctrine that the debt of punishment could be paid vicariously, by drawing on the superabundant treasury of Christ's merit and the works of the saints.]

"The Questors whose business it was to read these Indulgences aloud to assembled congregations were sometimes simple monks or priests; these were the amateurs. There were also professional Questors, like Chaucer's Pardoner, who were laymen and were paid a salary. No doubt most of the amateurs and some of the professionals were reasonably honest. But there were also imposters, fully equipped with fake papal documents, indulgences, and relics.

"Abuses flourished; the Church struggled against them in vain. The Pardoners preached, they gave pardon irrespective of repentance; they absolved men of murder and perjury. They were notably drunk and lustful; they lied about miracles and openly exhibited the bones of brute-beasts, pretending they were the relics of Saints. By terrorism, hypocrisy, cajolery, bribery, and blackmail, the Pardoners amassed a fortune."

110 No, let me drink the liquor of the grape
And keep a jolly wench in every town!
"But listen, gentlemen; to bring things down
To a conclusion, would you like a tale?
Now as I've drunk a draught of corn-ripe ale,
115 By God it stands to reason I can strike
On some good story that you all will like.
For though I am a wholly vicious man
Don't think I can't tell moral tales. I can!
Here's one I often preach when out for winning;
120 Now please be quiet. Here is the beginning."

The Pardoner's Tale

IN Flanders once there was a company
Of youngsters haunting vice and ribaldry,
Riot and gambling, stews[1] and public-houses
Where each with harp, guitar or lute carouses,
5 Dancing and dicing day and night, and bold
To eat and drink far more than they can hold,
Doing thereby the devil sacrifice
Within that devil's temple of cursed vice,
Abominable in superfluity,
10 With oaths so damnable in blasphemy
That it's a grisly thing to hear them swear. . . .
Seneca[2] has a thought worth pondering on;
No difference, he says, that he can find
Between a madman who has lost his mind
15 And one who is habitually mellow
Except that madness when it takes a fellow
Lasts longer, on the whole, than drunkenness.
O cursed gluttony, our first distress!
Cause of our first confusion, first temptation,
20 The very origin of our damnation,
Till Christ redeemed us with his blood again!
O infamous indulgence! Cursed stain
So dearly bought! And what has it been worth?
Gluttony has corrupted all the earth.
25 Adam, our father, and his wife no less,
From Paradise to labour and distress
Were driven for that vice, they were indeed.
While she and Adam fasted, so I read,
They were in Paradise; when he and she
30 Ate of the fruit of that forbidden tree
They were at once cast forth in pain and woe.
O gluttony, it is to thee we owe
Our griefs! O if we knew the maladies
That follow on excess and gluttonies,
35 Sure we would diet, we would temper pleasure
In sitting down at table, show some measure! . . .
Alas, the filth of it! If we contemn
The name, how far more filthy is the act!
A man who swills down vintages in fact
40 Makes a mere privy of his throat, a sink
For cursed superfluities of drink! . . .
Wine is a lecherous thing and drunkenness
A squalor of contention and distress.
O drunkard, how disfigured is thy face,
45 How foul thy breath, how filthy thy embrace!
And through thy drunken nose a stertorous snort
Like "*samson-samson*"—something of the sort.
Yet Samson never was a man to swig.
You totter, lurch, and fall like a stuck pig,
50 Your manhood's lost, your tongue is in a burr.
Drunkenness is the very sepulchre
Of human judgement and articulation.
He that is subject to the domination
Of drink can keep no secrets, be it said.
55 Keep clear of wine, I tell you, white or red,
Especially Spanish wines which they provide
And have on sale in Fish Street and Cheapside. . . .
But seriously, my lords, attention, pray!
All the most notable acts, I dare to say,
60 And victories in the Old Testament,
Won under God who is omnipotent,
Were won in abstinence, were won in prayer.
Look in the Bible, you will find it there.
Or else take Attila the Conqueror;[3]
65 Died in his sleep, a manner to abhor,
In drunken shame and bleeding at the nose.
A general should live sober, I suppose. . . .
Having put gluttony in its proper setting
I wish to warn you against dice and betting.
70 Gambling's the very mother of robbed purses,
Lies, double-dealing, perjury, and curses,
Manslaughter, blasphemy of Christ, and waste
Of time and money. Worse, you are debased
In public reputation, put to shame.
75 "A common gambler" is a nasty name.
The more exalted such a man may be
So much the more contemptible is he.
A gambling prince would be incompetent
To frame a policy of government,

1. *stews,* brothels.
2. *Seneca,* a Roman philosopher who died A.D. 65. References are to his Epistles.
3. *Attila the Conqueror,* leader of the Huns, who died A.D. 453.

80 And he will sink in general opinion
As one unfit to exercise dominion. . . .
Now let me speak a word or two of swearing
And perjury; the Bible is unsparing.
It's an abominable thing to curse
85 And swear, it says; but perjury is worse.
Almighty God has said, "Swear not at all," . . .
Behold and see the tables of the Law
Of God's Commandments, to be held in awe;
Look at the third where it is written plain,
90 "Thou shalt not take the name of God in vain."
You see He has forbidden swearing first;
Not murder, no, nor other thing accurst
Comes before that, I say, in God's commands.
That is the order; he who understands
95 Knows that the third commandment is just that.
And in addition, let me tell you flat,
Vengeance on him and all his house shall fall
That swears outrageously, or swears at all.
"God's precious heart and passion, by God's nails
100 And by the blood of Christ that is at Hailes.[4]
Seven's my luck, and yours is five and three;
God's blessed arms! If you play false with me
I'll stab you with my dagger!" Overthrown
By two small dice, two bitching bits of bone,
105 They reach rage, perjury, cheating, homicide.
O for the love of Jesu Christ who died
For us, abandon curses, small or great!
But, sirs, I have a story to relate.
It's of three rioters I have to tell
110 Who long before the morning service bell
Were sitting in a tavern for a drink.
And as they sat, they heard the hand-bell clink
Before a coffin going to the grave;
One of them called the little tavern-knave
115 And said "Go and find out at once—look spry!—
Whose corpse is in that coffin passing by;
And see you get the name correctly too."
"Sir," said the boy, "no need, I promise you;
Two hours before you came here I was told.
120 He was a friend of yours in days of old,
And suddenly, last night, the man was slain,
Upon his bench, face up, dead drunk again.
There came a privy thief, they call him Death,
Who kills us all round here, and in a breath
125 He speared him through the heart, he never stirred.
And then Death went his way without a word.
He's killed a thousand in the present plague,

4. *Hailes,* an abbey in Gloucestershire, which possessed a phial of what was claimed to be the blood of Christ.

OF LITERARY INTEREST

Origin of the Pardoner's Tale

The *Pardoner's Tale* is customarily referred to as "The Tale of Death and the Three Revelers." It is of Oriental origin, the earliest known analog being one of the birth-tales of Buddha. The basic story occurs in the folk literature of many countries. Kipling included a modern version in his *Jungle Books.* The character of the Old Man, however, seems to be original with Chaucer.

And, sir, it doesn't do to be too vague
If you should meet him; you had best be wary.
130 Be on your guard with such an adversary,
Be primed to meet him everywhere you go,
That's what my mother said. It's all I know."
The publican joined in with, "By St Mary.
What the child says is right; you'd best be wary,
135 This very year he killed, in a large village
A mile away, man, woman, serf at tillage,
Page in the household, children—all there were.
Yes, I imagine that he lives round there.
It's well to be prepared in these alarms,
140 He might do you dishonour!" "Huh, God's arms!"
The rioter said, "Is he so fierce to meet?
I'll search for him, by Jesus, street by street.
God's blessed bones! I'll register a vow!
Here, chaps! The three of us together now,
145 Hold up your hands, like me, and we'll be brothers
In this affair, and each defend the others,
And we will kill this traitor Death, I say!
Away with him as he has made away
With all our friends. God's dignity! To-night!"
150 They made their bargain, swore with appetite,
These three, to live and die for one another
As brother-born might swear to his born brother.
And up they started in their drunken rage
And made towards this village which the page
155 And publican had spoken of before.
Many and grisly were the oaths they swore,
Tearing Christ's blessed body to a shred;
"If we can only catch him, Death is dead!"
When they had gone not fully half a mile,
160 Just as they were about to cross a stile,
They came upon a very poor old man
Who humbly greeted them and thus began,
"God look to you, my lords, and give you quiet!"
To which the proudest of these men of riot

TAVERN SCENE FROM THE LUTTRELL PSALTER. COURTESY OF THE TRUSTEES OF THE BRITISH MUSEUM.

165 Gave back the answer, "What, old fool? Give place!
Why are you all wrapped up except your face?
Why live so long? Isn't it time to die?"
The old, old fellow looked him in the eye
And said, "Because I never yet have found,
170 Though I have walked to India, searching round
Village and city on my pilgrimage,
One who would change his youth to have my age.
And so my age is mine and must be still
Upon me, for such time as God may will.
175 "Not even Death, alas, will take my life;
So, like a wretched prisoner at strife
Within himself, I walk alone and wait
About the earth, which is my mother's gate,[5]
Knock-knocking with my staff from night to noon
180 And crying, 'Mother, open to me soon!
Look at me, mother, won't you let me in?
See how I wither, flesh and blood and skin!
Alas! When will these bones be laid to rest?
Mother, I would exchange—for that were best—
185 The wardrobe in my chamber, standing there
So long, for yours! Aye, for a shirt of hair
To wrap me in!' She has refused her grace,
Whence comes the pallor of my withered face.
"But it dishonoured you when you began
190 To speak so roughly, sir, to an old man,
Unless he had injured you in word or deed.
It says in holy writ, as you may read,
'Thou shalt rise up before the hoary head
And honour it.' And therefore be it said
195 'Do no more harm to an old man than you,
Being now young, would have another do
When you are old'—if you should live till then.
And so may God be with you, gentlemen,
For I must go whither I have to go."
200 "By God," the gambler said, "you shan't do so,
You don't get off so easy, by St John!
I heard you mention, just a moment gone,
A certain traitor Death who singles out
And kills the fine young fellows hereabout.
205 And you're his spy, by God! You wait a bit.
Say where he is or you shall pay for it,
By God and by the Holy Sacrament!
I say you've joined together by consent
To kill us younger folk, you thieving swine!"
210 "Well, sirs," he said, "if it be your design
To find out Death, turn up this crooked way
Towards that grove. I left him there to-day

5. *mother's gate,* the grave, entrance to "mother earth."

Under a tree, and there you'll find him waiting.
He isn't one to hide for all your prating.
215 You see that oak? He won't be far to find.
And God protect you that redeemed mankind,
Aye, and amend you!" Thus that ancient man.
At once the three young rioters began
To run, and reached the tree, and there they found
220 A pile of golden florins[6] on the ground,
New-coined, eight bushels of them as they thought.
No longer was it Death those fellows sought,
For they were all so thrilled to see the sight,
The florins were so beautiful and bright,
225 That down they sat beside the precious pile.
The wickedest spoke first after a while.
"Brothers," he said, "you listen to what I say.
I'm pretty sharp although I joke away.
It's clear that Fortune has bestowed this treasure
230 To let us live in jollity and pleasure.
Light come, light go! We'll spend it as we ought.
God's precious dignity! Who would have thought
This morning was to be our lucky day?
"If one could only get the gold away,
235 Back to my house, or else to yours, perhaps—
For as you know, the gold is ours, chaps—
We'd all be at the top of fortune, hey?
But certainly it can't be done by day.
People would call us robbers—a strong gang,
240 So our own property would make us hang.
No, we must bring this treasure back by night
Some prudent way, and keep it out of sight.
And so as a solution I propose
We draw for lots and see the way it goes.
245 The one who draws the longest, lucky man,
Shall run to town as quickly as he can
To fetch us bread and wine—but keep things dark—
While two remain in hiding here to mark
Our heap of treasure. If there's no delay,
250 When night comes down we'll carry it away,
All three of us, wherever we have planned."
He gathered lots and hid them in his hand
Bidding them draw for where the luck should fall.
It fell upon the youngest of them all,
255 And off he ran at once towards the town.
As soon as he had gone the first sat down
And thus began a parley with the other:
"You know that you can trust me as a brother;
Now let me tell you where your profit lies;
260 You know our friend has gone to get supplies

6. *florins,* coins worth a third of a pound sterling.

And here's a lot of gold that is to be
Divided equally amongst us three.
Nevertheless, if I could shape things thus
So that we shared it out—the two of us—
265 Wouldn't you take it as a friendly turn?"
"But how?" the other said with some concern,
"Because he knows the gold's with me and you;
What can we tell him? What are we to do?"
"Is it a bargain," said the first, "or no?
270 For I can tell you in a word or so
What's to be done to bring the thing about."
"Trust me," the other said, "you needn't doubt
My word. I won't betray you, I'll be true."
"Well," said his friend, "you see that we are two,
275 And two are twice as powerful as one.
Now look; when he comes back, get up in fun
To have a wrestle; then, as you attack,
I'll up and put my dagger through his back
While you and he are struggling, as in game;
280 Then draw your dagger too and do the same.
Then all this money will be ours to spend,
Divided equally of course, dear friend.
Then we can gratify our lusts and fill
The day with dicing at our own sweet will."
285 Thus these two miscreants agreed to slay
The third and youngest, as you heard me say.
The youngest, as he ran towards the town,
Kept turning over, rolling up and down
Within his heart the beauty of those bright
290 New florins, saying, "Lord, to think I might
Have all that treasure to myself alone!
Could there be anyone beneath the throne
Of God so happy as I then should be?"
And so the Fiend, our common enemy,
295 Was given power to put it in his thought
That there was always poison to be bought,
And that with poison he could kill his friends.
To men in such a state the Devil sends
Thoughts of this kind, and has a full permission
300 To lure them on to sorrow and perdition;
For this young man was utterly content
To kill them both and never to repent.
And on he ran, he had no thought to tarry,
Came to the town, found an apothecary
305 And said, "Sell me some poison if you will,
I have a lot of rats I want to kill
And there's a polecat too about my yard
That takes my chickens and it hits me hard;
But I'll get even, as is only right,
310 With vermin that destroy a man by night."
The chemist answered, "I've a preparation
Which you shall have, and by my soul's salvation
If any living creature eat or drink
A mouthful, ere he has the time to think,
315 Though he took less than makes a grain of wheat,
You'll see him fall down dying at your feet;
Yes, die he must, and in so short a while
You'd hardly have the time to walk a mile,
The poison is so strong, you understand."
320 This cursed fellow grabbed into his hand
The box of poison and away he ran
Into a neighbouring street, and found a man
Who lent him three large bottles. He withdrew
And deftly poured the poison into two.
325 He kept the third one clean, as well he might,
For his own drink, meaning to work all night
Stacking the gold and carrying it away.
And when this rioter, this devil's clay,
Had filled his bottles up with wine, all three,
330 Back to rejoin his comrades sauntered he.
Why make a sermon of it? Why waste breath?
Exactly in the way they'd planned his death
They fell on him and slew him, two to one.
Then said the first of them when this was done,
335 "Now for a drink. Sit down and let's be merry,
For later on there'll be the corpse to bury."
And, as it happened, reaching for a sup,
He took a bottle full of poison up
And drank; and his companion, nothing loth,
340 Drank from it also, and they perished both.
There is, in Avicenna's long relation[7]
Concerning poison and its operation,
Trust me, no ghastlier section to transcend
What these two wretches suffered at their end.
345 Thus these two murderers received their due,
So did the treacherous young poisoner too.

O cursed sin! O blackguardly excess!
O treacherous homicide! O wickedness!
O gluttony that lusted on and diced!
350 O blasphemy that took the name of Christ
With habit-hardened oaths that pride began!
Alas, how comes it that a mortal man,
That thou, to thy Creator, Him that wrought thee,
That paid His precious blood for thee and bought
thee,
355 Art so unnatural and false within?
Dearly beloved, God forgive your sin

7. *Avicenna's long relation,* a work on medicine by an Arabian physician (A.D. 980–1037).

And keep you from the vice of avarice!
My holy pardon frees you all of this,
Provided that you make the right approaches,
360 That is with sterling, rings, or silver brooches.
Bow down your heads under this holy bull!
Come on, you women, offer up your wool!
I'll write your name into my ledger; so!
Into the bliss of Heaven you shall go.
365 For I'll absolve you by my holy power,
You that make offering, clean as at the hour
When you were born. . . . That, sirs, is how I preach
And Jesu Christ, soul's healer, aye, the leech
Of every soul, grant pardon and relieve you
370 Of sin, for that is best, I won't deceive you.
One thing I should have mentioned in my tale,
Dear people. I've some relics in my bale
And pardons too, as full and fine, I hope,
As any in England, given me by the Pope.
375 If there be one among you that is willing
To have my absolution for a shilling
Devoutly given, come! and do not harden
Your hearts but kneel in humbleness for pardon;
Or else, receive my pardon as we go.
380 You can renew it every town or so
Always provided that you still renew
Each time, and in good money, what is due.
It is an honour to you to have found
A pardoner with his credentials sound
385 Who can absolve you as you ply the spur
In any accident that may occur.
For instance—we are all at Fortune's beck—
Your horse may throw you down and break your neck.
What a security it is to all
390 To have me here among you and at call
With pardon for the lowly and the great
When soul leaves body for the future state!
And I advise our Host here to begin,
The most enveloped of you all in sin.
395 Come forward, Host, you shall be first to pay.
And kiss my holy relics right away.
Only a groat. Come on, unbuckle your purse!"
"No, no," said he, "not I, and may the curse
Of Christ descend upon me if I do!
400 You'll have me kissing your old breeches too
And swear they were the relic of a saint. . . ."
The Pardoner said nothing, not a word;
He was so angry that he couldn't speak.
"Well," said our Host, "if you're for showing pique,
405 I'll joke no more, not with an angry man."
The worthy Knight immediately began,
Seeing the fun was getting rather rough,
And said, "No more, we've all had quite enough.
Now, Master Pardoner, perk up, look cheerly!
410 And you, Sir Host, whom I esteem so dearly,
I beg of you to kiss the Pardoner.
"Come, Pardoner, draw nearer, my dear sir.
Let's laugh again and keep the ball in play."
They kissed, and we continued on our way.

DISCUSSION

1. How sound is the psychology used by the Pardoner to extort money? See, for example, lines 51–62 of his *Prologue*, describing the trick "worth a hundred marks a year" to him.

2. How do the Revelers' actions reinforce the points the Pardoner is trying to make?

3. The Old Man whom the three Revelers encounter has been called one of the most striking figures in all poetry. Most critics think that he is a symbolic figure. What do you think he signifies?

4. The Pardoner admits (*Prologue*, line 83) that he always uses the same text or moral in his sermons. What is the irony in his use of this text?

5. After revealing all his tricks to the other pilgrims and relating his tale, the Pardoner offers to sell them the same pardon he has already admitted is worthless. How do you account for this?

6. Some critics claim that the Pardoner is the only pilgrim whom Chaucer thoroughly detests. Do you agree? Give the evidence on which you base your opinion.

WRITING

1. Write a brief description of the Pardoner preaching in the pulpit, either from the standpoint of a parishioner who believes him to be a holy and honorable man, or from the standpoint of one who sees through his tricks.

2. The Pardoner says that all his sermons are based on one text, "Avarice is the root of all evil." Devise a vignette (a very short story) to illustrate this text. Or, if you prefer, substitute a word of your own choice for "avarice."

3. F. N. Robinson, a distinguished editor of Chaucer, wrote: "In spite of his contemptible nature, physical and moral, the Pardoner is one of the most intellectual figures among the pilgrims and his performance is worthy of his powers." React to this comment in a brief composition.

THE WIFE OF BATH'S TALE

The Wife of Bath's Prologue

IF there were no authority on earth
Except experience, mine, for what it's worth,
And that's enough for me, all goes to show
That marriage is a misery and a woe;
5 For let me say, if I may make so bold,
My lords, since when I was but twelve years old,
Thanks be to God Eternal evermore,
Five husbands have I had at the church door;
Yes, it's a fact that I have had so many,
10 All worthy in their way, as good as any. . . .
Welcome the sixth, whenever he appears.
I can't keep continent for years and years.
No sooner than one husband's dead and gone
Some other christian man shall take me on,
15 For then, so says the Apostle,[1] I am free
To wed, o'God's name, where it pleases me.
Wedding's no sin, so far as I can learn.
Better it is to marry than to burn. . . .
Show me a time or text where God disparages,
20 Or sets a prohibition upon marriages
Expressly, let me have it! Show it me!
And where did He command virginity?
I know as well as you do, never doubt it,
All the Apostle Paul has said about it;
25 He said that as for precepts he had none.
One may advise a woman to be one;
Advice is no commandment in my view.
He left it in our judgement what to do. . . .
And as for being married, he lets me do it
30 Out of indulgence, so there's nothing to it
In marrying me, suppose my husband dead;
There's nothing bigamous in such a bed. . . .
"I grant it you. I'll never say a word
Decrying maidenhood although preferred
35 To frequent marriage; there are those who mean
To live in their virginity, as clean
In body as in soul, and never mate.
I'll make no boast about my own estate.
As in a noble household, we are told,
40 Not every dish and vessel's made of gold,
Some are of wood, yet earn their master's praise,
God calls His folk to Him in many ways.
To each of them God gave His proper gift,
Some this, some that, and left them to make shift.
45 Virginity is indeed a great perfection,
And married continence, for God's dilection,
But Christ, who of perfection is the well,
Bade not that everyone should go and sell
All that he had and give it to the poor
50 To follow in His footsteps, that is sure.
He spoke to those that would live perfectly,
And by your leave, my lords, that's not for me.
I will bestow the flower of life, the honey,
Upon the acts and fruit of matrimony.
55 ". . . I'll have a husband yet
Who shall be both my debtor and my slave
And bear his tribulation to the grave
Upon his flesh, as long as I'm his wife.
For mine shall be the power all his life
60 Over his proper body, and not he,
Thus the Apostle Paul has told it me,
And bade our husbands they should love us well;
There's a command on which I like to dwell. . . ."
The Pardoner started up, and thereupon
65 "Madam," he said, "by God and by St John,
That's noble preaching no one could surpass!
I was about to take a wife; alas!
Am I to buy it on my flesh so dear?
There'll be no marrying for me this year!"
70 "You wait," she said, "my story's not begun.
You'll taste another brew before I've done;
You'll find it isn't quite so nice as beer.
For while the tale is telling you shall hear
Of all the tribulations man and wife
75 Can have; I've been an expert all my life,
That is to say, myself have been the whip.
So please yourself whether you want to sip
At that same cask of marriage I shall broach;
Be cautious before making the approach. . . ."
80 "Madam, I put it to you as a prayer,"
The Pardoner said, "go on as you began!
Tell us your tale, spare not for any man.
Instruct us younger men in your technique."
"Gladly," she answered, "if I am to speak.
85 But still I hope the company won't reprove me
Though I should speak as fantasy may move me,
And please don't be offended at my views;
They're really only offered to amuse.
"Now, gentlemen, I'll on and tell my tale
90 And as I hope to drink good wine and ale
I'll tell the truth. Those husbands that I had,
Three of them were good and two were bad.

---

1. *Apostle,* St. Paul. In the passages that follow, the Wife quotes scripture freely—but not always accurately—to support her arguments.

The three that I call 'good' were rich and old. . . .
I governed them so well and held the rein
95 So firmly they were rapturously fain
To go and buy me pretty things to wear;
They were delighted if I spoke them fair.
God knows how spitefully I used to scold them.
"Listen, I'll tell you how I used to hold them,
100 You knowing women, who can understand.
First put them in the wrong, and out of hand.
No one can be so bold—I mean no man—
At lies and swearing as a woman can.
This is no news, as you'll have realized,
105 To knowing ones, but to the misadvised.
A knowing wife if she is worth her salt
Can always prove her husband is at fault,
And even though the fellow may have heard
Some story told him by a little bird
110 She knows enough to prove the bird is crazy
And get her maid to witness she's a daisy,
With full agreement, scarce solicited.
But listen. Here's the sort of thing I said:
"'Now, sir old dotard, what is that you say?
115 Why is my neighbour's wife so smart and gay?
She is respected everywhere she goes.
I sit at home and have no decent clothes.
Why haunt her house? What are you doing there?
Are you so amorous? Is she so fair?
120 What, whispering secrets to our maid? For shame,
Sir ancient lecher! Time you dropped that game.
And if I see my gossip or a friend
You scold me like a devil! There's no end
If I as much as stroll towards his house.
125 Then you come home as drunken as a mouse,
You mount your throne and preach, chapter and
verse
—All nonsense—and you tell me it's a curse
To marry a poor woman—she's expensive;
Or if her family's wealthy and extensive
130 You say it's torture to endure her pride
And melancholy airs, and more beside. . . .
"'You say that some desire us for our wealth,
Some for our shapeliness, our looks, our health,
Some for our singing, others for our dancing,
135 Some for our gentleness and dalliant glancing,
And some because our hands are soft and small;
By your account the devil gets us all.
"'You say what castle wall can be so strong
As to hold out against a siege for long?
140 And if her looks are foul you say that she
Is hot for every man that she can see,
Leaping upon them with a spaniel's airs
Until she finds a man to buy her wares.
Never was goose upon the lake so grey
145 But that she found a gander, so you say.
You say it's hard to keep a girl controlled
If she's the kind that no one wants to hold.
That's what you say as you stump off to bed,
You brute! You say no man of sense would wed,
150 That is, not if he wants to go to Heaven.
Wild thunderbolts and fire from the seven
Planets descend and break your withered neck!
"'You say that buildings falling into wreck,
And smoke, and scolding women, are the three
155 Things that will drive a man from home. Dear me!
What ails the poor old man to grumble so?
"'We women hide our faults to let them show
Once we are safely married, so you say.
There's a fine proverb for a popinjay![2]
160 "'You say that oxen, asses, hounds and horses
Can be tried out on various ploys and courses;
And basins too, and dishes when you buy them,
Spoons, chairs and furnishings, a man can try them
As he can try a suit of clothes, no doubt,
165 But no one ever tries a woman out
Until he's married her; old dotard crow!
And then you say she lets her vices show.
"'You also say we count it for a crime
Unless you praise our beauty all the time,
170 Unless you're always poring on our faces
And call us pretty names in public places;
Or if you fail to treat me to a feast
Upon my birthday—presents at the least—
Or to respect my nurse and her grey hairs,
175 Or be polite to all my maids upstairs
And to my father's cronies and his spies.
That's what you say, old barrelful of lies!
"'Then there's our young apprentice, handsome
Johnny;
Because he has crisp hair that shines as bonny
180 As finest gold, and squires me up and down
You show your low suspicions in a frown.
I wouldn't have him, not if you died to-morrow!
"'And tell me this, God punish you with sorrow,
Why do you hide the keys of coffer doors?
185 It's just as much my property as yours.
Do you want to make an idiot of your wife?
Now, by the Lord that gave me soul and life,
I think you'd like to lock me in your coffer!

2. *popinjay,* parrot.

"Go where you please, dear wife," you ought to offer,
190 "Amuse yourself! I shan't give ear to malice,
I know you for a virtuous wife, Dame Alice."
We cannot love a husband who takes charge
Of where we go. We like to be at large. . . .
"'And when a woman tries a mild display
195 In dress or costly ornament, you say
It is a danger to her chastity,
And then, bad luck to you, start making free
With Bible tags in the Apostle's name;[3]
"And in like manner, chastely and with shame,
200 You women should adorn yourselves," said he,
"And not with braided hair or jewelry
With pearl or golden ornament." What next!
I'll pay as much attention to your text
And rubric in such things as would a gnat.
205 "'And once you said that I was like a cat,
For if you singe a cat it will not roam
And that's the way to keep a cat at home.
But when she feels her fur is sleek and gay
She can't be kept indoors for half a day
210 But off she takes herself as dusk is falling
To show her fur and go a-caterwauling.
Which means if I feel gay, as you suppose,
I shall run out to show my poor old clothes.
"'Silly old fool! You and your private spies!
215 Go on, beg Argus[4] with his hundred eyes
To be my bodyguard, that's better still!
But yet he shan't, I say, against my will.
I'll pull him by the beard, believe you me!
"'And once you said that principally three
220 Misfortunes[5] trouble earth, east, west and north,
And no man living could endure a fourth.
My dear sir shrew, Jesu cut short your life!
You preach away and say a hateful wife
Is reckoned to be one of these misfortunes.
225 Is there no other trouble that importunes
The world and that your parables could condemn?
Must an unhappy wife be one of them?
"'Then you compared a woman's love to Hell,

PRIORESS, FROM THE ELLESMERE CHAUCER. BY PERMISSION OF THE HUNTINGTON LIBRARY, SAN MARINO, CALIFORNIA.

To barren land where water will not dwell,
230 And you compared it to a quenchless fire,
The more it burns the more is its desire
To burn up everything that burnt can be.
You say that just as worms destroy a tree
A wife destroys her husband and contrives,
235 As husbands know, the ruin of their lives.'
"Such was the way, my lords, you understand
I kept my older husbands well in hand.
I told them they were drunk and their unfitness
To judge my conduct forced me to take witness
240 That they were lying. Johnny and my niece
Would back me up. O Lord, I wrecked their peace,
Innocent as they were, without remorse!
For I could bite and whinney like a horse
And launch complaints when things were all my fault;
245 I'd have been lost if I had called a halt.
First to the mill is first to grind your corn;

3. *Apostle's name.* The reference is to Timothy I.ii.9. Note that the Wife is accusing her husband of using the same tactics that she constantly uses herself.
4. *Argus,* in Greek legend, a hundred-eyed giant who never closed all his eyes in sleep at the same time and therefore kept constant watch.
5. *three/Misfortunes.* She is alluding to Proverbs xxx, 21–23: "For three things the earth is disquieted, and for four which it cannot bear: for a servant when he reigneth; and a fool when he is filled with meat; for an odious woman when she is married; and an handmaid that is heir to her mistress."

I attacked first and they were overborne,
Glad to apologize and even suing
Pardon for what they'd never thought of doing.
250 "I'd tackle one for wenching, out of hand,
Although so ill the man could hardly stand,
Yet he felt flattered in his heart because
He thought it showed how fond of him I was.
I swore that all my walking out at night
255 Was just to keep his wenching well in sight.
That was a dodge that made me shake with mirth;
But all such wit is given us at birth.
Lies, tears, and spinning are the things God gives
By nature to a woman, while she lives.
260 So there's one thing at least that I can boast,
That in the end I always ruled the roast;
Cunning or force was sure to make them stumble,
And always keeping up a steady grumble. . . .
"I then would say, 'My dear, just take a peep!
265 What a meek look on Willikin our sheep!
Come nearer, husband, let me kiss your cheek;
You should be just as patient, just as meek;
Sweeten your heart. Your conscience needs a probe.
You're fond of preaching patience out of Job,
270 And so be patient; practise what you preach,
And if you don't, my dear, we'll have to teach
You that it's nice to have a quiet life.
One of us must be master, man or wife,
And since a man's more reasonable, he
275 Should be the patient one, you must agree. . . .
"That's how my first three husbands were undone.
Now let me tell you of my last but one.
"He was a reveller, was number four;
That is to say he kept a paramour.
280 And I was young, ah, ragery's the word,
Stubborn and strong and jolly as a bird.
Play me the harp and I would dance and sing,
Believe me, like a nightingale in spring,
If I had had a draught of sweetened wine. . . .
285 "But Christ! Whenever it comes back to me,
When I recall my youth and jollity,
It fairly warms the cockles of my heart!
This very day I feel a pleasure start,
Yes, I can feel it tickling at the root.
290 Lord, how it does me good! I've had my fruit,
I've had my world and time, I've had my fling!
But age that comes to poison everything
Has taken all my beauty and my pith.
Well, let it go, the devil go therewith!
295 The flour is gone, there is no more to say,
And I must sell the bran as best I may;
But still I mean to find my way to fun. . . .
Now let me tell you of my last but one.
"I told you how it filled my heart with spite
300 To see another woman his delight,
By God and all His saints I made it good!
I carved him out a cross of the same wood,
Not with my body in a filthy way,
But certainly by seeming rather gay
305 To others, frying him in his own grease
Of jealousy and rage; he got no peace.
By God on earth I was his purgatory,
For which I hope his soul may be in glory.
God knows he sang a sorry tune, he flinched,
310 And bitterly enough, when the shoe pinched.
And God and he alone can say how grim,
How many were the ways I tortured him.
"He died when I came back from Jordan Stream[6]
And he lies buried under the rood-beam,[7]
315 Albeit that his tomb can scarce supply us
With such a show as that of King Darius
—Apelles sculped it in a sumptuous taste—
But costly burial would have been mere waste.
Farewell to him, God give his spirit rest!
320 He's in his grave, he's nailed up in his chest.
"Now of my fifth, last husband let me tell.
God never let his soul be sent to Hell!
And yet he was my worst, and many a blow
He struck me still can ache along my row
325 Of ribs, and will until my dying day. . . .
I think I loved him best, I'll tell no lie.
He was disdainful in his love, that's why.
We women have a curious fantasy
In such affairs, or so it seems to me.
330 When something's difficult, or can't be had,
We crave and cry for it all day like mad.
Forbid a thing, we pine for it all night,
Press fast upon us and we take to flight;
We use disdain in offering our wares.
335 A throng of buyers sends prices up at fairs,
Cheap goods have little value, they suppose;
And that's a thing that every woman knows.
"My fifth and last—God keep his soul in health!
The one I took for love and not for wealth,
340 Had been at Oxford not so long before
But had left school and gone to lodge next door,

6. *When I . . . Jordan Stream,* when she returned from one of her pilgrimages to the Holy Land.
7. *rood-beam,* a beam usually between the chancel and the nave of a church, on which was placed a rood or crucifix. Burial within the chancel itself would have been more expensive.

Yes, it was to my godmother's he'd gone.
God bless her soul! *Her* name was Alison.
She knew my heart and more of what I thought
345 Than did the parish priest, and so she ought! . . .
"And so one time it happened that in Lent,
As I so often did, I rose and went
To see her, ever wanting to be gay
And go a-strolling, March, April, and May,
350 From house to house for chat and village malice.
"Johnny (the boy from Oxford) and Dame Alice
And I myself, into the fields we went.
My husband was in London all that Lent;
All the more fun for me—I only mean
355 The fun of seeing people and being seen
By cocky lads; for how was I to know
Where or what graces Fortune might bestow?
And so I made a round of visitations,
Went to processions, festivals, orations,
360 Preachments and pilgrimages, watched the carriages
They use for plays and pageants, went to marriages,
And always wore my gayest scarlet dress.
"These worms, these moths, these mites, I must confess,
Got little chance to eat it, by the way.
365 Why not? Because I wore it every day.
"Now let me tell you all that came to pass.
We sauntered in the meadows through the grass
Toying and dallying to such extent,
Johnny and I, that I grew provident
370 And I suggested, were I ever free
And made a widow, he should marry me.
And certainly—I do not mean to boast—
I ever was more provident than most
In marriage matters and in other such.
375 I never think a mouse is up to much
That only has one hole in all the house;
If that should fail, well, it's good-bye the mouse. . . .
"Well, let me see . . . what had I to explain?
Aha! By God, I've got the thread again.
380 "When my fourth husband lay upon his bier
I wept all day and looked as drear as drear,
As widows must, for it is quite in place,
And with a handkerchief I hid my face.
Now that I felt provided with a mate
385 I wept but little, I need hardly state.
"To church they bore my husband on the morrow
With all the neighbours round him venting sorrow,
And one of them of course was handsome Johnny.
So help me God, I thought he looked so bonny
390 Behind the coffin! Heavens, what a pair
Of legs he had! Such feet, so clean and fair!
I gave my whole heart up, for him to hold.
He was, I think, some twenty winters old,
And I was forty then, to tell the truth.
395 But still, I always had a coltish tooth.
Yes, I'm gap-toothed; it suits me well I feel,
It is the print of Venus and her seal. . . .
"What shall I say? Before the month was gone
This gay young student, my delightful John,
400 Had married me in solemn festival.
I handed him the money, lands, and all
That ever had been given me before;
This I repented later, more and more.
None of my pleasures would he let me seek.
405 By God, he smote me once upon the cheek
Because I tore a page out of his book,
And that's the reason why I'm deaf. But look,
Stubborn I was, just like a lioness;
As to my tongue, a very wrangleness.
410 I went off gadding as I had before

OF CRITICAL INTEREST

Opinions of the Wife

"I translated Chaucer . . . and, amongst the rest, pitched on the *Wife of Bath's Tale;* not daring, as I have said, to adventure on her *Prologue* because 'tis too licentious."

John Dryden, in his Preface to *Fables,* 1700.

"The Characters of Women Chaucer has divided into two classes, the Lady Prioress and the Wife of Bath. Are not these leaders of the ages of men? The lady prioress, in some ages, predominates; and in some the wife of Bath, in whose character Chaucer has been . . . minute and exact, because she is . . . a scourge and a blight. I shall say no more of her, nor expose what Chaucer has left hidden; let the young reader study what he has said of her: it is useful as a scare-crow. There are of such characters born too many for the peace of the world."

William Blake, in *A Descriptive Catalogue of Pictures, Poetical and Historical Inventions,* 1809.

"The Wife of Bath is without doubt the most outrageous woman who ever walked into immortality. . . . Chaucer has given her his own irrepressible delight in living, and her whole discourse is one whoop of satisfaction over the fun she has had."

Marchette Chute in *Geoffrey Chaucer of England,* 1946.

From house to house, however much he swore.
Because of that he used to preach and scold,
Drag Roman history up from days of old,
How one Simplicius Gallus left his wife,
415 Deserting her completely all his life,
Only for poking out her head one day
Without a hat, upon the public way.
"Some other Roman—I forget his name—
Because his wife went to a summer's game
420 Without his knowledge, left her in the lurch.
"And he would take the Bible up and search
For proverbs in Ecclesiasticus,
Particularly one that has it thus:
'Suffer no wicked woman to gad about.'
425 And then would come the saying (need you doubt?)
A man who seeks to build his house of sallows,
A man who spurs a blind horse over fallows,
Or lets his wife make pilgrimage to Hallows,
Is worthy to be hanged upon the gallows.[8]
430 But all for naught. I didn't give a hen
For all his proverbs and his wise old men.
Nor would I take rebuke at any price;
I hate a man who points me out my vice,
And so, God knows, do many more than I.
435 That drove him raging mad, you may rely.
No more would I forbear him, I can promise.
"Now let me tell you truly by St Thomas
About that book and why I tore the page
And how he smote me deaf in very rage.
440 "He had a book, he kept it on his shelf,
And night and day he read it to himself
And laughed aloud, although it was quite serious.
He called it *Theophrastus and Valerius.*[9] . . .
"Now to my purpose as I told you; look,
445 Here's how I got a beating for a book.
One evening Johnny, glowering with ire,
Sat with his book and read it by the fire.
And first he read of Eve whose wickedness
Brought all mankind to sorrow and distress,
450 Root-cause why Jesus Christ Himself was slain
And gave His blood to buy us back again.
Aye, there's the text where you expressly find
That woman brought the loss of all mankind.
"He read me then how Samson as he slept
455 Was shorn of all his hair by her he kept,
And by that treachery Samson lost his eyes.
And then he read me, if I tell no lies,
All about Hercules and Deianire;
She tricked him into setting himself on fire.
460 "He left out nothing of the miseries
Occasioned by his wives to Socrates. . . .
"And then he told how one Latumius
Lamented to his comrade Arrius
That in his orchard-plot there grew a tree
465 On which his wives had hanged themselves, all
three,
Or so he said, out of some spite or other;
To which this Arrius replied, 'Dear brother,
Give me a cutting from that blessed tree
And planted in my garden it shall be!' . . .
470 "Who could imagine, who could figure out
The torture in my heart? It reached the top
And when I saw that he would never stop
Reading this cursed book, all night no doubt,
I suddenly grabbed and tore three pages out
475 Where he was reading, at the very place,
And fisted such a buffet in his face
That backwards down into our fire he fell.
"Then like a maddened lion, with a yell
He started up and smote me on the head,
480 And down I fell upon the floor for dead.
"And when he saw how motionless I lay
He was aghast and would have fled away,
But in the end I started to come to.
'O have you murdered me, you robber, you,
485 To get my land?' I said. 'Was that the game?
Before I'm dead I'll kiss you all the same.'
"He came up close and kneeling gently down
He said, 'My love, my dearest Alison,
So help me God, I never again will hit
490 You, love; and if I did, you asked for it.
Forgive me!' But for all he was so meek
I up at once and smote him on the cheek
And said, 'Take that to level up the score!
Now let me die. I can't speak any more.'
495 "We had a mort of trouble and heavy weather
But in the end we made it up together.
He gave the bridle over to my hand,
Gave me the government of house and land,
Of tongue and fist, indeed of all he'd got.
500 I made him burn that book upon the spot.
And when I'd mastered him, and out of deadlock
Secured myself the sovereignty in wedlock,
And when he said, 'My own and truest wife,

8. *A man . . . gallows,* a proverbial saying that apparently reflects Johnny's opinion of the Wife's pilgrimages. *Sallows* are willow twigs; *fallows* are fields that have been plowed but left unseeded.
9. *Theophrastus and Valerius,* a satire on matrimony attributed to Walter Map, a wit and cynic who lived about A.D. 1200.

Do as you please for all the rest of life,
505 But guard your honour and my good estate,'
From that day forward there was no debate.
So help me God I was as kind to him
As any wife from Denmark to the rim
Of India, and as true. And he to me.
510 And I pray God that sits in majesty
To bless his soul and fill it with his glory.
Now, if you'll listen, I will tell my story."

Words between the Summoner and the Friar

The Friar laughed when he had heard all this.
"Well, Ma'am," he said, "as God may send me bliss,
This is a long preamble to a tale!"
But when the Summoner heard the Friar rail,
5 "Just look at that!" he cried. "God's arms and skin!
These meddling friars are always butting in!
Don't we all know a friar and a fly
Go buzzing into every dish and pie!
What do you mean with your 'preambulation'?
10 Amble yourself, trot, do a meditation!
You're spoiling all our fun with your commotion."
The Friar smiled and said, "Is that your notion?
I promise on my word before I go
To find occasion for a tale or so
15 About a summoner that will make us laugh."
"Well, damn your eyes, and on my own behalf,"
The Summoner answered, "mine be damned as well
If I can't think of several tales to tell
About the friars that will make you mourn
20 Before we get as far as Sittingbourne.
Have you no patience? Look, he's in a huff!"
Our Host called out, "Be quiet, that's enough!
Shut up, and let the woman tell her tale.
You must be drunk, you've taken too much ale.
25 Now, Ma'am, you go ahead and no demur."
"All right," she said, "it's just as you prefer,
If I have licence from this worthy friar."
"Nothing," said he, "that I should more desire."

The Wife of Bath's Tale

WHEN good King Arthur ruled in ancient days,
(A king that every Briton loves to praise)
This was a land brim-full of fairy folk.
The Elf-Queen and her courtiers joined and broke
5 Their elfin dance on many a green mead,
Or so was the opinion once, I read,
Hundreds of years ago, in days of yore.
But no one now sees fairies any more,
For now the saintly charity and prayer
10 Of holy friars seem to have purged the air;
They search the countryside through field and stream
As thick as motes that speckle a sunbeam,
Blessing the halls, the chambers, kitchens, bowers,
Cities and boroughs, castles, courts, and towers,
15 Thorpes,[1] barns and stables, outhouses and dairies,
And that's the reason why there are no fairies. . . .
Now it so happened, I began to say,
Long, long ago in good King Arthur's day,
There was a knight who was a lusty liver.
20 One day as he came riding from the river
He saw a maiden walking all forlorn
Ahead of him, alone as she was born.
And of that maiden, spite of all she said,
By very force he took her maidenhead.
25 This act of violence made such a stir,
So much petitioning of the king for her,
That he condemned the knight to lose his head
By course of law. He was as good as dead
(It seems that then the statutes took that view)
30 But that the queen, and other ladies too,
Implored the king to exercise his grace
So ceaselessly, he gave the queen the case
And granted her his life, and she could choose
Whether to show him mercy or refuse.
35 The queen returned him thanks with all her might,
And then she sent a summons to the knight
At her convenience, and expressed her will:
"You stand, for such is the position still,
In no way certain of your life," said she,
40 "Yet you shall live if you can answer me:
What is the thing that women most desire?
Beware the axe and say as I require.
"If you can't answer on the moment, though,
I will concede you this: you are to go
45 A twelve month and a day to seek and learn
Sufficient answer, then you shall return.
I shall take gages[2] from you to extort
Surrender of your body to the court."
Sad was the knight and sorrowfully sighed,
50 But there! All other choices were denied,
And in the end he chose to go away
And to return after a year and day

1. *thorpes*, agricultural villages.
2. *gages*, pledges, guarantees.

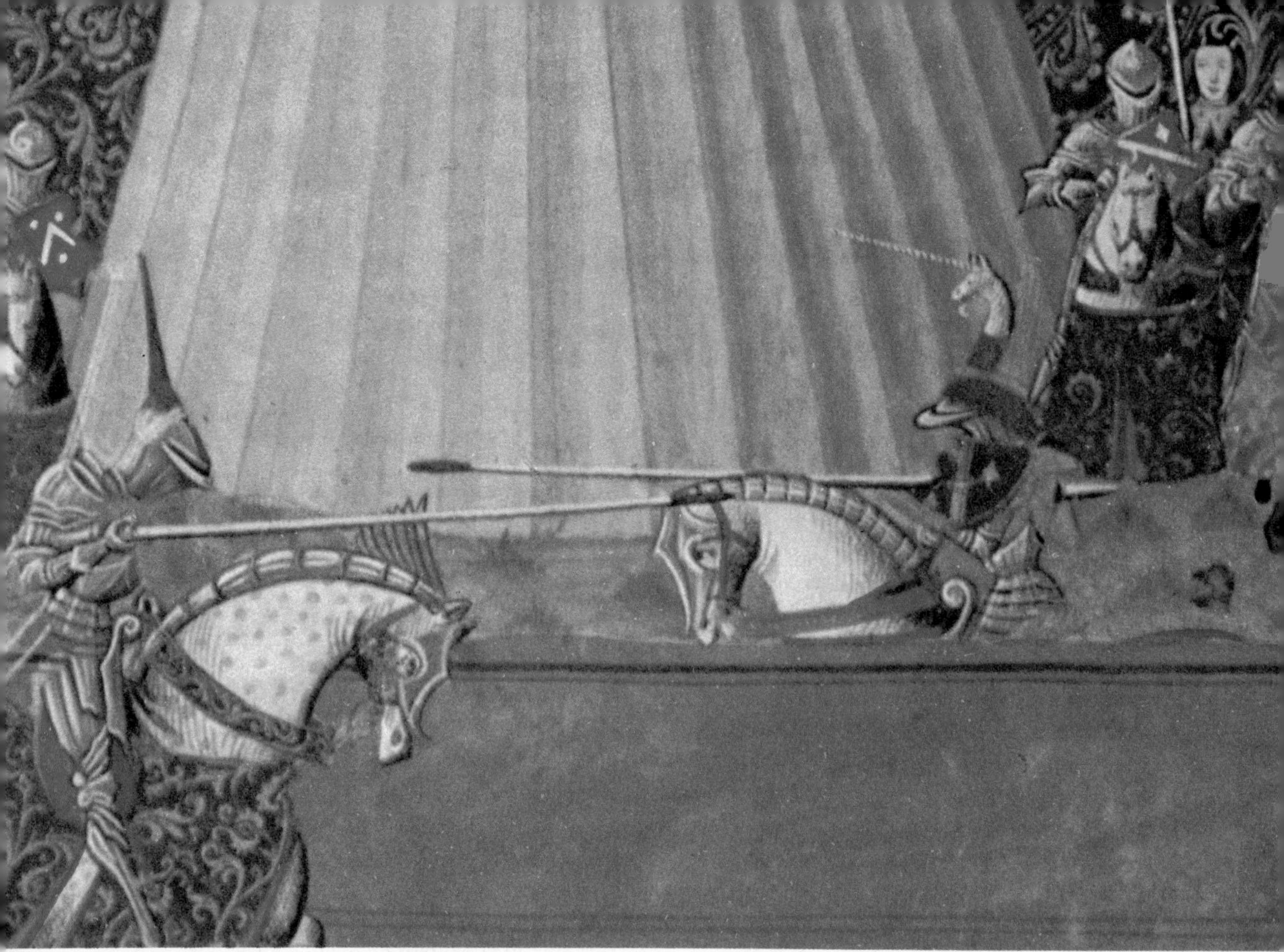

KNIGHTS IN FRONT OF A TENT, FROM THE HARLEY MANUSCRIPT, FOL. 23. COURTESY TRUSTEES OF THE BRITISH MUSEUM.

Armed with such answer as there might be sent
To him by God. He took his leave and went.
55 He knocked at every house, searched every place,
Yes, anywhere that offered hope of grace.
What could it be that women wanted most?
But all the same he never touched a coast,
Country, or town in which there seemed to be
60 Any two people willing to agree.
Some said that women wanted wealth and treasure,
"Honour," said some, some "Jollity and pleasure,"
Some "Gorgeous clothes" and others "Fun in bed,"
"To be oft widowed and remarried," said
65 Others again, and some that what most mattered
Was that we should be cossetted and flattered.
That's very near the truth, it seems to me;
A man can win us best with flattery.
To dance attendance on us, make a fuss,
70 Ensnares us all, the best and worst of us.
Some say the things we most desire are these:
Freedom to do exactly as we please,
With no one to reprove our faults and lies,
Rather to have one call us good and wise.
75 Truly there's not a woman in ten score
Who has a fault, and someone rubs the sore,
But she will kick if what he says is true;
You try it out and you will find so too.
However vicious we may be within
80 We like to be thought wise and void of sin.
Others assert we women find it sweet
When we are thought dependable, discreet
And secret, firm of purpose and controlled,
Never betraying things that we are told.
85 But that's not worth the handle of a rake;
Women conceal a thing? For Heaven's sake!
Remember Midas?[3] Will you hear the tale?
Among some other little things, now stale,
Ovid relates that under his long hair

3. *Midas.* The source is Ovid's *Metamorphoses,* in which, however, the secret is known by Midas' barber, not his wife.

90 The unhappy Midas grew a splendid pair
Of ass's ears; as subtly as he might,
He kept his foul deformity from sight;
Save for his wife, there was not one that knew.
He loved her best, and trusted in her too.
95 He begged her not to tell a living creature
That he possessed so horrible a feature.
And she—she swore, were all the world to win,
She would not do such villainy and sin
As saddle her husband with so foul a name;
100 Besides to speak would be to share the shame.
Nevertheless she thought she would have died
Keeping this secret bottled up inside;
It seemed to swell her heart and she, no doubt
Thought it was on the point of bursting out.
105 Fearing to speak of it to woman or man
Down to a reedy marsh she quickly ran
And reached the sedge. Her heart was all on fire
And, as a bittern bumbles in the mire,
She whispered to the water, near the ground
110 "Betray me not, O water, with thy sound!
To thee alone I tell it: it appears
My husband has a pair of ass's ears!
Ah! My heart's well again, the secret's out!
I could no longer keep it, not a doubt."
115 And so you see, although we may hold fast
A little while, it must come out at last.
We can't keep secrets; as for Midas, well,
Read Ovid for his story; he will tell.
This knight that I am telling you about
120 Perceived at last he never would find out
What it could be that women loved the best.
Faint was the soul within his sorrowful breast
As home he went, he dared no longer stay;
His year was up and now it was the day.
125 As he rode home in a dejected mood,
Suddenly, at the margin of a wood,
He saw a dance upon the leafy floor
Of four and twenty ladies,[4] nay, and more.
Eagerly he approached, in hope to learn
130 Some words of wisdom ere he should return;
But lo! Before he came to where they were,
Dancers and dance all vanished into air!
There wasn't a living creature to be seen
Save one old woman crouched upon the green.
135 A fouler-looking creature I suppose
Could scarcely be imagined. She arose
And said, "Sir knight, there's no way on from here.
Tell me what you are looking for, my dear,
For peradventure that were best for you;
140 We old, old women know a thing or two."
"Dear Mother," said the knight, "alack the day!
I am as good as dead if I can't say
What thing it is that women most desire;
If you could tell me I would pay your hire."
145 "Give me your hand," she said, "and swear to do
Whatever I shall next require of you
—If so to do should lie within your might—
And you shall know the answer before night."
"Upon my honour," he answered, "I agree."
150 "Then," said the crone, "I dare to guarantee
Your life is safe; I shall make good my claim.
Upon my life the queen will say the same.
Show me the very proudest of them all
In costly coverchief or jewelled caul[5]
155 That dare say no to what I have to teach.
Let us go forward without further speech."
And then she crooned her gospel in his ear
And told him to be glad and not to fear.
They came to court. This knight, in full array,
160 Stood forth and said, "O Queen, I've kept my day
And kept my word and have my answer ready."
There sat the noble matrons and the heady
Young girls, and widows too, that have the grace
Of wisdom, all assembled in that place,
165 And there the queen herself was throned to hear
And judge his answer. Then the knight drew near
And silence was commanded through the hall.
The queen then bade the knight to tell them all
What thing it was that women wanted most.
170 He stood not silent like a beast or post,
But gave his answer with the ringing word
Of a man's voice and the assembly heard:
"My liege and lady, in general," said he,
"A woman wants the self-same sovereignty
175 Over her husband as over her lover,
And master him; he must not be above her.
That is your greatest wish, whether you kill
Or spare me; please yourself. I wait your will."
In all the court not one that shook her head
180 Or contradicted what the knight had said;
Maid, wife, and widow cried, "He's saved his life!"
And on the word up started the old wife,
The one the knight saw sitting on the green,
And cried, "Your mercy, sovereign lady queen!

4. *dance . . . ladies,* the fairy ring, a familiar element in Celtic folklore.

5. *caul,* a netted cap worn by women.

185 Before the court disperses, do me right!
'Twas I who taught this answer to the knight,
For which he swore, and pledged his honour to it,
That the first thing I asked of him he'd do it,
So far as it should lie within his might.
190 Before this court I ask you then, sir knight,
To keep your word and take me for your wife;
For well you know that I have saved your life.
If this be false, deny it on your sword!"
"Alas!" he said, "Old lady, by the Lord
195 I know indeed that such was my behest,
But for God's love think of a new request,
Take all my goods, but leave my body free."
"A curse on us," she said, "if I agree!
I may be foul, I may be poor and old,
200 Yet will not choose to be, for all the gold
That's bedded in the earth or lies above,
Less than your wife, nay, than your very love!"
"My love?" said he. "By Heaven, my damnation!
Alas that any of my race and station
205 Should ever make so foul a misalliance!"
Yet in the end his pleading and defiance
All went for nothing, he was forced to wed.
He takes his ancient wife and goes to bed.
Now peradventure some may well suspect
210 A lack of care in me since I neglect
To tell of the rejoicings and display
Made at the feast upon their wedding-day.
I have but a short answer to let fall;
I say there was no joy or feast at all,
215 Nothing but heaviness of heart and sorrow.
He married her in private on the morrow
And all day long stayed hidden like an owl,
It was such torture that his wife looked foul.
Great was the anguish churning in his head
220 When he and she were piloted to bed;
He wallowed back and forth in desperate style.
His ancient wife lay smiling all the while;
At last she said "Bless us! Is this, my dear,
How knights and wives get on together here?
225 Are these the laws of good King Arthur's house?
Are knights of his all so contemptuous?
I am your own beloved and your wife,
And I am she, indeed, that saved your life;
And certainly I never did you wrong.
230 Then why, this first of nights, so sad a song?
You're carrying on as if you were half-witted!
Say, for God's love, what sin have I committed?
I'll put things right if you will tell me how."
"Put right?" he cried. "That never can be now!
235 Nothing can ever be put right again!
You're old, and so abominably plain,
So poor to start with, so low-bred to follow;
It's little wonder if I twist and wallow!
God, that my heart would burst within my breast!"
240 "Is that," said she, "the cause of your unrest?"
"Yes, certainly," he said, "and can you wonder?"
"I could set right what you suppose a blunder,
That's if I cared to, in a day or two,
If I were shown more courtesy by you.
245 Just now," she said, "you spoke of gentle birth,
Such as descends from ancient wealth and worth.
If that's the claim you make for gentlemen
Such arrogance is hardly worth a hen.
Whoever loves to work for virtuous ends,
250 Public and private, and who most intends
To do what deeds of gentleness he can,
Take him to be the greatest gentleman.
Christ wills we take our gentleness from Him,
Not from a wealth of ancestry long dim,
255 Though they bequeath their whole establishment
By which we claim to be of high descent.
Our fathers cannot make us a bequest
Of all those virtues that became them best
And earned for them the name of gentleman,
260 But bade us follow them as best we can. . . .
For of our parents nothing can we claim
Save temporal things, and these may hurt and maim.
"But everyone knows this as well as I;
For if gentility were implanted by
265 The natural course of lineage down the line,
Public or private, could it cease to shine

OF HUMAN INTEREST

Chaucer's worry about scribal errors and their distortions of meaning is apparent in this half-humorous curse addressed to the man who copied his manuscripts.

Chaucers Wordes unto Adam, His Owne Scriveyn

Adam scriveyn, if ever it thee bifalle
Boece or Troilus to wryten newe,
Under thy long lokkes° thou most have the scalle°, — locks/mange
But after my makyn thou wryte more trewe;
So oft a-days I mot thy werk renewe,
It to correcte and eek to rubbe and scrape°; — erase
And al is thorough thy negligence and rape.° — haste

In doing the fair work of gentle deed?
No vice or villainy could then bear seed. . . .
"Gentility is only the renown
270 For bounty that your fathers handed down,
Quite foreign to your person, not your own;
Gentility must come from God alone.
That we are gentle comes to us by grace
And by no means is it bequeathed with place. . . .
275 And therefore, my dear husband, I conclude
That even if my ancestors were rude,
Yet God on high—and so I hope He will—
Can grant me grace to live in virtue still,
A gentlewoman only when beginning
280 To live in virtue and to shrink from sinning.
"As for my poverty which you reprove,
Almighty God Himself in whom we move,
Believe, and have our being, chose a life
Of poverty, and every man or wife,
285 Nay, every child can see our Heavenly King
Would never stoop to choose a shameful thing.
No shame in poverty if the heart is gay,
As Seneca and all the learned say.
He who accepts his poverty unhurt
290 I'd say is rich although he lacked a shirt.
But truly poor are they who whine and fret
And covet what they cannot hope to get.
And he that, having nothing, covets not,
Is rich, though you may think he is a sot. . . .
295 And since it's no offence, let me be plain;
Do not rebuke my poverty again.
"Lastly you taxed me, sir, with being old.
Yet even if you never had been told
By ancient books, you gentlemen engage
300 Yourselves in honour to respect old age.
To call an old man 'father' shows good breeding,
And this could be supported from my reading.
"You say I'm old and fouler than a fen.
You need not fear to be a cuckold, then.
305 Filth and old age, I'm sure you will agree,
Are powerful wardens upon chastity.
Nevertheless, well knowing your delights,
I shall fulfil your worldly appetites.
"You have two choices; which one will you try?
310 To have me old and ugly till I die,
But still a loyal, true, and humble wife
That never will displease you all her life,
Or would you rather I were young and pretty
And chance your arm what happens in a city
315 Where friends will visit you because of me,
Yes, and in other places too, maybe.
Which would you have? The choice is all your own."
The knight thought long, and with a piteous groan
At last he said, with all the care in life,
320 "My lady and my love, my dearest wife,
I leave the matter to your wise decision.
You make the choice yourself, for the provision
Of what may be agreeable and rich
In honour to us both, I don't care which;
325 Whatever pleases you suffices me."
"And have I won the mastery?" said she,
"Since I'm to choose and rule as I think fit?"
"Certainly, wife," he answered her, "that's it."
"Kiss me," she cried. "No quarrels! On my oath
330 And word of honour, you shall find me both,
That is, both fair and faithful as a wife;
May I go howling mad and take my life
Unless I prove to be as good and true
As ever wife was since the world was new!
335 And if tomorrow when the sun's above
I seem less fair than any lady-love,
Than any queen or empress east or west,
Do with my life and death as you think best.
Cast up the curtain, husband. Look at me!"
340 And when indeed the knight had looked to see,
Lo, she was young and lovely, rich in charms.
In ecstasy he caught her in his arms,
His heart went bathing in a bath of blisses
And melted in a hundred thousand kisses,
345 And she responded in the fullest measure
With all that could delight or give him pleasure.
So they lived ever after to the end
In perfect bliss; and may Christ Jesus send
Us husbands meek and young and fresh in bed,
350 And grace to overbid them when we wed.
And—Jesu hear my prayer!—cut short the lives
Of those who won't be governed by their wives;
And all old, angry niggards of their pence,
God send them soon a very pestilence!

FROM THE LUTTRELL PSALTER. COURTESY OF THE TRUSTEES OF THE BRITISH MUSEUM.

SQUIRE, FROM THE ELLESMERE CHAUCER. BY PERMISSION OF THE HUNTINGTON LIBRARY, SAN MARINO, CALIFORNIA.

DISCUSSION

1. It seems fairly obvious that one reason for the Wife's going on pilgrimage is to search for a sixth husband. Which of the pilgrims might she set out to entice, and what might be her chance of success?

2. In both her *Prologue* and *Tale*, the Wife expresses ideas that were far ahead of the conventional thinking of her day. Point out examples.

3. Both the *Prologue* and *Tale* are rich in epigrams and apothegms (pointed maxims). List some that you think are especially effective. What do they all tell you about her attitude toward life?

4. Some critics maintain that as the Wife tells her tale, she becomes so engrossed in it that she comes to identify herself with the old woman. Point out instances where the old woman speaks or acts as though she were the Wife of Bath.

5. Do you find yourself more inclined to like or to dislike the Wife of Bath? Justify your answer.

READERS' THEATER

Take a short extract from *The Wife of Bath's Prologue* and make whatever changes and adjustments are necessary to present it as a dramatic duologue—a quarrel between Dame Alice and one of her five husbands.

WRITING

1. Prepare a "link" of your own (it may be in prose) in which one or two other pilgrims react to the *Wife of Bath's Tale*. Examples of Chaucer's links are the remarks of the Host and "gentlefolk" preceding the *Pardoner's Prologue*, the end of the *Pardoner's Tale*, and the "Words Between the Summoner and the Friar" following the *Wife of Bath's Prologue*.

2. Assume that the Wife of Bath has been asked to prepare a short speech in support of a women's liberation movement (medieval or modern), and that you are her ghost writer. Prepare a prose speech for her, trying to capture some of the vigor so evident in her utterances.

OF HUMAN INTEREST

Chaucer enjoyed a joke at his own expense. In one of his poems, *The House of Fame*, he tells of a dream he had in which a huge eagle carried him high into the sky, to deposit him eventually at the House of Fame, where he could listen to the tales of lovers. En route, the eagle speaks to the terrified Chaucer, describing how the poet lives, and incidentally making a passing reference to Chaucer's appetite:

For when thy labour doon al ys,
And hast mad alle thy rekenynges,
In stede or reste and newe thynges,
Thou goost hom to thy hous anoon;
And, also domb as any stoon,
Thou sittest at another book
Tyl fully daswed° ys thy look, — dazed
And lyvest thus as an heremyte°, — hermit
Although thyn abstynence ys lyte.

II. LYRICS

During the Middle Ages the work, not its creator, was considered the important thing, and the authors of these lyrics are unknown. All the poems were originally intended to be sung. To give an idea of the melody of the language, a number of them are given in their original Middle English. Many words whose spelling looks odd will, when pronounced, sound enough like familiar modern words to enable you to recognize them. (Try different vowel sounds.) Most final *e*'s were pronounced with a light neutral or schwa sound.

In number 2 and number 4, some spellings have been modernized. Numbers 5, 6, 8, 9, and 10 are translations.

1. TELL ME, WIGHT IN THE BROOM
(14th century)

"Say me, wight[1] *in the broom,*
What is me for to doon?
Ich° have the werste bonde° — I / husband
That is in any londe°." — land

5 *"If thy bonde is ille°,* — bad
Hold thy tonge stille."

"Tell me, wight in the broom,
Teach me what I must do
So that my husband
Will love me true."

5 "Hold thy tongue still,
And thou'lt have all thy will."

Translated by Mabel Van Duzee.

1. *wight,* a supernatural or unearthly being, good or bad.

2. MAIDEN IN THE MOOR
(Early 14th century)

Maiden in the moor lay—
In the moor lay
Seven nights full, seven nights full,
Maiden in the moor lay—
5 *In the moor lay—*
Seven nights full and a day.

Well was her meat°. — Good was her food.
What was her meat?
The primrose and the—
10 The primrose and the—
Well was her meat.
What was her meat?
The primrose and the violet.

Well was her drink.
15 What was her drink?
The chilled water of the—
The chilled water of the—
Well was her drink.
What was her drink?
20 The chilled water of the well-spring.

Well was her bower°. — abode
What was her bower?
The red rose and the—
The red rose and the—
25 Well was her bower.
What was her bower?
The red rose and the lily flower.

OF LITERARY INTEREST

How were the lyrics preserved?

The earliest Middle English lyrics that have been preserved are in manuscripts dating from the thirteenth century, but there are scraps of evidence suggesting that long before that, there existed popular poetry which is now lost. There is, for example, the scandalous episode mentioned by a writer in the twelfth century. A parish priest in Worcestershire, having been kept awake all night by revellers dancing and singing in the churchyard, next morning began the service not by intoning *Dominus vobiscum,* but by singing the refrain that had been ringing all night in his ears: "Swete lemman, thin are" ("Sweetheart, have mercy").

A fairly large number of medieval lyrics have survived, especially from the fourteenth and fifteenth centuries. Yet, as one authority points out, "all that has been preserved may be regarded as a fragment of all there must have been. We owe most of the finest lyrics that we do have to a few windfalls, about half a dozen outstanding manuscript collections. The losses in the indigenous song verse must certainly have been the heaviest. The more elaborate lyrics composed by men of letters from Chaucer onwards for reading privately or to a select company would be more esteemed than the traditional songs by the kind of persons who could read or write. They would have been written when composed, and once written would be the more likely to be copied. The traditional songs, besides being more lightly regarded by lettered persons, would in any case be more easily remembered and would therefore be less likely to be written down. What was being sung by many people—and had long been sung—might also be more easily taken for granted."[1]

Most of the surviving Middle English poems are religious, as one would expect, since they are mainly in manuscripts copied and preserved in religious houses. Some secular poems, however, were found scribbled on fly-leaves of religious works, in blank spaces on government documents, or as graffiti scratched on columns and walls of medieval churches. (Parchment for writing was scarce and expensive.) Other bits of secular poetry survived because they were mentioned in sermons inveighing against the songs and dances—survivals of pagan Britain—which the people continued to find irresistible in spite of the opposition of the Church.

Secular lyrics have also been found in "commonplace books" belonging to laymen—miscellaneous ragbag collections that might contain prose chronicles, medical prescriptions, genealogies, and deeds, in addition to poems. Other poems are in manuscript collections that must have been the repertories of professional minstrels.

"Tell me, wight in the broom" is quoted in an early thirteenth-century sermon. It refers to the pagan custom of consulting soothsayers. The broom plant was considered to have magical properties.

"Maiden in the moor" is one of several poems found written on a narrow strip of vellum bound up, as if by accident, with completely different material in a manuscript of the early fourteenth century. It appears to be a dance-song intended for group performance. Who the maiden is who has been keeping a week-long vigil beside a well—whether she is human or faery—can only be conjectured. If she is human, she may have been undergoing some rite of purification or initiation, perhaps in connection with a pagan ritual designed to influence nature through magic.

The riddling song "I have a young sister" is from a minstrel collection, and was probably old when the minstrel wrote it down.

3. I HAVE A YOUNG SISTER
(Early 15th century)

I have a yong suster
Fer° biyonde the see; — far
Manye be the druries° — love-tokens
That she sente me.

5 She sente me the cherye° — cherry
Withouten any stoon°, — stone
And so she dide the dove
Withouten any boon°. — bone

She sente me the brere° — briar
10 Withouten any rinde°; — bark
She bad me love my lemman° — sweetheart
Withoute longinge.

How sholde any cherye
Be withoute stoon?
15 And how sholde any dove
Be withoute boon?

How sholde any brere
Be withoute rinde?
How sholde I love my lemman
20 Withoute longinge?

Whan the cherye was a flowr,
Thanne hadde it no stoon;
Whan the dove was an ey°, — egg
Thanne hadde it no boon.

25 Whan the brere was unbred°, — unripe
Thanne hadde it no rinde;
Whan the maiden hath that° she loveth, — what
She is withoute longinge.

1. From "Carols and Other Songs and Lyrics" from *Medieval English Poetry* by John Speirs. Reprinted by permission of Faber and Faber Limited.

4. ADAM LAY IN BONDAGE
(Early 15th century)

(Adam represents mankind, in bondage to Satan through the Fall. According to popular tradition of the time, the Creation and the Fall took place around 4000 B.C.)

Adam lay i-bounden, bounden in a bond,
Four thousand winter thought he not too long;
And all was for an apple, an apple that he took,
As clerkes finden written in here book.

5 Ne hadde the apple take be, the apple taken ben,
Ne hadde never our Lady a ben Hevene Queen.
Blessed be the time that apple take was!
Therfore we moun singen: "Deo gracias!"[1]

1. *Deo gracias,* thanks be to God.

5. *From* THE LAND OF COCKAYNE
(Late 13th century)

Far in the sea and west of Spain
There is a country called Cockayne.
No other land beneath the skies
So many kinds of joy supplies.
5 Though Paradise be merry and bright,
Cockayne is yet a fairer sight.
What is there in Paradise to see
But grass and flowers and greenery?
Though doubtless there the joy is great,
10 There is naught but fruit to eat.
There is no hall nor bower nor bench,
And only water thirst to quench.
But two men live there, I've heard say,
Enoch and Elijah they.
15 It is a doleful place to be,
With so little company.
In Cockayne there's ample fare
Without trouble, toil, or care.
The food is choice, the drink is bright
20 At noon, late afternoon, and night.
I say in sooth—ye need not fear—
There is no land on earth its peer.
There is no land beneath the sun
Where there is so much joy and fun.
25 There is many a pleasant sight;
All is day, there is no night.
There is no quarreling or strife;
There is no death but ever life.
There is no lack of meat or cloth;
30 There is no man or woman wroth.
There is no serpent, wolf, or fox,
No horse or nag or cow or ox;
There is no sheep, no swine, no goat.
There is no filthiness, God wot!
35 No cattle breeding and no studs.
The land is full of other goods.
There is no fly or flea or louse
In clothing, farmyard, bed, or house.
There is no thunder, sleet, or hail,
40 No vile worm crawls, or any snail.
No tempest rages, rain or wind.
No man or woman there is blind.
But all is mirth and joy and glee.
Well he fares who there may be!
45 There are rivers great and fine
Of oil and honey, milk and wine.
Water is never used at all,
Save to look at or wash withal.
There is fruit of every sort,
50 And all is frolic and disport.
There is an abbey fair and gay,
Where white monks dwell and also gray.
There are chambers good and halls;
All of pasties are the walls,
55 Of flesh and fish and tender meat,
The most delicious man may eat.
Flour-cakes are the shingles all
Of cloister, chamber, church, and hall.
The pinnacles are puddings fat,
60 No prince or king could cavil at.
One may eat thereof his fill,
And yet be guilty of no ill.
All is common to young and old,
To stern and haughty, meek and bold.
65 There is a cloister fair and bright,
Broad and long, a noble sight.
The pillars of the fine arcade
Are every one of crystal made;

Each base and capital, 'tis said,
70 Of jasper and of coral red. . . .
There are birds in every bush,
Throstle, nightingale, and thrush,
The lark and the green woodpecker,—
Hard to name them all it were.
75 Never ceasing, with all their might
They gaily sing both day and night.
There are other birds, to wit:
Geese ready roasted on the spit
Fly to that abbey—God it wot—
80 And cry out, "Geese, all hot! all hot!"
They bring too garlick plenteously,
The best dressing that one could see.
The larks, it is a well known truth,
Light adown in a man's mouth,
85 Stewed daintily and right well done,
Sprinkled with cloves and cinnamon.
For drink there is no need to ask;
To take it is the only task.
When the monks proceed to mass
90 All the windows made of glass
Are turned into crystal bright,
To give the monks the greater light.
When the masses are all said
And the books aside are laid,
95 The crystal turns to glass once more,
Into the state it was before.
The younger monks go every day
After meat to have their play.
There is no hawk or bird that flies
100 With greater swiftness through the skies
Than these young monks in sportive mood
With their long sleeves and their hood.
When the abbot sees their flight,
In it he takes great delight,
105 Nevertheless with charges strong
Bids them alight at evensong.
The monks, however, will not obey
And in a covey soar away. . . .
And the monk who slumbers best
110 And gives his body ample rest,
There is a goodly certainty
That he'll be abbot speedily.
Whoso will come that land unto,
Full great penance he must do.
115 For seven years, as it is said,
Through dung of swine he must needs wade,
Sunk up to the very chin.
Thus he may to that land win.

OF LITERARY INTEREST

Poems against women

Witty satires on women were common from the twelfth century on. Some of them were written by celibate churchmen who regarded women as the deceiving descendants of Eve, but others simply grew out of a long tradition of humorous verbal exchanges between the sexes.

All three poems included here are from collections of carols or dance-songs. From illustrations in old manuscripts, as well as descriptions in literature, it appears that the dance known as the *carole* consisted of a chain of male and female dancers who stepped in a circle to the accompaniment of the voice. A leader sang the stanzas of the song while the ring moved to the left. At the close of the stanza the entire company would respond with the refrain or burden, dancing in place the while. Then the circle would revolve again while the leader sang the next stanza, and so on. The refrain or burden sung by the entire group appears at the beginning of the poem and was repeated after each stanza.

In medieval times the term *carol* was used for a poem on any subject that was made up of uniform stanzas and included a burden. Later the term came to be applied only to joyous songs for holidays like Christmas and May Day.

6. WHEN TO TRUST WOMEN
(15th century)

When the following things are done to our intent,
Then give a woman your trust and confidence!

When nettles in winter bring forth roses red,
And thorns of all sorts bear figs naturally,
5 And broom-shrubs bear apples in every mead,
And laurels bear cherries abundantly,
And oaks bear dates very plenteously,
And leeks produce honey in superfluence—
Then give a woman your trust and confidence!

10 When swine are masters of all kinds of music,
And asses are doctors of every science,
And cats heal men by practicing of physic,
And buzzards to scripture give any credence,
And merchants buy with honor and not pounds
and pence,
15 And crows are made poets for their eloquence—
Then give a woman your trust and confidence!

7. WHAT WOMEN ARE NOT
(Late 15th century)

Of all creatures women be best;
Cuius contrarium verum est.[1]

In every place ye may well see
That women be trewe as tirtyll° on tree; — turtle dove
5 Not liberall in langage but ever in secrete,
And gret joye among them is for to be.

The stedfastnes of women will never be don,
So jentyll°, so curtes, they be everichon°, — gentle / everyone
Meke as a lambe, still as a stone;
10 Croked nor crabbed find ye none.

Men be more cumbers° a thousand fold, — troublesome
And I mervayll° how they dare be so bold — marvel
Against women for to hold,
Seeing them so pascient, softe, and cold.

15 For tell a woman all your counsayle°, — secrets
And she can kepe it wonderly well;
She had lever° go quik to hell — rather
Than to her neighbour she wold it tell.

Now say well by women, or elles be still,
20 For they never displesed man by ther will;
To be angry or wroth they can no skill,
For I dare say they think non° ill. — no

1. Latin, meaning "Of which the opposite is true."

8. THE HENPECKED HUSBAND'S COMPLAINT
(15th century)

How! Hey! No lie is this:
I dare not speak when she shouts "Peace!"

Young men, I warn you every one:
Old wives take you none!
5 For I myself have one at home—
I dare not speak when she shouts "Peace!"

When I come from the plow at noon,
In a broken dish my food's slung down,
I dare not ask our dame for a spoon—
10 I dare not speak when she shouts "Peace!"

If I ask our dame for bread,
She grabs her broom and breaks my head,
And chases me clear under the bed—
I dare not speak when she shouts "Peace!"

15 If I ask our dame for meat,
About the ears with the dish I'm beat;
"Boy, you don't deserve to eat!"—
I dare not speak when she shouts "Peace!"

If I ask our dame for cheese,
20 "Boy," says she, all at her ease,
"You aren't worth two unshelled peas!"—
I dare not speak when she shouts "Peace!"

9. THE BLACKSMITHS
(14th–15th century)

Swart, sweaty smiths, smutched with smoke,
Drive me to death with din of their dints.[1]
Such noise a-nights heard a man never:
What criminal cries, what clatter and clanging!
5 The cursed cow-carpenters[2] cry after "Coal! coal!"
And blow their bellows till their brains burst.
"Huff puff," says the one, "Hoff poff," the other.
They spit and sprawl and spell many spells;
They gnaw and gnash, they groan together,
10 And hold hot at it with hard hammers.
Of a bull's hide is their bellies' covering;[3]
Their shanks are shackled[4] for the spattering sparks;
Heavy hammers they have, that are handled hard.
Stark strokes they strike on a steel-stock
15 And batter out a burden: "Loos boos! las das!"
Such a damnable din is due only the devil.
The master lays into the links, lashing with his
hammer,
Twists them together, and taps out a treble:
"Tic tock, hic hock, tiket taket, tic tock—
20 Loos boos, las das!" *This* is the life they lead,
These mare-clothers.[5] Christ give them curses!
Not a man these nights can have his rest!

From *Fourteenth-Century Verse and Prose*, by Kenneth Sisam. Reprinted by permission of the Clarendon Press, Oxford.

1. *dints*, blows.
2. *cow-carpenters*. The term used in the original ("cammede kongons") has given translators trouble. Others render it as "snub-nosed no-goods" or "crooked changelings, misshapen creatures."
3. *bellies' covering*, smiths' aprons.
4. *shackled*, protectively covered.
5. *mare-clothers*, smiths who clothe horses in armor.

"CRAFTSMEN AND GUILDMASTER."
COURTESY THE TRUSTEES OF THE BRITISH MUSEUM.

OF LITERARY INTEREST

Alliterative verse

While Chaucer and other sophisticated court poets were writing rhymed verse in the French and Italian style, some poets in the north and west of England were composing alliterative poetry in the Anglo-Saxon oral tradition. The excellence of the alliterative poems that have happened to survive—and they include masterpieces like *Sir Gawayne and the Grene Knight, The Pearl, Piers Plowman,* and various Arthurian romances—leads some scholars to believe there must have been a continuous tradition of poetry in this style dating from Anglo-Saxon times. "The Blacksmiths" is one of the few surviving short lyrics in the old alliterative style.

10. THREE SORROWFUL THINGS
(13th century)

When I think upon things three,
Never may I happy be.
The one is that I must away;
Another, I know not the day;
5 The third one is my greatest care,
I know not whither I must fare.

Translated by Mabel Van Duzee.

11. JESU! SEND US PEACE
(Late 15th century)

Jesu! for thy mercy endelesse,
Save thy pepill and sende us pesse.

Jesu! for thy wondes fife,[1]
Save fro sheding Christain blode;
Sese alle grete trobill[2] of malice and strife,
5 And of oure neybores sende us tidinges gode.

Blessed Jesu!
Blessed Jesu!

1. five wounds.
2. Cease all great trouble.

12. WESTRON WIND
(Late 15th century)

Westron winde, when will thou blow
The smalle raine downe can raine?
Christ if my love were in my armes,
And I in my bed againe.

(Fragment from a songbook)

The spring-welcoming song below, one of the oldest surviving English lyrics, is a round for six voices. It may have been preserved because a Latin hymn was set to its music.

13. CUCKOO SONG
(Early 13th century)

Sing, cuccu, nu! Sing, cuccu!
Sing, cuccu! Sing, cuccu, nu!

Sumer is icumen in;° — spring has come in
Lhude° sing, cuccu! — loud
5 Groweth sed and bloweth med,
And springth the wude° nu. — woods
Sing, cuccu!

Awe° bleteth after lomb, — ewe
Lhouth° after calve cu, — lows
10 Bulluc sterteth°, bucke verteth°, — starts / breaks wind
Murie sing, cuccu!
Cuccu! Cuccu!
Well singes thu, cuccu;
Ne swik° thu naver nu! — cease

DISCUSSION

1. Of "Westron Wind" one critic has said, "Rarely have such passion and pain been compressed into so few words." Discuss the appropriateness of this assessment.

2. "The Land of Cockayne" describes an earthly paradise where all life's forbidden pleasures can be enjoyed.
(a) What can you infer about the person who composed it? Give as many specific details as you can.
(b) Find a copy of the American song "The Big Rock Candy Mountains." In what respects does it resemble "The Land of Cockayne"? In what ways is it different?

3. Discuss whether the alliterative verse form of "The Blacksmiths" fits its subject.

4. Paradoxes and riddles appealed to the medieval mind. Discuss the use of these devices in "Adam lay in bondage," "I have a young sister," and "When to Trust Women." Which lyric uses these devices with greatest effect?

5. Assume that, instead of telling tales on the journey home from Canterbury, Chaucer's pilgrims are to sing songs. To which pilgrim would you assign each of the following, and why? "Cuckoo Song," "The Henpecked Husband's Complaint," "The Land of Cockayne," "The Blacksmiths," "Adam lay in bondage."

III. POPULAR BALLADS

LORD RANDAL

1

"O where hae ye been, Lord Randal, my son?
O where hae ye been, my handsome young man?"
"I hae been to the wild wood; mother, make my bed soon,
For I'm weary wi hunting, and fain wald lie down."

2

"Where gat ye your dinner, Lord Randal, my son?
Where gat ye your dinner, my handsome young man?"
"I din'd wi my true-love; mother, make my bed soon,
For I'm weary wi hunting, and fain wald lie down."

3

"What gat ye to your dinner, Lord Randal, my son?
10 What gat ye to your dinner, my handsome young man?"
"I gat eels boild in broo; mother, make my bed soon,
For I'm weary wi hunting, and fain wald lie down."

4

"What became of your bloodhounds, Lord Randal, my son?
What became of your bloodhounds, my handsome young man?"
15 "O they swelld and they died; mother, make my bed soon,
For I'm weary wi hunting, and fain wald lie down."

5

"O I fear ye are poisond, Lord Randal, my son!
O I fear ye are poisond, my handsome young man!"
"O yes! I am poisond; mother, make my bed soon,
20 For I'm sick at the heart, and I fain wald lie down."

From Scott's *Minstrelsy of the Scottish Border,* 1803.

OF LITERARY INTEREST

The ballad stanza

The so-called ballad stanza, used in many folk or popular ballads, consists of four lines, the first and third of which contain four accented syllables, the second and fourth, three. The rhyme scheme is usually *abcb,* sometimes *abab,* and the rhyme is often only approximate. Although in its purest state the ballad stanza is in iambic meter, the addition of a variable number of unaccented syllables is common. Some authentic ballads (like "Lord Randal") display further variations.

THE UNQUIET GRAVE

1

"The wind doth blow today, my love,
And a few small drops of rain;
I never had but one true-love,
In cold grave she was lain.

2

"I'll do as much for my true-love
As any young man may;
I'll sit and mourn all at her grave
For a twelvemonth and a day."

3

The twelvemonth and a day being up,
The dead began to speak:
"Oh who sits weeping on my grave,
And will not let me sleep?"

4

"'Tis I, my love, sits on your grave,
And will not let you sleep;
For I crave one kiss of your clay-cold lips,
And that is all I seek."

5

"You crave one kiss of my clay-cold lips;
But my breath smells earthy strong;
If you have one kiss of my clay-cold lips,
Your time will not be long.

6

"'Tis down in yonder garden green,
Love, where we used to walk,
The finest flower that ere was seen
Is withered to a stalk.

7

"The stalk is withered dry, my love,
So will our hearts decay;
So make yourself content, my love,
Till God calls you away."

Communicated orally by a young
girl in Sussex; published 1868.

OF HUMAN INTEREST

The folk belief that excessive grieving for the dead disturbs their rest has been found in wide areas of the Western world. Usually it asserts that the tears wet the grave-clothes or shroud and do not dry, causing the corpse much discomfort.

GET UP AND BAR THE DOOR

1

It fell about the Martinmas time,
And a gay time it was then,
When our goodwife got puddings[1] to make,
And she's boild them in the pan.

2

The wind sae cauld blew south and north,
And blew into the floor;
Quoth our goodman to our goodwife,
"Gae out and bar the door."

3

"My hand is in my hussyfskap,[2]
Goodman, as ye may see;
An it shoud nae be barrd this hundred year,
It's no be barrd for me."

4

They made a paction tween them twa,[3]
They made it firm and sure,
That the first word whaeer shoud speak,
Shoud rise and bar the door.

5

Then by there came two gentlemen,
At twelve o clock at night,
And they could neither see house nor hall,
Nor coal nor candle-light.

6

"Now whether is this a rich man's house,
Or whether is it a poor?"
But neer a word wad ane o them speak,
For barring of the door.

7

And first they[4] ate the white puddings,
And then they ate the black;
Tho muckle[5] thought the goodwife to hersel,
Yet neer a word she spake.

8

Then said the one unto the other,
"Here, man, tak ye my knife;
Do ye tak aff the auld man's beard,
And I'll kiss the goodwife."

---

1. *puddings,* sausages.
2. *hussyfskap,* housewife's work.
3. *paction . . . twa,* agreement between themselves.
4. *they,* the gentlemen.
5. *muckle,* a great deal.

9

"But there's nae water in the house,
  And what shall we do than?"
35 "What ails ye at the pudding-broo,
  That boils into the pan?"

10

O up then started our goodman,
  An angry man was he:
"Will ye kiss my wife before my een,
40 And scad me wi pudding-bree?"

11

Then up and started our goodwife,
  Gied three skips on the floor:
"Goodman, you've spoken the foremost word,
  Get up and bar the door."

Herd, *The Ancient and Modern Scots Songs*, 1769.

SIR PATRICK SPENCE[1]

1

The king sits in Dumferling[2] toune,
  Drinking the blude-reid wine:
"O whar will I get guid sailor,
  To sail this schip of mine?"

2

5 Up and spak an eldern knicht,
  Sat at the kings richt kne:
"Sir Patrick Spence is the best sailor
  That sails upon the se."

3

The king has written a braid letter,[3]
10 And signed it wi his hand,
And sent it to Sir Patrick Spence,
  Was walking on the sand.

4

The first line that Sir Patrick red,
  A loud lauch[4] lauched he;
15 The next line that Sir Patrick red,
  The teir blinded his ee.

5

"O wha is this has don this deid,
  This ill deid don to me,
To send me out this time o' the yeir,
20 To sail upon the se!

6

"Mak hast, mak haste, my mirry men all,
  Our guid schip sails the morne":
"O say na sae, my master deir,
  For I feir a deadlie storme.

7

25 "Late late yestreen I saw the new moone,
  Wi the auld moone in hir arme,
And I feir, I feir, my deir master,
  That we will cum to harme."

8

O our Scots nobles wer richt laith
30 To weet their cork-heild schoone;
But lang owre a' the play wer playd,
  Their hats they swam aboone.[5]

9

O lang, lang may their ladies sit,
  Wi their fans into their hand,
35 Or eir they se Sir Patrick Spence
  Cum sailing to the land.

10

O lang, lang may the ladies stand,
  Wi their gold kems in their hair,
Waiting for thair ain deir lords,
40 For they'll se thame na mair.

11

Haf owre, haf owre to Aberdour,[6]
  It's fiftie fadom deip,
And thair lies guid Sir Patrick Spence,
  Wi the Scots lords at his feit.

From Percy's *Reliques*, 1765.

---

1. Some scholars think this ballad is based on actual historical events. In 1281, the Scottish king's daugher Margaret was married to Eric, King of Norway. She crossed safely to Norway in August, but on the return journey the ship, carrying many knights and nobles, was lost.
2. *Dumferling,* residence of the Scottish kings.
3. *braid letter,* letter of command.

4. *lauch,* laugh.
5. *laith . . . aboone.* The sense of this passage is that the Scottish nobles did not want to get their feet (cork-heeled shoes) wet, but before the voyage was over, they were in water over their heads (their hats swam about).
6. *Haf . . . Aberdour,* halfway home to Aberdeen.

THE LAILY WORM AND THE MACHREL OF THE SEA

1

"I was but seven year auld
When my mither she did die;
My father married the ae warst woman
The warld did ever see.

2

5 "For she has made me the laily worm,[1]
That lies at the fit[2] o the tree,
An my sister Masery she's made
The machrel[3] of the sea.

3

"An every Saturday at noon
10 The machrel comes to me,
An she takes my laily head
An lays it on her knee,
She kaims it wi a siller kaim,[4]
An washes 't in the sea.

4

15 "Seven knights hae I slain,
Sin I lay at the fit of the tree,
An ye war na my ain father,
The eight ane ye should be."[5]

5

"Sing on your song, ye laily worm,
20 That ye did sing to me":
"I never sung that song but what
I would it sing to thee."

(Stanzas 6–9 are repetitions of 1–4.)

10

He sent for his lady,
As fast as send could he:
25 "Whar is my son that ye sent frae me,
And my daughter, Lady Masery?"

11

"Your son is at our king's court,
Serving for meat an fee,
An your daughter's at our queen's court,
30 . . . .

12

"Ye lie, ye ill woman,
Sae loud as I hear ye lie;
My son's the laily worm,
That lies at the fit o the tree,
35 And my daughter, Lady Masery,
Is the machrel of the sea!"

13

She has tane a siller wan,[6]
An gien him[7] strokes three,
And he has started up the bravest knight,
40 That ever your eyes did see.

14

She has taen a small horn,
An loud an shrill blew she,
An a' the fish came her untill
But the proud machrel of the sea:
45 "Ye shapeit me ance an unseemly shape,
An ye's never mare shape me."

15

He has sent to the wood
For whins[8] and for hawthorn,
And he has taen that gay lady,
50 And there he did her burn.

Taken down from recitation in
northern Scotland, 1802–1803.

---

1. *laily worm,* lowly worm; snake.
2. *fit,* foot.
3. *machrel,* mackerel.
4. *siller kaim,* silver comb.
5. Professor Child, the great ballad collector, comments: "It is an aggravation of stepmother malice that the victim of enchantment, however amiable and inoffensive before, should become truculent and destructive."
6. *siller wan,* silver wand.
7. *him,* the laily worm, not the father.
8. *whins,* furze or gorse (evergreen shrubs), which would ignite quickly.

DISCUSSION

1. (a) At what point in "Lord Randal" do you begin to guess what has happened? When are you certain?

(b) What is the effect of the change in wording in line 4 of the final stanza?

2. (a) What details in "The Unquiet Grave" contribute to the feeling of longing and loss?

(b) Why does this ballad seem so much more poignant than the other ballads of domestic tragedy?

(c) What similarities can you see between "The Unquiet Grave" and the lyric "Westron Wind"? What possible explanation can you suggest for the similarities?

3. In folk ballads, actions or exterior appearances are often given rather than feelings or abstract ideas. Find examples of this technique in the ballads.

4. "Sir Patrick Spence" is often cited as an example of the artistic heights to which the popular ballad can rise.

(a) What does "blude-reid wine" in line 2 add to the emotional tone? What would be the effect of using "clear-white wine" instead?

(b) Find other examples of emotionally-weighted words and phrases in the ballads.

(c) Although descriptive details in "Sir Patrick Spence" are minimal, most readers form a clear impression of the characters of Sir Patrick, the King, and the Scots nobles. Do any of the other ballads give you a similarly clear picture of the characters?

5. "Get Up and Bar the Door" is an example of a rare type, the humorous ballad.

(a) In what does its humor lie?

(b) Why might the number of tragic ballads far exceed the number of humorous ballads?

6. The wording of "The Laily Worm" has apparently suffered distortion and loss as the ballad was passed down orally.

(a) Point out examples of illogicalities or loose ends that may reflect the ballad's imperfect condition.

(b) Find similar imperfections in other ballads.

(c) Do these artistic lapses spoil your enjoyment of the ballads?

7. However the ballads were composed, they are folk poetry in the sense that they were transmitted orally by uneducated people and made no attempt at literary flourishes. Do you feel that the emotions come through less clearly than in more formally composed poems? Explain.

8. Would it be legitimate to say that *Beowulf* is just an extended ballad? Or is it something more? Explain.

9. Choose a modern popular ballad and compare it to one of the ballads in this section. In what ways have ballads remained the same? In what ways have they changed?

READERS' THEATER

All the ballads lend themselves well to dramatic reading, especially if someone in the class can strum a guitar for accompaniment. The number of voices required ranges from two to five.

WRITING

Write a modern ballad dealing with a contemporary event or problem. Follow the form of the traditional popular ballad.

SEE ALSO THE ARTICLE "THE POPULAR BALLADS" ON PAGE 125.

KITCHEN SCENE FROM THE LUTTRELL PSALTER. COURTESY OF THE TRUSTEES OF THE BRITISH MUSEUM.

IV. SIR THOMAS MALORY (1395–1471)

SLANDER AND STRIFE[1]

IN May, when every heart flourishes and burgeons (for, as the season is pleasant to behold and comfortable, so man and woman rejoice and are glad of summer coming with his fresh flowers, for winter with his rough winds and blasts causes lusty men and women to cower and to sit by fires), so this season there befell in the month of May a great vexation and ill-fortune that did not end till the flower of chivalry of all the world was destroyed and slain.

And all was due to two unhappy knights who were named Sir Aggravain and Sir Mordred, that were brothers to Sir Gawain. For this Sir Aggravain and Sir Mordred had ever a secret hate unto the queen, Dame Guenevere, and to Sir Lancelot; and daily and nightly they ever watched upon Sir Lancelot.

So it misfortuned that Sir Gawain and all his brothers[2] were in King Arthur's chamber, and then Sir Aggravain said openly and not in council, that many knights might hear: "I am astonished that we all be not ashamed both to see and to know how Sir Lancelot lies daily and nightly by the queen. And all we know well that it is so, and it is shameful of us all that we should suffer so noble a king as King Arthur to be shamed."

Then spoke Sir Gawain and said, "Brother, Sir Aggravain, I pray you and charge you, bring no such matters no more before me, for wit you well, I will not be on your side."

"So God me help," said Sir Gaheris and Sir Gareth, "we will not be a party to your deeds."

"Then will I!" said Sir Mordred.

"I believe you well," said Sir Gawain, "for ever unto all mischief will you consent. And I would that you cease all this and make you not so busy, for I know," said Sir Gawain, "what will fall of it."

"Fall whatsoever fall may," said Sir Aggravain, "I will disclose it to the king."

"Not by my consent," said Sir Gawain, "for if there arise war and strife betwixt Sir Lancelot and us, wit you well, brother, there will be many kings and great lords who will hold with Sir Lancelot. Also, brother Sir Aggravain," said Sir Gawain, "you must remember how oftentimes Sir Lancelot has come to the help of the king and queen; and the best of us all had been full cold at the heart-root had not Sir Lancelot been more worthy than we, and that has he proved himself full oft. And as for my part," said Sir Gawain, "I will never be against Sir Lancelot, for one day's deed, and that was when he rescued me from King Carados of the Dolorous Tower and slew him and saved my life. Also, brother, Sir Aggravain and Sir Mordred, in like wise Sir Lancelot rescued you both and three score and two from Sir Tarquin. And therefore, brother, methinks such noble deeds and kindness should be remembered."

"Do as you list," said Sir Aggravain, "for I will conceal it no longer."

Then with these words came in Sir Arthur.

"Now, brother," said Sir Gawain, "put an end to your strife."

"That will I not," said Sir Aggravain and Sir Mordred.

"Well! Will you so?" said Sir Gawain. "Then God speed you, for I will not hear of your tales, nor be of your counsel."

"No more will I," said Sir Gaheris.

"Nor I," said Sir Gareth, "for I shall never say evil of that man that made me knight."

And therewithal they three departed making great dole.

"Alas!" said Sir Gawain and Sir Gareth, "now is this realm wholly destroyed and put to shame, and the noble fellowship of the Round Table shall be disparbeled [dispersed]."

So they departed, and then King Arthur asked them [the others] what complaint they made.

"My lord," said Sir Aggravain, "I shall tell you,

1. Part I of *The Most Piteous Tale of The Morte Arthur Saunz Guerdon*, slightly modernized, from the Winchester MS. version in *The Works of Sir Thomas Malory* edited by Eugène Vinaver (Oxford University Press, 1947, 1967).

2. *Sir Gawain . . . brothers.* Sir Aggravain, Sir Mordred, Sir Gaheris, and Sir Gareth are all brothers of Sir Gawain. Mordred is also the natural son of King Arthur.

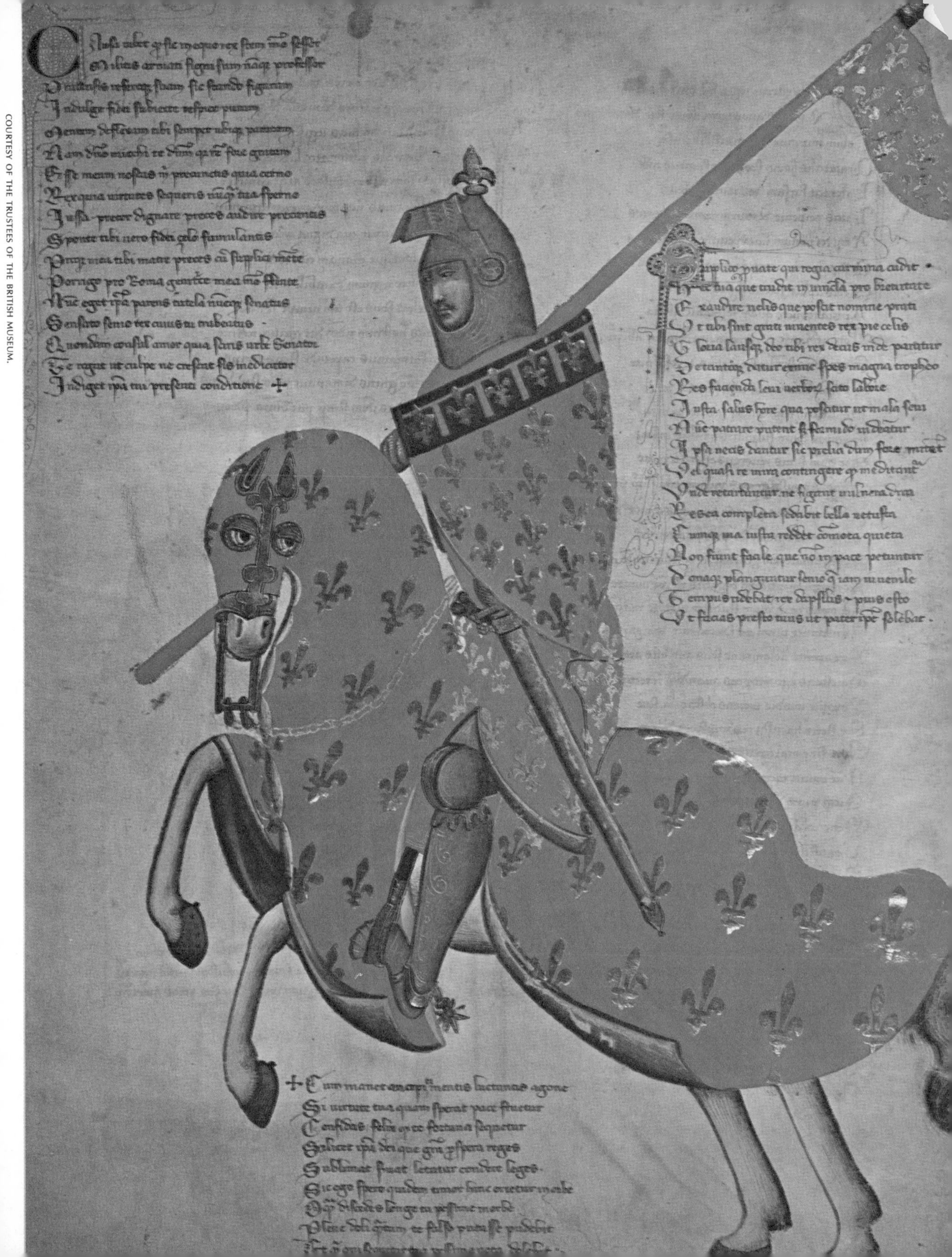

for I may keep it no longer. I and my brother Sir Mordred just broke to my brother Sir Gawain, Sir Gaheris, and Sir Gareth—for this is all, to make it short—that we know that Sir Lancelot loves your queen, and has done so for long. And we are your sister's sons—we may suffer it no longer. And all we know that you should be above Sir Lancelot, and you are the king that made him knight, and therefore we will prove it that he is a traitor to your person."

"If it be so," said the king, "wit you well, he is none other. But I would be loath to begin such a thing unless I might have proof of it, for Sir Lancelot is an hardy knight, and all you know that he is the best knight among us all, and unless he be taken in the deed he will fight with him that brings up the scandal, and I know of no knight that is able to match him.[3] Therefore, if it be true as you say, I would that he were taken with the deed."

For, as the French book says, the king was full loath that such a scandal should be upon Sir Lancelot and his queen. For the king had a suspicion of it, but he would not hear thereof, for Sir Lancelot had done so much for him and for the queen so many times that wit you well the king loved him passing well.

"My lord," said Sir Aggravain, "you shall ride tomorrow a-hunting, and doubt you not, Sir Lancelot will not go with you. And so when it draws toward night you may send the queen word that you will lie out all that night, and so may you send for your cooks. And then, upon pain of death, that night we shall take him with the queen, and we shall bring him unto you, quick or dead."

"I will well," said the king. "Then I counsel you to take with you trusty companions."

"Sir," said Sir Aggravain, "my brother Sir Mordred and I will take with us twelve knights of the Round Table."

"Beware," said King Arthur, "for I warn you, you shall find him strong."

"Let us deal!" said Sir Aggravain and Sir Mordred.

So on the morn King Arthur rode a-hunting and sent word to the queen that he would be out all that night. Then Sir Aggravain and Sir Mordred took with them twelve knights and hid themselves in a chamber in the castle of Carlyle.

When night came, Sir Lancelot told Sir Bors how he intended to go that night and speak with the queen.

"Sir," said Sir Bors, "you shall not go this night by my advice."

"Why?" said Sir Lancelot.

"Sir, for I dread me ever of Sir Aggravain that lies in wait for you daily to do you shame and us all. And never gave my heart so much warning as now against your going to the queen (because peradventure he has laid some watch for you and the queen). Therefore I dread me sore of some treason."

"Have no dread," said Sir Lancelot, "for I shall go and come again and make no tarrying."

"Sir," said Sir Bors, "I am sorry for that, for I dread me sore that your going this night will injure us all."

"Fair nephew," said Sir Lancelot, "I marvel why you speak thus, since the queen has sent for me. And wit you well, I will not be so much a coward, but she shall understand I will see her good grace."

"God speed you well," said Sir Bors, "and send you sound and safe again!"

Then Sir Lancelot departed and took his sword under his arm, and so he walked in his mantle, that noble knight, and put himself in great jeopardy. And so he passed on till he came to the queen's chamber, and so quickly he was let into the chamber.

And thus as they were together there came Sir Aggravain and Sir Mordred with twelve knights with them of the Round Table, and they said with great crying and terrifying voice, "Thou traitor, Sir Lancelot, now thou art taken!"[4]

And thus they cried with a loud voice, so that all the court might hear it. And these fourteen knights all were armed at all points, as if they were to fight in a battle.

"Alas!" said Queen Guenevere, "now are we both put to shame!"

"Madam," said Sir Lancelot, "is there here in your chamber any armour with which I might cover my body? If there be any, give it to me and I shall put an end to their malice, by the grace of God!"

"Now truly," said the queen, "I have no armour,

3. *he will fight . . . to match him.* King Arthur is referring to trial by single combat. The knight who brings up the scandal must, if challenged, fight the knight against whom he made the charges (or, if the charged person is a woman, against a knight who volunteers to serve as her champion). The victor is presumed to have had right on his side. King Arthur, recognizing Sir Lancelot's strength, says he wants more proof than a mere accusation that can be overturned by Sir Lancelot's victory over his accuser.

4. Sir Aggravain and Sir Mordred deliberately insult Sir Lancelot by addressing him as "thee" and "thou," the pronoun they would use in speaking to servants or inferiors.

neither helm, shield, sword, nor spear, wherefore I dread me sore our long love is come to a shameful end. For I hear by their noise there be many noble knights, and well I know they are well armed, and against them you may make no resistance. Wherefore you are likely to be slain, and then shall I be burned! Because if you might escape them," said the queen, "I would not doubt but that you would rescue me, no matter in what danger that I ever stood in."

"Alas!" said Sir Lancelot, "in all my life thus was I never bestead that I should be thus shamefully slain for lack of mine armour."

But ever Sir Aggravain and Sir Mordred cried, "Traitor knight, come out of the queen's chamber! For wit thou well thou art beset so that thou shalt not escape."

"Ah, Jesu mercy!" said Sir Lancelot. "This shameful cry and noise I may not suffer, for better were death at once than thus to endure this distress."

Then he took the queen in his arms and kissed her and said, "Most noblest Christian queen, I beseech you, as you have been ever my special good lady, and I at all times your humble knight and true to my utmost, and as I never failed you in right nor in wrong since the first day King Arthur made me knight, that you will pray for my soul if that I be slain. For well I am assured that Sir Bors, my nephew, and all the remnant of my kin, with Sir Lavain and Sir Urré, that they will not fail to rescue you from the fire. And therefore, mine own lady, take courage again. Whatever comes of me, go with Sir Bors, my nephew, and Sir Urré and they will do you all the pleasure that they may, and you shall live like a queen upon my lands."

"Nay, Sir Lancelot, nay!" said the queen. "Wit you well that I will not live long after your days. If you are slain I will take my death as meekly as ever did martyr take his death for Jesu Christ's sake."

"Well, madam," said Sir Lancelot, "since it is so that the day is come that our love must depart, wit you well I shall sell my life as dear as I may. And a thousandfold," said Sir Lancelot, "I am more sorrowful for you than for myself! And now I had rather than to be lord of all Christendom that I had sure armour upon me, that men might speak of my deeds before I were slain."

"Truly," said the queen, "if it might please God, I wish that they would take me and slay me and suffer you to escape."

OF LITERARY INTEREST

Early in the development of the Arthurian cycle, King Arthur himself was the center of interest. Later, however, he faded into the background as the exploits of various knights of the Round Table were added. Among these additions are the quest for the Holy Grail and two of the most famous love stories of all time, those of Tristram and Iseult and of Lancelot and Guinevere.

"That shall never be," said Sir Lancelot. "God defend me from such a shame! But, Jesu Christ, be Thou my shield and mine armour!"

And therewith Sir Lancelot wrapped his mantle about his arm well and surely; and by then they had gotten a great bench out of the hall, and therewith they all rushed at the door.

"Now, fair lords," said Sir Lancelot, "leave your shouting and your knocking, and I shall set open this door, and then may you do with me what you like."

"Come off, then," said they all, "and do it, for it avails thee not to strive against us all! And therefore let us into this chamber, and we shall save thy life until thou come to King Arthur."

Then Sir Lancelot unbarred the door, and with his left hand he held it open a little, so that but one man might come in at one time. And now there came striding a good knight, a broad man and large, and his name was Sir Collgrevance of Gore. And he with a sword struck at Sir Lancelot mightily. But he put aside the stroke, and gave him such a buffet upon the helmet that he fell groveling, dead, within the chamber door.

Then Sir Lancelot with great might drew the knight within the chamber door. And then Sir Lancelot, with help of the queen and her ladies, was quickly armed in Collgrevance's armour. And ever stood Sir Aggravain and Sir Mordred, crying, "Traitor knight! Come forth out of the queen's chamber!"

"Sirs, leave your noise," said Sir Lancelot, "for wit you well, Sir Aggravain, you shall not take me prisoner this night! Therefore, take my advice, go you all from this chamber door and do not make such an uproar. For I promise you by my knighthood, if you will depart and make no more noise, I shall tomorrow appear before you all and before the king, and then let it be seen which of you or else all of you will convict me of treason. And there shall I answer you, as a knight should, that I came hither to the queen for no manner of evil design, and I will prove and make it good upon you with my hands."

"Fie upon thee, traitor," said Sir Aggravain and Sir Mordred, "for we will take thee whether thou wish it or not and slay thee, if we please! For we let thee know that we have the choice from King Arthur to save thee or to slay thee."

"Ah, sirs," said Sir Lancelot, "is there no other choice with you? Then guard youselves!"

And then Sir Lancelot opened wide the chamber door, and mightily and gallantly he strode in among them. And anon with the first stroke he slew Sir Aggravain, and immediately after twelve of his fellows. Within a while he had laid them down cold to the earth, for there was not one of the twelve knights who might withstand Sir Lancelot one buffet. And also he wounded Sir Mordred, and therewithal he [Mordred] fled with all his might. Then Sir Lancelot returned again unto the queen and said, "Madam, now wit you well, all our true love is brought to an end, for now will King Arthur ever be my foe. And therefore, madam, if it please you that I may have you with me, I shall save you from all manner of dangers."

"Sir, that is not wise," said the queen, "me seems, for now you have done so much harm it will be best that you hold you still with this. And if you see that tomorrow they will put me to death, then may you rescue me as you think best."

"I will well," said Sir Lancelot, "for do not doubt, while I am a man living I shall rescue you."

And then he kissed her, and either of them gave the other a ring, and so he left the queen there and went to his lodging. . . .

Then that noble knight Sir Lancelot told [Sir Bors and his other friends] how he was hard-pressed in the queen's chamber, and how and in what manner he escaped from them.

"And therefore wit you well, my fair lords, I am sure there is nothing but war unto me and mine. And

OF HISTORICAL INTEREST

Was there a real King Arthur?

The earliest documentary reference to a historic Arthur is in a Welsh poem, the *Gododdin* (about A.D. 600), in which a Briton is praised for his fighting prowess, "though he was not Arthur." Arthur's real-life prototype was probably a sixth-century Celtic military leader, not a king, who won many battles against the Anglo-Saxon invaders. Several tenth-century Welsh histories mention him by name and give the dates of great battles in which he fought. The Arthurian cycle received its greatest impetus in Geoffrey of Monmouth's Latin *History of the Kings of Britain* (1137), now believed to be more fiction than fact. Sometime during the height of the Middle Ages Arthur became associated with the code of chivalry and with medieval French romances about Lancelot and the Holy Grail. Through these diverse sources Arthur ultimately emerged in song and story as the embodiment of the ideal knight and king.

Interest in the Arthurian stories spread far and wide. A twelfth-century scholar declared in astonishment that Arthur was known in Asia and the East—in Egypt, the Bosporus, Carthage, Antioch, Armenia, and Palestine. Twelfth-century cathedrals in Italy contain Arthurian figures and names.

During the Middle Ages many Englishmen believed that King Arthur had not died but had been carried to the Isle of Avalon where he would remain until England needed him again, at which time he would return to unite the country. The "Isle of Avalon" in southwest England is today a series of small hills projecting into the marshes of Somerset, site of the impressive ruins of the early medieval abbey of Glastonbury. In earlier days the site undoubtedly was surrounded by water. Scholars think the island was a sacred place of the Celts even in pagan times, used over a long period as a burial ground. In A.D. 1191, the monks at Glastonbury Abbey uncovered a deep grave containing the remains of a man and a woman, and a leaden cross bearing the Latin inscription "Here lies buried the renowned King Arthur, with Guinevere his second wife, in the Isle of Avalon." However, modern research has tended to disprove that the remains were really those of Arthur and Guinevere—which leaves the whole matter still open.

because I have slain this night Sir Aggravain, Sir Gawain's brother, and at least twelve of his fellows, for this cause now I am sure of war to the death. For these knights were sent by King Arthur to betray me, and therefore the king will in his anger and malice condemn the queen unto burning, and that may not I suffer that she should be burnt for my sake. For if I may be heard and if my offer is accepted, I will fight for the queen, because she is a true lady unto her lord. But the king in his anger, I fear, will not accept me as a champion as I ought to be."

"My lord, Sir Lancelot," said Sir Bors, "by my advice, you should take the woe with the weal. And since it is befallen as it is I advise you to guard yourself, for if you will, there is no fellowship of knights christened that shall do you wrong. And also I will counsel you, my lord, that my lady Queen Guenevere, if she be in any distress, inasmuch as she is in pain for your sake, that you gallantly rescue her; for if you did otherwise all the world would speak you shame to the world's end. Inasmuch as you were taken with her, whether you did right or wrong, it is now your part to protect the queen, that she be not slain and put to a shameful death. For if she so dies, the shame shall be evermore yours."

"Now Jesu defend me from shame," said Sir Lancelot, "and keep and save my lady the queen from villainy and shameful death, and that she never be destroyed through my failure to take up the challenge! Wherefore, my fair lords, my kin and my friends," said Sir Lancelot, "what will you do?" . . .

So, to make short tale, they were all agreed that, for better or for worse, if so were that the queen were brought on that morn to the fire, promptly they all would rescue her. And so by the advice of Sir Lancelot they put them all in a wood as near Carlyle as possible, and there they abode quietly to find out what the king would do.

(Meanwhile, the wounded Mordred has hastened to tell King Arthur what had happened. Arthur regrets that Sir Lancelot will be ranged against him, for he foresees that this will mean the end of the fellowship of the Round Table. He is grieved, too, that to preserve his honor he must order the queen's death. Sir Gawain advises him against being over-hasty, pointing out that he does not yet know the whole story. When King Arthur persists, Sir Gawain refuses to have any part in the execution. On a direct order from the king, his younger brothers Sir Gaheris and Sir Gareth reluctantly agree to be present, but, as a show of solidarity with Sir Lancelot, they refuse to wear armour.

Next morning Queen Guenevere is led out to be burned to death in the presence of the lords and ladies of the court.)

Then was there one that Sir Lancelot had sent to that place, who went to espy what time the queen should go to her death. And as soon as he saw the queen despoiled into her smock and shriven, then he quickly gave Sir Lancelot warning. Then was there but spurring and urging forward of horse, and right so they came to the fire. And whoever stood against them, there were they slain, full many a noble knight.

And so in this hurlyburly, as Sir Lancelot pressed here and there, it misfortuned him to slay Sir Gaheris and Sir Gareth, the noble knight, for they were unarmed and unaware. As the French book says, Sir Lancelot smote Sir Gaheris and Sir Gareth upon the brain-pans, wherethrough they were slain in the field. Howbeit in very truth Sir Lancelot saw them not. And so were they found dead among the thickest of the press.

Then Sir Lancelot, when he had thus done, and slain and put to flight all that would withstand him, then he rode straight to Queen Guenevere and threw a gown about her, and then he made her to be set behind him and prayed her to be of good cheer. Now wit you well the queen was glad that she was at that time escaped from the death, and then she thanked God and Sir Lancelot.

And so he rode his way with the queen, as the French book says, to Joyous Garde, and there he kept her as a noble knight should. And many great lords and many good knights were sent him, and many full noble knights drew unto him. When they heard that King Arthur and Sir Lancelot were at strife, many knights were glad, but many were sorry of their strife. □

DISCUSSION

1. If one person were to be blamed for the dissolution of the fellowship of the Round Table, who would it be? Why?
2. One reader has remarked, "In his approach to the events that he describes, Malory places the ideals of chivalry above normal human emotions." Do you agree? Explain why you do or do not.
3. In the preface to the first edition of Malory's work (1485), William Caxton, the publisher, claims that his intent is "that noble men may see and learn the noble acts of chivalry, the gentle and virtuous deeds that some knights used in those days, by which they came to honor, and how they that were vicious were punished and oft put to shame and rebuke." Based on the story you have read, discuss the validity of Caxton's statement.
4. Occasionally Malory interrupts his narrative with a personal comment or explanation. Find a few examples. In more recent times, some authors (e.g. Hemingway) have hesitated to intrude themselves into their readers' consciousness. What is your reaction to Malory's technique?

WRITING

1. Prepare a script, a prose narrative, or an imaginary conversation of a confrontation between King Arthur and Sir Lancelot, keeping in mind that Arthur had liked Lancelot and did not want to see the fellowship of the Round Table dispersed.
2. Follow the suggestions in 1 above, but make the confrontation between King Arthur and Queen Guinevere.

READERS' THEATER

Rewrite part of Malory's dialogue in idiomatic modern English. Two groups of students might then do dramatic readings, the first group presenting the material in Malory's words (the version in this text), the second presenting the modern version. What does each version achieve that the other does not?

EXTENSION

Modern interests differ somewhat from those of the Medieval Age or the Victorian Age. In this extract from T. H. White's book, the author concentrates on psychological factors rather than physical action or sentiment.

From THE ONCE AND FUTURE KING

LANCELOT knew that the King had gone to hunt in the New Forest, so he was sure that the Queen would send for him. It was dark in his bedroom, except for the one light in front of the holy picture, and he was pacing the floor in a dressing-gown. Except for the gay dressing-gown, and a sort of turban wound round his head, he was ready for bed: that is, he was naked.

Chapter VI of Book IV, "The Candle in the Wind" from *The Once and Future King* by T. H. White. Copyright 1939, 1940 by T. H. White © 1958 by T. H. White. Reprinted by permission of G. P. Putnam's Sons and David Higham Associates, Ltd. for Jonathan Cape Ltd.

It was a sombre room, without luxuries. The walls were bare and there was no canopy over the small hard couch. The windows were unglazed. They had some sort of oiled, opaque linen stretched over them. Great commanders often have these plain, campaigning bedrooms—they say that the Duke of Wellington used to sleep on a camp bed at Walmer Castle—with nothing in them except perhaps a chair, or an old trunk. Lancelot's room had one coffin-like, metal-bound chest. Apart from that, and from the bed, there was nothing to be seen—except his huge sword which stood against the wall, its straps hanging about it.

There was a kettle-hat lying on the chest. After

LANCELOT SAVING GUENEVERE. BIBLIOTHEQUE NATIONALE, SERVICE PHOTOGRAPHIQUE, PARIS.

some time, he picked it up and carried it to the picture light, where he stood with the same puzzled expression which the boy had had so long ago—looking at his reflection in the steel. He put it down, and began to march once more.

When the tap came on the door, he thought it was the signal. He was picking up the sword, and stretching his hand to the latch, when the door opened on its own account. Gareth came in.

"May I come?"

"Gareth!"

He looked at him in surprise, then said without enthusiasm: "Come in. It is nice to see you."

"Lancelot, I have come to warn you."

After a close look, the old man grinned.

"Gracious!" he said. "I hope you are not going to warn me about anything serious?"

"Yes, it is serious."

"Well, come in, and shut the door."

"Lancelot, it is about the Queen. I don't know how to begin."

"Don't trouble to begin then."

He took the younger man by the shoulders, began propelling him back to the door.

"It was charming of you to warn me," he said, squeezing the shoulders, "but I don't expect you can tell me anything I don't know."

"Oh, Lancelot, you know I would do anything to help you. I don't know what the others will say when they hear I have been to you. But I couldn't stay away."

"What is the trouble?"

He stopped their progress to look at him again.

"It is Agravaine and Mordred. They hate you. Or Agravaine does. He is jealous. Mordred hates Arthur most. We tried our best to stop them, but they would go on. Gawaine says he won't have anything to do with it, either way, and Gaheris was never good at making up his mind. So I had to come myself. I had to come, even if it is against my own brothers and the clan, because I owe everything to you, and I couldn't let it happen."

"My poor Gareth! What a state you have got yourself in!"

"They have been to the King and told him outright that you—that you go to the Queen's bedroom. We tried to stop them, and we wouldn't stay to listen, but that is what they told."

Lancelot released the shoulder. He took two paces through the room.

"Don't be upset about it," he said, coming back. "Many people have said so before, but nothing came of it. It will blow over."

"Not this time. I can feel it won't, inside me."

"Nonsense."

"It is not nonsense, Lancelot. They hate you. They won't try a combat this time, not after Meliagrance. They are too cunning. They will do something to trap you. They will go behind your back."

But the veteran only smiled and patted him.

"You are imagining things," he announced. "Go home to bed, my friend, and forget it. It was nice of you to come—but go home now and cheer up, and have a good sleep. If the King had been going to make a fuss, he would never have gone off hunting."

Gareth bit his fingers, plucking up the face to speak directly.

At last he said: "Please don't go to the Queen tonight."

Lancelot lifted one of his extraordinary eyebrows—but lowered it on second thoughts.

"Why not?"

"I am sure it is a trap. I am sure the King has gone away for the night on purpose that you should go to her, and then Agravaine will be there to catch you."

"Arthur would never do a thing like that."

"He has."

"Nonsense. I have known Arthur since you were in the nursery, and he wouldn't do it."

"But it is a risk!"

"If it is a risk, I shall enjoy it."

"Please!"

This time he put his hand in the small of Gareth's back, and began moving him seriously to the door

"Now, my dear kitchen page, just listen. In the first place, I know Arthur: in the second place, I know Agravaine. Do you think I ought to be afraid of him?"

"But treachery . . ."

"Gareth, once when I was a young fellow a lady came skipping past me, chasing after a peregrine which had snapped its creance. The trailing part of the creance got wound up in a tree, and the peregrine hung there at the top. The lady persuaded me to climb the tree, to get her hawk. I was never much of a climber. When I did get to the top, and had freed the hawk, the lady's husband turned up in full armour and said he was going to chop my head off. All the hawk business had been a trap to get me out of my armour, so that he would have me at his mercy. I was in the tree in my shirt, without even a dagger."

"Yes?"

"Well, I knocked him on the head with a branch. And he was a much better man than poor old Agravaine, even if we have grown rheumaticky since those bright days."

"I know you can deal with Agravaine. But suppose he attacks you with an armed band?"

"He won't do anything."

"He will."

There was a scratch at the door, a gentle drumming. A mouse might have made it, but Lancelot's eyes grew vague.

"Well, if he does," he said shortly, "then I shall have to fight the band. But the situation is imaginary."

"Couldn't you stay away tonight?"

They had reached the door, and the King's captain spoke decisively.

"Look," he said, "if you must know, the Queen has sent for me. I could hardly refuse, once I was sent for, could I?"

"So my treachery to the Old Ones will be useless?"

"Not useless. Anybody who knew would love you for facing it. But we can trust Arthur."

"And you will go in spite of everything?"

"Yes, kitchen page, and I shall go this minute. Good gracious, don't look so tragic about it. Leave it to the practised scoundrel and run away to bed."

"It means Good-bye."

"Nonsense, it means Good night. And, what is more, the Queen is waiting."

The old man swung a mantle over his shoulder, as easily as if he were still in the pride of youth. He lifted the latch and stood in the doorway, wondering what he had forgotten.

"If only I could stop you!"

"Alas, you can't."

He stepped into the darkness of the passage, dismissing the subject from his mind, and disappeared. What he had forgotten was his sword. □

SIR GEORGE LUTTRELL, FROM THE LUTTRELL PSALTER. COURTESY OF THE TRUSTEES OF THE BRITISH MUSEUM.

V. BACKGROUND

The Medieval Age

THE medieval age in England was a time of turbulence and change. In 1066, when William the Conqueror invaded England with his Norman armies, the country was still largely Anglo-Saxon in outlook. By 1485, when Henry VII took the throne after thirty years of civil strife known as the Wars of the Roses, England was on the brink of her Renaissance, an unparalleled flowering of the arts and of nationalistic feeling.

At the time, the invasion brought about a sudden disruption of English culture. The Normans brought in new blood, new ideas, and a new language. William made changes in law and government, and imposed the Norman feudal system, a rigid hierarchy of rights and duties according to social station. At the lowest end of the scale were the Anglo-Saxon serfs who went with the land, had few rights, and lived lives of almost incredible burden, owing to their feudal overseers the greater share of their worldly goods and services. Norman French became the language of the court and the nobility.

The cleavages between Saxon and Norman immediately after the Conquest seemed insurmountable, yet within three centuries they had almost disappeared. The Norman nobles who settled in Britain began to look on that land as their home. The chivalric code of honor and the conventions of courtly love—both Norman imports—had a softening effect on the Anglo-Saxon code of gift-loyalties and warrior virtues; and the melancholy, fatalistic view of life shared in the mead-hall communities was gradually infused with a lighter, gayer Norman strain. Though it did not entirely disappear, the somber, alliterative Anglo-Saxon verse was gradually replaced by a lyric poetry capable of a broader range of emotional and aesthetic effects.

At the same time, the power of the feudal system began to be slowly undermined. The absolute power of the king, never really secure in an age of warring feudal states, was brought to an end when King John was forced by his barons and knights to sign the Magna Carta in 1215. This Great Charter assured certain basic rights to all Englishmen of birth, and made even the king subject to the laws of the land. The rights granted by the Charter were broadened further in 1295, when Edward I called together the first parliament which extended recognition to representatives of each county and borough in the land.

In the mid-fourteenth century a visitation of plague —the Black Death—killed more than thirty percent of the population. Many serfs, left without masters or work, were forced into the towns to seek a livelihood. Following the plague years, the growing wool trade between England and Flanders caused sheep grazing to replace land tilling, again forcing serfs into the towns, where conditions grew critical. In 1381 the peasants staged a revolt which, although it was savagely suppressed, marked the end of their abject acceptance of a place at the bottom of the social ladder. During this same period, the power of the guilds—associations of merchants and craftsmen—grew tremendously, and the middle class began to assert itself.

Throughout the Middle Ages the Church exercised almost as much power as the king; it controlled not only vast treasuries and tracts of land, but also the sources of education and learning, the monasteries. Religion and the teaching of the Church circumscribed the life of the average man in a way which would seem incredible today. In a world of war and plague, where a man was considered to have reached old age by his middle thirties, the Church's promise of a better life to come seemed the only hope. The faith generated by the Church was manifested in almost every aspect of medieval life, and most notably in the magnificent cathedrals of the age. The two centuries of holy war—the Crusades —which began in 1095 when an army of devout soldiers, commoner and noble alike, marched forth to rescue the Holy Land from the infidel, were an aspect of that faith. So also were the great pilgrimages to holy shrines, such as the one to Canterbury which forms the background for Chaucer's *Tales*. In a world where man accepted his place because it was part of the divine scheme, excommunication from the Church signified not only eternal damnation but absolute separation from the community of men.

Yet the Church's combination of worldly and spiritual power was in process of fragmentation as well, particularly in the later medieval period. In the twelfth and thirteenth centuries the first colleges at Oxford and Cambridge, later to become vast centers of secular education, were established. John Wycliffe translated the Bible into English (around 1384) and made it accessible for the first time to those who could not read Latin. Caxton's introduction of the printing press in England (1476) signaled the end of the monasteries as sole transmitters of learning. Those men who survived the Crusades or returned from the numerous military expeditions of the Hundred Years' War (1337-1453), brought with them experiences of foreign realms and new points of view. At the close of the Middle Ages, the gradual erosion of the feudal system, with its accompanying social turmoil, was also weakening the Church's foundations. Finally, the long-standing friction between Church and king culminated in Henry VIII's outright attack on Church power and property and the establishment of the Church of England in the sixteenth century.

The particular vigor of the medieval period comes down to us largely through its literature. Chaucer's portraits of wayfaring pilgrims gives us a sampling of the medieval visage, warts and all; his view is both panoramic and unsparingly microscopic. The anonymous lyrics present a variety of voices, alternately plaintive, vindictive, or joyous. Malory tells us of mythic treacheries and the clank of battle gear—themes and sounds as familiar to us now as they were to the readers of his tales five hundred years ago. □

HOW ORIGINAL WAS CHAUCER?

by F. N. Robinson

THERE has been much speculation as to what suggested to Chaucer the idea of a pilgrimage. He may, of course, have been describing an actual experience. At all events he had no occasion to resort to books for knowledge of the pilgrimage as an institution. In the general device of a frame story, or series of tales within an enclosing narrative, it has often been thought that he imitated the *Decameron.*[1] But it now appears improbable that Chaucer knew Boccaccio's great collection of tales, and the idea of tales within a tale was so familiar that no particular model need be sought. Popular from antiquity in the Orient (from which Europe derived in modern times one of the most famous examples, *The Thousand and One Nights*), the type was well known in classical and medieval literature. But the *Canterbury Tales* are unlike most collections of the sort in the fact that the enclosing narrative is not formal or mechanical or merely introductory, but provides, and keeps in action, a social group engaged naturally in mutual entertainment.

Whatever the reason for its adoption, the device of the pilgrimage is one of the happiest ever employed in a collection of stories. It afforded Chaucer an opportunity to bring together a representative group of various classes of society, united by a common religious purpose, yet not so dominated by that purpose as to be unable to give themselves over to enjoyment. Whether such a company would ever have mingled as Chaucer's pilgrims do, or would have entered upon such a round of storytelling, it is idle to discuss, as idle as to question whether the speakers could have been heard from horseback on the road. Literal truth to fact the *Canterbury Tales* obviously do not represent. In their very metrical form there is, if one chooses to be literal-minded, a convention of unreality. But there is essential poetic truth in the portrayal of the characters, in their sentiments and personal relations, and, no less, in the representation of the pilgrimage as a social assemblage.

For the General Prologue, as for the general device of the Canterbury pilgrimage, no real model has been found. Individual sketches of knights or priests or peasants are common enough in medieval literature of France and England, and some of them—like the lazy priest in *Piers Plowman,*[2] who knew his Robin Hood better than his paternoster—have often been adduced to illustrate one or another of Chaucer's characters. Whole works, too, were devoted to the description of the various orders of society, and others to the classification of men and women by physical and temperamental characteristics. With this lore of the physiognomists and social philosophers Chaucer was doubtless familiar. But in none of his predecessors has there been found a gallery of portraits like that in the *Prologue,* and there is very little that is comparable in later English poetry except in Chaucer's avowed imitators.

Chaucer's pilgrims are far more vivid and personal than the usual personified types in medieval allegories. This is perhaps sufficiently accounted for by Chaucer's creative imagination. But it is hard to believe that his men and women were not in some measure drawn from life, and a number of facts confirm this suspicion. Harry Bailly, the Host, has the same name as a contemporary innkeeper in Southwark. In several other instances, details of locality, occupation, and character are given with so much particularity that the temptation has proved irresistible to look for historical counterparts. The probability is strong that Chaucer had contemporary models for his characters. And curiosity on this subject, it is proper to add, is not merely trivial. Such inquiries and conjectures, like the search for literary sources, help toward an understanding of the poet's imagination and of the material on which it worked.

Individual as the pilgrims are, they are also representative. Many of them exhibit types of character or of professional conduct—the gentle Knight, the venal Friar, the hypocrite in the person of the Pardoner—such as were familiar in the literature of

---

Condensed and slightly adapted from Editor's Preface to *The Works of Geoffrey Chaucer* by F. N. Robinson. Reprinted by permission of the publisher, Houghton Mifflin Company.

1. *Decameron,* a collection of tales by the Italian writer Giovanni Boccaccio, written 1351–1353. The frame story tells how ten young people who have gone to the country to escape the Black Death pass away the time by telling stories for ten days.

2. *Piers Plowman,* a long allegorical poem, contemporary with Chaucer's work, but written in alliterative verse. It is a moral and social satire in the familiar medieval form of a dream-vision. Though usually attributed to a hypothetical William Langland, it seems to be by at least two, perhaps even five, different writers.

the age. And taken together, they cover nearly the whole range of life in Chaucer's England. The circle of royalty and the higher nobility, to be sure, is not directly represented. Men of such rank and station could hardly have been included in the company. But the mind and manners of courtly society are well expressed by the Knight, who had seen honorable service at home and abroad; by his son the Squire, the typical courtly lover; again, from a different angle, by the Prioress; and, best of all, by Chaucer himself, the accomplished courtier and man of the world, who as author creates the atmosphere and medium of the whole narrative. The clergy, regular and secular, are included in liberal number, and there are also represented the learned professions of law and medicine, the merchants and the craftsmen of the guild, officials of the manor, the sailor, and the common peasant farmer. It would be hard to find such a description of English society between the *Beowulf*, with its picture of the heroic age, and the broader canvas of the Elizabethan drama.

In keeping with the miscellaneous character of the company is the wide range of tastes and interests represented by the stories they relate. Nearly every type of medieval fiction appears, and appears at its best. In almost every case Chaucer assigned to a pilgrim a tale suited to his character and vocation. He represents the party as engaged in free and natural social intercourse, and oftener than not the tales are evoked by the talks along the way. In fact, from one point of view, the pilgrimage is a continuous and lively drama, in which the stories themselves contribute to the action. □

CHAUCER AND HIS TRANSLATORS

Chaucer (lines 469–478 of *Wife of Bath's Prologue*)

But, Lord Crist! whan that it remembereth me
Upon my yowthe, and on my jolitee,
It tikleth me aboute myn herte roote.
Unto this day it doth myn herte boote
That I have had my world as in my tyme.
But age, allas! that al wole envenyme,
Hath me biraft my beautee and my pith.
Lat go, farewel! the devel go therwith!
The flour is goon, thar is namoore to telle;
The bren, as I best kan, now moste I selle.

Alexander Pope (1714)

But oh good Gods! whene'er a thought I cast
On all the joys of youth and beauty past,
To find in pleasures I have had my part
Still warms me to the bottom of my heart.
This wicked world was once my dear delight;
Now all my conquests, all my charms good night!
The flour consumed, the best that now I can
Is e'en to make my market of the bran.

Coghill (see lines 285–296)

Chaucer (lines 1–5 of *Wife of Bath's Tale*)

In th'olde dayes of the Kyng Arthour,
Of which that Britons speken greet honour,
Al was this land fulfild of fayerye.
The elf-queene, with hir joly compaignye,
Daunced ful ofte in many a grene mede.

John Dryden (1700)

In days of old, when Arthur fill'd the throne,
Whose acts and fame to foreign lands were
 blown,
The king of elfs and little fairy queen
Gambol'd on heaths, and danc'd on ev'ry green;
And where the jolly troop had led the round,
The grass unbidden rose, and mark'd the ground:
Nor darkling did they dance; the silver light
Of Phoebe served to guide their steps aright,
And, with their tripping pleas'd, prolong'd the
 night.
Her beams they follow'd, where at full she
 play'd,
Nor longer then she shed her horns they stay'd,

From thence with airy flight to foreign lands
conveyʼd.
Above the rest our Britain held they dear;
More solemnly they kept their sabbaths here,
And made more spacious rings, and revel'd half
the year.

Coghill (1952)

When good King Arthur ruled in ancient days,
(A king that every Briton loves to praise)
This was a land brim-full of fairy folk.
The Elf-Queen and her courtiers joined and broke
Their elfin dance on many a green mead.

FROM THE LUTTRELL PSALTER. COURTESY OF THE TRUSTEES OF THE BRITISH MUSEUM.

THE POPULAR BALLADS

by M. J. C. Hodgart

A ballad is a narrative song which bears the stamp of folklore. There are many kinds of poetry which have been called ballads—the broadside ballads of the Elizabethans, literary imitations like Coleridge's *Rime of the Ancient Mariner*—but the only ones to be discussed here are the traditional English and Scottish ballads as collected in F. J. Child's monumental work.[1] These ballads are short narratives, in stanzas of two or four lines, which tell their stories in a highly characteristic way; they are dramatic, using a high proportion of dialogue to stage direction, usually beginning in the fifth act and presenting the story in a series of rapid flashes which may be compared with the technique of the cinema. They are impersonal in their attitude, and there is little comment or moralizing. They are free from the rhetorical devices of most "learned" poetry but possess a rhetoric of their own, using repetition, stock phrases, and a stylized description of heroes and heroines—all this in common with folk-literature of other kinds and of other peoples. Their special narrative technique carries a folk-view of life, an ironic acceptance of tragedy, and a rich background of popular myth, of ghosts and fairies. The result if often poetry of a high order.

The ballads, like the lyrics, were sung, and they too must be taken with their musical settings. Not only does their full poetic effect come over when they are sung, but their history is only explicable by reference to the history of folk-song. Their metrical forms are essentially musical forms and their special narrative technique arises naturally from the dividing up of the story into clearly defined stanzas.

How did ballads begin? A great deal of discussion of this point has taken place, much of it to no purpose. The most probable explanation of the origin of the ballad form lies in the medieval dance-song, the *carole*. The stories of the ballads, on the other hand, have originated in a variety of ways. Some ballads are part of the international treasury of folklore (especially the supernatural and romantic ballads); some were drawn from Arthurian and other romances by minstrels of the late Middle Ages, while minstrels must also have had a hand in the Robin Hood cycle; the Border ballads were composed by local poets about local incidents of the sixteenth and seventeenth centuries; the more properly historical ballads are based rather on chronicles. The theory of communal composition can account for certain kinds of primitive folksong, but not for any ballad as we know it. Ballads are comparatively late in date.

Nor are the ballads pure examples of folk-art. On the one hand they contain a great deal of folkbelief and primitive survivals (a rich body of lore about fairies and ghosts, tabu, enchantment and marvels). On the other hand, their texts have been greatly altered by printing as popular broadsides and by remaking by educated poets, mainly of the eighteenth century. When the images, narrative technique, and outlook of folk-tradition have been combined with a poet's skill, the ballads have become great poetry. □

Condensed and adapted from *Medieval Lyrics and the Ballads* by M. J. C. Hodgart, from *The Pelican Guide to English Literature*, Vol. I, edited by Boris Ford.

1. *The English and Scottish Popular Ballads*, edited by Francis James Child. In five volumes, published 1882–1898 by Houghton Mifflin Company.

The Changing English Language

THE Norman invasion in 1066 had abrupt and dramatic consequences in the development of the English language. Norman French then became the official language of the governing classes of England; within a short time it was also adopted by the English nobility, as the English and Norman upper classes gradually intermingled. However, Old English remained the language of the masses, and the social distinction between those who spoke French and those who spoke English persisted until the beginning of the thirteenth century.

The continued use of French by the upper classes was promoted by the close ties between England and France. After the Conquest, the Anglo-Norman kings retained their titles as Dukes of Normandy, and, through contractual marriages between English and Norman nobility, Englishmen began to acquire land and conduct business in Normandy. Had the political ties across the English Channel remained unbroken, it is possible that all of us today might be speaking some form of French. However, shortly after 1200, relations between Normandy and England deteriorated. Families which held land in both countries were forced to surrender their rights in one or the other. In consequence, the nobles of Norman descent who chose to retain their land-holdings in England began to think of France as an alien land and of themselves as Englishmen. A growing suspicion of things "foreign" by those descendants of the original Norman invaders who had become firmly invested in England created a growing nationalistic spirit and an increased tolerance of things English, including the language.

The revival of the English language was also aided by the rise of a middle class of tradesmen and craftsmen, together with a slow but general improvement in economic and social conditions for the mass of native Englishmen. As the English-speaking majority gradually became more influential, the use of English in government and trade became both natural and necessary. Early in the fourteenth century writers began turning from Latin and French (which were considered the languages of scholarship and literature respectively) to English. In 1362 English was declared, by royal decree, the official language of the courts of law.

By 1400 English was totally restored as the language of the realm, but it had been substantially altered and expanded by three and a half centuries of contact with French. For the first two centuries (1066-1250) the incursion of French vocabulary was relatively slight. Words adopted from the French during this period reflect the relationships between the ruling and subordinate classes (*noble, dame, servant, messenger*) or religious concerns (*sermon, communion, confession, clergy, convent*). By 1250, when ties between England and Normandy had loosened and English nationalism was making itself felt, many more French words began to be assimilated into English—particularly words associated with government, law, and business, such as *crown, state, reign, authority, tax, judge, pardon.* Also notable are the number of words from literature (*poet, tragedy, story*), art (the word *art* itself, *music*), medicine (*physician, pain*), fashion (*gown, boot, robe*), and those concerning food (*beef, bacon, olives*) and social life (*dance, recreation*), which were borrowed from French during this period. The dimensions of the change in cultural outlook which accompanied the changes in language during this period can perhaps be inferred from these and the numerous other additions to English vocabulary, concerned as they are, in the main, with beauty, style, comfort, and the good life.

The structure of the language, too, was changing. Between 1066 and 1400 Old English, originally a highly inflected language, became greatly simplified. Inflections were dropped or were merged into the few surviving forms which are familiar today (for instance, *sing, sang, sung*). The Old English verb *help,* for example, had originally four principal parts (*healpan, healp, hulpon, -holpen*) with five or more additional endings to indicate person and number. Today, of course, it has only two principal parts (*help, helped*), with one additional ending (*-s*) in the present tense. As the Old English inflections and endings gradually disappeared, the grammatical relationships which they expressed were taken over by the pattern and order of words, so that English became an increasingly phrasal language.

During approximately the same period of time, the distinct Anglo-Saxon dialects merged and evolved into four Middle English dialect groups. The most prominent of these was East Midland, the dialect spoken by the people between the Thames and the Humber rivers. This area included the city of London, rapidly developing as a center of government and commerce. Because of London's importance, the East Midland dialect gradually came to be looked on as "the King's English." Around 1370 Geoffrey Chaucer wrote in this dialect, giving it literary status; and when William Caxton introduced printing to England a century later, he used the speech of London as his standard. The speech of the East Midland area thus became a sort of early "standard English" from which both modern English and American English are directly descended.

The changes in the English language which occurred during the three or four centuries following the Norman Conquest were so all-encompassing that few if any of Chaucer's contemporaries would have been able to comprehend the Old English of *Beowulf*. Dramatic as these changes were, they did not take place swiftly; they evolved slowly over the course of generations, and were the result of complex political and social changes in a turbulent age. □

FROM THE LUTTRELL PSALTER. TRUSTEES OF THE BRITISH MUSEUM.

BIOGRAPHIES

Geoffrey Chaucer 1340? / 1400

The son of a prosperous London wine merchant, Chaucer was trained from an early age for a court career. By 1357 he was a page in the service of the wife of King Edward III's third son. While serving with the army in France in 1359 he was taken prisoner, but was freed the following year upon payment of a ransom to which the king made a sizable contribution. He married one of the queen's ladies-in-waiting, and from that time on was in the employ of the king. He was frequently sent abroad on diplomatic missions, notably to France, the Low Countries, and Italy.

His earliest works were translations from the French *(The Romaunt of the Rose)* or showed the influence of French authors *(The Book of the Duchess, The House of Fame)*. In these long poems, as well as in a later work, *The Legend of Good Women*, Chaucer used a form popular with medieval French writers, the dream vision.

During his first trip to Italy, Chaucer became acquainted with the writings of Dante, Petrarch, and Boccaccio. In his greatest works, *Troilus and Criseyde* and *The Canterbury Tales*, he used stories by Boccaccio and other Italian storytellers.

Chaucer was buried in Westminster Abbey (an honor accorded him because of his government appointments), in the part that has since come to be known as the Poets' Corner.

Sir Thomas Malory c.1395 / 1471

The author Sir Thomas Malory is usually identified with a Warwickshire knight of that name. Malory lived during the turbulent period of the Wars of the Roses, a series of vicious conflicts which split England into two factions organized around the rival houses of York and Lancaster. He spent most of the last twenty years of his life in prison on one charge or another. During his imprisonment he worked on his compilation of the Arthurian legends. Newgate, where he was imprisoned, was near the house of the Grey Friars, which had a large library. Probably Malory obtained his source materials from that library.

His writings contain several references to his imprisonment. In particular, he ends his book on the Arthurian legends with these words: "I pray you all, gentlemen and gentlewomen, that readeth this book of Arthur and his knights from the beginning to the ending, pray for me while I am on live that God send me good deliverance [from prison]; and when I am dead, I pray you all pray for my soul." When Malory died, he was buried in the chapel of the Grey Friars.

(OVERLEAF) EMBROIDERY DEPICTING LADY CATHERINE STAFFORD WITH HER 13 CHILDREN.
BY COURTESY OF THE VICTORIA AND ALBERT MUSEUM, LONDON, CROWN COPYRIGHT.

chapter three

THE ELIZABETHAN AGE
1485–1625

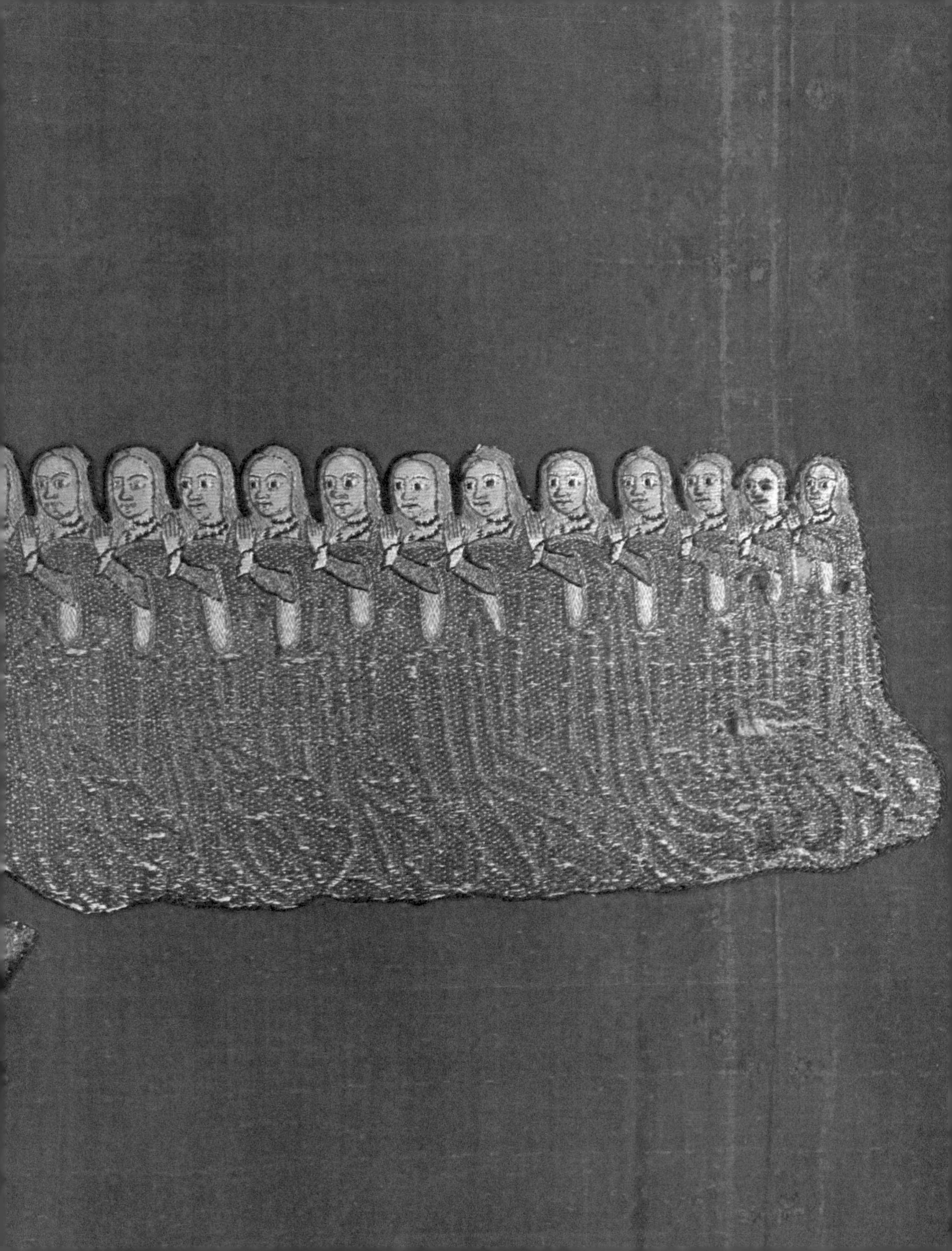

I. ELIZABETH AND THE COURTLY POETS

Although Queen Elizabeth reigned only from 1558 to 1603, her name has been appropriated by historians to identify an age—the Elizabethan—that actually begins before her birth in 1533 and extends beyond her death in 1603. For whatever happy combination of reasons, the arts flourished under her reign. It was a period of great poetry, prose, and drama. England has not seen its like since, and most countries have never experienced such an age.

Something of Queen Elizabeth's attitude toward the arts is indicated by her own efforts as a poet, and by the efforts of the men of action who surrounded her at court. Some examples of this courtly poetry are presented here. Sir Walter Raleigh and the Earl of Essex were Elizabeth's two most influential advisers. Raleigh, who was first in the Queen's favor, fell out when Essex became a favorite, and then returned to his position when Essex fell. Both men were dashing adventurers, soldier-statesmen, and poets.

WHEN I WAS FAIR AND YOUNG

by Queen Elizabeth

When I was fair and young, and favor gracèd me,
Of many was I sought, their mistress for to be;
But I did scorn them all, and answered them therefore,
"Go, go, go, seek some otherwhere,
Impòrtune me no more!" 5

How many weeping eyes I made to pine with woe,
How many sighing hearts, I have no skill to show;
Yet I the prouder grew, and answered them therefore,
"Go, go, go, seek some otherwhere,
Impòrtune me no more!" 10

Then spake fair Venus' son, that proud victorious boy,
And said, "Fine dame, since that you be so coy,
I will so pluck your plumes that you shall say no more,
'Go, go, go, seek some otherwhere,
Impòrtune me no more!'" 15

When he had spake these words, such change grew in my breast,
That neither night nor day since that, I could take any rest.
Then lo! I did repent that I had said before,
"Go, go, go, seek some otherwhere,
Impòrtune me no more!" 20

OF HUMAN INTEREST

The death of Raleigh

"A Scaffold was erected in the old Palace yard, upon which after 14 yeares reprivement, [Sir Walter Raleigh's] head was cutt off; at which time, such abundance of bloud issued from his veines, that shewed he had stock of nature enough left to have continued him many yeares in life, though now above three score yeares old, if it had not been taken away by the hand of Violence. And this was the end of the great Sir Walter Raleigh: great sometimes in the favour of Queen Elizabeth, and next to Sir Francis Drake, the great Scourge and hate of the Spaniard. . . ."

WHAT IS OUR LIFE?
by Sir Walter Raleigh

What is our life? a play of passion;
Our mirth, the music of division;[1]
Our mothers' wombs the tiring-houses[2] be
Where we are dressed for this short comedy.
5 Heaven the judicious sharp spectator is,
That sits and marks still[3] who doth act amiss;
Our graves that hide us from the searching sun
Are like drawn curtains when the play is done.
Thus march we playing to our latest rest;
10 Only we die in earnest—that's no jest.

---

1. *music of division,* the more rapid accompaniment to, or variation on, a musical theme.
2. *tiring-houses,* dressing rooms.
3. *still,* continuously.

TO HIS SON
by Sir Walter Raleigh

Three things there be that prosper all apace
And flourish, while they are asunder far;
But on a day they meet all in a place,
And when they meet, they one another mar.
And they be these: the wood, the weed, the wag.[1]
The wood is that that makes the gallows tree;
The weed is that that strings the hangman's bag;
The wag, my pretty knave, betokens thee.
Now mark, dear boy: while these assemble not,
Green springs the tree, hemp grows, the wag is wild;
But when they meet, it makes the timber rot,
It frets the halter, and it chokes the child.
God bless the child!

---

1. *wag,* mischievous boy. The word is a shortened form of the old word *waghalter,* "gallows bird."

TO PLEAD MY FAITH WHERE FAITH HAD NO REWARD
by Robert Devereux, Earl of Essex

To plead my faith where faith had no reward,
To move remorse where favor is not borne,
To heap complaints where she doth not regard—
Were fruitless, bootless, vain, and yield but scorn.

5 I lovèd her whom all the world admired,
I was refused of her that can love none;
And my vain hopes, which far too high aspired,
Is dead, and buried, and for ever gone.

Forget my name, since you have scorned my love,
10 And womanlike do not too late lament;
Since for your sake I do all mischief prove,
I none accuse nor nothing do repent.

I was as fond as ever she was fair,
Yet loved I not more than I now despair.

DISCUSSION

1. Characterize the speaker in Queen Elizabeth's poem. What does Cupid's threat (to pluck her plumes) in the third stanza mean? Is the action justified?

2. Relate the last words of Raleigh's "What Is Our Life?" ("Only we die in earnest—that's no jest") to the rest of the poem.

3. In "To His Son," Raleigh uses alliteration to call attention to the important items he enumerates in line 5: "the wood, the weed, the wag."

(a) What does each of the items refer to? To what extent is Raleigh's use of these particular words justified (aside from the alliterative effect)?

(b) What is the general impact of their use—serious or comic?

4. Queen Elizabeth never married—some say for reasons of state—but down through the ages rumors have persisted, romantically linking her and Essex. How may "To Plead My Faith" be read in the light of these rumors?

II. SONNETS AND SONNET SEQUENCES

The Elizabethan age might be called the age of the sonnet, for it was during this period that this short, highly structured poetic form was introduced into England, and flourished.

The sonnet form originated in Italy, probably in the thirteenth century, and was used by two Italian masters, Dante (1265–1321) and Petrarch (1304–1374). Sir Thomas Wyatt and Henry Howard, Earl of Surrey, are credited with introducing and promoting the form in England early in the sixteenth century. It soon became fashionable in England to write love sonnets to a beloved—usually idealized—lady, after the manner of Petrarch's sonnets to his mistress, Laura. As the sonnets accumulated, they became sequences, and in addition to expressing ardent emotions, began to sketch out a fragmentary narrative—of falling in love, pursuing the beloved, losing the beloved, finding the beloved, celebrating the beauty of the beloved. Nearly every poet of the Elizabethan period wrote a sonnet sequence to the lady he most admired: Sir Philip Sidney to Penelope Devereux in *Astrophel and Stella;* Edmund Spenser to Elizabeth Boyle in *Amoretti;* William Shakespeare to his mysterious "dark lady."

In later English literature, the sonnet was to become a form useful for expressing a variety of themes, including social criticism, liberty, alienation; indeed, other themes were expressed in this form during the sixteenth century. But by and large, to the Elizabethan poet the sonnet proved best suited as a vehicle for expressing the immense range of emotions of love and passion. The dominance of this theme should not surprise anyone familiar with popular music of the twentieth century.

I FIND NO PEACE

by Thomas Wyatt

I find no peace and all my wár is done,
I fear and hope, I burn and freeze like ice,
I fly above the wind, yet can I not arise,
And naught I have and all the world I seize on;
5 That looseth nor locketh[1] holdeth me in prison,
And holdeth me not; yet can I 'scape nowise;
Nor letteth me live nor die at my devise,[2]
And yet of death it giveth none occasion.
Without eye, I see; and without tongue, I plain:[3]
10 I desire to perish, and yet I ask health;
I love another, and thus I hate myself;
I feed me in sorrow, and laugh in all my pain.
Likewise displeaseth me both death and life,
And my delight is causer of this strife.

1. *That looseth nor locketh,* what neither sets me free nor locks me up; i.e., love.
2. *devise,* wish.
3. *plain,* complain.

WHOSO LIST TO HUNT

by Thomas Wyatt

Whoso list[1] to hunt, I know where is an hind,[2]
But as for me, alas, I may no more.
The vain travail hath wearied me so sore
I am of them that furthest come behind.
5 Yet may I, by no means, my wearied mind
Draw from the deer: but as she fleeth afore
Fainting I follow. I leave off therefore,
Since in a net I seek to hold the wind.
Whoso list her hunt, I put him out of doubt,
10 As well as I, may spend his time in vain:
And graven with diamonds in letters plain
There is written, her fair neck round about,
"*Noli me tangere,*[3] for Caesar's I am,
And wild for to hold, though I seem tame."

1. *list,* likes.
2. *hind,* female deer.
3. *Noli me tangere,* do not touch me (Latin).

A LOVER'S VOW

by Henry Howard, Earl of Surrey

Set me whereas the sun doth parch the green,
Or where his beams may not dissolve the ice,
In temperate heat, where he is felt and seen;
With proud people, in presence sad and wise,
5 Set me in base, or yet in high degree;
In the long night, or in the shortest day;
In clear weather, or where mists thickest be;
In lusty youth, or when my hairs be gray;
Set me in earth, in heaven, or yet in hell;
10 In hill, in dale, or in the foaming flood;
Thrall,[1] or at large, alive whereso I dwell;
Sick or in health, in ill fame or in good;
Yours will I be, and with that only thought
Comfort myself when that my hap[2] is naught.

1. *Thrall,* enslaved.
2. *hap,* good fortune.

DISCUSSION

1. Paradox—the conjunction of conflicting elements—is a frequently used technique in poetry of wit. What paradoxes can you find in Wyatt's "I Find No Peace"?

2. Sonneteers liked to speak in elaborate metaphors, in which one set of terms stands for another. What is the central metaphor in Wyatt's "Whoso List to Hunt" and how far is it extended?

3. The last two lines of Surrey's "A Lover's Vow" appear to explain the somewhat frenzied tone of the preceding lines. What is the explanation, and how persuasive is it?

OF LITERARY INTEREST

The sonnet

Writers have long been fascinated by literary forms that impose a rigorous discipline—forms whose rhythmical patterns, rhyme schemes, and limited number of lines force meticulous shaping of material. The Japanese, for example, love to write the ultrabrief Haiku, composed of only seventeen carefully chosen syllables. In English, the sonnet has been the most popular and durable short poetic form.

All sonnets (except some maverick modern ones) are made up of fourteen lines of *iambic pentameter*—five two-syllable feet, each foot made up of an unstressed syllable followed by a stressed syllable.

Sonnets fall into two groups, according to their rhyme scheme. The Italian sonnet is usually rhymed abbaabba/cdecde, forming basically a two-part poem of eight lines and six lines respectively. These two parts are played off against each other in an infinite variety of ways. Sometimes the latter part extends or narrows the first; sometimes it opposes or reverses it. This form of sonnet is sometimes called Petrarchan, after the Italian poet Francesco Petrarch who perfected the form and wrote extensively in it.

The Shakespearean or English sonnet is usually rhymed abab/cdcd/efef/gg, presenting a four-part structure in which an idea or theme is developed in three stages (through variation, extension, alternation, etc.) and then brought to a conclusion in the final or fourth part. This final couplet may be used in a variety of ways: to summarize, to emphasize, to make quick application, to suddenly narrow focus, or even to pull a surprise reversal. It is perhaps most effective when it presents the unexpected, leaving the reader with a comic twist or a tragic reminder that has strong emotional impact.

The sonnet has endured because it does a great deal in little space. Because of the discipline it demands, it challenges the writer and rewards the reader. Its attraction for both writer and reader is in the strictness of the form, but the form is pleasurable, ultimately, not for itself but for what it can do in shaping and conveying significant experience.

Sir Philip Sidney 1554 / 1586

From ASTROPHEL AND STELLA

1

Loving in truth, and fain in verse my love to show,
That she, dear she, might take some pleasure of my pain,
Pleasure might cause her read, reading might make her know,
Knowledge might pity win, and pity grace obtain—
5 I sought fit words to paint the blackest face of woe;
Studying inventions[1] fine, her wits to entertain,
Oft turning others' leaves to see if thence would flow
Some fresh and fruitful showers upon my sun-burned brain.
But words came halting forth, wanting invention's stay,[2]
10 Invention, nature's child, fled step-dame Study's blows,
And others' feet still seemed but strangers in my way.
Thus, great with child to speak, and helpless in my throes,
Biting my truant pen, beating myself for spite,
"Fool," said my muse to me, "look in thy heart and write."

1. *inventions,* rhetorical devices.
2. *wanting invention's stay,* lacking the help of imagination.

31

With how sad steps, O moon, thou climb'st the skies!
How silently, and with how wan a face!
What! may it be that even in heavenly place
That busy archer[1] his sharp arrows tries?
5 Sure, if that long-with-love-acquainted eyes
Can judge of love, thou feel'st a lover's case;
I read it in thy looks—thy languished grace
To me, that feel the like, thy state descries.[2]
Then, even of fellowship, O moon, tell me,
10 Is constant love deemed there but want of wit?
Are beauties there as proud as here they be?
Do they above love to be loved, and yet
Those lovers scorn whom that love doth possess?
Do they call virtue there ungratefulness?[3]

1. *archer,* Cupid.
2. *descries,* reveals.
3. *Do . . . ungratefulness?* Do they call ungratefulness a virtue there?

OF HUMAN INTEREST

Sir Philip Sidney

"He was not only of an excellent witt, but extremely beautifull: he much resembled his sister, but his Haire was not red, but a little inclining, viz. a darke ambor colour. If I were to find a fault in it, methinks 'tis not masculine enough; yett he was a person of great courage. . . .

"He was of a very munificent spirit, and liberall to all Lovers of Learning, and to those that pretended to any acquaintance with Parnassus: in so much that he was cloyed and surfeited with the Poetasters of those dayes. Among others, Mr. Edmund Spenser made his addresse to him, and brought his *Faery Queen.* Sir Philip was busy at his Study, and his servant delivered Mr. Spencer's booke to his master, who layd it by, thinking it might be such kind of Stuffe as he was frequently troubled with. Mr. Spencer stayed so long that his patience was wearied, and went his way discontented, and never intended to come again. When Sir Philip perused it, he was so exceedingly delighted with it that he was extremely sorry he was gonne, and where to send for him he knew not. After much enquiry he learned his lodgeing, and sent for him, mightily caressed him, and ordered his servant to give him so many pounds in gold. His servant sayd that that was too much. No, sayd Sir Philip, and ordered an addition. From this time there was a great friendship between them, to his dying day."

39

Come sleep! O sleep, the certain knot of peace,
The baiting place[1] of wit, the balm of woe,
The poor man's wealth, the prisoner's release,
Th'indifferent[2] judge between the high and low;
5 With shield of proof[3] shield me from out the prease[4]
Of those fierce darts despair at me doth throw;
O make in me those civil wars to cease;
I will good tribute pay, if thou do so.
Take thou of me smooth pillows, sweetest bed,
10 A chamber deaf to noise and blind to light,
A rosy garland and a weary head;
And if these things, as being thine by right,
Move not thy heavy grace, thou shalt in me,
Livelier than elsewhere, Stella's image see.

---

1. *baiting place,* place where travelers stop for food and rest.
2. *indifferent,* impartial.
3. *shield of proof,* proven strength.
4. *prease,* press, crowd.

54

Because I breathe not love to every one,
Nor do not use set colors for to wear,
Nor nourish special locks of vowèd hair,
Nor give each speech a full point of a groan,
5 The courtly nymphs, acquainted with the moan
Of them who in their lips Love's standard bear,
"What, he!" say they of me, "Now I dare swear
He cannot love; no, no, let him alone."
And think so still, so Stella know my mind;
10 Profess indeed I do not Cupid's art;
But you, fair maids, at length this true shall find,
That his right badge is but worn in the heart;
Dumb swans, not chatt'ring pies,[1] do lovers prove;
They love indeed who quake to say they love.

---

1. *pies,* magpies (birds).

63

O grammar-rules, O now your virtues show;
So children still read you with awful[1] eyes,
As my young dove may, in your precepts wise,
Her grant to me by her own virtue know;
5 For late, with heart most high, with eyes most low,
I craved the thing which ever she denies;
She, lightning Love displaying Venus' skies,
Lest once should not be heard, twice said, "No, No!"
Sing then, my muse, now Io Paean[2] sing;
10 Heav'ns envy not at my high triumphing,
But grammar's force with sweet success confirm;
For grammar says—O this, dear Stella, weigh—
For grammar says—to grammar who says nay?
That in one speech two negatives affirm!

---

1. *awful,* respectful.
2. *Io Paean,* in Greek antiquity, a song of triumph after victory, addressed to Apollo.

DISCUSSION

1. Show how the thought of Sonnet 1 reflects the 4/4/4/2 line-structure of the English sonnet. How does the thought shift in each of these groups of lines?

2. Compare the thought structure of Sonnet 31 with the structure of 1. Is there a weakness in the couplet, especially in the turn "and yet" coming at the end of the twelfth line rather than at the beginning of the thirteenth?

3. Sometimes a sonnet writer seems to be carried away by his central organizing principle or subject, and forgets that his poem is supposed to function as a love poem in a sonnet sequence. Discuss the treatment of sleep in Sonnet 39 in this light.

4. Explain and relate to the rest of the poem line 13 of Sonnet 54: "Dumb swans, not chatt'ring pies, do lovers prove."

5. There is an old grammatical rule that a double negative makes a positive; the logic of Sonnet 63, therefore, appears impeccable. Will Stella be convinced?

HEART EXCHANGE

by Sir Philip Sidney

My true love hath my heart, and I have his,
By just exchange one for the other given:
I hold his dear, and mine he cannot miss;
There never was a bargain better driven.
5 His heart in me keeps me and him in one;
My heart in him his thoughts and senses guides:
He loves my heart, for once it was his own;
I cherish his, because in me it bides.
His heart his wound received from my sight;
10 My heart was wounded with his wounded heart;
For, as from me on him his hurt did light,
So still me-thought in me his hurt did smart:
Both equal hurt in this change sought our bliss:
My true love hath my heart and I have his.

From *Arcadia* (1590).

PORTRAIT BY HANS HOLBEIN. BY COURTESY OF THE VICTORIA AND ALBERT MUSEUM, LONDON, CROWN COPYRIGHT.

EXTENSION

The modern American poet, E. E. Cummings (1894–1962) has written a poem astonishingly close in meaning and metaphor to Sidney's "Heart Exchange":

i carry your heart with me(i carry it in
my heart)i am never without it(anywhere
i go you go,my dear;and whatever is done
by only me is your doing,my darling)
i fear
5 no fate(for you are my fate,my sweet)i want
no world(for beautiful you are my world,my true)
and it's you are whatever a moon has always meant
and whatever a sun will always sing is you

here is the deepest secret nobody knows
10 (here is the root of the root and the bud of the bud
and the sky of the sky of a tree called life;which grows
higher than soul can hope or mind can hide)
and this is the wonder that's keeping the stars apart

i carry your heart(i carry it in my heart)

DISCUSSION

Both the Sidney and the Cummings poem make use of a single *conceit* (a fanciful and sometimes far-fetched image) in which there is much play on the word "heart," moving without warning from its metaphorical to its physical and then back to its metaphorical meaning.

1. Explore the ways in which the two poems are alike and how they differ in wittily developing this conceit.

2. Explain line 4 in the Sidney poem: "His heart in me keeps me and him in one."

3. Explain lines 3-4 in the Cummings poem: "whatever is done/by only me is your doing, my darling)."

4. Discuss the effect of the typography of the Cummings poem (uncapitalized letters, crowding of sentence elements, absence of punctuation).

Edmund Spenser 1552 / 1599

From AMORETTI

30

My love is like to ice, and I to fire:
How comes it then that this her cold so great
Is not dissolved through my so hot desire,
But harder grows the more I her entreat?
5 Or how comes it that my exceeding heat
Is not allayed by her heart-frozen cold,
But that I burn much more in boiling sweat,
And feel my flames augmented manifold?
10 What more miraculous thing may be told,
That fire, which all things melts, should harden ice,
And ice, which is congeal'd with senseless cold,
Should kindle fire by wonderful device?
Such is the power of love in gentle mind,
That it can alter all the course of kind.[1]

1. *kind,* nature.

54

Of this world's Theatre in which we stay,
My love like the Spectator idly sits
Beholding me that all the pageants[1] play,
Disguising diversely my troubled wits.
Sometimes I joy when glad occasion fits,
And mask in mirth like to a Comedy;
Soon after when my joy to sorrow flits,
I wail and make my woes a Tragedy.
Yet she beholding me with constant eye,
10 Delights not in my mirth nor rues my smart.
But when I laugh she mocks, and when I cry
She laughs, and hardens evermore her heart.
What then can move her? If nor mirth nor moan,
She is no woman, but a senseless stone.

1. *pageants,* roles.

67

Like as a huntsman, after weary chase,
Seeing the game from him escaped away,
Sits down to rest him in some shady place,
With panting hounds beguilèd of their prey—
5 So after long pursuit and vain assay,
When I all weary had the chase forsook,
The gentle deer returned the selfsame way,
Thinking to quench her thirst at the next brook.
There she, beholding me with milder look,
10 Sought not to fly, but fearless still did bide:
Till I in hand her yet half trembling took,
And with her own good will her firmly tied.
Strange thing, me seemed, to see a beast so wild,
So goodly won, with her own will beguiled.

75

One day I wrote her name upon the strand,
But came the waves and washèd it away:
Again I wrote it with a second hand,
But came the tide and made my pains his prey.
5 "Vain man," said she, "that dost in vain assay
A mortal thing so to immortalize,
For I myself shall like to this decay,
And eke my name be wipèd out likewise."
"Not so," quoth I, "let baser things devise
10 To die in dust, but you shall live in fame;
My verse your virtues rare shall eternize,
And in the heavens write your glorious name.
Where, whenas death shall all the world subdue,
Our love shall live, and later life renew."

DISCUSSION

1. The central paradoxical metaphor of "My love is like to ice" is clear enough (she is ice, he is fire). The wonder is that it sustains the poem for fourteen lines. How?

2. Is the couplet in Sonnet 75 simply a lover's exaggeration, or is there some truth in it?

3. (a) Compare the central metaphors of Sonnets 54 and 67 and assess their suitability to the emotions expressed in the two sonnets.

(b) What evidence can you find in Sonnet 54, in which the lover is rejected, that the lady might eventually be won over, as in Sonnet 67?

III. THE FAERIE QUEENE by Spenser

Edmund Spenser's plan for his allegorical epic, *The Faerie Queene* (published 1590–1595), was remarkably elaborate: there were to be twelve books, each book to be devoted to one of the twelve virtues of chivalry, such as Holiness, Temperance, Chastity. Spenser completed only half of his projected plan, or a total of six books with twelve cantos each. Even so, the poem is the longest noteworthy poem in the English language.

In order to illustrate moral virtues, Spenser fashioned his poem as an *allegory*, letting his characters stand for particular abstract qualities. But the allegorical purposes fused with political and other purposes, and the characters became identifiable not only with virtues but with historical personages. The Faerie Queene herself, Gloriana, is a guiding presence throughout the work who dispatches her knights on errands and quests in the service of virtue. Gloriana represents glory in a general sense, but she also represents Queen Elizabeth.

But it is a mistake to get bogged down in allegorical and political references when reading *The Faerie Queene*. Spenser's poetry has a vivid, physical quality that gives it tremendous force on a simple narrative level. The poem should be read first for this quality and the allegory left to fend for itself. As an example, note the way Spenser describes the monster as it is strangled by the knight in the episode printed in this book:

> Therewith she spewed out of her filthy maw
> A flood of poison horrible and black,
> Full of great lumps of flesh and gobbets raw. . . .

The reader does not need to know that the knight is both Holiness and St. George, patron saint of England, and that the monster represents the supposed error of Catholicism (then attacking the Protestantism of Queen Elizabeth) in order to feel the impact of Spenser's images. *The Faerie Queene* is filled with poetic riches, splendor, fireworks; it should be read for its sheer exuberance, robust action, and its magic, astonishingly abundant creation.

THE KNIGHT SLAYS A MONSTER *(from Canto I)*

The Faerie Queene opens with a description of a knight riding his steed across a plain. He is followed by a lovely lady who is attended by a dwarf carrying her "needments" on his back. The knight is venturing forth to prove his power in battle and thus to win the favor of his queen and the admiration of the lady. This strange group soon loses its way and comes by accident upon an ominous-looking cave. Inside lurks an ugly monster, half serpent, half woman—"most loathsome, filthy, foul." Thus the knight is given his first opportunity to test his strength and bravery.

10

Led with delight, they thus beguile the way,
Until the blustering storm is overblown;
When weening[1] to return, whence they did stray,
They cannot find that path, which first was shown,
5 But wander to and fro in ways unknown,
Furthest from end then, when they nearest ween,
That makes them doubt, their wits be not their own:
So many paths, so many turnings seen,
That which of them to take, in diverse doubt they been.

11

10 At last resolving forward still to fare,
Till that some end they find or in or out,
That path they take, that beaten seemed most bare,
And like to lead the labyrinth about;
Which when by tract[2] they hunted had throughout,
15 At length it brought them to a hollow cave,
Amid the thickest woods. The Champion stout
Eftsoons[3] dismounted from his courser brave,
And to the Dwarf a while his needless spear he gave.

1. *weening,* intending.
2. *by tract,* by following the track.
3. *Eftsoons,* immediately.

12

"Be well aware," quoth then that Lady mild,
20 "Lest sudden mischief ye too rash provoke:
The danger hid, the place unknown and wilde,
Breeds dreadful doubts: Oft fire is without smoke,
And peril without show: therefore your stroke,
Sir Knight, withhold, till further trial made."
25 "Ah Lady," said he, "shame were to revoke
The forward footing for an hidden shade:
Virtue gives herself light, through darkness for to wade."

13

"Yea but," quoth she, "the peril of this place
I better wot[4] then you, though now too late
30 To wish you back return with foul disgrace.
Yet wisdom warns, whilst foot is in the gate,
To stay the step, ere forced to retreat.
This is the wandering wood, this Error's den,
A monster vile, whom God and man does hate:
35 Therefore I read[5] beware." "Fly, fly," quoth then
The fearful Dwarf: "this is no place for living men."

14

But full of fire and greedy hardiment,[6]
The youthful knight could not for aught be stayed,
But forth unto the darksome hole he went,
40 And looked in: his glistering armor made
A little glooming light, much like a shade,
By which he saw the ugly monster plain,
Half like a serpent horribly displayed,
But th'other half did woman's shape retain,
45 Most loathsome, filthy, foul, and full of vile disdain.

15

And as she lay upon the dirty ground,
Her huge long tail her den all overspread,
Yet was in knots and many boughtes[7] upwound,
Pointed with mortal sting. Of her there bred
50 A thousand young ones, which she daily fed,
Sucking upon her poisonous dugs, each one
Of sundry shapes, yet all ill favored:
Soon as that uncouth light upon them shone,
Into her mouth they crept, and sudden all were gone.

4. *wot,* know.
5. *read,* advise, warn.
6. *greedy hardiment,* eager courage.
7. *boughtes,* coils.

16

55 Their dam upstart, out of her den affrayed,[8]
And rushed forth, hurling her hideous tail
About her cursed head, whose folds displayed
Were stretched now forth at length without entrail.[9]
She looked about, and seeing one in mail
60 Armed to point,[10] sought back to turn again;
For light she hated as the deadly bale,
Ay wont in desert darkness to remain,
Where plain none might her see, nor she see any plain.

17

Which when the valiant Elf[11] perceived, he leapt
65 As lion fierce upon the flying prey,
And with his trenchant blade her boldly kept
From turning back, and forced her to stay:
Therewith enraged she loudly 'gan to bray,
And turning fierce, her speckled tail advanced,
70 Threatening her angry sting, him to dismay:
Who naught aghast, his mighty hand enhanced:[12]
The stroke down from her head unto her shoulder glanced.

18

Much daunted with that dint,[13] her sense was dazed,
Yet kindling rage, herself she gathered round,
75 And all at once her beastly body raised
With doubled forces high above the ground:
Then wrapping up her wreathed stern around,
Leaped fierce upon his shield, and her huge train[14]
All suddenly about his body wound,
80 That hand or foot to stir he strove in vain:
God help the man so wrapped in Error's endless train.[15]

19

His Lady sad to see his sore constraint,
Cried out, "Now, now, Sir knight, show what ye be.
Add faith unto your force, and be not faint:

8. *affrayed,* frightened away.
9. *entrail,* coiling, folding.
10. *to point,* completely.
11. *Elf,* the knight; he was described as coming from Faerie Land.
12. *enhanced,* lifted.
13. *dint,* blow.
14. *train,* long trailing tail.
15. *train,* snare.

85 Strangle her, else she sure will strangle thee."
That when he heard, in great perplexity,
His gall did grate for grief[16] and high disdain,
And knitting all his force got one hand free,
Wherewith he gripped her gorge with so great pain,
90 That soon to loose her wicked bands did her constrain.

20

Therewith she spewed out of her filthy maw
A flood of poison horrible and black,
Full of great lumps of flesh and gobbets raw,
Which stunk so vilely, that it forced him slack
95 His grasping hold, and from her turn him back:
Her vomit full of books and papers was,
With loathly frogs and toads, which eyes did lack,
And creeping sought way in the weedy grass:
Her filthy parbreake[17] all the place defiled has.

21

100 As when old father Nilus 'gins to swell
With timely pride above the Egyptian vale,
His fatty waves do fertile slime outwell,
And overflow each plain and lowly dale:
But when his later spring 'gins to avale,[18]
105 Huge heaps of mud he leaves, wherein there breed
Ten thousand kinds of creatures, partly male
And partly female of his fruitful seed;
Such ugly monstrous shapes elsewhere may no man reed.[19]

22

The same so sore annoyed has the knight,
110 That well nigh choked with the deadly stink,
His forces fail, nor can no longer fight.
Whose courage when the fiend perceived to shrink,
She poured forth out of her hellish sink
Her fruitful cursed spawn of serpents small,
115 Deformed monsters, foul, and black as ink,
Which swarming all about his legs did crawl,
And him encumbered sore, but could not hurt at all.

16. *His gall . . . grief,* his anger was stirred.
17. *parbreake,* vomit.
18. *avale,* subside.
19. *reed,* see.

23

As gentle Shepherd in sweet eventide,
When ruddy Phoebus[20] 'gins to welke[21] in west,
120 High on an hill, his flock to viewen wide,
Marks which do bite their hasty supper best;
A cloud of cumbrous[22] gnats do him molest,
All striving to infix their feeble stings,
That from their 'noyance he no where can rest,
125 But with his clownish hands their tender wings
He brusheth oft, and oft doth mar their murmurings.

24

Thus ill bestead,[23] and fearful more of shame,
Than of the certain peril he stood in,
Half furious unto his foe he came,
130 Resolved in mind all suddenly to win,
Or soon to lose, before he once would lin;[24]
And struck at her with more than manly force,
That from her body full of filthy sin
He raft[25] her hateful head without remorse;
135 A stream of coal-black blood forth gushed from her corse.[26]

20. *Phoebus,* Apollo, the Greek god of the sun.
21. *welke,* diminish.
22. *cumbrous,* bothersome, annoying.
23. *bestead,* situated.
24. *lin,* stop.
25. *raft,* took off.
26. *corse,* body.

OF LITERARY INTEREST

The Spenserian stanza

Edmund Spenser devised a special stanza for *The Faerie Queene*. It has a total of nine lines, the first eight in *iambic pentameter* (five feet of unaccented-accented syllables), and the last an *Alexandrine*, made of *iambic hexameter* (i.e., with one additional foot). The rhyme scheme is highly interlocking: ababbcbcc. The tightness of the form, and especially the finality of the long last line, tends to make each stanza self-contained. The result, when used in narrative poetry (at least in Spenser's hands) is a sequence of densely packed, richly woven images, almost like miniatures flashing by one at a time, vividly present and then gone. Many poets after Spenser have tried to write in this stanza form, but none with so much success as John Keats in "The Eve of St. Agnes." (See "The Romantics.")

25

Her scattered brood, soon as their Parent dear
They saw so rudely falling to the ground,
Groaning full deadly, all with troublous fear,
Gathered themselves about her body round,
140 Weening their wonted entrance to have found
At her wide mouth: but being there withstood
They flocked all about her bleeding wound,
And sucked up their dying mother's blood,
Making her death their life, and eke[27] her hurt their good.

26

145 That detestable sight him much amazed,
To see th'unkindly Imps of heaven accursed,
Devour their dam; on whom while so he gazed,
Having all satisfied their bloody thirst,
Their bellies swollen he saw with fullness burst,
150 And bowels gushing forth: well worthy end
Of such as drunk her life, the which them nursed:
Now needeth him no longer labor spend,
His foes have slain themselves, with whom he should contend.

27. *eke,* also.

27

His Lady seeing all that chanced, from far
155 Approached in haste to greet his victory,
And said, "Fair knight, born under happy star,
Who see your vanquished foes before you lie:
Well worthy be you of that Armory,[28]
Wherein you have great glory won this day,
160 And proved your strength on a strong enemy,
Your first adventure: many such I pray,
And henceforth ever wish, that like succeed it may."

28

Then mounted he upon his Steed again,
And with the Lady backward sought to wend;
165 That path he kept, which beaten was most plain,
Nor ever would to any byway bend,
But still did follow one unto the end,
The which at last out of the wood them brought.
So forward on his way (with God to friend)[29]
170 He passed forth, and new adventure sought;
Long way he traveled, before he heard of aught. ☐

28. *Armory,* i.e., the armor of a Christian man (a reference to Ephesians 6:13–14).
29. *to friend,* as a friend.

OF LITERARY INTEREST

Allegory

An allegory is a narrative in which the characters, events, or settings stand for something other than simply themselves—most frequently abstract ideas such as Faith, Honor, Virtue, but sometimes political, religious, or professional attitudes, beliefs, or personages. Allegory is not, therefore, a literary type in the sense of "sonnet" or "short story." It is, rather, a strategy or technique that can be used in any literary type, poetry or prose. The most famous allegories in English literature are the medieval morality play, *Everyman,* Edmund Spenser's long poem, *The Faerie Queene,* and John Bunyan's prose narrative, *Pilgrim's Progress.*

An allegorical meaning or an allegorical dimension may be found in works that do not comply fully with the traditional definition of allegory, such as the Bible (Jonah and the whale), Herman Melville's *Moby Dick,* or Joseph Heller's *Catch-22.* George Orwell's *Animal Farm* is an allegory in the form of a satire, ridiculing an entire political system. The modern theater of the absurd is strongly allegorical. Samuel Beckett's *Waiting for Godot,* Eugene Ionesco's *The Bald Soprano,* Harold Pinter's *The Caretaker,* and Edward Albee's *The Zoo Story* all contain enigmatic situations that appear to stand for the enigmatic situation of modern man; or they portray events which appear to stand for the horrible or meaningless events of modern life; or they exhibit relationships—rather, nonrelationships—that seem to symbolize the alienation of contemporary man. Allegory or the allegorical impulse appears, then, to be durable and enduring, serving, informing, and shaping literature from the beginning down to the present age.

DISCUSSION

1. First read this passage as an exciting action, ignoring for the moment the allegorical elements.

(a) Many readers of *The Faerie Queene* have noted its dreamlike quality. Possibly the events make more sense when conceived as a dream. What elements in this passage suggest a dream?

(b) Are the characters individuals or types? The knight, the lady, and the dwarf all are involved in some way in the action. Do their deeds or speeches give them individuality?

2. The knight represents Holiness, the lady Truth, the monster Error. Holiness, with the aid of Truth, crushes Error. Look at this passage now as allegory.

(a) In stanza 16, why is the monster afraid of light?

(b) Discuss the children of the monster—their creation and their death—in allegorical terms.

3. The form, imagery, and language of *The Faerie Queene* are in large part the secret of its success.

(a) What is the effect in the Spenserian stanza (see above) of the long last (ninth) line, with six feet (an *Alexandrine*)? Does it convey a sense of rapidity and openness, or the opposite? How does this sense affect the narrative flow?

(b) Stanzas 25 and 26 present a repulsive sight of the monster's children thriving on their mother's death and then expiring. Examine the imagery and diction to discover how Spenser achieves this effect.

(c) Show how the Shepherd metaphor in Stanza 23 functions in the passage.

4. *The Faerie Queene* has continued to interest readers for over three centuries.

(a) Does the action have any meaning or relevance for us today? Explain.

(b) Is the allegory obsolete, inasmuch as it is related largely to the religious and other controversies of Spenser's day? Discuss.

WRITING

1. Try your hand at writing the first three stanzas of a narrative using the Spenserian stanza. For the proper mood, you might need to construct your plot out of the materials of an older, more heroic time. (Note John Keats' "The Eve of St. Agnes.")

2. Write a realistic account of the crushing of a major Error, based on either fiction or fact. Use your own (modern) prose style.

3. Write a short allegory in which you work out precise equivalents for your characters and incidents. Relate the allegory to some contemporary conflict, debate, or controversy. (Perhaps: the Politician as magician, the Voters as audience, Government as a vaudeville act.)

IV. SONGS AND LYRICS

"If music be the food of love, play on,
Give me excess of it. . . ."

These lines open William Shakespeare's *Twelfth Night,* and may be taken almost literally as representing the universal feelings of the Elizabethan age. The whole world seemed to sing, and sang of love. But there were songs about other subjects, too—when the poets and musicians could bear to take their minds off love.

The Elizabethan world came alive with the sound of music. For the Elizabethan gentleman skill in music was as indispensable as skill in sports or reading Latin. Ordinary men and women were ashamed if they could not take part in the singing of a madrigal. As one writer of the time put it, even a journeyman shoemaker had to be able "to sound the trumpet, to play upon the flute, and bear his part in a three-man's song, and readily reckon his tools in rhyme."

Some Elizabethan songs are beautifully clear; others are fantastic and elaborate. Some are gay and frivolous; others sober and serious. There seem to be, in fact, enough kinds to suit every possible taste or mood.

THE PASSIONATE SHEPHERD TO HIS LOVE

by Christopher Marlowe

Come live with me and be my Love,
And we will all the pleasures prove
That hills and valleys, dales and fields,
Or woods or steepy mountain yields.

5 And we will sit upon the rocks,
And see the shepherds feed their flocks
By shallow rivers, to whose falls
Melodious birds sing madrigals.

And I will make thee beds of roses
10 And a thousand fragrant posies;
A cap of flowers, and a kirtle
Embroidered all with leaves of myrtle;

A gown made of the finest wool
Which from our pretty lambs we pull;
15 Fair-linèd slippers for the cold,
With buckles of the purest gold;

A belt of straw and ivy buds
With coral clasps and amber studs—
And if these pleasures may thee move,
20 Come live with me and be my Love.

The shepherd swains shall dance and sing
For thy delight each May morning—
If these delights thy mind may move,
Then live with me and be my Love.

THE NYMPH'S REPLY TO THE SHEPHERD

by Sir Walter Raleigh

If all the world and love were young,
And truth in every shepherd's tongue,
These pretty pleasures might me move,
To live with thee and be thy love.

5 Time drives the flocks from field to fold,
When rivers rage, and rocks grow cold;
And Philomel[1] becometh dumb;
The rest complain of cares to come.

The flowers do fade, and wanton fields
10 To wayward winter reckoning yields;
A honey tongue, a heart of gall,
Is fancy's spring, but sorrow's fall.

Thy gowns, thy shoes, thy bed of roses,
Thy cap, thy kirtle, and thy posies,
15 Soon break, soon wither, soon forgotten;
In folly ripe, in reason rotten.

Thy belt of straw and ivy buds,
Thy coral clasps and amber studs,
All these in me no means can move,
20 To come to thee and be thy love.

But could youth last, and love still breed,
Had joys no date, nor age no need,
Then these delights my mind might move
To live with thee and be thy love.

---

1. *Philomel* (fil′ə mel), the nightingale.

MY SWEETEST LESBIA

by Thomas Campion

My sweetest Lesbia, let us live and love,
And though the sager sort our deeds reprove,
Let us not weigh them. Heaven's great lamps do
dive
Into their west, and straight again revive,
5 But soon as once set is our little light,
Then must we sleep one ever-during[1] night.

If all would lead their lives in love like me,
Then bloody swords and armor should not be;
No drum nor trumpet peaceful sleeps should move,
10 Unless alarm came from the camp of love.
But fools do live, and waste their little light,
And seek with pain their ever-during night.

When timely death my life and fortune ends,
Let not my hearse be vexed with mourning friends,
15 But let all lovers, rich in triumph, come
And with sweet pastimes grace my happy tomb;
And Lesbia, close up thou my little light,
And crown with love my ever-during night.

1. *ever-during*, ever-enduring or everlasting.

LOVE IS A SICKNESS

by Samuel Daniel

Love is a sickness full of woes,
All remedies refusing,
A plant that with most cutting grows,
Most barren with best using.
5 Why so?
More we enjoy it, more it dies,
If not enjoyed it sighing cries,
Hey ho.[1]

Love is a torment of the mind,
10 A tempest everlasting,
And Jove hath made it of a kind
Not well, nor full, nor fasting.[2]
Why so?
More we enjoy it, more it dies,
15 If not enjoyed it sighing cries,
Hey ho.

1. *Hey ho,* used to express sadness and dejection (as well as joy).
2. *Not well . . . fasting,* not well, whether it is indulged (full) or denied (fasting).

DISCUSSION

1. Explain the central paradox expressed in "Love Is a Sickness," and discuss its accuracy.
2. What is the major "argument" of "My Sweetest Lesbia"? How persuasive is it?
3. In "The Passionate Shepherd to His Love," what dramatic situation do you envision: what is the setting, where is the boy, where is the girl, what are they doing? How would you place the scene for the movies?
4. If you were directing the dramatic scene in which the nymph replied to the shepherd, what instructions as to movement, business, etc. would you give the actress playing the nymph for the delivery of her lines?

WRITING

Write a script for a modern version of the shepherd-nymph exchange, in prose or poetry, in formal language or in whatever is the current style. Describe the setting for the dramatic scene, and provide instructions for your actors.

SONGS BY SHAKESPEARE

Dirge from Cymbeline

Fear no more the heat o' the sun,
  Nor the furious winter's rages;
Thou thy worldly task hast done,
  Home art gone, and ta'en thy wages:
5 Golden lads and girls all must,
As chimney-sweepers, come to dust.

Fear no more the frown o' the great;
  Thou art past the tyrant's stroke;
Care no more to clothe and eat;
10 To thee the reed is as the oak:
The scepter, learning, physic, must
All follow this, and come to dust.

Fear no more the lightning-flash,
  Nor the all-dreaded thunder-stone;[1]
15 Fear not slander, censure rash;
  Thou hast finished joy and moan:
All lovers young, all lovers must
Consign[2] to thee, and come to dust.

No exorciser harm thee!
20 Nor no witchcraft charm thee!
Ghost unlaid forbear thee!
  Nothing ill come near thee!
Quiet consummation[3] have;
And renownèd be thy grave!

1. *thunder-stone*, thunderbolt, the supposed solid body accompanying a stroke of lightning.
2. *Consign*, come to the same end as.
3. *consummation*, end, death.

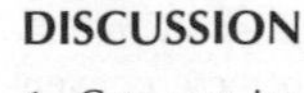

MINIATURE BY NICHOLAS HILLIARD, CIRCA 1588. BY COURTESY OF THE VICTORIA AND ALBERT MUSEUM, LONDON, CROWN COPYRIGHT.

Song from The Tempest

Full fathom five thy father lies;
  Of his bones are coral made;
Those are pearls that were his eyes:
  Nothing of him that doth fade,
5 But doth suffer a sea change
Into something rich and strange.
Sea nymphs hourly ring his knell:
  Ding-dong.
Hark! now I hear them—Ding-dong, bell.

1. Sung by the spirit Ariel as he lures the shipwrecked Ferdinand to shore, making him believe his father has drowned.

DISCUSSION

1. Can you imagine (perhaps by improvising) what kind of music might have accompanied the words of these songs?

2. In the lament, "Fear No More," is there any kind of progression of thought through the stanzas, or is there merely repetition?

3. "Full Fathom Five" is, in a sense, a mysterious description of a drowned man. What has happened to him?

V. SHAKESPEARE'S SONNETS

Although primarily a dramatist, Shakespeare tried various other literary forms and was something of a master of all.

Shakespeare's sonnets were published in 1609, probably without the poet's permission. They appear to have been written some ten or more years earlier. The 154 sonnets form a sequence which tells a fragmentary story involving a young man, a "dark lady," and the poet himself, together with a "rival poet." In Sonnets 1-126, the young man has the principal role, while in the remainder, the dark lady becomes prominent. Scholars and critics have made many attempts to untangle all the mysteries of Shakespeare's sonnets as they may shed light on his life, but generally to no avail. For a fictionalized account making full use of the sonnets, see Anthony Burgess' novel, *Nothing Like the Sun* (1964).

18

Shall I compare thee to a summer's day?
Thou art more lovely and more temperate.
Rough winds do shake the darling buds of May,
And summer's lease hath all too short a date.
5 Sometime too hot the eye of heaven shines,
And often is his gold complexion dimmed.
And every fair from fair sometimes declines,
By chance or nature's changing course untrimmed.[1]
But thy eternal summer shall not fade,
10 Nor lose possession of that fair thou owest,[2]
Nor shall Death brag thou wander'st in his shade,
When in eternal lines to time thou growest.
So long as men can breathe, or eyes can see,
So long lives this, and this gives life to thee.

1. *untrimmed,* reduced; shorn of beauty.
2. *fair thou owest,* beauty you own.

130

My mistress' eyes are nothing like the sun,
Coral is far more red than her lips' red.
If snow be white, why then her breasts are dun,
If hairs be wires, black wires grow on her head.
5 I have seen roses damasked,[1] red and white,
But no such roses see I in her cheeks.
And in some perfumes is there more delight
Than in the breath that from my mistress reeks.
I love to hear her speak, yet well I know
10 That music hath a far more pleasing sound.
I grant I never saw a goddess go,[2]
My mistress, when she walks, treads on the ground.
And yet, by Heaven, I think my love as rare
As any she[3] belied with false compare.

1. *damasked,* mingled.
2. *go,* walk.
3. *any she,* any woman.

DISCUSSION

During the Elizabethan period, love poetry tended to follow certain conventions, one of which was an exaggerated description of the beauty of the beloved. A poet generally felt obligated to work within these conventions, but he tried to achieve originality in spite of them—through ingenuity in devising comparisons, through cleverness of phrasing, or even by turning the conventions upside down.

1. (a) In Sonnet 18, why does Shakespeare begin by asking a question?

(b) How consistent is he in carrying through the comparison of his love with a summer's day?

(c) In the last line, what does "this" refer to, and how does it give life to the beloved?

(d) Some readers believe that Shakespeare was, in this and other sonnets, paying greater tribute to his poetry than to his love. Explain. What do you think?

2. (a) What conventions are turned upside down in Sonnet 130?

(b) Explore the effect of the use of "dun" in line 3; of "reeks" in line 8.

(c) The final couplet opens "And yet," signifying a reversal of some sort. Explain the impact of this couplet on the preceding 12 lines.

WRITING

1. Try your hand at writing a poem, perhaps even a sonnet, using the conventional comparisons referred to in Shakespeare's Sonnet 130.

2. Write a comic poem, or sonnet, in which you stand a convention on its head.

3. "Poetry with ingenious comparisons, far-fetched assertions, and extraordinarily clever phrasing may be interesting but cannot be sincere as genuine love poetry because it does not express deep feeling or profound emotion." Defend or attack this statement, using examples from the poetry of the Elizabethan period.

DETAIL FROM A PAINTING SHOWING A NOBLEMAN'S FEAST. NATIONAL PORTRAIT GALLERY, LONDON.

29

When in disgrace with fortune and men's eyes
I all alone beweep my outcast state,
And trouble deaf Heaven with my bootless[1] cries
And look upon myself and curse my fate,
5 Wishing me like to one more rich in hope,
Featured like him, like him with friends possessed,
Desiring this man's art and that man's scope,
With what I most enjoy contented least—
Yet in these thoughts myself almost despising,
10 Haply I think on thee, and then my state,
Like to the lark at break of day arising
From sullen earth, sings hymns at Heaven's gate.
For thy sweet love remembered such wealth brings
That then I scorn to change my state with kings.

1. *bootless,* useless.

30

When to the sessions[1] of sweet silent thought
I summon up remembrance of things past,
I sigh the lack of many a thing I sought,
And with old woes new wail my dear time's waste.
5 Then can I drown an eye, unused to flow,
For precious friends hid in death's dateless[2] night,
And weep afresh love's long since canceled woe,
And moan the expense[3] of many a vanished sight.
Then can I grieve at grievances foregone,[4]
10 And heavily from woe to wŏe tell o'er
The sad account of forebemoanèd moan,
Which I new-pay as if not paid before.
But if the while I think on thee, dear friend,
All losses are restored and sorrows end.

1. *sessions,* literally, the sittings of a law court.
2. *dateless,* endless.
3. *expense,* loss.
4. *foregone,* past.

55

Not marble, nor the gilded monuments
Of princes, shall outlive this powerful rhyme.
But you shall shine more bright in these contents
Than unswept stone,[1] besmeared with sluttish time.
5 When wasteful war shall statues overturn,
And broils root out the work of masonry,
Nor Mars his sword nor war's quick fire shall burn
The living record of your memory.
'Gainst death and all-oblivious enmity
10 Shall you pace forth. Your praise shall still find room
Even in the eyes of all posterity
That wear this world out to the ending doom.
So, till the judgment[2] that[3] yourself arise,
You live in this, and dwell in lovers' eyes.

1. *unswept stone,* dusty slab over a grave (in the floor of a church, where prominent people were often buried).
2. *judgment,* Day of Judgment at the end of the world.
3. *that,* when.

60

Like as the waves make toward the pebbled shore,
So do our minutes hasten to their end,
Each changing place with that which goes before,
In sequent toil all forward do contend.
5 Nativity,[1] once in the main of light,[2]
Crawls to maturity, wherewith being crowned,
Crooked eclipses 'gainst his glory fight,
And Time that gave doth now his gift confound.
Time doth transfix the flourish set on youth
10 And delves the parallels in beauty's brow,
Feeds on the rarities of nature's truth,
And nothing stands but for his scythe to mow.
And yet to times in hope my verse shall stand,
Praising thy worth, despite his cruel hand.

1. *nativity,* i.e., the newborn baby.
2. *main of light,* bright daylight.

71

No longer mourn for me when I am dead
Than you shall hear the surly sullen bell
Give warning to the world that I am fled
From this vile world, with vilest worms to dwell.
5 Nay, if you read this line, remember not
The hand that writ it, for I love you so
That I in your sweet thoughts would be forgot
If thinking on me then should make you woe.
Oh, if, I say, you look upon this verse
10 When I perhaps compounded am with clay,
Do not so much as my poor name rehearse,
But let your love even with my life decay,
Lest the wise world should look into your moan,
And mock you with me after I am gone.

73

That time of year thou mayst in me behold
When yellow leaves, or none, or few, do hang
Upon those boughs which shake against the cold,
Bare ruined choirs[1] where late the sweet birds sang.
5 In me thou see'st the twilight of such day
As after sunset fadeth in the west,
Which by and by black night doth take away,
Death's second self, that seals up[2] all in rest.
In me thou see'st the glowing of such fire,
10 That on the ashes of his youth doth lie
As the deathbed whereon it must expire,
Consumed with that which it was nourished by.
This thou perceivest, which makes thy love more strong,
To love that well which thou must leave ere long.

1. *choir,* part of a cathedral where services are held.
2. *seals up,* ends, concludes.

116

Let me not to the marriage of true minds
Admit impediments. Love is not love
Which alters when it alteration finds,
Or bends with the remover to remove.[1]
5 Oh no! It is an ever-fixèd mark,
That looks on tempests and is never shaken.
It is the star to every wandering bark,
Whose worth's unknown, although his height be
taken.
Love's not Time's fool, though rosy lips and cheeks
10 Within his bending sickle's compass come.
Love alters not with his brief hours and weeks,
But bears it out even to the edge of doom.
If this be error and upon me proved,
I never writ, nor no man ever loved.

1. *Or bends . . . remove:* or changes when the loved one is inconstant.

144

Two loves I have of comfort and despair,
Which like two spirits do suggest[1] me still.
The better angel is a man right fair,
The worser spirit a woman colored ill.
5 To win me soon to Hell, my female evil
Tempteth my better angel from my side,
And would corrupt my saint to be a devil,
Wooing his purity with her foul pride.[2]
And whether that my angel be turned fiend
10 Suspect I may, yet not directly tell,
But being both from me, both to each friend,
I guess one angel in another's Hell.
Yet this shall I ne'er know, but live in doubt
Till my bad angel fire my good one out.

1. *suggest,* prompt.
2. *pride,* sexual desire.

DISCUSSION

1. Compare the thought structures of Sonnets 29 and 30. Note that in Sonnet 29, line 9 begins with "Yet," suggesting a turn, while the turn does not seem to appear in Sonnet 30 until line 13, which begins with "But." How do the different structures achieve different effects?

2. Explain the following lines and relate them to their sonnets:

(a) Sonnet 55, line 14: "You live in this, and dwell in lovers' eyes."

(b) Sonnet 60, line 8: "And Time that gave doth now his gift confound."

(c) Sonnet 71, line 12: "But let your love even with my life decay."

3. Trace through the thought structure of Sonnet 73, showing why the images appear in the order they do.

4. Explore the reason for the word choice in the first line of Sonnet 116: "the marriage of *true minds.*"

5. In Sonnet 144, a conventional love triangle seems to be sketched. What are the relationships, and what is the poet's attitude? (See introductory note to this section for an account of the sonnets as related to Shakespeare's biography.)

VI. MACBETH

William Shakespeare

Characters

DUNCAN, *king of Scotland*

MALCOLM, DONALBAIN — *his sons*

MACBETH, BANQUO — *generals of the king's army*

MACDUFF, LENNOX, ROSS, MENTEITH, ANGUS, CAITHNESS — *noblemen of Scotland*

FLEANCE, *son to Banquo*
SIWARD, *Earl of Northumberland, general of the English forces*
YOUNG SIWARD, *his son*
SEYTON, *an officer attending on Macbeth*
BOY, *son to Macduff*
AN ENGLISH DOCTOR
A SCOTCH DOCTOR
A SOLDIER
A PORTER
AN OLD MAN
THREE MURDERERS
LADY MACBETH
LADY MACDUFF
GENTLEWOMAN *attending on Lady Macbeth*
HECATE
THREE WITCHES
APPARITIONS
LORDS, GENTLEMEN, OFFICERS, SOLDIERS, ATTENDANTS, AND MESSENGERS

Act One

SCENE 1. *A desert place. Thunder and lightning. Enter three* WITCHES.

FIRST WITCH. When shall we three meet again
In thunder, lightning, or in rain?
SECOND WITCH. When the hurlyburly's done,
When the battle's lost and won.
5 THIRD WITCH. That will be ere the set of sun.
FIRST WITCH. Where the place?
SECOND WITCH. Upon the heath.
THIRD WITCH. There to meet with Macbeth.
FIRST WITCH. I come, Graymalkin!°
SECOND WITCH. Paddock° calls.
10 THIRD WITCH. Anon.
ALL. Fair is foul, and foul is fair,[1]
Hover through the fog and filthy air.[2]

Graymalkin: a gray cat.
Paddock: a toad.
1. *Line 11:* What does this line mean? Be alert for characters and events which illustrate this apparent contradiction.
2. What is the purpose of this scene? In some stage presentations it has been omitted. If you were staging *Macbeth,* would you include it? Why or why not?

SCENE 2. *A camp near Forres°. (Played on the Platform.) Alarum within°. Enter* DUNCAN, MALCOLM, DONALBAIN, LENNOX, *with* ATTENDANTS, *meeting a bleeding* SERGEANT.

DUNCAN.[3] What bloody° man is that? He can report,
As seemeth by his plight, of the revolt
The newest state.
MALCOLM. This is the sergeant
Who like a good and hardy soldier fought
5 'Gainst my captivity.[4] Hail, brave friend!
Say to the King the knowledge of the broil
As thou didst leave it.
SERGEANT. Doubtful it stood,
As two spent swimmers that do cling together
And choke their art°. The merciless Macdonwald—
10 Worthy to be a rebel, for to that
The multiplying villainies of nature
Do swarm upon him—from the western isles°
Of kerns° and gallowglasses° is supplied;
And Fortune, on his damnèd quarrel smiling,
15 Showed like a rebel's whore.° But all's too weak;
For brave Macbeth—well he deserves that name—
Disdaining Fortune, with his brandished steel,
Which smoked with bloody execution,
Like valor's minion° carvèd out his passage

Forres: a town north of Edinburgh.
Alarum within: offstage noises indicating that a battle is going on. An alarum usually consisted of confused sounds of trumpets, drum, clash of arms, and men yelling.

3. In reading the speeches of Duncan, consider whether he has the characteristics of a strong king.
bloody: Blood is one of the significant motifs that recur in the play. Others are sleeplessness, animal and bird imagery, clothing metaphors (usually of borrowed or ill-fitting garments), darkness and light, hell and devils, and reversal of accepted values. Note throughout what purpose these motifs might serve.
4. About how old do you guess Malcolm is?
choke their art: hinder their ability to swim.

the western isles: Ireland and the Hebrides.
kerns: lightly-armed Irish footsoldiers.
gallowglasses: Irish footsoldiers armed with axes.

Fortune . . . whore: Fortune falsely seemed to favor Macdonwald. (Fortune was often described as a harlot who was fickle and granted her favors to anyone, regardless of worth.)

minion: darling or favorite.

All comments and suggestions in the side-notes about Shakespeare's staging are from *On Producing Shakespeare* by Ronald Watkins. From the Benjamin Blom Inc. 1967 edition. Used with permission. The suggestions are based on clues in early printings of the play and the conjectures of scholars, and assume a stage like that of the Globe Theater.

20 Till he faced the slave°;
Which ne'er shook hands, nor bade farewell to him,
Till he unseamed him from the nave to the chaps,°
And fixed his head upon our battlements.

DUNCAN. O valiant cousin! Worthy gentleman!

25 SERGEANT. As whence the sun 'gins his reflection
Shipwrecking storms and direful thunders break,
So from that spring whence comfort seemed to come
Discomfort swells. Mark, King of Scotland, mark:
No sooner justice had, with valor armed,
30 Compelled these skipping kerns to trust their heels,
But the Norweyan° lord, surveying vantage,
With furbished arms and new supplies of men,
Began a fresh assault.

DUNCAN. Dismayed not this
Our captains, Macbeth and Banquo?

SERGEANT. Yes—
35 As sparrows eagles, or the hare the lion.
If I say sooth, I must report they were
As cannons overcharged with double cracks,° so they
Doubly redoubled strokes upon the foe;
Except they meant to bathe in reeking wounds,
40 Or memorize another Golgotha,°
I cannot tell.[5]
But I am faint; my gashes cry for help.

DUNCAN. So well thy words become thee as thy wounds;
They smack of honor both. Go get him surgeons.

(Exit SERGEANT, *attended.)*

45 Who comes here?

(Enter ROSS.*)*

MALCOLM. The worthy thane° of Ross.

LENNOX. What a haste looks through his eyes! So should he look
That seems to speak things strange.

ROSS. God save the King!

DUNCAN. Whence cam'st thou, worthy thane?

ROSS. From Fife, great King,
Where the Norweyan banners flout the sky
50 And fan our people cold. Norway himself°
With terrible numbers,
Assisted by that most disloyal traitor,
The thane of Cawdor, began a dismal conflict,
Till that Bellona's bridegroom°, lapped in proof,°
55 Confronted him with self-comparisons,°
Point against point rebellious, arm 'gainst arm,
Curbing his lavish spirit; and, to conclude,
The victory fell on us.

DUNCAN. Great happiness!

ROSS. That now
Sweno, the Norways' King, craves composition°;
60 Nor would we deign him burial of his men

slave: Macdonwald.

unseamed him . . . chaps: split him from navel to jaws.

Norweyan: Norwegian.

double cracks: doubly charged with powder.

memorize . . . Golgotha (gol′gə thə): make the area as memorable for bloodshed as the place where Christ was crucified.

5. *Lines 7-41:* What do the Sergeant's comments indicate about Macbeth as soldier and leader?

thane: a Scottish title, just below an earl.

Norway himself: the king of Norway.

Bellona's bridegroom: Macbeth. Bellona was the Roman goddess of war.

lapped in proof: dressed in armor.

confronted . . . comparisons: matched him man-to-man.

composition: a peace treaty.

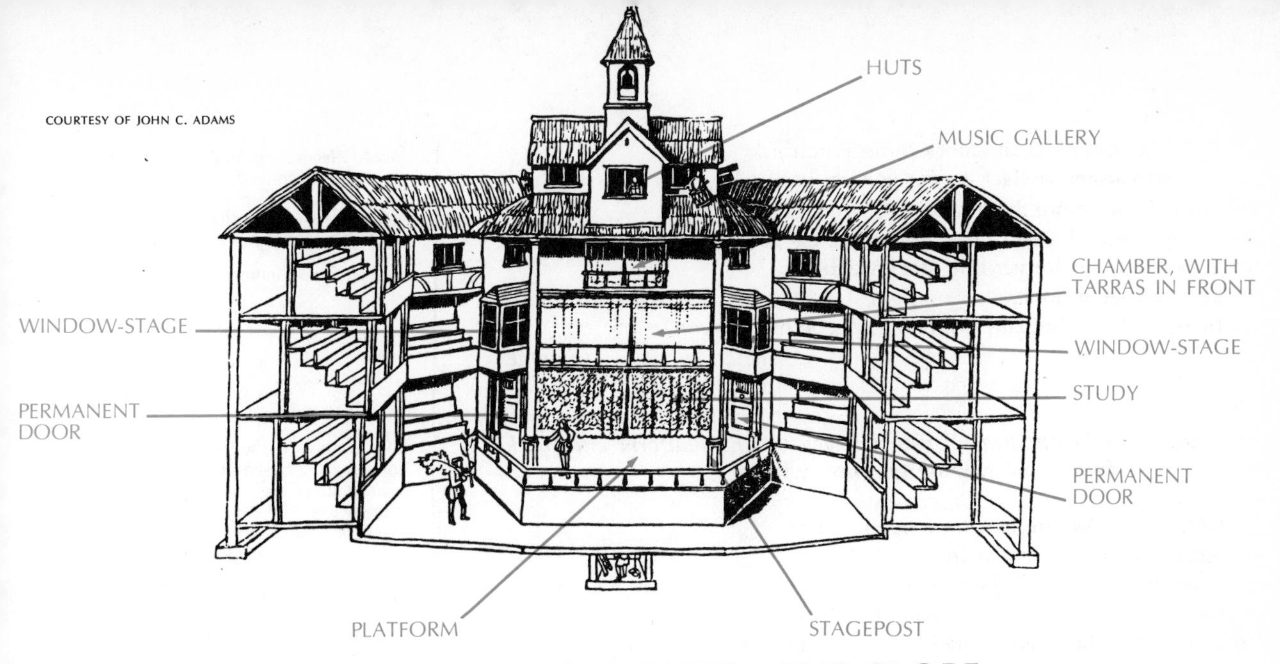

SHAKESPEARE'S THEATER—THE GLOBE

AFTER 1599, Shakespeare probably wrote most of his plays with the Globe Theater in mind. This multiple-story structure may strike us as complicated, but in fact it simplified production because it suited the conventions of Elizabethan drama.

According to the conjectures of scholars, the outside diameter of the theater was about 84 feet, and its three tiers of seats, plus an open area for standees, could accommodate about 2000 spectators.

The main acting area was the Platform which extended out into the audience and was probably some 24 feet across the front, 41 feet across the widest part at the back, and 29 feet deep. Because it was so large, battle scenes, processions, or simultaneous unrelated actions could be convincingly presented.

At the back of the Platform was a recess known as the Study which was usually used for interior scenes. To the audience, an actor in the Study would seem quite remote from action going on at the front of the Platform. At either side of the Study were large permanent doors, similar to the street doors of Elizabethan town houses. These were the main stage entrances. In the floor of the Platform were a number of trap doors leading to the area below stage known as Hell. From these traps arose apparitions, smoke, and fog, and through them actors descended when the action required them to go underground.

On the second level there was another curtained recess called the Chamber, generally used for domestic settings, especially scenes involving women. In front of the Chamber was a narrow balcony called the Tarras (terrace) which connected with two small bay windows or window stages that flanked it. The Tarras was often used in conjunction with the Platform—for example, to represent a hill, battlements, or a gallery from which observers watched action below.

The third level contained a narrow musicians' gallery which could also be used as an acting area. Above it was a canopied roof supported by two large stage posts that rose from the Platform. Sound effects such as thunder or battle "alarums" were produced in the Huts above the Canopy. The Huts also housed a pulley system used for lowering apparitions or objects supposed to appear from midair.

This entire three-story structure which formed the back of the stage and gave the effect of a large Elizabethan town house was known as the Tiring House. It was the Globe's permanent set.

With its many-level stage and variety of acting areas, the Globe was ideally suited for presenting the numerous short scenes which followed each other without break in Shakespeare's plays. Changes in location could be made obvious by a shift in playing area or by manipulating the curtains of the Study or the Chamber.

Till he disbursed, at Saint Colme's Inch°,
Ten thousand dollars° to our general use.

DUNCAN. No more that thane of Cawdor shall deceive
Our bosom interest°. Go pronounce his present death,
65 And with his former title greet Macbeth.

ROSS. I'll see it done.

DUNCAN. What he hath lost noble Macbeth hath won.

(Exeunt.)

Saint Colme's Inch: an island off the coast of Scotland.

dollars: either Dutch thalers or Spanish pieces-of-eight.

bosom interest: intimate trust.

SCENE 3. *A heath° near Forres. (Played on the Platform and in the Study.) Thunder. Enter the three* WITCHES.

(The heath-set in the Study might contain gaunt bushes, their shape indicating that the wind is blowing strongly toward the point of Macbeth's entry. The grave-trap may be open—perhaps disguised with a stone or a turf-bank—ready to receive one of the disappearing sisters.)

FIRST WITCH. Where hast thou been, sister?

SECOND WITCH. Killing swine.

THIRD WITCH. Sister, where thou?

FIRST WITCH. A sailor's wife had chestnuts in her lap,
5 And munched, and munched, and munched—"Give me," quoth I.
"Aroint thee,° witch!" the rump-fed ronyon° cries.
Her husband's to Aleppo° gone, master o' the *Tiger*,
But in a sieve I'll thither sail,
And, like a rat without a tail,°
10 I'll do, I'll do, and I'll do.

SECOND WITCH. I'll give thee a wind.

FIRST WITCH. Thou'rt kind.

THIRD WITCH. And I another.

FIRST WITCH. I myself have all the other,
15 And the very ports they blow,
All the quarters that they know
I' the shipman's card°.
I will drain him dry as hay;
Sleep shall neither night nor day
20 Hang upon his penthouse lid°;
He shall live a man forbid°;
Weary se'nnights nine times nine
Shall he dwindle, peak, and pine;
Though his bark cannot be lost,
25 Yet it shall be tempest-tossed.[6]
Look what I have.

SECOND WITCH. Show me, show me.

FIRST WITCH. Here I have a pilot's thumb,
Wrecked as homeward he did come.

(Drum within.)

30 THIRD WITCH. A drum, a drum!
Macbeth doth come!

ALL. The weird sisters, hand in hand
Posters of° the sea and land,
Thus do go about, about;
35 Thrice to thine, and thrice to mine,

Aroint thee: begone.
rump-fed ronyon: mangy creature, fed on refuse.
Aleppo: city in NW Syria, famous as a trading center.
without a tail: It was believed that witches could change themselves into animals, but could be detected by some deformity.

shipman's card: compass card or chart.

penthouse lid: eyelid.
forbid: accursed.

6. *Lines 24-25:* What do these lines indicate about the extent of the witches' power?

Posters of: travelers over.

And thrice again to make up nine.°
Peace! the charm's wound up.°

(Enter MACBETH *and* BANQUO.*)*

MACBETH. So foul and fair a day I have not seen.[7]
BANQUO. How far is 't to Forres?° What are these
40 So withered, and so wild in their attire,
That look not like the inhabitants o' the earth,
And yet are on 't? Live you?° Or are you aught
That man may question? You seem to understand me,
By each at once her choppy finger laying
45 Upon her skinny lips.[8] You should be women,
And yet your beards forbid me to interpret
That you are so.
MACBETH. Speak, if you can; what are you?°
FIRST WITCH. All hail, Macbeth! hail to thee, thane of Glamis!
SECOND WITCH. All hail, Macbeth! hail to thee, thane of Cawdor!
50 THIRD WITCH. All hail, Macbeth, that shalt be king hereafter!
BANQUO. Good sir, why do you start,[9] and seem to fear
Things that do sound so fair? I' the name of truth,
Are ye fantastical, or that indeed
Which outwardly ye show? My noble partner
55 You greet with present grace and great prediction
Of noble having and of royal hope,
That he seems rapt withal°; to me you speak not.
If you can look into the seeds of time,
And say which grain will grow and which will not,
60 Speak then to me, who neither beg nor fear
Your favors nor your hate.
FIRST WITCH. Hail!
SECOND WITCH. Hail!
THIRD WITCH. Hail!
65 FIRST WITCH. Lesser than Macbeth, and greater.
SECOND WITCH. Not so happy, yet much happier.
THIRD WITCH. Thou shalt get° kings, though thou be none.
So all hail, Macbeth and Banquo!
FIRST WITCH. Banquo and Macbeth, all hail!
70 MACBETH. Stay, you imperfect speakers, tell me more.
By Sinel's° death I know I am thane of Glamis;
But how of Cawdor? The thane of Cawdor lives,
A prosperous gentleman. And to be king
Stands not within the prospect of belief,
75 No more than to be Cawdor. Say from whence
You owe this strange intelligence? Or why
Upon this blasted heath you stop our way
With such prophetic greeting? Speak, I charge you.

(WITCHES *vanish.*)°

BANQUO. The earth hath bubbles, as the water has,
80 And these are of them. Whither are they vanished?
MACBETH. Into the air, and what seemed corporal melted
As breath into the wind. Would they had stayed!

(*The weird sisters . . . nine:* This incantation might accompany a ritual dance with which the witches mark out in the center of the Platform a charmed circle for Macbeth to step into.)

(*Peace! . . . up:* They retreat hastily to the perimeter outside the Stage-Post on the opposite side from the door of Macbeth's entry.)

7. *Line 38:* What earlier lines is Macbeth echoing? What does he mean? Why might Shakespeare have given him this line?

(*How . . . Forres?* Shouted through fog to the distant figures.)

(*Live you?* Spoken at close range.)

8. *Lines 44-45:* The witches gesture "silence" in response to Banquo's question, yet they answer Macbeth at once. What does this show about the nature of their spell?

(*Speak, . . you?* As he enters, Macbeth might move into the charmed circle the witches have made, reacting from the spell with a shudder. Banquo's course would be in front of the circle. Macbeth would then speak from the circle.)

9. Why *does* Macbeth start? As you read on, compare his reaction to the witches' prophecies with Banquo's reaction. What do the reactions of the two men reveal? What might this suggest about the future action of the play?

rapt withal: completely lost in thought.

get: beget.

Sinel: Macbeth's father. Macbeth had inherited the title.

(*vanish:* through the grave-trap in the Study.)

BANQUO. Were such things here as we do speak about?
Or have we eaten on the insane root°
85 That takes the reason prisoner?

MACBETH. Your children shall be kings.

BANQUO. You shall be king.

MACBETH. And thane of Cawdor, too; went it not so?

BANQUO. To the selfsame tune and words. Who's here?

(Enter ROSS *and* ANGUS.*)*

ROSS. The King hath happily received, Macbeth,
90 The news of thy success; and when he reads
Thy personal venture in the rebels' fight,
His wonders and his praises do contend
Which should be thine or his. Silenced° with that,
In viewing o'er the rest o' the selfsame day,
95 He finds thee in the stout Norweyan ranks,
Nothing afeared of what thyself didst make,
Strange images of death.° As thick as hail
Came post with post,° and everyone did bear
Thy praises in his kingdom's great defense,
100 And poured them down before him.

ANGUS. We are sent
To give thee from our royal master thanks;
Only to herald thee into his sight,
Not pay thee.

ROSS. And, for an earnest° of a greater honor,
He bade me, from him, call thee thane of Cawdor;
105 In which addition, hail, most worthy thane!
For it is thine.

BANQUO. What, can the devil speak true?

MACBETH. The thane of Cawdor lives; why do you dress me
In borrowed robes?

ANGUS. Who was the thane lives yet;
But under heavy judgment bears that life
110 Which he deserves to lose. Whether he was combined
With those of Norway, or did line° the rebel
With hidden help and vantage, or that with both
He labored in his country's wreck, I know not;
But treasons capital, confessed and proved,
115 Have overthrown him.

MACBETH *(aside).* Glamis, and thane of Cawdor!
The greatest is behind°.[10] *(to* ROSS *and* ANGUS*)* Thanks for your pains.
(to BANQUO*)* Do you not hope your children shall be kings,
When those that gave the thane of Cawdor to me
Promised no less to them?

BANQUO. That, trusted home,
120 Might yet enkindle you unto the crown,°
Besides the thane of Cawdor. But 'tis strange;
And oftentimes, to win us to our harm,
The instruments of darkness tell us truths,

insane root: root of hemlock, which was thought to cause hallucinations.

Silenced: speechless with admiration.

Nothing . . . death: Macbeth killed, but did not fear death for himself.

post with post: one newsbearer after another.

earnest: pledge; promise.

line: support.

behind: to come.

10. What has Ross said earlier that would allow Macbeth to say, "The greatest is behind"—even if he hadn't had the confrontation with the witches? Contrast Macbeth's reactions with Banquo's.

That . . . crown: Complete belief in the witches may arouse in you the ambition to become king. (Note the word "enkindle.")

Win us with honest trifles, to betray 's
125 In deepest consequence.
Cousins, a word, I pray you.

MACBETH *(aside).* Two truths are told,
As happy prologues to the swelling act
Of the imperial theme. —I thank you, gentlemen.
(aside) This supernatural soliciting
130 Cannot be ill, cannot be good; if ill,
Why hath it given me earnest of success,
Commencing in a truth? I am thane of Cawdor;
If good, why do I yield to that suggestion
Whose horrid image doth unfix my hair
135 And make my seated heart knock at my ribs,
Against the use of nature? Present fears
Are less than horrible imaginings;
My thought, whose murder yet is but fantastical,
Shakes so my single state of man that function
140 Is smothered in surmise, and nothing is
But what is not.°[11]

My thought . . . is not: My thought, in which the murder is still only a fantasy, so disturbs me that all power of action is smothered by imagination, and only unreal imaginings seem real to me.

11. Note the ambivalent feelings Macbeth expresses in this aside. Which side of his nature seems to predominate here?

BANQUO. Look, how our partner's rapt.

MACBETH *(aside).* If chance will have me king, why, chance may crown me,
Without my stir.

BANQUO. New honors come upon him,
Like our strange garments°, cleave not to their mold
145 But with the aid of use.

strange garments: new clothes.

MACBETH *(aside).* Come what come may,
Time and the hour runs through the roughest day.[12]

12. *Lines 116-146:* In his asides, Macbeth tells the audience, but not the other characters, his secret thoughts. What are they? Read the asides without the intervening comments to get their full impact.

BANQUO. Worthy Macbeth, we stay upon your leisure.°

MACBETH. Give me your favor; my dull brain was wrought
With things forgotten. Kind gentlemen, your pains
150 Are registered where every day I turn
The leaf to read them.° Let us toward the King.
Think upon what hath chanced, and, at more time,
The interim having weighed it, let us speak
Our free hearts each to other.[13]

we stay . . . leisure: we await your convenience.

where . . . read them: in my mind and heart.

13. *Lines 152-154:* To whom is Macbeth addressing these lines?

BANQUO. Very gladly.

155 MACBETH. Till then, enough. Come, friends.

(Exeunt.)

SCENE 4. *Forres. The palace. (Played on the Platform.) Flourish°. Enter* DUNCAN, MALCOLM, DONALBAIN, LENNOX, *and* ATTENDANTS.

Flourish: a blast of trumpets used to announce the entry of a royal personage.

DUNCAN. Is execution done on Cawdor? Are not
Those in commission yet returned?

MALCOLM. My liege,
They are not yet come back. But I have spoke
With one that saw him die; who did report
5 That very frankly he confessed his treasons,

Implored your Highness' pardon, and set forth
A deep repentance. Nothing in his life
Became him like the leaving it; he died
As one that had been studied in his death
10 To throw away the dearest thing he owed,
As 'twere a careless trifle.

DUNCAN. There's no art
To find the mind's construction in the face.°
He was a gentleman on whom I built
An absolute trust.[14]

(Enter MACBETH, BANQUO, ROSS, *and* ANGUS.*)*

O worthiest cousin!
15 The sin of my ingratitude even now
Was heavy on me; thou art so far before
The swiftest wing of recompense is slow
To overtake thee. Would thou hadst less deserved,
That the proportion both of thanks and payment
20 Might have been mine! Only I have left to say,
More is thy due than more than all can pay.[15]

MACBETH. The service and the loyalty I owe,
In doing it, pays itself. Your Highness' part
Is to receive our duties; and our duties
25 Are to your throne and state, children and servants,
Which do but what they should, by doing every thing
Safe toward your love and honor.[16]

DUNCAN. Welcome hither;
I have begun to plant thee, and will labor
To make thee full of growing.[17] Noble Banquo,
30 That hast no less deserved, nor must be known
No less to have done so, let me enfold thee
And hold thee to my heart.

BANQUO. There if I grow,
The harvest is your own.

DUNCAN. My plenteous joys,
Wanton in fullness, seek to hide themselves
35 In drops of sorrow.[18] Sons, kinsmen, thanes,
And you whose places are the nearest, know
We will establish our estate upon°
Our eldest, Malcolm, whom we name hereafter
The Prince of Cumberland;[19] which honor must
40 Not unaccompanied invest him only,
But signs of nobleness, like stars, shall shine
On all deservers. From hence to Inverness°,
And bind us further to you.

MACBETH. The rest is labor which is not used for you.°
45 I'll be myself the harbinger, and make joyful
The hearing of my wife with your approach;
So humbly take my leave.

DUNCAN. My worthy Cawdor!

There's no art . . . face: There is no way of judging a man's thoughts from his appearance.

14. About whom is Duncan speaking? What possible dramatic irony might there be in Macbeth's entrance immediately after this speech? Be alert for other examples of Shakespeare's use of this technique.

15. *Lines 20-21:* Considering Duncan's previous message to Macbeth, what might Macbeth expect from Duncan with respect to the succession to the crown?

16. *Lines 22-27:* This speech makes explicit the proper relationship between king and thane. Why do you think Shakespeare gave Macbeth this speech?

17. *I have begun . . . growing:* What does Duncan mean?

18. *My plenteous joys . . . sorrow:* What does Duncan say in his physical reaction?

establish . . . upon: name as heir to the throne.

19. *Lines 35-39a:* How should the actor playing Macbeth react here? Why might Duncan pick this moment and this company to name Malcolm his successor?

Inverness: Macbeth's castle.

The rest . . . you: Resting is work for me, when I am doing nothing to help you.

MACBETH *(aside)*. The Prince of Cumberland! that is a step
On which I must fall down, or else o'erleap,
50 For in my way it lies. Stars, hide your fires;
Let not light see my black and deep desires;
The eye wink at the hand; yet let that be
Which the eye fears, when it is done, to see.[20]

(Exit.)

20. *Lines 48-53:* Is Macbeth's reaction at all surprising? Is it justified? What does his speech suggest may be his "black and deep desires"?

DUNCAN. True, worthy Banquo; he is full so valiant,[21]
55 And in his commendations I am fed;
It is a banquet to me. Let's after him,
Whose care is gone before to bid us welcome.
It is a peerless kinsman.

(Flourish. Exeunt.)

21. To whom is Duncan referring? What do you think Banquo has just been saying to Duncan?

SCENE 5. *Inverness.* MACBETH'*s castle. (Played in the Chamber.) Enter* LADY MACBETH, *reading a letter.*

LADY MACBETH. "They met me in the day of success; and I have learned by the perfectest report they have more in them than mortal knowledge. When I burned in desire to question them further, they made themselves air, into which they vanished. Whiles I stood rapt in the
5 wonder of it, came missives° from the King, who all-hailed me 'Thane of Cawdor'; by which title, before, these weird sisters saluted me, and referred me to the coming-on of time, with 'Hail, king that shalt be!' This have I thought good to deliver thee, my dearest partner of greatness, that thou mightst not lose the dues of rejoicing,
10 by being ignorant of what greatness is promised thee. Lay it to thy heart, and farewell."[22]

missives: messengers.

Glamis thou art, and Cawdor; and shalt be
What thou art promised. Yet do I fear thy nature;
It is too full o' the milk of human kindness
15 To catch the nearest way.[23] Thou wouldst be great;
Art not without ambition, but without
The illness° should attend it. What thou wouldst highly,
That wouldst thou holily; wouldst not play false,
And yet wouldst wrongly win. Thou 'ldst have, great Glamis,
20 That which cries, "Thus thou must do, if thou have it";
And that which rather thou dost fear to do
Than wishest should be undone. Hie thee hither,
That I may pour my spirits in thine ear,
And chastise with the valor of my tongue
25 All that impedes thee from the golden round°,
Which fate and metaphysical aid doth seem
To have thee crowned withal.[24]

22. What does the letter reveal about their relationship? Which phrases in the letter are especially significant?

23. How does Lady Macbeth's first reaction to the witches' prophecies differ from Macbeth's?

illness: unscrupulousness.

golden round: the crown.

(Enter a MESSENGER.*)*

What is your tidings?

MESSENGER. The King comes here tonight.

LADY MACBETH. Thou'rt mad to say it![25]
Is not thy master with him? Who, were't so,
30 Would have informed for preparation.

24. In what ways does Lady Macbeth's description of her husband reinforce your impression of the ambivalence of his character?

25. In what tone of voice would she say this? What would be her tone in the next sentence? Why?

MESSENGER. So please you, it is true; our thane is coming;
One of my fellows had the speed of him,°
Who, almost dead for breath, had scarcely more
Than would make up his message.

had the speed of him: outdistanced him.

LADY MACBETH. Give him tending;
35 He brings great news.[26]

(Exit MESSENGER.*)*

The raven° himself is hoarse
That croaks the fatal entrance of Duncan
Under my battlements. Come, you spirits
That tend on mortal thoughts°, unsex me here,
And fill me from the crown to the toe top full
40 Of direst cruelty! make thick my blood;
Stop up the access and passage to remorse,
That no compunctious visitings of nature°
Shake my fell[27] purpose, nor keep peace between
The effect and it!° Come to my woman's breasts,
45 And take my milk for gall, you murdering ministers,
Wherever in your sightless substances
You wait on nature's mischief! Come, thick night,
And pall° thee in the dunnest° smoke of hell,
That my keen knife see not the wound it makes,[28]
50 Nor heaven peep through the blanket of the dark,
To cry, "Hold, hold!"[29]

26. *Line 35a:* What thought has just occurred to Lady Macbeth?
raven: Long believed to be a bird of ill omen, the raven was said to foretell death by its croaking.

mortal thoughts: murderous thoughts.

compunctious . . . nature: natural feelings of compassion.
27. The word *fell* has many meanings. What "reverberations" does it set up in your mind? Which meaning(s) applies?
keep peace . . . and it: come between my intention and my carrying out of it.
pall: wrap.
dunnest: darkest; murkiest.
28. At this point, who does Lady Macbeth think will commit the murder?
29. *Lines 35-51a:* What is Lady Macbeth trying to do in this speech? What conflict in her character is revealed by the conflict between her expressed desires and the nurturing metaphor she uses?

(Enter MACBETH.*)*

Great Glamis! Worthy Cawdor!
Greater than both, by the all-hail hereafter!
Thy letters have transported me beyond
This ignorant present, and I feel now
55 The future in the instant.

MACBETH. My dearest love,
Duncan comes here tonight.

LADY MACBETH. And when goes hence?

MACBETH. Tomorrow, as he purposes.[30]

30. How does Macbeth say this? (firmly? tentatively?)

LADY MACBETH. O never
Shall sun that morrow see!
Your face, my thane, is as a book where men
60 May read strange matters. To beguile the time,
Look like the time;° bear welcome in your eye,
Your hand, your tongue. Look like the innocent flower,
But be the serpent under 't. He that's coming
Must be provided for[31]; and you shall put
65 This night's great business into my dispatch°,
Which shall to all our nights and days to come
Give solely sovereign sway and masterdom.

To beguile . . . time: to deceive the world, appear as it demands or expects.

31. In what senses does she use the phrase "provided for"?
dispatch: care.

MACBETH. We will speak further.[32]

32. Is Macbeth completely convinced?

LADY MACBETH. Only look up clear;
To alter favor ever is to fear°—
70 Leave all the rest to me.

To alter . . . fear: to change facial expression shows fear.

(Exeunt.)

SCENE 6. *Before* MACBETH'S *castle. (Played on the Platform.) Hautboys*° *and torches. Enter* DUNCAN, MALCOLM, DONALBAIN, BANQUO, LENNOX, MACDUFF, ROSS, ANGUS, *and* ATTENDANTS.

Hautboys: a band of oboelike instruments, generally used by Shakespeare in connection with a procession or a banquet.

DUNCAN. This castle hath a pleasant seat; the air
Nimbly and sweetly recommends itself
Unto our gentle senses.[33]

BANQUO. This guest of summer,
The temple-haunting martlet°, does approve°,
5 By his loved mansionry, that the heaven's breath
Smells wooingly here. No jutty, frieze,
Buttress, nor coign of vantage but this bird
Hath made his pendent bed and procreant cradle;
Where they most breed and haunt, I have observed,
10 The air is delicate.[34]

(Enter LADY MACBETH.*)*

33. Note that almost all Duncan's lines may be read in an ominous, ironic sense.
martlet: martin, a bird of the swallow family.
approve: demonstrate.

34. *Lines 1-10:* Contrast these lines with Lady Macbeth's reference to the raven in Act One, Scene 5, 35b-37a.

DUNCAN. See, see, our honored hostess!
The love that follows us sometime is our trouble,
Which still we thank as love. Herein I teach you
How you shall bid God 'ild° us for your pains,
And thank us for your trouble.°

LADY MACBETH. All our service
15 In every point twice done and then done double[35]
Were poor and single business to contend
Against those honors deep and broad wherewith
Your Majesty loads our house; for those of old,
And the late dignities heaped up to them,
20 We rest your hermits.°

God 'ild: literally "God yield," used in returning thanks.
The love . . . your trouble: Duncan means that, since he is there because he loves them, they should thank him even for the trouble he causes them.
35. What sort of "double" does she have in mind?

We rest your hermits: Like hermits, we will pray for you.

DUNCAN. Where's the thane of Cawdor?
We coursed him at the heels, and had a purpose
To be his purveyor°; but he rides well,
And his great love, sharp as his spur, hath holp him
To his home before us. Fair and noble hostess,
25 We are your guests tonight.

purveyor: forerunner.

LADY MACBETH. Your servants ever
Have theirs, themselves, and what is theirs, in compt,
To make their audit at your Highness' pleasure,
Still to return your own.°

Your servants . . . own: Since we are your servants, all that we have is subject to account and ready to be delivered to you.

DUNCAN. Give me your hand;
Conduct me to mine host. We love him highly,
30 And shall continue our graces toward him.
By your leave, hostess.

(Exeunt.)

SCENE 7. *Outside a banqueting hall in* MACBETH'*s castle. (Played on the Platform.) Hautboys and torches. Enter a* SEWER°, *and divers* SERVANTS *with dishes and service, and pass over the stage. Then enter* MACBETH.

Sewer: servant who arranges the dining table. (Stage business: ". . . the comedy gang of the company make a brief appearance, one no doubt unpunctual, another caught tasting the dish he carries. They will form up for inspection by the Sewer, before marching into the banquet-hall [the Chamber]: noises of merriment from inside will become suddenly louder and more hilarious as they disappear, and will be hushed all at once as an unseen door bangs shut. Macbeth comes swiftly onto the empty Platform in the sudden silence."—Watkins)

MACBETH. If it were done when 'tis done, then 'twere well
It were done quickly; if the assassination
Could trammel up the consequence, and catch
With his surcease° success; that but this blow
5 Might be the be-all and the end-all here,
But here, upon this bank and shoal of time,
We 'ld jump° the life to come. But in these cases
We still have judgment here; that we but teach
Bloody instructions, which, being taught, return
10 To plague the inventor; this even-handed justice
Commends the ingredients of our poisoned chalice
To our own lips. He's here in double trust:
First, as I am his kinsman and his subject,
Strong both against the deed; then, as his host,
15 Who should against his murderer shut the door,
Not bear the knife myself.[36] Besides, this Duncan
Hath borne his faculties° so meek, hath been
So clear in his great office, that his virtues
Will plead like angels, trumpet-tongued, against
20 The deep damnation of his taking-off°,
And pity, like a naked, new-born babe,
Striding the blast,° or heaven's cherubim, horsed
Upon the sightless couriers of the air°,
Shall blow the horrid deed in every eye,
25 That tears shall drown the wind. I have no spur
To prick the sides of my intent, but only
Vaulting ambition, which o'erleaps itself
And falls on the other.°[37]

surcease: death.
jump: disregard.

36. Who does Macbeth think will be committing the murder?
faculties: royal power.

taking-off: departure from earth.

Striding the blast: riding the wind.
couriers of the air: winds.

I have . . . the other: I have nothing to stimulate me to the execution of my purpose but ambition, which is apt to overreach itself. ("Overreaching" is expressed here by the image of a person meaning to vault into his saddle who takes too great a leap and falls on the other side of his horse.)
37. In what specific ways does this soliloquy support Lady Macbeth's estimate of Macbeth?

(*Enter* LADY MACBETH.)

How now! what news?
LADY MACBETH. He has almost supped; why have you left the chamber?
30 MACBETH. Hath he asked for me?
LADY MACBETH. Know you not he has?
MACBETH. We will proceed no further in this business.
He hath honored me of late; and I have bought
Golden opinions from all sorts of people,
Which would be worn now in their newest gloss,
35 Not cast aside so soon.[38]
LADY MACBETH.[39] Was the hope drunk
Wherein you dressed yourself? Hath it slept since?
And wakes it now, to look so green and pale
At what it did so freely? From this time
Such I account thy love. Art thou afeard
40 To be the same in thine own act and valor
As thou art in desire? Wouldst thou have that

38. What does Macbeth give as his reason for not proceeding with the murder? Is this explanation in accord with what he said in his soliloquy (lines 1-28)? If not, why does he offer a different reason to his wife?
39. Trace through the arguments by which she works to convince her husband to go through with the murder. Is this a plausible scene? Why or why not?

Which thou esteem'st the ornament of life°,
And live a coward in thine own esteem,
Letting "I dare not" wait upon "I would,"
45 Like the poor cat i' the adage?°

ornament of life: the crown.

cat . . . adage: The adage is "The cat would eat fish, but would not wet her feet."

MACBETH. Prithee, peace.
I dare do all that may become a man;
Who dares do more is none.[40]

LADY MACBETH. What beast was't, then,
That made you break this enterprise to me?[41]
When you durst do it, then you were a man;
50 And, to be more than what you were, you would
Be so much more the man. Nor time nor place
Did then adhere,° and yet you would make both;
They have made themselves, and that their fitness now
Does unmake you. I have given suck, and know
55 How tender 'tis to love the babe that milks me;

40. How does Macbeth say this: pleadingly? mildly? defensively? angrily?
41. Did he explicitly "break it" to her, or did he merely suggest it?

Nor time . . . adhere: There was no suitable time or place to commit the murder.

I would, while it was smiling in my face,
Have plucked my nipple from his boneless gums,
And dashed the brains out,[42] had I so sworn as you
Have done to this.

MACBETH. If we should fail?

LADY MACBETH. We fail![43]

60 But screw your courage to the sticking-place,°
And we'll not fail.[44] When Duncan is asleep—
Whereto the rather shall this day's hard journey
Soundly invite him—his two chamberlains
Will I with wine and wassail so convince
65 That memory, the warder of the brain,
Shall be a fume, and the receipt of reason
A limbeck only.° When in swinish sleep
Their drenchèd natures lie as in a death,
What cannot you and I perform upon
70 The unguarded Duncan?[45] What not put upon
His spongy° officers, who shall bear the guilt
Of our great quell?°

MACBETH. Bring forth men-children only·
For thy undaunted mettle should compose
Nothing but males. Will it not be received,
75 When we have marked with blood those sleepy two
Of his own chamber and used their very daggers,
That they have done 't?

LADY MACBETH. Who dares receive it other,
As we shall make our griefs and clamor roar
Upon his death?

MACBETH. I am settled, and bend up
80 Each corporal agent to this terrible feat.°
Away, and mock the time with fairest show;
False face must hide what the false heart doth know.[46]

(Exeunt.)

42. *Lines 54-59a:* To what earlier speech by Lady Macbeth do these lines bear a resemblance?

43. Editors of *Macbeth* have punctuated this line variously as either "We fail!" or "We fail?" How would the change in punctuation affect the meaning?

But screw . . . place: The image is drawn from the mechanical device used to prepare a crossbow for firing.

44. Lady Macbeth has been angry. How does her tone change here? Why?

memory . . . only: memory and reason both will dissipate, like the vapor of the alcohol they drink. This complicated image compares the human brain to the apparatus used in distilling alcohol.

45. Who does Lady Macbeth now say will commit the murder?

spongy: drunken.

quell: murder.

bend up . . . feat: direct all my bodily powers to executing the murder.

46. Macbeth has made up his mind to commit the murder. Has he convinced himself that what he is about to do is morally justified?

Act Two

SCENE 1. *Court of* MACBETH*'s castle. (Played on the Platform.) Enter* BANQUO, *and* FLEANCE *bearing a torch before him.*

BANQUO. How goes the night, boy?

FLEANCE. The moon is down; I have not heard the clock.

BANQUO. And she goes down at twelve.

FLEANCE. I take 't, 'tis later, sir.

BANQUO. Hold, take my sword. There's husbandry° in heaven;
5 Their candles are all out. Take thee that,[47] too.
A heavy summons lies like lead upon me,

husbandry: economy.

47. What might "that" be?

And yet I would not sleep; merciful powers,
Restrain in me the cursèd thoughts that nature
Gives way to in repose![48]

(Enter MACBETH, *and a* SERVANT *with a torch.)*

Give me my sword.

10 Who's there?

MACBETH. A friend.

BANQUO. What, sir, not yet at rest? The King's abed.
He hath been in unusual pleasure, and
Sent forth great largess to your offices.°
15 This diamond he greets your wife withal,[49]
By the name of most kind hostess; and shut up
In measureless content.°

MACBETH. Being unprepared,
Our will became the servant to defect,
Which else should free have wrought.°

BANQUO. All's well.
20 I dreamt last night of the three weird sisters;
To you they have showed some truth.

MACBETH. I think not of them;
Yet, when we can entreat an hour to serve,
We would spend it in some words upon that business,
If you would grant the time.

BANQUO. At your kind'st leisure.

25 MACBETH. If you shall cleave to my consent, when 'tis,°
It shall make honor for you.

BANQUO. So I lose none
In seeking to augment it, but still keep
My bosom franchised and allegiance clear,
I shall be counseled.°[50]

MACBETH. Good repose the while!

30 BANQUO. Thanks, sir. The like to you!

(Exeunt BANQUO *and* FLEANCE.*)*

MACBETH. Go bid thy mistress, when my drink is ready,
She strike upon the bell. Get thee to bed.

(Exit SERVANT.*)*

Is this a dagger which I see before me,
The handle toward my hand? Come, let me clutch thee.
35 I have thee not, and yet I see thee still.
Art thou not, fatal vision, sensible
To feeling as to sight? Or art thou but
A dagger of the mind, a false creation,
Proceeding from the heat-oppressèd brain?[51]
40 I see thee yet, in form as palpable
As this which now I draw.
Thou marshal'st me° the way that I was going,
And such an instrument I was to use.
Mine eyes are made the fools o' the other senses,
45 Or else worth all the rest; I see thee still,
And on thy blade and dudgeon° gouts of blood,

48. What is bothering Banquo? What might his "cursed thoughts" be?

great largess . . . offices: many gifts of money to be distributed among your servants.

49. Why does Shakespeare have Banquo instead of Duncan give the diamond?

shut up . . . content: has ended his day greatly contented.

Being unprepared . . . wrought: The unexpectedness of Duncan's visit has prevented us from entertaining him as we would have liked.

If you . . . when 'tis: If you ally yourself with me, when the time comes.

So I . . . counseled: As long as I do not lose my honor in trying to increase it, and keep myself free and my loyalty to Duncan unstained, I will listen to you.

50. *Lines 26-29:* Why might Banquo be suspicious at this point? What do these lines tell you about his character?

51. (a) If you were directing a stage production of *Macbeth,* would you have the dagger physically appear before Macbeth, or would you have him address the empty air?

(b) What does the imaginary dagger reveal about Macbeth's character in general, and his feelings about the murder specifically?

thou marshal'st me: you conduct, lead me.

dudgeon: hilt.

Which was not so before. There's no such thing;
It is the bloody business which informs°
Thus to mine eyes. Now o'er the one half world
50 Nature seems dead, and wicked dreams abuse
The curtained sleep; witchcraft celebrates
Pale Hecate's° offerings, and withered murder,
Alarumed by his sentinel, the wolf,
Whose howl's his watch, thus with his stealthy pace,
55 With Tarquin's° ravishing strides, toward his design
Moves like a ghost. Thou sure and firm-set earth,
Hear not my steps, which way they walk, for fear
Thy very stones prate of my whereabout,
And take the present horror from the time,
60 Which now suits with it. Whiles I threat, he lives;
Words to the heat of deeds too cold breath gives.

(A bell rings.)

I go, and it is done; the bell invites me.
Hear it not, Duncan; for it is a knell
That summons thee to heaven or to hell.

(Exit.)°

informs: appears.

Hecate: goddess of witchcraft.

Tarquin: one of the tyrannical kings of early Rome, who ravished the chaste Lucrece.

(Macbeth exits through the Study, which presumably leads to Duncan's chamber.)

SCENE 2. *The same. (Played in the Study and on the Platform.) Enter* LADY MACBETH.°

LADY MACBETH. That which hath made them drunk hath made me bold;
What hath quenched them hath given me fire. Hark! Peace!
It was the owl that shrieked, the fatal bellman°,
Which gives the stern'st good-night. He is about it.
5 The doors are open; and the surfeited grooms
Do mock their charge with snores. I have drugged their possets°,
That death and nature do contend about them,
Whether they live or die.

MACBETH *(within)*. Who's there? What, ho!°

10 LADY MACBETH. Alack, I am afraid they have awaked,
And 'tis not done. The attempt and not the deed
Confounds us. Hark! I laid their daggers ready;
He could not miss 'em. Had he not resembled
My father as he slept, I had done 't.[52]

(Enter MACBETH.*)*°

My husband!

15 MACBETH. I have done the deed. Didst thou not hear a noise?

LADY MACBETH. I heard the owl scream and the crickets cry.
Did not you speak?

MACBETH. When?

LADY MACBETH. Now.

MACBETH. As I descended?

LADY MACBETH. Aye.

MACBETH. Hark!
20 Who lies i' the second chamber?

(Lady Macbeth enters in the Study. Through the center door might be seen the beginning of a flight of stairs leading to Duncan's apartment.)

owl . . . bellman: The screech of an owl was often interpreted as an omen of death. In Elizabethan times, the bellman or town-crier announced to condemned prisoners the time of their execution.

possets: drinks made of hot milk curdled with wine or ale.

(Macbeth may momentarily appear on the Tarras as he speaks this line.)

52. Is Lady Macbeth's weakness here expected? How do you account for it? What might be her tone here: frightened? irritated? angry? shaken?

(Macbeth descends the stairs into the Study.)

LADY MACBETH. Donalbain.
MACBETH *(Looking on his hands).* This is a sorry sight.
LADY MACBETH. A foolish thought, to say a sorry sight.
MACBETH. There's one did laugh in 's sleep, and one cried, "Murder!"[53]
That they did wake each other; I stood and heard them;
25 But they did say their prayers, and addressed them
Again to sleep.
LADY MACBETH. There are two° lodged together.
MACBETH. One cried, "God bless us!" and "Amen" the other,
As they had seen me with these hangman's hands.
Listening their fear, I could not say, "Amen,"
30 When they did say, "God bless us!"
LADY MACBETH. Consider it not so deeply.
MACBETH. But wherefore could not I pronounce "Amen"?
I had most need of blessing, and "Amen"
Stuck in my throat.
LADY MACBETH. These deeds must not be thought
After these ways; so, it will make us mad.
35 MACBETH. Methought I heard a voice cry, "Sleep no more!
Macbeth does murder sleep," the innocent sleep,
Sleep that knits up the raveled sleave° of care,
The death of each day's life, sore labor's bath,
Balm of hurt minds, great nature's second course,
40 Chief nourisher in life's feast—
LADY MACBETH. What do you mean?
MACBETH. Still it cried, "Sleep no more!" to all the house;
"Glamis hath murdered sleep, and therefore Cawdor
Shall sleep no more; Macbeth shall sleep no more."
LADY MACBETH. Who was it that thus cried? Why, worthy thane,
45 You do unbend your noble strength, to think
So brainsickly of things.[54] Go get some water,
And wash this filthy witness from your hand.
Why did you bring these daggers from the place?
They must lie there. Go carry them, and smear
50 The sleepy grooms with blood.
MACBETH. I'll go no more;
I am afraid to think what I have done;
Look on 't again I dare not.
LADY MACBETH. Infirm of purpose!
Give me the daggers. The sleeping and the dead
Are but as pictures; 'tis the eye of childhood
55 That fears a painted devil. If he do bleed,
I'll gild the faces of the grooms withal.
For it must seem their guilt.°[55]
(Exit. Knocking within.)
MACBETH. Whence is that knocking?
How is 't with me, when every noise appals me?
What hands are here? Ha! they pluck out mine eyes.
60 Will all great Neptune's ocean wash this blood
Clean from my hand? No, this my hand will rather

53. Is Macbeth responding to Lady Macbeth here? Where should the actor's attention be directed as he speaks? Think about this as the scene continues.

two: Malcolm and Donalbain.

raveled sleave: tangled thread.

54. At what point does Macbeth again become aware of Lady Macbeth?

I'll gild . . . guilt: a pun on the words *gild* and *guilt*. The pun would have been more obvious to an Elizabethan audience, for *gold* was often used synonymously with *red*.

55. *Lines 15-57:* What is Macbeth's state of mind after the murder? Lady Macbeth's? What mistake has Macbeth made? What is illogical about Lady Macbeth's proposed method of remedying it? How do you account for her failure to think straight?

The multitudinous seas incarnadine°,
Making the green one red.°

(*Reënter* LADY MACBETH.)

LADY MACBETH. My hands are of your color; but I shame
65 To wear a heart so white. (*Knocking within.*) I hear a knocking
At the south entry; retire we to our chamber;
A little water clears us of this deed.
How easy is it, then![56] Your constancy
Hath left you unattended.° (*Knocking within.*) Hark! more
knocking.
70 Get on your nightgown°, lest occasion call us,
And show us to be watchers°. Be not lost
So poorly in your thoughts.[57]

MACBETH. To know my deed, 'twere best not know myself.°

(*Knocking within.*)

Wake Duncan with thy knocking! I would thou couldst!

(*Exeunt.*)[58]

incarnadine: redden.

Making . . . red: making the green sea red.

56. *Lines 64-68a:* Both now have blood on their hands. Do you agree that "a little water" can "clear them" of the murder? In what sense might it? In what sense not? Contrast Lady Macbeth's words with Macbeth's in lines 60-63.
Your constancy . . . unattended: Your composure has left you.
nightgown: dressing gown.
watchers: awake.
57. How has Macbeth been reacting? In what manner does Lady Macbeth say "Be not lost . . ."?
To know . . . myself: It is better to be lost in my thoughts than to be aware of what I have done.
58. At what pace should this scene be played? What clues in the dialogue tell you?

SCENE 3. *The same. (Played in the Study and on the Platform.) Knocking within. Enter a* PORTER.

PORTER. Here's a knocking indeed! If a man were porter of hell-gate, he should have old° turning the key. (*Knocking within.*) Knock, knock, knock! Who's there, i' the name of Beelzebub°? Here's a farmer, that hanged himself on the expectation of plenty.° Come in 5 time; have napkins enow° about you; here you'll sweat for 't. (*Knocking within.*) Knock, knock! Who's there, in the other devil's name? Faith, here's an equivocator[59] that could swear in both the scales against either scale; who committed treason enough for God's sake, yet could not equivocate to heaven. O come in, equi- 10 vocator. (*Knocking within.*) Knock, knock, knock! Who's there? Faith, here's an English tailor come hither for stealing out of a French hose.° Come in, tailor; here you may roast your goose°. (*Knocking within.*) Knock, knock; never at quiet! What are you? But this place is too cold for hell. I'll devil-porter it no further. I had 15 thought to have let in some of all professions that go the primrose way to the everlasting bonfire.° (*Knocking within.*) Anon, anon! I pray you, remember the porter.

(*Opens the gate.*)

(*Enter* MACDUFF *and* LENNOX.)

MACDUFF. Was it so late, friend, ere you went to bed,
That you do lie so late?

20 PORTER. 'Faith, sir, we were carousing till the second cock°: and drink, sir, is a great provoker of three things.

MACDUFF. What three things does drink especially provoke?

PORTER. Marry, sir, nose-painting, sleep, and urine. Lechery, sir, it provokes, and unprovokes; it provokes the desire, but it takes away 25 the performance: therefore, much drink may be said to be an equivocator with lechery: it makes him, and it mars him; it sets him on,

old: dialect for "plenty of."
Beelzebub: the Devil.
expectation of plenty: because he expected large crops and therefore low prices.
napkins enow: enough handkerchiefs to wipe off the sweat caused by the heat of Hell.
59. This is usually taken as an allusion to the trial of the Jesuit Henry Garnet for treason in the spring of 1606, and to the doctrine of equivocation used in his defense: that a lie was not a lie if the speaker had in mind a different meaning which made the statement true. Watch for examples of equivocation which follow.
stealing . . . hose: Tailors were often accused of stealing cloth. Since French hose (breeches) at this period were short and tight, it would take a clever tailor to cut them smaller and steal the excess cloth.
goose: a pressing iron used by a tailor. There may also be a play on the expression "cook your goose."
primrose . . . bonfire: path of pleasure leading to everlasting damnation in Hell.

second cock: about three o'clock in the morning.

and it takes him off; it persuades him, and disheartens him; makes him stand to, and not stand to; in conclusion, equivocates him in a sleep, and, giving him the lie, leaves him.

30 MACDUFF. I believe drink gave thee the lie last night.

PORTER. That it did, sir, i' the very throat on me; but I requited him for his lie; and, I think, being too strong for him, though he took up my legs sometime, yet I made a shift to cast him.[60]

MACDUFF. Is thy master stirring?

(Enter MACBETH.*)*

35 Our knocking has awakened him; here he comes.

LENNOX. Good-morrow, noble sir.

MACBETH. Good-morrow, both.

MACDUFF. Is the King stirring, worthy thane?

MACBETH. Not yet.

MACDUFF. He did command me to call timely° on him;
I have almost slipped the hour.

MACBETH. I'll bring you to him.

40 MACDUFF. I know this is a joyful trouble to you;
But yet 'tis one.

MACBETH. The labor we delight in physics° pain.
This is the door.

MACDUFF. I'll make so bold to call,
For 'tis my limited° service. *(Exit.)*

45 LENNOX. Goes the King hence today?

MACBETH. He does; he did appoint so.

LENNOX. The night has been unruly; where we lay,
Our chimneys were blown down; and, as they say,
Lamentings heard i' the air; strange screams of death,
And prophesying with accents terrible
50 Of dire combustion and confused events
New hatched to the woeful time; the obscure bird°
Clamored the livelong night. Some say the earth
Was feverous and did shake.

MACBETH. 'Twas a rough night.[61]

LENNOX. My young remembrance cannot parallel
55 A fellow to it.

(Reënter MACDUFF.*)*

MACDUFF. O horror, horror, horror! Tongue nor heart
Cannot conceive nor name thee![62]

MACBETH, LENNOX. What's the matter?

MACDUFF. Confusion now hath made his masterpiece!
Most sacrilegious murder hath broke ope
60 The Lord's anointed temple°, and stole thence
The life o' the building!

MACBETH. What is 't you say? The life?[63]

LENNOX. Mean you his Majesty?

MACDUFF. Approach the chamber, and destroy your sight
With a new Gorgon°. Do not bid me speak;
65 See, and then speak yourselves.

(Exeunt MACBETH *and* LENNOX.*)*

60. Many of the expressions in this passage refer to wrestling. "Gave thee the lie" means "floored you and put you to sleep." "Took up my leg" means "got my feet off the ground." "Cast" is a pun meaning both "throw down" and "vomit."
What is the dramatic effect of having this comical scene follow immediately after the encounter between Macbeth and Lady Macbeth after the murder?

timely: early.

physics: cures.

limited: appointed.

obscure bird: the owl.

61. How would Macbeth say this?

62. Is Macduff's response a plausible one?

Lord's . . . temple: an allusion to the idea that the king is God's representative. The metaphorical temple is the king's body.

63. Is Macbeth's response a plausible one?

Gorgon: a horrible monster of Greek legend. Whoever looked at her was turned to stone.

Awake, awake!
Ring the alarum-bell. Murder and treason!
Banquo and Donalbain! Malcolm! awake!
Shake off this downy sleep, death's counterfeit,
And look on death itself! Up, up, and see
70 The great doom's image!° Malcolm! Banquo!
As from your graves rise up, and walk like sprites,
To countenance this horror! Ring the bell.

(Bell rings.)

(Enter LADY MACBETH.*)*

LADY MACBETH. What's the business,
That such a hideous trumpet calls to parley
75 The sleepers of the house? Speak, speak!

MACDUFF. O gentle lady,
'Tis not for you to hear what I can speak;
The repetition, in a woman's ear,
Would murder as it fell.

(Enter BANQUO.*)*

O Banquo, Banquo,
Our royal master's murdered!

LADY MACBETH. Woe, alas!
80 What, in our house?[64]

BANQUO. Too cruel anywhere.
Dear Duff, I prithee, contradict thyself,
And say it is not so.[65]

(Reënter MACBETH *and* LENNOX, *with* ROSS.*)*

MACBETH. Had I but died an hour before this chance,
I had lived a blessed time; for, from this instant,
85 There's nothing serious in mortality°;
All is but toys; renown and grace is dead;
The wine of life is drawn, and the mere lees
Is left this vault° to brag of.[66]

(Enter MALCOLM *and* DONALBAIN.*)*

DONALBAIN. What is amiss?

MACBETH. You are, and do not know 't.
90 The spring, the head, the fountain of your blood
Is stopped; the very source of it is stopped.

MACDUFF. Your royal father's murdered.

MALCOLM. Oh, by whom?[67]

LENNOX. Those of his chamber, as it seemed, had done 't;
Their hands and faces were all badged° with blood;
95 So were their daggers, which unwiped we found
Upon their pillows.
They stared, and were distracted; no man's life
Was to be trusted with them.

MACBETH. Oh, yet I do repent me of my fury,
100 That I did kill them.[68]

MACDUFF. Wherefore did you so?

MACBETH. Who can be wise, amazed, temperate and furious,

great doom's image: a sight as awful as Judgment Day.

64. Is Lady Macbeth's response what you would expect? How do you account for it?

65. Is Banquo surprised at what has happened? What does he think of Lady Macbeth's response?

mortality: human life.

this vault: the universe.

66. How many meanings can you read into this speech? Consider what it might mean to the assembled lords, to Macbeth himself, and to the reader.

67. How might Malcolm say this?

badged: marked; splotched.

68. How should the actor playing Macduff react to this announcement? the actor playing Banquo?

Loyal and neutral, in a moment? No man.
The expedition° of my violent love
Outrun the pauser, reason. Here lay Duncan,
105 His silver skin laced with his golden blood;
And his gashed stabs looked like a breach in nature
For ruin's wasteful entrance; there, the murderers,
Steeped in the colors of their trade, their daggers
Unmannerly breeched with gore. Who could refrain,
110 That had a heart to love, and in that heart
Courage to make 's love known?

LADY MACBETH. Help me hence, ho![69]

MACDUFF. Look to the lady.

MALCOLM (*aside to* DONALBAIN). Why do we hold our tongues,
That most may claim this argument for ours?°

DONALBAIN (*aside to* MALCOLM). What should be spoken here, where our fate,
115 Hid in an auger-hole°, may rush, and seize us?
Let's away;
Our tears are not yet brewed.

MALCOLM (*aside to* DONALBAIN). Nor our strong sorrow
Upon the foot of motion.

BANQUO. Look to the lady;

(LADY MACBETH *is carried out.*)

And when we have our naked frailties hid,°
120 That suffer in exposure, let us meet,
And question this most bloody piece of work,
To know it further. Fears and scruples° shake us;
In the great hand of God I stand, and thence
Against the undivulged pretense I fight
125 Of treasonous malice.°

MACDUFF. And so do I.

ALL. So all.

MACBETH. Let's briefly put on manly readiness,°
And meet i' the hall together.

ALL. Well contented.

(*Exeunt all but* MALCOLM *and* DONALBAIN.)

MALCOLM. What will you do? Let's not consort with them.
To show an unfelt sorrow is an office
130 Which the false man does easy.[71] I'll to England.

DONALBAIN. To Ireland, I; our separated fortune
Shall keep us both the safer; where we are,
There's daggers in men's smiles; the near in blood,
The nearer bloody.°

MALCOLM. This murderous shaft that's shot
135 Hath not yet lighted, and our safest way
Is to avoid the aim. Therefore, to horse;
And let us not be dainty of° leave-taking,
But shift away; there's warrant in that theft
Which steals itself, when there's no mercy left.°

(*Exeunt.*)[72]

---

expedition: haste.

(". . . a fine wild scene with the thanes in dishabille; the servants half naked. The fainting lady is one focal point upstage and surrounded by Thanes and servants, so as not to distract from the whispered conversation of Malcolm and Donalbain, right forward at the center of the octagon; Macbeth no doubt prominent on the perimeter, outside one of the Stage-Posts, with a grim eye of menace on the two princes. . . ."—Watkins)

69. Some commentators maintain that Lady Macbeth really faints; others claim she only pretends to. Which theory seems more likely? Justify your answer in terms of what you know about Macbeth and Lady Macbeth, and the dialogue immediately preceding.

That most . . . ours: who are most concerned.

auger-hole: obscure hiding place.

when . . . hid: gotten dressed.

scruples: doubts.

Against . . . malice: I will fight against the unknown purpose which prompted this act of treason.

70. Why did Shakespeare give this speech to Banquo rather than to Macduff?

put . . . readiness: get dressed.

71. How does Malcolm's speech relate to "Foul is fair"?

the near . . . bloody: the closer the kinship to Duncan, the greater the chance of being murdered.

dainty of: ceremonious about.

there's warrant . . . left: we are justified in stealing away in these merciless times.

72. What initially makes Malcolm and Donalbain suspicious? (Macbeth's windy remarks? what Banquo and Macduff have just said? or what?)

SCENE 4. *Outside* MACBETH'S *castle. (Played on the Platform.) Enter* ROSS *and an* OLD MAN.

OLD MAN. Threescore and ten I can remember well;
Within the volume of which time I have seen
Hours dreadful and things strange; but this sore night
Hath trifled° former knowings.

trifled: made trivial.

ROSS. Ah, good father,
5 Thou seest, the heavens, as troubled with man's act,
Threaten his bloody stage; by the clock, 'tis day,
And yet dark night strangles the traveling lamp°.
Is 't night's predominance, or the day's shame,
That darkness does the face of earth entomb,
10 When living light should kiss it?

traveling lamp: the sun.

OLD MAN. 'Tis unnatural,[73]
Even like the deed that's done. On Tuesday last
A falcon, towering in her pride of place,
Was by a mousing owl hawked at and killed.[74]

ROSS. And Duncan's horses—a thing most strange and certain—
15 Beauteous and swift, the minions of their race,
Turned wild in nature—broke their stalls, flung out,
Contending 'gainst obedience, as they would make
War with mankind.

73. The Elizabethans saw nature as existing in a strictly ordered state. Ross and the Old Man describe events which indicate that the order in nature is awry. Be alert for further indications of unnatural workings in the universe. What might they reflect?
74. What is the symbolic meaning of the falcon-owl incident? Watch for specific symbolic significance in other unnatural acts mentioned.

OLD MAN. 'Tis said they eat each other.

ROSS. They did so, to the amazement of mine eyes,
20 That looked upon it.

(Enter MACDUFF.*)*

Here comes the good Macduff.
How goes the world, sir, now?

MACDUFF. Why, see you not?

ROSS. Is 't known who did this more than bloody deed?

MACDUFF. Those that Macbeth hath slain.

ROSS. Alas, the day!
What good could they pretend?°

MACDUFF. They were suborned.°
25 Malcolm and Donalbain, the King's two sons,
Are stol'n away and fled; which puts upon them
Suspicion of the deed.

What . . . pretend: What profit could they have aimed at?
suborned: hired or bribed.

ROSS. 'Gainst nature still!
Thriftless ambition, that will ravin up°
Thine own life's means°! Then 'tis most like
30 The sovereignty will fall upon Macbeth.

ravin up: devour.
own life's means: parent.

MACDUFF. He is already named, and gone to Scone°
To be invested.

Scone: ancient residence of Scottish kings.

ROSS. Where is Duncan's body?

MACDUFF. Carried to Colmekill°,
The sacred storehouse of his predecessors,
35 And guardian of their bones.

Colmekill (kōm′ kil): Iona Island.

ROSS. Will you to Scone?

MACDUFF. No, cousin, I'll to Fife.

ROSS. Well, I will thither.
MACDUFF. Well, may you see things well done there; adieu!
Lest our old robes sit easier than our new![75]
ROSS. Farewell, father.
40 OLD MAN. God's benison° go with you; and with those
That would make good of bad, and friends of foes!

(Exeunt.)[76]

75. Why might Macduff be suspicious of Macbeth?

benison: blessing.

76. What is the dramatic purpose of this scene?

Act Three

SCENE 1. *Forres. The palace. (Played on the Platform and in the Study.)*
Enter BANQUO.

BANQUO. Thou hast it now—king, Cawdor, Glamis, all—[77]
As the weird women promised; and, I fear,
Thou play'dst most foully for 't. Yet it was said
It should not stand in thy posterity,
5 But that myself should be the root and father
Of many kings. If there come truth from them—
As upon thee, Macbeth, their speeches shine—
Why, by the verities on thee made good,
May they not be my oracles as well,
10 And set me up in hope? But hush! no more.[78]

(Sennet° sounded. Enter MACBETH, *as king,* LADY MACBETH, *as queen,* LENNOX, ROSS, LORDS, LADIES, *and* ATTENDANTS.*)*

MACBETH. Here's our chief guest.
LADY MACBETH. If he had been forgotten,
It had been as a gap in our great feast,
And all-thing unbecoming.
MACBETH. Tonight we hold a solemn supper, sir,
15 And I'll request your presence.
BANQUO. Let your Highness
Command upon me; to the which my duties
Are with a most indissoluble tie
Forever knit.[79]
MACBETH. Ride you this afternoon?
20 BANQUO. Aye, my good lord.
MACBETH. We should have else desired your good advice,
Which still hath been both grave and prosperous,°
In this day's council; but we'll take tomorrow.
Is 't far you ride?[80]
25 BANQUO. As far, my lord, as will fill up the time
'Twixt this and supper. Go not my horse the better,
I must become a borrower of the night
For a dark hour or twain.
MACBETH. Fail not our feast.
BANQUO. My lord, I will not.

77. How much time has passed by now?

78. Banquo alone of the lords knows about the witches' prophecies, but he has said nothing about them. Why hasn't he? Does he have any plans for immediate action?

Sennet: musical piece played by cornets, generally used to grace a formal procession. It indicates here that Macbeth has achieved the object of his ambition.

79. In what tone does Banquo speak?

Which . . . prosperous: which always has been thoughtful and fruitful.

80. Why does Macbeth ask this question (and later ones) about Banquo's plans?

30 MACBETH. We hear our bloody cousins are bestowed
In England and in Ireland, not confessing
Their cruel parricide, filling their hearers
With strange invention;[81] but of that tomorrow,
When therewithal we shall have cause of state
35 Craving us jointly.° Hie you to horse; adieu,
Till you return at night. Goes Fleance with you?[82]
BANQUO. Aye, my good lord; our time does call upon 's.
MACBETH. I wish your horses swift and sure of foot;
And so I do commend you to their backs.
40 Farewell. *(Exit* BANQUO.*)*
Let every man be master of his time
Till seven at night. To make society
The sweeter welcome, we will keep ourself
Till supper-time alone; while then, God be with you.
(Exeunt all but MACBETH *and an* ATTENDANT.*)*

81. How should the actor playing Banquo react when Macbeth tells him about Malcolm and Donalbain?
cause . . . jointly: affairs of state demanding the attention of both of us.
82. In what tone of voice does Macbeth ask this question?

45 Sirrah, a word with you; attend those men
Our pleasure?

ATTENDANT. They are, my lord, without the palace gate.

MACBETH. Bring them before us.

(Exit ATTENDANT.*)*

To be thus is nothing,
But to be safely thus.—Our fears in Banquo
50 Stick deep; and in his royalty of nature
Reigns that which would be feared. 'Tis much he dares;
And, to that dauntless temper of his mind,
He hath a wisdom that doth guide his valor
To act in safety. There is none but he
55 Whose being I do fear; and, under him,
My Genius is rebuked; as, it is said,
Mark Antony's was by Caesar.° He chid the sisters
When first they put the name of king upon me,
And bade them speak to him; then prophetlike
60 They hailed him father to a line of kings.
Upon my head they placed a fruitless crown,
And put a barren scepter in my gripe,
Thence to be wrenched with an unlineal hand,[83]
No son of mine succeeding. If 't be so,
65 For Banquo's issue have I filed° my mind;
For them the gracious Duncan have I murdered;
Put rancors in the vessel of my peace
Only for them; and mine eternal jewel
Given to the common enemy of man,°
70 To make them kings, the seed of Banquo kings!
Rather than so, come fate into the list°,
And champion me to the utterance!°[84] Who's there?

(Reënter ATTENDANT, *with two* MURDERERS.*)*

Now go to the door, and stay there till we call.

(Exit ATTENDANT.*)*

Was it not yesterday we spoke together?

75 FIRST MURDERER. It was, so please your Highness.

MACBETH. Well, then, now
Have you considered of my speeches? Know
That it was he in the times past which held you
So under fortune,° which you thought had been
Our innocent self; this I made good to you
80 In our last conference, passed in probation° with you,
How you were borne in hand°, how crossed, the instruments,
Who wrought with them, and all things else that might
To half a soul and to a notion crazed°
Say, "Thus did Banquo."

FIRST MURDERER. You made it known to us.

85 MACBETH. I did so, and went further, which is now
Our point of second meeting. Do you find
Your patience so predominant in your nature
That you can let this go? Are you so gospeled°

("There can be no better background for this soliloquy than the royal 'state' on which Macbeth sits in his King's robes, wearing his fruitless crown, and grasping his barren sceptre. The setting is more properly one of circumstance than of locality."—Watkins)

There is none . . . Caesar: Macbeth's insatiable ambition is silently rebuked by Banquo's innate loyalty. Mark Antony feared Octavius Caesar as a political, not personal, enemy, and this is how Macbeth regards Banquo.

83. *Wrenched* has connotations of violence. How has Macbeth interpreted Banquo's loyalty and his silence about the witches' prophecies? What does he fear Banquo may do?
filed: defiled.

mine eternal . . . man: given my soul to the Devil.
list: battlefield.
champion . . . utterance: fight me to the death.

84. *Lines 47-72:* How does this soliloquy compare with the earlier one (Act One, Scene 7, 1-28) in which he contemplated the murder of Duncan?

Know . . . fortune: It is usually assumed that the First and Second Murderers are former retainers of Banquo's.
passed in probation: gave detailed proof.
borne in hand: deceived.

notion crazed: half-wit.

gospeled: religious.

To pray for this good man and for his issue
90 Whose heavy hand hath bowed you to the grave
And beggared yours forever?

FIRST MURDERER. We are men, my liege.

MACBETH. Aye, in the catalogue ye go for men;
As hounds and greyhounds, mongrels, spaniels, curs,
Shoughs, water-rugs, and demi-wolves are clept°
95 All by the name of dogs. The valued file°
Distinguishes the swift, the slow, the subtle,
The housekeeper, the hunter, every one
According to the gift which bounteous nature
Hath in him closed, whereby he does receive
100 Particular addition, from the bill
That writes them all alike;° and so of men.
Now if you have a station in the file,
Not i' the worst rank of manhood, say 't;
And I will put that business in your bosoms
105 Whose execution takes your enemy off,
Grapples you to the heart and love of us,
Who wear our health but sickly in his life,
Which in his death were perfect.

SECOND MURDERER. I am one, my liege,
Whom the vile blows and buffets of the world
110 Have so incensed that I am reckless what
I do to spite the world.

FIRST MURDERER. And I another
So weary with disasters, tugged with° fortune,
That I would set my life on any chance,
To mend it, or be rid on 't.

MACBETH. Both of you
115 Know Banquo was your enemy.

BOTH MURDERERS. True, my lord.

MACBETH. So is he mine; and in such bloody distance°
That every minute of his being thrusts
Against my near'st of life;° and though I could
With barefaced power sweep him from my sight
120 And bid my will avouch it,° yet I must not,
For certain friends that are both his and mine,
Whose loves I may not drop, but wail his fall°
Who I myself struck down; and thence it is
That I to your assistance do make love,
125 Masking the business from the common eye
For sundry weighty reasons.

SECOND MURDERER. We shall, my lord,
Perform what you command us.

FIRST MURDERER. Though our lives—

MACBETH. Your spirits shine through you. Within this hour at most
I will advise you where to plant yourselves;
130 Acquaint you with the perfect spy o' the time,°
The moment on 't; for 't must be done tonight,

Shoughs . . . clept: shaggy dogs, water dogs, and half-wolves are called.

valued file: list according to worth.

Particular . . . alike: specific qualifications along with the general attributes.

tugged with: pulled about by.

such bloody distance: with such hostility.

thrusts . . . life: threatens my very existence.

bid . . . avouch it: justify it as an act of royal will.

but . . . fall: I must pretend to lament his death.

Acquaint . . . time: Critics still puzzle over the exact meaning of this passage. A plausible interpretation is that Macbeth will give them the most accurate report available as to the time when they should begin watching for Banquo.

And something from the palace; always thought
That I require a clearness°. And with him—
To leave no rubs nor botches in the work—
135 Fleance his son, that keeps him company,
Whose absence is no less material to me
Than is his father's, must embrace the fate
Of that dark hour. Resolve yourselves° apart;
I'll come to you anon.

clearness: freedom from suspicion.

Resolve yourselves: make up your minds.

BOTH MURDERERS. We are resolved, my lord.
140 MACBETH. I'll call upon you straight; abide within.

(Exeunt MURDERERS.*)*

It is concluded. Banquo, thy soul's flight,
If it find heaven, must find it out tonight.

(Exit.)

SCENE 2. *The palace. (Played in the Chamber.) Enter* LADY MACBETH *and a* SERVANT.

LADY MACBETH. Is Banquo gone from court?
SERVANT. Aye, madam, but returns again tonight.
LADY MACBETH. Say to the King I would attend his leisure
For a few words.
SERVANT. Madam, I will. *(Exit.)*
LADY MACBETH. Naught's had, all's spent,
5 Where our desire is got without content.
'Tis safer to be that which we destroy
Than by destruction dwell in doubtful joy.[85]

85. In what way has Lady Macbeth changed?

(Enter MACBETH.*)*

How now, my lord! why do you keep alone,
Of sorriest fancies your companions making,
10 Using those thoughts which should indeed have died
With them they think on? Things without all remedy
Should be without regard; what's done is done.
MACBETH. We have scotched° the snake, not killed it;
She'll close and be herself, whilst our poor malice
15 Remains in danger of her former tooth.
But let the frame of things° disjoint, both the worlds suffer,°
Ere we will eat our meal in fear, and sleep
In the affliction of these terrible dreams
That shake us nightly; better be with the dead,
20 Whom we, to gain our peace, have sent to peace,
Than on the torture of the mind to lie
In restless ecstasy°. Duncan is in his grave;
After life's fitful fever he sleeps well.
Treason has done his worst; nor steel, nor poison,
25 Malice domestic,° foreign levy°, nothing,
Can touch him further.[86]
LADY MACBETH. Come on,
Gentle my lord, sleek o'er your rugged looks;

scotched: cut, gashed.

frame of things: the universe.
both . . . suffer: earth and heaven perish.

restless ecstasy: suffering, torment.

Malice domestic: civil war.
levy: invasion.
86. *Lines 4-26:* How do you judge Macbeth and Lady Macbeth now feel about the murder of Duncan?

Be bright and jovial among your guests tonight.

MACBETH. So shall I, love; and so, I pray, be you.

30 Let your remembrance apply to Banquo;
Present him eminence,° both with eye and tongue;
Unsafe the while, that we
Must lave our honors in these flattering streams,
And make our faces vizards° to our hearts,
35 Disguising what they are.°

LADY MACBETH. You must leave this.

MACBETH. Oh, full of scorpions is my mind, dear wife!
Thou know'st that Banquo, and his Fleance, lives.

LADY MACBETH. But in them nature's copy's not eterne.°

MACBETH. There's comfort yet; they are assailable;
40 Then be thou jocund. Ere the bat hath flown
His cloistered flight, ere to black Hecate's summons
The shard-borne° beetle with his drowsy hums
Hath rung night's yawning peal, there shall be done
A deed of dreadful note.

LADY MACBETH. What's to be done?[87]

45 MACBETH. Be innocent of the knowledge, dearest chuck,
Till thou applaud the deed. Come, seeling° night,
Scarf up° the tender eye of pitiful day;
And with thy bloody and invisible hand
Cancel and tear to pieces that great bond°
50 Which keeps me pale! Light thickens, and the crow
Makes wing to the rooky wood;
Good things of day begin to droop and drowse,
Whiles night's black agents to their preys do rouse.
Thou marvel'st at my words; but hold thee still;
55 Things bad begun make strong themselves by ill.
So, prithee, go with me. *(Exeunt.)*[88]

SCENE 3. *A park near the palace. (Played on the Platform.) Enter three* MURDERERS.[89]

FIRST MURDERER. But who did bid thee join with us?

THIRD MURDERER. Macbeth.

SECOND MURDERER. He needs not our mistrust, since he delivers
Our offices and what we have to do
To the direction just.°

FIRST MURDERER. Then stand with us.°

5 The west yet glimmers with some streaks of day;
Now spurs the lated traveler apace
To gain the timely inn; and near approaches
The subject of our watch.

THIRD MURDERER. Hark! I hear horses.

BANQUO *(within)*. Give us a light there, ho!

SECOND MURDERER. Then 'tis he; the rest
10 That are within the note of expectation°

Present him eminence: show him special favor.

vizards: masks.

Unsafe . . . are: We are unsafe so long as we must flatter and appear to be what we are not.

But . . . eterne: They will not live forever.

shard-borne: borne on rough wings.

87. Who is now taking the lead in planning?

seeling: blinding. To seel is a technical term used in falconry for sewing up the eyelids of a young hawk to make him used to the hood. (Macbeth is now speaking from the Tarras outside Lady Macbeth's chamber.)

Scarf up: blindfold.

great bond: Banquo's bond of life (?).

88. Compare the planning of Banquo's murder with the planning of Duncan's. What indications are there that the relationship between Macbeth and his wife has changed?

89. How many murderers were present in Macbeth's first interview with them? Why might Macbeth involve a third murderer in the plot?

The third murderer has been variously identified as: a confidential servant of Macbeth's; the character called Attendant in Scene 1; Ross; Macbeth himself. On the basis of evidence in the play, which seems most likely? (Watkins points out: "There is a purely mechanical reason why a third murderer is necessary: Banquo's body must be carried off, and it takes two to carry him off expeditiously; not only that, but the light struck from the hand of Fleance must also be removed before the change of locality to the ensuing banquet scene. One of the trio must pick up the light.")

He needs not . . . just: We need not distrust him, since he reports accurately what we are to do.

(*Then stand with us:* The murderers might use the Stage-Posts for their ambush.)

note of expectation: list of expected guests.

Already are i' the court.

FIRST MURDERER. His horses go about.°

THIRD MURDERER. Almost a mile; but he does usually,
So all men do, from hence to the palace gate
Make it their walk.

SECOND MURDERER. A light, a light!

(Enter BANQUO, *and* FLEANCE *with a torch.)*

THIRD MURDERER. 'Tis he.

15 FIRST MURDERER. Stand to 't.

BANQUO. It will be rain tonight.

FIRST MURDERER. Let it come down.

(They set upon BANQUO.*)*

BANQUO. Oh, treachery! Fly, good Fleance, fly, fly, fly!
Thou mayest revenge. O slave!

(Dies. FLEANCE *escapes.)*

THIRD MURDERER. Who did strike out the light?

go about: take the long way to the castle. (Shakespeare had to find some plausible excuse for not bringing the horses onstage.)

FIRST MURDERER. Was 't not the way?

20 THIRD MURDERER. There's but one down; the son is fled.

SECOND MURDERER. We have lost
Best half of our affair.

FIRST MURDERER. Well, let's away, and say how much is done.
(Exeunt.)[90]

90. What are some of the circumstances that contributed to Fleance's escape?

SCENE 4. *Hall in the palace. (Played on the Platform and in the Study.) A banquet prepared. Enter* MACBETH, LADY MACBETH, ROSS, LENNOX, LORDS, *and* ATTENDANTS.

MACBETH. You know your own degrees°; sit down. At first
And last the hearty welcome.

degrees: rank. Guests at state banquets were seated according to rank.

LORDS. Thanks to your Majesty.

MACBETH. Ourself will mingle with society
And play the humble host.
5 Our hostess keeps her state,° but in best time
We will require her welcome.

keeps her state: remains seated on her throne (in the Study).

LADY MACBETH. Pronounce it for me, sir, to all our friends;
For my heart speaks they are welcome.
(FIRST MURDERER *appears at the door.)*

MACBETH. See, they encounter thee with their hearts' thanks.
10 Both sides are even. Here I'll sit i' the midst.°
Be large in mirth; anon we'll drink a measure
The table round. *(Moves toward* MURDERER *at door.)*° There's blood upon thy face.

i' the midst: Macbeth's place at the table is in the middle facing the audience.
(*Moves . . . door:* Because of the size of the Platform, this whispered conversation could plausibly take place at one side, outside one of the Stage-Posts.)

MURDERER. 'Tis Banquo's then.

MACBETH. 'Tis better thee without than he within.°
15 Is he dispatched?

'Tis better . . . within: The blood is better on you than in him.

MURDERER. My lord, his throat is cut; that I did for him.

MACBETH. Thou art the best o' the cutthroats; yet he's good
That did the like for Fleance. If thou didst it,
Thou art the nonpareil°.

nonpareil: one without equal.

MURDERER. Most royal sir,
20 Fleance is 'scaped.

MACBETH *(aside)*.[91] Then comes my fit again; I had else been perfect,
Whole as the marble, founded as the rock,
As broad and general as the casing° air.
But now I am cabined, cribbed, confined, bound in
25 To saucy doubts and fears. But Banquo's safe?

91. Macbeth must react in some way before he speaks. What would be appropriate?
casing: enveloping.

MURDERER. Aye, my good lord; safe in a ditch he bides,
With twenty trenchèd gashes on his head,
The least a death to nature.

MACBETH. Thanks for that;
There the grown serpent lies. The worm that's fled
30 Hath nature that in time will venom breed,
No teeth for the present. Get thee gone; tomorrow
We'll hear ourselves again. *(Exit* MURDERER.)

LADY MACBETH. My royal lord,
You do not give the cheer; the feast is sold

That is not often vouched, while 'tis a-making,
35 'Tis given with welcome; to feed were best at home;
From thence the sauce to meat is ceremony;
Meeting were bare without it.°

MACBETH. Sweet remembrancer!
Now good digestion wait on appetite,
And health on both!

LENNOX. May't please your Highness sit.

(The GHOST OF BANQUO *enters, and sits in* MACBETH*'s place.)*[92]

40 MACBETH. Here had we now our country's honor roofed,°
Were the graced person of our Banquo present;
Who may I rather challenge for unkindness
Than pity for mischance!°

ROSS. His absence, sir,
Lays blame upon his promise. Please 't your Highness
45 To grace us with your royal company.

MACBETH. The table's full.

LENNOX. Here is a place reserved, sir.

MACBETH. Where?

LENNOX. Here, my good lord. What is 't that moves your Highness?

MACBETH. Which of you have done this?

LORDS. What, my good lord?

50 MACBETH. Thou canst not say I did it; never shake
Thy gory locks at me.[93]

ROSS. Gentlemen, rise; his Highness is not well.

LADY MACBETH. Sit, worthy friends. My lord is often thus,
And hath been from his youth. Pray you, keep seat;
55 The fit is momentary; upon a thought°
He will again be well. If much you note him,
You shall offend him and extend his passion;°
Feed, and regard him not.[94] Are you a man?

MACBETH. Aye, and a bold one, that dare look on that
60 Which might appal the devil.

LADY MACBETH. O proper stuff!
This is the very painting of your fear;
This is the air-drawn dagger which, you said,
Led you to Duncan.[95] Oh, these flaws and starts,
Imposters to° true fear, would well become
65 A woman's story at a winter's fire,
Authorized by her grandam. Shame itself!
Why do you make such faces? When all's done,
You look but on a stool.[96]

MACBETH. Prithee, see there! behold! look! lo! how say you?
70 Why, what care I? If thou canst nod, speak, too.
If charnel houses and our graves must send
Those that we bury back, our monuments
Shall be the maws of kites.° *(*GHOST *vanishes.)*

LADY MACBETH. What, quite unmanned in folly?

MACBETH. If I stand here, I saw him.

LADY MACBETH. Fie, for shame!

the feast is . . . it: Unless a host keeps his guests assured of their welcome, the meal is like one bought at an inn, and one might as well dine at home. When one is away from home, ceremony should accompany the meal.

92. Watch for the point when Macbeth becomes aware of the ghost.
If you were staging a modern production, would you have the ghost physically on stage? Explain.

Here had . . . roofed: We would have all our country's most honored men here.

Who may I . . . mischance: Who is, I hope, absent because he has chosen not to attend rather than because he has been prevented from coming by some misfortune.

93. To whom is Macbeth speaking? What is the "it" he denies doing?

upon a thought: in a moment.

extend his passion: prolong his fit.

94. *Lines 53-58a:* What tone of voice would Lady Macbeth use here? To whom does she then say "Are you a man?" How would her tone change here?

95. Where on the stage would Macbeth and Lady Macbeth be positioned at this point?

imposters to: imitations of.

96. Does Lady Macbeth see the ghost?

If charnel . . . kites: If morgues and graves cannot keep our bodies buried, our burial place should be the stomachs of birds of prey.

75 MACBETH. Blood hath been shed ere now, i' the olden time,
Ere humane statute purged the gentle weal;°
Aye, and since, too, murders have been performed
Too terrible for the ear. The time has been,
That, when the brains were out, the man would die,
80 And there an end; but now they rise again,
With twenty mortal murders on their crowns,°
And push us from our stools; this is more strange
Than such a murder is.

LADY MACBETH. My worthy lord,
Your noble friends do lack you.

MACBETH. I do forget.
85 Do not muse at me, my most worthy friends;
I have a strange infirmity, which is nothing
To those that know me. Come, love and health to all;
Then I'll sit down. Give me some wine; fill full.
I drink to the general joy o' the whole table,
90 And to our dear friend Banquo, whom we miss;
Would he were here! To all, and him, we thirst°,
And all to all.

LORDS. Our duties, and the pledge.

(Reënter GHOST.*)*

MACBETH. Avaunt! and quit my sight! Let the earth hide thee!
Thy bones are marrowless, thy blood is cold;
95 Thou has no speculation° in those eyes
Which thou dost glare with!

LADY MACBETH. Think of this, good peers,
But as a thing of custom; 'tis no other;
Only it spoils the pleasure of the time.[97]

MACBETH. What man dare, I dare.
100 Approach thou like the rugged Russian bear,
The armed rhinoceros, or the Hyrcan tiger;
Take any shape but that, and my firm nerves
Shall never tremble. Or be alive again,
And dare me to the desert with thy sword;
105 If trembling I inhabit then,° protest me
The baby of a girl°. Hence, horrible shadow!
Unreal mockery, hence!

(GHOST *vanishes.)*[98]

Why, so; being gone,
I am a man again. Pray you, sit still.

LADY MACBETH. You have displaced the mirth, broke the good meeting,
110 With most admired° disorder.

MACBETH. Can such things be,
And overcome us like a summer's cloud,
Without our special wonder? You make me strange
Even to the disposition that I owe,°
When now I think you can behold such sights,
115 And keep the natural ruby of your cheeks,
When mine is blanched with fear.

Ere . . . weal: before laws purged violence from society.

mortal . . . crowns: deadly wounds on their heads.

thirst: wish to drink.

speculation: light of living intelligence.

97. Who hears Macbeth's tirades? How do Macbeth and Lady Macbeth explain his behavior? Do you think the lords accept the explanation?

If . . . then: If I then still tremble.

The baby of a girl: puny infant of an immature mother. (Some editors interpret it as "a girl's doll.")

98. Who has seen the ghost? What similar hallucination occurs earlier in the play, and what purpose do both incidents serve?

admired: wondered at.

You make . . . owe: You make me wonder at my own disposition.

ROSS. What sights, my Lord?

LADY MACBETH. I pray you, speak not; he grows worse and worse;
Question enrages him. At once, good night;
Stand not upon the order of your going,°
120 But go at once.

Stand not . . . going: Do not wait to leave in formal order.

LENNOX. Good night; and better health
Attend his Majesty!

LADY MACBETH. A kind good-night to all![99]

(Exeunt all but MACBETH *and* LADY MACBETH.*)*

99. Macbeth has not explicitly told Lady Macbeth of his plot to murder Banquo. At what point in this scene do you think she realizes what has happened? How might an actress convey this knowledge to an audience?

MACBETH. It will have blood; they say blood will have blood.
Stones have been known to move and trees to speak;
Augurs and understood relations have
125 By magot-pies and choughs and rooks brought forth
The secret'st man of blood.° What is the night?

Augurs . . . blood: Through talking birds, omens correctly interpreted have led to the discovery of the most secretive of murderers. Magot-pies are magpies; choughs, a type of crow.

LADY MACBETH. Almost at odds with morning, which is which.

MACBETH. How say'st thou, that Macduff denies his person
At our great bidding?

LADY MACBETH. Did you send to him, sir?

130 MACBETH. I hear it by the way; but I will send.
There's not a one of them but in his house
I keep a servant feed°. I will tomorrow,
And betimes I will, to the weird sisters.°
More shall they speak; for now I am bent to know,
135 By the worst means, the worst. For mine own good,
All causes shall give way; I am in blood
Stepped in so far that, should I wade no more,
Returning were as tedious as go o'er.
Strange things I have in head, that will to hand;
140 Which must be acted ere they may be scanned.°

feed: paid [in fee] to spy.

I will . . . sisters: I will send for Macduff tomorrow, and very early I will go to the witches.

Which . . . scanned: which must be done before they can be discussed or considered.

LADY MACBETH. You lack the season of all natures, sleep.

MACBETH. Come, we'll to sleep. My strange and self-abuse
Is the initiate fear that wants hard use;°
We are yet but young in deed.[100]

(Exeunt.)

My strange . . . use: My peculiar actions arise from the fact that I am a novice at crime, not yet hardened.

100. (a) Do you agree with Macbeth's explanation for his agitation and sleeplessness? How well would you say he knows himself?
(b) What should the pace and mood be for this part of the scene?

SCENE 5. *A heath.*[101] *Thunder. Enter the three* WITCHES, *meeting* HECATE.

101. It is generally accepted that this scene was not written by Shakespeare. Do you see anything in the style of the writing which may have led to this opinion?

FIRST WITCH. Why, how now, Hecate! you look angerly.

HECATE. Have I not reason, beldams as you are,
Saucy and overbold? How did you dare
To trade and traffic with Macbeth
5 In riddles and affairs of death;
And I, the mistress of your charms,
The close contriver of all harms,
Was never called to bear my part,
Or show the glory of our art?
10 And, which is worse, all you have done
Hath been but for a wayward son,
Spiteful and wrathful, who, as others do,
Loves for his own ends, not for you.

But make amends now. Get you gone,
15 And at the pit of Acheron°
Meet me i' the morning. Thither he
Will come to know his destiny.
Your vessels and your spells provide,
Your charms and everything beside.
20 I am for the air; this night I'll spend
Unto a dismal and a fatal end;
Great business must be wrought ere noon.
Upon the corner of the moon
There hangs a vaporous drop profound;
25 I'll catch it ere it come to ground;
And that, distilled by magic sleights,
Shall raise such artificial sprites
As by the strength of their illusion
Shall draw him on to his confusion.
30 He shall spurn fate, scorn death, and bear
His hopes 'bove wisdom, grace, and fear;
And you all know security°
Is mortals' chiefest enemy.
(Music and a song within, "Come away, come away," etc.)
Hark! I am called; my little spirit, see,
35 Sits in a foggy cloud, and stays for me.
(Exit.)

Acheron: a river in Hell.

security: overconfidence.

FIRST WITCH. Come, let's make haste; she'll soon be back again.
(Exeunt.)

SCENE 6. *Forres. The palace. (Played on the Tarras.) Enter* LENNOX *and another* LORD.

LENNOX. My former speeches have but hit your thoughts,
Which can interpret further;° only, I say,
Things have been strangely borne°. The gracious Duncan
Was pitied of Macbeth; marry, he was dead.
5 And the right-valiant Banquo walked too late;
Whom, you may say, if 't please you, Fleance killed,
For Fleance fled; men must not walk too late.
Who cannot want the thought how monstrous
It was for Malcolm and for Donalbain
10 To kill their gracious father? Damnèd fact!
How it did grieve Macbeth! Did he not straight
In pious rage the two delinquents tear,
That were the slaves of drink and thralls of sleep?
Was not that nobly done? Aye, and wisely, too;
15 For 'twould have angered any heart alive
To hear the men deny 't. So that, I say,
He has borne all things well. And I do think
That had he Duncan's sons under his key—
As, an 't please heaven, he shall not—they should find
20 What 'twere to kill a father; so should Fleance.
But, peace! for from broad words° and 'cause he failed

My former . . . further: My earlier speeches have only given you ideas, from which you can draw your own conclusions.

borne: conducted.

from broad words: because he spoke frankly.

His presence at the tyrant's feast, I hear
Macduff lives in disgrace; sir, can you tell
Where he bestows himself?[102]

LORD. The son of Duncan,
25 From whom this tyrant holds the due of birth,
Lives in the English court, and is received
Of the most pious Edward° with such grace
That the malevolence of fortune nothing
Takes from his high respect. Thither Macduff
30 Is gone to pray the holy King, upon his aid
To wake Northumberland and warlike Siward;
That by the help of these—with Him above
To ratify the work—we may again
Give to our tables meat, sleep to our nights,
35 Free from our feasts and banquets bloody knives,
Do faithful homage and receive free honors,
All which we pine for now; and this report
Hath so exasperate the King that he
Prepares for some attempt of war.

LENNOX. Sent he to Macduff?°

40 LORD. He did; and with an absolute "Sir, not I,"
The cloudy° messenger turns me his back,
And hums, as who should say, "You'll rue the time
That clogs° me with this answer."

LENNOX. And that well might
Advise him° to a caution, to hold what distance
45 His wisdom can provide. Some holy angel
Fly to the court of England and unfold
His message ere he come, that a swift blessing
May soon return to this our suffering country
Under a hand accursed!

LORD. I'll send my prayers with him.

(Exeunt.)[103]

102. Note the indirect suggestion in Lennox's speech. Why is he less than forthright?
At what points does his tone of voice change? What is the dramatic effect of these changes?

Edward: Edward the Confessor, King of England 1042–1066.

Sent he . . . ? Did he send for Macduff?

cloudy: sullen.

clogs: obstructs.

him: Macduff.

103. What is the dramatic purpose of this scene? What earlier scene does it parallel?
Some scholars believe this scene should follow Act Four, Scene 1, where it seems to make better sense. It may have been shifted to its present position when Scene 5 was added, to avoid having two scenes with the witches come together.

Act Four

SCENE 1. *A cavern.° In the middle, a boiling caldron. Thunder. Enter the three* WITCHES.

(*cavern:* probably set in the Study.)

FIRST WITCH. Thrice the brinded cat hath mewed.
SECOND WITCH. Thrice and once the hedgepig° whined.
THIRD WITCH. Harpier° cries, "'Tis time, 'tis time."
FIRST WITCH. Round about the caldron go;
5 In the poisoned entrails throw.
Toad, that under cold stone
Days and nights has thirty-one
Sweltered venom sleeping got,
Boil thou first i' the charmèd pot.

hedgepig: hedgehog.

Harpier: the Third Witch's familiar spirit.

10 ALL. Double, double toil and trouble;
Fire burn and caldron bubble.
SECOND WITCH. Fillet of a fenny snake,
In the caldron boil and bake;
Eye of newt and toe of frog,
15 Wool of bat and tongue of dog,
Adder's fork and blind-worm's° sting,
Lizard's leg and howlet's wing,
For a charm of powerful trouble,
Like a hell-broth boil and bubble.
20 ALL. Double, double toil and trouble;
Fire burn and caldron bubble.
THIRD WITCH. Scale of dragon, tooth of wolf,
Witches' mummy, maw and gulf°
Of the ravined° salt-sea shark,
25 Root of hemlock digged i' the dark,
Liver of blaspheming Jew,
Gall of goat, and slips of yew°
Slivered in the moon's eclipse,
Nose of Turk and Tartar's lips,
30 Finger of birth-strangled babe
Ditch-delivered by a drab°,
Make the gruel thick and slab°;
Add thereto a tiger's chaudron°,
For the ingredients of our caldron.
35 ALL. Double, double toil and trouble;
Fire burn and caldron bubble.
SECOND WITCH. Cool it with a baboon's blood,
Then the charm is firm and good.

(Enter HECATE *to the other three* WITCHES.*)*°

HECATE. Oh, well done! I commend your pains;
40 And everyone shall share i' the gains.
And now about the caldron sing,
Like elves and fairies in a ring,
Enchanting all that you put in.

(Music and a song, "Black spirits," etc.)
*(*HECATE *retires.)*

SECOND WITCH. By the pricking of my thumbs,
45 Something wicked this way comes.
Open, locks,
Whoever knocks!

(Enter MACBETH.*)*

MACBETH. How now, you secret, black, and midnight hags!
What is 't you do?[104]
ALL. A deed without a name.
50 MACBETH. I conjure you, by that which you profess,
Howe'er you come to know it, answer me.
Though you untie the winds and let them fight
Against the churches; though the yesty° waves
Confound and swallow navigation up;

blind-worm: a small snakelike lizard, thought to be poisonous.

maw and gulf: stomach and gullet.

ravined: ravenous.

yew: evergreen tree, thought to be poisonous.

drab: whore.

slab: slimy.

chaudron: entrails.

The appearance of Hecate is believed to be a later addition, not by Shakespeare—perhaps to provide an excuse for a dance and a song.

104. How has Macbeth's attitude toward the witches changed since his first meeting with them (Act One, Scene 3)? What might this suggest about changes in his character?

yesty: foamy.

55 Though bladed corn be lodged° and trees blown down;
Though castles topple on their warders' heads;
Though palaces and pyramids do slope
Their heads to their foundations; though the treasure
Of nature's germens° tumble all together,
60 Even till destruction sicken°; answer me
To what I ask you.

FIRST WITCH. Speak.

SECOND WITCH. Demand.

THIRD WITCH. We'll answer.

FIRST WITCH. Say, if thou'dst rather hear it from our mouths,
Or from our masters?

MACBETH. Call 'em; let me see 'em.

FIRST WITCH. Pour in sow's blood, that hath eaten
65 Her nine farrow; grease that's sweaten
From the murderer's gibbet throw
Into the flame.

ALL. Come, high or low;
Thyself and office deftly show!

(Thunder. FIRST APPARITION: *an armed Head.)*[105]

MACBETH. Tell me, thou unknown power—

FIRST WITCH. He knows thy thought;
70 Hear his speech, but say thou naught.

FIRST APPARITION. Macbeth! Macbeth! Macbeth! beware Macduff;
Beware the thane of Fife. Dismiss me. Enough.°

(Descends.)

MACBETH. Whate'er thou art, for thy good caution, thanks;
Thou hast harped° my fear aright; but one word more—

75 FIRST WITCH. He will not be commanded; here's another,
More potent than the first.

(Thunder. SECOND APPARITION: *a bloody Child.)*°

SECOND APPARITION. Macbeth! Macbeth! Macbeth!

MACBETH. Had I three ears, I 'ld hear thee.

SECOND APPARITION. Be bloody, bold, and resolute; laugh to scorn
80 The power of man, for none of woman born
Shall harm Macbeth. *(Descends.)*

MACBETH. Then live, Macduff; what need I fear of thee?
But yet I'll make assurance double sure,
And take a bond of fate,° thou shalt not live;
85 That I may tell pale-hearted fear it lies,
And sleep in spite of thunder.

(Thunder. THIRD APPARITION: *a Child crowned, with a tree in his hand.)*°

What is this,
That rises like the issue of a king,
And wears upon his baby-brow the round
And top of sovereignty?

ALL. Listen, but speak not to 't.

90 THIRD APPARITION. Be lion-mettled, proud, and take no care
Who chafes, who frets, or where conspirers are.
Macbeth shall never vanquished be until

Though . . . lodged: Though grain, still green, be beaten down.

nature's germens: the seeds or elements through which nature operates.

sicken: is surfeited.

105. In Shakespeare's time, the apparition of a helmeted head came up (presumably from Hell below) through the caldron, which was placed over a trap door. If you were directing a modern production, how would you solve the problems of staging the appearance of the apparitions? What modern equipment might you use?

Dismiss . . . enough: Note that this is the only apparition that does not equivocate with Macbeth. (Explained in Act Five, Scene 8.)

harped: guessed.

bloody Child: Macduff as a child. (Explained in Act Five, Scene 8.)

take . . . fate: make sure that fate's promise is fulfilled.

child . . . hand: Malcolm. (Explained in Act Five, Scene 4.)

Great Birnam wood to high Dunsinane hill
Shall come against him. *(Descends.)*

MACBETH. That will never be;

95 Who can impress° the forest, bid the tree
Unfix this earth-bound root? Sweet bodements!° good!
Rebellion's head, rise never till the wood
Of Birnam rise, and our high-placed Macbeth
Shall live the lease of nature, pay his breath
100 To time and mortal custom.° Yet my heart
Throbs to know one thing; tell me, if your art
Can tell so much—shall Banquo's issue ever
Reign in this kingdom?

ALL. Seek to know no more.

MACBETH. I will be satisfied; deny me this,
105 And an eternal curse fall on you! Let me know.
Why sinks that caldron? and what noise° is this?

(Hautboys.)

FIRST WITCH. Show!

SECOND WITCH. Show!

THIRD WITCH. Show!

110 ALL. Show his eyes, and grieve his heart,
Come like shadows, so depart!

(A show of EIGHT KINGS°, *the last with a glass° in his hand;* BANQUO'S GHOST *following.)*

MACBETH. Thou art too like the spirit of Banquo; down!
Thy crown does sear mine eyeballs.° And thy hair,
Thou other gold-bound brow, is like the first.
115 A third is like the former. Filthy hags!
Why do you show me this? A fourth! Start, eyes!
What, will the line stretch out to the crack of doom?
Another yet! A seventh! I'll see no more;
And yet the eighth appears, who bears a glass
120 Which shows me many more; and some I see
That twofold balls and treble scepters° carry.
Horrible sight! Now, I see, 'tis true;
For the blood-boltered° Banquo smiles upon me,
And points at them for his. *(*APPARITIONS *vanish.)* What, is this so?

125 FIRST WITCH. Aye, sir, all this is so; but why
Stands Macbeth thus amazedly?
Come, sisters, cheer we up his sprites,
And show the best of our delights.
I'll charm the air to give a sound,
130 While you perform your antic round°;
That this great King may kindly say
Our duties did his welcome pay.

(Music. The WITCHES *dance, and then vanish, with* HECATE.*)*

MACBETH. Where are they? Gone? Let this pernicious hour
Stand aye accursèd in the calendar!
135 Come in, without there!°

impress: conscript; force to serve as soldiers.

bodements: prophecies.

pay his breath . . . custom: die a natural death.

noise: music.

A show . . . Kings: The eight Stuart kings of Scotland, descending from Banquo and succeeding down to James I, the present king, walk in turn across the back of the stage.

glass: a magic mirror showing the future.

Thou . . . eyeballs: Spoken as the first king passes. Macbeth continues to comment as each king passes in turn.

twofold . . . scepters: The balls or orbs and scepters symbolize the sovereignty of England and Scotland, and the kingdoms of England, Scotland, and Ireland which were united for the first time under James I, eighth of the Stuart kings.

blood-boltered: having hair matted with blood.

antic round: grotesque [or ancient?] round dance.

Lines 125-135: This passage is also considered to be a later interpolation, not by Shakespeare.

(Enter LENNOX.*)*

LENNOX. What's your grace's will?

MACBETH. Saw you the weird sisters?

LENNOX. No, my lord.

MACBETH. Came they not by you?

LENNOX. No, indeed, my lord.

MACBETH. Infected be the air whereon they ride;
And damned all those that trust them![106] I did hear
140 The galloping of horse; who was 't came by?

LENNOX. 'Tis two or three, my lord, that bring you word
Macduff is fled to England.

MACBETH. Fled to England!

LENNOX. Aye, my good lord.

MACBETH. Time, thou anticipatest my dread exploits;
145 The flighty purpose never is o'ertook
Unless the deed go with it; from this moment
The very firstlings of my heart shall be
The firstlings of my hand.° And even now,
To crown my thoughts with acts, be it thought and done.
150 The castle of Macduff I will surprise;
Seize upon Fife; give to the edge o' the sword
His wife, his babes, and all unfortunate souls
That trace him in his line. No boasting like a fool;
This deed I'll do before this purpose cool.
155 But no more sights!—Where are these gentlemen?
Come, bring me where they are. *(Exeunt.)*

106. What is the irony of this line?

The flighty . . . hand: One must act at once if one is to accomplish one's purpose. From now on I shall put my thoughts into immediate action.

SCENE 2. *Fife.* MACDUFF'S *castle. (Played in the Chamber.) Enter* LADY MACDUFF, *her* SON, *and* ROSS.

LADY MACDUFF. What had he done, to make him fly the land?[107]

ROSS. You must have patience, madam.

LADY MACDUFF. He had none;
His flight was madness. When our actions do not,
Our fears do make us traitors.

ROSS. You know not
5 Whether it was his wisdom or his fear.

LADY MACDUFF. Wisdom! to leave his wife, to leave his babes,
His mansion and his titles in a place
From whence himself does fly? He loves us not;
He wants the natural touch;° for the poor wren
10 The most diminutive of birds, will fight,
Her young ones in her nest, against the owl.
All is the fear and nothing is the love;
As little is the wisdom, where the flight
So runs against all reason.

ROSS. My dearest coz,°
15 I pray you, school° yourself; but, for your husband,
He is noble, wise, judicious, and best knows

107. What message has Ross apparently just brought to Lady Macduff?

He wants . . . touch: He lacks natural human affection.

coz: cousin.
school: control.

The fits o' the season.° I dare not speak much further;
But cruel are the times, when we are traitors
And do not know ourselves,° when we hold rumor
20 From what we fear,° yet know not what we fear,
But float upon a wild and violent sea
Each way and move. I take my leave of you;
Shall not be long but I'll be here again;
Things at the worst will cease, or else climb upward
25 To what they were before. My pretty cousin°,
Blessing upon you!

LADY MACDUFF. Fathered he is, and yet he's fatherless.

ROSS. I am so much a fool, should I stay longer,
It would be my disgrace and your discomfort;°
30 I take my leave at once.

LADY MACDUFF. Sirrah°, your father's dead;
And what will you do now? How will you live?

SON. As birds do, mother.

LADY MACDUFF. What, with worms and flies?

SON. With what I get, I mean; and so do they.

LADY MACDUFF. Poor bird! thou'ldst never fear the net nor lime°,
35 The pitfall nor the gin°.

SON. Why should I, mother? Poor birds they are not set for.
My father is not dead, for all your saying.

LADY MACDUFF. Yes, he is dead; how wilt thou do for a father?

SON. Nay, how will you do for a husband?

40 LADY MACDUFF. Why, I can buy me twenty at any market.

SON. Then you'll buy 'em to sell again.

LADY MACDUFF. Thou speak'st with all thy wit; and yet, i' faith,
With wit enough for thee.

SON. Was my father a traitor, mother?

45 LADY MACDUFF. Aye, that he was.

SON. What is a traitor?

LADY MACDUFF. Why, one that swears and lies.°

SON. And be all traitors that do so?

LADY MACDUFF. Every one that does so is a traitor, and must be hanged.

50 SON. And must they all be hanged that swear and lie?

LADY MACDUFF. Every one.

SON. Who must hang them?

LADY MACDUFF. Why, the honest men.

SON. Then the liars and swearers are fools, for there are liars and
55 swearers enow to beat the honest men and hang up them.

LADY MACDUFF. Now, God help thee, poor monkey! But how wilt thou do for a father?

SON. If he were dead, you'ld weep for him; if you would not, it were a good sign that I should quickly have a new father.

60 LADY MACDUFF. Poor prattler, how thou talk'st![108]

(Enter a MESSENGER.*)*[109]

MESSENGER. Bless you, fair dame! I am not to you known,
Though in your state of honor I am perfect.°
I doubt° some danger does approach you nearly.

fits . . . season: violence of the times.

do not . . . ourselves: do not know ourselves (or each other) to be traitors.

hold rumor . . . fear: believe rumors that grow out of fears.

My . . . cousin: Macduff's small son.

It would be . . . discomfort: Ross feels like weeping; in Shakespeare's time it was considered disgraceful for a man to weep.

Sirrah: ordinary form of address used in speaking to children and servants.

lime: birdlime, a sticky substance used to catch birds.

gin: snare.

swears and lies: swears allegiance and then breaks his oath.

108. *Macbeth* has only two humorous scenes: the broad comedy of the drunken porter, and the light comedy of this scene. What was Shakespeare's dramatic purpose in placing Lady Macduff's scene here?

109. It has been suggested that the messenger may have been sent by Lady Macbeth. Does this seem possible? Be alert for possible clues later in the play.

in your . . . perfect: I know of your honorable rank.

doubt: suspect.

If you will take a homely man's advice,
65 Be not found here; hence, with your little ones.
To fright you thus, methinks I am too savage;
To do worse to you were fell cruelty,
Which is too nigh your person. Heaven preserve you!
I dare abide no longer.

(Exit.)

LADY MACDUFF. Whither should I fly?
70 I have done no harm. But I remember now
I am in this earthly world, where to do harm
Is often laudable, to do good sometime
Accounted dangerous folly; why, then, alas,
Do I put up that womanly defense,
75 To say I have done no harm?

(Enter MURDERERS.*)*

What are these faces?

FIRST MURDERER. Where is your husband?

LADY MACDUFF. I hope in no place so unsanctified
Where such as thou mayst find him.

FIRST MURDERER. He's a traitor.

SON. Thou liest, thou shag-haired villain!

FIRST MURDERER. What, you egg!
(Stabbing him)

80 Young fry of treachery!

SON. He has killed me, mother;
Run away, I pray you! *(Dies.)*

(Exit LADY MACDUFF, *crying "Murder!" Exeunt* MURDERERS, *following her.)*[110]

110. Trace the murders committed by Macbeth up to this point in terms of their justifiability. What is revealed about changes in his character?

SCENE 3.° *England. Before the King's palace. (Played on the Platform and in the Study.) Enter* MALCOLM *and* MACDUFF.

(The unusual length of Scene 3 may be explained by the fact that it was customary to give the chief actor a rest during the fourth act, or thereabouts, of a tragedy.)

MALCOLM. Let us seek out some desolate shade, and there
Weep our sad bosoms empty.

MACDUFF. Let us rather
Hold fast the mortal sword and, like good men,
Bestride our downfall'n birthdom.° Each new morn
5 New widows howl, new orphans cry, new sorrows
Strike heaven on the face,[111] that it resounds
As if it felt with Scotland and yelled out
Like syllable of dolor.

Bestride . . . birthdom: defend our fallen fatherland.

111. What is the irony in Macduff's saying this?

MALCOLM. What I believe, I'll wail;
What know, believe, and what I can redress,
10 As I shall find the time to friend°, I will.
What you have spoke, it may be so perchance,
This tyrant, whose sole name blisters our tongues,
Was once thought honest; you have loved him well.
He hath not touched you yet. I am young; but something
15 You may deserve of him through me,° and wisdom
To offer up a weak poor innocent lamb
To appease an angry god.

to friend: suitable.

but something . . . me: but you may win favor from Macbeth by betraying me.

MACDUFF. I am not treacherous.

MALCOLM. But Macbeth is.
A good and virtuous nature may recoil
20 In an imperial charge.° But I shall crave your pardon;
That which you are my thoughts cannot transpose°;
Angels are bright still, though the brightest fell;
Though all things foul would wear the brows of grace,
Yet grace must still look so.

recoil . . . charge: reverse itself through loyalty to the king.

transpose: change.

MACDUFF. I have lost my hopes.

25 MALCOLM. Perchance even there where I did find my doubts,
Why in that rawness left you wife and child,
Those precious motives, those strong knots of love,
Without leave-taking? I pray you,

Let not my jealousies be your dishonors,
30 But mine own safeties.° You may be rightly just,
Whatever I shall think.

MACDUFF. Bleed, bleed, poor country!
Great tyranny! lay thou thy basis sure,
For goodness dare not check thee; wear thou thy wrongs;
The title is affeered!° Fare thee well, lord.
35 I would not be the villain that thou think'st
For the whole space that's in the tyrant's grasp,
And the rich East to boot.

MALCOLM. Be not offended;
I speak not as in absolute fear of you.
I think our country sinks beneath the yoke;
40 It weeps, it bleeds; and each new day a gash
Is added to her wounds. I think withal
There would be hands uplifted in my right;
And here from gracious England° have I offer
Of goodly thousands; but, for all this,
45 When I shall tread upon the tyrant's head,
Or wear it on my sword, yet my poor country
Shall have more vices than it had before,
More suffer, and more sundry ways than ever,
By him that shall succeed.

MACDUFF. What should he be?

50 MALCOLM. It is myself I mean; in whom I know
All the particulars of vice so grafted
That, when they shall be opened, black Macbeth
Will seem as pure as snow, and the poor state
Esteem him as a lamb, being compared
55 With my confineless harms.°

MACDUFF. Not in the legions
Of horrid hell can come a devil more damned
In evils to top Macbeth.

MALCOLM. I grant him bloody,
Luxurious°, avaricious, false, deceitful,
Sudden°, malicious, smacking of every sin
60 That has a name; but there's no bottom, none,
In my voluptuousness. Your wives, your daughters,
Your matrons and your maids, could not fill up
The cistern of my lust and my desire.
All continent impediments would o'erbear
65 That did oppose my will. Better Macbeth
Than such an one to reign.[112]

MACDUFF. Boundless intemperance
In nature is a tyranny; it hath been
The untimely emptying of the happy throne
And fall of many kings. But fear not yet
70 To take upon you what is yours; you may
Convey° your pleasures in a spacious plenty,
And yet seem cold, the time° you may so hoodwink.

Let not . . . safeties: I am suspicious not to dishonor you but because I wish to assure my own safety.

The title . . . affeered: Your title of tyranny is confirmed.

England: the king of England.

confineless harms: unlimited evil.

Luxurious: lustful.
Sudden: violent.

112. Why does Malcolm make this confession?

Convey: obtain secretly.
the time: the world.

We have willing dames enough; there cannot be
That vulture in you, to devour so many
75 As will to greatness dedicate themselves,
Finding it so inclined.

MALCOLM. With this there grows
In my most ill-composed affection° such
A stanchless° avarice that, were I king,
I should cut off the nobles for their lands,
80 Desire his jewels and this other's house;
And my more-having would be as a sauce
To make me hunger more; that I should forge
Quarrels unjust against the good and loyal,
Destroying them for wealth.

MACDUFF. This avarice
85 Sticks deeper, grows with more pernicious root
Than summer-seeming° lust, and it hath been
The sword of our slain kings. Yet do not fear;
Scotland hath foisons° to fill up your will,
Of your mere own. All these are portable,
90 With other graces weighed.°

MALCOLM. But I have none; the king-becoming graces,
As justice, verity, temperance, stableness,
Bounty, perseverance, mercy, lowliness,
Devotion, patience, courage, fortitude,
95 I have no relish of them, but abound
In the division of each several crime,
Acting it many ways. Nay, had I power, I should
Pour the sweet milk of concord into hell,
Uproar the universal peace, confound
100 All unity on earth.

MACDUFF. O Scotland, Scotland!

MALCOLM. If such a one be fit to govern, speak;
I am as I have spoken.

MACDUFF. Fit to govern!
No, not to live. O nation miserable,
With an untitled tyrant bloody-sceptered,
105 When shalt thou see thy wholesome days again,
Since that the truest issue of thy throne
By his own interdiction° stands accursed,
And does blaspheme his breed? Thy royal father
Was a most sainted king. The queen that bore thee,
110 Oftener upon her knees than on her feet,
Died every day she lived.° Fare thee well!
These evils thou repeat'st upon thyself
Have banished me from Scotland. O my breast,
Thy hope ends here!

MALCOLM. Macduff, this noble passion,
115 Child of integrity, hath from my soul
Wiped the black scruples, reconciled my thoughts,
To thy good truth and honor. Devilish Macbeth

ill-composed affection: evil disposition.
stanchless: insatiable.

summer-seeming: short-lived.

foisons: plenty.

All these . . . weighed: These weaknesses are bearable, considering your other virtues.

interdiction: decree.

Died . . . lived: prepared for death by daily prayers and self-sacrifice.

By many of these trains° hath sought to win me
Into his power, and modest wisdom plucks me
120 From overcredulous haste. But God above
Deal between thee and me! For even now
I put myself to thy direction, and
Unspeak mine own detraction, here abjure
The taints and blames I laid upon myself,
125 For strangers to my nature. I am yet
Unknown to woman, never was forsworn,
Scarcely have coveted what was mine own,
At no time broke my faith, would not betray
The devil to his fellow, and delight
130 No less in truth than life; my first false speaking
Was this upon myself. What I am truly
Is thine and my poor country's to command;
Whither indeed, before thy here-approach,
Old Siward, with ten thousand warlike men,
135 Already at a point,° was setting forth.
Now we'll together; and the chance of goodness
Be like our warranted quarrel!° Why are you silent?

MACDUFF. Such welcome and unwelcome things at once
'Tis hard to reconcile.

(Enter a DOCTOR.*)*

140 MALCOLM. Well, more anon.—Comes the King forth, I pray you?

DOCTOR. Aye, sir; there are a crew of wretched souls
That stay his cure.° Their malady convinces
The great assay of art;° but at his touch—
Such sanctity hath Heaven given his hand—
145 They presently amend.

MALCOLM. I thank you, doctor.

(Exit DOCTOR.*)*

MACDUFF. What's the disease he means?

MALCOLM. 'Tis called the evil:°
A most miraculous work in this good King;
Which often, since my here-remain in England,
I have seen him do. How he solicits Heaven,
150 Himself best knows; but strangely-visited people,
All swoln and ulcerous, pitiful to the eye,
The mere despair of surgery, he cures,
Hanging a golden stamp about their necks,
Put on with holy prayers. And 'tis spoken,
155 To the succeeding royalty he leaves
The healing benediction. With this strange virtue,
He hath a heavenly gift of prophecy,
And sundry blessings hang about his throne,
That speak him full of grace.

(Enter ROSS.*)*

MACDUFF. See, who comes here?

160 MALCOLM. My countryman; but yet I know him not.

MACDUFF. My ever-gentle cousin, welcome hither.

trains: devices.

at a point: prepared.

and the chance . . . quarrel: and may our chance of success be as strong as the justness of our cause.

stay his cure: wait for him to cure them.

convinces . . . art: defies cure by any medical skill.

the evil: scrofula, a disease characterized by swelling of the lymphatic glands. It was called "the king's evil" because of a belief that it could be healed by the touch of a king. This curing power was first attributed to Edward the Confessor and later to his successors. This passage was obviously intended to flatter James I, who believed he had this power.

MALCOLM. I know him now. Good God, betimes remove
The means that makes us strangers!

ROSS. Sir, amen.

MACDUFF. Stands Scotland where it did?

ROSS. Alas, poor country!

165 Almost afraid to know itself. It cannot
Be called our mother, but our grave; where nothing,
But who knows nothing, is once seen to smile;
Where sighs and groans and shrieks that rend the air
Are made, not marked; where violent sorrow seems
170 A modern ecstasy°. The dead man's knell
Is there scarce asked for who; and good men's lives
Expire before the flowers in their caps,
Dying or ere they sicken.

MACDUFF. Oh, relation
Too nice,° and yet too true!

MALCOLM. What's the newest grief?

175 ROSS. That of an hour's age doth hiss the speaker°;
Each minute teems° a new one.

MACDUFF. How does my wife?

ROSS. Why, well.[113]

MACDUFF. And all my children?

ROSS. Well, too.

MACDUFF. The tyrant has not battered at their peace?

ROSS. No; they were well at peace when I did leave 'em.

180 MACDUFF. Be not a niggard of your speech; how goes 't?

ROSS. When I came hither to transport the tidings,
Which I have heavily borne, there ran a rumor
Of many worthy fellows that were out°;
Which was to my belief witnessed the rather,
185 For that I saw the tyrant's power afoot.
Now is the time of help; your eye in Scotland
Would create soldiers, make our women fight,
To doff their dire distresses.

MALCOLM. Be 't their comfort
We are coming thither. Gracious England hath
190 Lent us good Siward and ten thousand men;
An older and a better soldier none
That Christendom gives out.

ROSS. Would I could answer
This comfort with the like! But I have words
That would be howled out in the desert air,
195 Where hearing should not latch° them.

MACDUFF. What concern they?
The general cause? Or is it a fee-grief°
Due to some single breast?

ROSS. No mind that's honest
But in it shares some woe; though the main part
Pertains to you alone.

MACDUFF. If it be mine,

A modern ecstasy: ordinary feeling.

relation too nice: report too exact.

doth hiss the speaker: causes the speaker to be hissed because he is already out of date.

teems: brings forth.

113. How does Ross speak: quickly, or hesitantly?

out: in arms.

latch: catch the sound of.

fee-grief: private grief.

200 Keep it not from me; quickly let me have it.
ROSS. Let not your ears despise my tongue forever,
Which shall possess them with the heaviest sound
That ever yet they heard.
MACDUFF. Hum! I guess at it.
ROSS. Your castle is surprised; your wife and babes
205 Savagely slaughtered.[114] To relate the manner
Were, on the quarry° of these murdered deer,
To add the death of you.
MALCOLM. Merciful heaven!
What, man! ne'er pull your hat upon your brows;
Give sorrow words: the grief that does not speak
210 Whispers the o'er-fraught heart, and bids it break.
MACDUFF. My children, too?
ROSS. Wife, children, servants, all
That could be found.
MACDUFF. And I must be from thence!
My wife killed, too?
ROSS. I have said.
MALCOLM. Be comforted;
Let's make us medicines of our great revenge,
215 To cure his deadly grief.
MACDUFF. He has no children.[115] All my pretty ones?
Did you say all? O hell-kite! All?
What, all my pretty chickens and their dam
At one fell swoop?
220 MALCOLM. Dispute it like a man.
MACDUFF. I shall do so;
But I must also feel it as a man.
I cannot but remember such things were,
That were most precious to me. Did Heaven look on
And would not take their part? Sinful Macduff,
225 They were all struck for thee! Naught, that I am,
Not for their own demerits, but for mine,
Fell slaughter on their souls. Heaven rest them now!
MALCOLM. Be this the whetstone of your sword; let grief
Convert to anger; blunt not the heart, enrage it.
230 MACDUFF. Oh, I could play the woman with mine eyes
And braggart with my tongue! But, gentle Heavens,
Cut short all intermission; front to front
Bring thou this fiend of Scotland and myself;
Within my sword's length set him; if he 'scape,
235 Heaven forgive him, too!
MALCOLM. This tune goes manly.
Come, go we to the King; our power is ready;
Our lack is nothing but our leave.° Macbeth
Is ripe for shaking, and the powers above
Put on their instruments. Receive what cheer you may;
240 The night is long that never finds the day.

(Exeunt.)[116]

114. What has happened that might prompt Ross now to tell Macduff the truth about his wife and children?
quarry: heap of dead bodies.

115. To whom is Macduff referring? What does he mean? (Several interpretations are possible.)

Our lack . . . leave: We only need the King's permission to depart.

116. Why do you think Shakespeare had Macduff learn of Lady Macduff's murder *after* he had convinced Malcolm of his loyalty?

OF CRITICAL INTEREST

How does a psychoanalyst interpret Lady Macbeth's sleepwalking?

"A case of hysterical somnambulism, and conforming to all the known laws of the psychological phenomena of the somnambulistic mental states. . . .

"In the somnambulistic crises, there is a rehearsal of all the emotional experiences which originally caused the mental dissociation. This rehearsal is a literal one, all words, gestures, sounds, scenes, being faithfully reproduced and acted out in a most dramatic manner. Each crisis exactly resembles the preceding one. . . .

"There is a form of nervous disease known as a compulsive neurosis in which the subject has an almost continuous compulsion to either wash the hands or to repeat other actions almost indefinitely. The compulsion may arise from the idea that the hands are soiled or contaminated. . . . The act of washing the hands is a compromise for self-reproach and repressed experience. The mechanism here in the sleepwalking scene is the same as in the compulsive neurosis, a proof of Shakespeare's remarkable insight into the workings of the human mind. . . ."

From *The Hysteria of Lady Macbeth*
by Isador H. Coriat, M.D. (1912).

Shakespeare, the poet of all mankind

"Shakespeare is above all writers, at least above all modern writers, the poet of nature; the poet that holds up to his readers a faithful mirror of manners and of life. His characters are not modified by the customs of particular places, unpractised by the rest of the world; by the peculiarities of studies or professions, which can operate but upon small numbers; or by the accidents of transient fashions or temporary opinions: they are the genuine progeny of common humanity, such as the world will always supply, and observation will always find. His persons act and speak by the influence of those general passions and principles by which all minds are agitated, and the whole system of life is continued in motion. In the writings of other poets a character is too often an individual; in those of Shakespeare it is commonly a species."

From Dr. Samuel Johnson's Preface to his
edition of Shakespeare's Plays (1765).

OF HUMAN INTEREST

What was it like to act Lady Macbeth?

The famous actress Sarah Kemble Siddons made a powerful impression on early nineteenth-century audiences with her interpretation of the role of Lady Macbeth. She wrote: "It was my custom to study my characters at night, when all the domestic cares and business of the day were over. On the night preceding that in which I was to appear in this part for the first time, I shut myself up, as usual, when all the family were retired, and commenced my study of Lady Macbeth. As the character is very short, I thought I should soon accomplish it. Being then only twenty years of age, I believed, as many others do believe, that little more was necessary than to get the words into my head; for the necessity of discrimination and the development of character, at that time of my life, had scarcely entered into my imagination. But, to proceed. I went on with tolerable composure, in the silence of the night (a night I can never forget), till I came to the assassination scene, when the horrors of the scene rose to a degree that made it impossible for me to get farther. I snatched up my candle and hurried out of the room in a paroxysm of terror. My dress was of silk, and the rustling of it, as I ascended the stairs to go to bed, seemed to my panic-struck fancy like the movement of a spectre pursuing me. At last I reached my chamber, where I found my husband fast asleep. I clapt my candlestick down upon the table, without the power of putting the candle out, and threw myself on my bed, without daring to stay even to take off my clothes. At peep of day I rose to resume my task; but so little did I know of my part when I appeared in it, at night, that my shame and confusion cured me of procrastinating my business for the remainder of my life."

From Remarks on the Character of Lady Macbeth,
by Mrs. Siddons, in *Life of Mrs. Siddons* by
T. Campbell (1834).

Act Five

SCENE 1. *Dunsinane. Anteroom in the castle. (Played in the Chamber.)*
Enter a DOCTOR OF PHYSIC° *and a* WAITING-GENTLEWOMAN.

Physic: medicine.

DOCTOR. I have two nights watched with you, but can perceive no truth in your report. When was it she last walked?[117]

117. Note that this scene is in prose—perhaps because the disjointed remarks of Lady Macbeth's sleepwalking do not seem suitable for poetry; the Doctor and Gentlewoman, who speak on a less intense emotional plane, could not very well be given poetry to speak if Lady Macbeth was not.

GENTLEWOMAN. Since his Majesty went into the field, I have seen her rise from her bed, throw her nightgown upon her, unlock her closet,
5 take forth paper, fold it, write upon 't, read it, afterwards seal it, and again return to bed; yet all this while in a most fast sleep.

DOCTOR. A great perturbation in nature, to receive at once the benefit of sleep, and do the effects of watching! In this slumbery agitation, besides her walking and other actual performances, what, at any
10 time, have you heard her say?

GENTLEWOMAN. That, sir, which I will not report after her.

DOCTOR. You may to me; and 'tis most meet you should.

GENTLEWOMAN. Neither to you nor anyone, having no witness to confirm my speech.

(Enter LADY MACBETH, *with a taper.)*

15 Lo, you, here she comes! This is her very guise; and, upon my life, fast asleep. Observe her; stand close.

DOCTOR. How came she by that light?

GENTLEWOMAN. Why, it stood by her; she has light by her continually, 'tis her command.

20 DOCTOR. You see, her eyes are open.

GENTLEWOMAN. Aye, but their sense is shut.

DOCTOR. What is it she does now? Look how she rubs her hands.

GENTLEWOMAN. It is an accustomed action with her, to seem thus washing her hands. I have known her continue in this a quarter of an hour.

25 LADY MACBETH. Yet here's a spot.

DOCTOR. Hark! she speaks. I will set down what comes from her, to satisfy my remembrance the more strongly.

LADY MACBETH. Out, damned spot! out, I say!—One; two. Why, then 'tis time to do 't.—Hell is murky! Fie, my lord, fie! a soldier, and
30 afeard? What need we fear who knows it, when none can call our power to account?—Yet who would have thought the old man to have had so much blood in him?

DOCTOR. Do you mark that?

LADY MACBETH. The thane of Fife had a wife; where is she now?—What,
35 will these hands ne'er be clean?—No more o' that, my lord, no more o' that; you mar all with this starting.

DOCTOR. Go to, go to; you have known what you should not.

GENTLEWOMAN. She has spoke what she should not, I am sure of that. Heaven knows what she has known.

40 LADY MACBETH. Here's the smell of the blood still; all the perfumes of Arabia will not sweeten this little hand. Oh, oh, oh!

DOCTOR. What a sigh is there! The heart is sorely charged.

GENTLEWOMAN. I would not have such a heart in my bosom for the dignity of the whole body.

45 DOCTOR. Well, well, well—

GENTLEWOMAN. Pray God it be, sir.

DOCTOR. This disease is beyond my practice; yet I have known those which have walked in their sleep who have died holily in their beds.

LADY MACBETH. Wash your hands, put on your nightgown; look not so 50 pale.—I tell you yet again, Banquo's buried; he cannot come out on 's grave.

DOCTOR. Even so?

LADY MACBETH. To bed, to bed! There's knocking at the gate. Come, come, come, come, give me your hand. What's done cannot be 55 undone.—To bed, to bed, to bed![118]

DOCTOR. Will she go now to bed?

GENTLEWOMAN. Directly.

DOCTOR. Foul whisperings are abroad! unnatural deeds
Do breed unnatural troubles; infected minds
60 To their deaf pillows will discharge their secrets.
More needs she the divine than the physician.
God, God forgive us all! Look after her;
Remove from her the means of all annoyance°,
And still keep eyes upon her. So, good night.
65 My mind she has mated°, and amazed my sight.
I think, but dare not speak.

GENTLEWOMAN. Good night, good doctor.

(Exeunt.)[119]

118. (a) Can you connect each phrase of Lady Macbeth's speeches with some specific aspect of the crimes in which she has been involved?

(b) Lady Macbeth is obviously in process of emotional collapse. Have there been signs earlier in the play that this might happen? Note especially her speeches at her last appearance, the end of Act Three, Scene 4.

annoyance: injury to herself.

mated: checkmated. The doctor cannot betray his patient.

119. How convincingly has Shakespeare portrayed emotional illness?

SCENE 2.[120] *The country near Dunsinane. (Played on the Platform.) Drum and colors. Enter* MENTEITH, CAITHNESS, ANGUS, LENNOX, *and* SOLDIERS.

120. Note that this act is made up of a series of short scenes which take place alternately at Dunsinane Castle and on the battlefields. On the stage of the Globe, this could easily be managed. If you were making a film of *Macbeth,* how would you handle the frequent shifts? How might they be dealt with in a modern stage production?

MENTEITH. The English power is near, led on by Malcolm,
His uncle Siward, and the good Macduff.
Revenges burn in them; for their dear causes
Would to the bleeding and the grim alarm
5 Excite the mortified man.°

ANGUS. Near Birnam wood
Shall we well meet them; that way are they coming.

CAITHNESS. Who knows if Donalbain be with his brother?

LENNOX. For certain, sir, he is not. I have a file
Of all the gentry: there is Siward's son,[121]
10 And many unrough° youths that even now
Protest their first of manhood.°

MENTEITH. What does the tyrant?

CAITHNESS. Great Dunsinane he strongly fortifies.
Some say he's mad; others that lesser hate him
Do call it valiant fury; but, for certain,
15 He cannot buckle his distempered cause
Within the belt of rule.°

ANGUS. Now does he feel
His secret murders sticking on his hands;
Now minutely revolts upbraid his faith-breach;°

their dear causes . . . man: their deeply-felt causes would arouse a dead man to bloody battle.

121. Follow young Siward's activities. Why did Shakespeare introduce this episode?

unrough: beardless.

Protest . . . manhood: call themselves men for the first time.

He cannot . . . rule: He cannot control the situation.

Now . . . faith-breach: Every minute, those who revolt against him blame his faithlessness.

Those he commands move only in command,
20 Nothing in love; now does he feel his title
Hang loose about him, like a giant's robe
Upon a dwarfish thief.

MENTEITH. Who then shall blame
His pestered senses to recoil and start,
When all that is within him does condemn
25 Itself for being there?

CAITHNESS. Well, march we on,
To give obedience where 'tis truly owed.
Meet we the medicine of the sickly weal,
And with him pour we in our country's purge
Each drop of us.°

LENNOX. Or so much as it needs,
30 To dew the sovereign flower and drown the weeds.
Make we our march toward Birnam.

(Exeunt, marching.)

Meet we . . . us: We go to meet Malcolm, who will heal the sickness of our country, and to offer our lives in the curing process.

SCENE 3. *Dunsinane. A room in the castle. (Played in the Chamber.)*
Enter MACBETH, DOCTOR, *and* ATTENDANTS.

MACBETH. Bring me no more reports; let them° fly all.
Till Birnam wood remove to Dunsinane,
I cannot taint° with fear. What's the boy Malcolm?
Was he not born of woman? The spirits that know
5 All mortal consequences have pronounced me thus:
"Fear not, Macbeth; no man that's born of woman
Shall e'er have power upon thee." Then fly, false thanes,
And mingle with the English epicures.
The mind I sway by° and the heart I bear
10 Shall never sag with doubt nor shake with fear.

(Enter a SERVANT.*)*

The devil damn thee black, thou cream-faced loon!
Where got'st thou that goose look?

SERVANT. There is ten thousand—

MACBETH. Geese, villain?

SERVANT. Soldiers, sir.

MACBETH. Go prick thy face, and over-red° thy fear,
15 Thou lily-livered boy. What soldiers, patch?°
Death of thy soul! those linen cheeks of thine
Are counselors to fear. What soldiers, whey-face?

SERVANT. The English force, so please you.

MACBETH. Take thy face hence.

(Exit SERVANT.*)*

Seyton!—I am sick at heart,
20 When I behold—Seyton, I say!—This push°
Will cheer me ever, or disseat me now.
I have lived long enough; my way of life
Is fall'n into the sear, the yellow leaf;
And that which should accompany old age,

them: the thanes.

taint: become infected with.

I sway by: I am directed by.

over-red: redden. The implication is that the servant's blood has gone to his lower body on account of his fear. He is pale, and there is no blood in his liver, where his courage should have resided—hence, *lily-livered.*
patch: fool.

push: attack.

25 As honor, love, obedience, troops of friends,
I must not look to have; but, in their stead,
Curses, not loud but deep, mouth-honor, breath,
Which the poor heart would fain deny, and dare not.
Seyton![122]

(Enter SEYTON.*)*

30 SEYTON. What is your gracious pleasure?
MACBETH. What news more?

122. What *appears* to be Macbeth's emotional state at the beginning of the scene? How is he actually feeling? What tells you?

SEYTON. All is confirmed, my lord, which was reported.
MACBETH. I'll fight till from my bones my flesh be hacked.
Give me my armor.
SEYTON. 'Tis not needed yet.
MACBETH. I'll put it on.
35 Send out moe horses, skirr° the country round;
Hang those that talk of fear. Give me mine armor.
How does your patient, doctor?[123]

skirr: scour.

123. What do Macbeth's remarks about his wife's illness reveal about the state of their relationship at this point?

DOCTOR. Not so sick, my lord,
As she is troubled with thick-coming fancies,
That keep her from her rest.
MACBETH. Cure her of that.
40 Canst thou not minister to a mind diseased,
Pluck from the memory a rooted sorrow,
Raze out the written troubles of the brain,
And with some sweet oblivious antidote
Cleanse the stuffed bosom of that perilous stuff°
45 Which weighs upon the heart?

stuff: Some scholars think this word is a printer's error and should be *grief*.

DOCTOR. Therein the patient
Must minister to himself.
MACBETH. Throw physic to the dogs; I'll none of it.
Come, put mine armor on; give me my staff.
Seyton, send out.° Doctor, the thanes fly from me.
50 Come sir, dispatch. If thou couldst, doctor, cast
The water of my land,° find her disease
And purge it to a sound and pristine health,
I would applaud thee to the very echo,
That should applaud again.—Pull 't off,° I say.—
55 What rhubarb, senna, or what purgative drug,
Would scour these English hence? Hear'st thou of them?

send out: send out more scouts.

cast . . . land: diagnose my country's illness.

Pull 't off: referring to some part of his armor.

DOCTOR. Aye, my good lord; your royal preparation
Makes us hear something.
MACBETH. Bring it° after me.
I will not be afraid of death and bane
60 Till Birnam forest come to Dunsinane.
DOCTOR *(aside)*. Were I from Dunsinane away and clear,
Profit again should hardly draw me here.

it: the armor.

(Exeunt.)

SCENE 4. *Country near Birnam wood. (Played on the Platform.) Drum and colors. Enter* MALCOLM, OLD SIWARD *and his* SON, MACDUFF, MENTEITH, CAITHNESS, ANGUS, LENNOX, ROSS, *and* SOLDIERS, *marching.*

MALCOLM. Cousins, I hope the days are near at hand
That chambers will be safe.°

That chambers . . . safe: when people can sleep safely.

MENTEITH. We doubt it nothing.
SIWARD. What wood is this before us?
MENTEITH. The wood of Birnam.
MALCOLM. Let every soldier hew him down a bough,
5 And bear 't before him; thereby shall we shadow
The numbers of our host, and make discovery°
Err in report of us.°

discovery: Macbeth's scouts.

Lines 3-7: Here the equivocations of the apparitions begin to be revealed.

SOLDIERS. It shall be done.
SIWARD. We learn no other but the confident tyrant
Keeps still in Dunsinane, and will endure
10 Our setting down before 't.°

setting down . . . : laying siege to it.

MALCOLM. 'Tis his main hope;
For where there is advantage to be given,
Both more and less° have given him the revolt,
And none serve with him but constrainèd things
Whose hearts are absent, too.

Both more and less: both nobles and common people.

MACDUFF. Let our just censures
15 Attend the true event,° and put we on
Industrious soldiership.

Let . . . event: Let our judgment await the actual outcome of the battle.

SIWARD. The time approaches
That will with due decision make us know
What we shall say we have and what we owe.
Thoughts speculative their unsure hopes relate,
20 But certain issue strokes must arbitrate;°
Toward which advance the war.

Thoughts . . . arbitrate: We are now speculating on the basis of our hopes; only after the battle will we know the real outcome.

(Exeunt, marching.)

SCENE 5. *Dunsinane. Within the castle. (Played on the Tarras and in the Chamber.) Enter°* MACBETH, SEYTON, *and* SOLDIERS, *with drum and colors.*

(They enter on the Tarras.)

MACBETH. Hang out our banners on the outward walls;
The cry is still "They come!" Our castle's strength
Will laugh a seige to scorn; here let them lie
Till famine and the ague eat them up.
5 Were they not forced° with those that should be ours,
We might have met them dareful, beard to beard,
And beat them backward home.

forced: reinforced.

(A cry of women within.)

What is that noise?
SEYTON. It is the cry of women, my good lord.

(Exit.)°

(Exits into the Chamber.)

MACBETH. I have almost forgot the taste of fears.

10 The time has been[124] my senses would have cooled
To hear a night-shriek, and my fell° of hair
Would at a dismal treatise° rouse and stir
As life were in 't. I have supped full with horrors;
Direness, familiar to my slaughterous thoughts,
15 Cannot once start me.

(Reënter SEYTON.*)*°

Wherefore was that cry?

SEYTON. The Queen, my lord, is dead.

MACBETH.[125] She should have died hereafter;
There would have been a time for such a word.
Tomorrow, and tomorrow, and tomorrow,
20 Creeps in this petty pace from day to day.
To the last syllable of recorded time,
And all our yesterdays have lighted fools
The way to dusty death. Out, out, brief candle!
Life's but a walking shadow, a poor player
25 That struts and frets his hour upon the stage
And then is heard no more; it is a tale
Told by an idiot, full of sound and fury,
Signifying nothing.[126]

(Enter a MESSENGER.*)*

Thou comest to use thy tongue; thy story quickly.

30 MESSENGER. Gracious my lord,
I should report that which I say I saw,
But know not how to do it.

MACBETH. Well, say, sir.

MESSENGER. As I did stand my watch upon the hill,
I looked toward Birnam, and anon, methought,
35 The wood began to move.

MACBETH. Liar and slave!

MESSENGER. Let me endure your wrath, if 't be not so.
Within this three mile may you see it coming;
I say, a moving grove.

MACBETH. If thou speak'st false,
Upon the next tree shalt thou hang alive,
40 Till famine cling° thee; if thy speech be sooth,
I care not if thou dost for me as much.
I pull in resolution,° and begin
To doubt the equivocation° of the fiend
That lies like truth: "Fear not, till Birnam wood
45 Do come to Dunsinane"; and now a wood
Comes toward Dunsinane. Arm, arm, and out![127]
If this which he avouches does appear,
There is nor flying hence nor tarrying here.
I 'gin to be aweary of the sun,
50 And wish the estate o' the world were now undone.
Ring the alarum-bell! Blow, wind! come, wrack!°
At least we'll die with harness on our back.

(Exeunt.)

124. When was the time he refers to? What does the rest of the speech suggest about changes in his character?
fell: covering.
dismal treatise: horrible story.

(He reënters from the Chamber.)

125. How might Macbeth react before he speaks?

126. What does Macbeth mean by "She should have died hereafter"? Which lines in the soliloquy are most helpful in providing clues? What does the soliloquy say about life in general? about Macbeth's life specifically?

cling: shrivel up.

I pull in resolution: I weaken in confidence. With these words begins Macbeth's awareness that he has been duped by the witches.
doubt the equivocation: fear the deception.

127. *Line 46:* Compare these words with lines 2-7 of this scene. What has caused Macbeth to change his plans?

wrack: ruin; destruction.

SCENE 6. *Dunsinane. Before the castle. (Played on the Platform.) Drum and colors. Enter* MALCOLM, OLD SIWARD, MACDUFF, *and their* ARMY, *with boughs.*

MALCOLM. Now near enough; your leavy screens throw down,
And show like those you are. You, worthy uncle,
Shall, with my cousin, your right noble son,
Lead our first battle°; worthy Macduff and we
5 Shall take upon 's what else remains to do,
According to our order.

battle: division of troops.

SIWARD. Fare you well.
Do we but find the tyrant's power tonight,
Let us be beaten, if we cannot fight.
MACDUFF. Make all our trumpets speak; give them all breath,
10 Those clamorous harbingers of blood and death.

(Exeunt.)

SCENE 7. *Another part of the field. (Played on the Platform.)° Alarums. Enter* MACBETH.

(At this point, the Study curtains may have been thrown open to reveal the gate of Macbeth's castle, with perhaps a portcullis hanging under the Tarras. Macbeth stands at bay before the gates.)

MACBETH. They have tied me to a stake; I cannot fly,
But, bearlike, I must fight the course.° What's he
That was not born of woman? Such a one
Am I to fear, or none.

They have . . . course: In bearbaiting, a popular sport in Shakespeare's time, a bear was tied to a stake and forced to fight rounds with dogs set upon it in relays.

(Enter YOUNG SIWARD.*)*

5 YOUNG SIWARD. What is thy name?
MACBETH. Thou'lt be afraid to hear it.
YOUNG SIWARD. No; though thou call'st thyself a hotter name
Than any is in hell.
MACBETH. My name's Macbeth.
YOUNG SIWARD. The devil himself could not pronounce a title
More hateful to mine ear.
MACBETH. No, nor more fearful.
10 YOUNG SIWARD. Thou liest, abhorrèd tyrant; with my sword
I'll prove the lie thou speak'st.

(They fight, and YOUNG SIWARD *is slain.)*

MACBETH. Thou wast born of woman.
But swords I smile at, weapons laugh to scorn,
Brandished by man that's of a woman born.

(Exit.)

(Alarums. Enter MACDUFF.*)*

MACDUFF. That way the noise is. Tyrant, show thy face!
15 If thou be'st slain and with no stroke of mine,
My wife and children's ghosts will haunt me still.
I cannot strike at wretched kerns, whose arms
Are hired to bear their staves; either thou, Macbeth,
Or else my sword with an unbattered edge
20 I sheathe again undeeded. There thou shouldst be;

By this great clatter, one of greatest note
Seems bruited°. Let me find him, fortune!
And more I beg not. *(Exit. Alarums.)*

(Enter MALCOLM *and* OLD SIWARD.*)*

SIWARD. This way, my lord; the castle's gently rendered°;
25 The tyrant's people on both sides do fight;
The noble thanes do bravely in the war;
The day almost itself professes yours,
And little is to do.

MALCOLM. We have met the foes
That strike beside us.

SIWARD. Enter, sir, the castle.

(Exeunt. Alarums.)

bruited: announced by a great noise.

rendered: surrendered.
(The formal entry into the castle, after surrender, might be made through gates visible in the Study. Victorious soldiers might appear in the window-stages and dip the tyrant's banners, planting those of Malcolm and Siward on the Tarras. Macbeth's next entry and that of Macduff would probably be made through the two stage-doors on the Platform.)

SCENE 8. *Another part of the field. (Played on the Platform.) Enter* MACBETH.

MACBETH. Why should I play the Roman fool and die
On mine own sword?° Whiles I see lives°, the gashes
Do better upon them.

(Enter MACDUFF.*)*

MACDUFF. Turn, hell-hound, turn!

MACBETH. Of all men else I have avoided thee.
5 But get thee back; my soul is too much charged
With blood of thine already.

MACDUFF. I have no words;
My voice is in my sword, thou bloodier villain
Than terms can give thee out! *(They fight.)*

MACBETH. Thou losest labor;
As easy mayst thou the intrenchant° air
10 With thy keen sword impress as make me bleed.
Let fall thy blade on vulnerable crests;
I bear a charmèd life, which must not yield
To one of woman born.

MACDUFF. Despair thy charm;
And let the angel whom thou still hast served
15 Tell thee Macduff was from his mother's womb
Untimely ripped.

MACBETH. Accursèd be that tongue that tells me so,
For it hath cowed my better part of man!
And be these juggling fiends no more believed
20 That palter with us in a double sense;
That keep the word of promise to our ear,
And break it to our hope. I'll not fight with thee.

MACDUFF. Then yield thee, coward,
And live to be the show and gaze o' the time.
25 We'll have thee, as our rarer monsters are,
Painted upon a pole,° and underwrit,
"Here may you see the tyrant."

Why . . . sword: The Romans considered suicide more honorable than capture.
lives: living persons.

intrenchant: invulnerable.

Painted . . . pole: your picture painted on a board which will be suspended on a pole.

MACBETH. I will not yield,
To kiss the ground before young Malcolm's feet,
And to be baited with the rabble's curse.
30 Though Birnam wood be come to Dunsinane,
And thou opposed, being of no woman born,
Yet I will try the last. Before my body
I throw my warlike shield. Lay on, Macduff,
And damned be him that first cries, "Hold, enough!"[128]

(Exeunt, fighting. Alarums.)

(Retreat. Flourish. Enter, with drum and colors, MALCOLM, OLD SIWARD, ROSS, *the other* THANES, *and* SOLDIERS.*)*

35 MALCOLM. I would the friends we miss were safe arrived.
SIWARD. Some must go off°; and yet, by these I see,
So great a day as this is cheaply bought.
MALCOLM. Macduff is missing, and your noble son.
ROSS. Your son, my lord, has paid a soldier's debt;
40 He only lived but till he was a man;
The which no sooner had his prowess confirmed
In the unshrinking station where he fought,
But like a man he died.
SIWARD. Then he is dead?[129]
ROSS. Aye, and brought off the field; your cause of sorrow
45 Must not be measured by his worth, for then
It hath no end.
SIWARD. Had he his hurts before?
ROSS. Aye, on the front.
SIWARD. Why then, God's soldier be he![130]
Had I as many sons as I have hairs,
I would not wish them to a fairer death;
50 And so, his knell is knolled.
MALCOLM. He's worth more sorrow,
And that I'll spend for him.
SIWARD. He's worth no more.
They say he parted well, and paid his score;
And so, God be with him! Here comes newer comfort.

(Reënter MACDUFF, *with* MACBETH*'s head.)*

MACDUFF. Hail, King! for so thou art. Behold, where stands
55 The usurper's cursèd head. The time is free;
I see thee compassed with thy kingdom's pearl,°
That speak my salutation in their minds;
Whose voices I desire aloud with mine—
Hail, King of Scotland!
ALL. Hail, King of Scotland!
60 MALCOLM. We shall not spend a large expense of time
Before we reckon with your several loves,
And make us even with you. My thanes and kinsmen,
Henceforth be earls, the first that ever Scotland
In such an honor named. What's more to do,
65 Which would be planted newly with the time,

128. *Lines 27-34:* How do Macbeth's last lines in the play relate to his character as described by the Sergeant in Act One, Scene 2?

go off: die.

129. Compare Siward's reaction to his son's death (a) to the way Macbeth reacted at the news of Duncan's death (Act Two, Scene 3); and (b) to Macduff's reaction when he heard of the murder of his family.

130. Why does Siward say this?

compassed . . . pearl: surrounded by the nobles of your kingdom.

As calling home our exiled friends abroad
That fled the snares of watchful tyranny;
Producing forth the cruel ministers
Of this dead butcher and his fiendlike queen,
70 Who, as 'tis thought, by self and violent hands
Took off her life;[131] this, and what needful else
That calls upon us, by the grace of Grace
We will perform in measure, time, and place;
So, thanks to all at once and to each one,
75 Whom we invite to see us crowned at Scone.

(Flourish. Exeunt.)

THE END

131. *Lines 69-71:* What other indications are there that Lady Macbeth has committed suicide?

(Watkins: "The finale a fully crowded scene. Malcolm center, with Macduff and Siward near him; the Thanes grouped by the two Stage-Posts; some soldiers around the perimeter, others on the Tarras with Macbeth's head and banners. The departure is processional through the Castle gates in the Study, to the accompaniment of a Flourish. The tyrant's head remains when all others have withdrawn into the Tiring-House.")

Illustrations on pages 150, 158, 164, 175, 177, 181, 193, and 208 by Charles Ricketts for *The Tragedie of Macbeth* reproduced in the Players' Shakespeare, after the Folio of 1623, Ernest Benn, 1923.

DISCUSSION

1. According to the classical view, the undoing or downfall of the main character in a tragedy is brought about through a tragic flaw in his character, or through a tragic error. What brought about Macbeth's downfall? Lady Macbeth's?

2. According to the classical view, tragedy should arouse feelings of pity and fear in its audience. Is this true of the play *Macbeth?* Explain.

3. Compare Macbeth and Lady Macbeth as they appear in Act One with the way they appear in Act Five. How has each of them changed with respect to strength of character? How do you account for this?

4. Lady Macbeth fades out of the play almost completely (except for the sleepwalking scene) after Act Three. What dramatic effect is achieved by her absence and her final reappearance?

5. Do you agree with Malcolm's dismissal of Macbeth and Lady Macbeth as "this dead butcher and his fiendlike queen"? Explain.

6. What sort of king was Duncan? (Note what he says, what he does, and what others say about him.) Is Shakespeare's portrayal of his character consistent?

7. Duncan said of the traitorous Thane of Cawdor: "There's no art / To find the mind's construction in the face." The ability to go beneath the surface to interpret character and motivation—in others and in oneself—is universally important, on the stage and off.

(a) How sound a judge was Lady Macbeth of Macbeth's character?

(b) How sound a judge was Macbeth of Lady Macbeth's character?

(c) How well did Macbeth and Lady Macbeth understand themselves and their own psychological limitations?

8. In literature, characters are frequently used as foils; that is, the characteristics of one point up by contrast the characteristics of another.

(a) What traits of Macbeth are thrown into relief by contrast with

Duncan? with young Siward? with Malcolm?

(b) What characteristics of Lady Macbeth are pointed up by contrast with Lady Macduff?

9. The article "The Character of Macbeth" on pages 214–216 presents a widely accepted view by a distinguished Shakespearian scholar. The American writer Mary McCarthy disagrees with Bradley. In an essay entitled "General Macbeth" she claims that Macbeth is simply a commonplace man, literal-minded, superstitious, overcredulous, and completely lacking in imagination. Rather, she suggests, it is Lady Macbeth who is imaginative.

Which opinion seems most convincing to you? Support your choice with evidence from the play.

WRITING

1. Commentators have pointed out that three forces are at work to destroy Macbeth: flaws in his own character, the forces of evil or the Devil as represented by the Three Weird Sisters, and Lady Macbeth. Select the force that you think was most responsible for his downfall and show how that force was predominant. You may wish to note that the other forces existed, but that the one you select was the major one.

2. To equivocate means "to use ambiguous expressions, especially to mislead." Discuss equivocation as a theme in *Macbeth,* citing specific examples from the text.

3. Children play a major role in *Macbeth,* not only as actors but also in the imagery. Discuss their use in both these ways.

4. Assume that Macbeth and Lady Macbeth have both been taken prisoner, and that a decision has been made to execute the one found more guilty and to free the other. Do *one* of the following:

(a) Assume that you are the prosecutor and prepare the case against Lady Macbeth.

(b) Assume that you are the prosecutor and prepare the case against Macbeth.

5. (a) Choose one of Lady Macbeth's major soliloquies and discuss what it reveals about her character. Consider the sleepwalking scene as a soliloquy.

(b) Do the same for Macbeth.

6. Select any symbol or other unifying device and trace its use throughout the play. (As an example, note Caroline Spurgeon's discussion of clothing imagery in the article "The Imagery in *Macbeth.*") Suggestions: blood, birds, reality-illusion, sleep and sleeplessness, night and darkness. However, you are not limited to these.

7. Write a filmscript for a short scene (or part of a scene) from *Macbeth.* Include acting suggestions and directions for camera angles, lighting, sets, etc.

READERS' THEATER

Imagine you are staging any one scene in *Macbeth.* Plan the setting, the costumes, and any special effects that you feel would increase the dramatic tension. Prepare one major speech from the scene for reading to the class.

For your class presentation, first "set the stage" by explaining your ideas about sets, costumes, and special effects, then read your speech.

THE IMAGERY IN MACBETH

by Caroline T. E. Spurgeon

THE imagery in *Macbeth* appears to be more rich and varied, more highly imaginative, more unapproachable by any other writer, than that of any other single play. It is particularly so, I think, in the continuous use made of the simplest, humblest, everyday things, drawn from the daily life in a small house, as a vehicle for sublime poetry.

Few simple things—harmless in themselves—have such a curiously humiliating and degrading effect as the spectacle of a notably small man enveloped in a coat far too big for him. Comic actors know this well, and it is by means of this homely picture that Shakespeare shows us his imaginative view of the hero, and expresses the fact that the honors for which the murders were committed are, after all, of very little worth to him.

The idea constantly recurs that Macbeth's new honors sit ill upon him, like a loose and badly fitting garment, belonging to someone else. Macbeth himself first expresses it, quite early in the play, when, immediately following the first appearance of the witches and their prophecies, Ross arrives from the king, and greets him as thane of Cawdor, to which Macbeth quickly replies,

> The thane of Cawdor lives: why do you dress me
> In borrowed robes?

And a few minutes later, when he is rapt in ambitious thoughts suggested by the confirmation of two out of the three "prophetic greetings," Banquo, watching him, murmurs,

> New honors come upon him,
> Like our strange garments, cleave not to their mould
> But with the aid of use.

When Duncan is safely in the castle, Macbeth's better nature for a moment asserts itself, and, in debate with himself, he revolts from the contemplated deed for a threefold reason: because of its incalculable results, the treachery of such an action from one who is both kinsman and host, and Duncan's own virtues and greatness as king.

When his wife joins him, his repugnance to the deed is as great, but it is significant that he gives three quite different reasons for not going ahead with it, reasons which he hopes may appeal to her, for he knows the others would not. . . .

There is irony in the fact that to express the position he uses the same metaphor of clothes:

> I have bought
> Golden opinions from all sorts of people,
> Which would be worn now in their newest gloss,
> Not cast aside so soon.

To which Lady Macbeth, quite unmoved, retorts contemptuously:

> Was the hope drunk
> Wherein you dressed yourself?

After the murder, when Ross says he is going to Scone for Macbeth's coronation, Macduff uses the same simile:

> Well, may you see things well done there: adieu!
> Lest our old robes sit easier than our new!

And, at the end, when the tyrant is at bay at Dunsinane, and the English troops are advancing, the Scottish lords still have this image in their minds. Caithness sees him as a man vainly trying to fasten a large garment on him with too small a belt:

> He cannot buckle his distempered cause
> Within the belt of rule;

while Angus, in a similar image, vividly sums up the essence of what they all have been thinking ever since Macbeth's accession to power:

> now does he feel his title
> Hang loose about him, like a giant's robe
> Upon a dwarfish thief.

Slightly abrided from *Shakespeare's Imagery and What It Tells Us* by Caroline T. E. Spurgeon. Reprinted by permission of Cambridge University Press.

THE CHARACTER OF MACBETH

by A. C. Bradley

THE way to be untrue to Shakespeare is to conventionalise, to conceive Macbeth, for example, as a half-hearted cowardly criminal, and Lady Macbeth as a wholehearted fiend.

These two characters are fired by one and the same passion of ambition; and to a considerable extent they are alike. The disposition of each is high, proud, and commanding. They are peremptory or contemptuous to their inferiors. We observe in them no love of country, and no interest in the welfare of anyone outside their family. And though in both there is something, and in one much, of what is higher—honor, conscience, humanity—they do not live consciously in the light of these things or speak their language.

So far there is much likeness between them. Otherwise they are contrasted, and the action is built upon this contrast. Their attitudes toward the projected murder of Duncan are quite different; and it produces in them equally different effects. In consequence, they appear in the earlier part of the play as of equal importance, if indeed Lady Macbeth does not overshadow her husband; but afterwards she retires more and more into the background, and he becomes unmistakably the leading figure. His is indeed the more complex character.

Macbeth is introduced to us as a general of extraordinary prowess, who has covered himself with glory in putting down a rebellion and repelling the invasion of a foreign army. In these conflicts he showed great personal courage, a quality which he continues to display throughout the drama in regard to all plain dangers. It is difficult to be sure of his customary demeanor, for in the play we see him in exceptional circumstances; but from his *later* conversations with Lady Macbeth, and from his language to the murderers of Banquo and to others, we imagine him as a great warrior, somewhat masterful, rough, and abrupt, a man to inspire some fear and much admiration. He was thought "honest," or honorable; Macduff, a man of the highest integrity, "loved him well." And there was, in fact, much good in him. . . .certainly he was far from devoid of humanity and pity.

At the same time he was exceedingly ambitious. The tendency must have been greatly strengthened by his marriage. When we see him, it has been further stimulated by his remarkable success. It becomes a passion. The course of action suggested by it is extremely perilous: it sets his good name, his position, and even his life on the hazard. It is also abhorrent to his better feelings. Their defeat in the struggle with ambition leaves him utterly wretched, and would have kept him so, however complete had been his outward success and security. On the other hand, his passion for power and his instinct for self-assertion are so vehement that no inward misery could persuade him to relinquish the fruits of crime, or to advance from remorse to repentance.

In the character so far sketched there is nothing very peculiar. But there is in Macbeth one marked peculiarity, the true apprehension of which is the key to Shakespeare's conception. This bold ambitious man of action has, within certain limits, the imagination of a poet—an imagination on the one hand extremely sensitive to impressions of a certain kind, and, on the other, productive of violent disturbance both of mind and body. Through it he is kept in contact with supernatural impressions and is liable to supernatural fears. And through it, especially, come to him the intimations of conscience and honor. Macbeth's better nature—to put the matter for clearness' sake too broadly—instead of speaking to him in the overt language of moral ideas, commands, and prohibitions, incorporates itself in images which alarm and horrify. His imagination is thus the best of him, something usually deeper and higher than his conscious thoughts. But his wife quite misunderstands it, and he himself understands it only in part. The terrifying images which deter him from crime and follow its commission, and which are really the protest of his deepest self, seem to his wife the creations of mere nervous fear, and are sometimes referred by himself to the dread of vengeance or the restlessness of insecurity. His conscious or reflective mind, that is, moves chiefly among considerations of outward success and failure, while his inner being is convulsed by conscience. . . .

It is of the first importance to realise the strength,

Condensed and slightly adapted from *Lecture IX, Shakespearean Tragedy* by A. C. Bradley. Reprinted by permission of St. Martin's Press, Inc., Macmillan & Co., Ltd. and Macmillan London and Basingstoke.

and also the limits, of Macbeth's imagination. He shows no sign of any unusual sensitiveness to the glory or beauty in the world or the soul. His imagination is excitable and intense, but narrow. That which stimulates it is, almost solely, that which thrills with sudden, startling, and often supernatural fear. There is a famous passage late in the play which is here very significant, because it refers to a time before his conscience was burdened, and so shows his native disposition:

> The time has been, my senses would have cooled
> To hear a night-shriek; and my fell of hair
> Would at a dismal treatise rise and stir
> As life were in't.

In the drama, everything which terrifies him is of this character, only it has now a deeper and a moral significance. Palpable dangers leave him unmoved or fill him with fire. What appals him is always the image of his own guilty heart or bloody deed, or some image which derives from them its terror or gloom. As the first "horrid image" of Duncan's murder—of himself murdering Duncan—rises from unconsciousness and confronts him, his hair stands on end and the outward scene vanishes from his eyes. Why? For fear of "consequences"? The idea is ridiculous. Or because the deed is bloody? The man who with his "smoking" steel "carved out his passage" to the rebel leader, and "unseamed him from the nave to the chaps," would hardly be frightened by blood. How could fear of consequences make the dagger he is to use hang suddenly glittering before him in the air, and then as suddenly dash it with gouts of blood? Even when he *talks* of consequences, and declares that if he were safe against them he would "jump the life to come," his imagination bears witness against him, and shows us that what really holds him back is the hideous vileness of the deed:

> He's here in double trust;
> First, as I am his kinsman and his subject . . .

and so on. It may be said that he is here thinking of the horror that others will feel at the deed. Yes, but could he realise thus how horrible the deed would look to others if it were not equally horrible to himself?

It is the same when the murder is done. He is well-nigh mad with horror, but it is not the horror of detection. It is not he who thinks of washing his hands or getting his nightgown on. He has brought away the daggers he should have left on the pillows of the grooms, but what does he care for that? What *he* thinks of is that, when he heard one of the men awaked from sleep say "God bless us," he could not say "Amen"; for his imagination presents to him the parching of his throat as an immediate judgment from heaven. His wife heard the owl scream and the crickets cry; but what *he* heard was the voice that first cried "Macbeth doth murder sleep," and then, a minute later, with a change of tense, denounced on him, as if his three names gave him three personalities to suffer in, the doom of sleeplessness:

> Glamis hath murdered sleep, and therefore Cawdor
> Shall sleep no more, Macbeth shall sleep no more.

There comes a sound of knocking. It should be perfectly familiar to him; but he knows not whence, or from what world, it comes. He looks down at his hands, and starts violently: "What hands are here?" For they seem alive, they move, they mean to pluck out his eyes. He looks at one of them again; it does not move; but the blood upon it is enough to dye the whole ocean red. What has all this to do with "consequences"? It is his soul speaking in the only shape in which it can speak freely, that of imagination.

So long as Macbeth's imagination is active, we watch him fascinated; we feel suspense, horror, awe; in which are latent, also, admiration and sympathy. But so soon as it is quiescent these feelings vanish. He is no longer "infirm of purpose": he becomes domineering, even brutal, or he becomes a cool pitiless hypocrite. He is generally said to be a very bad actor, but this is not wholly true. Whenever his imagination stirs, he acts badly. It so possesses him, and is so much stronger than his reason, that his face betrays him, and his voice utters the most improbable untruths[1] or the most artificial rhetoric.[2] But when it is asleep he is firm, self-controlled, and practical, as in the conversation where he skilfully elicits from Banquo that information about his movements which is required for the successful arrangement of his murder. Here he is hate-

1. E.g., in Act One, Scene 3, where he excuses his abstraction by saying that his "dull brain was wrought with things forgotten," when nothing could be more natural than that he should be thinking of his new honor.

2. E.g., in Act One, Scene 4. This is so also in Act Two, Scene 3, lines 114 ff., though here there is some real imaginative excitement mingled with the rhetorical antitheses and balanced clauses and forced bombast.

ful; and so he is in the conversation with the murderers. On the other hand, we feel much pity as well as anxiety in the scene where his wife overcomes his opposition to the murder; and we feel it (though his imagination is not specially active) because this scene shows us how little he understands himself. Not that he fails to realise in reflection the baseness of the deed. But he has never, to put it pedantically, accepted as the principle of his conduct the morality which takes shape in his imaginative fears. Had he done so, and said plainly to his wife, "The thing is vile, and, however much I have sworn to do it, I will not," she would have been helpless.

. . . As it is, the deed is done in horror and without the faintest desire or sense of glory—done, one may almost say, as if it were an appalling duty; and, the instant it is finished, its futility is revealed to Macbeth as clearly as its vileness had been revealed beforehand. As he staggers from the scene he mutters in despair, "Wake Duncan with thy knocking! I would thou could'st." When, half an hour later, he returns with Lennox from the room of the murder, he breaks out:

> Had I but died an hour before this chance,
> I had lived a blessed time. . . .

and so on. This is no mere acting. The language here has none of the false rhetoric of his merely hypocritical speeches. It is meant to deceive, but it utters at the same time his profoundest feeling. And this he can henceforth never hide from himself for long. However he may try to drown it in further enormities, he hears it murmuring "Duncan is in his grave:/After life's fitful fever he sleeps well"; or, ". . . better be with the dead"; or, "I have lived long enough." And it speaks its last words on the last day of his life:

> Out, out, brief candle!
> Life's but a walking shadow, a poor player
> That struts and frets his hour upon the stage
> And then is heard no more: . . .

How strange that this judgment on life, the despair of a man who had knowingly made mortal war on his own soul, should be frequently quoted as Shakespeare's own judgment, and should even be adduced, in serious criticism, as a proof of his pessimism! □

THE WITCH-SCENES IN MACBETH

by A. C. Bradley

ON THE one hand the Witches are credited by some critics with far too great an influence upon the action; sometimes they are described as goddesses, or even as fates, whom Macbeth is powerless to resist. On the other hand, we are told that, great as is their influence on the action, it is so because they are merely symbolic representations of the unconscious or half-conscious guilt in Macbeth.

(1) As to the former, Shakespeare took as material for his purposes, the ideas about witchcraft that he found existing in people around him and in books like Reginald Scot's *Discovery* (1584). And he used these ideas without changing their substance at all. He selected and improved, avoiding the merely ridiculous, dismissing the sexually loathsome or stimulating, rehandling and heightening whatever could touch the imagination with fear, horror, and mysterious attraction. The Witches, that is to say, are not goddesses, or fates, or, in any way whatever, supernatural beings. They are old women, poor and ragged, skinny and hideous, full of vulgar spite, occupied in killing their neighbours' swine or revenging themselves on sailors' wives who have refused them chestnuts. There is not a syllable in *Macbeth* to imply that they are anything but women. But they have received from evil spirits certain supernatural powers.

Next, while the influence of the Witches' prophecies on Macbeth is very great, it is quite clearly shown to be an influence and nothing more. There is no sign whatever in the play that Shakespeare meant the actions of Macbeth to be forced on him by an external power. The prophecies of the Witches are presented simply as dangerous circumstances with which Macbeth has to deal. Macbeth is, in the ordinary sense, perfectly free in regard to them. That the influence of the first prophecies upon him came

Abridged from *Lecture IX, Shakespearean Tragedy* by A. C. Bradley. Reprinted by permission of St. Martin's Press, Inc., Macmillan & Co., Ltd. and Macmillan London and Basingstoke.

as much from himself as from them, is made abundantly clear by the obviously intentional contrast between him and Banquo. Banquo, ambitious but perfectly honest, is scarcely even startled by them, and he remains throughout the scene indifferent to them. But when Macbeth heard them he was not an innocent man. Precisely how far his mind was guilty may be a question; but no innocent man would have started, as he did, with a start of *fear* at the mere prophecy of a crown, or have conceived thereupon *immediately* the thought of murder. Either this thought was not new to him, or he had cherished at least some vaguer dishonorable dream. In either case not only was he free to accept or resist the temptation, but the temptation was already within him. And we are admitting, again, too much when we use the word "temptation" in reference to the first prophecies of the Witches. Speaking strictly we must affirm that he was tempted only by himself. *He* speaks indeed of their "supernatural soliciting"; but in fact they did not solicit. They merely announced events: they hailed him as Thane of Glamis, Thane of Cawdor, and King hereafter. No connection of these announcements with any actions of his was even hinted by them.

When Macbeth sees the Witches again, after the murders of Duncan and Banquo, we observe, however, a striking change. They no longer need to go and meet him; he seeks them out. He has committed himself to his course of evil. Now accordingly they do "solicit." They prophesy, but they also give advice: they bid him be bloody, bold, and secure. We have no hope that he will reject their advice; but so far are they from having, even now, any power to compel him to accept it, that they make careful preparations to deceive him into doing so. And, almost as though to intimate how entirely the responsibility for his deeds still lies with Macbeth, Shakespeare makes his first act after this interview one for which his tempters gave him not a hint—the slaughter of Macduff's wife and children.

To all this we must add that Macbeth himself nowhere betrays a suspicion that his action is, or has been, thrust on him by an external power. He curses the Witches for deceiving him, but he never attempts to shift to them the burden of his guilt.

(2) We may deal more briefly with the opposite interpretation. According to it the Witches and their prophecies are to be taken merely as symbolical representations of thoughts and desires which have slumbered in Macbeth's breast and now rise into consciousness and confront him. With this idea, which springs from the wish to get rid of a mere external supernaturalism, and to find a psychological and spiritual meaning in that which the groundlings probably received as hard facts, one may feel sympathy. But it is evident that it is rather a "philosophy" of the Witches than an immediate dramatic apprehension of them; and even so it will be found both incomplete and, in other respects, inadequate.

It is incomplete because it cannot possibly be applied to all the facts. Let us grant that it will apply to the most important prophecy, that of the crown; and that the later warning which Macbeth receives, to beware of Macduff, also answers to something in his own breast and "harps his fear aright." But there we have to stop. Macbeth had evidently no suspicion of that treachery in Cawdor through which he himself became Thane; and who will suggest that he had any idea, however subconscious, about Birnam Wood or the man not born of woman?

The theory under consideration is inadequate here chiefly because it is much too narrow. The Witches and their prophecies, if they are to be taken symbolically, must represent not only the evil slumbering in the hero's soul, but all those obscurer influences of the evil around him in the world which aid his own ambition and the incitements of his wife. Such influences, even if we put aside all belief in evil "spirits," are as certain, momentous, and terrifying facts as the presence of inchoate evil in the soul itself; and if we exclude all reference to these facts from our idea of the Witches, it will be greatly impoverished and will certainly fail to correspond with the imaginative effect. The words of the Witches are fatal to the hero only because there is in him something which leaps into light at the sound of them; but they are at the same time the witness of forces which never cease to work in the world around him, and, on the instant of his surrender to them, entangle him inextricably in the web of Fate. If the inward connection is once realised (and Shakespeare has left us no excuse for missing it), we need not fear, and indeed shall scarcely be able, to exaggerate the effect of the Witch-scenes in heightening and deepening the sense of fear, horror, and mystery which pervades the atmosphere of tragedy. □

VII. ELIZABETHAN PROSE

During the Elizabethan period, Latin gradually gave way to English as the language of learning, and English prose finally achieved its maturity. Sir Thomas More wrote his *Utopia* (1516) in Latin. When Sir Francis Bacon wrote his account of a Utopian society, *The New Atlantis* (1626), he wrote in English. Two events, one just before and one at the end of the Elizabethan age, contributed immensely to the stabilization of the English language: the introduction of the printing press into England in 1476, and the King James translation of the Bible, published in 1611. It is no exaggeration to say that what Shakespeare did for poetry and drama, the King James Bible did for prose. The models they set have been the standards by which all later poetry, drama, and prose have been judged.

The Essays of Sir Francis Bacon 1561 / 1626

Sir Francis Bacon's *Essays* were published in three installments over a period of a quarter-century (1597–1625) to a total of fifty-eight essays. Bacon introduced the essay form into England, and through his genius with the language made it popular. His essays were short, treated a variety of subjects of universal interest, and were written in epigrammatic, sharply honed style. His individual sentences are memorable and are still frequently quoted.

7. OF PARENTS AND CHILDREN

THE joys of parents are secret, and so are their griefs and fears; they cannot utter the one, nor they will not utter the other. Children sweeten labours, but they make misfortunes more bitter; they increase the cares of life, but they mitigate the remembrance of death. The perpetuity by generation is common to beasts; but memory, merit, and noble works are proper to men; and surely a man shall see the noblest works and foundations have proceeded from childless men, which have sought to express the images of their minds where those of their bodies have failed; so the care of posterity is most in them that have no posterity. They that are the first raisers of their houses are most indulgent towards their children, beholding them as the continuance not only of their kind, but of their work; and so both children and creatures.

The difference in affection of parents towards their several children is many times unequal, and sometimes unworthy, especially in the mother; as Solomon saith, "A wise son rejoiceth the father, but an ungracious one shames the mother." A man shall see, where there is a house full of children, one or two of the eldest respected and the youngest made wantons;[1] but in the midst some that are as it were forgotten, who many times, nevertheless, prove the best.

The illiberality of parents in allowance towards their children is an harmful error—makes them base, acquaints them with shifts,[2] makes them sort[3] with mean company, and makes them surfeit more when they come to plenty; and therefore the proof[4] is best when men keep their authority towards their children, but not their purse. Men have a foolish manner (both parents and schoolmasters and servants) in creating and breeding an emulation between brothers during childhood, which many times sorteth to discord when they are men, and disturbeth families.

1. *wantons,* spoiled pets.
2. *shifts,* underhanded schemes.
3. *sort,* consort.
4. *proof,* result.

IN THE COLLECTIONS AT GORHAMBURY, ST. ALBANS, HERTFORDSHIRE.

The Italians make little difference between children and nephews or near kinsfolks; but so they be of the lump,[5] they care not though they pass not through their own body. And, to say truth, in nature it is much a like matter; insomuch that we see a nephew sometimes resembleth an uncle or a kinsman more than his own parent, as the blood happens.

Let parents choose betimes the vocations and courses they mean their children should take, for then they are most flexible; and let them not too much apply themselves to the disposition of their children, as thinking they will take best to that which they have most mind to. It is true that if the affection or aptness of the children be extraordinary, then it is good not to cross it; but generally the precept is good, *Optimum elige, suave et facile illud faciet consuetudo*.[6] Younger brothers are commonly fortunate,[7] but seldom or never where the elder are disinherited. □

---

5. *lump*, extended family group.
6. *Optimum . . . consuetudo*. Choose the best; custom will make it pleasant and easy.
7. *fortunate*, i.e., in that they must depend on their own efforts. In English law, only the oldest son inherited property and title.

OF HUMAN INTEREST

Sir Francis Bacon

"At every meale, according to the season of the yeare, he had his Table strewed with Sweet Herbes and Flowers, which he sayd did refresh his spirits and memorie. . . .

"His Lordship would many times have Musique in the next roome where he meditated. I have now forgott what Mr. Bushel sayd, whether his Lordship enjoyed his Muse best at night or in the Morning. . . .

"His Lordship would often drinke a good draught of strong Beer (March-beer) to-bedwards, to lay his working Fancy asleep, which otherwise would keepe him from sleeping great part of the night."

OF LITERARY INTEREST

The essay

The essay is a prose work of moderate length in which the author develops his ideas on a subject, expresses an opinion or point of view, or attempts to persuade the reader to a particular belief. The length, subject matter, and structure are all quite flexible, depending on the judgment or whim of the writer.

Although essays had been written since the time of the ancient Greeks and Romans, it was not until 1580, when the French writer Montaigne called his prose pieces *essais* or "attempts," that the form received its name. His essays were translated into English in 1603 by John Florio, and were an important influence on William Shakespeare and Sir Francis Bacon.

Essays are sometimes classified as *formal* or *informal*, although the classifications are not strict ones. The formal essay (Bacon's tend to fall into this category) is generally impersonal, logically organized, and filled with serious purpose. The informal essay (like Montaigne's) is personal in tone, with the presence of the author felt, and is often whimsical, frequently humorous, occasionally digressive. Charles Lamb is the most accomplished writer of informal or familiar essays in English (see the section on "The Romantics").

50. OF STUDIES

STUDIES serve for delight, for ornament, and for ability. Their chief use for delight is in privateness and retiring; for ornament, is in discourse; and for ability, is in the judgment and disposition of business; for expert[1] men can execute, and perhaps judge of particulars, one by one; but the general counsels, and the plots and marshaling of affairs come best from those that are learned. To spend too much time in studies is sloth; to use them too much for ornament is affectation; to make judgment wholly by their rules is the humor[2] of a scholar. They perfect nature, and are perfected by experience; for natural abilities are like natural plants, that need pruning by study; and studies themselves do give forth directions too much at large, except they be bounded in by experience. Crafty[3] men contemn studies, simple men admire them, and wise men use them; for they teach not their own use; but that is a wisdom without them and above them, won by observation.

Read not to contradict and confute, nor to believe and take for granted, nor to find talk and discourse, but to weigh and consider. Some books are to be tasted, others to be swallowed, and some few to be chewed and digested; that is, some books are to be read only in parts; others to be read but not curiously,[4] and some few to be read wholly, and with diligence and attention. Some books also may be read by deputy, and extracts made of them by others; but that would be only in the less important arguments and the meaner sort of books; else distilled books are, like common distilled waters, flashy[5] things.

Reading maketh a full man; conference a ready man; and writing an exact man. And, therefore, if a man write little, he had need have a great memory; if he confer little, he had need have a present wit;[6] and if he read little, he had need have much cunning, to seem to know what he doth not. Histories make men wise; poets, witty; the mathematics, subtile; natural philosophy, deep; moral, grave; logic and rhetoric, able to contend: *Abeunt studia in mores!*[7] Nay, there is no stand or impediment in the wit but may be wrought out by fit studies; like as diseases of the body may have appropriate exercises. Bowling is good for the stone[8] and reins, shooting for the lungs and breast, gentle walking for the stomach, riding for the head, and the like. So if a man's wit be wandering, let him study mathematics; for in demonstrations, if his wit be called away never so little, he must begin again. If his wit be not apt to distinguish or find differences, let him study the schoolmen,[9] for they are *cymini sectores!*[10] If he be not apt to beat over matters, and to call up one thing to prove and illustrate another, let him study the lawyers' cases. So every defect of the mind may have a special receipt. □

1. *expert,* experienced; practical.
2. *humor,* whim, disposition.
3. *Crafty,* skilled in crafts; practical.
4. *curiously,* thoroughly.
5. *flashy,* tasteless, flat.
6. *wit,* intelligence; the word is used throughout the essay in this sense.
7. *Abeunt . . . mores!* Studies develop into habits.
8. *stone,* a disease of the kidneys (reins).
9. *schoolmen,* medieval scholars.
10. *cymini sectores,* hairsplitters (literally, splitters of cuminseeds).

DISCUSSION

1. *"Of Parents and Children":*

(a) Discuss the style exhibited in the second sentence: "Children sweeten labours, but they make misfortunes more bitter; they increase the cares of life, but they mitigate the remembrance of death."

(b) Discuss the meaning and truth of Bacon's assertion: "so the care of posterity is most in them that have no posterity."

(c) Are Bacon's opinions about the oldest, middle, and youngest children in accord with your experience or observation?

(d) What do you think of Bacon's advice that "men keep their authority towards their children, but not their purse"?

2. *"Of Studies":*

(a) Explain Bacon's opening statement: "Studies serve for delight, for ornament, and for ability."

(b) What kind of people do you know who read for the wrong reasons, as suggested in Bacon's statement: "Read not to contradict and confute, nor to believe and take for granted, nor to find talk and discourse, but to weigh and consider"?

(c) Discuss books that you would put in the following categories: "Some books are to be tasted, others to be swallowed, and some few to be chewed and digested."

From

THE UNFORTUNATE TRAVELLER

by Thomas Nashe

Scholars have variously pronounced *The Unfortunate Traveller* (1594) to be the first historical novel, the prototype picaresque novel, and the first novel in the English language. Certainly this piece of popular literature is rollicking and English; it is also historically innovative in that it places an imaginary protagonist, Jack Wilton, among actual historical figures and events.

Wilton is a shrewd social observer and a rogue, who journeys around Europe, sometimes with his master, Henry Howard, the Earl of Surrey, sometimes disguised as his master. He witnesses historic battles, encounters such great men of the age as Erasmus, Thomas More, and Martin Luther—as well as some beguiling courtesans—and visits Rome during a plague.

This excerpt presents part of an early adventure, when young Jack Wilton is a page in the camp of King Henry VIII at the siege of Tournay, in France.

OVER sea with my implements I got me, where hearing the King of France and the Switzers[1] were together by the ears, I made towards them as fast as I could, thinking to thrust myself into that faction that was strongest. It was my good luck or my ill (I know not which) to come just to the fighting of the battle; where I saw a wonderful spectacle of bloodshed on both sides: here unwieldy Switzers wallowing in their gore, like an ox in his dung, there the sprightly French sprawling and turning on the stained grass, like a roach new-taken out of the stream: all the ground was strewed as thick with battleaxes as the carpenter's yard with chips; the plain appeared like a quagmire, overspread as it was with trampled dead bodies. In one place might you behold a heap of dead murthered men overwhelmed with a falling steed instead of a tombstone, in another place a bundle of bodies fettered together in their own bowels; and as the tyrant Roman emperors used to tie condemned living captives face to face to dead corpses, so were the half living here mixed with squeezed carcasses long putrefied. Any man might give arms that was an actor in that battle, for there were more arms and legs scattered in the field that day than will be gathered up till doomsday: the French king himself in this conflict was much distressed, the brains of his own men sprinkled in his face, thrice was his courser slain under him, and thrice was he struck on the breast with a spear: but in the end, by the help of the Venetians, the Helvetians or Switzers were subdued, and he crowned a victor, a peace concluded, and the city of Milan surrendered unto him as a pledge of reconciliation.

That war thus blown over, and the several bands dissolved, like a crow that still follows aloof where there is carrion, I flew me over to Münster in Germany, which an Anabaptistical brother,[2] named John Leyden, kept at that instant against the Emperor and the Duke of Saxony. Here I was in good hope to set up my staff for some reasonable time, deeming that no city would drive it to a siege, except they were able to hold out: and prettily well had these Münsterians held out, for they kept the Emperor and the Duke of Saxony play for the space of a year; and longer would have done, but that Dame Famine came amongst them; whereupon they were forced by messengers to agree upon a day of fight, when according to their Anabaptistical error they might all be new-christened in their own blood.

That day come, flourishing entered John Leyden the botcher[3] into the field, with a scarf made of lists[4] like a bowcase, a cross on his breast like a thread-

1. *Switzers*, Swiss.
2. *Anabaptistical brother*. Anabaptist was the general name for various Protestant sects interested in social revolution that appeared in Germany in the 16th century.
3. *botcher*, cobbler.
4. *lists*, edgings of cloth.

bottom,[5] a round twilted[6] tailor's cushion buckled like a tankard-bearer's device to his shoulders for a target, the pike whereof was a packneedle, a tough prentice's club for his spear, a great brewer's cow[7] on his back for a corselet, and on his head for a helmet a huge high shoe with the bottom turned upwards, embossed as full of hobnails as ever it might stick: his men were all base handicrafts, as cobblers and curriers and tinkers, whereof some had bars of iron, some hatchets, some cool-staves,[8] some dung-forks, some spades, some mattocks, some wood-knives, some addises[9] for their weapons: he that was best provided had but a piece of a rusty brown bill bravely fringed with cobwebs to fight for him. Perchance here and there you might see a fellow that had a canker-eaten skull on his head, which served him and his ancestors for a chamber pot two hundred years, and another that had bent a couple of iron dripping pans armor-wise, to fence his back and his belly; another that had thrust a pair of dry old boots as a breastplate before his belly of his doublet, because he would not be dangerously hurt; another that had twilted all his truss full of counters, thinking, if the enemy should take him, he would mistake them for gold, and so save his life for his money. Very devout asses they were, for all they were so dunstically[10] set forth, and such as thought they knew as much of God's mind as richer men: why, inspiration was their ordinary familiar, and buzzed in their ears like a bee in a box every hour what news from heaven, hell, and the land of Whipperginnie:[11] displease them who durst, he should have his mittimus to damnation *extempore;* they would vaunt there was not a pea's difference betwixt them and the Apostles; they were as poor as they, of as base trades as they, and no more inspired than they, and with God there is no respect of persons; only herein may seem some little diversity to lurk, that Peter wore a sword, and they count it flat hell-fire for any man to wear a dagger; nay, so grounded and graveled were they in this opinion, that now when they should come to battle, there's never a one of them would bring a blade (no, not an onion blade) about him, to die for it. It was not lawful, said they, for any man to draw the sword but the magistrate; and in fidelity, (which I had well-nigh forgot,) Jack Leyden, their magistrate, had the image or likeness of a piece of a rusty sword, like a lusty lad, by his side: now I remember me, it was but a foil neither, and he wore it to shew that he should have the foil of his enemies, which might have been an oracle for his two-hand interpretation. *Quid plura?*[12] His battle is pitched: by pitched, I do not mean set in order, for that was far from their order, only as sailors do pitch their apparel to make it storm-proof, so had most of them pitched their patched clothes to make them impierceable: a nearer way than to be at the charges of armour by half. And in another sort he might be said to have pitched the field, for he had pitched or rather set up his rest whither to fly if they were discomfited.

Peace, peace there in the belfry,[13] service begins: upon their knees before they join falls John Leyden and his fraternity very devoutly, they pray, they howl, they expostulate with God to grant them victory, and use such unspeakable vehemence a man would think them the only well-bent men under heaven. Wherein let me dilate a little more gravely than the nature of his history requires, or will be expected of so young a practitioner in divinity: that not those that intermissively cry, "Lord, open unto us, Lord, open unto us," enter first into the kingdom; that not the greatest professors have the greatest portion in grace; that all is not gold that glisters. When Christ said, "The kingdom of heaven must suffer violence," he meant not the violence of long babbling prayers, nor the violence of tedious invective sermons without wit, but the violence of faith, the violence of good works, the violence of patient suffering. The ignorant arise and snatch the kingdom of heaven to themselves with greediness, when we with all our learning sink down into hell. □

---

5. *thread bottom,* card or paper on which thread is wound.
6. *twilted,* padded like a quilt.
7. *cow,* covering of a large tub.
8. *cool-staves,* carrying rods for tubs.
9. *addises,* adzes.
10. *dunstically,* stupidly.
11. *Whipperginnie,* an imaginary land with unsavory connotations.
12. *Quid plura?* What more?
13. *belfry,* under the church tower, where the poorer part of the congregation sat.

DISCUSSION

In this passage, Nashe describes two separate scenes. Characterize the episodes and explain what details give each its distinctive effect.

The King James Bible

No complete translation of the Bible was made into English until the late fourteenth century, when John Wycliffe, a theologian and church reformer who was condemned as a heretic, oversaw a translation. Other "unauthorized" translations appeared in the early sixteenth century, including versions by William Tyndale and Miles Coverdale. Finally, in 1539, the "Great Bible" appeared, under the auspices of the reigning monarch, Henry VIII. This was the first English Bible with official endorsement.

In 1604, James I convened a conference at Hampton Court at which plans were laid for a new version of the Bible by a group of translators. Some fifty or so theologians and scholars began work in various centers of learning (Oxford, Cambridge, Westminster), making extensive use of previous translations, especially the Tyndale and Wycliffe. The work was issued in 1611 as the "Authorized Version" and has fixed itself so firmly in the imagination of the English speaking world that no other translation seems able to challenge it.

The King James Bible has been called "the noblest monument of English prose," and deserves the epithet because of the sheer brilliance of its language. Its extensive use of concrete terms and images, its straightforward phrases and sentences, its balance and parallelism in many passages—all make for a dignified simplicity eminently compatible with religious feeling and ritual. Indeed, the language of the King James Bible has so profoundly affected succeeding generations of writers and has so thoroughly stamped itself in the minds of ordinary people that today it forms a basic part of our everyday speech.

(For a comparison of translations of the Bible, see the various versions of the Twenty-third Psalm on page 226.)

THE CREATION OF THE WORLD

(Genesis, Chapters 1-3)

In the beginning God created the heaven and the earth. And the earth was without form, and void; and darkness was upon the face of the deep. And the Spirit of God moved upon the face of the waters. And God said, "Let there be light": and there was light. And God saw the light, that it was good: and God divided the light from the darkness. And God called the light Day, and the darkness he called Night. And the evening and the morning were the first day.

And God said, "Let there be a firmament in the midst of the waters, and let it divide the waters from the waters." And God made the firmament, and divided the waters which were under the firmament from the waters which were above the firmament: and it was so. And God called the firmament Heaven. And the evening and the morning were the second day.

And God said, "Let the waters under the heaven be gathered together unto one place, and let the dry land appear": and it was so. And God called the dry land Earth; and the gathering together of the waters called he Seas: and God saw that it was good. And God said, "Let the earth bring forth grass, the herb yielding seed, and the fruit tree yielding fruit after his kind, whose seed is in itself, upon the earth": and it was so. And the earth brought forth grass, and herb yielding seed after his kind, and the tree yielding fruit, whose seed was in itself, after his kind: and God saw that it was good. And the evening and the morning were the third day.

And God said, "Let there be lights in the firmament of the heaven to divide the day from the night; and let them be for signs, and for seasons, and for days, and years: and let them be for lights in the firmament of the heaven to give light upon the earth": and it was so. And God made two great lights; the greater light to rule the day, and the lesser light to rule the night: he made the stars also. And God set them in the firmament of the heaven to give light upon the earth. And to rule over the day and over the night, and to divide the light from the darkness: and God saw that it was good. And the evening and the morning were the fourth day.

And God said, "Let the waters bring forth abundantly the moving creature that hath life, and fowl that may fly above the earth in the open firmament of heaven." And God created great whales, and every living creature that moveth, which the waters brought forth abundantly, after their kind, and every winged fowl after his kind: and God saw that it was good. And God blessed them, saying, "Be fruitful, and multiply, and fill the waters in the seas, and let fowl multiply in the earth." And the evening and the morning were the fifth day.

And God said, "Let the earth bring forth the living creature after his kind, cattle, and creeping thing, and beast of the earth after his kind": and it was so. And God made the beast of the earth after his kind, and cattle after their kind, and every thing that creepeth upon the earth after his kind: and God saw that it was good.

And God said, "Let us make man in our image, after our likeness: and let them have dominion over the fish of the sea, and over the fowl of the air, and over the cattle, and over all the earth, and over every creeping thing that creepeth upon the earth." So God created man in his own image, in the image of God created he him; male and female created he them. And God blessed them, and God said unto them, "Be fruitful, and multiply, and replenish the earth, and subdue it: and have dominion over the fish of the sea, and over the fowl of the air, and over every living thing that moveth upon the earth."

And God said, "Behold, I have given you every herb bearing seed, which is upon the face of all the earth, and every tree, in the which is the fruit of a tree yielding seed; to you it shall be for meat. And to every beast of the earth, and to every fowl of the air, and to every thing that creepeth upon the earth, wherein there is life, I have given every green herb for meat": and it was so.

And God saw every thing that he had made, and, behold, it was very good. And the evening and the morning were the sixth day.

Thus the heavens and the earth were finished, and all the host of them. And on the seventh day God ended his work which he had made; and he rested on the seventh day from all his work which he had made. And God blessed the seventh day, and sanctified it: because that in it he had rested from all his work which God created and made.

The Creation of Adam and Eve

These are the generations of the heavens and of the earth when they were created, in the day that the Lord God made the earth and the heavens, and every plant of the field before it grew: for the Lord God had not caused it to rain upon the earth, and there was not a man to till the ground. But there went up a mist from the earth, and watered the whole face of the ground. And the Lord God formed man of the dust of the ground, and breathed into his nostrils the breath of life; and man became a living soul.

And the Lord God planted a garden eastward in Eden; and there he put the man whom he had formed. And out of the ground made the Lord God to grow every tree that is pleasant to the sight, and good for food; the tree of life also in the midst of the garden, and the tree of knowledge of good and evil. . . .

And the Lord God took the man, and put him into the garden of Eden to dress it and to keep it. And the Lord God commanded the man, saying, "Of every tree of the garden thou mayest freely eat: but of the tree of the knowledge of good and evil, thou shalt not eat of it: for in the day that thou eatest thereof thou shalt surely die."

And the Lord God said, "It is not good that the man should be alone; I will make him an help meet for him." And out of the ground the Lord God formed every beast of the field, and every fowl of the air; and brought them unto Adam to see what he would call them: and whatsoever Adam called every living creature, that was the name thereof. And Adam gave names to all cattle, and to the fowl of the air, and to every beast of the field; but for Adam there was not found an help meet for him.

And the Lord God caused a deep sleep to fall upon Adam, and he slept: and he took one of his ribs, and closed up the flesh instead thereof; and the rib, which the Lord God had taken from man, made he a woman, and brought her unto the man.

And Adam said, "This is now bone of my bones, and flesh of my flesh: she shall be called Woman, because she was taken out of Man."

Therefore shall a man leave his father and his mother, and shall cleave unto his wife: and they shall be one flesh. And they were both naked, the man and his wife, and were not ashamed.

The Fall of Man

Now the serpent was more subtil than any beast of the field which the Lord God had made.

And he said unto the woman, "Yea, hath God said, 'Ye shall not eat of every tree of the garden'?"

And the woman said unto the serpent, "We may eat of the fruit of the trees of the garden: but of the fruit of the tree which is in the midst of the garden, God hath said, 'Ye shall not eat of it, neither shall ye touch it, lest ye die.' "

And the serpent said unto the woman, "Ye shall not surely die: for God doth know that in the day ye eat thereof, then your eyes shall be opened, and ye shall be as gods, knowing good and evil."

And when the woman saw that the tree was good for food, and that it was pleasant to the eyes, and a tree to be desired to make one wise, she took of the fruit thereof, and did eat, and gave also unto her husband with her; and he did eat. And the eyes of them both were opened, and they knew that they were naked; and they sewed fig leaves together, and made themselves aprons.

And they heard the voice of the Lord God walking in the garden in the cool of the day: and Adam and his wife hid themselves from the presence of the Lord God amongst the trees of the garden.

And the Lord God called unto Adam, and said unto him, "Where art thou?"

And he said, "I heard thy voice in the garden, and I was afraid, because I was naked; and I hid myself."

And he said, "Who told thee that thou wast naked? Hast thou eaten of the tree, whereof I commanded thee that thou shouldest not eat?"

And the man said, "The woman whom thou gavest to be with me, she gave me of the tree, and I did eat."

And the Lord God said unto the woman, "What is this that thou hast done?"

And the woman said, "The serpent beguiled me, and I did eat."

And the Lord God said unto the serpent, "Because thou hast done this, thou art cursed above all cattle, and above every beast of the field; upon thy belly shalt thou go, and dust shalt thou eat all the days of thy life: and I will put enmity between thee and the woman, and between thy seed and her seed; it shall bruise thy head, and thou shalt bruise his heel."

Unto the woman he said, "I will greatly multiply thy sorrow and thy conception; in sorrow thou shalt bring forth children; and thy desire shall be to thy husband, and he shall rule over thee."

And unto Adam he said, "Because thou hast hearkened unto the voice of thy wife, and hast eaten of the tree, of which I commanded thee, saying, 'Thou shalt not eat of it': cursed is the ground for thy sake; in sorrow shalt thou eat of it all the days of thy life. Thorns also and thistles shall it bring forth to thee; and thou shalt eat the herb of the field; in the sweat of thy face shalt thou eat bread, till thou return unto the ground; for out of it wast thou taken: for dust thou art, and unto dust shalt thou return."

And Adam called his wife's name Eve; because she was the mother of all living. Unto Adam also and to his wife did the Lord God make coats of skins, and clothed them.

And the Lord God said, "Behold, the man is become as one of us, to know good and evil: and now, lest he put forth his hand, and take also of the tree of life, and eat, and live for ever": therefore the Lord God sent him forth from the garden of Eden, to till the ground from whence he was taken. So he drove out the man; and he placed at the east of the garden of Eden Cherubims, and a flaming sword which turned every way, to keep the way of the tree of life. □

DISCUSSION

1. Imagine that a child, beginning to be fully conscious of the world that surrounds him, asks: "Who created the world? How? Why? How long did it take? What about whales? How about man himself?" Show how the opening of Genesis answers these questions.

2. Do some research on other stories of the creation. (For example, Ovid's *Metamorphoses,* Book I, gives the Greek conception of the beginning of the world. For an American Indian version of creation, see John G. Neihardt's *Black Elk Speaks,* Chapter III: "The Great Vision." You will be able to find others, too.)

3. According to Genesis, why did God create man? woman?

4. Analyze the behavior of Adam and Eve after the Fall, and indicate how they have changed.

5. Compare the story of the Fall in Genesis with the treatment of the story by Milton in *Paradise Lost* (see "The Seventeenth Century").

6. The style of the King James Bible has appeared to be unsurpassable. Find a passage you consider particularly effective and explore the reasons for its effectiveness. For example, analyze: "In the beginning God created the heaven and the earth."

TRANSLATIONS OF THE BIBLE

The Bible has been the best-seller of all time, and translations of it have been numerous. The achievement of the King James version can best be judged by comparing it with some of the others. Here are four versions of the Twenty-third Psalm: the King James translation, one published before it, and two published later.

From *The Great Bible (1539)*

The Lord is my shepherd; therefore can I lack nothing. He shall feed me in a green pasture, and lead me forth beside the waters of comfort. He shall convert my soul, and bring me forth in the paths of righteousness for his name's sake. Yea, though I walk through the valley of the shadow of death, I will fear no evil, for thou art with me. Thy rod and thy staff comfort me. Thou shalt prepare a table before me against them that trouble me; thou has anointed my head with oil, and my cup shall be full. But thy loving-kindness and mercy shall follow me all the days of my life and I will dwell in the house of the Lord forever.

From *The King James Bible (1611)*

The Lord is my shepherd: I shall not want.
He maketh me to lie down in green pastures: he leadeth me beside the still waters.
He restoreth my soul: he leadeth me in the paths of righteousness for his name's sake.
Yea, though I walk through the valley of the shadow of death, I will fear no evil: for thou art with me; thy rod and thy staff they comfort me.
Thou preparest a table before me in the presence of mine enemies: thou anointest my head with oil; my cup runneth over.
Surely goodness and mercy shall follow me all the days of my life: and I will dwell in the house of the Lord forever.

From *The Bay Psalm Book (1640)*[1]

The Lord to me a shepherd is,
want therefore shall not I.
He in the folds of tender grass,
doth cause me down to lie:
To waters calm me gently leads,
Restore my soul doth he:
He doth in paths of righteousness
for his name's sake lead me.
Yea though in valley of death's shade
I walk, none ill I'll fear:
Because thou art with me, thy rod
and staff my comfort are.
For me a table thou hast spread,
in presence of my foes:
Thou dost anoint my head with oil,
my cup it overflows.
Goodness and mercy surely shall
all my days follow me:
And in the Lord's house I shall dwell
so long as days shall be.

1. The Bay Psalm Book was the first book published in the American Colonies.

From *The New English Bible (1970)*

The LORD is my shepherd; I shall want nothing.
He makes me lie down in green pastures,
and leads me beside the waters of peace;
he renews life within me,
and for his name's sake guides me in the right path.
Even though I walk through a valley dark as death
I fear no evil, for thou art with me,
thy staff and thy crook are my comfort.

Thou spreadest a table for me in the sight of my enemies;
thou hast richly bathed my head with oil,
and my cup runs over.
Goodness and love unfailing, these will follow me all the days of my life,
and I shall dwell in the house of the LORD
my whole life long.

PORTRAIT OF QUEEN ELIZABETH FROM THE PRINT DIVISION, NEW YORK PUBLIC LIBRARY.

VIII. BACKGROUND

The Elizabethan Age

WHEN Henry VIII came to the throne in 1509, there was little reason to think that England had entered the most glorious century of its history. The atmosphere of civil strife still lingered, although the Wars of the Roses had technically ended at the Battle of Bosworth Field in 1485. The great religious question—whether the Protestant or the Catholic worship should become the authorized mode—remained still aggravated and unsettled. Although Henry VIII declared himself the head of the Church of England in 1534, the Anglican Church was not firmly established until 1571, and religious issues were to remain unresolved well into the seventeenth century.

It was Queen Elizabeth I, the daughter of Henry VIII in both body and spirit, who brought to England a measure of tolerance and religious compromise. A master politician and a brilliant and unscrupulous strategist, she gathered about her during her reign (1558–1603) a court of learned and adventurous men and created in England a feeling of national purpose which truly unified the country. She deftly maneuvered the ship of state through a prolonged duel with Spain, foiling an attempted invasion of England by sending Drake and Hawkins out to sink and disperse the Spanish Armada in 1588. Her words upon that occasion are notable: ". . . I know I have the body of a weak feeble woman, but I have the heart and stomach of a king—and a King of England, too, and think foul scorn that. . .Spain or any Prince of Europe should dare to invade the borders of my realm." This same "weak feeble woman" nosed her rival and cousin, Mary, Queen of Scots, out of power and set in motion a series of events that led to Mary's beheading. By the time of her death in 1603 (she died a spinster, having manipulated many proposals of marriage from foreign royalty to her country's advantage), England had experienced a vast expansion of military and economic power and a surprising rejuvenation of all the fine arts.

The roots of this unexpected renaissance are complex. By the time of Elizabeth's reign, England had begun to recover from the ravages of centuries of warfare and to achieve a new stability. The population increased, creating new markets and bringing about the exploitation of new sources of raw materials, among them those of the New World. The commercial ventures of the Virginia Company in North America and of the East India Company in the Orient were aspects of this expansion. Another source of riches were ventures like those of the pirate-patriot Sir Francis Drake, whom Elizabeth commissioned to intercept Spanish treasure ships on the high seas and relieve them of the heavy burden of gold they had stolen from the Indians of South America. With such ventures generating as much as 5000% return on investment, the royal treasury grew fat, as did the pockets of those who found favor at Court and formed their own successful syndicates.

Elizabeth's reign was the age of courtiers. Almost every aspect of English life centered around the activities of Elizabeth's entourage. Her court, bustling with foreign ambassadors and ministers of trade, buzzing with intrigue, was the source of power and influence, and a share of her sometimes whimsical favor was the ultimate goal of every ambitious man in the kingdom.

The age was also one of contrasts. By Elizabeth's time the new Humanism and the surge of interest in the arts that characterized the Italian Renaissance had made itself felt in England. Medieval contempt of worldly things, still common at the end of the fifteenth century, was offset by an exuberant acceptance of the world and its possibilities. The medieval view of man as repentant sinner, vulnerable to a variety of spiritual and physical ills, was revised by English Renaissance idealism to read, in the words of Shakespeare's Hamlet: "What a piece of work is man! how noble in reason! how infinite in faculty! in form and moving how express and admirable! in action how like an angel! in apprehension how like a god!" But this idealism rarely found an expression untarnished by irony; the same Elizabethan who believed in the infinite capabilities of man also saw quite clearly his precarious position between heaven and hell in the ordered scheme of things. If man was "infinite in faculty" he was also "the quintessence of dust." The dualities of the Elizabethan imagination allowed not only a vision of the human form divine, but the skull and skeleton under it.

The particular exuberance of the Elizabethan period owes much to similar sets of contrasts. Men who rationally discussed the implications of the newly rediscovered Greek philosophers also piously attended witch burnings. Courtiers, garmented in the finest silks, who insisted that the mark of a true gentleman was his touch at the lute or his taste in poetry, howled with pleasure at the bear pits, as mastiffs tore chunks from the chained animal. Elizabeth, herself usually a woman of regal wit and deportment, deft in elevated conversation and intricate argument, occasionally slapped and spat at her associates. The age was a mixture of the earthy and the refined, and the two never did seem to blend.

The literature of the sixteenth century, not surprisingly, reflects the national preoccupation with style, wit, courtly demeanor, beauty, and rich ornamentation, and encompasses both the earthy and the elevated aspects of the age. The hallmark of Elizabethan literature is its superabundant eloquence, its concern with decorative effects, and its philosophical focus on man as the measure of all things. Elizabethan language, with few changes, is still ours, and the literature of the age still works on our imaginations. In good measure we have today borne out the Elizabethan ideal of man infinite in faculties and capabilities, as well as underscored the paradox of man's frailty—a duality of which the Elizabethans were perhaps more mindful. □

The Changing English Language

THE last years of the fifteenth century mark the end of the Middle English period and the beginning of what is called the early Modern English period. The development of the language during the sixteenth century seems at first both paradoxical and chaotic. On the one hand, there was a movement to make the language more uniform; on the other hand, it continued to be, in both its spoken and written forms, more plastic than it is now, and it was commonly molded to suit the requirements of individual expression.

Some of the confusion during the sixteenth century was due to the persistence of regional dialects. William Caxton, England's first printer, commented on the problem with some exasperation:

". . . That comyn englysshe that is spoken in one shyre varyeth from another. In so moche that in my dayes happened that certayn marchaũtes were in a ship in tamyse for to haue sayled ouer the see into zelande/and for lacke of wynde thei taryed atte forlond. and wente to land for to refreshe them And one of thaym named sheffelde a mercer came in to an hows and axed for mete and specyally he axyd after eggys And the goode wyf answerde that she coude speke no frenshe. And the marchaũt was angry for he also coude speke no frenshe. but wolde haue hadde egges/ and she vnderstode hym not/ And thenne at laste a nother sayd that he wolde haue eyren/ then the good wyf sayd that she vnderstod hym wel/ Loo what sholde a man in thyse dayes now wryte. egges or eyren/ certynly it is harde to playse euery man/ by cause of dyuersitie & chaũge of langage."

Contributing to the problem of regional variations was the lack of any standard system of spelling and pronunciation. A writer spelled according to his own tastes, and a reader had to have a certain amount of agility and imagination. The word *fellow*, for example, was spelled variously as *fallow*, *felowe*, *felow*, *fallowe;* and *where* might be spelled *wher*, *whear*, *were*, *wheare*, *whair*. Strangely, with all these variations, the Elizabethans seem to have had little difficulty in communicating.

But problems existed, and of these the Elizabethans seem to have been very conscious; during the sixteenth century the first attempts to "improve" and regulate the language were made. Among the forces promoting regulation was the printing press, which eliminated the vagaries and mistakes in handwritten manuscripts and greatly enlarged the number of books and pamphlets available. With the growth of printing came a renewed interest in education (a word, by the way, first used in English in 1531). By Shakespeare's time about half the population of London could at least read, and that number continued to grow.

Among the tens of thousands of items run off the presses during the latter part of the century were numerous "how to" books on spelling and usage, and many pamphlets and introductions defending the English vernacular over Latin as the language for all occasions. The preoccupation with a uniform language grew out of the strong sense of national identity; the experimentation with new vocabulary and new means of expression grew out of the adventurous spirit of the Elizabethans and also out of the concern for elegance and style; there was a realization that, in the newly flexible social structure, an elegant style could contribute to upward social mobility.

Of necessity the language had to grow to accommodate the new discoveries being made in scholarship and science. During the later years of the sixteenth century, English vocabulary was tremendously expanded by energetic and sometimes indiscriminate adaptation of words from Latin, Greek, French, Italian, and Spanish to supply terms the native idiom lacked. (Experts estimate that more than ten thousand words were added to English during this period.) So widespread was the importation of foreign terms that the first dictionaries printed in England were listings not of English but of foreign terms. Some of the new coinings from other languages, such as *obstupefact*, *splendidious*, *deruncinate* (to weed), *illecebrous* (delicate), and *aspectable* (visible), died by the wayside as the language developed, but many of the borrowings survived.

Latin and Greek contributed thousands of words, among them *antipathy*, *catastrophe*, *external*, *erupt*, *halo*, *anachronism*, *encyclopedia*, *appendix*, *emphasis*, *submerge*, *strenuous*, *inflate*, *infringement*. From French came *bigot*, *alloy*, *chocolate*, and *detail*, while *balcony*, *cameo*, *stanza*, and *violin* were borrowed from Italian. Spanish and Portuguese added *alligator*, *negro*, *potato*, *tobacco*, *cannibal*, and many others.

Together with, and partially in reaction to, this habit of borrowing and experimenting with foreign terms, there arose a movement to revive and adapt Old English words, adding to the language such forms as *wolfish, briny, astound, doom, filch,* and *freak.* It was largely through scholarly writing and literature that most of the new terms gained admittance to the language. The poets of the period—particularly Spenser and Shakespeare—were notorious coiners and borrowers of words.

In contrast to the tremendous embellishment of its vocabulary, the grammatical structure of English underwent relatively few changes in the sixteenth century. Some time in the last part of the century, a shift in the pronunciation of long vowels settled the pronunciation of English close to what it is today.

Irregularities and variations within the language remained, however. Elizabethan idiom observed no rigid grammatical rules. Shakespeare could, for instance, use phrases like "stranger'd with an oath," "nor this is not my nose neither," "it dislikes me." The grammar seems foreign, but the sense does not. *Kneen* and *knees, shoon* and *shoes, have wrote* or *have written, most boldest* or *most bold*—all were equally correct. *Service* could be pronounced "sarvice," *smart* could be pronounced "smert." Not surprisingly, the major focus of the following centuries was to be on the continuing movement to standardize English. □

BIOGRAPHIES

Sir Francis Bacon 1561 / 1626

Bacon was a courtier to the manner born. His father had been one of Queen Elizabeth's important ministers, and he was kinsman to the influential and noble Cecil family. Throughout his life, Bacon successfully coördinated a life of politics with the life of the mind. He rose from a minor embassy post, during Elizabeth's reign, to the position of Lord Chancellor under James I. He was one of the first English essayists, and also wrote a fictional account of an ideal state, *The New Atlantis.* Scientific thinking, with its logical, empirical, and inductive reasoning, was championed by Bacon. His *Instauration Magna,* or Great Renewal of Science, proposed a revision of the field of exact knowledge through experimentation and observation—the background for modern science.

Bacon's devotion to science was literally the death of him. After stuffing a chicken with snow, as an experiment in preserving meat by freezing, he contracted a fatal case of pneumonia.

Thomas Campion 1567 / 1620

Physician, lawyer, poet, musicologist, and outstanding songwriter, Campion embodied the idea of the "renaissance man." He disliked meaningless rhyming for sheer style, and his sensitivity to both music and language is illustrated in his poetic work. He also wrote a prose discourse, *Observations on the Art of English Poesy,* in which he argued against "the vulgar and unartificial[1] custom of riming," and in favor of rhymeless verse in the classical Latin style.

1. *unartificial,* without art or skill.

Samuel Daniel 1562 / 1619

A traditionalist, Samuel Daniel believed in a strong monarchy, and in the traditional role of the poet—a belief illustrated by his eight-volume epic poem on the War of the Roses. Though he also wrote plays, he is most noted for his sonnets.

Daniel was tutor to William Herbert (later one of Shakespeare's patrons), and it was Herbert's mother, Lady Pembroke, who started him writing poetry.

In 1603, James I appointed him Inspector of the Children of the Queen's Revels—a post which allowed him to retire to the country and write. Daniel's two major prose works were the *Defence of Rime,* written in answer to Campion's *Observations on the Art of English Poesy,* and a *History of England.*

Robert Devereux, Earl of Essex 1566 / 1601

Devereux is probably best known as one of Queen Elizabeth's favorites. Like many of the other gallant young men at Court, he was both a military adventurer and a poet. He was more childish and impetuous than others in his relations with the Queen, and this resulted in his ultimate disfavor.

In 1599, after being involved in military adventures in France and Spain, he was sent to Ireland to command an army against the rebels. Hearing reports of the popularity of his rivals at Court, he made a hasty and unauthorized treaty with the leader of the rebellion and rushed back to the Queen, hoping to regain the status he feared he had lost. Elizabeth banished him from Court for disobeying orders, and also deprived him of his license to collect a tax on sweet wines, the mainstay of his finances. Resentful, Devereux organized a plot against the Queen which was discovered. He was charged with treason and executed—a sentence which Elizabeth decreed only reluctantly.

Christopher Marlowe 1564 / 1593

Marlowe's unconventional life ended at twenty-nine; all his writings were produced in a period of four years.

He was a professional writer, a University Wit (see Shakespeare), and a classical scholar who produced works—both translations and original writings—that were very popular in his day. Among his most powerful plays are *Tamburlaine, The Tragical History of Dr. Faustus,* and *The Jew of Malta.* Some scholars think he may have had a hand in some of Shakespeare's plays. He was also an occasional actor for the Lord Admiral's Men.

In addition to being a professional dramatist, Marlowe is believed to have been a secret agent for the government. One reason for this theory is that the hesitancy of Cambridge University to grant him an M.A. degree (because of his long absences from his studies) was overridden by an order from the Queen's Privy Council. Another supporting fact is that on the day he was killed he was in the company of proven spies.

Some of the details of Marlowe's death are still mysterious. He died of stab wounds inflicted at an inn. Many scholars believe he was the victim of a political murder. Others think his death may simply have been the result of a quarrel. Still a third theory holds that the scene at the inn was actually a plot to produce the rumor of his death, enabling him to go on a secret mission of espionage.

Thomas Nashe 1567 / 1601

Nashe was the unconventional son of a poor Herefordshire clergyman. He earned a B. A. degree at Cambridge, but left without finishing his work for the M. A. degree. Throughout his life he was frequently in trouble with the authorities.

Besides being a poet and dramatist, he was a witty satirist who became embroiled in many acrimonious pamphlet-battles with other writers. A satire on almanac-makers by one "Adam Fouleweather" has been attributed to him. His exuberant book *The Unfortunate Traveller* is still considered a classic example of picaresque literature. Like many professional writers of all periods, he occasionally found it necessary to do hack writing as a source of income. Nashe composed what he called "toys for gentlemen"—indecent poems and lyrics, one of which was so obscene that it was not published for over two centuries.

Sir Walter Raleigh 1552 / 1618

Raleigh was an outstanding example of the versatile renaissance man. Though he was active in the service of Queen Elizabeth for over ten years, his importance lies more in his other accomplishments than in his influence upon her. He was a poet, a dabbler in music and science, a historian, a pirate, a landowner, a member of Parliament, and a colonizer of the New World.

He was several times imprisoned in the Tower of London —the first time, in 1692, at the Queen's displeasure over his having seduced one of her ladies-in-waiting. Later, during James I's reign, he spent fifteen years in the Tower on a charge of treason. While there, he wrote and performed scientific experiments. He finally obtained his release to go on an expedition to find gold in South America. Raleigh disobeyed instructions on the journey, and also failed to find gold. Upon returning to England he was again charged with treason, and beheaded.

William Shakespeare 1564 / 1616

Shakespeare's ancestors were Warwickshire farmers. His father moved to the town of Stratford-on-Avon, took up glove-making, married into a distinguished family, and became the town's high bailiff—an office similar to mayor. Shakespeare probably attended Stratford's excellent free grammar school and received a classical education there. It is also probable that he was apprenticed to a local trade at age thirteen as a result of his father's declining fortune. At eighteen he married Anne Hathaway, eight years his senior, and they had three children.

Little is known about Shakespeare from the time of his Stratford life in the mid-1580's until he emerged as a rising London playwright in 1592.

This was an exciting period in the English theater, mainly because of a group known as the University Wits, which included Marlowe, Nashe, and others. These brilliant young men turned out sophisticated plays for the courtiers and sensational plays for the general public. Though not a university man like the rest, Shakespeare stepped into this tradition and carried it forward with great success, producing a tremendous variety of plays—thirty-seven in all—within two decades.

Play-writing as such, however, was usually a poorly paid business, but because of his success as a playwright, Shakespeare held a full share in the profits of the Lord Chamberlain's Men, an acting company later called the King's Men. He occasionally acted with the company, taking minor parts (e.g., King Duncan in *Macbeth*). When Shakespeare retired to Stratford a few years before his death, it was to the second-largest house in town and proudly displaying the family's coat-of-arms.

Sir Philip Sidney 1554 / 1586

Though Wyatt and Surrey were responsible for introducing the sonnet into England, the great popularity of the form was the result of the publication, in 1591, of Sidney's *Astrophel and Stella.*

Sidney came from an intellectual and aristocratic background and was well-connected in England and on the continent. He was a soldier, scholar, poet, critic, courtier, and diplomat.

Sidney's *Defense of Poesie*, written in reply to a Puritan fanatic's attack on literature, is considered the best critical work written in the Elizabethan period. His *Arcadia,* a florid prose romance interspersed with lyrics, was an early forerunner of the modern novel.

Sidney's last act, according to his friend and biographer, Fulke Greville, was typically gallant. Though fatally wounded in a battle in Holland, Sidney passed his water bottle to a wounded foot-soldier, saying "Thy necessity is greater than mine."

Edmund Spenser 1552 / 1599

Spenser was born in London of middle-class parents, but early in his career, through his literary interests and talents, became associated with members of the nobility. In 1580 he won a government post in Ireland. There he pursued his literary career, and published the first three books of *The Faerie Queene* in 1590. Like other writers of the period, Spenser composed a sonnet sequence—*Amoretti,* dedicated to his future bride, Elizabeth Boyle. Along with other works, he finished another three books of *The Faerie Queene* by 1596. Although he did not live to complete the additional six books planned, *The Faerie Queene* is considered one of the great works of English poetry, and has influenced many of the major English poets who followed him.

Henry Howard, Earl of Surrey 1517 / 1547

The aristocratic Howard family boasted two of the queens of Henry VIII, a Tudor in-law, and an assortment of dukes and earls. Among the latter was the poet Henry Howard. His father, the Duke of Norfolk, was a close adviser of Henry VIII, and Surrey himself was considered as a possible husband for the princess Mary (later queen), at the suggestion of his cousin, Ann Boleyn.

Henry Howard is known, along with Thomas Wyatt, as being one of the first English sonnet writers and for having established the English or Shakespearean sonnet form. He was an early proponent of blank verse (unrhymed lines of iambic pentameter). At this time it was customary for poetry to be circulated in manuscript, and Howard's works were not published until ten years after his death.

The Howard family's rivalry with the equally powerful Seymour family was probably responsible for Surrey's several political imprisonments during the last ten years of his life, and for his eventual execution.

Sir Thomas Wyatt 1503? / 1542

Thomas Wyatt had a gentleman's background. He attended Cambridge University (B. A. and M. A.), was knighted in 1537, held an ambassadorial post, was elected to Parliament, and was welcome at Court. He grew up with Anne Boleyn and later wrote poems to her.

Along with Surrey, Wyatt is known as an early and innovative sonnet writer. It is uncertain whether the two actually knew each other, however. Like Surrey, he was in and out of prison on political charges, but unlike him, he died a natural death.

THREE CENTURIES OF ENGLISH LITERATURE

(OVERLEAF) MAP CIRCA 1646. BAYTON-WILLIAMS, 18 LOWNDES STREET, BELGRAVIA, LONDON, S.W. 1.

chapter four

THE SEVENTEENTH CENTURY 1625–1700

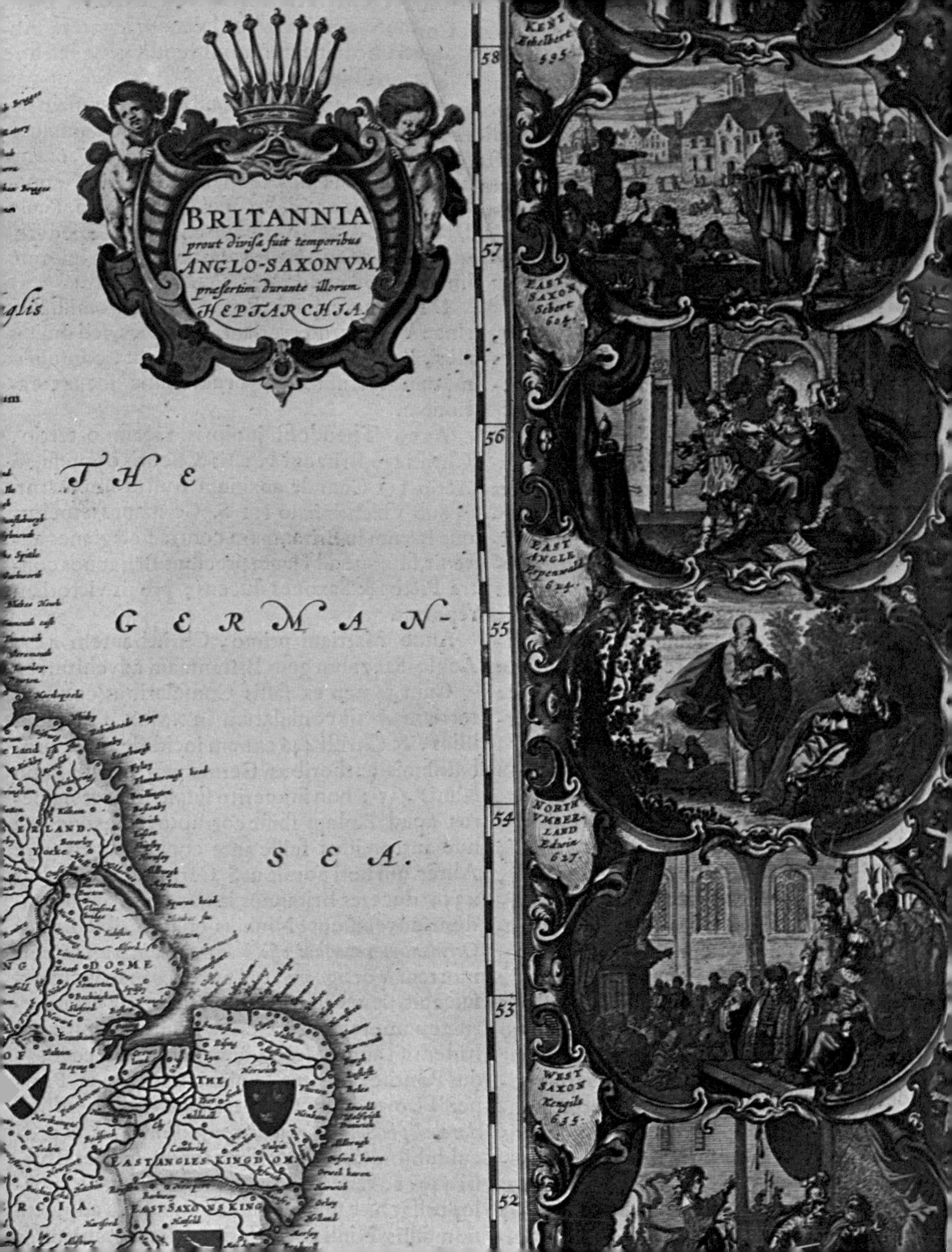

BRITANNIA
prout divisa fuit temporibus
ANGLO-SAXONVM,
praesertim durante illorum
HEPTARCHIA.
THE
GERMAN-
SEA.
KENT
Æthelbert
595.
EAST
SAXON
Sebert
604.
EAST
ANGLE
624.
NORTH
VMBERLAND
Edwin
627.
WEST
SAXON
Kengils
635.
58
57
56
55
54
53
52
Yorke
Beverley
Scarbrough
Flamborough head
Spurne head
EAST ANGLES KINGDOM

I. THE METAPHYSICAL POETS

Dr. Samuel Johnson, the great eighteenth-century literary figure, following a suggestion by John Dryden, labeled a school of poets of the early seventeenth century the *metaphysical* poets, because of their emphasis on the intellect or wit as against feeling and emotion. (See the article on page 271.) Johnson was not alone in believing these poets defective. But contemporary poets, particularly T. S. Eliot, have praised and imitated the metaphysical poets, and their reputations (especially that of John Donne) are much higher now than they were before the twentieth century.

Metaphysical poetry has come to be defined by its style rather than its content. The emphasis is on paradox: as Dr. Johnson put it, "The most heterogeneous ideas are yoked by violence together." The method of development is frequently the ingenious, often witty, elaboration of a *conceit* (a metaphor or analogy carried to great lengths). Other characteristics are the use of puns, the use of surprising comparisons, and the use of learned or scientific allusions. The total effect of a metaphysical poem at its best is to startle the reader into seeing and knowing what he has not *really* noticed or thought about before.

John Donne 1572 / 1631

SONG

Go and catch a falling star,
Get with child a mandrake root,[1]
Tell me where all past years are,
Or who cleft the devil's foot;
5 Teach me to hear mermaids singing,
Or to keep off envy's stinging,
And find
What wind
Serves to advance an honest mind.

10 If thou be'st born to strange sights,
Things invisible to see,
Ride ten thousand days and nights,
Till Age snow white hairs on thee;
Thou, when thou return'st, will tell me
15 All strange wonders that befell thee,
And swear
No where
Lives a woman true, and fair.

If thou find'st one, let me know;
20 Such a pilgrimage were sweet.
Yet do not; I would not go,
Though at next door we might meet.
Though she were true, when you met her,
And last, till you write your letter,
25 Yet she
Will be
False, ere I come, to two or three.

1. *Get . . . mandrake root.* Mandrake is a European herb with a forked root, fancied to resemble the figure of a man. Recognizing the resemblance but the impossibility of a plant's reproducing as humans do, Donne includes this in his catalogue of impossibilities.

OF CRITICAL INTEREST

ON DONNE'S POETRY
by Samuel T. Coleridge

With Donne, whose muse on dromedary trots,
Wreathe from pokers into truelove knots;
Rhyme's sturdy cripple, fancy's maze and clue,
Wit's forge and fire-blast, meaning's press and screw.
1836

THE BAIT

Come live with me, and be my love,
And we will some new pleasures prove
Of golden sands, and crystal brooks,
With silken lines, and silver hooks.

5 There will the river whispering run
Warmed by thy eyes, more than the sun.
And there th' enamoured fish will stay,
Begging themselves they may betray.

When thou wilt swim in that live bath,
10 Each fish, which every channel hath,
Will amorously to thee swim,
Gladder to catch thee, than thou him.

If thou, to be so seen, be'st loath,
By sun, or moon, thou darkenest both,
15 And if myself have leave to see,
I need not their light, having thee.

Let others freeze with angling reeds,
And cut their legs, with shells and weeds,
Or treacherously poor fish beset,
20 With strangling snare, or windowy net:

Let coarse bold hands, from slimy nest
The bedded fish in banks out-wrest,
Or curious traitors, sleave silk flies
Bewitch poor fishes' wandering eyes.

25 For thee, thou need'st no such deceit,
For thou thyself art thine own bait;
That fish, that is not catched thereby,
Alas, is wiser far than I.

THE INDIFFERENT

I can love both fair and brown,
Her whom abundance melts, and her whom want
 betrays,
Her who loves loneness best, and her who masks and
 plays,[1]

Her whom the country formed, and whom the town,
5 Her who believes, and her who tries,
Her who still weeps with spongy eyes,
And her who is dry cork, and never cries;
I can love her, and her, and you, and you,
I can love any, so she be not true.

10 Will no other vice content you?
Will it not serve your turn to do as did your mothers?
Or have you all old vices spent, and now would find
 out others?
Or doth a fear that men are true torment you?
O we are not, be not you so;
15 Let me, and do you, twenty know.
Rob me, but bind me not, and let me go.
Must I, who came to travail[2] thorough[3] you
Grow your fixed subject, because you are true?

Venus heard me sigh this song,
20 And by love's sweetest part, variety, she swore
She heard not this till now; and that it should be so
 no more.
She went, examined, and returned ere long,
And said, "Alas, some two or three
Poor heretics in love there be,
25 Which think to 'stablish dangerous constancy.
But I have told them, 'Since you will be true,
You shall be true to them who are false to you.'"

---

1. *masks and plays,* i.e., loves social pleasures.
2. *travail.* In the 17th century our words *travel* and *travail* ("pain and trouble; labor") were spelled the same; either spelling was used for either meaning.
3. *thorough,* through.

THE CANONIZATION[1]

For God's sake, hold your tongue, and let me love,
Or chide my palsy, or my gout,
My five gray hairs, or ruined fortune flout,
With wealth your state, your mind with arts improve,
5 Take you a course,[2] get you a place,[3]
Observe his Honor, or his Grace,[4]
Or the King's real, or his stampèd face[5]
Contèmplate; what you will, approve,[6]
So you will let me love.

10 Alas, alas, who's injured by my love?
What merchant's ships have my sighs drowned?
Who says my tears have overflowed his ground?
When did my colds a forward spring remove?[7]
When did the heats which my veins fill
15 Add one more to the plaguy bill?[8]
Soldiers find wars, and lawyers find out still
Litigious men, which quarrels move,
Though she and I do love.

Call us what you will, we are made such by love;
20 Call her one, me another fly,
We are tapers too, and at our own cost die,[9]
And we in us find the eagle and the dove,[10]
The phoenix riddle[11] hath more wit[12]
By us; we two being one, are it.
25 So to one neutral thing both sexes fit.
We die and rise the same, and prove
Mysterious by this love.[13]

We can die by it, if not live by love,
And if unfit for tombs and hearse
30 Our legend be, it will be fit for verse;
And if no piece of chronicle we prove,
We'll build in sonnets pretty rooms;
As well a well-wrought urn becomes
The greatest ashes, as half-acre tombs,
35 And by these hymns, all shall approve
Us canonized for love:

And thus invoke us; "You whom reverend love
Made one another's hermitage;[14]
You, to whom love was peace, that now is rage;
40 Who did the whole world's soul contract, and drove
Into the glasses of your eyes
(So made such mirrors and such spies,
That they did all to you epitomize)
Countries, towns, courts: beg from above
45 A pattern of your love!"[15]

1. *Canonization,* declaring a deceased person to be a saint; also, to make something divine.
2. *Take you a course,* follow some way of advancing yourself.
3. *place,* position at Court.
4. *Observe . . . Grace,* cultivate some lord or bishop.
5. *stampèd face,* the face of the king stamped on coins.
6. *approve,* try out.
7. *a forward spring remove,* hold back an early spring.
8. *plaguy bill,* list of plague victims, published weekly.
9. *at our . . . die.* Dying was a widely-used metaphor for the consummation of physical love. The expression refers to the popular belief that each indulgence in sexual relations shortened one's life by a day.
10. *eagle . . . dove.* The eagle symbolized strength or the masculine quality; the dove, gentleness or the feminine element.
11. *phoenix riddle,* the mystery of the legendary bird which was said to burn itself to death every five hundred years and then rise again from its own ashes. It is used as a symbol both of immortality and of desire rising from its own exhaustion.
12. *hath more wit,* makes more sense.
13. *We die . . . this love.* Because physical consummation does not change or diminish our love, we are different from ordinary humans (as saints are).
14. *hermitage,* refuge from the world.
15. *beg . . . love.* The poet and his mistress, having died and become saints, are implored by the world to beg from Heaven a pattern of their love, so that later lovers may model their loves on this one.

A VALEDICTION: FORBIDDING MOURNING

As virtuous men pass mildly away,
  And whisper to their souls to go,
Whilst some of their sad friends do say
  The breath goes now, and some say, No:

5 So let us melt, and make no noise,
  No tear-floods, nor sigh-tempests move,
'Twere profanation of our joys
  To tell the laity our love.

Moving of th' earth brings harms and fears,
10 Men reckon what it did and meant,
But trepidation of the spheres,
  Though greater far, is innocent.[1]

Dull sublunary[2] lovers' love
  (Whose soul is sense) cannot admit
15 Absence, because it doth remove
  Those things which elemented[3] it.

But we by a love so much refined
  That our selves know not what it is,
Inter-assurèd of the mind,
20 Care less, eyes, lips, and hands to miss.

Our two souls therefore, which are one,
  Though I must go, endure not yet
A breach, but an expansion,
  Like gold to aery thinness beat.

25 If they be two, they are two so
  As stiff twin compasses[4] are two;
Thy soul, the fixed foot, makes no show
  To move, but doth, if th' other do.

And though it in the centre sit,
30 Yet when the other far doth roam,
It leans and hearkens after it,
  And grows erect, as that comes home.

Such wilt thou be to me, who must
  Like th' other foot, obliquely run;
35 Thy firmness makes my circle[5] just,
  And makes me end where I begun.

1. *trepidation . . . innocent.* Movements (trepidation) of the heavenly spheres, though greater than those of an earthquake, provoke no fears in (nor danger to) man.
2. *sublunary,* beneath the moon; i.e., earthly and subject to change.
3. *elemented,* composed.
4. *compasses.* The image is of the instrument used for describing a circle. One branch or leg of the compass is held steady, as a pivot, while the other leg is rotated to draw the circle.
5. *circle.* The circle was a symbol of perfection.

DISCUSSION

1. *"Song":*

(a) Why are so many images and orders crowded into the first stanza?

(b) What is the state of mind of the speaker of the poem, and what do you think has happened to him?

2. *"The Indifferent":*

(a) What is startling about the attitude of the speaker in this poem?

(b) What role does Venus play in the poem, and why?

(c) Do you see any similarity between this poem and Shakespeare's Sonnet 130 (page 146)?

3. *"The Canonization":*

(a) Reconstruct the conversation that has led the speaker of the poem to say what he does.

(b) Explain the title of the poem.

4. *"The Bait":*

(a) Compare this poem with the poem by Christopher Marlowe which opens with the same line (page 143).

(b) Explain line 26: "For thou thyself art thine own bait."

5. *"A Valediction: Forbidding Mourning":*

(a) How do the lovers of this poem differ from the "dull sublunary lovers" of stanza 4?

(b) Explain the next-to-last line of the poem: "Thy firmness makes my circle just."

From HOLY SONNETS

6

This is my play's last scene; here heavens appoint
My pilgrimage's last mile; and my race
Idly yet quickly run, hath this last pace,
My span's last inch, my minute's latest point;
5 And gluttonous death will instantly unjoint
My body and my soul, and I shall sleep a space;
But my ever-waking part shall see that face
Whose fear already shakes my every joint;
Then as my soul to heaven, her first seat, takes
flight,
10 And earth-born body in the earth shall dwell,
So fall my sins, that all may have their right,
To where they are bred, and would press me—
to Hell.
Impute me righteous,[1] thus purged of evil,
For thus I leave the world, the flesh, and devil.

1. *Impute me righteous.* According to Christian doctrine, even after a man's soul has been purged (through repentance) of sins he himself has committed, he still is burdened with the original sin of Adam and has to be saved ("imputed righteous") by the merit of Christ.

10

Death, be not proud, though some have callèd thee
Mighty and dreadful, for thou art not so;
For those whom thou think'st thou dost overthrow
Die not, poor Death, nor yet canst thou kill me.
5 From rest and sleep, which but thy pictures be,
Much pleasure; then from thee much more must
flow,
And soonest our best men with thee do go,
Rest of their bones, and soul's delivery.
Thou art slave to fate, chance, kings, and
desperate men,
10 And dost with poison, war, and sickness dwell,
And poppy[1] or charms can make us sleep as well
And better than thy stroke; why swell'st[2] thou then?
One short sleep past, we wake eternally,
And death shall be no more; Death, thou shalt die.

1. *poppy,* the source of various narcotic drugs.
2. *swell'st,* puff up with pride.

7

At the round earth's imagined corners, blow
Your trumpets, angels; and arise, arise
From death, you numberless infinities
Of souls, and to your scattered bodies go;
5 All whom the flood did, and fire shall, o'erthrow,
All whom war, dearth, age, agues, tyrannies,
Despair, law, chance, hath slain, and you whose
eyes
Shall behold God, and never taste death's woe.[1]
But let them sleep, Lord, and me mourn a space;
10 For, if above all these, my sins abound,
'Tis late to ask abundance of Thy grace
When we are there. Here on this lowly ground,
Teach me how to repent; for that's as good
As if Thou hadst sealed my pardon with Thy blood.

1. *and you . . . woe,* those still alive at the Last Judgment and the end of the world, who will be judged without having experienced death.

14

Batter my heart, three-personed God; for You
As yet but knock, breathe, shine, and seek to mend;
That I may rise and stand, o'erthrow me, and bend
Your force to break, blow, burn, and make me new.
5 I, like an usurped town, to another due,
Labour to admit You, but O, to no end;
Reason, Your viceroy in me, me should defend,
But is captived, and proves weak or untrue.
Yet dearly I love You, and would be lovèd fain,
10 But am betrothed unto Your enemy.
Divorce me, untie or break that knot again;
Take me to You, imprison me, for I,
Except You enthral me, never shall be free,
Nor ever chaste, except You ravish me.

MEDITATION 17

Nunc lento sonitu dicunt, morieris.
(Now this bell tolling softly for another, says to me, Thou must die.)

PERCHANCE he for whom this bell tolls may be so ill as that he knows not it tolls for him; and perchance I may think myself so much better than I am, as that they who are about me and see my state may have caused it to toll for me, and I know not that. The church is catholic, universal, so are all her actions; all that she does belongs to all. When she baptizes a child, that action concerns me; for that child is thereby connected to that head which is my head too, and ingrafted into that body whereof I am a member.[1] And when she buries a man, that action concerns me: all mankind is of one author and is one volume; when one man dies, one chapter is not torn out of the book, but translated into a better language; and every chapter must be so translated. God employs several translators; some pieces are translated by age, some by sickness, some by war, some by justice; but God's hand is in every translation, and his hand shall bind up all our scattered leaves again for that library where every book shall lie open to one another. As therefore the bell that rings to a sermon calls not upon the preacher only, but upon the congregation to come, so this bell calls us all; but how much more me, who am brought so near the door by this sickness.

There was a contention as far as a suit[2] (in which piety and dignity, religion and estimation,[3] were mingled) which of the religious orders should ring to prayers first in the morning; and it was determined that they should ring first that rose earliest. If we understand aright the dignity of this bell that tolls for our evening prayer, we would be glad to make it ours by rising early, in that application, that it might be ours as well as his whose indeed it is. The bell doth toll for him that thinks it doth; and though it intermit again, yet from that minute that that occasion wrought upon him, he is united to God. Who casts not up his eye to the sun when it rises? but who takes off his eye from a comet when that breaks out? Who bends not his ear to any bell which upon any occasion rings? but who can remove it from that bell which is passing a piece of himself out of this world? No man is an island, entire of itself; every man is a piece of the continent, a part of the main. If a clod be washed away by the sea, Europe is the less, as well as if a promontory were, as well as if a manor of thy friend's or of thine own were. Any man's death diminishes me because I am involved in mankind, and therefore never send to know for whom the bell tolls; it tolls for thee. . . .

1. *head . . . member.* That is, the Christian church is the head of all men, as well as a body made up of its members.
2. *contention . . . suit,* a controversy that went as far as a lawsuit.
3. *estimation,* self-esteem.

DISCUSSION

1. *Holy Sonnet 6:*
Explain how the speaker "distributes" himself after death.

2. *Holy Sonnet 7:*
What is the reversal introduced in line 9, beginning with "But let them sleep . . ."?

3. *Holy Sonnet 10:*
(a) Is this sonnet somewhat like whistling in the dark, or is there some truth to the main argument?
(b) In what sense will death ever die?

4. *Holy Sonnet 14:*
Explain the striking paradoxes of the last two lines—enthrallment leading to freedom, ravishing to chastity.

5. *Meditation 17:*
Discuss the meaning and effectiveness of the two main metaphors: (a) man as a chapter in a book; (b) man as a piece of a continent.

TO HIS COY MISTRESS

by Andrew Marvell

Had we but world enough, and time,
This coyness, lady, were no crime.
We would sit down, and think which way
To walk, and pass our long love's day.
5 Thou by the Indian Ganges' side
Shouldst rubies find: I by the tide
Of Humber[1] would complain[2] I would
Love you ten years before the flood,[3]
And you should, if you please, refuse
10 Till the conversion of the Jews;[4]
My vegetable love should grow
Vaster than empires and more slow;
An hundred years should go to praise
Thine eyes, and on thy forehead gaze;
15 Two hundred to adore each breast,
But thirty thousand to the rest;
An age at least to every part,
And the last age should show your heart.
For, lady, you deserve this state;[5]
20 Nor would I love at lower rate.

But at my back I always hear
Time's wingèd chariot hurrying near;
And yonder all before us lie
Deserts of vast eternity.
25 Thy beauty shall no more be found,
Nor in thy marble vault shall sound
My echoing song; then worms shall try
That long preserved virginity;
And your quaint[6] honor turn to dust,
30 And into ashes all my lust:
The grave's a fine and private place,
But none, I think, do there embrace.

Now therefore, while the youthful hue
Sits on thy skin like morning dew,
35 And while thy willing soul transpires[7]
At every pore with instant fires,
Now let us sport us while we may,
And now, like amorous birds of prey,
Rather at once our time devour
40 Than languish in his slow-chapped[8] power,
Let us roll all our strength and all
Our sweetness up into one ball,
And tear our pleasures with rough strife
Thorough the iron gates of life:
45 Thus, though we cannot make our sun
Stand still, yet we will make him run.

1. *Humber,* a river that flows through Marvell's home town of Hull.
2. *complain,* i.e., sing plaintive love songs.
3. *flood,* the Biblical flood.
4. *conversion of the Jews.* It was a popular belief that this would occur just before the Last Judgment and the end of the world.
5. *state,* dignity.
6. *quaint,* fastidious; out-of-fashion.
7. *transpires,* breathes out.
8. *slow-chapped,* slow-jawed.

OF HUMAN INTEREST

Andrew Marvell

"He was of middling stature, pretty strong sett, roundish faced, cherry cheek't, hazell eie, browne haire. He was in his conversation very modest, and of very few words: and though he loved wine he would never drinke hard in company, and was wont to say that, he would not play the good-fellow in any man's company in whose hands he would not trust his life. He had not a generall acquaintance. . . .

"He kept bottles of wine at his lodgeing, and many times he would drinke liberally by himselfe to refresh his spirits, and exalt his Muse. . . .

"Obiit Londini, Aug. 18, 1678; and is buried in St. Giles church in-the-fields about the middle of the south aisle. Some suspect that he was poysoned by the Jesuits, but I cannot be positive."

EXTENSION

Contemporary writers have found Marvell's "To His Coy Mistress" a fascinating poem—not so much about love as about time. (For example, there is a reference to it in Part III of T. S. Eliot's *The Waste Land,* and in the title of Robert Penn Warren's novel *World Enough and Time.*) The contemporary American poet Archibald MacLeish was moved to write a poem directly to Marvell.

YOU, ANDREW MARVELL

by Archibald MacLeish

And here face down beneath the sun
And here upon earth's noonward height
To feel the always coming on
The always rising of the night:

5 To feel creep up the curving east
The earthy chill of dusk and slow
Upon those under lands the vast
And ever climbing shadow grow

And strange at Ecbatan[1] the trees
10 Take leaf by leaf the evening strange
The flooding dark about their knees
The mountains over Persia change

And now at Kermanshah[2] the gate
Dark empty and the withered grass
15 And through the twilight now the late
Few travelers in the westward pass

And Baghdad[3] darken and the bridge
Across the silent river gone
And through Arabia the edge
20 Of evening widen and steal on

And deepen on Palmyra's[4] street
The wheel rut in the ruined stone
And Lebanon fade out and Crete[5]
High through the clouds and overblown

25 And over Sicily the air
Still flashing with the landward gulls
And loom and slowly disappear
The sails above the shadowy hulls

And Spain go under and the shore
30 Of Africa the gilded sand
And evening vanish and no more
The low pale light across that land

Nor now the long light on the sea:

And here face downward in the sun
35 To feel how swift how secretly
The shadow of the night comes on . . .

From *Collected Poems 1917–1952* by Archibald MacLeish. Reprinted by permission of the publisher, Houghton Mifflin Company.

1. *Ecbatan,* city in old Persia, now in modern Iran. (Note that MacLeish names cities from east to west, just as the sun seems to move and the shadow of dusk moves.)
2. *Kermanshah,* ancient province and town in Iran.
3. *Baghdad,* most important city in Mesopotamia, now the capital of Iraq.
4. *Palmyra,* ancient city of central Syria.
5. *Crete,* an island of Greece, in the Mediterranean.

DISCUSSION

1. Lines 21–22 of "To His Coy Mistress" are two of the most famous lines of English poetry: "But at my back I always hear/Time's wingèd chariot hurrying near."

(a) Discuss the meaning and effect of the lines.

(b) How do they relate to Archibald MacLeish's poem?

2. Explain the meaning of the last two lines of "To His Coy Mistress" ("Thus, though we cannot make our sun/Stand still, yet we will make him run") and relate them to the rest of the poem.

3. Why does the MacLeish poem seem to begin in the middle of something, opening with the conjunction *And,* and to break off without actually concluding?

EASTER WINGS

by George Herbert

Lord, who createdst man in wealth and store,[1]
Though foolishly he lost the same,
Decaying more and more
Till he became
5 Most poor:
With thee
O let me rise
As larks, harmoniously,
And sing this day thy victories:
10 Then shall the fall further the flight in me.

My tender age in sorrow did begin;
And still with sicknesses and shame
Thou didst so punish sin,
That I became
15 Most thin.
With thee
Let me combine,
And feel this day thy victory;
For, if I imp[2] my wing on thine,
20 Affliction shall advance the flight in me.

1. *store*, abundance.
2. *imp*, a technical term used in falconry. Additional feathers were grafted (imped) onto a falcon's wings to improve its ability to fly.

DRINKING

by Abraham Cowley

From some copies of verses translated paraphrastically out of Anacreon[1]

The thirsty earth soaks up the rain,
And drinks, and gapes for drink again.
The plants suck in the earth, and are
With constant drinking fresh and fair.
5 The sea itself, which one would think
Should have but little need of drink,
Drinks ten thousand rivers up,
So filled that they o'erflow the cup.
The busy sun—and one would guess
10 By's drunken, fiery face no less—
Drinks up the sea, and when he's done,
The moon and stars drink up the sun.
They drink and dance by their own light;
They drink and revel all the night.
15 Nothing in nature's sober found,
But an eternal health goes round.
Fill up the bowl, then, fill it high,
Fill all the glasses there, for why
Should every creature drink but I?
20 Why, man of morals, tell me why?

1. *Anacreon,* Greek lyric poet (c. 563–478 B.C.) whose poems praised love and wine. Cowley's poem is a paraphrase of the original Latin.

DISCUSSION

1. Explore the ways in which George Herbert makes the physical shape of his poem reflect its content, and vice versa.

2. (a) What progression do you find in the series of images in Abraham Cowley's "Drinking"?

(b) Would you say that Samuel Johnson's remarks about metaphysical wit (page 271) apply in any way to this poem?

II. SONGS AND LYRICS— CLASSICAL, CAVALIER, CAREFREE

The two major sides in the religious struggle which divided England in the seventeenth century differed markedly in their life-styles. The somber Puritans came to be known as Roundheads because they habitually wore their hair short. The Anglicans of the established church, supporters of the Stuart kings, were more dashing and brightly attired and were known as Cavaliers (because of their resemblance to the courtiers of the King's cavalry). The Cavalier Poets flourished during the reign of Charles I (1625–1649). Ben Jonson was an earlier poet, of course, and not one of their group, but his poetry inspired both their admiration and their imitation. Prominent among them were Sir John Suckling, Richard Lovelace, Robert Herrick, and George Wither. Their poetry tended to follow classical models of elegance, and was written in support of wine, women, and the carefree life. If metaphysical poetry emphasized intellect and wit, Cavalier poetry stressed grace and charm.

COME, MY CELIA

by Ben Jonson

Come, my Celia, let us prove,[1]
While we can, the sports of love;
Time will not be ours forever;
He at length our good will sever.
5 Spend not then his gifts in vain.
Suns that set may rise again;
But if once we lose this light,
'Tis with us perpetual night.
Why should we defer our joys?
10 Fame and rumor are but toys.
Cannot we delude the eyes
Of a few poor household spies,
Or his easier ears beguile,
So removèd by our wile?
15 'Tis no sin love's fruit to steal;
But the sweet thefts to reveal,
To be taken, to be seen,
These have crimes accounted been.

From the play *Volpone.* Volpone is attempting to seduce Celia, whose husband he has temporarily gotten out of the way.
1. *prove,* experience.

IT IS NOT GROWING LIKE A TREE

by Ben Jonson

It is not growing like a tree
In bulk, doth make men better be;
Or standing long an oak, three hundred year,
To fall a log at last, dry, bald, and sear:
5 A lily of a day
Is fairer far in May;
Although it fall and die that night,
It was the plant and flower of light.
In small proportions we just beauties see,
And in short measures life may perfect be.

THE CONSTANT LOVER

by Sir John Suckling

Out upon it! I have loved
Three whole days together;
And am like to love three more,
If it prove fair weather.

5 Time shall molt away his wings
Ere he shall discover,
In the whole wide world again,
Such a constant lover.

But the spite on't is, no praise
10 Is due at all to me:
Love with me had made no stays
Had it any been but she.

Had it any been but she,
And that very face,
15 There had been at least ere this
A dozen dozen in her place.

WHAT CARE I?

by George Wither

Shall I, wasting in despair,
Die because a woman's fair?
Or my cheeks make pale with care
'Cause another's rosy are?
5 Be she fairer than the day
Or the flowery meads in May—
If she be not so to me,
What care I how fair she be?

Shall my foolish heart be pined
10 'Cause I see a woman kind?
Or a well disposèd nature
Joinèd with a lovely feature?
Be she meeker, kinder, than
Turtle-dove or pelican,
15 If she be not so to me,
What care I how kind she be?

Shall a woman's virtues move
Me to perish for her love?
Or her merits' value known
20 Make me quite forget mine own?
Be she with that goodness blest
Which may gain her name of Best;
If she seem not such to me,
What care I how good she be?

25 'Cause her fortune seems too high,
Shall I play the fool and die?
Those that bear a noble mind
Where they want of riches find,
Think what with them they would do
30 Who without them dare to woo;
And unless that mind I see,
What care I how great she be?

Great or good, or kind or fair,
I will ne'er the more despair;
35 If she love me, this believe,
I will die ere she shall grieve;
If she slight me when I woo,
I can scorn and let her go.
For if she be not for me,
40 What care I for whom she be?

TO ALTHEA, FROM PRISON

by Richard Lovelace

When Love with unconfinèd wings
Hovers within my gates,
And my divine Althea brings
To whisper at the grates;
5 When I lie tangled in her hair
And fettered to her eye,
The birds that wanton in the air
Know no such liberty.

When flowing cups run swiftly round
10 With no allaying Thames,[1]
Our careless heads with roses bound,
Our hearts with loyal flames;
When thirsty grief in wine we steep,
When healths and drafts go free,
15 Fishes that tipple in the deep
Know no such liberty.

When, like committed linnets, I
With shriller throat will sing
The sweetness, mercy, majesty,
20 And glories of my King;
When I shall voice aloud how good
He is, how great should be,
Enlargèd winds, that curl the flood,
Know no such liberty.

25 Stone walls do not a prison make,
Nor iron bars a cage;
Minds innocent and quiet take
That for an hermitage;
If I have freedom in my love
30 And in my soul am free,
Angels alone, that soar above,
Enjoy such liberty.

---

1. *no allaying Thames,* no diluting water from the Thames River.

TO LUCASTA, ON GOING TO THE WARS

by Richard Lovelace

Tell me not, sweet, I am unkind,
  That from the nunnery
Of thy chaste breast and quiet mind
  To war and arms I fly.

5 True, a new mistress now I chase,
  The first foe in the field;
And with a stronger faith embrace
  A sword, a horse, a shield.

Yet this inconstancy is such
10 As thou too shalt adore;
I could not love thee, dear, so much
  Loved I not honor more.

UPON JULIA'S CLOTHES

by Robert Herrick

Whenas in silks my Julia goes,
Then, then, methinks, how sweetly flows
That liquefaction of her clothes.

Next, when I cast mine eyes, and see
That brave[1] vibration, each way free,
O, how that glittering taketh me!

1. *brave*, splendid.

TO THE VIRGINS, TO MAKE MUCH OF TIME

by Robert Herrick

Gather ye rosebuds while ye may,
  Old time is still a-flying;
And this same flower that smiles today
  Tomorrow will be dying.

5 The glorious lamp of heaven, the sun,
  The higher he's a-getting
The sooner will his race be run,
  And nearer he's to setting.

That age is best which is the first,
10 When youth and blood are warmer;
But being spent, the worse, and worst
  Times still succeed the former.

Then be not coy, but use your time,
  And, while ye may, go marry;
15 For, having lost but once your prime,
  You may forever tarry.

DISCUSSION

1. *Ben Jonson:*

(a) Explore the truth of the last line of "It Is Not Growing Like a Tree": "And in short measures life may perfect be."

(b) Discuss the morality or justness of the last four lines of "Come, My Celia."

2. *George Wither:*

Discuss the state of mind of the speaker in "What Care I?" Does he seem to protest too much?

3. *Sir John Suckling:*

In "The Constant Lover," a reversal of sentiment seems to begin in stanza 3. What is it, and how genuine is it?

4. *Richard Lovelace:*

(a) In "To Lucasta," why does the speaker say that his beloved will "adore" his "inconstancy"?

(b) Each stanza of "To Althea" ends with a different image—birds, fishes, winds, angels. Explain their function in the poem.

5. *Robert Herrick:*

(a) In "Upon Julia's Clothes," discuss the effect of the word *liquefaction*.

(b) Compare "To the Virgins" with Marvell's "To His Coy Mistress," especially in the handling of the theme of time's swift passage.

III. JOHN MILTON 1608 / 1674

ON HIS HAVING ARRIVED AT THE AGE OF TWENTY-THREE

How soon hath Time, the subtle thief of youth
Stolen on his wing my three and twentieth year!
My hasting days fly on with full career,
But my late spring no bud or blossom shew'th.[1]
5 Perhaps my semblance[2] might deceive the truth
That I to manhood am arrived so near;
And inward ripeness doth much less appear,
That some more timely-happy spirits endu'th.[3]
Yet be it less or more, or soon or slow,
10 It shall be still in strictest measure even[4]
To that same lot, however mean or high,
Toward which Time leads me, and the will of Heaven;
All is, if I have grace to use it so,
As ever in my great Task-Master's eye.

1. *shew'th,* shows.
2. *semblance,* youthful appearance.
3. *endu'th,* endows.
4. *even,* adequate; i.e., his "inward ripeness" or inner readiness will be adequate to whatever destiny Time and Heaven are leading him.

ON HIS BLINDNESS

When I consider how my light is spent
Ere half my days in this dark world and wide,
And that one talent[1] which is death to hide
Lodged with me useless, though my soul more bent
5 To serve therewith my Maker, and present
My true account, lest He returning chide;
"Doth God exact day-labor, light denied?"
I fondly[2] ask. But Patience, to prevent
That murmur, soon replies, "God doth not need
10 Either man's work or His own gifts. Who best
Bear His mild yoke, they serve Him best. His state
Is kingly: thousands at His bidding speed,
And post o'er land and ocean without rest;
They also serve who only stand and wait."

1. *talent,* the gift of writing. This refers to Jesus' parable of the talents, or coins, which tells of the "unprofitable servant" who was condemned for hiding his one talent in the earth instead of spending it. (Mathew 25: 15–30)
2. *fondly,* foolishly.

OF LITERARY INTEREST

Milton's sonnets

Although Milton wrote only twenty-three sonnets during a period of approximately thirty years, he was an expert in the use of this literary form. "On His Having Arrived at the Age of Twenty-Three" was found among his Cambridge manuscripts. He had inserted it in a letter to a friend who had apparently remonstrated with him upon his aimless student life. In reply, Milton wrote: "That you may see that I am something suspicious of myself, or do take notice of a certain belatedness in me, I am the bolder to send you some of my nightward thoughts some little while ago, made up in a Petrarchan stanza which I told you of."

Milton became completely blind at the age of forty-five. "On His Blindness" was written shortly after this personal catastrophe.

DISCUSSION

1. In "On His Having Arrived at the Age of Twenty-Three," how does Milton reconcile himself to his meager accomplishments?
2. Compare "On His Blindness" with the sonnet written at the age of twenty-three (more than two decades earlier), both of which are concerned with Milton's achievements.

PARADISE LOST

FROM BOOK I—INVOCATION

Of man's first disobedience, and the fruit
Of that forbidden tree, whose mortal taste
Brought death into the world, and all our woe,
With loss of Eden, till one greater man[1]
5 Restore us, and regain the blissful seat,
Sing heavenly muse,[2] that on the secret top
Of Oreb, or of Sinai, didst inspire
That shepherd,[3] who first taught the chosen seed,
In the beginning how the heavens and earth
10 Rose out of chaos: Or if Sion hill[4]
Delight thee more, and Siloa's brook[4] that flowed
Fast by the oracle of God; I thence
Invoke thy aid to my adventurous song,
That with no middle flight intends to soar
15 Above the Aonian mount,[5] while it pursues
Things unattempted yet in prose or rhyme.
And chiefly thou, O spirit,[6] that dost prefer
Before all temples the upright heart and pure,
Instruct me, for thou knowest; thou from the first
20 Wast present, and, with mighty wings outspread
Dove-like satest brooding on the vast abyss
And madest it pregnant: What in me is dark
Illumine, what is low raise and support;
That to the height of this great argument
25 I may assert eternal providence,
And justify the ways of God to men.

The action of Paradise Lost *begins in* medias res *(in the midst of things), after Satan's rebellion and after he and his legions are driven from Heaven and thrown into Chaos. The opening episodes show the fallen angels "rolling in the fiery gulf" until Satan rises and addresses his companions.*

1. *greater man,* Christ.
2. *heavenly muse,* the spirit that spoke to Moses on Mount Sinai and Mount Horeb (Oreb) in the wilderness.
3. *that shepherd,* Moses.
4. *Sion hill, Siloa's brook,* sacred places in Jerusalem.
5. *Aonian mount,* Mount Helicon in Greece, home of the Muses.
6. *spirit,* the Holy Spirit, the third person of the Holy Trinity, or God.

PORTRAIT OF MILTON COURTESY PRINCETON UNIVERSITY LIBRARY.

"... Farewell happy fields
250 Where joy forever dwells: Hail horrors, hail
Infernal world, and thou profoundest Hell
Receive thy new possessor: One who brings
A mind not to be changed by place or time.
The mind is its own place, and in itself
255 Can make a heaven of Hell, a hell of Heaven.
What matter where, if I be still the same,
And what I should be, all but less than[7] he
Whom thunder hath made greater? Here at least
We shall be free; the Almighty hath not built
260 Here for his envy, will not drive us hence:
Here we may reign secure, and in my choice
To reign is worth ambition though in Hell:
Better to reign in Hell, than serve in Heaven."

Satan rallies his legions and they build their kingdom in Hell. Bent on revenge, Satan searches throughout Chaos to find man and his world. He learns that God has forbidden Adam and Eve to eat of the fruit of the Tree of Knowledge, and decides that he will lure them into disobedience. He slips into the Garden of Eden, enters the body of the serpent, and finds Eve alone. He approaches her, rendering himself "pleasing" in shape and "lovely," with the purpose of flattering and thus tricking her.

FROM BOOK IX

Oft he bowed
525 His turret crest, and sleek enameled neck,
Fawning, and licked the ground whereon she trod.
His gentle dumb expression turned at length

7. *all but less than,* less only than.

The eye of Eve to mark his play; he glad
Of her attention gained, with serpent tongue
530 Organic, or impulse of vocal air,
His fraudulent temptation thus began.

SATAN:
"Wonder not, sovereign mistress, if perhaps
Thou canst, who art sole wonder, much less arm
Thy looks, the heaven of mildness, with disdain,
535 Displeased that I approach thee thus, and gaze
Insatiate, I thus single, nor have feared
Thy awful brow, more awful thus retired.
Fairest resemblance of thy maker fair,
Thee all things living gaze on, all things thine
540 By gift, and thy celestial beauty adore
With ravishment beheld, there best beheld
Where universally admired; but here
In this enclosure wild, these beasts among,
Beholders rude, and shallow to discern
545 Half what in thee is fair, one man except,
Who sees thee? (and what is one?) who shouldst be seen
A goddess among gods, adored and served
By angels numberless, thy daily train."
So glozed[8] the tempter, and his proem[9] tuned;
550 Into the heart of Eve his words made way,
Though at the voice much marveling; at length
Not unamazed she thus in answer spake.

EVE:
"What may this mean? Language of man pronounced
By tongue of brute, and human sense expressed?
555 The first at least of these I thought denied
To beasts, whom God on their creation-day
Created mute to all articulate sound;
The latter I demur,[10] for in their looks
Much reason, and in their actions oft appears.
560 Thee, serpent, subtlest beast of all the field
I knew, but not with human voice endued;
Redouble then this miracle, and say,
How camest thou speakable of mute, and how
To me so friendly grown above the rest
565 Of brutal kind, that daily are in sight?
Say, for such wonder claims attention due."
To whom the guileful tempter thus replied.

SATAN:
"Empress of this fair world, resplendent Eve,
Easy to me it is to tell thee all
570 What thou commandest, and right thou shouldst be obeyed:
I was at first as other beasts that graze
The trodden herb, of abject thoughts and low,
As was my food, nor aught but food discerned
Or sex, and apprehended nothing high:
575 Till on a day roving the field, I chanced
A goodly tree far distant to behold
Laden with fruit of fairest colors mixed,
Ruddy and gold: I nearer drew to gaze;
When from the boughs a savory odor blown,
580 Grateful to appetite, more pleased my sense
Than smell of sweetest fennel or the teats
Of ewe or goat dropping with milk at even,
Unsucked of lamb or kid, that tend their play
To satisfy the sharp desire I had
585 Of tasting those fair apples, I resolved
Not to defer; hunger and thirst at once,
Powerful persuaders, quickened at the scent
Of that alluring fruit, urged me so keen.
About the mossy trunk I wound me soon,
590 For high from ground the branches would require
Thy utmost reach or Adam's: Round the tree
All other beasts that saw, with like desire
Longing and envying stood, but could not reach.
Amid the tree now got, where plenty hung
595 Tempting so nigh, to pluck and eat my fill
I spared not, for such pleasure till that hour
At feed or fountain never had I found.
Sated at length, erelong I might perceive
Strange alteration in me, to degree
600 Of reason in my inward powers, and speech
Wanted not long, though to this shape retained.
Thenceforth to speculations high or deep
I turned my thoughts, and with capacious mind
Considered all things visible in heaven,
605 Or Earth, or Middle,[11] all things fair and good;
But all that fair and good in thy divine
Semblance, and in thy beauty's heavenly ray
United I beheld; no fair[12] to thine
Equivalent or second, which compelled
610 Me thus, though importune perhaps, to come
And gaze, and worship thee of right declared
Sovereign of creatures, universal dame."
So talked the spirited[13] sly snake; and Eve

8. *glozed,* flattered.
9. *proem,* prologue.
10. *demur,* question; i.e., I doubt that rational sense was denied to animals.
11. *Middle,* the air.
12. *fair,* beauty.
13. *spirited,* possessed by a spirit.

Yet more amazed unwary thus replied.
EVE:
615 "Serpent, thy overpraising leaves in doubt
The virtue of that fruit, in thee first proved:
But say, where grows the tree, from hence how far?
For many are the trees of God that grow
In Paradise, and various, yet unknown
620 To us, in such abundance lies our choice,
As leaves a greater store of fruit untouched,
Still hanging incorruptible, till men
Grow up to their provision, and more hands
Help to disburden nature of her birth."
625 To whom the wily adder, blithe and glad.
SATAN:
"Empress, the way is ready, and not long,
Beyond a row of myrtles, on a flat,
Fast by a fountain, one small thicket past
Of blowing[14] myrrh and balm; if thou accept
630 My conduct, I can bring thee thither soon."
"Lead then," said Eve. He leading swiftly rolled
In tangles, and made intricate seem straight,
To mischief swift. Hope elevates, and joy
Brightens his crest, as when a wandering fire,
635 Compact of unctuous vapor,[15] which the night
Condenses, and the cold environs round,
Kindled through agitation to a flame,
Which oft, they say, some evil spirit attends
Hovering and blazing with delusive light,
640 Misleads the amazed night-wanderer from his way
To bogs and mires, and oft through pond or pool,
There swallowed up and lost, from succor far.
So glistered the dire snake, and into fraud
Led Eve our credulous mother, to the tree
645 Of prohibition,[16] root of all our woe;
Which when she saw, thus to her guide she spake.
EVE:
"Serpent, we might have spared our coming
hither,
Fruitless to me, though fruit be here to excess,
The credit of whose virtue rest with thee,
650 Wondrous indeed, if cause of such effects.
But of this tree we may not taste nor touch;
God so commanded, and left that command
Sole daughter of his voice:[17] the rest, we live
Law to ourselves, our reason is our law."

14. *blowing,* blooming.
15. *Compact . . . vapor,* made of oily mist.
16. *tree/Of prohibition,* forbidden tree.
17. *Sole . . . voice,* his only command.

OF HUMAN INTEREST

John Milton

"His harmonicall and ingeniose Soul did lodge in a beautifull and well proportioned body. He was a spare man. He was scarce so tall as I am (*quaere,* quot feet I am high: *resp.,* of middle stature).

"He had abroun hayre. His complexion exceeding faire—he was so faire that they called him *the Lady of Christ's College.* Ovall face. His eie a darke gray.

"He was very healthy and free from all diseases: seldome tooke any physique (only sometimes he tooke manna): only towards his latter end he was visited with the Gowte, Spring and Fall.

"He had a delicate tuneable Voice, and had good skill. His father instructed him. He had an Organ in his howse; he played on that most. Of a very cheerfull humour. He would be chearfull even in his Gowte fitts, and sing.

"He had a very good Memorie; but I believe that his excellent Method of thinking and disposing did much to helpe his Memorie."

From *Aubrey's Brief Lives* (1690), edited by Oliver Lawson Dick. [First published in 1690.]

655 To whom the tempter guilefully replied.
SATAN:
"Indeed? hath God then said that of the fruit
Of all these garden trees ye shall not eat,
Yet lords declared of all in earth or air?"
To whom thus Eve yet sinless.
EVE:
"Of the fruit
660 Of each tree in the garden we may eat,
But of the fruit of this fair tree amidst
The garden, God hath said, 'Ye shall not eat
Thereof, nor shall ye touch it, lest ye die.'"
She scarce had said, though brief, when now
more bold
665 The tempter, but with show of zeal and love
To man, and indignation at his wrong,
New part puts on,[18] and as to passion moved,
Fluctuates disturbed, yet comely and in act
Raised,[19] as of some great matter to begin.
670 As when of old some orator renowned
In Athens or free Rome, where eloquence

18. *New part puts on,* assumes a new role.
19. *in act raised,* poised in stance.

Flourished, since mute, to some great cause
addressed,
Stood in himself collected, while each part,
Motion, each act won audience ere the tongue,
675 Sometimes in height began, as no delay
Of preface brooking through his zeal of right.[20]
So standing, moving, or to height upgrown
The tempter all impassioned thus began.

SATAN:

"O sacred, wise, and wisdom-giving plant,
680 Mother of science,[21] now I feel thy power
Within me clear, not only to discern
Things in their causes, but to trace the ways
Of highest agents, deemed however wise.
Queen of this universe, do not believe
685 Those rigid threats of death; ye shall not die:
How should ye? by the fruit? it gives you life
To knowledge. By the threatener, look on me,
Me who have touched and tasted, yet both live,
And life more perfect have attained than fate
690 Meant me, by venturing higher than my lot.
Shall that be shut to man, which to the beast
Is open? or will God incense his ire
For such a petty trespass, and not praise
Rather your dauntless virtue, whom the pain
695 Of death denounced,[22] whatever thing death be,
Deterred not from achieving what might lead
To happier life, knowledge of good and evil;
Of good, how just? of evil, if what is evil
Be real, why not known, since easier shunned?
700 God therefore cannot hurt ye, and be just;
Not just, not God;[23] not feared then, nor obeyed:
Your fear itself of death removes the fear.
Why then was this forbid? Why but to awe,
Why but to keep ye low and ignorant,
705 His worshipers; he knows that in the day
Ye eat thereof, your eyes that seem so clear,
Yet are but dim, shall perfectly be then
Opened and cleared, and ye shall be as gods,
Knowing both good and evil as they know.
710 That ye should be as gods, since I as man,
Internal man,[24] is but proportion meet,
I of brute human, ye of human gods.
So ye shall die perhaps, by putting off
Human, to put on gods, death to be wished,
715 Though threatened, which no worse than this can
bring.
And what are gods that man may not become
As they, participating[25] godlike food?
The gods are first, and that advantage use
On our belief, that all from them proceeds;
720 I question it, for this fair earth I see,
Warmed by the sun, producing every kind,
Them nothing: If they all things, who enclosed
Knowledge of good and evil in this tree,
That whoso eats thereof, forthwith attains
725 Wisdom without their leave? and wherein lies
The offense, that man should thus attain to know?
What can your knowledge hurt him, or this tree
Impart against his will if all be his?
Or is it envy, and can envy dwell
730 In heavenly breasts? these, these and many more
Causes import[26] your need of this fair fruit.
Goddess humane, reach then, and freely taste."
He ended, and his words replete with guile
Into her heart too easy entrance won:
735 Fixed on the fruit she gazed, which to behold
Might tempt alone, and in her ears the sound
Yet rung of his persuasive words, impregned[27]
With reason, to her seeming, and with truth;
Meanwhile the hour of noon drew on, and waked
740 An eager appetite, raised by the smell
So savory of that fruit, which with desire,
Inclinable now grown to touch or taste,
Solicited her longing eye; yet first
Pausing a while, thus to herself she mused.

EVE:

745 "Great are thy virtues, doubtless, best of fruits,
Though kept from man, and worthy to be admired,
Whose taste, too long forborne, at first assay[28]
Gave elocution to the mute, and taught
The tongue not made for speech to speak thy
praise:
750 Thy praise he also who forbids thy use,
Conceals not from us, naming thee the tree
Of knowledge, knowledge both of good and evil;
Forbids us then to taste, but his forbidding

---

20. *Sometimes in height . . . right.* As if too agitated to begin at the beginning, the speaker burst into the middle of his speech.
21. *science,* knowledge.
22. *denounced,* threatened.
23. *God therefore . . . God.* The serpent reasons that for God to punish Eve with death would be unjust, and if God were unjust He would not be God.
24. *Internal man,* like man inside (intellectually) but not in appearance.
25. *participating,* sharing.
26. *import,* prove.
27. *impregned,* impregnated.
28. *assay,* try.

Commends thee more, while it infers the good
755 By thee communicated, and our want:
For good unknown, sure is not had, or had
And yet unknown, is as not had at all.
In plain then, what forbids he but to know,
Forbids us good, forbids us to be wise?
760 Such prohibitions bind not. But if death
Bind us with after-bands, what profits then
Our inward freedom? In the day we eat
Of this fair fruit, our doom is, we shall die.
How dies the serpent? he hath eaten and lives,
765 And knows, and speaks, and reasons, and discerns,
Irrational till then. For us alone
Was death invented? or to us denied
This intellectual food, for beasts reserved?
For beasts it seems: yet that one beast which first
770 Hath tasted, envies not, but brings with joy
The good befallen him, author unsuspect,[29]
Friendly to man, far from deceit or guile.
What fear I then, rather what know to fear
Under this ignorance of good and evil,
775 Of God or death, of law or penalty?
Here grows the cure of all, this fruit divine,
Fair to the eye, inviting to the taste,
Of virtue to make wise: what hinders then
To reach, and feed at once both body and mind?"

780 So saying, her rash hand in evil hour
Forth reaching to the fruit, she plucked, she eat:
Earth felt the wound, and nature from her seat
Sighing through all her works gave signs of woe,
That all was lost. Back to the thicket slunk
785 The guilty serpent, and well might, for Eve
Intent now wholly on her taste, naught else
Regarded, such delight till then, as seemed,
In fruit she never tasted, whether true
Or fancied so, through expectation high
790 Of knowledge, nor was godhead from her thought.
Greedily she engorged without restraint,
And knew not eating death . . . .

Eve offers the fruit to Adam, who eats out of love for her. They immediately fall to accusing each other. Sin and death enter the world. God orders Adam and Eve expelled from Eden, and sends the Angel Michael to execute His will. Michael shows the future to Adam, and then Adam goes to wake Eve and depart from Paradise.

29. *author unsuspect,* a reliable authority.

FROM BOOK XII

Descended, Adam to the bower where Eve
Lay sleeping ran before, but found her waked;
And thus with words not sad she him received.
610 "Whence thou returnest, and whither wentest, I know;
For God is also in sleep, and dreams advise,
Which he hath sent propitious, some great good
Presaging, since with sorrow and heart's distress
Wearied I fell asleep: but now lead on;
615 In me is no delay; with thee to go,
Is to stay here; without thee here to stay,
Is to go hence unwilling; thou to me
Art all things under heaven, all places thou,
Who for my willful crime art banished hence.
620 This further consolation yet secure
I carry hence; though all by me is lost,
Such favor I unworthy am vouchsafed,
By me the promised seed shall all restore."
So spake our mother Eve, and Adam heard
625 Well pleased, but answered not; for now too nigh
The archangel stood, and from the other hill
To their fixed station, all in bright array
The cherubim descended; on the ground
Gliding meteorous, as evening mist
630 Risen from a river o'er the marish[30] glides,
And gathers ground fast at the laborer's heel
Homeward returning. High in front advanced,
The brandished sword of God before them blazed
Fierce as a comet; which with torrid heat,
635 And vapor as the Libyan air adust,[31]
Began to parch that temperate clime; whereat
In either hand the hastening angel caught
Our lingering parents, and to the eastern gate
Led them direct, and down the cliff as fast
640 To the subjected plain; then disappeared.
They looking back, all the eastern side beheld
Of Paradise, so late their happy seat,
Waved over by that flaming brand, the gate
With dreadful faces thronged and fiery arms:
645 Some natural tears they dropped, but wiped them soon;
The world was all before them, where to choose
Their place of rest, and providence their guide:
They hand in hand with wandering steps and slow,
Through Eden took their solitary way. □

30. *marish,* marsh.
31. *Libyan air adust,* hot desert winds of Libya.

EXTENSION

It is perhaps a paradox that the fall of man should ever be called "fortunate," but there is a long tradition in which the original sin of Adam and Eve is seen as proving ultimately beneficial for mankind: only through the fall was man enabled to win God's grace. (See, for example, "Adam Lay in Bondage" in the Medieval section.) In Book XII of *Paradise Lost*, lines 469–478, Adam reflects on the idea of the fortunate fall in a speech he makes to the Archangel Michael:

O goodness infinite, goodness immense!
That all this good of evil shall produce,
And evil turn to good; more wonderful
Then that which by creation first brought forth
Light out of darkness! full of doubt I stand,
Whether I should repent me now of sin
By me done and occasioned, or rejoice
Much more, that much more good thereof shall spring,
To God more glory, more good will to men
From God, and over wrath grace shall abound.

A contemporary British poet has written his own version of this idea:

THE FORTUNATE FALL

by A. Alvarez

Perhaps Eve in the garden knew the sun
With her whole flesh; and pruned the rose's soul—
The thing was thornless, pliable, like Eve—
And she the garden whence all flowers sprung.

5 But Adam knew her as the fruit he stole,
The apple, sleeping, God made him conceive.
His side and eyes were opened. They were bare,
The tree despoiled and knowledge risen whole.

Before she even fumbled with the leaves
10 Adam was finished. Of course, she had a flair
For fumbling that was folly to oppose,
Tricky, pleading, knowing. Why should he grieve?

So he chose for her, chose his own despair.
Her hair, like rain, closed on the thorny rose.

(1953)

DISCUSSION

1. In the Invocation, Milton asserts that his purpose in *Paradise Lost* is to "justify the ways of God to men." Does he accomplish this purpose in the parts you have read?
2. Explain and explore these famous quotations:
"The mind is its own place, and in itself / Can make a heaven of Hell, a hell of Heaven."
"Better to reign in Hell, than serve in Heaven."
3. How does Satan lure Eve into eating the forbidden fruit?
4. Just before Eve eats the fruit, she meditates and persuades herself that she should go ahead and eat. Examine the lines (745–779) and discuss the plausibility of her reasoning.
5. What consolation does Eve have in the closing lines of the poem?
6. How does Milton's version of the story differ from the King James Version in the Bible (pages 223–225 in this text)?

READER'S THEATER

Assign the parts of Eve, Satan, and the narrator, and do a dramatic reading of the temptation scene. How would you design the tree and the fruit for today's theater?

WRITING

Check over the King James Version and the Milton presentation of the temptation scene, and rewrite it in modern language; or simply improvise the scene and see how it all comes out.

IV. John Dryden 1631 / 1700

A SONG FOR ST. CECILIA'S DAY

From harmony, from heavenly harmony,
This universal frame began:
When Nature underneath a heap
Of jarring atoms lay,
5 And could not heave her head,
The tuneful voice was heard from high:
"Arise, ye more than dead."

Then cold and hot and moist and dry[1]
In order to their stations leap,
10 And Music's power obey.
From harmony, from heavenly harmony,
This universal frame began:
From harmony to harmony
Through all the compass of the notes it ran,
15 The diapason closing full in Man.

What passion cannot Music raise and quell!
When Jubal struck the chorded shell,[2]
His listening brethren stood around,
And wondering, on their faces fell
20 To worship that celestial sound.
Less than a god they thought there could not dwell
Within the hollow of that shell
That spoke so sweetly and so well.
What passion cannot Music raise and quell!

25 The trumpet's loud clangor
Excites us to arms
With shrill note of anger
And mortal alarms.
The double, double, double beat
30 Of the thundering drum
Cries: "Hark! the foes come;
Charge, charge, 'tis too late to retreat!"

The soft complaining flute
In dying notes discovers[3]
35 The woes of hopeless lovers
Whose dirge is whispered by the warbling lute.
Sharp violins proclaim
Their jealous pangs and desperation,
Fury, frantic indignation,
40 Depth of pain, and height of passion
For the fair, disdainful dame.

But oh! what art can teach,
What human voice can reach
The sacred organ's praise?
45 Notes inspiring holy love,
Notes that wing their heavenly ways
To mend the choirs above.
Orpheus[4] could lead the savage race;
And trees unrooted left their place,
50 Sequacious[5] of the lyre;
But bright Cecilia raised the wonder higher:
When to her organ vocal breath was given,
An angel heard, and straight appeared,
Mistaking earth for heaven.

GRAND CHORUS

55 As from the power of sacred lays
The spheres began to move,[6]
And sung the great Creator's praise
To all the blessed above;
So when the last and dreadful hour
60 This crumbling pageant shall devour,
The trumpet shall be heard on high,
The dead shall live, the living die,
And Music shall untune the sky.

---

1. *cold . . . dry,* air, fire, water, and earth, which were the four elements of the universe according to classical and medieval natural philosophy.
2. *Jubal . . . shell.* Jubal is referred to in the Bible as "the father of all such as handle the harp and pipe." (Genesis 4:21). Dryden pictures Jubal's lyre as made of a tortoise shell.
3. *discovers,* reveals; expresses.
4. *Orpheus.* In Greek mythology, Orpheus was such a wonderful musician that animals and even inanimate objects followed him when he played on his lyre.
5. *Sequacious,* following after.
6. *spheres . . . move.* It was believed that the stars made music as they revolved in their spheres.

OF LITERARY INTEREST

St. Cecilia and her praise

St. Cecilia, a Christian martyr of the third century, is the patron saint of music and by tradition the inventor of the pipe organ. At an annual London music festival held on St. Cecilia's Day (November 22), it was customary to present an original ode set to music. Dryden, in his ode, tried to translate the effects of various instruments into poetry.

Alexander Pope, Dryden's disciple, also wrote an ode to St. Cecilia, and a number of modern poets, including W. H. Auden, have likewise done so. George Barker has recently written an "Ode Against St. Cecilia's Day," a bitter antiwar poem invoking silence and grief rather than joyful music.

The ode

An ode (for example, "A Song for St. Cecilia's Day") is an exalted, often rapturous, lyric poem on a lofty subject, with complex or irregular stanzas. The form of the ode grew out of Greek drama, in which the chorus, accompanied by music, chanted a strophe when moving to the left on the stage, an antistrophe when moving to the right, and an epode when standing still. The Greek poet Pindar established the regular pattern for the ode, with fixed forms for the various parts. However, the English ode has tended almost always to be irregular, with stanzaic structure shifting readily to accommodate shifts of thought and mood. Some odes tend to be primarily eulogistic, others meditative. Most odes are written to praise someone or to commemorate some event. An ode may also be inspired by an object or creature; see, for example, Shelley's "Ode to the West Wind" or Keats's "Ode to a Nightingale."

OF HUMAN INTEREST

Dryden's marriage

In his early thirties, Dryden married Lady Elizabeth Howard, somewhat older than himself. The marriage was not a happy one, and Dryden almost never mentioned the subject of marriage without attacking it. He wrote this epitaph even before his wife died:

Here lies my wife: here let her lie!
Now she's at rest. And so am I.

COURTESY OF THE TRUSTEES OF THE BRITISH MUSEUM.

DISCUSSION

1. (a) What does Dryden mean by "universal frame" in line 2?

(b) What idea does he develop in the first two stanzas of the poem?

(c) Explain lines 14-15.

2. (a) What idea is developed in the third stanza?

(b) How are stanzas 4-6 related to this idea?

(c) What comparison of pagan and Christian music does Dryden make in stanza 6?

(d) What is the concluding idea of the poem?

V. THE DIARY OF SAMUEL PEPYS

Samuel Pepys (1633–1703), from the vantage point of his post in the Naval Office in London, was able to observe society, government, and mankind during an exciting period of English history—the Restoration of the monarchy beginning in 1660. He kept a diary in a secret code from 1660 to 1669, revealing as much about himself as about his times. He apparently wrote for himself, without intending to publish his work. It was not until 1825 that the diary was examined and the code deciphered. His diary (along with John Evelyn's covering the same period) has served ever since to give glimpses and insights into the intimate and domestic, as well as the public and official, life of the period.

At the time he was writing the entries that are excerpted below, Pepys was thirty years old. Since June 1660 he had been a Commissioner and a Principal Officer of the Navy Board as Clerk of the Acts, a position gained through the influence of the Earl of Sandwich, his cousin by marriage. Pepys, along with fellow members of the Board, lived in official Navy housing adjacent to their office.

NATIONAL PORTRAIT GALLERY, LONDON

APRIL 1663

Sat. 18th. Up betimes and to my office, where all the morning. At noon to dinner. With us Mr. Creed,[1] who has been deeply engaged at the office this day about the ending of his accounts, wherein he is most unhappy to have to do with a company of fools who after they have signed his accounts and made bills upon them yet dare not boldly assert to the Treasurer that they are satisfied with his accounts. Hereupon all dinner, and walking in the garden the afternoon, he and I talking of the ill management of our office, which God knows is very ill for the King's advantage. I would I could make it better. In the evening to my office, and at night home to supper and bed.

Sun. 19th (Easter day). Up and this day put on my close-kneed coloured suit, which, with new stockings of the colour, with belt, and new gilt-handled sword, is very handsome. To church alone, and so to dinner, where my father and brother Tom dined with us, and after dinner to church again, my father sitting below in the chancel. After church done, where the young Scotchman preaching I slept all the while, my father and I to see my uncle and aunt Wight, and after a stay of an hour there my father to my brother's and I home to supper, and after supper fell in discourse of dancing, and I find that Ashwell[2] hath a very fine carriage, which makes my wife almost ashamed of herself to see herself so outdone, but to-morrow she begins to learn to dance for a month or two. So to prayers and to bed.

Mon. 20th. Up betimes as I use to do, and in my chamber begun to look over my father's accounts, which he brought out of the country with him by my desire, whereby I may see what he has received and spent, and I find that he is not anything extravagant, and yet it do so far outdo his estate that he must either think of lessening his charge, or I must be forced to spare money out of my purse to help him through, which I would willing do as far as £20 goes. . . .

After dinner, it raining very hard, by coach to Whitehall, where, after Sir G. Carteret, Sir J. Minnes, Mr. Coventry[3] and I had been with the Duke,[4] we to the Committee of Tangier and did matters there, and so broke up. With Sir G. Carteret and Sir John Minnes by coach to my Lord Treasurer's, thinking to have spoken about getting money for paying the Yards; but we found him with some ladies at cards: and so,

1. *Creed,* John Creed, Deputy-Treasurer of the Fleet.

2. *Ashwell,* Mary Ashwell, recently hired as maid-companion to Mrs. Pepys.
3. *Carteret, Minnes, Coventry,* older members of the Navy Board.
4. *Duke,* the Duke of York, the king's brother, and Lord Admiral of the Navy. He later became King James II.

it being a bad time to speak, we parted, and Sir J. Minnes and I home, and after walking with my wife in the garden late, to supper and to bed, being somewhat troubled at Ashwell's desiring and insisting over eagerly upon her going to a ball to meet some of her old companions at a dancing school here in town next Friday, but I am resolved she shall not go. So to bed. . . .

Wed. 22nd. Up betimes and to my office very busy all the morning there. . . . So to my uncle Wight's, by invitation, whither my father, wife, and Ashwell came, where we had but a poor dinner, and not well dressed,[5] besides, the very sight of my aunt's hands and greasy manner of carving, did almost turn my stomach. After dinner by coach to the King's Playhouse, where we saw but part of "Witt without mony," which I do not like much, but coming late put me out of tune, and it costing me four halfcrowns for myself and company. So, the play done, home, and I to my office a while and so home, where my father (who is so very melancholy) and we played at cards, and so to supper and to bed.

Thurs. 23rd. St. George's day and Coronacion, the King and Court being at Windsor, at the installing of the King of Denmark by proxy and the Duke of Monmouth. I up betimes, and with my father, having a fire made in my wife's new closet[6] above, it being a wet and cold day, we sat there all the morning looking over his country accounts. . . . We resolve upon sending for Will Stankes[7] up to town to give us a right understanding in all that we have in Brampton, and before my father goes to settle every thing so as to resolve how to find a living for my father and to pay debts and legacies. . . .

At cards till late, and being at supper, my boy being sent for some mustard to a neat's tongue, the rogue staid half an hour in the streets, it seems at a bonfire, at which I was very angry, and resolve to beat him to-morrow.

Fri. 24th. Up betimes, and with my salt eel[8] went down in the parler and there got my boy and did beat him till I was fain to take breath two or three times, yet for all I am afeard it will make the boy never the better, he is grown so hardened in his tricks, which I am sorry for, he being capable of making a brave man, and is a boy that I and my wife love very well.

So made me ready, and to my office, where all the morning, and at noon home, whither came Captain Holland, who is lately come home from sea, and has been much harassed in law about the ship which he has bought, so that it seems in a despair he endeavoured to cut his own throat, but is recovered it; and it seems—whether by that or any other persuasion (his wife's mother being a great zealot) he is turned almost a Quaker, his discourse being nothing but holy, and that impertinent, that I was weary of him. At last pretending to go to the Change[9] we walked thither together, and there I left him and home to dinner, sending my boy by the way to enquire after two dancing masters at our end of the town for my wife to learn, of whose names the boy brought word.

After dinner all the afternoon fiddling upon my viallin (which I have not done many a day) while Ashwell danced above in my upper best chamber, which is a rare room for musique, expecting this afternoon my wife to bring my cozen Scott and Stradwick, but they came not, and so in the evening we by ourselves to Half-way house to walk, but did not go in there, but only a walk and so home again and to supper, my father with us, and had a good lobster intended for part of our entertainment to these people to-day, and so to cards, and then to bed, being the first day that I have spent so much to my pleasure a great while.

Sat. 25th. Up betimes and to my vyall and song book a pretty while, and so to my office, and there we sat all the morning. . . .

At noon we rose, Sir W. Batten[10] ashamed and vexed [because of a dispute with Pepys], and so home to dinner, and after dinner walked to the old Exchange and so all along to Westminster Hall, White Hall, my Lord Sandwich's lodgings, and going by water back to the Temple did pay my debts in several places in order to my examining my accounts to-morrow to my great content. So in the evening home, and after supper (my father at my brother's) and merrily practising to dance, which my wife hath begun to learn this day of Mr. Pembleton, but I fear

---

5. *dressed,* prepared; cooked.
6. *closet,* small private room. Pepys had recently added an upper story to his house.
7. *Will Stankes,* manager of a family property in the country from which Pepys' father received income.
8. *salt eel,* piece of rope used as a whip.
9. *Change,* the Royal Exchange, a building where merchants assembled to transact business.
10. *Sir W. Batten,* an older colleague on the Navy Board, and a neighbor. Pepys disliked him and considered him dishonest.

will hardly do any great good at it, because she is conceited that she do well already, though I think no such thing. So to bed. . . .

Lastly I did hear that the Queen is much grieved of late at the King's neglecting her, he having not supped once with her this quarter of a year, and almost every night with my Lady Castlemaine; who hath been with him this St. George's feast at Windsor, and came home with him last night; and, which is more, they say is removed as to her bed from her own home to a chamber in White Hall, next to the King's own; which I am sorry to hear, though I love her much.

Sun. 26th (Lord's-day). Lay pretty long in bed talking with my wife, and then up and set to the making up of my monthly accounts, but Tom[11] coming, with whom I was angry for botching my camlott[12] coat, to tell me that my father and he would dine with me, and that my father was at our church, I got me ready and had a very good sermon of a country minister upon "How blessed a thing it is for brethren to live together in unity!" So home and all to dinner, and then would have gone by coach to have seen my Lord Sandwich at Chelsey if the man would have taken us, but he denying it we staid at home, and I all the afternoon upon my accounts, and find myself worth full £700, for which I bless God, it being the most I was ever yet worth in money.

In the evening (my father being gone to my brother's to lie to-night) my wife, Ashwell, and the boy and I, and the dogg, over the water and walked to Half-way house, and beyond into the fields, gathering of cowslipps, and so to Half-way house, with some cold lamb we carried with us, and there supped, and had a most pleasant walk back again, Ashwell all along telling us some parts of their mask at Chelsey School, which was very pretty, and I find she hath a most prodigious memory, remembering so much of things acted six or seven years ago. So home, and after reading my vows, being sleepy, without prayers to bed, for which God forgive me!

Mon. 27th. Up betimes and to my office, where doing business alone a good while till people came about business to me. Will Griffin tells me this morning that Captain Browne, Sir W. Batten's brother-in-law, is dead of a blow given him two days ago by a seaman, a servant of his, being drunk, with a stone striking him on the forehead, for which I am sorry, he having a good woman and several small children. . . . Home by coach, where I found Mary[13] gone from my wife, she being too high for her, though a very good servant, and my boy too will be going in a few days, for he is not for my family, he is grown so out of order and not to be ruled, and do himself, against his brother's counsel, desire to be gone, which I am sorry for, because I love the boy and would be glad to bring him to good. At home with my wife and Ashwell talking of her going into the country this year, wherein we had like to have fallen out, she thinking that I have a design to have her go, which I have not, and to let her stay here I perceive will not be convenient, for she expects more pleasure than I can give her here, and I fear I have done very ill in letting her begin to learn to dance. . . .

Tues. 28th. Up betimes and to my office, and there all the morning, only stepped up to see my wife and her dancing master at it, and I think after all she will do pretty well at it. . . .

Thurs. 30th. [Will Stankes had arrived the previous day from the country.] Lord! what a stir Stankes makes with his being crowded in the streets and wearied in walking in London, and would not be wooed by my wife and Ashwell to go to a play, nor to White Hall, or to see the lyons,[14] though he was carried in a coach. I never could have thought there had been upon earth a man so little curious in the world as he is. . . .

MAY 1663

Fri. May 1st. Up betimes and my father with me, and he and I all the morning and Will Stankes private, in my wife's closet above, settling our matters concerning our Brampton estate, &c., and I find that there will be, after all debts paid within £100, £50 per annum clear coming towards my father's maintenance, besides £25 per annum annuities to my Uncle Thomas and Aunt Perkins. Of which, though I was in my mind glad, yet thought it not fit to let my father know it thoroughly, but after he had gone out to visit my uncle Thomas and brought him to dinner with him, and after dinner I got my father, brother Tom, and myself together, I did make the

11. *Tom,* his brother, who had recently taken over their father's tailoring business.
12. *camlott,* expensive imported fabric made of camel's hair.
13. *Mary,* not Mary Ashwell, but a previous servant.
14. *lyons* (lions), in the menagerie at the Tower of London, one of the chief sights of the city.

business worse to them, and did promise £20 out of my own purse to make it £50 a year to my father, propounding that Stortlow may be sold to pay £200 for his satisfaction therein and the rest to go towards payment of debts and legacies. The truth is I am fearful lest my father should die before debts are paid, and then the land goes to Tom and the burden of paying all debts will fall upon the rest of the land. Not that I would do my brother any real hurt. I advised my father to good husbandry and to living within the compass of £50 a year, and all in such kind words, as not only made them but myself to weep, and I hope it will have a good effect.

That being done, and all things agreed on, we went down, and after a glass of wine we all took horse, and I, upon a horse hired of Mr. Game, saw him out of London, at the end of Bishopsgate Street, and so I turned and rode, with some trouble, through the fields towards Hide Park, whither all the world, I think, are going; and in my going, met W. Howe[15] coming galloping upon a little crop black nag; it seems one that was taken in some ground of my Lord's, by some mischance being left by his master, a thief; this horse being found with black cloth ears on, and a false mayne, having none of his own. . . .

By and by, about seven or eight o'clock, homeward. . . . In my way, in Leadenhall Street, there was morris-dancing which I have not seen a great while. So set my horse up at Game's, paying 5*s.* for him. And so home to see Sir J. Minnes, who is well again, and after staying talking with him awhile, I took leave and went to hear Mrs. Turner's daughter, at whose house Sir J. Minnes lies, play on the harpsicon;[16] but, Lord! it was enough to make any man sick to hear her; yet I was forced to commend her highly. So home to supper and to bed, Ashwell playing upon the tryangle[17] very well before I went to bed. . . .

Sat. 2nd. Being weary last night, I slept till almost seven o'clock, a thing I have not done many a day. So up and to my office (being come to some angry words with my wife about neglecting the keeping of the house clean, I calling her beggar, and she me pricklouse, which vexed me) and there all the morning. So to the Exchange and then home to dinner, and very merry and well pleased with my wife, and so to the office again, where we met extraordinary upon drawing up the debts of the Navy to my Lord Treasurer. So rose and up to Sir W. Pen[18] to drink a glass of bad syder in his new far low dining room, which is very noble, and so home, where Captain Ferrers and his lady are come to see my wife. . . .

Sun. 3rd (Lord's day). Up before 5 o'clock and alone at setting my Brampton papers to rights according to my father's and my computation . . . . So made myself ready and to church, where Sir W. Pen showed me the young lady which young Dawes, that sits in the new corner-pew in the church, hath stole away from Sir Andrew Rickard, her guardian, worth £1,000 per annum present, good land, and some money, and a very well-bred and handsome lady: he, I doubt, but a simple fellow. However, he got this good luck to get her, which methinks I could envy him with all my heart.

Home to dinner with my wife, who not being very well did not dress herself but staid at home all day, and so I to church in the afternoon and so home again, and up to teach Ashwell the grounds of time and other things on the tryangle, and made her take out a Psalm very well, she having a good ear and hand. And so a while to my office, and then home to supper and prayers, to bed, my wife and I having a little falling out because I would not leave my discourse below with her and Ashwell to go up and talk with her alone upon something she has to say. She reproached me but I had rather talk with any body than her, by which I find I think she is jealous of my freedom with Ashwell, which I must avoid giving occasion of.

Mon. 4th. Up betimes and to setting my Brampton papers in order and looking over my wardrobe against summer, and laying things in order to send to my brother to alter. By and by took boat intending to have gone down to Woolwich,[19] but seeing I could not get back time enough to dinner, I returned and home. Whither by and by the dancing-master came, whom standing by, seeing him instructing my wife, when he had done with her, he would needs have me try the steps of a coranto, and what with his desire and my wife's importunity, I did begin, and then was obliged to give him entry-money 10*s.*, and am become his scholler. The truth

15. *W. Howe,* also in the service of Pepys' cousin and patron, the Earl of Sandwich.

16. *harpsicon,* harpsichord.

17. *tryangle,* probably a triangular spinet.

18. *Sir W. Pen* (Penn), a neighbor and fellow member of the Navy Board. His son was William Penn who founded Pennsylvania.

19. *Woolwich,* an important naval dockyard.

is, I think it a thing very useful for a gentleman, and sometimes I may have occasion of using it, and though it cost me what I am heartily sorry it should, besides that I must by my oath[20] give half as much more to the poor. . . .

Tues. 5th. Up betimes and to my office, and there busy all the morning, among other things walked a good while up and down with Sir J. Minnes, he telling many old stories of the Navy, and of the state of the Navy at the beginning of the late troubles,[21] and I am troubled at my heart to think, and shall hereafter cease to wonder, at the bad success of the King's cause, when such a knave as he (if it be true what he says) had the whole management of the fleet. . . .

Wed. 6th. Up betimes and to my office a good while at my new rulers, then to business, and towards noon to the Exchange with Creed, where we met with Sir J. Minnes coming in his coach from Westminster, who tells us, in great heat, that, by God, the Parliament will make mad work; that they will render all men incapable of any military or civil employment that have borne arms in the late troubles against the King, excepting some persons; which, if it be so, as I hope it is not, will give great cause of discontent, and I doubt will have but bad effects. I left them at the Exchange and walked to Paul's Churchyard to look upon a book or two, and so back, and thence to the Trinity House, and there dined, where among other discourse worth hearing among the old seamen, they tell us that they have catched often in Greenland in fishing whales with the iron grapnells that had formerly been struck into their bodies covered over with fat; that they have had eleven hogsheads of oyle out of the tongue of a whale.

Thence after dinner home to my office, and there busy till the evening. Then home and to supper, and while at supper comes Mr. Pembleton, and after supper we up to our dancing room and there danced three or four country dances, and after that a practice of my coranto I began with him the other day, and I begin to think that I shall be able to do something at it in time. Late and merry at it, and so weary to bed.

Sat. 9th. Up betimes and to my office, whither sooner than ordinary comes Mr. Hater[22] desiring to speak a word to me alone, which I was from the disorder of his countenance amused at, and so the poor man began telling me [that he was in difficulties

20. *oath.* Pepys was trying to cure himself of too much devotion to pleasure through a system of self-imposed fines.

21. *late troubles,* the execution of King Charles I and the establishment of the Puritan Commonwealth under Cromwell.

22. *Mr. Hater,* Tom Hater, Pepys' chief clerk.

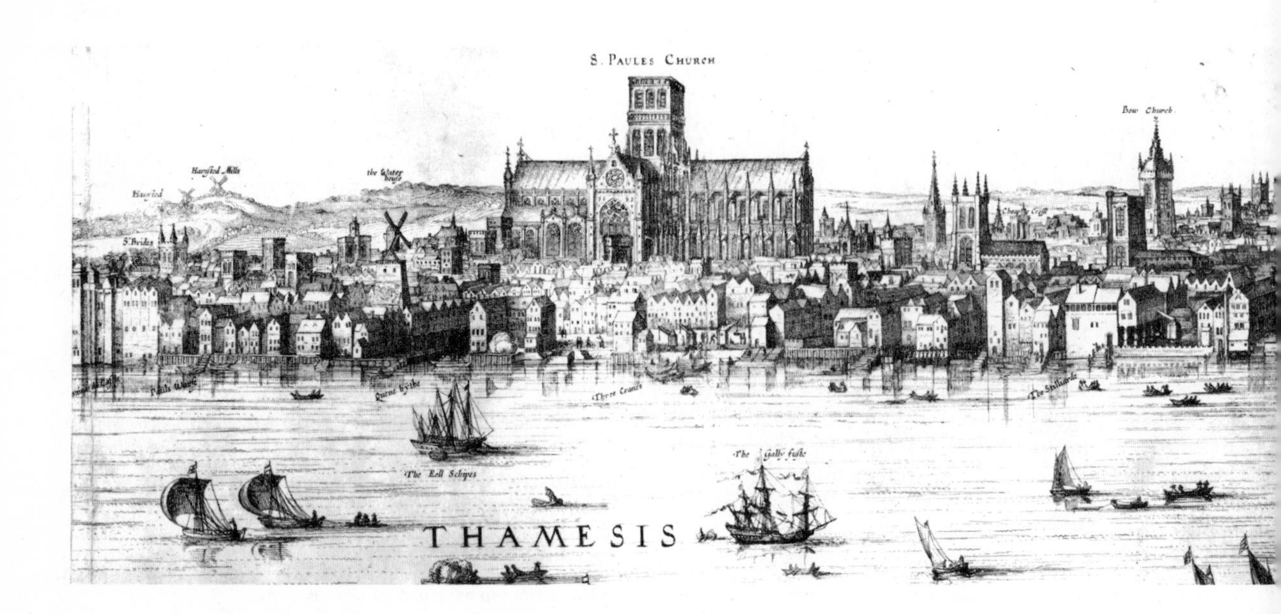

with the authorities for attending a Quaker meeting, which was then illegal. Pepys promised to intercede for him with Mr. Coventry, an influential member of the Board.] At noon dined at home with a heavy heart for the poor man, and after dinner went out to my brother's, and thence to Westminster, where at Mr. Jervas's, my old barber, I did try two or three borders and perriwiggs, meaning to wear one; and yet I have no stomach [for it,] but that the pains of keeping my hair clean is so great. He trimmed me, and at last I parted, but my mind was almost altered from my first purpose, from the trouble that I foresee will be in wearing them also. Thence by water home and to the office, where busy late, and so home to supper and bed, with my mind much troubled about T. Hater.

Mon. 11th. Up betimes, and by water to Woolwich on board the Royall James, to see in what dispatch she is to be carried about to Chatham. So to the yard a little, and thence on foot to Greenwich, where going I was set upon by a great dogg, who got hold of my garters, and might have done me hurt; but, Lord, to see in what a maze I was, that, having a sword about me, I never thought of it, or had the heart to make use of it, but might, for want of that courage, have been worried. . . .

Fri. 15th. [Pepys first details extensive items of gossip about the Court and members of the nobility, all illustrating "the unhappy posture of things at this time."]

Sir Thomas [Crew] showed me his picture and Sir Anthony Vandike's, in crayon in little, done exceedingly well. Having thus freely talked with him, and of many more things, I took leave . . . and so well pleased home, where I found it almost night, and my wife and the dancing-master alone above, not dancing but talking. Now so deadly full of jealousy I am that my heart and head did so cast about and fret that I could not do any business possibly, but went out to my office, and anon late home again and ready to chide at every thing, and then suddenly to bed and could hardly sleep, yet durst not say any thing, but was forced to say that I had bad news from the Duke concerning Tom Hater as an excuse to my wife, who by my folly has too much opportunity given her with the man, who is a pretty neat black man,[23] but married. But it is a deadly folly and plague that I bring upon myself to be so jealous and by giving myself such an occasion more than my wife desired of giving her another month's dancing. Which however shall be ended as soon as I can possibly. . . .

Sat. 16th. Up with my mind disturbed and with my last night's doubts upon me, for which I deserve to be

23. *black man,* dark-haired man.

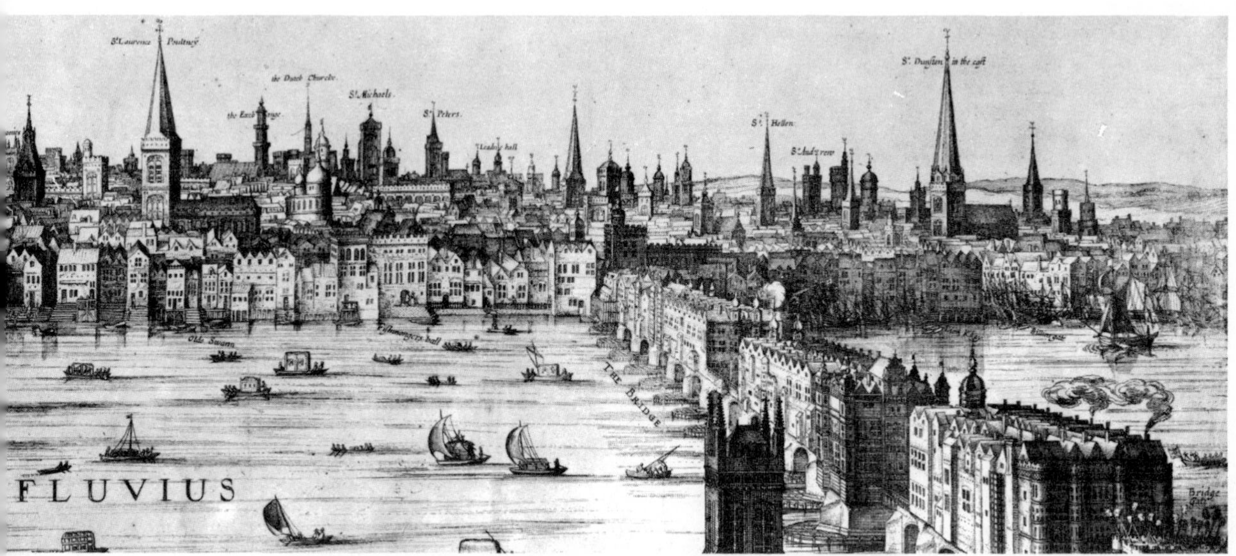

SEVENTEENTH-CENTURY LONDON. COURTESY OF THE TRUSTEES OF THE BRITISH MUSEUM.

beaten if not really served as I am fearful of being, especially since God knows that I do not find honesty enough in my own mind but that upon a small temptation I could be false to her, and therefore ought not to expect more justice from her, but God pardon both my sin and my folly herein. To my office and there sitting all the morning, and at noon dined at home. After dinner comes Pembleton, and I being out of humour would not see him, pretending business, but, Lord! with what jealousy did I walk up and down my chamber listening to hear whether they danced or no, which they did, notwithstanding I afterwards knew and did then believe that Ashwell was with them. So to my office awhile, and, my jealousy still reigning, I went in and, not out of any pleasure but from that only reason, did go up to them to practice, and did make an end of "La Duchesse," which I think I should, with a little pains, do very well. So broke up and saw him gone. . . .
Sun. 17th (Lord's day). Up and in my chamber all the morning, preparing my great letters to my father, stating to him the perfect condition of our estate. My wife and Ashwell to church, and after dinner they to church again, and I all the afternoon making an end of my morning's work, which I did about evening, and then to talk with my wife till after supper, and so to bed having another small falling out and myself vexed with my old fit of jealousy about her dancing-master. But I am a fool for doing it. So to bed by daylight, I having a very great cold, so as I doubt whether I shall be able to speak to-morrow at our attending the Duke, being now so hoarse.
Wed. 20th. Up and to my office, and anon home and to see my wife dancing with Pembleton about noon, and I to the Trinity House to dinner and after dinner home, and there met Pembleton, who I perceive has dined with my wife, which she takes no notice of, but whether that proceeds out of design, or fear to displease me I know not, but it put me into a great disorder again. . . .
Thurs. 21st. Up, but cannot get up so early as I was wont, nor my mind to business as it should be and used to be before this dancing. However, to my office, where most of the morning talking of Captain Cox of Chatham about his and the whole yard's difference against Mr. Barrow the storekeeper. . . . After much good advice and other talk I home and danced with Pembleton, and then the barber trimmed me, and so to dinner, my wife and I having high words about her dancing to that degree that I did enter and make a vow to myself not to oppose her or say anything to dispraise or correct her therein as long as her month lasts, in pain of *2s. 6d.* for every time, which, if God pleases, I will observe, for this roguish business has brought us more disquiett than anything [that] has happened a great while. After dinner to my office, where late, and then home; and Pembleton being there again, we fell to dance a country dance or two, and so to supper and bed. But being at supper my wife did say something that caused me to oppose her in, she used the word devil, which vexed me, and among other things I said I would not have her to use that word, upon which she took me up most scornfully, which, before Ashwell and the rest of the world, I know not now-a-days how to check, as I would heretofore, for less than that would have made me strike her. So that I fear without great discretion I shall go near to lose too my command over her, and nothing do it more than giving her this occasion of dancing and other pleasures, whereby her mind is taken up from her business and finds other sweets besides pleasing of me, and so makes her that she begins not at all to take pleasure in me or study to please me as heretofore. . . .
Fri. 22nd. Up pretty betimes, and shall, I hope, come to myself and business again, after a small playing the truant, for I find that my interest and profit do grow daily, for which God be praised and keep me to my duty. To my office, and anon one tells me that Rundall, the house-carpenter of Deptford, hath sent me a fine blackbird, which I went to see. He tells me he was offered *20s.* for him as he came along, he do so whistle. So to my office, and busy all the morning, among other things, learning to understand the course of the tides, and I think I do now do it. At noon Mr. Creed comes to me, and he and I to the Exchange, where I had much discourse with several merchants, and so home with him to dinner, and then by water to Greenwich, and calling at the little alehouse at the end of the town to wrap a rag about my little left toe, being new sore with walking, we walked pleasantly to Woolwich, in our way hearing the nightingales sing. . . .
Sat. 23rd. Waked this morning between four and five by my blackbird, which whistles as well as ever I heard any; only it is the beginning of many tunes very well, but there leaves them, and goes no further. So up and to my office, where we sat, and among other things I had a fray with Sir J. Minnes

in defence of my Will[24] in a business where the old coxcomb would have put a foot upon him, which was only in Jack Davis and in him a downright piece of knavery in procuring a double ticket and getting the wrong one paid as well as the second was to the true party. But it appeared clear enough to the board that Will was true in it. . . .

Sun. 24th (Lord's day). . . . forebore going to church this morning, but staid at home looking over my papers about Tom Trice's business, and so at noon dined, and my wife telling me that there was a pretty lady come to church with Peg Pen to-day, I against my intention had a mind to go to church to see her, and did so, and she is pretty handsome. But over against our gallery I espied Pembleton, and saw him leer upon my wife all the sermon, I taking no notice of him, and my wife upon him, and I observed she made a curtsey to him at coming out without taking notice to me at all of it, which with the consideration of her being desirous these two last Lord's days to go to church both forenoon and afternoon do really make me suspect something more than ordinary, though I am loth to think the worst, but yet it put and do still keep me at a great loss in my mind, and makes me curse the time that I consented to her dancing. . . . But I must have patience and get her into the country, or at least to make an end of her learning to dance as soon as I can.

After sermon to Sir W. Pen's, with Sir J. Minnes to do a little business to answer Mr. Coventry to-night. And so home and with my wife and Ashwell into the garden walking a great while, discoursing what this pretty wench should be by her garb and deportment; with respect to Mrs. Pen she may be her woman, but only that she sat in the pew with her, which I believe he would not let her do. So home, and read to my wife a fable or two in Ogleby's Æsop, and so to supper, and then to prayers and to bed. My wife this evening discoursing of making clothes for the country, which I seem against, pleading lack of money, but I am glad of it in some respects because of getting her out of the way from this fellow, and my own liberty to look after my business more than of late I have done. So to prayers and to bed. . . .

Mon. 25th. I staid within most of the morning, and by and by the barber came and Sarah Kite my cozen, poor woman, came to see me and borrow 40*s*. of me, telling me she will pay it at Michaelmas again to me. I was glad it was no more, being indifferent whether she pays it me or no, but it will be a good excuse to lend her nor give her any more. So I did freely at first word do it, and give her a crown more freely to buy her child something, she being a good-natured and painful wretch, and one that I would do good for as far as I can that I might not be burdened. . . .

Ashwell did by and by come to me with an errand from her mistress to desire money to buy a country suit for her against she goes as we talked last night, and so I did give her £4, and believe it will cost me the best part of 4 more to fit her out, but with peace and honour I am willing to spare anything so as to be able to keep all ends together, and my power over her undisturbed. So to my office and by and by home, where my wife and her master were dancing, and so I staid in my chamber till they had done, and sat down myself to try a little upon the Lyra viall,[25] my hand being almost out, but easily brought to again.

Tues. 26th. Lay long in bed talking with my wife. So up and to my office a while and then home, where I found Pembleton, and by many circumstances I am led to conclude that there is something more than ordinary between my wife and him, which do so trouble me that I know not at this very minute that I now write this almost what either I write or am doing, nor how to carry myself to my wife in it, being unwilling to speak of it to her for making of any breach and other inconveniences, nor let it pass for fear of her continuing to offend me and the matter grow worse thereby. So that I am grieved at the very heart, but I am very unwise in being so.

There dined with me Mr. Creed and Captain Grove, and before dinner I had much discourse in my chamber with Mr. Deane, the builder of Woolwich, about building of ships. But nothing could get the business out of my head, I fearing that this afternoon by my wife's sending every [one] abroad and knowing that I must be at the office she has appointed him to come. This is my devilish jealousy, which I pray God may be false, but it makes a very hell in my mind, which the God of heaven remove, or I shall be very unhappy. So to the office, where we sat awhile. By and by my mind being in great trouble I went home to see how things were, and there I found as I doubted Mr. Pembleton with my wife, and nobody else in the house, which made me almost mad, and going up to my chamber after a turn or

24. *Will* (Hewer), Pepys' chief clerk.

25. *Lyra viall* (viol), a stringed musical instrument.

two I went out again and called somebody on pretence of business and left him in my little room at the door (it was the Dutchman, commander of the King's pleasure boats, who having been beat by one of his men sadly, was come to the office to-day to complain) telling him I would come again to him to speak with him about his business. So in great trouble and doubt to the office, and Mr. Coventry nor Sir G. Carteret being there I made a quick end of our business and desired leave to be gone, pretending to go to the Temple, but it was home, and so up to my chamber, and as I think if they had any intention of hurt I did prevent doing anything at that time, but I continued in my chamber vexed and angry till he went away, pretending aloud, that I might hear, that he could not stay, and Mrs. Ashwell not being within they could not dance. And, Lord! to see how my jealousy wrought so far that I went softly up to see whether any of the beds were out of order or no, which I found not, but that did not content me, but I staid all the evening walking, and though anon my wife came up to me and would have spoke of business to me, yet I construed it to be but impudence, and though my heart full yet I did say nothing, being in a great doubt what to do. So at night, suffered them to go all to bed, and late put myself to bed in great discontent, and so to sleep.

Wed. 27th. So I waked by 3 o'clock, my mind being troubled, and after having lain till past 4 o'clock seemed going to rise, though I did it only to see what my wife would do, and so going out of the bed she took hold of me and would know what ailed me, and after many kind and some cross words I began to tax her discretion in yesterday's business, but she quickly told me my own, knowing well enough that it was my old disease of jealousy, which I denied, but to no purpose. After an hour's discourse, sometimes high and sometimes kind, I found very good reason to think that her freedom with him is very great and more than was convenient, but with no evil intent, and so after awhile I caressed her and parted seeming friends, but she crying in a great discontent. So I up and by water to the Temple, and thence with Commissioner Pett to St. James's. . . .

This day there was great thronging to Banstead Downs, upon a great horse-race and foot-race. I am sorry I could not go thither. So home back as I came, to London Bridge, and so home, where I find my wife in a musty humour, and tells me before Ashwell that Pembleton had been there, and she would not have him come in unless I was there, which I was ashamed of; but however, I had rather it should be so than the other way. So to my office, to put things in order there, and by and by comes Pembleton, and word is brought me from my wife thereof that I might come home. So I sent word that I would have her go dance, and I would come presently. So being at a great loss whether I should appear to Pembleton or no, and what would most proclaim my jealousy to him, I at last resolved to go home, and took Tom Hater with me, and staid a good while in my chamber, and there took occasion to tell him how I hear that Parliament is putting an act out against all sorts of conventicles,[26] and did give him good counsel, not only in his own behalf, but my own, that if he did hear or know anything that could be said to my prejudice, that he would tell me, for in this wicked age . . . a man ought to be prepared to answer for himself in all things that can be inquired concerning him. After much discourse of this nature to him I sent him away, and then went up, and there we danced country dances, and single, my wife and I; and my wife paid him off for this month also, and so he is cleared. After dancing we took him down to supper, and were very merry, and I made myself so, and kind to him as much as I could, to prevent his discourse, though I perceive to my trouble that he knows all, and may do me the disgrace to publish it as much as he can. Which I take very ill, and if too much provoked shall witness it to her. After supper and he gone we to bed.

Thurs. 28th. . . . after dinner by water to the Royall Theatre; but that was so full they told us we could have no room. And so to the Duke's House; and there saw "Hamlett" done, giving us fresh reason never to think enough of Betterton.[27] Who should we see come upon the stage but Gosnell, my wife's maid? but neither spoke, danced, nor sung; which I was sorry for. But she becomes the stage very well. . . .

Fri. 29th. This day is kept strictly as a holy-day, being the King's Coronation. We lay long in bed, and it rained very hard, rain and hail, almost all the morning. By and by Creed and I abroad, and called at several churches; and it is a wonder to see, and by that to guess the ill temper of the City at this time, either to religion in general, or to the King, that in some churches there was hardly ten people in the whole church, and those poor people. So to a coffee-house, and there in discourse hear the King of France is likely to be well again. So home to dinner, and out by water to the Royall Theatre, but they not acting to-day, then to the Duke's house, and there saw "The Slighted Mayde," wherein Gosnell acted Pyramena, a great part, and did it very well, and I believe will do it better and better, and prove a good actor. I to my brother's, and thence to my uncle Fenner's to have seen my aunt James (who has been long in town and goes away to-morrow and I not seen her), but did find none of them within, which I was glad of, and so back to my brother's to speak with him, and so home, and in my way did take two turns forwards and backwards through the Fleete Ally to see a couple of pretty [strumpets] that stood off the doors there, and God forgive me I could scarce stay myself from going into their houses with them, so apt is my nature to evil after once, as I have these two days, set upon pleasure again. . . .

Sun. 31st (Lord's day). Lay long in bed talking with my wife, and do plainly see that her distaste (which is beginning now in her again) against Ashwell arises from her jealousy of me and her, and my neglect of herself, which indeed is true, and I to blame; but for the time to come I will take care to remedy all. So up and to church, where I think I did see Pembleton, whatever the reason is I did not perceive him to look up towards my wife, nor she much towards him; however, I could hardly keep myself from being troubled that he was there, which is a madness not to be excused now that his coming to my house is past, and I hope all likelyhood of her having occasion to converse with him again. Home to dinner, and after dinner up and read part of the new play of "The Five Houres' Adventures," which though I have seen it twice, yet I never did admire or understand it enough, it being a play of the greatest plot that ever I expect to see, and of great vigour quite through the whole play, from beginning to the end. To church again after dinner (my wife finding herself ill . . . did not go), and there the Scot preaching I slept most of the sermon. This day Sir W. Batten's son's child is christened in the country, whither Sir J. Minnes, and Sir W. Batten, and Sir W. Pen are all gone. I wonder, and take it highly ill that I am not invited by the

26. *conventicles,* unlawful religious assemblies (as of the Quakers) where worship was conducted not according to the rites of the Church of England.

27. *Betterton,* Thomas Betterton, famous Shakespearean actor. He was especially noted for his portrayal of Hamlet, a role he played for over 50 years.

father, though I know his father and mother, with whom I am never likely to have much kindness, but rather I study the contrary, are the cause of it, and in that respect I am glad of it.

Being come from church, I to make up my month's accounts, and find myself clear worth £726, for which God be praised, but yet I might have been better by £20 almost had I forborne some layings out in dancing and other things upon my wife, and going to plays and other things merely to ease my mind as to the business of the dancing-master, which I bless God is now over. . . .

This month the greatest news is, the height and heat that the Parliament is in, in enquiring into the revenue, which displeases the Court, and their backwardness to give the King any money. Their enquiring into the selling of places do trouble a great many; among the chief, my Lord Chancellor (against whom particularly it is carried), and Mr. Coventry; for which I am sorry. The King of France was given out to be poisoned and dead; but it proves to be the measles: and he is well, or likely to be soon well again. I find myself growing in the esteem and credit that I have in the office, and I hope falling to my business again will confirm me in it, and the saving of money, which God grant! So to supper, prayers, and bed. □

DISCUSSION

1. What aspect of Pepys' diary do you find interesting? What seemed boring? trivial? shameful?
2. Discuss Pepys' relationship with his wife:

(a) How would you characterize his feelings about his wife?

(b) How well did he understand his own feelings?

(c) How does his own behavior compare with his wife's?

3. More than any other kind of writing, a diary reveals the character of the man who writes it. Point out passages that reveal aspects of Pepys' character. Was he a good man, a bad man, or simply human?
4. What insights does Pepys' diary offer into the society of his day? Point out passages that reveal social customs or structures different from those prevailing today.

WRITING

1. Use your imagination and write a day's entry for Pepys' diary, perhaps a day on which he discovered his wife in the arms of another man, or a day on which she discovered him giving way to temptation.
2. Write a day's entry for your own diary, choosing the most interesting day of the past week. Be as honest as you can in describing your feelings about events and people.
3. Keep a diary for a week, modeling it after Pepys', and see what you can discover about yourself in the process of close examination of your life and yourself.

THE GREAT FIRE OF 1666. COURTESY OF THE MASTER AND COURT OF THE WORSHIPFUL COMPANY OF GOLDSMITHS OF LONDON.

VI. BACKGROUND

The Seventeenth Century

WITH Queen Elizabeth's death in 1603, the uneasy peace which she had imposed on the contentious religious factions of the realm began to dissolve. James I, Elizabeth's successor to the throne, lacked both her quick political touch and her flexibility; he was a stubborn Anglican who was determined to make both Catholic and Puritan "conform" to the official religion of the state—a policy which, as continued by Charles I, his son, was to prove disastrous. The general belief in an ordered universe and the shared feelings of national unity and destiny, which had provided domestic peace and social stability during Elizabeth's long reign, also began to crumble. The history of the seventeenth century was consequently one of violence and upheaval. By the end of the century England had witnessed seven years of bloody civil war which terminated in the beheading of King Charles I in 1649, the overthrow of the monarchy and the establishment of a totalitarian Puritan Commonwealth (1649–1660), the restoration of the monarchy (Charles II, 1660–1685), the deposing of another king (James II, 1685–1688), and the establishment on the throne of a foreign monarch (William III, who reigned with his wife, Mary, 1689–1702).

If the conflict between Anglicans and Puritans—Cavalier elegance and decadence on the one side arrayed against Puritan sobriety and fanaticism on the other—dominates the age, there were other forces at work which were of equal importance. The religious conflicts gave birth to new modes of worship, producing a multiplicity of religious sects and forcing men to rely on their own moral and religious intuitions. The old, static order of social station and duty was disrupted, not only by the armed conflicts which swept the land, but also by the spiritual trauma which followed the execution of Charles I, whom many viewed as God's true representative on earth (although the Puritans obviously dissented). Men were forced, amid a welter of arguments and counterarguments, to decide for themselves what direction their lives should take. The cruel conflicts and persecutions of the age forced the growth of individualism.

Contributing to the development of individualism and to the decay of the old hierarchical order were a number of scientific developments. The astronomer Galileo conducted experiments in Italy which confirmed the Copernican theory that the earth was not, as the Elizabethans believed, the center of the universe, but was, in fact, only one of the planets that revolved around the sun. Other scientific experiments and discoveries—principally those of William Harvey on the circulation of the blood, and of Sir Isaac Newton on the theory of gravity—radically changed the ways men looked at themselves and their world.

The development of a strong and prosperous middle class also challenged the old views and ways. Tradesmen flourished, and by the end of the century had become competitive with members of the Court as leaders of society. The rise of the middle class and its growing representation in Parliament no doubt helped transform the government into the constitutional monarchy it was by the end of the century.

Other events contributed to the passing of the old order. In 1665, shortly after the restoration of Charles II, a ferocious outbreak of bubonic plague killed a quarter of the population of London. In the following year the Great Fire destroyed whole sections of the city, leaving more than thirteen thousand buildings and many public monuments in ashes. The rebuilding of the capital city represents only one aspect of the vast restructuring and slow healing that the nation was to undergo in the last half of the century.

Much of seventeenth-century literature was born of the uncertainties and intense questioning of the time. Donne's famous religious sonnet, "Batter my heart, three-person'd God," for instance, has about it a fierce intensity, a sort of barely controlled violence, which must in some manner portray the personal force behind contemporary religious issues. In general the poets of the seventeenth century seem to be engaged in an earnest search for the essential elements of man's relationship with the world and his fellow men; there is in much of their writing a sense of urgency, a startling impatience with the constrictions of time and circumstance, a strenuous arguing against the inglorious facts of the human condition, particularly against the ultimate curb on all human striving, death. The poetry of the Cavaliers is on the lighter and more elegant side of these concerns; and the poetry of Puritan Milton more solemn and somber-hued, but the urgency and argument are there (Milton's argument "to justify the ways of God to man" perhaps the most ambitious of all). Pepys' orientation is more worldly, his concerns as a man on the make in Restoration London more pedestrian; but the earnestness is there, and no detail of the contemporary scene is too trivial or too personal for his record.

Beneath the chaotic surface of the seventeenth century vital changes in individual outlook, religious attitudes, and governmental policies took place. The image of the age is one of difficult and painful change, of prejudices, hostilities, abrupt reversals in fortune, and finally of deep-rooted tensions and uncertainties not unlike those of our own time. □

METAPHYSICAL WIT

by Samuel Johnson

WIT, like all other things subject by their nature to the choice of man, has its changes and fashions, and at different times takes different forms. About the beginning of the seventeenth century appeared a race of writers that may be termed the metaphysical poets. . . .

The metaphysical poets were men of learning, and to show their learning was their whole endeavor; but, unluckily resolving to show it in rhyme, instead of writing poetry they only wrote verses, and very often such verses as stood the trial of the finger better than of the ear; for the modulation was so imperfect that they were only found to be verses by counting the syllables. . . .

If wit be well described by Pope as being "that which has been often thought, but was never before so well expressed,"[1] they certainly never attained nor ever sought it, for they endeavored to be singular in their thoughts, and were careless of their diction. But Pope's account of wit is undoubtedly erroneous; he depresses it below its natural dignity, and reduces it from strength of thought to happiness of language.

If by a more noble and more adequate conception that be considered as wit which is at once natural and new, that which though not obvious is, upon its first production, acknowledged to be just;[2] if it be that which he that never found it, wonders how he missed; to wit of this kind the metaphysical poets have seldom risen. Their thoughts are often new, but seldom natural; they are not obvious, but neither are they just; and the reader, far from wondering that he missed them, wonders more frequently by what perverseness of industry they were ever found.

But wit, abstracted from its effects upon the hearer, may be more rigorously and philosophically considered as a kind of *discordia concors*,[3] a combination of dissimilar images, or discovery of occult resemblances in things apparently unlike. Of wit, thus defined, they have more than enough. The most heterogeneous ideas are yoked by violence together: nature and art are ransacked for illustrations, comparisons, and allusions; their learning instructs, and their subtlety surprises; but the reader commonly thinks his improvement dearly bought, and, though he sometimes admires, is seldom pleased.

From this account of their compositions it will be readily inferred that they were not successful in representing or moving the affections. As they were wholly employed on something unexpected and surprising, they had no regard to that uniformity of sentiment which enables us to conceive and to excite the pains and the pleasure of other minds. . . . Their wish was only to say what they hoped had been never said before.

. . .Those writers who lay on the watch for novelty could have little hope of greatness; for great things cannot have escaped former observation. Their attempts were always analytic: they broke every image into fragments, and could no more represent by their slender conceits and labored particularities the prospects of nature or the scenes of life, than he who dissects a sunbeam with a prism can exhibit the wide effulgence of a summer noon. . . .

Yet great labor directed by great abilities is never wholly lost: if they frequently threw away their wit upon false conceits, they likewise sometimes struck out unexpected truth: if their conceits were farfetched, they were often worth the carriage. To write on their plan it was at least necessary to read and think. . . .

From "Cowley," in *The Lives of the English Poets* by Samuel Johnson (1779).

1. From Alexander Pope's *Essay on Criticism*. Excerpts appear in the section on the Eighteenth Century.

2. *just*, exact; proper.

3. *discordia concors*, literally, "a harmonious discord."

The Changing English Language

THE desire for order and certainty which emerged amidst the turmoil of the seventeenth century was reflected in the development of the language. Particularly in the latter half of the century, Englishmen, reacting against the novelties and unregulated spontaneity which characterized Elizabethan expression, began to call for an ordered, rational language.

English was discovered to have no body of grammatical rules that could serve as a systematic and unfailing guide to "correct" expression, and therefore Latin models were turned to once more. John Dryden, who was one of the loudest in his outcries against the unruly language of his predecessors ("we . . . have not so much as a tolerable dictionary, or a grammar, so that our language is in a manner barbarous," he wrote) is said at one point in his career to have translated his thoughts first into Latin to discover their most proper form of expression in English.

The Royal Society, founded in 1660 by a group of learned man and scientists, objected to the Elizabethan love of verbal gymnastics on the ground that it was unscientific, and demanded of its members instead "a close, naked, natural way of speaking; positive expressions, clear senses, a native easiness, bringing as near the mathematical plainness as they can." The scientists were supported in this matter by the Puritans, who objected to display of any kind, whether in matters of religion, dress, or language.

As Englishmen expanded their interests abroad in the seventeenth century, their language continued to absorb foreign words. Increased commercial rivalry with the Dutch brought in such terms as *bowsprit, brandy, cruise, freight, keel, smack,* and *sloop*. From the American colonies came such words as *canoe, maize, papoose,* and *squaw*. The popularity of Italian music in the latter half of the century gave rise to terms such as *aria, allegro, contralto, cantata, opera, oratorio, piano, soprano,* and *trombone*. The main change, however, was the growing emphasis on ease and clearness of expression, which came to full bloom in attempts to standardize, refine, and give permanent order and status to English in the eighteenth century.

Cavalier (left) from Battles of the English Civil War, by Austin Woolrych, B. T. Botsford, London. Roundhead (right) by courtesy of the Trustees of The London Museum.

BIOGRAPHIES

Abraham Cowley 1618 / 1667

During his lifetime Cowley was most admired for long and learned poems embroidered with bold conceits. He published his first book of poetry at fifteen, and the bulk of his later work was in imitation of classical poets, both Greek and Roman.

A royalist, Cowley served as secretary to the exiled Queen during the Civil Wars, coding and decoding her correspondence. He was probably a spy, and he journeyed about the continent and England on royal missions.

Returning to England after the Restoration, he became one of the charter members of the Royal Society, and finally retired to his country estate to write.

John Donne 1572 / 1631

The dichotomy of flesh and spirit found in Donne's work reflects the sequence of styles in his own life. He came from a prosperous Catholic family, studied at both Oxford and Cambridge, and began to read law. As a young man his main interests seem to have been the theater, women, and the writing of bawdy and cynical verse. In 1596 he joined a military campaign and journeyed to Cadiz; the following year he went on another campaign to the Azores. In 1598 he was appointed secretary to one of the Queen's ministers, but he eloped with the minister's niece three years later and lost favor and his position.

Among the various means by which Donne tried to support his growing family (he eventually fathered twelve children) was pamphlet writing, and some of his tracts were in support of the Anglican Church. In 1607 King James, impressed by these works, urged Donne to take holy orders. (Donne had converted to the established Church before 1600.) Since the King refused to grant him any other position, Donne finally joined the clergy in 1615.

Donne preached regularly before members of the court and London's wealthy merchant class, and the literary and dramatic flair of his sermons made him widely admired. In 1621 he was appointed Dean of St. Paul's Cathedral, and he was in line for a bishopric when he died.

During his later years, Donne became obsessed with the idea of death. He is said to have preached his own funeral oration several weeks before his death, and he posed, wrapped in a shroud, for the effigy on his own tomb.

John Dryden 1631 / 1700

Dryden lived in a time of political and religious turmoil, and his own beliefs seemed to shift with the times. Coming from a family with Puritan and anti-Royalist leanings, he began his literary career in 1659 with a poem in praise of Cromwell. After the Restoration the next year, he came out in favor of the Anglican Church and the monarchy by publishing a poem in praise of Charles II. When the Crown became Catholic with the accession of James II in 1685, Dryden became a convert to Catholicism. One of his most celebrated poems, *The Hind and the Panther,* was a defense of the Catholic religion. He remained a Catholic after the Protestants William and Mary came to power three years later, even at the cost of the royal pensions and offices he had held. From then on, he had to depend entirely upon his pen for a living.

Dryden wrote poetry, verse satire, prose prefaces, and literary criticism, but his chief source of income was the stage. One of the most prolific dramatists of the Restoration, he turned out comedies, tragedies, and heroic plays for the newly opened theaters. His best play was *All for Love,* a version of the story of Antony and Cleopatra. He also translated Vergil, revised Chaucer, collaborated on an adaptation of Shakespeare's *The Tempest,* and made *Paradise Lost* into an opera.

Dryden was one of the first writers to break away from the extravagant style of the late metaphysical poets and to write in a more restrained and natural style. The heroic couplet he used in many of his satires and plays became the dominant poetic style for a century.

George Herbert 1593 / 1633

Herbert was a member of an ancient and distinguished Welsh family. He was an outstanding scholar at Cambridge, and in 1619 was made orator of the university, a post which required him to express, in florid Latin, the sentiments of the university on public occasions. The post also required him to spend much time at court. However, it did not lead to the political advancement he had hoped for, and in 1630 he followed the practice of many younger sons from highly connected families and took holy orders. He accepted appointment as a country priest. Unlike many others, however, he actually did the work of a priest, preaching and praying, visiting the poor and sick, and rebuilt his church out of his own pocket. He died of consumption after a ministry of only three years. A collection of the religious poetry for which he is known was published after his death.

Robert Herrick 1591 / 1674

Like Donne and Herbert, Herrick turned from a worldly life to holy orders. He loved London and the society of poets and wits like Ben Jonson, and when in 1629 he was appointed to a country parish in Devonshire, he considered it a bitter exile. Gradually, though, he came to delight in the life and customs of the West Country. As a Royalist, he lost his post during the Puritan upheaval and returned to London in 1647. The next year he published his only book, a collection of 1200 poems. Because the times were tempestuous (the country was obsessed with the trial and execution of King Charles I), Herrick's book was soon lost to public view. After the Restoration, Herrick was reinstated in his parish and resumed his quiet country life. His poetry was rediscovered only in the 19th century.

Ben Jonson 1572 / 1637

Jonson was a charismatic person who fascinated his contemporaries. His work was scholarly, the result, perhaps, of several years of classical schooling he received as a boy and many years of self-tutelage in later life. He never went to university (though both Oxford and Cambridge later awarded him honorary degrees). Instead he took up his stepfather's trade, bricklaying, and then entered the army. During service in Flanders he killed a Spaniard in single-handed combat as both English and Spanish armies looked on.

On his return to London in 1595 he became an actor and a playwright. He produced his first successful play, *Every Man in His Humour,* in 1598 (Shakespeare, a friend, acted in it). Shortly after this, Jonson, always hot-headed, was imprisoned and nearly executed for killing a fellow actor in a duel. Once released, he continued his career in the theater, gained the favor of James I, and became a writer of court masques—elaborate spectacles which involved music, dancing, and pageantry. During this period he also wrote a number of satiric comedies, two of which—*Volpone* and *The Alchemist*—are still considered among the supreme satiric achievements of the English stage.

After the death of James I, Jonson was neglected by both the public and the court, for Charles I patronized painters rather than writers. Nevertheless, he became the center of a circle of young poets who dubbed themselves "The Tribe of Ben" and regularly joined him at the Mermaid Tavern for feasts of wine and wit. At his death Jonson was widely mourned as the last of the great Elizabethans. He lies buried in Westminster Abbey under the inscription "O Rare Ben Jonson."

Richard Lovelace 1618 / 1658

Handsome and clever, the eldest son of a wealthy family, Richard Lovelace was very much the courtly Cavalier poet. When King Charles and his queen visited Oxford in 1636, they were so favorably impressed by undergraduate Lovelace's demeanor that they commanded he be given an M.A. on the spot. However, his allegiance to King Charles during the Civil Wars caused him several stays in prison (during the first of which he wrote "To Althea").

His periods of imprisonment and his adventures in the French campaign against the Spanish, during which he was wounded, exhausted his inheritance. He spent the last years of his life impoverished and depressed, and died at the age of 39 in a London slum.

Andrew Marvell 1621 / 1678

Marvell was a quiet and sensible man with Puritan leanings who became devoted to Cromwell's cause. Yet he was so extremely tolerant of others' opinions that as a student at Cambridge he allowed a Jesuit to persuade him to quit his studies. (The senior Marvell, an Anglican minister, found his son in a London bookshop and convinced him to return to the university.) After earning his degree, he traveled abroad for several years and then became a tutor to the daughter of Sir Thomas Fairfax, Lord-General of the Parliamentary Forces.

In 1657 Marvell was appointed assistant to Milton, who was then Latin Secretary. Two years later Marvell was elected to the House of Commons, where he served his constituents conscientiously, refusing all bribes and writing frequent newsletters. These newsletters, together with some satires and religious tracts, made up most of the writings for which he was known during his lifetime. Three years after his death a volume of his poetry was published by a woman who claimed to be his widow, but who later turned out to be his housekeeper.

John Milton 1608 / 1674

In his parents' cultured Puritan home, Milton began to write poetry at the age of ten. After finishing his formal education with an M.A. from Cambridge, he returned to his family's country home at Horton to study under his own direction. There he read almost everything available in Latin, Greek, Italian, and English, and wrote the elegy *Lycidas* and the masque *Comus*. After five years at Horton, Milton embarked on a two-year tour of Europe, where he found his literary reputation had already begun to spread. With the outbreak of the Civil Wars, he returned to England, where he tutored and wrote pamphlets. When his first marriage went awry, he became an early and vehement advocate of divorce on the grounds of incompatibility, a cause which he championed in his pamphlets and which many people in Puritan England found reprehensible. (Milton was married three times, widowed twice.)

Under the new Commonwealth, Milton was appointed Latin Secretary (a post comparable to Secretary of Foreign Affairs). While he held this office, eyestrain from years of reading late into the night caused him to become totally blind.

Despite a brief imprisonment, the seizure of most of his property, and the destruction of some of his pamphlets, Milton survived the Restoration essentially unharmed. He and his daughters retired to a quiet life. Accounts tell of tension between the stern and dictatorial Milton and his unsympathetic daughters, who resented having to read aloud in languages they did not understand and take dictation for hours on end, but the final years of Milton's life were productive, if not completely peaceful. During his last decade he wrote (through dictation) *Paradise Lost, Paradise Regained,* and *Samson Agonistes.*

Samuel Pepys 1633 / 1703

In his *Diary,* Pepys probably revealed more about himself and his society than any biographer or historian has done. He had the knack of being at the center of important events: as a schoolboy he was an eyewitness to the beheading of Charles I; years later, he was with the fleet that brought Charles II back to England to restore the monarchy. A shrewd observer and a meticulous businessman, he noted in his *Diary* everything from daily trivia and personal intimacies to the most dramatic of public events—the Plague of 1665 and the Fire of London in 1666. He was a conscientious public servant who eventually achieved, through deft use of social influence and incessant politicking, the high office of Secretary to the Navy in 1673.

Though his years in high office were not uneventful (he was imprisoned twice, and released both times due largely to the influence of powerful friends), his public career ended with the Glorious Revolution of 1688. He spent the rest of his years in retirement at Clapham, publishing in 1690 his *Memoirs of the Navy,* the only work other than his official reports which he ever intended the public or posterity to read.

Sir John Suckling 1609 / 1642

Suckling, like Lovelace, was a graceful and carefree Cavalier dandy. Living mainly off a sizable inheritance, he cut a dashing figure at court. He preferred women, music, and gambling to the refinements of wit and intellect. During the Civil Wars he raised a gaudily outfitted company of "gentlemen" for a campaign against the Scots, but the whole company withdrew swiftly if not graciously on first contact with the enemy.

In 1641 Suckling, a Loyalist, became involved in a plot to free one of the King's imprisoned ministers. The plot was discovered; Suckling was accused of conspiracy to overthrow Parliament. Realizing that the King could no longer provide protection, he fled to France. There he died in poverty the following year, possibly by his own hand.

George Wither 1588 / 1667

Wither first made his reputation as a poet and satirist. His satires were considered libelous and several times landed him in prison. He was in London during the plague of 1625 and wrote a lengthy poem about it. During the Civil Wars he served as a military commander, first on the side of King Charles I, later on the side of the Puritans. In 1642 he sold his estate to raise a troop of horse and was placed in charge of Farnham Castle. A few days later he set off for London, leaving the castle undefended, and was captured by Royalists. He would have been hanged except for the intervention of Sir John Denham, who said that so long as Wither lived, he himself would not be the worst poet in England.

As a convinced Puritan, Wither wrote many hymns and religious tracts. After the Restoration he spent another three years in jail, but passed the last years of his life quietly in London.

chapter five

THE EIGHTEENTH CENTURY 1700–1798

WILLIAM HOGARTH, "THE BENCH" (1758). COURTESY OF THE TRUSTEES OF THE BRITISH MUSEUM.

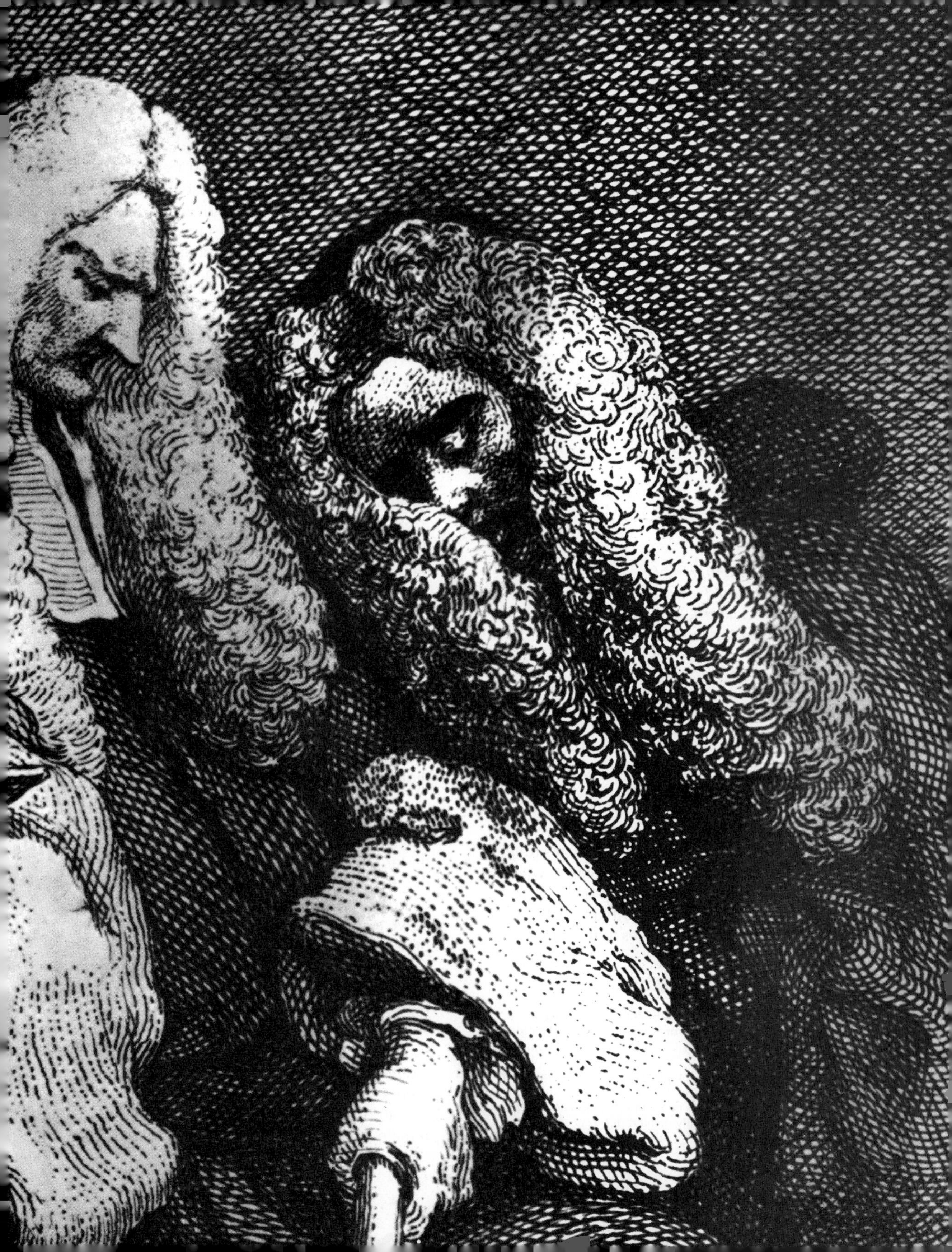

Jonathan Swift
1667 / 1745

The eighteenth century—at least the first half of it—was the Age of Reason, for it had rigid rules for everything from the "taming" of Shakespeare to the pruning of gardens and the way people should conduct themselves. Men of the age looked upon their forefathers as rude barbarians and themselves as the first civilized Englishmen.

Yet to some it was painfully clear that, actually, their society was still as irrational and crude as ever. And thus, in literature, satire became the dominant form; it varied with the temperaments of the men producing it—from the mild and smiling admonitions of Joseph Addison to the bitterly disillusioned condemnations of Jonathan Swift.

A MODEST PROPOSAL

For Preventing the Children of Poor People in Ireland from Being a Burden to Their Parents or Country, and for Making Them Beneficial to the Public

IT is a melancholy object to those who walk through this great town,[1] or travel in the country, when they see the streets, the roads, and cabin doors crowded with beggars of the female sex, followed by three, four, or six children, all in rags and importuning every passenger for an alms. These mothers, instead of being able to work for their honest livelihood, are forced to employ all their time in strolling to beg sustenance for their helpless infants; who as they grow up either turn thieves, for want of work, or leave their dear native country to fight for the pretender[2] in Spain, or sell themselves to the Barbados.[3]

I think it is agreed by all parties that this prodigious number of children in the arms, or on the backs, or at the heels of their mothers, and frequently of their fathers, is, in the present deplorable state of the kingdom, a very great additional grievance; and therefore whoever could find out a fair, cheap, and easy method of making these children sound, useful members of the commonwealth would deserve so well of the public as to have his statue set up for a preserver of the nation.

But my intention is very far from being confined to provide only for the children of professed beggars: it is of a much greater extent and shall take in the whole number of infants at a certain age who are born of parents in effect as little able to support them as those who demand our charity in the streets.

As to my own part, having turned my thoughts for many years upon this important subject and maturely weighed the several schemes of our projectors, I have always found them grossly mistaken in their computation. It is true, a child just dropped from its dam may be supported by her milk for a solar year, with little other nourishment: at most not above the value of two shillings which the mother may certainly get, or the value in scraps, by her lawful occupation of begging; and it is exactly at one year old that I propose to provide for them in such a manner, as, instead of being a charge upon their parents or the parish, or wanting food and raiment for the rest of their lives, they shall, on the contrary, contribute to the feeding and partly to the clothing of many thousands.

There is likewise another great advantage in my scheme, that it will prevent those voluntary abortions and that horrid practice of women murdering their bastard children, alas! too frequent among us, sacrificing the poor innocent babes, I doubt more to avoid the expense than the shame, which would move tears and pity in the most savage and inhuman breast.

The number of souls in this kingdom being usually reckoned one million and a half, of these I calculate there may be about two hundred thousand couple, whose wives are breeders; from which number I subtract thirty thousand couple, who are able to maintain their own children (although I apprehend there cannot be so many, under the present distresses of the kingdom), but this being granted, there will remain an hundred and seventy thousand breeders.

---

1. *this great town,* Dublin.
2. *the pretender,* James Stuart (1688–1766), son of King James II, "pretender" or claimant to the throne which his father had lost in the Revolution of 1688. He was Catholic, and Ireland was loyal to him.
3. *sell . . . Barbados.* Because of extreme poverty, many of the Irish bound or "sold" themselves to obtain passage to the West Indies or other British possessions in North America. They agreed to work for their new masters, usually planters, for a specified number of years.

I again subtract fifty thousand for those women who miscarry, or whose children die by accident or disease within the year. There only remains one hundred and twenty thousand children of poor parents annually born. The question therefore is, How this number shall be reared and provided for? which, as I have already said, under the present situation of affairs, is utterly impossible by all the methods hitherto proposed. For we can neither employ them in handicraft or agriculture; we neither build houses (I mean in the country) nor cultivate land: they can very seldom pick up a livelihood by stealing till they arrive at six years old, except where they are of towardly[4] parts; although I confess they learn the rudiments much earlier; during which time they can, however, be properly looked upon only as probationers; as I have been informed by a principal gentleman in the county of Cavan, who protested to me that he never knew above one or two instances under the age of six, even in a part of the kingdom so renowned for the quickest proficiency in that art.

I am assured by our merchants that a boy or a girl before twelve years old is no salable commodity; and even when they come to this age they will not yield above three pounds, or three pounds and half a crown at most, on the exchange; which cannot turn to account either to the parents or kingdom, the charge of nutriment and rags having been at least four times that value.

I shall now therefore humbly propose my own thoughts, which I hope will not be liable to the least objection.

I have been assured by a very knowing American of my acquaintance in London that a young healthy child well nursed is at a year old a most delicious, nourishing, and wholesome food, whether stewed, roasted, baked, or boiled; and I make no doubt that it will equally serve in a fricassee or a ragout.[5]

I do therefore humbly offer it to public consideration that of the hundred and twenty thousand children already computed, twenty thousand may be reserved for breed, whereof only one-fourth part to be males; which is more than we allow to sheep, black cattle, or swine; and my reason is that these children are seldom the fruits of marriage, a circumstance not much regarded by our savages; therefore one male will be sufficient to serve four females. That the remaining hundred thousand may, at a year old, be offered in sale to the persons of quality and fortune through the kingdom; always advising the mother to let them suck plentifully in the last month, so as to render them plump and fat for a good table. A child will make two dishes at an entertainment for friends; and when the family dines alone, the fore or hind quarter will make a reasonable dish, and seasoned with a little pepper or salt will be very good boiled on the fourth day, especially in winter.

I have reckoned upon a medium that a child just born will weigh twelve pounds, and in a solar year, if tolerably nursed, will increase to twenty-eight pounds.

I grant this food will be somewhat dear, and therefore very proper for landlords, who, as they have already devoured most of the parents, seem to have the best title to the children.

Infant's flesh will be in season throughout the year, but more plentifully in March, and a little before and after: for we are told by a grave author, an eminent French physician,[6] that fish being a prolific diet, there are more children born in Roman Catholic countries about nine months after Lent than at any other season; therefore, reckoning a year after Lent, the markets will be more glutted than usual, because the number of popish infants is at least three to one in this kingdom: and therefore it will have one other collateral advantage, by lessening the number of papists among us.

I have already computed the charge of nursing a beggar's child (in which list I reckon all cottagers, laborers, and four-fifths of the farmers) to be about two shillings per annum, rags included; and I believe no gentleman would repine to give ten shillings for the carcass of a good fat child, which, as I have said, will make four dishes of excellent nutritive meat, when he has only some particular friend or his own family to dine with him. Thus the squire will learn to be a good landlord and grow popular among his tenants; the mother will have eight shillings net profit and be fit for work till she produces another child.

Those who are more thrifty (as I must confess the times require) may flay the carcass; the skin of which artificially[7] dressed will make admirable gloves for ladies and summer boots for fine gentlemen.

4. *towardly,* dutiful; easily managed.
5. *ragout,* a highly seasoned meat stew.
6. *grave author . . . physician,* François Rabelais (c.1494–1553), who was anything but a "grave author."
7. *artificially,* artfully; skillfully.

As to our city of Dublin, shambles[8] may be appointed for this purpose in the most convenient parts of it, and butchers we may be assured will not be wanting; although I rather recommend buying the children alive and dressing them hot from the knife as we do roasting pigs.

A very worthy person, a true lover of his country, and whose virtues I highly esteem, was lately pleased, in discoursing on this matter, to offer a refinement upon my scheme. He said that many gentlemen of this kingdom, having of late destroyed their deer, he conceived that the want of venison might be well supplied by the bodies of young lads and maidens, not exceeding fourteen years of age nor under twelve; so great a number of both sexes in every country being now ready to starve for want of work and service; and these to be disposed of by their parents, if alive, or otherwise by their nearest relations. But with due deference to so excellent a friend and so deserving a patriot, I cannot be altogether in his sentiments; for as to the males, my American acquaintance assured me from frequent experience that their flesh was generally tough and lean, like that of our schoolboys, by continual exercise, and their taste disagreeable; and to fatten them would not answer the charge. Then as to the females, it would, I think, with humble submission be a loss to the public, because they soon would become breeders themselves: and besides, it is not improbable that some scrupulous people might be apt to censure such a practice (although indeed very unjustly), as a little bordering upon cruelty; which, I confess, has always been with me the strongest objection against any project, however so well intended.

But in order to justify my friend, he confessed that this expedient was put into his head by the famous Psalmanazar,[9] a native of the island Formosa, who came from thence to London above twenty years ago: and in conversation told my friend that in his country when any young person happened to be put to death, the executioner sold the carcass to persons of quality as a prime dainty; and that in his time the body of a plump girl of fifteen, who was crucified for an attempt to poison the emperor, was sold to his imperial majesty's prime minister of state, and other great mandarins of the court, in joints from the gibbet, at four hundred crowns. Neither indeed can I deny that if the same use were made of several plump girls in this town, who, without one single groat to their fortunes, cannot stir abroad without a chair, and appear at a playhouse and assemblies in foreign fineries which they never will pay for, the kingdom would not be the worse.

Some persons of a desponding spirit are in great concern about that vast number of poor people, who are aged, diseased, or maimed; and I have been desired to employ my thoughts, what course may be taken to ease the nation of so grievous an incumbrance. But I am not in the least pain upon that matter, because it is very well known that they are every day dying and rotting, by cold and famine, and filth and vermin, as fast as can be reasonably expected. And as to the young laborers, they are now in almost as hopeful a condition: they cannot get work, and consequently pine away for want of nourishment to a degree that if at any time they are accidentally hired to common labor, they have not strength to perform it; and thus the country and themselves are happily delivered from the evils to come.

I have too long digressed and therefore shall return to my subject. I think the advantages, by the proposal which I have made, are obvious and many, as well as of the highest importance.

For first, as I have already observed, it would greatly lessen the number of papists, with whom we are yearly overrun, being the principal breeders of the nation, as well as our most dangerous enemies;

OF HUMAN INTEREST

Was Swift a misanthrope?

Swift was often accused of being a hater of mankind. Here is his own statement, from a letter to Alexander Pope: ". . . when you think of the world, give it one lash the more at my Request. I have ever hated all Nations, Professions, and Communities; and all my love is towards Individuals; for instance, I hate the Tribe of Lawyers, Physicians . . . Soldiers, English, Scotch, French, and the rest. But principally I hate and detest that animal called Man, although I heartily love John, Peter, Thomas, and so forth. . . ."

8. *shambles*, slaughterhouses.
9. *Psalmanazar*, the imposter George Psalmanazar (c.1679–1763), a Frenchman who passed himself off in England as a Formosan, and wrote a totally fictional "true" account of Formosa, in which he described cannibalism.

and who stay at home on purpose to deliver the kingdom to the pretender, hoping to take their advantage by the absence of so many good protestants, who have chosen rather to leave their country than stay at home and pay tithes against their conscience to an episcopal curate.[10]

Secondly, the poorer tenants will have something valuable of their own, which by law may be made liable to distress,[11] and help to pay their landlord's rent; their corn and cattle being already seized, and money a thing unknown.

Thirdly, whereas the maintenance of a hundred thousand children, from two years old and upwards, cannot be computed at less than ten shillings a piece per annum, the nation's stock will be thereby increased fifty thousand pounds per annum, beside the profit of a new dish introduced to the tables of all gentlemen of fortune in the kingdom, who have any refinement in taste. And the money will circulate among ourselves, the goods being entirely of our own growth and manufacture.

Fourthly, the constant breeders, beside the gain of eight shillings sterling per annum by the sale of their children, will be rid of the charge of maintaining them after the first year.

Fifthly, this food would likewise bring great custom to taverns: where the vintners will certainly be so prudent as to procure the best receipts for dressing it to perfection, and consequently have their houses frequented by all the fine gentlemen, who justly value themselves upon their knowledge in good eating: and a skilful cook, who understands how to oblige his guests, will contrive to make it as expensive as they please.

Sixthly, this would be a great inducement to marriage, which all wise nations have either encouraged by rewards or enforced by laws and penalties. It would increase the care and tenderness of mothers toward their children, when they were sure of a settlement for life to the poor babes, provided in some sort by the public, to their annual profit instead of expense. We should see an honest emulation among the married women, which of them could bring the fattest child to the market. Men would become as fond of their wives during the time of their pregnancy as they are now of their mares in foal, their cows in calf, or sows when they are ready to farrow; nor offer to beat or kick them (as is too frequent a practice) for fear of a miscarriage.

Many other advantages might be enumerated. For instance, the addition of some thousand carcasses in our exportation of barreled beef, the propagation of swine's flesh, and improvement in the art of making good bacon, so much wanted among us by the great destruction of pigs, too frequent at our tables; which are no way comparable in taste or magnificence to a well-grown, fat, yearling child, which roasted whole will make a considerable figure at a lord mayor's feast, or any other public entertainment. But this and many others I omit, being studious of brevity.

Supposing that one thousand families in this city would be constant customers for infants' flesh, besides others who might have it at merry-meetings, particularly weddings and christenings, I compute that Dublin would take off annually about twenty thousand carcasses; and the rest of the kingdom (where probably they will be sold somewhat cheaper) the remaining eighty thousand.

I can think of no one objection that will possibly be raised against this proposal, unless it should be urged that the number of people will be thereby much lessened in the kingdom. This I freely own, and it was indeed one principal design in offering it to the world. I desire the reader will observe that I calculate my remedy for this one individual kingdom of Ireland, and for no other that ever was, is, or, I think, ever can be upon earth. Therefore let no man talk to me of other expedients: of taxing our absentees at five shillings a pound: of using neither clothes nor household furniture, except what is of our own growth and manufacture: of utterly rejecting the materials and instruments that promote foreign luxury: of curing the expensiveness of pride, vanity, idleness, and gaming in our women: of introducing a vein of parsimony, prudence, and temperance: of learning to love our country in the want of which we differ even from LAPLANDERS and the inhabitants of TOPINAMBOO:[12] of quitting our animosities and factions, nor acting any longer like the Jews, who were murdering one another at the very moment their city was taken:[13] of being a little cautious not to sell our country and conscience for nothing: of teaching landlords to have at least one

10. *protestants . . . curate.* Swift is here attacking the absentee landlords.
11. *distress,* distraint, the legal seizure of property for payment of debts.

12. *Topinamboo,* a savage area of Brazil.
13. *city was taken.* While the Roman Emperor Titus was besieging Jerusalem, which he took and destroyed in A.D. 70, within the city factions of fanatics were waging bloody warfare.

degree of mercy toward their tenants: lastly, of putting a spirit of honesty, industry, and skill into our shop-keepers; who, if a resolution could now be taken to buy only our native goods, would immediately unite to cheat and exact upon us in the price, the measure, and the goodness, nor could ever yet be brought to make one fair proposal of just dealing, though often and earnestly invited to it.[14]

Therefore, I repeat, let no man talk to me of these and the like expedients, till he has at least some glimpse of hope that there will be ever some hearty and sincere attempt to put them in practice.

But as to myself, having been wearied out for many years with offering vain, idle, visionary thoughts, and at length utterly despairing of success, I fortunately fell upon this proposal; which, as it is wholly new, so it has something solid and real, of no expense and little trouble, full in our own power, and whereby we can incur no danger in disobliging ENGLAND. For this kind of commodity will not bear exportation, the flesh being of too tender a consistence to admit a long continuance in salt, although perhaps I could name a country which would be glad to eat up our whole nation without it.[15]

After all, I am not so violently bent upon my own opinion as to reject any offer proposed by wise men, which shall be found equally innocent, cheap, easy, and effectual. But before something of that kind shall be advanced in contradiction to my scheme, and offering a better, I desire the author or authors will be pleased maturely to consider two points. First, as things now stand, how they will be able to find food and raiment for an hundred thousand useless mouths and backs. And secondly, there being a round million of creatures in human figure throughout this kingdom, whose whole subsistence put into a common stock would leave them in debt two millions of pounds sterling, adding those who are beggars by profession to the bulk of farmers, cottagers, and laborers, with their wives and children, who are beggars in effect; I desire those politicians, who dislike my overture, and may perhaps be so bold as to attempt an answer, that they will first ask the parents of these mortals, whether they would not at this day think it a great happiness to have been sold for food at a year old in the manner I prescribe, and thereby have avoided such a perpetual scene of misfortunes as they have since gone through by the oppression of landlords, the impossibility of paying rent without money or trade, the want of common sustenance, with neither house nor clothes to cover them from the inclemencies of the weather, and the most inevitable prospect of entailing the like or greater miseries upon their breed for ever.

I profess, in the sincerity of my heart, that I have not the least personal interest in endeavoring to promote this necessary work, having no other motive than the public good of my country, by advancing our trade, providing for infants, relieving the poor, and giving some pleasure to the rich. I have no children by which I can propose to get a single penny; the youngest being nine years old, and my wife past child-bearing. (1729)

14. *invited to it.* Swift had already made all these proposals in various pamphlets.

15. *a country . . . without it.* England; this is another way of saying, "The British are devouring the Irish."

DISCUSSION

1. (a) At what point did you first realize that Swift was "putting you on"? What was your reaction?

(b) Why might Swift have used the word "Modest" in his title?

2. Paragraph 4 refers to "a child just dropped from the dam." The essay contains other examples of terms usually applied only to animals. Why does Swift use this device?

3. (a) List some of the shocking details of life in Ireland that the essay casually reveals.

(b) What is their cumulative effect?

4. (a) Who are the major targets of this satire?

(b) Does Swift suggest that the Irish themselves are in a way responsible for their plight? Explain.

5. (a) What sort of man would write an essay like this?

(b) What in today's world might such a man be moved to write about?

WRITING

1. Select a modern abuse and write a short satirical essay about it.

2. Assume that you are either (a) an Anglo-Irish absentee landlord, or (b) a literate native Irishman, and write Swift a letter expressing your opinion of his essay.

3. Prepare a dialogue in which two or three of Swift's contemporaries discuss his essay.

READERS' THEATER

Select key sections of "A Modest Proposal" for reading aloud by one or more students while another student, who holds a book in front of him, pantomimes a reader's reaction.

Daniel Defoe 1659 / 1731

ENGRAVINGS BY JOHN DUNSTALL SHOWING SCENES OF THE GREAT PLAGUE OF LONDON, 1665. FROM A CONTEMPORARY BROADSHEET. BY COURTESY OF THE TRUSTEES OF THE LONDON MUSEUM.

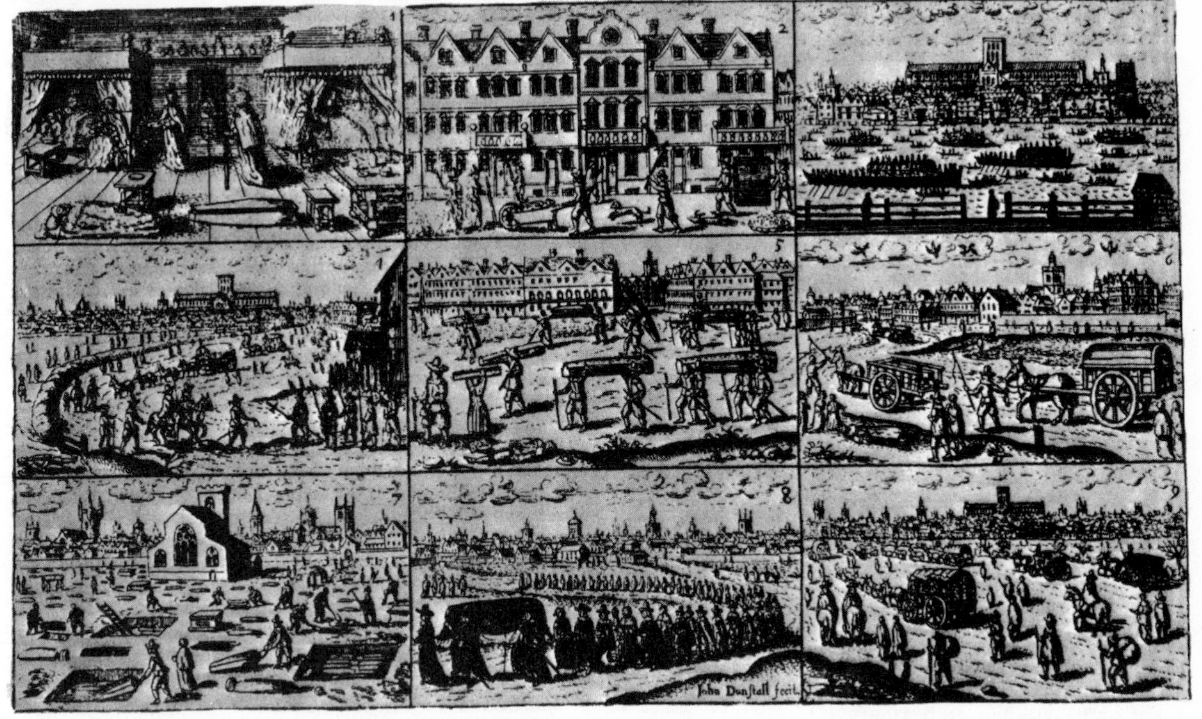

From JOURNAL OF THE PLAGUE YEAR

I

. . . IT pleased God that I was still spared, and very hearty and sound in health, but very impatient of being pent up within doors without air, as I have been for fourteen days or thereabouts, and I could not restrain myself, but I would go to carry a letter for my brother to the post-house. Then it was indeed that I observed a profound silence in the streets. When I came to the post-house, as I went to put in my letter, I saw a man stand in one corner of the yard and talking to another at a window, and a third had opened a door belonging to the office. In the middle of the yard lay a small leather purse with two keys hanging at it, with money in it, but nobody would meddle with it. I asked how long it had lain there; the man at the window said it had lain almost an hour, but that they had not meddled with it, because they did not know but the person who dropped it might come back to look for it. I had no such need of money, nor was the sum so big that I had any inclination to meddle with it, or to get the money at the hazard it might be attended with; so I seemed to go away, when the man who had opened the door said he would take it up, but so that if the right owner came for it he should be sure to have it. So he went in and fetched a pail of water, and set it down hard by the purse, then went again and fetched some gunpowder, and cast a good deal of powder upon the purse, and then made a train from that which he had thrown loose upon the purse. The train reached about two yards. After this he goes in a third time and fetches out a pair of tongs red hot, and which he had prepared, I suppose, on purpose, and first setting fire to the train of powder, that singed the purse, and also smoked the air sufficiently. But he was not content with that, but he then takes up the purse with the tongs, holding it so long till the tongs burnt through the purse, and then he shook the money out into the pail of water, so he carried it in. The money, as I remember, was about thirteen shillings and some smooth groats and brass farthings.

There might perhaps have been several poor people as I have observed above, that would have been hardy enough to have ventured for the sake of the money; but you may easily see by what I have observed that the few people who were spared were very careful of themselves at that time when the distress was so exceeding great. . . .

II

Passing through Tokenhouse Yard, in Lothbury, of a sudden a casement violently opened just over my head, and a woman gave three frightful screeches, and then cried, "Oh! death, death, death!" in a most inimitable tone, and which struck me with horror and a chillness in my very blood. There was nobody to be seen in the whole street, neither did any other window open, for people had no curiosity now in any case, nor could anybody help one another, so I went on to pass into Bell Alley.

Just in Bell Alley, on the right hand of the passage, there was a more terrible cry than that, though it was not so directed out at the window; but the whole family was in a terrible fright, and I could hear women and children run screaming about the rooms like distracted, when a garret-window opened, and somebody from a window on the other side the alley called and asked, "What is the matter?" upon which, from the first window it was answered, "O Lord, my old master has hanged himself!" The other asked again, "Is he quite dead?" and the first answered, "Ay, ay, quite dead; quite dead and cold!" This person was a merchant and a deputy alderman, and very rich. I care not to mention the name, though I knew his name too, but that would be an hardship to the family, which is now flourishing again.

But this is but one; it is scarce credible what dreadful cases happened in particular families every day. People in the rage of the distemper, or in the torment of their swellings, which was indeed intolerable, running out of their own government, raving and distracted, and oftentimes laying violent hands upon themselves, throwing themselves out at their windows, shooting themselves, &c.; mothers murdering their own children in their lunacy, some dying of mere grief as a passion, some of mere fright and surprise without any infection at all, others frighted into idiotism and foolish distractions, some into despair and lunacy, others into melancholy madness. . . .

III

. . . here I must observe also that the plague, as I suppose all distempers do, operated in a different manner on differing constitutions; some were immediately overwhelmed with it, and it came to violent fevers, vomitings, insufferable headaches, pains in the back, and so up to ravings and ragings with those pains; others with swellings and tumours in the neck or groin, or armpits, which till they could be broke put them into insufferable agonies and torment; while others, as I have observed, were silently infected, the fever preying upon their spirits insensibly, and they seeing little of it till they fell into swooning, and faintings, and death without pain.

I am not physician enough to enter into the particular reasons and manner of these differing effects of one and the same distemper. . . . I am only relating what I know, or have heard, or believe of the particular cases, and what fell within the compass of my view; but this may be added too, that though the former sort of those cases, namely, those openly visited, were the worst for themselves as to pain . . . yet the latter had the worst state of the disease; for in the former they frequently recovered, especially if the swellings broke, but the latter was inevitable death; no cure, no help could be possible, nothing could follow but death. . . .

IV

. . . the shutting up of houses, so as to confine those that were well with those that were sick, had very great inconveniences in it, and some that were very tragical. . . . But it was authorised by a law, it had the public good in view as the end chiefly aimed at, and all the private injuries that were done by the putting it in execution must be put to the account of the public benefit.

It is doubtful to this day whether, in the whole, it contributed anything to the stop of the infection. . . . Certain it is that if all the infected persons were effectually shut in, no sound person could have been infected by them, because they could not have come near them. But the case was this, and I shall only touch it here, namely, that the infection was propagated insensibly, and by such persons as were not visibly infected, who neither knew whom they infected or who they were infected by.

A house in Whitechapel was shut up for the sake of one infected maid, who had only spots, not the tokens come out upon her, and recovered; yet these people obtained no liberty to stir, neither for air or exercise forty days. Want of breath, fear, anger, vexation, and all the other griefs attending such an injurious treatment cast the mistress of the family into a fever, and visitors came into the house and said it was the plague, though the physicians declared it was not. However, the family were obliged to begin their quarantine anew on the report of the visitor or examiner, though their former quarantine wanted but a few days of being finished. This oppressed them so with anger and grief, and, as before, straitened them also so much as to room, and for want of breathing and free air, that most of the family fell sick, one of one distemper, one of another, chiefly *scorbutic*[1] ailments; only one a violent colic; till, after several prolongings of their confinement, some or other of those that came in with the visitors to inspect the persons that were ill, in hopes of releasing them, brought the distemper with them and infected the whole house, and all or most of them died, not of the plague as really upon them before, but of the plague that those people brought them, who should have been careful to have protected them from it. And this was a thing which frequently happened, and was, indeed, one of the worst consequences of shutting houses up. . . .

V

. . . the common people, who, ignorant and stupid in their reflections, as they were brutishly wicked and thoughtless before, were now led by their fright to extremes of folly; and, as I have said before that they ran to conjurers and witches, and all sorts of deceivers, to know what should become of them (who fed their fears, and kept them always alarmed and awake on purpose to delude them and pick their pockets), so they were as mad upon their running after quacks and mountebanks, and every practising old woman, for medicines and remedies; storing themselves with such multitudes of pills, potions, and preservatives, as they were called, that they not only spent their money, but even poisoned themselves beforehand, for fear of the poison of the infection, and prepared their bodies for the plague, instead of preserving them against it. On the other hand, it is incredible, and scarce to be imagined, how the posts of houses and corners of streets were plastered over with doctors' bills and papers of ignorant fellows, quacking and tampering in physic, and inviting the people to come to them for remedies, which was generally set off with such flourishes as these, viz.: "Infallible preventive pills against the plague." "Never-failing preservatives against the infection." "Sovereign cordials against the corruption of the air." "Exact regulations for the conduct of the body in case of an infection." "Anti-pestilential pills." "Incomparable drink against the plague, never found out before." "An universal remedy for the plague." "The only true plague water." "The royal antidote against all kinds of infection"; and such a number more that I cannot reckon up; and if I could, would fill a book of themselves to set them down.

Others set up bills to summon people to their lodgings for directions and advice in the case of infection. These had specious titles also, such as these:—

> "An eminent High Dutch physician, newly come over from Holland, where he resided during all the time of the great plague last year in Amsterdam, and cured multitudes of people that actually had the plague upon them."
>
> "An Italian gentlewoman just arrived from Naples, having a choice secret to prevent infection, which she found out by her great experience, and did wonderful cures with it in the late plague there, wherein there died 20,000 in one day."
>
> "An ancient gentlewoman, having practised with great success in the late plague in this city, anno 1636, gives her advice only to the female sex. To be spoke with," &c.
>
> "An experienced physician, who has long studied the doctrine of antidotes against all sorts of poison and infection, has, after forty years' practice, arrived to such skill as may, with God's blessing, direct persons how to prevent their being touched by any contagious distemper whatsoever. He directs the poor gratis."

I take notice of these by way of specimen. I could give you two or three dozen of the like and yet have abundance left behind. 'T is sufficient from these to apprise any one of the humour of those times, and how a set of thieves and pickpockets not only robbed

1. *scorbutic*, related to scurvy.

and cheated the poor people of their money, but poisoned their bodies with odious and fatal preparations; some with mercury, and some with other things as bad, perfectly remote from the thing pretended to, and rather hurtful than serviceable to the body in case an infection followed. . . .

VI

It is here to be observed that after the funerals became so many that people could not toll the bell, mourn or weep, or wear black for one another, as they did before; no, nor so much as make coffins for those that died; so after a while the fury of the infection appeared to be so increased that, in short, they shut up no houses at all. It seemed enough that all the remedies of that kind had been used till they were found fruitless, and that the plague spread itself with an irresistible fury; so that as the fire the succeeding year spread itself, and burned with such violence that the citizens, in despair, gave over their endeavours to extinguish it, so in the plague it came at last to such violence that the people sat still looking at one another, and seemed quite abandoned to despair; whole streets seemed to be desolated, and not to be shut up only, but to be emptied of their inhabitants; doors were left open, windows stood shattering with the wind in empty houses for want of people to shut them. In a word, people began to give up themselves to their fears, and to think that all regulations and methods were in vain, and that there was nothing to be hoped for but an universal desolation. . . .

VII

In the middle of their distress, when the condition of the city of London was so truly calamitous, just then it pleased God, as it were, by His immediate hand to disarm this enemy; the poison was taken out of the sting. It was wonderful; even the physicians themselves were surprised at it. Wherever they visited they found their patients better; either they had sweated kindly, or the tumours were broke, or the carbuncles went down, and the inflammations round them changed colour, or the fever was gone, or the violent headache was assuaged, or some good symptom was in the case; so that in a few days everybody was recovering, whole families that were infected and down, that had ministers praying with them, and expected death every hour, were revived and healed, and none died at all out of them.

Nor was this by any new medicine found out, or new method of cure discovered, or by any experience in the operation which the physicians or surgeons attained to; but it was evidently from the secret invisible hand of Him that had at first sent this disease as a judgment upon us; and let the atheistic part of mankind call my saying what they please, it is no enthusiasm; it was acknowledged at that time by all mankind. □

DISCUSSION

1. Defoe is regarded as a master of verisimilitude—the art of piling detail upon detail so that his fictional accounts have the authenticity of real life. From the *Journal,* select several examples of verisimilitude and show how Defoe's technique operates.
2. Does Defoe seem more concerned with the physical horrors of the plague, or with the psychological? Explain.
3. Why does Defoe's *Journal* ring more true than the usual account in a history book would?
4. Compare Defoe's style in the *Journal* with that of Samuel Pepys in his Diary, considering such factors as the following: Which seems more personal? more informal? designed more for a reading audience rather than for the author's own eyes?

WRITING

Choosing with care details that will establish a verisimilitude similar to Defoe's, write a brief fictional description of some event outside your immediate experience, such as the air raids of World War II, being trapped in a hijacked aircraft, or something similar.

Joseph Addison 1672 / 1719

NED SOFTLY THE POET

The Tatler, No. 163
Will's Coffee-house, April 24, 1710

I yesterday came hither about two hours before the company generally make their appearance, with a design to read over all the newspapers; but upon my sitting down, I was accosted by Ned Softly, who saw me from a corner in the other end of the room, where I found he had been writing something. "Mr. Bickerstaff," says he, "I observe by a late paper of yours that you and I are just of a humor; for you must know, of all impertinences, there is nothing which I so much hate as news. I never read a Gazette in my life, and never trouble my head about our armies, whether they win or lose, or in what part of the world they lie encamped." Without giving me time to reply, he drew a paper of verses out of his pocket, telling me that he had something which would entertain me more agreeably, and that he would desire my judgment upon every line, for that we had time enough before us till the company came in.

Ned Softly is a very pretty poet, and a great admirer of easy lines. Waller is his favorite; and as that admirable writer has the best and worst verses of any among our great English poets, Ned Softly has got all the bad ones without book, which he repeats upon occasion, to show his reading and garnish his conversation. Ned is indeed a true English reader, incapable of relishing the great and masterly strokes of this art, but wonderfully pleased with the little Gothic ornaments of epigrammatical conceits, turns, points, and quibbles, which are so frequent in the most admired of our English poets, and practised by those who want genius and strength to represent, after the manner of the ancients, simplicity in its natural beauty and perfection.

Finding myself unavoidably engaged in such a conversation, I was resolved to turn my pain into a pleasure, and to divert myself as well as I could with so very odd a fellow. "You must understand," says Ned, "that the sonnet I am going to read to you was written upon a lady, who showed me some verses of her own making, and is, perhaps, the best poet of our age. But you shall hear it."

Upon which he began to read as follows:

TO MIRA ON HER INCOMPARABLE POEMS

When dressed in laurel wreaths you shine,
And tune your soft melodious notes,
You seem a sister of the Nine,
Or Phœbus' self in petticoats.

I fancy, when your song you sing,
(Your song you sing with so much art)
Your pen was plucked from Cupid's wing;
For, ah! it wounds me like his dart.

"Why," says I, "this is a little nosegay of conceits, a very lump of salt: every verse has something in it that piques; and then the *dart* in the last line is certainly as pretty a sting in the tail of an epigram, for so I think you critics call it, as ever entered into the thought of a poet."

"Dear Mr. Bickerstaff," says he, shaking me by the hand, "everybody knows you to be a judge of these things; and to tell you truly, I read over Roscommon's translation of 'Horace's Art of Poetry,' three several times, before I sat down to write the sonnet which I have shown you. But you shall hear it again, and pray

OF LITERARY INTEREST

The Tatler and The Spectator

One day in 1709, there appeared in the London coffee houses a single news sheet called *The Tatler,* which bore the motto "Whatever men do is the subject of this book." Its author was Richard Steele, who had decided to make the education of the newly arrived middle class his main life task. *The Tatler's* news items and essays were soon being read by practically everybody.

One issue found its way to Ireland, where Joseph Addison, a former schoolmate of Steele, was employed in government service. Addison thought he recognized *The Tatler's* anonymous author and sent him a contribution for its columns. This was the beginning of a famous literary partnership.

When *The Tatler* was discontinued in 1711 because of political difficulties, Addison and Steele founded a daily paper called *The Spectator.* Still writing anonymously, the authors offered their comments on manners, morals, and literature through the character of "the Spectator."

observe every line of it; for not one of them shall pass without your approbation.

When dressed in laurel wreaths you shine.

"That is," says he, "when you have your garland on; when you are writing verses." To which I replied, "I know your meaning: a metaphor!" "The same," said he, and went on:

"And tune your soft melodious notes.

"Pray observe the gliding of that verse; there is scarce a consonant in it: I took care to make it run upon liquids. Give me your opinion of it."

"Truly," said I, "I think it as good as the former."

"I am very glad to hear you say so," says he; "but mind the next:

You seem a sister of the Nine.

"That is," says he, "you seem a sister of the Muses; for if you look into ancient authors, you will find it was their opinion that there were nine of them." "I remember it very well," said I; "but pray proceed."

"Or Phœbus' self in petticoats.

"Phœbus," says he, "was the God of Poetry. These little instances, Mr. Bickerstaff, show a gentleman's reading. Then to take off from the air of learning, which Phœbus and the Muses have given to this first stanza, you may observe how it falls all of a sudden into the familiar, 'in petticoats!'

Or Phœbus' self in petticoats."

"Let us now," says I, "enter upon the second stanza. I find the first line is still a continuation of the metaphor:

I fancy, when your song you sing."

"It is very right," says he; "but pray observe the turn of words in those two lines. I was a whole hour in adjusting of them, and have still a doubt upon me, whether in the second line it should be 'Your song you sing'; or, 'You sing your songs.' You shall hear them both:

I fancy when your song you sing
(Your song you sing with so much art).

Or,

I fancy, when your song you sing
(You sing your song with so much art.)"

"Truly," said I, "the turn is so natural either way that you have made me almost giddy with it."

"Dear sir," said he, grasping me by the hand, "you have a great deal of patience; but pray what do you think of the next verse:

A COFFEE HOUSE. RADIO TIMES HULTON PICTURE LIBRARY.

Your pen was plucked from Cupid's wing?"

"Think!" says I; "I think you have made Cupid look like a little goose."

"That was my meaning," says he; "I think the ridicule is well enough hit off. But we now come to the last, which sums up the whole matter:

For, ah! it wounds me like his dart.

"Pray, how do you like that 'Ah!' Does it not make a pretty figure in that place? *Ah!*——it looks as if I felt the dart, and cried out as being pricked with it!

For, ah! it wounds me like his dart.

"My friend Dick Easy," continued he, "assured me, he would rather have written that *Ah!* than to have been the author of the Æneid. He indeed objected, that I made Mira's pen like a quill in one of the lines, and like a dart in the other. But as to that——"

"Oh! as to that," says I, "it is but supposing Cupid to be like a porcupine, and his quills and darts will be the same thing."

He was going to embrace me for the hint; but half a dozen critics coming into the room, whose faces he did not like, he conveyed the sonnet into his pocket, and whispered me in the ear, "he would show it me again as soon as his man had written it over fair."

DISSECTION OF A BEAU'S HEAD

The Spectator, No. 275. *January 15, 1712*

I was yesterday engaged in an assembly of virtuosos,[1] where one of them produced many curious observations which he had lately made in the anatomy of an human body. Another of the company communicated to us several wonderful discoveries, which he had also made on the same subject, by the help of very fine glasses. This gave birth to a great variety of uncommon remarks, and furnished discourse for the remaining part of the day.

The different opinions which were started on this occasion presented to my imagination so many new ideas that, by mixing with those which were already there, they employed my fancy all the last night, and composed a very wild extravagant dream.

I was invited, methought, to the dissection of a beau's head, and of a coquette's heart, which were both of them laid on a table before us. An imaginary operator opened the first with a great deal of nicety, which, upon a cursory and superficial view, appeared like the head of another man; but, upon applying our glasses to it, we made a very odd discovery, namely, that what we looked upon as brains, were not such in reality, but an heap of strange materials wound up in that shape and texture, and packed together with wonderful art in the several cavities of the skull. For, as Homer tells us that the blood of the gods is not real blood, but only something like it; so we found that the brain of a beau is not real brain, but only something like it.

The pineal gland, which many of our modern philosophers suppose to be the seat of the soul, smelt very strong of essence and orange-flower water, and was encompassed with a kind of horny substance, cut into a thousand little faces or mirrors, which were imperceptible to the naked eye; insomuch that the soul, if there had been any here, must have been always taken up in contemplating her own beauties.

We observed a large antrum or cavity in the sinciput, that was filled with ribbons, lace, and embroidery, wrought together in a most curious piece of network, the parts of which were likewise imperceptible to the naked eye. Another of these antrums or cavities was stuffed with invisible billet-doux,[2] love-letters, pricked dances,[3] and other trumpery of the same nature. In another we found a kind of powder, which set the whole company a sneezing, and by the scent discovered itself to be right Spanish.[4] The several other cells were stored with commodities of the same kind, of which it would be tedious to give the reader an exact inventory.

There was a large cavity on each side of the head, which I must not omit. That on the right side was filled with fictions, flatteries, and falsehoods, vows, promises, and protestations; that on the left with oaths and imprecations. There issued out a duct from each of these cells, which ran into the root of the tongue, where both joined together, and passed forward in one common duct to the tip of it. We discovered several little roads or canals running from the ear into the brain, and took particular care to trace them out through their several passages. One of them extended itself to a bundle of sonnets and little musical instruments. Others ended in several bladders which were filled either with wind or froth. But the large canal entered into a great cavity of the skull, from whence there went another canal into the tongue. This great cavity was filled with a kind of spongy substance, which the French anatomists call *galimatias*, and the English nonsense.

The skins of the forehead were extremely tough and thick, and, what very much surprised us, had not in them any single blood-vessel that we were able to discover, either with or without our glasses; from whence we concluded that the party when alive must have been entirely deprived of the faculty of blushing.

The *os cribriforme* was exceedingly stuffed, and in some places damaged with snuff. We could not but take notice in particular of that small muscle, which is not often discovered in dissections, and draws the nose upwards, when it expresses the contempt which the owner of it has, upon seeing anything he does not like, or hearing anything he does not understand. I need not tell my learned reader, this is that muscle which performs the motion so often men-

1. *virtuosos,* men interested in science.

2. *billet-doux* (bil′ ā dü′), love letters (French).

3. *pricked dances,* dance-cards or dance programs marked to indicate which dances are taken.

4. *right Spanish,* a type of snuff.

tioned by the Latin poets, when they talk of a man's cocking his nose, or playing the rhinoceros.

We did not find anything very remarkable in the eye, saving only that the *musculi amatorii*, or as we may translate it into English, the ogling muscles, were very much worn and decayed with use; whereas on the contrary, the elevator, or the muscle which turns the eye toward heaven, did not appear to have been used at all.

I have only mentioned in this dissection such new discoveries as we were able to make, and have not taken any notice of those parts which are to be met with in common heads. As for the skull, the face, and indeed the whole outward shape and figure of the head, we could not discover any difference from what we observe in the heads of other men. We were informed, that the person to whom this head belonged, had passed for a man above five and thirty years; during which time he ate and drank like other people, dressed well, talked loud, laughed frequently, and on particular occasions had acquitted himself tolerably at a ball or an assembly; to which one of the company added, that a certain knot of ladies took him for a wit. He was cut off in the flower of his age by the blow of a paring-shovel, having been surprised by an eminent citizen, as he was tendering some civilities to his wife.

When we had thoroughly examined this head with all its apartments, and its several kinds of furniture, we put up the brain, such as it was, into its proper place, and laid it aside under a broad piece of scarlet cloth, in order to be prepared, and kept in a great repository of dissections; our operator telling us that the preparation would not be so difficult as that of another brain, for that he had observed several of the little pipes and tubes which ran through the brain were already filled with a kind of mercurial substance, which he looked upon to be true quicksilver.

He applied himself in the next place to the coquette's heart, which he likewise laid open with great dexterity. There occurred to us many particularities in this dissection; but, being unwilling to burden my reader's memory too much, I shall reserve this subject for the speculation of another day. □

DISCUSSION

1. Both *The Tatler* and *The Spectator* aimed at correcting some of the follies of their age.

(a) What follies are treated in the selections included here?

(b) Which selection is more effective? Why?

(c) Which selection is most relevant to modern readers? Why?

2. To avoid boring their readers, the periodical essayists used a variety of literary forms, such as fables, allegories, visions, conversational anecdotes, tales, and letters from real or imaginary correspondents.

(a) Which of the forms can you identify in the selections included here?

(b) Would either of the selections be more effective in a different form? Explain.

3. How does the beau's head indicate his character and the life he lived?

4. (a) Based on Ned Softly's explication of his sonnet, what sort of English teacher would he make?

(b) What is your reaction to Bickerstaff's ironical comments?

(c) Is Softly aware of any of them? Explain.

WRITING

1. Try your hand at a periodical essay satirizing one of the follies of the modern world. The class may wish to collect and reproduce the best of these in a modern *Tatler* or *Spectator*.

2. Try a literary dissection of the head of a modern beau, or any other modern character type.

3. According to Addison and Steele, the objectives of their literary periodicals were "to enliven morality with wit, and to temper wit with morality." In a short paper, discuss how well the selections you have read carry out these objectives.

Alexander Pope 1688 / 1744

THE RAPE OF THE LOCK

An Heroi-Comical Poem

The Rape of the Lock was written to help end a quarrel between two families that resulted when a young lord cut off a lock of a young lady's hair. The poem follows the epic form, but it is a "mock epic," a kind of burlesque, treating trivial matters in ultraserious or elevated language and style. In traditional epics such as *Beowulf* or Homer's *Iliad* and *Odyssey* or Milton's *Paradise Lost,* impressive creatures of supernatural powers (gods, monsters, angels) enter into and affect the action. Pope introduced in their stead small creatures such as sylphs and gnomes. He explained: "The gnomes, or daemons of earth, delight in mischief; but the sylphs, whose habituation is in the air, are the best-conditioned creatures imaginable." In the poem the sylphs are assigned the task of defending the heroine, Belinda, and her precious locks of hair.

CANTO I

What dire offense from am'rous causes springs,
What mighty contests rise from trivial things,
I sing—This verse to Caryll,[1] Muse! is due;
This, ev'n Belinda may vouchsafe to view:
5 Slight is the subject, but not so the praise,
If she inspire, and he approve my lays.
  Say what strange motive, Goddess! could compel
A well-bred lord t' assault a gentle belle?
O say what stranger cause, yet unexplored,
10 Could make a gentle belle reject a lord?
In tasks so bold, can little men engage,
And in soft bosoms dwells such mighty rage?
  Sol through white curtains shot a tim'rous ray,
And oped those eyes that must eclipse the day;
15 Now lap dogs give themselves the rousing shake.
And sleepless lovers, just at twelve, awake:
Thrice rung the bell, the slipper knocked the ground,
And the pressed watch returned a silver sound.[2]
Belinda still her downy pillow pressed,
20 Her guardian Sylph prolonged the balmy rest.
'Twas he had summoned to her silent bed
The morning dream that hovered o'er her head.
A youth more glittering than a Birth-night beau,[3]
(That ev'n in slumber caused her cheek to glow)
25 Seemed to her ear his winning lips to lay,
And thus in whispers said, or seemed to say. . . .

(As Belinda dreams, her guardian sylph, Ariel, delivers a long speech explaining the life of the sylphs, and concludes with a grave warning.)

  "Of these am I, who thy protection claim,
A watchful sprite, and Ariel is my name.
Late, as I ranged the crystal wilds of air,
30 In the clear mirror of thy ruling star
I saw, alas! some dread event impend,
Ere to the main this morning sun descend,
But heav'n reveals not what, or how, or where:
Warned by the Sylph, oh pious maid, beware!
35 This to disclose is all thy guardian can:
Beware of all, but most beware of man!"
  He said; when Shock, who thought she slept too long,
Leaped up, and waked his mistress with his tongue.
'Twas then, Belinda, if report say true,
40 Thy eyes first opened on a billet-doux;
Wounds, charms, and ardors were no sooner read,
But all the vision vanished from thy head.
  And now, unveiled, the toilet[4] stands displayed,
Each silver vase in mystic order laid.
45 First, robed in white, the nymph intent adores,
With head uncovered, the cosmetic powers.
A heav'nly image in the glass appears,
To that she bends, to that her eye she rears;
Th' inferior priestess, at her altar's side,
50 Trembling, begins the sacred rites of pride.
Unnumbered treasures ope at once, and here
The various off'rings of the world appear;
From each she nicely culls with curious toil,
And decks the goddess with the glitt'ring spoil.
55 This casket India's glowing gems unlocks,
And all Arabia breathes from yonder box.
The tortoise here and elephant unite,
Transformed to combs, the speckled and the white.

1. *Caryll,* John Caryll, who suggested that Pope write the poem to heal the breach between the two families.
2. *pressed . . . sound,* a type of watch in which a pressure on the stem would cause the watch to strike the last hour again.
3. *Birth-night beau,* a gentleman dressed in fine clothes for the sovereign's birthday ball.
4. *toilet,* dressing table.

Here files of pins extend their shining rows,
60 Puffs, powders, patches, Bibles, billet-doux.
Now awful Beauty puts on all its arms;
The fair each moment rises in her charms,
Repairs her smiles, awakens ev'ry grace,
And calls forth all the wonders of her face;
65 Sees by degrees a purer blush arise,
And keener lightnings quicken in her eyes.
The busy Sylphs surround their darling care;
These set the head, and those divide the hair,
Some fold the sleeve, while others plait the gown;
70 And Betty's[5] praised for labors not her own.

CANTO II

(After her elaborate preparations at the dressing table, Belinda sets out, "launched on the bosom of the silver Thames," on her way to Hampton Court, one of the royal palaces near London, and the center of her delightful, sophisticated, and trivial social life.)

This nymph, to the destruction of mankind,
Nourished two locks, which graceful hung behind
In equal curls, and well conspired to deck
With shining ringlets the smooth iv'ry neck.
75 Love in these labyrinths his slaves detains,
And mighty hearts are held in slender chains.
With hairy springes[6] we the birds betray,
Slight lines of hair surprise the finny prey,
Fair tresses man's imperial race ensnare,
80 And beauty draws us with a single hair.
Th' adventurous Baron the bright locks admired;
He saw, he wished, and to the prize aspired.
Resolved to win, he meditates the way,
By force to ravish, or by fraud betray;
85 For when success a lover's toils attends,
Few ask, if fraud or force attained his ends.

(The sylph Ariel, aware of the threat to Belinda, summons his fellow sylphs and sends them to their various stations about Belinda to guard her every precious possession.)

"This day, black omens threat the brightest Fair
That e'er deserved a watchful spirit's care;
Some dire disaster, or by force, or slight;
90 But what, or where, the Fates have wrapped in night.
Whether the nymph shall break Diana's law,[7]
Or some frail china jar receive a flaw;
Or stain her honor, or her new brocade;
Forget her prayers, or miss a masquerade;
95 Or lose her heart, or necklace, at a ball;
Or whether Heav'n has doomed that Shock must fall.
Haste, then, ye spirits! to your charge repair:
The fluttering fan be Zephyretta's care;
The drops[8] to thee, Brillante, we consign;
100 And, Momentilla, let the watch be thine:
Do thou, Crispissa, tend her fav'rite lock;
Ariel himself shall be the guard of Shock.
"To fifty chosen Sylphs, of special note,
We trust th' important charge, the petticoat:
105 Oft have we known that sev'nfold fence to fail,
Though stiff with hoops, and armed with ribs of whale;
Form a strong line about the silver bound,
And guard the wide circumference around.
"Whatever spirit, careless of his charge,
110 His post neglects, or leaves the fair at large,
Shall feel sharp vengeance soon o'ertake his sins,
Be stopped in vials, or transfixed with pins;
Or plunged in lakes of bitter washes lie,
Or wedged whole ages in a bodkin's eye:
115 Gums and pomatums[9] shall his flight restrain,
While clogged he beats his silken wings in vain;
Or alum styptics[10] with contracting power
Shrink his thin essence like a rivelled flower:
Or, as Ixion[11] fixed, the wretch shall feel
120 The giddy motion of the whirling mill,
In fumes of burning chocolate shall glow,
And tremble at the sea that froths below!"
He spoke; the spirits from the sails descend;
Some, orb in orb, around the nymph extend,
125 Some thrid[12] the mazy ringlets of her hair,
Some hang upon the pendants of her ear;
With beating hearts the dire event they wait,
Anxious, and trembling for the birth of Fate.

CANTO III

Close by those meads, for ever crowned with flow'rs,
130 Where Thames with pride surveys his rising tow'rs,
There stands a structure of majestic frame,

---

5. *Betty,* Belinda's maid.
6. *springes,* nooses to catch birds.
7. *Diana's law,* chastity. Diana was the goddess of maidenhood.
8. *drops,* pendant earrings.
9. *pomatums,* perfumed ointments to keep the hair in place.
10. *alum styptics,* astringents.
11. *Ixion,* in Greek myth, fastened to an endlessly revolving wheel in Hades as punishment for making love to Juno, queen of the gods.
12. *thrid,* thread; pass through.

Which from the neighb'ring Hampton takes its name.
Here Britain's statesmen oft the fall foredoom
Of foreign tyrants, and of nymphs at home;
135 Here thou, great Anna![13] whom three realms obey,
Dost sometimes counsel take—and sometimes tea.
Hither the heroes and the nymphs resort,
To taste awhile the pleasures of a court;
In various talk th' instructive hours they passed,
140 Who gave the ball, or paid the visit last;
One speaks the glory of the British Queen,
And one describes a charming Indian screen;
A third interprets motions, looks, and eyes;
At ev'ry word a reputation dies.
145 Snuff, or the fan, supply each pause of chat,
With singing, laughing, ogling, and all that.
Meanwhile, declining from the noon of day,
The sun obliquely shoots his burning ray;
The hungry judges soon the sentence sign,
150 And wretches hang that jurymen may dine; . . .
(Belinda joins the pleasure-seekers at Hampton Court, and wins at a card game, ombre, *over the Baron who covets her locks. But as the game ends, and they all partake of refreshments, the Baron seizes his opportunity.)*
But when to mischief mortals bend their will,
How soon they find fit instruments of ill!
Just then, Clarissa drew with tempting grace
A two-edged weapon[14] from her shining case;
155 So ladies in romance assist their knight,
Present the spear, and arm him for the fight.
He takes the gift with rev'rence, and extends
The little engine on his fingers' ends;
This just behind Belinda's neck he spread,
160 As o'er the fragrant steams she bends her head:
Swift to the lock a thousand sprites repair,
A thousand wings, by turns, blow back the hair;
And thrice they twitched the diamond in her ear;
Thrice she looked back, and thrice the foe drew near.
165 Just in that instant, anxious Ariel sought
The close recesses of the virgin's thought;
As on the nosegay in her breast reclined,
He watched th' ideas rising in her mind,
Sudden he viewed, in spite of all her art,
170 An earthly lover lurking at her heart.

13. *Anna,* Queen Anne (1702–1714).

14. *two-edged weapon,* scissors.

OF LITERARY INTEREST

Satire

Satire is the literary art of making a subject ridiculous by arousing towards it feelings of contempt, amusement, and scorn. While humor has the evocation of amusement as its sole end, satire often employs the comic to the end of pointing up human faults and effecting some improvement in humanity or human institutions. The butt of satire may be an individual (as in Dryden's *MacFlecknoe,* a mock epic whose victim is playwright Thomas Shadwell), a type of person (Addison's "Dissection of a Beau's Head"), a particular social evil (as in Swift's *A Modest Proposal*), or even the entire race of mankind (Swift's *Gulliver's Travels).*

The most frequently used satirical techniques are *irony, sarcasm, burlesque,* and *parody. Irony* is a technique in which the attitudes stated differ from what is really meant. For example, words of praise can be used to imply blame. *A Modest Proposal* is one of the most effective and savage examples of sustained ironic tone in English literature.

Sarcasm is more caustic, crude, and heavy-handed than irony, of which it is a form. Sarcasm also tends to be more personally directed than irony.

Burlesque is an imitation of a person or subject which, by ridiculous exaggeration or distortion, aims to amuse. The quality which characterizes this technique is a discrepancy between the subject matter and the style in which it is treated. For example, a frivolous subject may be treated with mock dignity, or, conversely, a weighty subject might be handled in a trivial style. Mock epics, such as Pope's *The Rape of the Lock,* use the elaborate and elevated style of the epic to make a trivial subject laughable.

Parody differs from burlesque in that it derides not a person or subject, but a specific literary work or style, by imitating features and applying them to trivial or incongruous materials. The poem "Father William" in *Alice in Wonderland* (page 454) is a funny and successful parody of Southey's poem "The Old Man's Comforts."

Satire has existed at least since the classical literature of Greece and Rome. It achieved a golden age in eighteenth-century England, when poetry, drama, essays, and criticism all took on the satiric tone at the hands of such masters as Dryden, Pope, Addison, Steele, and Swift. Satire continues to be an important medium for social commentary in our time. A well-known modern example is George Orwell's *Animal Farm.* The English satiric spirit has also been maintained by such authors as G. B. Shaw, Evelyn Waugh, and Aldous Huxley and such magazines as *Punch;* in the United States, periodicals like *Mad* and *The National Lampoon* present social and political satire.

Amazed, confused, he found his pow'r expired,
Resigned to fate, and with a sigh retired.
The peer now spreads the glittering forfex[15] wide,
T' inclose the lock; now joins it, to divide.
175 Ev'n then, before the fatal engine closed,
A wretched Sylph too fondly interposed;
Fate urged the shears, and cut the Sylph in twain
(But airy substance soon unites again).
The meeting points the sacred hair dissever
180 From the fair head, for ever, and for ever!
Then flashed the living lightning from her eyes,
And screams of horror rend th' affrighted skies.
Not louder shrieks to pitying Heav'n are cast,
When husbands or when lap dogs breathe their last;
185 Or when rich China vessels fallen from high,
In glitt'ring dust and painted fragments lie!
"Let wreaths of triumph now my temples twine,"
(The victor cried) "the glorious prize is mine!
While fish in streams, or birds delight in air,
190 Or in a coach and six the British fair,
As long as *Atalantis*[16] shall be read,
Or the small pillow grace a lady's bed,
While visits shall be paid on solemn days,
When numerous wax-lights in bright order blaze,
195 While nymphs take treats, or assignations give,
So long my honor, name, and praise shall live!

15. *forfex,* scissors.
16. *Atalantis,* a popular book of court scandal and gossip.

What time would spare, from steel receives its date,
And monuments, like men, submit to fate!
Steel could the labor of the gods destroy,
200 And strike to dust th' imperial tow'rs of Troy;
Steel could the works of mortal pride confound,
And hew triumphal arches to the ground.
What wonder then, fair nymph! thy hairs should feel
The conquering force of unresisted steel?"

CANTO IV

(Confusion and hysteria result from the Baron's dastardly deed of cutting off Belinda's lock of hair, and Belinda delivers to the Baron a speech of elevated indignation.)

205 "For ever curs'd be this detested day,
Which snatched my best, my fav'rite curl away!
Happy! ah ten times happy had I been,
If Hampton Court these eyes had never seen!
Yet am not I the first mistaken maid,
210 By love of courts to num'rous ills betrayed.
Oh had I rather unadmired remained
In some lone isle, or distant northern land;
Where the gilt chariot never marks the way,
Where none learn ombre, none e'er taste bohea!
215 There kept my charms concealed from mortal eye,
Like roses that in deserts bloom and die.

DANCING THE MINUET AT A FASHIONABLE BALL. RADIO TIMES HULTON PICTURE LIBRARY.

OF HUMAN INTEREST

What finally happened?

Pope's mock epic apparently succeeded in its purpose of healing the breach between the families involved. Only one of the minor characters depicted was offended; in fact, Arabella Fermor ("Belinda") was pleased with the attention given her. While it would have made the story complete if the real-life hero and heroine had married and lived happily ever after, this was not to be. The "Baron" (Lord Petre) married a younger and richer heiress, but died of smallpox within a year. Arabella married another gentleman and became the mother of six children.

What moved my mind with youthful lords to roam?
Oh had I stayed, and said my prayers at home!
'Twas this, the morning omens seemed to tell:
220 Thrice from my trembling hand the patchbox fell;
The tottering china shook without a wind,
Nay, Poll sat mute, and Shock was most unkind!
A Sylph too warned me of the threats of fate,
In mystic visions, now believed too late!
225 See the poor remnants of these slighted hairs!
My hands shall rend what ev'n thy rapine spares:
These, in two sable ringlets taught to break,
Once gave new beauties to the snowy neck.
The sister-lock now sits uncouth, alone,
230 And in its fellow's fate foresees its own;
Uncurled it hangs, the fatal shears demands;
And tempts, once more, thy sacrilegious hands.
Oh hadst thou, cruel! been content to seize
Hairs less in sight, or any hairs but these!"

CANTO V

(Such a treacherous deed as the rape of a lock of lady's hair inevitably results in an "epic" battle.)

235 "To arms, to arms!" the fierce virago cries,
And swift as lightning to the combat flies.
All side in parties, and begin th' attack;
Fans clap, silks rustle, and tough whalebones crack;
Heroes' and heroines' shouts confus'dly rise,
240 And bass, and treble voices strike the skies.
No common weapons in their hands are found,
Like gods they fight, nor dread a mortal wound.

(Belinda attacks the Baron, but to no avail. They are both deprived of the precious lock as it rises into the skies immortalized and transfigured into a heavenly body.)

See fierce Belinda on the Baron flies,
With more than usual lightning in her eyes;
245 Nor feared the chief th' unequal fight to try,
Who sought no more than on his foe to die.
But this bold lord, with manly strength endued,
She with one finger and a thumb subdued:
Just where the breath of life his nostrils drew,
250 A charge of snuff the wily virgin threw;
The Gnomes direct, to every atom just,
The pungent grains of titillating dust.
Sudden, with starting tears each eye o'erflows,
And the high dome re-echoes to his nose.
255 "Now meet thy fate," incensed Belinda cried,
And drew a deadly bodkin[17] from her side.
(The same, his ancient personage to deck,
Her great-great-grandsire wore about his neck
In three seal rings; which after, melted down,
260 Formed a vast buckle for his widow's gown:
Her infant grandame's whistle next it grew,
The bells she jingled, and the whistle blew;
Then in a bodkin graced her mother's hairs,
Which long she wore, and now Belinda wears.)
265 "Boast not my fall" (he cried) "insulting foe!
Thou by some other shalt be laid as low.
Nor think, to die dejects my lofty mind;
All that I dread is leaving you behind!
Rather than so, ah let me still survive,
270 And burn in Cupid's flames—but burn alive."
"Restore the lock!" she cries; and all around
"Restore the lock!" the vaulted roofs rebound.
Not fierce Othello in so loud a strain
Roared for the handkerchief that caused his pain.[18]
275 But see how oft ambitious aims are crossed,
And chiefs contend till all the prize is lost!
The lock, obtained with guilt, and kept with pain,
In ev'ry place is sought, but sought in vain:
With such a prize no mortal must be blest,
280 So Heav'n decrees! with Heav'n who can contest?
Some thought it mounted to the lunar sphere,
Since all things lost on earth, are treasured there.
There heroes' wits are kept in pond'rous vases,
And beaux' in snuffboxes and tweezer-cases.
285 There broken vows, and deathbed alms are found,
And lovers' hearts with ends of riband bound;

17. *bodkin,* ornamental hairpin shaped like a stiletto.
18. *Othello . . . pain.* In Shakespeare's play, Othello becomes enraged when his wife Desdemona fails to produce a highly-prized handkerchief and is convinced she has given it to her supposed lover.

The courtier's promises and sick man's prayers,
The smiles of harlots, and the tears of heirs.
Cages for gnats, and chains to yoke a flea,
290 Dried butterflies, and tomes of casuistry.[19]
But trust the Muse—she saw it upward rise,
Though marked by none but quick poetic eyes:
(So Rome's great founder to the heav'ns withdrew,
To Proculus alone confessed in view.)[20]
295 A sudden star, it shot through liquid air,
And drew behind a radiant trail of hair.
Not Berenice's lock[21] first rose so bright,
The heav'ns bespangling with disheveled light.
The Sylphs behold it kindling as it flies,
300 And pleased pursue its progress through the skies.
This the beau monde shall from the Mall[22] survey,
And hail with music its propitious ray.
This, the blest lover shall for Venus take,
And send up vows from Rosamonda's lake.[23]
305 This Partridge soon shall view in cloudless skies,
When next he looks through Galileo's eyes;
And hence th' egregious wizard shall foredoom
The fate of Louis, and the fall of Rome.[24]
Then cease, bright nymph! to mourn thy ravished hair
310 Which adds new glory to the shining sphere!
Not all the tresses that fair head can boast
Shall draw such envy as the lock you lost.
For, after all the murders of your eye,
When, after millions slain, your self shall die;
315 When those fair suns shall set, as set they must,
And all those tresses shall be laid in dust;
This lock, the Muse shall consecrate to fame,
And 'midst the stars inscribe Belinda's name. □

19. *tomes of casuistry,* books of oversubtle reasoning about conscience and conduct.
20. *So Rome's . . . view.* Proculus, a Roman senator, saw Romulus, the founder of Rome, taken to heaven.
21. *Berenice's lock.* The Egyptian queen Berenice dedicated a lock of her beautiful hair to Venus for the safe return of her husband from war; the hair was turned into a comet. There is a constellation known as *Coma Berenicis,* Berenice's hair.
22. *Mall,* a promenade in St. James's Park in London.
23. *Rosamonda's lake,* in St. James's Park.
24. *Partridge . . . Rome.* John Partridge (1644–1715) was an astrologer and almanac-maker who annually predicted the downfall of the King of France and of the Pope.

DISCUSSION

1. (a) In *The Rape of the Lock,* what devices are used to make Belinda seem like a goddess? to seem like an Amazon or other female warrior?
(b) How does Pope make these appropriate to a *mock* epic?
2. The Baron's feelings about Belinda are clear. What are her feelings about him?
3. How important are the Sylphs to the plot of the poem? to the atmosphere? Explain.
4. In what respects has the war between the sexes remained unchanged from the time of *The Rape of the Lock* to the present day? In what respects has it changed?
5. Explain how *The Rape of the Lock* could be popular with the real-life principals involved, at the same time that it pointed out the ridiculousness of their quarrel.
6. Pope's mock epic depends for its effect on the juxtaposition of the serious and the trivial. Cite at least five instances.

WRITING

1. Prepare a newspaper story describing the loss of Belinda's lock.
2. Write a letter of apology from the Baron to Belinda, and her reply to it.
3. In a paper of about 500 words, discuss how Pope adapted some of the following devices of the epic for his mock epic: invocation to the muse; statement of theme; statement of the epic question; elevated language; intervention of supernatural beings; a hero who seems "larger than life"; boastful speeches by great warriors; descriptions of armor; detailed history of heroes' weapons; great battles; personal combats.

READERS' THEATER

Join with other students in presenting a dramatic reading of this version of *The Rape of the Lock.* You will need the following parts: narrator, Ariel, Belinda, the Baron. You may wish to divide the narrator's lines. If the entire poem seems too ambitious a project, select portions of it.

QUOTABLE POPE

Next to Shakespeare, Pope is probably the most frequently quoted of English poets. The following remarks are from his *Essay on Criticism,* a long poem which expressed in polished heroic couplets (pairs of rhyming lines in iambic pentameter) the eighteenth century's basic rules for poetry.

1. 'Tis with our judgments as our watches; none
   Go just alike, yet each believes his own.

2. Let such teach others who themselves excel,
   And censure freely who have written well.

3. Music resembles poetry; in each
   Are nameless graces which no methods teach.

4. Those oft are stratagems which errors seem,
   Nor is it Homer nods, but we that dream.

5. Of all the causes which conspire to blind
   Man's erring judgment, and misguide the mind,
   What the weak head with strongest bias rules,
   Is pride, the never-failing vice of fools.

6. Trust not yourself: but your defects to know,
   Make use of every friend—and every foe.

7. A little learning is a dangerous thing;
   Drink deep, or taste not the Pierian spring.[1]
   There shallow draughts intoxicate the brain,
   And drinking largely sobers us again.

8. 'Tis not a lip, or eye, we beauty call,
   But the joint force and full result of all.

9. True wit is Nature to advantage dressed,
   What oft was thought, but ne'er so well expressed.

10. As shades more sweetly recommend the light,
    So modest plainness sets off sprightly wit.

11. Words are like leaves; and where they most abound,
    Much fruit of sense beneath is rarely found.

12. True ease in writing comes from art, not chance,
    As those move easiest who have learned to dance.

13. Those heads, as stomachs, are not sure the best
    Which nauseate all, and nothing can digest.

14. Be not the first by whom the new are tried,
    Nor yet the last to lay the old aside.

15. Where'er you find "the cooling western breeze,"
    In the next line, it "whispers through the trees";
    If crystal streams "with pleasing murmurs creep,"
    The reader's threatened (not in vain) with "sleep."

16. Some praise at morning what they blame at night,
    But always think the last opinion right.

17. We think our fathers fools, so wise we grow;
    Our wiser sons, no doubt, will think us so.

18. Envy will merit, as its shade, pursue.
    But like a shadow, proves the substance true.

19. Good nature and good sense must ever join;
    To err is human, to forgive divine.

1. *Pierian spring,* i.e. inspiration; from Pieria, where the Muses were born.

KNOW THEN THYSELF

From AN ESSAY ON MAN

Know then thyself, presume not God to scan:
The proper study of mankind is man.
Placed on this isthmus of a middle state,
A being darkly wise, and rudely great:
5 With too much knowledge for the skeptic side,
With too much weakness for the Stoic's pride,
He hangs between: in doubt to act, or rest;
In doubt to deem himself a god, or beast;
In doubt his mind or body to prefer;
10 Born but to die, and reas'ning but to err;
Alike in ignorance, his reason such,
Whether he thinks too little, or too much:
Chaos of thought and passion, all confused;
Still by himself abused, or disabused;
15 Created half to rise, and half to fall;
Great lord of all things, yet a prey to all;
Sole judge of truth, in endless error hurled:
The glory, jest, and riddle of the world!

EPIGRAM

Engraved on the Collar of a Dog Which I Gave to His Royal Highness

I am his Highness' dog at Kew;
Pray tell me sir, whose dog are you?

DISCUSSION

1. Many of the excerpts from *An Essay on Criticism* can be read in two senses: as advice to writers or critics, and as general maxims for living. Select three of them and explain their use in both senses.

2. Everyone agrees that Pope's "Epigram Engraved on the Collar of a Dog" is clever, but just where *does* its cleverness lie?

3. What is the tone of "Know Then Thyself"? Does the speaker think that man will ever be able to understand himself? Explain.

WRITING

1. Select any of the excerpts from *An Essay on Criticism* and use it as the basis for a composition in which you draw on your own experience to explain and illustrate its applicability.

2. Try your hand at writing some two-line epigrams. Current news events or public figures are good targets for this sort of writing.

Samuel Johnson 1709 / 1784

NATIONAL PORTRAIT GALLERY, LONDON

Johnson's reputation as a scholar and writer was established in 1755 with the publication of his *Dictionary*, which was as much a revelation of its author's personality as an attempt to stabilize the English language.

From
THE DICTIONARY

alliga′tor. The crocodile. This name is chiefly used for the crocodile of America, between which, and that of Africa, naturalists have laid down this difference, that one moves the upper, and the other the lower jaw; but this is now known to be chimerical, the lower jaw being equally moved by both.

bu′lly. (Skinner derives this word from *burly*, as a corruption in the pronunciation; which is very probably right; or from *bulky*, or *bull-eyed;* which are less probable. May it not come from *bull*, the pope's letter, implying the insolence of those who came invested with authority from the papal court?) A noisy, blustering, quarrelling fellow: it is generally taken for a man that has only the appearance of courage.

bu′tterfly. A beautiful insect, so named because it first appears at the beginning of the season for butter.

chi′cken. (3) A term for a young girl.

chiru′rgeon. One that cures ailments, not by internal medicines, but outward applications. It is now generally pronounced, and by many written, *surgeon*.

cough. A convulsion of the lungs, vellicated by some sharp serosity. It is pronounced *coff*.

cu′ckoo. (1) A bird which appears in the spring; and is said to suck the eggs of other birds, and lay her own to be hatched in their place; from which practice, it was usual to alarm a husband at the approach of an adulterer by calling *cuckoo*, which, by mistake, was in time applied to the husband. This bird is remarkable for the uniformity of his note, from which his name in most tongues seems to have been formed.

to cu′rtail. (*curto*, Latin. It was anciently written *curtal*, which perhaps is more proper; but dogs that had their tails cut, being called *curtal* dogs, the word was vulgarly conceived to mean originally *to cut the tail*, and was in time written according to that notion.) (1) To cut off; to cut short; to shorten.

dedica′tion. (2) A servile address to a patron.

den. (1) A cavern or hollow running horizontally, or with a small obliquity, under ground; distinct from a hole, which runs down perpendicularly.

dull. (8) Not exhilarating; not delightful; as, *to make dictionaries is* dull *work.*

e′ssay. (2) A loose sally of the mind; an irregular indigested piece; not a regular and orderly composition.

exci′se. A hateful tax levied upon commodities, and adjudged not by the common judges of property, but wretches hired by those to whom excise is paid.[1]

fa′vourite. (2) One chosen as a companion by his superiour; a mean wretch whose whole business is by any means to please.

fun. (A low cant word.) Sport; high merriment; frolicksome delight.

ga′mbler. (A cant word, I suppose, for *game,* or *gamester.*) A knave whose practice it is to invite the unwary to game and cheat them.

to gi′ggle. To laugh idly; to titter; to grin with merry levity. It is retained in Scotland.

goat. A ruminant animal that seems a middle species between deer and sheep.

gob. A small quantity. A low word.

gra′vy. The serous juice that runs from flesh not much dried by the fire.

gru′bstreet. Originally the name of a street in Moorfields in London, much inhabited by writers of small histories, dictionaries, and temporary poems; whence any mean production is called grubstreet.

to hiss. To utter a noise like that of a serpent and some other animals. It is remarkable, that this word cannot be pronounced without making the noise which it signifies.

itch. (1) A cutaneous disease extremely contagious, which overspreads the body with small pustules filled with a thin serum, and raised as microscopes have discovered by a small animal. It is cured by sulphur.

lexico′grapher. A writer of dictionaries; a harmless drudge, that busies himself in tracing the original, and detailing the signification of words.

lunch, lu′ncheon. As much food as one's hand can hold.

1. *excise.* Johnson's father had had trouble with the commissioners of excise, in the conduct of his business as a bookseller and maker of parchment.

ne′twork. Any thing reticulated or decussated, at equal distances, with interstices between the intersections.

oats. A grain, which in England is generally given to horses, but in Scotland supports the people.

pa′rasite. One that frequents rich tables, and earns his welcome by flattery.

pa′stern. (1) The knee of an horse.[2]

pa′tron. (1) One who countenances, supports, or protects. Commonly a wretch who supports with insolence, and is paid with flattery.

pe′nsioner. (2) A slave of state hired by a stipend to obey his master.

sa′tire. A poem in which wickedness or folly is censured. Proper *satire* is distinguished, by the generality of the reflections, from a *lampoon* which is aimed against a particular person; but they are too frequently confounded.

shre′wmouse. A mouse of which the bite is generally supposed venomous, and to which vulgar tradition assigns such malignity, that she is said to lame the foot over which she runs. I am informed that all these reports are calumnious, and that her feet and teeth are equally harmless with those of any other little mouse. Our ancestors however looked on her with such terrour, that they are supposed to have given her name to a scolding woman, whom for her venom they call a *shrew.*

so′nnet. (1) A short poem consisting of fourteen lines, of which the rhymes are adjusted by a particular rule. It is not very suitable to the English language, and has not been used by any man of eminence since Milton.

to′ry. (A cant term, derived, I suppose, from an Irish word signifying a savage.) One who adheres to the ancient constitution of the state, and the apostolical hierarchy of the church of England, opposed to a whig.[3]

whig. (2) The name of a faction.

wi′tticism. A mean attempt at wit.

to worm. (2) To deprive a dog of something, nobody knows what, under his tongue, which is said to prevent him, nobody knows why, from running mad.

2. *pastern.* (1) In fact, part of the foot of a horse. When a lady asked Johnson how he came to define the word in this way, he answered, "Ignorance, Madam, pure ignorance." But he didn't bother to correct his definition until eighteen years later.

3. Johnson himself was a Tory.

JOHNSON'S LETTER TO CHESTERFIELD

NATIONAL PORTRAIT GALLERY, LONDON

When Johnson, in 1746, first proposed the idea of compiling a dictionary, he discussed the project with Lord Chesterfield, one of the most cultivated noblemen of the age and a man with some scholarly knowledge of language and literature. Chesterfield expressed interest, and in accordance with the custom of literary patronage, gave Johnson a gift of £10. Johnson then addressed to him a detailed *Plan of a Dictionary,* in which Chesterfield is referred to as the patron of the project. Chesterfield read and approved the document before it was published, and apparently promised Johnson his continued assistance and financial support. This, however, never materialized. When the *Dictionary* finally appeared in 1755, Chesterfield expressed the desire to be regarded as its patron. This is the letter Johnson wrote him.

To the Right Honorable
the Earl of Chesterfield

February 7, 1755.

My Lord: I have lately been informed by the proprietor of *The World,*[1] that two papers, in which my *Dictionary* is recommended to the public, were written by your lordship. To be so distinguished is an honor which, being very little accustomed to favors from the great, I know not well how to receive, or in what terms to acknowledge.

When, upon some slight encouragement, I first visited your lordship, I was overpowered, like the rest of mankind, by the enchantment of your address; and I could not forbear to wish that I might boast myself *"Le vainqueur du vainqueur de la terre"*,[2] that I might obtain that regard for which I saw the world contending; but I found my attendance so little encouraged, that neither pride nor modesty would suffer me to continue it. When I had once addressed your lordship in public, I had exhausted all the art of pleasing which a retired and uncourtly scholar can possess. I had done all that I could; and no man is well pleased to have his all neglected, be it ever so little.

Seven years, my lord, have now passed, since I waited in your outward rooms, or was repulsed from your door; during which time I have been pushing on my work through difficulties, of which it is useless to complain, and have brought it at last to the verge of publication, without one act of assistance, one word of encouragement, or one smile of favor. Such treatment I did not expect, for I never had a patron before.

The shepherd in Vergil grew at last acquainted with Love, and found him a native of the rocks.[3]

Is not a patron, my lord, one who looks with unconcern on a man struggling for life in the water, and, when he has reached ground, encumbers him with help? The notice which you have been pleased to take of my labors, had it been early, had been kind; but it has been delayed till I am indifferent and cannot enjoy it; till I am solitary, and cannot impart it; till I am known, and do not want it. I hope it is no very cynical asperity not to confess obligations where no benefit has been received, or to be unwilling that the public should consider me as owing that to a patron, which Providence has enabled me to do for myself.

Having carried on my work thus far with so little obligation to any favorer of learning, I shall not be disappointed though I should conclude it, if less be possible, with less; for I have been long wakened from that dream of hope, in which I once boasted myself with so much exaltation,

My Lord,
Your Lordship's most humble,
Most Obedient servant,

SAM. JOHNSON

1. *The World,* a newspaper run by a friend of Johnson.
2. *Le vainqueur . . . de la terre.* The conqueror of the conqueror of the world (French).
3. *The shepherd . . . rocks.* Johnson is referring to a pastoral poem by Vergil which speaks of the cruelty and inhumanity of love.

VULTURES TALK ABOUT MEN

The Idler, No. 22—September 9, 1758

"The Idler" was a weekly essay which Johnson wrote for *The Universal Chronicle,* a weekly newspaper, from 1758–1760. The essays were twice collected and reprinted during Johnson's lifetime, but both editions omitted No. 22, possibly because of the unsavory picture it presents of mankind.

MANY naturalists are of opinion that the animals which we commonly consider as mute have the power of imparting their thoughts to one another. That they can express general sensations is very certain; every being that can utter sounds has a different voice for pleasure and for pain. The hound informs his fellows when he scents his game; the hen calls her chickens to their food by her cluck, and drives them from danger by her scream.

Birds have the greatest variety of notes; they have indeed a variety which seems almost sufficient to make a speech adequate to the purposes of a life which is regulated by instinct and can admit little change or improvement. To the cries of birds curiosity or superstition has been always attentive; many have studied the language of the feathered tribes, and some have boasted that they understood it.

The most skilful or most confident interpreters of the silvan dialogues have been commonly found among the philosophers of the East, in a country where the calmness of the air and the mildness of the seasons allow the student to pass a great part of the year in groves and bowers. But what may be done in one place by peculiar opportunities, may be performed in another by peculiar diligence. A shepherd of Bohemia has, by long abode in the forests, enabled himself to understand the voice of birds; at least he relates with great confidence a story of which the credibility may be considered by the learned.

"As I was sitting, (said he) within a hollow rock, and watching my sheep that fed in the valley, I heard two vultures interchangeably crying on the summit of the cliff. Both voices were earnest and deliberate. My curiosity prevailed over my care of the flock; I climbed slowly and silently from crag to crag, concealed among the shrubs, till I found a cavity where I might sit and listen without suffering or giving disturbance.

"I soon perceived that my labour would be well repaid; for an old vulture was sitting on a naked prominence, with her young about her, whom she was instructing in the arts of a vulture's life and preparing, by the last lecture, for their final dismission to the mountains and the skies.

"'My children,' said the old vulture, 'you will the less want my instructions because you have had my practice before your eyes; you have seen me snatch from the farm the household fowl, you have seen me seize the leveret in the bush, and the kid in the pasture; you know how to fix your talons, and how to balance your flight when you are laden with your prey. But you remember the taste of more delicious food; I have often regaled you with the flesh of man.'

"'Tell us,' said the young vultures, 'where man may be found, and how he may be known; his flesh is surely the natural food of a vulture. Why have you never brought a man in your talons to the nest?'

"'He is too bulky,' said the mother; 'when we find a man, we can only tear away his flesh and leave his bones upon the ground.'

"'Since man is so big,' said the young ones, 'how do you kill him? You are afraid of the wolf and of the bear; by what power are vultures superior to man, is man more defenseless than a sheep?'

"'We have not the strength of man,' returned the mother, 'and I am sometimes in doubt whether we have the subtilty; and the vultures would seldom feast upon his flesh, had not nature, that devoted him to our uses, infused into him a strange ferocity, which I have never observed in any other being that feeds

---

OF HUMAN INTEREST

Johnson's pride

Lord Chesterfield maintained repeatedly that he had never knowingly refused to see Dr. Johnson. Some Johnson biographers believe that if Johnson had persisted, Chesterfield no doubt would have received him. But Johnson, once rebuffed, was too proud to continue efforts to see Chesterfield. Boswell, in his *Life of Johnson,* reports: "[Dr. Adams] insisted on Lord Chesterfield's general affability and easiness of access, especially to literary men. 'Sir, (said Johnson) that is not Lord Chesterfield; he is the proudest man this day existing.' 'No, (said Dr. Adams) there is one person, at least, as proud; I think, by your own account you are the prouder man of the two.' 'But mine (replied Johnson instantly) was *defensive* pride.'"

upon the earth. Two herds of men will often meet and shake the earth with noise, and fill the air with fire. When you hear noise and see fire which flashes along the ground, hasten to the place with your swiftest wing, for men are surely destroying one another; you will then find the ground smoking with blood and covered with carcasses, of which many are dismembered and mangled for the convenience of the vulture.'

"'But when men have killed their prey,' said the pupil, 'why do they not eat it? When the wolf has killed a sheep he suffers not the vulture to touch it till he has satisfied himself. Is not man another kind of wolf?'

"'Man,' said the mother, 'is the only beast who kills that which he does not devour, and this quality makes him so much a benefactor to our species.'

"'If men kill our prey and lay it in our way,' said the young one, 'what need shall we have of labouring for ourselves?'

"'Because man will, sometimes,' replied the mother, 'remain for a long time quiet in his den. The old vultures will tell you when you are to watch his motions. When you see men in great numbers moving close together, like a flight of storks, you may conclude that they are hunting, and that you will soon revel in human blood.'

"'But still,' said the young one, 'I would gladly know the reason of this mutual slaughter. I could never kill what I could not eat.'

"'My child,' said the mother, 'this is a question which I cannot answer, tho' I am reckoned the most subtile bird of the mountain. When I was young I used frequently to visit the ayry of an old vulture who dwelt upon the Carpathian rocks; he had made many observations; he knew the places that afforded prey round his habitation, as far in every direction as the strongest wing can fly between the rising and setting of the summer sun; he had fed year after year on the entrails of men. His opinion was that men had only the appearance of animal life, being really vegetables with the power of motion; and that as the boughs of an oak are dashed together by the storm, that swine may fatten upon the falling acorns, so men are by some unaccountable power driven one against another, till they lose their motion, that vultures may be fed. Others think they have observed something of contrivance and policy among these mischievous beings, and those that hover more closely round them pretend that there is, in every herd, one that gives directions to the rest, and seems to be more eminently delighted with a wide carnage. What it is that entitles him to such preëminence we know not; he is seldom the biggest or the swiftest, but he shews by his eagerness and diligence that he is, more than any of the others, a friend to vultures.'" □

DISCUSSION

1. The excerpts from the *Dictionary* provide a cross-section of Johnson's personality as well as his work. Find examples that:

(a) illustrate his whimsy.

(b) show his learning.

(c) display the beliefs of his age.

(d) have undergone great change in meaning or in acceptability since his day.

(e) indicate the timelessness of some colloquial or substandard words or expressions.

(f) demonstrate his thoroughness.

(g) reveal his prejudices.

(h) show his ability to enjoy a joke at his own expense.

2. (a) Which of the expressions in Johnson's letter to Chesterfield do you consider to be "masterful put-downs"?

(b) Compare the *Dictionary* definition of *patron* with that in the letter. Which do you prefer?

(c) How do you suppose Lord Chesterfield reacted to Johnson's letter? To see how successful a guesser you are, consult Boswell's *Life of Johnson* or an encyclopedia or literary history to find what Chesterfield's reaction was.

3. (a) In "Vultures Talk about Men," the Bohemian shepherd's account uses a device popular with all story-tellers: that of the naive narrator (in this case the old vulture) whose simplicity increases the impact of the moral of the story. Explain specifically how this device operates in "The Idler" No. 22.

(b) Reread Johnson's definition of *essay*. How well does it apply to "Vultures Talk about Men"?

WRITING

1. Take a dozen or so words of your own choice and prepare personalized definitions of them in the manner of Johnson's *Dictionary*.

2. Assume you are Lord Chesterfield and write an answer to Johnson's letter.

3. Compose a fable exposing some evil or folly of the modern world, in the manner of "The Idler" No. 22.

LLOYD'S COFFEE HOUSE. LLOYD'S, LONDON.

From LONDON

The year after he came to the city, Johnson published, anonymously, a long satirical poem which he labeled "A poem in imitation of the third satire of Juvenal." Juvenal was a Roman (A.D. 60?–130?) who wrote bitter denunciations of the society, culture, and politics of his day.

By numbers, here, from shame or censure free,[1]
All crimes are safe, but hated poverty.
This, only this, the rigid law pursues,
This, only this, provokes the snarling Muse;
5 The sober trader, at a tattered cloak,
Wakes from his dream and labors for a joke;
With brisker air the silken courtiers gaze,
And turn the varied taunt a thousand ways.
Of all the griefs that harass the distressed
10 Sure the most bitter is a scornful jest
Fate never wounds more deep the gen'rous heart
Than when a blockhead's insult points the dart. . . .

Prepare for death, if here at night you roam,
And sign your will before you sup from home.
15 Some fiery fop, with new commission vain,
Who sleeps on brambles till he kills his man;[2]
Some frolic drunkard, reeling from a feast,
Provokes a broil and stabs you for a jest.
Yet ev'n these heroes, mischievously gay,
20 Lords of the street and terrors of the way,
Flushed as they are with folly, youth and wine,
Their prudent insults to the poor confine:
Afar they mark the flambeau's bright approach,
And shun the shining train and golden coach.
25 In vain, these dangers past, your doors you close,
And hope the balmy blessings of repose:
Cruel with guilt, and daring with despair,
The midnight murd'rer bursts the faithless bar,
Invades the sacred hour of silent rest,
30 And plants, unseen, a dagger in your breast.
Scarce can our fields—such crowds at Tyburn[3] die—
With hemp the gallows and the fleet supply.
Propose your schemes, ye senatorian band,
Whose "Ways and Means"[4] support the sinking land,
35 Lest ropes be wanting, in the tempting Spring,
To rig another convoy for the King.

1. *By numbers . . . free,* free from shame or censure because they (crimes) are so frequent.
2. *Who sleeps . . . man,* who cannot rest until he kills his man.
3. *Tyburn,* place where criminals were executed.
4. *Ways and Means,* term used in the House of Commons for methods of raising money.

DISCUSSION

1. (a) Compare the evils described in "London" with those described by Swift in "A Modest Proposal."

(b) How does the modern age compare with the age described in "London"?

2. Keeping in mind the violence that Johnson describes, write either, in prose or in rhymed couplets a satire on the violence of our modern age (perhaps "Ten Suggestions for Staying Alive in America Today").

James Boswell 1740 / 1795

From
THE LIFE OF SAMUEL JOHNSON, LL.D.

As I had the honor and happiness of enjoying Dr. Johnson's friendship for upwards of twenty years; as I had the scheme of writing his life constantly in view; as he was well apprised of this circumstance, and from time to time obligingly satisfied my inquiries by communicating to me the incidents of his early years; as I acquired a facility in recollecting, and was very assiduous in recording, his conversation, of which the extraordinary vigor and vivacity constituted one of the first features of his character; and as I have spared no pains in obtaining materials concerning him from every quarter where I could discover that they were to be found, and have been favored with the most liberal communications by his friends, I flatter myself that few biographers have entered upon such a work as this with more advantages; independent of literary abilities, in which I am not vain enough to compare myself with some great names who have gone before me in this kind of writing. . . .

Boswell's Introduction to Johnson (1763)

This is to me a memorable year, for in it I had the happiness to obtain the acquaintance of that extraordinary man whose memoirs I am now writing; an acquaintance which I shall ever esteem as one of the most fortunate circumstances in my life. . . .

Mr. Thomas Davies the actor, who then kept a bookseller's shop in Russel-street, Covent-garden, told me that Johnson was very much his friend, and came frequently to his house, where he more than once invited me to meet him; but by some unlucky accident or other he was prevented from coming to us.

At last, on Monday the 16th of May, when I was sitting in Mr. Davies's back-parlor, after having drunk tea with him and Mrs. Davies, Johnson unexpectedly came into the shop; and Mr. Davies having perceived him through the glass-door in the room in which we were sitting, advancing towards us—he announced his aweful approach to me, somewhat in the manner of an actor in the part of Horatio, when he addresses Hamlet on the appearance of his father's ghost, "Look, my Lord, it comes."

I found that I had a very perfect idea of Johnson's figure, from the portrait of him painted by Sir Joshua Reynolds soon after he had published his *Dictionary*, in the attitude of sitting in his easy chair in deep meditation, which was the first picture his friend did for him, which Sir Joshua kindly presented to me. Mr. Davies mentioned my name, and respectfully introduced me to him. I was much agitated, and recollecting his prejudice against the Scotch, of which I had heard much, I said to Davies, "Don't tell where I come from."

"From Scotland," cried Davies roguishly.

"Mr. Johnson, (said I) I do indeed come from Scotland, but I cannot help it." I am willing to flatter myself that I meant this as light pleasantry to soothe and conciliate him, and not as an humiliating abasement at the expense of my country. But however that might be, this speech was somewhat unlucky, for with that quickness of wit for which he was so remarkable, he seized the expression "come from Scotland" which I used in the sense of being of that country, and, as if I had said that I had come away from it, or left it, retorted, "That, Sir, I find, is what a very great many of your countrymen cannot help."

This stroke stunned me a good deal; and when we had sat down, I felt myself not a little embarrassed, and apprehensive of what might come next. He then addressed himself to Davies: "What do you think of Garrick?[1] He has refused me an order for the play

In these excerpts, punctuation and paragraphing have been slightly modernized.

1. *Garrick*, David Garrick, the most famous actor of his day, and a former pupil of Johnson's.

for Miss Williams,[2] because he knows the house will be full, and that an order would be worth three shillings."

Eager to take any opening to get into conversation with him, I ventured to say, "O, Sir, I cannot think Mr. Garrick would grudge such a trifle to you."

"Sir (said he, with a stern look), I have known David Garrick longer than you have done: and I know no right you have to talk to me on the subject."

Perhaps I deserved this check, for it was rather presumptuous in me, an entire stranger, to express any doubt of the justice of his animadversion upon his old acquaintance and pupil. I now felt myself much mortified, and began to think that the hope which I had long indulged of obtaining his acquaintance was blasted. And, in truth, had not my ardor been uncommonly strong, and my resolution uncommonly persevering, so rough a reception might have deterred me for ever from making any further attempts. Fortunately, however, I remained upon the field not wholly discomfited; and was soon rewarded by hearing some of his conversation, of which I preserved the following short minute, without marking the questions and observations by which it was produced.

"People (he remarked) may be taken in once, who imagine that an author is greater in private life than other men. Uncommon parts[3] require uncommon opportunities for their exertion."

"In barbarous society, superiority of parts is of real consequence. Great strength or great wisdom is of much value to an individual. But in more polished times there are people to do every thing for money; and then there are a number of other superiorities, such as those of birth and fortune, and rank, that dissipate men's attention, and leave no extraordinary share of respect for personal and intellectual superiority. This is wisely ordered by Providence, to preserve some equality among mankind.". . .

I was highly pleased with the extraordinary vigor of his conversation, and regretted that I was drawn away from it by an engagement at another place. I had, for a part of the evening, been left alone with him, and had ventured to make an observation now and then, which he received very civilly; so that I was satisfied that though there was a roughness in his manner, there was no ill-nature in his disposition. Davies followed me to the door, and when I complained to him a little of the hard blows which the great man had given me, he kindly took upon him to console me by saying, "Don't be uneasy. I can see he likes you very well."

A few days afterwards I called on Davies, and asked him if he thought I might take the liberty of waiting on Mr. Johnson at his Chambers in the Temple. He said I certainly might, and that Mr. Johnson would take it as a compliment. So upon Tuesday the 24th of May, I boldly repaired to Johnson. His Chambers were on the first floor of No. 1, Inner-Temple-lane, and I entered them with an impression given me by the Reverend Dr. Blair, of Edinburgh, who had been introduced to him not long before, and described his having "found the Giant in his den"; an expression which, when I came to be pretty well acquainted with Johnson, I repeated to him, and he was diverted by this picturesque account of himself.

He received me very courteously; but it must be confessed that his apartment, and furniture, and morning dress were sufficiently uncouth. His brown suit of clothes looked very rusty; he had on a little old shrivelled unpowdered wig, which was too small for his head; his shirt-neck and knees of his breeches were loose; his black worsted stockings ill drawn up; and he had a pair of unbuckled shoes by way of slippers. But all these slovenly peculiarities were forgotten the moment that he began to talk. Some gentlemen whom I do not recollect were sitting with him; and when they went away, I also rose; but he said to me, "Nay, don't go."

"Sir, (said I) I am afraid that I intrude upon you. It is benevolent to allow me to sit and hear you."

He seemed pleased with this compliment, which I sincerely paid him, and answered, "Sir, I am obliged to any man who visits me." I have preserved the following short minute of what passed this day:

"Madness frequently discovers itself merely by unnecessary deviation from the usual modes of the world. My poor friend Smart shewed the disturbance of his mind by falling upon his knees and saying his prayers in the street or in any other unusual place. Now although, rationally speaking, it is greater madness not to pray at all than to pray as Smart did, I am afraid there are so many who do not pray that their understanding is not called in question."

---

2. *Miss Williams,* an indigent elderly lady who lived in Johnson's household and on his bounty.

3. *parts,* personal qualities; abilities or talents.

Concerning this unfortunate poet, Christopher Smart, who was confined in a mad-house, he had, at another time, the following conversation with Dr. Burney:

BURNEY. "How does poor Smart do, Sir; is he likely to recover?"

JOHNSON. "It seems as if his mind had ceased to struggle with the disease, for he grows fat upon it."

BURNEY. "Perhaps, Sir, that may be from want of exercise."

JOHNSON. "No, Sir; he has partly as much exercise as he used to have, for he digs in the garden. Indeed, before his confinement, he used for exercise to walk to the ale-house; but he was *carried* back again. I did not think he ought to be shut up. His infirmities were not noxious to society. He insisted on people praying with him; and I'd as lief pray with Kit Smart as any one else. Another charge was that he did not love clean linen; and I have no passion for it."

Johnson continued, "Mankind have a great aversion to intellectual labor; but even supposing knowledge to be easily attainable, more people would be content to be ignorant than would take even a little trouble to acquire it."

"The morality of an action depends on the motive from which we act. If I fling half a crown to a beggar with intention to break his head, and he picks it up and buys victuals with it, the physical effect is good; but, with respect to me, the action is very wrong."

Johnson on Fathers and Sons (July 1763)

Feeling myself now quite at ease as his companion, though I had all possible reverence for him, I expressed a regret that I could not be so easy with my father, though he was not much older than Johnson, and certainly however respectable had not more learning and greater abilities to depress me. I asked him the reason of this.

JOHNSON. "Why, Sir, I am a man of the world. I live in the world, and I take, in some degree, the color of the world as it moves along. Your father is a Judge in a remote part of the island, and all his notions are taken from the old world. Besides, Sir, there must always be a struggle between a father and son, while one aims at power and the other at independence."

I said I was afraid my father would force me to be a lawyer.

JOHNSON. "Sir, you need not be afraid of his forcing you to be a laborious practising lawyer; that is not in his power. For as the proverb says, 'One man may lead a horse to the water, but twenty cannot make him drink.' He may be displeased that you are not what he wishes you to be; but that displeasure will not go far. If he insists only on your having as much law as is necessary for a man of property, and then endeavors to get you into Parliament, he is quite right."

On Young People

At night Mr. Johnson and I supped in a private room at the Turk's Head coffee-house in the Strand. "I encourage this house (said he) for the mistress of it is a good civil woman, and has not much business."

"Sir, I love the acquaintance of young people; because, in the first place, I don't like to think myself growing old. In the next place, young acquaintances must last longest, if they do last; and then, Sir, young men have more virtue than old men; they have more generous sentiments in every respect. I love the young dogs of this age: they have more wit and humor and knowledge of life than we had; but then the dogs are not so good scholars. Sir, in my early years I read very hard. It is a sad reflection, but a true one, that I knew almost as much at eighteen as I do now. My judgment, to be sure, was not so good; but I had all the facts. I remember very well, when I was at Oxford, an old gentleman said to me, 'Young man, ply your book diligently now, and acquire a stock of knowledge; for when years come upon you, you will find that poring upon books will be but an irksome task.'"

On Eating (August 1763)

At supper this night he talked of good eating with uncommon satisfaction. "Some people (said he) have a foolish way of not minding, or pretending not to mind, what they eat. For my part, I mind my belly very studiously, and very carefully; for I look upon it that he who does not mind his belly will hardly mind anything else."

He now appeared to me *Jean Bull philosophe,*[4] and he was, for the moment, not only serious but

4. *Jean Bull philosophe,* John Bull the philosopher (French). John Bull is the personification of the English nation, the typical Englishman. Boswell probably means that Johnson was philosophizing in the English vein.

vehement. Yet I have heard him, upon other occasions, talk with great contempt of people who were anxious to gratify their palates; and the 206th number of his *Rambler* is a masterly essay against gulosity. His practice, indeed, I must acknowledge, may be considered as casting the balance of his different opinions upon this subject, for I never knew any man who relished good eating more than he did. When at table, he was totally absorbed in the business of the moment; his looks seemed rivetted to his plate; nor would he, unless when in very high company, say one word, or even pay the least attention to what was said by others, till he had satisfied his appetite, which was so fierce, and indulged with such intenseness, that while in the act of eating, the veins of his forehead swelled, and generally a strong perspiration was visible. To those whose sensations were delicate, this could not but be disgusting; and it was doubtless not very suitable to the character of a philosopher, who should be distinguished by self-command. But it must be owned that Johnson, though he could be rigidly *abstemious,* was not a *temperate* man either in eating or drinking. He could refrain, but he could not use moderately. He told me that he had fasted two days without inconvenience, and that he had never been hungry but once. They who beheld with wonder how much he eat upon all occasions when his dinner was to his taste could not easily conceive what he must have meant by hunger, and not only was he remarkable for the extraordinary quantity which he eat, but he was, or affected to be, a man of very nice discernment in the science of cookery. He used to descant critically on the dishes which had been at table where he had dined or supped, and to recollect minutely what he had liked.

When invited to dine, even with an intimate friend, he was not pleased if something better than a plain dinner was not prepared for him. I have heard him say on such an occasion, "This was a good dinner enough, to be sure; but it was not a dinner to *ask* a man to." On the other hand, he was wont to express, with great glee, his satisfaction when he had been entertained quite to his mind.

On Equality of the Sexes (April 1778)

Mrs. Knowles affected to complain that men had much more liberty allowed them than women.

JOHNSON. "Why, Madam, women have all the liberty they should wish to have. We have all the labor and the danger, and the women all the ad-

vantage. We go to sea, we build houses, we do everything, in short, to pay our court to the women."

MRS. KNOWLES. "The Doctor reasons very wittily, but not convincingly. Now, take the instance of building; the mason's wife, if she is ever seen in liquor, is ruined; the mason may get himself drunk as often as he pleases, with little loss of character; nay, may let his wife and children starve."

JOHNSON. "Madam, you must consider, if the mason does get himself drunk, and let his wife and children starve, the parish will oblige him to find security for their maintenance. We have different modes of restraining evil. Stocks for the men, a ducking-stool for women, and a pound for beasts. If we require more perfection from women than from ourselves, it is doing them honor. And women have not the same temptations that we have: they may always live in virtuous company; men must mix in the world indiscriminately. If a woman has no inclination to do what is wrong, being secured from it is no restraint to her. I am at liberty to walk into the Thames; but if I were to try it, my friends would restrain me in Bedlam, and I should be obliged to them."

MRS. KNOWLES. "Still, Doctor, I cannot help thinking it a hardship that more indulgence is allowed to men than to women. It gives a superiority to men, to which I do not see how they are entitled."

JOHNSON. "It is plain, Madam, one or other must have the superiority. As Shakespeare says, 'If two men ride on a horse, one must ride behind.'"

DILLY. "I suppose, Sir, Mrs. Knowles would have them to ride in panniers, one on each side."

JOHNSON. "Then, Sir, the horse would throw them both."

MRS. KNOWLES. "Well, I hope that in another world the sexes will be equal."

BOSWELL. "That is being too ambitious, Madam. *We* might as well desire to be equal with the angels. We shall all, I hope, be happy in a future state, but we must not expect to be all happy in the same degree. It is enough if we be happy according to our several capacities. A worthy carman will get to heaven as well as Sir Isaac Newton. Yet, though equally good, they will not have the same degrees of happiness."

JOHNSON. "Probably not." □

SEE ALSO THE ARTICLE "BOSWELL AS BIOGRAPHER" BEGINNING ON PAGE 332.

BOSWELL AND JOHNSON AS TRAVEL WRITERS

In 1773, Johnson and Boswell made an extended journey from Edinburgh through the more remote parts of Scotland to the Hebrides, or Western Islands, a region then almost totally isolated from the rest of Europe. Both men wrote of their experiences. Johnson's account, *A Journey to the Western Islands of Scotland,* was published in 1775. In 1785, after Johnson's death, Boswell published a heavily edited version of the journal he had kept on the tour. The version used here, however, is from the recently recovered manuscript journal (see the article beginning on page 332), and presents, in Boswell's natural, private style, what he actually wrote in 1773.

Excerpts from the beginning of Boswell's journal are given here, and then parallel passages from Boswell's and Johnson's accounts of the same events.

From Boswell's *Journal of a Tour to the Hebrides with Samuel Johnson, LL.D.*

DR. Johnson had for many years given me hopes that we should go together and visit the Hebrides. Martin's Account of those islands had impressed us with a notion that we might there contemplate a system of life almost totally different from what we had been accustomed to see; and to find simplicity and wildness, and all the circumstances of remote time or place, so near to our native great island, was an object within the reach of reasonable curiosity. . . . We reckoned there would be some inconveniences and hardships, and perhaps a little danger; but these we were persuaded were magnified in the imagination of everybody. When I was at Ferney in 1764, I mentioned our design to Voltaire.[1] He looked at me as if I had talked of going to the North Pole, and said, "You do not insist on my accompanying you?" "No, sir." "Then I am very willing you should go." I was not afraid that our curious expedition would be prevented by such apprehensions, but I doubted that it would not be possible to prevail on Dr. Johnson to relinquish for some time the felicity of a London life. . . .

He had disappointed my expectations so long that I began to despair; but in spring, 1773, he talked of coming to Scotland that year with so much firmness that I hoped he was at last in earnest. I knew that if he were once launched from the metropolis, he would go forward very well; and I got our common friends there to assist in setting him afloat. To Mrs. Thrale in particular, whose enchantment over him seldom failed, I was much obliged. . . .

Dr. Johnson's prejudice against Scotland was announced almost as soon as he began to appear in the world of letters. . . . The truth is, like the ancient Greeks and Romans, he allowed himself to look upon all nations but his own as barbarians. If he was particularly prejudiced against the Scots, it was because they were more in his way; because he thought their success in England rather exceeded the due proportion of their real merit. . . .

To Scotland, however, he ventured; and he returned from it in great good humor, with his prejudices much lessened, and with very grateful feelings of the hospitality with which he was treated, as is evident from that admirable work, his *Journey to the Western Islands of Scotland*. . . .

[*Boswell and Johnson arrived separately in Edinburgh, Johnson traveling there in post-chaises with a Mr. Scott of Oxford.*]

On Saturday the fourteenth of August, 1773, late in the evening, I received a note from him that he was arrived at Boyd's Inn, at the head of the Canongate. I went to him directly. He embraced me cordially, and I exulted in the thought that I now had him actually in Caledonia.[2] Mr. Scott's amiable manners and attachment to our Socrates at once united me to him. He told me that before I came in the Doctor had unluckily had a bad specimen of Scottish cleanliness. He then drank no fermented liquor. He asked to have his lemonade made sweeter, upon which the waiter with his greasy fingers lifted a lump of sugar and put it into it. The Doctor in indignation threw it out of the window. Scott said

1. *Voltaire,* (1694–1778), French satirist, philosopher, historian, dramatist, and poet, considered one of the most influential men in the history of thought and very famous in his own day.

2. *Caledonia,* Latin name for Scotland.

he was afraid he would have knocked the waiter down. Mr. Johnson told me that such another trick was played him at the house of a lady in Paris.

He was to do me the honour to lodge under my roof. I regretted sincerely that I had not also a room for Mr. Scott. Mr. Johnson and I walked arm-in-arm up the High Street to my house in James's Court; it was a dusky night; I could not prevent his being assailed by the evening effluvia of Edinburgh. I heard a late baronet of some distinction in the political world in the beginning of the present reign observe that "walking the streets of Edinburgh at night was pretty perilous and a good deal odoriferous." The peril is much abated by the care which the magistrates have taken to enforce the city laws against throwing foul water from the windows; but, from the structure of the houses in the old town, which consist of many storeys in each of which a different family lives, and there being no covered sewers, the odor still continues. . . .

ANOCH—TUESDAY 31 AUGUST, 1773

BETWEEN twelve and one we set out and travelled eleven wild miles till we came to a house in Glenmoriston kept by one Macqueen. Our landlord was a sensible fellow. He had learnt his grammar,[3] and Dr. Johnson justly observed that a man is the better for that as long as he lives. There were some books here: a treatise against drunkenness, translated from the French, a volume of the *Spectator*, a volume of Prideaux' *Connexion, Cyrus's Travels.* Macqueen said he had more volumes, and his pride seemed to be piqued that we were surprised at his having books.

Near to this, we had passed a party of soldiers under a sergeant at work upon the road. We gave them two shillings to drink. They came to this house and made merry in the barn. We went out, Mr. Johnson saying, "Come, let's go and give 'em another shilling apiece." We did so, and he was saluted "My Lord" by all of 'em. He is really generous, loves influence, and has the way of gaining it. He said he was quite feudal. Here I agree with him. I said I regretted I was not head of a clan. I would make my tenants follow me. I could not be a *patriarchal* chief. But I'd be a *feudal* chief.

The poor soldiers got too much liquor. Some of 'em fought and left blood upon the spot, and cursed whisky next morning. The house here was built of thick turfs and thatched with thinner turfs and heath. It had three rooms in length, and a little room projected. Where we sat, the side-walls were *wainscotted,* as Mr. Johnson said, with wands very well plaited. Our landlord had made all with his own hand. We had a broiled chicken, mutton collops or chops, mutton sausage, and eggs, of which Mr. Johnson eat five and nothing else. I eat four, some chicken and some sausage, and drank some rum and water and sugar. Joseph had lemons for Mr. Johnson, so he had lemonade. Mr. Johnson said he was a fine fellow: a civil man and a wise man.

Macqueen, our landlord, sat by us awhile and talked with us. He said all Glenmoriston's people would bleed for him if they were well used. But

DR. JOHNSON IN HIS TRAVELLING DRESS. FROM A CONTEMPORARY ENGRAVING.

3. *learnt his grammar,* i.e., he had studied Latin.

that seventy men had gone out of the Glen to America. That he himself intended to go next year, for that his farm, which twenty-five years ago was only £5 a year, was now raised to £20. That he could pay £10 and live, but no more. Mr. Johnson said he wished Macqueen Laird of Glenmoriston, and Glenmoriston to go to America. Macqueen very generously said he should be sorry for it, for Glenmoriston could not shift for himself in America as he could do.

I talked of the officers whom we had left today: how much service they had seen and how little they got for it, even of fame. Mr. Johnson said, "Sir, a soldier gets as little as any man can get." I observed that Goldsmith had more fame than all the officers last war who were not generals. JOHNSON. "Why, sir, you will get ten thousand to do what they did before you get one who does what Goldsmith has done. You must consider a thing is valued according to its rarity. A pebble that paves the street is in itself more useful than the diamond upon a lady's finger." I wish Goldie had heard this.

He said yesterday when I wondered how John Hay, one of our guides, who had been pressed aboard a man-of-war, did not choose to continue longer than nine months, after which time he got off: "Why, sir, no man will be a sailor who has contrivance to get himself into a jail, for being in a ship is being in a jail with the chance of being drowned."

We had tea in the afternoon, and our landlord's daughter, a modest civil girl very neatly dressed, made it to us. She told us she had been a year at Inverness and learnt reading and writing, sewing, knotting, working lace, and pastry. Mr. Johnson made her a present of a book of arithmetic which he had bought at Inverness.

The room had some deals laid as a kind of ceiling. There were two beds in the room. A woman's gown was hung on a rope to make a curtain of separation between them. Joseph had the sheets which we brought with us laid on them. We had much hesitation whether to undress or lie down with our clothes on. I said at last, "I'll plunge in! I shall have less room for vermin to settle about me when I strip!" Mr. Johnson said he was like one hesitating whether to go into the cold bath. At last he resolved too. I observed he might serve a campaign. Said he, "I could do all that can be done by patience. Whether I should have strength enough, I know not." He was in excellent humor. To see the Rambler as I saw him tonight was really a curiosity. . . .

Tonight each offered up his private devotions. After we had chatted a little from our beds, Dr. Johnson said, "God bless us both for Jesus Christ's sake. Good night." I pronounced "Amen." Mr. Johnson fell asleep immediately. I could not have that good fortune for a long time. I fancied myself bit by innumerable vermin under the clothes, and that a spider was travelling from the *wainscot* towards my mouth. At last I fell into insensibility.

WEDNESDAY 1 SEPTEMBER. I awaked very early. I began to imagine that the landlord, being about to emigrate, might murder us to get our money and lay it upon the soldiers in the barn. Such groundless fears will arise in the mind before it has resumed its vigour after sleep! Mr. Johnson had had the same kind of ideas; for he told me afterwards that he considered so many soldiers, having seen us, would be witnesses should any harm be done; and the thought of that, I suppose, he considered would make us secure. When I got up, I found him sound asleep in his miserable sty, I may say, with a coloured handkerchief tied round his head. With difficulty could I get him up. . . .

From Johnson's JOURNEY TO THE WESTERN ISLANDS OF SCOTLAND

EARLY in the afternoon we came to Anoch, a village in *Glenmollison* of three huts, one of which is distinguished by a chimney. Here we were to dine and lodge, and were conducted through the first room, that had the chimney, into another lighted by a small glass window. The landlord attended us with great civility, and told us what he could give us to eat and drink. I found some books on a shelf, among which were a volume or more of Prideaux's Connection.[1]

This I mentioned as something unexpected, and perceived that I did not please him. I praised the propriety of his language, and was answered that I need not wonder, for he had learned it by grammar.

By subsequent opportunities of observation, I found that my host's diction had nothing peculiar. Those Highlanders that can speak English, commonly speak it well, with few of the words and little of the tone by which a Scotchman is distinguished. Their language seems to have been learned in the army or the navy, or by some communication with those who could give them good examples of accent and pronunciation. By their Lowland neighbours they would not willingly be taught; for they have long considered them as a mean and degenerate race. These prejudices are wearing fast away; but so much of them still remains, that when I asked a very learned minister in the islands which they considered as their most savage clans: "*Those,* said he, *that live next the lowlands.*"

As we came hither early in the day, we had time sufficient to survey the place. The house was built like other huts of loose stones, but the part in which we dined and slept was lined with turf and wattled with twigs, which kept the earth from falling. Near it was a garden of turnips and a field of potatoes. It stands in a glen, or valley, pleasantly watered by a winding river. But this country, however it may delight the gazer or amuse the naturalist, is of no great advantage to its owners. Our landlord told us of a gentleman who possesses lands eighteen Scotch miles in length and three in breadth, a space containing at least a hundred square English miles. He has raised his rents, to the danger of depopulating his farms, and he fells his timber, and by exerting every art of augmentation, has obtained an yearly revenue of four hundred pounds, which for a hundred square miles is three halfpence an acre.

Some time after dinner we were surprised by the entrance of a young woman, not inelegant either in mien or dress, who asked us whether we would have tea. We found that she was the daughter of our host, and desired her to make it. Her conversation, like her appearance, was gentle and pleasing. We knew that the girls of the Highlands are all gentlewomen, and treated her with great respect, which she received as customary and due, and was neither elated by it, nor confused, but repaid my civilities without embarrassment, and told me how much I honoured her country by coming to survey it.

She had been at *Inverness* to gain the common female qualifications, and had, like her father, the English pronunciation. I presented her with a book, which I happened to have about me, and should not be pleased to think that she forgets me.

In the evening the soldiers whom we had passed on the road came to spend at our inn the little money that we had given them. They had the true military impatience of coin in their pockets, and had marched at least six miles to find the first place where liquor could be bought. Having never been before in a place so wild and unfrequented, I was glad of their arrival, because I knew that we had made them friends, and to gain still more of their good will, we went to them, where they were carousing in the barn, and added something to our former gift. All that we gave was not much, but it detained them in the barn, either merry or quarrelling, the whole night, and in the morning they went back to their work, with great indignation at the bad qualities of whisky.

We had gained so much the favour of our host that, when we left his house in the morning, he walked by us a great way, and entertained us with conversation both on his own condition, and that of the country. His life seemed to be merely pastoral, except that he differed from some of the ancient Nomades in having a settled dwelling. His wealth consists of one hundred sheep, as many goats,

1. *Prideaux's Connection.* Humphrey Prideaux (1648–1728) was a cleric and oriental scholar whose *Connection* was a scholarly work on the interval between the Old and New Testaments.

twelve milk-cows, and twenty-eight beeves ready for the drover.

From him we first heard of the general dissatisfaction which is now driving the Highlanders into the other hemisphere; and when I asked him whether they would stay at home if they were well treated, he answered with indignation that no man willingly left his native country. Of the farm which he himself occupied, the rent had, in twenty-five years, been advanced from five to twenty pounds, which he found himself so little able to pay that he would be glad to try his fortune in some other place. Yet he owned the reasonableness of raising the Highland rents in a certain degree, and declared himself willing to pay ten pounds for the ground which he had formerly had for five.

Our host having amused us for a time, resigned us to our guides. . . . ☐

DISCUSSION

1. In *The Life of Samuel Johnson,* Boswell's professed objective is to write Johnson's biography so that "he will be seen as he really was," to "delineate him without reserve."

(a) To what extent did he carry out this intent?

(b) What are some of the unpleasant aspects of the picture of Johnson that Boswell presents? What is your reaction to these aspects of Johnson?

(c) What seems to be Boswell's attitude toward Johnson?

(d) Does Boswell succeed in making Johnson come alive for you? Explain.

2. Reread for comparison the parallel passages on Anoch from Johnson's and Boswell's journals.

(a) In what respects are they similar? In what ways are they different?

(b) What differences in the characters of the two narrators emerge from these accounts?

(c) Which account do you prefer? Why?

WRITING

1. Some of the ideas Johnson expounded to Boswell are still being talked about today. Select one or two of these and write a brief essay in which you discuss the extent to which our ideas are similar to or different from those of Johnson's day. Possibilities: the generation gap as discussed in the "On Fathers and Sons" section of the *Life*; "Women's Lib" as presented by Mrs. Knowles, and the validity of Johnson's reactions.

2. Assume you are a modern Boswell and write a description of an imaginary meeting between yourself and some modern figure you admire.

3. The American critic J. Donald Adams has commented on Johnson's *Dictionary:* "Steeped in prejudice and tinged with mulishness as some of the definitions were, they are at least always the product of a sharp and honest mind. It is one of Johnson's great—and one of his most engaging—qualities, that he never indulged in double talk, that he never soft-soaped anyone. . . . Behind this book there is a man." In a brief essay, discuss the applicability of this statement, not only to the *Dictionary,* but to the picture of Johnson that emerges from all the writings by or about him in this section.

READERS' THEATER

1. Prepare and present a dramatized version of Boswell's first meeting with Johnson.

2. Prepare and present an original conversation between Johnson and Boswell dealing with some topic of current interest.

Thomas Gray

1716 / 1771

ELEGY WRITTEN IN A COUNTRY CHURCHYARD

The curfew tolls the knell of parting day,
  The lowing herd wind slowly o'er the lea,
The plowman homeward plods his weary way,
  And leaves the world to darkness and to me.

Now fades the glimmering landscape on the sight,
  And all the air a solemn stillness holds,
Save where the beetle wheels his droning flight,
  And drowsy tinklings lull the distant folds;

Save that from yonder ivy-mantled tower
  The moping owl does to the moon complain
Of such as, wandering near her secret bower,
  Molest her ancient solitary reign.

Beneath those rugged elms, that yew-tree's shade,
  Where heaves the turf in many a moldering heap,
Each in his narrow cell forever laid,
  The rude forefathers of the hamlet sleep.

The breezy call of incense-breathing Morn,
  The swallow twittering from the strawbuilt shed,
The cock's shrill clarion, or the echoing horn,[1]
  No more shall rouse them from their lowly bed.

For them no more the blazing hearth shall burn,
  Or busy housewife ply her evening care;
No children run to lisp their sire's return,
  Or climb his knees the envied kiss to share.

Oft did the harvest to their sickle yield,
  Their furrow oft the stubborn glebe has broke;
How jocund did they drive their team afield!
  How bowed the woods beneath their sturdy
    stroke!

Let not Ambition mock their useful toil,
  Their homely joys, and destiny obscure;
Nor Grandeur hear, with a disdainful smile,
  The short and simple annals of the poor.

The boast of heraldry, the pomp of power,
  And all that beauty, all that wealth e'er gave,
Awaits alike the inevitable hour:
  The paths of glory lead but to the grave.

Nor you, ye proud, impute to these the fault,
  If Memory o'er their tomb no trophies raise,
Where through the long-drawn aisle and fretted vault
  The pealing anthem swells the note of praise.

Can storied urn[2] or animated[3] bust
  Back to its mansion call the fleeting breath?
Can Honor's voice provoke the silent dust,
  Or Flattery soothe the dull cold ear of Death?

Perhaps in this neglected spot is laid
  Some heart once pregnant with celestial fire;
Hands that the rod of empire might have swayed,
  Or waked to ecstasy the living lyre.

But Knowledge to their eyes her ample page
  Rich with the spoils of time did ne'er unroll;
Chill Penury repressed their noble rage,
  And froze the genial current of the soul.

Full many a gem of purest ray serene
  The dark unfathomed caves of ocean bear;
Full many a flower is born to blush unseen,
  And waste its sweetness on the desert air.

1. *horn,* the huntsman's horn.
2. *storied urn,* an urn decorated with pictures that tell a story.
3. *animated,* lifelike.

Some village Hampden[4] that with dauntless breast
The little tyrant of his fields withstood;
Some mute inglorious Milton here may rest,
60 Some Cromwell guiltless of his country's blood.

The applause of listening senates to command,
The threats of pain and ruin to despise,
To scatter plenty o'er a smiling land,
And read their history in a nation's eyes,

65 Their lot forbade; nor circumscribed alone
Their growing virtues, but their crimes confined;
Forbade to wade through slaughter to a throne,
And shut the gates of mercy on mankind,

The struggling pangs of conscious truth to hide,
70 To quench the blushes of ingenuous shame,
Or heap the shrine of Luxury and Pride
With incense kindled at the Muse's flame.

Far from the madding crowd's ignoble strife,
Their sober wishes never learned to stray;
75 Along the cool sequestered vale of life
They kept the noiseless tenor of their way.

Yet ev'n these bones from insult to protect
Some frail memorial still erected nigh,
With uncouth[5] rimes and shapeless sculpture decked,
80 Implores the passing tribute of a sigh.

Their name, their years, spelt by the unlettered Muse,
The place of fame and elegy supply;
And many a holy text around she strews,
That teach the rustic moralist to die.

85 For who, to dumb Forgetfulness a prey,
This pleasing anxious being e'er resigned,
Left the warm precincts of the cheerful day,
Nor cast one longing, lingering look behind?

On some fond breast the parting soul relies,
90 Some pious drops the closing eye requires;
Ev'n from the tomb the voice of Nature cries,
Ev'n in our ashes live their wonted fires.

For thee,[6] who mindful of the unhonored dead
Dost in these lines their artless tale relate;
95 If chance, by lonely Contemplation led,
Some kindred spirit shall inquire thy fate,

Haply some hoary-headed swain may say,
"Oft have we seen him at the peep of dawn
Brushing with hasty steps the dews away
100 To meet the sun upon the upland lawn,

"There at the foot of yonder nodding beech,
That wreathes its old fantastic roots so high,
His listless length at noontide would he stretch,
And pore upon the brook that babbles by.

105 "Hard by yon wood, now smiling as in scorn,
Muttering his wayward fancies he would rove,
Now drooping, woeful wan, like one forlorn,
Or crazed with care, or crossed in hopeless love.

"One morn I missed him on the customed hill,
110 Along the heath, and near his favorite tree;
Another came; nor yet beside the rill,
Nor up the lawn, nor at the wood was he;

"The next with dirges due in sad array
Slow through the church-way path we saw him borne.
115 Approach and read (for thou canst read) the lay,
Graved on the stone beneath yon aged thorn."

THE EPITAPH

Here rests his head upon the lap of Earth
A youth to Fortune and to Fame unknown.
Fair Science frowned not on his humble birth,
120 *And Melancholy marked him for her own.*

Large was his bounty, and his soul sincere,
Heaven did a recompense as largely send;
He gave to Misery all he had, a tear,
He gained from Heaven ('twas all he wished) a friend.

125 *No farther seek his merits to disclose,*
Or draw his frailties from their dread abode.
(There they alike in trembling hope repose),
The bosom of his Father and his God.

4. *Hampden,* John Hampden (1594–1643), member of the Puritan or Roundhead party who spoke out against royal taxes.
5. *uncouth,* strange, odd.
6. *thee,* Gray himself.

ODE ON THE DEATH OF A FAVOURITE CAT, DROWNED IN A TUB OF GOLD FISHES

'Twas on a lofty vase's side,
Where China's gayest art had dyed
  The azure flowers, that blow;
Demurest of the tabby kind,
5 The pensive Selima reclined,
  Gazed on the lake below.

Her conscious tail her joy declared;
The fair round face, the snowy beard,
  The velvet of her paws,
10 Her coat, that with the tortoise vies,
Her ears of jet, and emerald eyes,
  She saw; and purred applause.

Still had she gazed; but 'midst the tide
Two angel forms were seen to glide,
15   The Genii of the stream:
Their scaly armour's Tyrian hue
Thro' richest purple to the view
  Betrayed a golden gleam.

The hapless Nymph with wonder saw:
20 A whisker first and then a claw,
  With many an ardent wish,
She stretched in vain to reach the prize.
What female heart can gold despise?
  What Cat's averse to fish?

25 Presumptuous Maid! with looks intent
Again she stretched, again she bent,
  Nor knew the gulf between.
(Malignant Fate sat by, and smiled)
The slipp'ry verge her feet beguiled,
30   She tumbled headlong in.

Eight times emerging from the flood
She mewed to ev'ry wat'ry God,
  Some speedy aid to send.
No Dolphin came, no Nereid stirred:
35 Nor cruel *Tom*, nor *Susan* heard.
  A Fav'rite has no friend!

From hence, ye Beauties, undeceived,
Know, one false step is ne'er retrieved,
  And be with caution bold.
40 Not all that tempts your wand'ring eyes
And heedless hearts, is lawful prize;
  Nor all, that glisters, gold.

DISCUSSION

1. (a) What words in the first stanza of the Elegy contribute to the air of melancholy that pervades the poem?

(b) How do the second and third stanzas add to this melancholy?

2. The fourth stanza introduces the subject of the poem, the "rude forefathers of the hamlet."

(a) What is the speaker's attitude toward them as contrasted with his attitude toward the great of the world?

(b) To what extent were the rude forefathers' poverty and lack of education a handicap?

(c) To what extent were they a blessing?

3. One critical opinion holds that Gray's poem is "an elegy for Man, or at least for all 'average' and obscure men." Comment on this opinion.

4. If the "rude forefathers of the hamlet" may be said to be the protagonists of the poem, who or what are the antagonists?

5. Reread the poem and list lines and phrases that strike you as most quotable. To what do you attribute this preponderance of quotable material?

6. According to the epitaph which ends the poem, how satisfactory a life did the speaker live?

7. (a) At what points in "Ode on the Death of a Favorite Cat" does Gray turn aside from the cat to point a moral for his female readers?

(b) Comment on the appropriateness of the form and tone to the subject matter of the "Ode."

(c) Compare and contrast Gray's adaptation of a traditional ode with Pope's adaptation of a traditional epic in "The Rape of the Lock."

WRITING

1. Write a free verse poem or prose composition in which you celebrate the virtues of some humble moderns who, like Gray's villagers, would otherwise be overlooked and forgotten.

2. Write a short paper in which you discuss Gray's careful selection of words for their sounds and connotations so that they contribute actively to the theme and mood of his Elegy.

3. Write a brief parody of Gray's Elegy. Suggestions: "The hall-bell clangs the end of history . . ." or "The alarm shrieks the start of blue Monday. . . ." You can probably think of better subjects.

Robert Burns 1759 / 1796

A RED, RED ROSE

O my luve is like a red, red rose
  That's newly sprung in June.
O my luve is like the melodie
  That's sweetly played in tune.

5 As fair art thou, my bonie lass,
  So deep in luve am I,
And I will luve thee still, my dear,
  Till a' the seas gang dry.

Till a' the seas gang dry, my dear,
10 And the rocks melt wi' the sun!
And I will luve thee still, my dear,
  While the sands o' life shall run.

And fare thee weel, my only luve,
  And fare thee weel a while!
15 And I will come again, my luve,
  Tho' it were ten thousand mile!

TO A MOUSE

on turning her up in her nest
with the plow, November, 1785

WEE, sleekit,° cow'rin', tim'rous beastie, — sleek
O what a panic's in thy breastie!
Thou need na start awa sae hasty,
    Wi' bickering brattle!° — short race
5 I wad be laith to rin an' chase thee
    Wi' murd'ring pattle!° — plow-spade

I'm truly sorry man's dominion
Has broken Nature's social union,
An' justifies that ill opinion
10 Which makes thee startle
At me, thy poor earth-born companion,
    An' fellow-mortal!

I doubt na, whiles,° but thou may thieve; — sometimes
What then? poor beastie, thou maun live!
15 A daimen-icker in a thrave[1]
    'S a sma' request:
I'll get a blessin' wi' the lave,° — the rest
    And never miss 't!

Thy wee bit housie, too, in ruin!
20 Its silly wa's° the win's are strewin'! — simple walls
An' naething, now, to big° a new ane, — build
    O' foggage° green! — coarse grass
An' bleak December's win's ensuin',
    Baith snell° an' keen! — biting

25 Thou saw the fields laid bare and waste.
An' weary winter comin' fast,
An' cozie here, beneath the blast,
    Thou thought to dwell,
Till crash! the cruel coulter° past — plowshare
30 Out-thro' thy cell.

That wee bit heap o' leaves an' stibble
Has cost thee mony a weary nibble!
Now thou's turn'd out, for a' thy trouble,
    But house or hald,° — abode
35 To thole the winter's sleety dribble,
    An' cranreuch° cauld! — hoarfrost

But, Mousie, thou art no thy lane,° — alone
In proving foresight may be vain:
The best laid schemes o' mice an' men
40 Gang aft a-gley,° — go awry
An' lea'e us nought but grief an' pain
    For promis'd joy.

Still thou art blest compar'd wi' me!
The present only toucheth thee:
45 But oh! I backward cast my e'e
    On prospects drear!
An' forward tho' I canna see,
    I guess an' fear!

1. *A daimen-icker in a thrave,* an occasional ear or head of grain in a shock.

TO A LOUSE

on seeing one on a lady's bonnet at church

1

HA! wh'are ye gaun, ye crowlin' ferlie!° — crawling wonder
Your impudence protects you sairly;° — greatly
I canna say but ye strunt° rarely, — strut
Owre gauze and lace;
5 Tho' faith! I fear ye dine but sparely
On sic a place.

2

Ye ugly, creepin', blastit wonner,
Detested, shunned by saunt an' sinner!
How dare ye set your fit° upon her, — foot
10 Sae fine a lady?
Gae somewhere else, and seek your dinner
On some poor body.

3

Swith! in some beggar's haffet squattle;[1]
There ye may creep, and sprawl, and sprattle° — struggle
15 Wi' ither kindred jumping cattle,
In shoals and nations;
Where horn nor bane° ne'er dare unsettle — comb nor poison
Your thick plantations.

4

Now haud° ye there, ye're out o' sight, — hold
20 Below the fatt'rels,° snug an' tight; — ribbon-ends
Na, faith ye yet! ye'll no be right
Till ye've got on it,
The very tapmost tow'ring height
O' Miss's bonnet.

5

25 My sooth! right bauld ye set your nose out,
As plump and gray as onie grozet;° — gooseberry
O for some rank mercurial rozet,° — rosin
Or fell red smeddum!° — dust
I'd gie you sic a hearty doze o't,
30 Wad dress your droddum![2]

6

I wad na been surprised to spy
You on an auld wife's flannen toy;° — flannel cap
Or aiblins° some bit duddie° boy, — perhaps / ragged
On 's wyliecoat;° — undervest
35 But Miss's fine Lunardi![3] fie,
How daur ye do't?

7

O Jenny, dinna toss your head,
An' set your beauties a' abread!
Ye little ken what cursèd speed
40 The blastie's makin'!
Thae winks and finger-ends, I dread,
Are notice takin'!

8

O wad some Power the giftie gie us
To see oursels as others see us!
45 It wad frae mony a blunder free us,
And foolish notion:
What airs in dress an' gait wad lea'e us,
And ev'n devotion!

---

1. *Swith! . . squattle.* Quick! on some beggar's temple sprawl.

2. *Wad dress your droddum,* would fix you proper.
3. *Lunardi,* balloon bonnet, named after a famous balloonist.

EPITAPHS AND EPIGRAMS

EPITAPH ON A SCHOOLMASTER

HERE lie Willie Michie's banes;
  O Satan, when ye tak him,
Gie him the schoolin' of your weans,° (children)
  For clever deils° he'll mak them! (devils)

ON THE DEATH OF A LAP-DOG *named Echo*

In wood and wild, ye warbling throng,
  Your heavy loss deplore;
Now half-extinct your powers of song,
  Sweet Echo is no more.

5 Ye jarring, screeching things around,
  Scream your discordant joys;
Now half your din of tuneless sound
  With Echo silent lies.

POVERTY

IN politics if thou wouldst mix,
  And mean thy fortunes be;
Bear this in mind,—be deaf and blind,
  Let great folks hear and see.

THE BOOK-WORMS

THROUGH and through the inspired leaves,
  Ye maggots, make your windings;
But, oh! respect his lordship's taste,
  And spare his golden bindings.

IMPROMPTU

How daur ye ca' me howlet-face,° (owl-face)
  Ye ugly, glowering spectre?
My face was but the keekin' glass,° (mirror)
  An' there ye saw your picture.

TO AN ARTIST

DEAR —, I'll gie ye some advice
  You'll tak it no uncivil:
You shouldna paint at angels mair,
  But try and paint the devil.
5 To paint an angel's kittle° wark, (ticklish)
  Wi' auld Nick there's less danger;
You'll easy draw a weel-kent° face, (well-known)
  But no sae weel a stranger.

THE SELKIRK GRACE

SOME hae meat, and canna eat,
  And some was eat that want it,
But we hae meat and we can eat,
  And sae the Lord be thankit.

ON HEARING THAT THERE WAS FALSEHOOD IN THE REV. DR. BABINGTON'S VERY LOOKS

THAT there is falsehood in his looks
  I must and will deny;
They say their master is a knave—
  And sure they do not lie.

EXTEMPORE *on passing a lady's carriage*

IF you rattle along like your mistress's tongue,
  Your speed will out-rival the dart:
But, a fly for your load, you'll break down on the
    road,
  If your stuff be as rotten's her heart.

EPITAPH ON A HENPECKED COUNTRY SQUIRE

As father Adam first was fooled
  (A case that's still too common),
Here lies a man a woman ruled,
  —The Devil ruled the woman.

ON SCARING SOME WATER FOWL

in Loch-Turit, a wild scene
among the hills of Ochtertyre

WHY, ye tenants of the lake,
For me your wat'ry haunt forsake?
Tell me, fellow-creatures, why
At my presence thus you fly?
5 Why disturb your social joys,
Parent, filial, kindred ties?—
Common friend to you and me,
Nature's gifts to all are free:
Peaceful keep your dimpling wave,
10 Busy feed, or wanton lave;
Or, beneath the sheltering rock,
Bide the surging billow's shock.
Conscious, blushing for our race,
Soon, too soon, your fears I trace.
15 Man, your proud, usurping foe,
Would be lord of all below;
Plumes himself in Freedom's pride,
Tyrant stern to all beside.
The eagle, from the cliffy brow,
20 Marking you his prey below,
In his breast no pity dwells,
Strong necessity compels.
But man, to whom alone is giv'n
A ray direct from pitying Heav'n,
25 Glories in his heart humane—
And creatures for his pleasure slain.
In these savage, liquid plains,
Only known to wand'ring swains,
Where the mossy riv'let strays,
30 Far from human haunts and ways;
All on Nature you depend,
And life's poor season peaceful spend.
Or, if man's superior might
Dare invade your native right,
35 On the lofty ether borne,
Man with all his pow'rs you scorn;
Swiftly seek, on clanging wings,
Other lakes and other springs;
And the foe you cannot brave,
40 Scorn at least to be his slave.

DISCUSSION

1. (a) What has occasioned the writing of "A Red, Red Rose"?
(b) How old do the lovers appear to be?
(c) How serious is the speaker? Explain.
2. (a) What bit of philosophy is contained in the second stanza of "To a Mouse"? in the seventh? in the eighth?
(b) What is gained by having such philosophical thoughts initiated by the plight of the mouse?
3. (a) Contrast "To a Louse" with "To a Mouse" with regard to situation, tone of speaker, and mood of poem.
(b) Which of the two poems comes across to you more strongly? Why?
4. About whom is "To a Louse" really written—the louse? Jenny? the speaker? all of these? something more than all of these?
5. (a) In what respects is "On Scaring Some Water Fowl" as topical today as it was when Burns wrote it?
(b) With what other Burns poem you have read may it best be compared?
6. (a) Which of the "Epigrams and Epitaphs" are *not* satirical in intent?
(b) Which are most satirical? Explain.
(c) Which are most humorous?
(d) Are you conscious of any difference between those written in Scots dialect and those written in English? Explain.

WRITING

1. Recast the ideas conveyed in one (or more) of Burns' poems in prose form. For instance, "To a Mouse" might be retold as a fable, "To a Louse" as a gossip item for a local newspaper, "A Red, Red Rose" as a short love story.
2. Develop a brief essay in which you discuss the ways in which Burns' life as a poor farmer enriched his poetry.
3. Although Burns is the most famous of the Scots poets, he is by no means the only one. Investigate and write a report on some other Scots poets, ancient or modern.
4. Discuss the ways in which Burns' songs and poems continue the tradition of the medieval lyric and ballad.

William Blake 1757 / 1827

From SONGS OF INNOCENCE

INTRODUCTION

Piping down the valleys wild,
Piping songs of pleasant glee
On a cloud I saw a child,
And he laughing said to me:

5 Pipe a song about a Lamb!
So I piped with merry cheer.
Piper pipe that song again—
So I piped, he wept to hear.

Drop thy pipe thy happy pipe
10 Sing thy songs of happy cheer.
So I sung the same again
While he wept with joy to hear.

Piper sit thee down and write
In a book that all may read—
15 So he vanished from my sight,
And I plucked a hollow reed,

And I made a rural pen,
And I stained the water clear,
And I wrote my happy songs,
20 Every child may joy to hear.

THE LAMB

Little Lamb, who made thee?
Dost thou know who made thee?
Gave thee life, & bid thee feed
By the stream & o'er the mead;
5 Gave thee clothing of delight,
Softest clothing, wooly, bright;
Gave thee such a tender voice,
Making all the vales rejoice?
Little Lamb, who made thee?
10 Dost thou know who made thee?

Little Lamb, I'll tell thee,
Little Lamb, I'll tell thee:
He is callèd by thy name,
For he calls himself a Lamb.
15 He is meek, & he is mild;
He became a little child.
I a child, & thou a lamb,
We are callèd by his name.
Little Lamb, God bless thee!
20 Little Lamb, God bless thee!

OF LITERARY INTEREST

Blake—the first multimedia artist?

Songs of Innocence first appeared in 1789. Blake completed Songs of Experience five years later, and combined the two sets of poems into a single volume which he called *Songs of Innocence and Experience: Shewing the Two Contrary States of the Human Soul.* Although not all the Songs of Innocence have counterparts in Songs of Experience, Blake obviously intended that many of the poems be matched.

Not only did Blake compose the poems, but he prepared his own illustrative engravings by a process he himself developed, inscribed the poems in his own handwriting instead of resorting to movable type, reproduced each engraved page by hand, and either himself tinted, or had his wife tint, each illustration. The result was something comparable to the illuminated manuscripts of medieval times.

THE CHIMNEY SWEEPER

When my mother died I was very young,
And my father sold me while yet my tongue
Could scarcely cry "'weep! 'weep! 'weep! 'weep!"
So your chimneys I sweep, & in soot I sleep.

5 There's little Tom Dacre, who cried when his head,
That curled like a lamb's back, was shav'd: so I said
"Hush, Tom! never mind it, for when your head's bare
You know that the soot cannot spoil your white hair."

And so he was quiet, & that very night,
10 As Tom was a-sleeping, he had such a sight!
That thousands of sweepers, Dick, Joe, Ned, & Jack,
Were all of them locked up in coffins of black.

And by came an Angel who had a bright key,
And he opened the coffins & set them all free;
15 Then down a green plain leaping, laughing, they run,
And wash in a river, and shine in the Sun.

Then naked & white, all their bags left behind,
They rise upon clouds and sport in the wind;
And the Angel told Tom, if he'd be a good boy,
20 He'd have God for his father, & never want joy.

And so Tom awoke; and we rose in the dark,
And got with our bags & our brushes to work.
Tho' the morning was cold, Tom was happy & warm;
So if all do their duty they need not fear harm.

THE LITTLE BOY LOST

"Father! father! where are you going?
O do not walk so fast.
Speak, father, speak to your little boy,
Or else I shall be lost."

5 The night was dark, no father was there;
The child was wet with dew;
The mire was deep, & the child did weep,
And away the vapour flew.

THE LITTLE BOY FOUND

The little boy lost in the lonely fen,
Led by the wand'ring light,
Began to cry; but God, ever nigh,
Appeared like his father in white.

5 He kissed the child & by the hand led
And to his mother brought,
Who in sorrow pale, thro' the lonely dale,
Her little boy weeping sought.

THE DIVINE IMAGE

To Mercy, Pity, Peace, and Love
All pray in their distress;
And to these virtues of delight
Return their thankfulness.

5 For Mercy, Pity, Peace, and Love
Is God, our father dear,
And Mercy, Pity, Peace, and Love
Is Man, his child and care.

For Mercy has a human heart,
10 Pity a human face,
And Love, the human form divine,
And Peace, the human dress.

Then every man, of every clime,
That prays in his distress,
15 Prays to the human form divine,
Love, Mercy, Pity, Peace.

And all must love the human form,
In heathen, turk, or jew;
Where Mercy, Love, & Pity dwell
20 There God is dwelling too.

HOLY THURSDAY

'Twas on a Holy Thursday,[1] their innocent faces clean,
The children walking two & two, in red & blue & green,
Grey-headed beadles walked before, with wands as white as snow,
Till into the high dome of Paul's they like Thames' waters flow.

5 O what a multitude they seemed, these flowers of London town!
Seated in companies they sit with radiance all their own.
The hum of multitudes was there, but multitudes of lambs,
Thousands of little boys & girls raising their innocent hands.

Now like a mighty wind they raise to heaven the voice of song,
10 Or like harmonious thunderings the seats of Heaven among.
Beneath them sit the agèd men, wise guardians of the poor;
Then cherish pity, lest you drive an angel from your door.

1. *Holy Thursday*, Ascension Day, the 40th day after Easter, when children in orphanages were brought to St. Paul's Cathedral to give thanks for the charity of God, of which human charity is supposedly a reflection.

INFANT JOY

I have no name
I am but two days old.—
What shall I call thee?
I happy am
5 Joy is my name,—
Sweet joy befall thee!

Pretty joy!
Sweet joy but two days old.
Sweet joy I call thee:
10 Thou dost smile.
I sing the while
Sweet joy befall thee.

NURSE'S SONG

When the voices of children are heard on the green
And laughing is heard on the hill,
My heart is at rest within my breast
And everything else is still.

5 "Then come home, my children, the sun is gone down
And the dews of night arise;
Come, come, leave off play, and let us away
Till the morning appears in the skies."

"No, no, let us play, for it is yet day
10 And we cannot go to sleep;
Besides, in the sky the little birds fly
And the hills are all covered with sheep."

"Well, well, go & play till the light fades away
And then go home to bed."
15 The little ones leaped & shouted & laughed
And all the hills ecchoed.

OF HUMAN INTEREST

Blake's obscurities

Few people of his own day understood or appreciated Blake's writings or his drawings. In a letter to a Dr. Trusler whose writings he was asked to illustrate and who objected to the obscurity of his designs, he wrote: "You say that I want somebody to Elucidate my Ideas. What is Grand is necessarily obscure to Weak men. That which can be made Explicit to the Idiot is not worthy my care. The wisest of the Ancients considered what is not too Explicit as the fittest for Instruction, because it rouzes the faculties to act. I name Moses, Solomon, Esop, Homer, Plato."

But in the same letter he also says: "But I am happy to find a Great Majority of Fellow Mortals who can Elucidate My Visions, & Particularly they have been elucidated by Children, who have taken a greater delight in contemplating my Pictures than I even hoped. Neither Youth nor Childhood is Folly or Incapacity."

From SONGS OF EXPERIENCE

INTRODUCTION

Hear the voice of the Bard!
Who Present, Past, and Future sees
Whose ears have heard
The Holy Word,
5 That walk'd among the ancient trees.

Calling the lapsed Soul[1]
And weeping in the evening dew:
That might controll
The starry pole:
10 And fallen fallen light renew!

O Earth O Earth return!
Arise from out the dewy grass:
Night is worn,
And the morn
15 Rises from the slumberous mass.

Turn away no more:
Why wilt thou turn away
The starry floor
The wat'ry shore
20 Is giv'n thee till the break of day.

---

1. *lapsed Soul,* soul fallen from grace after the fall of Adam and Eve.

NURSE'S SONG

When the voices of children are heard on the green
And whisp'rings are in the dale,
The days of my youth rise fresh in my mind,
My face turns green and pale.

5 Then come home, my children, the sun is gone down,
And the dews of night arise;
Your spring & your day are wasted in play,
And your winter and night in disguise.

THE TYGER

Tyger! Tyger! burning bright
In the forests of the night,
What immortal hand or eye
Could frame thy fearful symmetry?

5 In what distant deeps or skies
Burnt the fire of thine eyes?
On what wings dare he aspire?
What the hand dare sieze the fire?

And what shoulder, & what art,
10 Could twist the sinews of thy heart?
And when thy heart began to beat,
What dread hand? & what dread feet?

What the hammer? what the chain?
In what furnace was thy brain?
15 What the anvil? what dread grasp
Dare its deadly terrors clasp?

When the stars threw down their spears,
And watered heaven with their tears,
Did he smile his work to see?
20 Did he who made the Lamb make thee?

Tyger! Tyger! burning bright
In the forests of the night,
What immortal hand or eye
Dare frame thy fearful symmetry?

FROM BLAKE'S ORIGINAL ENGRAVING

THE CHIMNEY SWEEPER

A little black thing among the snow,
Crying "'weep! 'weep!" in notes of woe!
"Where are thy father & mother? say?"
"They are both gone up to the church to pray.

5 "Because I was happy upon the heath,
And smiled among the winter's snow,
They clothed me in the clothes of death,
And taught me to sing the notes of woe.

"And because I am happy & dance & sing,
10 They think they have done me no injury,
And are gone to praise God & his Priest & King,
Who make up a heaven of our misery."

A LITTLE BOY LOST

"Nought loves another as itself,
Nor venerates another so,
Nor is it possible to Thought
A greater than itself to know:

5 "And Father, how can I love you
Or any of my brothers more?
I love you like the little bird
That picks up crumbs around the door."

The Priest sat by and heard the child,
10 In trembling zeal he siezed his hair:
He led him by his little coat,
And all admired the Priestly care.

And standing on the altar high,
"Lo! what a fiend is here!" said he,
15 "One who sets reason up for judge
Of our most holy Mystery."

The weeping child could not be heard,
The weeping parents wept in vain;
They stripped him to his little shirt,
20 And bound him in an iron chain;

And burned him in a holy place,
Where many had been burned before:
The weeping parents wept in vain.
Are such things done on Albion's shore?

THE HUMAN ABSTRACT

Pity would be no more
If we did not make somebody Poor;
And Mercy no more could be
If all were as happy as we.

5 And mutual fear brings peace,
Till the selfish loves increase:
Then Cruelty knits a snare,
And spreads his baits with care.

He sits down with holy fears,
10 And waters the ground with tears;
Then Humility takes its root
Underneath his foot.

Soon spreads the dismal shade
Of Mystery over his head;
15 And the Catterpiller and Fly
Feed on the Mystery.

And it bears the fruit of Deceit,
Ruddy and sweet to eat;
And the Raven his nest has made
20 In its thickest shade.

The Gods of the earth and sea
Sought thro' Nature to find this Tree;
But their search was all in vain:
There grows one in the Human Brain.

HOLY THURSDAY

Is this a holy thing to see
In a rich and fruitful land,
Babes reduced to misery,
Fed with cold and usurous hand?

Is that trembling cry a song?
Can it be a song of joy?
And so many children poor?
It is a land of poverty!

And their sun does never shine,
And their fields are bleak & bare,
And their ways are filled with thorns:
It is eternal winter there.

For where-e'er the sun does shine,
And where-e'er the rain does fall,
Babe can never hunger there,
Nor poverty the mind appall.

LONDON

I wander thro' each chartered street,
Near where the chartered Thames does flow,
And mark in every face I meet
Marks of weakness, marks of woe.

In every cry of every Man,
In every Infant's cry of fear,
In every voice, in every ban,
The mind-forged manacles I hear.

How the Chimney-sweeper's cry
Every black'ning Church appalls;
And the hapless Soldier's sigh
Runs in blood down Palace walls.

But most thro' midnight streets I hear
How the youthful Harlot's curse
Blasts the new born Infant's tear,
And blights with plagues the Marriage hearse.

THE FLY

Little Fly,
Thy summer's play
My thoughtless hand
Has brushed away.

Am not I
A fly like thee?
Or art not thou
A man like me?

For I dance,
And drink, & sing,
Till some blind hand
Shall brush my wing.

If thought is life
And strength & breath,
And the want
Of thought is death;

Then am I
A happy fly,
If I live
Or if I die.

THE CLOD AND THE PEBBLE

"Love seeketh not Itself to please,
Nor for itself hath any care,
But for another gives its ease,
And builds a Heaven in Hell's despair."

So sung a little Clod of Clay
Trodden with the cattle's feet,
But a Pebble of the brook
Warbled out these metres meet:

"Love seeketh only Self to please,
To bind another to Its delight,
Joys in another's loss of ease,
And builds a Hell in Heaven's despite."

INFANT SORROW

My mother groaned! my father wept,
Into the dangerous world I leapt:
Helpless, naked, piping loud:
Like a fiend hid in a cloud.

5 Struggling in my father's hands:
Striving against my swaddling bands:
Bound and weary I thought best
To sulk upon my mother's breast.

THE SICK ROSE

O rose, thou art sick!
The invisible worm
That flies in the night,
In the howling storm,

5 Has found out thy bed
Of crimson joy,
And his dark secret love
Does thy life destroy.

A DIVINE IMAGE

Cruelty has a Human Heart,
And Jealousy a Human Face;
Terror the Human Form Divine,
And Secrecy the Human Dress.

5 The Human Dress is forged Iron,
The Human Form a fiery Forge,
The Human Face a Furnace sealed,
The Human Heart its hungry Gorge.

A POISON TREE

I was angry with my friend:
I told my wrath, my wrath did end.
I was angry with my foe:
I told it not, my wrath did grow.

5 And I watered it in fears,
Night & morning with my tears;
And I sunned it with smiles,
And with soft deceitful wiles.

And it grew both day and night,
10 Till it bore an apple bright;
And my foe beheld it shine,
And he knew that it was mine,

And into my garden stole
When the night had veiled the pole:
15 In the morning glad I see
My foe outstretched beneath the tree.

FROM BLAKE'S ORIGINAL ENGRAVING

PROVERBS OF HELL

From The Marriage of Heaven and Hell

In seed time learn, in harvest teach, in winter enjoy.
Drive your cart and your plow over the bones of the dead.
The road of excess leads to the palace of wisdom.
Prudence is a rich, ugly old maid courted by Incapacity.
5 The cut worm forgives the plow.
A fool sees not the same tree that a wise man sees.
He whose face gives no light, shall never become a star.
Eternity is in love with the productions of time.
All wholesome food is caught without a net or a trap.
10 No bird soars too high, if he soars with his own wings.
If the fool would persist in his folly he would become wise.
Shame is pride's cloak.
Excess of sorrow laughs. Excess of joy weeps.
The roaring of lions, the howling of wolves, the raging of the stormy sea, and the destructive sword, are portions of eternity, too great for the eye of man.
15 Let man wear the fell of the lion, woman the fleece of the sheep.
The bird a nest, the spider a web, man friendship.
What is now proved was once only imagined.
Every thing possible to be believed is an image of truth.
The fox provides for himself, but God provides for the lion.
20 Think in the morning. Act in the noon. Eat in the evening. Sleep in the night.
The tygers of wrath are wiser than the horses of instruction.
Expect poison from the standing water.
You never know what is enough unless you know what is more than enough.
The weak in courage is strong in cunning.
25 Damn braces. Bless relaxes.
The crow wished every thing was black, the owl that every thing was white.
Improvement makes strait roads; but the crooked roads without improvement are roads of Genius.
Truth can never be told so as to be understood, and not be believed.

OF LITERARY INTEREST

Blake's ideas

There is no use denying the difficulties of Blake's poetry—though they should no longer keep anyone from discovering its exuberant beauty. All the tangled ramifications of Blake's thought spring from a single idea . . . that man, born free, is everywhere in chains. But this is only one aspect of Blake's multidimensioned view of human experience—of mankind once whole and happy, now fallen into discord and tyranny, from which it must be rescued by some revolutionary or apocalyptic upheaval. In theological terms, this is the familiar story of man's fall from Eden into a world of sin—which Blake, a dissenting Protestant, saw also in ecclesiastical terms, as the negation of Christ's "Everlasting Gospel" by the dogmas of the church. In intellectual terms, it is the decline from the wisdom of the ancients to the dead logic of Locke, the dead science of Newton; in artistic terms, from the sublime example of the Bible to the "stolen and perverted" tradition of the classics. In society, it is the change from universal brotherhood to the inequalities of monarchy; in economics, from the primitive state in which every man was an "earth-owner" to the present divisions of rich and poor; in technology, from the craftsmanship of the guild system to the factory methods of capitalism. Fundamentally, it is an inner or psychological fall, from the unself-conscious integrity of "Infant Joy" with its innocent sensuality to the self-tormenting self-divisions of adulthood and the battle of the sexes.

Blake's insight into the evils of his time was extraordinary in its scope; his dedication to the struggle against them was heroic. But as with all prophets, the times seemed to belie his vision, and he remained without honor in his country for many years after his death.

From "The Framing of His Fearful Symmetry" by Aileen Ward as taken from *Book Week* (January 23, 1966). Used by permission of the *Chicago Tribune*.

DISCUSSION

1. (a) In the Introduction to *Songs of Innocence,* the speaker is both piper and poet. In the Introduction to *Songs of Experience,* there is no identifiable speaker, but the reader is instructed to listen to the voice of the bard, who is also a prophet. How is each an appropriate figure for the group of poems he introduces?

(b) In the Introduction to *Innocence,* the child directs the poet; in the Introduction to *Experience,* the Holy Word calls the lapsed soul. How is each an appropriate figure for his subject matter?

(c) The setting of the Introduction to *Innocence* is daytime; that in the Introduction to *Experience* ranges from evening to daybreak. What do these settings connote?

(d) The Introduction to *Experience* contains indications, other than the setting, that the lapsed soul is not entirely lost, that the situation may be reversed. What are some of these indications?

2. "The Lamb" and "The Tyger" are also matched poems.

(a) How is each connected with the Introduction to its category?

(b) How are these two matched poems related to each other by content?

(c) Many theories have been advanced as to what the lamb and the tyger symbolize. What do they mean to you?

3. The matched "Chimney Sweeper" poems differ vastly in tone.

(a) How do their last stanzas contrast?

(b) Which is the more powerful poem? Why?

4. (a) Which of the two *Experience* poems, "A Divine Image" or "The Human Abstract," is a better contrast to "The Divine Image" in *Innocence?* Explain.

(b) "A Divine Image" is the last poem in *Experience.* Do you agree with its placement there? Explain.

5. (a) What effect does Blake gain through the contrasting views of the children in the matched "Holy Thursday" poems?

(b) When these poems are considered in conjunction with the matched "Chimney Sweeper" poems and "London" (*Experience*), what do they reveal about London in Blake's day?

6. Consider the matched "Nurse's Song" poems. Do both have the same speaker, or are two different speakers involved? Explain.

7. (a) What differences are there between the state of the infant in stanzas 1 and 2 of "Infant Sorrow"?

(b) Are there any such differences in "Infant Joy"?

(c) Do these matched poems represent the joyful and sorrowful infant, or the infancy of joy and sorrow? Explain.

8. "Little Boy Lost" and "Little Boy Found" (*Innocence*) may be read at several different levels. Give at least two plausible interpretations of them.

9. (a) Account for the placement of the following poems under *Experience:* "The Sick Rose," "The Fly," "The Clod and the Pebble," "A Poison Tree."

(b) Which poem do you find most impressive? Why?

10. If, as Blake claims, the "Proverbs of Hell" do "show the nature of Infernal wisdom," what *is* the nature of that wisdom?

WRITING

1. Write an overall comparison of *Songs of Innocence* and *Songs of Experience,* focusing on any one of the following: tone, major symbols, or verse forms and rhythm—or another area of focus approved by your teacher.

2. Select any of the "Proverbs of Hell" and write a composition illustrating it. If you wish, your composition may take the form of a fable or illustrative anecdote.

3. Write a paper discussing William Blake as a social critic, or as a humanitarian.

READERS' THEATER

1. Prepare the matched poems in *Songs of Innocence and of Experience* for dramatic reading in class. Be careful to select voices appropriate to each poem.

2. For a more ambitious undertaking, present a "Blake Poetry Festival," in which one student serves as Blake, introducing other students who read selected poems, perhaps with a musical background. Conclude the program with renditions of "Memo" and "Lullaby for William Blake" on the following page.

SEE ALSO THE ARTICLE "WHAT DID BLAKE MEAN BY INNOCENCE AND EXPERIENCE?" BEGINNING ON PAGE 335.

EXTENSIONS

Many modern poets have paid tribute to William Blake. Here are two examples.

MEMO

by Michael Horovitz

(from Wm Blake
to sundry psychedelinquent whizz kids
assuming his name in vain):

Stop bleating
5 about the bush
little lambs

Get wean'd
Or get stufft

(in some body
10 else's pram—

From *Children of Albion,* published by Penguin Books Ltd. Reprinted by permission of the author.

LULLABY FOR WILLIAM BLAKE

by Adrian Mitchell

Blakehead, babyhead,
Your head is full of light.
You sucked the sun like a gobstopper.
Blakehead, babyhead,
5 High as a satellite on sunflower seeds,
First man-powered man to fly the Atlantic,
Inventor of the poem which kills itself,
The poem which gives birth to itself,
The human form, jazz, Jerusalem
10 And other luminous, luminous galaxies.
You out-spat your enemies.
You irradiated your friends.
Always naked, you shaven, shaking tyger-lamb,
Moon-man, moon-clown, moon-singer, moon-drinker,
15 You never killed anyone.
Blakehead, babyhead,
Accept this mug of crude red wine—
I love you.

From *Out Loud,* published by Cape Goliard, distributed in America by Grossman Publishers, Inc. Reprinted by permission of Jonathan Cape Ltd.

"THE RANELAGH ROTUNDA" BY ANTONIO CANALE (CANALETTO). THE ROTUNDA WAS BUILT FOR CONCERTS AND FESTIVITIES BY THE EARL OF RANELAGH. ITS OPULENCE FITTED THE LIFE-STYLE OF AN EIGHTEENTH-CENTURY LORD. REPRODUCED BY COURTESY OF THE TRUSTEES, THE NATIONAL GALLERY, LONDON.

BACKGROUND

The Eighteenth Century

WHILE it was partly a reaction against the social and political chaos of the preceding century, the passion for order that characterized the first half of the eighteenth century was mainly the outgrowth of a new enlightenment in science (Newton) and in philosophy (Locke) which revived the old belief that the natural laws of the universe were discoverable and could be used by men for the better understanding and regulation of their lives. On the whole, the Augustan Age gives the impression of assured elegance and refinement, decorous social behavior, and propriety, grace, and a certain rigidity in the arts. But beneath the puffery of wigs and beribboned silks, beneath the restrained and witty conversation there remained a very human zest for living—at times even a touch of boorishness. There was also a pronounced uneasiness about the supposedly settled state of things.

This subsurface instability is evident in the contrasts of the age. While the beaux and belles were carried in their coaches or brocaded sedan chairs for an evening's entertainment, the poor lived with filth and stench and wondered what they would eat next day. The contrasts extended to the lofty figures of the age as well. The portrait of Dr. Johnson which comes to us, both through his own writings and the reports of Boswell and others, indicates that this great man of letters who had such a sure touch and such apparently set opinions was actually tortured by deep personal struggles. The satire of Dean Swift betrays distrust in reason, human nature, and social progress. Even the lighter satire of Pope and Addison hints at some misgivings about the settled nature of things and the ideals of reasonable human behavior.

There was an energetic restlessness in the age which pushed at established limits. The frontiers of the British empire were extended deeper into America, Africa, and Asia. London was growing into an ever greater urban center of trade, its creative and commercial life focusing on the smoky din of its coffee houses where merchants, lawyers, writers, brokers, and men of affairs, as well as the "pretty fellows" of fashion, gathered to bargain, argue, swear (with restraint, of course), laugh, gossip, and read the latest poem, pamphlet, or journal.

The eighteenth century was also a time of earnest party politics and shifting centers of political power. During the early years of the century the middle class, which had already begun to merge with the landed gentry through intermarriage and common concerns for wealth and property, moved into a position of political dominance. Representative of this enlarged and newly powerful group was the Whig party which gained great power in Parliament. When Queen Anne, the last of the Stuart monarchs, died without an heir in 1714, the Whigs threw the Tory or conservative party out of office and granted the royal succession to Anne's cousins from the small German kingdom of Hanover.

The first kings of the House of Hanover—George I (1714–1727) and George II (1727–1760)—were, contrary to common belief, competent if limited rulers, but their power rested to a large extent in the hands of their cabinet ministers, Townshend, Walpole, and the two Pitts, who were masterful wielders of political influence and effective in keeping Parliament in line. When George III came to the throne in 1760 he tried unsuccessfully to reëstablish the Tory party and to loosen Parliamentary curbs on monarchial power. His obstinacy in asserting himself over Parliament and in insisting on Parliament's power over the American colonies caused a long period of political instability in England and a prolonged war in America. By 1788 George III had already begun to show signs of progressive blindness and madness, and for the last two decades of his reign his life was enshrouded in the darkness of insanity.

By the end of the eighteenth century England had already suffered the first major loss to her colonial empire; war with America had drawn her into war with France; the industrial revolution which was to blacken Britain's skies had already begun; and the truths which had seemed so self-evident at the beginning of the century were being questioned by those with a new vision of man's role in the world. □

BOSWELL AS BIOGRAPHER

by James L. Clifford

BOSWELL'S *Life of Johnson* has been universally acknowledged as one of the great books of the Western world. Yet only in the last half century have we had any clear idea of the nature of Boswell's achievement, or of the way in which he worked. Generally accepted for most of the nineteenth century was Macaulay's theory that the *Life* was an accidental masterpiece, produced by a fool who happened to have a perfect subject. No one ever thought of him as a major creative artist.

In the 1920's, following the fantastic discovery of a portion of Boswell's archives at Malahide Castle outside Dublin, and the subsequent further discoveries there and in Scotland, the emphasis gradually began to change. For one thing, Boswell's reputation as a revealing diarist steadily mounted. His London journal, discovered at Fettercairn House in Scotland in 1930, but not published until twenty years later, became a best seller and was widely hailed as one of the most fascinating autobiographical documents in all literature.

In addition to changing Boswell's reputation as a

creative writer, the new discoveries provide extensive evidence concerning Boswell's method of recording conversations, the question of basic accuracy, and his particular technique in combining all his diverse material into a readable biography.

Boswell and Johnson

When Boswell met Samuel Johnson in May 1763, the pensioned lexicographer and essayist was thirty years his senior. Inevitably the relationship was that of a youthful admirer to an eccentric middle-aged celebrity. But it soon became more than that, for the youthful Scot, for all his levity and rakish propensities, had a serious side. This Johnson soon found out, as he grew to respect the keen intelligence behind Boswell's gay exterior. Through Boswell's revealing accounts it is fascinating to watch the development of their close friendship.

It is not certain when Boswell first considered writing the life of Johnson. The earliest indication comes in an entry in his journal for October 12, 1780. But it was not until after Johnson's death in December 1784 that Boswell began seriously to consider the actual writing of the biography. Even then he was slow in starting. Despite the solicitation of his publisher, who was eager to have him provide at once a rival volume to the numerous journalistic lives which were beginning to appear, he refused to be hurried. Nevertheless, he was eager to give the public a taste of what was coming. The obvious answer was to bring out a version of the journal he had kept during the tour to the Hebrides in 1773, the longest single period during which he had been in close contact with Johnson. The volume appeared in the early fall of 1785. It was an immediate sensation, stirring up intense controversy, largely on ethical grounds concerned with his revelations of Johnson's casual conversations.

Happily, the attacks did not turn Boswell from his main purpose, though they may have induced him to be a little more careful when including material about persons who were extremely sensitive to publicity. But he was now certain of just what he wanted to do, and in a leisurely fashion he set about his task.

Boswell interviewed many of Johnson's old friends; he sent a special questionnaire to Edmund Hector, Johnson's old schoolmate, with blanks left for the answers. He gathered all the letters of Johnson he could find. He got what he could from Frank Barber, Johnson's servant, and most of the Club members, as well as many others, cooperated with Boswell's efforts. Thus he gradually assembled a huge mass of material.

When a first version was finally prepared, it was then rigorously revised, further corrections being made in proof. At last *The Life of Samuel Johnson, LL.D.* was published on May 16, 1791, exactly twenty-eight years after the first meeting in 1763. It was widely read, and was a definite financial success.

Boswell's Method of Keeping a Journal

When Boswell came to London in 1762, the last thing before he went to bed or the first thing in the morning, he was accustomed to write out short memoranda to himself outlining what he intended to do during the day. Every so often he would arrange to stay home and write up his full journal, and no doubt these little memoranda helped to remind him of what had happened. Yet there were obvious discrepancies. For example, on May 16, 1763, the surviving memorandum contains various items about sending out his breeches to be mended, about what to eat for breakfast, about getting money and seeing people, and even what frame of mind to be in, but there is no mention whatsoever of what has been called "the most important single event in Boswell's life"—his meeting with Samuel Johnson.

Once Boswell recognized that these notes were not of much use in writing up his journal, he changed his practice. Normally he waited until the end of the day, and then summed up briefly what had actually occurred. These notes were vital to him when he came to write a full account in his journal.

In the later 1770's what survives is often a sequence of very brief notations, some of the most cryptic kind, along with others (the majority) fairly long and quite intelligible. When Boswell fell behind, instead of going back and trying to catch up, he would write a long entry for the day before, or for a few days before, and then cover up the gap with rough notes. There are long periods when there are only intermittent entries. Thus sometimes we have fully written journals, sometimes only the condensed, suggestive notes or half-expanded versions, and sometimes nothing at all.

The Question of Accuracy of Reporting

So long as the old theory was accepted—that Boswell was little more than an energetic reporter—the matter of the verbal accuracy of his versions did not stir up much controversy. Other evidence which was available seemed to confirm his reports, and that was that. But now, with the general agreement on Boswell's remarkable creative gifts, there are some questions which need to be discussed. Exactly how did Boswell's memory work? What part of the dramatic scenes in the *Life* represents Boswell's imaginative coloring, and how much is purely factual?

Frederick A. Pottle, who knows more about Boswell than anyone today, believes that Boswell had a very special kind of mind. Once it was given a jog —by a note or in some other way—the whole of an earlier event came back to him in great detail. Given the proper reminder, Boswell was just as capable of bringing back little details after ten years as after two weeks. Pottle cites various evidence to support his position, including the findings of modern psychologists who have studied people with similar memories.

Some readers may wonder if there are any dependable ways of checking Boswell's reporting of Johnson's conversation. The answer is that there are. Occasionally other people were present who also had the itch to write down what was said by the Doctor, and some of these other reports catch the same "Johnsonian aether." In general when two accounts are compared, there is surprising agreement as to the main ideas expressed, although inevitably there are variations in wording.

Gathering Material for the Life

That Boswell had a keen interest in securing accurate facts has never been doubted. As he bragged in the "Advertizement" to the first edition of the *Life,* he was quite ready to "run half over London" to verify a date. And it is now evident that he used admirable skepticism in regard to casual anecdotes which he secured from others.

The wealth of evidence now available makes clear that Boswell did not use all the material he collected, even when it was relevant. Thus he omitted an amusing story told him by Hector of a night in Birmingham when Johnson as a young man may have been drunk. Other small details which Boswell felt were either irrelevant or not characteristic of the great moralist he was describing were silently omitted.

This does not mean that Boswell was consciously distorting character or falsifying evidence. Like all great biographers, he was presenting the essential truth as he saw it.

Contemporary Reception

Because the *Tour to the Hebrides* and the *Life of Johnson* have for so long been recognized as masterpieces, we sometimes forget that when they first appeared they were subjected to the same kind of abuse that is leveled against some candid biographers today. The *Tour* when it appeared in 1785 was constantly under attack in the newspapers.

In fashionable and conservative circles what shocked many readers was Boswell's willingness to report exactly what people said in private conversation. This attitude was summed up by one letter-writer: "Johnson's faults were balanced by many and great virtues; and when that is the case, the virtues only should be remembered, and the faults entirely forgotten." Biography according to this position should embalm, not re-create.

On the appearance of the *Life,* almost six years later, there was the same kind of shock over the frankness of the personal revelations it contained. We now know that Boswell tried hard not to hurt the feelings of Johnson's close friends, and had been willing to do some significant censoring, but none of this was apparent to the general reader. On the surface it appeared that he was indiscreetly telling everything. And many thought that such lack of taste not only hurt others, but was injurious to the reputation of Johnson himself. There is even some indication that in later years Boswell himself was not graciously received in certain circles, for fear that he would write down what was said and perhaps publish it.

At the same time, many general readers were quite ready to accept the new approach with enthusiasm. A writer in the *Monthly Review* replied to objectors as follows:

> . . . where the biographer has for his subject the life and sentiments of so eminent an instructor of mankind as Samuel Johnson, and so immense a store-house of mental treasure to open and disclose . . . there can be no just exception taken against the number and variety of the ob-

jects exhibited. . . . To the reporter, would he not say "Give us *all;* suppress nothing; lest, in rejecting that which, in your estimation, may seem to be of inferior value, you unwarily throw away gold with the dross."

Before the late eighteenth century, there was little significant criticism concerning the art and ethical principles of biography. Life-writing had simply not been accepted as a major literary genre. It was not until the extended arguments stirred up by Boswell's thorough and revealing coverage of Johnson's private life that biography gradually took its place as one of the important kinds of writing worthy of searching critical examination.

With the argument over Boswell's *Life of Johnson* the whole issue as to how much a biographer should tell was finally brought into the open. Even though the next century kept insisting on reticence and good taste, the possibilities of three-dimensional re-creation of character, both psychological and factual, were now apparent. □

WHAT DID BLAKE MEAN BY INNOCENCE AND EXPERIENCE?

by Morton D. Paley

WHAT are the two Contrary States and what is the relationship between them? *Innocence* and *Experience* are not, first of all, a direct record of Blake's spiritual autobiography. Anyone who thinks the *Songs of Innocence* reflect Blake's own world view at the time of composition should carefully read the prose satire *An Island in the Moon,* which Blake wrote in 1784 and in which versions of three *Songs of Innocence* first appear. In this anything-but-innocent narrative, the simplicity of "Holy Thursday," "Nurse's Song," and "Little Boy Lost" contrast sharply with the egotism and pretentiousness of the characters. Of course we cannot know whether Blake had the *Songs of Experience* in mind when he wrote the *Songs of Innocence,* but we do know that four of the earlier group seemed to him sufficiently poems of Experience to be shifted to the latter group in 1794: "The School Boy," "The Little Girl Lost," "The Little Girl Found," and "The Voice of the Ancient Bard." These poems had already burst the bounds of the state of Innocence, all of them presenting themes more appropriate to the Contrary State—institutional restraint, the prophetic function of the poet, the growth of self-awareness. Innocence *demands* Experience: both are phases in the spiritual development of man and, at the same time, perennial ways of looking at the world.

The state of Innocence is compounded of the pagan Age of Gold and the Judeo-Christian Eden. Externally and generically, it applies to the condition of man before the Fall; internally and psychologically to the child who has not yet experienced the inner divisions of human life. Its literary forebears are the worlds of the pastoral and the Psalms. Blake's Innocence also has a special relationship to the thought of the Swedish visionary Emanuel Swedenborg, whose works Blake annotated with great interest in the 1780's and who conceived of Innocence in terms peculiarly appropriate to Blake's: as an inner state, taking images such as the child and the lamb as correspondences.

Experience, too, is an inner state externalized in a

Abridged from the Introduction by Morton D. Paley, Ed., *Twentieth Century Interpretations of Songs of Innocence and of Experience:* A Collection of Critical Essays, © 1969. By permission of Prentice-Hall, Inc., Englewood Cliffs, New Jersey.

world of images—chains, thorns, spears, graves, briars, blood, and roots, to name a few—all of which correspond to felt qualities in life. In Experience, which is the world of normal adult life, people try to analyze and codify their feelings, and as a result they become incapable of spontaneity. The traditional hierarchy of society, seen as benevolent in *Innocence*, is now regarded as a vast exploitative deceit. With all this suffering, however, Experience also brings a bitter wisdom. Experience, then, is not wholly negative. The harmony of Innocence has been lost, but insight comes in its place. In the wisdom of Experience, as embodied in the voice of the prophetic Bard of the second group of Songs, lies the possibility of reorganizing man's divided self and, if not of regaining the lost world of Innocence, then of forging a new unity. "Man is so created," Swedenborg wrote, "as to be during his childhood in external innocence, and when he becomes old in internal innocence, to the end that he may come by means of the former into the latter, and from the latter into the former." "Unorganized Innocence," according to Blake, is "an Impossibility. Innocence dwells with Wisdom, but never with Ignorance."

The transition from Innocence to Experience may be seen as a version of what medieval theologians call The Fortunate Fall—the idea that the fall of Adam and Eve was in a paradoxical sense a "happy sin," in that otherwise Christ would not have been born to save mankind. For Blake, the fall into Experience was if not happy at least necessary.

As Blake tells us in *The Marriage of Heaven and Hell*, "without Contraries is no progression." In this case, progression is toward a condition of being in which the harmony lost in the fall from Innocence is regained. The agent of regeneration is Energy. In the fallen world of Experience, this Energy is present as the wrath of the Tyger.

The Victorians at times mistook Blake's simplicity for naivete and were, accordingly, disposed toward an overly literal view of the poems. We, by contrast, may be tempted to find complexities that are not there, to over-read, to discover myths hidden in the shrubbery as if the poem were an ingenious puzzle. □

The Changing English Language

IN KEEPING with the spirit of the Age of Reason, the movement in language in the eighteenth century was toward greater regulation of expression and greater precision in word usage and pronunciation. By the beginning of the century there had already grown up among those in fashionable society a disdain for the extravagant flourishes and conceits of seventeenth-century speech; emphasis came to be placed on refined, polite discourse based on "common sense." Those caught in the surge toward refinement—among them Swift, Steele, Addison, Johnson, and Lord Chesterfield—tended to disparage what they called "cant" or "low speech" with an assurance in the rightness of their judgments which today strikes us as immodest. However, these arbiters of language realized, as did many of their time, that the English language was in a muddle that the disputes over grammar of the previous centuries had failed to solve: words still had widely variant meanings, spellings, and pronunciations, and the general instability of the language was a barrier to clear communication. In the mishandling of the language the educated and well-to-do seem to have been as guilty as any. Defoe complained in one of his works that "gentlemen of fortunes and families . . . can hardly write their own names" and when they can write they "can't spell their mother tongue." A favorite point made by satirists of the day was that the one member of a great household most likely to read and write the King's English was either the butler or the serving woman.

The urge to bring the language more into accord with Natural Law is evident in hundreds of projects undertaken during the course of the century and typified by this statement of Lord Chesterfield's published in *The World* in 1754, a year before the appearance of Johnson's *Dictionary*:

It must be owned that our language is, at present, in a state of anarchy, and hitherto, perhaps, it may not have been the worse for it. During our free and open trade, many words and expressions have been imported, adopted, and naturalized from other languages, which have greatly enriched our own. . . . The time for discrimination seems to be now come. Toleration, adoption, and naturalization, have run their lengths. Good order and authority are now necessary. But where shall we find them, and at the same time, the obedience due to them? We must have recourse to the old Roman expedient in times of confusion, and choose a dictator. Upon this principle, I give my vote for Mr. Johnson to fill that great and arduous post. . . .

Johnson's ponderous two-volume *Dictionary*, great achievement though it was, offered only a partial solution to the problems of normalizing the language, and before the century ended there were many other attempts. The efforts at standardization spilled over into literary texts. One mid-eighteenth-century editor announced that Shakespeare's works were an "unweeded Garden grown to Seed," and confidently set about the cultivation and pruning he thought necessary. Another overearnest reformer named Bentley tackled Milton's poetry, and got for his pains Pope's ridicule for being a scribbler "whose unwearied pains / Made Horace dull, and humbled Milton's strains." If there was widespread agreement that the English language needed polishing, there was little agreement about how it should be done, and the controversy continued throughout the century.

One characteristic of the many arguments for purification of English was a sort of intellectual elitism that rejected the living language of the mob (the word *mob* is itself an eighteenth-century coinage used by those who wished to emphasize their social exclusivity). The more common words of Anglo-Saxon derivation were frowned upon as low, slangy, or imprecise, and in their place many Latinisms were substituted (see Johnson's definition of *network* on page 299), largely because words derived from Latin were supported by the "authority" of classical writers, and also because they were suited for expressing the abstractions that dominated eighteenth-century thinking.

While neoclassicism did much to tone down the bizarre and freakish aspects of seventeenth-century speech, it did not, in spite of its insistence on rules and rigidity, stamp out the rich variety which makes English a vital instrument of communication. Although both Johnson and Swift objected to the use of such words as *humbug, prig, doodle, bamboozle, fib, bully, fop, banter, stingy, fun, prude,* they continued in use then as they do today, evidence of the fact that people, not grammar books or dictionaries, make and perpetuate language. □

BIOGRAPHIES

Joseph Addison 1672 / 1719

An Oxford graduate and classical scholar of some note, Addison was also a Member of Parliament from 1708 until his death, and briefly held the office of Secretary of State in the last years of his life. He varied his political activity with literary endeavors, contributing periodical essays to Richard Steele's *Tatler,* and later joining with Steele to produce the *Spectator* (1711–1712). Addison's life was the epitome of Neoclassical virtues: he sought in his writings to reform the manners and tastes of his time, he was politically active, and he was a model of reasonableness and rationality. His periodical essays are polished, gently humorous, and unobtrusively moral in tone.

William Blake 1757 / 1827

William Blake was not only a poet, but a painter, an engraver, and a spiritual visionary. He claimed to have seen the prophet Ezekiel in a tree when only a child, and believed that much of his later poetry was dictated to him by a spiritual amanuensis. He lived all but three years of his life in London, where he earned a moderate—sometimes barely sufficient—income as an engraver. Between 1783 and 1793 he wrote, illustrated, and printed his most famous lyrics, *Songs of Innocence and Experience,* and also one major prose work, *The Marriage of Heaven and Hell.*

From 1800 to 1803 he lived at Flepham on the Sussex coast, under the patronage of a wealthy amateur artist,

William Hayley, who tried to convert him into a more conventional craftsman. Blake, always temperamental about his personal freedom, soon quarreled with Hayley and returned to London, but not before an event occurred which left a permanent mark on his life. He was charged with sedition by a soldier who had a personal grudge against him. Though he was acquitted after a harrowing trial and escaped hanging, he lived for the rest of his life under the conviction that dark and uncontrollable powers were at work in the world, a view that affected his later prophetic poems, *Milton* (1804) and *Jerusalem* (1820).

Blake's later years were largely happy and peaceful; after the age of sixty he gave up poetry in favor of painting, illustrating the poetry of Dante and Chaucer and the Book of Job. During his lifetime, Blake's visual productions were almost unknown to the public, and his poetry was entirely ignored. The recent increase in his popularity can probably be attributed to recognition of his humanitarian (even revolutionary) beliefs, and interest in his mysticism.

James Boswell 1740 / 1795

The discovery and recent publication of Boswell's personal journals have done much to correct the caricature of Boswell, pencil in hand and ear cocked, dancing attendance on the great Samuel Johnson and his circle. It is now clear that there was mutual respect and affection between the two, in spite of Boswell's sometimes absurd antics which drew harsh words from Johnson.

The son of a judge with the honorary title Lord Auchinleck, Boswell studied law at the University of Edinburgh, traveled widely on the continent, where he met and captivated Rousseau and Voltaire, and was technically a member of the gentry who could meet Johnson's circle on equal footing. He was also a man of genius with a remarkable memory and an instinct for unsparing portrayal of himself and others. His *Life of Johnson* (1791) and *Journal of a Tour to the Hebrides* (1785) reveal Johnson the whole man, not only the public figure in its most favorable aspects.

Robert Burns 1759 / 1796

When Burns' first volume of poetry appeared in 1786, he was immediately hailed as a "plowman poet," a rude untutored singer of Scottish native song. The realities of his early life in Ayreshire, Scotland, were harsh enough: in his early teens he was called upon to do a man's work as a farmer to help support his six younger brothers and sisters, his mother, and his ailing father. But Burns was no uneducated country bumpkin. He had received the foundations of an education and had read widely on his own, even teaching himself French. When the popularity of his first poetry thrust him into public light, he became known in Edinburgh social circles as a charming and brilliant conversationalist. However, his liberal views and irreverent attitude toward the stern Scottish Presbyterian morality of the times (he had several illegitimate children) so outraged the good citizens of Edinburgh that his social success was brief. In 1788 he secured a government post and settled down with Jean Armour as a married man. He tried his hand at farming to supplement his government salary, failed, and died in his mid thirties, his constitution weakened by the rigors of his early life.

Burns wrote or rewrote over 200 songs in Scots dialect, as well as some in English. His longer poems reveal a versatile lyrical talent, a sharp and sometimes merciless sense of humor, and deep sensitivity to the natural world.

Daniel Defoe 1659 / 1731

The son of a butcher named Foe, Daniel Defoe was a man who seized, without undue scruples, whatever opportunities presented themselves. A Presbyterian, he was hampered his whole life long by his dissenting views. As a young man he set up business as a merchant but soon found himself bankrupt. He then turned to writing political verses and pamphlets, and was pilloried, fined, and jailed for a stinging satire on the Church of England's methods of treating nonconformists like himself. In his middle years he was a political adventurer, a spy and informer, serving one Robert Harley with his journalistic talents. A Whig by conviction, Defoe had few misgivings about switching parties when Harley became head of the Tory ministry in 1710. When the Tories fell from power in 1714, Defoe switched back to the Whig side with equal ease.

From a total of more than 250 works, Defoe is best known for those he wrote in later life, among them *Robinson Crusoe* (1719), *Moll Flanders* (1722), and *A Journal of the Plague Year* (1722). Purporting to be not fiction but true accounts, they have a realistic bite that makes them read like fact.

Thomas Gray 1716 / 1771

Gray is known today primarily for his "Elegy Written in a Country Churchyard" which, when it was published in 1750, immediately established his reputation. Its supposed setting, the churchyard of Stoke Poges, a village in Buckinghamshire, became Gray's own final resting place.

Gray studied at Cambridge, left without a degree to travel abroad, and then returned to the university where he completed his studies and lived for the rest of his life. In his later years he was appointed Professor of Modern History, but he never felt called upon to give a lecture in that subject, devoting himself instead to a life of quiet retirement and various scholarly pursuits. His poetic output was relatively small. His shy, affectionate nature and gentle humor are preserved in his letters, now considered among the best from an age in which letter writing was an art.

Samuel Johnson 1709 / 1784

Boswell's *Life* presents a picture of Johnson that is at least life-size—and Johnson was a huge man. Perhaps part of his future was shaped by his being the son of a Lichfield bookseller; perhaps still more, by his contracting scrofula, probably from his nurse, when he was barely out of infancy. The disease impaired his eyesight and left his face horribly marred. He attended Oxford but did not take a degree because family financial crises recalled him to Lichfield. When he was 26 he married a widow considerably older than himself, to whom he remained devoted for years after her death in 1752. For a while he operated a private school, but when that failed he went to London with one of his pupils, David Garrick, who was destined to become the greatest actor of his day. After doing some periodical writing, and publishing several works independently, among them *London* (1738), he issued the plan for his great *Dictionary,* a work which he finally finished in 1755. While working on the *Dictionary* he continued to write, and in 1750 started the *Rambler,* which ran for two years. Publication of the *Dictionary* won him a leading place among English men of letters. From 1758 to 1760 he wrote the "Idler" essays for the *Universal Chronicle.* In 1765 he completed his second extended project, the editing of Shakespeare's works. In 1763 he met Boswell, and in 1764 founded the Literary Club, which numbered among its members Goldsmith, Garrick, and Boswell. Johnson's trip to the Hebrides with Boswell in 1773 resulted in the publication of his *Journey to the Western Islands of Scotland* (1775). From 1777 to 1781 he was engaged in his third and last extended project: writing *The Lives of the English Poets.*

Alexander Pope 1688 / 1744

Despite personal handicaps that would have caused a man of less determination to give up, Pope rose to be the leading literary figure of his day. He was a Roman Catholic in an age when adherence to the "Old Faith" prevented him from receiving a university education, voting, or holding public office, and when the tax burden on Roman Catholics was sufficiently high to drive many once well-to-do families into bankruptcy. In addition, at the age of 12 Pope was stricken with a disease that left him dwarfed, crippled, and in almost constant pain. By sheer power of will, he managed to educate himself and to become admired as a poet and feared as a satirist. Pope earned a large income through his poetry, editorial work, and translations of the *Iliad* and the *Odyssey.* He was instrumental in forming the Scriblerus Club, a group of writers (including Swift) who met on occasion to satirize the pretensions of learned men. In an age of satire Pope was often subjected to vituperous literary attacks, but he always gave at least as good as he got, cutting down his enemies with sharply honed heroic couplets. Among his best-known works are *Essay on Criticism* (1711), published when he was only 23; *The Rape of the Lock* (1714); *Essay on Man* (1733–34); and *Moral Essays* (1731–35), all written in heroic couplets.

Jonathan Swift 1667 / 1745

Born in Dublin of English parents, Swift was educated in Ireland, receiving his degree from Trinity College, Dublin, "by special grace" after he had been censured for offenses against college discipline. He fled with many of his fellow Anglo-Irish when James II invaded Ireland, and took refuge in England in the household of a kinsman, Sir William Temple. There he remained, with only a few visits to Ireland, from 1689 to 1699, reading widely and writing his first powerful satires. At some point during his stay with Temple he decided, with some reluctance, to make the Church his career, and so was ordained an Anglican minister in 1694.

Swift soon became a convinced churchman and upheld in spirited pamphlets and conversation the causes of both the Anglican Church and the Crown against all dissenters. In 1710 he became a Tory, and in 1713 was appointed Dean of St. Patrick's Cathedral in Dublin. There he established himself as an able administrator, though he disliked living in Ireland, largely because he had formed friendships with many prominent men in England and found his Irish friends less polished.

In his later years, Swift was afflicted with a rare disease which caused dizziness, deafness, and nausea. Nevertheless he continued to write prolifically, and kept his wit and his extraordinarily keen eye for human foibles and social corruption until the last few years of his life, when disease and old age closed in. *Gulliver's Travels* (1726), the only work for which he ever received payment, and *A Modest Proposal* (1729) were written at the height of his mature years.

chapter six

THE ROMANTICS 1798–1837

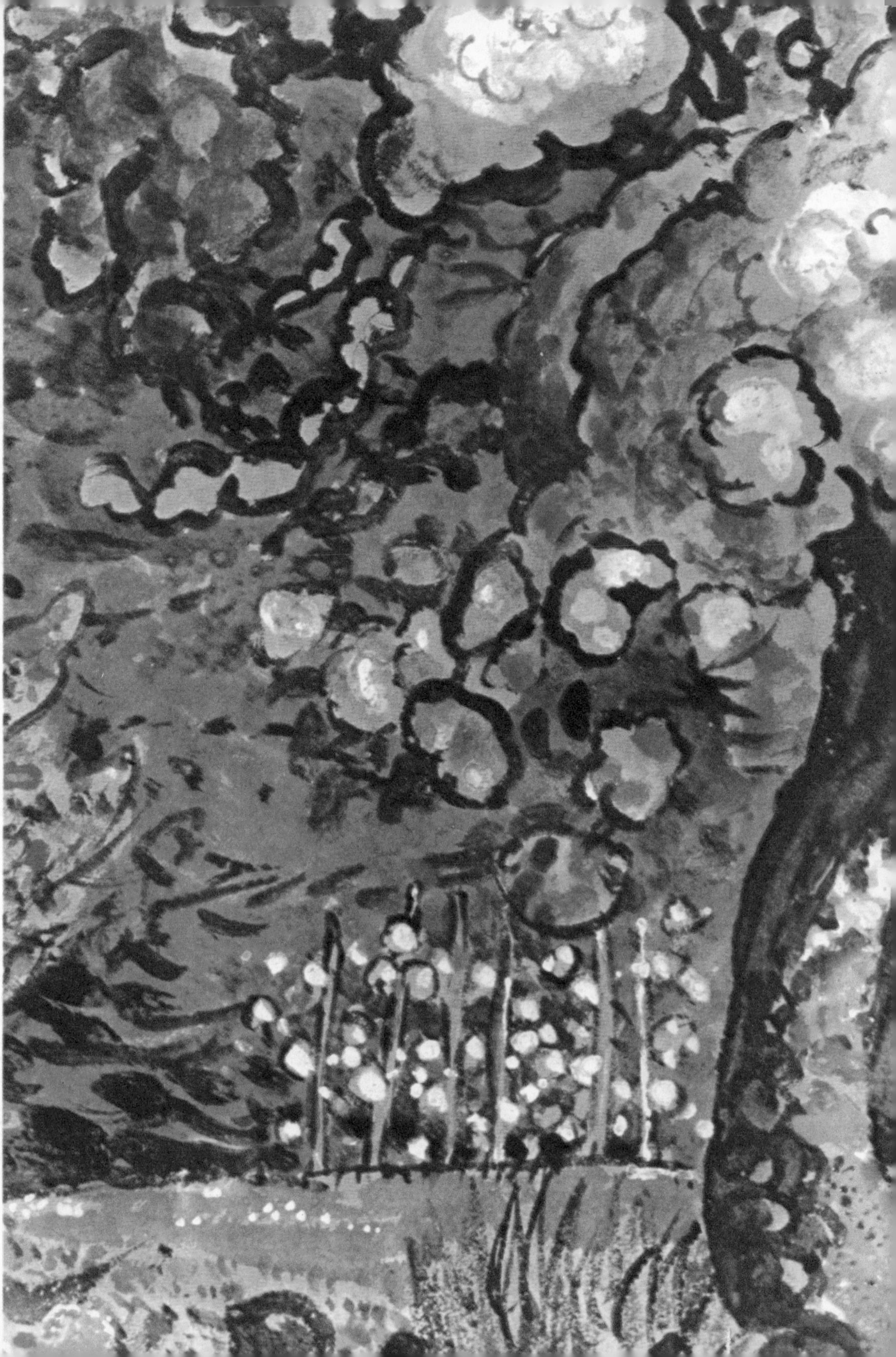

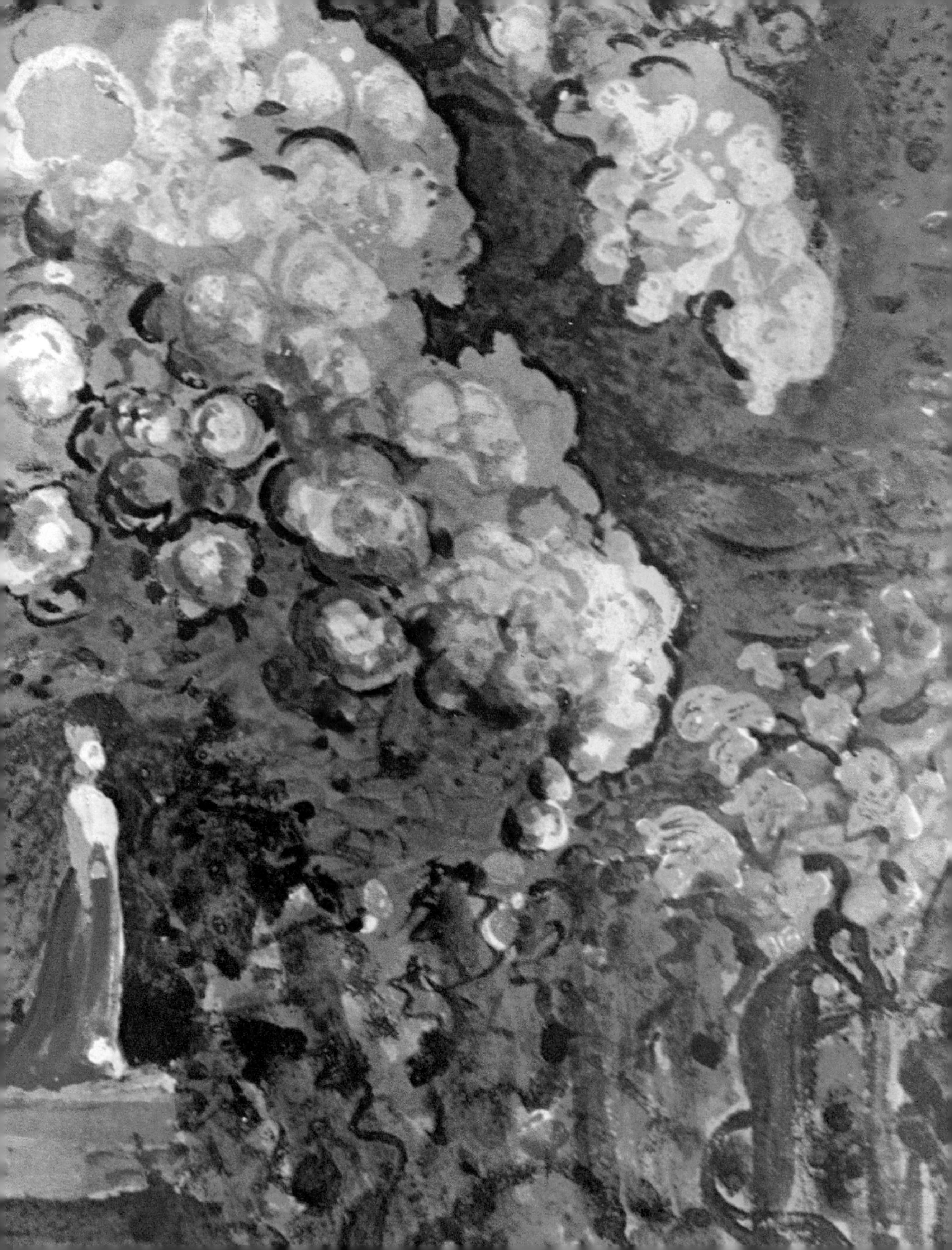

William Wordsworth

1770 / 1850

COMPOSED UPON WESTMINSTER BRIDGE, SEPTEMBER 3, 1802

Earth has not anything to show more fair:
Dull would he be of soul who could pass by
A sight so touching in its majesty:
This City now doth, like a garment, wear
5 The beauty of the morning; silent, bare,
Ships, towers, domes, theaters, and temples lie
Open unto the fields, and to the sky;
All bright and glittering in the smokeless air.
Never did sun more beautifully steep
10 In his first splendor, valley, rock, or hill;
Ne'er saw I, never felt, a calm so deep!
The river glideth at his own sweet will:
Dear God! the very houses seem asleep;
And all that mighty heart is lying still!

THE WORLD IS TOO MUCH WITH US

The world is too much with us; late and soon,
Getting and spending, we lay waste our powers:
Little we see in Nature that is ours;
We have given our hearts away, a sordid boon!
5 The sea that bares her bosom to the moon;
The winds that will be howling at all hours,
And are up-gathered now like sleeping flowers;
For this, for everything, we are out of tune;
It moves us not.—Great God! I'd rather be
10 A Pagan suckled in a creed outworn;
So might I, standing on this pleasant lea,
Have glimpses that would make me less forlorn;
Have sight of Proteus rising from the sea;
Or hear old Triton[1] blow his wreathèd horn.

1. *Proteus . . . Triton,* sea gods in Greek mythology.

LONDON, 1802

Milton! thou shouldst be living at this hour.
England hath need of thee; she is a fen
Of stagnant waters: altar, sword, and pen,
Fireside, the heroic wealth of hall and bower,
5 Have forfeited their ancient English dower
Of inward happiness. We are selfish men;
Oh! raise us up, return to us again,
And give us manners, virtue, freedom, power.
Thy soul was like a star, and dwelt apart:
10 Thou hadst a voice whose sound was like the sea;
Pure as the naked heavens, majestic, free,
So didst thou travel on life's common way,
In cheerful godliness; and yet thy heart
The lowliest duties on herself did lay.

IT IS A BEAUTEOUS EVENING

It is a beauteous evening, calm and free,
The holy time is quiet as a Nun
Breathless with adoration; the broad sun
Is sinking down in its tranquillity;
5 The gentleness of heaven broods o'er the Sea:
Listen! the mighty Being is awake,
And doth with his eternal motion make
A sound like thunder—everlastingly.
Dear Child![1] dear Girl; that walkest with me here,
10 If thou appear untouched by solemn thought,
Thy nature is not therefore less divine:
Thou liest in Abraham's bosom[2] all the year;
And worshipp'st at the temple's inner shrine,
God being with thee when we know it not.

1. *Dear Child,* Wordsworth's French daughter, Caroline.
2. *in Abraham's bosom,* in the presence or favor of God. See Luke 16:22.

NUNS FRET NOT

Nuns fret not at their convent's narrow room;
And hermits are contented with their cells;
And students with their pensive citadels;
Maids at the wheel, the weaver at his loom,
5 Sit blithe and happy; bees that soar for bloom,
High as the highest Peak of Furness-fells,
Will murmur by the hour in foxglove bells:
In truth the prison, unto which we doom
Ourselves, no prison is: and hence for me,
10 In sundry moods, 'twas pastime to be bound
Within the Sonnet's scanty plot of ground;
Pleased if some Souls (for such there needs must be)
Who have felt the weight of too much liberty,
Should find brief solace there, as I have found.

PERSUASION

"Man's life is like a Sparrow, mighty King!
That—while at banquet with your Chiefs you sit
Housed near a blazing fire—is seen to flit
Safe from the wintry tempest. Fluttering,
5 Here did it enter; there, on hasty wing,
Flies out, and passes on from cold to cold;
But whence it came we know not, nor behold
Whither it goes. Even such, that transient Thing,
The human Soul; not utterly unknown
10 While in the Body lodged, her warm abode;
But from what world She came, what woe or weal
On her departure waits, no tongue hath shown;
This mystery if the Stranger[1] can reveal,
His be a welcome cordially bestowed!"

1. *Stranger,* Paulinus, who converted King Edwin. See Bede's account on page 51.

DISCUSSION

Composed upon Westminster Bridge

1. What qualities in the sleeping city would you describe as natural rather than artificial? How is Wordsworth's view of the sleeping city related to his view of nature?

2. Compare this sonnet with William Blake's "London" (page 326). What similar features of the city do both poems note? What differences in tone are there between the two poems?

The World Is Too Much with Us

1. What aspects of the world does Wordsworth view as positive, and what as negative? With what aspects are we "out of tune"? What aspects are "too much with us"? Do you feel that Wordsworth's theme has as much validity today?

2. Where in the sonnet does the most dramatic break occur? How would you read the sonnet aloud to give this break maximum effect?

3. What personifications does Wordsworth use to present various aspects of nature? Does his use of personification make the natural world seem more intimate, or more distant?

London, 1802

1. What qualities does Wordsworth ascribe to Milton? What qualities of life in 1802 does he mention as contrast?

It Is a Beauteous Evening

1. List the words in the sonnet which most directly convey its mood and discuss the sonnet in terms of them.

2. How does the mood of this sonnet compare with "Composed upon Westminster Bridge"?

3. What effect does Wordsworth create through the evening-nun simile?

4. How are the last six lines connected with the preceding eight? What "solemn thoughts" make Wordsworth turn to address his daughter?

Nuns Fret Not

1. What paradox is Wordsworth working out in this sonnet? How is it related to the constraints of the sonnet form?

2. Wordsworth notes that there must be some who have felt the "weight of too much liberty." What does he mean here? Is there such a thing as "too much liberty"?

3. Discuss the implications of the statement "In truth the prison, unto which we doom / Ourselves, no prison is."

Persuasion

Compare this sonnet with the words of "another of the king's chief men" as reported by Bede on page 53. Which presentation do you prefer? Why? Does Wordsworth's use of the sonnet form improve the original?

WRITING

Write your own version of "The World Is Too Much with Us" (in free verse), commenting on aspects of the modern world with which you feel we are "out of tune."

LUCY POEMS

STRANGE FITS OF PASSION HAVE I KNOWN

Strange fits of passion have I known:
And I will dare to tell,
But in the Lover's ear alone,
What once to me befell.

5 When she I loved looked every day
Fresh as a rose in June,
I to her cottage bent my way,
Beneath an evening-moon.

Upon the moon I fixed my eye,
10 All over the wide lea;
With quickening pace my horse drew nigh
Those paths so dear to me.

And now we reached the orchard-plot;
And, as we climbed the hill,
15 The sinking moon to Lucy's cot
Came near, and nearer still.

In one of those sweet dreams I slept,
Kind Nature's gentlest boon!
And all the while my eyes I kept
20 On the descending moon.

My horse moved on; hoof after hoof
He raised, and never stopped:
When down behind the cottage roof,
At once, the bright moon dropped.

25 What fond and wayward thoughts will slide
Into a Lover's head!
"O mercy!" to myself I cried,
"If Lucy should be dead!"

SHE DWELT AMONG THE UNTRODDEN WAYS

She dwelt among the untrodden ways
Beside the springs of Dove,
A Maid whom there were none to praise
And very few to love:

5 A violet by a mossy stone
Half hidden from the eye!
—Fair as a star, when only one
Is shining in the sky.

She lived unknown, and few could know
10 When Lucy ceased to be;
But she is in her grave, and, oh,
The difference to me!

I TRAVELLED AMONG UNKNOWN MEN

I travelled among unknown men,
In lands beyond the sea;
Nor, England! did I know till then
What love I bore to thee.

5 'Tis past, that melancholy dream!
Nor will I quit thy shore
A second time; for still I seem
To love thee more and more.

Among thy mountains did I feel
10 The joy of my desire;
And she I cherished turned her wheel
Beside an English fire.

Thy mornings showed, thy nights concealed,
The bowers where Lucy played;
15 And thine too is the last green field
That Lucy's eyes surveyed.

A SLUMBER DID MY SPIRIT SEAL

A slumber did my spirit seal;
I had no human fears:
She seemed a thing that could not feel
The touch of earthly years.

5 No motion has she now, no force;
She neither hears nor sees;
Rolled round in earth's diurnal course,
With rocks, and stones, and trees.

OF CRITICAL INTEREST

"She dwelt among the untrodden ways"

Samuel Butler, nineteenth-century author and critic, wrote the following speculations on the meaning of Wordsworth's poem. Is he serious or spoofing?

"Anyone imbued with the spirit of modern science will read Wordsworth's poem with different eyes from those of a mere literary critic. He will note that Wordsworth is most careful not to explain the nature of the difference which the death of Lucy will occasion to him. He tells us that there will be a difference; but there the matter ends. The superficial reader takes it that he was very sorry she was dead; it is, of course, possible that he may have actually been so, but he has not said this. On the contrary, he has hinted plainly that she was ugly, and generally disliked; she was only like a violet when she was half-hidden from the view, and only fair as a star when there were so few stars out that it was practically impossible to make an invidious comparison. If there were as many as even two stars the likeness was felt to be at an end. If Wordsworth had imprudently promised to marry this young person during a time when he had been unusually long in keeping to good resolutions, and had afterwards seen someone whom he liked better, then Lucy's death would undoubtedly have made a considerable difference to him, and this is all that he has ever said that it would do. What right have we to put glosses upon the masterly reticence of a poet, and credit him with feelings possibly the very reverse of those he actually entertained?

"Sometimes, indeed, I have been inclined to think that a mystery is being hinted at more dark than any critic has suspected. I do not happen to possess a copy of the poem, but the writer, if I am not mistaken, says that 'few could know when Lucy ceased to be.' 'Ceased to be' is a suspiciously euphemistic expression, and the words 'few could know' are not applicable to the ordinary peaceful death of a domestic servant such as Lucy appears to have been. No matter how obscure the deceased, any number of people commonly can know the day and hour of his or her demise, whereas in this case we are expressly told it would be impossible for them to do so. Wordsworth was nothing if not accurate, and would not have said that few could know, but that few actually did know, unless he was aware of circumstances that precluded all but those implicated in the crime of her death from knowing the precise moment of its occurrence. If Lucy was the kind of person not obscurely portrayed in the poem; if Wordsworth had murdered her, either by cutting her throat or smothering her, in concert, perhaps, with his friends Southey and Coleridge; and if he had thus found himself released from an engagement which had become irksome to him, or possibly from the threat of an action for breach of promise, then there is not a syllable in the poem with which he crowns his crime that is not alive with meaning. On any other supposition to the general reader it is unintelligible. . . ."

From "Quis Desiderio . . . ?" by Samuel Butler. First published in the *Universal Review*, July 1888.

DISCUSSION

1. Discuss how the Lucy poems differ from each other, taking into account the mood (how do the natural objects mentioned fit the mood of each poem?) and the emotional tone (what kinds of feelings—determination, grief, consolation, fear, foreboding, etc.—does each poem deal with?).
2. The first poem ("Strange Fits of Passion") has been called "hallucinatory." What kind of hallucination takes place? How is it induced? What is the suggestion behind the line "At once, the bright moon dropped"?

WRITING

1. Can you detect any progression in action and time—a plot—implied in the Lucy poems presented here? Construct a hypothetical story around them. What is your reaction to Samuel Butler's hypothesis in the Extension?
2. The Lucy poems have been parodied many times. Choose one poem and write a parody of it.

EXPOSTULATION AND REPLY

"Why, William, on that old grey stone,
Thus for the length of half a day,
Why, William, sit you thus alone,
And dream your time away?

"Where are your books?—that light bequeathed
To Beings else forlorn and blind!
Up! up! and drink the spirit breathed
From dead men to their kind.

"You look round on your Mother Earth,
As if she for no purpose bore you;
As if you were her first-born birth,
And none had lived before you!"

One morning thus, by Esthwaite lake,
When life was sweet, I knew not why,
To me my good friend Matthew spake,
And thus I made reply:

"The eye—it cannot choose but see;
We cannot bid the ear be still;
Our bodies feel, where'er they be,
Against or with our will.

"Nor less I deem that there are Powers
Which of themselves our minds impress;
That we can feed this mind of ours
In a wise passiveness.

"Think you, 'mid all this mighty sum
Of things for ever speaking,
That nothing of itself will come,
But we must still be seeking?

"—Then ask not wherefore, here, alone,
Conversing as I may,
I sit upon this old grey stone,
And dream my time away."

THE SOLITARY REAPER

Behold her, single in the field,
Yon solitary Highland lass!
Reaping and singing by herself;
Stop here, or gently pass!
Alone she cuts and binds the grain,
And sings a melancholy strain;
O listen! for the vale profound
Is overflowing with the sound.

No nightingale did ever chaunt
More welcome notes to weary bands
Of travelers in some shady haunt,
Among Arabian sands:
A voice so thrilling ne'er was heard
In springtime from the cuckoo-bird,
Breaking the silence of the seas
Among the farthest Hebrides.

Will no one tell me what she sings?—
Perhaps the plaintive numbers flow
For old, unhappy, far-off things,
And battles long ago;
Or is it some more humble lay,
Familiar matter of today?
Some natural sorrow, loss, or pain,
That has been, and may be again?

Whate'er the theme, the maiden sang
As if her song could have no ending;
I saw her singing at her work,
And o'er the sickle bending;—
I listened, motionless and still;
And, as I mounted up the hill,
The music in my heart I bore,
Long after it was heard no more.

From

PREFACE TO LYRICAL BALLADS

Partly to answer the criticisms which met the first edition of *Lyrical Ballads* (see the biography of Wordsworth on page 385), and partly to explain his own theories of poetry, Wordsworth wrote a Preface to the second (1800) edition. Here are two passages from this Preface.

THE principal object . . . proposed in these Poems was to choose incidents and situations from common life, and to relate or describe them throughout, as far as was possible, in a selection of language really used by men, and, at the same time, to throw over them a certain colouring of imagination, whereby ordinary things should be presented to the mind in an unusual aspect; and further, and above all, to make these incidents and situations interesting by tracing in them, truly though not ostentatiously, the primary laws of our nature: chiefly, as far as regards the manner in which we associate ideas in a state of excitement. Humble and rustic life was generally chosen, because in that condition the essential passions of the heart find a better soil in which they can attain their maturity, are less under restraint, and speak a plainer and more emphatic language; because in that condition of life our elementary feelings coexist in a state of greater simplicity, and, consequently, may be more accurately contemplated, and more forcibly communicated; because the manners of rural life germinate from those elementary feelings, and, from the necessary character of rural occupations, are more easily comprehended, and are more durable; and, lastly, because in that condition the passions of men are incorporated with the beautiful and permanent forms of nature. The language, too, of these men has been adopted (purified indeed from what appear to be its real defects, from all lasting and rational causes of dislike or disgust) because such men hourly communicate with the best objects from which the best part of language is originally derived; and because, from their rank in society and the sameness and narrow circle of their intercourse, being less under the influence of social vanity, they convey their feelings and notions in simple and unelaborated expressions. Accordingly, such a language, arising out of repeated experience and regular feelings, is a more permanent, and a far more philosophical language, than that which is frequently substituted for it by Poets, who think that they are conferring honour upon themselves and their art, in proportion as they separate themselves from the sympathies of men, and indulge in arbitrary and capricious habits of expression, in order to furnish food for fickle tastes and fickle appetites of their own creation.

. . . .

Poetry is the spontaneous overflow of powerful feelings: it takes its origin from emotion recollected in tranquillity: the emotion is contemplated till, by a species of reaction, the tranquillity gradually disappears, and an emotion, kindred to that which was before the subject of contemplation, is gradually produced, and does itself actually exist in the mind.

DISCUSSION

Expostulation and Reply

What "Powers" or "things forever speaking" do you think Wordsworth had in mind when he wrote this poem? What are these "Powers" contrasted with?

The Solitary Reaper

1. Describe in as much detail as you can *imagine* (you won't find much explicit detail in the poem) the setting in which the lone woman reaps the grain. What overtones of mood does Wordsworth give the scene?

2. Read the excerpt from Wordsworth's "Preface to Lyrical Ballads" on this page. To what extent, in this poem, has he used the "language really used by men" or a situation taken from "humble and rustic" life?

LINES COMPOSED A FEW MILES ABOVE TINTERN ABBEY

FIVE years have past; five summers,
with the length
Of five long winters! and again I hear
These waters, rolling from their mountain springs
With a soft inland murmur. Once again
5 Do I behold these steep and lofty cliffs
That on a wild secluded scene impress
Thoughts of more deep seclusion and connect
The landscape with the quiet of the sky.
The day is come when I again repose
10 Here, under this dark sycamore, and view
These plots of cottage ground, these orchard tufts,
Which at this season, with their unripe fruits,
Are clad in one green hue, and lose themselves
Mid groves and copses. Once again I see
15 These hedgerows, hardly hedgerows, little lines
Of sportive wood run wild; these pastoral farms,
Green to the very door; and wreaths of smoke
Sent up, in silence, from among the trees,
With some uncertain notice, as might seem
20 Of vagrant dwellers in the houseless woods,
Or of some hermit's cave, where by his fire
The hermit sits alone.

These beauteous forms,
Through a long absence, have not been to me
As is a landscape to a blind man's eye;
25 But oft, in lonely rooms, and 'mid the din
Of towns and cities, I have owed to them,
In hours of weariness, sensations sweet,
Felt in the blood, and felt along the heart;
And passing even into my purer mind,
30 With tranquil restoration—feelings too
Of unremembered pleasure, such, perhaps,
As have no slight or trivial influence
On that best portion of a good man's life,
His little, nameless, unremembered acts
35 Of kindness and of love. Nor less, I trust,
To them I may have owed another gift,
Of aspect more sublime; that blessèd mood,
In which the burthen of the mystery,
In which the heavy and the weary weight
40 Of all this unintelligible world,
Is lightened—that serene and blessèd mood,
In which the affections gently lead us on—
Until, the breath of this corporeal frame
And even the motion of our human blood
45 Almost suspended, we are laid asleep
In body, and become a living soul;
While with an eye made quiet by the power
Of harmony, and the deep power of joy,
We see into the life of things.

If this
50 Be but a vain belief, yet, oh! how oft—
In darkness and amid the many shapes
Of joyless daylight; when the fretful stir
Unprofitable, and the fever of the world,
Have hung upon the beatings of my heart—
55 How oft, in spirit, have I turned to thee,
O sylvan Wye! thou wanderer through the woods,
How often has my spirit turned to thee!
And now, with gleams of half-extinguished thought,
With many recognitions dim and faint,
60 And somewhat of a sad perplexity,
The picture of the mind revives again;
While here I stand, not only with the sense
Of present pleasure, but with pleasing thoughts
That in this moment there is life and food
65 For future years. And so I dare to hope,
Though changed, no doubt, from what I was when
first
I came among these hills, when like a roe
I bounded o'er the mountains, by the sides
Of the deep rivers, and the lonely streams,
70 Wherever nature led—more like a man
Flying from something that he dreads than one
Who sought the thing he loved. For nature then
(The coarser pleasures of my boyish days,
And their glad animal movements all gone by)
75 To me was all in all. —I cannot paint
What then I was. The sounding cataract
Haunted me like a passion; the tall rock,
The mountain, and the deep and gloomy wood,
Their colors and their forms, were then to me
80 An appetite, a feeling and a love,
That had no need of a remoter charm,
By thought supplied, nor any interest
Unborrowed from the eye. —That time is past,
And all its aching joys are now no more,
85 And all its dizzy raptures. Not for this
Faint I, nor mourn nor murmur; other gifts
Have followed; for such loss, I would believe,
Abundant recompense. For I have learned
To look on nature, not as in the hour
90 Of thoughtless youth, but hearing often times
The still, sad music of humanity,
Nor harsh nor grating, though of ample power

To chasten and subdue. And I have felt
A presence that disturbs me with the joy
95 Of elevated thoughts; a sense sublime
Of something far more deeply interfused,
Whose dwelling is the light of setting suns,
And the round ocean and the living air,
And the blue sky, and in the mind of man;
100 A motion and a spirit, that impels
All thinking things, all objects of all thought,
And rolls through all things. Therefore am I still
A lover of the meadows and the woods,
And mountains; and of all that we behold
105 From this green earth; of all the mighty world
Of eye, and ear—both what they half create,
And what perceive; well pleased to recognize
In nature and the language of the sense
The anchor of my purest thoughts, the nurse,
110 The guide, the guardian of my heart, and soul
Of all my moral being.

Nor perchance,
If I were not thus taught, should I the more
Suffer my genial spirits to decay;
For thou art with me here upon the banks
115 Of this fair river; thou my dearest friend,[1]
My dear, dear friend; and in thy voice I catch
The language of my former heart, and read
My former pleasures in the shooting lights
Of thy wild eyes. Oh! yet a little while
120 May I behold in thee what I was once,
My dear, dear sister! and this prayer I make,
Knowing that nature never did betray
The heart that loved her; 'tis her privilege,
Through all the years of this our life, to lead
125 From joy to joy; for she can so inform
The mind that is within us, so impress
With quietness and beauty, and so feed
With lofty thoughts, that neither evil tongues,
Rash judgments, nor the sneers of selfish men,
130 Nor greetings where no kindness is, nor all
The dreary intercourse of daily life,
Shall e'er prevail against us, or disturb
Our cheerful faith, that all which we behold
Is full of blessings. Therefore let the moon
135 Shine on thee in thy solitary walk;
And let the misty mountain winds be free
To blow against thee; and, in after years,
When these wild ecstasies shall be matured
Into a sober pleasure, when thy mind
140 Shall be a mansion for all lovely forms,
Thy memory be as a dwelling place
For all sweet sounds and harmonies; oh! then,
If solitude, or fear, or pain, or grief,
Should be thy portion, with what healing thoughts
145 Of tender joy wilt thou remember me,
And these my exhortations! Nor, perchance—
If I should be where I no more can hear
Thy voice, nor catch from thy wild eyes these gleams
Of past existence—wilt thou then forget
150 That on the banks of this delightful stream
We stood together; and that I, so long
A worshiper of nature, hither came
Unwearied in that service—rather say
With warmer love—oh! with far deeper zeal
155 Of holier love. Nor wilt thou then forget
That after many wanderings, many years
Of absence, these steep woods and lofty cliffs,
And this green pastoral landscape, were to me
More dear, both for themselves and for thy sake! □

1. *my dearest friend,* Wordsworth's sister, Dorothy.

DISCUSSION

1. How is nature presented in the first twenty-two lines of the poem? Are there any signs of human habitation? How are these presented?
2. Read the sonnet "The World Is Too Much with Us" against lines 23–65. What similarities of theme can you detect? What "gifts" or sustenance does Wordsworth find in nature? How does he view city life?
3. How is Wordsworth's affection for his sister connected with the themes of the poem?
4. Do you think we can in any way view nature today as Wordsworth does in this poem? What, if anything, has changed in the natural world and our view of it?

WRITING

1. In a sense this poem is about the passage of time and the changes in attitude toward nature that Wordsworth experienced between boyhood and manhood. In lines 65–111, trace the stages of his development. What did nature mean to him as a boy? as a grown man? (In your essay, you might use the contrast between "powerful feelings" and "tranquility" which Wordsworth brings up in his definition of poetry in the "Preface to Lyrical Ballads.")
2. In prose or poetry, write a description of your feelings on returning, after an absence of months or years, to some place you have felt close to.

From THE PRELUDE, Book I

Wordsworth referred to *The Prelude,* on which he worked for almost fifty years, as "a history of the author's mind." This excerpt describes boyhood adventures which made a profound impression on him.

FAIR seed-time had my soul, and I grew up
Fostered alike by beauty and by fear:
Much favoured in my birth-place, and no less
In that belovèd Vale[1] to which erelong
5 We were transplanted;—there were we let loose
For sports of wider range. Ere I had told
Ten birth-days, when among the mountain slopes
Frost, and the breath of frosty wind, had snapped
The last autumnal crocus, 't was my joy
10 With store of springes[2] o'er my shoulder hung
To range the open heights where woodcocks run
Along the smooth green turf. Through half the night,
Scudding away from snare to snare, I plied
That anxious visitation;—moon and stars
15 Were shining o'er my head. I was alone,
And seemed to be a trouble to the peace
That dwelt among them. Sometimes it befell
In these night wanderings, that a strong desire
O'erpowered my better reason, and the bird
20 Which was the captive of another's toil
Became my prey; and when the deed was done
I heard among the solitary hills
Low breathings coming after me, and sounds
Of undistinguishable motion, steps
25 Almost as silent as the turf they trod.

Nor less, when spring had warmed the cultured Vale,
Moved we as plunderers where the mother-bird
Had in high places built her lodge; though mean
Our object and inglorious, yet the end
30 Was not ignoble. Oh! when I have hung
Above the raven's nest, by knots of grass
And half-inch fissures in the slippery rock
But ill sustained, and almost (so it seemed)
Suspended by the blast that blew amain,
35 Shouldering the naked crag, oh, at that time
While on the perilous ridge I hung alone,
With what strange utterance did the loud dry wind
Blow through my ear! the sky seemed not a sky
Of earth—and with what motion moved the clouds!

40 Dust as we are, the immortal spirit grows
Like harmony in music; there is a dark
Inscrutable workmanship that reconciles
Discordant elements, makes them cling together
In one society. How strange, that all
45 The terrors, pains, and early miseries,
Regrets, vexations, lassitudes interfused
Within my mind, should e'er have borne a part,
And that a needful part, in making up
The calm existence that is mine when I
50 Am worthy of myself! Praise to the end!
Thanks to the means which Nature deigned to employ;
Whether her fearless visitings, or those
That came with soft alarm, like hurtless light
Opening the peaceful clouds; or she would use
55 Severer interventions, ministry
More palpable, as best might suit her aim.

One summer evening (led by her) I found
A little boat tied to a willow tree
Within a rocky cove, its usual home.
60 Straight I unloosed her chain, and stepping in
Pushed from the shore. It was an act of stealth
And troubled pleasure, nor without the voice
Of mountain-echoes did my boat move on;
Leaving behind her still, on either side,
65 Small circles glittering idly in the moon,
Until they melted all into one track
Of sparkling light. But now, like one who rows,
Proud of his skill, to reach a chosen point
With an unswerving line, I fixed my view
70 Upon the summit of a craggy ridge,
The horizon's utmost boundary; far above
Was nothing but the stars and the grey sky.
She was an elfin pinnace; lustily
I dipped my oars into the silent lake,
75 And, as I rose upon the stroke, my boat
Went heaving through the water like a swan;
When, from behind that craggy steep till then
The horizon's bound, a huge peak, black and huge,
As if with voluntary power instinct,
80 Upreared its head. I struck and struck again,
And growing still in stature the grim shape
Towered up between me and the stars, and still,
For so it seemed, with purpose of its own
And measured motion like a living thing,
85 Strode after me. With trembling oars I turned,

1. *Vale,* Esthwaite Vale in Lancashire, near Wordsworth's boyhood home.
2. *springes,* snares for catching birds.

And through the silent water stole my way
Back to the covert of the willow tree;
There in her mooring-place I left my bark,—
And through the meadows homeward went, in grave
90 And serious mood; but after I had seen
That spectacle, for many days, my brain
Worked with a dim and undetermined sense
Of unknown modes of being; o'er my thoughts
There hung a darkness, call it solitude
95 Or blank desertion. No familiar shapes
Remained, no pleasant images of trees,
Of sea or sky, no colours of green fields;
But huge and mighty forms, that do not live
Like living men, moved slowly through the mind
100 By day, and were a trouble to my dreams. □

DISCUSSION

1. What guises does nature take as the "teacher" of young Wordsworth? Is nature presented as pleasant and harmless, or as a threatening force? What imagery in the passage supports your view?
2. What feelings of guilt are evident in this passage? How and where are they presented?

Samuel Taylor Coleridge

1772 / 1834

NATIONAL PORTRAIT GALLERY, LONDON

COLOGNE

In Köhln,[1] a town of monks and bones,
And pavements fanged with murderous stones
And rags, and hags, and hideous wenches;
I counted two and seventy stenches,
5 All well defined, and several stinks!
Ye Nymphs that reign o'er sewers and sinks,
The river Rhine, it is well known,
Doth wash your city of Cologne;
But tell me, Nymphs, what power divine
10 Shall henceforth wash the river Rhine?

1. *Köhln,* the German name for Cologne.

THE EXCHANGE

We pledged our hearts, my love and I,—
I in my arms the maiden clasping;
I could not guess the reason why,
But, oh! I trembled like an aspen.

5 Her father's love she bade me gain;
I went, but shook like any reed!
I strove to act the man—in vain!
We had exchanged our hearts indeed.

SONG

Though veiled in spires of myrtle-wreath,
Love is a sword which cuts its sheath,
And through the clefts itself has made,
We spy the flashes of the blade!

5 But through the clefts itself has made
We likewise see Love's flashing blade,
By rust consumed, or snapt in twain;
And only hilt and stump remain.

KUBLA KHAN

In Xanadu did Kubla Khan
A stately pleasure dome decree:
Where Alph, the sacred river, ran
Through caverns measureless to man
5 Down to a sunless sea.
So twice five miles of fertile ground
With walls and towers were girdled round:
And there were gardens bright with sinuous rills,
Where blossomed many an incense-bearing tree;
10 And here were forests ancient as the hills,
Enfolding sunny spots of greenery.

But oh! that deep romantic chasm which slanted
Down the green hill athwart a cedarn cover!
A savage place! as holy and enchanted
15 As e'er beneath a waning moon was haunted
By woman wailing for her demon lover!
And from this chasm, with ceaseless turmoil seething,
As if this earth in fast thick pants were breathing,
A mighty fountain momently was forced:
20 Amid whose swift half-intermitted burst
Huge fragments vaulted like rebounding hail,
Or chaffy grain beneath the thresher's flail:
And 'mid these dancing rocks at once and ever
It flung up momently the sacred river.
25 Five miles meandering with a mazy motion
Through wood and dale the sacred river ran,
Then reached the caverns measureless to man,
And sank in tumult to a lifeless ocean:
And 'mid this tumult Kubla heard from far
30 Ancestral voices prophesying war!
The shadow of the dome of pleasure
Floated midway on the waves;
Where was heard the mingled measure
From the fountain and the caves.
35 It was a miracle of rare device,
A sunny pleasure dome with caves of ice!

A damsel with a dulcimer
In a vision once I saw:
It was an Abyssinian maid,
40 And on her dulcimer she played,
Singing of Mount Abora.
Could I revive within me
Her symphony and song,
To such a deep delight 'twould win me,
45 That with music loud and long,
I would build that dome in air,
That sunny dome! those caves of ice!
And all who heard should see them there,
And all should cry, Beware! Beware!
50 His flashing eyes, his floating hair!
Weave a circle round him thrice,
And close your eyes with holy dread,
For he on honeydew hath fed,
And drunk the milk of Paradise.

OF LITERARY INTEREST

Coleridge's remarks about "Kubla Khan"

The following fragment is here published at the request of a poet of great and deserved celebrity,[1] and, as far as the author's own opinions are concerned, rather as a psychological curiosity, than on the ground of any supposed *poetic* merits.

In the summer of the year 1797, the author, then in ill health, had retired to a lonely farmhouse between Porlock and Linton, on the Exmoor confines of Somerset and Devonshire. In consequence of a slight indisposition, an anodyne had been prescribed, from the effects of which he fell asleep in his chair at the moment that he was reading the following sentence, or words of the same substance, in *Purchas's Pilgrimage:* "Here the Khan Kubla commanded a palace to be built, and a stately garden thereunto. And thus ten miles of fertile ground were inclosed with a wall."[2] The author continued for about three hours in a profound sleep, at least of the external senses, during which time he has the most vivid confidence that he could not have composed less than from two to three hundred lines; if that

1. *poet . . . celebrity,* Byron.

2. *"Here the Khan . . . with a wall."* The actual sentence in *Purchas his Pilgrimage* (1613) reads "In Xamdu did Cublai Can build a stately Palace, encompassing sixteene miles of plaine ground with a wall, wherein are fertile Meddowes, pleasant springs, delightfull Streames, and all sorts of beasts of chase and game, and in the middest thereof a sumptuous house of pleasure, which may be removed from place to place." The historical Kubla Khan founded the Mongol dynasty in China in the thirteenth century.

FROST AT MIDNIGHT

The Frost performs its secret ministry,
Unhelped by any wind. The owlet's cry
Came loud—and hark, again! loud as before.
The inmates of my cottage, all at rest,
5 Have left me to that solitude, which suits
Abstruser musings: save that at my side
My cradled infant[1] slumbers peacefully.
'Tis calm indeed! so calm, that it disturbs
And vexes meditation with its strange
10 And extreme silentness. Sea, hill, and wood,
This populous village! Sea, and hill, and wood,
With all the numberless goings-on of life,
Inaudible as dreams! the thin blue flame
Lies on my low-burnt fire, and quivers not;
15 Only that film,[2] which fluttered on the grate,
Still flutters there, the sole unquiet thing.
Methinks its motion in this hush of nature
Gives it dim sympathies with me who live,
Making it a companionable form,

1. *My cradled infant,* Coleridge's son, Hartley.
2. *film,* a film of soot. Coleridge's note on this reads: "In all parts of the kingdom these films are called *strangers* and are supposed to portend the arrival of some absent friend."

---

indeed can be called composition in which all the images rose up before him as *things,* with a parallel production of the correspondent expressions, without any sensation or consciousness of effort. On awaking he appeared to himself to have a distinct recollection of the whole, and taking his pen, ink, and paper, instantly and eagerly wrote down the lines that are here preserved. At this moment he was unfortunately called out by a person on business from Porlock, and detained by him above an hour, and on his return to his room, found, to his no small surprise and mortification, that though he still retained some vague and dim recollection of the general purport of the vision, yet, with the exception of some eight or ten scattered lines and images, all the rest had passed away like the images on the surface of a stream into which a stone has been cast. . . .

20 Whose puny flaps and freaks the idling Spirit
By its own moods interprets, everywhere
Echo or mirror seeking of itself,
And makes a toy of Thought.

But O! how oft,
How oft, at school, with most believing mind,
25 Presageful, have I gazed upon the bars,
To watch that fluttering *stranger!* and as oft
With unclosed lids, already had I dreamt
Of my sweet birthplace, and the old church tower,
Whose bells, the poor man's only music, rang
30 From morn to evening, all the hot fair-day,
So sweetly, that they stirred and haunted me
With a wild pleasure, falling on mine ear
Most like articulate sounds of things to come!
So gazed I, till the soothing things, I dreamt,
35 Lulled me to sleep, and sleep prolonged my dreams!
And so I brooded all the following morn,
Awed by the stern preceptor's face, mine eye
Fixed with mock study on my swimming book:
Save if the door half opened, and I snatched
40 A hasty glance, and still my heart leaped up,
For still I hoped to see the *stranger's* face,
Townsman, or aunt, or sister more beloved,
My playmate when we both were clothed alike![3]

Dear Babe, that sleepest cradled by my side,
45 Whose gentle breathings, heard in this deep calm,
Fill up the interspersèd vacancies
And momentary pauses of the thought!
My babe so beautiful! it thrills my heart
With tender gladness, thus to look at thee,
50 And think that thou shalt learn far other lore,
And in far other scenes! For I was reared
In the great city, pent 'mid cloisters dim,
And saw nought lovely but the sky and stars.
But *thou,* my babe! shalt wander like a breeze
55 By lakes and sandy shores, beneath the crags
Of ancient mountain, and beneath the clouds,

3. *when we both were clothed alike,* i.e., when both Coleridge and his sister Ann wore infant clothes.

Which image in their bulk both lakes and shores
And mountain crags: so shalt thou see and hear
The lovely shapes and sounds intelligible
60 Of that eternal language, which thy God
Utters, who from eternity doth teach
Himself in all, and all things in himself.
Great universal Teacher! he shall mold
Thy spirit, and by giving make it ask.

65 Therefore all seasons shall be sweet to thee,
Whether the summer clothe the general earth
With greenness, or the redbreast sit and sing
Betwixt the tufts of snow on the bare branch
Of mossy apple tree, while the nigh thatch
70 Smokes in the sun-thaw; whether the eave-drops fall
Heard only in the trances of the blast,
Or if the secret ministry of frost
Shall hang them up in silent icicles,
Quietly shining to the quiet Moon. □

OF HUMAN INTEREST

A son's reply

In this sonnet, Coleridge's son Hartley alludes to "Frost at Midnight."

Dedicatory Sonnet To S. T. Coleridge

Father, and Bard revered! to whom I owe,
Whate'er it be, my little art of numbers,
Thou, in thy night-watch o'er my cradled slumbers,
Didst meditate the verse that lives to show,
5 (And long shall live, when we alike are low)
Thy prayer how ardent, and thy hope how strong,
That I should learn of Nature's self the song,
The lore which none but Nature's pupils know.

The prayer was heard I "wandered like a breeze,"
10 By mountain brooks and solitary meres,[1]
And gathered there the shapes and phantasies
Which, mixed with passions of my sadder years,
Compose this book. If good therein there be,
That good, my sire, I dedicate to thee.

1. *meres,* lakes.

DISCUSSION

Kubla Khan

1. What instances of exotic imagery do you find in this poem? Can you factually describe or explain them—for example, can you describe what a "pleasure dome" is? Or do you *feel* the meaning, rather than "see" it in detail? What qualities of language add to your impression?

2. Readers of "Kubla Khan" have often commented that in spite of the luxuriance of the scenes described, the poem has foreboding or sinister undertones. Do you find any? What lines or phrases suggest them to you?

3. What does Coleridge suggest, in the last thirteen lines of the poem, as possible effects of reviving or completing his dream vision?

Frost at Midnight

1. What is the pervasive mood of this poem? What types of imagery help convey this mood?

2. What role does the "stranger" play? What memories does it recall?

3. What do Coleridge's memories suggest about his boyhood? In what ways are they related to (or contrasted with) his wishes for his infant son?

4. In the first and last lines of the poem, Coleridge refers to the "secret ministry of frost." What are the implications of this phrase? What particular overtones do you find in the word "ministry"? What does the phrase suggest about Coleridge's attitude toward nature?

WRITING

Read Hartley Coleridge's "Dedicatory Sonnet" and the words addressed to him in "Frost at Midnight." What do the two poems together suggest regarding the relationship between father and son?

George Gordon, Lord Byron

1788 / 1824

WHEN WE TWO PARTED

When we two parted
  In silence and tears,
Half broken-hearted
  To sever for years,
5 Pale grew thy cheek and cold,
  Colder thy kiss;
Truly that hour foretold
  Sorrow to this.

The dew of the morning
10 Sunk chill on my brow—
It felt like the warning
  Of what I feel now.
Thy vows are all broken,
  And light is thy fame;
15 I hear thy name spoken,
  And share in its shame.

They name thee before me,
  A knell to mine ear;
A shudder comes o'er me—
20 Why wert thou so dear?
They know not I knew thee,
  Who knew thee too well:—
Long, long shall I rue thee,
  Too deeply to tell.

25 In secret we met—
  In silence I grieve
That thy heart could forget,
  Thy spirit deceive.
If I should meet thee
30 After long years,
How should I greet thee?—
  With silence and tears.

SO WE'LL GO NO MORE A-ROVING

So we'll go no more a-roving
  So late into the night,
Though the heart be still as loving,
  And the moon be still as bright.

5 For the sword outwears its sheath,
  And the soul wears out the breast,
And the heart must pause to breathe,
  And Love itself have rest.

Though the night was made for loving,
10 And the day returns too soon,
Yet we'll go no more a-roving
  By the light of the moon.

SHE WALKS IN BEAUTY

She walks in beauty, like the night,
  Of cloudless climes and starry skies;
And all that's best of dark and bright
  Meet in her aspect and her eyes:
5 Thus mellowed to that tender light
  Which heaven to gaudy day denies.

One shade the more, one ray the less,
  Had half impaired the nameless grace
Which waves in every raven tress,
10 Or softly lightens o'er her face;
Where thoughts serenely sweet express
  How pure, how dear their dwelling place.

And on that cheek, and o'er that brow,
  So soft, so calm, yet eloquent,
15 The smiles that win, the tints that glow,
  But tell of days in goodness spent,
A mind at peace with all below,
  A heart whose love is innocent!

DARKNESS

I HAD a dream, which was not all a dream.
The bright sun was extinguished, and the stars
Did wander darkling in the eternal space,
Rayless, and pathless, and the icy earth
5 Swung blind and blackening in the moonless air;
Morn came and went—and came, and brought no day,
And men forgot their passions in the dread
Of this their desolation; and all hearts
Were chilled into a selfish prayer for light:
10 And they did live by watchfires—and the thrones,
The palaces of crownèd kings—the huts,
The habitations of all things which dwell,
Were burnt for beacons; cities were consumed,
And men were gathered round their blazing homes
15 To look once more into each other's face;
Happy were those who dwelt within the eye
Of the volcanoes, and their mountain torch:
A fearful hope was all the world contained;
Forests were set on fire—but hour by hour
20 They fell and faded—and the crackling trunks
Extinguished with a crash—and all was black.
The brows of men by the despairing light
Wore an unearthly aspect, as by fits
The flashes fell upon them; some lay down
25 And hid their eyes and wept; and some did rest
Their chins upon their clenchèd hands, and smiled;
And others hurried to and fro, and fed
Their funeral piles with fuel, and looked up
With mad disquietude on the dull sky,
30 The pall of a past world; and then again
With curses cast them down upon the dust,
And gnashed their teeth and howled: the wild birds shrieked
And, terrified, did flutter on the ground,
And flap their useless wings; the wildest brutes
35 Came tame and tremulous; and vipers crawled
And twined themselves among the multitude,
Hissing, but stingless—they were slain for food;
And War, which for a moment was no more,
Did glut himself again—a meal was bought
40 With blood, and each sate sullenly apart
Gorging himself in gloom: no love was left;
All earth was but one thought—and that was death
Immediate and inglorious; and the pang
Of famine fed upon all entrails—men
45 Died, and their bones were tombless as their flesh;
The meager by the meager were devoured,
Even dogs assailed their masters, all save one,
And he was faithful to a corse, and kept
The birds and beasts and famished men at bay,
50 Till hunger clung them, or the dropping dead
Lured their lank jaws; himself sought out no food,
But with a piteous and perpetual moan,
And a quick desolate cry, licking the hand
Which answered not with a caress—he died.
55 The crowd was famished by degrees; but two
Of an enormous city did survive,
And they were enemies: they met beside
The dying embers of an altar place.
Where had been heaped a mass of holy things
60 For an unholy usage; they raked up,
And shivering scraped with their cold skeleton hands
The feeble ashes, and their feeble breath
Blew for a little life, and made a flame
Which was a mockery; then they lifted up
65 Their eyes as it grew lighter, and beheld
Each other's aspects—saw, and shrieked, and died—
Even of their mutual hideousness they died,
Unknowing who he was upon whose brow
Famine had written Fiend. The world was void,
70 The populous and the powerful was a lump
Seasonless, herbless, treeless, manless, lifeless—
A lump of death—a chaos of hard clay.
The rivers, lakes, and ocean all stood still,
And nothing stirred within their silent depths;
75 Ships sailorless lay rotting on the sea,
And their masts fell down piecemeal: as they dropped
They slept on the abyss without a surge—
The waves were dead; the tides were in their grave,
The Moon, their mistress, had expired before;
80 The winds were withered in the stagnant air,
And the clouds perished; Darkness had no need
Of aid from them—She was the Universe. □

DISCUSSION

She Walks in Beauty

What quality of beauty does Byron emphasize in this portrait? Is it physical or spiritual beauty?

When We Two Parted

What words or phrases most vividly convey the feelings experienced by the speaker? What specifically is that feeling—has the speaker completely rejected the person addressed in the poem?

Darkness

1. Do you find anything in this poem which relieves its pessimism? What?
2. What sound effects make this poem so powerful in expression? Select six lines and examine them closely in terms of word choice, assonance, and alliteration.

WRITING

Darkness

Write a paragraph or two on the overtones of meaning you find in the first line. What aspects of possible reality are there in this poem for modern readers?

From DON JUAN, CANTO 1

1

I WANT a hero: an uncommon want,
When every year and month sends forth a new one,
Till, after cloying the gazettes with cant,
The age discovers he is not the true one;
5 Of such as these I should not care to vaunt,
I'll therefore take our ancient friend Don Juan—
We all have seen him, in the pantomime,
Sent to the devil somewhat ere his time.

6

Most epic poets plunge "in medias res"
10 (Horace makes this the heroic turnpike road),
And then your hero tells, whene'er you please,
What went before—by way of episode,
While seated after dinner at his ease,
Beside his mistress in some soft abode,
15 Palace, or garden, paradise, or cavern,
Which serves the happy couple for a tavern.

7

That is the usual method, but not mine—
My way is to begin with the beginning;
The regularity of my design
20 Forbids all wandering as the worst of sinning,
And therefore I shall open with a line
(Although it cost me half an hour in spinning)
Narrating somewhat of Don Juan's father,
And also of his mother, if you'd rather.

8

25 In Seville was he born, a pleasant city,
Famous for oranges and women—he
Who has not seen it will be much to pity,
So says the proverb—and I quite agree;
Of all the Spanish towns is none more pretty,
30 Cadiz, perhaps—but that you soon may see:—
Don Juan's parents lived beside the river,
A noble stream, and called the Guadalquivir.

9

His father's name was Jóse—*Don*, of course,
A true Hidalgo,[1] free from every stain
35 Of Moor or Hebrew blood, he traced his source
Through the most Gothic gentlemen of Spain;
A better cavalier ne'er mounted horse,
Or, being mounted, e'er got down again,
Than Jóse, who begot our hero, who
40 Begot—but that's to come—Well, to renew:

10

His mother was a learned lady, famed
For every branch of every science known—
In every Christian language ever named,
With virtues equalled by her wit alone:
45 She made the cleverest people quite ashamed,
And even the good with inward envy groan,
Finding themselves so very much exceeded
In their own way by all the things that she did.

1. *Hidalgo*, a member of the lower Spanish nobility.

13

She knew the Latin—that is, "the Lord's prayer,"
50 And Greek—the alphabet—I'm nearly sure;
She read some French romances here and there,
Although her mode of speaking was not pure;
For native Spanish she had no great care,
At least her conversation was obscure;
55 Her thoughts were theorems, her words a problem,
As if she deemed that mystery would ennoble 'em.

15

Some women use their tongues—she *looked* a lecture,
Each eye a sermon, and her brow a homily,
An all-in-all sufficient self-director,
60 Like the lamented late Sir Samuel Romilly,[2]
The Law's expounder, and the State's corrector,
Whose suicide was almost an anomaly—
One sad example more, that "All is vanity,"—
(The jury brought their verdict in "Insanity.")

17

65 Oh! she was perfect past all parallel—
Of any modern female saint's comparison;
So far above the cunning powers of hell,
Her guardian angel had given up his garrison;
Even her minutest motions went as well
70 As those of the best time-piece made by Harrison:[3]
In virtues nothing earthly could surpass her,
Save thine "incomparable oil," Macassar![4]

18

Perfect she was, but as perfection is
Insipid in this naughty world of ours,
75 Where our first parents never learned to kiss
Till they were exiled from their earlier bowers,
Where all was peace, and innocence, and bliss
(I wonder how they got through the twelve hours),
Don Jóse, like a lineal son of Eve,
80 Went plucking various fruit without her leave.

19

He was a mortal of the careless kind,
With no great love for learning, or the learned,
Who chose to go where'er he had a mind,
And never dreamed his lady was concerned;
85 The world, as usual, wickedly inclined
To see a kingdom or a house o'erturned,
Whispered he had a mistress, some said *two*,
But for domestic quarrels *one* will do.

20

Now Donna Inez had, with all her merit,
90 A great opinion of her own good qualities;
Neglect, indeed, requires a saint to bear it,
And such, indeed, she was in her moralities;
But then she had a devil of a spirit,
And sometimes mixed up fancies with realities,
95 And let few opportunities escape
Of getting her liege lord into a scrape.

23

Don Jóse and his lady quarrelled—*why*,
Not any of the many could divine,
Though several thousand people chose to try,
100 'Twas surely no concern of theirs nor mine;
I loathe that low vice—curiosity;
But if there's anything in which I shine,
'Tis in arranging all my friends' affairs,
Not having, of my own, domestic cares.

24

105 And so I interfered, and with the best
Intentions, but their treatment was not kind;
I think the foolish people were possessed,
For neither of them could I ever find,
Although their porter afterwards confessed—
110 But that's no matter, and the worst's behind,
For little Juan o'er me threw, down stairs,
A pail of housemaid's water unawares.

25

A little curly-headed, good-for-nothing,
And mischief-making monkey from his birth;
115 His parents ne'er agreed except in doting
Upon the most unquiet imp on earth;
Instead of quarrelling, had they been but both in
Their senses, they'd have sent young master forth
To school, or had him soundly whipped at home,
120 To teach him manners for the time to come.

26

Don Jóse and the Donna Inez led
For some time an unhappy sort of life,
Wishing each other, not divorced, but dead;
They lived respectably as man and wife,

2. *Sir Samuel Romilly*, an English lawyer who represented Byron's wife in her suit for divorce; he committed suicide in 1818.
3. *Harrison*, John Harrison (1693–1776), watchmaker and scientific inventor.
4. *Macassar*, a fragrant oil used as hair dressing.

125 Their conduct was exceedingly well-bred,
And gave no outward signs of inward strife,
Until at length the smothered fire broke out,
And put the business past all kind of doubt.

27

For Inez called some druggists and physicians,
130 And tried to prove her loving lord was *mad*,
But as he had some lucid intermissions,
She next decided he was only *bad;*
Yet when they asked her for her depositions,
No sort of explanation could be had,
135 Save that her duty both to man and God
Required this conduct—which seemed very odd.

32

Their friends had tried at reconciliation,
Then their relations, who made matters worse,
('Twere hard to tell upon a like occasion
140 To whom it may be best to have recourse—
I can't say much for friend or yet relation):
The lawyers did their utmost for divorce,
But scarce a fee was paid on either side
Before, unluckily, Don Jóse died.

33

145 He died: and most unluckily, because,
According to all hints I could collect
From counsel learned in those kinds of laws
(Although their talk's obscure and circumspect),
His death contrived to spoil a charming cause;
150 A thousand pities also with respect
To public feeling, which on this occasion
Was manifested in a great sensation.

37

Dying intestate, Juan was sole heir
To a chancery suit, and messuages,[5] and lands,
155 Which, with a long minority and care,
Promised to turn out well in proper hands:
Inez became sole guardian, which was fair,
And answered but to nature's just demands;
An only son left with an only mother
160 Is brought up much more wisely than another.

38

Sagest of women, even of widows, she
Resolved that Juan should be quite a paragon,
And worthy of the noblest pedigree:
(His sire was of Castile, his dam from Aragon).
165 Then for accomplishments of chivalry,
In case our lord the king should go to war again,
He learned the arts of riding, fencing, gunnery,
And how to scale a fortress—or a nunnery.

39

But that which Donna Inez most desired,
170 And saw into herself each day before all
The learned tutors whom for him she hired,
Was, that his breeding should be strictly moral:
Much into all his studies she inquired,
And so they were submitted first to her, all,
175 Arts, sciences, no branch was made a mystery
To Juan's eyes, excepting natural history.

40

The languages, especially the dead,
The sciences, and most of all the abstruse,
The arts, at least all such as could be said
180 To be the most remote from common use,
In all these he was much and deeply read;
But not a page of anything that's loose,
Or hints continuation of the species,
Was ever suffered, lest he should grow vicious.

41

185 His classic studies made a little puzzle,
Because of filthy loves of gods and goddesses,
Who in the earlier ages raised a bustle,
But never put on pantaloons or bodices;
His reverend tutors had at times a tussle,
190 And for their Æneids, Iliads, and Odysseys,
Were forced to make an odd sort of apology,
For Donna Inez dreaded the Mythology.

44

Juan was taught from out the best edition,
Expurgated by learned men, who place,
195 Judiciously, from out the schoolboy's vision,
The grosser parts; but, fearful to deface
Too much their modest bard by this omission,
And pitying sore this mutilated case,
They only add them all in an appendix,
200 Which saves, in fact, the trouble of an index;

45

For there we have them all "at one fell swoop,"
Instead of being scattered through the pages;

5. *messuages,* houses together with adjacent buildings.

They stand forth marshalled in a handsome troop,
  To meet the ingenuous youth of future ages,
205 Till some less rigid editor shall stoop
  To call them back into their separate cages,
Instead of standing staring all together,
Like garden gods—and not so decent either.

47

Sermons he read, and lectures he endured,
210 And homilies, and lives of all the saints;
To Jerome and to Chrysostom inured,
  He did not take such studies for restraints;
But how faith is acquired, and then ensured,
  So well not one of the aforesaid paints
215 As Saint Augustine in his fine Confessions,[6]
Which make the reader envy his transgressions.

48

This, too, was a sealed book to little Juan—
  I can't but say that his mamma was right,
If such an education was the true one.
220 She scarcely trusted him from out her sight;
Her maids were old, and if she took a new one,
  You might be sure she was a perfect fright;
She did this during even her husband's life—
I recommend as much to every wife.

49

225 Young Juan waxed in godliness and grace;
  At six a charming child, and at eleven
With all the promise of as fine a face
  As e'er to man's maturer growth was given:
He studied steadily and grew apace,
230 And seemed, at least, in the right road to heaven,
For half his days were passed at church, the other
Between his tutors, confessor, and mother.

50

At six, I said, he was a charming child,
  At twelve he was a fine, but quiet boy;
235 Although in infancy a little wild,
  They tamed him down amongst them: to destroy
His natural spirit not in vain they toiled.
  At least it seemed so; and his mother's joy
Was to declare how sage, and still, and steady,
240 Her young philosopher was grown already.

6. *Saint Augustine . . . Confessions.* In his *Confessions* Saint Augustine describes a variety of his youthful sins.

54

Young Juan now was sixteen years of age,
  Tall, handsome, slender, but well knit: he seemed
Active, though not so sprightly, as a page;
  And everybody but his mother deemed
245 Him almost man; but she flew in a rage
  And bit her lips (for else she might have screamed)
If any said so, for to be precocious
Was in her eyes a thing the most atrocious.

55

Amongst her numerous acquaintance, all
250 Selected for discretion and devotion,
There was the Donna Julia, whom to call
  Pretty were but to give a feeble notion
Of many charms in her as natural
  As sweetness to the flower, or salt to ocean,
255 Her zone to Venus, or his bow to Cupid,
(But this last simile is trite and stupid).

60

Her eye (I'm very fond of handsome eyes)
  Was large and dark, suppressing half its fire
Until she spoke, then through its soft disguise
260 Flashed an expression more of pride than ire,
And love than either; and there would arise
  A something in them which was not desire,
But would have been, perhaps, but for the soul
Which struggled through and chastened down the
    whole.

61

265 Her glossy hair was clustered o'er a brow
  Bright with intelligence, and fair, and smooth;
Her eyebrow's shape was like the aërial bow,
  Her cheek all purple with the beam of youth,
Mounting, at times, to a transparent glow,
270 As if her veins ran lightning; she, in sooth,
Possessed an air and grace by no means common:
Her stature tall—I hate a dumpy woman.

62

Wedded she was some years, and to a man
  Of fifty, and such husbands are in plenty;
275 And yet, I think, instead of such a ONE
  'Twere better to have TWO of five-and-twenty,
Especially in countries near the sun:
  And now I think on't, "mi vien in mente,"[7]

7. *mi vien in mente,* it comes to mind (Italian).

Ladies even of the most uneasy virtue
280 Prefer a spouse whose age is short of thirty.

69

Juan she saw, and, as a pretty child,
Caressed him often—such a thing might be
Quite innocently done, and harmless styled,
When she had twenty years, and thirteen he;
285 But I am not so sure I should have smiled
When he was sixteen, Julia twenty-three;
These few short years make wondrous alterations,
Particularly amongst sun-burnt nations.

70

Whate'er the cause might be, they had become
290 Changed; for the dame grew distant, the youth shy,
Their looks cast down, their greetings almost dumb,
And much embarrassment in either eye;
There surely will be little doubt with some
That Donna Julia knew the reason why,
295 But as for Juan, he had no more notion
Than he who never saw the sea of ocean.

71

Yet Julia's very coldness still was kind,
And tremulously gentle her small hand
Withdrew itself from his, but left behind
300 A little pressure, thrilling, and so bland
And slight, so very slight, that to the mind
'Twas but a doubt; but ne'er magician's wand
Wrought change with all Armida's[8] fairy art
Like what this light touch left on Juan's heart.

72

305 And if she met him, though she smiled no more,
She looked a sadness sweeter than her smile,
As if her heart had deeper thoughts in store
She must not own, but cherished more the while
For that compression in its burning core;
310 Even innocence itself has many a wile,
And will not dare to trust itself with truth,
And love is taught hypocrisy from youth.

75

Poor Julia's heart was in an awkward state;
She felt it going, and resolved to make
315 The noblest efforts for herself and mate,
For honour's, pride's, religion's, virtue's sake.
Her resolutions were most truly great,
And almost might have made a Tarquin[9] quake:
She prayed the Virgin Mary for her grace,
320 As being the best judge of a lady's case.

76

She vowed she never would see Juan more,
And next day paid a visit to his mother,
And looked extremely at the opening door,
Which, by the Virgin's grace, let in another;
325 Grateful she was, and yet a little sore—
Again it opens, it can be no other,
'Tis surely Juan now—No! I'm afraid
That night the Virgin was no further prayed.

77

She now determined that a virtuous woman
330 Should rather face an overcome temptation,
That flight was base and dastardly, and no man
Should ever give her heart the least sensation;
That is to say, a thought beyond the common
Preference, that we must feel upon occasion,
335 For people who are pleasanter than others,
But then they only seem so many brothers.

78

And even if by chance—and who can tell?
The devil's so very sly—she should discover
That all within was not so very well,
340 And, if still free, that such or such a lover
Might please perhaps, a virtuous wife can quell
Such thoughts, and be the better when they're over;
And if the man should ask, 'tis but denial:
I recommend young ladies to make trial.

79

345 And then there are such things as love divine,
Bright and immaculate, unmixed and pure,
Such as the angles think so very fine,
And matrons, who would be no less secure,
Platonic, perfect, "just such love as mine":
350 Thus Julia said—and thought so, to be sure;
And so I'd have her think, were I the man
On whom her reveries celestial ran.

8. *Armida,* a sorceress mentioned in the work of Torquato Tasso, Italian Renaissance poet (1544–1595).

9. *a Tarquin,* one of the legendary kings of ancient Rome noted for their lustiness.

86

So much for Julia. Now we'll turn to Juan.
Poor little fellow! he had no idea
355 Of his own case, and never hit the true one;
In feelings quick as Ovid's Miss Medea,[10]
He puzzled over what he found a new one,
But not as yet imagined it could be a
Thing quite in course, and not at all alarming,
360 Which, with a little patience, might grow charming.

87

Silent and pensive, idle, restless, slow,
His home deserted for the lonely wood,
Tormented with a wound he could not know,
His, like all deep grief, plunged in solitude:
365 I'm fond myself of solitude or so,
But then, I beg it may be understood,
By solitude I mean a Sultan's, not
A hermit's, with a haram for a grot.

90

Young Juan wandered by the glassy brooks,
370 Thinking unutterable things; he threw
Himself at length within the leafy nooks
Where the wild branch of the cork forest grew;
There poets find materials for their books,
And every now and then we read them through,
375 So that their plan and prosody are eligible,
Unless, like Wordsworth, they prove unintelligible.

91

He, Juan (and not Wordsworth), so pursued
His self-communion with his own high soul,
Until his mighty heart, in its great mood,
380 Had mitigated part, though not the whole
Of its disease; he did the best he could
With things not very subject to control,
And turned, without perceiving his condition,
Like Coleridge, into a metaphysician.

92

385 He thought about himself, and the whole earth,
Of man the wonderful, and of the stars,
And how the deuce they ever could have birth;
And then he thought of earthquakes, and of wars,
How many miles the moon might have in girth,
390 Of air-balloons, and of the many bars
To perfect knowledge of the boundless skies;—
And then he thought of Donna Julia's eyes.

There are 132 more stanzas in the remainder of Canto I of Don Juan. *Between 1819 and 1823 Byron added fifteen more cantos to the poem.*

10. *Ovid's Miss Medea.* In the *Metamorphoses,* Ovid presents Medea as a quick-tempered woman who took dreadful revenge on Jason for deserting her.

DISCUSSION

1. In stanza 7 Byron states that the regularity of his plans for his epic poem "Forbids all wandering as the worst of sinning." Is his poem that formal? Does he digress? Does he make "asides" or off-the-cuff remarks? How is the formality or informality of the poem reflected in his "poetic" diction?

2. Reread the portrait of Donna Inez (Don Juan's mother) in stanzas 10–18. Byron says "Oh! she was perfect past all parallel." Was she?

3. What plans does Donna Inez have for her son? What is Byron's attitude toward these plans? Is there any suggestion that Don Juan might become the kind of "paragon" his mother has in mind? that he might become another type of "paragon"?

4. Which do you feel is the most sympathetic portrait Byron paints in these stanzas from *Don Juan*? On what do you base your opinion?

5. Most of Byron's stanzas contain some sort of "punch line." Locate a few examples. What is their effect? Describe the effect in terms of any of the following words: mild, sharp, stinging, savage, childish, merely clever, showy, profound.

WRITING

1. In Canto IV of *Don Juan,* Byron writes "if I laugh at any mortal thing / 'Tis that I may not weep." Write a short essay classifying the selection in this book from *Don Juan:* is it merely designed for amusement, or is it an earnest criticism of human weaknesses, or is it something in between?

2. "Beneath each quick and glittering wit lies a vast, dark chasm of despair." Explore the meaning of this statement in reference to Byron and also in reference to your personal observations of everyday wit and humor.

3. Byron said that poetry is "the lava of the imagination whose eruption prevents an earthquake." Write a short paper in which you discuss the poems in this volume that he may have written for emotional release.

4. *Don Juan* is a mock epic (note its beginning: "I want a hero"). Compare and contrast it with *The Rape of the Lock,* another mock epic.

Percy Bysshe Shelley 1792 / 1822

ENGLAND IN 1819

An old, mad, blind, despised, and dying king[1]—
Princes, the dregs of their dull race, who flow
Through public scorn—mud from a muddy spring;
Rulers who neither see, nor feel, nor know,
5 But leechlike to their fainting country cling,
Till they drop, blind in blood, without a blow;
A people starved and stabbed in the untilled field—
An army, which liberticide and prey
Makes as a two-edged sword to all who wield;
10 Golden and sanguine laws which tempt and slay;
Religion Christless, Godless—a book sealed;
A Senate—Time's worst statute[2] unrepealed—
Are graves, from which a glorious Phantom[3] may
Burst, to illumine our tempestuous day.

---

1. *An old . . . king,* George III, who died in 1820, blind and insane.
2. *Time's worst statute,* the law restricting the civil liberties of Roman Catholics, which was not repealed until 1829.
3. *Phantom,* revolution.

OZYMANDIAS

I met a traveller from an antique land
Who said: Two vast and trunkless legs of stone
Stand in the desert . . . Near them, on the sand,
Half sunk, a shattered visage lies, whose frown,
5 And wrinkled lip, and sneer of cold command,
Tell that its sculptor well those passions read
Which yet survive, stamped on these lifeless things,
The hand that mocked them, and the heart that fed:
And on the pedestal these words appear:
10 "My name is Ozymandias, king of kings:
Look on my works, ye Mighty, and despair!"
Nothing beside remains. Round the decay
Of that colossal wreck, boundless and bare
The lone and level sands stretch far away.

SONG TO THE MEN OF ENGLAND

1

Men of England, wherefore plow
For the lords who lay ye low?
Wherefore weave with toil and care
The rich robes your tyrants wear?

2

5 Wherefore feed, and clothe, and save,
From the cradle to the grave,
Those ungrateful drones who would
Drain your sweat—nay, drink your blood?

3

Wherefore, Bees of England, forge
10 Many a weapon, chain, and scourge,
That these stingless drones may spoil
The forced produce of your toil?

4

Have ye leisure, comfort, calm,
Shelter, food, love's gentle balm?
15 Or what is it ye buy so dear
With your pain and with your fear?

5

The seed ye sow, another reaps;
The wealth ye find, another keeps;
The robes ye weave, another wears;
20 The arms ye forge, another bears.

6

Sow seed—but let no tyrant reap;
Find wealth—let no impostor heap;
Weave robes—let not the idle wear;
Forge arms—in your defense to bear.

7

25 Shrink to your cellars, holes, and cells;
In halls ye deck another dwells.
Why shake the chains ye wrought? Ye see
The steel ye tempered glance on ye.

8

With plow and spade, and hoe and loom,
30 Trace your grave, and build your tomb,
And weave your winding-sheet, till fair
England be your sepulcher.

MUTABILITY

We are as clouds that veil the midnight moon;
How restlessly they speed, and gleam, and quiver,
Streaking the darkness radiantly!—yet soon
Night closes round, and they are lost for ever:

5 Or like forgotten lyres, whose dissonant strings
Give various response to each varying blast,
To whose frail frame no second motion brings
One mood or modulation like the last.

We rest.—A dream has power to poison sleep;
10 We rise.—One wandering thought pollutes the day;
We feel, conceive or reason, laugh or weep;
Embrace fond woe, or cast our cares away:

It is the same!—For, be it joy or sorrow,
The path of its departure still is free:
15 Man's yesterday may ne'er be like his morrow;
Nought may endure but Mutability.

MUSIC, WHEN SOFT VOICES DIE

Music, when soft voices die,
Vibrates in the memory—
Odours, when sweet violets sicken,
Live within the sense they quicken.

5 Rose leaves, when the rose is dead,
Are heaped for the belovèd's bed;
And so thy thoughts, when thou art gone,
Love itself shall slumber on.

A DIRGE

Rough wind, that moanest loud
Grief too sad for song;
Wild wind, when sullen cloud
Knells all the night long;
5 Sad storm, whose tears are vain,
Bare woods, whose branches strain,
Deep caves and dreary main—
Wail, for the world's wrong!

DETAIL FROM "CALAIS PIER, WITH FRENCH POISSARDS PREPARING FOR SEA: AN ENGLISH PACKET ARRIV BY JOSEPH M. W. TURNER (EXHIBITED IN 1803). REPRODUCED BY COURTESY OF THE TRUSTEES, THE NATIONAL GALLERY, LONDON.

ODE TO THE WEST WIND

1

O WILD West Wind, thou breath of Autumn's being,
Thou, from whose unseen presence the leaves dead
Are driven, like ghosts from an enchanter fleeing,

Yellow, and black, and pale, and hectic red,
5 Pestilence-stricken multitudes: O thou,
Who chariotest to their dark wintry bed

The wingèd seeds, where they lie cold and low,
Each like a corpse within its grave, until
Thine azure sister of the Spring shall blow

10 Her clarion o'er the dreaming earth, and fill
(Driving sweet buds like flocks to feed in air)
With living hues and odors plain and hill:

Wild Spirit, which art moving everywhere;
Destroyer and preserver; hear, oh, hear!

2

15 Thou on whose stream, mid the steep sky's commotion,
Loose clouds like earth's decaying leaves are shed,
Shook from the tangled boughs of Heaven and Ocean,

Angels of rain and lightning: there are spread
On the blue surface of thine aëry surge,
20 Like the bright hair uplifted from the head

Of some fierce Maenad,[1] even from the dim verge
Of the horizon to the zenith's height,
The locks of the approaching storm. Thou dirge

Of the dying year, to which this closing night
25 Will be the dome of a vast sepulcher,
Vaulted with all thy congregated might

Of vapors, from whose solid atmosphere
Black rain, and fire, and hail will burst: oh hear!

3

Thou who didst waken from his summer dreams
30 The blue Mediterranean, where he lay,
Lulled by the coil of his crystalline streams,

Beside a pumice isle in Baiae's bay,[2]
And saw in sleep old palaces and towers
Quivering within the wave's intenser day,

35 All overgrown with azure moss and flowers
So sweet, the sense faints picturing them! Thou
For whose path the Atlantic's level powers

Cleave themselves into chasms, while far below
The sea-blooms and the oozy woods which wear
40 The sapless foliage of the ocean, know

Thy voice, and suddenly grow gray with fear,
And tremble and despoil themselves: oh, hear!

4

If I were a dead leaf thou mightest bear,
If I were a swift cloud to fly with thee;
45 A wave to pant beneath thy power, and share

The impulse of thy strength, only less free
Than thou, O uncontrollable! If even
I were as in my boyhood, and could be

The comrade of thy wanderings over Heaven,
50 As then, when to outstrip thy skyey speed
Scarce seemed a vision; I would ne'er have striven

As thus with thee in prayer in my sore need.
Oh, lift me as a wave, a leaf, a cloud!
I fall upon the thorns of life! I bleed!

(more)

1. *Maenad* (mē′nad), a priestess of Bacchus, god of wine.

2. *Baiae's* (bä′yäz) *bay*. The village of Baia is a seaport about ten miles from Naples in Italy.

55 A heavy weight of hours has chained and bowed
One too like thee: tameless, and swift, and proud.

5

Make me thy lyre, even as the forest is:
What if my leaves are falling like its own!
The tumult of thy mighty harmonies

60 Will take from both a deep, autumnal tone,
Sweet though in sadness. Be thou, Spirit fierce,
My spirit! Be thou me, impetuous one!

Drive my dead thoughts over the universe
Like withered leaves to quicken a new birth!
65 And, by the incantation of this verse,

Scatter, as from an unextinguished hearth
Ashes and sparks, my words among mankind!
Be through my lips to unawakened earth

The trumpet of a prophecy! O Wind,
70 If Winter comes, can Spring be far behind?

DISCUSSION

England in 1819

1. What is the literal "argument" of this sonnet?
2. What imagery in the sonnet gives the argument its strongest impact, in your opinion?

Ozymandias

1. What is the irony of the inscription on the pedestal?
2. How does the imagery of the poem reinforce the double meaning of the word "despair"?

Song to the Men of England

1. What in your opinion is Shelley's general attitude toward the men of England? Is he sympathetic, or contemptuous?
2. Compare this song with the sonnet "England in 1819." Is there any similarity of tone or theme between the two? Which uses the stronger imagery?

Mutability

Which of the following statements do you think best embodies the theme of "Mutability"? (a) Tomorrow and tomorrow and tomorrow creeps in its petty pace from day to day. (b) The only certainty is change. (c) Sad today, glad tomorrow. Support your choice by referring to the poem.

A Dirge

Reread "Westron Wind" on page 105 and compare it with this lyric. What differences do you find? Which poem do you prefer? Why?

Ode to the West Wind

1. What two contradictory forces does the West Wind represent? What echoes of this paradox do you find throughout the poem? In what sense is the West Wind a spirit "moving everywhere"?
2. Choose from the poem what you consider the two or three most dramatic images of the West Wind's intensity. What qualities of language or physical description convey the idea or feeling of force?

John Keats 1795 / 1821

NATIONAL PORTRAIT GALLERY, LONDON

WHEN I HAVE FEARS

When I have fears that I may cease to be
Before my pen has gleaned my teeming brain,
Before high-pilèd books, in charact'ry,
Hold like rich garners the full-ripened grain;
5 When I behold, upon the night's starred face,
Huge cloudy symbols of a high romance,
And think that I may never live to trace
Their shadows, with the magic hand of chance;
And when I feel, fair creature of an hour,
10 That I shall never look upon thee more,
Never have relish in the faery power
Of unreflecting love!—then on the shore
Of the wide world I stand alone, and think
Till Love and Fame to nothingness do sink.

BRIGHT STAR, WOULD I WERE STEDFAST

Bright star, would I were stedfast as thou art—
Not in lone splendour hung aloft the night
And watching, with eternal lids apart,
Like nature's patient, sleepless Eremite,[1]
5 The moving waters at their priestlike task
Of pure ablution round earth's human shores,
Or gazing on the new soft-fallen mask
Of snow upon the mountains and the moors—
No—yet still stedfast, still unchangeable,
10 Pillowed upon my fair love's ripening breast,
To feel for ever its soft fall and swell,
Awake for ever in a sweet unrest,
Still, still to hear her tender-taken breath,
And so live ever—or else swoon to death.

1. *Eremite,* hermit; guardian.

THIS LIVING HAND[1]

This living hand, now warm and capable
Of earnest grasping, would, if it were cold
And in the icy silence of the tomb,
So haunt thy days and chill thy dreaming nights
5 That thou would[st] wish thine own heart dry of
blood
So in my veins red life might stream again,
And thou be conscience-calm'd—see here it is—
I hold it towards you.

1. This poem was supposedly written for Fanny Brawne, with whom Keats was in love.

ON FIRST LOOKING INTO CHAPMAN'S HOMER

Much have I travelled in the realms of gold,
And many goodly states and kingdoms seen;
Round many western islands have I been
Which bards in fealty to Apollo hold.
5 Oft of one wide expanse had I been told
That deep-brow'd Homer ruled as his demesne;[1]
Yet did I never breathe its pure serene
Till I heard Chapman speak out loud and bold:
Then felt I like some watcher of the skies
10 When a new planet swims into his ken;
Or like stout Cortez when with eagle eyes
He stared at the Pacific—and all his men
Looked at each other with a wild surmise—
Silent, upon a peak in Darien.

1. *demesne*, domain.

OF CRITICAL INTEREST

Did Keats make an ignorant blunder?

The fact that Balboa, not Cortez, first discovered the Pacific has disturbed commentators on Keats's sonnet "On First Looking into Chapman's Homer" for many years. Why does Keats, who was a voracious reader from boyhood and acquainted with most of the available literature on historic voyages, use Cortez as his symbol of discovery? Perhaps he deliberately chose Cortez to imply that one need not be "the first" to make a discovery for that discovery to have profound personal significance. After all, Keats was not the first to read Chapman's famous translation of Homer (which had been in print for two centuries), nor was his discovery of Chapman's version his first contact with Homer (he had read Pope's translation). Yet the force of his discovery was such that it left him overwhelmed by a kind of personal illumination grasped for the first time.

The story is that Keats stayed up the whole night reading the translation with his friend and former teacher, Charles Cowden Clarke. Keats walked home at dawn, and Clarke received the sonnet in the mail later the same morning.

We who live in a competitive age of rapidly proliferating "firsts"—first man on the moon, first heart transplant—may think it strange of Keats to mention Cortez, who was second. But Keats was not talking about outward accomplishments; he was talking about the satisfactions of an inner voyage, where "first" no longer counts.

TO AUTUMN

1

Season of mists and mellow fruitfulness,
Close bosom-friend of the maturing sun;
Conspiring with him how to load and bless
With fruit the vines that round the thatch-eaves run;
5 To bend with apples the mossed cottage-trees,
And fill all fruit with ripeness to the core;
To swell the gourd, and plump the hazel shells
With a sweet kernel; to set budding more,
And still more, later flowers for the bees,
10 Until they think warm days will never cease,
For Summer has o'er-brimmed their clammy cells.

2

Who hath not seen thee oft amid thy store?
Sometimes whoever seeks abroad may find
Thee sitting careless on a granary floor,
15 Thy hair soft-lifted by the winnowing wind;
Or on a half-reaped furrow sound asleep,
Drowsed with the fume of poppies, while thy hook
Spares the next swath and all its twinèd flowers:
And sometimes like a gleaner thou dost keep
20 Steady thy laden head across a brook;
Or by a cider-press, with patient look,
Thou watchest the last oozings hours by hours.

3

Where are the songs of Spring? Aye, where are they?
Think not of them, thou hast thy music too—
25 While barred clouds bloom the soft-dying day,
And touch the stubble-plains with rosy hue;
Then in a wailful choir the small gnats mourn
Among the river sallows,[1] borne aloft
Or sinking as the light wind lives or dies;
30 And full-grown lambs loud bleat from hilly bourn;
Hedge crickets sing; and now with treble soft
The redbreast whistles from a garden croft;
And gathering swallows twitter in the skies.

---

1. *sallows*, willows.

DISCUSSION

This Living Hand

Compare these lines with the sonnet "When I Have Fears." Which is the more direct statement of "unreflecting love"? Which is more convincing?

Bright Star. . . .

What is the one word in this sonnet which emphasizes its theme? State that theme in one or two sentences.

On First Looking into Chapman's Homer

What does the last line—"Silent, upon a peak in Darien"—suggest about the feelings Keats experienced when he first read the book?

To Autumn

1. Shortly after this poem was composed on September 19, 1819, Keats wrote to a friend: "I never liked stubble fields so much as now—Aye, better than the chilly green of the spring. Somehow a stubble field looks warm. . . ." What in the poem would explain Keats's preference?

2. Compare Keats's attitude toward autumn with Shelley's in "Ode to the West Wind." What differences do you find?

3. Discuss "To Autumn" in the context of Keats's life and in terms of this opinion: "Keats's Ode overflows with all the sensations of those warm and drowsy days just before the onslaught of winter, when the world and one's relation to it seem a promise totally fulfilled. During that short season one lives every day as if it were an unexpected reprieve, knowing full well what it will be like after the first killing frost."

WRITING

The poet symbolizes Autumn as a mythic person; yet describes the signs of Fall in very real terms. How would you describe or personify this season? Write a brief essay or poem, using an image that seems to you to best portray Autumn. Let your imagination run free.

ODE ON A GRECIAN URN

THOU still unravished bride of quietness,
Thou foster child of Silence and slow Time,
Sylvan historian, who canst thus express
A flowery tale more sweetly than our rime—
5 What leaf-fringed legend haunts about thy shape
Of deities or mortals, or of both,
In Tempe[1] or the dales of Arcady?[2]
What men or gods are these? What maidens loath?
What mad pursuit? What struggle to escape?
10 What pipes and timbrels? What wild ecstasy?

Heard melodies are sweet, but those unheard
Are sweeter; therefore, ye soft pipes, play on;
Not to the sensual ear, but, more endeared,
Pipe to the spirit ditties of no tone.
15 Fair youth, beneath the trees, thou canst not leave
Thy song, nor ever can those trees be bare;
Bold lover, never, never canst thou kiss,
Though winning near the goal—yet, do not grieve;
She cannot fade, though thou hast not thy bliss,
20 Forever wilt thou love, and she be fair!

Ah, happy, happy boughs! that cannot shed
Your leaves, nor ever bid the spring adieu;
And, happy melodist, unweariėd,
Forever piping songs forever new.
25 More happy love! more happy, happy love!
Forever warm and still to be enjoyed,
Forever panting, and forever young;
All breathing human passion far above,
That leaves a heart high-sorrowful and cloyed,
30 A burning forehead, and a parching tongue.

Who are these coming to the sacrifice?
To what green altar, O mysterious priest,
Lead'st thou that heifer lowing at the skies,
And all her silken flanks with garlands dressed?
35 What little town by river or seashore,
Or mountain-built with peaceful citadel,
Is emptied of this folk, this pious morn?
And, little town, thy streets forevermore
Will silent be; and not a soul to tell
40 Why thou art desolate, can e'er return.

O Attic shape![3] Fair attitude! with brede[4]
Of marble men and maidens overwrought,
With forest branches and the trodden weed;
Thou, silent form! dost tease us out of thought
45 As doth eternity: Cold pastoral!
When old age shall this generation waste,
Thou shalt remain, in midst of other woe
Than ours, a friend to man, to whom thou say'st,
"Beauty is truth, truth beauty—that is all
50 Ye know on earth, and all ye need to know."

1. *Tempe,* a beautiful valley in Thessaly in Greece.
2. *Arcady,* Arcadia, a part of ancient Greece, celebrated in pastoral poetry as the home of an ideal shepherd life.
3. *Attic shape,* a shape representing the simple, elegant taste of Athens.
4. *brede,* embroidery.

DISCUSSION

1. What specifically is the source of the "happiness" that Keats sees in the scene depicted on the urn? How is such "happiness" related to the statement: "Heard melodies are sweet, but those unheard / Are sweeter"? Why might Keats's final judgment of the urn be: "*Cold* pastoral"?

2. Describe the scenes depicted on the urn in as much detail as the poem allows. Do you get a clear picture, or an indistinct one?

3. What truths do you think the urn conveys about the human condition? What might Keats mean by "beauty"?

LA BELLE DAME SANS MERCI[1]

1

O what can ail thee, Knight at arms,
Alone and palely loitering?
The sedge has withered from the Lake
And no birds sing!

2

5 O what can ail thee, Knight at arms,
So haggard, and so woebegone?
The squirrel's granary is full
And the harvest's done.

3

I see a lily on thy brow
10 With anguish moist and fever dew,
And on thy cheeks a fading rose
Fast withereth too.

4

I met a Lady in the Meads,
Full beautiful, a faery's child,
15 Her hair was long, her foot was light
And her eyes were wild.

5

I made a Garland for her head,
And bracelets too, and fragrant Zone;[2]
She looked at me as she did love
20 And made sweet moan.

6

I set her on my pacing steed
And nothing else saw all day long,
For sidelong would she bend and sing
A faery's song.

7

25 She found me roots of relish sweet,
And honey wild, and manna dew,
And sure in language strange she said
"I love thee true."

8

She took me to her elfin grot
30 And there she wept and sighed full sore,
And there I shut her wild wild eyes
With kisses four.

9

And there she lullèd me asleep,
And there I dreamed, Ah Woe betide!
35 The latest dream I ever dreamt
On the cold hill side.

10

I saw pale Kings, and Princes too,
Pale warriors, death-pale were they all;
They cried, "La belle dame sans merci
40 Thee hath in thrall!"

11

I saw their starved lips in the gloam
With horrid warning gapèd wide,
And I awoke, and found me here
On the cold hill's side.

12

45 And this is why I sojourn here,
Alone and palely loitering;
Though the sedge is withered from the Lake
And no birds sing.

1. The title means "The Lovely Lady Without Pity."
2. *Zone,* girdle.

DISCUSSION

1. What kind of "enthrallment" does the lady impose? Is it the imprisonment of physical love, or the confinements of a world of misleading fancy? Might it be the confines of a temporal world where youth and youthful love grow into withered old age? Other theories?

2. What effects has this "enthrallment" had on the knight? What are the overtones of the last two lines of the poem in respect to his condition?

ODE TO A NIGHTINGALE

MY heart aches, and a drowsy numbness pains
My sense, as though of hemlock[1] I had drunk,
Or emptied some dull opiate to the drains
One minute past, and Lethe-wards[2] had sunk.
5 'Tis not through envy of thy happy lot,
But being too happy in thine happiness—
That thou, light-wingèd Dryad[3] of the trees,
In some melodious plot
Of beechen green, and shadows numberless,
10 Singest of summer in full-throated ease.

O for a draft of vintage! that hath been
Cooled a long age in the deep-delvèd earth,
Tasting of Flora[4] and the country green,
Dance, and Provencal song,[5] and sunburnt mirth!
15 O for a beaker full of the warm South,
Full of the true, the blushful Hippocrene,[6]
With beaded bubbles winking at the brim,
And purple-stainèd mouth;
That I might drink, and leave the world unseen,
20 And with thee fade away into the forest dim—

Fade far away, dissolve, and quite forget
What thou among the leaves hast never known,
The weariness, the fever, and the fret
Here, where men sit and hear each other groan;
25 Where palsy shakes a few, sad, last gray hairs,
Where youth grows pale, and specter-thin, and dies;
Where but to think is to be full of sorrow
And leaden-eyed despairs,
Where Beauty cannot keep her lustrous eyes,
30 Or new love pine at them beyond tomorrow.

Away! away! for I will fly to thee,
Not charioted by Bacchus[7] and his pards,
But on the viewless[8] wings of poesy,
Though the dull brain perplexes and retards.
35 Already with thee! tender is the night,
And haply the Queen-Moon is on her throne,
Clustered around by all her starry fays;
But here there is no light,
Save what from heaven is with the breezes blown
40 Through verdurous glooms and winding mossy ways.

I cannot see what flowers are at my feet,
Nor what soft incense hangs upon the boughs,
But, in embalmèd darkness, guess each sweet
Wherewith the seasonable month endows
45 The grass, the thicket, and the fruit tree wild;
White hawthorn, and the pastoral eglantine;
Fast fading violets covered up in leaves;
And mid-May's eldest child,
The coming muskrose, full of dewy wine,
50 The murmurous haunt of flies on summer eves.

Darkling I listen; and, for many a time,
I have been half in love with easeful Death,
Called him soft names in many a musèd rime,
To take into the air my quiet breath;
55 Now more than ever seems it rich to die,
To cease upon the midnight with no pain,
While thou art pouring forth thy soul abroad
In such an ecstasy!
Still wouldst thou sing, and I have ears in vain—
60 To thy high requiem become a sod.

Thou wast not born for death, immortal Bird!
No hungry generations tread thee down;
The voice I hear this passing night was heard
In ancient days by emperor and clown;[9]
65 Perhaps the selfsame song that found a path
Through the sad heart of Ruth, when sick for home,
She stood in tears amid the alien corn;[10]
The same that ofttimes hath
Charmed magic casements, opening on the foam
70 Of perilous seas, in faery lands forlorn.

---

1. *hemlock,* a poison.
2. *Lethe-wards,* towards Lethe, the river of forgetfulness in Hades.
3. *Dryad,* a tree nymph.
4. *Flora,* goddess of the flowers and the spring.
5. *Provençal song.* Provence in southern France was famous in the Middle Ages for the songs of its troubadours.
6. *Hippocrene,* a fountain on Mt. Helicon in Greece, sacred to the Muses.
7. *Bacchus,* god of wine, who was often represented as riding in a carriage drawn by leopards (pards).
8. *viewless,* invisible.
9. *clown,* peasant.
10. *Ruth . . . corn.* According to the Bible story, Ruth left her homeland to go with Naomi, her mother-in-law, to Judah, a foreign country to her, where she worked in the corn (wheat) fields (Ruth 2:1–23).

Forlorn! the very word is like a bell
  To toll me back from thee to my sole self.
Adieu! the fancy cannot cheat so well
  As she is famed to do, deceiving elf.
75 Adieu! adieu! thy plaintive anthem fades
  Past the near meadows, over the still stream,
    Up the hillside; and now 'tis buried deep
      In the next valley glades.
  Was it a vision, or a waking dream?
80 Fled is that music.—Do I wake or sleep? □

DISCUSSION

1. What are the probable causes of Keats's sense of "heartache" and "drowsy numbness" as given in the poem?

2. In what sense can this poem be called a reverie about "escaping" from the world? What possible means of escape are suggested? Why does Keats finally reject them all?

3. What role do the poet, the nightingale, and Ruth play?

4. What does Keats mean by lines 73–74: "the fancy cannot cheat so well / As she is famed to do"? How is this related to his "forlorn" state?

THE EVE OF ST. AGNES

St. Agnes, who was martyred in Rome around A.D. 300 at the age of thirteen, was the patron saint of virgins. In the Middle Ages there developed the legend on which this poem is based—that by following a certain ritual on St. Agnes' Eve (January 20), a virtuous maiden might see her future husband in a dream.

1

ST. AGNES' Eve—Ah, bitter chill it was!
The owl, for all his feathers, was a-cold;
The hare limped trembling through the frozen grass,
And silent was the flock in woolly fold:
5 Numb were the Beadsman's[1] fingers while he told
His rosary, and while his frosted breath,
Like pious incense from a censer old,
Seemed taking flight for heaven, without a death,
Past the sweet Virgin's picture, while his prayer he
    saith.

2

10 His prayer he saith, this patient, holy man;
Then takes his lamp, and riseth from his knees,
And back returneth, meager, barefoot, wan,
Along the chapel aisle by slow degrees:
The sculptured dead, on each side, seem to freeze,
15 Imprisoned in black, purgatorial rails:
Knights, ladies, praying in dumb orat'ries,
He passeth by, and his weak spirit fails
To think how they may ache in icy hoods and mails.

3

Northward he turneth through a little door,
20 And scarce three steps, ere Music's golden tongue
Flattered to tears this aged man and poor;
But no—already had his death-bell rung:
The joys of all his life were said and sung;
His was harsh penance on St. Agnes' Eve:
25 Another way he went, and soon among
Rough ashes sat he for his soul's reprieve,
And all night kept awake, for sinners' sake to grieve.

4

That ancient Beadsman heard the prelude soft;
And so it chanced, for many a door was wide,
30 From hurry to and fro. Soon, up aloft,
The silver, snarling trumpets 'gan to chide:
The level chambers, ready with their pride,
Were glowing to receive a thousand guests.

1. *Beadsman*, a dependent whose whole duty was to pray for his benefactor.

The carved angels, ever eager-eyed,
35 Stared, where upon their heads the cornice rests,
With hair blown back, and wings put crosswise on
their breasts.

5

At length burst in the argent revelry,
With plume, tiara, and all rich array,
Numerous as shadows haunting faerily
40 The brain new-stuffed, in youth, with triumphs gay
Of old romance. These let us wish away,
And turn, sole-thoughted, to one Lady there,
Whose heart had brooded, all that wintry day,
On love, and winged St. Agnes' saintly care,
45 As she had heard old dames full many times declare.

6

They told her how, upon St. Agnes' Eve,
Young virgins might have visions of delight,
And soft adorings from their loves receive
Upon the honeyed middle of the night,
50 If ceremonies due they did aright;
As, supperless to bed they must retire,
And couch supine their beauties, lily white;
Nor look behind, nor sideways, but require
Of Heaven with upward eyes for all that they desire.

7

55 Full of this whim was thoughtful Madeline:
The music, yearning like a God in pain,
She scarcely heard: her maiden eyes divine,
Fixed on the floor, saw many a sweeping train
Pass by—she heeded not at all: in vain
60 Came many a tiptoe, amorous cavalier,
And back retired; not cooled by high disdain,
But she saw not: her heart was otherwhere;
She sighed for Agnes' dreams, the sweetest of the
year.

8

She danced along with vague, regardless eyes,
65 Anxious her lips, her breathing quick and short:
The hallowed hour was near at hand: she sighs
Amid the timbrels, and the thronged resort
Of whisperers in anger or in sport;
'Mid looks of love, defiance, hate, and scorn,
70 Hoodwinked with faery fancy; all amort,[2]
Save to St. Agnes and her lambs unshorn,[3]
And all the bliss to be before tomorrow morn.

---

2. *amort,* deadened.
3. *St. Agnes and her lambs unshorn.* St. Agnes' day was originally celebrated by the sacrifice of two lambs, their wool to be woven later by chosen nuns.

9

So, purposing each moment to retire,
She lingered still. Meantime, across the moors,
75 Had come young Porphyro, with heart on fire
For Madeline. Beside the portal doors,
Buttressed from moonlight, stands he, and implores
All saints to give him sight of Madeline,
But for one moment in the tedious hours,
80 That he might gaze and worship all unseen;
Perchance speak, kneel, touch, kiss—in sooth such
things have been.

10

He ventures in: let no buzzed whisper tell,
All eyes be muffled, or a hundred swords
Will storm his heart, Love's feverous citadel:
85 For him, those chambers held barbarian hordes,
Hyena foemen, and hot-blooded lords,
Whose very dogs would execrations howl
Against his lineage; not one breast affords
Him any mercy in that mansion foul,
90 Save one old beldame, weak in body and in soul.

11

Ah, happy chance! the aged creature came,
Shuffling along with ivory-headed wand,
To where he stood, hid from the torch's flame,
Behind a broad hall pillar, far beyond
95 The sound of merriment and chorus bland.
He startled her: but soon she knew his face,
And grasped his fingers in her palsied hand,
Saying, "Mercy, Porphyro! hie thee from this place;
They are all here tonight, the whole blood-thirsty
race!

12

100 "Get hence! get hence! there's dwarfish Hildebrand:
He had a fever late, and in the fit
He cursed thee and thine, both house and land:
Then there's that old Lord Maurice, not a whit
More tame for his gray hairs—Alas me! flit!
105 Flit like a ghost away."—"Ah, Gossip[4] dear,
We're safe enough; here in this arm-chair sit,
And tell me how—" "Good saints! not here, not here!
Follow me, child, or else these stones will be
thy bier."

13

He followed through a lowly archèd way,
110 Brushing the cobwebs with his lofty plume;

---

4. *Gossip,* friend.

And as she muttered "Well-a—well-a-day!"
He found him in a little moonlight room,
Pale, latticed, chill, and silent as a tomb.
"Now tell me where is Madeline," said he,
115 "O tell me, Angela, by the holy loom
Which none but secret sisterhood may see,
When they St. Agnes' wool are weaving piously."

14

"St. Agnes! Ah! it is St. Agnes' Eve—
Yet men will murder upon holy days.
120 Thou must hold water in a witch's sieve,[5]
And be liege-lord of all the Elves and Fays
To venture so: it fills me with amaze
To see thee, Porphyro!—St. Agnes' Eve!
God's help! my lady fair the conjurer plays
125 This very night: good angels her deceive!
But let me laugh awhile,—I've mickle time to grieve."

15

Feebly she laugheth in the languid moon,
While Porphyro upon her face doth look,
Like puzzled urchin on an aged crone
130 Who keepeth closed a wondrous riddlebook,
As spectacled she sits in chimney nook.
But soon his eyes grew brilliant, when she told
His lady's purpose; and he scarce could brook
Tears, at the thought of those enchantments cold,
135 And Madeline asleep in lap of legends old.

16

Sudden a thought came like a full-blown rose,
Flushing his brow, and in his pained heart
Made purple riot: then doth he propose
A stratagem, that makes the beldame start:
140 "A cruel man and impious thou art!
Sweet lady, let her pray, and sleep and dream
Alone with her good angels, far apart
From wicked men like thee. Go, go! I deem
Thou canst not surely be the same that thou didst
seem."

17

145 "I will not harm her, by all saints I swear!"
Quoth Porphyro: "O may I ne'er find grace
When my weak voice shall whisper its last prayer,
If one of her soft ringlets I displace,
Or look with ruffian passion in her face.
150 Good Angela, believe me, by these tears;
Or I will, even in moment's space,
Awake, with horrid shout, my foemen's ears,
And beard them, though they be more fanged than
wolves and bears."

18

"Ah! why wilt thou affright a feeble soul?
155 A poor, weak, palsy-stricken, churchyard thing,
Whose passing-bell may ere the midnight toll;
Whose prayers for thee, each morn and evening,
Were never missed." Thus plaining, doth she bring
A gentler speech from burning Porphyro;
160 So woeful, and of such deep sorrowing,
That Angela gives promise she will do
Whatever he shall wish, betide her weal or woe.

19

Which was, to lead him, in close secrecy,
Even to Madeline's chamber, and there hide
165 Him in a closet, of such privacy
That he might see her beauty unespied,
And win perhaps that night a peerless bride,
While legioned fairies paced the coverlet,
And pale enchantment held her sleepy-eyed.
170 Never on such a night have lovers met,
Since Merlin paid his Demon all the monstrous debt.[6]

20

"It shall be as thou wishest," said the Dame:
"All cates and dainties shall be stored there
Quickly on this feast-night: by the tambour frame
175 Her own lute thou wilt see: no time to spare,
For I am slow and feeble, and scarce dare
On such a catering trust my dizzy head.
Wait here, my child, with patience: kneel in prayer
The while. Ah! thou must needs the lady wed,
180 Or may I never leave my grave among the dead."

21

So saying she hobbled off with busy fear.
The lover's endless minutes slowly passed;
The dame returned, and whispered in his ear
To follow her; with aged eyes aghast
185 From fright of dim espial. Safe at last
Through many a dusky gallery, they gain
The maiden's chamber, silken, hushed and chaste;

5. *hold water . . . sieve,* a sign of supernatural power.

6. *Since Merlin . . . debt.* Merlin, the famous wizard of King Arthur's court, was the son of a demon. He was killed by the sorceress Vivien who used a spell he himself had taught her.

Where Porphyro took covert, pleased amain.
His poor guide hurried back with agues in her brain.

22

190 Her faltering hand upon the balustrade,
Old Angela was feeling for the stair,
When Madeline, St. Agnes' charmed maid,
Rose, like a missioned spirit, unaware:
With silver taper's light, and pious care,
195 She turned and down the aged gossip led
To a safe level matting. Now prepare,
Young Porphyro, for gazing on that bed;
She comes, she comes again, like ring-dove frayed[7]
and fled.

23

Out went the taper as she hurried in;
200 Its little smoke, in pallid moonshine, died:
She closed the door, she panted, all akin
To spirits of the air, and visions wide:
No uttered syllable, or, woe betide!
But to her heart, her heart was voluble,
205 Paining with eloquence her balmy side;
As though a tongueless nightingale should swell
Her throat in vain, and die, heart-stifled, in her dell.

24

A casement high and triple-arched there was,
All garlanded with carven imageries,
210 Of fruits, and flowers, and bunches of knotgrass,
And diamonded with panes of quaint device,
Innumerable of stains and splendid dyes,
As are the tiger-moth's deep-damasked wings,
And in the midst, 'mong thousand heraldries,
215 And twilight saints, and dim emblazonings,
A shielded scutcheon blushed with blood of queens
and kings.

25

Full on this casement shone the wintry moon,
And threw warm gules[8] on Madeline's fair breast,
As down she knelt for Heaven's grace and boon;
220 Rose-bloom fell on her hands, together prest,
And on her silver cross soft amethyst,
And on her hair a glory, like a saint:
She seemed a splendid angel, newly drest,
Save wings, for heaven:—Porphyro grew faint:
225 She knelt, so pure a thing, so free from mortal taint.

7. *frayed,* frightened.
8. *gules,* red colors from the stained glass.

26

Anon his heart revives: her vespers done,
Of all its wreathed pearls her hair she frees;
Unclasps her warmed jewels one by one;
Loosens her fragrant bodice; by degrees
230 Her rich attire creeps rustling to her knees:
Half-hidden, like a mermaid in sea-weed,
Pensive awhile she dreams awake, and sees,
In fancy, fair St. Agnes in her bed,
But dares not look behind, or all the charm is fled.

27

235 Soon, trembling in her soft and chilly nest,
In sort of wakeful swoon, perplexed she lay,
Until the poppied warmth of sleep oppressed
Her soothed limbs, and soul fatigued away;
Flown, like a thought, until the morrow-day;
240 Blissfully havened both from joy and pain;
Clasped like a missal where swart Paynims pray;[9]
Blinded alike from sunshine and from rain,
As though a rose should shut, and be a bud again.

28

Stolen to this paradise, and so entranced,
245 Porphyro gazed upon her empty dress,
And listened to her breathing, if it chanced
To wake into a slumberous tenderness;
Which when he heard, that minute did he bless,
And breathed himself: then from the closet crept,
250 Noiseless as fear in a wide wilderness,
And over the hushed carpet, silent, stept,
And 'tween the curtains peeped, where, lo!—how
fast she slept.

29

Then by the bed-side, where the faded moon
Made a dim, silver twilight, soft he set
255 A table, and, half anguished, threw thereon
A cloth of woven crimson, gold and jet:—
O for some drowsy Morphean amulet![10]
The boisterous, midnight, festive clarion,
The kettle-drum, and far-heard clarinet,
260 Affray his ears, though but in dying tone:—
The hall-door shuts again, and all the noise is gone.

9. *Clasped . . . pray,* shut like a prayer book which pagans would have no occasion to open.
10. *Morphean amulet,* a sleep-producing charm. Morpheus was the god of sleep.

30

And still she slept an azure-lidded sleep,
In blanched linen, smooth, and lavendered,
While he from forth the closet brought a heap
265 Of candied apple, quince, and plum, and gourd;
With jellies soother than the creamy curd,
And lucent syrops, tinct with cinnamon;
Manna and dates, in argosy transferred
From Fez; and spiced dainties, every one,
270 From silken Samarcand to cedared Lebanon.

31

These delicates he heaped with glowing hand
On golden dishes and in baskets bright
Of wreathed silver: sumptuous they stand
In the retired quiet of the night,
275 Filling the chilly room with perfume light.—
"And now, my love, my seraph fair, awake!
Thou art my heaven, and I thine eremite:[11]
Open thine eyes, for meek St. Agnes' sake,
Or I shall drowse beside thee, so my soul doth ache."

32

280 Thus whispering, his warm, unnerved arm
Sank in her pillow. Shaded was her dream
By the dusk curtains:—'twas a midnight charm
Impossible to melt as iced stream:
The lustrous salvers in the moonlight gleam;
285 Broad golden fringe upon the carpet lies:
It seemed he never, never could redeem
From such a stedfast spell his lady's eyes;
So mused awhile, entoiled in woofed phantasies.

33

Awakening up, he took her hollow lute,—
290 Tumultuous,—and, in chords that tenderest be,
He played an ancient ditty, long since mute,
In Provence called, "La belle dame sans mercy":
Close to her ear touching the melody;—
Wherewith disturbed, she uttered a soft moan;
295 He ceased—she panted quick—and suddenly
Her blue affrayed eyes wide open shone:
Upon his knees he sank, pale as smooth-sculptured
stone.

34

Her eyes were open, but she still beheld,
Now wide awake, the vision of her sleep:

11. *eremite,* devoted follower.

300 There was a painful change, that nigh expelled
The blisses of her dream so pure and deep
At which fair Madeline began to weep,
And moan forth witless words with many a sigh,
While still her gaze on Porphyro would keep:
305 Who knelt, with joined hands and piteous eye,
Fearing to move or speak, she looked so dreamingly.

35

"Ah, Porphyro!" said she, "but even now
Thy voice was at sweet tremble in mine ear,
Made tuneable with every sweetest vow;
310 And those sad eyes were spiritual and clear:
How changed thou art! how pallid, chill, and drear!
Give me that voice again, my Porphyro,
Those looks immortal, those complainings dear!
Oh, leave me not in this eternal woe,
315 For if thou diest, my Love, I know not where to go."

36

Beyond a mortal man impassioned far
At these voluptuous accents, he arose,
Ethereal, flushed, and like a throbbing star
Seen 'mid the sapphire heaven's deep repose;
320 Into her dream he melted, as the rose
Blendeth its odor with the violet,—
Solution sweet: meantime the frost-wind blows
Like Love's alarum, pattering the sharp sleet
Against the window-panes; St. Agnes' moon hath set.

37

325 'Tis dark: quick pattereth the flaw-blown sleet.
"This is no dream, my bride, my Madeline!"
'Tis dark: the iced gusts still rave and beat:
"No dream, alas! alas! and woe is mine!
Porphyro will leave me here to fade and pine.
330 Cruel! what traitor could thee hither bring?
I curse not, for my heart is lost in thine,
Though thou forsakest a deceived thing;—
A dove forlorn and lost with sick unpruned wing."

38

"My Madeline! sweet dreamer! lovely bride!
335 Say, may I be for aye thy vassal blest?
Thy beauty's shield, heart-shaped and vermeil-dyed?
Ah, silver shrine, here will I take my rest
After so many hours of toil and quest,
A famished pilgrim,—saved by miracle.
340 Though I have found, I will not rob thy nest,
Saving of thy sweet self; if thou think'st well
To trust, fair Madeline, to no rude infidel.

39

"Hark! 'tis an elfin-storm from faery land,
Of haggard seeming, but a boon indeed:
345 Arise—arise! the morning is at hand;—
The bloated wassailers will never heed;—
Let us away, my love, with happy speed;
There are no ears to hear, or eyes to see,—
Drowned all in Rhenish and the sleepy mead:
350 Awake! arise! my love, and fearless be,
For o'er the southern moors I have a home for thee."

40

She hurried at his words, beset with fears,
For there were sleeping dragons all around,
At glaring watch, perhaps, with ready spears—
355 Down the wide stairs a darkling way they found;
In all the house was heard no human sound.
A chain-drooped lamp was flickering by each door;
The arras, rich with horseman, hawk, and hound,
Fluttered in the besieging wind's uproar;
360 And the long carpets rose along the gusty floor.

41

They glide, like phantoms, into the wide hall;
Like phantoms, to the iron porch they glide,
Where lay the Porter, in uneasy sprawl,
With a huge empty flagon by his side:
365 The wakeful bloodhound rose, and shook his hide,
But his sagacious eye an inmate owns:
By one, and one the bolts full easy slide:—
The chains lie silent on the footworn stones;
The key turns, and the door upon its hinges groans.

42

370 And they are gone: aye, ages long ago
These lovers fled away into the storm.
That night the Baron dreamt of many a woe,
And all his warrior-guests with shade and form
Of witch, and demon, and large coffin-worm,
375 Were long be-nightmared. Angela the old
Died palsy-twitched, with meager face deform;
The Beadsman, after thousand aves told,
For aye unsought-for slept among his ashes cold. □

DISCUSSION

1. What kinds of images appear most frequently in the first three stanzas? What general effect do these stanzas have on you?

2. What might the Beadsman represent? What one other character in the poem is most closely associated with him? In what ways? With whom are these two most strongly contrasted?

3. Choose the one passage which you think most effectively brings out the rich texture and coloring of the medieval scene, and show how imagery and language are used to create these effects.

4. If you had to interpret this poem as either "dream" or "reality," which would you choose? What elements contribute to the poem's dreamlike quality? to its realistic qualities?

5. How do you interpret the ending? Are the two lovers stepping out into a future that is to be lived "happily ever after" or are they headed for a different fate? What in the poem supports your view?

6. The theme of "La Belle Dame Sans Merci" is raised at one point in this poem. Is Madeline in any way comparable to the fair lady without pity in Keats's other poem? Are there any similarities between the poems as a whole?

7. There are hints of cruelty in the poem. Where do you find them? Would you characterize Porphyro as cruel in any way?

WRITING

The Eve of St. Agnes touches on themes that run through much English and continental literature, from folk tales like "Sleeping Beauty" to high tragedy like Shakespeare's *Romeo and Juliet.* Discuss the similarities of these and other works you can think of to *The Eve of St. Agnes.* How are they parallel, how different?

Charles Lamb 1775 / 1834

Although the romantic spirit found its most striking expression in lyric poetry, prose was also affected by the new influence. An essayist like Charles Lamb, for example, no longer felt he had to write in the scholarly style of the classicists. His writing became personal, whimsical, full of figure and fancy. His subjects bore no resemblance to those of eighteenth-century essays—they became only launching pads for the expression of personality. This new approach to prose writing is known as the *familiar essay.* Lamb was a master of this new art.

DREAM CHILDREN

CHILDREN love to listen to stories about their elders, when *they* were children; to stretch their imagination to the conception of a traditionary great-uncle, or grandame, whom they never saw. It was in this spirit that my little ones crept about me the other evening to hear about their great-grandmother Field, who lived in a great house in Norfolk (a hundred times bigger than that in which they and papa lived) which had been the scene—so at least it was generally believed in that part of the country—of the tragic incidents which they had lately become familiar with from the ballad of "The Children in the Wood." Certain it is that the whole story of the children and their cruel uncle was to be seen fairly carved out in wood upon the chimney piece of the great hall, the whole story down to the Robin Redbreasts,[1] till a foolish rich person pulled it down to set up a marble one of modern invention in its stead, with no story upon it. Here Alice put out one of her dear mother's looks, too tender to be called upbraiding.

Then I went on to say how religious and how good their great-grandmother Field was, how beloved and respected by everybody, though she was not indeed the mistress of this great house, but had only the charge of it (and yet in some respects she might be said to be mistress of it too) committed to her by the owner, who preferred living in a newer and more fashionable mansion which he had purchased somewhere in the adjoining county; but still she lived in it in a manner as if it had been her own and kept up the dignity of the great house in a sort while she lived, which afterward came to decay and was nearly pulled down, and all its old ornaments were stripped and carried away to the owner's other house, where they were set up and looked as awkward as if someone were to carry away the old tombs they had seen lately at the Abbey[2] and stick them up in Lady C.'s tawdry gilt drawing room. Here John smiled, as much as to say, "That would be foolish, indeed."

And then I told how, when she came to die, her funeral was attended by a concourse of all the poor, and some of the gentry too, of the neighborhood for many miles round, to show their respect for her memory, because she had been such a good and religious woman—so good indeed, that she knew all the Psaltery[3] by heart, aye, and a great part of the Testament besides. Here little Alice spread her hands.

Then I told what a tall, upright, graceful person their great-grandmother Field once was, and how in her youth she was esteemed the best dancer—here Alice's little right foot played an involuntary move-

1. *Robin Redbreasts.* At the end of the ballad the robins cover the bodies of the murdered children with leaves.

2. *Abbey,* Westminster Abbey in London, where many famous Englishmen are buried.

3. *Psaltery,* the version of the Psalms in the *Book of Common Prayer.*

ment, till upon my looking grave, it desisted—the best dancer, I was saying, in the county, till a cruel disease, called a cancer, came and bowed her down with pain; but it could never bend her good spirits, or make them stoop, because she was so good and religious.

Then I told how she was used to sleep by herself in a lone chamber of the great lone house, and how she believed that an apparition of two infants was to be seen at midnight gliding up and down the great staircase near where she slept, but she said "those innocents would do her no harm"; and how frightened I used to be, because I was never half so good or religious as she—and yet I never saw the infants. Here John tried to look courageous.

Then I told how good she was to all her grandchildren, having us to the great house in the holidays, where I in particular used to spend many hours by myself in gazing upon the old busts of the twelve Caesars that had been emperors of Rome, till the old marble heads would seem to live again or I to be turned into marble with them; how I never could be tired with roaming about that huge mansion with its vast, empty rooms, with their worn-out hangings, fluttering tapestry, and carved oaken panels, with the gliding almost rubbed out—sometimes in the spacious old-fashioned gardens, which I had almost to myself, unless when now and then a solitary gardening man would cross me—and how the nectarines and peaches hung upon the walls without my ever offering to pluck them, because they were forbidden fruits, unless now and then—and because I had more pleasure in strolling about among the old melancholy-looking yew trees, or the firs, and picking up the red berries and the fir apples,[4] which were good for nothing but to look at—or in lying about upon the fresh grass, with all the fine garden smells around me—or basking in the orangery, till I could almost fancy myself ripening too along with the oranges and the limes in that grateful warmth—or in watching the dace that darted to and fro in the fishpond, at the bottom of the garden, with here and there a great sulky pike hanging midway down the water in silent state, as if it mocked at their impertinent friskings—I had more pleasure in these busy-idle diversions than in all the sweet flavors of peaches, nectarines, oranges, and suchlike common baits of children. Here John slyly deposited back upon the plate a bunch of grapes which, not unobserved by Alice, he had meditated dividing with her, and both seemed willing to relinquish them for the present as irrelevant.

Then in somewhat a more heightened tone, I told how, though their great-grandmother Field loved all her grandchildren, yet in an especial manner she might be said to love their uncle, John L______,[5] because he was so handsome and spirited a youth,

4. *fir apples,* pine cones.

5. *John L______,* Lamb's brother John.

OF HUMAN INTEREST

Lamb's family tragedy

On September 27, 1796, Charles Lamb wrote this disconnected letter with its strange postscript to his friend Samuel Coleridge:

My dearest friend—White or some of my friends or the public papers by this time may have informed you of the terrible calamities that have fallen on our family. I will only give you the outlines. My poor dear dearest sister in a fit of insanity has been the death of her own mother. I was at hand only time enough to snatch the knife out of her grasp. She is at present in a mad house, from whence I fear she must be moved to an hospital. God has preserved to me my senses,—I eat and drink and sleep, and have my judgment I believe very sound.

My poor father was slightly wounded, and I am left to take care of him and my aunt. Mr. Norris of the Bluecoat school has been very kind to us, and we have no other friend, but thank God I am very calm and composed and able to do the best that remains to do. Write,—as religious a letter as possible—but no mention of what is gone and done with—with me the former things are passed away, and I have something more to do that [than] to feel——

God almighty
have us all in
his keeping.——

C. LAMB.

mention nothing of poetry. I have destroyed every vestige of past vanities of that kind. Do as you please, but if you publish, publish mine (I give free leave) without name or initial, and never send me a book, I charge you, you [your] own judgment will convince you not to take any notice of this yet to your dear wife.—You look after your family,—I have my reason and strength left to take care of mine. I charge you don't think of coming to see me. Write. I will not see you if you come. God almighty love you and all of us——

and a king to the rest of us; and, instead of moping about in solitary corners, like some of us, he would mount the most mettlesome horse he could get, when but an imp no bigger than themselves, and make it carry him half over the county in a morning, and join the hunters when there were any out—and yet he loved the old great house and gardens too, but had too much spirit to be always pent up within their boundaries—and how their uncle grew up to man's estate as brave as he was handsome, to the admiration of everybody, but of their great-grandmother Field most especially; and how he used to carry me upon his back when I was a lame-footed boy—for he was a good bit older than me—many a mile when I could not walk for pain; and how in afterlife he became lame-footed too, and I did not always (I fear) make allowance enough for him when he was impatient, and in pain, nor remember sufficiently how considerate he had been to me when I was lame-footed; and how when he died, though he had not been dead an hour, it seemed as if he had died a great while ago, such a distance there is betwixt life and death; and how I bore his death as I thought pretty well at first, but afterward it haunted and haunted me; and though I did not cry or take it to heart as some do, and as I think he would have done if I had died, yet I missed him all day long, and knew not till then how much I had loved him. I missed his kindness, and I missed his crossness, and wished him to be alive again, to be quarreling with him (for we quarreled sometimes), rather than not have him again, and was as uneasy without him as he, their poor uncle, must have been when the doctor took off his limb. Here the children fell a-crying and asked if their little mourning, which they had on, was not for Uncle John; and they looked up and prayed me not to go on about their uncle, but to tell them some stories about their pretty dead mother.

Then I told how for seven long years, in hope sometimes, sometimes in despair, yet persisting ever, I courted the fair Alice W______n; and, as much as children could understand, I explained to them what coyness and denial meant in maidens—when suddenly, turning to Alice, the soul of the first Alice looked out at her eyes with such a reality of representment, that I became in doubt which of them stood there before me, or whose that bright hair was; and while I stood gazing, both the children gradually grew fainter to my view, receding, and still receding, till nothing at last but two mournful features were seen in the uttermost distance, which, without speech, strangely impressed upon me the effects of speech: "We are not of Alice, nor of thee, nor are we children at all. We are nothing; less than nothing, and dreams. We are only what might have been, and must wait upon the tedious shores of Lethe millions of ages before we have existence and a name"—and immediately awaking, I found myself quietly seated in my bachelor armchair, where I had fallen asleep, with the faithful Bridget unchanged by my side—but John L. (or James Elia)[6] was gone forever.

6. *Bridget . . . James Elia,* names given by Lamb to his sister Mary and his brother John.

DISCUSSION

1. Explain the title of this essay.
2. "Lamb's reverie is not much more than the sentimental musings of a pathetic and aging bachelor." Agree or disagree with this opinion, supporting your argument with details from the essay.
3. What qualities of spirit do Grandmother Field and Uncle John represent? What similarities are there between the two portraits?

WRITING

"Every man is beset, his whole life long, with the difficulty of accepting what has been and what is and reconciling these realities with what might have been." Discuss Lamb's essay in terms of this statement and the biographical sketch of his life on pages 384–385.

BACKGROUND

JOSEPH M. W. TURNER, "PEACE: BURIAL AT SEA" EXHIBITED 1842. THE TATE GALLERY, LONDO

The Romantic Age

TOWARD the end of the eighteenth century the certainties and rigidities of the Augustan Age began to crumble under the influence of revolutionary and humanitarian ideals which swept across America, Europe, and England. The serene and symmetrical neoclassical facade had already toppled by the time Frenchmen stormed the Bastille in 1789. By the last decades of the century the Romantic literary movement in England was well under way; it had been foreshadowed by the nature poets Goldsmith, Gray, and Burns, and been given its first intense thrust by the visionary William Blake. By 1815, when Napoleon was finally defeated at the Battle of Waterloo, the revolutionary fervor which inspired English Romanticism had already begun to cool.

The Romantic period was thus one of very short duration. The bulk of its great poetry was written between 1795 and 1830. Each of the major figures in it knew, or knew of, the others. Wordsworth and Coleridge collaborated on a volume of poetry; Shelley and Byron spent time together on the continent; and the cross-fertilization of minds in conversation, letters, reviews, and criticism that took place during these short decades was to change, as no previous period had, the shape and nature of literature. As a revolutionary period it had its eccentrics, some of whom displayed outright disregard for social convention, others who were quiet renegades. It was, in short, an age of individualists who seem to have taken their cue from the French Romantic philosopher Rousseau who said, "I may not be better than other people, but at least I'm different."

An even more prominent trait was the high seriousness and vigorous humanitarianism of the period. By the end of the eighteenth century the abuses of the Industrial Revolution and the need for social reform had become clear. Although legislative reforms were slow in coming—most were established in the late nineteenth century—the reforming spirit is evident in most Romantic writing, in its concern for the humble lives of the poor and its outright rejection of materialism and rationalism. It became clear to the Romantic that all was not right with the world, as the eighteenth-century rationalist had professed, and for merely logical reasoning he substituted personal "feeling" and conviction. The chief characteristic of the period was thus a tremendous increase in awareness (what the Romantics called "sensibility") not only of the sublime power and beauty of nature unsullied by man's hand, but also of man's intimate connection with the natural world, and of the social ills that result when that world is corrupted or man's "first-born affinities" with it are severed.

The literature of this brief period is richer and more powerful in the statement of these basic themes than any which preceded or followed it. It has about it a deep personal earnestness, a sensuous delight in the most common and natural (and most overlooked) things of this world, a blend of intensely lived joy and dejection, a yearning for ideal states of being and a probing interest in mysterious and mystical experience. If the Romantic vision of the world was occasionally tinged with bitterness or outrage, it was because the Romantic confronted the implications of a mechanical and materialistic society which threatened to extinguish man's awareness of his vital relationship with his fellow men and with the rhythms of nature that mold his life. Romantic protests, in fact, remain as persuasive today as they did a century and a half ago, and the challenges and questions implied in Romantic literature remain still valid, and still unanswered. □

BIOGRAPHIES

George Noel Gordon, Lord Byron 1788 / 1824

Lord Byron was born lame, a fate to which he was never able to reconcile himself. Born only remotely to nobility, he inherited his title at age 11 on the death of a great-uncle. When he entered Cambridge at 17, he was well-read in Latin and Greek, excelled in swimming and boxing, and had already fallen in love twice. After graduation he traveled throughout Europe and Asia Minor. Returning to London when he was 23, he published the first two cantos of *Childe Harold,* made a brilliant speech in the House of Lords defending workers who had wrecked machinery that threatened their jobs, and became famous overnight.

He relished his role as the favorite of London society. After several love affairs, he married the nobly born, very proper Annabella Milbanke, but at the end of the first year of marriage Annabella took their newborn daughter and returned to her parents. Byron was outraged. Londoners, appalled at Byron's egotistical conduct, ostracized him. Bitter about the hypocricies of society, he left England in 1816, never to return.

Byron wandered about the continent, doing precisely as he pleased, hobnobbing with prominent people, befriending Shelley, and carrying on intrigues with ladies, one of whom, Claire Claremont, bore him a daughter. He finished *Childe Harold,* began his masterpiece, *Don Juan,* and wrote many shorter poems. His verses sold well, but while his fortunes prospered, his health, always poor, began to fail.

A foe of despotism anywhere, Byron in 1823 joined the Greek war for independence from the Turks, devoting much time and money to the effort. But before he could see battle, he caught fever and died in camp at Missolonghi, embittered and old at 36.

To his contemporaries Byron was more a colorful and scandalous personality than a poet. His poetry reflects the paradoxes of his life. He was a fiery rebel and a conventional aristocrat, an idealist and a cynic, a cad to his countrymen and a hero to the Greeks. His power as a poet is due to his sharp eye for human foibles and hypocrisy; his satire was the best produced in England since Pope's.

Samuel Taylor Coleridge 1772 / 1834

The youngest of twelve children, Coleridge was an imaginative and precocious child. Although his family was poor, he was sent to Cambridge, where he read everything he thought worth while and fascinated the students with eloquent monologues, full of mysticism and radical politics. ("Charles, did you ever hear me preach?" he once asked his friend Lamb. "I never heard you do anything else," Lamb replied.) However, he found university life boring, ran up debts, and recklessly left school in his second year to join His Majesty's Fifteenth Light Dragoons under the name of Silas Tomkyn Comberbacke. The harsh discipline of military life was too much for him; fortunately his brothers and friends rescued him, paid his debts, and had him reinstated in college. But he was not to remain at the university.

In June 1794, Coleridge met Robert Southey, a young poet who had become inspired by the French Revolution. The two made elaborate plans to migrate to America and found a colony based on brotherly love, simple living, and high thinking. But they never reached America. Southey settled in Lisbon; Coleridge, newly married to Sara Fricker and practically destitute, wandered about the English countryside. He started a magazine and wrote a play. The magazine failed within two months; the play was not published.

In 1797 he met Wordsworth; stimulated by his encouragement and their shared plans for *Lyrical Ballads,* he produced in one year almost all his greatest poetry, including "The Rime of the Ancient Mariner," "Christabel," and "Kubla Khan." At about this time he began taking opium, first for relief from the excruciating pains of neuralgia and other ailments, then compulsively to allay the frustrations of a marriage gone sour (he fell in love with Sara Hutchinson, sister of Wordsworth's wife) and recurrent feelings of personal inadequacy. By the age of 30 he was no longer capable of sustained creative effort; at 35 he separated from his wife. The remainder of his life was an agonizing struggle against the addictive grip of opium. Nevertheless, in his later years he managed to produce significant works of literary criticism and philosophy and established a reputation as a brilliant lecturer and conversationalist.

John Keats 1795 / 1821

John Keats was born in London, the oldest son of a cockney stable keeper. His father was killed in a riding accident when the boy was 9; six years later his mother died of tuberculosis. That same year he was taken out of school and apprenticed to a physician. Although he spent some time in London hospitals and qualified to practice as an apothecary, he finally abandoned medicine for literature.

With support from such people as Wordsworth and Lamb, the 21-year-old Keats began his literary career in earnest, full of the exuberance of youth. Suddenly came disappointment and tragedy: one brother left for America, the other died of tuberculosis. The publication of *Endymion,* his first sustained poetic effort, was met with vicious and unwarranted criticism. His cockney heritage and medical training were ridiculed. Bad publicity kept his poetry from selling and Keats was soon destitute; in 1818 his suspicion that he had tuberculosis was confirmed. Ill, depressed, Keats fell in love with Fanny Brawne, but knowing he could never marry, and under orders from his physician to give up all work, he left England for the warmer climate of Italy in a last desperate attempt to regain his health. There he died in 1821. He was buried in the Protestant Cemetery in Rome under the epitaph he himself had composed: "Here lies one whose name was writ in water."

Unlike Wordsworth and Shelley, Keats was not caught up in the zeal for reform that accompanied the French Revolution. Throughout his short creative life he was chary of poetry "that has designs upon us." Instead of using poetry to state ideas, he struggled for an intuitive vision of truth in poetic beauty. Hence the lushness of the imagery in his best poetry, its sustained melodious flow. In the course of his short life, Keats learned to use language with a range and felicity equalled only by the greatest poets.

Charles Lamb 1775 / 1834

Born in a medieval quarter of old London, Lamb drew as much inspiration from the city as Wordsworth found in the countryside. London was the center of his world; there he lived, worked, and died. He was miserable only when well-meaning friends took him for visits to the country. An easy-going, light-hearted man, his personal life was marred by frustration. Because of a stammer, he was unable to take an examination at his preparatory school to qualify for a university. Lack of education forced him to take a job as a low-salaried clerk for The East India Company, where he worked until 1825. His sister Mary had several attacks of madness, during one of which she killed their mother. Rather than confine her to a miserable life in a sanitarium, Lamb abandoned hope of marriage and devoted the rest of his life to her care and comfort.

Lamb did not really begin to find himself as a writer until he reached middle age. His first book of familiar essays, entitled *Essays of Elia,* was published when he was 48. The book's humor, whimsy, and faint overtones of sadness made Lamb immediately popular with nineteenth-century readers. It is from this first volume that "Dream Children" comes.

Percy Bysshe Shelley 1792 / 1822

Percy Shelley was the black sheep of a conventional, wealthy family; he stepped lightly over religious, political, social, and moral boundaries, seemingly unaware of their existence. He was a brilliant student, but resentful of all authority, and did not hesitate to express nonconformist views while at Eton, a fashionable boys' school, where he was at odds with everyone. He fared no better at Oxford, where he published a pamphlet entitled "The Necessity of Atheism," for which he was expelled.

By the time he was 21 he was married (to Harriet Westbrooke) and a father, and had already published his first important poem, *Queen Mab,* a diatribe against orthodox religion and morality. After several years he began to find his marriage dull, and eloped with Mary Godwin, daughter of the radical William Godwin, whose revolutionary zeal Shelley shared. In 1816 Harriet committed suicide, and shortly thereafter Shelley married Mary (who had already borne two of his children), but he never fully recovered from the scorn the English public heaped upon him for his actions. In 1818 he and Mary left for Italy. In 1822 he was drowned while sailing in a small boat off the Italian coast. His body was discovered some ten days later and was cremated on the beach. As the funeral pyre burned low, Mary, according to some accounts, snatched her husband's heart from the ashes. The heart is buried in the Protestant Cemetery in Rome under the inscription "Cor Cordium!" (Heart of Hearts!).

Shelley wrote most of his greatest poetry in the four years he spent in Italy. Throughout his lifetime he was filled with schemes for reforming the world, and he remained a firm believer in the purity of his intentions and the soundness of his views. However, his greatness lies not so much in the themes of reform and revolution that run through much of his poetry as in his powerful imagination and his overbrimming lyric power.

William Wordsworth 1770 / 1850

As a restless young man Wordsworth became caught up in the radical causes of the French Revolution; as an old man, established as poet laureate of England, he became an ultraconservative whose rigid opinions many found unattractive.

Wordsworth's life was not untroubled. His mother died when he was 7, his father when he was 13. Yet his boyhood days were free, perhaps the happiest of his life. He attended the village school at Hawkshead and ranged through the countryside during vacations. He read widely on his own; his sensibilities became sharpened, his sympathies enlarged, his intimate knowledge of natural things strengthened. At Cambridge he found the classical curriculum a bore, and graduated in 1791 without distinction and with no particular plans.

During a European walking tour in the summer of 1790 his sympathies for the French Revolution had been aroused. After graduation he set out again for France, where he met and fell in love with Annette Vallon, who bore him a daughter, Caroline. In 1792, he was unexpectedly summoned to England, and when war broke out between France and England it was impossible for him to return to France. He did not see Annette or Caroline again until 1802, when he made arrangements for Caroline's financial support. Then he married Mary Hutchinson, a friend since boyhood days.

From 1797 to 1807, a period considered his most productive, Wordsworth worked closely with Coleridge, a relationship quickened by Wordsworth's sister Dorothy. *Lyrical Ballads,* published anonymously in 1798, contained poems by both men, according to the following scheme: Wordsworth was to "give the charm of novelty to subjects of everyday life"; Coleridge was to let his imagination roam over more unusual and supernatural subject matter. Though the book included such poems as Coleridge's "Rime of the Ancient Mariner" and Wordsworth's "Tintern Abbey" (now considered among the finest in the English language), it was at first contemptuously received by critics. In 1800 an expanded edition was published with a preface written by Wordsworth to explain his theories of poetry.

By 1810 Wordsworth's extraordinary powers of awareness had begun to fade. He became estranged from Coleridge for several years; his revolutionary fervor dulled; and he never again achieved the intensity of his earlier work. Yet when he died at the age of 80 he had not lost his fierce dedication to his role as poet and visionary which gives his best lines their unequaled power.

chapter seven

THE VICTORIANS 1837–1901

"AN ENGLISH AUTUMN AFTERNOON" BY FORD MADOX BROWN. BY PERMISSION OF THE BIRMINGHAM MUSEUM AND ART GALLERY.

I. EARLY VICTORIAN POETS

Alfred, Lord Tennyson

1809 / 1892

ULYSSES

IT LITTLE profits that an idle king,
By this still hearth, among these barren crags,
Matched with an aged wife, I mete and dole
Unequal laws unto a savage race,
5 That hoard, and sleep, and feed, and know not me.
I cannot rest from travel; I will drink
Life to the lees. All times I have enjoyed
Greatly, have suffered greatly, both with those
That loved me, and alone; on shore, and when
10 Through scudding drifts the rainy Hyades[1]
Vexed the dim sea. I am become a name;
For always roaming with a hungry heart
Much have I seen and known—cities of men
And manners, climates, councils, governments,
15 Myself not least, but honored of them all—
And drunk delight of battle with my peers,
Far on the ringing plains of windy Troy.
I am part of all that I have met;
Yet all experience is an arch wherethrough
20 Gleams that untraveled world whose margin fades
Forever and forever when I move.
How dull it is to pause, to make an end,
To rust unburnished, not to shine in use!
As though to breathe were life! Life piled on life
25 Were all too little, and of one to me
Little remains; but every hour is saved
From that eternal silence, something more,
A bringer of new things; and vile it were
For some three suns to store and hoard myself,
30 And this gray spirit yearning in desire
To follow knowledge like a sinking star,
Beyond the utmost bound of human thought.
This is my son, mine own Telemachus,
To whom I leave the scepter and the isle—
35 Well-loved of me, discerning to fulfill
This labor, by slow prudence to make mild
A rugged people, and through soft degrees
Subdue them to the useful and the good.
Most blameless is he, centered in the sphere
40 Of common duties, decent not to fail
In offices of tenderness, and pay
Meet adoration to my household gods,
When I am gone. He works his work, I mine.
There lies the port; the vessel puffs her sail;
45 There gloom the dark, broad seas. My mariners,
Souls that have toiled, and wrought, and thought
with me—
That ever with a frolic welcome took
The thunder and the sunshine, and opposed
Free hearts, free foreheads—you and I are old;
50 Old age hath yet his honor and his toil.
Death closes all; but something ere the end,
Some work of noble note, may yet be done,
Not unbecoming men that strove with gods.
The lights begin to twinkle from the rocks;
55 The long day wanes; the slow moon climbs; the
deep
Moans round with many voices. Come, my friends.
'Tis not too late to seek a newer world.
Push off, and sitting well in order smite
The sounding furrows; for my purpose holds
60 To sail beyond the sunset, and the baths
Of all the western stars, until I die.
It may be that the gulfs will wash us down;
It may be we shall touch the Happy Isles,[2]
And see the great Achilles, whom we knew.
65 Though much is taken, much abides; and though
We are not now that strength which in old days
Moved earth and heaven, that which we are, we
are—
One equal temper of heroic hearts,
Made weak by time and fate, but strong in will
70 To strive, to seek, to find, and not to yield.

1. *rainy Hyades* (hī′ ə dēz), a group of seven stars once associated with the rainy season.

2. *Happy Isles,* the mythical Islands of the Blessed where the souls of the good were supposed to dwell after death.

BREAK, BREAK, BREAK

Break, break, break,
  On thy cold gray stones, O Sea!
And I would that my tongue could utter
  The thoughts that arise in me.

5 O well for the fisherman's boy,
  That he shouts with his sister at play!
O well for the sailor lad,
  That he sings in his boat on the bay!

And the stately ships go on
10 To their haven under the hill;
But O for the touch of a vanished hand,
  And the sound of a voice that is still!

Break, break, break,
  At the foot of thy crags, O Sea!
15 But the tender grace of a day that is dead
  Will never come back to me.

CROSSING THE BAR

Sunset and evening star,
  And one clear call for me!
And may there be no moaning of the bar,[1]
  When I put out to sea,

5 But such a tide as moving seems asleep,
  Too full for sound and foam,
When that which drew from out the boundless deep
  Turns again home.

Twilight and evening bell,
10 And after that the dark!
And may there be no sadness of farewell,
  When I embark;

For though from out our bourn of time and place
  The flood may bear me far,
15 I hope to see my Pilot face to face
  When I have crossed the bar.

1. *no moaning of the bar.* A sandbar sometimes obstructs the passage of a ship from the harbor into open water. An old superstition held that, whenever a death occurred, the outgoing tide moaned as it rolled over the bar.

From IN MEMORIAM

7

Dark house, by which once more I stand
  Here in the long unlovely street,
  Doors, where my heart was used to beat
So quickly, waiting for a hand,

5 A hand that can be clasped no more—
  Behold me, for I cannot sleep,
  And like a guilty thing I creep
At earliest morning to the door.

He is not here; but far away
10 The noise of life begins again,
  And ghastly thro' the drizzling rain
On the bald street breaks the blank day.

34

My own dim life should teach me this,
  That life shall live for evermore,
15 Else earth is darkness at the core,
And dust and ashes all that is;

This round of green, this orb of flame,
  Fantastic beauty; such as lurks
  In some wild poet, when he works
20 Without a conscience or an aim.

What then were God to such as I?
  'T were hardly worth my while to choose
  Of things all mortal, or to use
A little patience ere I die;

25 'T were best at once to sink to peace,
  Like birds the charming serpent draws,
  To drop head-foremost in the jaws
Of vacant darkness and to cease.

96

You say, but with no touch of scorn,
30 Sweet-hearted, you, whose light blue eyes
  Are tender over drowning flies,
You tell me, doubt is Devil-born.

I know not: one indeed I knew
  In many a subtle question versed,
35 Who touched a jarring lyre at first,
But ever strove to make it true;

Perplext in faith, but pure in deeds,
At last he beat his music out.
There lives more faith in honest doubt,
40 Believe me, than in half the creeds.

He fought his doubts and gathered strength,
He would not make his judgment blind,
He faced the spectres of the mind
And laid them; thus he came at length

45 To find a stronger faith his own,
And Power was with him in the night,
Which makes the darkness and the light,
And dwells not in the light alone,

But in the darkness and the cloud,
50 As over Sinai's peaks of old,
While Israel made their gods of gold,
Altho' the trumpet blew so loud.

THE DAWN

"You are but children"
—EGYPTIAN PRIEST TO SOLON

Red of the Dawn!
Screams of a babe in the red-hot palms of a Moloch[1] of Tyre,
Man with his brotherless dinner on man in the tropical wood,
Priests in the name of the Lord passing souls through fire to the fire,
5 Head-hunters and boats of Dahomey[2] that float upon human blood.

Red of the Dawn!
Godless fury of peoples, and Christless frolic of kings,
And the bolt of war dashing down upon cities and blazing farms,
For Babylon was a child newborn, and Rome was a babe in arms,
10 And London and Paris and all the rest are as yet but in leading strings.

Dawn not Day,
While scandal is mouthing a bloodless name at *her* cannibal feast,
And rake-ruined bodies and souls go down in a common wreck,
And the Press of a thousand cities is prized for it smells of the beast,
15 Or easily violates virgin Truth for a coin or a check.

Dawn not Day!
Is it Shame, so few should have climbed from the dens in the level below,
Men, with a heart and a soul, no slaves of a four-footed will?
But if twenty million of summers are stored in the sunlight still,
20 We are far from the noon of man, there is time for the race to grow.

Red of the Dawn!
Is it turning a fainter red? So be it, but when shall we lay
The Ghost of the Brute that is walking and haunting us yet, and be free?
In a hundred, a thousand winters? Ah, what will *our* children be?
25 The men of a hundred thousand, a million summers away?

---

1. *Moloch,* a god to whom children were sacrificed.
2. *Dahomey,* a West African country in which human sacrifice still existed in the 19th century.

From GUINEVERE

In his *Idylls of the King,* Alfred, Lord Tennyson rewrote some of Malory's Arthurian tales in nineteenth-century Victorian verse infused with Victorian sensibility. His treatment of the love story of Lancelot and Guinevere, less robust and more delicate than that of Malory, places emphasis on Guinevere's ultimate retreat to a nunnery. In the passage quoted here, Tennyson opens with the scheming Modred [Mordred], eager to discredit Sir Lancelot and improve his own chances of succeeding his natural father as king, spying on Guinevere in hopes of catching her with her lover. The incidents that follow are essentially the same as those related in the Malory passage on pages 112–117. But note how Tennyson has shifted the emphasis.

For thus it chanced one morn when all the court,
Green-suited, but with plumes that mock'd the may,
Had been—their wont—a-maying and return'd,
That Modred still in green, all ear and eye,
25 Climb'd to the high top of the garden-wall
To spy some secret scandal if he might,
And saw the Queen who sat betwixt her best
Enid and lissome Vivien, of her court
The wiliest and the worst; and more than this
30 He saw not, for Sir Lancelot passing by
Spied where he couch'd, and as the gardener's hand
Picks from the colewort a green caterpillar,
So from the high wall and the flowering grove
Of grasses Lancelot pluck'd him by the heel,
35 And cast him as a worm upon the way;
But when he knew the prince tho' marr'd with dust,
He, reverencing king's blood in a bad man,
Made such excuses as he might, and these
Full knightly without scorn: for in those days
40 No knight of Arthur's noblest dealt in scorn;
But, if a man were halt, or hunch'd, in him
By those whom God had made full-limb'd and tall,
Scorn was allow'd as part of his defect,
And he was answer'd softly by the King
45 And all his Table. So Sir Lancelot holp
To raise the prince, who rising twice or thrice
Full sharply smote his knees, and smiled, and went:
But, ever after, the small violence done
Rankled in him and ruffled all his heart,
50 As the sharp wind that ruffles all day long
A little bitter pool about a stone
On the bare coast.

But when Sir Lancelot told
This matter to the Queen, at first she laugh'd
Lightly, to think of Modred's dusty fall,
55 Then shudder'd, as the village wife who cries,
"I shudder, some one steps across my grave";
Then laugh'd again, but faintlier, for indeed
She half-foresaw that he, the subtle beast,
Would track her guilt until he found, and hers
60 Would be for evermore a name of scorn.
Henceforward rarely could she front in hall,
Or elsewhere, Modred's narrow foxy face,
Heart-hiding smile, and gray persistent eye.
Henceforward too, the Powers that tend the soul,
65 To help it from the death that cannot die,
And save it even in extremes, began
To vex and plague her. Many a time for hours,
Beside the placid breathings of the King,
In the dead night, grim faces came and went
70 Before her, or a vague spiritual fear—
Like to some doubtful noise of creaking doors,
Heard by the watcher in a haunted house,
That keeps the rust of murder on the walls—
Held her awake: or if she slept she dream'd
75 An awful dream; for then she seem'd to stand
On some vast plain before a setting sun,
And from the sun there swiftly made at her
A ghastly something, and its shadow flew
Before it till it touch'd her, and she turn'd—
80 When lo! her own, that broadening from her feet,
And blackening, swallow'd all the land, and in it
Far cities burnt, and with a cry she woke.
And all this trouble did not pass but grew,
Till even the clear face of the guileless King,
85 And trustful courtesies of household life,
Became her bane; and at last she said,
"O Lancelot, get thee hence to thine own land,
For if thou tarry we shall meet again,
And if we meet again some evil chance
90 Will make the smouldering scandal break and blaze
Before the people and our lord the King."
And Lancelot ever promised, but remain'd,
And still they met and met. Again she said,
"O Lancelot, if thou love me get thee hence."
95 And then they were agreed upon a night—
When the good King should not be there—to meet
And part for ever. Vivien, lurking, heard.
She told Sir Modred. Passion-pale they met
And greeted. Hands in hands, and eye to eye,
100 Low on the border of her couch they sat
Stammering and staring. It was their last hour,
A madness of farewells. And Modred brought

His creatures to the basement of the tower
For testimony; and crying with full voice,
105 "Traitor, come out, ye are trapt at last," aroused
Lancelot, who rushing outward lionlike
Leapt on him, and hurl'd him headlong, and he fell
Stunn'd, and his creatures took and bare him off,
And all was still. Then she, "The end is come,
110 And I am shamed for ever"; and he said:
"Mine be the shame; mine was the sin: but rise,
And fly to my strong castle over-seas:
There will I hide thee till my life shall end,
There hold thee with my life against the world."
115 She answer'd: "Lancelot, wilt thou hold me so?
Nay, friend, for we have taken our farewells.
Would God that thou couldst hide me from myself!
Mine is the shame, for I was wife, and thou
Unwedded; yet rise now, and let us fly,
120 For I will draw me into sanctuary,
And bide my doom." So Lancelot got her horse,
Set her thereon, and mounted on his own,
And then they rode to the divided way,
There kiss'd, and parted weeping: for he past,
125 Love-loyal to the least wish of the Queen,
Back to his land; but she to Almesbury
Fled all night long by glimmering waste and weald,
And heard the spirits of the waste and weald
Moan as she fled, or thought she heard them moan:
130 And in herself she moan'd, "Too late, too late!"
Till in the cold wind that foreruns the morn,
A blot in heaven, the raven, flying high,
Croak'd, and she thought, "He spies a field of death;
For now the heathen of the Northern Sea,
135 Lured by the crimes and frailties of the court,
Begin to slay the folk and spoil the land."

And when she came to Almesbury she spake
There to the nuns, and said, "Mine enemies
Pursue me, but, O peaceful Sisterhood,
140 Receive and yield me sanctuary, nor ask
Her name to whom ye yield it till her time
To tell you"; and her beauty, grace, and power
Wrought as a charm upon them, and they spared
To ask it. . . .

□

DISCUSSION

1. (a) What emotional experience has the speaker of "Break, Break, Break" undergone, and how has it affected him?

(b) Which words in the poem intensify the effect of that experience?

(c) Evaluate the appropriateness of the poem's setting as a background for the speaker's emotion.

2. (a) What details in "Crossing the Bar" evoke a mood of peacefulness?

(b) What is the speaker's attitude toward death?

(c) How does this feeling contrast with that of "Break, Break, Break"? In which of the two poems do you think the emotion is more sincere?

3. (a) In "Guinevere," by what details is Modred made to appear repulsive?

(b) In general, how does Tennyson's account differ from that of Malory in "Slander and Strife" (page 114)?

4. (a) In "The Dawn," what is the Red of the Dawn? What is the Ghost of the Brute (line 23)?

(b) What does the speaker think of the past? the present?

(c) What is his unspoken hope for the future?

(d) How does this poem show the effect of the scientific thought of the Victorian Age?

(e) What appeal is the speaker making?

5. (a) In "Ulysses," how does Ulysses feel about his quiet life as ruler of Ithaca?

(b) What in his past might have made him feel that way?

(c) Do you agree with his philosophy of life? Explain.

(d) The last line of "Ulysses" has always been thought to be powerful. Analyze the ways in which the line achieves its effect, and show how this line has been prepared for by the rest of the poem.

6. Tennyson himself said that "In Memoriam" began with a funeral and ended with a wedding. This memorial to his friend Arthur Henry Hallam consists of 131 short poems written over a period of many years. The three included here (Nos. 7, "Dark House," 34, "My Own Dim Life," and 96, "You Say") come from the beginning, middle, and end of the series. Explain how they show the successive stages in the poet's first grief and slow recovery.

Robert Browning
1812 / 1889

PORPHYRIA'S LOVER

The rain set early in tonight,
The sullen wind was soon awake,
It tore the elm-tops down for spite,
And did its worst to vex the lake:
5 I listened with heart fit to break.
When glided in Porphyria; straight
She shut the cold out and the storm,
And kneeled and made the cheerless grate
Blaze up, and all the cottage warm;
10 Which done, she rose, and from her form
Withdrew the dripping cloak and shawl,
And laid her soiled gloves by, untied
Her hat and let the damp hair fall,
And, last, she sat down by my side
15 And called me. When no voice replied,
She put my arm about her waist,
And made her smooth white shoulder bare,
And all her yellow hair displaced,
And, stooping, made my cheek lie there,
20 And spread, o'er all, her yellow hair,
Murmuring how she loved me—she
Too weak, for all her heart's endeavor,
To set its struggling passion free
From pride, and vainer ties dissever,
25 And give herself to me forever.
But passion sometimes would prevail,
Nor could tonight's gay feast restrain
A sudden thought of one so pale
For love of her, and all in vain:
30 So, she was come through wind and rain.
Be sure I looked up at her eyes
Happy and proud; at last I knew
Porphyria worshiped me: surprise
Made my heart swell, and still it grew
35 While I debated what to do.
That moment she was mine, mine, fair,
Perfectly pure and good: I found
A thing to do, and all her hair
In one long yellow string I wound
40 Three times her little throat around,
And strangled her. No pain felt she;
I am quite sure she felt no pain.
As a shut bud that holds a bee,
I warily oped her lids: again
45 Laughed the blue eyes without a stain.
And I untightened next the tress
About her neck; her cheek once more
Blushed bright beneath my burning kiss:
I propped her head up as before,
50 Only, this time my shoulder bore
Her head, which droops upon it still:
The smiling rosy little head,
So glad it has its utmost will,
That all it scorned at once is fled,
55 And I, its love, am gained instead!
Porphyria's love: she guessed not how
Her darling one wish would be heard.
And thus we sit together now,
And all night long we have not stirred,
60 And yet God has not said a word!

MEMORABILIA

Ah, did you once see Shelley plain,
And did he stop and speak to you
And did you speak to him again?
How strange it seems and new!

5 But you were living before that,
And also you are living after;
And the memory I started at—
My starting moves your laughter.

I crossed a moor, with a name of its own
10 And a certain use in the world no doubt,
Yet a hand's-breadth of it shines alone
'Mid the blank miles round about:

For there I picked up on the heather
And there I put inside my breast
15 A moulted feather, an eagle-feather!
Well, I forget the rest.

MY LAST DUCHESS

The time is the 16th century, the scene the city of Ferrara in northern Italy. The speaker is the Duke of Ferrara.

THAT'S my last duchess painted on the wall,
Looking as if she were alive. I call
That piece a wonder, now: Frà Pandolf's hands
Worked busily a day, and there she stands.
5 Will 't please you sit and look at her? I said
"Frà Pandolf" by design, for never read
Strangers like you that pictured countenance,
The depth and passion of its earnest glance,
But to myself they turned (since none puts by
10 The curtain I have drawn for you, but I)
And seemed as they would ask me, if they durst,
How such a glance came there; so, not the first
Are you to turn and ask thus. Sir, 'twas not
Her husband's presence only, called that spot
15 Of joy into the Duchess' cheek: perhaps
Frà Pandolf chanced to say "Her mantle laps
Over my lady's wrist too much," or "Paint
Must never hope to reproduce the faint
Half-flush that dies along her throat": such stuff
20 Was courtesy, she thought, and cause enough
For calling up that spot of joy. She had
A heart—how shall I say?—too soon made glad,
Too easily impressed; she liked whate'er
She looked on, and her looks went everywhere.
25 Sir, 'twas all one! My favor at her breast,
The dropping of the daylight in the West,
The bough of cherries some officious fool
Broke in the orchard for her, the white mule
She rode with round the terrace—all and each
30 Would draw from her alike the approving speech,
Or blush, at least. She thanked men—good! but thanked
Somehow—I know not how—as if she ranked
My gift of a nine-hundred-years-old name
With anybody's gift. Who'd stoop to blame
35 This sort of trifling? Even had you skill
In speech—which I have not—to make your will
Quite clear to such an one, and say, "Just this
Or that in you disgusts me; here you miss,
Or there exceed the mark"—and if she let
40 Herself be lessoned so, nor plainly set
Her wits to yours, forsooth, and made excuse—
E'en then would be some stooping; and I choose
Never to stoop. Oh sir, she smiled, no doubt,
Whene'er I passed her; but who passed without
45 Much the same smile? This grew; I gave commands;
Then all smiles stopped together. There she stands
As if alive. Will 't please you rise? We'll meet
The company below, then. I repeat,
The Count your master's known munificence
50 Is ample warrant that no just pretense
Of mine for dowry will be disallowed;
Though his fair daughter's self, as I avowed
At starting, is my object. Nay, we'll go
Together down, sir. Notice Neptune, though,
55 Taming a sea-horse, thought a rarity,
Which Claus of Innsbruck cast in bronze for me!

SUMMUM BONUM[1]

All the breath and bloom of the year in the bag of one bee;
All the wonder and wealth of the mine in the heart of one gem;
In the core of one pearl all the shade and the shine of the sea:
Breath and bloom, shade and shine—wonder, wealth, and—how far above them—
5 Truth, that's brighter than gem,
Trust, that's purer than pearl—
Brightest truth, purest trust in the universe—all were for me
In the kiss of one girl.

1. *Summum Bonum,* the highest good (Latin).

PROSPICE[1]

Fear death?—to feel the fog in my throat,
  The mist in my face,
When the snows begin, and the blasts denote
  I am nearing the place,
5 The power of the night, the press of the storm,
  The post of the foe;
Where he stands, the Arch Fear in a visible form;
  Yet the strong man must go:
For the journey is done and the summit attained,
10 And the barriers fall,
Though a battle's to fight ere the guerdon be gained,
  The reward of it all.
I was ever a fighter, so—one fight more,
  The best and the last!

15 I would hate that Death bandaged my eyes, and
    forbore,
  And bade me creep past.
No! let me taste the whole of it, fare like my peers,
  The heroes of old,
Bear the brunt, in a minute pay glad life's arrears
20 Of pain, darkness and cold.
For sudden the worst turns the best to the brave.
  The black minute's at end,
And the elements' rage, the fiend voices that rave,
  Shall dwindle, shall blend,
25 Shall change, shall become first a peace out of
    pain.
  Then a light, then thy breast,
O thou soul of my soul! I shall clasp thee again,
  And with God be the rest![2]

1. *Prospice* (pros′ pi chē), look forward (Latin).

2. *Then a light . . . be the rest.* These last three lines refer to Mrs. Browning, who had died shortly before the poem was written.

DISCUSSION

1. (a) Reread lines 1–15 of "Porphyria's Lover." What do Porphyria's actions indicate about her feelings for the speaker?

(b) What do lines 26–30 add to the portrait of Porphyria?

(c) What, then, prompts the speaker to strangle her?

(d) What is the meaning of the last line of the poem?

(e) What does the dramatic monologue reveal about Porphyria's lover?

2. (a) In "My Last Duchess," the only person we hear speak is the Duke, yet we come to dislike him. What devices has Browning used to cause the Duke inadvertently to reveal his evil nature?

(b) What is the situation in the poem —who is speaking to whom, what have they been discussing, where are they?

(c) Why has Browning selected this particular moment to present the Duke speaking?

(d) How much meaning may be read into the words in the opening lines that are here italicized: "That's *my last duchess* painted on the wall/ Looking *as if she were alive*"?

(e) Why does Browning include the remark about "Neptune. . . / Taming a sea horse" at the end of the poem?

3. (a) Compare the attitude toward death expressed in "Prospice" with that in Tennyson's "Crossing the Bar" and with John Donne's in "Death, be not proud." Which poem do you prefer? Why?

(b) To what extent is "Prospice" a love poem? What difference would there be if it ended with line 25?

(c) To what does Browning compare death in lines 1–12?

(d) Explain the meaning of *Arch Fear* (line 7), *journey* (line 9), and *guerdon* (line 11).

(e) The poem opens with a question, "Fear death?" which is not finally answered until line 17. Show how the poem is structured by this device of question and answer.

4. (a) In "Memorabilia," what is the speaker's attitude toward Shelley?

(b) Is the man to whom he is speaking successful in destroying his hero-worship? Explain.

(c) How do the last two stanzas of the poem illuminate the first two?

5. (a) One reader has dismissed "Summum Bonum" as "a bit of verbal fluff"; another has claimed it was "motivated by honest passion." With which reader do you agree, and why?

(b) Browning uses "the bag of one bee" to symbolize all the delights of fragrance and color that summer brings. Why is this an apt choice to symbolize all of summer? Explain the other natural symbols the poet uses. What relationship does he develop between the natural symbols in lines 1–4 and the rest of the poem?

(c) Why might Browning have used one word order in lines 1 and 2 and then reversed it in line 3?

WRITING

What report do you think the Count's emissary will bring back with him about the Duke in "My Last Duchess?" Write his report.

Matthew Arnold
1822 / 1888

TO MARGUERITE

Yes! in the sea of life enisled,
With echoing straits between us thrown,
Dotting the shoreless watery wild,
We mortal millions live *alone.*
5 The islands feel the enclasping flow,
And then their endless bounds they know.

But when the moon their hollows lights,
And they are swept by balms of spring,
And in their glens, on starry nights,
10 The nightingales divinely sing;
And lovely notes, from shore to shore,
Across the sounds and channels pour—

Oh! then a longing like despair
Is to their farthest caverns sent;
15 For surely once, they feel, we were
Parts of a single continent!
Now round us spreads the watery plain—
Oh, might our marges meet again!

Who ordered, that their longing's fire
20 Should be, as soon as kindled, cooled?
Who renders vain their deep desire?—
A god, a god their severance ruled!
And bade betwixt their shores to be
The unplumbed, salt, estranging sea.

THE LAST WORD

Creep into thy narrow bed,
Creep, and let no more be said!
Vain thy onset! all stands fast.
Thou thyself must break at last.

5 Let the long contention cease!
Geese are swans, and swans are geese.
Let them have it how they will!
Thou art tired; best be still.

They out-talked thee, hissed thee, tore thee?
10 Better men fared thus before thee;
Fired their ringing shot and passed,
Hotly charged—and sank at last.

Charge once more, then, and be dumb!
Let the victors, when they come,
15 When the forts of folly fall,
Find thy body by the wall.

WEST LONDON

Crouched on the pavement, close by Belgrave
  Square,
A tramp I saw, ill, moody, and tongue-tied.
A babe was in her arms, and at her side
A girl; their clothes were rags, their feet were bare.
Some labouring men, whose work lay somewhere
  there,
Passed opposite; she touched her girl, who hied
Across, and begged, and came back satisfied.
The rich she had let pass with frozen stare.
Thought I: "Above her state this spirit towers;
She will not ask of aliens, but of friends,
Of sharers in a common human fate.
She turns from that cold succour, which attends
The unknown little from the unknowing great,
And points us to a better time than ours."

DOVER BEACH

The sea is calm tonight,
The tide is full, the moon lies fair
Upon the straits; on the French coast the light
Gleams and is gone; the cliffs of England stand,
5 Glimmering and vast, out in the tranquil bay.
Come to the window, sweet is the night air!

Only, from the long line of spray
Where the sea meets the moon-blanched land,
Listen! you hear the grating roar
10 Of pebbles which the waves draw back, and fling,
At their return, up the high strand,
Begin, and cease, and then again begin,
With tremulous cadence slow, and bring
The eternal note of sadness in.

15 Sophocles[1] long ago
Heard it on the Aegean, and it brought
Into his mind the turbid ebb and flow
Of human misery; we
Find also in the sound a thought,
20 Hearing it by this distant northern sea.

The Sea of Faith
Was once, too, at the full, and round earth's shore
Lay like the folds of a bright girdle furled.
But now I only hear
25 Its melancholy, long, withdrawing roar,
Retreating, to the breath
Of the night wind, down the vast edges drear
And naked shingles[2] of the world.

Ah, love, let us be true
30 To one another! for the world, which seems
To lie before us like a land of dreams,
So various, so beautiful, so new,
Hath really neither joy, nor love, nor light,
Nor certitude, nor peace, nor help for pain;
35 And we are here as on a darkling plain
Swept with confused alarms of struggle and flight,
Where ignorant armies clash by night.

---

1. *Sophocles,* Greek dramatist (495–406 B.C.).
2. *shingles,* beaches.

SELF-DEPENDENCE

1

Weary of myself, and sick of asking
What I am, and what I ought to be,
At this vessel's prow I stand, which bears me
Forwards, forwards o'er the starlit sea.

2

5 And a look of passionate desire
O'er the sea and to the stars I send:
"Ye who from my childhood up have calmed me,
Calm me, ah, compose me to the end!

3

"Ah, once more," I cried, "ye stars, ye waters,
10 On my heart your mighty charm renew;
Still, still let me, as I gaze upon you,
Feel my soul becoming vast like you!"

4

From the intense, clear, star-sown vault of heaven,
Over the lit sea's unquiet way,
15 In the rustling night-air came the answer:
"Wouldst thou *be* as these are? *Live* as they.

5

"Unaffrighted by the silence round them,
Undistracted by the sights they see,
These demand not that the things without them
20 Yield them love, amusement, sympathy.

6

"And with joy the stars perform their shining,
And the sea its long moon-silvered roll;
For self-poised they live, nor pine with noting
All the fever of some differing soul.

7

25 "Bounded by themselves, and unregardful
In what state God's other works may be,
In their own tasks all their powers pouring,
These attain the mighty life you see."

8

O air-born voice! long since, severely clear,
30 A cry like thine in mine own heart I hear:
"Resolve to be thyself; and know that he
Who finds himself loses his misery!"

DISCUSSION

1. (a) According to the speaker in "To Marguerite," how do humans resemble islands?

(b) Does he feel these "islands" will ever be joined one to another?

(c) Compare his sentiments with those expressed by John Donne in "Meditation 17" (page 241).

2. Suppose that "The Last Word" is a soliloquy—that the speaker and "thou" are the same person. How would you interpret it?

3. In an Italian sonnet the first eight lines pose the proposition or problem, and the last six lines resolve it. Discuss how "West London" either follows or fails to follow this pattern.

4. (a) "Dover Beach" opens with a peaceful description; then the word *Only* (line 7) introduces a complete change in mood. What is that change?

(b) Trace further changes in mood which occur in the last two stanzas.

(c) What personal solution is suggested in the last stanza? Will the speaker find it satisfactory?

(d) "Dover Beach" is sometimes called "the first modern poem." Account for this comment.

(e) Is this predominantly a love poem, a philosophic poem, a meditative poem, or a combination? Explain.

5. (a) In "Self-Dependence" there are a number of speeches. Who is speaking in each case?

(b) Explore the meaning of the last two lines in stanza 6: "For self-poised they live, nor pine with noting / All the fever of some differing soul." Begin by defining the precise reference for "they." Relate these lines to the title and conclusion of the poem.

II. OTHER VICTORIAN POETS

From SONNETS FROM THE PORTUGUESE by Elizabeth Barrett Browning

22

WHEN our two souls stand up erect and strong,
Face to face, silent, drawing nigh and nigher,
Until the lengthening wings break into fire
At either curvèd point—what bitter wrong
5 Can the earth do to us, that we should not long
Be here contented? Think. In mounting higher,
The angels would press on us and aspire
To drop some golden orb of perfect song
Into our deep, dear silence. Let us stay
10 Rather on earth, Beloved—where the unfit
Contrarious moods of men recoil away
And isolate pure spirits, and permit
A place to stand and love in for a day,
With darkness and the death-hour rounding it.

28

My letters! all dead paper, mute and white!
And yet they seem alive and quivering
Against my tremulous hands which loose the string
And let them drop down on my knee to-night.
5 This said—he wished to have me in his sight
Once, as a friend: this fixed a day in spring
To come and touch my hand . . . a simple thing,
Yet I wept for it!—this, . . . the paper's light . . .
Said, *Dear I love thee;* and I sank and quailed
10 As if God's future thundered on my past.
This said, *I am thine*—and so its ink has paled
With lying at my heart that beat too fast.
And this . . . O Love, thy words have ill availed
If, what this said, I dared repeat at last!

43

How do I love thee? Let me count the ways.
I love thee to the depth and breadth and height
My soul can reach, when feeling out of sight
For the ends of Being and ideal Grace.
5 I love thee to the level of everyday's
Most quiet need, by sun and candlelight.
I love thee freely, as men strive for Right;
I love thee purely, as they turn from Praise.
I love thee with the passion put to use
10 In my old griefs, and with my childhood's faith,
I love thee with a love I seemed to lose
With my lost saints—I love thee with the breadth,
Smiles, tears, of all my life!—and, if God choose,
I shall but love thee better after death.

FALL, LEAVES, FALL

by Emily Brontë

Fall, leaves, fall; die, flowers, away;
Lengthen night and shorten day;
Every leaf speaks bliss to me
Fluttering from the autumn tree.
5 I shall smile when wreaths of snow
Blossom where the rose should grow;
I shall sing when night's decay
Ushers in a drearier day.

THE LATEST DECALOGUE

by Arthur Hugh Clough

Thou shalt have one God only; who
Would be at the expense of two?
No graven images may be
Worshipped, except the currency:
5 Swear not at all; for, for thy curse
Thine enemy is none the worse:
At church on Sunday to attend
Will serve to keep the world thy friend:
Honour thy parents; that is, all
10 From whom advancement may befall;
Thou shalt not kill; but need'st not strive
Officiously to keep alive:
Do not adultery commit;
Advantage rarely comes of it:
15 Thou shalt not steal; an empty feat,
When it's so lucrative to cheat:
Bear not false witness; let the lie
Have time on its own wings to fly:
Thou shalt not covet, but tradition
20 Approves all forms of competition.

THE FIRST DAY

by Christina Rossetti

I wish I could remember that first day,
First hour, first moment of your meeting me,
If bright or dim the season, it might be
Summer or Winter for aught I can say;
5 So unrecorded did it slip away,
So blind was I to see and to foresee,
So dull to mark the budding of my tree
That would not blossom yet for many a May.
If only I could recollect it, such
10 A day of days! I let it come and go
As traceless as a thaw of bygone snow;
It seemed to mean so little, meant so much;
If only now I could recall that touch,
First touch of hand in hand—Did one but know!

UP-HILL

by Christina Rossetti

Does the road wind up-hill all the way?
Yes, to the very end.
Will the day's journey take the whole long day?
From morn to night, my friend.

5 But is there for the night a resting-place?
A roof for when the slow dark hours begin.
May not the darkness hide it from my face?
You cannot miss that inn.

Shall I meet other wayfarers at night?
10 Those who have gone before.
Then must I knock, or call when just in sight?
They will not keep you standing at that door.

Shall I find comfort, travel-sore and weak?
Of labor you shall find the sum.
15 Will there be beds for me and all who seek?
Yea, beds for all who come.

THE GARDEN OF PROSERPINE[1]

by Algernon Charles Swinburne

HERE, where the world is quiet;
Here, where all trouble seems
Dead winds' and spent waves' riot
In doubtful dreams of dreams;
5 I watch the green field growing
For reaping folk and sowing,
For harvest-time and mowing,
A sleepy world of streams.

I am tired of tears and laughter,
10 And men that laugh and weep;
Of what may come hereafter
For men that sow to reap:
I am weary of days and hours,
Blown buds of barren flowers,
15 Desires and dreams and powers
And everything but sleep.

Here life has death for neighbor,
And far from eye or ear
Wan waves and wet winds labor,
20 Weak ships and spirits steer;
They drive adrift, and whither
They wot not who make thither;
But no such winds blow hither,
And no such things grow here.

25 No growth of moor or coppice,
No heather-flower or vine,
But bloomless buds of poppies,
Green grapes of Proserpine,
Pale beds of blowing rushes
30 Where no leaf blooms or blushes
Save this whereout she crushes
For dead men deadly wine.

Pale, without name or number,
In fruitless fields of corn,
35 They bow themselves and slumber
All night till light is born;
And like a soul belated,
In hell and heaven unmated,
By cloud and mist abated
40 Comes out of darkness morn.

Though one were strong as seven,
He too with death shall dwell,
Nor wake with wings in heaven,
Nor weep for pains in hell;
45 Though one were fair as roses,
His beauty clouds and closes;
And well though love reposes,
In the end it is not well.

Pale, beyond porch and portal,
50 Crowned with calm leaves, she stands
Who gathers all things mortal
With cold immortal hands;
Her languid lips are sweeter
Than love's who fears to greet her
55 To men that mix and meet her
From many times and lands.

She waits for each and other,
She waits for all men born;
Forgets the earth her mother,
60 The life of fruits and corn;
And spring and seed and swallow
Take wing for her and follow
Where summer song rings hollow
And flowers are put to scorn.

65 There go the loves that wither,
The old loves with wearier wings;
And all dead years draw thither,
And all disastrous things;
Dead dreams of days forsaken,
70 Blind buds that snows have shaken,
Wild leaves that winds have taken,
Red strays of ruined springs.

We are not sure of sorrow,
And joy was never sure;
75 Today will die tomorrow;
Time stoops to no man's lure,
And love, grown faint and fretful,
With lips but half regretful
Sighs, and with eyes forgetful
80 Weeps that no love endures.

---

1. *Proserpine* (pros′ ər pīn), in Roman mythology, the daughter of Zeus and the earth goddess Demeter, who was abducted by the god of the underworld and ruled with him there. Her Greek name is Persephone.

From too much love of living,
From hope and fear set free,
We thank with brief thanksgiving
Whatever gods may be
85 That no life lives for ever;
That dead men rise up never;
That even the weariest river
Winds somewhere safe to sea.

Then star nor sun shall waken,
90 Nor any change of light;
Nor sound of waters shaken,
Nor any sound or sight;
Nor wintry leaves nor vernal,
Nor days nor things diurnal;
95 Only the sleep eternal
In an eternal night. □

SYMPHONY IN YELLOW
by Oscar Wilde

An omnibus across the bridge
Crawls like a yellow butterfly,
And, here and there, a passer-by
Shows like a little restless midge.

5 Big barges full of yellow hay
Are moved against the shadowy wharf,
And, like a yellow silken scarf,
The thick fog hangs along the quay.

The yellow leaves begin to fade
10 And flutter from the Temple elms,
And at my feet the pale green Thames
Lies like a rod of rippled jade.

REQUIEM
by Robert Louis Stevenson

Under the wide and starry sky,
Dig the grave and let me lie.
Glad did I live and gladly die.
And I laid me down with a will.

This be the verse you grave for me:
Here he lies where he longed to be;—
Home is the sailor, home from the sea,
And the hunter home from the hill.

DISCUSSION

Elizabeth Barrett Browning

1. (a) In Sonnet 22, which facets of earthly love does the speaker praise most?

(b) Why doesn't she wish this love to mount any higher?

2. Describe in your own words the progress of the romance in Sonnet 28, "My letters all dead paper. . . ."

3. (a) Can you "count the ways" in which the speaker loves the person to whom Sonnet 43 is addressed? Is there any order or arrangement to the "ways"?

(b) What are "my lost saints" in line 12?

Emily Brontë

1. How does "Fall, Leaves" epitomize the feeling of pessimism that is characteristic of much Victorian literature?

Arthur Hugh Clough

1. Explore the source of the irony that permeates this modern "adaptation" of the Ten Commandments.

Christina Rossetti

1. "The First Day" is quite specific in its utterances. On a deeper, generalized level, what is it referring to?

2. "Uphill" progresses in a series of questions and answers.

(a) Who might be asking the questions?

(b) Who is answering them?

(c) What does the poem mean?

Algernon Charles Swinburne

1. (a) In "The Garden of Proserpine," what comparison is made between life on earth and life in the underworld?

(b) Is this poem an expression of the universal death-wish, the desire for total oblivion?

Oscar Wilde

1. (a) In "Symphony in Yellow," what similes are used, and with what effect? What is the effect of the change in color in the last two lines?

(b) Compare the mood of this poem with that of Keats's "To Autumn."

Robert Louis Stevenson

1. "Requiem" is a poem about the speaker's death, yet it does not seem gloomy. Why?

From THE RUBÁIYÁT OF OMAR KHAYYÁM

by Edward Fitzgerald

"The Rubáiyát" is a translation of a work by the Persian poet and mathematician Omar Khayyám, who died around the year 1123. The original contained more than 400 quatrains, of which Fitzgerald translated 101. Experts agree that the translation is faithful to the original in spirit and idea, but very different in formal effect.

1

WAKE! For the Sun, who scattered into flight
The Stars before him from the Field of Night
Drives Night along with them from Heav'n and strikes
The Sultàn's Turret with a Shaft of Light.

2

Come, fill the Cup, and in the fire of Spring
Your Winter garment of Repentance fling;
The Bird of Time has but a little way
To flutter—and the Bird is on the Wing.

3

A Book of Verses underneath the Bough,
A Jug of Wine, a Loaf of Bread—and Thou (10)
Beside me singing in the Wilderness—
Oh, Wilderness were Paradise enow!

4

Some for the Glories of This World, and some
Sigh for the Prophet's[1] Paradise to come;
Ah, take the Cash, and let the Credit go, (15)
Nor heed the rumble of a distant Drum!

5

Look to the blowing[2] Rose about us—"Lo,
Laughing," she says, "into the world I blow,
At once the silken tassel of my Purse
Tear, and its Treasure on the Garden throw." (20)

6

And those who husbanded the Golden Grain,
And those who flung it to the winds like Rain,
Alike to no such aureate Earth are turned
As, buried once, Men want dug up again.

7

Think, in this battered Caravanserai[3] (25)
Whose Portals are alternate Night and Day,
How Sultàn after Sultàn with his Pomp
Abode his destined Hour, and went his way.

8

I sometimes think that never blows so red
The Rose as where some buried Caesar bled; (30)
That every Hyacinth[4] the Garden wears
Dropped in her Lap from some once lovely Head.

9

And this reviving Herb whose tender Green
Fledges the River-Lip on which we lean—
Ah, lean upon it lightly! for who knows (35)
From what once lovely Lip it springs unseen!

10

Ah, make the most of what we yet may spend,
Before we too into the Dust descend;
Dust into Dust, and under Dust, to lie,
Sans[5] Wine, sans Song, sans Singer, and—sans End! (40)

11

Why, all the Saints and Sages who discussed
Of the Two Worlds so wisely—they are thrust
Like foolish Prophets forth; their Words to Scorn
Are scattered, and their Mouths are stopped with Dust.

1. *Prophet's,* Mohammed's.
2. *blowing,* blossoming.
3. *Caravanserai,* an inn in the Orient where caravans put up for the night.
4. *Hyacinth,* the flower named after Hyacinthus, a youth killed by the god Apollo, and from whose blood the flower sprang.
5. *Sans,* without (French).

12

45 Myself when young did eagerly frequent
Doctor and Saint, and heard great argument
About it and about; but evermore
Came out by the same door where in I went.

13

With them the seed of Wisdom did I sow,
50 And with mine own hand wrought to make it grow;
And this was all the Harvest that I reaped—
"I came like Water, and like Wind I go."

14

I sent my Soul through the Invisible,
Some letter of that Afterlife to spell;
55 And by and by my Soul returned to me,
And answered, "I Myself am Heav'n and Hell"—

15

Heav'n but the Vision of fulfilled Desire,
And Hell the Shadow from a Soul on fire
Cast on the Darkness into which Ourselves,
60 So late emerged from, shall so soon expire.

16

We are no other than a moving row
Of Magic Shadow-shapes that come and go
Round with the Sun-illumined Lantern held
In Midnight by the Master of the Show;

17

65 But helpless Pieces of the Game He plays
Upon this Checkerboard of Nights and Days;
Hither and thither moves, and checks, and slays,
And one by one back in the Closet lays.

18

The Moving Finger writes, and, having writ,
70 Moves on; nor all your Piety nor Wit
Shall lure it back to cancel half a line,
Nor all your Tears wash out a Word of it.

19

Oh, Thou, who Man of Baser Earth didst make,
And ev'n with Paradise devise the Snake,
75 For all the Sin wherewith the Face of Man
Is blackened—Man's forgiveness give—and take!

20

Yet, Ah, that Spring should vanish with the Rose!
That Youth's sweet-scented manuscript should close!
The Nightingale that in the branches sang,
80 Ah whence, and whither flown again, who knows!

21

Would but some wingèd Angel ere too late
Arrest the yet unfolded Roll of Fate,
And make the stern Recorder otherwise
Enregister, or quite obliterate!

22

85 Ah, Love! could you and I with Him conspire
To grasp this sorry Scheme of Things entire,
Would not we shatter it to bits—and then
Remold it nearer to the Heart's Desire!

DISCUSSION

1. Discuss the symbolism of the imagery in stanza 3—the book of verses, the bough, the jug of wine, and "thou."

2. Relate "Ozymandias" (page 363) to some of the stanzas in this poem (especially stanza 7).

3. Discuss the meaning of line 48. Explain the aptness of the figure of the door.

4. Discuss the appropriateness and value of the metaphors of the "Magic Shadow-shapes" in line 62 and the "Moving Finger" in line 69.

III. LATE VICTORIAN POETS

Thomas Hardy
1840 / 1928

NATURE'S QUESTIONING

When I look forth at dawning, pool,
Field, flock, and lonely tree,
All seem to gaze at me
Like chastened children sitting silent in a school;

5 Their faces dulled, constrained, and worn,
As though the master's ways
Through the long teaching days
Had cowed them till their early zest was overborne.

Upon them stirs in lippings mere
10 (As if once clear in call,
But now scarce breathed at all)—
"We wonder, ever wonder, why we find us here!

"Has some Vast Imbecility,
Mighty to build and blend,
15 But impotent to tend,
Framed us in jest, and left us now to hazardry?

"Or come we of an Automaton
Unconscious of our pains? . . .
Or are we live remains
20 Of Godhead dying downwards, brain and eye now gone?

"Or is it that some high Plan betides,
As yet not understood,
Of Evil stormed by Good,
We the Forlorn Hope over which Achievement strides?"

25 Thus things around. No answerer I. . .
Meanwhile the winds, and rains,
And Earth's old glooms and pains
Are still the same, and Life and Death are neighbours nigh.

HAP

If but some vengeful god would call to me
From up the sky, and laugh: "Thou suffering thing,
Know that thy sorrow is my ecstasy,
That thy love's loss is my hate's profiting!"

5 Then would I bear it, clench myself, and die,
Steeled by the sense of ire unmerited;
Half-eased in that a Powerfuller than I
Had willed and meted me the tears I shed.

But not so. How arrives it joy lies slain,
10 And why unblooms the best hope ever sown?
—Crass Casualty obstructs the sun and rain,
And dicing Time for gladness casts a moan. . .
These purblind Doomsters had as readily strown
Blisses about my pilgrimage as pain.

HIS IMMORTALITY

I saw a dead man's finer part
Shining with each faithful heart
Of those bereft. Then said I: "This must be
His immortality."

5 I looked there as the seasons wore,
And still his soul continuously bore
A life in theirs. But less its shine excelled
Than when I first beheld.

His fellow-yearsmen passed, and then
10 In later hearts I looked for him again;
And found him—shrunk, alas! into a thin
And spectral mannikin.

Lastly I ask—now old and chill—
If aught of him remain unperished still;
15 And find, in me alone, a feeble spark,
Dying amid the dark.

"AH, ARE YOU DIGGING ON MY GRAVE?"

"Ah, are you digging on my grave
My loved one?—planting rue?"
—"No: yesterday he went to wed
One of the brightest wealth has bred.
5 'It cannot hurt her now,' he said,
'That I should not be true.'"

"Then who is digging on my grave?
My nearest dearest kin?"
—"Ah, no: they sit and think, 'What use!
10 What good will planting flowers produce?
No tendance of her mound can loose
Her spirit from Death's gin.'"

"But some one digs upon my grave?
My enemy?—prodding sly?"
15 —"Nay: when she heard you had passed the Gate
That shuts on all flesh soon or late,
She thought you no more worth her hate,
And cares not where you lie."

"Then, who is digging on my grave?
20 Say—since I have not guessed!"
—"O it is I, my mistress dear,
Your little dog, who still lives near,
And much I hope my movements here
Have not disturbed your rest?"

25 "Ah, yes! *You* dig upon my grave . . .
Why flashed it not on me
That one true heart was left behind!
What feeling do we ever find
To equal among human kind
30 A dog's fidelity!"

"Mistress, I dug upon your grave
To bury a bone, in case
I should be hungry near this spot
When passing on my daily trot.
35 I am sorry, but I quite forgot
It was your resting-place."

THE DARKLING THRUSH

I leant upon a coppice gate
When Frost was spectre-gray,
And Winter's dregs made desolate
The weakening eye of day.
5 The tangled bine-stems scored the sky
Like strings of broken lyres,
And all mankind that haunted nigh
Had sought their household fires.

The land's sharp features seemed to be
10 The Century's corpse outleant;
His crypt the cloudy canopy,
The wind his death-lament.
The ancient pulse of germ and birth
Was shrunken hard and dry,
15 And every spirit upon earth
Seemed fervourless as I.

At once a voice arose among
The bleak twigs overhead
In a full-hearted evensong
20 Of joy illimited;
An aged thrush, frail, gaunt and small,
In blast-beruffled plume,
Had chosen thus to fling his soul
Upon the growing gloom.

25 So little cause for carolings
Of such ecstatic sound
Was written on terrestrial things
Afar or nigh around,
That I could think there trembled through
30 His happy good-night air
Some blessed Hope, whereof he knew
And I was unaware.

EPITAPH ON A PESSIMIST

I'm Smith of Stoke, aged sixty-odd,
I've lived without a dame
From youth-time on; and would to God
My dad had done the same.

From the French.

AT CASTLE BOTEREL

As I drive to the junction of lane and highway,
  And the drizzle bedrenches the waggonette,
I look behind at the fading byway,
  And see on its slope, now glistening wet,
5   Distinctly yet

Myself and a girlish form benighted
  In dry March weather. We climb the road
Beside a chaise. We had just alighted
  To ease the sturdy pony's load
10   When he sighed and slowed.

What we did as we climbed, and what we talked of
  Matters not much, nor to what it led—
Something that life will not be balked of
  Without rude reason till hope is dead,
15   And feeling fled.

It filled but a minute. But was there ever
  A time of such quality, since or before,
In that hill's story? To one mind never,
  Though it has been climbed, foot-swift, foot-sore,
20   By thousands more.

Primaeval rocks form the road's steep border,
  And much have they faced there, first and last,
Of the transitory in Earth's long order;
  But what they record in colour and cast
25   Is—that we two passed.

And to me, though Time's unflinching rigour,
  In mindless rote, has ruled from sight
The substance now, one phantom figure
  Remains on the slope, as when that night
30   Saw us alight.

I look and see it there, shrinking, shrinking,
  I look back at it amid the rain
For the very last time; for my sand is sinking,
  And I shall traverse old love's domain
35   Never again.

DISCUSSION

1. (a) What indications are there in the first three stanzas of "Nature's Questioning" that the world is old? How does the last stanza support this?

(b) The speaker mentions four aspects of the questions he imagines as being posed by the natural world: that it was created by "some Vast Imbecility," "an Automaton," "Godhead dying downwards," or "some high Plan." Explain each of these aspects.

(c) How does the speaker view life?

2. (a) What does the speaker in "Hap" find even worse than the hatred of some vengeful god? Do you agree with him?

(b) Look up the meaning of the title in a dictionary and explain how it applies to the poem.

3. (a) In "Ah, Are You Digging on My Grave," has anyone—lover, family, enemy, or dog—really betrayed the buried girl, or are all behaving true to life's plans for them?

(b) This poem piles irony upon irony. Which do you think is the greatest irony?

(c) What does Hardy gain by keeping the tone of this poem so objective?

4. Comment on the character of Smith of Stoke in "Epitaph on a Pessimist." Limit yourself to 48 words—twice the number in the poem.

5. (a) In "The Darkling Thrush," contrast the speaker's mood with that of the thrush.

(b) Does the thrush affect the speaker's mood to any extent?

(c) Comment on the use of the word *darkling* in the title.

(d) What words and phrases suggest death?

6. How does the theme of "His Immortality" compare with the theme of immortality as treated by conventional sonneteers?

7. (a) In "At Castle Boterel," the speaker is revisiting a scene he knew years before. What happened on that earlier occasion?

(b) Was it something passing, or something relatively permanent? Explain.

(c) What is the point of bringing in the "Primaeval rocks" and the reference to "Time's unflinching rigour"?

(d) What is the theme of the poem?

Gerard Manley Hopkins 1844 / 1889

PIED BEAUTY

Glory be to God for dappled things—
For skies of couple-color as a brinded cow;
For rose-moles all in stipple upon trout that swim;
Fresh-firecoal chestnut-falls;[1] finches' wings;
Landscape plotted and pieced[2]—fold, fallow, and plow;
And all trades, their gear and tackle and trim.

All things counter,[3] original, spare, strange;
Whatever is fickle, freckled (who knows how?)
With swift, slow; sweet, sour; adazzle, dim;
He fathers-forth whose beauty is past change:
Praise him.

1. *chestnut-falls,* chestnuts newly stripped of their husks.
2. *plotted and pieced,* divided into fields.
3. *counter,* contrary to what is expected.

GOD'S GRANDEUR

The world is charged with the grandeur of God.
It will flame out, like shining from shook foil;
It gathers to a greatness, like the ooze of oil
Crushed.[1] Why do men then now not reck his rod?
Generations have trod, have trod, have trod;
And all is seared with trade; bleared, smeared with toil;
And wears man's smudge and shares man's smell: the soil
Is bare now, nor can foot feel, being shod.

And for[2] all this, nature is never spent;
There lives the dearest freshness deep down things;
And though the last lights off the black West went
Oh, morning, at the brown brink eastward, springs—
Because the Holy Ghost over the bent
World broods with warm breast and with ah! bright wings.

1. *ooze . . . /Crushed,* oil from crushed olives.
2. *for,* despite.

SPRING AND FALL

to a young child

Márgarét, are you gríeving
Over Goldengrove unleaving?
Leáves, líke the things of man, you
With your fresh thoughts care for, can you?
Áh! ás the heart grows older
It will come to such sights colder
By and by, nor spare a sigh
Though worlds of wanwood leafmeal lie;
And yet you wíll weep and know why.
Now no matter, child, the name:
Sórrow's spríngs áre the same.
Nor mouth had, no nor mind, expressed
What heart heard of, ghost guessed:
It ís the blight man was born for,
It is Margaret you mourn for.

THOU ART INDEED JUST, LORD

Thou art indeed just, Lord, if I contend
With thee; but, sir, so what I plead is just.
Why do sinners' ways prosper? and why must
Disappointment all I endeavour end?
Wert thou my enemy, O thou my friend,
How wouldst thou worse, I wonder, than thou dost
Defeat, thwart me? Oh, the sots and thralls of lust
Do in spare hours more thrive than I that spend,
Sir, life upon thy cause. See, banks and brakes
Now, leavèd how thick! lacèd they are again
With fretty chervil, look, and fresh wind shakes
Them; birds build—but not I build; no, but strain,
Time's eunuch, and not breed one work that wakes.
Mine, O thou lord of life, send my roots rain.

THE WINDHOVER[1]

To Christ Our Lord

I caught this morning morning's minion, king-
  dom of daylight's dauphin, dapple-dawn-drawn Falcon, in his riding
  Of the rolling level underneath him steady air, and striding
High there, how he rung upon the rein of a wimpling wing
5 In his ecstasy! then off, off forth on swing,
  As a skate's heel sweeps smooth on a bow-bend—the hurl and gliding
  Rebuffed the big wind. My heart in hiding
Stirred for a bird—the achieve of, the mastery of the thing!

Brute beauty and valor and act, oh, air, pride, plume, here
10 Buckle! AND the fire that breaks from thee then, a billion
Times told lovelier, more dangerous, O my chevalier!
  No wonder of it: shéer plód makes plow down sillion
Shine, and blue-bleak embers, ah, my dear,
  Fall, gall themselves, and gash gold-vermilion.

From *Poems of Gerard Manley Hopkins,* 4th Edition. Edited by W. H. Gardner and N. H. Mackenzie, 1967, published by Oxford University Press by arrangement with The Society of Jesus. Reprinted by permission.

1. *Windhover,* a kestrel or sparrow-hawk.

DISCUSSION

1. (a) In "Pied Beauty," what specific aspects of nature are being praised?

(b) What physical characteristics do they have in common that causes Hopkins to praise them?

(c) What is the deeper reason for his praise?

2. (a) What is the complaint raised in the first eight lines of "God's Grandeur"?

(b) What is Hopkins' point in using words and images drawn from modern technology?

(c) How do the concluding six lines contrast with the first eight?

(d) Is the end result pessimistic or optimistic? Explain.

3. (a) According to "Spring and Fall," what is "the blight man was born for"?

(b) Explain how the poet uses the child's sorrow at seeing the falling autumn leaves to point out a universal truth.

(c) The words "Sorrow's springs" (line 11) have a dual function, based on two different meanings of the word *spring*. Explain this dual function.

(d) Discuss Hopkins' use of assonance (matching of vowel sounds), alliteration, and coined words such as *wanwood* (suggestive of *wan* and *wormwood*) and *leafmeal* (suggestive of *leaf* and *piecemeal*).

(e) What similarities can you find between "Spring and Fall" and Anglo-Saxon poetry?

4. (a) How does "The Windhover" try to capture the soaring, wheeling flight of the bird?

(b) Explain the subtitle, "To Christ our Lord."

(c) One reader has remarked that Hopkins' poems are like birdsong or the music of woodwinds—an ecstatic, trilling sigh, shaped and tempered by occasional plosive consonant sounds (d, g, k, t, p, b). Do you agree?

5. (a) What are the speaker's major complaints in "Thou Art Indeed Just"?

(b) How are these complaints similar to those expressed by Hardy in "Hap"?

(c) How are they different from Hardy's?

A. E. Housman
1859 / 1936

LOVELIEST OF TREES

Loveliest of trees, the cherry now
Is hung with bloom along the bough,
And stands about the woodland ride,
Wearing white for Eastertide.

5 Now, of my threescore years and ten,
Twenty will not come again,
And take from seventy springs a score,
It only leaves me fifty more.

And since to look at things in bloom
10 Fifty springs are little room,
About the woodlands I will go
To see the cherry hung with snow.

WHEN I WAS ONE-AND-TWENTY

When I was one-and-twenty
  I heard a wise man say,
"Give crowns and pounds and guineas
  But not your heart away;
5 Give pearls away and rubies
  But keep your fancy free."
But I was one-and-twenty,
  No use to talk to me.

When I was one-and-twenty
10   I heard him say again,
"The heart out of the bosom
  Was never given in vain;
'Tis paid with sighs a plenty
  And sold for endless rue."
15 And I am two-and-twenty,
  And oh, 'tis true, 'tis true.

TO AN ATHLETE DYING YOUNG

The time you won your town the race
We chaired you through the market place;
Man and boy stood cheering by,
And home we brought you shoulder-high.

5 Today, the road all runners come,
Shoulder-high we bring you home,
And set you at your threshold down,
Townsman of a stiller town.

Smart lad, to slip betimes away
10 From fields where glory does not stay,
And early though the laurel grows
It withers quicker than the rose.

Eyes the shady night has shut
Cannot see the record cut,
15 And silence sounds no worse than cheers
After earth has stopped the ears.

Now you will not swell the rout
Of lads that wore their honors out,
Runners whom renown outran
20 And the name died before the man.

So set, before its echoes fade,
The fleet foot on the sill of shade,
And hold to the low lintel up
The still-defended challenge cup.

25 And round that early-laureled head
Will flock to gaze the strengthless dead,
And find unwithered on its curls
The garland briefer than a girl's.

TERENCE, THIS IS STUPID STUFF

"Terence,[1] this is stupid stuff:
You eat your victuals fast enough;
There can't be much amiss, 'tis clear,
To see the rate you drink your beer.
5 But ho, good Lord, the verse you make,
It gives a chap the belly-ache.
The cow, the old cow, she is dead;
It sleeps well, the horned head:
We poor lads, 'tis our turn now
10 To hear such tunes as killed the cow.[2]
Pretty friendship 'tis to rhyme
Your friends to death before their time
Moping melancholy mad:
Come, pipe a tune to dance to, lad."

15 Why, if 'tis dancing you would be,
There's brisker pipes than poetry.
Say, for what were hop-yards meant,
Or why was Burton built on Trent?[3]
Oh many a peer of England brews
20 Livelier liquor than the Muse,
And malt does more than Milton can
To justify God's ways to man.
Ale, man, ale's the stuff to drink
For fellows whom it hurts to think:
25 Look into the pewter pot
To see the world as the world's not.
And faith, 'tis pleasant till 'tis past:
The mischief is that 'twill not last.
Oh I have been to Ludlow fair
30 And left my necktie God knows where,
And carried half-way home, or near,
Pints and quarts of Ludlow beer:
Then the world seemed none so bad,
And I myself a sterling lad;
35 And down in lovely muck I've lain,
Happy till I woke again.
Then I saw the morning sky:
Heigho, the tale was all a lie;
The world, it was the old world yet,
40 I was I, my things were wet,
And nothing now remained to do
But begin the game anew.

Therefore, since the world has still
Much good, but much less good than ill,
45 And while the sun and moon endure
Luck's a chance, but trouble's sure,
I'd face it as a wise man would,
And train for ill and not for good.
'Tis true, the stuff I bring for sale
50 Is not so brisk a brew as ale:
Out of a stem that scored the hand
I wrung it in a weary land.
But take it: if the smack is sour,
The better for the embittered hour;
55 It should do good to heart and head
When your soul is in my soul's stead;
And I will friend you, if I may,
In the dark and cloudy day.

There was a king reigned in the East:
60 There, when kings will sit to feast,
They get their fill before they think
With poisoned meat and poisoned drink.
He gathered all that springs to birth
From the many venomed earth;
65 First a little, thence to more,
He sampled all her killing store;
And easy, smiling, seasoned sound,
Sate the king when healths went round.
They put arsenic in his meat
70 And stared aghast to watch him eat;
They poured strychnine in his cup
And shook to see him drink it up:
They shook, they stared as white's their shirt:
Them it was their poison hurt.
75 —I tell the tale that I heard told.
Mithridates, he died old.[4]

1. *Terence,* the imagined character through whom Housman speaks in the poems in *A Shropshire Lad.*
2. *such tunes as killed the cow,* a reference to the traditional expression "the tune which the old cow died of," which refers to a boring or badly performed piece of music.
3. Burton-on-Trent is a famous English brewing town.
4. *Mithridates, he died old.* Mithridates VI, King of Pontus (120–63 B.C.) is reported to have taken the precautions against assasination by his enemies which are described here. It is said that after his country was defeated by Rome, Mithridates tried to commit suicide, but his body was so inured that poison had no effect. He finally had to command a soldier to kill him with a sword.

IS MY TEAM PLOUGHING

"Is my team ploughing,
  That I was used to drive
And hear the harness jingle
  When I was man alive?"

5 Ay, the horses trample,
  The harness jingles now;
No change though you lie under
  The land you used to plough.

"Is football playing
10 Along the river shore,
With lads to chase the leather,
  Now I stand up no more?"

Ay, the ball is flying,
  The lads play heart and soul;
15 The goal stands up, the keeper
  Stands up to keep the goal.

"Is my girl happy,
  That I thought hard to leave,
And has she tired of weeping
20 As she lies down at eve?"

Ay, she lies down lightly,
  She lies not down to weep:
Your girl is well contented.
  Be still, my lad, and sleep.

25 "Is my friend hearty,
  Now I am thin and pine,
And has he found to sleep in
  A better bed than mine?"

Yes, lad, I lie easy,
30 I lie as lads would choose;
I cheer a dead man's sweetheart,
  Never ask me whose.

DISCUSSION

1. (a) How old is the speaker in "Loveliest of Trees"?

(b) Are the mathematical computations about his age out of keeping with the general tone of the poem? Explain.

(c) Some critics claim that this brief lyric epitomizes springtime. Do you agree?

2. How seriously is the reader supposed to take the complaint of the speaker in "When I Was One-and-Twenty"? Justify your answer.

3. Several poems in this book concern a person who is dead and buried, among them "The Unquiet Grave" (page 108), "Ah, Are You Digging on My Grave," and "Is My Team Ploughing?" Compare these three poems with regard to the feelings of the survivors and the general tone of the poems. Does there appear to be any change across the centuries? Explain.

4. (a) What is the mood of the speaker in "To an Athlete Dying Young"?

(b) Are his words intended to relieve his own grief, to console the spirit of the dead athlete, to have an even wider application—or to do all of these? Explain.

(c) What is meant by the lines "And early though the laurel grows/ It withers quicker than the rose"?

5. (a) What contrasting qualities of poetry and ale are implied in "Terence, This Is Stupid Stuff"?

(b) What does the story of Mithridates have to do with Terence's view of the world? Which lines in stanza 3 best express the point Terence is making?

(c) What does this poem have in common with such poems in the *carpe diem* tradition as Marlowe's "The Passionate Shepherd to His Love" (page 143), Jonson's "Come, My Celia" (page 245), and "The Rubáiyát"? How is it different?

WRITING

1. Tennyson's poems express some measure of religious doubt and the disorientation that accompanied it. Reread the selections by Tennyson in this book (as well as others, if you wish); then write a short paper in which you compare his feelings about religious belief with your own or with those you have observed generally in your experience as representative of today.

2. Reread Robert Browning's "Summum Bonum," "Prospice," and the Sonnets of Elizabeth Barrett Browning and discuss the strength of their mutual love, as revealed in their poetry, in giving purpose to their lives.

3. Matthew Arnold seemed to concern himself with the feelings of alienation that resulted from the weakening of traditional faith. Discuss both "To Marguerite" and "Dover Beach" in the light of that alienation.

4. Write a short paper comparing your personal responses to Tennyson, Browning, and Arnold. You may wish to concentrate on which of the three appears most modern, which wrote what seems to you the most relevant poetry, which wrote the most universal poetry, or which you personally like best.

5. Using the poems of the "Other Victorians" as your basis, write a paper describing matters that seemed to be of prime concern to them—universals such as life, love, and death as well as the more particular problems of the age: loss of faith, concern over growing industrialization, disorientation as traditional values crumbled.

6. Imagine that "Loveliest of Trees," "When I Was One-and-Twenty," and "Is My Team Ploughing" all deal with the same young man, and write an account of what happened to him.

7. One critic has described Hopkins' faith as "ecstatically anguished." Discuss the extent to which the poems included in this section bear out that evaluation.

8. Thomas Hardy is sometimes called "the artist of the ironic in both poetry and fiction." Write a short paper in which you discuss the irony in some of his poems, and, if you wish, also in his short story "The Three Strangers."

9. Consider the three early Victorians—Tennyson, Browning, and Arnold—and the three late Victorians—Housman, Hardy, and Hopkins—and write a paper in which you make a general comparison of the prominent early figures with the prominent late figures.

READERS' THEATER

Many of the poems in this section are dramatic monologues or poems for two voices. Select some of these and present an all-Victorian poetry reading program.

IV. SHORT FICTION

HORATIO SPARKINS

by Charles Dickens

"INDEED, my love, he paid Teresa very great attention on the last assembly night," said Mrs. Malderton, addressing her spouse, who, after the fatigues of the day in the City, was sitting with a silk handkerchief over his head, and his feet on the fender, drinking his port;—"very great attention; and I say again, every possible encouragement ought to be given him. He positively must be asked down here to dine."

"Who must?" inquired Mr. Malderton.

"Why, you know whom I mean, my dear—the young man with the black whiskers and the white cravat, who has just come out at our assembly, and whom all the girls are talking about. Young—— dear me! what's his name?—Marianne, what *is* his name?" continued Mrs. Malderton, addressing her youngest daughter, who was engaged in netting a purse, and looking sentimental.

"Mr. Horatio Sparkins, ma," replied Miss Marianne, with a sigh.

"Oh! yes, to be sure—Horatio Sparkins," said Mrs. Malderton. "Decidedly the most gentleman-like young man I ever saw. I am sure in the beautifully-made coat he wore the other night, he looked like—like——"

"Like Prince Leopold, ma—so noble, so full of sentiment!" suggested Marianne, in a tone of enthusiastic admiration.

"You should recollect, my dear," resumed Mrs. Malderton, "that Teresa is now eight-and-twenty; and that it really is very important that something should be done."

Miss Teresa Malderton was a very little girl, rather fat, with vermilion cheeks, but good-humoured, and still disengaged, although, to do her justice, the misfortune arose from no lack of perseverance on her part. In vain had she flirted for ten years; in vain had Mr. and Mrs. Malderton assiduously kept up an extensive acquaintance among the young eligible bachelors of Camberwell, and even of Wandsworth and Brixton; to say nothing of those who "dropped in" from town. Miss Malderton was as well known as the lion on the top of Northumberland House, and had an equal chance of "going off."

"I am quite sure you'd like him," continued Mrs. Malderton, "he is so gentlemanly!"

"So clever!" said Miss Marianne.

"And has such a flow of language!" added Miss Teresa.

"He has a great respect for you, my dear," said Mrs. Malderton to her husband. Mr. Malderton coughed, and looked at the fire.

"Yes, I'm sure he's very much attached to pa's society," said Miss Marianne.

"No doubt of it," echoed Miss Teresa.

"Indeed, he said as much to me in confidence," observed Mrs. Malderton.

"Well, well," returned Mr. Malderton, somewhat flattered; "if I see him at the assembly to-morrow, perhaps I'll ask him down. I hope he knows we live at Oak Lodge, Camberwell, my dear?"

"Of course—and that you keep a one-horse carriage."

"I'll see about it," said Mr. Malderton, composing himself for a nap; "I'll see about it."

Mr. Malderton was a man whose whole scope of ideas was limited to Lloyd's, the Exchange, the India House, and the Bank. A few successful speculations had raised him from a situation of obscurity and comparative poverty, to a state of affluence. As frequently happens in such cases, the ideas of himself and his family became elevated to an extraordinary pitch as their means increased; they affected fashion, taste, and many other fooleries, in imitation of their betters, and had a very decided and becoming horror of anything which could, by possibility, be considered *low*. He was hospitable from ostentation, illiberal from ignorance, and prejudiced from conceit. Egotism and the love of display induced him to keep an excellent table: convenience, and a love of good things of this life, ensured him plenty of guests. He liked to have clever men, or what he considered such, at his table, because it was a great thing to talk about; but he never could endure what he called "sharp fellows." Probably, he cherished this feeling out of compliment to his two sons, who gave their respected parent no uneasiness in that particular. The family were ambitious of forming acquaintances and connexions in some sphere of society superior to that in which they themselves moved; and one of the necessary consequences of this desire, added to their utter ignorance of the world beyond their own small circle, was, that any one who could lay claim to an acquaintance with people of rank and title, had a sure passport to the table at Oak Lodge, Camberwell.

The appearance of Mr. Horatio Sparkins at the assembly, had excited no small degree of surprise and curiosity among its regular frequenters. Who could he be? He was evidently reserved, and apparently melancholy. Was he a clergyman?—He danced too well. A barrister?—He said he was not called. He used very fine words, and talked a great deal. Could he be a distinguished foreigner, come to England for the purpose of describing the country, its manners and customs; and frequenting public balls and public dinners, with the view of becoming acquainted with high life, polished etiquette, and English refinement?—No, he had not a foreign accent. Was he a surgeon, a contributor to the magazines, a writer of fashionable novels, or an artist?—No; to each and all of these surmises, there existed some valid objection.—"Then," said everybody, "he must be *somebody*."—"I should think he must be," reasoned Mr. Malderton, within himself, "because he perceives our superiority, and pays us so much attention."

The night succeeding the conversation we have just recorded, was "assembly night." The double-fly was ordered to be at the door of Oak Lodge at nine o'clock precisely. The Miss Maldertons were dressed in sky-blue satin trimmed with artificial flowers; and Mrs. M. (who was a little fat woman), in ditto ditto, looked like her eldest daughter multiplied by two. Mr. Frederick Malderton, the eldest son, in full-dress costume, was the very *beau idéal* of a smart waiter; and Mr. Thomas Malderton, the youngest, with his white dress-stock, blue coat, bright buttons, and red watch-ribbon, strongly resembled the portrait of that interesting, but rash young gentleman, George Barnwell. Every member of the party had made up his or her mind to cultivate the acquaintance of Mr. Horatio Sparkins. Miss Teresa, of course, was to be as amiable and interesting as ladies of eight-and-twenty on the look-out for a husband, usually are. Mrs. Malderton would be all smiles and graces. Miss Marianne would request the favour of some verses for her album. Mr. Malderton would patronise the great unknown by asking him to dinner. Tom intended to ascertain the extent of his information on the interesting topics of snuff and cigars. Even Mr. Frederick Malderton himself, the family authority on all points of taste, dress, and fashionable arrangement; who had lodgings of his own in town; who had a free admission to Covent-garden theatre; who always dressed according to the fashions of the months; who went up the water twice a-week in the season; and who actually had an intimate friend who once knew a gentleman who formerly lived in the Albany,—even he had determined that Mr. Horatio Sparkins must be a devilish good fellow, and that he would do him the honour of challenging him to a game at billiards.

The first object that met the anxious eyes of the expectant family on their entrance into the ball-room, was the interesting Horatio, with his hair brushed off his forehead, and his eyes fixed on the ceiling, reclining in a contemplative attitude on one of the seats.

"There he is, my dear," whispered Mrs. Malderton to Mr. Malderton.

"How like Lord Byron!" murmured Miss Teresa.

"Or Montgomery!" whispered Miss Marianne.

"Or the portraits of Captain Cook!" suggested Tom.

"Tom—don't be an ass!" said his father, who checked him on all occasions, probably with a view to prevent his becoming "sharp"—which was very unnecessary.

The elegant Sparkins attitudinised with admirable effect, until the family had crossed the room. He then started up, with the most natural appearance of surprise and delight; accosted Mrs. Malderton with the utmost cordiality; saluted the young ladies in the most enchanting manner; bowed to, and shook hands with, Mr. Malderton, with a degree of respect amounting almost to veneration; and returned the greetings of the two young men in a half-gratified, half-patronising manner, which fully convinced them that he must be an important, and, at the same time, condescending personage.

"Miss Malderton," said Horatio, after the ordinary salutations, and bowing very low, "may I be permitted to presume to hope that you will allow me to have the pleasure——"

"I don't *think* I am engaged," said Miss Teresa, with a dreadful affectation of indifference—"but, really—so many——"

Horatio looked handsomely miserable.

"I shall be most happy," simpered the interesting Teresa, at last. Horatio's countenance brightened up, like an old hat in a shower of rain.

"A very genteel young man, certainly!" said the gratified Mr. Malderton, as the obsequious Sparkins and his partner joined the quadrille which was just forming.

"He has a remarkably good address," said Mr. Frederick.

"Yes, he is a prime fellow," interposed Tom, who always managed to put his foot in it—"he talks just like an auctioneer."

"Tom!" said his father solemnly, "I think I desired you, before, not to be a fool." Tom looked as happy as a cock on a drizzly morning.

"How delightful!" said the interesting Horatio to his partner, as they promenaded the room at the conclusion of the set—"how delightful, how refreshing it is, to retire from the cloudy storms, the vicissitudes, and the troubles, of life, even if it be but for a few short fleeting moments: and to spend those moments, fading and evanescent though they be, in the delightful, the blessed society of one individual—whose frowns would be death, whose coldness would be madness, whose falsehood would be ruin, whose constancy would be bliss; the possession of whose affection would be the brightest and best reward that Heaven could bestow on man?"

"What feeling! what sentiment!" thought Miss Teresa, as she leaned more heavily on her companion's arm.

"But enough—enough!" resumed the elegant Sparkins, with a theatrical air. "What have I said? what have I—I—to do with sentiments like these! Miss Malderton"—here he stopped short—"may I hope to be permitted to offer the humble tribute of ——"

"Really, Mr. Sparkins," returned the enraptured Teresa, blushing in the sweetest confusion, "I must refer you to papa. I never can, without his consent, venture to——"

"Surely he cannot object——"

"Oh, yes. Indeed, indeed, you know him not!" interrupted Miss Teresa, well knowing there was nothing to fear, but wishing to make the interview resemble a scene in some romantic novel.

"He cannot object to my offering you a glass of negus," returned the adorable Sparkins, with some surprise.

"Is that all?" thought the disappointed Teresa. "What a fuss about nothing!"

"It will give me the greatest pleasure, sir, to see you to dinner at Oak Lodge, Camberwell, on Sunday next at five o'clock, if you have no better engagement," said Mr. Malderton, at the conclusion of the evening, as he and his sons were standing in conversation with Mr. Horatio Sparkins.

Horatio bowed his acknowledgments, and accepted the flattering invitation.

"I must confess," continued the father, offering his snuff-box to his new acquaintance, "that I don't enjoy these assemblies half so much as the comfort—I had almost said the luxury—of Oak Lodge. They have no great charms for an elderly man."

"And after all, sir, what is man?" said the metaphysical Sparkins. "I say, what is man?"

"Ah! very true," said Mr. Malderton; "very true."

"We know that we live and breath," continued Horatio; "that we have wants and wishes, desires and appetites——"

"Certainly," said Mr. Frederick Malderton, looking profound.

"I say, we know that we exist," repeated Horatio, raising his voice, "but there we stop; there, is an end to our knowledge; there, is the summit of our attainments; there, is the termination of our ends. What more do we know?"

"Nothing," replied Mr. Frederick—than whom no one was more capable of answering for himself in that particular. Tom was about to hazard something, but, fortunately for his reputation, he caught his father's angry eye, and slunk off like a puppy convicted of petty larceny.

"Upon my word," said Mr. Malderton the elder, as they were returning home in the fly, "that Mr. Sparkins is a wonderful young man. Such surprising knowledge! such extraordinary information! and such a splendid mode of expressing himself!"

"I think he must be somebody in disguise," said Miss Marianne. "How charmingly romantic!"

"He talks very loud and nicely," timidly observed Tom, "but I don't exactly understand what he means."

"I almost begin to despair of *your* understanding anything, Tom," said his father, who, of course, had been much enlightened by Mr. Horatio Sparkins's conversation.

"It strikes me, Tom," said Miss Teresa, "that you have made yourself very ridiculous this evening."

"No doubt of it," cried everybody—and the unfortunate Tom reduced himself into the least possible space. That night, Mr. and Mrs. Malderton had a long conversation respecting their daughter's prospects and future arrangements. Miss Teresa went to bed, considering whether, in the event of her marrying a title, she could conscientiously encourage the visits of her present associates; and dreamed, all night, of disguised noblemen, large routs, ostrich plumes, bridal favours, and Horatio Sparkins.

Various surmises were hazarded on the Sunday morning, as to the mode of conveyance which the anxiously-expected Horatio would adopt. Did he keep a gig?—was it possible he could come on horseback?—or would he patronize the stage? These, and other various conjectures of equal importance, engrossed the attention of Mrs. Malderton and her daughters during the whole morning after church.

"Upon my word, my dear, it's a most annoying thing that that vulgar brother of yours should have invited himself to dine here to-day," said Mr. Malderton to his wife. "On account of Mr. Sparkins's coming down, I purposely abstained from asking any one but Flamwell. And then to think of your brother—a trades-man—it's insufferable. I declare I wouldn't have him mention his shop, before our new guest—no, not for a thousand pounds! I wouldn't care if he had the good sense to conceal the disgrace he is to the family; but he's so fond of his horrible business, that he *will* let people know what he is."

Mr. Jacob Barton, the individual alluded to, was a large grocer; so vulgar, and so lost to all sense of feeling, that he actually never scrupled to avow that he wasn't above his business: "he'd made his money by it, and he didn't care who know'd it."

"Ah! Flamwell, my dear fellow, how d'ye do?" said Mr. Malderton, as a little spoffish man, with green spectacles, entered the room. "You got my note?"

"Yes, I did; and here I am in consequence."

"You don't happen to know this Mr. Sparkins by name? You know everybody?"

Mr. Flamwell was one of those gentlemen of remarkably extensive information whom one occasionally meets in society, who pretend to know everybody, but in reality know nobody. At Malderton's, where any stories about great people were received with a greedy ear, he was an especial favourite; and, knowing the kind of people he had to deal with, he carried his passion of claiming acquaintance with everybody, to the most immoderate length. He had rather a singular way of telling his greatest lies in a parenthesis, and with an air of self-denial, as if he feared being thought egotistical.

"Why, no, I don't know him by that name," returned Flamwell, in a low tone, and with an air of immense importance. "I have no doubt I know him, though. Is he tall?"

"Middle-sized," said Miss Teresa.

"With black hair?" inquired Flamwell, hazarding a bold guess.

"Yes," returned Miss Teresa, eagerly.

"Rather a snub nose?"

"No," said the disappointed Teresa, "he has a Roman nose."

"I said a Roman nose, didn't I?" inquired Flamwell. "He's an elegant young man?"

"Oh, certainly."

"With remarkably prepossessing manners?"

"Oh, yes!" said all the family together. "You must know him."

"Yes, I thought you knew him, if he was anybody," triumphantly exclaimed Mr. Malderton. "Who d'ye think he is?"

"Why, from your description," said Flamwell, ruminating, and sinking his voice, almost to a whisper, "he bears a strong resemblance to the Honourable Augustus Fitz-Edward Fitz-John Fitz-Osborne. He's a very talented young man, and rather eccentric. It's extremely probable he may have changed his name for some temporary purpose."

Teresa's heart beat high. Could he be the Honourable Augustus Fitz-Edward Fitz-John Fitz-Osborne! What a name to be elegantly engraved upon two glazed cards, tied together with a piece of white satin ribbon! "The Honourable Mrs. Augustus Fitz-Edward Fitz-John Fitz-Osborne!" The thought was transport.

"It's five minutes to five," said Mr. Malderton,

looking at his watch: "I hope he's not going to disappoint us."

"There he is!" exclaimed Miss Teresa, as a loud double-knock was heard at the door. Everybody endeavoured to look—as people when they particularly expect a visitor always do—as if they were perfectly unsuspicious of the approach of anybody.

The room-door opened—"Mr. Barton!" said the servant.

"Confound the man!" murmured Malderton. "Ah! my dear sir, d'ye do! Any news?"

"Why no," returned the grocer, in his usual bluff manner. "No, none partickler. None that I am much aware of. How d'ye do, gals and boys? Mr. Flamwell, sir—glad to see you."

"Here's Mr. Sparkins!" said Tom, who had been looking out at the window, "on *such* a black horse!" There was Horatio, sure enough, on a large black horse, curvetting and prancing along, like an Astley's supernumerary. After a great deal of reining in, and pulling up, with the accompaniments of snorting, rearing, and kicking, the animal consented to stop at about a hundred yards from the gate, where Mr. Sparkins dismounted, and confided him to the care of Mr. Malderton's groom. The ceremony of introduction was gone through, in all due form. Mr. Flamwell looked from behind his green spectacles at Horatio with an air of mysterious importance; and the gallant Horatio looked unutterable things at Teresa.

"Is he the Honourable Mr. Augustus What's-his-name?" whispered Mrs. Malderton to Flamwell, as he was escorting her to the dining-room.

"Why, no—at least not exactly," returned that great authority—"not exactly."

"Who *is* he then?"

"Hush!" said Flamwell, nodding his head with a grave air, importing that he knew very well; but was prevented, by some grave reasons of state, from disclosing the important secret. It might be one of the ministers making himself acquainted with the views of the people.

"Mr. Sparkins," said the delighted Mrs. Malderton, "pray divide the ladies. John, put a chair for the gentleman between Miss Teresa and Miss Marianne." This was addressed to a man who, on ordinary occasions, acted as half-groom, half-gardener; but who, as it was important to make an impression on Mr. Sparkins, had been forced into a white neckerchief and shoes, and touched up, and brushed, to look like a second footman.

The dinner was excellent; Horatio was most attentive to Miss Teresa, and every one felt in high spirits, except Mr. Malderton, who, knowing the propensity of his brother-in-law, Mr. Barton, endured that sort of agony which the newspapers inform us is experienced by the surrounding neighbourhood when a pot-boy hangs himself in a hay-loft, and which is "much easier to be imagined than described."

"Have you seen your friend, Sir Thomas Noland, lately, Flamwell?" inquired Mr. Malderton, casting a sidelong look at Horatio, to see what effect the mention of so great a man had upon him.

"Why, no—not very lately. I saw Lord Gubbleton the day before yesterday."

"Ah! I hope his lordship is very well?" said Malderton, in a tone of the greatest interest. It is scarcely necessary to say that, until that moment, he had been quite innocent of the existence of such a person.

"Why, yes; he was very well—very well indeed. He's a devilish good fellow. I met him in the City, and had a long chat with him. Indeed, I'm rather intimate with him. I couldn't stop to talk to him as long as I could wish, though, because I was on my way to a banker's, a very rich man, and a member of Parliament, with whom I am also rather, indeed I may say very, intimate."

"I know whom you mean," returned the host, consequentially—in reality knowing as much about the matter as Flamwell himself. "He has a capital business."

This was touching on a dangerous topic.

"Talking of business," interposed Mr. Barton, from the centre of the table. "A gentleman whom you knew very well, Malderton, before you made that first lucky spec of yours, called at our shop the other day, and——"

"Barton, may I trouble you for a potato?" interrupted the wretched master of the house, hoping to nip the story in the bud.

"Certainly," returned the grocer, quite insensible of his brother-in-law's object—"and he said in a very plain manner——"

"*Floury*, if you please," interrupted Malderton again; dreading the termination of the anecdote, and fearing a repetition of the word "shop."

"He said, says he," continued the culprit, after despatching the potato; "says he, how goes on your business? So I said, jokingly—you know my way—

says I, I'm never above my business, and I hope my business will never be above me. Ha, ha!"

"Mr. Sparkins," said the host, vainly endeavouring to conceal his dismay, "a glass of wine?"

"With the utmost pleasure, sir."

"Happy to see you."

"Thank you."

"We were talking the other evening," resumed the host, addressing Horatio, partly with the view of displaying the conversational powers of his new acquaintance, and partly in the hope of drowning the grocer's stories—"we were talking the other night about the nature of man. Your argument struck me very forcibly."

"And me," said Mr. Frederick. Horatio made a graceful inclination of the head.

"Pray, what is your opinion of woman, Mr. Sparkins?" inquired Mrs. Malderton. The young ladies simpered.

"Man," replied Horatio, "man, whether he ranged the bright, gay, flowery plains of a second Eden, or the more sterile, barren, and I may say, commonplace regions, to which we are compelled to accustom ourselves, in times such as these; man, under any circumstances, or in any place—whether he were bending beneath the withering blasts of the frigid zone, or scorching under the rays of a vertical sun—man, without woman, would be—alone."

"I am very happy to find you entertain such honourable opinions, Mr. Sparkins," said Mrs. Malderton.

"And I," added Miss Teresa. Horatio looked his delight, and the young lady blushed.

"Now, it's my opinion——" said Mr. Barton.

"I know what you're going to say," interposed Malderton, determined not to give his relation another opportunity, "and I don't agree with you."

"What!" inquired the astonished grocer.

"I am sorry to differ from you, Barton," said the host, in as positive a manner as if he really were contradicting a position which the other had laid down, "but I cannot give my assent to what I consider a very monstrous proposition."

"But I meant to say——"

"You never can convince me," said Malderton, with an air of obstinate determination. "Never."

"And I," said Mr. Frederick, following up his father's attack, "cannot entirely agree in Mr. Sparkins's argument."

"What!" said Horatio, who became more metaphysical, and more argumentative, as he saw the female part of the family listening in wondering delight—"what! Is effect the consequence of cause? Is cause the precursor of effect?"

"That's the point," said Flamwell.

"To be sure," said Mr. Malderton.

"Because, if effect is the consequence of cause, and if cause does precede effect, I apprehend you are wrong," added Horatio.

"Decidedly," said the toad-eating Flamwell.

"At least, I apprehend that to be the just and logical deduction?" said Sparkins, in a tone of interrogation.

"No doubt of it," chimed in Flamwell again. "It settles the point."

"Well, perhaps it does," said Mr. Frederick; "I didn't see it before."

"I don't exactly see it now," thought the grocer; "but I suppose it's all right."

"How wonderfully clever he is!" whispered Mrs. Malderton to her daughters, as they retired to the drawing-room.

"Oh, he's quite a love!" said both the young ladies together; "he talks like an oracle. He must have seen a great deal of life."

The gentlemen being left to themselves, a pause ensued, during which everybody looked very grave, as if they were quite overcome by the profound nature of the previous discussion. Flamwell, who had made up his mind to find out who and what Mr. Horatio Sparkins really was, first broke silence.

"Excuse me, sir," said that distinguished personage, "I presume you have studied for the bar? I thought of entering once, myself—indeed, I'm rather intimate with some of the highest ornaments of that distinguished profession."

"N—no!" said Horatio, with a little hesitation; "not exactly."

"But you have been much among the silk gowns, or I mistake?" inquired Flamwell, deferentially.

"Nearly all my life," returned Sparkins.

The question was thus pretty well settled in the mind of Mr. Flamwell. He was a young gentleman "about to be called."

"I shouldn't like to be a barrister," said Tom, speaking for the first time, and looking round the table to find somebody who would notice the remark.

No one made any reply.

"I shouldn't like to wear a wig," said Tom, hazarding another observation.

"Tom, I beg you will not make yourself ridiculous," said his father. "Pray listen, and improve yourself by the conversation you hear, and don't be constantly making these absurd remarks."

"Very well, father," replied the unfortunate Tom, who had not spoken a word since he had asked for another slice of beef at a quarter-past five o'clock, P.M., and it was then eight.

"Well, Tom," observed his good-natured uncle, "never mind! *I* think with you. *I* shouldn't like to wear a wig. I'd rather wear an apron."

Mr. Malderton coughed violently. Mr. Barton resumed—"For if a man's above his business——"

The cough returned with tenfold violence, and did not cease until the unfortunate cause of it, in his alarm, had quite forgotten what he intended to say.

"Mr. Sparkins," said Flamwell, returning to the charge, "do you happen to know Mr. Delafontaine, of Bedford-square?"

"I have exchanged cards with him; since which, indeed, I have had an opportunity of serving him considerably," replied Horatio, slightly colouring; no doubt, at having been betrayed into making the acknowledgment.

"You are very lucky, if you have had an opportunity of obliging that great man," observed Flamwell, with an air of profound respect.

"I don't know who he is," he whispered to Mr. Malderton, confidentially, as they followed Horatio up to the drawing-room. "It's quite clear, however, that he belongs to the law, and that he is somebody of great importance, and very highly connected."

"No doubt, no doubt," returned his companion.

The remainder of the evening passed away most delightfully. Mr. Malderton, relieved from his apprehensions by the circumstance of Mr. Barton's falling into a profound sleep, was as affable and gracious as possible. Miss Teresa played the "Fall of Paris," as Mr. Sparkins declared, in a most masterly manner, and both of them, assisted by Mr. Frederick, tried over glees and trios without number; they having made the pleasing discovery that their voices harmonised beautifully. To be sure, they all sang the first part; and Horatio, in addition to the slight drawback of having no ear, was perfectly innocent of knowing a note of music; still, they passed the time very agreeably, and it was past twelve o'clock before Mr. Sparkins ordered the mourning-coach-looking steed to be brought out—an order which was only complied with, on the distinct understanding that he was to repeat his visit on the following Sunday.

"But, perhaps, Mr. Sparkins will form one of our party to-morrow evening?" suggested Mrs. M. "Mr. Malderton intends taking the girls to see the pantomime." Mr. Sparkins bowed, and promised to join the party in box 48, in the course of the evening.

"We will not tax you for the morning," said Miss Teresa, bewitchingly; "for ma is going to take us to all sorts of places, shopping. I know that gentlemen have a great horror of that employment." Mr. Sparkins bowed again, and declared that he should be delighted, but business of importance occupied him in the morning. Flamwell looked at Malderton significantly—"It's term time!" he whispered.

At twelve o'clock on the following morning, the "fly" was at the door of Oak Lodge, to convey Mrs. Malderton and her daughters on their expedition for the day. They were to dine and dress for the play at a friend's house. First, driving thither with their band-boxes, they departed on their first errand to make some purchases at Messrs. Jones, Spruggins, and Smith's, of Tottenham-court-road; after which, they were to go to Redmayne's in Bond-street; thence, to innumerable places that no one ever heard of. The young ladies beguiled the tediousness of the ride by eulogising Mr. Horatio Sparkins, scolding their mamma for taking them so far to save a shilling, and wondering whether they should ever reach their destination. At length, the vehicle stopped before a dirty-looking ticketed linen-draper's shop, with goods of all kinds, and labels of all sorts and sizes, in the window. There were dropsical figures of seven with a little three-farthings in the corner; "perfectly invisible to the naked eye"; three hundred and fifty thousand ladies' boas, *from* one shilling and a penny halfpenny; real French kid shoes, at two and ninepence per pair; green parasols, at an equally cheap rate; and "every description of goods," as the proprietors said—and they must know best—"fifty percent under cost price."

"Lor! ma, what a place you have brought us to!" said Miss Teresa; "what *would* Mr. Sparkins say if he could see us!"

"Ah! what, indeed!" said Miss Marianne, horrified at the idea.

"Pray be seated, ladies. What is the first article?" inquired the obsequious master of the ceremonies of the establishment, who, in his large white neckcloth and formal tie, looked like a bad "portrait of a gentleman" in the Somerset-house exhibition.

"I want to see some silks," answered Mrs. Malderton.

"Directly, ma'am.—Mr. Smith! Where *is* Mr. Smith?"

"Here, sir," cried a voice at the back of the shop.

"Pray make haste, Mr. Smith," said the M.C. "You never are to be found when you're wanted, sir."

Mr. Smith, thus enjoined to use all possible despatch, leaped over the counter with great agility, and placed himself before the newly-arrived customers. Mrs. Malderton uttered a faint scream; Miss Teresa, who had been stooping down to talk to her sister, raised her head, and beheld—Horatio Sparkins!

"We will draw a veil," as novel-writers say, over the scene that ensued. The mysterious, philosophical, romantic, metaphysical Sparkins—he who, to the interesting Teresa, seemed like the embodied idea of the young dukes and poetical exquisites in blue silk dressing-gowns, and ditto ditto slippers, of whom she had read and dreamed, but had never expected to behold, was suddenly converted into Mr. Samuel Smith, the assistant at a "cheap shop"; the junior partner in a slippery firm of some three weeks' existence. The dignified evanishment of the hero of Oak Lodge, on this unexpected recognition, could only be equalled by that of a furtive dog with a considerable kettle at his tail. All the hopes of the Maldertons were destined at once to melt away, like the lemon ices at a Company's dinner; Almack's was still to them as distant as the North Pole; and Miss Teresa had as much chance of a husband as Captain Ross had of the north-west passage.

Years have elapsed since the occurrence of this dreadful morning. The daisies have thrice bloomed on Camberwell-green; the sparrows have thrice repeated their vernal chirps in Camberwell-grove; but the Miss Maldertons are still unmated. Miss Teresa's case is more desperate than ever; but Flamwell is yet in the zenith of his reputation; and the family have the same predilection for aristocratic personages, with an increased aversion to anything *low*. □

DISCUSSION

1. "Horatio Sparkins" is obviously an attack on social climbing and its concomitant vice, snobbery. How many different aspects of this snobbery can you identify in the story?

2. Are any characters portrayed favorably? Explain.

3. Although much of the humor of this story lies in its surprise ending, it does contain other humorous touches. Discuss some of these, including the use of stylistic devices such as far-flown similes.

THE THREE STRANGERS

by Thomas Hardy

Among the few features of agricultural England which retain an appearance but little modified by the lapse of centuries, may be reckoned the long, grassy and furzy downs, coombs, or ewe leases,[1] as they are called according to their kind, that fill a large area of certain counties in the south and southwest. If any mark of human occupation is met with hereon, it usually takes the form of the solitary cottage of some shepherd.

Fifty years ago such a lonely cottage stood on such a down, and may possibly be standing there now. In spite of its loneliness, however, the spot, by actual measurement, was not more than five

From *Wessex Tales* by Thomas Hardy. By permission of the Hardy Estate; Macmillan London & Basingstoke; The Macmillan Company of Canada Limited, and St. Martin's Press, Incorporated.

1. *furzy downs . . . ewe leases.* Furzy downs are rolling lands overgrown with furze, a low evergreen shrub with yellow flowers; coombs are small valleys or hollows; ewe leases are sheep pastures.

miles from a county-town. Yet that affected it little. Five miles of irregular upland, during the long inimical seasons, with their sleets, snows, rains, and mists, afford withdrawing space enough to isolate a Timon or a Nebuchadnezzar[2]; much less, in fair weather, to please that less repellent tribe, the poets, philosophers, artists and others who "conceive and meditate of pleasant things."

Some old earthen camp or barrow, some clump of trees, at least some starved fragment of ancient hedge is usually taken advantage of in the erection of these forlorn dwellings. But, in the present case, such a kind of shelter had been disregarded. Higher Crowstairs, as the house was called, stood quite detached and undefended. The only reason for its precise situation seemed to be the crossing of two footpaths at right angles hard by, which may have crossed there and thus for a good five hundred years. Hence the house was exposed to the elements on all sides. But, though the wind up here blew unmistakably when it did blow, and the rain hit hard whenever it fell, the various weathers of the winter season were not quite so formidable on the down as they were imagined to be by dwellers on low ground. The raw rimes were not so pernicious as in the hollows, and the frosts were scarcely so severe. When the shepherd and his family who tenanted the house were pitied for their sufferings from the exposure, they said that upon the whole they were less inconvenienced by "wuzzes and flames" (hoarses and phlegms) than when they had lived by the stream of a snug neighboring valley.

The night of March 28, 182–, was precisely one of the nights that were wont to call forth these expressions of commiseration. The level rainstorm smote walls, slopes and hedges like the clothyard shafts of Senlac and Crecy.[3] Such sheep and outdoor animals as had no shelter stood with their buttocks to the winds; while the tails of little birds trying to roost on some scraggy thorn were blown inside out like umbrellas. The gable end of the cottage was stained with wet, and the eavesdroppings flapped against the wall. Yet never was commiseration for the shepherd more misplaced. For that cheerful rustic was entertaining a large party in glorification of the christening of his second girl.

The guests had arrived before the rain began to fall, and they were all now assembled in the chief or living room of the dwelling. A glance into the apartment at eight o'clock on this eventful evening would have resulted in the opinion that it was as cosy and comfortable a nook as could be wished for in boisterous weather. The calling of its inhabitant was proclaimed by a number of highly polished sheepcrooks without stems that were hung ornamentally over the fireplace, the curl of each shining crook varying from the antiquated type engraved in the patriarchal pictures of old family Bibles to the most approved fashion of the last local sheep fair. The room was lighted by half-a-dozen candles, having wicks only a trifle smaller than the grease which enveloped them, in candlesticks that were never used but at high days, holy days, and family feasts. The lights were scattered about the room, two of them standing on the chimney piece. This position of candles was in itself significant. Candles on the chimney piece always meant a party.

On the hearth, in front of a back brand to give substance, blazed a fire of thorns, that crackled "like the laughter of the fool."

Nineteen persons were gathered here. Of these, five women, wearing gowns of various bright hues, sat in chairs along the wall; girls shy and not shy filled the window bench; four men, including Charley Jake the hedge carpenter, Elijah New the parish clerk, and John Pitcher, a neighboring dairyman, the shepherd's father-in-law, lolled in the settle; a young man and maid, who were blushing over tentative *pourparlers*[4] on a life companionship, sat beneath the corner cupboard; and an elderly engaged man of fifty or upward moved restlessly about from spots where his betrothed was not to the spot where she was. Enjoyment was pretty general, and so much the more prevailed in being unhampered by conventional restrictions. Absolute confidence in each other's good opinion begat perfect ease, while the finishing stroke of manner, amounting to a truly princely serenity, was lent to the majority by the absence of any expression or trait denoting that they wished to get on in the world, enlarge their minds, or do any eclipsing thing whatever—which nowadays so generally

2. *Timon or a Nebuchadnezzar.* Timon, in Shakespeare's *Timon of Athens,* mistrusted his fellowmen and lived as a hermit. Nebuchadnezzar, ancient king of Babylon, spent four years alone in the wilderness living on grass.

3. *clothyard shafts of Senlac and Crecy,* yard-long arrows used in two famous battles.

4. *pourparlers* (pür′ pär′ lā′), discussions preliminary to negotiations (French).

nips the bloom and *bonhomie* of all except the two extremes of the social scale.

Shepherd Fennel had married well, his wife being a dairyman's daughter from a vale at a distance, who brought fifty guineas in her pocket—and kept them there, till they should be required for ministering to the needs of a coming family. This frugal woman had been somewhat exercised as to the character that should be given to the gathering. A sit-still party had its advantages; but an undisturbed position of ease in chairs and settles was apt to lead on the men to such an unconscionable deal of toping that they would sometimes fairly drink the house dry. A dancing party was the alternative; but this, while avoiding the foregoing objection on the score of good drink, had a counterbalancing disadvantage in the matter of good victuals, the ravenous appetites engendered by the exercise causing immense havoc in the buttery. Shepherdess Fennel fell back upon the intermediate plan of mingling short dances with short periods of talk and singing, so as to hinder any ungovernable rage in either. But this scheme was entirely confined to her own gentle mind: the shepherd himself was in the mood to exhibit the most reckless phases of hospitality.

The fiddler was a boy of those parts, about twelve years of age, who had a wonderful dexterity in jigs and reels, though his fingers were so small and short as to necessitate a constant shifting for the high notes, from which he scrambled back to the first position with sounds not of unmixed purity of tone. At seven the shrill tweedle-dee of this youngster had begun, accompanied by a booming ground bass from Elijah New, the parish clerk, who had thoughtfully brought with him his favorite musical instrument, the serpent.[5] Dancing was instantaneous, Mrs. Fennel privately enjoining the players on no account to let the dance exceed the length of a quarter of an hour.

But Elijah and the boy in the excitement of their position quite forgot the injunction. Moreover, Oliver Giles, a man of seventeen, one of the dancers, who was enamored of his partner, a fair girl of thirty-three rolling years, had recklessly handed a new crown piece to the musicians, as a bribe to keep going as long as they had muscle and wind. Mrs. Fennel, seeing the steam begin to generate on the countenances of her guests, crossed over and touched the fiddler's elbow and put her hand on the serpent's mouth. But they took no notice, and fearing she might lose her character of genial hostess if she were to interfere too markedly, she retired and sat down helpless. And so the dance whizzed on with cumulative fury, the performers moving in their planet-like courses, direct and retrograde, from apogee to perigee, till the hand of the well-kicked clock at the bottom of the room had traveled over the circumference of an hour.

While these cheerful events were in the course of enactment within Fennel's pastoral dwelling an incident having considerable bearing on the party had occurred in the gloomy night without. Mrs. Fennel's concern about the growing fierceness of the dance corresponded in point of time with the ascent of a human figure to the solitary hill of Higher Crowstairs from the direction of the distant town. This personage strode on through the rain without a pause, following the little-worn path which, further on its course, skirted the shepherd's cottage.

It was nearly the time of full moon, and on this account, though the sky was lined with a uniform sheet of dripping cloud, ordinary objects out of doors were readily visible. The sad wan light revealed the lonely pedestrian to be a man of supple frame; his gait suggested that he had somewhat passed the period of perfect and instinctive agility, though not so far as to be otherwise than rapid of motion when occasion required. At a rough guess, he might have been about forty years of age. He appeared tall, but a recruiting sergeant, or other person accustomed to the judging of men's heights by the eye, would have discerned that this was chiefly owing to his gauntness, and that he was not more than five-feet-eight or nine.

Notwithstanding the regularity of his tread there was caution in it, as in that of one who mentally feels his way; and despite the fact that it was not a black coat nor a dark garment of any sort that he wore, there was something about him which suggested that he naturally belonged to the black-coated tribes of men. His clothes were of fustian, and his boots hobnailed, yet in his progress he showed not the mud-accustomed bearing of hobnailed and fustianed peasantry.

By the time that he had arrived abreast of the shepherd's premises the rain came down, or rather came along, with yet more determined violence.

5. *serpent,* a low-toned wind instrument made of wood, now obsolete.

The outskirts of the little settlement partially broke the force of wind and rain, and this induced him to stand still. The most salient of the shepherd's domestic erections was an empty sty at the forward corner of his hedgeless garden, for in these latitudes the principle of masking the homelier features of your establishment by a conventional frontage was unknown. The traveler's eye was attracted to this small building by the pallid shine of the wet slates that covered it. He turned aside, and, finding it empty, stood under the pent roof for shelter.

While he stood the boom of the serpent within the adjacent house, and the lesser strains of the fiddler, reached the spot as an accompaniment to the surging hiss of the flying rain on the sod, its louder beating on the cabbage leaves of the garden, on the straw hackles of eight or ten beehives just discernible by the path, and its dripping from the eaves into a row of buckets and pans that had been placed under the walls of the cottage. For at Higher Crowstairs, as at all such elevated domiciles, the grand difficulty of housekeeping was an insufficiency of water; and a casual rainfall was utilized by turning out, as catchers, every utensil that the house contained. Some queer stories might be told of the contrivances for economy of suds and dish-waters that are absolutely necessitated in upland habitations during the droughts of summer. But at this season there were no such exigencies; a mere acceptance of what the skies bestowed was sufficient for an abundant store.

At last the notes of the serpent ceased and the house was silent. This cessation of activity aroused the solitary pedestrian from the reverie into which he had lapsed, and, emerging from the shed, with an apparently new intention, he walked up the path to the house door. Arrived here, his first act was to kneel down on a large stone beside the row of vessels, and to drink a copious draught from one of them. Having quenched his thirst he rose and lifted his hand to knock, but paused with his eye upon the panel. Since the dark surface of the wood revealed absolutely nothing, it was evident that he must be mentally looking through the door, as if he wished to measure thereby all the possibilities that a house of this sort might include, and how they might bear upon the question of his entry.

In his indecision he turned and surveyed the scene around. Not a soul was anywhere visible. The garden path stretched downward from his feet, gleaming like the track of a snail; the roof of the little well (mostly dry), the well cover, the top rail of the garden gate, were varnished with the same dull liquid glaze; while, far away in the vale, a faint whiteness of more than usual extent showed that the rivers were high in the meads. Beyond all this winked a few bleared lamplights through the beating drops—lights that denoted the situation of the county town from which he had appeared to come. The absence of all notes of life in that direction seemed to clinch his intentions, and he knocked at the door.

Within, a desultory chat had taken the place of movement and musical sound. The hedge carpenter was suggesting a song to the company, which nobody just then was inclined to undertake, so that the knock afforded a not unwelcome diversion.

"Walk in!" said the shepherd promptly.

The latch clicked upward, and out of the night our pedestrian appeared upon the doormat. The shepherd arose, snuffed two of the nearest candles, and turned to look at him.

Their light disclosed that the stranger was dark in complexion and not unprepossessing as to feature. His hat, which for a moment he did not remove, hung low over his eyes, without concealing that they were large, open, and determined, moving with a flash rather than a glance round the room. He seemed pleased with his survey, and, baring his shaggy head, said, in a rich deep voice, "The rain is so heavy, friends, that I ask leave to come in and rest awhile."

"To be sure, stranger," said the shepherd. "And faith, you've been lucky in choosing your time, for we are having a bit of a fling for a glad cause—though, to be sure, a man could hardly wish that glad cause to happen more than once a year."

"Nor less," spoke up a woman. "For 'tis best to get your family over and done with, as soon as you can, so as to be all the earlier out of the fag o't."

"And what may be this glad cause?" asked the stranger.

"A birth and christening," said the shepherd.

The stranger hoped his host might not be made unhappy either by too many or too few of such episodes, and being invited by a gesture to pull at the mug, he readily acquiesced. His manner, which, before entering, had been so dubious, was now altogether that of a careless and candid man.

"Late to be traipsing athwart this coomb—hey?" said the engaged man of fifty.

"Late it is, master, as you say. I'll take a seat in the chimney corner, if you have nothing to urge against it, ma'am; for I am a little moist on the side that was next the rain."

Mrs. Shepherd Fennel assented, and made room for the self-invited comer, who, having got completely inside the chimney corner, stretched out his legs and his arms with the expansiveness of a person quite at home.

"Yes, I am rather cracked in the vamp," he said freely, seeing that the eyes of the shepherd's wife fell upon his boots, "and I am not well fitted either. I have had some rough times lately, and have been forced to pick up what I can get in the way of wearing, but I must find a suit better fit for working days when I reach home."

"One of hereabouts?" she inquired.

"Not quite that—further up the country."

"I thought so. And so be I; and by your tongue you come from my neighborhood."

"But you would hardly have heard of me," he said quickly. "My time would be long before yours, ma'am, you see."

This testimony to the youthfulness of his hostess had the effect of stopping her cross-examination.

"There is only one thing more wanted to make me happy," continued the newcomer. "And that is a little baccy, which I am sorry to say I am out of."

"I'll fill your pipe," said the shepherd.

"I must ask you to lend me a pipe likewise."

"A smoker, and no pipe about 'ee?"

"I have dropped it somewhere on the road."

The shepherd filled and handed him a new clay pipe, saying, as he did so, "Hand me your baccy box—I'll fill that too, now I am about it."

The man went through the movement of searching his pockets.

"Lost that too?" said his entertainer, with some surprise.

"I am afraid so," said the man with some confusion. "Give it to me in a screw of paper." Lighting his pipe at the candle with a suction that drew the whole flame into the bowl, he resettled himself in the corner and bent his looks upon the faint steam from his damp legs, as if he wished to say no more.

Meanwhile the general body of guests had been taking little notice of this visitor by reason of an absorbing discussion in which they were engaged with the band about a tune for the next dance. The matter being settled, they were about to stand up when an interruption came in the shape of another knock at the door.

At sound of the same the man in the chimney corner took up the poker and began stirring the brands as if doing it thoroughly were the one aim of his existence; and a second time the shepherd said, "Walk in!" In a moment another man stood upon the straw-woven doormat. He too was a stranger.

This individual was one of a type radically different from the first. There was more of the commonplace in his manner, and a certain jovial cosmopolitanism sat upon his features. He was several years older than the first arrival, his hair being slightly frosted, his eyebrows bristly, and his whiskers cut back from his cheeks. His face was rather full and flabby, and yet it was not altogether a face without power. A few grog blossoms marked the neighborhood of his nose. He flung back his long drab greatcoat, revealing that beneath it he wore a suit of cinder-gray shade throughout, large heavy seals, of some metal or other that would take a polish, dangling from his fob as his only personal ornament. Shaking the waterdrops from his low-crowned glazed hat, he said, "I must ask for a few minutes' shelter, comrades, or I shall be wetted to my skin before I get to Casterbridge."

"Make yourself at home, master," said the shepherd, perhaps a trifle less heartily than on the first occasion. Not that Fennel had the least tinge of niggardliness in his composition; but the room was far from large, spare chairs were not numerous, and damp companions were not altogether desirable at close quarters for the women and girls in their bright-colored gowns.

However, the second comer, after taking off his greatcoat, and hanging his hat on a nail in one of the ceiling beams as if he had been specially invited to put it there, advanced and sat down at the table. This had been pushed so closely into the chimney corner, to give all available room to the dancers, that its inner edge grazed the elbow of the man who had ensconced himself by the fire; and thus the two strangers were brought into close companionship. They nodded to each other by way of breaking the ice of unacquaintance, and the first stranger handed his neighbor the family mug—a huge vessel of brown ware, having its upper edge worn away like a threshold by the rub of whole generations of thirsty lips that had gone the way of all flesh, and bearing the following inscription burnt upon its rotund side in yellow letters:

THERE IS NO FUN
UNTiLL i CUM.

The other man, nothing loth, raised the mug to his lips, and drank on, and on, and on—till a curious blueness overspread the countenance of the shepherd's wife, who had regarded with no little surprise the first stranger's free offer to the second of what did not belong to him to dispense.

"I knew it!" said the toper to the shepherd with much satisfaction. "When I walked up your garden before coming in, and saw the hives all of a row, I said to myself, 'Where there's bees there's honey, and where there's honey there's mead.' But mead of such a truly comfortable sort as this I really didn't expect to meet in my older days." He took yet another pull at the mug, till it assumed an ominous elevation.

"Glad you enjoy it!" said the shepherd warmly.

"It is goodish mead," assented Mrs. Fennel, with an absence of enthusiasm which seemed to say that it was possible to buy praise for one's cellar at too heavy a price. "It is trouble enough to make—and really I hardly think we shall make any more. For honey sells well, and we ourselves make shift with a drop o' small mead and metheglin for common use from the comb washings."[6]

"O, but you'll never have the heart!" reproachfully cried the stranger in cinder gray, after taking up the mug a third time, and setting it down empty. "I love mead, when 'tis old like this, as I love to go to church o' Sundays, or to relieve the needy any day of the week."

"Ha, ha, ha!" said the man in the chimney corner, who, in spite of the taciturnity induced by the pipe of tobacco, could not or would not refrain from this slight testimony to his comrade's humor.

Now the old mead of those days, brewed of the purest first year or maiden honey, four pounds to the gallon—with its due complement of white of eggs, cinnamon, ginger, cloves, mace, rosemary, yeast, and processes of working, bottling, and cellaring—tasted remarkably strong; but it did not taste so strong as it actually was. Hence, presently, the stranger in cinder gray at the table, moved by its creeping influence, unbuttoned his waistcoat, threw himself back in his chair, spread his legs, and made his presence felt in various ways.

"Well, well, as I say," he resumed, "I am going to Casterbridge, and to Casterbridge I must go. I should have been almost there by this time; but the rain drove me into your dwelling, and I'm not sorry for it."

"You don't live in Casterbridge?" said the shepherd.

"Not as yet; though I shortly mean to move there."

"Going to set up in trade, perhaps?"

"No, no," said the shepherd's wife. "It is easy to see that the gentleman is rich, and don't want to work at anything."

The cinder-gray stranger paused, as if to consider whether he would accept that definition of himself. He presently rejected it by answering, "Rich is not quite the word for me, dame. I do work, and I must work. And even if I only get to Casterbridge by midnight I must begin work there at eight tomorrow morning. Yes, het or wet, blow or snow, famine or sword, my day's work tomorrow must be done."

"Poor man! Then, in spite o' seeming, you be worse off than we?" replied the shepherd's wife.

"'Tis the nature of my trade, men and maidens. 'Tis the nature of my trade more than my poverty. . . . But really and truly I must up and off, or I shan't get a lodging in the town." However, the speaker did not move, and directly added, "There's time for one more draught of friendship before I go; and I'd perform it at once if the mug were not dry."

"Here's a mug o' small," said Mrs. Fennel. "Small, we call it, though to be sure 'tis only the first wash o' the combs."

"No," said the stranger disdainfully. "I won't spoil your first kindness by partaking o' your second."

"Certainly not," broke in Fennel. "We don't increase and multiply every day, and I'll fill the mug again." He went away to the dark place under the stairs where the barrel stood. The shepherdess followed him.

"Why should you do this?" she said reproachfully, as soon as they were alone. "He's emptied it once though it held enough for ten people; and now he's not contented wi' the small, but must

6. *small mead . . . comb washings,* drinks less potent than mead, made by pouring water over honeycomb after the salable honey has been removed.

needs call for more o' the strong! And a stranger unbeknown to any of us. For my part, I don't like the look o' the man at all."

"But he's in the house, my honey; and 'tis a wet night, and a christening. Daze it, what's a cup of mead more or less? There'll be plenty more next bee-burning."[7]

"Very well—this time, then," she answered, looking wistfully at the barrel. "But what is the man's calling, and where is he one of, that he should come in and join us like this?"

"I don't know. I'll ask him again."

The catastrophe of having the mug drained dry at one pull by the stranger in cinder gray was effectually guarded against this time by Mrs. Fennel. She poured out his allowance in a small cup, keeping the large one at a discreet distance from him. When he had tossed off his portion the shepherd renewed his inquiry about the stranger's occupation.

The latter did not immediately reply, and the man in the chimney corner, with sudden demonstrativeness, said, "Anybody may know my trade—I'm a wheelwright."

"A very good trade for these parts," said the shepherd.

"And anybody may know mine—if they've the sense to find it out," said the stranger in cinder gray.

"You may generally tell what a man is by his claws," observed the hedge carpenter, looking at his own hands. "My fingers be as full of thorns as an old pincushion is of pins."

The hands of the man in the chimney corner instinctively sought the shade, and he gazed into the fire as he resumed his pipe. The man at the table took up the hedge carpenter's remark, and added smartly, "True; but the oddity of my trade is that, instead of setting a mark upon me, it sets a mark upon my customers."

No observation being offered by anybody in elucidation of this enigma the shepherd's wife once more called for a song. The same obstacles presented themselves as at the former time—one had no voice, another had forgotten the first verse. The stranger at the table, whose soul had now risen to a good working temperature, relieved the difficulty by exclaiming that, to start the company, he would sing himself. Thrusting one thumb into the armhole of his waistcoat, he waved the other hand in the air, and, with an extemporizing gaze at the shining sheepcrooks above the mantelpiece, began:

O my trade it is the rarest one, simple shepherds all—
My trade is a sight to see;
For my customers I tie, and take them up on high,
And waft 'em to a far countree!

The room was silent when he had finished the verse—with one exception, that of the man in the chimney corner, who, at the singer's word, "Chorus!" joined him in a deep bass voice of musical relish—

And waft 'em to a far countree!

Oliver Giles, John Pitcher the dairyman, the parish clerk, the engaged man of fifty, the row of young women against the wall, seemed lost in thought not of the gayest kind. The shepherd looked meditatively on the ground, the shepherdess gazed keenly at the singer, and with some suspicion; she was doubting whether this stranger were merely singing an old song from recollection, or was composing one there and then for the occasion. All were as perplexed at the obscure revelation as the guests at Belshazzar's Feast,[8] except the man in the chimney corner, who quietly said, "Second verse, stranger," and smoked on.

The singer thoroughly moistened himself from his lips inwards, and went on with his next stanza as requested:

My tools are but common ones, simple shepherds all—
My tools are no sight to see:
A little hempen string, and a post whereon to swing,
Are implements enough for me!

Shepherd Fennel glanced round. There was no longer any doubt that the stranger was answering his question rhythmically. The guests one and all started back with suppressed exclamations. The young woman engaged to the man of fifty fainted halfway, and would have proceeded, but finding him wanting in alacrity for catching her she sat down trembling.

"O, he's the——!" whispered the people in the background, mentioning the name of an ominous public officer. "He's come to do it! 'Tis to

7. *bee-burning.* Bee keepers use smoke as protection while taking honey from the beehive.

8. *perplexed . . . Feast.* According to the Old Testament story, handwriting appeared on the wall at Belshazzar's Feast, forecasting doom (Daniel 5:1–24).

be at Casterbridge jail tomorrow—the man for sheep stealing—the poor clock-maker we heard of, who used to live away at Shottsford and had no work to do—Timothy Summers, whose family were astarving, and so he went out of Shottsford by the highroad, and took a sheep in open daylight, defying the farmer and the farmer's wife and the farmer's lad, and every man jack among 'em. He" (and they nodded towards the stranger of the deadly trade) "is come from up the country to do it because there's not enough to do in his own county town, and he's got the place here now our own county man's dead; he's going to live in the same cottage under the prison wall."

The stranger in cinder gray took no notice of this whispered string of observations, but again wetted his lips. Seeing that his friend in the chimney corner was the only one who reciprocated his joviality in any way, he held out his cup towards that appreciative comrade, who also held out his own. They clinked together, the eyes of the rest of the room hanging upon the singer's actions. He parted his lips for the third verse; but at that moment another knock was audible upon the door. This time the knock was faint and hesitating.

The company seemed scared; the shepherd looked with consternation towards the entrance, and it was with some effort that he resisted his alarmed wife's deprecatory glance, and uttered for the third time the welcoming words, "Walk in!"

The door was gently opened, and another man stood upon the mat. He, like those who had preceded him, was a stranger. This time it was a short, small personage, of fair complexion, and dressed in a decent suit of dark clothes.

"Can you tell me the way to——?" he began: when, gazing round the room to observe the nature of the company amongst whom he had fallen, his eyes lighted on the stranger in cinder gray. It was just at the instant when the latter, who had thrown his mind into his song with such a will that he scarcely heeded the interruption, silenced all whispers and inquiries by bursting into his third verse:

Tomorrow is my working day, simple shepherds all—
Tomorrow is a working day for me:
For the farmer's sheep is slain, and the lad who did it ta'en,
And on his soul may God ha' merc-y!

The stranger in the chimney corner, waving cups with the singer so heartily that his mead splashed over on the hearth, repeated in his bass voice as before:

And on his soul may God ha' merc-y!

All this time the third stranger had been standing in the doorway. Finding now that he did not come forward or go on speaking, the guests particularly regarded him. They noticed to their surprise that he stood before them the picture of abject terror—his knees trembling, his hand shaking so violently that the door latch by which he supported himself rattled audibly: his white lips were parted, and his eyes fixed on the merry officer of justice in the middle of the room. A moment more and he had turned, closed the door, and fled.

"What a man can it be?" said the shepherd.

The rest, between the awfulness of their late discovery and the odd conduct of this third visitor, looked as if they knew not what to think, and said nothing. Instinctively they withdrew further and further from the grim gentleman in their midst, whom some of them seemed to take for the Prince of Darkness himself, till they formed a remote circle, an empty space of floor being left between them and him—". . . *circulus, cujus centrum diabolus.*"[9] The room was so silent—though there were more than twenty people in it—that nothing could be heard but the patter of the rain against the window shutters, accompanied by the occasional hiss of a stray drop that fell down the chimney into the fire, and the steady puffing of the man in the corner, who had now resumed his pipe of long clay.

The stillness was unexpectedly broken. The distant sound of a gun reverberated through the air—apparently from the direction of the county town.

"Be jiggered!" cried the stranger who had sung the song, jumping up.

"What does that mean?" asked several.

"A prisoner escaped from the jail—that's what it means."

All listened. The sound was repeated, and none of them spoke but the man in the chimney corner, who said quietly, "I've often been told that in this county they fire a gun at such times; but I never heard it till now."

"I wonder if it is *my* man?" murmured the personage in cinder gray.

9. *circulus . . . diabolus,* a circle in the center of which was the devil (Latin).

"Surely it is!" said the shepherd involuntarily. "And surely we've zeed him! That little man who looked in at the door by now, and quivered like a leaf when he zeed ye and heard your song!"

"His teeth chattered, and the breath went out of his body," said the dairyman.

"And his heart seemed to sink within him like a stone," said Oliver Giles.

"And he bolted as if he'd been shot at," said the hedge carpenter.

"True—his teeth chattered, and his heart seemed to sink; and he bolted as if he'd been shot at," slowly summed up the man in the chimney corner.

"I didn't notice it," remarked the hangman.

"We were all a-wondering what made him run off in such a fright," faltered one of the women against the wall, "and now 'tis explained!"

The firing of the alarm gun went on at intervals, low and sullenly, and their suspicions became a certainty. The sinister gentleman in cinder gray roused himself. "Is there a constable here?" he asked, in thick tones. "If so, let him step forward."

The engaged man of fifty stepped quavering out from the wall, his betrothed beginning to sob on the back of the chair.

"You are a sworn constable?"

"I be, sir."

"Then pursue the criminal at once, with assistance, and bring him back here. He can't have gone far."

"I will, sir, I will—when I've got my staff. I'll go home and get it, and come sharp here, and start in a body."

"Staff! Never mind your staff; the man'll be gone!"

"But I can't do nothing without my staff—can I, William, and John, and Charles Jake? No; for there's the king's royal crown a painted on en in yaller and gold, and the lion and the unicorn, so as when I raise en up and hit my prisoner, 'tis made a lawful blow thereby. I wouldn't 'tempt to take up a man without my staff—no, not I. If I hadn't the law to gie me courage, why, instead o' my taking up him he might take up me!"

"Now, I'm a king's man myself, and can give you authority enough for this," said the formidable officer in gray. "Now then, all of ye, be ready. Have ye any lanterns?"

"Yes—have ye any lanterns? I demand it!" said the constable.

"And the rest of you able-bodied——"

"Able-bodied men—yes—the rest of ye!" said the constable.

"Have you some good stout staves and pitchforks——"

"Staves and pitchforks—in the name o' the law! And take 'em in yer hands and go in quest, and do as we in authority tell ye!"

Thus aroused, the men prepared to give chase. The evidence was, indeed, though circumstantial, so convincing, that but little argument was needed to show the shepherd's guests that after what they had seen it would look very much like connivance if they did not instantly pursue the unhappy third stranger, who could not as yet have gone more than a few hundred yards over such uneven country.

A shepherd is always well provided with lanterns; and, lighting these hastily, and with hurdle-staves in their hands, they poured out of the door, taking a direction along the crest of the hill, away from town, the rain having fortunately a little abated.

Disturbed by the noise, or possibly by unpleasant dreams of her baptism, the child who had been christened began to cry heartbrokenly in the room overhead. These notes of grief came down through the chinks of the floor to the ears of the women below, who jumped up one by one, and seemed glad of the excuse to ascend and comfort the baby, for the incidents of the last half-hour greatly oppressed them. Thus in the space of two or three minutes the room on the ground floor was deserted quite.

But it was not for long. Hardly had the sound of footsteps died away when a man returned round the corner of the house from the direction the pursuers had taken. Peeping in at the door, and seeing nobody there, he entered leisurely. It was the stranger of the chimney corner, who had gone out with the rest. The motive of his return was shown by his helping himself to a cut piece of skimmer cake that lay on a ledge beside where he had sat, and which he had apparently forgotten to take with him. He also poured out half a cup more mead from the quantity that remained, ravenously eating and drinking these as he stood. He had not finished when another figure came in just as quietly—his friend in cinder gray.

"O—you here?" said the latter, smiling. "I thought you had gone to help in the capture." And this speaker also revealed the object of his return by looking solicitously round for the fascinating mug of old mead.

"And I thought you had gone," said the other, continuing his skimmer cake with some effort.

"Well, on second thoughts, I felt there were enough without me," said the first confidentially, "and such a night as it is, too. Besides, 'tis the business o' the Government to take care of its criminals—not mine."

"True; so it is. And I felt as you did, that there were enough without me."

"I don't want to break my limbs running over the humps and hollows of this wild country."

"Nor I neither, between you and me."

"These shepherd people are used to it—simple-minded souls, you know, stirred up to anything in a moment. They'll have him ready for me before the morning, and no trouble to me at all."

"They'll have him, and we shall have saved ourselves all labor in the matter."

"True, true. Well, my way is to Casterbridge; and 'tis as much as my legs will do to take me that far. Going the same way?"

"No, I am sorry to say! I have to get home over there" (he nodded indefinitely to the right), "and I feel as you do, that it is quite enough for my legs to do before bedtime."

The other had by this time finished the mead in the mug, after which, shaking hands heartily at the door, and wishing each other well, they went their several ways.

In the meantime the company of pursuers had reached the end of the hog's-back elevation which dominated this part of the down. They had decided on no particular plan of action; and, finding that the man of the baleful trade was no longer in their company, they seemed quite unable to form any such plan now. They descended in all directions down the hill, and straightway several of the party fell into the snare set by nature for all misguided midnight ramblers over this part of the cretaceous formation. The "lanchets," or flint slopes, which belted the escarpment at intervals of a dozen yards, took the less cautious ones unawares, and losing their footing on the rubbly steep they slid sharply downwards, the lanterns rolling from their hands to the bottom, and there lying on their sides till the horn was scorched through.

When they had again gathered themselves together the shepherd, as the man who knew the country best, took the lead, and guided them round these treacherous inclines. The lanterns, which seemed rather to dazzle their eyes and warn the fugitive than to assist them in the exploration, were extinguished, due silence was observed; and in this more rational order they plunged into the vale. It was a grassy, briery, moist defile, affording some shelter to any person who had sought it; but the party perambulated it in vain, and ascended on the other side. Here they wandered apart, and after an interval closed together again to report progress. At the second time of closing in they found themselves near a lonely ash, the single tree on this part of the coomb, probably sown there by a passing bird some fifty years before. And here, standing a little to one side of the trunk, as motionless as the trunk itself, appeared the man they were in quest of, his outline being well defined against the sky beyond. The band noiselessly drew up and faced him.

"Your money or your life!" said the constable sternly to the still figure.

"No, no," whispered John Pitcher. "'Tisn't our side ought to say that. That's the doctrine of vagabonds like him, and we be on the side of the law."

"Well, well," replied the constable impatiently; "I must say something, mustn't I? And if you had all the weight o' this undertaking upon your mind, perhaps you'd say the wrong thing too! Prisoner at the bar, surrender, in the name of the Father—the Crown, I mane!"

The man under the tree seemed now to notice them for the first time, and, giving them no opportunity whatever for exhibiting their courage, he strolled slowly towards them. He was, indeed, the little man, the third stranger; but his trepidation had in a great measure gone.

"Well, travelers," he said, "did I hear ye speak to me?"

"You did: you've got to come and be our prisoner at once!" said the constable. "We arrest 'ee on the charge of not biding in Casterbridge jail in a decent proper manner to be hung tomorrow morning. Neighbors, do your duty, and seize the culpet!"

On hearing the charge the man seemed enlightened, and, saying not another word, resigned himself with preternatural civility to the search party, who, with their staves in their hands, surrounded him on all sides, and marched him back towards the shepherd's cottage.

It was eleven o'clock by the time they arrived.

The light shining from the open door, a sound of men's voices within, proclaimed to them as they approached the house that some new events had arisen in their absence. On entering they discovered the shepherd's living room to be invaded by two officers from Casterbridge jail, and a well-known magistrate who lived at the nearest country seat, intelligence of the escape having become generally circulated.

"Gentlemen," said the constable, "I have brought back your man—not without risk and danger; but every one must do his duty! He is inside this circle of able-bodied persons, who have lent me useful aid, considering their ignorance of Crown work. Men, bring forward your prisoner!" And the third stranger was led to the light.

"Who is this?" said one of the officials.

"The man," said the constable.

"Certainly not," said the turnkey; and the first corroborated his statement.

"But how can it be otherwise?" asked the constable. "Or why was he so terrified at sight o' the singing instrument of the law who sat there?" Here he related the strange behavior of the third stranger on entering the house during the hangman's song.

"Can't understand it," said the officer coolly. "All I know is that it is not the condemned man. He's quite a different character from this one; a gauntish fellow with dark hair and eyes, rather good-looking, and with a musical bass voice that if you heard once you'd never mistake as long as you lived."

"Why, souls—'twas the man in the chimney corner!"

"Hey—what?" said the magistrate, coming forward after inquiring particulars from the shepherd in the background. "Haven't you got the man after all?"

"Well, sir," said the constable, "he's the man we were in search of, that's true; and yet he's not the man we were in search of. For the man we were in search of was not the man we wanted, sir, if you understand my everyday way; for 'twas the man in the chimney corner!"

"A pretty kettle of fish altogether!" said the magistrate. "You had better start for the other man at once."

The prisoner now spoke for the first time. The mention of the man in the chimney corner seemed to have moved him as nothing else could do. "Sir," he said, stepping forward to the magistrate, "take no more trouble about me. The time is come when I may as well speak. I have done nothing; my crime is that the condemned man is my brother. Early this afternoon I left home at Shottsford to tramp it all the way to Casterbridge jail to bid him farewell. I was benighted, and called here to rest and ask the way. When I opened the door I saw before me the very man, my brother, that I thought to see in the condemned cell at Casterbridge. He was in this chimney corner; and jammed close to him, so that he could not have got out if he had tried, was the executioner who'd come to take his life, singing a song about it and not knowing that it was his victim who was close by, joining in to save appearances. My brother threw a glance of agony at me, and I knew he meant, 'Don't reveal what you see; my life depends on it.' I was so terror-struck that I could hardly stand, and, not knowing what I did, I turned and hurried away."

The narrator's manner and tone had the stamp of truth, and his story made a great impression on all around. "And do you know where your brother is at the present time?" asked the magistrate.

"I do not. I have never seen him since I closed this door."

"I can testify to that, for we've been between ye ever since," said the constable.

"Where does he think to fly to? What is his occupation?"

"He's a watch-and-clock-maker, sir."

"'A said 'a was a wheelwright—a wicked rogue," said the constable.

"The wheels of clocks and watches he meant, no doubt," said Shepherd Fennel. "I thought his hands were palish for 's trade."

"Well, it appears to me that nothing can be gained by retaining this poor man in custody," said the magistrate; "your business lies with the other, unquestionably."

And so the little man was released offhand; but he looked nothing the less sad on that account, it being beyond the power of magistrate or constable to raze out the written troubles in his brain, for they concerned another whom he regarded with more solicitude than himself. When this was done, and the man had gone his way, the night was found to be so far advanced that it was deemed useless to renew the search before the next morning.

Next day, accordingly, the quest for the clever

sheep stealer became general and keen, to all appearance at least. But the intended punishment was cruelly disproportioned to the transgression, and the sympathy of a great many country folk in that district was strongly on the side of the fugitive. Moreover, his marvelous coolness and daring in hob-and-nobbing with the hangman, under the unprecedented circumstances of the shepherd's party, won their admiration. So that it may be questioned if all those who ostensibly made themselves so busy in exploring woods and fields and lanes were quite so thorough when it came to the private examination of their own lofts and outhouses. Stories were afloat of a mysterious figure being occasionally seen in some old overgrown trackway or other, remote from turnpike roads; but when a search was instituted in any of these suspected quarters nobody was found. Thus the days and weeks passed without tidings.

In brief, the bass-voiced man of the chimney corner was never recaptured. Some said that he went across the sea, others that he did not, but buried himself in the depths of a populous city. At any rate, the gentleman in cinder gray never did his morning's work at Casterbridge, nor met anywhere at all, for business purposes, the genial comrade with whom he had passed an hour of relaxation in the lonely house on the slope of the coomb.

The grass has long been green on the graves of Shepherd Fennel and his frugal wife, the guests who made up the christening party have mainly followed their entertainers to the tomb; the baby in whose honor they all had met is a matron in the sere and yellow leaf. But the arrival of the three strangers at the shepherd's that night, and the details connected therewith, is a story as well known as ever in the country about Higher Crowstairs. □

DISCUSSION

1. Does any one person stand out clearly as the protagonist in this story? Explain.

2. Could the three strangers have arrived at Shepherd Fennel's in any different order?

3. Discuss the importance of the setting, especially the stormy night and the occasion (a christening party).

4. Characterize one of the following:

(a) Timothy Summers
(b) The hangman
(c) Timothy's brother
(d) Shepherd Fennel
(e) Shepherdess Fennel

5. Discuss some of the humorous touches in this story. Are they fitting, or do they interfere with the suspense?

6. (a) Comment on the severity of the sentence meted out to Timothy Summers. Does he have anything of the criminal about him?

(b) How do the local people feel about his sentence?

7. One reader has criticized this story for overuse of coincidence; another has praised it for its supreme irony. With which do you agree?

WRITING

1. One school of criticism feels that the real protagonist in Hardy's works is Egdon Heath—the countryside he describes in his fiction. Some critics have expanded this idea even further to say that in the pages of his works he has preserved a bygone way of life for future generations. Read one of his novels (perhaps *The Mayor of Casterbridge* or *Tess of the D'Urbervilles*), and write an essay commenting on these suggestions.

2. In a brief essay discuss the importance of the ending of "Horatio Sparkins" to the point that Dickens is attempting to make. Or, as an alternative, write your own ending to the story.

3. The short stories in this unit describe life in two different areas of Victorian England: "The Three Strangers" that of Hardy's Egdon Heath or Wessex, and "Horatio Sparkins" that of the environs of London. Write an essay in which you do either of the following:

(a) Compare the two settings and their effect on the life of the characters.

(b) Explain which area you would prefer to live in, using the stories as the basis for your decision.

INDUSTRIOUS FLEAS?
ASTLEY'S
THE BATTLE
ENGLISH OPERAHOUSE
TRIUMPHANT SUCCESS of NATIVE TALE
NOURJAHAD!
MOUNTAIN SYLPH
HERMANN!
KING ARTHUR EVERY EVENING THIS WEEK
EXTRAORDINARY HIT.
THE LAST DAYS OF
POMPEII!
MADAME
VESTRIS
having recovered from her severe indisposition will appear
THIS EVENING!
THE POWERFUL AND MAGNIFICENT STEAM SHIP
FAVORITE
OSTEND.
CARRYING HIS MAJESTY'S MAILS.
SPREAD EAGLE
PARIS
LANE.
SPECTACLE
RTHUR
ST. JAMES'S THEATRE
BRAHAM
M. HARLEY!!
OBERON
ENCHANTED HORN!
TOM THUMB
Feast of Apollo
STOP
JOHN PARRY
THE SHAM PRINCE
ST. JAMES'S THEATRE
OTELLO
ADELPHI.
ROBERT MACAIRE
TOM&JERRY
THE CHRISTENING!!!
!!!!!!
EVERY EVENING
GUSTAVUS the THIRD!
MASK'D BALL.
ON MONDAY
POSTILLION
WATERMAN
FRA DIAVOLO
TWO LECTURES
will be delivered in
BULL MOUTH!!!
16 WELSH GOATS.
10 COWS, 13 HOGS,
SALE.
TO BE SOLD
A FEMALE DONKEY.
FARM
10 HORSES!
COWS.
LOUNG
HIGH
SHADOW WALL
READ !!!
FOR ONE
ROYAL
FOR SALE
JIM CROW
COME VERY EARLY

BACKGROUND

The Victorian Age

THE familiar stereotype of the Victorians as smug, prudish, and inflexibly formal is largely false. Far from exhibiting a single style, the time spanned by the reign of Queen Victoria (1837–1901) was one of the most varied and diverse periods in the history of English life and letters. More than any period which preceded, it was a time in which great issues—social, moral, scientific, and religious—were earnestly, often heatedly, debated. The fact that it was a time characterized by energetic change and a belief in progress made settlement of these issues urgent.

By the beginning of Victoria's reign, a rigid code of conduct had indeed come into vogue. Those who wished to be thought respectable (appearances were very important) observed the Sabbath with strict prohibitions against amusements, and spent the rest of the week in quiet and pious domesticity. Women were expected to be frail and sheltered creatures, silent, obedient, and decorative, mothers of children equally silent and obedient. The model male could and often did rule his household with an iron will; but gambling, swearing, intemperance, and sometimes even smoking were enough to remove him from the ranks of the respectable.

Yet respectability did not for long remain a static code. The feminist movement, already under way in the 1790's, had by the last part of the nineteenth century created a revolution in women's dress and deportment. Between 1870 and 1880 campaigners for women's rights formed societies in most large English towns and flooded Parliament with petitions containing nearly three million signatures, requesting that the right to vote be extended to women. Because of Queen Victoria's unexplained hostility toward the idea, and the widely held view that women were incapable of casting an intelligent vote, such motions were defeated. But by 1882, with the passage of the Married Women's Property Act, which gave married women the right to own property and to keep what they earned, large gains for women's rights had been won. Also, novelists like the Brontë sisters and Mary Ann Evans (George Eliot) presented love and marriage honestly from the woman's point of view, and probably persuaded many young women that the choice of a husband was theirs by right, even though marriages still were often arranged by ambitious parents.

By 1851, when Victoria opened the first world's fair at the gigantic Crystal Palace in London, the Industrial Revolution had come of age. Ushered in by improved textile manufacturing equipment in the late eighteenth century, the Industrial Revolution had quickly gathered momentum and by the mid-1800's had begun to work profound changes on the face of the land and the personalities of English people. By the late 1800's the quiet mood of much of rural England had given way to the frenetic pace of factory towns, and a new social phenomenon had arisen: the industrial working class. Probably the most pressing and apparently insoluble problem which confronted concerned Victorians was the condition of the workers, who frequently labored inhumanly long hours, for low wages, in filthy, dangerous factories, who lived in inadequate housing, and were subject to recurrent unemployment. Among the most horrifying of the abuses were the brutalities of child labor.

Responses to the problems of the Industrial Revolution were varied. Those who owned mines and factories supported a policy of *laissez-faire*, or no government regulation; those who sympathized with the workers, notably the Socialists, recommended not only government regulation but government ownership. The debate fluctuated between extremes but produced at least moderate results. Of the vast number of reform bills passed by Victorian parliaments, the two most significant were those of 1867 and 1884–1885, the first extending the franchise to urban workers, the second enfranchising workers in agricultural districts. (However, the franchise did not extend to women, who had to wait until 1928 to gain equal voting rights.) By 1911 the House of Lords had been deprived of all power except a delaying veto, and England was on its way to becoming a modern democracy in which the people, through their representatives in the House of Commons, were politically sovereign.

More sudden and dramatic were the changes in attitude wrought by the publication, in 1859, of Charles Darwin's *Origin of Species*, a book which proposed a theory of evolution that was to have far-reaching impact. When the book appeared, most people still accepted the Biblical account of creation as literal truth. To them Darwin's proposal gave a particular shock, for he theorized that the species now on earth had evolved over a period of hundreds of thousands of years through a harsh struggle for existence which only the hardiest survived. Many eventually came to see that there was no necessary conflict between the new biology and the interpretations of religion, but initially Darwin's theories cast many into doubt, even despair, about their traditional faith. Whether accepted or rejected, Darwin's ideas worked on the imagination of the age. Industrial owners and managers were not dismayed to hear that the key to evolutionary development was the "survival of the fittest," for they were able to interpret this as reason enough why some should be at the top of the heap and others on the bottom. Imperialists leaned on Darwin to explain why the British should dominate an empire five times the size of England itself. For others, particularly Marxians, Darwin's theories lent support to political views which emphasized the inevitability of class struggle. But the depersonalized view of life suggested by both Darwinian theory and the realities of industrialization tinged the essentially optimistic Victorian belief in progress with a pervasive unease.

Victorian literature reflects the mixture of opposites so characteristic of the age: hope and despair, faith and doubt, radical social theory and conservative social practice, the espousal of Christian love and gentleness combined with the ruthless use of power.

Queen Victoria herself was the calm and stable center in these times of change. Quiet, prudent, conservative in speech and behavior, she exemplified the domestic virtues of this thoroughly middle-class age. She bore her husband Prince Albert nine children, and preferred to leave most of the business of governing to her able ministers Gladstone and Disraeli. By the time she died after more than six decades as queen, England had entered a more complex and turbulent century, but it was still innocent of the horrors of global war and the dehumanization of a fully mechanized society. □

FEMININE FASHION. BY COURTESY OF THE VICTORIA AND ALBERT MUSEUM, LONDON, CROWN COPYRIGHT.

FEMINIST FASHION. RADIO TIMES HULTON PICTURE LIBRARY.

BIOGRAPHIES

Matthew Arnold 1822 / 1888

Matthew Arnold was not only a poet, but an educator, a classical scholar, and one of the most brilliant literary and social critics of the Victorian age. His interest in education came naturally, for his father, Thomas Arnold, was the renowned headmaster of Rugby School who in the first half of the 19th century did much to revolutionize secondary-school education in England.

Shortly after leaving Oxford, Arnold became a government inspector of schools, a post he held until two years before his death. He also made an extensive study of school systems in Europe for the government and wrote several books on continental education. In 1857 he was appointed to the Professorship of Poetry at Oxford (a part-time post) and lectured there for ten years.

Arnold was sharply critical of the materialism and narrow-mindedness of the Victorian middle classes (whom he called Philistines), and preached the gospel of culture as a corrective. He defined culture as a compound of "sweetness and light" consisting of a knowledge of "the best that has been thought and said in the world." He maintained that no work of art could be great that did not possess both artistic merit and moral power.

Emily Brontë 1818 / 1848

Novelist and poet Emily Brontë was the middle of the three famous Brontë sisters (the others were Charlotte and Anne, both novelists). Except for brief and unhappy periods in boarding schools, she was educated at home and spent her entire life in her father's parsonage.

The Brontë children, much on their own, created an imaginary country which they called "Gondal" and composed poems and legends about it. In 1845, Charlotte discovered Emily's carefully guarded poems (some of them "Gondal" poems) and published them with her own and Anne's as *Poems by Currer, Ellis, and Acton Bell.* Not until the publication and enormous success of Charlotte's novel *Jane Eyre* and Emily's *Wuthering Heights* (both in 1847) did the poems attract any attention. Emily died of tuberculosis the following year.

Elizabeth Barrett Browning 1806 / 1861

Up to her 41st year, Elizabeth Barrett was a semi-invalid, confined to her gloomy home by an overly possessive and tyrannical father. Her secluded life gave her time to study and write, and by the time she met her future husband, Robert Browning, she had become famous enough as a poet to be considered a rival to Tennyson.

Browning admired her poetry, and corresponded with her for several months before they met. When they did, they both fell deeply in love. A little over a year later they were secretly married and Browning swept her off to Italy.

In poems like "The Cry of the Children" she showed her deep social sympathy; her scholarship was displayed in translations of Aeschylus. Her long blank-verse romance *Aurora Leigh* was immensely popular with Victorian readers. But her works that are best known today are the *Sonnets from the Portuguese,* a set of love-poems addressed to her husband.

Robert Browning 1812 / 1889

During the years of his marriage, Robert Browning was sometimes referred to as "Mrs. Browning's husband," for his wife was more famous than he. Only in middle age did he win wide acclaim. To many of his contemporaries his poetry seemed crude, for he was one of the first to use the diction of ordinary speech. His work was condemned as difficult and obscure, probably because he assumed that the reading public shared his enormous erudition, acquired from private tutoring and intensive reading in his father's excellent library. Yet these qualities, along with the psychological insights he displayed, particularly in his dramatic monologues, are what make him seem almost modern to readers today.

Browning was the son of a well-to-do banker, and at the age of 22 made the "grand tour" of Europe, spending much time in Russia and Italy. His first important work, the dramatic poem *Paracelsus* (1835) is based on the life of a 15th-century magician and alchemist; in it he showed both the interest in the Renaissance and in men and their motives that became dominant strains in his work. Other volumes followed, but gained little attention.

His romantic love affair with the poet Elizabeth Barrett has been celebrated in story and drama. After their marriage in 1846, the Brownings moved to Italy, where they spent 15 years of idyllic happiness. After his wife's death in 1861, Browning returned to England with their son. He continued to publish major works of poetry, and his reputation steadily rose. His greatest single work, the novel-length *The Ring and the Book,* appeared in 1868. He spent the last years of his life in Venice, and died there. He is buried in the Poets' Corner at Westminster Abbey, not far from the tomb of Tennyson.

Arthur Hugh Clough 1819 / 1861

Clough was troubled all his life by the religious doubts which agitated so many thoughtful people of the time, and in 1848 he resigned his post as a fellow and tutor at Oriel College, Oxford, where he was expected to subscribe to the doctrines of the Church of England. The next few restless years were spent in Italy, in London, and in the United States in various educational posts. Later he worked in the Education Office in London, until ill health drove him to travel. He died in Italy of malarial fever.

Charles Dickens 1812 / 1870

When Charles Dickens was 12, his father was imprisoned for debt. Forced to live by himself, the boy found employment in a factory where, for a few shillings a week, he labeled blacking bottles. A sensitive child, he was deeply affected by the time he spent in the London underworld, and later modeled many of the descriptions, characters, and events in his novels on his childhood observations. This traumatic period ended when his father received a legacy which permitted him to pay his debts and go free. Charles was sent to school for three years and, at the age of 15, became a solicitor's clerk. He taught himself shorthand and became a newspaper reporter in the House of Commons.

His first sketches, which he signed "Boz," appeared in popular periodicals and then in book form in 1836. These were immediately followed by the *Pickwick Papers,* published in twenty monthly installments beginning in April 1836, and an immediate success. For the next 34 years Dickens wrote an uninterrupted stream of novels, most of which originally appeared in serial form. Among them were *Oliver Twist, Nicholas Nickleby, A Christmas Carol, David Copperfield, Bleak House, A Tale of Two Cities,* and *Great Expectations.*

In 1842, Dickens traveled to America, where his disgust with the institution of slavery and his advocation of international copyright laws aroused much resentment. (His own books were widely pirated.) After a short stint at acting —a profession which had always fascinated him—he founded and edited a succession of popular periodicals.

Although in increasingly poor health, he began giving public readings in 1858, making a second visit to America in 1867–68. After his return to England, he began a novel, *Edwin Drood,* but died suddenly before it was completed. He was buried in Westminster Abbey.

Edward Fitzgerald 1809 / 1883

Fitzgerald is known today only for his "translation" of the Persian poem *The Rubáiyát,* but he made similar free translations of the plays of the 17th-century Spanish dramatist Calderon, and paraphrases of plays by Aeschylus and Sophocles which were remarkably successful in transferring the spirit of the originals into English.

After graduating from Trinity College, Cambridge, he settled down on his country estate in Suffolk where he studied Greek, Spanish, and Persian and lived the life of a country gentleman. After the publication of *The Rubáiyát,* he bought a yacht and spent much of the rest of his life cruising on the North Sea.

Thomas Hardy 1840 / 1928

Thomas Hardy was born in Dorsetshire, the county in southwest England which he used as the "Wessex" setting for his novels. At the age of 16 he was apprenticed to a church architect. While pursuing his architectural career in London, he wrote poetry in his spare time. After unsuccessfully trying to get his poetry published, he turned to writing fiction. Although his first novel was rejected by publishers, his second, *Desperate Remedies* (1871), was well received, and he gave up his architectural practice to devote himself to writing.

The best of his prose works are those he classified as "novels of environment and character": *Under the Greenwood Tree* (1872), *Far from the Madding Crowd* (1874), *The Return of the Native* (1878), *The Mayor of Casterbridge* (1886), *The Woodlanders* (1887), *Tess of the D'Urbervilles* (1891), and *Jude the Obscure* (1896). Hardy's realistic representation of people and his fatalistic, pessimistic view of life offended many of his contemporaries. When his last novel was denounced and referred to as *Jude the Obscene,* he turned from the writing of prose to his first love, poetry.

His most ambitious poetic work was *The Dynasts,* an epic-drama about the Napoleonic wars and their impact on England, published in three parts 1904–1908. He wrote and published a great deal of fine poetry until the end of his life.

When he died at the age of 88, his heart was buried in his native Dorset in accordance with his wishes, but his ashes were placed in Westminster Abbey.

Gerard Manley Hopkins 1844 / 1889

Gerard Manley Hopkins entered Oxford in 1863 with the intention of becoming a minister in the Anglican Church, but instead he was converted to Roman Catholicism and was ordained as a Jesuit priest in 1877. After serving in several parishes, including one in the working-class slums of Liverpool where he was distressed by the poverty and squalor, he was appointed Professor of Classics at University College, Dublin.

Hopkins was a sensitive and innovative poet who sometimes had difficulty reconciling his religious vocation with his poetic art. After his conversion, he burned all his early poems (though working copies survive) and did not write poetry again until 1875, when he composed his long poem "The Wreck of the Deutschland," a memorial to five German nuns who had drowned in the disaster.

When he died, Hopkins left his manuscripts to his friend and fellow poet Robert Bridges. Convinced that Hopkins' poetry would be ignored if introduced too early, Bridges held up its publication for 29 years. When Hopkins' collected *Poems* appeared in 1918, they caused a sensation, and the poet was hailed as a brilliant innovator whose spirit was closer to that of the 20th century than to his own age.

A(lfred) E(dward) Housman 1859 / 1936

Housman's best-known work, *A Shropshire Lad,* was written mostly in a burst of creativity in 1895 and published the next year. His next small collection of poems appeared in 1922, and a few additional poems were published after his death.

Housman began writing poetry while a student at Oxford, and it has been suggested that his failure to pass his final examinations in classical studies—though he had been an excellent scholar—was due to his greater devotion to poetry.

For the next ten years he worked in the Royal Patent Office and pursued his classical studies alone. He gradually built up a reputation as a scholar on the strength of contributions to learned journals. In 1892 he became a professor of Latin at University College, London, and in 1911 became a professor at Cambridge. His most important scholarly work was a translation of the minor Latin poet Manilius.

Christina Georgina Rossetti 1830 / 1894

Christina Rossetti was the daughter of an Italian political exile and sister to the poet and painter Dante Gabriel Rossetti. She was content to live within the circle of her family and their friends, many of them artists and writers. She was a devout Anglican, and in her later years spent much of her time in religious devotions. Although she shunned publicity, she became well known for her poetry after the publication of *Goblin Market* (1862) and succeeding books of verse. She also wrote short stories and devotional books.

Robert Louis Stevenson 1850 / 1894

Although he was in poor health all his life, Scottish novelist, poet, and essayist Robert Louis Stevenson had a great love for the sea and for travel. He studied law and passed his bar exams, but found writing more to his taste. He first attracted attention with accounts of his travels: *An Inland Voyage* and *Travels with a Donkey.* While on the continent, he met an American woman whom he married in California in 1880. For the next seven years, his health rapidly declined, and he moved about the British Isles and the continent, seeking a healthful climate. His literary reputation was established at this time with the publication of *Treasure Island, A Child's Garden of Verses, The Strange Case of Dr. Jekyll and Mr. Hyde,* and *Kidnapped.*

After a brief stay at Saranac Lake in the Adirondacks, the Stevensons set sail for the South Seas, settling in 1890 in Samoa. He found both the climate and the character of the Samoans to his liking; he was called "Tusitala" (teller of tales) by the people. He died suddenly in 1894, not from his lung ailment, but from a cerebral hemorrhage.

Algernon Charles Swinburne 1837 / 1909

Algernon Charles Swinburne shocked Victorian England with his unconventional religious ideas (he was an atheist), his political views (he was a liberal republican dedicated to the overthrow of governments), and his frankly sensual poetry. He came from a distinguished family and attended Eton and Oxford. He already had some reputation as a poet when he came to the university, and continued to write while there, but indiscretions in conduct forced him to withdraw. He then traveled on the continent and was attracted to bohemian circles in Paris and London. His play *Atalanta in Calydon* (1865) won critical acclaim; his volume *Poems and Ballads* (1866) created a furor throughout England for its frank sensuousness and paganism. Older Victorians almost universally condemned him (Carlyle called his poetry "the miaulings of a delirious cat"), but he was almost a god to the young rebels of his day. In the years that followed, his increasingly dissipated life took its toll on his frail physique, and in 1879, when he was on the point of dying of delirium tremens, he put himself into the care of his friend Theodore Watts-Dunton, who kept him sober, subdued, and writing for the next thirty years.

Alfred, Lord Tennyson 1809 / 1892

Alfred Tennyson was the fourth of the twelve children of a village rector. His father, a talented but moody man, brought up his family in an atmosphere of high thinking and lofty aspirations. Even before Alfred entered Trinity College, Cambridge, in 1828, he had published a book of verse with his brothers. In 1829 he won the Cambridge Poetry Prize for his poem "Timbuctoo," and in the next few years published several collections of poems. His works won enough public favor to encourage him in pursuing a career in poetry.

At Cambridge, Tennyson had formed a close friendship with Arthur Hallam, who later became engaged to Alfred's sister Emily. In 1833, Hallam died unexpectedly in Vienna —a shattering blow to Tennyson. Under the influence of this loss, he began work on his long poem *In Memoriam,* in which he explored some of the questions that were troubling many thinkers of the age, in particular the conflict between orthodox religious faith and the doubts which followed on new scientific theories such as Darwin's theories of evolution. *In Memoriam* was not completed until 1850; in the meantime, Tennyson also worked on other poems, including his second major work, *The Idylls of the King,* a series of twelve narrative poems which retell the Arthurian tales collected centuries earlier by Thomas Malory.

The publication of *In Memoriam* brought Tennyson fame, and in the same year he was appointed poet laureate to succeed Wordsworth. His popularity was firmly established as he continued to publish major poetic works. He was raised to the peerage in 1884.

Tennyson's work was out of favor for a time, but today he is considered the greatest poet of the Victorian age, who dealt, in poetry of great technical variety and complexity, with the basic moral questions of his and every age: Who am I? What can I believe?

Oscar Wilde 1854 / 1900

Irish dramatist, novelist, and poet Oscar Wilde was as famous—or notorious—as a personality and a wit as he was as a writer. His brilliant conversation, eccentric dress (he often wore a velvet jacket and knee breeches) and his activities as leader of the "Aesthetic" movement ("Art for Art's sake") earned him much attention. His first dramatic success was *Lady Windemere's Fan* (1892); he appeared onstage after the opening performance to congratulate the audience on the intelligence of their appreciation. In the next three years, *A Woman of No Importance, Salome* (which was refused a license in England), and *The Importance of Being Earnest* were produced. His novel *The Picture of Dorian Gray* appeared in 1891.

In 1895 Wilde imprudently filed a libel suit against the Marquess of Queensberry, who had objected to Wilde's liaison with his son, Lord Alfred Douglas. Wilde lost the case and was himself condemned to prison. Upon his release he went to France, where he wrote *The Ballad of Reading Gaol.* He died two years later of cerebral meningitis.

Alice in Wonderland

by Lewis Carroll

chapter eight

IN the little more than a hundred years since *Alice in Wonderland* was first published it has received an amount of attention and critical acclaim far surpassing that accorded to any other "children's story." It has been translated into more than forty languages, and has brought delight to millions. Many of Alice's most devoted fans have, in fact, not been children at all. Bertrand Russell, the late British mathematician and philosopher, once suggested that the *Alice* stories were unfit for anyone under fifteen years of age.

What is behind Alice's almost universal appeal? That depends on who you are, what you are looking for, and what your "porpoise" is, as the Mock Turtle would say. The literary critics have linked Alice's experiences in Wonderland with the descent and return archetype, the picaresque novel, and the English pastoral tradition, among other things. Psychoanalysts have commented at length about Alice's "identity crises" and her maturing behavior and growing self-control as the story unfolds. Scientists have puzzled over the improbabilities of Alice's free fall down the rabbit hole; mathematicians have pondered the Einsteinian implications of the White Rabbit's unusual watch; historians and biographers have speculated on Wonderland's veiled references to the contemporary Victorian scene; and linguists have unearthed with evident glee Carroll's complicated word play and his sometimes outrageous puns.

There is something else about the Alice stories that every reader feels: beneath the gauzy surface of innocent fantasy—the Wonderland where animals argue and philosophize, where lobsters dance and turtles sing, where croquet balls are hedgehogs—there are other, more significant, levels, and the reader emerges from Alice's world with a peculiar feeling that perhaps events there are no more zany than events in the world of everyday reality. In the real world, as in Alice's, there are people whose unmodulated response to every unpleasant or complicated social situation is, like that of the Queen of Hearts, "Off with their heads!"

Perhaps the last word on *Alice in Wonderland* should go to its author. "The why of this book," Lewis Carroll wrote, "cannot, and need not, be put into words. Those for whom a child's mind is a sealed book, and who see no divinity in a child's smile, would read such words in vain; while for anyone who has ever loved one true child, no words are needed." Through the eyes of Alice, the world for all of us—eight to eighty—is still wild and full of marvels.

The following introductory verses refer to a boating trip taken by Lewis Carroll and his friend, the Reverend Robinson Duckworth, with the three Liddell sisters in 1862. They rowed up the Thames river from Oxford to a small village, had tea, and returned before evening. The gently mock-heroic poem refers to the Liddell sisters as the "cruel Three": Lorina Liddell, Prima, *was the eldest; Alice,* Secunda, *was younger; and Edith,* Tertia, *was youngest. Their demands for a story inspired* Alice in Wonderland.

All in the golden afternoon
  Full leisurely we glide;
For both our oars, with little skill,
  By little arms are plied.
While little hands make vain pretence
  Our wanderings to guide.

Ah, cruel Three! In such an hour,
  Beneath such dreamy weather,
To beg a tale of breath too weak
  To stir the tiniest feather!
Yet what can one poor voice avail
  Against three tongues together?

Imperious Prima flashes forth
  Her edict "to begin it"—
In gentler tone Secunda hopes
  "There will be nonsense in it!"—
While Tertia interrupts the tale
  Not *more* than once a minute.

Anon, to sudden silence won,
  In fancy they pursue
The dream-child moving through a land
  Of wonders wild and new,
In friendly chat with bird or beast—
  And half believe it true.

And ever, as the story drained
  The wells of fancy dry,
And faintly strove that weary one
  To put the subject by,
"The rest next time—" "It *is* next time!"
  The happy voices cry.

Thus grew the tale of Wonderland:
  Thus slowly, one by one,
Its quaint events were hammered out—
  And now the tale is done,
And home we steer, a merry crew,
  Beneath the setting sun.

Alice! a childish story take,
  And with a gentle hand
Lay it where Childhood's dreams are twined
  In Memory's mystic band,
Like pilgrim's wither'd wreath of flowers
  Plucked in a far-off land.

1 DOWN THE RABBIT-HOLE

ALICE was beginning to get very tired of sitting by her sister on the bank, and of having nothing to do: once or twice she had peeped into the book her sister was reading, but it had no pictures or conversations in it, "and what is the use of a book," thought Alice, "without pictures or conversations?"

So she was considering in her own mind, (as well as she could, for the hot day made her feel very sleepy and stupid), whether the pleasure of making a daisy-chain would be worth the trouble of getting up and picking the daisies, when suddenly a white rabbit with pink eyes ran close by her.

There was nothing so *very* remarkable in that; nor did Alice think it so *very* much out of the way to hear the Rabbit say to itself, "Oh dear! Oh dear! I shall be too late!" (when she thought it over afterwards, it occurred to her that she ought to have wondered at this, but at the time it all seemed quite natural); but when the Rabbit actually *took a watch out of its waistcoat-pocket,* and looked at it, and then hurried on, Alice started to her feet, for it flashed across her mind that she had never before seen a rabbit with either a waistcoat-pocket or a watch to take out of it, and, burning with curiosity, she ran across the field after it, and was just in time to see it pop down a large rabbit-hole under the hedge.

In another moment down went Alice after it, never once considering how in the world she was to get out again.

The rabbit-hole went straight on like a tunnel for

some way, and then dipped suddenly down, so suddenly that Alice had not a moment to think about stopping herself before she found herself falling down what seemed to be a very deep well.

Either the well was very deep, or she fell very slowly, for she had plenty of time as she went down to look about her, and to wonder what was going to happen next. First, she tried to look down and make out what she was coming to, but it was too dark to see anything: then she looked at the sides of the well, and noticed that they were filled with cupboards and bookshelves: here and there she saw maps and pictures hung upon pegs. She took down a jar from one of the shelves as she passed; it was labelled "ORANGE MARMALADE," but to her great disappointment it was empty: she did not like to drop the jar for fear of killing somebody underneath, so managed to put it into one of the cupboards as she fell past it.

"Well!" thought Alice to herself, "after such a fall as this, I shall think nothing of tumbling down stairs! How brave they'll all think me at home! Why, I wouldn't say anything about it, even if I fell off the top of the house!" (Which was very likely true.)

Down, down, down. Would the fall *never* come to an end? "I wonder how many miles I've fallen by this time?" she said aloud. "I must be getting somewhere near the centre of the earth. Let me see: that would be four thousand miles down, I think—" (for, you see, Alice had learnt several things of this sort in her lessons in the schoolroom, and though this was not a *very* good opportunity for showing off her knowledge, as there was no one to listen to her, still it was good practice to say it over) "—yes, that's about the right distance—but then I wonder what Latitude or Longitude I've got to?" (Alice had not the slightest idea what Latitude was, or Longitude either, but she thought they were nice grand words to say.)

Presently she began again. "I wonder if I shall fall right *through* the earth! How funny it'll seem to come out among the people that walk with their heads downwards! The Antipathies, I think—" (she was rather glad there *was* no one listening, this time, as it didn't sound at all the right word) "—but I shall have to ask them what the name of the country is, you know. Please, Ma'am, is this New Zealand or Australia?" (and she tried to curtsey as she spoke —fancy *curtseying* as you're falling through the air! Do you think you could manage it?) "And what an ignorant little girl she'll think me for asking! No, it'll never do to ask: perhaps I shall see it written up somewhere."

Down, down, down. There was nothing else to do, so Alice soon began talking again. "Dinah'll miss me very much to-night, I should think!" (Dinah was the cat.) "I hope they'll remember her saucer of milk at teatime. Dinah, my dear! I wish you were down here with me! There are no mice in the air, I'm afraid, but you might catch a bat, and that's very like a mouse, you know. But do cats eat bats, I wonder?" And here Alice began to get rather sleepy, and went on saying to herself, in a dreamy sort of way, "Do cats eat bats? Do cats eat bats?" and sometimes, "Do bats eat cats?" for, you see, as she couldn't answer either question, it didn't much matter which way she put it. She felt that she was dozing off, and had just begun to dream that she was walking hand in hand with Dinah, and was saying to her very earnestly, "Now, Dinah, tell me the truth: did you ever eat a bat?" when suddenly, thump! thump! down she came upon a heap of sticks and dry leaves, and the fall was over.

Alice was not a bit hurt, and she jumped up on to her feet in a moment: she looked up, but it was all dark overhead; before her was another long passage, and the White Rabbit was still in sight, hurrying down it. There was not a moment to be lost: away went Alice like the wind, and was just in time to hear it say, as it turned a corner, "Oh my ears and whiskers, how late it's getting!" She was close behind it when she turned the corner, but the Rabbit was no longer to be seen: she found herself in a long, low hall, which was lit up by a row of lamps hanging from the roof.

There were doors all around the hall, but they were all locked, and when Alice had been all the way down one side and up the other, trying every door, she walked sadly down the middle, wondering how she was ever to get out again.

Suddenly she came upon a little three-legged table, all made of solid glass; there was nothing on it but a tiny golden key, and Alice's first idea was that this might belong to one of the doors of the hall; but, alas! either the locks were too large, or the key was too small, but at any rate it would not open any of them. However, on the second time round, she came upon a low curtain she had not noticed before, and behind it was a little door about fifteen inches high: she tried the little golden key in the lock, and to her great delight it fitted!

Alice opened the door and found that it led into a small passage, not much larger than a rathole: she knelt down and looked along the passage into the loveliest garden you ever saw. How she longed to get out of that dark hall, and wander about among those beds of bright flowers and those cool fountains, but she could not even get her head through the doorway; "and even if my head would go through," thought poor Alice, "it would be of very little use without my shoulders. Oh, how I wish I could shut up like a telescope! I think I could, if I only knew how to begin." For, you see, so many out-of-the-way things had happened lately that Alice had begun to think that very few things indeed were really impossible.

There seemed to be no use in waiting by the little door, so she went back to the table, half hoping she might find another key on it, or at any rate a book of rules for shutting people up like telescopes: this time she found a little bottle on it, ("which certainly was not here before," said Alice,) and tied round the neck of the bottle was a paper label with the words "DRINK ME" beautifully printed on it in large letters.

It was all very well to say "Drink me," but the wise little Alice was not going to do *that* in a hurry: "no, I'll look first," she said, "and see whether it's marked *'poison'* or not": for she had read several nice little stories about children who had got burnt, and eaten up by wild beasts, and other unpleasant things, all because they *would* not remember the simple rules their friends had taught them, such as, that a red-hot poker will burn you if you hold it too long; and that if you cut your finger *very* deeply with a knife, it usually bleeds; and she had never forgotten that, if you drink much from a bottle marked "poison," it is almost certain to disagree with you, sooner or later.

However, this bottle was *not* marked "poison," so Alice ventured to taste it, and finding it very nice, (it had, in fact, a sort of mixed flavour of cherry-tart, custard, pineapple, roast turkey, toffy, and hot buttered toast), she very soon finished it off.

"What a curious feeling!" said Alice, "I must be shutting up like a telescope."

And so it was indeed: she was now only ten inches high, and her face brightened up at the thought that she was now the right size for going through the little door into that lovely garden. First, however, she waited for a few minutes to see if she was going to shrink any further: she felt a little nervous about this, "for it might end, you know," said Alice to herself, "in my going out altogether, like a candle. I wonder what I should be like then?" And she tried to fancy what the flame of a candle looks like after the candle is blown out, for she could not remember ever having seen such a thing.

After a while, finding that nothing more happened, she decided on going into the garden at once, but, alas for poor Alice! when she got to the door, she found she had forgotten the little golden key, and when she went back to the table for it, she found she could not possibly reach it: she could see it quite plainly through the glass, and she tried her best to climb up one of the legs of the table, but it was too slippery, and when she had tired herself out with trying, the poor little thing sat down and cried.

"Come, there's no use in crying like that!" said Alice to herself, rather sharply, "I advise you to leave off this minute!" She generally gave herself very good advice, (though she very seldom followed it), and sometimes she scolded herself so severely as to bring tears into her eyes, and once she remembered trying to box her own ears for having cheated herself in a game of croquet she was playing against herself, for this curious child was very fond of pretending to be two people. "But it's no use now," thought poor Alice, "to pretend to be two people! Why, there's hardly enough of me left to make *one* respectable person!"

Soon her eye fell on a little glass box that was lying under the table: she opened it, and found in it a very small cake, on which the words "EAT ME" were beautifully marked in currants. "Well, I'll eat it," said Alice, "and if it makes me grow larger, I can reach the key; and if it makes me grow smaller, I can creep under the door; so either way I'll get into the garden, and I don't care which happens!"

She ate a little bit, and said anxiously to herself "Which way? Which way?" holding her hand on the top of her head to feel which way it was growing, and she was quite surprised to find that she remained the same size: to be sure, this is what generally happens when one eats cake, but Alice had got so much into the way of expecting nothing but out-of-the-way things to happen, that it seemed quite dull and stupid for life to go on in the common way.

So she set to work, and very soon finished off the cake.

2

THE POOL OF TEARS

"CURIOUSER and curiouser!" cried Alice (she was so much surprised, that for the moment she quite forgot how to speak good English): "now I'm opening out like the largest telescope that ever was! Good-bye feet!" (for when she looked down at her feet, they seemed to be almost out of sight, they were getting so far off). "Oh, my poor little feet, I wonder who will put on your shoes and stockings for you now, dears? I'm sure *I* shan't be able! I shall be a great deal too far off to trouble myself about you: you must manage the best way you can;—but I must be kind to them," thought Alice, "or perhaps they won't walk the way I want to go! Let me see: I'll give them a new pair of boots every Christmas."

And she went on planning to herself how she would manage it. "They must go by the carrier," she thought; "and how funny it'll seem, sending presents to one's own feet! And how odd the directions will look!

> *"Alice's Right Foot Esq.,*
> *Hearthrug, near the Fender*[1]
> *(with Alice's love.)*

"Oh dear, what nonsense I'm talking!"

Just at this moment her head struck against the roof of the hall: in fact she was now rather more than nine feet high, and she at once took up the little golden key and hurried off to the garden door.

Poor Alice! It was as much as she could do, lying down on one side, to look through into the garden with one eye; but to get through was more hopeless than ever: she sat down and began to cry again.

"You ought to be ashamed of yourself," said Alice, "a great girl like you," (she might well say this), "to go on crying in this way! Stop this moment, I tell you!" But she went on all the same, shedding gallons of tears, until there was a large pool round her, about four inches deep and reaching half down the hall.

After a time she heard a little pattering of feet in the distance, and she hastily dried her eyes to see what was coming. It was the White Rabbit returning, splendidly dressed, with a pair of white kid gloves in one hand and a large fan in the other: he came trotting along in a great hurry, muttering to himself as he came, "Oh! the Duchess, the Duchess! Oh! won't she be savage if I've kept her waiting!" Alice felt so desperate that she was ready to ask help of any one; so when the Rabbit came near her, she began, in a low, timid voice, "If you please, sir—" The Rabbit started violently, dropped the white kid gloves and the fan, and scurried away into the darkness as hard as he could go.

Alice took up the fan and gloves, and, as the hall was very hot, she kept fanning herself all the time she went on talking: "Dear, dear! How queer everything is to-day! And yesterday things went on just as usual. I wonder if I've been changed in the night? Let me think: was I the same when I got up this morning? I almost think I can remember feeling a little different. But if I'm not the same, the next question is, Who in the world am I? Ah, *that's* the great puzzle!" And she began thinking over all the children she knew, that were of the same age as herself, to see if she could have been changed for any of them.

"I'm sure I'm not Ada," she said, "for her hair goes in such long ringlets, and mine doesn't go in ringlets at all; and I'm sure I can't be Mabel, for I know all sorts of things, and she, oh! she knows such a very little! Besides, *she's* she, and *I'm* I, and—oh dear, how puzzling it all is! I'll try if I know all the things I used to know. Let me see: four times five is twelve, and four times six is thirteen, and four times seven is—oh dear! I shall never get to twenty at that rate! However, the Multiplication Table don't signify: let's try Geography. London is the capital of Paris, and Paris is the capital of Rome, and Rome —no, *that's* all wrong, I'm certain! I must have been changed for Mabel! I'll try and say *'How doth the little—'*" and she crossed her hands on her lap, as if she were saying lessons, and began to repeat it, but her voice sounded hoarse and strange, and the

1. *Fender,* a metal screen that separated the fireplace from the hearth, and kept live coals or sparks from spilling out onto the hearthrug.

words did not come the same as they used to do:—

"How doth the little crocodile[2]
Improve his shining tail,
And pour the waters of the Nile
On every golden scale!

How cheerfully he seems to grin,
How neatly spreads his claws,
And welcomes little fishes in
With gently smiling jaws!

"I'm sure those are not the right words," said poor Alice, and her eyes filled with tears again as she went on, "I must be Mabel after all, and I shall have to go and live in that poky little house, and have next to no toys to play with, and oh! ever so many lessons to learn! No, I've made up my mind about it: if I'm Mabel, I'll stay down here! It'll be no use their putting their heads down and saying, 'Come up again, dear!' I shall only look up and say, 'Who am I, then? Tell me that first, and then, if I like being that person, I'll come up: if not, I'll stay down here till I'm somebody else'—but, oh dear!" cried Alice with a sudden burst of tears, "I do wish they *would* put their heads down! I am so *very* tired of being all alone here!"

As she said this, she looked down at her hands, and was surprised to see that she had put on one of the Rabbit's little white kid gloves while she was talking. "How *can* I have done that?" she thought. "I must be growing small again." She got up and went to the table to measure herself by it, and found that, as nearly as she could guess, she was now about two feet high, and was going on shrinking rapidly: she soon found out that the cause of this was the fan she was holding, and she dropped it hastily, just in time to save herself from shrinking away altogether.

"That *was* a narrow excape!" said Alice, a good deal frightened at the sudden change, but very glad to find herself still in existence; "and now for the garden!" and she ran with all speed back to the little door: but alas! the little door was shut again, and the little golden key was lying on the glass table as before, "and things are worse than ever," thought the poor child, "for I never was so small as this before, never! And I declare it's too bad, that it is!"

As she said these words her foot slipped, and in another moment, splash! she was up to her chin in salt water. Her first idea was that she had somehow fallen into the sea, "and in that case I can go back by railway," she said to herself. (Alice had been to the seaside once in her life, and had come to the general conclusion, that wherever you go to on the English coast you find a number of bathing machines[3] in the sea, some children digging in the sand with wooden spades, then a row of lodging houses, and behind them a railway station.) However she soon made out that she was in the pool of tears which she had wept when she was nine feet high.

"I wish I hadn't cried so much!" said Alice, as she swam about, trying to find her way out. "I shall be punished for it now, I suppose, by being drowned in my own tears! That *will* be a queer thing, to be sure! However, everything is queer to-day."

Just then she heard something splashing about in the pool a little way off, and she swam nearer to make out what it was: at first she thought it must be a walrus or hippopotamus, but then she remembered how small she was now, and she soon made out that it was only a mouse, that had slipped in like herself.

"Would it be of any use, now," thought Alice, "to speak to this mouse? Everything is so out-of-the-way down here, that I should think very likely it can talk: at any rate there's no harm in trying." So she began: "O Mouse, do you know the way out of this pool? I am very tired of swimming about here, O Mouse!" (Alice thought this must be the right way of speaking to a mouse: she had never done such a thing before, but she remembered having seen in her brother's Latin Grammar, "A mouse—of a mouse—to a mouse—a mouse—O mouse!") The Mouse looked at her rather inquisitively, and seemed to her to wink with one of its little eyes, but it said nothing.

"Perhaps it doesn't understand English," thought Alice; "I daresay it's a French mouse, come over with William the Conqueror." (For, with all her knowledge of history, Alice had no very clear notion how long ago anything had happened.) So she began again: "Où est ma chatte?"[4] which was the first

2. This is the first of many parodies that appear in *Alice in Wonderland*. See page 482 for the original.

3. *Bathing machines,* typically Victorian inventions designed to give the bather (swimmer) privacy. They were small wooden locker rooms on wheels. The bather entered and changed into his bathing costume while the contraption was on the beach; it was then drawn by horses into the sea, where the occupant could emerge and bathe out of public view.

4. *French:* "Where is my cat?"

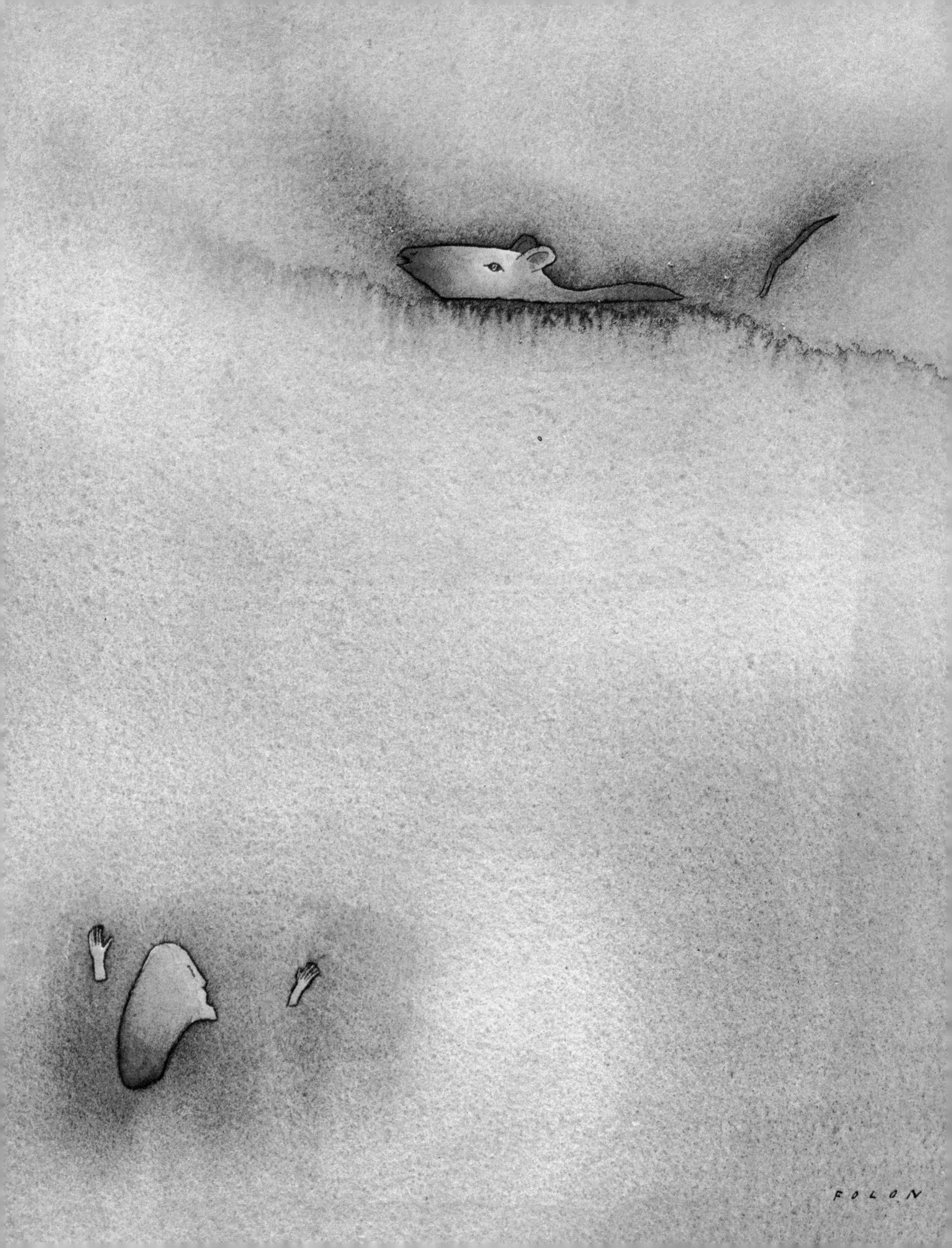
FOLON

sentence in her French lesson-book. The Mouse gave a sudden leap out of the water, and seemed to quiver all over with fright. "Oh, I beg your pardon!" cried Alice hastily, afraid that she had hurt the poor animal's feelings. "I quite forgot you didn't like cats."

"Not like cats!" cried the Mouse, in a shrill, passionate voice. "Would *you* like cats if you were me?"

"Well, perhaps not," said Alice in a soothing tone: "don't be angry about it. And yet I wish I could show you our cat Dinah: I think you'd take a fancy to cats if you could only see her. She is such a dear quiet thing," Alice went on, half to herself, as she swam lazily about in the pool, "and she sits purring so nicely by the fire, licking her paws and washing her face—and she is such a nice soft thing to nurse—and she's such a capital one for catching mice—oh, I beg your pardon!" cried Alice again, for this time the Mouse was bristling all over, and she felt certain it must be really offended. "We won't talk about her any more if you'd rather not."

"We, indeed!" cried the Mouse, who was trembling down to the end of his tail. "As if *I* would talk on such a subject! Our family always *hated* cats: nasty, low, vulgar things! Don't let me hear the name again!"

"I won't indeed!" said Alice, in a great hurry to change the subject of conversation. "Are you—are you fond—of—of dogs?" The mouse did not answer, so Alice went on eagerly: "There is such a nice little dog near our house I should like to show you! A little bright-eyed terrier, you know, with oh! such long curly brown hair! And it'll fetch things when you throw them, and it'll sit up and beg for its dinner, and all sorts of things—I can't remember half of them—and it belongs to a farmer, you know, and he says it's so useful, it's worth a hundred pounds! He says it kills all the rats and—oh dear!" cried Alice in a sorrowful tone. "I'm afraid I've offended it again!" For the Mouse was swimming away from her as hard as it could go, and making quite a commotion in the pool as it went.

So she called softly after it: "Mouse dear! Do come back again, and we won't talk about cats or dogs either, if you don't like them!" When the Mouse heard this, it turned round and swam slowly back to her: its face was quite pale (with passion, Alice thought), and it said in a low trembling voice, "Let us get to the shore, and then I'll tell you my history, and you'll understand why it is I hate cats and dogs."

It was high time to go, for the pool was getting quite crowded with the birds and animals that had fallen into it: there was a Duck and a Dodo, a Lory and an Eaglet,[5] and several other curious creatures. Alice led the way, and the whole party swam to the shore.

3

A CAUCUS RACE AND A LONG TALE

THEY were indeed a queer-looking party that assembled on the bank—the birds with draggled feathers, the animals with their fur clinging close to them, and all dripping wet, cross, and uncomfortable.

The first question of course was, how to get dry again: they had a consultation about this, and after a few minutes it seemed quite natural to Alice to find herself talking familiarly with them, as if she had known them all her life. Indeed, she had quite a long argument with the Lory, who at last turned sulky, and would only say, "I am older than you, and must know better"; and this Alice would not allow, without knowing how old it was, and as the Lory positively refused to tell its age, there was no more to be said.

At last the Mouse, who seemed to be a person of some authority among them, called out, "Sit down, all of you, and listen to me! *I'll* soon make you dry enough!" They all sat down at once, in a large ring, with the Mouse in the middle. Alice kept her eyes anxiously fixed on it, for she felt sure she would catch a bad cold if she did not get dry very soon.

"Ahem!" said the Mouse with an important air, "are you all ready? This is the driest thing I know. Silence all round, if you please! 'William the Conqueror, whose cause was favoured by the pope, was

5. The animals mentioned are thinly disguised representations of members of the party which boated on the Thames in 1862. The Duck is the Reverend Duckworth; the Dodo (a flightless bird already extinct by the 1860's) is Lewis Carroll (Charles Dodgson); the Lory (an Australian parrot) is Lorina Liddell; the Eaglet, Edith Liddell.

soon submitted to by the English, who wanted leaders, and had been of late much accustomed to usurpation and conquest. Edwin and Morcar, the earls of Mercia and Northumbria—' "[6]

"Ugh!" said the Lory, with a shiver.

"I beg your pardon?" said the Mouse, frowning, but very politely: "Did you speak?"

"Not I!" said the Lory, hastily.

"I thought you did," said the Mouse. "I proceed. 'Edwin and Morcar, the earls of Mercia and Northumbria, declared for him; and even Stigand, the patriotic archbishop of Canterbury, found it advisable—' "

"Found *what?*" said the Duck.

"Found *it*," the Mouse replied rather crossly: "of course you know what 'it' means."

"I know what 'it' means well enough, when *I* find a thing," said the Duck: "It's generally a frog or a worm. The question is, what did the archbishop find?"

The Mouse did not notice this question, but hurriedly went on, " '—found it advisable to go with Edgar Atheling to meet William and offer him the crown. William's conduct at first was moderate. But the insolence of his Normans—' How are you getting on now, my dear?" it continued, turning to Alice as it spoke.

"As wet as ever," said Alice in a melancholy tone: "it doesn't seem to dry me at all."

"In that case," said the Dodo solemnly, rising to its feet, "I move that the meeting adjourn, for the immediate adoption of more energetic remedies—"

"Speak English!" said the Eaglet. "I don't know the meaning of half those long words, and what's more, I don't believe you do either!" And the Eaglet bent down its head to hide a smile: some of the other birds tittered audibly.

"What I was going to say," said the Dodo in an offended tone, "was, that the best thing to get us dry would be a Caucus-race."[7]

"What *is* a Caucus-race?" said Alice; not that she much wanted to know, but the Dodo had paused as if it thought that *somebody* ought to speak, and no one else seemed inclined to say anything.

"Why," said the Dodo, "the best way to explain it is to do it." (And as you might like to try the thing yourself, some winter day, I will tell you how the Dodo managed it.)

First it marked out a race-course, in a sort of circle, ("the exact shape doesn't matter," it said,) and then all the party were placed along the course, here and there. There was no "One, two, three, and away," but they began running when they liked, and left off when they liked, so that it was not easy to know when the race was over. However, when they had been running half-an-hour or so, and were quite dry again, the Dodo suddenly called out, "The race is over!" and they all crowded round it, panting, and asking, "But who has won?"

This question the Dodo could not answer without a great deal of thought, and it sat for a long time with one finger pressed upon its forehead, (the position in which you usually see Shakespeare, in the pictures of him,) while the rest waited in silence. At last the Dodo said, "*Everybody* has won, and all must have prizes."

"But who is to give the prizes?" quite a chorus of voices asked.

"Why, *she*, of course," said the Dodo, pointing to Alice with one finger; and the whole party at once crowded round her, calling out in a confused way: "Prizes! Prizes!"

Alice had no idea what to do, and in despair she put her hand into her pocket, and pulled out a box of comfits,[8] (luckily the salt water had not got into it,) and handed them round as prizes. There was exactly one a-piece, all round.

"But she must have a prize herself, you know," said the Mouse.

"Of course," the Dodo replied very gravely. "What else have you got in your pocket?" he went on, turning to Alice.

"Only a thimble," said Alice sadly.

"Hand it over here," said the Dodo.

Then they all crowded round her once more, while the Dodo solemnly presented the thimble, saying, "We beg your acceptance of this elegant thimble"; and, when it had finished this short speech, they all cheered.

Alice thought the whole thing very absurd, but they all looked so grave that she did not dare to laugh, and as she could not think of anything to say,

---

6. The passage that the mouse recites is probably from a contemporary English history textbook.

7. Although the term "caucus" originated in the United States and meant simply a gathering of political figures to select a candidate, the term, as it was used in Victorian England, carried harsher overtones of organizational confusion and political greed.

8. *Comfits*, a type of candy made by covering dried fruits or seeds with sugar.

she simply bowed, and took the thimble, looking as solemn as she could.

The next thing was to eat the comfits: this caused some noise and confusion, as the large birds complained that they could not taste theirs, and the small ones choked and had to be patted on the back. However it was over at last, and they sat down again in a ring, and begged the Mouse to tell them something more.

"You promised to tell me your history, you know," said Alice, "and why it is you hate—C and D," she added in a whisper, half afraid that it would be offended again.

"Mine is a long and sad tale!" said the Mouse, turning to Alice, and sighing.

"It *is* a long tail, certainly," said Alice, looking down with wonder at the Mouse's tail; "but why do you call it sad?" And she kept on puzzling about it while the Mouse was speaking, so that her idea of the tale was something like this:——"Fury
said to a mouse, That
he met in the house,
'Let us both go
to law: *I* will prose-
cute *you*.—Come,
I'll take no denial:
We must have the
trial; for really
this morning I've
nothing to do.'
Said the mouse
to the cur,
'Such a trial,
dear sir,
with no
jury
or judge,
would be
wasting our
breath.' 'I'll be
judge, I'll
be jury,'
said cun-
ning old
Fury: 'I'll
try the
whole
cause,
and
con-
demn
you
to death'."

"You are not attending!" said the Mouse to Alice, severely. "What are you thinking of?"

"I beg your pardon," said Alice very humbly: "you had got to the fifth bend, I think?"

"I had *not!*" cried the Mouse, sharply and very angrily.

"A knot!" said Alice, always ready to make herself useful, and looking anxiously about her. "Oh, do let me help to undo it!"

"I shall do nothing of the sort," said the Mouse, getting up and walking away. "You insult me by talking such nonsense!"

"I didn't mean it!" pleaded poor Alice. "But you're so easily offended, you know!"

The Mouse only growled in reply.

"Please come back, and finish your story!" Alice called after it; and the others all joined in chorus, "Yes, please do!" but the Mouse only shook its head impatiently, and walked a little quicker.

"What a pity it wouldn't stay!" sighed the Lory, as soon as it was quite out of sight; and an old crab took the opportunity of saying to her daughter, "Ah, my dear! Let this be a lesson to you never to lose *your* temper!"

"Hold your tongue, Ma!" said the young crab, a little snappishly. "You're enough to try the patience of an oyster!"

"I wish I had our Dinah here, I know I do!" said Alice aloud, addressing nobody in particular. "She'd soon fetch it back!"

"And who is Dinah, if I might venture to ask the question?" said the Lory.

Alice replied eagerly, for she was always ready to talk about her pet. "Dinah's our cat. And she's such a capital one for catching mice, you can't think! And oh, I wish you could see her after the birds! Why, she'll eat a little bird as soon as look at it!"

This speech caused a remarkable sensation among the party. Some of the birds hurried off at once: one old magpie began wrapping itself up very carefully, remarking, "I really must be getting home; the night-air doesn't suit my throat!" and a canary called out in a trembling voice to its children, "Come away, my dears! It's high time you were all in bed!" On various pretexts they all moved off, and Alice was soon left alone.

"I wish I hadn't mentioned Dinah!" she said to herself in a melancholy tone. "Nobody seems to like her, down here, and I'm sure she's the best cat in the world! Oh, my dear Dinah! I wonder if I shall ever see you any more!" And here poor Alice began to cry again, for she felt very lonely and low-spirited. In a little while, however, she again heard a little pattering of footsteps in the distance, and she looked up eagerly, half hoping that the Mouse had changed his mind, and was coming back to finish his story.

4

THE RABBIT SENDS IN A LITTLE BILL

IT was the White Rabbit, trotting slowly back again, and looking anxiously about as it went as if it had lost something; and she heard it muttering to itself, "The Duchess! The Duchess! Oh my dear paws! Oh my fur and whiskers! She'll get me executed, as sure as ferrets are ferrets! Where *can* I have dropped them, I wonder!" Alice guessed in a moment that it was looking for the fan and the pair of white kid gloves, and she very goodnaturedly began hunting about for them, but they were nowhere to be seen—everything seemed to have changed since her swim in the pool, and the great hall, with the glass table and the little door, had vanished completely.

Very soon the Rabbit noticed Alice, as she went hunting about, and called out to her in an angry tone, "Why, Mary Ann, what *are* you doing out here? Run home this moment, and fetch me a pair of gloves and a fan! Quick, now!" And Alice was so much frightened that she ran off at once in the direction it pointed to, without trying to explain the mistake that it had made.

"He took me for his housemaid," she said to herself as she ran. "How surprised he'll be when he finds out who I am! But I'd better take him his fan and gloves—that is, if I can find them." As she said this, she came upon a neat little house, on the door of which was a bright brass plate with the name "W. RABBIT," engraved upon it. She went in without knocking, and hurried upstairs, in great fear lest she should meet the real Mary Ann, and be turned out of the house before she had found the fan and gloves.

"How queer it seems," Alice said to herself, "to be going messages for a rabbit! I suppose Dinah'll be sending me on messages next!" And she began fancying the sort of thing that would happen: "'Miss Alice! Come here directly, and get ready for your walk!' 'Coming in a minute, nurse! But I've got to watch this mousehole till Dinah comes back, and see that the mouse doesn't get out.' Only I don't think," Alice went on, "that they'd let Dinah stop in the house if it began ordering people about like that!"

By this time she had found her way into a tidy little room with a table in the window, and on it (as she had hoped) a fan and two or three pairs of tiny white kid gloves: she took up the fan and a pair of the gloves, and was just going to leave the room, when her eye fell upon a little bottle that stood near the looking-glass. There was no label this time with the words "DRINK ME," but nevertheless she uncorked it and put it to her lips. "I know *something* interesting is sure to happen," she said to herself, "whenever I eat or drink anything; so I'll just see what this bottle does. I do hope it'll make me grow large again, for really I'm quite tired of being such a tiny little thing!"

It did so indeed, and much sooner than she had expected: before she had drunk half the bottle, she found her head pressing against the ceiling, and had to stoop to save her neck from being broken. She hastily put down the bottle, saying to herself, "That's quite enough—I hope I shan't grow any more—As it is, I can't get out at the door—I do wish I hadn't drunk quite so much!"

Alas! It was too late to wish that! She went on growing and growing, and very soon had to kneel down on the floor: in another minute there was not even room for this, and she tried the effect of lying down, with one elbow against the door, and the other arm curled round her head. Still she went on growing, and, as a last resource, she put one arm out of the window, and one foot up the chimney, and said to herself, "Now I can do no more, whatever happens. What *will* become of me?"

Luckily for Alice, the little magic bottle had now had its full effect, and she grew no larger: still it was very uncomfortable, and, as there seemed to be no sort of chance of her ever getting out of the room again, no wonder she felt unhappy.

"It was much pleasanter at home," thought poor Alice, "when one wasn't always growing larger and smaller, and being ordered about by mice and rab-

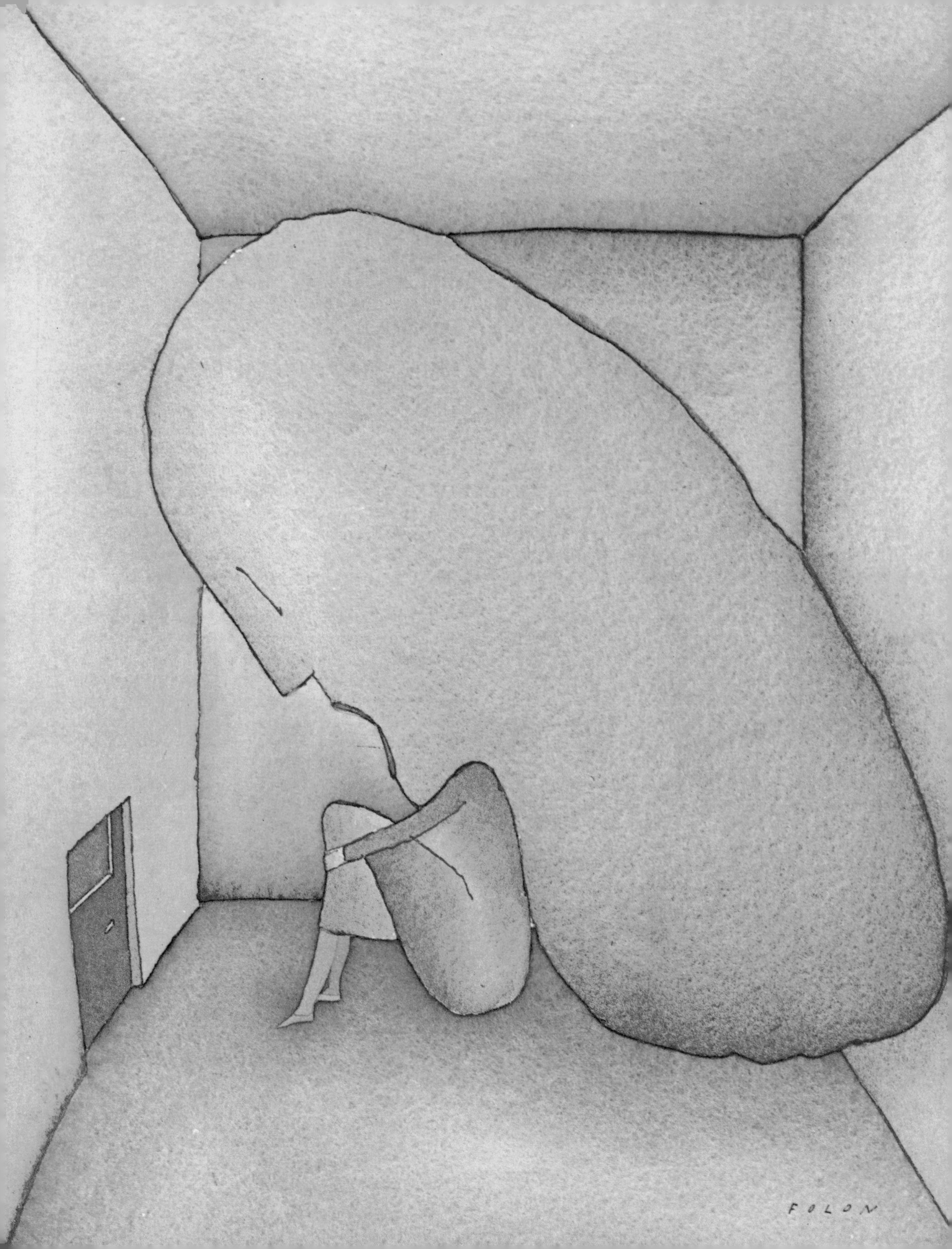
FOLON

bits. I almost wish I hadn't gone down that rabbit-hole—and yet—and yet—it's rather curious, you know, this sort of life! I do wonder what *can* have happened to me! When I used to read fairy-tales, I fancied that kind of thing never happened, and now here I am in the middle of one! There ought to be a book written about me, that there ought! And when I grow up, I'll write one—but I'm grown up now," she added in a sorrowful tone, "at least there's no room to grow up any more *here*."

"But then," thought Alice, "shall I *never* get any older than I am now? That'll be a comfort, one way—never to be an old woman—but then—always to have lessons to learn! Oh, I shouldn't like *that!*"

"Oh, you foolish Alice!" she answered herself. "How can you learn lessons in here? Why, there's hardly room for you, and no room at all for any lesson-books!"

And so she went on, taking first one side and then the other, and making quite a conversation of it altogether, but after a few minutes she heard a voice outside, and stopped to listen.

"Mary Ann! Mary Ann!" said the voice, "fetch me my gloves this moment!" Then came a little pattering of feet on the stairs. Alice knew it was the Rabbit coming to look for her, and she trembled till she shook the house, quite forgetting that she was now about a thousand times as large as the Rabbit, and had no reason to be afraid of it.

Presently the Rabbit came up to the door, and tried to open it, but as the door opened inwards, and Alice's elbow was pressed hard against it, that attempt proved a failure. Alice heard it say to itself, "Then I'll go round and get in at the window."

"*That* you won't!" thought Alice, and, after waiting till she fancied she heard the Rabbit just under the window, she suddenly spread our her hand, and made a snatch in the air. She did not get hold of anything, but she heard a little shriek and a fall, and a crash of broken glass, from which she concluded that it was just possible it had fallen into a cucumber-frame,[9] or something of the sort.

Next came an angry voice—the Rabbit's—"Pat! Pat! Where are you?" And then a voice she had never heard before, "Sure then I'm here! Digging for apples, yer honour!"

"Digging for apples, indeed!" said the Rabbit angrily. "Here! Come and help me out of *this!*" (Sounds of more broken glass.)

"Now tell me, Pat, what's that in the window?"

"Sure, it's an arm, yer honour!" (He pronounced it "arrum.")

"An arm, you goose! Who ever saw one that size? Why, it fills the whole window!"

"Sure, it does, yer honour: but it's an arm for all that."

"Well, it's got no business there, at any rate: go and take it away!"

There was a long silence after this, and Alice could only hear whispers now and then, such as, "Sure, I don't like it, yer honour, at all at all!" "Do as I tell you, you coward!" and at last she spread out her hand again and made another snatch in the air. This time there were *two* little shrieks, and more sounds of broken glass. "What a number of cucumber-frames there must be!" thought Alice. "I wonder what they'll do next! As for pulling me out of the window, I only wish they *could!* I'm sure *I* don't want to stay in here any longer!"

She waited for some time without hearing anything more: at last came a rumbling of little cart-wheels, and the sound of a good many voices all talking together: she made out the words, "Where's the other ladder?—Why, I hadn't to bring but one: Bill's got the other—Bill! fetch it here, lad!—Here, put 'em up at this corner—No, tie 'em together first—they don't reach half high enough yet—Oh! they'll do well enough; don't be particular—Here, Bill! catch hold of this rope—Will the roof bear? —Mind that loose slate—Oh, it's coming down! Heads below!" (a loud crash)—"Now, who did that?—It was Bill, I fancy—Who's to go down the chimney?—Nay, *I shan't! You* do it!—*That* I won't then! Bill's got to go down—Here, Bill! the master says you've got to go down the chimney!"

"Oh, so Bill's got to come down the chimney, has he?" said Alice to herself. "Why, they seem to put everything upon Bill! I wouldn't be in Bill's place for a good deal: this fireplace is narrow, to be sure, but I *think* I can kick a little!"

She drew her foot as far down the chimney as she could, and waited till she heard a little animal (she couldn't guess of what sort it was) scratching and scrambling about in the chimney close above her: then, saying to herself, "This is Bill," she gave one sharp kick and waited to see what would happen next. The first thing she heard was a general chorus of

9. *cucumber-frame,* a sort of small hot-house or glass-enclosed structure for growing plants in cold weather.

"there goes Bill!" then the Rabbit's voice alone: "catch him, you by the hedge!" —then silence, and then another confusion of voices—"Hold up his head—Brandy now—Don't choke him—How was it, old fellow? What happened to you? Tell us all about it!"

Last came a little feeble squeaking voice, ("That's Bill," thought Alice). "Well, I hardly know—No more, thank ye, I'm better now—but I'm a deal too flustered to tell you—all I know is, something comes at me like a Jack-in-the-box, and up I goes like a sky-rocket!"

"So you did, old fellow!" said the others.

"We must burn the house down!" said the Rabbit's voice, and Alice called out as loud as she could:

"If you do, I'll set Dinah at you!"

There was a dead silence instantly, and Alice thought to herself, "I wonder what they *will* do next! If they had any sense, they'd take the roof off." After a minute or two they began moving about again, and Alice heard the Rabbit say, "A barrowful will do, to begin with."

"A barrowful of *what?*" thought Alice; but she had not long to doubt, for the next moment a shower of little pebbles came rattling in at the window, and some of them hit her in the face. "I'll put a stop to this," she said to herself and shouted out:

"You'd better not do that again!" which produced another dead silence.

Alice noticed with some surprise that the pebbles were all turning into little cakes as they lay on the floor, and a bright idea came into her head.

"If I eat one of these cakes," she thought, "it's sure to make some change in my size: and as it can't possibly make me larger, it must make me smaller, I suppose."

So she swallowed one of the cakes, and was delighted to find that she began shrinking directly. As soon as she was small enough to get through the door, she ran out of the house, and found quite a crowd of little animals and birds waiting outside. The poor little Lizard, Bill, was in the middle, being held up by two guinea pigs, who were giving it something out of a bottle. They all made a rush at Alice the moment she appeared, but she ran off as hard as she could, and soon found herself safe in a thick wood.

"The first thing I've got to do," said Alice to herself, as she wandered about in the wood, "is to grow to my right size again; and the second thing is to find my way into that lovely garden. I think that will be the best plan."

It sounded an excellent plan, no doubt, and very neatly and simply arranged; the only difficulty was, that she had not the smallest idea how to set about it; and while she was peering about anxiously among the trees, a little sharp bark just over her head made her look up in a great hurry.

An enormous puppy was looking down at her with large round eyes, and feebly stretching out one paw, trying to touch her. "Poor little thing!" said Alice in a coaxing tone, and she tried hard to whistle to it, but she was terribly frightened all the time at the thought that it might be hungry, in which case it would be very likely to eat her up in spite of all her coaxing.

Hardly knowing what she did, she picked up a little bit of stick, and held it out to the puppy; whereupon the puppy jumped into the air off all its feet at once, with a yelp of delight, and rushed at the stick, and made believe to worry it; then Alice dodged behind a great thistle, to keep herself from being run over, and, the moment she appeared on the other side, the puppy made another rush at the stick, and tumbled head over heels in its hurry to get hold of it; then Alice, thinking it was very like having a game of play with a cart-horse, and expecting every moment to be trampled under its feet, ran round the thistle again; then the puppy began a series of short charges at the stick, running a very little way forwards each time and a long way back, and barking hoarsely all the while, till at last it sat down a good way off, panting, with its tongue hanging out of its mouth, and its great eyes half shut.

This seemed to Alice a good opportunity for making her escape, so she set off at once, and ran till she was quite tired and out of breath, and till the puppy's bark sounded quite faint in the distance. "And yet what a dear little puppy it was!" said Alice, as she leant against a buttercup to rest herself, and fanned herself with one of the leaves; "I should have liked teaching it tricks very much, if—if I'd only been the right size to do it! Oh dear! I'd nearly forgotten that I've got to grow up again! Let me see—how *is* it to be managed? I suppose I ought to eat or drink something or other; but the great question is, what?"

The great question certainly was, what? Alice looked all round her at the flowers and the blades of grass, but she could not see anything that looked like the right thing to eat or drink under the circumstances. There was a large mushroom growing near her, about the same height as herself, and when she had looked under it, and on both sides of it, and behind it, it occurred to her that she might as well look and see what was on the top of it.

She stretched herself up on tiptoe, and peeped over the edge of the mushroom, and her eyes immediately met those of a large blue caterpillar, that was sitting on the top with its arms folded, quietly smoking a long hookah,[10] and taking not the smallest notice of her or of anything else.

5

ADVICE FROM A CATERPILLAR

THE Caterpillar and Alice looked at each other for some time in silence: at last the Caterpillar took the hookah out of its mouth, and addressed her in a languid, sleepy voice.

"Who are *you?*" said the Caterpillar.

This was not an encouraging opening for a conversation. Alice replied, rather shyly, "I—I hardly know, sir, just at present—at least I know who I *was* when I got up this morning, but I think I must have been changed several times since then."

"What do you mean by that?" said the Caterpillar sternly. "Explain yourself!"

"I can't explain *myself,* I'm afraid, sir," said Alice, "because I'm not myself, you see."

"I don't see," said the Caterpillar.

"I'm afraid I can't put it more clearly," Alice replied very politely, "for I can't understand it myself to begin with; and being so many different sizes in one day is very confusing."

"It isn't," said the Caterpillar.

"Well, perhaps you haven't found it so yet," said Alice; "but when you have to turn into a chrysalis—you will some day, you know—and then after that into a butterfly, I should think you'll feel it a little queer, won't you?"

"Not a bit," said the Caterpillar.

"Well, perhaps your feelings may be different," said Alice; "all I know is, it would feel very queer to *me.*"

"You!" said the Caterpillar contemptuously. "Who are *you?*"

Which brought them back again to the beginning of the conversation. Alice felt a little irritated at the Caterpillar's making such *very* short remarks, and she drew herself up and said, very gravely, "I think you ought to tell me who *you* are, first."

"Why?" said the Caterpillar.

Here was another puzzling question; and, as Alice could not think of any good reason, and as the Caterpillar seemed to be in a *very* unpleasant state of mind, she turned away.

"Come back!" the Caterpillar called after her. "I've something important to say!"

This sounded promising, certainly: Alice turned and came back again.

"Keep your temper," said the Caterpillar.

"Is that all?" said Alice, swallowing down her anger as well as she could.

"No," said the Caterpillar.

Alice thought she might as well wait, as she had nothing else to do, and perhaps after all it might tell her something worth hearing. For some minutes it puffed away without speaking, but at last it unfolded its arms, took the hookah out of its mouth again, and said:

"So you think you're changed, do you?"

"I'm afraid I am, sir," said Alice; "I can't remember things as I used—and I don't keep the same size for ten minutes together!"

"Can't remember *what* things?" said the Caterpillar.

"Well, I've tried to say 'How doth the little busy bee,' but it all came different!" Alice replied in a very melancholy voice.

"Repeat '*You Are Old, Father William,*'"[11] said the Caterpillar.

Alice folded her hands, and began:—

---

10. *hookah,* a water pipe.

11. The poem being parodied is given on page 482.

"You are old, father William," the young man said,
"And your hair has become very white;
And yet you incessantly stand on your head—
Do you think, at your age, it is right?"

"In my youth," father William replied to his son,
"I feared it might injure the brain;
But now that I'm perfectly sure I have none,
Why, I do it again and again."

"You are old," said the youth, "as I mentioned before,
And have grown most uncommonly fat;
"Yet you turned a back-somersault in at the door—
Pray, what is the reason of that?"

"In my youth," said the sage, as he shook his grey locks,
"I kept all my limbs very supple
By the use of this ointment—one shilling the box—
Allow me to sell you a couple."

"You are old," said the youth, "and your jaws are too weak
For anything tougher than suet;
Yet you finished the goose, with the bones and the beak—
Pray, how did you manage to do it?"

"In my youth," said his father, "I took to the law,
And argued each case with my wife;
And the muscular strength, which it gave to my jaw,
Has lasted the rest of my life."

"You are old," said the youth; "one would hardly suppose
That your eye was as steady as ever;
Yet you balanced an eel on the end of your nose—
What made you so awfully clever?"

"I have answered three questions, and that is enough,"
Said his father; "don't give yourself airs!
Do you think I can listen all day to such stuff?
Be off, or I'll kick you downstairs!"

"That is not said right," said the Caterpillar.

"Not *quite* right, I'm afraid," said Alice timidly; "some of the words have got altered."

"It is wrong from beginning to end," said the Caterpillar decidedly, and there was silence for some minutes.

The Caterpillar was the first to speak.

"What size do you want to be?" it asked.

"Oh, I'm not particular as to size," Alice hastily replied; "only one doesn't like changing so often, you know."

"I *don't* know," said the Caterpillar.

Alice said nothing: she had never been so much contradicted in all her life before, and she felt that she was losing her temper.

"Are you content now?" said the Caterpillar.

"Well, I should like to be a *little* larger, sir, if you wouldn't mind," said Alice: "three inches is such a wretched height to be."

"It is a very good height indeed!" said the Caterpillar angrily, rearing itself upright as it spoke (it was exactly three inches high).

"But I'm not used to it!" pleaded poor Alice in a piteous tone. And she thought to herself, "I wish the creatures wouldn't be so easily offended!"

"You'll get used to it in time," said the Caterpillar; and it put the hookah into its mouth and began smoking again.

This time Alice waited patiently until it chose to speak again. In a minute or two the Caterpillar took the hookah out of its mouth, and yawned once or twice, and shook itself. Then it got down off the mushroom, and crawled away into the grass, merely remarking as it went, "One side will make you grow taller, and the other side will make you grow shorter."

"One side of *what?* The other side of *what?*" thought Alice to herself.

"Of the mushroom," said the Caterpillar, just as if she had asked it aloud; and in another moment it was out of sight.

Alice remained looking thoughtfully at the mushroom for a minute, trying to make out which were the two sides of it; and, as it was perfectly round, she found this a very difficult question. However, at last she stretched her arms round it as far as they would go, and broke off a bit of the edge with each hand.

"And now which is which?" she said to herself, and nibbled a little of the right-hand bit to try the effect: the next moment she felt a violent blow underneath her chin; it had struck her foot!

She was a good deal frightened by this very sudden change, but she felt that there was no time to be

FOLON

lost, as she was shrinking rapidly; so she set to work at once to eat some of the other bit. Her chin was pressed so closely against her foot, that there was hardly room to open her mouth; but she did it at last, and managed to swallow a morsel of the left-hand bit.

"Come, my head's free at last!" said Alice in a tone of delight, which changed into alarm in another moment, when she found that her shoulders were nowhere to be found: all she could see, when she looked down, was an immense length of neck, which seemed to rise like a stalk out of a sea of green leaves that lay far below her.

"What *can* all that green stuff be?" said Alice. "And where *have* my shoulders got to? And oh, my poor hands, how is it I can't see you?" She was moving them about as she spoke, but no result seemed to follow, except a little shaking among the distant green leaves.

As there seemed to be no chance of getting her hands up to her head, she tried to get her head down to them, and she was delighted to find that her neck would bend about easily in any direction, like a serpent. She had just succeeded in curving it down into a graceful zig-zag, and was going to dive in among the leaves, which she found to be nothing but the tops of the trees under which she had been wandering, when a sharp hiss made her draw back in a hurry: a large pigeon had flown into her face, and was beating her violently with its wings.

"Serpent!" screamed the Pigeon.

"I'm *not* a serpent!" said Alice indignantly. "Let me alone!"

"Serpent, I say again!" repeated the Pigeon, but in a more subdued tone, and added with a kind of sob, "I've tried every way, and nothing seems to suit them!"

"I haven't the least idea what you're talking about," said Alice.

"I've tried the roots of trees, and I've tried banks, and I've tried hedges," the Pigeon went on, without attending to her; "but those serpents! There's no pleasing them!"

Alice was more and more puzzled, but she thought there was no use in saying anything more till the Pigeon had finished.

"As if it wasn't trouble enough hatching the eggs," said the Pigeon, "but I must be on the look-out for serpents night and day! Why, I haven't had a wink of sleep, these three weeks!"

"I'm very sorry you've been annoyed," said Alice, who was beginning to see its meaning.

"And just as I'd taken the highest tree in the wood," continued the Pigeon, raising its voice to a shriek, "and just as I was thinking I should be free of them at last, they must needs come wriggling down from the sky! Ugh! Serpent!"

"But I'm *not* a serpent, I tell you!" said Alice, "I'm —I'm a—"

"Well! *What* are you?" said the Pigeon. "I can see you're trying to invent something."

"I—I'm a little girl," said Alice, rather doubtfully, as she remembered the number of changes she had gone through that day.

"A likely story indeed!" said the Pigeon in a tone of the deepest contempt. "I've seen a good many little girls in my time, but never one with such a neck as that! No, no! You're a serpent; and there's no use denying it. I suppose you'll be telling me next that you've never tasted an egg!"

"I *have* tasted eggs, certainly," said Alice, who was a very truthful child; "but little girls eat eggs quite as much as serpents do, you know."

"I don't believe it," said the Pigeon; "but if they do, why then they're a kind of serpent, that's all I can say."

This was such a new idea to Alice, that she was quite silent for a minute or two, which gave the Pigeon the opportunity of adding, "You're looking for eggs, I know *that* well enough; and what does it matter to me whether you're a little girl or a serpent?"

"It matters a good deal to *me*," said Alice hastily; "but I'm not looking for eggs, as it happens; and if I was, I shouldn't want *yours:* I don't like them raw."

"Well, be off, then!" said the Pigeon in a sulky tone, as it settled down again into its nest. Alice crouched down among the trees as well as she could, for her neck kept getting entangled among the branches, and every now and then she had to stop and untwist it. After a while she remembered that she still held the pieces of mushroom in her hands, and she set to work very carefully, nibbling first at one and then at the other, and growing sometimes taller and sometimes shorter, until she had succeeded in bringing herself down to her usual height.

It was so long since she had been anything near the right size, that it felt quite strange at first, but she got used to it in a few minutes, and began talking to herself as usual. "Come, there's half my plan done now! How puzzling all these changes are! I'm never sure what I'm going to be, from one minute to another! However, I've got back to my right size: the next thing is, to get into that beautiful garden—how *is* that to be done, I wonder?" As she said this, she came suddenly upon an open place, with a little house in it about four feet high. "Whoever lives there," thought Alice, "it'll never do to come upon them *this* size: why, I should frighten them out of their wits!" So she began nibbling at the right-hand bit again, and did not venture to go near the house till she had brought herself down to nine inches high.

6

PIG AND PEPPER

FOR a minute or two she stood looking at the house, and wondering what to do next, when suddenly a footman in livery came running out of the wood—(she considered him to be a footman because he was in livery: otherwise, judging by his face only, she would have called him a fish)—and rapped loudly at the door with his knuckles. It was opened by another footman in livery, with a round face and large eyes like a frog; and both footmen, Alice noticed, had powdered hair that curled all over their heads. She felt very curious to know what it was all about, and crept a little way out of the wood to listen.

The Fish-Footman began by producing from under his arm a great letter, nearly as large as himself, and this he handed over to the other, saying in a solemn tone, "For the Duchess. An invitation from the Queen to play croquet." The Frog-Footman repeated, in the same solemn tone, only changing the order of the words a little, "From the Queen. An invitation for the Duchess to play croquet." Then they both bowed low, and their curls got entangled together.

Alice laughed so much at this that she had to run back into the wood for fear of their hearing her, and when she next peeped out the Fish-Footman was gone, and the other was sitting on the ground near the door, staring stupidly up into the sky.

Alice went timidly up to the door, and knocked.

"There's no sort of use in knocking," said the Footman, "and that for two reasons. First, because I'm on the same side of the door as you are; secondly, because they're making such a noise inside, no one could possibly hear you." And certainly there *was* a most extraordinary noise going on within—a constant howling and sneezing, and every now and then a great crash, as if a dish or kettle had been broken to pieces.

"Please, then," said Alice, "how am I to get in?"

"There might be some sense in your knocking," the Footman went on without attending to her, "if we had the door between us. For instance, if you were *inside*, you might knock, and I could let you out, you know." He was looking up into the sky all the time he was speaking, and this Alice thought decidedly uncivil. "But perhaps he can't help it," she said to herself; "his eyes are so *very* nearly at the top of his head. But at any rate he might answer questions—How am I to get in?" she repeated, aloud.

"I shall sit here," the Footman remarked, "till tomorrow—"

At this moment the door of the house opened, and a large plate came skimming out, straight at the Footman's head: it just grazed his nose, and broke to pieces against one of the trees behind him.

"—or next day, maybe," the Footman continued in the same tone, exactly as if nothing had happened.

"How am I to get in?" Alice asked again in a louder tone.

"*Are* you to get in at all?" said the Footman. "That's the first question, you know."

It *was*, no doubt: only Alice did not like to be told so. "It's really dreadful," she muttered to herself, "the way all the creatures argue. It's enough to drive one crazy!"

The Footman seemed to think this a good opportunity for repeating his remark, with variations. "I shall sit here," he said, "on and off, for days and days."

"But what am *I* to do?" said Alice.

"Anything you like," said the Footman, and began whistling.

"Oh, there's no use in talking to him," said Alice desperately: "he's perfectly idiotic!" And she opened the door and went in.

The door led right into a large kitchen, which was full of smoke from one end to the other: the Duchess was sitting on a three-legged stool in the middle, nursing a baby; the cook was leaning over the fire, stirring a large cauldron which seemed to be full of soup.

"There's certainly too much pepper in that soup!" Alice said to herself, as well as she could for sneezing.

There was certainly too much of it in the air. Even the Duchess sneezed occasionally; and as for the baby, it was sneezing and howling alternately without a moment's pause. The only two creatures in the kitchen that did not sneeze, were the cook, and a large cat which was sitting on the hearth and grinning from ear to ear.

"Please, would you tell me," said Alice, a little timidly, for she was not quite sure whether it was good manners for her to speak first, "why your cat grins like that?"

"It's a Cheshire Cat," said the Duchess, "and that's why. Pig!"

She said the last word with such sudden violence that Alice quite jumped; but she saw in another moment that it was addressed to the baby, and not to her, so she took courage, and went on again:—

"I didn't know that Cheshire Cats always grinned; in fact, I didn't know that cats *could* grin."

"They all can," said the Duchess; "and most of 'em do."

"I don't know of any that do," Alice said very politely, feeling quite pleased to have got into a conversation.

"You don't know much," said the Duchess; "and that's a fact."

Alice did not at all like the tone of this remark, and thought it would be as well to introduce some other subject of conversation. While she was trying to fix on one, the cook took the cauldron of soup off the fire, and at once set to work throwing everything within her reach at the Duchess and the baby—the fire-irons came first; then followed a shower of saucepans, plates, and dishes. The Duchess took no notice of them, even when they hit her; and the baby was howling so much already, that it was quite impossible to say whether the blows hurt it or not.

"Oh, *please* mind what you're doing!" cried Alice, jumping up and down in an agony of terror. "Oh, there goes his *precious* nose!" as an unusually large saucepan flew close by it, and very nearly carried it off.

"If everybody minded their own business," said the Duchess in a hoarse growl, "the world would go round a deal faster than it does."

"Which would *not* be an advantage," said Alice, who felt very glad to get an opportunity of showing off a little of her knowledge. "Just think what work it would make with the day and night! You see the earth takes twenty-four hours to turn round on its axis—"

"Talking of axes," said the Duchess, "chop off her head!"

Alice glanced rather anxiously at the cook, to see if she meant to take the hint; but the cook was busily stirring the soup, and seemed not to be listening, so she went on again: "Twenty-four hours, I *think;* or is it twelve? I—"

"Oh, don't bother *me,*" said the Duchess; "I never could abide figures." And with that she began nursing her child again, singing a sort of lullaby to it as she did so, and giving it a violent shake at the end of every line:—

"Speak roughly to your little boy,[12]
And beat him when he sneezes;
He only does it to annoy,
Because he knows it teases."

CHORUS
(in which the cook and the baby joined)
"Wow! wow! wow!"

While the Duchess sang the second verse of the song, she kept tossing the baby violently up and down, and the poor little thing howled so, that Alice could hardly hear the words:—

"I speak severely to my boy,
I beat him when he sneezes;
For he can thoroughly enjoy
The pepper when he pleases!"

CHORUS
"Wow! wow! wow!"

"Here! you may nurse it a bit, if you like!" said the Duchess to Alice, flinging the baby at her as she spoke. "I must go and get ready to play croquet with the Queen," and she hurried out of the room. The

12. See page 482 for the poem which Carroll was parodying.

cook threw a fryingpan after her as she went, but it just missed her.

Alice caught the baby with some difficulty, as it was a queer-shaped little creature, and held out its arms and legs in all directions, "just like a star-fish," thought Alice. The poor little thing was snorting like a steam-engine when she caught it, and kept doubling itself up and straightening itself out again, so that altogether, for the first minute or two, it was as much as she could do to hold it.

As soon as she had made out the proper way of nursing it, (which was to twist it up into a sort of knot, and then keep tight hold of its right ear and left foot, so as to prevent its undoing itself,) she carried it out into the open air. "If I don't take this child away with me," thought Alice, "they're sure to kill it in a day or two: wouldn't it be murder to leave it behind?" She said the last words out loud, and the little thing grunted in reply (it had left off sneezing by this time). "Don't grunt," said Alice: "that's not at all a proper way of expressing yourself."

The baby grunted again, and Alice looked very anxiously into its face to see what was the matter with it.

There could be no doubt that it had a *very* turn-up nose, much more like a snout than a real nose; also its eyes were getting extremely small, for a baby: altogether Alice did not like the look of the thing at all, "—but perhaps it was only sobbing," she thought, and looked into its eyes again, to see if there were any tears.

No, there were no tears. "If you're going to turn into a pig, my dear," said Alice, seriously, "I'll have nothing more to do with you. Mind now!" The poor little thing sobbed again, (or grunted, it was impossible to say which,) and they went on for some while in silence.

Alice was just beginning to think to herself, "Now, what am I to do with this creature when I get it home?" when it grunted again, so violently, that she looked down into its face in some alarm. This time there could be *no* mistake about it: it was neither more nor less than a pig, and she felt that it would be quite absurd for her to carry it any further.

So she set the little creature down, and felt quite relieved to see it trot away quietly into the wood. "If it had grown up," she said to herself, "it would have been a dreadfully ugly child: but it makes rather a handsome pig, I think." And she began thinking over other children she knew, who might do very well as pigs, and was just saying to herself, "if one only knew the right way to change them—" when she was a little startled by seeing the Cheshire Cat sitting on a bough of a tree a few yards off.

The Cat only grinned when it saw Alice. It looked goodnatured, she thought: still it had *very* long claws and a great many teeth, so she felt it ought to be treated with respect.

"Cheshire Puss," she began, rather timidly, as she did not at all know whether it would like the name: however, it only grinned a little wider. "Come, it's pleased so far," thought Alice, and she went on, "Would you tell me, please, which way I ought to walk from here?"

"That depends a good deal on where you want to get to," said the Cat.

"I don't care much where—" said Alice.

"Then it doesn't matter which way you walk," said the Cat.

"—so long as I get *somewhere,*" Alice added as an explanation.

"Oh, you're sure to do that," said the Cat, "if you only walk long enough."

Alice felt that this could not be denied, so she tried another question. "What sort of people live about here?"

"In *that* direction," the Cat said, waving its right paw round, "lives a Hatter: and in *that* direction," waving the other paw, "lives a March Hare. Visit either you like: they're both mad."[13]

"But I don't want to go among mad people," Alice remarked.

"Oh, you can't help that," said the Cat: "we're all mad here. I'm mad. You're mad."

"How do you know I'm mad?" said Alice.

"You must be," said the Cat, "or you wouldn't have come here."

Alice didn't think that proved it at all; however, she went on: "and how do you know that you're mad?"

"To begin with," said the Cat, "a dog's not mad. You grant that?"

"I suppose so," said Alice.

"Well then," the Cat went on, "you see a dog

---

13. The March Hare is so named because of its crazy antics during its mating season, March. The phrase, "mad as a hatter," probably derives from the fact that nineteenth-century makers of hats used mercury for curing and shaping the felt from which gentlemen's hats were commonly made. Continuous contact with mercury caused tremors, hallucinations, and in some cases madness.

growls when it's angry, and wags its tail when it's pleased. Now *I* growl when I'm pleased, and wag my tail when I'm angry. Therefore I'm mad."

"*I* call it purring, not growling," said Alice.

"Call it what you like," said the Cat. "Do you play croquet with the Queen to-day?"

"I should like it very much," said Alice, "but I haven't been invited yet."

"You'll see me there," said the Cat, and vanished. Alice was not much surprised at this, she was getting so well used to queer things happening. While she was still looking at the place where it had been, it suddenly appeared again.

"By-the-bye, what became of the baby?" said the Cat. "I'd nearly forgotten to ask."

"It turned into a pig," Alice answered very quietly, just as if the Cat had come back in a natural way.

"I thought it would," said the Cat, and vanished again.

Alice waited a little, half expecting to see it again, but it did not appear, and after a minute or two she walked on in the direction in which the March Hare was said to live. "I've seen hatters before," she said to herself: "the March Hare will be much the most interesting, and perhaps as this is May it won't be raving mad—at least not so mad as it was in March." As she said this, she looked up, and there was the Cat again, sitting on a branch of a tree.

"Did you say pig, or fig?" said the Cat.

"I said pig," replied Alice; "and I wish you wouldn't keep appearing and vanishing so suddenly: you make one quite giddy."

"All right," said the Cat; and this time it vanished quite slowly, beginning with the end of the tail, and ending with the grin, which remained some time after the rest of it had gone.

"Well! I've often seen a cat without a grin," thought Alice; "but a grin without a cat! It's the most curious thing I ever saw in all my life!"

She had not gone much farther before she came in sight of the house of the March Hare: she thought it must be the right house, because the chimneys were shaped like ears and the roof was thatched with fur. It was so large a house, that she did not like to go nearer till she had nibbled some more of the left-hand bit of mushroom, and raised herself to about two feet high: even then she walked up towards it rather timidly, saying to herself, "Suppose it should be raving mad after all! I almost wish I'd gone to see the Hatter instead!"

7

A MAD TEA-PARTY

THERE was a table set out under a tree in front of the house, and the March Hare and the Hatter were having tea at it: a Dormouse[14] was sitting between them, fast asleep, and the other two were using it as a cushion, resting their elbows on it, and talking over its head. "Very uncomfortable for the Dormouse," thought Alice; "only, as it's asleep, I suppose it doesn't mind."

The table was a large one, but the three were all crowded together at one corner of it. "No room! No room!" they cried out when they saw Alice coming. "There's *plenty* of room!" said Alice indignantly, and she sat down in a large arm-chair at one end of the table.

"Have some wine," the March Hare said in an encouraging tone.

Alice looked all round the table, but there was nothing on it but tea. "I don't see any wine," she remarked.

"There isn't any," said the March Hare.

"Then it wasn't very civil of you to offer it," said Alice angrily.

"It wasn't very civil of you to sit down without being invited," said the March Hare.

"I didn't know it was *your* table," said Alice; "it's laid for a great many more than three."

"Your hair wants cutting," said the Hatter. He had been looking at Alice for some time with great curiosity, and this was his first speech.

"You should learn not to make personal remarks," Alice said with some severity: "it's very rude."

The Hatter opened his eyes very wide on hearing this; but all he *said* was, "Why is a raven like a writing-desk?"

"Come, we shall have some fun now!" thought Alice. "I'm glad they've begun asking riddles—I believe I can guess that," she added aloud.

"Do you mean that you think you can find out the answer to it?" said the March Hare.

"Exactly so," said Alice.

"Then you should say what you mean," the March Hare went on.

14. The Dormouse is not a mouse but a kind of small squirrel.

"I do," Alice hastily replied; "at least—at least I mean what I say—that's the same thing, you know."

"Not the same thing a bit!" said the Hatter. "Why, you might just as well say that 'I see what I eat' is the same thing as 'I eat what I see'!"

"You might just as well say," added the March Hare, "that 'I like what I get' is the same thing as 'I get what I like'!"

"You might just as well say," added the Dormouse, who seemed to be talking in his sleep, "that 'I breathe when I sleep' is the same thing as 'I sleep when I breathe'!"

"It *is* the same thing with you," said the Hatter, and here the conversation dropped, and the party sat silent for a minute, while Alice thought over all she could remember about ravens and writing-desks, which wasn't much.

The Hatter was the first to break the silence. "What day of the month is it?" he said, turning to Alice: he had taken his watch out of his pocket, and was looking at it uneasily, shaking it every now and then, and holding it to his ear.

Alice considered a little, and said, "The fourth."

"Two days wrong!" sighed the Hatter. "I told you butter wouldn't suit the works!" he added, looking angrily at the March Hare.

"It was the *best* butter," the March Hare meekly replied.

"Yes, but some crumbs must have got in as well," the Hatter grumbled: "you shouldn't have put it in with the bread-knife."

The March Hare took the watch and looked at it gloomily: then he dipped it into his cup of tea, and looked at it again: but he could think of nothing better to say than his first remark, "It was the *best* butter, you know."

Alice had been looking over his shoulder with some curiosity. "What a funny watch!" she remarked. "It tells the day of the month, and doesn't tell what o'clock it is!"

"Why should it?" muttered the Hatter. "Does *your* watch tell you what year it is?"

"Of course not," Alice replied very readily: "but that's because it stays the same year for such a long time together."

"Which is just the case with *mine*," said the Hatter.

Alice felt dreadfully puzzled. The Hatter's remark seemed to her to have no sort of meaning in it, and yet it was certainly English. "I don't quite understand you," she said as politely as she could.

"The Dormouse is asleep again," said the Hatter, and he poured a little hot tea on to its nose.

The Dormouse shook its head impatiently, and said, without opening its eyes, "Of course, of course: just what I was going to remark myself."

"Have you guessed the riddle yet?" the Hatter said, turning to Alice again.

"No, I give it up," Alice replied: "what's the answer?"

"I haven't the slightest idea," said the Hatter.

"Nor I," said the March Hare.

Alice sighed wearily. "I think you might do something better with the time," she said, "than wasting it in asking riddles that have no answers."[15]

"If you knew Time as well as I do," said the Hatter, "you wouldn't talk about wasting *it*. It's *him*."

"I don't know what you mean," said Alice.

"Of course you don't!" the Hatter said, tossing his head contemptuously. "I dare say you never even spoke to Time!"

"Perhaps not," Alice cautiously replied: "but I know I have to beat time when I learn music."

"Ah! that accounts for it," said the Hatter. "He won't stand beating. Now, if you only kept on good terms with him, he'd do almost anything you liked with the clock. For instance, suppose it were nine o'clock in the morning, just time to begin lessons: you'd only have to whisper a hint to Time, and round goes the clock in a twinkling! Half-past one, time for dinner!"

("I only wish it was," the March Hare said to itself in a whisper.)

"That would be grand, certainly," said Alice thoughtfully: "but then—I shouldn't be hungry for it, you know."

"Not at first, perhaps," said the Hatter: "but you could keep it to half-past one as long as you liked."

"Is that the way *you* manage?" Alice asked.

The Hatter shook his head mournfully. "Not I!" he replied. "We quarrelled last March—just before *he* went mad, you know—" (pointing with his teaspoon at the March Hare,) "—it was at the great concert given by the Queen of Hearts, and I had to sing

15. Although the answer to this riddle is not given in the Alice stories, Carroll later supplied this answer: "Because it can produce a few notes, tho they are *very* flat; and it is never put with the wrong end in front." Among other well-known suggestions are: (1) Because Poe wrote on them both. (2) Bills and tails are their features. (3) Because they both stand on legs, and should be made to shut up.

'Twinkle, twinkle, little bat!
How I wonder what you're at!'

You know the song, perhaps?"

"I've heard something like it," said Alice.

"It goes on, you know," the Hatter continued, "in this way:—

'Up above the world you fly,
Like a teatray in the sky.
Twinkle, twinkle—'"

Here the Dormouse shook itself, and began singing in its sleep "*Twinkle, twinkle, twinkle, twinkle—*" and went on so long that they had to pinch it to make it stop.

"Well, I'd hardly finished the first verse," said the Hatter, "when the Queen bawled out 'He's murdering the time! Off with his head!'"

"How dreadfully savage!" exclaimed Alice.

"And ever since that," the Hatter went on in a mournful tone, "he won't do a thing I ask! It's always six o'clock now."

A bright idea came into Alice's head. "Is that the reason so many tea-things are put out here?" she asked.

"Yes, that's it," said the Hatter with a sigh: "it's always tea-time, and we've no time to wash the things between whiles."

"Then you keep moving round, I suppose?" said Alice.

"Exactly so," said the Hatter: "as the things get used up."

"But when you come to the beginning again?" Alice ventured to ask.

"Suppose we change the subject," the March Hare interrupted, yawning. "I'm getting tired of this. I vote the young lady tells us a story."

"I'm afraid I don't know one," said Alice, rather alarmed at the proposal.

"Then the Dormouse shall!" they both cried. "Wake up, Dormouse!" And they pinched it on both sides at once.

The Dormouse slowly opened his eyes. "I wasn't asleep," he said in a hoarse, feeble voice: "I heard every word you fellows were saying."

"Tell us a story!" said the March Hare.

"Yes, please do!" pleaded Alice.

"And be quick about it," added the Hatter, "or you'll be asleep again before it's done."

"Once upon a time there were three little sisters," the Dormouse began in a great hurry; "and their names were Elsie, Lacie, and Tillie;[16] and they lived at the bottom of a well—"

"What did they live on?" said Alice, who always took a great interest in questions of eating and drinking.

"They lived on treacle,"[17] said the Dormouse, after thinking a minute or two.

"They couldn't have done that, you know," Alice gently remarked: "they'd have been ill."

"So they were," said the Dormouse; "*very* ill."

Alice tried a little to fancy to herself what such an extraordinary way of living would be like, but it puzzled her too much, so she went on: "But why did they live at the bottom of a well?"

"Take some more tea," the March Hare said to Alice, very earnestly.

"I've had nothing yet," Alice replied in an offended tone, "so I can't take more."

"You mean, you can't take *less*," said the Hatter: "it's very easy to take *more* than nothing."

"Nobody asked *your* opinion," said Alice.

"Who's making personal remarks now?" the Hatter asked triumphantly.

Alice did not quite know what to say to this: so she helped herself to some tea and bread-and-butter, and then turned to the Dormouse, and repeated her question.

"Why did they live at the bottom of a well?"

The Dormouse again took a minute or two to think about it, and then said, "It was a treacle-well."

"There's no such thing!" Alice was beginning very angrily, but the Hatter and the March Hare went "Sh! sh!" and the Dormouse sulkily remarked, "If you can't be civil, you'd better finish the story for yourself."

"No, please go on!" Alice said very humbly: "I won't interrupt you again. I dare say there may be *one*."

"One, indeed!" said the Dormouse indignantly. However, he consented to go on. "And so these three little sisters—they were learning to draw, you know—"

"What did they draw?" said Alice, quite forgetting her promise.

---

16. Another reference to the three Liddell sisters. Elsie stands for L. C. or Lorina C. Liddell; Lacie is an anagram for Alice; Tillie is a form of Matilda, Edith's nickname.

17. *treacle,* molasses.

"Treacle," said the Dormouse, without considering at all this time.

"I want a clean cup," interrupted the Hatter: "let's all move one place on."

He moved on as he spoke, and the Dormouse followed him: the March Hare moved into the Dormouse's place, and Alice rather unwillingly took the place of the March Hare. The Hatter was the only one who got any advantage from the change: and Alice was a good deal worse off than before, as the March Hare had just upset the milk-jug into his plate.

Alice did not wish to offend the Dormouse again, so she began very cautiously: "But I don't understand. Where did they draw the treacle from?"

"You can draw water out of a water-well," said the Hatter: "so I should think you could draw treacle out of a treacle-well—eh, stupid?"

"But they were *in* the well," Alice said to the Dormouse, not choosing to notice this last remark.

"Of course they were," said the Dormouse, "—well in." This answer so confused poor Alice, that she let the Dormouse go on for some time without interrupting it.

"They were learning to draw," the Dormouse went on, yawning and rubbing its eyes, for it was getting very sleepy; "and they drew all manner of things—everything that begins with an M—"

"Why with an M?" said Alice.

"Why not?" said the March Hare.

Alice was silent.

The Dormouse had closed its eyes by this time, and was going off into a doze, but on being pinched by the Hatter, it woke up again with a little shriek, and went on: "—that begins with an M, such as mousetraps, and the moon, and memory, and muchness—you know you say things are 'much of a muchness'[18]—did you ever see such a thing as a drawing of a muchness?"

"Really, now you ask me," said Alice, very much confused, "I don't think—"

"Then you shouldn't talk," said the Hatter.

This piece of rudeness was more than Alice could bear: she got up in great disgust, and walked off: the Dormouse fell asleep instantly, and neither of the others took the least notice of her going, though she looked back once or twice, half hoping that they would call after her: the last time she saw them, they were trying to put the Dormouse into the teapot.

"At any rate I'll never go *there* again!" said Alice as she picked her way through the wood. "It's the stupidest tea-party I ever was at in all my life!"

Just as she said this, she noticed that one of the trees had a door leading right into it. "That's very curious!" she thought. "But everything's curious today. I think I may as well go in at once." And in she went.

Once more she found herself in the long hall, and close to the little glass table. "Now, I'll manage better this time," she said to herself, and began by taking the little golden key, and unlocking the door that led into the garden. Then she set to work nibbling at the mushroom (she had kept a piece of it in her pocket) till she was about a foot high: then she walked down the little passage: and *then* she found herself at last in the beautiful garden, among the bright flowerbeds and the cool fountains.

18. The British phrase "much of a muchness" means "things are pretty much the same."

8

THE QUEEN'S CROQUET-GROUND

A large rose-tree stood near the entrance of the garden: the roses growing on it were white, but there were three gardeners at it, busily painting them red. Alice thought this a very curious thing, and she went nearer to watch them, and just as she came up to them she heard one of them say, "Look out now, Five![19] Don't go splashing paint over me like that!"

"I couldn't help it," said Five in a sulky tone; "Seven jogged my elbow."

On which Seven looked up and said, "That's right, Five! Always lay the blame on others!"

"*You'd* better not talk!" said Five. "I heard the Queen say only yesterday you deserved to be beheaded!"

19. The organization of various characters in this chapter, as well as in Chapter 12, is ingeniously modeled on a deck of playing cards. The gardeners, for instance, are the two, five, and seven of spades. The clubs are soldiers; the diamonds are courtiers; the hearts are the royal children. The royal cards are, of course, kings and queens, among them the King and Queen of Hearts. The Knave is the jack.

"What for?" said the one who had spoken first.

"That's none of *your* business, Two!" said Seven.

"Yes, it *is* his business!" said Five, "and I'll tell him—it was for bringing the cook tulip-roots instead of onions."

Seven flung down his brush, and had just begun, "Well, of all the unjust things—" when his eye chanced to fall upon Alice as she stood watching them, and he checked himself suddenly: the others looked round also, and all of them bowed low.

"Would you tell me, please," said Alice, a little timidly, "why you are painting those roses?"

Five and Seven said nothing, but looked at Two. Two began, in a low voice, "Why, the fact is, you see, Miss, this here ought to have been a *red* rose-tree, and we put a white one in by mistake, and if the Queen was to find it out, we should all have our heads cut off, you know. So you see, Miss, we're doing our best, afore she comes, to—" At this moment Five, who had been anxiously looking across the garden, called out "The Queen! The Queen!" and the three gardeners instantly threw themselves flat upon their faces. There was a sound of many footsteps, and Alice looked round, eager to see the Queen.

First came ten soldiers carrying clubs; these were all shaped like the three gardeners, oblong and flat, with their hands and feet at the corners; next the ten courtiers: these were ornamented all over with diamonds and walked two and two, as the soldiers did. After these came the royal children; there were ten of them, and the little dears came jumping merrily along hand in hand, in couples: they were all ornamented with hearts. Next came the guests, mostly Kings and Queens, and among them Alice recognized the White Rabbit: it was talking in a hurried nervous manner, smiling at everything that was said, and went by without noticing her. Then followed the Knave of Hearts, carrying the King's crown on a crimson velvet cushion; and, last of all this grand procession, came THE KING AND QUEEN OF HEARTS.

Alice was rather doubtful whether she ought not to lie down on her face like the three gardeners, but she could not remember ever having heard of such a rule at processions: "and besides, what would be the use of a procession," she thought, "if people had all to lie down on their faces, so that they couldn't see it?" So she stood where she was and waited.

When the procession came opposite to Alice, they all stopped and looked at her, and the Queen said severely, "Who is this?" She said it to the Knave of Hearts, who only bowed and smiled in reply.

"Idiot!" said the Queen, tossing her head impatiently; and turning to Alice, she went on, "What's your name, child?"

"My name is Alice, so please your Majesty," said Alice very politely; but she added, to herself, "Why, they're only a pack of cards, after all. I needn't be afraid of them!"

"And who are *these?*" said the Queen, pointing to the three gardeners who were lying round the rose-tree; for you see, as they were lying on their faces, and the pattern on their backs was the same as the rest of the pack, she could not tell whether they were gardeners, or soldiers, or courtiers, or three of her own children.

"How should *I* know?" said Alice, surprised at her own courage. "It's no business of *mine*." The Queen turned crimson with fury, and after glaring at her for a moment like a wild beast, began screaming, "Off with her head! Off—"

"Nonsense!" said Alice, very loudly and decidedly, and the Queen was silent.

The King laid his hand upon her arm, and timidly said, "Consider, my dear: she is only a child!"

The Queen turned angrily away from him, and said to the Knave, "Turn them over!"

The Knave did so, very carefully, with one foot.

"Get up!" said the Queen in a shrill, loud voice, and the three gardeners instantly jumped up, and began bowing to the King, the Queen, the royal children, and everybody else.

"Leave off that!" screamed the Queen. "You make me giddy." And then, turning to the rose-tree, she went on, "What *have* you been doing here?"

"May it please your Majesty," said Two, in a very humble tone, getting down on one knee as he spoke, "we were trying—"

"*I* see!" said the Queen, who had meanwhile been examining the roses. "Off with their heads!" and the procession moved on, three of the soldiers remaining behind to execute the unfortunate gardeners, who ran to Alice for protection.

"You shan't be beheaded!" said Alice, and she put them into a large flower-pot that stood near. The three soldiers wandered about for a minute or two, looking for them, and then quietly marched off after the others.

"Are their heads off?" shouted the Queen.

"Their heads are gone, if it please your Majesty!" the soldiers shouted in reply.

"That's right!" shouted the Queen. "Can you play croquet?"

The soldiers were silent, and looked at Alice, as the question was evidently meant for her.

"Yes!" shouted Alice.

"Come on then!" roared the Queen, and Alice joined the procession, wondering very much what would happen next.

"It's—it's a very fine day!" said a timid voice at her side. She was walking by the White Rabbit, who was peeping anxiously into her face.

"Very," said Alice: "where's the Duchess?"

"Hush! Hush!" said the Rabbit in a low, hurried tone. He looked anxiously over his shoulder as he spoke, and then raised himself upon tiptoe, put his mouth close to her ear, and whispered, "She's under sentence of execution."

"What for?" said Alice.

"Did you say 'What a pity?'" the Rabbit asked.

"No, I didn't," said Alice: "I don't think it's at all a pity. I said 'What for?'"

"She boxed the Queen's ears—" the Rabbit began. Alice gave a little scream of laughter. "Oh, hush!" the Rabbit whispered in a frightened tone. "The Queen will hear you! You see she came rather late, and the Queen said—"

"Get to your places!" shouted the Queen in a voice of thunder, and people began running about in all directions, tumbling up against each other: however, they got settled down in a minute or two, and the game began.

Alice thought she had never seen such a curious croquet-ground in her life: it was all ridges and furrows; the croquet-balls were live hedgehogs,[20] and the mallets live flamingoes, and the soldiers had to double themselves up and stand on their hands and feet to make the arches.

The chief difficulty Alice found at first was in managing her flamingo: she succeeded in getting its body tucked away, comfortably enough, under her arm, with its legs hanging down, but generally, just as she had got its neck nicely straightened out, and was going to give the hedgehog a blow with its head, it *would* twist itself round and look up into her face, with such a puzzled expression that she could not help bursting out laughing: and when she had got its head down, and was going to begin again, it was very provoking to find that the hedgehog had unrolled itself, and was in the act of crawling away: besides all this, there was generally a ridge or a furrow in the way wherever she wanted to send the hedgehog to, and, as the doubled-up soldiers were always getting up and walking off to other parts of the ground, Alice soon came to the conclusion that it was a very difficult game indeed.

The players all played at once without waiting for turns, quarrelling all the while, and fighting for the hedgehogs; and in a very short time the Queen was in a furious passion, and went stamping about, and shouting, "Off with his head!" or "Off with her head!" about once in a minute.

Alice began to feel very uneasy: to be sure, she had not as yet had any dispute with the Queen, but she knew that it might happen any minute, "and then," thought she, "what would become of me? They're dreadfully fond of beheading people here: the great wonder is that there's any one left alive!"

She was looking about for some way of escape, and wondering whether she could get away without being seen, when she noticed a curious appearance in the air: it puzzled her very much at first, but after watching it a minute or two she made it out to be a grin, and she said to herself, "It's the Cheshire Cat: now I shall have somebody to talk to."

"How are you getting on?" said the Cat, as soon as there was mouth enough for it to speak with.

Alice waited till the eyes appeared, and then nodded. "It's no use speaking to it," she thought, "till its ears have come, or at least one of them." In another minute the whole head appeared, and then Alice put down her flamingo, and began an account of the game, feeling very glad she had some one to listen to her. The Cat seemed to think that there was enough of it now in sight, and no more of it appeared.

"I don't think they play at all fairly," Alice began, in rather a complaining tone, "and they all quarrel so dreadfully one can't hear one's self speak—and they don't seem to have any rules in particular; at least, if there are, nobody attends to them—and you've no idea how confusing it is all the things being alive; for instance, there's the arch I've got to go through next walking about at the other end of the ground—and I should have croqueted the

---

20. Hedgehogs are harmless, porcupine-like animals which roll themselves into a tight ball when alarmed, hence their rôle here as croquet balls.

Queen's hedgehog just now, only it ran away when it saw mine coming!"

"How do you like the Queen?" said the Cat in a low voice.

"Not at all," said Alice: "she's so extremely—" Just then she noticed that the Queen was close behind her, listening: so she went on "—likely to win, that it's hardly worth while finishing the game."

The Queen smiled and passed on.

"Who *are* you talking to?" said the King, coming up to Alice, and looking at the Cat's head with great curiosity.

"It's a friend of mine—a Cheshire Cat," said Alice: "allow me to introduce it."

"I don't like the look of it at all," said the King: "however, it may kiss my hand if it likes."

"I'd rather not," the Cat remarked.

"Don't be impertinent," said the King, "and don't look at me like that!" He got behind Alice as he spoke.

"A cat may look at a king," said Alice. "I've read that in some book, but I don't remember where."

"Well, it must be removed," said the King very decidedly, and he called to the Queen, who was passing at the moment, "My dear! I wish you would have this cat removed!"

The Queen had only one way of settling all difficulties, great or small. "Off with his head!" she said without even looking round.

"I'll fetch the executioner myself," said the King eagerly, and he hurried off.

Alice thought she might as well go back and see how the game was going on, as she heard the Queen's voice in the distance, screaming with passion. She had already heard her sentence three of the players to be executed for having missed their turns, and she did not like the look of things at all, as the game was in such confusion that she never knew whether it was her turn or not. So she went off in search of her hedgehog.

The hedgehog was engaged in a fight with another hedgehog, which seemed to Alice an excellent opportunity for croqueting one of them with the other; the only difficulty was, that her flamingo was gone across to the other side of the garden, where Alice could see it trying in a helpless sort of way to fly up into a tree.

By the time she had caught the flamingo and brought it back, the fight was over, and both the hedgehogs were out of sight: "but it doesn't matter much," thought Alice, "as all the arches are gone from this side of the ground." So she tucked it away under her arm, that it might not escape again, and went back to have a little more conversation with her friend.

When she got back to the Cheshire Cat, she was surprised to find quite a large crowd collected round it: there was a dispute going on between the executioner, the King, and the Queen, who were all talking at once, while all the rest were quite silent, and looked very uncomfortable.

The moment Alice appeared, she was appealed to by all three to settle the question and they repeated their arguments to her, though, as they all spoke at once, she found it very hard to make out exactly what they said. The executioner's argument was, that you couldn't cut off a head unless there was a body to cut it off from: that he had never had to do such a thing before, and he wasn't going to begin at *his* time of life.

The King's argument was, that anything that had a head could be beheaded, and that you weren't to talk nonsense.

The Queen's argument was, that if something wasn't done about it in less than no time, she'd have everybody executed, all round. (It was this last remark that had made the whole party look so grave and anxious.)

Alice could think of nothing else to say but "It belongs to the Duchess: you'd better ask *her* about it."

"She's in prison," the Queen said to the executioner: "fetch her here." And the executioner went off like an arrow.

The Cat's head began fading away the moment he was gone, and, by the time he had come back with the Duchess, it had entirely disappeared: so the King and the executioner ran wildly up and down looking for it, while the rest of the party went back to the game.

9

THE MOCK TURTLE'S STORY

YOU can't think how glad I am to see you again, you dear old thing!" said the Duchess, as she tucked her arm affectionately into Alice's, and they walked off together.

Alice was very glad to find her in such a pleasant temper, and thought to herself that perhaps it was only the pepper that had made her so savage when they met in the kitchen. "When *I'm* a Duchess," she said to herself (not in a very hopeful tone though,) "I won't have any pepper in my kitchen *at all.* Soup does very well without. —Maybe it's always pepper that makes people hot-tempered," she went on, very much pleased at having found out a new kind of rule, "and vinegar that makes them sour—and camomile[21] that makes them bitter—and—and barley-sugar and such things that make children sweet-tempered. I only wish people knew *that:* then they wouldn't be so stingy about it, you know—"

She had quite forgotten the Duchess by this time, and was a little startled when she heard her voice close to her ear. "You're thinking about something, my dear, and that makes you forget to talk. I can't tell you just now what the moral of that is, but I shall remember it in a bit."

"Perhaps it hasn't one," Alice ventured to remark.

"Tut, tut, child!" said the Duchess. "Everything's got a moral, if only you can find it." And she squeezed herself up closer to Alice's side as she spoke.

Alice did not much like her keeping so close to her: first, because the Duchess was *very* ugly, and secondly, because she was exactly the right height to rest her chin on Alice's shoulder, and it was an uncomfortably sharp chin. However, she did not like to be rude, so she bore it as well as she could.

"The game's going on rather better now," she said, by way of keeping up the conversation a little.

"'Tis so," said the Duchess: "and the moral of that is—'Oh, 'tis love, 'tis love, that makes the world go round!'"

"Somebody said," Alice whispered, "that it's done by everybody minding their own business!"

"Ah well! It means much the same thing," said the Duchess, digging her sharp little chin into Alice's shoulder as she added, "and the moral of *that* is—'Take care of the sense, and the sounds will take care of themselves.'"[22]

"How fond she is of finding morals in things!" Alice thought to herself.

"I dare say you're wondering why I don't put my arm round your waist," said the Duchess after a pause: "the reason is, that I'm doubtful about the temper of your flamingo. Shall I try the experiment?"

"He might bite," Alice cautiously replied, not feeling at all anxious to have the experiment tried.

"Very true," said the Duchess: "flamingoes and mustard both bite. And the moral of that is—'Birds of a feather flock together.'"

"Only mustard isn't a bird," Alice remarked.

"Right as usual," said the Duchess: "what a clear way you have of putting things!"

"It's a mineral, I *think,*" said Alice.

"Of course it is," said the Duchess, who seemed ready to agree to everything that Alice said; "there's a large mustard-mine near here. And the moral of that is—'The more there is of mine, the less there is of yours.'"

"Oh, I know!" exclaimed Alice, who had not attended to this last remark, "it's a vegetable. It doesn't look like one, but it is."

"I quite agree with you," said the Duchess, "and the moral of that is—'Be what you would seem to be' —or, if you'd like it put more simply—'Never imagine yourself not to be otherwise than what it might appear to others that what you were or might have been was not otherwise than what you had been would have appeared to them to be otherwise.'"

"I think I should understand that better," Alice said very politely, "if I had it written down: but I can't quite follow it as you say it."

"That's nothing to what I could say if I chose," the Duchess replied in a pleased tone.

"Pray don't trouble yourself to say it any longer than that," said Alice.

"Oh, don't talk about trouble!" said the Duchess. "I make you a present of everything I've said as yet."

"A cheap sort of present!" thought Alice. "I'm

---

21. *camomile,* a bitter medicine used in Victorian times, extracted from a flower of the same name.

22. The Duchess' maxim is a pun on the English proverb, "Take care of the pence, and the pounds will take care of themselves."

glad they don't give birthday presents like that!" But she did not venture to say it out loud.

"Thinking again?" the Duchess asked, with another dig of her sharp little chin.

"I've a right to think," said Alice sharply, for she was beginning to feel a little worried.

"Just about as much right," said the Duchess, "as pigs have to fly: and the m—"

But here, to Alice's great surprise, the Duchess' voice died away, even in the middle of her favourite word "moral," and the arm that was linked into hers began to tremble. Alice looked up, and there stood the Queen in front of them, with her arms folded, frowning like a thunderstorm.

"A fine day, your Majesty!" the Duchess began in a low, weak voice.

"Now, I give you fair warning," shouted the Queen, stamping on the ground as she spoke; "either you or your head must be off, and that in about half no time! Take your choice!"

The Duchess took her choice, and was gone in a moment.

"Let's go on with the game," the Queen said to Alice, and Alice was too much frightened to say a word, but slowly followed her back to the croquet-ground.

The other guests had taken advantage of the Queen's absence, and were resting in the shade: however, the moment they saw her, they hurried back to the game, the Queen merely remarking that a moment's delay would cost them their lives.

All the time they were playing the Queen never left off quarrelling with the other players, and shouting "Off with his head!" or "Off with her head!" Those whom she sentenced were taken into custody by the soldiers, who of course had to leave off being arches to do this, so that by the end of half an hour or so there were no arches left, and all the players, except the King, the Queen, and Alice, were in custody, and under sentence of execution.

Then the Queen left off, quite out of breath, and said to Alice, "Have you seen the Mock Turtle yet?"

"No," said Alice. "I don't even know what a Mock Turtle is."

"It's the thing Mock Turtle Soup[23] is made from," said the Queen.

"I never saw one, or heard of one," said Alice.

"Come on, then," said the Queen, "and he shall tell you his history."

As they walked off together, Alice heard the King say in a low voice, to the company generally, "You are all pardoned." "Come, *that's* a good thing!" she said to herself, for she had felt quite unhappy at the number of executions the Queen had ordered.

They very soon came upon a Gryphon,[24] lying fast asleep in the sun. "Up, lazy thing!" said the Queen, "and take this young lady to see the Mock Turtle, and to hear his history. I must go back and see after some executions I have ordered"; and she walked off, leaving Alice alone with the Gryphon. Alice did not quite like the look of the creature, but on the whole she thought it would be quite as safe to stay with it as to go after that savage Queen: so she waited.

The Gryphon sat up and rubbed its eyes: then it watched the Queen till she was out of sight: then it chuckled. "What fun!" said the Gryphon, half to itself, half to Alice.

"What *is* the fun?" said Alice.

"Why, *she*," said the Gryphon. "It's all her fancy, that: they never executes nobody, you know. Come on!"

"Everybody says 'come on!' here," thought Alice, as she went slowly after it: "I never was so ordered about before in all my life, never!"

They had not gone far before they saw the Mock Turtle in the distance, sitting sad and lonely on a little ledge of rock, and, as they came nearer, Alice could hear him sighing as if his heart would break. She pitied him deeply.

"What is his sorrow?" she asked the Gryphon, and the Gryphon answered, very nearly in the same words as before, "It's all his fancy, that: he hasn't got no sorrow, you know. Come on!"

So they went up to the Mock Turtle, who looked at them with large eyes full of tears, but said nothing.

"This here young lady," said the Gryphon, "She wants for to know your history, she do."

"I'll tell it her," said the Mock Turtle in a deep, hollow tone: "sit down both of you, and don't speak a word till I've finished."

So they sat down, and nobody spoke for some minutes. Alice thought to herself, "I don't see how he can

---

23. Mock turtle soup is made from veal. One of Tenniel's original illustrations for *Alice in Wonderland* shows the Mock Turtle with the head, tail, and hooves of a calf, along with a sea-turtle's shell and flippers.

24. The Gryphon is a mythical beast, half lion and half eagle.

ever finish, if he doesn't begin." But she waited patiently.

"Once," said the Mock Turtle at last, with a deep sigh, "I was a real Turtle."

These words were followed by a very long silence, broken only by an occasional exclamation of "Hjckrrh!" from the Gryphon, and the constant heavy sobbing of the Mock Turtle. Alice was very nearly getting up and saying, "Thank you, sir, for your interesting story," but she could not help thinking there *must* be more to come, so she sat still and said nothing.

"When we were little," the Mock Turtle went on at last, more calmly, though still sobbing a little now and then, "we went to school in the sea. The master was an old Turtle—we used to call him Tortoise—"

"Why did you call him Tortoise, if he wasn't one?" Alice asked.

"We called him Tortoise because he taught us," said the Mock Turtle angrily; "really you are very dull!"

"You ought to be ashamed of yourself for asking such a simple question," added the Gryphon; and then they both sat silent and looked at poor Alice, who felt ready to sink into the earth. At last the Gryphon said to the Mock Turtle, "Drive on, old fellow! Don't be all day about it!" and he went on in these words: "Yes, we went to school in the sea, though you mayn't believe it—"

"I never said I didn't!" interrupted Alice.

"You did," said the Mock Turtle.

"Hold your tongue!" added the Gryphon, before Alice could speak again. The Mock Turtle went on.

"We had the best of educations—in fact, we went to school every day—"

"*I've* been to a day-school too," said Alice; "you needn't be so proud as all that."

"With extras?" asked the Mock Turtle a little anxiously.

"Yes," said Alice, "we learned French and music."

"And washing?" said the Mock Turtle.

"Certainly not!" said Alice indignantly.

"Ah! Then yours wasn't a really good school," said the Mock Turtle in a tone of great relief. "Now at *ours* they had at the end of the bill, 'French, music, *and washing*—extra.'"[25]

25. English boarding schools frequently charged extra for courses not in the normal curriculum, such as music and French, as well as for laundry done at the school.

"You couldn't have wanted it much," said Alice; "living at the bottom of the sea."

"I couldn't afford to learn it," said the Mock Turtle with a sigh. "I only took the regular course."

"What was that?" enquired Alice.

"Reeling and Writhing, of course, to begin with," the Mock Turtle replied: "and then the different branches of Arithmetic—Ambition, Distraction, Uglification, and Derision."

"I never heard of 'Uglification,'" Alice ventured to say. "What is it?"

The Gryphon lifted up both its paws in surprise. "Never heard of uglifying!" it exclaimed. "You know what to beautify is, I suppose?"

"Yes," said Alice, doubtfully: "it means—to—make—anything—prettier."

"Well then," the Gryphon went on, "if you don't know what to uglify is, you *are* a simpleton.'"

Alice did not feel encouraged to ask any more questions about it, so she turned to the Mock Turtle, and said, "What else had you to learn?"

"Well, there was Mystery," the Mock Turtle replied, counting off the subjects on his flappers,—"Mystery, ancient and modern, with Seography,—then Drawling—the Drawling-master was an old conger-eel, that used to come once a week: *he* taught us Drawling, Stretching, and Fainting in Coils."

"What was *that* like?" said Alice.

"Well, I can't show it to you, myself," the Mock Turtle said: "I'm too stiff. And the Gryphon never learnt it."

"Hadn't time," said the Gryphon: "I went to the Classical master, though. He was an old crab, *he* was."

"I never went to him," the Mock Turtle said with a sigh: "he taught Laughing and Grief, they used to say."

"So he did, so he did," said the Gryphon, sighing in his turn, and both creatures hid their faces in their paws.

"And how many hours a day did you do lessons?" said Alice, in a hurry to change the subject.

"Ten hours the first day," said the Mock Turtle: "nine the next, and so on."

"What a curious plan!" exclaimed Alice.

"That's the reason they're called lessons," the Gryphon remarked: "because they lessen from day to day."

This was quite a new idea to Alice, and she

thought it over a little before she made her next remark. "Then the eleventh day must have been a holiday?"

"Of course it was," said the Mock Turtle.

"And how did you manage on the twelfth?" Alice went on eagerly.

"That's enough about lessons," the Gryphon interrupted in a very decided tone: "tell her something about the games now."

10

THE LOBSTER QUADRILLE

THE Mock Turtle sighed deeply, and drew the back of one flapper across his eyes. He looked at Alice and tried to speak, but for a minute or two sobs choked his voice. "Same as if he had a bone in his throat," said the Gryphon, and it set to work shaking him and punching him in the back. At last the Mock Turtle recovered his voice, and, with tears running down his cheeks, he went on again:—

"You may not have lived much under the sea—" ("I haven't," said Alice)—"and perhaps you were never introduced to a lobster—" (Alice began to say "I once tasted—" but checked herself hastily, and said, "No, never")—"so you can have no idea what a delightful thing a Lobster-Quadrille[26] is!"

"No, indeed," said Alice. "What sort of a dance is it?"

"Why," said the Gryphon, "you first form into a line along the seashore—"

"Two lines!" cried the Mock Turtle. "Seals, turtles, salmon, and so on: then, when you've cleared all the jelly-fish out of the way—"

"*That* generally takes some time," interrupted the Gryphon.

"—you advance twice—"

"Each with a lobster as a partner!" cried the Gryphon.

26. The quadrille was a kind of square dance fashionable in Victorian England.

"Of course," the Mock Turtle said: "advance twice, set to partners—"

"—change lobsters, and retire in same order," continued the Gryphon.

"Then, you know," the Mock Turtle went on, "you throw the—"

"The Lobsters!" shouted the Gryphon, with a bound into the air.

"—as far out to sea as you can—"

"Swim after them!" screamed the Gryphon.

"Turn a somersault in the sea!" cried the Mock Turtle, capering wildly about.

"Change lobsters again!" yelled the Gryphon at the top of its voice.

"Back to land again, and—that's all the first figure," said the Mock Turtle, suddenly dropping his voice, and the two creatures, who had been jumping about like mad things all this time, sat down again very sadly and quietly, and looked at Alice.

"It must be a very pretty dance," said Alice timidly.

"Would you like to see a little of it?" said the Mock Turtle.

"Very much indeed," said Alice.

"Come, let's try the first figure!" said the Mock Turtle to the Gryphon. "We can do it without lobsters, you know. Which shall sing?"

"Oh, *you* sing," said the Gryphon. "I've forgotten the words." So they began solemnly dancing round and round Alice, every now and then treading on her toes when they passed too close, and waving their fore-paws to mark the time, while the Mock Turtle sang this, very slowly and sadly:—

"Will you walk a little faster?" said a whiting to a snail,[27]
"There's a porpoise close behind us, and he's treading on my tail.
See how eagerly the lobsters and the turtles all advance!
They are waiting on the shingle—will you come and join the dance?
Will you, won't you, will you, won't you, will you join the dance?
Will you, won't you, will you, won't you, won't you join the dance?

27. See page 482.

"You can really have no notion how delightful it will be
When they take us up and throw us, with the lobsters, out to sea!"
But the snail replied "Too far, too far!" and gave a look askance—
Said he thanked the whiting kindly, but he would not join the dance.
Would not, could not, would not, could not, would not join the dance.
Would not, could not, would not, could not, could not join the dance.

"What matters it how far we go?" his scaly friend replied,
"There is another shore, you know, upon the other side.
The further off from England the nearer is to France—
Then turn not pale, beloved snail, but come and join the dance.
Will you, won't you, will you, won't you, will you join the dance?
Will you, won't you, will you, won't you, won't you join the dance?"

"Thank you, it's a very interesting dance to watch," said Alice, feeling very glad that it was over at last; "and I do so like that curious song about the whiting!"

"Oh, as to the whiting," said the Mock Turtle, "they—you've seen them, of course?"

"Yes," said Alice, "I've often seen them at dinn—" she checked herself hastily.

"I don't know where Dinn may be," said the Mock Turtle, "but if you've seen them so often, of course you know what they're like."

"I believe so," Alice replied thoughtfully. "They have their tails in their mouths;—and they're all over crumbs."[28]

"You're wrong about the crumbs," said the Mock Turtle: "crumbs would all wash off in the sea. But they *have* their tails in their mouths; and the reason is—" here the Mock Turtle yawned and shut his eyes.—"Tell her about the reason and all that," he said to the Gryphon.

"The reason is," said the Gryphon, "that they *would* go with the lobsters to the dance. So they got thrown out to sea. So they had to fall a long way. So they got their tails fast in their mouths. So they couldn't get them out again. That's all."

"Thank you," said Alice, "it's very interesting. I never knew so much about a whiting before."

"I can tell you more than that, if you like," said the Gryphon. "Do you know why it's called a whiting?"

"I never thought about it," said Alice. "Why?"

"It does the boots and shoes," the Gryphon replied very solemnly.

Alice was thoroughly puzzled. "Does the boots and shoes!" she repeated in a wondering tone.

"Why, what are *your* shoes done with?" said the Gryphon. "I mean, what makes them so shiny?"

Alice looked down at them, and considered a little before she gave her answer. "They're done with blacking, I believe."

"Boots and shoes under the sea," the Gryphon went on in a deep voice, "are done with whiting. Now you know."

"And what are they made of?" Alice asked in a tone of great curiosity.

"Soles and eels, of course," the Gryphon replied rather impatiently: "any shrimp could have told you that."

"If I'd been the whiting," said Alice, whose thoughts were still running on the song, "I'd have said to the porpoise, 'Keep back, please: we don't want *you* with us!'"

"They were obliged to have him with them," the Mock Turtle said: "no wise fish would go anywhere without a porpoise."

"Wouldn't it really?" said Alice in a tone of great surprise.

"Of course not," said the Mock Turtle: "why, if a fish came to *me*, and told me he was going a journey, I should say 'With what porpoise?'"

"Don't you mean 'purpose?'" said Alice.

"I mean what I say," the Mock Turtle replied in an offended tone. And the Gryphon added "Come, let's hear some of *your* adventures."

"I could tell you my adventures—beginning from this morning," said Alice a little timidly: "but it's no use going back to yesterday, because I was a different person then."

"Explain all that," said the Mock Turtle.

"No, no! the adventures first," said the Gryphon in

28. Whiting, a fish related to cod, was displayed for sale by Victorian fish-vendors with its tail inserted through its eye socket. Whiting is often cooked in bread crumbs. Hence Alice's observations.

an impatient tone: "explanations take such a dreadful time."

So Alice began telling them her adventures from the time when she first saw the White Rabbit: she was a little nervous about it just at first, the two creatures got so close to her, one on each side, and opened their eyes and mouths so *very* wide, but she gained courage as she went on. Her listeners were perfectly quiet till she got to the part about her repeating "*You are old, Father William,*" to the Caterpillar, and the words all coming different, and then the Mock Turtle drew a long breath, and said, "That's very curious."

"It's all about as curious as it can be," said the Gryphon.

"It all came different!" the Mock Turtle repeated thoughtfully. "I should like to hear her try and repeat something now. Tell her to begin." He looked at the Gryphon as if he thought it had some kind of authority over Alice.

"Stand up and repeat '*'Tis the voice of the sluggard,*'" said the Gryphon.

"How the creatures order one about, and make one repeat lessons!" thought Alice, "I might just as well be at school at once." However, she got up, and began to repeat it, but her head was so full of the Lobster-Quadrille, that she hardly knew what she was saying, and the words came very queer indeed:—

"'Tis the voice of the lobster; I heard him declare,[29]
'You have baked me too brown, I must sugar my
hair.'
As a duck with its eyelids, so he with his nose
Trims his belt and his buttons, and turns out his
toes.
When the sands are all dry, he is gay as a lark,
And will talk in contemptuous tones of the Shark:
But, when the tide rises and sharks are around,
His voice has a timid and tremulous sound."

"That's different from what *I* used to say when I was a child," said the Gryphon.

"Well, I never heard it before," said the Mock Turtle; "but it sounds uncommon nonsense."

Alice said nothing: she had sat down again with her face in her hands, wondering if anything would *ever* happen in a natural way again.

"I should like to have it explained," said the Mock Turtle.

"She can't explain it," said the Gryphon hastily. "Go on with the next verse."

"But about his toes?" the Mock Turtle persisted. "How *could* he turn them out with his nose, you know?"

"It's the first position in dancing," Alice said; but she was dreadfully puzzled by the whole thing, and longed to change the subject.

"Go on with the next verse," the Gryphon repeated impatiently: "it begins '*I passed by his garden.*'"

Alice did not dare to disobey, though she felt sure it would all come wrong, and she went on in a trembling voice:—

"I passed by his garden, and marked, with one eye,
How the Owl and the Panther were sharing a pie:
The Panther took pie-crust, and gravy, and meat,
While the Owl had the dish as its share of the treat.
When the pie was all finished, the Owl, as a boon,
Was kindly permitted to pocket the spoon:
While the Panther received knife and fork with a
growl,
And concluded the banquet by—"

"What *is* the use of repeating all that stuff," the Mock Turtle interrupted, "if you don't explain it as you go on? It's by far the most confusing thing *I* ever heard!"

"Yes, I think you'd better leave off," said the Gryphon, and Alice was only too glad to do so.

"Shall we try another figure of the Lobster-Quadrille?" the Gryphon went on. "Or would you like the Mock Turtle to sing you a song?"

"Oh, a song please, if the Mock Turtle would be so kind," Alice replied, so eagerly that the Gryphon said, in a rather offended tone, "Hm! No accounting for tastes! Sing her '*Turtle Soup,*' will you, old fellow?"

The Mock Turtle sighed deeply, and began, in a voice sometimes choked with sobs, to sing this:—

"Beautiful Soup, so rich and green,[30]
Waiting in a hot tureen!
Who for such dainties would not stoop?
Soup of the evening, beautiful Soup!

29. See page 482.

30. See page 484.

Soup of the evening, beautiful Soup!
Beau—ootiful Soo—oop!
Beau—ootiful Soo—oop!
Soo—oop of the e—e—evening,
Beautiful, beautiful Soup!

"Beautiful Soup! Who cares for fish,
Game, or any other dish?
Who would not give all else for two p
ennyworth only of beautiful Soup?
Pennyworth only of beautiful Soup?
Beau—ootiful Soo—oop!
Beau—ootiful Soo—oop!
Soo—oop of the e—e—evening,
Beautiful, beauti—FUL SOUP!"

"Chorus again!" cried the Gryphon, and the Mock Turtle had just begun to repeat it, when a cry of "The trial's beginning!" was heard in the distance.

"Come on!" cried the Gryphon, and, taking Alice by the hand, it hurried off, without waiting for the end of the song.

"What trial is it?" Alice panted as she ran, but the Gryphon only answered "Come on!" and ran the faster while more and more faintly came, carried on the breeze that followed them, the melancholy words:—

"Soo—oop of the e—e—evening,
Beautiful, beautiful Soup!"

11

WHO STOLE THE TARTS?

THE King and Queen of Hearts were seated on their throne when they arrived, with a great crowd assembled about them—all sorts of little birds and beasts, as well as the whole pack of cards: the Knave was standing before them, in chains, with a soldier on each side to guard him; and near the King was the White Rabbit, with a trumpet in one hand, and a scroll of parchment in the other. In the very middle of the court was a table, with a large dish of tarts upon it: they looked so good, that it made Alice quite hungry to look at them—"I wish they'd get the trial done," she thought, "and hand round the refreshments!" But there seemed to be no chance of this, so she began looking at everything about her to pass away the time.

Alice had never been in a court of justice before, but she had read about them in books, and she was quite pleased to find that she knew the name of nearly everything there. "That's the judge," she said to herself, "because of his great wig."

The judge, by the way, was the King, and as he wore his crown over the wig, he did not look at all comfortable, and it was certainly not becoming.

"And that's the jury-box," thought Alice, "and those twelve creatures," (she was obliged to say "creatures," you see, because some of them were animals, and some were birds,) "I suppose they are the jurors." She said this last word two or three times over to herself, being rather proud of it: for she thought, and rightly too, that very few little girls of her age knew the meaning of it at all. However, "jurymen" would have done just as well.

The twelve jurors were all writing very busily on slates. "What are they doing?" Alice whispered to the Gryphon. "They can't have anything to put down yet, before the trial's begun."

"They're putting down their names," the Gryphon whispered in reply, "for fear they should forget them before the end of the trial."

"Stupid things!" Alice began in a loud indignant voice, but she stopped herself hastily, for the White Rabbit cried out, "Silence in the court!" and the King put on his spectacles and looked anxiously round, to make out who was talking.

Alice could see, as well as if she were looking over their shoulders, that all the jurors were writing down "stupid things!" on their slates, and she could even make out that one of them didn't know how to spell "stupid," and that he had to ask his neighbour to tell him. "A nice muddle their slates'll be in before the trial's over!" thought Alice.

One of the jurors had a pencil that squeaked. This, of course, Alice could *not stand*, and she went round the court and got behind him, and very soon found an opportunity of taking it away. She did it so quickly that the poor little juror (it was Bill, the Lizard) could not make out at all what had become of it; so, after hunting all about for it, he was obliged to write with one finger for the rest of the day; and this was of very little use, as it left no mark on the slate.

"Herald, read the accusation!" said the King.

On this the White Rabbit blew three blasts on the trumpet, and then unrolled the parchment scroll, and read as follows:—

"The Queen of Hearts, she made some tarts,
All on a summer day:
The Knave of Hearts, he stole those tarts,
And took them quite away!"

"Consider your verdict," the King said to the jury.

"Not yet, not yet!" the Rabbit hastily interrupted. "There's a great deal to come before that!"

"Call the first witness," said the King; and the White Rabbit blew three blasts on the trumpet, and called out, "First witness!"

The first witness was the Hatter. He came in with a teacup in one hand, and a piece of bread-and-butter in the other. "I beg pardon, your Majesty," he began, "for bringing these in: but I hadn't quite finished my tea when I was sent for."

"You ought to have finished," said the King. "When did you begin?"

The Hatter looked at the March Hare, who had followed him into the court, arm-in-arm with the Dormouse. "Fourteenth of March, I *think* it was," he said.

"Fifteenth," said the March Hare.

"Sixteenth," added the Dormouse.

"Write that down," the King said to the jury, and the jury eagerly wrote down all three dates on their slates, and then added them up, and reduced the answer to shillings and pence.

"Take off your hat," the King said to the Hatter.

"It isn't mine," said the Hatter.

"Stolen!" the King exclaimed, turning to the jury, who instantly made a memorandum of the fact.

"I keep them to sell," the Hatter added as an explanation: "I've none of my own. I'm a hatter."

Here the Queen put on her spectacles, and began staring hard at the Hatter, who turned pale and fidgeted.

"Give your evidence," said the King; "and don't be nervous, or I'll have you executed on the spot."

This did not seem to encourage the witness at all: he kept shifting from one foot to the other, looking uneasily at the Queen, and in his confusion he bit a large piece out of his teacup instead of the bread-and-butter.

Just at this moment Alice felt a very curious sensation, which puzzled her a good deal until she made out what it was: she was beginning to grow larger again, and she thought at first she would get up and leave the court; but on second thoughts she decided to remain where she was as long as there was room for her.

"I wish you wouldn't squeeze so," said the Dormouse, who was sitting next to her. "I can hardly breathe."

"I can't help it," said Alice very meekly: "I'm growing."

"You've no right to grow *here,*" said the Dormouse.

"Don't talk nonsense," said Alice more boldly: "you know you're growing too."

"Yes, but *I* grow at a reasonable pace," said the Dormouse: "not in that ridiculous fashion." And he got up very sulkily and crossed over to the other side of the court.

All this time the Queen had never left off staring at the Hatter, and, just as the Dormouse crossed the court, she said to one of the officers at the court, "Bring me the list of the singers in the last concert!" on which the wretched Hatter trembled so, that he shook both his shoes off.[31]

"Give your evidence," the King repeated angrily, "or I'll have you executed, whether you're nervous or not."

"I'm a poor man, your Majesty," the Hatter began in a trembling voice, "and I hadn't but just begun my tea—not above a week or so—and what with the bread-and-butter getting so thin—and the twinkling of the tea—"

"The twinkling of *what?"* said the King.

"It *began* with the tea," the Hatter replied.

"Of course twinkling begins with a T!" said the King sharply. "Do you take me for a dunce? Go on!"

"I'm a poor man," the Hatter went on, "and most things twinkled after that—only the March Hare said—"

"I didn't!" the March Hare interrupted in a great hurry.

"You did!" said the Hatter.

---

31. The Hatter trembles because he "murdered the time" (i.e. forgot the meter) when he sang before the Queen. (See his report of the affair in Chapter 7.)

"I deny it!" said the March Hare.

"He denies it," said the King: "leave out that part."

"Well, at any rate, the Dormouse said—" the Hatter went on, looking anxiously round to see if he would deny it too: but the Dormouse denied nothing, being fast asleep.

"After that," continued the Hatter, "I cut some more bread-and-butter—"

"But what did the Dormouse say?" one of the jury asked.

"That I can't remember," said the Hatter.

"You *must* remember," remarked the King, "or I'll have you executed."

The miserable Hatter dropped his teacup and bread-and-butter, and went down on one knee. "I'm a poor man, your Majesty," he began.

"You're a *very* poor *speaker,*" said the King.

Here one of the guinea-pigs cheered, and was immediately suppressed by the officers of the court.

(As that is rather a hard word, I will just explain to you how it was done. They had a large canvas bag, which tied up at the mouth with strings: into this they slipped the guinea-pig, head first, and then sat upon it.)

"I'm glad I've seen that done," thought Alice. "I've so often read in the newspapers, at the end of trials, 'There was some attempt at applause, which was immediately suppressed by the officers of the court,' and I never understood what it meant till now."

"It that's all you know about it, you may stand down," continued the King.

"I can't go no lower," said the Hatter: "I'm on the floor as it is."

"Then you may *sit* down," the King replied.

Here the other guinea-pig cheered, and was suppressed.

"Come, that finishes the guinea-pigs!" thought Alice. "Now we shall get on better."

"I'd rather finish my tea," said the Hatter with an anxious look at the Queen, who was reading the list of singers.

"You may go," said the King, and the Hatter hurriedly left the court, without even waiting to put his shoes on.

"—and just take his head off outside," the Queen added to one of the officers; but the Hatter was out of sight before the officer could get to the door.

"Call the next witness!" said the King.

The next witness was the Duchess' cook. She carried the pepper-box in her hand, and Alice guessed who it was, even before she got into the court, by the way the people near the door began sneezing all at once.

"Give your evidence," said the King.

"Shan't," said the cook.

The King looked anxiously at the White Rabbit, who said in a low voice, "Your Majesty must cross-examine *this* witness."

"Well, if I must, I must," the King said with a melancholy air, and, after folding his arms and frowning at the cook till his eyes were nearly out of sight, he said in a deep voice, "What are tarts made of?"

"Pepper, mostly," said the cook.

"Treacle," said a sleepy voice behind her.

"Collar that Dormouse!" the Queen shrieked out. "Behead that Dormouse! Turn that Dormouse out of court! Suppress him! Pinch him! Off with his whiskers!"

For some minutes the whole court was in confusion, getting the Dormouse turned out, and, by the time they had settled down again, the cook had disappeared.

"Never mind!" said the King, with an air of great relief. "Call the next witness." And he added in an under-tone to the Queen, "Really my dear, *you* must cross-examine the next witness. It quite makes my forehead ache!"

Alice watched the White Rabbit as he fumbled over the list, feeling very curious to see what the next witness would be like, "—for they haven't got much evidence *yet,*" she said to herself. Imagine her surprise, when the White Rabbit read out, at the top of his shrill little voice, the name "Alice!"

FOLON

12

ALICE'S EVIDENCE

HERE!" cried Alice, quite forgetting in the flurry of the moment how large she had grown in the last few minutes, and she jumped up in such a hurry that she tipped over the jury-box with the edge of her skirt, upsetting all the jurymen onto the heads of the crowd below, and there they lay sprawling about, reminding her very much of a globe of goldfish she had accidentally upset the week before.

"Oh, I *beg* your pardon!" she exclaimed in a tone of great dismay, and began picking them up again as quickly as she could, for the accident of the goldfish kept running in her head, and she had a vague sort of idea that they must be collected at once and put back into the jury-box, or they would die.

"The trial cannot proceed," said the King in a very grave voice, "until all the jurymen are back in their proper places—*all*," he repeated with great emphasis, looking hard at Alice as he said so.

Alice looked at the jury-box, and saw that, in her haste, she had put the Lizard in head downwards, and the poor little thing was waving its tail about in a melancholy way, being quite unable to move. She soon got it out again, and put it right; "not that it signifies much," she said to herself; "I should think it would be *quite* as much use in the trial one way up as the other."

As soon as the jury had a little recovered from the shock of being upset, and their slates and pencils had been found and handed back to them, they set to work very diligently to write out a history of the accident, all except the Lizard, who seemed too much overcome to do anything but sit with its mouth open, gazing up into the roof of the court.

"What do you know about this business?" the King said to Alice.

"Nothing," said Alice.

"Nothing *whatever?*" persisted the King.

"Nothing whatever," said Alice.

"That's very important," the King said, turning to the jury. They were just beginning to write this down on their slates, when the White Rabbit interrupted: "*Un*important, your Majesty means, of course," he said in a very respectful tone, but frowning and making faces at him as he spoke.

"*Un*important, of course, I meant," the King hastily said, and went on to himself in an undertone, "important—unimportant—unimportant—important—" as if he were trying which word sounded best.

Some of the jury wrote it down "important," and some "unimportant." Alice could see this, as she was near enough to look over their slates; "but it doesn't matter a bit," she thought to herself.

At this moment the King, who had been for some time busily writing in his note-book, called out "Silence!" and read out from his book, "Rule Forty-two. *All persons more than a mile high to leave the court.*"

Everybody looked at Alice.

"*I'm* not a mile high," said Alice.

"You are," said the King.

"Nearly two miles high," added the Queen.

"Well, I shan't go at any rate," said Alice; "besides, that's not a regular rule: you invented it just now."

"It's the oldest rule in the book," said the King.

"Then it ought to be Number One," said Alice.

The King turned pale, and shut his notebook hastily. "Consider your verdict," he said to the jury, in a low trembling voice.

"There's more evidence to come yet, please your Majesty," said the White Rabbit, jumping up in a great hurry; "this paper has just been picked up."

"What's in it?" said the Queen.

"I haven't opened it yet," said the White Rabbit, "but it seems to be a letter, written by the prisoner to—to somebody."

"It must have been that," said the King, "unless it was written to nobody, which isn't usual, you know."

"Who is it directed to?" said one of the jurymen.

"It isn't directed at all," said the White Rabbit; "in fact, there's nothing written on the *outside*." He unfolded the paper as he spoke, and added, "it isn't a letter after all: it's a set of verses."

"Are they in the prisoner's handwriting?" asked another of the jurymen.

"No, they're not," said the White Rabbit, "and that's the queerest thing about it." (The jury all looked puzzled.)

"He must have imitated somebody else's hand," said the King. (The jury all brightened up again.)

"Please your Majesty," said the Knave: "I didn't

write it, and they can't prove I did: there's no name signed at the end."

"If you didn't sign it," said the King, "that only makes the matter worse. You *must* have meant some mischief, or else you'd have signed your name like an honest man."

There was a general clapping of hands at this: it was the first really clever thing the King had said that day.

"That *proves* his guilt," said the Queen.

"It proves nothing of the sort!" said Alice. "Why, you don't even know what they're about!"

"Read them," said the King.

The White Rabbit put on his spectacles. "Where shall I begin, please your Majesty?" he asked.

"Begin at the beginning," the King said, gravely, "and go on till you come to the end: then stop."

These were the verses the White Rabbit read:—

"They told me you had been to her,
And mentioned me to him:
She gave me a good character,
But said I could not swim.

He sent them word I had not gone
(We know it to be true):
If she should push the matter on,
What would become of you?

I gave her one, they gave him two,
You gave us three or more;
They all returned from him to you,
Though they were mine before.

If I or she should chance to be
Involved in this affair,
He trusts to you to set them free,
Exactly as we were.

My notion was that you had been
(Before she had this fit)
An obstacle that came between
Him, and ourselves, and it.

Don't let him know she liked them best,
For this must ever be
A secret, kept from all the rest,
Between yourself and me."

"That's the most important piece of evidence we've heard yet," said the King, rubbing his hands; "so now let the jury—"

"If any one of them can explain it," said Alice, (she had grown so large in the last few minutes that she wasn't a bit afraid of interrupting him,) "I'll give him sixpence. *I* don't believe there's an atom of meaning in it."

The jury all wrote down on their slates, "*She* doesn't believe there's an atom of meaning in it," but none of them attempted to explain the paper.

"If there's no meaning in it," said the King, "that saves a world of trouble, you know, as we needn't try to find any. And yet I don't know," he went on, spreading out the verses on his knee, and looking at them with one eye; "I seem to see some meaning in them, after all. '*—said I could not swim—*' you can't swim, can you?" he added, turning to the Knave.

The Knave shook his head sadly. "Do I look like it?" he said (which he certainly did *not*, being made entirely of cardboard).

"All right, so far," said the King, and he went on muttering over the verses to himself: "'*We know it to be true—*' that's the jury of course—'*I gave her one, they gave him two—*' why, that must be what he did with the tarts, you know—"

"But it goes on '*they all returned from him to you*,'" said Alice.

"Why, there they are!" said the King triumphantly, pointing to the tarts on the table. "Nothing can be clearer than that. Then again—'*before she had this fit—*' you never had fits, my dear, I think?" he said to the Queen.

"Never!" said the Queen furiously, throwing an inkstand at the Lizard as she spoke.

(The unfortunate little Bill had left off writing on his slate with one finger, as he found it made no mark; but he now hastily began again, using the ink, that was trickling down his face, as long as it lasted.)

"Then the words don't *fit* you," said the King, looking round the court with a smile. There was a dead silence.

"It's a pun!" the King added in an angry tone, and everybody laughed. "Let the jury consider their verdict," the King said, for about the twentieth time that day.

"No, no!" said the Queen. "Sentence first—verdict afterwards."

"Stuff and nonsense!" said Alice loudly. "The idea of having the sentence first!"

FOLON

"Hold your tongue!" said the Queen, turning purple.

"I won't!" said Alice.

"Off with her head!" the Queen shouted at the top of her voice. Nobody moved.

"Who cares for you?" said Alice, (she had grown to her full size by this time). "You're nothing but a pack of cards!"

At this the whole pack rose up into the air, and came flying down upon her; she gave a little scream, half of fright and half of anger, and tried to beat them off, and found herself lying on the bank, with her head in the lap of her sister, who was gently brushing away some dead leaves that had fluttered down from the trees on to her face.

"Wake up, Alice dear!" said her sister; "why, what a long sleep you've had!"

"Oh, I've had such a curious dream!" said Alice, and she told her sister, as well as she could remember, all these strange Adventures of hers that you have just been reading about; and when she had finished, her sister kissed her, and said, "It *was* a curious dream, dear, certainly: but now run in to your tea; it's getting late." So Alice got up and ran off, thinking while she ran, as well she might, what a wonderful dream it had been.

But her sister sat still just as she left her, leaning her head on her hand, watching the setting sun, and thinking of little Alice and all her wonderful Adventures, till she too began dreaming after a fashion, and this was her dream:—

First, she dreamed of little Alice herself:—once again the tiny hands were clasped upon her knee, and the bright eager eyes were looking up into hers —she could hear the very tones of her voice, and see that queer little toss of her head, to keep back the wandering hair that *would* always get into her eyes—and still as she listened, or seemed to listen, the whole place around her became alive with the strange creatures of her little sister's dream.

The long grass rustled at her feet as the White Rabbit hurried by—the frightened Mouse splashed his way through the neighbouring pool—she could hear the rattle of the teacups as the March Hare and his friends shared their never-ending meal, and the shrill voice of the Queen ordering off her unfortunate guests to execution—once more the pig-baby was sneezing on the Duchess' knee, while plates and dishes crashed around it—once more the shriek of the Gryphon, the squeaking of the Lizard's slate-pencil, and the choking of the suppressed guinea-pigs, filled the air, mixed up with the distant sob of the miserable Mock Turtle.

So she sat on, with closed eyes, and half believed herself in Wonderland, though she knew she had but to open them again and all would change to dull reality—the grass would be only rustling in the wind, and the pool rippling to the waving of the reeds—the rattling teacups would change to tinkling sheep-bells, and the Queen's shrill cries to the voice of the shepherd boy—and the sneeze of the baby, the shriek of the Gryphon, and all the other queer noises, would change (she knew) to the confused clamour of the busy farm-yard—while the lowing of the cattle in the distance would take the place of the Mock Turtle's heavy sobs.

Lastly, she pictured to herself how this same little sister of hers would, in the aftertime, be herself a grown woman; and how she would keep, through all her riper years, the simple and loving heart of her childhood: and how she would gather about her other little children, and make *their* eyes bright and eager with many a strange tale, perhaps even with the dream of Wonderland of long-ago: and how she would feel with all their simple sorrows, and find a pleasure in all their simple joys, remembering her own child-life, and the happy summer days.

THE END

NOTES

2. The poems and songs parodied by Carroll were well known to his contemporary readers. Victorian children were often required to memorize them as part of their lessons. The original of the parody on page 444 is a moralistic poem by Isaac Watts (1674–1748), titled "Against Idleness and Mischief." It runs as follows:

How doth the little busy bee
  Improve each shining hour
And gather honey all the day
  From every opening flower!

How skillfully she builds her cell!
  How neat she spreads her wax!
And labours hard to store it well
  With the sweet food she makes.

In works of labour or of skill,
  I would be busy too;
For Satan finds some mischief still
  For idle hands to do.

In books, or work, or healthful play
  Let my first years be passed,
That I may give for every day
  Some good account at last.

11. The verses on page 454 are a parody of Robert Southey's (1774–1843) didactic poem, "The Old Man's Comforts and How He Gained Them."

"You are old, father William," the young man cried,
"The few locks which are left you are grey;
You are hale, father William, a hearty old man;
Now tell me the reason, I pray."

"In the days of my youth," father William replied,
"I remember'd that youth would fly fast,
And abus'd not my health and my vigour at first,
That I never might need them at last."

"You are old, father William," the young man cried,
"And pleasures with youth pass away.
And yet you lament not the days that are gone;
Now tell me the reason, I pray."

"In the days of my youth," father William replied,
"I remember'd that youth could not last;
I thought of the future, whatever I did,
That I never might grieve for the past."

"You are old, father William," the young man cried,
"And life must be hast'ning away;
You are cheerful and love to converse upon death;
Now tell me the reason, I pray."

"I am cheerful, young man," father William replied,
"Let the cause thy attention engage;
In the days of my youth I remember'd my God!
And He hath not forgotten my age."

12. The verses on page 458 are a parody of a poem attributed to David Bates, a nineteenth-century versifier from Philadelphia. The original was titled "Speak Gently." Below are several stanzas selected from it:

Speak gently! It is better far
  To rule by love than fear;
Speak gently; let no harsh words mar
  The good we might do here!

Speak gently! Love doth whisper low
  The vows that true hearts bind;
And gently Friendship's accents flow;
  Affection's voice is kind.

Speak gently to the little child!
  Its love be sure to gain;
Teach it in accents soft and mild;
  It may not long remain.

Speak gently to the young, for they
  Will have enough to bear;
Pass through this life as best they may,
  'Tis full of anxious care!

27. The song of the Mock Turtle is patterned on, and parodies the first line of a poem by Mary Howitt, "The Spider and the Fly." The first stanza of the original reads:

"Will you walk into my parlour?" said the spider to the fly.
"'Tis the prettiest little parlour that ever you did spy.
The way into my parlour is up a winding stair,
And I've got many curious things to show when you are
  there."
"Oh, no, no," said the little fly, "to ask me is in vain.
For who goes up your winding stair can ne'er come down
  again."

29. Alice's poem is a parody of a moralistic poem by Isaac Watts, "The Sluggard," which reads in part as follows:

'Tis the voice of the sluggard; I heard him complain,
"You have wak'd me too soon, I must slumber again."
As the door on its hinges, so he on his bed,

On this page are a few of the original illustrations for *Alice in Wonderland,* drawn by John Tenniel, a cartoonist on the staff of the British humor magazine *Punch.* He worked closely with Lewis Carroll, and his interpretations of the characters have defined the way most readers visualize them. Since then, however, many other artists—including Arthur Rackham, N. C. Wyeth, and Salvador Dali—have pictured the characters in a variety of styles.

The illustrations in this volume were painted especially for it by the young Belgian artist Jean Michel Folon.

Turns his sides and his shoulders and his heavy head.

"A little more sleep, and a little more slumber,"
Thus he wastes half his days, and his hours without number,
And when he gets up, he sits folding his hands,
Or walks about sauntering, or trifling he stands.

I pass'd by his garden, and saw the wild brier,
The thorn and the thistle grow broader and higher;
The clothes that hang on him are turning to rags;
And his money still wastes till he starves or he begs.

30. The Mock Turtle's paean to real turtle soup is a parody of a popular contemporary song, "Star of the Evening," with words and music by James Sayles. The first verse of the original runs as follows:

Beautiful star in heav'n so bright,
Softly falls thy silv'ry light,
As thou movest from earth afar,
Star of the evening, beautiful star.

CHORUS:
Beautiful star,
Beautiful star,
Star of the evening, beautiful star.

DISCUSSION

1. Various critics of *Alice in Wonderland* have interpreted Alice's troubles with her variations in size, her confusion and forgetfulness, her slips of the tongue, etc., as representative of the "problems of growing up." Argue for or against such an interpretation, using the following questions as guidelines:

(a) Specifically, what types of problems in communication and self-control does she experience?

(b) Do any aspects of these problems have symbolic overtones? (For example, what do Alice's troubles with the golden key, her struggles to get through the small door into the beautiful garden, suggest?)

(c) In what instances does she muse over or struggle with questions about her identity? How are these questions answered?

(d) Does Alice seem to gain in self-control as the story progresses? (Is she, for instance, more sure of herself, more socially adept, in her second encounter with the Duchess on the croquet field than when she first met her in the kitchen?)

(e) Would you go so far as to say that *Alice* is primarily a story of "growing up"? Would you deny such a statement altogether?

2. Wonderland is full of improbabilities: the hierarchy of men and animals is reversed; the rules of time, space, orderly sequence, and cause and effect are broken; events and conversations sometimes have little pattern or sense. This state of affairs has led more than one interpreter to suggest that Alice's dream is actually a "nightmare" vision of a purposeless and chaotic universe which threatens and contradicts the conscious and seemingly logical assumptions we live by. Does *Alice in Wonderland* have this darker aspect, or is it merely a story of a child's innocent travels through a whimsical but harmless realm? Can you identify any points in the story where the chaos of Wonderland actually threatens Alice?

3. How might the White Rabbit, the Frog-Footman, the Pigeon, the Caterpillar, and the Mock Turtle be satirical reflections of certain human characteristics or tendencies?

4. Which of all the remarkable characters in Wonderland does Alice feel most comfortable with? Why?

5. (a) *Alice in Wonderland* has been called a view of the incomprehensible adult world as seen through the eyes of a child. To what extent is Alice childlike? Is there anything in her behavior that seems precocious?

(b) To what extent is Alice the obedient, polite, prim and proper model of Victorian girlhood? Does she ever break the rules of proper behavior? Does Carroll at any point reveal a critical attitude toward contemporary standards of child-rearing? How?

6. What aspects of the trial scene in the last two chapters seem most pointed as social satire? Are the satirical elements increased or decreased by Alice's naivete?

7. Psychoanalytic critics are fond of remarking that the male characters in Wonderland are generally weak and timid, dominated by the female characters. Which would you list among the "weakest" and "strongest" characters? Does your listing bear out such an interpretation? Into which category do you put Alice? Who dominates her? Whom does she dominate? Do these roles shift?

8. Is the Queen of Hearts merely a harmless blusterer, or do her actions and words hint at something more ominous?

9. A parody is defined as a composition imitating another, usually serious, work with intent to ridicule or criticize. The success of a parody depends largely on the cleverness with which the imitator has used a form similar to the original to convey an entirely different (and often irreverent) meaning. Using this definition as a point of departure, choose the one parody in *Alice* which you think is most successful, and explain why.

10. "You're nothing but a pack of cards!" Alice exclaims at the end of the story, and up to this point the reader has perhaps forgotten that most of the characters in the last four chapters are really nothing but animated playing cards. What devices has Carroll used to give them such successful animation? What is there about their actions and speech that makes them convincing? Which among them is the most fully characterized?

11. Compare the poem recited by the White Rabbit in Chapter 12 with "Jabberwocky," which appears in *Through the Looking Glass*. Does either poem finally make any kind of sense? Why might one poem make some sort of sense and the other none at all? What linguistic elements contribute to the sense or nonsense of each?

JABBERWOCKY

'T was brillig, and the slithy toves
  Did gyre and gimble in the wabe:
All mimsy were the borogoves,
  And the mome raths outgrabe.

"Beware the Jabberwock, my son!
  The jaws that bite, the claws that catch!
Beware the Jubjub bird, and shun
  The frumious Bandersnatch!"

He took his vorpal sword in hand:
  Long time the manxome foe he sought—
So rested he by the Tumtum tree,
  And stood awhile in thought.

And, as in uffish thought he stood,
  The Jabberwock, with eyes of flame,
Came whiffling through the tulgey wood,
  And burbled as it came!

One, two! One, two! And through and through
  The vorpal blade went snicker-snack!
He left it dead, and with its head
  He went galumphing back.

"And hast thou slain the Jabberwock?
  Come to my arms, my beamish boy!
O frabjous day! Callooh! Callay!"
  He chortled in his joy.

'T was brillig, and the slithy toves
  Did gyre and gimble in the wabe:
All mimsy were the borogoves,
  And the mome raths outgrabe.

12. Alice's dream and all the elements of her fantasy world are "framed" by scenes from the real world. In the beginning Alice grows drowsy and falls asleep by the river bank; in the end she is awakened by some dead leaves that have fluttered down onto her face. What relationships are there between these elements of the real world and Alice's dream world? How does Carroll explain one in terms of the other, and what devices does he use to submerge his heroine into the realm of dreams and then extract her? Do you find his transition effective? Is it at all like the experience of sleeping and waking?

13. If there is anything that can be called plot in *Alice in Wonderland* it concerns Alice's attempts to enter the beautiful garden. How does the garden look to her when she first looks at it longingly through the small door? What is it like when she finally comes to inspect it closely? What might the garden symbolize?

EXTENSIONS (1)

Puns and other forms of word-play

A professor of English is once supposed to have boasted to friends (during a five-course dinner) that he had a most unusual collection of literature. He had, he said, Burns in the kitchen, Dryden in the laundry, Lamb in the pantry, Frost in the refrigerator, and De la Mare in the barn. Whereupon one of his guests rose from the table, remarking that he had had enough and "was groaning board" as well as suffering from "authoritis." "Wait!" cried the professor, "We have not Donne!" Thereupon everybody got in his Wordsworth, and the remainder of the evening, as afterwards described by one survivor of it, was "cruel and unusual punishment."

The same verdict might be given to Chapters 9 and 10 of *Alice in Wonderland,* which contain as prickly a thicket of puns as one could hope to find anywhere in English literature.

Puns have been called the lowest form of wit. Yet among the dabblers in this form of word-play are Shakespeare and James Joyce. The tradition of the pun, in fact, has its roots in the earliest English literature (notably the Anglo-Saxon riddles), and continues to the present—John Lennon, the Liverpool musician and wit, being one of the most visible modern practitioners.

Puns are a form of word-play made technically possible by the abundance of homonyms in the English language—words which sound alike but have variant meanings (and sometimes spellings). Puns are not restricted to established vocabulary, and often make use of nonsense verbiage, portmanteau (blend) words, dialect, and other vagaries of speech. Anything is fair game in punning, so long as there is a recognizable sound (some would say *unsound*) connection between the double or multiple meanings. Here is an example that runs the whole gamut:

NICELY NICELY CLIVE

by John Lennon

To Clive Barrow it was just an ordinary day nothing unusual or strange about it, everything quite novel, nothing outstanley just another day but to Roger it was something special, a day amongst days . . . a red lettuce day . . . because Roger was getting married and as he dressed that morning he thought about the gay batchelor soups he'd had with all his pals. And Clive said nothing. To Roger everything was different, wasn't this the day his Mother had told him about, in his best suit and all that, grimming and shakeing hands, people tying boots and ricebudda on his car.

To have and to harm . . . till death duty part . . . he knew it all off by hertz. Clive Barrow seemed oblivious. Roger could visualise Anne in her flowing weddy drag, being wheeled up the aisle, smiling a blessing. He had butterfield in his stomarce as he fastened his bough tie and brushed his hairs. "I hope I'm doing the right thing" he thought looking in the mirror, "Am I good enough for her?" Roger need not have worried because he was. "Should I have flowers all round the spokes?" said Anne polishing her foot rest. "Or should I keep it syble?" she continued looking down on her grain haired Mother.

"Does it really matter?" repaid her Mother wearily wiping her sign. "He won't be looking at your spokes anyway." Anne smiled the smile of someone who's seen a few laughs.

Then luckily Anne's father came home from sea and cancelled the husband.

First cousin to the pun is the malapropism—the use of an inappropriate word which bears some similarity to the correct one. Malapropisms also have a long history; Shakespeare, for instance, delighted in making his comic characters abuse language. The prime practitioner of this form of tongue-tied derangement, and the source of its name, is Mrs. Malaprop in Richard Sheridan's play *The Rivals* (1775). She describes one character as being "as headstrong as an allegory on the banks of the Nile," and calls another "the pineapple of politeness." When Lewis Carroll wrote the scene in which the Mock Turtle and the Gryphon discuss their schooling, perhaps he had this monologue by Mrs. Malaprop in mind:

MRS. MALAPROP. Observe me, Sir Anthony. I would by no means wish a daughter of mine to be a progeny of learning; I don't think so much learning becomes a young woman; for instance, I would never let her meddle with Greek, or Hebrew, or Algebra, or simony, or fluxions, or paradoxes, or such inflammatory branches of learning—neither would it be necessary for her to handle any of your mathematical, astronomical, diabolical instruments.—But, Sir Anthony, I would send her, at nine years old, to a boarding-school, in order to learn a little ingenuity and artifice. Then, sir, she should have a supercilious knowledge in accounts;—and as she grew up, I would have her instructed in geometry, that she might know something of the contagious countries;—but above all, Sir Anthony, she should be mistress of orthodoxy, that she might not misspell, and mispronounce words so shamefully as girls usually do; and likewise that she might reprehend the true meaning of what she is saying. This, Sir Anthony, is what I would have a woman know;—and I don't think there is a superstitious article in it. □

EXTENSIONS (2)

Alice and Gulliver

The scene in which Alice grows to Gargantuan proportions and finds herself wedged inside the White Rabbit's house calls to mind the scene from Jonathan Swift's *Gulliver's Travels,* when Gulliver wakes up in Lilliput. The abnormal size of both Alice and Gulliver is not the only similarity. Gulliver, like Alice, is trapped and almost totally immobilized; both are pelted with missiles, both bellow and send their captors flying; both scenes are suffused in confused action and noise.

. . . When I awaked, it was just daylight. I attempted to rise, but was not able to stir: for, as I happened to lie on my back, I found my arms and legs were strongly fastened on each side to the ground; and my hair, which was long and thick, tied down in the same manner. I likewise felt several slender ligatures across my body, from my armpits to my thighs. I could only look upwards; the sun began to grow hot, and the light offended mine eyes. I heard a confused noise about me, but in the posture I lay, could see nothing except the sky.

In a little time I felt something alive moving on my left leg, which advancing gently forward over my breast, came almost up to my chin; when bending eyes downwards as much as I could, I perceived it to be a human creature not six inches high, with a bow and arrow in his hands, and a quiver at his back. In the meantime, I felt at least forty more of the same kind (as I conjectured) following the first.

I was in the utmost astonishment, and roared so loud, that they all run back in a fright; and some of them, as I was afterwards told, were hurt with the falls they got by leaping from my sides upon the ground. However, they soon returned; and one of them, who ventured so far as to get a full sight of my face, lifting up his hands and eyes by way of admiration, cried out in a shrill, but distinct voice, "Hekina degul"; the others repeated the same words several times, but I then knew not what they meant.

I lay all this while, as the reader may believe, in great uneasiness; at length, struggling to get loose, I had the fortune to break the strings, and wrench out the pegs that fastened my left arm to the ground: for by lifting it up to my face, I discovered the methods they had taken to bind me; and, at the same time, with a violent pull, which gave me excessive pain, I a little loosened the strings that tied down my hair on the left side; so that I was just able to turn my head about two inches. But the creatures ran off a second time, before I could seize them; whereupon there was a great shout in a very shrill accent; and after it ceased, I heard one of them cry aloud, "Tolgo Phonac"; when in an instant, I felt above an hundred arrows discharged on my left hand, which pricked me like so many needles. . . . □

EXTENSIONS (3)

From REMINISCENCES OF CHILDHOOD

by Dylan Thomas

The memories of childhood have no order, and so I remember that never was there such a dame school as ours, so firm and kind and smelling of galoshes, with the sweet and fumbled music of the piano lessons drifting down from upstairs to the lonely schoolroom, where only the sometimes tearful wicked sat over undone sums, or to repeat a little crime—the pulling of a little girl's hair during geography, the sly shin kick under the table during English literature. Behind the school was a narrow lane where only the oldest and boldest threw pebbles at windows, scuffled and boasted, fibbed about their relations—

"My father's got a chauffeur."

"What's he want a chauffeur for? He hasn't got a car."

"My father's the richest man in town."

"My father's the richest man in Wales."

"My father owns the world."

And swapped gob-stoppers for slings, old knives for marbles, kite strings for foreign stamps.

The lane was always the place to tell your secrets; if you did not have any, you invented them. Occasionally now I dream that I am turning out of school into the lane of confidences when I say to the boys of my class, "At last, I have a real secret."

"What is it—what is it?"

"I can fly."

And when they do not believe me, I flap my arms and slowly leave the ground only a few inches at first, then gaining air until I fly waving my cap level with the upper windows of the school, peering in until the mistress at the piano screams and the metronome falls to the ground and stops, and there is no more time.

And I fly over the trees and chimneys of my town, over the dockyards skimming the masts and funnels, over Inkerman Street, Sebastopol Street, and the street where all the women wear men's caps, over the trees of the everlasting park, where a brass band shakes the leaves and sends them showering down on to the nurses and the children, the cripples and the idlers, and the gardeners, and the shouting boys: over the yellow seashore, and the stone-chasing dogs, and the old men, and the singing sea.

The memories of childhood have no order, and no end. □

BETTMANN ARCHIVE, INC.

BIOGRAPHY

Charles Lutwidge Dodgson
1832 / 1898

While he is known today primarily as Lewis Carroll, the author of *Alice in Wonderland, Through the Looking-Glass,* and *The Hunting of the Snark,* Charles Lutwidge Dodgson was for the greater part of his life a Lecturer in Mathematics at Christ Church, one of the colleges of Oxford University. He was also a member of the Anglican clergy, though he never served a parish. He was the author of abstruse works on mathematics and logic, booklets of games and puzzles, some light poetry, and a variety of witty pamphlets on contemporary affairs at Oxford.

Shortly after the first publication of *Alice in Wonderland* in 1865, so the anecdote runs, Queen Victoria, who was delighted with the story, graciously suggested that the author might dedicate his next book to her. He did, but it was a mathematical work titled *An Elementary Treatise on Determinants.* The anecdote is challenged by at least one Carroll biographer, but it underscores the fact that Dodgson's life was almost wholly academic.

Yet there were other facets to Dodgson's donnish existence. He was an expert photographer who took exceptional portraits of children and adults at a time when photography was a new art. He was personally acquainted with Tennyson, Rossetti, Thackeray, Ruskin, and other notables of the day. He regularly walked a dozen miles before retiring. But his favorite pastime was the entertainment of young children, particularly young girls, towards whom he demonstrated strong and intensely idealistic affection. Retiring academic though he was, there was in him a vein of childlike playfulness, as on one occasion when he was invited to tea with some of his young friends. Punctual as always, attired in clerical black, he mistakenly entered the house next door where a group of elderly ladies were taking afternoon tea. He flung open the door and entered on all fours, growling, hoping to surprise the children. Realizing his mistake, he rose, bowed to the astonished ladies, and departed without a word of apology.

Alice in Wonderland grew out of Dodgson's affection for one little girl, Alice Liddell, daughter of the Dean of Christ Church. On July 4, 1862, Dodgson and a friend, the Reverend Duckworth, took three of the Liddell girls, Alice among them, boating on the river Thames. As they rowed along, Dodgson began to tell extemporaneous stories of Alice's adventures underground; at the end of the day, Alice Liddell asked him to write out the adventures for her. By the end of 1863 he had finished a hand-written copy with his own illustrations, which he presented to her. Two years later, at the urging of friends, he revised and polished the original, added several chapters, commissioned illustrations by John Tenniel, and published the story under the pen name of Lewis Carroll.

Early reviews of *Alice in Wonderland* were mixed, but it soon became popular and has not been out of print since. It represented a remarkable departure from the generally sober and moralistic children's literature of the time. Throughout the rest of his life Dodgson only grudgingly admitted his link with Lewis Carroll, writer of whimsical stories, although he continued to publish other works under that name. Alice, of course, grew up and married (she became Mrs. Hargreaves, and raised three sons), but the memory of that sunny afternoon on the river Thames remained with Dodgson to give purpose and poignancy to his stories, which he doubtless considered only a minor part of his life's work.

THE TWENTIETH CENTURY

(OVERLEAF) "KING AND QUEEN," BY HENRY MOORE. FROM HENRY MOORE BY JOHN HEDGECOE/HENRY MOORE, THOMAS NELSON AND SONS, LTD.

THE TWENTIETH CENTURY

chapter nine

MODERN SHORT STORIES

PHOTO BY ROBERT AMFT

YOUTH

by Joseph Conrad

THIS could have occurred nowhere but in England, where men and sea interpenetrate, so to speak—the sea entering into the life of most men, and the men knowing something or everything about the sea, in the way of amusement, of travel, or of breadwinning.

We were sitting round a mahogany table that reflected the bottle, the claret-glasses, and our faces as we leaned on our elbows. There was a director of companies, an accountant, a lawyer, Marlow, and myself. The director had been a *Conway* boy, the accountant had served four years at sea, the lawyer—a fine crusted Tory, High Churchman, the best of old fellows, the soul of honour—had been chief officer in the P. & O. service in the good old days when mail-boats were square-rigged at least on two masts, and used to come down the China Sea before a fair monsoon with stun'-sails set alow and aloft. We all began life in the merchant service. Between the five of us there was the strong bond of the sea, and also the fellowship of the craft, which no amount of enthusiasm for yachting, cruising, and so on can give, since one is only the amusement of life and the other is life itself.

Marlow (at least I think that is how he spelt his name) told the story, or rather the chronicle, of a voyage:—

"Yes, I have seen a little of the Eastern seas; but what I remember best is my first voyage there. You fellows know there are those voyages that seem ordered for the illustration of life, that might stand for a symbol of existence. You fight, work, sweat, nearly kill yourself, sometimes do kill yourself, trying to accomplish something—and you can't. Not from any fault of yours. You simply can do nothing, neither great nor little—not a thing in the world—not even marry an old maid, or get a wretched 600-ton cargo of coal to its port of destination.

"It was altogether a memorable affair. It was my first voyage to the East, and my first voyage as second mate; it was also my skipper's first command. You'll admit it was time. He was sixty if a day; a little man, with a broad, not very straight back, with bowed shoulders and one leg more bandy than the other, he had that queer twisted-about appearance you see so often in men who work in the fields. He had a nutcracker face—chin and nose trying to come together over a sunken mouth—and it was framed in iron-gray fluffy hair, that looked like a chin-strap of cotton-wool sprinkled with coal-dust. And he had blue eyes in that old face of his, which were amazingly like a boy's, with that candid expression some quite common men preserve to the end of their days by a rare internal gift of simplicity of heart and rectitude of soul. What induced him to accept me was a wonder. I had come out of a crack Australian clipper, where I had been third officer, and he seemed to have a prejudice against crack clippers as aristocratic and high-toned. He said to me, 'You know, in this ship you will have to work.' I said I had to work in every ship I had ever been in. 'Ah, but this is different, and you gentlemen out of them big ships; . . . but there! I dare say you will do. Join to-morrow.'

"I joined to-morrow. It was twenty-two years ago; and I was just twenty. How time passes! It was one of the happiest days of my life. Fancy! Second mate for the first time—a really responsible officer! I wouldn't have thrown up my new billet for a fortune. The mate looked me over carefully. He was also an old chap, but of another stamp. He had a Roman nose, a snow-white, long beard, and his name was Mahon, but he insisted that it should be pronounced Mann. He was well connected; yet there was something wrong with his luck, and he had never got on.

"As to the captain, he had been for years in coasters, then in the Mediterranean, and last in the West Indian trade. He had never been round the Capes. He could just write a kind of sketchy hand, and didn't care for writing at all. Both were thorough good seamen of course, and between those two old chaps I felt like a small boy between two grandfathers.

"The ship also was old. Her name was the *Judea.* Queer name, isn't it? She belonged to a man Wilmer, Wilcox—some name like that; but he has been bankrupt and dead these twenty years or more, and his name don't matter. She had been laid up in Shadwell basin for ever so long. You may imagine her state. She was all rust, dust, grime—soot aloft, dirt on deck. To me it was like coming out of a palace into a ruined cottage. She was about 400 tons, had a primitive windlass, wooden latches to the doors, not a bit of brass about her, and a big square stern. There was on it, below her name in big letters, a lot of scrollwork, with the gilt off, and some sort of a coat of arms, with the motto 'Do or Die' underneath. I remember it took my fancy immensely. There was a touch of romance in it, something that made me love the old thing—something that appealed to my youth!

"We left London in ballast—sand ballast—to load a cargo of coal in a northern port for Bankok. Bankok! I thrilled. I had been six years at sea, but had only seen Melbourne and Sydney, very good places, charming places in their way—but Bankok!

"We worked out of the Thames under canvas, with a North Sea pilot on board. His name was Jermyn, and he dodged all day long about the galley drying his handkerchief before the stove. Apparently he never slept. He was a dismal man, with a perpetual tear sparkling at the end of his nose, who either had been in trouble, or was in trouble, or expected to be in trouble—couldn't be happy unless something went wrong. He mistrusted my youth, my common-sense, and my seamanship, and made a point of showing it in a hundred little ways. I dare say he was right. It seems to me I knew very little then, and I know not much more now; but I cherish a hate for that Jermyn to this day.

"We were a week working up as far as Yarmouth Roads, and then we got into a gale—the famous October gale of twenty-two years ago. It was wind, lightning, sleet, snow, and a terrific sea. We were flying light, and you may imagine how bad it was when I tell you we had smashed bulwarks and a flooded deck. On the second night she shifted her ballast into the lee bow, and by that time we had been blown off somewhere on the Dogger Bank. There was nothing for it but go below with shovels and try to right her, and there we were in that vast hold, gloomy like a cavern, the tallow dips stuck and flickering on the beams, the gale howling above, the ship tossing about like mad on her side; there we all were, Jermyn, the captain, every one, hardly able to keep our feet, engaged on that gravedigger's work, and trying to toss shovelfuls of wet sand up to windward. At every tumble of the ship you could see vaguely in the dim light men falling down with a great flourish of shovels. One of the ship's boys (we had two), impressed by the weirdness of the scene, wept as if his heart would break. We could hear him blubbering somewhere in the shadows.

"On the third day the gale died out, and by and by a north-country tug picked us up. We took sixteen days in all to get from London to the Tyne! When we got into dock we had lost our turn for loading, and they hauled us off to a tier where we remained for a month. Mrs. Beard (the captain's name was Beard) came from Colchester to see the old man. She lived on board. The crew of runners had left, and there remained only the officers, one boy, and the steward, a mulatto who answered to the name of Abraham. Mrs. Beard was an old woman, with a face all wrinkled and ruddy like a winter apple, and the figure of a young girl. She caught sight of me once, sewing on a button, and insisted on having my shirts to repair. This was something different from the captains' wives I had known on board crack clippers. When I brought her the shirts, she said: 'And the socks? They want mending, I am sure, and John's—Captain Beard's—things are all in order now. I would be glad of something to do.' Bless the old woman. She overhauled my outfit for me, and meantime I read for the first time *Sartor Resartus* and Burnaby's *Ride to Khiva*. I didn't understand much of the first then; but I remember I preferred the soldier to the philosopher at the time; a preference which life has only confirmed. One was a man, and the other was either more—or less. However, they are both dead and Mrs. Beard is dead, and youth, strength, genius, thoughts, achievements, simple hearts—all die. . . . No matter.

"They loaded us at last. We shipped a crew. Eight able seamen and two boys. We hauled off one evening to the buoys at the dock-gates, ready to go out, and with a fair prospect of beginning the voyage next day. Mrs. Beard was to start for home by a late train. When the ship was fast we went to tea. We sat rather silent through the meal—Mahon, the old couple, and I. I finished first, and slipped away for a smoke, my cabin being in a deck-house just against the poop. It was high water, blowing fresh with a drizzle; the double dock-gates were opened, and the steam-colliers were going in and out in the darkness with their lights burning bright, a great plashing of propellers, rattling of winches, and a lot of hailing on the pier-heads. I watched the procession of head-lights gliding high and of green lights gliding low in the night, when suddenly a red gleam flashed at me, vanished, came into view again, and remained. The fore-end of a steamer loomed up close. I shouted down the cabin, 'Come up, quick!' and then heard a startled voice saying afar in the dark, 'Stop her, sir.' A bell jingled. Another voice cried warningly, 'We are going right into that barque, sir.' The answer to this was a gruff 'All right,' and the next thing was a heavy crash as the steamer struck a glancing blow with the bluff of her bow about our fore-rigging. There was a moment of confusion, yelling, and running about. Steam roared. Then somebody was heard saying, 'All clear, sir.' . . . 'Are you all right?' asked the gruff voice. I had jumped forward to see the damage, and hailed back, 'I think so.' 'Easy astern,' said the gruff voice. A bell jingled. 'What steamer is that?' screamed Mahon. By that time she was no more to us than a bulky shadow manœuvring a little way off. They shouted at us some name—a woman's name, Miranda or Melissa—or some such thing. 'This means another month in this beastly hole,' said Mahon to me, as we peered with lamps about the splintered bulwarks and broken braces. 'But where's the captain?'

"We had not heard or seen anything of him all that time. We went aft to look. A doleful voice arose hailing somewhere in the middle of the dock, '*Judea* ahoy!' . . . How the devil did he get there? . . .

'Hallo!' we shouted. 'I am adrift in our boat without oars,' he cried. A belated water-man offered his services, and Mahon struck a bargain with him for half-a-crown to tow our skipper alongside; but it was Mrs. Beard that came up the ladder first. They had been floating about the dock in that mizzly cold rain for nearly an hour. I was never so surprised in my life.

"It appears that when he heard my shout 'Come up' he understood at once what was the matter, caught up his wife, ran on deck, and across, and down into our boat, which was fast to the ladder. Not bad for a sixty-year-old. Just imagine that old fellow saving heroically in his arms that old woman—the woman of his life. He set her down on a thwart and was ready to climb back on board when the painter came adrift somehow, and away they went together. Of course in the confusion we did not hear him shouting. He looked abashed. She said cheerfully, 'I suppose it does not matter my losing the train now?' 'No, Jenny—you go below and get warm,' he growled. Then to us: 'A sailor has no business with a wife—I say. There I was, out of the ship. Well, no harm done this time. Let's go and look at what that fool of a steamer smashed.'

"It wasn't much, but it delayed us three weeks. At the end of that time, the captain being engaged with his agents, I carried Mrs. Beard's bag to the railway-station and put her all comfy into a third-class carriage. She lowered the window to say, 'You are a good young man. If you see John—Captain Beard—without his muffler at night, just remind him from me to keep his throat well wrapped up.' 'Certainly, Mrs. Beard,' I said. 'You are a good young man: I noticed how attentive you are to John—to Captain—' The train pulled out suddenly; I took my cap off to the old woman: I never saw her again. . . . Pass the bottle.

"We went to sea next day. When we made that start for Bankok we had been already three months out of London. We had expected to be a fortnight or so—at the outside.

"It was January, and the weather was beautiful—the beautiful sunny winter weather that has more charm than in the summer-time, because it is unexpected, and crisp, and you know it won't, it can't, last long. It's like a windfall, like a godsend, like an unexpected piece of luck.

"It lasted all down the North Sea, all down Channel; and it lasted till we were three hundred miles or so to the westward of the Lizards: then the wind went round to the sou'west and began to pipe up. In two days it blew a gale. The *Judea*, hove to, wallowed on the Atlantic like an old candle-box. It blew day after day: it blew with spite, without interval, without mercy, without rest. The world was nothing but an immensity of great foaming waves rushing at us, under a sky low enough to touch with the hand and dirty like a smoked ceiling. In the stormy space surrounding us there was as much flying spray as air. Day after day and night after night there was nothing round the ship but the howl of the wind, the tumult of the sea, the noise of water pouring over her deck. There was no rest for her and no rest for us. She tossed, she pitched, she stood on her head, she sat on her tail, she rolled, she groaned, and we had to hold on while on deck and cling to our bunks when below, in a constant effort of body and worry of mind.

"One night Mahon spoke through the small window of my berth. It opened right into my very bed, and I was lying there sleepless, in my boots, feeling as though I had not slept for years, and could not if I tried. He said excitedly—

"'You got the sounding-rod in here, Marlow? I can't get the pumps to suck. By God! it's no child's play.'

"I gave him the sounding-rod and lay down again, trying to think of various things—but I thought only of the pumps. When I came on deck they were still at it, and my watch relieved at the pumps. By the light of the lantern brought on deck to examine the sounding-rod I caught a glimpse of their weary, serious faces. We pumped all the four hours. We pumped all night, all day, all the week—watch and watch. She was working herself loose, and leaked badly—not enough to drown us at once, but enough to kill us with the work at the pumps. And while we pumped the ship was going from us piecemeal: the bulwarks went, the stanchions were torn out, the ventilators smashed, the cabin-door burst in. There was not a dry spot in the ship. She was being gutted bit by bit. The long-boat changed, as if by magic, into matchwood where she stood in her gripes. I had lashed her myself, and was rather proud of my handiwork, which had withstood so long the malice of the sea. And we pumped. And there was no break in the weather. The sea was white like a sheet of foam, like a caldron of boiling milk; there was not a break in the clouds, no—not the size of a man's hand—no, not for so much as ten seconds. There was for us no sky, there were for us no stars, no sun, no universe—nothing but angry clouds and an infuriated sea. We pumped watch and watch, for dear life; and it seemed to last for months, for years, for all eternity, as though we had been dead and gone to a hell for sailors. We forgot the day of the week, the name of the month, what year it was, and whether we had ever been ashore. The sails blew away, she lay broadside on under a weather-cloth, the ocean poured over her, and we did not care. We turned those handles, and had the eyes of idiots. As soon as we had crawled on deck I used to take a round turn with a rope about the men, the pumps, and the mainmast, and we turned, we turned incessantly, with the water to our waists, to our necks, over our heads. It was all one. We had forgotten how it felt to be dry.

"And there was somewhere in me the thought: By Jove! this is the deuce of an adventure—something you read about; and it is my first voyage as second mate—and I am only twenty—and here I am lasting it out as well as any of these men, and keeping my chaps up to the mark. I was pleased. I would not have given up the experience for worlds. I had moments of exultation. Whenever the old dismantled craft pitched heavily with her counter high in the air, she seemed to me to throw up, like an appeal, like a defiance, like a cry to the clouds without mercy, the words written on her stern: '*Judea,* London. Do or Die.'

"O youth! The strength of it, the faith of it, the imagination of it! To me she was not an old rattletrap carting about the world a lot of coal for a freight —to me she was the endeavour, the test, the trial of life. I think of her with pleasure, with affection, with regret—as you would think of someone dead you have loved. I shall never forget her. . . . Pass the bottle.

"One night when tied to the mast, as I explained, we were pumping on, deafened with the wind, and without spirit enough in us to wish ourselves dead, a heavy sea crashed aboard and swept clean over us. As soon as I got my breath I shouted, as in duty bound, 'Keep on, boys!' when suddenly I felt something hard floating on deck strike the calf of my leg. I made a grab at it and missed. It was so dark we could not see each other's faces within a foot—you understand.

"After that thump that ship kept quiet for a while, and the thing, whatever it was, struck my leg again. This time I caught it—and it was a saucepan. At first, being stupid with fatigue and thinking of nothing but the pumps, I did not understand what I had in my hand. Suddenly it dawned upon me, and I shouted, 'Boys, the house on deck is gone. Leave this, and let's look for the cook.'

"There was a deck-house forward, which contained the galley, the cook's berth, and the quarters of the crew. As we had expected for days to see it swept away, the hands had been ordered to sleep in the cabin—the only safe place in the ship. The steward, Abraham, however, persisted in clinging to his berth, stupidly, like a mule—from sheer fright I believe, like an animal that won't leave a stable falling in an earthquake. So we went to look for him. It was chancing death, since once out of our lashings we were as exposed as if on a raft. But we went. The house was shattered as if a shell had exploded inside. Most of it had gone overboard—stove, men's quarters, and their property, all was gone; but two posts, holding a portion of the bulkhead to which Abraham's bunk was attached, remained as if by a miracle. We groped in the ruins and came upon this, and there he was, sitting in his bunk, surrounded by foam and wreckage, jabbering cheerfully to himself. He was out of his mind; completely and for ever mad, with this sudden shock coming upon the fag-end of his endurance. We snatched him up, lugged him aft, and pitched him head-first down the cabin companion. You understand there was no time to carry him down with infinite precautions and wait to see how he got on. Those below would pick him up at the bottom of the stairs all right. We were in a hurry to go back to the pumps. That business could not wait. A bad leak is an inhuman thing.

"One would think that the sole purpose of that fiendish gale had been to make a lunatic of that poor devil of a mulatto. It eased before morning, and next day the sky cleared, and as the sea went down the leak took up. When it came to bending a fresh set of sails the crew demanded to put back—and really there was nothing else to do. Boats gone, decks swept clean, cabin gutted, men without a stitch but what they stood in, stores spoiled, ship strained. We put her head for home, and—would you believe it? The wind came east right in our teeth. It blew fresh, it blew continuously. We had to beat up every inch of the way, but she did not leak so badly, the water keeping comparatively smooth. Two hours' pumping in every four is no joke—but it kept her afloat as far as Falmouth.

"The good people there live on casualties of the sea, and no doubt were glad to see us. A hungry crowd of shipwrights sharpened their chisels at the sight of that carcass of a ship. And, by Jove! they had pretty pickings off us before they were done. I fancy the owner was already in a tight place. There were delays. Then it was decided to take part of the cargo out and caulk her topsides. This was done, the repairs finished, cargo reshipped; a new crew came on board, and we went out—for Bankok. At the end of a week we were back again. The crew said they weren't going to Bankok—a hundred and fifty days' passage—in a something hooker that wanted pumping eight hours out of the twenty-four; and the nautical papers inserted again the little paragraph: '*Judea*. Barque. Tyne to Bankok; coals; put back to Falmouth leaky and with crew refusing duty.'

"There were more delays—more tinkering. The owner came down for a day, and said she was as right as a little fiddle. Poor old Captain Beard looked like the ghost of a Geordie skipper—through the worry and humiliation of it. Remember he was sixty, and it was his first command. Mahon said it was a foolish business, and could end badly. I loved the ship more than ever, and wanted awfully to get to Bankok. To Bankok! Magic name, blessed name. Mesopotamia wasn't a patch on it. Remember I was twenty, and it was my first second-mate's billet, and the East was waiting for me.

"We went out and anchored in the outer roads with a fresh crew—the third. She leaked worse than ever. It was as if those confounded shipwrights had actually made a hole in her. This time we did not even go outside. The crew simply refused to man the windlass.

"They towed us back to the inner harbour, and we became a fixture, a feature, an institution of the place. People pointed us out to visitors as 'That 'ere barque that's going to Bankok—has been here six months—put back three times.' On holidays the small boys pulling about in boats would hail, '*Judea*, ahoy!' and if a head showed above the rail shouted, 'Where you bound to?—Bankok?' and jeered. We were only three on board. The poor old skipper mooned in the cabin. Mahon undertook the cooking, and unexpectedly developed all a Frenchman's genius for preparing nice little messes. I looked languidly after the rigging. We became citizens of Falmouth. Every shopkeeper knew us. At the barber's or tobacconist's they asked familiarly, 'Do you think you will ever get to Bankok?' Meantime the owner, the underwriters, and the charterers squabbled amongst themselves in London, and our pay went on. . . . Pass the bottle.

"It was horrid. Morally it was worse than pumping for life. It seemed as though we had been forgotten by the world, belonged to nobody, would get nowhere; it seemed that, as if bewitched, we would have to live for ever and ever in that inner harbour, a derision and a byword to generations of long-shore loafers and dishonest boatmen. I obtained three months' pay and a five days' leave, and made a rush for London. It took me a day to get there and pretty well another to come back—but three months' pay went all the same. I don't know what I did with it. I went to a music-hall, I believe, lunched, dined, and supped in a swell place in Regent Street, and was back to time, with nothing but a complete set of Byron's works and a new railway rug to show for three months' work. The boatman who pulled me off to the ship said: 'Hallo! I thought you had left the old thing. *She* will never get to Bankok.' 'That's all *you* know about it,' I said scornfully—but I didn't like that prophecy at all.

"Suddenly a man, some kind of agent to somebody, appeared with full powers. He had grog-blossoms all over his face, an indomitable energy, and was a jolly soul. We leaped into life again. A hulk came alongside, took our cargo, and then we went into dry dock to get our copper stripped. No wonder she leaked. The poor thing, strained beyond endurance by the gale, had, as if in disgust, spat out all the oakum of her lower seams. She was recaulked, new coppered, and made as tight as a bottle. We went back to the hulk and reshipped our cargo.

"Then, on a fine moonlight night, all the rats left the ship.

"We had been infested with them. They had destroyed our sails, consumed more stores than the crew, affably shared our beds and our dangers, and now, when the ship was made seaworthy, concluded to clear out. I called Mahon to enjoy the spectacle. Rat after rat appeared on our rail, took a last look over his shoulder, and leaped with a hollow thud into the empty hulk. We tried to count them, but soon lost the tale. Mahon said: 'Well, well! don't talk to me about the intelligence of rats. They ought to have left before, when we had that narrow squeak from foundering. There you have the proof how silly is the superstition about them. They leave a good ship for an old rotten hulk, where there is nothing to eat, too, the fools! . . . I don't believe they know what is safe or what is good for them, any more than you or I.'

"And after some more talk we agreed that the wisdom of rats had been grossly overrated, being in fact no greater than that of men.

"The story of the ship was known, by this, all up the Channel from Land's End to the Forelands, and we could get no crew on the south coast. They sent us one all complete from Liverpool, and we left once more—for Bankok.

"We had fair breezes, smooth water right into the tropics, and the old *Judea* lumbered along in the sunshine. When she went eight knots everything cracked aloft, and we tied our caps to our heads; but mostly she strolled on at the rate of three miles an hour. What could you expect? She was tired—that old ship. Her youth was where mine is—where yours is—you fellows who listen to this yarn; and what friend would throw your years and your weariness in your face? We didn't grumble at her. To us aft, at least, it seemed as though we had been born in her, reared in her, had lived in her for ages, had never known any other ship. I would just as soon have abused the old village church at home for not being a cathedral.

"And for me there was also my youth to make me patient. There was all the East before me, and all life, and the thought that I had been tried in that ship and had come out pretty well. And I thought of men of old who, centuries ago, went that road in ships that sailed no better, to the land of palms, and spices, and yellow sands, and of brown nations ruled by kings more cruel than Nero the Roman, and more splendid than Solomon the Jew. The old bark lumbered on, heavy with her age and the burden of her cargo, while I lived the life of youth in ignorance and hope. She lumbered on through an interminable procession of days; and the fresh gilding flashed back at the setting sun, seemed to cry out over the darkening sea the words painted on her stern, '*Judea*, London. Do or Die.'

"Then we entered the Indian Ocean and steered northerly for Java Head. The winds were light. Weeks slipped by. She crawled on, do or die, and people at home began to think of posting us as overdue.

"One Saturday evening, I being off duty, the men asked me to give them an extra bucket of water or so—for washing clothes. As I did not wish to screw on the fresh-water pump so late, I went forward whistling, and with a key in my hand to unlock the forepeak scuttle, intending to serve the water out of a spare tank we kept there.

"The smell down below was as unexpected as it was frightful. One would have thought hundreds of paraffin-lamps had been flaring and smoking in that hole for days. I was glad to get out. The man with me coughed and said, 'Funny smell, sir.' I answered negligently, 'It's good for the health they say,' and walked aft.

"The first thing I did was to put my head down the square of the midship ventilator. As I lifted the lid a visible breath, something like a thin fog, a puff of faint haze, rose from the opening. The ascending air was hot, and had a heavy, sooty, paraffiny smell. I gave one sniff, and put down the lid gently. It was no use choking myself. The cargo was on fire.

"Next day she began to smoke in earnest. You see it was to be expected, for though the coal was of a safe kind, that cargo had been so handled, so broken up with handling, that it looked more like smithy coal than anything else. Then it had been wetted—more than once. It rained all the time we were taking it back from the hulk, and now with this long passage it got heated, and there was another case of spontaneous combustion.

"The captain called us into the cabin. He had a chart spread on the table, and looked unhappy. He said, 'The coast of West Australia is near, but I mean to proceed to our destination. It is the hurricane month, too; but we will just keep her head for Bankok, and fight the fire. No more putting back anywhere, if we all get roasted. We will try first to stifle this 'ere damned combustion by want of air.'

"We tried. We battened down everything, and still she smoked. The smoke kept coming out through imperceptible crevices; it forced itself through bulkheads and covers; it oozed here and there and everywhere in slender threads, in an invisible film, in an incomprehensible manner. It made its way into the cabin, into the forecastle; it poisoned the sheltered places on the deck, it could be sniffed as high as the mainyard. It was clear that if the smoke came out the air came in. This was disheartening. This combustion refused to be stifled.

"We resolved to try water, and took the hatches off. Enormous volumes of smoke, whitish, yellowish, thick, greasy, misty, choking, ascended as high as the trucks. All hands cleared out aft. Then the poisonous cloud blew away, and we went back to work in a smoke that was no thicker now than that of an ordinary factory chimney.

"We rigged the force-pump, got the hose along, and by and by it burst. Well, it was as old as the ship—a prehistoric hose, and past repair. Then we pumped with the feeble head pump, drew water with buckets, and in this way managed in time to pour lots of Indian Ocean into the main hatch. The bright stream flashed in sunshine, fell into a layer of white crawling smoke, and vanished on the black surface of coal. Steam ascended mingling with the smoke. We poured salt water as into a barrel without a bottom. It was our fate to pump in that ship, to pump out of her, to pump into her; and after keeping water out of her to save ourselves from being drowned, we frantically poured water into her to save ourselves from being burnt.

"And she crawled on, do or die, in the serene weather. The sky was a miracle of purity, a miracle of azure. The sea was polished, was blue, was pellucid, was sparkling like a precious stone, extending on all sides, all round to the horizon—as if the whole terrestrial globe had been one jewel, one colossal sapphire, a single gem fashioned into a planet. And on the lustre of the great calm waters the *Judea* glided imperceptibly, enveloped in languid and unclean vapours, in a lazy cloud that drifted to leeward, light and slow; a pestiferous cloud defiling the splendour of sea and sky.

"All this time of course we saw no fire. The cargo smouldered at the bottom somewhere. Once Mahon, as we were working side by side, said to me with a queer smile: 'Now, if she only would spring a tidy leak—like that time when we first left the Channel—it would put a stopper on this fire. Wouldn't it?' I remarked irrelevantly, 'Do you remember the rats?'

"We fought the fire and sailed the ship too as carefully as though nothing had been the matter. The steward cooked and attended on us. Of the other twelve men, eight worked while four rested. Everyone took his turn, captain included. There was equality, and if not exactly fraternity, then a deal of good feeling. Sometimes a man, as he dashed a bucketful of water down the hatchway, would yell out, 'Hurrah for Bankok!' and the rest laughed. But generally we were taciturn and serious—and thirsty. Oh! how thirsty! And we had to be careful with the water. Strict allowance. The ship smoked, the sun blazed. . . . Pass the bottle.

"We tried everything. We even made an attempt to dig down to the fire. No good, of course. No man could remain more than a minute below. Mahon, who went first, fainted there, and the man who went to fetch him out did likewise. We lugged them out on deck. Then I leaped down to show how easily it could be done. They had learned wisdom by that time, and contented themselves by fishing for me with a chain-hook tied to a broom-handle, I believe. I did not offer to go and fetch up my shovel, which was left down below.

"Things began to look bad. We put the long-boat into the water. The second boat was ready to swing out. We had also another, a 14-foot thing, on davits aft, where it was quite safe.

"Then, behold, the smoke suddenly decreased. We redoubled our efforts to flood the bottom of the ship. In two days there was no smoke at all. Everybody was on the broad grin. This was on a Friday. On Saturday no work, but sailing the ship, of course, was done. The men washed their clothes and their faces for the first time in a fortnight, and had a special dinner given them. They spoke of spontaneous combustion with contempt, and implied *they* were the boys to put out combustions. Somehow we all felt as though we each had inherited a large fortune. But a beastly smell of burning hung about the ship. Captain Beard had hollow eyes and sunken cheeks. I had never noticed so much before how twisted and bowed he was. He and Mahon prowled soberly about hatches and ventilators, sniffing. It struck me suddenly poor Mahon was a very, very old chap. As to me, I was as pleased and proud as though I had helped to win a great naval battle. O! Youth!

"The night was fine. In the morning a homeward-bound ship passed us hull down—the first we had seen for months; but we were nearing the land at last, Java Head being about 190 miles off, and nearly due north.

"Next day it was my watch on deck from eight to twelve. At breakfast the captain observed, 'It's wonderful how that smell hangs about the cabin.' About ten, the mate being on the poop, I stepped down on the main-deck for a moment. The carpenter's bench stood abaft the mainmast: I leaned against it sucking at my pipe, and the carpenter, a young chap, came to talk to me. He remarked, 'I think we have done very well, haven't we?' and then I perceived with annoyance the fool was trying to tilt the bench. I said curtly, 'Don't, Chips,' and immediately became aware of a queer sensation, of an absurd delusion,—I seemed somehow to be in the air. I heard all round me like a pent-up breath released—as if a thousand giants simultaneously had said Phoo!—and felt a dull concussion which made my ribs ache suddenly. No doubt about it—I was in the air, and my body was describing a short parabola. But short as it was, I had the time to think several thoughts in, as far as I can remember, the following order: 'This can't be the carpenter—What is it?—Some accident—Submarine volcano?—Coals, gas!—By Jove! we are being blown up—Everybody's dead—I am falling into the after-hatch—I see fire in it.'

"The coal-dust suspended in the air of the hold had glowed dull-red at the moment of the explosion. In the twinkling of an eye, in an infinitesimal fraction of a second since the first tilt of the bench, I was full length on the cargo. I picked myself up and scrambled out. It was quick like a rebound. The deck was a wilderness of smashed timber, lying crosswise like trees in a wood after a hurricane; an immense curtain of soiled rags waved gently before me—it was the main-sail blown to strips. I thought, The masts will be toppling over directly; and to get out of the way bolted on all-fours towards the poop-ladder. The first person I saw was Mahon, with eyes like saucers, his mouth open, and the long white hair standing straight on end round his head like a silver halo. He was just about to go down when the sight of the main-deck stirring, heaving up, and changing into splinters before his eyes, petrified him on the top step. I stared at him in unbelief, and he stared at me with a queer kind of shocked curiosity. I did not know that I had no hair, no eyebrows, no eyelashes, that my young moustache was burnt off, that my face was black, one cheek laid open, my nose cut, and my chin bleeding. I had lost my cap, one of my slippers, and my shirt was torn to rags. Of all this I was not aware. I was amazed to see the ship still afloat, the poop-deck whole—and, most of all, to see anybody alive. Also the peace of the sky and the serenity of the sea were distinctly surprising. I suppose I expected to see them convulsed with horror. . . . Pass the bottle.

"There was a voice hailing the ship from somewhere—in the air, in the sky—I couldn't tell, Presently I saw the captain—and he was mad. He asked me eagerly, 'Where's the cabin-table?' and to hear such a question was a frightful shock. I had just been blown up, you understand, and vibrated with that experience,—I wasn't quite sure whether I was alive. Mahon began to stamp with both feet and yelled at him 'Good God! don't you see the deck's blown out of her?' I found my voice, and stammered out as if conscious of some gross neglect of duty, 'I don't know where the cabin-table is.' It was like an absurd dream.

"Do you know what he wanted next? Well, he wanted to trim the yards. Very placidly, and as if lost in thought, he insisted on having the foreyard squared. 'I don't know if there's anybody alive,' said Mahon, almost tearfully. 'Surely,' he said, gently, 'there will be enough left to square the foreyard.'

"The old chap, it seems, was in his own berth winding up the chronometers, when the shock sent him spinning. Immediately it occurred to him—as he said afterwards—that the ship had struck something, and he ran out into the cabin. There, he saw, the cabin-table had vanished somewhere. The deck being blown up, it had fallen down into the lazarette of course. Where we had our breakfast that morning he saw only a great hole in the floor. This appeared to him so awfully mysterious, and impressed him so immensely, that what he saw and heard after he got on deck were mere trifles in comparison. And, mark, he noticed directly the wheel deserted and his barque off her course—and his only thought was to get that miserable, stripped, undecked, smouldering shell of a ship back again with her head pointing at her port of destination. Bankok! That's what he was after. I tell you this quiet, bowed, bandy-legged, almost deformed little man was immense in the singleness of his idea and in his placid ignorance of our agitation. He motioned us forward with a commanding gesture, and went to take the wheel himself.

"Yes; that was the first thing we did—trim the yards of that wreck! No one was killed, or even disabled, but everyone was more or less hurt. You should have seen them! Some were in rags, with black faces, like coal-heavers, like sweeps, and had bullet heads that seemed closely cropped, but were in fact singed to the skin. Others, of the watch below, awakened by being shot out from their collapsing bunks, shivered incessantly, and kept on groaning even as we went about our work. But they all worked. That crew of Liverpool hard cases had in them the right stuff. It's my experience they always have. It is the sea that gives it—the vastness, the loneliness surrounding their dark stolid souls. Ah! Well! we stumbled, we crept, we fell, we barked our shins on the wreckage, we hauled. The masts stood, but we did not know how much they might be charred down below. It was nearly calm, but a long swell ran from the west and made her roll. They might go at any moment. We looked at them with apprehension. One could not foresee which way they would fall.

"Then we retreated aft and looked about us. The deck was a tangle of planks on edge, of planks on end, of splinters, of ruined woodwork. The masts rose from that chaos like big trees above a matted undergrowth. The interstices of that mass of wreckage were full of something whitish, sluggish, stirring —of something that was like a greasy fog. The smoke of the invisible fire was coming up again, was trailing, like a poisonous thick mist in some valley choked with dead wood. Already lazy wisps were beginning to curl upwards amongst the mass of splinters. Here and there a piece of timber, stuck upright, resembled a post. Half of a fife-rail had been shot through the foresail, and the sky made a patch of glorious blue in the ignobly soiled canvas. A portion of several boards holding together had fallen across the rail, and one end protruded overboard, like a gangway leading upon nothing, like a gangway leading over the deep sea, leading to death—as if inviting us to walk the plank at once and be done with our ridiculous troubles. And still the air, the sky—a ghost, something invisible was hailing the ship.

"Someone had the sense to look over, and there was the helmsman, who had impulsively jumped overboard, anxious to come back. He yelled and swam lustily like a merman, keeping up with the ship. We threw him a rope, and presently he stood amongst us streaming with water and very crestfallen. The captain had surrendered the wheel, and apart, elbow on rail and chin in hand, gazed at the sea wistfully. We asked ourselves, What next? I thought, Now, this is something like. This is great. I wonder what will happen. O youth!

"Suddenly Mahon sighted a steamer far astern. Captain Beard said, 'We may do something with her yet.' We hoisted two flags, which said in the international language of the sea, 'On fire. Want immediate assistance.' The steamer grew bigger rapidly, and by and by spoke with two flags on her foremast, 'I am coming to your assistance.'

"In half an hour she was abreast, to windward, within hail, and rolling slightly, with her engines stopped. We lost our composure, and yelled all together with excitement, 'We've been blown up.' A man in a white helmet, on the bridge, cried, 'Yes! All right! all right!' and he nodded his head, and smiled, and made soothing motions with his hand as though at a lot of frightened children. One of the boats dropped in the water, and walked towards us upon the sea with her long oars. Four Calashes pulled a swinging stroke. This was my first sight of Malay seamen. I've known them since, but what struck me then was their unconcern: they came alongside, and even the bowman standing up and holding to our main-chains with the boat-hook did not deign to lift his head for a glance. I thought people who had been blown up deserved more attention.

"A little man, dry like a chip and agile like a monkey, clambered up. It was the mate of the steamer. He gave one look, and cried, 'O boys—you had better quit.'

"We were silent. He talked apart with the captain for a time,—seemed to argue with him. Then they went away together to the steamer.

"When our skipper came back we learned that the steamer was the *Somerville*, Captain Nash, from West Australia to Singapore *via* Batavia with mails, and that the agreement was she should tow us to Anjer or Batavia, if possible, where we could extinguish the fire by scuttling, and then proceed on our voyage—to Bankok! The old man seemed excited. 'We will do it yet,' he said to Mahon, fiercely. He shook his fist at the sky. Nobody else said a word.

"At noon the steamer began to tow. She went ahead slim and high, and what was left of the *Judea* followed at the end of seventy fathom of tow-rope,— followed her swiftly like a cloud of smoke with mastheads protruding above. We went aloft to furl the sails. We coughed on the yards, and were careful about the bunts. Do you see the lot of us there, putting a neat furl on the sails of that ship doomed to arrive nowhere? There was not a man who didn't think that at any moment the masts would topple over. From aloft we could not see the ship for smoke, and they worked carefully, passing the gaskets with even turns. 'Harbour furl—aloft there!' cried Mahon from below.

"You understand this? I don't think one of those chaps expected to get down in the usual way. When we did I heard them saying to each other, 'Well, I thought we would come down overboard, in a lump —sticks and all—blame me if I didn't.' 'That's what I was thinking to myself,' would answer wearily another battered and bandaged scarecrow. And, mind, these were men without the drilled-in habit of obedience. To an onlooker they would be a lot of profane scallywags without a redeeming point. What made them do it—what made them obey me when I, thinking consciously how fine it was, made them drop the bunt of the foresail twice to try and do it better? What? They had no professional reputation—no examples, no praise. It wasn't a sense of duty; they all knew well enough how to shirk, and laze, and dodge—when they had a mind to it—and mostly they had. Was it the two pounds ten a-month that sent them there? They didn't think their pay half good enough. No; it was something in them, something inborn and subtle and everlasting. I don't say positively that the crew of a French or German merchantman wouldn't have done it, but I doubt whether it would have been done in the same way. There was a completeness in it, something solid like a principle, and masterful like an instinct—a disclosure of something secret—of that hidden something, that gift of good or evil that makes racial difference, that shapes the fate of nations.

"It was that night at ten that, for the first time since we had been fighting it, we saw the fire. The speed of the towing had fanned the smouldering destruction. A blue gleam appeared forward, shining below the wreck of the deck. It wavered in patches, it seemed to stir and creep like the light of a glowworm. I saw it first, and told Mahon. 'Then the game's up,' he said. 'We had better stop this towing, or she will burst out suddenly fore and aft before we can clear out.' We set up a yell; rang bells to attract their attention; they towed on. At last Mahon and I had to crawl forward and cut the rope with an axe. There was no time to cast off the lashings. Red tongues could be seen licking the wilderness of splinters under our feet as we made our way back to the poop.

"Of course they very soon found out in the steamer that the rope was gone. She gave a loud blast of her whistle, her lights were seen sweeping in a wide circle, she came up ranging close alongside, and stopped. We were all in a tight group on the poop looking at her. Every man had saved a little bundle or a bag. Suddenly a conical flame with a twisted top shot up forward and threw upon the black sea a circle of light, with the two vessels side by side and heaving gently in its centre. Captain Beard had been sitting on the gratings still and mute for hours, but now he rose slowly and advanced in front of us, to the mizzen-shrouds. Captain Nash hailed: 'Come along! Look sharp. I have mail-bags on board. I will take you and your boats to Singapore.'

"'Thank you! No!' said our skipper. 'We must see the last of the ship.'

"'I can't stand by any longer,' shouted the other. 'Mails—you know.'

"'Ay! ay! We are all right.'

"'Very well! I'll report you in Singapore. . . . Good-bye!'

"He waved his hand. Our men dropped their bundles quietly. The steamer moved ahead, and passing out of the circle of light, vanished at once from our sight, dazzled by the fire which burned fiercely. And then I knew that I would see the East first as commander of a small boat. I thought it fine; and the fidelity to the old ship was fine. We should see the last of her. Oh, the glamour of youth! Oh, the fire of it, more dazzling than the flames of the burning ship, throwing a magic light on the wide earth, leaping audaciously to the sky, presently to be quenched by time, more cruel, more pitiless, more bitter than the sea—and like the flames of the burning ship surrounded by an impenetrable night.

"The old man warned us in his gentle and inflexible way that it was part of our duty to save for the underwriters as much as we could of the ship's gear. Accordingly we went to work aft, while she blazed forward to give us plenty of light. We lugged out a lot of rubbish. What didn't we save? An old barometer fixed with an absurd quantity of screws nearly cost me my life: a sudden rush of smoke came upon me, and I just got away in time. There were various stores, bolts of canvas, coils of rope; the poop looked like a marine bazaar, and the boats were lumbered to the gunwales. One would have thought the old man wanted to take as much as he could of his first command with him. He was very, very quiet, but off his balance evidently. Would you believe it? He wanted to take a length of old stream-cable and a kedge-anchor with him in the long-boat. We said 'Ay, ay, sir,' deferentially, and on the quiet let the things slip overboard. The heavy medicine-chest went that way, two bags of green coffee, tins of paint—fancy, paint!—a whole lot of things. Then I was ordered with two hands into the boats to make a stowage and get them ready against the time it would be proper for us to leave the ship.

"We put everything straight, stepped the long-boat's mast for our skipper, who was to take charge of her, and I was not sorry to sit down for a moment. My face felt raw, every limb ached as if broken. I was aware of all my ribs, and would have sworn to a twist in the backbone. The boats, fast astern, lay in a deep shadow, and all around I could see the circle of the sea lighted by the fire. A gigantic flame arose forward straight and clear. It flared fierce, with noises like the whirr of wings, with rumbles as of thunder. There were cracks, detonations, and from the cone of flame the sparks flew upwards, as man is born to trouble, to leaky ships, and to ships that burn.

"What bothered me was that the ship, lying broadside to the swell and to such wind as there was—a mere breath—the boats would not keep astern where they were safe, but persisted, in a pig-headed way boats have, in getting under the counter and then swinging alongside. They were knocking about dangerously and coming near the flame, while the ship rolled on them, and, of course, there was always the danger of the masts going over the side at any moment. I and my two boat-keepers kept them off as best we could, with oars and boat-hooks; but to be constantly at it became exasperating, since there was no reason why we should not leave at once. We could not see those on board, nor could we imagine what caused the delay. The boat-keepers were swearing feebly, and I had not only my share of the work but also had to keep at it two men who showed a constant inclination to lay themselves down and let things slide.

"At last I hailed, 'On deck there,' and someone looked over. 'We're ready here,' I said. The head disappeared, and very soon popped up again. 'The captain says, All right, sir, and to keep the boats well clear of the ship.'

"Half an hour passed. Suddenly there was a frightful racket, rattle, clanking of chain, hiss of water, and millions of sparks flew up into the shivering column of smoke that stood leaning slightly above the ship. The cat-heads had burned away, and the two red-hot anchors had gone to the bottom, tearing out after them two hundred fathom of red-hot chain. The ship trembled, the mass of flame swayed as if ready to collapse, and the fore top-gallant-mast fell. It darted down like an arrow of fire, shot under, and instantly leaping up within an oar's-length of the boats, floated quietly, very black on the luminous sea. I hailed the deck again. After some time a man in an unexpectedly cheerful but also muffled tone, as though he had been trying to speak with his mouth shut, informed me, 'Coming directly, sir,' and vanished. For a long time I heard nothing but the whirr and roar of the fire. There were also whistling sounds. The boats jumped, tugged at the painters, ran at each other playfully, knocked their sides together, or, do what we would, swung in a bunch against the ship's side. I couldn't stand it any longer, and swarming up a rope, clambered aboard over the stern.

"It was as bright as day. Coming up like this, the sheet of fire facing me was a terrifying sight, and the heat seemed hardly bearable at first. On a settee cushion dragged out of the cabin Captain Beard, his legs drawn up and one arm under his head, slept with the light playing on him. Do you know what the rest were busy about? They were sitting on deck right aft, round an open case, eating bread and cheese and drinking bottled stout.

"On the background of flames twisting in fierce tongues above their heads they seemed at home like salamanders, and looked like a band of desperate pirates. The fire sparkled in the whites of their eyes, gleamed on patches of white skin seen through the torn shirts. Each had the marks as of a battle about him—bandaged heads, tied up arms, a strip of dirty rag round a knee—and each man had a bottle between his legs and a chunk of cheese in his hand. Mahon got up. With his handsome and disreputable head, his hooked profile, his long white beard, and with an uncorked bottle in his hand, he resembled one of those reckless sea-robbers of old making merry amidst violence and disaster. 'The last meal on board,' he explained solemnly. 'We had nothing to eat all day, and it was no use leaving all this.' He flourished the bottle and indicated the sleeping skipper. 'He said he couldn't swallow anything, so I got him to lie down,' he went on; and as I stared, 'I don't know whether you are aware, young fellow, the man had no sleep to speak of for days—and there will be dam' little sleep in the boats.' 'There will be no boats by-and-by if you fool about much longer,' I said, indignantly. I walked up to the skipper and shook him by the shoulder. At last he opened his eyes, but did not move. 'Time to leave her, sir,' I said quietly.

"He got up painfully, looked at the flames, at the sea sparkling round the ship, and black, black as ink farther away; he looked at the stars shining dim through a thin veil of smoke in a sky black, black as Erebus.

"'Youngest first,' he said.

"And the ordinary seaman, wiping his mouth with the back of his hand, got up, clambered over the taffrail, and vanished. Others followed. One, on the point of going over, stopped short to drain his bottle, and with a great swing of his arm flung it at the fire. 'Take this!' he cried.

"The skipper lingered disconsolately, and we left him to commune alone for a while with his first command. Then I went up again and brought him away at last. It was time. The ironwork on the poop was hot to the touch.

"Then the painter of the long-boat was cut, and the three boats, tied together, drifted clear of the ship. It was just sixteen hours after the explosion when we abandoned her. Mahon had charge of the second boat, and I had the smallest—the 14-foot thing. The long-boat would have taken the lot of us; but the skipper said we must save as much property as we could—for the underwriters—and so I got my first command. I had two men with me, a bag of biscuits, a few tins of meat, and a breaker of water. I was ordered to keep close to the long-boat, that in case of bad weather we might be taken into her.

"And do you know what I thought? I thought I would part company as soon as I could. I wanted to have my first command all to myself. I wasn't going to sail in a squadron if there were a chance for independent cruising. I would make land by myself. I would beat the other boats. Youth! All youth! The silly, charming, beautiful youth.

"But we did not make a start at once. We must see the last of the ship. And so the boats drifted about that night, heaving and setting on the swell. The men dozed, waked, sighed, groaned. I looked at the burning ship.

"Between the darkness of earth and heaven she was burning fiercely upon a disc of purple sea shot by the blood-red play of gleams; upon a disc of water glittering and sinister. A high, clear flame, an immense and lonely flame, ascended from the ocean, and from its summit the black smoke poured continuously at the sky. She burned furiously; mournful and imposing like a funeral pile kindled in the night, surrounded by the sea, watched over by the stars. A magnificent death had come like a grace, like a gift, like a reward to that old ship at the end of her laborious days. The surrender of her weary ghost to the keeping of stars and sea was stirring like the sight of a glorious triumph. The masts fell just before daybreak, and for a moment there was a burst and turmoil of sparks that seemed to fill with flying fire the night patient and watchful, the vast night lying silent upon the sea. At daylight she was only a charred shell, floating still under a cloud of smoke and bearing a glowing mass of coal within.

"Then the oars were got out, and the boats forming in a line moved round her remains as if in procession—the long-boat leading. As we pulled across her stern a slim dart of fire shot out viciously at us, and suddenly she went down, head first, in a great hiss of steam. The unconsumed stern was the last to sink; but the paint had gone, had cracked, had peeled off, and there were no letters, there was no word, no stubborn device that was like her soul, to flash at the rising sun her creed and her name.

"We made our way north. A breeze sprang up, and about noon all the boats came together for the last time. I had no mast or sail in mine, but I made a mast out of a spare oar and hoisted a boat-awning for a sail, with a boat-hook for a yard. She was certainly overmasted, but I had the satisfaction of knowing that with the wind aft I could beat the other two. I had to wait for them. Then we all had a look at the captain's chart, and, after a sociable meal of hard bread and water, got our last instructions. These were simple: steer north, and keep together as much as possible. 'Be careful with that jury-rig, Marlow,' said the captain; and Mahon, as I sailed proudly past his boat, wrinkled his curved nose and hailed, 'You will sail that ship of yours under water, if you don't look out, young fellow.' He was a malicious old man—and may the deep sea where he sleeps now rock him gently, rock him tenderly to the end of time!

"Before sunset a thick rain-squall passed over the two boats, which were far astern, and that was the last I saw of them for a time. Next day I sat steering my cockle-shell—my first command—with nothing but water and sky around me. I did sight in the afternoon the upper sails of a ship far away, but said nothing, and my men did not notice her. You see I was afraid she might be homeward bound, and I had no mind to turn back from the portals of the East. I was steering for Java—another blessed name—like Bankok, you know. I steered many days.

"I need not tell you what it is to be knocking about in an open boat. I remembered nights and days of calm, when we pulled, we pulled, and the boat seemed to stand still, as if bewitched within the circle of the sea horizon. I remember the heat, the deluge of rain-squalls that kept us baling for dear life (but filled our water-cask), and I remember sixteen hours on end with a mouth dry as a cinder and a steering-oar over the stern to keep my first command head on to a breaking sea. I did not know how good a man I was till then. I remember the drawn faces, the dejected figures of my two men, and I remember my youth and the feeling that will never come back any more—the feeling that I could last for ever, outlast the sea, the earth, and all men; the deceitful feeling that lures us on to joys, to perils, to love, to vain effort—to death; the triumphant conviction of strength, the heat of life in the handful of dust, the glow in the heart that with every year grows dim, grows cold, grows small, and expires—and expires, too soon, too soon—before life itself.

"And this is how I see the East. I have seen its secret places and have looked into its very soul; but now I see it always from a small boat, a high outline of mountains, blue and afar in the morning; like faint mist at noon; a jagged wall of purple at sunset. I have the feel of the oar in my hand, the vision of a scorching blue sea in my eyes. And I see a bay, a wide bay, smooth as glass and polished like ice, shimmering in the dark. A red light burns far off upon the gloom of the land, and the night is soft and warm. We drag at the oars with aching arms, and suddenly a puff of wind, a puff faint and tepid and laden with strange odours of blossoms, of aromatic wood, comes out of the still night—the first sigh of the East on my face. That I can never forget. It was impalpable and enslaving, like a charm, like a whispered promise of mysterious delight.

"We had been pulling this finishing spell for eleven hours. Two pulled, and he whose turn it was to rest sat at the tiller. We had made out the red light in that bay and steered for it, guessing it must mark some small coasting port. We passed two vessels, outlandish and high-sterned, sleeping at anchor, and, approaching the light, now very dim, ran the boat's nose against the end of a jutting wharf. We were blind with fatigue. My men dropped the oars and fell off the thwarts as if dead. I made fast to a pile. A current rippled softly. The scented obscurity of the shore was grouped into vast masses, a density of colossal clumps of vegetation, probably—mute and fantastic shapes. And at their foot the semicircle of a beach gleamed faintly, like an illusion. There was not a light, not a stir, not a sound. The mysterious East faced me, perfumed like a flower, silent like death, dark like a grave.

"And I sat weary beyond expression, exulting like a conqueror, sleepless and entranced as if before a profound, a fateful enigma.

"A splashing of oars, a measured dip reverberating on the level of water, intensified by the silence of the shore into loud claps, made me jump up. A boat, a European boat, was coming in. I invoked the name of the dead: I hailed: *Judea* ahoy! A thin shout answered.

"It was the captain. I had beaten the flagship by three hours, and I was glad to hear the old man's voice again, tremulous and tired. 'Is it you, Marlow?' 'Mind the end of that jetty, sir,' I cried.

"He approached cautiously, and brought up with the deep-sea lead line which we had saved—for the underwriters. I eased my painter and fell alongside. He sat, a broken figure at the stern, wet with dew, his hands clasped in his lap. His men were asleep already. 'I had a terrible time of it,' he murmured. 'Mahon is behind—not very far.' We conversed in whispers, in low whispers, as if afraid to wake up the land. Guns, thunder, earthquakes would not have awakened the men just then.

"Looking round as we talked, I saw away at sea a bright light travelling in the night. 'There's a steamer passing the bay,' I said. She was not passing, she was entering, and she even came close and anchored. 'I wish,' said the old man, 'you would find out whether she is English. Perhaps they could give us a passage somewhere.' He seemed nervously anxious. So by dint of punching and kicking I started one of my men into a state of somnambulism, and giving him an oar, took another and pulled towards the lights of the steamer.

"There was a murmur of voices in her, metallic hollow clangs of the engine-room, footsteps on the deck. Her ports shone, round like dilated eyes. Shapes moved about, and there was a shadowy man high up on the bridge. He heard my oars.

"And then, before I could open my lips, the East spoke to me, but it was in a Western voice. A torrent of words was poured into the enigmatical, the fateful silence; outlandish, angry words, mixed with words and even whole sentences of good English, less strange but even more surprising. The voice swore and cursed violently; it riddled the solemn peace of the bay by a volley of abuse. It began by calling me Pig, and from that went crescendo into unmentionable adjectives—in English. The man up there raged aloud in two languages, and with a sincerity in his fury that almost convinced me I had, in some way, sinned against the harmony of the universe. I could hardly see him, but began to think he would work himself into a fit.

"Suddenly he ceased, and I could hear him snorting and blowing like a porpoise. I said—

"'What steamer is this, pray?'

"'Eh? What's this? And who are you?'

"'Castaway crew of an English barque burnt at sea. We came here to-night. I am the second mate. The captain is in the long-boat, and wishes to know if you would give us a passage somewhere.'

"'Oh, my goodness! I say. . . . This is the *Celestial* from Singapore on her return trip. I'll arrange with your captain in the morning, . . . and, . . . I say, . . . did you hear me just now?'

"'I should think the whole bay heard you.'

"'I thought you were a shore-boat. Now, look here—this infernal lazy scoundrel of a caretaker has gone to sleep again—curse him. The light is out, and I nearly ran foul of the end of this damned jetty. This is the third time he plays me this trick. Now, I ask you, can anybody stand this kind of thing? It's enough to drive a man out of his mind. I'll report him. . . . I'll get the Assistant Resident to give him the sack, by . . . ! See—there's no light. It's out, isn't it? I take you to witness the light's out. There should be a light, you know. A red light on the——'

"'There was a light,' I said, mildly.

"'But it's out, man! What's the use of talking like this? You can see for yourself it's out—don't you? If you had to take a valuable steamer along this God-forsaken coast you would want a light, too. I'll kick him from end to end of his miserable wharf. You'll see if I don't. I will——'

"'So I may tell my captain you'll take us?' I broke in.

"'Yes, I'll take you. Good-night,' he said, brusquely.

"I pulled back, made fast again to the jetty, and then went to sleep at last. I had faced the silence of the East. I had heard some of its language. But when I opened my eyes again the silence was as complete as though it had never been broken. I was lying in a flood of light, and the sky had never looked so far, so high, before. I opened my eyes and lay without moving.

"And then I saw the men of the East—they were looking at me. The whole length of the jetty was full of people. I saw brown, bronze, yellow faces, the black eyes, the glitter, the colour of an Eastern crowd. And all these beings stared without a murmur, without a sigh, without a movement. They stared down at the boats, at the sleeping men who at night had come to them from the sea. Nothing moved. The fronds of palms stood still against the sky. Not a branch stirred along the shore, and the brown roofs of hidden houses peeped through the green foliage, through the big leaves that hung shining and still like leaves forged of heavy metal. This was the East of the ancient navigators, so old, so mysterious, resplendent and sombre, living and unchanged, full of danger and promise. And these were the men. I sat up suddenly. A wave of movement passed through the crowd from end to end, passed along the heads, swayed the bodies, ran along the jetty like a ripple on the water, like a breath of wind on a field—and all was still again. I see it now—the wide sweep of the bay, the glittering sands, the wealth of green infinite and varied, the sea blue like the sea of a dream, the crowd of attentive faces, the blaze of vivid colour —the water reflecting it all, the curve of the shore, the jetty, the high-sterned outlandish craft floating still, and the three boats with the tired men from the West sleeping, unconscious of the land and the people and of the violence of sunshine. They slept thrown across the thwarts, curled on bottom-boards, in the careless attitudes of death. The head of the old skipper, leaning back in the stern of the long-boat, had fallen on his breast, and he looked as though he would never wake. Farther out old Mahon's face was upturned to the sky, with the long white beard spread out on his breast, as though he had been shot where he sat at the tiller; and a man, all in a heap in the bows of the boat, slept with both arms embracing the stem-head and with his cheek laid on the gunwale. The East looked at them without a sound.

"I have known its fascination since; I have seen the mysterious shores, the still water, the lands of brown nations, where a stealthy Nemesis lies in wait, pursues, overtakes so many of the conquering race, who are proud of their wisdom, of their knowledge, of their strength. But for me all the East is contained in that vision of my youth. It is all in that moment when I opened my young eyes on it. I came upon it from a tussle with the sea—and I was young—and I saw it looking at me. And this is all that is left of it! Only a moment: a moment of strength, of romance, of glamour—of youth! . . . A flick of sunshine upon a strange shore, the time to remember, the time for a sigh, and—good-bye!—Night—Good-bye . . . !"

He drank.

"Ah! The good old time—the good old time. Youth and the sea. Glamour and the sea! The good, strong sea, the salt, bitter sea, that could whisper to you and roar at you and knock your breath out of you."

He drank again.

"By all that's wonderful it is the sea, I believe, the sea itself—or is it youth alone? Who can tell? But you here—you all had something out of life: money, love—whatever one gets on shore—and, tell me, wasn't that the best time, that time when we were young at sea; young and had nothing, on the sea that gives nothing, except hard knocks—and sometimes a chance to feel your strength—that only—what you all regret?"

And we all nodded at him: the man of finance, the man of accounts, the man of law, we all nodded at him over the polished table that like a still sheet of brown water reflected our faces, lined, wrinkled; our faces marked by toil, by deceptions, by success, by love; our weary eyes looking still, looking always, looking anxiously for something out of life, that while it is expected is already gone—has passed unseen, in a sigh, in a flash—together with the youth, with the strength, with the romance of illusions. □

DISCUSSION

1. Why do you think Conrad used a frame story narrated by Marlow, rather than telling the story directly?

2. (a) What is the significance of the name of the ship, the *Judea*, and of her motto, "Do or die"?

(b) To which character does the ship's motto best apply? Explain.

3. (a) What mishaps and other omens indicate that the *Judea* will come to a sorry end?

(b) Does Marlow consider her end a sorry one? Explain.

4. In the opening paragraph of his story, Marlow says: "You fellows know there are those voyages that seem ordered for the illustration of life, that might stand for a symbol of existence. You fight, work, sweat, nearly kill yourself, sometimes do kill yourself, trying to accomplish something—and you can't. Not from any fault of yours." In this statement Marlow captures the basic theme of the story. In what way does the story also transcend or go beyond Marlow's statement?

5. (a) How does the story capture the essence of the optimism and enthusiasm that are youth?

(b) How does it capture the glory and glamor of the sea and the seaman's life?

6. What is the point of making the captain and the first mate elderly men?

7. Discuss the importance of each of the following passages to the story as a whole:

(a) "O youth! The strength of it, the faith of it, the imagination of it! To me she was not an old rattletrap carting about the world a lot of coal for a freight—to me she was the endeavor, the test, the trial of life. I think of her with pleasure, with affection, with regret—as you would think of someone dead you have loved. I shall never forget her. . . ." (page 496a).

(b) "That crew of Liverpool hard cases had in them the right stuff. It's my experience they always have. It is the sea that gives it—the vastness, the loneliness surrounding their dark stolid souls" (page 500b).

(c) "Oh, the glamour of youth! Oh, the fire of it, more dazzling than the flames of the burning ship, throwing a magic light on the wide earth, leaping audaciously to the sky, presently to be quenched by time, more cruel, more pitiless, more bitter than the sea—and like the flames of the burning ship surrounded by an impenetrable night" (page 502b).

(d) "I would make land by myself. I would beat the other boats. Youth! All youth! The silly, charming, beautiful youth" (page 504a).

(e) "A magnificent death had come like a grace, like a gift, like a reward to that old ship at the end of her laborious days" (page 504a).

8. Conrad is known as a master of descriptive detail. Which of his descriptions stand out most clearly in your mind? Can you explain why they do?

WRITING

Because short stories are by definition limited in length, they often leave some thread untied, some problem unresolved, some character unaccounted for—deliberately or otherwise. Many of the writing suggestions in this unit will ask you to fill in material the author omitted.

1. Describe, either in narrative or dramatic form, the meeting that takes place between Captain Beard and his wife when he finally gets back to England.

2. Discuss the effect created by Conrad's masterful use of descriptive passages.

3. Read Conrad's story "The Secret Sharer" and discuss the elements it shares with "Youth."

TICKETS, PLEASE

by D. H. Lawrence

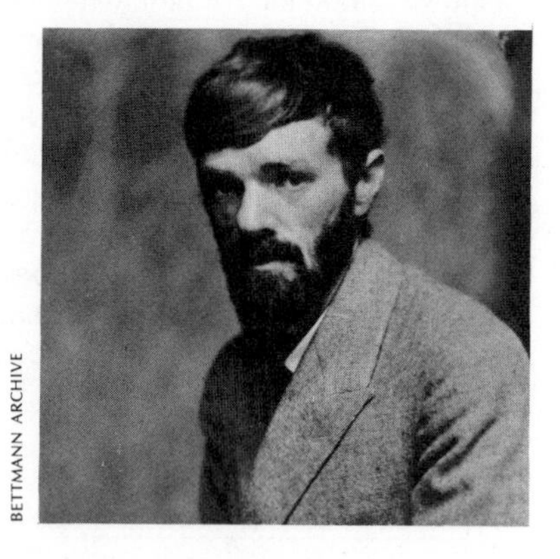
BETTMANN ARCHIVE

THERE is in the Midlands a single-line tramway system which boldly leaves the county town and plunges off into the black, industrial country-side, up hill and down dale, through the long ugly villages of workmen's houses, over canals and railways, past churches perched high and nobly over the smoke and shadows, through stark, grimy cold little market-places, tilting away in a rush past cinemas and shops down to the hollow where the collieries are, then up again, past a little rural church, under the ash trees, on in a rush to the terminus, the last little ugly place of industry, the cold little town that shivers on the edge of the wild, gloomy country beyond. There the green and creamy coloured tram-car seems to pause and purr with curious satisfaction. But in a few minutes—the clock on the turret of the Co-operative Wholesale Society's shops gives the time—away it starts once more on the adventure. Again there are the reckless swoops downhill, bouncing the loops: again the chilly wait in the hill-top market-place: again the breathless slithering round the precipitous drop under the church: again the patient halts at the loops, waiting for the outcoming car: so on and on, for two long hours, till at last the city looms beyond the fat gasworks, the narrow factories draw near, we are in the sordid streets of the great town, once more we sidle to a standstill at our terminus, abashed by the great crimson and cream-coloured city cars, but still perky, jaunty, somewhat dare-devil, green as a jaunty sprig of parsley out of a black colliery garden.

To ride on these cars is always an adventure. Since we are in war-time, the drivers are men unfit for active service: cripples and hunchbacks. So they have the spirit of the devil in them. The ride becomes a steeplechase. Hurray! we have leapt in a clear jump over the canal bridge—now for the four-lane corner. With a shriek and a trail of sparks we are clear again. To be sure, a tram often leaps the rails—but what matter! It sits in a ditch till other trams come to haul it out. It is quite common for a car, packed with one solid mass of living people, to come to a dead halt in the midst of unbroken blackness, the heart of nowhere on a dark night, and for the driver and the girl conductor to call: "All get off—car's on fire!" Instead, however, of rushing out in a panic, the passengers stolidly reply: "Get on—get on! We're not coming out. We're stopping where we are. Push on, George." So till flames actually appear.

The reason for this reluctance to dismount is that the nights are howlingly cold, black, and windswept, and a car is a haven of refuge. From village to village the miners travel, for a change of cinema, of girl, of pub. The trams are desperately packed. Who is going to risk himself in the black gulf outside, to wait perhaps an hour for another tram, then to see the forlorn notice "Depot Only," because there is something wrong! Or to greet a unit of three bright cars all so tight with people that they sail past with a howl of derision. Trams that pass in the night.

This, the most dangerous tram-service in England, as the authorities themselves declare, with pride, is entirely conducted by girls, and driven by rash young men, a little crippled, or by delicate young men, who creep forward in terror. The girls are fearless young hussies. In their ugly blue uniform, skirts up to their knees, shapeless old peaked caps on their heads, they have all the *sang-froid* of an old non-commissioned officer. With a tram packed with howling colliers, roaring hymns downstairs and a sort of antiphony of obscenities upstairs, the lasses are perfectly at their ease. They pounce on the youths who try to evade their ticket-machine. They push off the men at the end of their distance. They are not going to be done in the eye—not they. They fear nobody—and everybody fears them.

"Hello, Annie!"

"Hello, Ted!"

"Oh, mind my corn, Miss Stone. It's my belief you've got a heart of stone, for you've trod on it again."

"You should keep it in your pocket," replies Miss Stone, and she goes sturdily upstairs in her high boots.

"Tickets, please."

She is peremptory, suspicious, and ready to hit first. She can hold her own against ten thousand. The step of that tram-car is her Thermopylæ.[1]

Therefore, there is a certain wild romance aboard these cars—and in the sturdy bosom of Annie herself. The time for soft romance is in the morning, between ten o'clock and one, when things are rather slack: that is, except market-day and Saturday. Thus Annie has time to look about her. Then she often hops off her car and into a shop where she has spied something, while the driver chats in the main road. There is very good feeling between the girls and the drivers. Are they not companions in peril, shipments aboard this careering vessel of a tram-car, for ever rocking on the waves of a stormy land.

Then, also, during the easy hours, the inspectors are most in evidence. For some reason, everybody employed in this tram-service is young: there are no grey heads. It would not do. Therefore the inspectors are of the right age, and one, the chief, is also good-looking. See him stand on a wet, gloomy morning, in his long oilskin, his peaked cap well down over his eyes, waiting to board a car. His face ruddy, his small brown moustache is weathered, he has a faint impudent smile. Fairly tall and agile, even in his waterproof, he springs aboard a car and greets Annie.

"Hello, Annie! Keeping the wet out?"

"Trying to."

There are only two people in the car. Inspecting is soon over. Then for a long and impudent chat on the foot-board, a good, easy, twelve-mile chat.

The inspector's name is John Thomas Raynor—always called John Thomas, except sometimes, in malice, Coddy. His face sets in fury when he is addressed, from a distance, with this abbreviation. There is considerable scandal about John Thomas in half a dozen villages. He flirts with the girl conductors in the morning, and walks out with them in the dark night, when they leave their tram-car at the depôt. Of course, the girls quit the service frequently. Then he flirts and walks out with the newcomer: always providing she is sufficiently attractive, and that she will consent to walk. It is remarkable, however, that most of the girls are quite comely, they are all young, and this roving life aboard the car gives them a sailor's dash and recklessness. What matter how they behave when the ship is in port? To-morrow they will be aboard again.

Annie, however, was something of a Tartar, and her sharp tongue had kept John Thomas at arm's length for many months. Perhaps, therefore, she liked him all the more: for he always came up smiling, with impudence. She watched him vanquish one girl, then another. She could tell by the movement of his mouth and eyes, when he flirted with her in the morning, that he had been walking out with this lass, or the other, the night before. A fine cock-of-the-walk he was. She could sum him up pretty well.

In this subtle antagonism they knew each other like old friends, they were as shrewd with one another almost as man and wife. But Annie had always kept him sufficiently at arm's length. Besides, she had a boy of her own.

The Statutes fair, however, came in November, at Bestwood. It happened that Annie had the Monday night off. It was a drizzling ugly night, yet she dressed herself up and went to the fair-ground. She was alone, but she expected soon to find a pal of some sort.

The roundabouts were veering round and grinding out their music, the side-shows were making as much commotion as possible. In the coconut shies there were no coconuts, but artificial war-time substitutes, which the lads declared were fastened into the irons. There was a sad decline in brilliance and luxury. None the less, the ground was muddy as ever, there was the same crush, the press of faces lighted up by the flares and the electric lights, the same smell of naphtha and a few potatoes, and of electricity.

Who should be the first to greet Miss Annie on the showground but John Thomas. He had a black overcoat buttoned up to his chin, and a tweed cap pulled down over his brows, his face between was ruddy

1. *Thermopylae,* a narrow mountain pass in Greece where a small number of Greeks held back the Persian army in 480 B. C. until all the Greeks were slain.

and smiling and handy as ever. She knew so well the way his mouth moved.

She was very glad to have a "boy." To be at the Statutes without a fellow was no fun. Instantly, like the gallant he was, he took her on the Dragons, grim-toothed, roundabout switchbacks. It was not nearly so exciting as a tram-car actually. But, then, to be seated in a shaking, green dragon, uplifted above the sea of bubble faces, careering in a rickety fashion in the lower heavens, whilst John Thomas leaned over her, his cigarette in his mouth, was after all the right style. She was a plump, quick, alive little creature. So she was quite excited and happy.

John Thomas made her stay on for the next round. And therefore she could hardly for shame repulse him when he put his arm round her and drew her a little nearer to him, in a very warm and cuddly manner. Besides, he was fairly discreet, he kept his movement as hidden as possible. She looked down, and saw that his red, clean hand was out of sight of the crowd. And they knew each other so well. So they warmed up to the fair.

After the dragons they went on the horses. John Thomas paid each time, so she could but be complaisant. He, of course, sat astride on the outer horse—named "Black Bess"—and she sat sideways, towards him, on the inner horse—named "Wildfire." But of course John Thomas was not going to sit discreetly on "Black Bess," holding the brass bar. Round they spun and heaved, in the light. And round he swung on his wooden steed, flinging one leg across her mount, and perilously tipping up and down, across the space, half lying back, laughing at her. He was perfectly happy; she was afraid her hat was on one side, but she was excited.

He threw quoits on a table, and won for her two large, pale blue hat-pins. And then, hearing the noise of the cinemas, announcing another performance, they climbed the boards and went in.

Of course, during these performances pitch darkness falls from time to time, when the machine goes wrong. Then there is a wild whooping, and a loud smacking of simulated kisses. In these moments John Thomas drew Anne towards him. After all, he had a wonderfully warm, cosy way of holding a girl with his arm, he seemed to make such a nice fit. And, after all, it was pleasant to be so held: so very comforting and cosy and nice. He leaned over her and she felt his breath on her hair; she knew he wanted to kiss her on the lips. And, after all, he was so warm and she fitted in to him so softly. After all, she wanted him to touch her lips.

But the light sprang up; she also started electrically, and put her hat straight. He left his arm lying nonchalantly behind her. Well, it was fun, it was exciting to be at the Statutes with John Thomas.

When the cinema was over they went for a walk across the dark, damp fields. He had all the arts of love-making. He was especially good at holding a girl, when he sat with her on a stile in the black, drizzling darkness. He seemed to be holding her in space, against his own warmth and gratification. And his kisses were soft and slow and searching.

So Annie walked out with John Thomas, though she kept her own boy dangling in the distance. Some of the tram-girls chose to be huffy. But there, you must take things as you find them, in this life.

There was no mistake about it, Annie liked John Thomas a good deal. She felt so rich and warm in herself whenever he was near. And John Thomas really liked Annie, more than usual. The soft, melting way in which she could flow into a fellow, as if she melted into his very bones, was something rare and good. He fully appreciated this.

But with a developing acquaintance there began a developing intimacy. Annie wanted to consider him a person, a man: she wanted to take an intelligent interest in him, and to have an intelligent response. She did not want a mere nocturnal presence, which was what he was so far. And she prided herself that he could not leave her.

Here she made a mistake. John Thomas intended to remain a nocturnal presence; he had no idea of becoming an all-round individual to her. When she started to take an intelligent interest in him and his life and his character, he sheered off. He hated intelligent interest. And he knew that the only way to stop it was to avoid it. The possessive female was aroused in Annie. So he left her.

It is no use saying she was not surprised. She was at first startled, thrown out of her count. For she had been so *very* sure of holding him. For a while she was staggered, and everything became uncertain to her. Then she wept with fury, indignation, desolation, and misery. Then she had a spasm of despair. And then, when he came, still impudently, on to her car, still familiar, but letting her see by the movement of his head that he had gone away to somebody else for the time being, and was enjoying pastures new, then she determined to have her own back.

She had a very shrewd idea what girls John Thomas had taken out. She went to Nora Purdy. Nora was a tall, rather pale, but well-built girl, with beautiful yellow hair. She was rather secretive.

"Hey!" said Annie, accosting her; then softly: "Who's John Thomas on with now?"

"I don't know," said Nora.

"Why, tha does," said Annie, ironically lapsing into dialect. "Tha knows as well as I do."

"Well, I do, then," said Nora. "It isn't me, so don't bother."

"It's Cissy Meakin, isn't it?"

"It is, for all I know."

"Hasn't he got a face on him!" said Annie. "I don't half like his cheek. I could knock him off the foot-board when he comes round at me."

"He'll get dropped on one of these days," said Nora.

"Ay, he will, when somebody makes up their mind to drop it on him. I should like to see him taken down a peg or two, shouldn't you?"

"I shouldn't mind," said Nora.

"You've got quite as much cause to as I have," said Annie. "But we'll drop on him one of these days, my girl. What? Don't you want to?"

"I don't mind," said Nora.

But as a matter of fact, Nora was much more vindictive than Annie.

One by one Annie went the round of the old flames. It so happened that Cissy Meakin left the tramway service in quite a short time. Her mother made her leave. Then John Thomas was on the *qui vive.* He cast his eyes over his old flock. And his eyes lighted on Annie. He thought she would be safe now. Besides, he liked her.

She arranged to walk home with him on Sunday night. It so happened that her car would be in the depôt at half-past nine: the last car would come in at 10:15. So John Thomas was to wait for her there.

At the depôt the girls had a little waiting-room of their own. It was quite rough, but cosy, with a fire and an oven and a mirror, and table and wooden chairs. The half-dozen girls who knew John Thomas only too well had arranged to take service this Sunday afternoon. So, as the cars began to come in, early, the girls dropped into the waiting-room. And instead of hurrying off home, they sat around the fire and had a cup of tea. Outside was the darkness and lawlessness of war-time.

John Thomas came on the car after Annie, at about a quarter to ten. He poked his head easily into the girls' waiting-room.

"Prayer-meeting?" he asked.

"Ay," said Laura Sharp. "Ladies only."

"That's me!" said John Thomas. It was one of his favourite exclamations.

"Shut the door, boy," said Muriel Baggaley.

"Oh, which side of me?" said John Thomas.

"Which tha likes," said Polly Birkin.

He had come in and closed the door behind him. The girls moved in their circle, to make a place for him near the fire. He took off his great-coat and pushed back his hat.

"Who handles the teapot?" he said.

Nora Purdy silently poured him out a cup of tea.

"Want a bit o' my bread and drippin'?" said Muriel Baggaley to him.

"Ay, give us a bit."

And he began to eat his piece of bread.

"There's no place like home, girls," he said.

They all looked at him as he uttered this piece of impudence. He seemed to be sunning himself in the presence of so many damsels.

"Especially if you're not afraid to go home in the dark," said Laura Sharp.

"Me! By myself I am."

They sat till they heard the last tram come in. In a few minutes Emma Houselay entered.

"Come on, my old duck!" cried Polly Birkin.

"It *is* perishing," said Emma, holding her fingers to the fire.

"But—I'm afraid to, go home in, the dark," sang Laura Sharp, the tune having got into her mind.

"Who're you going with to-night, John Thomas?" asked Muriel Baggaley coolly.

"To-night?" said John Thomas. "Oh, I'm going home by myself to-night—all on my lonely-o."

"That's me!" said Nora Purdy, using his own ejaculation.

The girls laughed shrilly.

"Me as well, Nora," said John Thomas.

"Don't know what you mean," said Laura.

"Yes, I'm toddling," said he, rising and reaching for his overcoat.

"Nay," said Polly. "We're all here waiting for you."

"We've got to be up in good time in the morning," he said, in the benevolent official manner.

They all laughed.

"Nay," said Muriel. "Don't leave us all lonely,

John Thomas. Take one!"

"I'll take the lot, if you like," he responded gallantly.

"That you won't, either," said Muriel. "Two's company; seven's too much of a good thing."

"Nay—take one," said Laura. "Fair and square, all above board and say which."

"Ay," cried Annie, speaking for the first time. "Pick, John Thomas; let's hear thee."

"Nay," he said. "I'm going home quiet to-night. Feeling good, for once."

"Whereabouts?" said Annie. "Take a good 'un, then. But tha's got to take one of us!"

"Nay, how can I take one," he said, laughing uneasily. "I don't want to make enemies."

"You'd only make *one*," said Annie.

"The chosen *one*," added Laura.

"Oh, my! Who said girls!" exclaimed John Thomas, again turning, as if to escape. "Well—good-night."

"Nay, you've got to make your pick," said Muriel. "Turn your face to the wall, and say which one touches you. Go on—we shall only just touch your back—one of us. Go on—turn your face to the wall, and don't look, and say which one touches you."

He was uneasy, mistrusting them. Yet he had not the courage to break away. They pushed him to a wall and stood him there with his face to it. Behind his back they all grimaced, tittering. He looked so comical. He looked around uneasily.

"Go on!" he cried.

"You're looking—you're looking!" they shouted.

He turned his head away. And suddenly, with a movement like a swift cat, Annie went forward and fetched him a box on the side of the head that sent his cap flying and himself staggering. He started round.

But at Annie's signal they all flew at him, slapping him, pinching him, pulling his hair, though more in fun than in spite or anger. He, however, saw red. His blue eyes flamed with strange fear as well as fury, and he butted through the girls to the door. It was locked. He wrenched at it. Roused, alert, the girls stood round and looked at him. He faced them, at bay. At that moment they were rather horrifying to him, as they stood in their short uniforms. He was distinctly afraid.

"Come on, John Thomas! Come on! Choose!" said Annie.

"What are you after? Open the door," he said.

"We shan't—not till you've chosen!" said Muriel.

"Chosen what?" he said.

"Chosen the one you're going to marry," she replied.

He hesitated a moment.

"Open the blasted door," he said, "and get back to your senses." He spoke with official authority.

"You've got to choose!" cried the girls.

"Come on!" cried Annie, looking him in the eye. "Come on! Come on!"

He went forward, rather vaguely. She had taken off her belt, and swinging it, she fetched him a sharp blow over the head with the buckle end. He sprang and seized her. But immediately the other girls rushed upon him, pulling and tearing and beating him. Their blood was now thoroughly up. He was their sport now. They were going to have their own back, out of him. Strange, wild creatures, they hung on him and rushed at him to bear him down. His tunic was torn right up the back, Nora had hold at the back of his collar, and was actually strangling him. Luckily the button burst. He struggled in a wild frenzy of fury and terror, almost mad terror. His tunic was simply torn off his back, his shirt-sleeves were torn away, his arms were naked. The girls rushed at him, clenched their hands on him, and pulled at him: or they rushed at him and pushed him, butted him with all their might: or they struck him wild blows. He ducked and cringed and struck sideways. They became more intense.

At last he was down. They rushed on him, kneeling on him. He had neither breath nor strength to move. His face was bleeding with a long scratch, his brow was bruised.

Annie knelt on him, the other girls knelt and hung on to him. Their faces were flushed, their hair wild, their eyes were all glittering strangely. He lay at last quite still, with face averted, as an animal lies when it is defeated and at the mercy of the captor. Sometimes his eye glanced back at the wild faces of the girls. His breast rose heavily, his wrists were torn.

"Now, then, my fellow!" gasped Annie at length. "Now then—now—"

At the sound of her terrifying, cold triumph, he suddenly started to struggle as an animal might, but the girls threw themselves upon him with unnatural strength and power, forcing him down.

"Yes—now, then!" gasped Annie at length.

And there was a dead silence, in which the thud of heart-beating was to be heard. It was a suspense of pure silence in every soul.

"Now you know where you are," said Annie.

The sight of his white, bare arm maddened the girls. He lay in a kind of trance of fear and antagonism. They felt themselves filled with supernatural strength.

Suddenly Polly started to laugh—to giggle wildly—helplessly—and Emma and Muriel joined in. But Annie and Nora and Laura remained the same, tense, watchful, with gleaming eyes. He winced away from these eyes.

"Yes," said Annie, in a curious low tone, secret and deadly. "Yes! You've got it now. You know what you've done, don't you? You know what you've done."

He made no sound nor sign, but lay with bright, averted eyes, and averted, bleeding face.

"You ought to be *killed,* that's what you ought," said Annie, tensely. "You ought to be *killed.*" And there was a terrifying lust in her voice.

Polly was ceasing to laugh, and giving long-drawn Oh-h-hs and sighs as she came to herself.

"He's got to choose," she said vaguely.

"Oh, yes, he has," said Laura, with vindictive decision.

"Do you hear—do you hear?" said Annie. And with a sharp movement, that made him wince, she turned his face to her.

"Do you hear?" she repeated, shaking him.

But he was quite dumb. She fetched him a sharp slap on the face. He started, and his eyes widened. Then his face darkened with defiance, after all.

"Do you hear?" she repeated.

He only looked at her with hostile eyes.

"Speak!" she said, putting her face devilishly near his.

"What?" he said, almost overcome.

"You've got to *choose!*" she cried, as if it were some terrible menace, and as if it hurt her that she could not exact more.

"What?" he said, in fear.

"Choose your girl, Coddy. You've got to choose her now. And you'll get your neck broken if you play any more of your tricks, my boy. You're settled now."

There was a pause. Again he averted his face. He was cunning in his overthrow. He did not give in to them really—no, not if they tore him to bits.

"All right, then," he said, "I choose Annie." His voice was strange and full of malice. Annie let go of him as if he had been a hot coal.

"He's chosen Annie!" said the girls in chorus.

"Me!" cried Annie. She was still kneeling, but away from him. He was still lying prostrate, with averted face. The girls grouped uneasily around.

"Me!" repeated Annie, with a terrible bitter accent.

Then she got up, drawing away from him with strange disgust and bitterness.

"I wouldn't touch him," she said.

But her face quivered with a kind of agony, she seemed as if she would fall. The other girls turned aside. He remained lying on the floor, with his torn clothes and bleeding, averted face.

"Oh, if he's chosen—" said Polly.

"I don't want him—he can choose again," said Annie, with the same rather bitter hopelessness.

"Get up," said Polly, lifting his shoulder. "Get up."

He rose slowly, a strange, ragged, dazed creature. The girls eyed him from a distance, curiously, furtively, dangerously.

"Who wants him?" cried Laura, roughly.

"Nobody," they answered, with contempt. Yet each one of them waited for him to look at her, hoped he would look at her. All except Annie, and something was broken in her.

He, however, kept his face closed and averted from them all. There was a silence of the end. He picked up the torn pieces of his tunic, without knowing what to do with them. The girls stood about uneasily, flushed, panting, tidying their hair and their dress unconsciously, and watching him. He looked at none of them. He espied his cap in a corner, and went and picked it up. He put it on his head, and one of the girls burst into a shrill, hysteric laugh at the sight he presented. He, however, took no heed, but went straight to where his overcoat hung on a peg. The girls moved away from contact with him as if he had been an electric wire. He put on his coat and buttoned it down. Then he rolled his tunic-rags into a bundle, and stood before the locked door, dumbly.

"Open the door, somebody," said Laura.

"Annie's got the key," said one.

Annie silently offered the key to the girls. Nora unlocked the door.

"Tit for tat, old man," she said. "Show yourself a man, and don't bear a grudge."

But without a word or sign he had opened the door and gone, his face closed, his head dropped.

"That'll learn him," said Laura.

"Coddy!" said Nora.

"Shut up, for God's sake!" cried Annie fiercely, as if in torture.

"Well, I'm about ready to go, Polly. Look sharp!" said Muriel.

The girls were all anxious to be off. They were tidying themselves hurriedly, with mute, stupefied faces. □

DISCUSSION

1. (a) Does John Thomas deserve his fate? Explain.

(b) Is John Thomas ever in any real danger?

2. (a) What does the wartime setting have to do with the events of the story?

(b) What does the fact that the girls wear uniforms have to do with the events of the story?

3. (a) Why does Annie refuse John Thomas after he selects her?

(b) At the end of the story, why do the six girls behave so strangely after they have humiliated John Thomas?

4. (a) Do you think John Thomas will be back on the job the next day? Explain.

(b) Will all the girls be back?

5. Both "Tickets, Please" and "Youth" deal with the attainment of maturity.

(a) Compare the two selections with regard to their tone, the experiences that lead to maturity, and the state of mind of Marlow at the end of "Youth" and of Annie and John Thomas at the end of "Tickets, Please."

(b) In terms of their outcomes, would you say the maturing experiences were worth their cost to Marlow, to Annie, and to John Thomas?

(c) With which of these three characters was it easiest for you to identify? Why?

WRITING

Write an imaginary dialogue between Annie and John Thomas when they next meet.

TWO BLUE BIRDS

by D. H. Lawrence

THERE was a woman who loved her husband, but she could not live with him. The husband, on his side, was sincerely attached to his wife, yet he could not live with her. They were both under forty, both handsome, and both attractive. They had the most sincere regard for one another, and felt, in some odd way, eternally married to one another. They knew one another more intimately than they knew anybody else, they felt more known to one another than to any other person.

Yet they could not live together. Usually, they kept a thousand miles apart, geographically. But when he sat in the greyness of England, at the back of his

From *The Complete Short Stories: D. H. Lawrence, Vol. II.* Copyright 1922 by Thomas B. Seltzer, Inc., copyright renewed 1950 by Frieda Lawrence. Reprinted by permission of The Viking Press, Inc., Lawrence Pollinger Ltd. and the Estate of the Late Mrs. Frieda Lawrence.

mind, with a certain grim fidelity, he was aware of his wife, her strange yearning to be loyal and faithful, having her gallant affairs away in the sun, in the south. And she, as she drank her cocktail on the terrace over the sea, and turned her grey, sardonic eyes on the heavy dark face of her admirer, whom she really liked quite a lot, she was actually preoccupied with the clear-cut features of her handsome young husband, thinking of how he would be asking his secretary to do something for him, asking in that good-natured, confident voice of a man who knows that his request will be only too gladly fulfilled.

The secretary, of course, adored him. She was *very* competent, quite young, and quite good-looking. She adored him. But then all his servants always did, particularly his women-servants. His men-servants were likely to swindle him.

When a man has an adoring secretary, and you are the man's wife, what are you to do? Not that there was anything "wrong"—if you know what I mean!—between them. Nothing you could call adultery, to come down to brass tacks. No, no! They were just the young master and his secretary. He dictated to her, she slaved for him and adored him, and the whole thing went on wheels.

He didn't "adore" her. A man doesn't need to adore his secretary. But he depended on her. "I simply rely on Miss Wrexall." Whereas he could never rely on his wife. The one thing he knew finally about *her* was that she didn't intend to be relied on.

So they remained friends, in the awful unspoken intimacy of the once-married. Usually each year they went away together for a holiday, and, if they had not been man and wife, they would have found a great deal of fun and stimulation in one another. The fact that they were married, had been married for the last dozen years, and couldn't live together for the last three or four, spoilt them for one another. Each had a private feeling of bitterness about the other.

However, they were awfully kind. He was the soul of generosity, and held her in real tender esteem, no matter how many gallant affairs she had. Her gallant affairs were part of her modern necessity. "After all, I've got to *live.* I can't turn into a pillar of salt in five minutes just because you and I can't live together! It takes years for a woman like me to turn into a pillar of salt. At least I hope so!"

"Quite!" he replied. "Quite! By all means put them in pickle, make pickled cucumbers of them, before you crystallise out. That's my advice."

He was like that: so awfully clever and enigmatic. She could more or less fathom the idea of the pickled cucumbers, but the "crystallising out"—what did that signify?

And did he mean to suggest that he himself had been well pickled and that further immersion was for him unnecessary, would spoil his flavour? Was that what he meant? And herself, was she the brine and the vale of tears?

You never knew how catty a man was being, when he was really clever and enigmatic, withal a bit whimsical. He was adorably whimsical, with a twist of his flexible, vain mouth, that had a long upper lip, so fraught with vanity! But then a handsome, clear-cut, histrionic young man like that, how could he help being vain? The women made him so.

Ah, the women! How nice men would be if there were no other women!

And how nice the women would be if there were no other men! That's the best of a secretary. She may have a husband, but a husband is the mere shred of a man, compared to a boss, a chief, a man who dictates to you and whose words you faithfully write down and then transcribe. Imagine a wife writing down anything her husband said to her! But a secretary! Every *and* and *but* of his she preserves for ever. What are candied violets in comparison!

Now it is all very well having gallant affairs under the southern sun, when you know there is a husband whom you adore dictating to a secretary whom you are too scornful to hate yet whom you rather despise, though you allow she has her good points, away north in the place you ought to regard as home. A gallant affair isn't much good when you've got a bit of grit in your eye. Or something at the back of your mind.

What's to be done? The husband, of course, did not send his wife away.

"You've got your secretary and your work," she said. "There's no room for me."

"There's a bedroom and a sitting-room exclusively for you," he replied. "And a garden and half a motor-car. But please yourself entirely. Do what gives you most pleasure."

"In that case," she said, "I'll just go south for the winter."

"Yes, do!" he said. "You always enjoy it."

"I always do," she replied.

They parted with a certain relentlessness that had a touch of wistful sentiment behind it. Off she went to her gallant affairs, that were like the curate's egg, palatable in parts. And he settled down to work. He said he hated working, but he never did anything else. Ten or eleven hours a day. That's what it is to be your own master!

So the winter wore away, and it was spring, when the swallows homeward fly, or northward, in this case. This winter, one of a series similar, had been rather hard to get through. The bit of grit in the gallant lady's eye had worked deeper in the more she blinked. Dark faces might be dark, and icy cocktails might lend a glow; she blinked her hardest to blink that bit of grit away, without success. Under the spicy balls of the mimosa she thought of that husband of hers in his library, and of that neat, competent but *common* little secretary of his, for ever taking down what he said!

"How a man can *stand* it! How *she* can stand it, common little thing as she is, I don't know!" the wife cried to herself.

She meant this dictating business, this ten hours a day intercourse, *à deux,* with nothing but a pencil between them, and a flow of words.

What was to be done? Matters, instead of improving, had grown worse. The little secretary had brought her mother and sister into the establishment. The mother was a sort of cook-housekeeper, the sister was a sort of upper maid—she did the fine laundry, and looked after "his" clothes, and valeted him beautifully. It was really an excellent arrangement. The old mother was a splendid plain cook, the sister was all that could be desired as a valet de chambre, a fine laundress, an upper parlour-maid, and a table-waiter. And all economical to a degree. They knew his affairs by heart. His secretary flew to town when a creditor became dangerous, and she *always* smoothed over the financial crisis.

"He," of course, had debts, and he was working to pay them off. And if he had been a fairy prince who could call the ants to help him, he would not have been more wonderful than in securing this secretary and her family. They took hardly any wages. And they seemed to perform the miracle of loaves and fishes daily.

"She," of course, was the wife who loved her husband, but helped him into debt, and she still was an expensive item. Yet when she appeared at her "home," the secretarial family received her with most elaborate attentions and deference. The knight returning from the Crusades didn't create a greater stir. She felt like Queen Elizabeth at Kenilworth, a sovereign paying a visit to her faithful subjects. But perhaps there lurked always this hair in her soup! Won't they be glad to be rid of me again!

But they protested No! No! They had been waiting and hoping and praying she would come. They had been pining for her to be there, in charge: the mistress, "his" wife. Ah, "his" wife!

"His" wife! His halo was like a bucket over her head.

The cook-mother was "of the people," so it was the upper-maid daughter who came for orders.

"What will you order for to-morrow's lunch and dinner, Mrs. Gee?"

"Well, what do you usually have?"

"Oh, we want *you* to say."

"No, what do you *usually* have?"

"We don't have anything fixed. Mother goes out and chooses the best she can find, that is nice and fresh. But she thought you would tell her now what to get."

"Oh, I don't know! I'm not very good at that sort of thing. Ask her to go on just the same; I'm quite sure she knows best."

"Perhaps you'd like to suggest a sweet?"

"No, I don't care for sweets—and you know Mr. Gee doesn't. So don't make one for me."

Could anything be more impossible! They had the house spotless and running like a dream; how could an incompetent and extravagant wife dare to interfere, when she saw their amazing and almost inspired economy! But they ran the place on simply nothing!

Simply marvellous people! And the way they strewed palm branches under her feet!

But that only made her feel ridiculous.

"Don't you think the family manage very well?" he asked her tentatively.

"Awfully well! Almost romantically well!" she replied. "But I suppose you're perfectly happy?"

"I'm perfectly comfortable," he replied.

"I can see you are," she replied. "Amazingly so! I never knew such comfort! Are you sure it isn't bad for you?"

She eyed him stealthily. He looked very well, and extremely handsome, in his histrionic way. He was shockingly well-dressed and valeted. And he had that air of easy aplomb and good humour which is so becoming to a man, and which he only acquires when he is cock of his own little walk, made much of by his own hens.

"No!" he said, taking his pipe from his mouth and smiling whimsically round at her. "Do I look as if it were bad for me?"

"No, you don't," she replied promptly: thinking, naturally, as a woman is supposed to think nowadays, of his health and comfort, the foundation, apparently, of all happiness.

Then, of course, away she went on the backwash.

"Perhaps for your work, though, it's not so good as it is for *you*," she said in a rather small voice. She knew he couldn't bear it if she mocked at his work for one moment. And he knew that rather small voice of hers.

"In what way?" he said, bristles rising.

"Oh, I don't know," she answered indifferently. "Perhaps it's not good for a man's work if he is too comfortable."

"I don't know about *that!*" he said, taking a dramatic turn round the library and drawing at his pipe. "Considering I work, actually, by the clock, for twelve hours a day, and for ten hours when it's a short day, I don't think you can say I am deteriorating from easy comfort."

"No, I suppose not," she admitted.

Yet she did think it, nevertheless. His comfortableness didn't consist so much in good food and a soft bed, as in having nobody, absolutely nobody and nothing to contradict him. "I do like to think he's got nothing to aggravate him," the secretary had said to the wife.

"Nothing to aggravate him!" What a position for a man! Fostered by women who would let nothing "aggravate" him. If anything would aggravate his wounded vanity, this would!

So thought the wife. But what was to be done about it? In the silence of midnight she heard his voice in the distance, dictating away, like the voice of God to Samuel, alone and monotonous, and she imagined the little figure of the secretary busily scribbling shorthand. Then in the sunny hours of morning, while he was still in bed—he never rose till noon—from another distance came that sharp insect noise of the typewriter, like some immense grasshopper chirping and rattling. It was the secretary, poor thing, typing out his notes.

That girl—she was only twenty-eight—really slaved herself to skin and bone. She was small and neat, but she was actually worn out. She did far more work than he did, for she had not only to take down all those words he uttered, she had to type them out, make three copies, while he was still resting.

"What on earth she gets out of it," thought the wife, "I don't know. She's simply worn to the bone, for a very poor salary, and he's never kissed her, and never will, if I know anything about him."

Whether his never kissing her—the secretary, that is—made it worse or better, the wife did not decide. He never kissed anybody. Whether she herself—the wife, that is—wanted to be kissed by him, even that she was not clear about. She rather thought she didn't.

What on earth did she want then? She was his wife. What on earth did she want of him?

She certainly didn't want to take him down in shorthand, and type out again all those words. And she didn't really want him to kiss her; she knew him too well. Yes, she knew him too well. If you know a man too well, you don't want him to kiss you.

What then? What did she want? Why had she such an extraordinary hang-over about him? Just because she was his wife? Why did she rather "enjoy" other men—and she was relentless about enjoyment—without ever taking them seriously? And why must she take him so damn seriously, when she never really "enjoyed" him?

Of course she *had* had good times with him, in the past, before—ah! before a thousand things, all amounting really to nothing. But she enjoyed him no more. She never even enjoyed being with him. There was a silent, ceaseless tension between them, that never broke, even when they were a thousand miles apart.

Awful! That's what you call being married! What's to be done about it? Ridiculous, to know it all and not do anything about it!

She came back once more, and there she was, in her own house, a sort of super-guest, even to him. And the secretarial family devoting their lives to him.

Devoting their lives to him! But actually! Three women pouring out their lives for him day and night! And what did they get in return? Not one kiss! Very little money, because they knew all about his debts, and had made it their life business to get them paid off! No expectations! Twelve hours' work a day!

Comparative isolation, for he saw nobody!

And beyond that? Nothing! Perhaps a sense of uplift and importance because they saw his name and photograph in the newspaper sometimes. But would anybody believe that it was good enough?

Yet they adored it! They seemed to get a deep satisfaction out of it, like people with a mission. Extraordinary!

Well, if they did, let them. They were, of course, rather common, "of the people"; there might be a sort of glamour in it for them.

But it was bad for him. No doubt about it. His work was getting diffuse and poor in quality—and what wonder! His whole tone was going down—becoming commoner. Of course it was bad for him.

Being his wife, she felt she ought to do something to save him. But how could she? That perfectly devoted, marvelous secretarial family, how could she make an attack on them? Yet she'd love to sweep them into oblivion. Of course they were bad for him: ruining his work, ruining his reputation as a writer, ruining his life. Ruining him with their slavish service.

Of course she ought to make an onslaught on them! But how *could* she? Such devotion! And what had she herself to offer in their place? Certainly not slavish devotion to him, nor to his flow of words! Certainly not!

She imagined him stripped once more naked of secretary and secretarial family, and she shuddered. It was like throwing the naked baby in the dust-bin. Couldn't do that!

Yet something must be done. She felt it. She was almost tempted to get into debt for another thousand pounds, and send in the bill, or have it sent in to him, as usual.

But no! Something more drastic!

Something more drastic, or perhaps more gentle. She wavered between the two. And wavering, she first did nothing, came to no decision, dragged vacantly on from day to day, waiting for sufficient energy to take her departure once more.

It was spring! What a fool she had been to come up in spring! And she was forty! What an idiot of a woman to go and be forty!

She went down the garden in the warm afternoon, when birds were whistling loudly from the cover, the sky being low and warm, and she had nothing to do. The garden was full of flowers: he loved them for their theatrical display. Lilac and snowball bushes, and laburnum and red may, tulips and anemones and coloured daisies. Lots of flowers! Borders of forget-me-nots! Bachelor's buttons! What absurd names flowers had! She would have called them blue dots and yellow blobs and white frills. Not so much sentiment, after all!

There is a certain nonsense, something showy and stagey about spring, with its pushing leaves and chorus-girl flowers, unless you have something corresponding inside you. Which she hadn't.

Oh, heaven! Beyond the hedge she heard a voice, a steady rather theatrical voice. Oh, heaven! He was dictating to his secretary in the garden. Good God, was there nowhere to get away from it!

She looked around: there was indeed plenty of escape. But what was the good of escaping? He would go on and on. She went quietly towards the hedge, and listened.

He was dictating a magazine article about the modern novel. "What the modern novel lacks is architecture." Good God! Architecture! He might just as well say: What the modern novel lacks is whalebone, or a teaspoon, or a tooth stopped.

Yet the secretary took it down, took it down, took it down! No, this could not go on! It was more than flesh and blood could bear.

She went quietly along the hedge, somewhat wolf-like in her prowl, a broad, strong woman in an expensive mustard-coloured silk jersey and cream-coloured pleated skirt. Her legs were long and shapely, and her shoes were expensive.

With a curious wolf-like stealth she turned the hedge and looked across at the small, shaded lawn where the daisies grew impertinently. "He" was reclining in a coloured hammock under the pink-flowering horse-chestnut tree, dressed in white serge with a fine yellow-coloured linen shirt. His elegant hand dropped over the side of the hammock and beat a sort of vague rhythm to his words. At a little wicker table the little secretary, in a green knitted frock, bent her dark head over her note-book, and diligently made those awful shorthand marks. He was not difficult to take down, as he dictated slowly, and kept a sort of rhythm, beating time with his dangling hand.

"In every novel there must be one outstanding character with which we always sympathise—with *whom* we always sympathise—even though we recognise it—even when we are most aware of the human frailties—"

Every man his own hero, thought the wife grimly, forgetting that every woman is intensely her own heroine.

But what did startle her was a blue bird dashing about near the feet of the absorbed, shorthand-scribbling little secretary. At least it was a blue-tit, blue with grey and some yellow. But to the wife it seemed blue, that juicy spring day, in the translucent afternoon. The blue bird, fluttering round the pretty but rather *common* little feet of the little secretary.

The blue bird! The blue bird of happiness! Well, I'm blest,—thought the wife. Well, I'm blest!

And as she was being blest, appeared another blue bird—that is, another blue-tit—and began to wrestle with the first blue-tit. A couple of blue birds of happiness, having a fight over it! Well, I'm blest!

She was more or less out of sight of the human preoccupied pair. But "he" was disturbed by the fighting blue birds, whose little feathers began to float loose.

"Get out!" he said to them mildly, waving a dark-yellow handkerchief at them. "Fight your little fight, and settle your private affairs elsewhere, my dear little gentlemen."

The little secretary looked up quickly, for she had already begun to write it down. He smiled at her his twisted whimsical smile.

"No, don't take that down," he said affectionately. "Did you see those two tits laying into one another?"

"No!" said the little secretary, gazing brightly round, her eyes half-blinded with work.

But she saw the queer, powerful, elegant, wolf-like figure of the wife, behind her, and terror came into her eyes.

"I did!" said the wife, stepping forward with those curious, shapely, she-wolf legs of hers, under the very short skirt.

"Aren't they extraordinarily vicious little beasts?" said he.

"Extraordinarily!" she re-echoed, stooping and picking up a little breast-feather. "Extraordinarily! See how the feathers fly!"

And she got the feather on the tip of her finger, and looked at it. Then she looked at the secretary, then she looked at him. She had a queer, were-wolf expression between her brows.

"I think," he began, "these are the loveliest afternoons, when there's no direct sun, but all the sounds and the colours and the scents are sort of dissolved, don't you know, in the air, and the whole thing is steeped, steeped in spring. It's like being on the inside; you know how I mean, like being inside the egg and just ready to chip the shell."

"Quite like that!" she assented, without conviction.

There was a little pause. The secretary said nothing. They were waiting for the wife to depart again.

"I suppose," said the latter, "you're awfully busy, as usual?"

"Just about the same," he said, pursing his mouth deprecatingly.

Again the blank pause, in which he waited for her to go away again.

"I know I'm interrupting you," she said.

"As a matter of fact," he said, "I was just watching those two blue-tits."

"Pair of little demons!" said the wife, blowing away the yellow feather from her finger-tip.

"Absolutely!" he said.

"Well, I'd better go, and let you get on with your work," she said.

"No hurry!" he said, with benevolent nonchalance. "As a matter of fact, I don't think it's a great success, working out of doors."

"What made you try it?" said the wife. "You know you never could do it."

"Miss Wrexall suggested it might make a change. But I don't think it altogether helps, do you, Miss Wrexall?"

"I'm sorry," said the little secretary.

"Why should *you* be sorry?" said the wife, looking down at her as a wolf might look down half-benignly at a little black-and-tan mongrel. "You only suggested it for his good, I'm sure!"

"I thought the air might be good for him," the secretary admitted. "Why do people like you never think about yourselves?" the wife asked.

The secretary looked her in the eye.

"I suppose we do, in a different way," she said.

"A *very* different way!" said the wife ironically. "Why don't you make *him* think about *you?*" she added, slowly, with a sort of drawl. "On a soft spring afternoon like this, you ought to have him dictating poems to you, about the blue birds of happiness fluttering round your dainty little feet. I know *I* would, if I were his secretary."

There was a dead pause. The wife stood immobile and statuesque, in an attitude characteristic of her, half turning back to the little secretary, half averted. She half turned her back on everything.

The secretary looked at him.

"As a matter of fact," he said, "I was doing an article on the Future of the Novel."

"I know that," said the wife. "That's what's so awful! Why not something lively in the life of the novelist?"

There was a prolonged silence, in which he looked pained, and somewhat remote, statuesque. The little secretary hung her head. The wife sauntered slowly away.

"Just where were we, Miss Wrexall?" came the sound of his voice.

The little secretary started. She was feeling profoundly indignant. Their beautiful relationship, his and hers, to be so insulted!

But soon she was veering down-stream on the flow of his words, too busy to have any feelings, except one of elation at being so busy.

Tea-time came; the sister brought out the tea-tray into the garden. And immediately, the wife appeared. She had changed, and was wearing a chicory-blue dress of fine cloth. The little secretary had gathered up her papers and was departing, on rather high heels.

"Don't go, Miss Wrexall," said the wife.

The little secretary stopped short, then hesitated.

"Mother will be expecting me," she said.

"Tell her you're not coming. And ask your sister to bring another cup. I want you to have tea with us."

Miss Wrexall looked at the man, who was reared on one elbow in the hammock, and was looking enigmatical, Hamletish.

He glanced at her quickly, then pursed his mouth in a boyish negligence.

"Yes, stay and have tea with us for once," he said. "I see strawberries, and I know you're the bird for them."

She glanced at him, smiled wanly, and hurried away to tell her mother. She even stayed long enough to slip on a silk dress.

"Why, how smart you are!" said the wife, when the little secretary reappeared on the lawn, in chicory-blue silk.

"Oh, don't look at my dress, compared to yours!" said Miss Wrexall. They were of the same colour, indeed!

"At least you earned yours, which is more than I did mine," said the wife, as she poured tea. "You like it strong?"

She looked with her heavy eyes at the smallish, birdy, blue-clad, overworked young woman, and her eyes seemed to speak many inexplicable dark volumes.

"Oh, as it comes, thank you," said Miss Wrexall, leaning nervously forward.

"It's coming pretty black, if you want to ruin your digestion," said the wife.

"Oh, I'll have some water in it, then."

"Better, I should say."

"How'd the work go—all right?" asked the wife, as they drank tea, and the two women looked at each other's blue dresses.

"Oh!" he said. "As well as you can expect. It was a piece of pure flummery. But it's what they want. Awful rot, wasn't it, Miss Wrexall?"

Miss Wrexall moved uneasily on her chair.

"It interested me," she said, "though not so much as the novel."

"The novel? Which novel?" said the wife. "Is there another new one?"

Miss Wrexall looked at him. Not for words would she give away any of his literary activities.

"Oh, I was just sketching out an idea to Miss Wrexall," he said.

"Tell us about it!" said the wife. "Miss Wrexall, *you* tell us what it's about."

She turned on her chair, and fixed the little secretary.

"I'm afraid"—Miss Wrexall squirmed—"I haven't got it very clearly myself, yet."

"Oh, go along! Tell us what you *have* got then!"

Miss Wrexall sat dumb and very vexed. She felt she was being baited. She looked at the blue pleatings of her skirt.

"I'm afraid I can't," she said.

"Why are you afraid you can't? You're so *very* competent. I'm sure you've got it all at your finger-ends. I expect you write a good deal of Mr. Gee's books for him, really. He gives you the hint, and you fill it all in. Isn't that how you do it?" She spoke ironically, and as if she were teasing a child. And then she glanced down at the fine pleatings of her own blue skirt, very fine and expensive.

"Of course you're not speaking seriously?" said Miss Wrexall, rising on her mettle.

"Of course I am! I've suspected for a long time—at least for some time—that you write a good deal of Mr. Gee's books for him, from his hints."

It was said in a tone of raillery, but it was cruel.

"I should be terribly flattered," said Miss Wrexall,

straightening herself, "if I didn't know you were only trying to make me feel a fool."

"Make you feel a fool? My dear child!—why, nothing could be farther from me! You're twice as clever, and a million times as competent as I am. Why, my dear child, I've the greatest admiration for you! I wouldn't do what you do, not for all the pearls in India. I *couldn't* anyhow—"

Miss Wrexall closed up and was silent.

"Do you mean to say my books read as if—" he began, rearing up and speaking in a harrowed voice.

"I do!" said the wife. "*Just* as if Miss Wrexall had written them from your hints. I *honestly* thought she did—when you were too busy—"

"How very clever of you!" he said.

"Very!" she said. "Especially if I was wrong!"

"Which you were," he said.

"How very extraordinary!" she cried. "Well, I am once more mistaken!"

There was a complete pause.

It was broken by Miss Wrexall, who was nervously twisting her fingers.

"You want to spoil what there is between me and him, I can see that," she said bitterly.

"My dear, but what *is* there between you and him?" asked the wife.

"I was *happy* working with him, working for him! I was *happy* working for him!" cried Miss Wrexall, tears of indignant anger and chagrin in her eyes.

"My dear child!" cried the wife, with simulated excitement, "go *on* being happy working with him, go on being happy while you can! If it makes you happy, why then, enjoy it! Of course! Do you think I'd be so cruel as to want to take it away from you?—working with him? *I* can't do shorthand and type-writing and double-entrance book-keeping, or whatever it's called. I tell you, I'm utterly incompetent. I never earn anything. I'm the parasite of the British oak, like the mistletoe. The blue bird doesn't flutter round my feet. Perhaps they're too big and trampling."

She looked down at her expensive shoes.

"If I *did* have a word of criticism to offer," she said turning to her husband, "it would be to you, Cameron, for taking so much from her and giving her nothing."

"But he gives me everything, everything!" cried Miss Wrexall. "He gives me everything!"

"What do you mean by everything?" said the wife, turning on her sternly.

Miss Wrexall pulled up short. There was a snap in the air, and a change of currents.

"I mean nothing that *you* need begrudge me," said the little secretary rather haughtily. "I've never made myself cheap."

There was a blank pause.

"My God!" said the wife. "You don't call that being cheap? Why, I should say you got nothing out of him at all, you only give! And if you don't call that making yourself cheap—my God!"

"You see, we see things different," said the secretary.

"I should say we do!—*thank God!*" rejoined the wife.

"On whose behalf are you thanking God?" he asked sarcastically.

"Everybody's, I suppose! Yours, because you get everything for nothing, and Miss Wrexall's, because she seems to like it, and mine because I'm well out of it all."

"You *needn't* be out of it all," cried Miss Wrexall magnanimously, "if you didn't *put* yourself out of it all."

"Thank you, my dear, for your offer," said the wife, rising, "but I'm afraid no man can expect *two* blue birds of happiness to flutter round his feet, tearing out their little feathers!"

With which she walked away.

After a tense and desperate interim, Miss Wrexall cried:

"And *really*, need any woman be jealous of *me?*"

"Quite!" he said.

And that was all he did say. □

DISCUSSION

1. (a) Who is more to blame for the breakdown of the marriage, the husband or the wife? Support your answer by references to the text.

(b) According to the author, the husband and wife love each other. Why then are they unable to live together?

2. (a) What are Miss Wrexall's ultimate objectives?

(b) Do you think she ever attains any of them? Explain.

3. (a) What are the major personality differences between the wife and the secretary?

(b) Which of the two women does the husband find more attractive? Explain.

4. What is the symbolic function of the two blue birds?

5. Explain the meaning of each of the following passages:

(a) ". . . when you've got a bit of grit in your eye" (page 515b).

(b) "His halo was like a bucket over her head" (page 516b).

(c) "Perhaps it's not too good for a man's work if he is too comfortable" (page 517a)

(d) "She half turned her back on everything" (page 519b)

(e) "'. . . I'm the parasite of the British oak, like the mistletoe. The blue bird doesn't flutter round my feet. Perhaps they're too big and trampling" (page 521a)

6. "Tickets, Please" and "Two Blue Birds" show one of the greatest modern writers in two different fictional moods.

(a) Which story do you prefer? Why?

(b) What similarities can you detect in style, characterization, etc., in the two stories?

WRITING

1. Use narrative, dramatic, or expository writing to answer the question "What eventually becomes of Miss Wrexall?"

2. Write an imaginary conversation between the wife and Miss Wrexall when the two are alone, out of hearing of the husband or anyone else.

COURTESY OF ALFRED KNOPF

A CUP OF TEA

by Katherine Mansfield

ROSEMARY Fell was not exactly beautiful. No, you couldn't have called her beautiful. Pretty? Well, if you took her to pieces . . . But why be so cruel as to take anyone to pieces? She was young, brilliant, extremely modern, exquisitely well dressed, amazingly well read in the newest of the new books, and her parties were the most delicious mixture of the really important people and . . . artists—quaint creatures, discoveries of hers, some of them too terrifying for words, but others quite presentable and amusing.

Rosemary had been married two years. She had a duck of a boy. No, not Peter—Michael. And her husband absolutely adored her. They were rich, really rich, not just comfortably well off, which is odious and stuffy and sounds like one's grandparents. But if Rosemary wanted to shop she would go to Paris as you and I would go to Bond Street. If she wanted to buy flowers, the car pulled up at that perfect shop in Regent Street, and Rosemary inside the shop just gazed in her dazzled, rather exotic way, and said: "I want those and those and those. Give me four bunches of those. And that jar of roses. Yes, I'll have all the roses in the jar. No, no lilac. I hate lilac. It's got no shape." The attendant bowed and put the lilac out of sight, as though this was only too true; lilac was dreadfully shapeless. "Give me those stumpy little tulips. Those red and white ones." And she was followed to the car by a thin shopgirl staggering under an immense white paper armful that looked like a baby in long clothes. . . .

One winter afternoon she had been buying something in a little antique shop in Curzon Street. It was a shop she liked. For one thing, one usually had it to oneself. And then the man who kept it was ridiculously fond of serving her. He beamed whenever she came in. He clasped his hands; he was so gratified he could scarcely speak. Flattery, of course. All the same, there was something . . .

"You see, madam," he would explain in his low respectful tones, "I love my things. I would rather not part with them than sell them to someone who does not appreciate them, who has not that fine feeling which is so rare. . . ." And, breathing deeply, he unrolled a tiny square of blue velvet and pressed it on the glass counter with his pale finger-tips.

Today it was a little box. He had been keeping it for her. He had shown it to nobody as yet. An exquisite little enamel box with a glaze so fine it looked as though it had been baked in cream. On the lid a minute creature stood under a flowery tree, and a more minute creature still had her arms around his neck. Her hat, really no bigger than a geranium petal, hung from a branch; it had green ribbons. And there was a pink cloud like a watchful cherub floating above their heads. Rosemary took her hands out of her long gloves. She always took off her gloves to examine such things. Yes, she liked it very much. She loved it; it was a great duck. She must have it. And, turning the creamy box, opening and shutting it, she couldn't help noticing how charming her hands were against the blue velvet. The shopman, in some dim cavern of his mind, may have dared to think so too. For he took a pencil, leant over the counter, and his pale bloodless fingers crept timidly towards those rosy, flashing ones, as he murmured gently: "If I may venture to point out to madam, the flowers on the little lady's bodice."

"Charming!" Rosemary admired the flowers. But what was the price? For a moment the shopman did not seem to hear. Then a murmur reached her.

"Twenty-eight guineas, madame."

"Twenty-eight guineas." Rosemary gave no sign. She laid the little box down: she buttoned her gloves again. Twenty-eight guineas. Even if one is rich . . . She looked vague. She stared at a plump tea-kettle like a plump hen above the shopman's head, and her voice was dreamy as she answered: "Well, keep it for me—will you? I'll . . ."

But the shopman had already bowed as though keeping it for her was all any human being could ask. He would be willing, of course, to keep it for her for ever.

The discreet door shut with a click. She was outside on the step, gazing at the winter afternoon. Rain was falling, and with the rain it seemed the dark came too, spinning down like ashes. There was a cold bitter taste in the air, and the new-lighted lamps looked sad. Sad were the lights in the houses opposite. Dimly they burned as if regretting something. And people hurried by, hidden under their hateful umbrellas. Rosemary felt a strange pang. She pressed her muff to her breast; she wished she had the little box, too, to cling to. Of course, the car was there. She'd only to cross the pavement. But still she waited. There are moments, horrible moments in life, when one emerges from shelter and looks out, and it's awful. One oughtn't to give way to them. One ought to go home and have an extra-special tea. But at the very instant of thinking that, a young girl, thin, dark, shadowy—where had she come from?—was standing at Rosemary's elbow and a voice like a sigh, almost like a sob, breathed: "Madame, may I speak to you a moment?"

"Speak to me?" Rosemary turned. She saw a little battered creature with enormous eyes, someone quite young, no older than herself, who clutched at her coat-collar with reddened hands, and shivered as though she had just come out of the water.

"M-madam," stammered the voice. "Would you let me have the price of a cup of tea?"

"A cup of tea?" There was something simple, sincere in that voice; it wasn't in the least the voice of a beggar. "Then have you no money at all?" asked Rosemary.

"None, madam," came the answer.

"How extraordinary!" Rosemary peered through the dusk, and the girl gazed back at her. How more than extraordinary! And suddenly it seemed to Rosemary such an adventure. It was like something out of a novel by Dostoevsky, this meeting in the dusk. Supposing she took the girl home? Supposing she did do one of those things she was always reading about or seeing on the stage, what would happen? It would be thrilling. And she heard herself saying afterwards to the amazement of her friends: "I simply took her home with me," as she stepped forward and said to that dim person beside her: "Come home to tea with me."

The girl drew back startled. She even stopped shivering for a moment. Rosemary put out a hand and touched her arm. "I mean it," she said, smiling. And she felt how simple and kind her smile was. "Why won't you? Do. Come home with me now in my car and have tea."

"You—you don't mean it, madam," said the girl, and there was pain in her voice.

"But I do," cried Rosemary. "I want you to. To please me. Come along."

The girl put her fingers to her lips and her eyes devoured Rosemary. "You're—you're not taking me to the police station?" she stammered.

"The police station!" Rosemary laughed out. "Why should I be so cruel? No, I only want to make you warm and to hear—anything you care to tell me."

Hungry people are easily led. The footman held the door of the car open, and a moment later they were skimming through the dusk.

"There!" said Rosemary. She had a feeling of triumph as she slipped her hand through the velvet strap. She could have said, "Now I've got you," as she gazed at the little captive she had netted. But of course she meant it kindly. Oh, more than kindly. She was going to prove to this girl that—wonderful things did happen in life, that—fairy godmothers were real, that—rich people had hearts, and that women *were* sisters. She turned impulsively, saying: "Don't be frightened. After all, why shouldn't you come back with me? We're both women. If I'm the more fortunate, you ought to expect . . ."

But happily at that moment, for she didn't know how the sentence was going to end, the car stopped. The bell was rung, the door opened, and with a charming, protecting, almost embracing movement, Rosemary drew the other into the hall. Warmth, softness, light, a sweet scent, all those things so familiar to her she never even thought about them, she watched that other receive. It was fascinating. She was like the little rich girl in her nursery with all the cupboards to open, all the boxes to unpack.

"Come, come upstairs," said Rosemary, longing to begin to be generous. "Come up to my room." And, besides, she wanted to spare this poor little thing from being stared at by the servants; she decided as they mounted the stairs she would not even ring for Jeanne, but take off her things by herself. The great thing was to be natural!

And "There!" cried Rosemary again, as they reached her beautiful big bedroom with the curtains drawn, the fire leaping on her wonderful lacquer furniture, her gold cushions and the primrose and blue rugs.

The girl stood just inside the door; she seemed dazed. But Rosemary didn't mind that.

"Come and sit down," she cried, dragging her big chair up to the fire, "in this comfy chair. Come and get warm. You look so dreadfully cold."

"I daren't, madam," said the girl, and she edged backwards.

"Oh, please,"—Rosemary ran forward—"you mustn't be frightened, you mustn't, really. Sit down, and when I've taken off my things we shall go into the next room and have tea and be cosy. Why are you afraid?" And gently she half pushed the thin figure into its deep cradle.

But there was no answer. The girl stayed just as she had been put, with her hands by her sides and her mouth slightly open. To be quite sincere, she looked rather stupid. But Rosemary wouldn't acknowledge it. She leant over her, saying: "Won't you take off your hat? Your pretty hair is all wet. And one is so much more comfortable without a hat, isn't one?"

There was a whisper that sounded like "Very good, madam," and the crushed hat was taken off.

"Let me help you off with your coat, too," said Rosemary.

The girl stood up. But she held on to the chair with one hand and let Rosemary pull. It was quite an effort. The other scarcely helped her at all. She seemed to stagger like a child, and the thought came and went through Rosemary's mind, that if people wanted helping they must respond a little, just a little, otherwise it became very difficult indeed. And what was she to do with the coat now? She left it on the floor, and the hat too. She was just going to take a cigarette off the mantelpiece when the girl said quickly, but so lightly and strangely: "I'm very sorry, madam, but I'm going to faint. I shall go off, madam, if I don't have something."

"Good heavens, how thoughtless I am!" Rosemary rushed to the bell.

"Tea! Tea at once! And some brandy immediately!"

The maid was gone again, but the girl almost cried out. "No, I don't want no brandy. I never drink brandy. It's a cup of tea I want, madam." And she burst into tears.

It was a terrible and fascinating moment. Rosemary knelt beside her chair.

"Don't cry, poor little thing," she said. "Don't cry." And she gave the other her lace handkerchief. She really was touched beyond words. She put her arm round those thin, birdlike shoulders.

Now at last the other forgot to be shy, forgot everything except that they were both women, and gasped out: "I can't go on no longer like this. I can't bear it. I shall do away with myself. I can't bear no more."

"You shan't have to. I'll look after you. Don't cry any more. Don't you see what a good thing it was that you met me? We'll have tea and you'll tell me everything. And I shall arrange something. I promise. *Do* stop crying. It's so exhausting. Please!"

The other did stop just in time for Rosemary to get up before the tea came. She had the table placed between them. She plied the poor little creature with everything, all the sandwiches, all the bread and butter, and every time her cup was empty she filled it with tea, cream and sugar. People always said sugar was so nourishing. As for herself she didn't eat; she smoked and looked away tactfully so that the other should not be shy.

And really the effect of that slight meal was marvellous. When the tea-table was carried away a new being, a light, frail creature with tangled hair, dark lips, deep, lighted eyes, lay back in the big chair in a kind of sweet languor, looking at the blaze. Rosemary lit a fresh cigarette; it was time to begin.

"And when did you have your last meal?" she asked softly.

But at the moment the door-handle turned.

"Rosemary, may I come in?" It was Philip.

"Of course."

He came in. "Oh, I'm so sorry," he said, and stopped and stared.

"It's quite all right," said Rosemary smiling. "This is my friend, Miss—"

"Smith, madam," said the languid figure, who was strangely still and unafraid.

"Smith," said Rosemary. "We are going to have a little talk."

"Oh, yes," said Philip. "Quite," and his eye caught sight of the coat and hat on the floor. He came over to the fire and turned his back to it. "It's a beastly afternoon," he said curiously, still looking at that listless figure, looking at its hands and boots, and then at Rosemary again.

"Yes, isn't it?" said Rosemary enthusiastically. "Vile."

Philip smiled his charming smile. "As a matter of fact," said he, "I wanted you to come into the library for a moment. Would you? Will Miss Smith excuse us?"

The big eyes were raised to him, but Rosemary answered for her. "Of course she will." And they went out of the room together.

"I say," said Philip, when they were alone. "Explain. Who is she? What does it all mean?"

Rosemary, laughing, leaned against the door and said: "I picked her up in Curzon Street. Really. She's a real pick-up. She asked me for the price of a cup of tea, and I brought her home with me."

"But what on earth are you going to do with her?" cried Philip.

"Be nice to her," said Rosemary quickly. "Be frightfully nice to her. Look after her. I don't know how. We haven't talked yet. But show her—treat her—make her feel—"

"My darling girl," said Philip, "you're quite mad, you know. It simply can't be done."

"I knew you'd say that," retorted Rosemary. "Why not? I want to. Isn't that a reason? And besides, one's always reading about these things. I decided—"

"But," said Philip slowly, and he cut the end of a cigar, "she's so astonishingly pretty."

"Pretty?" Rosemary was so surprised that she blushed. "Do you think so? I—I hadn't thought about it."

"Good Lord!" Philip struck a match. "She's absolutely lovely. Look again, my child. I was bowled over when I came into your room just now. However . . . I think you're making a ghastly mistake. Sorry, darling, if I'm crude and all that. But let me know if Miss Smith is going to dine with us in time for me to look up *The Milliner's Gazette*."

"You absurd creature!" said Rosemary, and she went out of the library, but not back to her bedroom.

She went to her writing-room and sat down at her desk. Pretty! Absolutely lovely! Bowled over! Her heart beat like a heavy bell. Pretty! Lovely! She drew her cheque book towards her. But no, cheques would be no use, of course. She opened a drawer and took out five pound notes, looked at them, put two back, and holding the three squeezed in her hand, she went back to her bedroom.

Half an hour later Philip was still in the library, when Rosemary came in.

"I only wanted to tell you," said she, and she leaned against the door again and looked at him with her dazzled exotic gaze, "Miss Smith won't dine with us tonight."

Philip put down the paper. "Oh, what's happened? Previous engagement?"

Rosemary came over and sat down on his knee. "She insisted on going," said she, "so I gave the poor little thing a present of money. I couldn't keep her against her will, could I?" she added softly.

Rosemary had just done her hair, darkened her eyes a little, and put on her pearls. She put up her hands and touched Philip's cheeks.

"Do you like me?" said she, and her tone, sweet, husky, troubled him.

"I like you awfully," he said, and he held her tighter. "Kiss me."

There was a pause.

Then Rosemary said dreamily, "I saw a fascinating little box today. It cost twenty-eight guineas. May I have it?"

Philip jumped her on his knee. "You may, little wasteful one," said he.

But that was not really what Rosemary wanted to say.

"Philip," she whispered, and she pressed his head against her bosom, "am I *pretty?*" □

DISCUSSION

1. (a) What impels Rosemary to invite Miss Smith to her home?

(b) What changes Rosemary's mind about being of permanent help to Miss Smith?

(c) In the final analysis, is Rosemary's act in taking Miss Smith home merciful, or is it cruel?

(d) Does Rosemary ever consider Miss Smith as a human being in her own right?

2. Two superficially unrelated incidents have an important joint function in this story:

(a) In the antique shop, Rosemary admires and has set aside for probable purchase an exquisite little enamel box priced at 28 guineas (roughly $100).

(b) Upon stepping out of the antique shop into the desolate afternoon, Rosemary thinks, "There are moments, horrible moments in life, when one emerges from shelter and looks out, and it's awful."

Explain how these two incidents are related and how they are interwoven into the story.

3. (a) In what respects are the marriages in "Two Blue Birds" and "A Cup of Tea" similar?

(b) Which of the wives is more selfish?

(c) To what extent is each husband responsible for the weakness in his marriage?

WRITING

Write an ending to Miss Smith's story.

MILLIE

by Katherine Mansfield

MILLIE stood leaning against the verandah until the men were out of sight. When they were far down the road Willie Cox turned round on his horse and waved. But she didn't wave back. She nodded her head a little and made a grimace. Not a bad young fellow, Willie Cox, but a bit too free and easy for her taste. Oh, my word! it was hot. Enough to fry your hair!

Millie put her handkerchief over her head and shaded her eyes with her hand. In the distance along the dusty road she could see the horses, like brown spots dancing up and down, and when she looked away from them and over the burnt paddocks she could see them still—just before her eyes, jumping like mosquitoes. It was half-past two in the afternoon. The sun hung in the faded blue sky like a burning mirror, and away beyond the paddocks the blue mountains quivered and leapt like sea.

Sid wouldn't be back until half-past ten. He had ridden over to the township with four of the boys to help hunt down the young fellow who'd murdered Mr. Williamson. Such a dreadful thing! And Mrs. Williamson left all alone with those kids. Funny! she couldn't think of Mr. Williamson being dead! He was such a one for a joke. Always having a lark. Willie Cox said they found him in the barn, shot bang through the head, and the young English "johnny" who'd been on the station learning farming—disappeared. Funny! she couldn't think of anyone shooting Mr. Williamson, and him so popular and all. My word! when they caught that young man! Well, you couldn't be sorry for a young fellow like that. As Sid said, if he wasn't strung up where would they all be? A man like that doesn't stop at one go. There was blood all over the barn. And Willie Cox said he was that knocked out he picked a cigarette up out of the blood and smoked it. My word! he must have been half dotty.

Millie went back into the kitchen. She put some ashes on the stove and sprinkled them with water. Languidly, the sweat pouring down her face, and dropping off her nose and chin, she cleared away the dinner, and going into the bedroom, stared at herself in the fly-specked mirror, and wiped her face and neck with a towel. She didn't know what was the matter with herself that afternoon. She could have a good cry—just for nothing—and then change her blouse and have a good cup of tea. Yes, she felt like that!

She flopped down on the side of the bed and stared at the coloured print on the wall opposite, *Garden Party at Windsor Castle.* In the foreground emerald lawns planted with immense oak trees, and in their grateful shade, a muddle of ladies and gentlemen and parasols and little tables. The background was filled with the towers of Windsor Castle, flying three Union Jacks, and in the middle of the picture the old Queen, like a tea cosy with a head on top of it. "I wonder if it really looked like that." Millie stared at the flowery ladies, who simpered back at her. "I wouldn't care for that sort of thing. Too much side. What with the Queen an' one thing an' another."

Over the packing-case dressing-table there was a large photograph of her and Sid, taken on their wedding day. Nice picture that—if you *do* like. She was sitting down in a basket chair, in her cream cashmere and satin ribbons, and Sid, standing with one hand on her shoulder, looking at her bouquet. And behind them there were some fern trees, and a waterfall, and Mount Cook in the distance, covered with snow. She had almost forgotten her wedding day; time did pass so, and if you hadn't anyone to talk things over with, they soon dropped out of your mind. "I wunner why we never had no kids . . ." She shrugged her shoulders—gave it up. "Well, *I've* never missed them. I wouldn't be surprised if Sid had, though. He's softer than me."

And then she sat quiet, thinking of nothing at all, her red swollen hands rolled in her apron, her feet stuck out in front of her, her little head with the thick screw of dark hair drooped on her chest. *Tick-tick* went the kitchen clock, the ashes clinked in the grate, and the venetian blind knocked against the kitchen window. Quite suddenly Millie felt frightened. A queer trembling started inside her—in her stomach—and then spread all over to her knees and hands. "There's somebody about." She tiptoed to the door and peered into the kitchen. Nobody there; the verandah doors were closed, the blinds were down, and in the dusky light, the white face of the clock shone, and the furniture seemed to bulge and breathe . . . and listen, too. The clock—the ashes—and the venetian—and then again—something else, like steps in the back yard. "Go an' see what it is, Millie Evans."

She darted to the back door, opened it, and at the same moment someone ducked behind the wood pile. "Who's that?" she cried, in a loud, bold voice. "Come out o' that! I seen yer. I know where y'are. I got my gun. Come out from behind of that wood stack!" She was not frightened any more. She was furiously angry. Her heart banged like a drum. "I'll teach you to play tricks with a woman," she yelled, and she took a gun from the kitchen corner, and dashed down the verandah steps, across the glaring yard to the other side of the wood stack. A young man lay there, on his stomach, one arm across his face. "Get up! You're shamming!" Still holding the gun she kicked him in the shoulders. He gave no sign. "Oh my God, I believe he's dead." She knelt down, seized hold of him, and turned him over on his back. He rolled like a sack. She crouched back on her haunches, staring; her lips and nostrils fluttered with horror.

He was not much more than a boy, with fair hair, and a growth of fair down on his lips and chin. His eyes were open, rolled up, showing the whites, and his face was patched with dust caked with sweat. He wore a cotton shirt and trousers, with sandshoes on his feet. One of the trousers was stuck to his leg with a patch of dark blood. "I *can't*," said Millie, and then, "You've got to." She bent over and felt his heart. "Wait a minute," she stammered, "wait a minute," and she ran into the house for brandy and a pail of water. "What are you going to do, Millie Evans? Oh, I don't know. I never seen anyone in a dead faint before." She knelt down, put her arm under the boy's head and poured some brandy between his lips. It spilled down both sides of his mouth. She dipped a corner of her apron in the water and wiped his face and his hair and his throat, with fingers that trembled. Under the dust and sweat his face gleamed, white as her apron, and thin, and puckered in little lines. A strange dreadful feeling gripped Millie Evans' bosom—some seed that had never flourished there, unfolded and struck deep roots and burst into painful leaf. "Are yer coming round? Feeling all right again?" The boy breathed sharply, half choked, his eyelids quivered, and he moved his head from side to side. "You're better," said Millie, smoothing his hair. "Feeling fine now again, ain't you?" The pain in her bosom half suffocated her. "It's no good you crying, Millie Evans. You got to keep your head." Quite suddenly he sat up and leaned against the wood pile, away from her, staring on the ground. "There now!" cried Millie Evans, in a strange, shaking voice.

The boy turned and looked at her, still not speaking, but his eyes were so full of pain and terror that she had to shut her teeth and clench her hands to stop from crying. After a long pause he said in the little voice of a child talking in his sleep, "I'm hungry." His lips quivered. She scrambled to her feet and stood over him. "You come right into the house and have a sit-down meal," she said. "Can you walk?" "Yes," he whispered, and swaying he followed her across the glaring yard to the verandah. At the bottom step he paused, looking at her again. "I'm not coming in," he said. He sat on the verandah step in the little pool of shade that lay round the house. Millie watched him. "When did yer last 'ave anythink to eat?" He shook his head. She cut a chunk off the greasy corned beef and a round of bread plastered with butter; but when she brought it he was standing up, glancing round him, and paid no attention to the plate of food. "When are they coming back?" he stammered.

At that moment she knew. She stood, holding the plate, staring. He was Harrison. He was the English johnny who'd killed Mr. Williamson. "I know who you are," she said, very slowly, "yer can't fox me. That's who you are. I must have been blind in me two eyes not to 'ave known from the first." He made a movement with his hands as though that was all nothing. "When are they coming back?" And she meant to say, "Any minute. They're on their way now." Instead she said to the dreadful, frightened face, "Not till 'arf past ten." He sat down, leaning against one of the verandah poles. His face broke up into little quivers. He shut his eyes and tears streamed down his cheeks. "Nothing but a kid. An' all them fellows after 'im. 'E don't stand any more of a chance than a kid would." "Try a bit of beef," said Millie. "It's the food you want. Somethink to steady your stomach." She moved across the verandah and sat down beside him, the plate on her knees. "'Ere—try a bit." She broke the bread and butter into little pieces, and she thought, "They won't ketch him. Not if I can 'elp it. Men is all beasts. I don't care wot 'e's done, or wot 'e 'asn't done. See 'im through, Millie Evans. 'E's nothink but a sick kid."

Millie lay on her back, her eyes wide open, listening. Sid turned over, hunched the quilt round his shoulders, muttered "Good night, ole girl." She heard Willie Cox and the other chap drop their clothes on to the kitchen floor, and then their voices, and Willie Cox saying, "Lie down, Gumboil. Lie down, yer little devil," to his dog. The house dropped quiet. She lay and listened. Little pulses tapped in her body, listening, too. It was hot. She was frightened to move because of Sid. "'E must get off. 'E must. I don't care anythink about justice an' all the rot they've bin spoutin' to-night," she thought, savagely. "'Ow are yer to know what anythink's like till yer *do* know? It's all rot." She strained to the silence. He ought to be moving. . . . Before there was a sound from outside, Willie Cox's Gumboil got up and padded sharply across the kitchen floor and sniffed at the back door. Terror started up in Millie. "What's that dog doing? Uh! What a fool that young fellow is with a dog 'anging about. Why don't 'e lie down an' sleep?" The dog stopped, but she knew it was listening.

Suddenly, with a sound that made her cry out in horror the dog started barking and rushing to and fro. "What's that? What's up?" Sid flung out of bed. "It ain't nothink. It's only Gumboil. Sid, Sid!" She clutched his arm, but he shook her off. "My Christ, there's somethink up. My God!" Sid flung into his trousers. Willie Cox opened the back door. Gumboil in a fury darted out into the yard, round the corner of the house. "Sid, there's someone in the paddock," roared the other chap. "What is it—what's that?" Sid dashed out onto the front verandah. "'Ere, Millie, take the lantin. Willie, some skunk's got 'old of one of the 'orses." The three men bolted out of the house, and at the same moment Millie saw Harrison dash across the paddock on Sid's horse and down the road. "Millie, bring that blasted lantin." She ran in her bare feet, her nightdress flicking her legs. They were after him in a flash. And at the sight of Harrison in the distance, and the three men hot after, a strange mad joy smothered everything else. She rushed into the road—she laughed and shrieked and danced in the dust, jigging the lantern. "A—ah! Arter 'im, Sid! A—a—a—h! Ketch him, Willie. Go it! Go it! A—ah, Sid! Shoot 'im down. Shoot 'im!" □

DISCUSSION

1. (a) Why does Millie first try to help Harrison despite his crime?

(b) Is her behavior at the end of the story consistent with her earlier actions?

2. Would you call this a suspense story, or is it something else? Justify your answer.

3. (a) "A Cup of Tea" is set in London, "Millie" in New Zealand—both of them settings Katherine Mansfield knew from personal experience. Which setting do you think she used more effectively?

(b) Mansfield is regarded as an expert in characterization, especially through the use of small but graphic details. Which of the three women in these two stories—Rosemary, Miss Smith, or Millie—do you think is most skillfully drawn?

WRITING

Write an ending to Harrison's story.

EVELINE

by James Joyce

THE CROESSMANN COLLECTION OF JAMES JOYCE, SOUTHERN ILLINOIS UNIVERSITY AT CARBONDALE.

SHE sat at the window watching the evening invade the avenue. Her head was leaned against the window curtains and in her nostrils was the odor of dusty cretonne. She was tired.

Few people passed. The man out of the last house passed on his way home; she heard his footsteps clacking along the concrete pavement and afterwards crunching on the cinder path before the new red houses. One time there used to be a field there in which they used to play every evening with other people's children. Then a man from Belfast bought the field and built houses in it—not like their little brown houses but bright brick houses with shining roofs. The children of the avenue used to play together in that field—the Devines, the Waters, the Dunns, little Keogh the cripple, she and her brothers and sisters. Ernest, however, never played: he was too grown up. Her father used often to hunt them in out of the field with his blackthorn stick; but usually little Keogh used to keep *nix*[1] and call out when he saw her father coming. Still they seemed to have been rather happy then. Her father was not so bad then; and besides, her mother was alive. That was a long time ago; she and her brothers and sisters were all grown up; her mother was dead. Tizzie Dunn was dead, too, and the Waters had gone back to England. Everything changes. Now she was going to go away like the others, to leave her home.

Home! She looked round the room, reviewing all its familiar objects which she had dusted once a week for so many years, wondering where on earth all the dust came from. Perhaps she would never see again those familiar objects from which she had never dreamed of being divided. And yet during all those years she had never found out the name of the priest whose yellowing photograph hung on the wall above the broken harmonium beside the colored print of the promises made to Blessed Margaret Mary Alacoque. He had been a school friend of her father. Whenever he showed the photograph to a visitor her father used to pass it with a casual word: "He is in Melbourne now."

She had consented to go away, to leave her home. Was that wise? She tried to weigh each side of the question. In her home anyway she had shelter and food; she had those whom she had known all her life about her. Of course she had to work hard, both in the house and at business. What would they say of her in the Stores when they found out that she had run away with a fellow? Say she was a fool, perhaps; and her place would be filled up by advertisement. Miss Gavan would be glad. She had always had an edge on her, especially whenever there were people listening.

"Miss Hill, don't you see these ladies are waiting?"

"Look lively, Miss Hill, please."

She would not cry many tears at leaving the Stores.

But in her new home, in a distant unknown country, it would not be like that. Then she would be married—she, Eveline. People would treat her with respect then. She would not be treated as her mother had been. Even now, though she was over nineteen, she sometimes felt herself in danger of her father's violence. She knew it was that that had given her the palpitations. When they were growing up he had never gone for her, like he used to go for Harry and Ernest, because she was a girl; but latterly he had begun to threaten her and say what he would do to her only for her dead mother's sake. And now she had nobody to protect her. Ernest was dead and Harry, who was in the church decorating business,

---

From *Dubliners* by James Joyce. Originally published by B. W. Huebsch, Inc. in 1916.

1. *nix:* an old slang word, originally used by thieves, to refer to the member of a gang who kept watch.

was nearly always down somewhere in the country. Besides, the invariable squabble for money on Saturday nights had begun to weary her unspeakably. She always gave her entire wages—seven shillings—and Harry always sent up what he could but the trouble was to get any money from her father. He said she used to squander the money, that she had no head, that he wasn't going to give her his hard-earned money to throw about the streets, and much more, for he was usually fairly bad on Saturday night. In the end he would give her the money and ask her had she any intention of buying Sunday's dinner. Then she had to rush out as quickly as she could and do her marketing, holding her black leather purse tightly in her hand as she elbowed her way through the crowds and returning home late under her load of provisions. She had hard work to keep the house together and to see that the two young children who had been left to her charge went to school regularly and got their meals regularly. It was hard work—a hard life—but now that she was about to leave it she did not find it a wholly undesirable life.

She was about to explore another life with Frank. Frank was very kind, manly, open-hearted. She was to go away with him by the night boat to be his wife and to live with him in Buenos Aires where he had a home waiting for her. How well she remembered the first time she had seen him; he was lodging in a house on the main road where she used to visit. It seemed a few weeks ago. He was standing at the gate, his peaked cap pushed back on his head and his hair tumbled forward over a face of bronze. Then they had come to know each other. He used to meet her outside the Stores every evening and see her home. He took her to see *The Bohemian Girl* and she felt elated as she sat in an unaccustomed part of the theater with him. He was awfully fond of music and sang a little. People knew that they were courting and, when he sang about the lass that loves a sailor, she always felt pleasantly confused. He used to call her Poppens out of fun. First of all it had been an excitement for her to have a fellow and then she had begun to like him. He had tales of distant countries. He had started as a deck boy at a pound a month on a ship of the Allan Line going out to Canada. He told her the names of the ships he had been on and the names of the different services. He had sailed through the Straits of Magellan and he told her stories of the terrible Patagonians. He had fallen on his feet in Buenos Aires, he said, and had come over to the old country just for a holiday. Of course, her father had found out the affair and had forbidden her to have anything to say to him.

"I know these sailor chaps," he said.

One day he had quarreled with Frank and after that she had to meet her lover secretly.

The evening deepened in the avenue. The white of two letters in her lap grew indistinct. One was to Harry; the other was to her father. Ernest had been her favorite but she liked Harry too. Her father was becoming old lately, she noticed; he would miss her. Sometimes he could be very nice. Not long before, when she had been laid up for a day, he had read her out a ghost story and made toast for her at the fire. Another day, when their mother was alive, they had all gone for a picnic to the Hill of Howth. She remembered her father putting on her mother's bonnet to make the children laugh.

Her time was running out but she continued to sit by the window, leaning her head against the window curtain, inhaling the odor of dusty cretonne. Down far in the avenue she could hear a street organ playing. She knew the air. Strange that it should come that very night to remind her of the promise to her mother, her promise to keep the home together as long as she could. She remembered the last night of her mother's illness; she was again in the close dark room at the other side of the hall and outside she heard a melancholy air of Italy. The organ player had been ordered to go away and given six-pence. She remembered her father strutting back into the sickroom saying: "Damned Italians! coming over here!"

As she mused the pitiful vision of her mother's life laid its spell on the very quick of her being—that life of commonplace sacrifices closing in final craziness. She trembled as she heard again her mother's voice saying constantly with foolish insistence: "Derevaun Seraun! Derevaun Seraun!"[2]

She stood up in a sudden impulse of terror. Escape! She must escape! Frank would save her. He would give her life, perhaps love, too. But she wanted to live. Why should she be unhappy? She had a right to happiness. Frank would take her in his arms, fold her in his arms. He would save her.

She stood among the swaying crowd in the station

2. *"Derevaun . . . Seraun,"* possibly corrupt Gaelic for "the end of pleasure is pain."

at the North Wall. He held her hand and she knew that he was speaking to her, saying something about the passage over and over again. The station was full of soldiers with brown baggages. Through the wide doors of the sheds she caught a glimpse of the black mass of the boat, lying in beside the quay wall, with illumined portholes. She answered nothing. She felt her cheek pale and cold and, out of a maze of distress, she prayed to God to direct her, to show her what was her duty. The boat blew a long mournful whistle into the mist. If she went, tomorrow she would be on the sea with Frank, steaming toward Buenos Aires. Their passage had been booked. Could she still draw back after all he had done for her? Her distress awoke a nausea in her body and she kept moving her lips in silent fervent prayer.

A bell clanged upon her heart. She felt him seize her hand:

"Come!"

All the seas of the world tumbled about her heart. He was drawing her into them: he would drown her. She gripped with both hands at the iron railing.

"Come!"

No! No! No! It was impossible. Her hands clutched the iron in frenzy. Amid the seas she sent a cry of anguish.

"Eveline! Evvy!"

He rushed beyond the barrier and called to her to follow. He was shouted at to go on but he still called to her. She set her white face to him, passive, like a helpless animal. Her eyes gave him no sign of love or farewell or recognition. □

DISCUSSION

1. (a) Eveline thinks of Frank and his offer of marriage: "Escape! She must escape! Frank would save her. He would give her life, perhaps love, too. But she wanted to live. Why should she be unhappy? She had a right to happiness. Frank would take her in his arms, fold her in his arms. He would save her." What is wrong with this attitude toward marriage?

(b) Eveline, about to sail away from her homeland, probably for ever, thinks: "All the seas of the world tumbled about her heart. He was drawing her into them: he would drown her. She gripped with both hands at the iron railing. . . . She set her white face to him, passive, like a helpless animal. Her eyes gave him no sign of love or farewell or recognition." What had happened to her?

2. (a) Point out some of the small details that help create the atmosphere of Dublin over a half-century ago.

(b) Are they all visual details, or does Joyce involve the other senses? Give examples.

3. In his definitive biography of James Joyce, Richard Ellman reports that Eveline's real-life counterpart, Eveline Thornton, did not make the same decision as the girl in the story. Instead, Eveline Thornton married her sailor, settled down with him in Dublin, and bore him a number of children. Which version do you prefer?

4. (a) What parallels can you draw between the characters of Millie and Eveline?

(b) Suppose Eveline did marry Frank. Might her marriage have turned out to be like Millie's (in the story "Millie")?

WRITING

Write an explanatory letter from Eveline to Frank, or a letter from Frank to Eveline asking her to reconsider.

ARABY

by James Joyce

NORTH Richmond Street, being blind, was a quiet street except at the hour when the Christian Brothers' School set the boys free. An uninhabited house of two storeys stood at the blind end, detached from its neighbours in a square ground. The other houses of the street, conscious of decent lives within them, gazed at one another with brown imperturbable faces.

The former tenant of our house, a priest, had died in the back drawing-room. Air, musty from having been long enclosed, hung in all the rooms, and the waste room behind the kitchen was littered with old useless papers. Among these I found a few paper-covered books, the pages of which were curled and damp: *The Abbot,* by Walter Scott, *The Devout Communicant* and *The Memoirs of Vidocq.* I liked the last best because its leaves were yellow. The wild garden behind the house contained a central apple-tree and a few straggling bushes under one of which I found the late tenant's rusty bicycle-pump. He had been a very charitable priest; in his will he had left all his money to institutions and the furniture of his house to his sister.

When the short days of winter came, dusk fell before we had well eaten our dinners. When we met in the street the houses had grown somber. The space of sky above us was the color of everchanging violet and towards it the lamps of the street lifted their feeble lanterns. The cold air stung us and we played till our bodies glowed. Our shouts echoed in the silent street. The career of our play brought us through the dark muddy lanes behind the houses where we ran the gauntlet of the rough tribes from the cottages, to the back doors of the dark dripping gardens where odors arose from the ashpits, to the dark odorous stables where a coachman smoothed and combed the horse or shook music from the buckled harness. When we returned to the street, light from the kitchen windows had filled the areas. If my uncle was seen turning the corner we hid in the shadow until we had seen him safely housed. Or if Mangan's sister came out on the doorstep to call her brother in to his tea we watched her from our shadow peer up and down the street. We waited to see whether she would remain or go in and, if she remained, we left our shadow and walked up to Mangan's steps resignedly. She was waiting for us, her figure defined by the light from the half-opened door. Her brother always teased her before he obeyed and I stood by the railings looking at her. Her dress swung as she moved her body and the soft rope of her hair tossed from side to side.

Every morning I lay on the floor in the front parlor watching her door. The blind was pulled down to within an inch of the sash so that I could not be seen. When she came out on the doorstep my heart leaped. I ran to the hall, seized my books and followed her. I kept her brown figure always in my eye and, when we came near the point at which our ways diverged, I quickened my pace and passed her. This happened morning after morning. I had never spoken to her, except for a few casual words, and yet her name was like a summons to all my foolish blood.

Her image accompanied me even in places the most hostile to romance. On Saturday evenings when my aunt went marketing I had to go to carry some of the parcels. We walked through the flaring streets, jostled by drunken men and bargaining women, amid the curses of laborers, the shrill litanies of shop-boys who stood on guard by the barrels of pigs' cheeks, the nasal chanting of street-singers, who sang a *come-all-you* about O'Donovan Rossa, or a ballad about the troubles in our native land. These noises converged in a single sensation of life for me: I imagined that I bore my chalice safely through a throng of foes. Her name sprang to my lips at moments in strange prayers and praises which I myself did not understand. My eyes were often full of tears (I could not tell why) and at times a flood from my heart seemed to pour itself out into my bosom. I thought little of the future. I did not know whether I would ever speak to her or not or, if I spoke to her, how I could tell her of my confused adoration. But

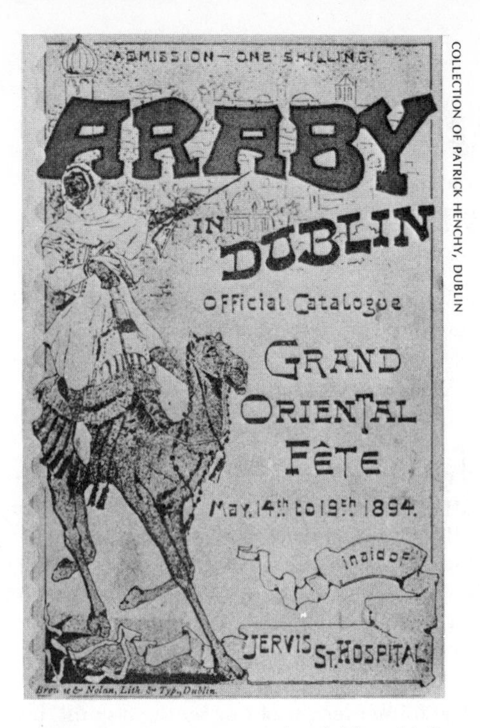

COLLECTION OF PATRICK HENCHY, DUBLIN

my body was like a harp and her words and gestures were like fingers running upon the wires.

One evening I went into the back drawing-room in which the priest had died. It was a dark rainy evening and there was no sound in the house. Through one of the broken panes I heard the rain impinge upon the earth, the fine incessant needles of water playing in the sodden beds. Some distant lamp or lighted window gleamed below me. I was thankful that I could see so little. All my senses seemed to desire to veil themselves and, feeling that I was about to slip from them, I pressed the palms of my hands together until they trembled, murmuring: "*O love! O love!*" many times.

At last she spoke to me. When she addressed the first words to me I was so confused that I did not know what to answer. She asked me was I going to *Araby*. I forgot whether I answered yes or no. It would be a splendid bazaar, she said she would love to go.

"And why can't you?" I asked.

While she spoke she turned a silver bracelet round and round her wrist. She could not go, she said, because there would be a retreat that week in her convent. Her brother and two other boys were fighting for their caps and I was alone at the railings. She held one of the spikes, bowing her head towards me. The light from the lamp opposite our door caught the white curve of her neck, lit up her hair that rested there and, falling, lit up the hand upon the railing. It fell over one side of her dress and caught the white border of a petticoat, just visible as she stood at ease.

"It's well for you," she said.

"If I go," I said, "I will bring you something."

What innumerable follies laid waste my waking and sleeping thoughts after that evening! I wished to annihilate the tedious intervening days. I chafed against the work of school. At night in my bedroom and by day in the classroom her image came between me and the page I strove to read. The syllables of the word *Araby* were called to me through the silence in which my soul luxuriated and cast an Eastern enchantment over me. I asked for leave to go to the bazaar on Saturday night. My aunt was surprised and hoped it was not some Freemason affair. I answered few questions in class. I watched my master's face pass from amiability to sternness; he hoped I was not beginning to idle. I could not call my wandering thoughts together. I had hardly any patience with the serious work of life which, now that it stood between me and my desire, seemed to me child's play, ugly monotonous child's play.

On Saturday morning I reminded my uncle that I wished to go to the bazaar in the evening. He was fussing at the hallstand, looking for the hat-brush, and answered me curtly:

"Yes, boy, I know."

As he was in the hall I could not go into the front parlor and lie at the window. I left the house in bad humor and walked slowly towards the school. The air was pitilessly raw and already my heart misgave me.

When I came home to dinner my uncle had not yet been home. Still it was early. I sat staring at the clock for some time and, when its ticking began to irritate me, I left the room. I mounted the staircase and gained the upper part of the house. The high, cold, empty gloomy rooms liberated me and I went from room to room singing. From the front window I saw my companions playing below in the street. Their cries reached me weakened and indistinct and, leaning my forehead against the cool glass, I looked over at the dark house where she lived. I may have stood there for an hour, seeing nothing but the brown-clad figure cast by my imagination, touched discreetly by the lamplight at the curved neck, at the hand upon the railings, and at the border below the dress.

When I came downstairs again I found Mrs. Mercer sitting at the fire. She was an old garrulous woman, a pawnbroker's widow, who collected used stamps for some pious purpose. I had to endure the gossip of the tea-table. The meal was prolonged beyond an hour and still my uncle did not come. Mrs. Mercer stood up to go: she was sorry she couldn't wait any longer, but it was after eight o'clock and she did not like to be out late, as the night air was bad for her. When she had gone I began to walk up and down the room, clenching my fists. My aunt said:

"I'm afraid you may put off your bazaar for this night of Our Lord."

At nine o'clock I heard my uncle's latchkey in the hall door. I heard him talking to himself and heard the hall stand rocking when it had received the weight of his overcoat. I could interpret these signs. When he was midway through his dinner I asked him to give me the money to go to the bazaar. He had forgotten.

"The people are in bed and after their first sleep now," he said.

I did not smile. My aunt said to him energetically:

"Can't you give him the money and let him go? You've kept him late enough as it is."

My uncle said he was very sorry he had forgotten. He said he believed in the old saying: "All work and no play makes Jack a dull boy." He asked me where I was going and, when I had told him a second time he asked me did I know *The Arab's Farewell to his Steed*. When I left the kitchen he was about to recite the opening lines of the piece to my aunt.

I held a florin tightly in my hand as I strode down Buckingham Street towards the station. The sight of the streets thronged with buyers and glaring with gas recalled to me the purpose of my journey. I took my seat in a third-class carriage of a deserted train. After an intolerable delay the train moved out of the station slowly. It crept onward among ruinous houses and over the twinkling river. At Westland Row Station a crowd of people pressed to the carriage doors; but the porters moved them back, saying that it was a special train for the bazaar. I remained alone in the bare carriage. In a few minutes the train drew up beside an improvised wooden platform. I passed out on to the road and saw by the lighted dial of a clock that it was ten minutes to ten. In front of me was a large building which displayed the magical name.

I could not find any sixpenny entrance and, fearing that the bazaar would be closed, I passed in quickly through a turnstile, handing a shilling to a weary-looking man. I found myself in a big hall girdled at half its height by a gallery. Nearly all the stalls were closed and the greater part of the hall was in darkness. I recognised a silence like that which pervades a church after a service. I walked into the center of the bazaar timidly. A few people were gathered about the stalls which were still open. Before a curtain, over which the words *Café Chantant* were written in colored lamps, two men were counting money on a salver. I listened to the fall of the coins.

Remembering with difficulty why I had come I went over to one of the stalls and examined porcelain vases and flowered tea-sets. At the door of the stall a young lady was talking and laughing with two young gentlemen. I remarked their English accents and listened vaguely to their conversation.

"O, I never said such a thing!"

"O, but you did!"

"O, but I didn't!"

"Didn't she say that?"

"Yes. I heard her."

"O, there's a . . . fib!"

Observing me the young lady came over and asked me did I wish to buy anything. The tone of her voice was not encouraging; she seemed to have spoken to me out of a sense of duty. I looked humbly at the great jars that stood like eastern guards at either side of the dark entrance to the stall and murmured:

"No, thank you."

The young lady changed the position of one of the vases and went back to the two young men. They began to talk of the same subject. Once or twice the young lady glanced at me over her shoulder.

I lingered before her stall, though I knew my stay was useless, to make my interest in her wares seem the more real. Then I turned away slowly and walked down the middle of the bazaar. I allowed the two pennies to fall against the sixpence in my pocket. I heard a voice call from one end of the gallery that the light was out. The upper part of the hall was now completely dark.

Gazing up into the darkness I saw myself as a creature driven and derided by vanity; and my eyes burned with anguish and anger. □

DISCUSSION

1. To members of Joyce's generation, the word "Araby" stood for all that was exotic and romantic. "Araby" is the theme, as well as the name, of the bazaar that the young speaker in Joyce's story goes to. How do the name and its implications add to his ultimate disappointment and disillusionment?

2. (a) How does Joyce manage to show the world of childhood as separate from, suspicious of, often in conflict with, the authority structure of the adult world?

(b) Does the narrator, at any point in the story, step across the gap that separates the two worlds? Explain.

3. At several points in the story, Joyce paints in a few words a panoramic scene of some aspect of Dublin life. Select any one of these scenes and point out how he makes it come to life for the modern reader.

4. Is the feeling the narrator has for Mangan's sister a mere adolescent crush, or something deeper? Explain.

5. Trace the various steps in the narrator's disillusionment, beginning with his uncle's failure to return home on time, and culminating in his realization that he is "a creature driven and derided by vanity."

6. Is the title of the story descriptive, ironic, or what? Explain.

7. Joyce himself claimed of his book *Dubliners*, from which "Eveline" and "Araby" are taken, that his purpose was "to write a chapter of the moral history of my country and I chose Dublin for the scene because that city seemed to me the centre of paralysis. . . ." (from a letter of May 5, 1906). Explain how both stories show this paralysis.

WRITING

Write an imaginary dialogue between the narrator and Mangan's sister on their next meeting.

SOLID OBJECTS

by Virginia Woolf

BETTMANN ARCHIVE

THE only thing that moved upon the vast semicircle of the beach was one small black spot. As it came nearer to the ribs and spine of the stranded pilchard boat, it became apparent from a certain tenuity in its blackness that this spot possessed four legs; and moment by moment it became more unmistakable that it was composed of the persons of two young men. Even thus in outline against the sand there was an unmistakable vitality in them; an indescribable vigour in the approach and withdrawal of the bodies, slight though it was, which proclaimed some violent argument issuing from the tiny mouths of the little round heads. This was corroborated on closer view by the repeated lunging of a walking-stick on the right-hand side. "You mean to tell me. . . . You actually believe . . ." thus the walking-stick on the right-hand side next the waves seemed to be asserting as it cut long straight stripes upon the sand.

"Politics be damned!" issued clearly from the body on the left-hand side, and, as these words were uttered, the mouths, noses, chins, little moustaches, tweed caps, rough boots, shooting coats, and check stockings of the two speakers became clearer and clearer; the smoke of their pipes went up into the air; nothing was so solid, so living, so hard, red, hirsute, and virile as these two bodies for miles and miles of sea and sandhill.

They flung themselves down by the six ribs and spine of the black pilchard boat. You know how the body seems to shake itself free from an argument, and to apologize for a mood of exaltation; flinging itself down and expressing in the looseness of its attitude a readiness to take up with something new—whatever it may be that comes next to hand. So Charles, whose stick had been slashing the beach for half a mile or so, began skimming flat pieces of slate over the water; and John, who had exclaimed "Politics be damned!" began burrowing his fingers down, down, into the sand. As his hand went further and further beyond the wrist, so that he had to hitch his sleeve a little higher, his eyes lost their intensity, or rather the background of thought and experience which gives an inscrutable depth to the eyes of grown people disappeared, leaving only the clear transparent surface, expressing nothing but wonder, which the eyes of young children display. No doubt the act of burrowing in the sand had something to do with it. He remembered that, after digging for a little, the water oozes round your finger-tips; the hole then becomes a moat; a well; a spring; a secret channel to the sea. As he was choosing which of these things to make it, still working his fingers in the water, they curled round something hard—a full drop of solid matter—and gradually dislodged a large irregular lump, and brought it to the surface. When the sand coating was wiped off, a green tint appeared. It was a lump of glass, so thick as to be almost opaque; the smoothing of the sea had completely worn off any edge or shape, so that it was impossible to say whether it had been bottle, tumbler, or window-pane; it was nothing but glass; it was almost a precious stone. You had only to enclose it in a rim of gold, or pierce it with a wire, and it became a jewel; part of a necklace, or a dull, green light upon a finger. Perhaps after all it was really a gem; something worn by a dark Princess trailing her finger in the water as she sat in the stern of the boat and listened to the slaves singing as they rowed her across the Bay. Or the oak sides of a sunk Elizabethan treasure-chest had split apart, and, rolled over and over, over and over, its emeralds had come at last to shore. John turned it in his hands; he held it to the light; he held it so that its irregular mass blotted out the body and extended right arm of his friend. The green thinned and thickened slightly as it was held against the sky or against the body. It pleased him; it puzzled him; it was so hard, so concentrated, so definite an object compared with the vague sea and the hazy shore.

Now a sigh disturbed him—profound, final, making him aware that his friend Charles had thrown all the flat stones within reach, or had come to the conclusion that it was not worth while to throw them. They ate their sandwiches side by side. When they had done, and were shaking themselves and rising to their feet, John took the lump of glass and looked at it in silence. Charles looked at it too. But he saw immediately that it was not flat, and filling his pipe he said with the energy that dismisses a foolish strain of thought:

"To return to what I was saying—"

He did not see, or if he had seen would hardly have noticed, that John, after looking at the lump for a moment, as if in hesitation, slipped it inside his pocket. That impulse, too, may have been the impulse which leads a child to pick up one pebble on a path strewn with them, promising it a life of warmth and security upon the nursery mantelpiece, delighting in the sense of power and benignity which such an action confers, and believing that the heart of the stone leaps with joy when it sees itself chosen from a million like it, to enjoy this bliss instead of a life of cold and wet upon the high road. "It might so easily have been any other of the millions of stones, but it was I, I, I!"

Whether this thought or not was in John's mind, the lump of glass had its place upon the mantelpiece, where it stood heavy upon a little pile of bills and letters, and served not only as an excellent paper-weight, but also as a natural stopping place for the young man's eyes when they wandered from his book. Looked at again and again half consciously by a mind thinking of something else, any object mixes itself so profoundly with the stuff of thought that it loses its actual form and recomposes itself a little differently in an ideal shape which haunts the brain when we least expect it. So John found himself attracted to the windows of curiosity shops when he was out walking, merely because he saw something which reminded him of the lump of glass. Anything, so long as it was an object of some kind, more or less round, perhaps with a dying flame deep sunk in its mass, anything—china, glass, amber, rock, marble—even the smooth oval egg of a prehistoric bird would do. He took, also, to keeping his eyes upon the ground, especially in the neighbourhood of waste land where the household refuse is thrown away. Such objects often occurred there—thrown away, of no use to anybody, shapeless, discarded. In a few months he had collected four or five specimens that took their place upon the mantelpiece. They were useful, too, for a man who is standing for Parliament upon the brink of a brilliant career has any number of papers to keep in order—addresses to constituents, declarations of policy, appeals for subscriptions, invitations to dinner, and so on.

One day, starting from his rooms in the Temple to catch a train in order to address his constituents, his eyes rested upon a remarkable object lying half-hidden in one of those little borders of grass which edge the bases of vast legal buildings. He could only touch it with the point of his stick through the railings; but he could see that it was a piece of china of the most remarkable shape, as nearly resembling a starfish as anything—shaped, or broken accidentally, into five irregular but unmistakable points. The colouring was mainly blue, but green stripes or spots of some kind overlaid the blue, and lines of crimson gave it a richness and lustre of the most attractive kind. John was determined to possess it; but the more he pushed, the further it receded. At length he was forced to go back to his rooms and improvise a wire ring attached to the end of a stick, with which, by dint of great care and skill, he finally drew the piece of china within reach of his hands. As he seized hold of it he exclaimed in triumph. At that moment the clock struck. It was out of the question that he should keep his appointment. The meeting was held without him. But how had the piece of china been broken into this remarkable shape? A careful examination put it beyond doubt that the star shape was accidental, which made it all the more strange, and it seemed unlikely that there should be another such in existence. Set at the opposite end of the mantelpiece from the lump of glass that had been dug from the sand, it looked like a creature from another world—freakish and fantastic as a harlequin. It seemed to be pirouetting through space, winking light like a fitful star. The contrast between the china so vivid and alert, and the glass so mute and contemplative, fascinated him, and wondering and amazed he asked himself how the two came to exist in the same world, let alone to stand upon the same narrow strip of marble in the same room. The question remained unanswered.

He now began to haunt the places which are most prolific of broken china, such as pieces of waste land between railway lines, sites of demolished houses, and commons in the neighbourhood of London. But china is seldom thrown from a great height; it is one of the rarest of human actions. You have to find in conjunction a very high house, and a woman of such reckless impulse and passionate prejudice that she flings her jar or pot straight from the window without thought of who is below. Broken china was to be found in plenty, but broken in some trifling domestic accident, without purpose or character. Nevertheless, he was often astonished, as he came to go into the question more deeply, by the immense variety of shapes to be found in London alone, and there was still more cause for wonder and speculation in the differences of qualities and designs. The finest specimens he would bring home and place upon his mantelpiece, where, however, their duty was more and more of an ornamental nature, since papers needing a weight to keep them down became scarcer and scarcer.

He neglected his duties, perhaps, or discharged them absent-mindedly, or his constituents when they visited him were unfavourably impressed by the appearance of his mantelpiece. At any rate he was not elected to represent them in Parliament, and his friend Charles, taking it much to heart and hurrying to condole with him, found him so little cast down by the disaster that he could only suppose that it was too serious a matter for him to realize all at once.

In truth, John had been that day to Barnes Common, and there under a furze bush had found a very remarkable piece of iron. It was almost identical with the glass in shape, massy and globular, but so cold and heavy, so black and metallic, that it was evidently alien to the earth and had its origin in one of the dead stars or was itself the cinder of a moon. It weighed his pocket down; it weighed the mantelpiece down; it radiated cold. And yet the meteorite stood upon the same ledge with the lump of glass and the star-shaped china.

As his eyes passed from one to another, the determination to possess objects that even surpassed these tormented the young man. He devoted himself more and more resolutely to the search. If he had not been consumed by ambition and convinced that one day some newly-discovered rubbish heap would reward him, the disappointments he had suffered, let alone the fatigue and derision, would have made him give up the pursuit. Provided with a bag and a long stick fitted with an adaptable hook, he ransacked all deposits of earth; raked beneath matted tangles of scrub; searched all alleys and spaces between walls where he had learned to expect to find objects of this kind thrown away. As his standard became higher and his taste more severe the disappointments were innumerable, but always some gleam of hope, some piece of china or glass curiously marked or broken, lured him on. Day after day passed. He was no longer young. His career—that is his political career—was a thing of the past. People gave up visiting him. He was too silent to be worth asking to dinner. He never talked to anyone about his serious ambitions; their lack of understanding was apparent in their behaviour.

He leaned back in his chair now and watched Charles lift the stones on the mantelpiece a dozen times and put them down emphatically to mark what he was saying about the conduct of the Government, without once noticing their existence.

"What was the truth of it, John?" asked Charles suddenly, turning and facing him. "What made you give it up like that all in a second?"

"I've not given it up," John replied.

"But you've not the ghost of a chance now," said Charles roughly.

"I don't agree with you there," said John with conviction. Charles looked at him and was profoundly uneasy; the most extraordinary doubts possessed him; he had a queer sense that they were talking about different things. He looked round to find some relief for his horrible depression, but the disorderly appearance of the room depressed him still further. What was that stick, and the old carpet bag hanging against the wall? And then those stones? Looking at John, something fixed and distant in his expression alarmed him. He knew only too well that his mere appearance upon a platform was out of the question.

"Pretty stones," he said as cheerfully as he could; and saying that he had an appointment to keep, he left John—for ever. □

DISCUSSION

1. Why might the author have chosen to open this story on a vast beach deserted except for John and Charles and the skeleton of a small fishing boat?

2. How do you account for John's giving up a budding political career in order to collect bits of glass and china: is he really an eccentric? Is "collector's itch" all that ails him? Or is it something more than either of these?

3. (a) "Pretty stones," says Charles, as he leaves John and their friendship behind forever. How does this comment show the vast difference between the two men?

(b) Which does the author seem to feel is more worth pursuing, politics or "solid objects"? Explain.

4. Both "Araby" and "Solid Objects" make extensive use of symbolism to treat of the difference between the real world and the world of illusion, yet the conclusions and feelings the authors lead us to are vastly different. Discuss these differences.

WRITING

Give your ideas as to what eventually happens to John.

THE DUCHESS AND THE JEWELLER

by Virginia Woolf

OLIVER BACON lived at the top of a house overlooking the Green Park. He had a flat; chairs jutted out at the right angles—chairs covered in hide. Sofas filled the bays of the windows—sofas covered in tapestry. The windows, the three long windows, had the proper allowance of discreet net and figured satin. The mahogany sideboard bulged discreetly with the right brandies, whiskeys, and liqueurs. And from the middle window he looked down upon the glossy roofs of fashionable cars packed in the narrow straits of Piccadilly. A more central position could not be imagined. And at eight in the morning he would have his breakfast brought in on a tray by a man-servant: the man-servant would unfold his crimson dressing-gown; he would rip his letters open with his long pointed nails and would extract thick white cards of invitation upon which the engraving stood up roughly from duchesses, countesses, viscountesses, and Honourable Ladies. Then he would wash; then he would eat his toast; then he would read his paper by the bright burning fire of electric coals.

"Behold Oliver," he would say, addressing himself. "You who began life in a filthy little alley, you who . . ." and he would look down at his legs, so shapely in their perfect trousers; at his boots; at his spats. They were all shapely, shining; cut from the best cloth by the best scissors in Savile Row. But he dismantled himself often and became again a little boy in a dark alley. He had once thought that the height of his ambition—selling stolen dogs to fashionable women in Whitechapel. And once he had been done.[1] "Oh, Oliver," his mother had wailed. "Oh, Oliver! When will you have sense, my son?" . . . Then he had gone behind a counter; had sold cheap watches; then he had taken a wallet to Amsterdam. . . . At that memory he would chuckle—the old Oliver remembering the young. Yes, he had done well with the three diamonds; also there was the commission on the emerald. After that he went into the private room behind the shop in Hatton Garden; the room with the scales, the safe, the thick magnifying glasses. And then . . . and then . . . He chuckled. When he passed through the knots of jewellers in the hot evening who were discussing prices, gold mines, diamonds, reports from South Africa, one of them would lay a finger to the side of his nose and murmur, "Hum—m—m," as he passed. It was no more than a murmur; no more than a nudge on the shoulder, a finger on the nose, a buzz that ran through the cluster of jewellers in Hatton Garden on a hot afternoon—oh, many years ago now! But still Oliver felt it purring down his spine, the nudge, the murmur that meant, "Look at him—young Oliver, the young jeweller—there he goes." Young he was then. And he dressed better and better; and had, first a hansom cab; then a car; and first he went up to the dress circle, then down into the stalls. And he had a villa at Richmond, overlooking the river, with trellises of red roses; and Mademoiselle used to pick one every morning and stick it in his buttonhole.

"So," said Oliver Bacon, rising and stretching his legs. "So . . ."

And he stood beneath the picture of an old lady on the mantelpiece and raised his hands. "I have kept my word," he said, laying his hands together, palm to palm, as if he were doing homage to her. "I have won my bet." That was so; he was the richest jeweller in England; but his nose, which was long and flexible, like an elephant's trunk, seemed to say

1. *done,* caught; arrested.

by its curious quiver at the nostrils (but it seemed as if the whole nose quivered, not only the nostrils) that he was not satisfied yet; still smelt something under the ground a little further off. Imagine a giant hog in a pasture rich with truffles; after unearthing this truffle and that, still it smells a bigger, a blacker truffle under the ground further off. So Oliver snuffed always in the rich earth of Mayfair another truffle, a blacker, a bigger further off.

Now then he straightened the pearl in his tie, cased himself in his smart blue overcoat; took his yellow gloves and his cane; and swayed as he descended the stairs and half snuffed, half sighed through his long sharp nose as he passed out into Piccadilly. For was he not still a sad man, a dissatisfied man, a man who seeks something that is hidden, though he had won his bet?

He swayed slightly as he walked, as the camel at the zoo sways from side to side when it walks along the asphalt paths laden with grocers and their wives eating from paper bags and throwing little bits of silver paper crumpled up on to the path. The camel despises the grocers; the camel is dissatisfied with its lot; the camel sees the blue lake and the fringe of palm trees in front of it. So the great jeweller, the greatest jeweller in the whole world, swung down Piccadilly, perfectly dressed, with his gloves, with his cane; but dissatisfied still, till he reached the dark little shop, that was famous in France, in Germany, in Austria, in Italy, and all over America—the dark little shop in the street off Bond Street.

As usual, he strode through the shop without speaking, though the four men, the two old men, Marshall and Spencer, and the two young men, Hammond and Wicks, stood straight and looked at him, envying him. It was only with one finger of the amber-coloured glove, waggling, that he acknowledged their presence. And he went in and shut the door of his private room behind him.

Then he unlocked the grating that barred the window. The cries of Bond Street came in; the purr of the distant traffic. The light from reflectors at the back of the shop struck upwards. One tree waved six green leaves, for it was June. But Mademoiselle had married Mr. Pedder of the local brewery—no one stuck roses in his buttonhole now.

"So," he half sighed, half snorted, "so—"

Then he touched a spring in the wall and slowly the panelling slid open, and behind it were the steel safes, five, no, six of them, all of burnished steel. He twisted a key; unlocked one; then another. Each was lined with a pad of deep crimson velvet; in each lay jewels—bracelets, necklaces, rings, tiaras, ducal coronets; loose stones in glass shells; rubies, emeralds, pearls, diamonds. All safe, shining, cool, yet burning, eternally, with their own compressed light.

"Tears!" said Oliver, looking at the pearls.

"Heart's blood!" he said, looking at the rubies.

"Gunpowder!" he continued, rattling the diamonds so that they flashed and blazed.

"Gunpowder enough to blow Mayfair—sky high, high, high!" He threw his head back and made a sound like a horse neighing as he said it.

The telephone buzzed obsequiously in a low muted voice on his table. He shut the safe.

"In ten minutes," he said. "Not before." And he sat down at his desk and looked at the heads of the Roman emperors that were graved on his sleeve links. And again he dismantled himself and became once more the little boy playing marbles in the alley where they sell stolen dogs on Sunday. He became that wily astute little boy, with lips like wet cherries. He dabbled his fingers in ropes of tripe; he dipped them in pans of frying fish; he dodged in and out among the crowds. He was slim, lissome, with eyes like licked stones. And now—now—the hands of the clock ticked on, one, two, three, four. . . . The Duchess of Lambourne waited his pleasure; the Duchess of Lambourne, daughter of a hundred Earls. She would wait for ten minutes on a chair at the counter. She would wait his pleasure. She would wait till he was ready to see her. He watched the clock in its shagreen case. The hand moved on. With each tick the clock handed him—so it seemed—pâté de foie gras, a glass of champagne, another of fine brandy, a cigar costing one guinea. The clock laid them on the table beside him as the ten minutes passed. Then he heard soft slow footsteps approaching; a rustle in the corridor. The door opened. Mr. Hammond flattened himself against the wall.

"Her Grace!" he announced.

And he waited there, flattened against the wall.

And Oliver, rising, could hear the rustle of the dress of the Duchess as she came down the passage. Then she loomed up, filling the door, filling the room with the aroma, the prestige, the arrogance, the pomp, the pride of all the Dukes and Duchesses swollen in one wave. And as a wave breaks, she broke, as she sat down, spreading and splashing and falling over Oliver Bacon, the great jeweller, covering him with sparkling bright colours, green, rose, violet; and odours; and iridescences; and rays shooting from fingers, nodding from plumes, flashing from silk; for she was very large, very fat, tightly girt in pink taffeta, and past her prime. As a parasol with many flounces, as a peacock with many feathers, shuts its flounces, folds its feathers, so she subsided and shut herself as she sank down in the leather armchair.

"Good morning, Mr. Bacon," said the Duchess. And she held out her hand which came through the slit of her white glove. And Oliver bent low as he shook it. And as their hands touched the link was forged between them once more. They were friends, yet enemies; he was master, she was mistress; each cheated the other, each needed the other, each feared the other, each felt this and knew this every time they touched hands thus in the little back room with the white light outside, and the tree with its six leaves, and the sound of the street in the distance and behind them the safes.

"And today, Duchess—what can I do for you today?" said Oliver, very softly.

The Duchess opened her heart, her private heart, gaped wide. And with a sigh but no words she took from her bag a long washleather pouch—it looked like a lean yellow ferret. And from a slit in the ferret's belly she dropped pearls—ten pearls. They rolled from the slit in the ferret's belly—one, two, three, four—like the eggs of some heavenly bird.

"All that's left me, dear Mr. Bacon," she moaned. Five, six, seven—down they rolled, down the slopes of the vast mountain sides that fell between her knees into one narrow valley—the eighth, the ninth, and the tenth. There they lay in the glow of the peach-blossom taffeta. Ten pearls.

"From the Appleby cincture," she mourned. "The last . . . the last of them all."

Oliver stretched out and took one of the pearls between finger and thumb. It was round, it was lustrous. But real was it, or false? Was she lying again? Did she dare?

She laid her plump padded finger across her lips. "If the Duke knew . . ." she whispered. "Dear Mr. Bacon, a bit of bad luck . . ."

Been gambling again, had she?

"That villain! That sharper!" she hissed.

The man with the chipped cheek bone? A bad 'un. And the Duke was straight as a poker; with side whiskers; would cut her off, shut her up down there if he knew—what I know, thought Oliver, and glanced at the safe.

"Araminta, Daphne, Diana," she moaned. "It's for *them.*"

The ladies Araminta, Daphne, Diana—her daughters. He knew them; adored them. But it was Diana he loved.

"You have all my secrets," she leered. Tears slid; tears fell; tears, like diamonds, collecting powder in the ruts of her cherry blossom cheeks.

"Old friend," she murmured, "old friend."

"Old friend," he repeated, "old friend," as if he licked the words.

"How much?" he queried.

She covered the pearls with her hand.

"Twenty thousand," she whispered.

But was it real or false, the one he held in his hand? The Appleby cincture—hadn't she sold it already? He would ring for Spencer or Hammond. "Take it and test it," he would say. He stretched to the bell.

"You will come down tomorrow?" she urged, she interrupted. "The Prime Minister—His Royal Highness . . ." She stopped. "And Diana . . ." she added.

Oliver took his hand off the bell.

He looked past her, at the backs of the houses in Bond Street. But he saw, not the houses in Bond Street, but a dimpling river; and trout rising and salmon; and the Prime Minister; and himself too, in white waistcoat; and then, Diana. He looked down at the pearl in his hand. But how could he test it, in the light of the river, in the light of the eyes of Diana? But the eyes of the Duchess were on him.

"Twenty thousand," she moaned. "My honour!"

The honour of the mother of Diana! He drew his cheque book towards him; he took out his pen.

"Twenty—" he wrote. Then he stopped writing. The eyes of the old woman in the picture were on him—of the old woman his mother.

"Oliver!" she warned him. "Have sense! Don't be a fool!"

"Oliver!" the Duchess entreated—it was "Oliver" now, not "Mr. Bacon." "You'll come for a long week-end?"

Alone in the woods with Diana! Riding alone in the woods with Diana!

"Thousand," he wrote, and signed it.

"Here you are," he said.

And there opened all the flounces of the parasol,

all the plumes of the peacock, the radiance of the wave, the swords and spears of Agincourt, as she rose from her chair. And the two old men and the two young men, Spencer and Marshall, Wicks and Hammond, flattened themselves behind the counter envying him as he led her through the shop to the door. And he waggled his yellow glove in their faces, and she held her honour—a cheque for twenty thousand pounds with his signature—quite firmly in her hands.

"Are they false or are they real?" asked Oliver, shutting his private door. There they were, ten pearls on the blotting-paper on the table. He took them to the window. He held them under his lens to the light. . . . This, then, was the truffle he had routed out of the earth! Rotten at the centre—rotten at the core!

"Forgive me, oh, my mother!" he sighed, raising his hand as if he asked pardon of the old woman in the picture. And again he was a little boy in the alley where they sold dogs on Sunday.

"For," he murmured, laying the palms of his hands together, "it is to be a long week-end." □

DISCUSSION

1. Who is the greater cheat, Oliver or the Duchess? Explain.

2. This story takes place in the upper-class London world of a bygone day. However, it deals with elements universal to human nature. What are some of these elements?

3. (a) Is Oliver to be pitied at all? Explain.

(b) Is the Duchess to be pitied at all?

4. Explain the significance of the following in the story:

(a) "For was he not still a sad man, a dissatisfied man, a man who seeks something that is hidden, though he had won his bet?" (page 541a).

(b) "'Tears,' said Oliver, looking at the pearls.

"'Heart's blood,' he said, looking at the rubies.

"'Gunpowder,' he continued, rattling the diamonds so that they flashed and blazed. 'Gunpowder enough to blow Mayfair—sky high, high, high!" (page 541b).

(c) "They were friends, yet enemies; he was master, she was mistress; each cheated the other, each needed the other, each feared the other, each felt this and knew this every time they touched hands thus in the little back room. . . ." (page 542a).

5. (a) What was Mademoiselle's role in Oliver's life?

(b) his mother's role?

(c) Diana's?

6. Both Oliver and the Duchess appear vain, but they differ in their vanity. How?

7. Oliver *Bacon* is, at one time or another, compared with an elephant, a hog, a camel, and a horse; the Duchess is compared to a peacock, her jewel pouch to a lean yellow ferret. What might be the author's purpose in using all this animal imagery?

8. Both John in "Solid Objects" and Oliver in "The Duchess and the Jeweller" find "stones" fascinating. How do they differ as to the values they place on these stones?

WRITING

Write Oliver Bacon's diary entries describing what happened at the house party.

TOBERMORY

by Saki

PHOTOGRAPH BY E. O. HOPPE, LONDON

IT was a chill, rain-washed afternoon of a late August day, that indefinite season when partridges are still in security or cold storage, and there is nothing to hunt—unless one is bounded on the north by the Bristol Channel, in which case one may lawfully gallop after fat red stags. Lady Blemley's house-party was not bounded on the north by the Bristol Channel, hence there was a full gathering of her guests round the tea-table on this particular afternoon. And, in spite of the blankness of the season and the triteness of the occasion, there was no trace in the company of that fatigued restlessness which means a dread of the pianola and a subdued hankering for auction bridge. The undisguised open-mouthed attention of the entire party was fixed on the homely negative personality of Mr. Cornelius Appin. Of all her guests, he was the one who had come to Lady Blemley with the vaguest reputation. Some one had said he was "clever," and he had got his invitation in the moderate expectation, on the part of his hostess, that some portion at least of his cleverness would be contributed to the general entertainment. Until tea-time that day she had been unable to discover in what direction, if any, his cleverness lay. He was neither a wit nor a croquet champion, a hypnotic force nor a begetter of amateur theatricals. Neither did his exterior suggest the sort of man in whom women are willing to pardon a generous measure of mental deficiency. He had subsided into mere Mr. Appin, and the Cornelius seemed a piece of transparent baptismal bluff. And now he was claiming to have launched on the world a discovery beside which the invention of gunpowder, of the printing-press, and of steam locomotion were inconsiderable trifles. Science had made bewildering strides in many directions during recent decades, but this thing seemed to belong to the domain of miracle rather than to scientific achievement.

"And do you really ask us to believe," Sir Wilfrid was saying, "that you have discovered a means for instructing animals in the art of human speech, and that dear old Tobermory has proved your first successful pupil?"

"It is a problem at which I have worked for the last seventeen years," said Mr. Appin, "but only during the last eight or nine months have I been rewarded with glimmerings of success. Of course I have experimented with thousands of animals, but latterly only with cats, those wonderful creatures which have assimilated themselves so marvellously with our civilization while retaining all their highly developed feral instincts. Here and there among cats one comes across an outstanding superior intellect, just as one does among the ruck of human beings, and when I made the acquaintance of Tobermory a week ago I saw at once that I was in contact with a 'Beyond-cat' of extraordinary intelligence. I had gone far along the road to success in recent experiments; with Tobermory, as you call him, I have reached the goal."

Mr. Appin concluded his remarkable statement in a voice which he strove to divest of a triumphant inflection. No one said "Rats," though Clovis's lips moved in a monosyllabic contortion which probably invoked those rodents of disbelief.

"And do you mean to say," asked Miss Resker, after a slight pause, "that you have taught Tobermory to say and understand easy sentences of one syllable?"

"My dear Miss Resker," said the wonder-worker patiently, "one teaches little children and savages and backward adults in that piecemeal fashion; when one has once solved the problem of making a beginning with an animal of highly developed intelligence one has no need for those halting methods. Tobermory can speak our language with perfect correctness."

This time Clovis very distinctly said, "Beyond-rats!" Sir Wilfrid was more polite, but equally sceptical.

"Hadn't we better have the cat in and judge for ourselves?" suggested Lady Blemley.

Sir Wilfrid went in search of the animal, and the company settled themselves down to the languid expectation of witnessing some more or less adroit drawing-room ventriloquism.

In a minute Sir Wilfrid was back in the room, his face white beneath its tan and his eyes dilated with excitement.

"By Gad, it's true!"

His agitation was unmistakably genuine, and his hearers started forward in a thrill of awakened interest.

Collapsing into an armchair he continued breathlessly: "I found him dozing in the smoking-room, and called out to him to come for his tea. He blinked at me in his usual way, and I said, 'Come on, Toby; don't keep us waiting'; and, by Gad! he drawled out in a most horribly natural voice that he'd come when he dashed well pleased! I nearly jumped out of my skin!"

Appin had preached to absolutely incredulous hearers; Sir Wilfrid's statement carried instant conviction. A Babel-like chorus of startled exclamation arose, amid which the scientist sat mutely enjoying the first fruit of his stupendous discovery.

In the midst of the clamour Tobermory entered the room and made his way with velvet tread and studied unconcern across to the group seated round the tea-table.

A sudden hush of awkwardness and constraint fell on the company. Somehow there seemed an element of embarrassment in addressing on equal terms a domestic cat of acknowledged mental ability.

"Will you have some milk, Tobermory?" asked Lady Blemley in a rather strained voice.

"I don't mind if I do," was the response, couched in a tone of even indifference. A shiver of suppressed excitement went through the listeners, and Lady Blemley might be excused for pouring out the saucerful of milk rather unsteadily.

"I'm afraid I've spilt a good deal of it," she said apologetically.

"After all, it's not my Axminster," was Tobermory's rejoinder.

Another silence fell on the group, and then Miss Resker, in her best district-visitor manner, asked if the human language had been difficult to learn. Tobermory looked squarely at her for a moment and then fixed his gaze serenely on the middle distance. It was obvious that boring questions lay outside his scheme of life.

"What do you think of human intelligence?" asked Mavis Pellington lamely.

"Of whose intelligence in particular?" asked Tobermory coldly.

"Oh, well, mine for instance," said Mavis, with a feeble laugh.

"You put me in an embarrassing position," said Tobermory, whose tone and attitude certainly did not suggest a shred of embarrassment. "When your inclusion in this house-party was suggested Sir Wilfrid protested that you were the most brainless woman of his acquaintance, and that there was a wide distinction between hospitality and the care of the feeble-minded. Lady Blemley replied that your lack of brain-power was the precise quality which had earned you your invitation, as you were the only person she could think of who might be idiotic enough to buy their old car. You know, the one they call 'The Envy of Sisyphus,'[1] because it goes quite nicely up-hill if you push it."

Lady Blemley's protestations would have had greater effect if she had not casually suggested to Mavis only that morning that the car in question would be just the thing for her down at her Devonshire home.

Major Barfield plunged in heavily to effect a diversion.

"How about your carryings-on with the tortoise-shell puss up at the stables, eh?"

The moment he had said it every one realized the blunder.

"One does not usually discuss these matters in public," said Tobermory frigidly. "From a slight observation of your ways since you've been in this house I should imagine you'd find it inconvenient if I were to shift the conversation on to your own little affairs."

The panic which ensued was not confined to the Major.

"Would you like to go and see if cook has got your dinner ready?" suggested Lady Blemley hurriedly,

---

1. *Sisyphus.* In Greek mythology, his punishment in Hades was to have to roll a huge stone up a hill, only to have it roll down again each time.

affecting to ignore the fact that it wanted at least two hours to Tobermory's dinner-time.

"Thanks," said Tobermory, "not quite so soon after my tea. I don't want to die of indigestion."

"Cats have nine lives, you know," said Sir Wilfrid heartily.

"Possibly," answered Tobermory; "but only one liver."

"Adelaide!" said Mrs. Cornett, "do you mean to encourage that cat to go out and gossip about us in the servants' hall?"

The panic had indeed become general. A narrow ornamental balustrade ran in front of most of the bedroom windows at the Towers, and it was recalled with dismay that this had formed a favourite promenade for Tobermory at all hours, whence he could watch the pigeons—and heaven knew what else besides. If he intended to become reminiscent in his present out-spoken strain the effect would be something more than disconcerting. Mrs. Cornett, who spent much time at her toilet table, and whose complexion was reputed to be of a nomadic though punctual disposition, looked as ill at ease as the Major. Miss Scrawen, who wrote fiercely sensuous poetry and led a blameless life, merely displayed irritation; if you are methodical and virtuous in private you don't necessarily want every one to know it. Bertie van Tahn, who was so depraved at seventeen that he had long ago given up trying to be any worse, turned a dull shade of gardenia white, but he did not commit the error of dashing out of the room like Odo Finsberry, a young gentleman who was understood to be reading for the Church and who was possibly disturbed at the thought of scandals he might hear concerning other people. Clovis had the presence of mind to maintain a composed exterior; privately he was calculating how long it would take to procure a box of fancy mice through the agency of the *Exchange and Mart* as a species of hush-money.

Even in a delicate situation like the present, Agnes Resker could not endure to remain too long in the background.

"Why did I ever come down here?" she asked dramatically.

Tobermory immediately accepted the opening.

"Judging by what you said to Mrs. Cornett on the croquet-lawn yesterday, you were out for food. You described the Blemleys as the dullest people to stay with that you knew, but said they were clever enough to employ a first-rate cook; otherwise they'd find it difficult to get any one to come down a second time."

"There's not a word of truth in it! I appeal to Mrs. Cornett—" exclaimed the discomfited Agnes.

"Mrs. Cornett repeated your remark afterwards to Bertie van Tahn," continued Tobermory, "and said, 'That woman is a regular Hunger Marcher; she'd go anywhere for four square meals a day,' and Bertie van Tahn said—"

At this point the chronicle mercifully ceased. Tobermory had caught a glimpse of the big yellow Tom from the Rectory working his way through the shrubbery towards the stable wing. In a flash he had vanished through the open French window.

With the disappearance of his too brilliant pupil Cornelius Appin found himself beset by a hurricane of bitter upbraiding, anxious inquiry, and frightened entreaty. The responsibility for the situation lay with him, and he must prevent matters from becoming worse. Could Tobermory impart his dangerous gift to other cats? was the first question he had to answer. It was possible, he replied, that he might have initiated his intimate friend the stable puss into his new accomplishment, but it was unlikely that his teaching could have taken a wider range as yet.

"Then," said Mrs. Cornett, "Tobermory may be a valuable cat and a great pet; but I'm sure you'll agree, Adelaide, that both he and the stable cat must be done away with without delay."

"You don't suppose I've enjoyed the last quarter of an hour, do you?" said Lady Blemley bitterly. "My husband and I are very fond of Tobermory—at least, we were before this horrible accomplishment was infused into him; but now, of course, the only thing is to have him destroyed as soon as possible."

"We can put some strychnine in the scraps he always gets at dinnertime," said Sir Wilfrid, "and I will go and drown the stable cat myself. The coachman will be very sore at losing his pet, but I'll say a very catching form of mange has broken out in both cats and we're afraid of it spreading to the kennels."

"But my great discovery!" expostulated Mr. Appin; "after all my years of research and experiment—"

"You can go and experiment on the short-horns at the farm, who are under proper control, said Mrs. Cornett, "or the elephants at the Zoological Gardens. They're said to be highly intelligent, and they have this recommendation, that they don't come creeping about our bedrooms and under chairs, and so forth."

An archangel ecstatically proclaiming the Millennium, and finding that it clashed unpardonably with Henley[2] and would have to be indefinitely postponed, could hardly have felt more crestfallen than Cornelius Appin at the reception of his wonderful achievement. Public opinion, however, was against him—in fact, had the general voice been consulted on the subject it is probable that a strong minority vote would have been in favour of including him in the strychnine diet.

Defective train arrangements and a nervous desire to see matters brought to a finish prevented an immediate dispersal of the party, but dinner that evening was not a social success. Sir Wilfrid had had rather a trying time with the stable cat and subsequently with the coachman. Agnes Resker ostentatiously limited her repast to a morsel of dry toast, which she bit as though it were a personal enemy; while Mavis Pellington maintained a vindictive silence throughout the meal. Lady Blemley kept up a flow of what she hoped was conversation, but her attention was fixed on the doorway. A plateful of carefully dosed fish scraps was in readiness on the sideboard, but sweets and savoury and dessert went their way, and no Tobermory appeared either in the dining-room or kitchen.

The sepulchral dinner was cheerful compared with the subsequent vigil in the smoking-room. Eating and drinking had at least supplied a distraction and cloak to the prevailing embarrassment. Bridge was out of the question in the general tension of nerves and tempers, and after Odo Finsberry had given a lugubrious rendering of "Melisande in the Wood" to a frigid audience, music was tacitly avoided. At eleven the servants went to bed, announcing that the small window in the pantry had been left open as usual for Tobermory's private use. The guests read steadily through the current batch of magazines, and fell back gradually on the "Badminton Library" and bound volumes of *Punch.* Lady Blemley made periodic visits to the pantry, returning each time with an expression of listless depression which forestalled questioning.

At two o'clock Clovis broke the dominating silence.

"He won't turn up tonight. He's probably in the local newspaper office at the present moment, dictating the first instalment of his reminiscences. Lady What's-her-name's book won't be in it. It will be the event of the day."

Having made this contribution to the general cheerfulness, Clovis went to bed. At long intervals the various members of the house-party followed his example.

The servants taking round the early tea made a uniform announcement in reply to a uniform question. Tobermory had not returned.

Breakfast was, if anything, a more unpleasant function than dinner had been, but before its conclusion the situation was relieved. Tobermory's corpse was brought in from the shrubbery, where a gardener had just discovered it. From the bites on his throat and the yellow fur which coated his claws it was evident that he had fallen in unequal combat with the big Tom from the Rectory.

By midday most of the guests had quitted the Towers, and after lunch Lady Blemley had sufficiently recovered her spirits to write an extremely nasty letter to the Rectory about the loss of her valuable pet.

Tobermory had been Appin's one successful pupil, and he was destined to have no successor. A few weeks later an elephant in the Dresden Zoological Garden, which had shown no previous signs of irritability, broke loose and killed an Englishman who had apparently been teasing it. The victim's name was variously reported in the papers as Oppin and Eppelin, but his front name was faithfully rendered Cornelius.

"If he was trying German irregular verbs on the poor beast," said Clovis, "he deserved all he got." □

2. *Henley,* the annual regatta (boat races) held at Henley-on-Thames. It is an extremely popular social and sporting event.

DISCUSSION

1. (a) What hadn't Cornelius Appin considered when he taught Tobermory to speak?

(b) Can you think of any other "great" inventions or discoveries that had unexpected side effects?

2. (a) Where does the humor lie in this story?

(b) To what extent is the story an attack on hypocrisy?

(c) To what extent is it true to human nature?

3. (a) Could "Tobermory" be said to present an insider's view of the sort of house party Oliver Bacon is so eager to attend in "The Duchess and the Jeweller"? Explain.

(b) What theme is common to both these stories?

(c) How do Saki and Woolf differ in their treatment of this theme?

WRITING

1. Write about an adventure that might have happened to Cornelius Appin between Tobermory's death and his own.

2. Write on any of the following topics, or a similar one of your choice: "Tobermory Tells About ______ High School," "Tobermory Visits Congress," "Tobermory Goes to War."

POISON

by Roald Dahl

IT must have been around midnight when I drove home, and as I approached the gates of the bungalow I switched off the head-lamps of the car so the beam wouldn't swing in through the window of the side bedroom and wake Harry Pope. But I needn't have bothered. Coming up the drive I noticed his light was still on, so he was awake anyway—unless perhaps he'd dropped off while reading.

I parked the car and went up the five steps to the balcony, counting each step carefully in the dark so I wouldn't take an extra one which wasn't there when I got to the top. I crossed the balcony, pushed through the screen doors into the house itself and switched on the light in the hall. I went across to the door of Harry's room, opened it quietly, and looked in.

He was lying on the bed and I could see he was awake. But he didn't move. He didn't even turn his head toward me, but I heard him say, "Timber, Timber, come here."

He spoke slowly, whispering each word carefully, separately, and I pushed the door right open and started to go quickly across the room.

"Stop. Wait a moment, Timber." I could hardly hear what he was saying. He seemed to be straining enormously to get the words out.

"What's the matter, Harry?"

"Sshhh!" he whispered. "Sshhh! For God's sake don't make a noise. Take your shoes off before you come nearer. *Please* do as I say, Timber."

The way he was speaking reminded me of George Barling after he got shot in the stomach when he stood leaning against a crate containing a spare airplane engine, holding both hands on his stomach and saying things about the German pilot in just the same hoarse straining half whisper Harry was using now.

"Quickly, Timber, but take your shoes off first."

I couldn't understand about taking off the shoes but I figured that if he was as ill as he sounded I'd better humor him, so I bent down and removed the shoes and left them in the middle of the floor. Then I went over to his bed.

"Don't touch the bed! For God's sake don't touch the bed!" He was still speaking like he'd been shot in the stomach and I could see him lying there on his back with a single sheet covering three quarters of his body. He was wearing a pair of pyjamas with blue, brown, and white stripes, and he was sweating terribly. It was a hot night and I was sweating a little myself, but not like Harry. His whole face was wet and the pillow around his head was sodden with moisture. It looked like a bad go of malaria to me.

"What is it, Harry?"

"A krait," he said.

"A *krait!* Oh, my God! Where'd it bite you? How long ago?"

"Shut up," he whispered.

"Listen, Harry," I said, and I leaned forward and touched his shoulder. "We've got to be quick. Come on now, quickly, tell me where it bit you." He was lying there very still and tense as though he were holding on to himself hard because of sharp pain.

"I haven't been bitten," he whispered. "Not yet. It's on my stomach. Lying there asleep."

I took a quick pace backward; I couldn't help it, and I stared at his stomach or rather at the sheet that covered it. The sheet was rumpled in several places and it was impossible to tell if there was anything underneath.

"You don't really mean there's a krait lying on your stomach now?"

"I swear it."

"How did it get there?" I shouldn't have asked the question because it was easy to see he wasn't fooling. I should have told him to keep quiet.

"I was reading," Harry said, and he spoke very slowly, taking each word in turn and speaking it carefully so as not to move the muscles of his stomach. "Lying on my back reading and I felt something on my chest, behind the book. Sort of tickling. Then out of the corner of my eye saw this little krait sliding over my pyjamas. Small, about ten inches. Knew I mustn't move. Couldn't have anyway. Lay there watching it. Thought it would go over top of the sheet." Harry paused and was silent for a few moments. His eyes looked down along his body toward the place where the sheet covered his stomach, and I could see he was watching to make sure his whispering wasn't disturbing the thing that lay there.

"There was a fold in the sheet," he said, speaking more slowly than ever now and so softly I had to lean close to hear him. "See it, it's still there. It went under that. I could feel it through my pyjamas, moving on my stomach. Then it stopped moving and now it's lying there in the warmth. Probably asleep. I've been waiting for you." He raised his eyes and looked at me.

"How long ago?"

"Hours," he whispered. "Hours and bloody hours and hours. I can't keep still much longer. I've been wanting to cough."

There was not much doubt about the truth of Harry's story. As a matter of fact it wasn't a surprising thing for a krait to do. They hang around people's houses and they go for the warm places. The surprising thing was that Harry hadn't been bitten. The bite is quite deadly except sometimes when you catch it at once and they kill a fair number of people each year in Bengal, mostly in the villages.

"All right, Harry," I said, and now I was whispering too. "Don't move and don't talk any more unless you have to. You know it won't bite unless it's frightened. We'll fix it in no time."

I went softly out of the room in my stocking feet and fetched a small sharp knife from the kitchen. I put it in my trouser pocket ready to use instantly in case something went wrong while we were still thinking out a plan. If Harry coughed or moved or did something to frighten the krait and got bitten, I was going to be ready to cut the bitten place and try to suck the venom out. I came back to the bedroom and Harry was still lying there very quiet and sweating all over his face. His eyes followed me as I moved across the room to his bed and I could see he was wondering what I'd been up to. I stood beside him, trying to think of the best thing to do.

"Harry," I said, and now when I spoke I put my mouth almost on his ear so I wouldn't have to raise my voice above the softest whisper, "I think the best thing to do is for me to draw the sheet back very, very gently. Then we could have a look first. I think I could do that without disturbing it."

"Don't be a damn' fool." There was no expression in his voice. He spoke each word too slowly, too carefully, and too softly for that. The expression was in the eyes and around the corners of the mouth.

"Why not?"

"The light would frighten him. It's dark under there now."

"Then how about whipping the sheet back quick

and brushing it off before it has time to strike?"

"Why don't you get a doctor?" Harry said. The way he looked at me told me I should have thought of that myself in the first place.

"A doctor. Of course. That's it. I'll get Ganderbai."

I tiptoed out to the hall, looked up Ganderbai's number in the book, lifted the phone and told the operator to hurry.

"Doctor Ganderbai," I said. "This is Timber Woods."

"Hello, Mr. Woods. You not in bed yet?"

"Look, could you come round at once? And bring serum—for a krait bite."

"Who's been bitten?" The question came so sharply it was like a small explosion in my ear.

"No one. No one yet. But Harry Pope's in bed and he's got one lying on his stomach—asleep under the sheet on his stomach."

For about three seconds there was silence on the line. Then speaking slowly, not like an explosion now but slowly, precisely, Ganderbai said, "Tell him to keep quite still. He is not to move or to talk. Do you understand?"

"Of course."

"I'll come at once!" He rang off and I went back to the bedroom. Harry's eyes watched me as I walked across to his bed.

"Ganderbai's coming. He said for you to lie still."

"What in God's name does he think I'm doing!"

"Look, Harry, he said no talking. Absolutely no talking. Either of us."

"Why don't you shut up then?" When he said this, one side of his mouth started twitching with rapid little downward movements that continued for a while after he finished speaking. I took out my handkerchief and very gently I wiped the sweat off his face and neck, and I could feel the slight twitching of the muscle—the one he used for smiling—as my fingers passed over it with the handkerchief.

I slipped out to the kitchen, got some ice from the icebox, rolled it up in a napkin, and began to crush it small. That business of the mouth, I didn't like that. Or the way he talked, either. I carried the ice pack back to the bedroom and laid it across Harry's forehead.

"Keep you cool."

He screwed up his eyes and drew breath sharply through his teeth. "Take it away," he whispered. "Make me cough." His smiling-muscle began to twitch again.

The beam of a head-lamp shone through the window as Ganderbai's car swung around to the front of the bungalow. I went out to meet him, holding the ice pack with both hands.

"How is it?" Ganderbai asked, but he didn't stop to talk; he walked on past me across the balcony and through the screen doors into the hall. "Where is he? Which room?"

He put his bag down on a chair in the hall and followed me into Harry's room. He was wearing soft-soled bedroom slippers and he walked across the floor noiselessly, delicately, like a careful cat. Harry watched him out of the sides of his eyes. When Ganderbai reached the bed he looked down at Harry and smiled, confident and reassuring, nodding his head to tell Harry it was a simple matter and he was not to worry but just to leave it to Dr. Ganderbai. Then he turned and went back to the hall and I followed him.

"First thing is to try to get some serum into him," he said, and he opened his bag and started to make preparations. "Intravenously. But I must do it neatly. Don't want to make him flinch."

We went into the kitchen and he sterilized a needle. He had a hypodermic syringe in one hand and a small bottle in the other and he stuck the needle through the rubber top of the bottle and began drawing a pale yellow liquid up into the syringe by pulling out the plunger. Then he handed the syringe to me.

"Hold that till I ask for it."

He picked up the bag and together we returned to the room. Harry's eyes were bright now and wide open. Ganderbai bent over Harry and very cautiously, like a man handling sixteenth-century lace, he rolled up the pyjama sleeve to the elbow without moving the arm. I noticed he stood well away from the bed.

He whispered, "I'm going to give you an injection. Serum. Just a prick but try not to move. Don't tighten your stomach muscles. Let them go limp."

Harry looked at the syringe.

Ganderbai took a piece of red rubber tubing from his bag and slid one end under and up and around Harry's bicep; then he tied the tubing tight with a knot. He sponged a small area of the bare forearm with alcohol, handed the swab to me and took the syringe from my hand. He held it up to the light, squinting at the calibrations, squirting out some of the yellow fluid. I stood still beside him, watching.

Harry was watching too and sweating all over his face so it shone like it was smeared thick with face cream melting on his skin and running down onto the pillow.

I could see the blue vein on the inside of Harry's forearm, swollen now because of the tourniquet, and then I saw the needle above the vein, Ganderbai holding the syringe almost flat against the arm, sliding the needle in sideways through the skin into the blue vein, sliding it slowly but so firmly it went in smooth as into cheese. Harry looked at the ceiling and closed his eyes and opened them again but he didn't move.

When it was finished Ganderbai leaned forward putting his mouth close to Harry's ear. "Now you'll be all right even if you *are* bitten. But don't move. Please don't move. I'll be back in a moment."

He picked up his bag and went out to the hall and I followed.

"Is he safe now?" I asked.

"No."

"How safe is he?"

The little Indian doctor stood there in the hall rubbing his lower lip.

"It must give some protection, mustn't it?" I asked.

He turned away and walked to the screen doors that led onto the veranda. I thought he was going through them but he stopped this side of the doors and stood looking out into the night.

"Isn't the serum very good?" I asked.

"Unfortunately not," he answered without turning round. "It might save him. It might not. I am trying to think of something else to do."

"Shall we draw the sheet back quick and brush it off before it has time to strike?"

"Never! We are not entitled to take a risk." He spoke sharply and his voice was pitched a little higher than usual.

"We can't very well leave him lying there," I said. "He's getting nervous."

"Please! Please!" he said, turning round, holding both hands up in the air. "Not so fast, please. This is not a matter to rush into bald-headed." He wiped his forehead with his handkerchief and stood there, frowning, nibbling his lip.

"You see," he said at last. "There is a way to do this. You know what we must do—we must administer an anesthetic to the creature where it lies."

It was a splendid idea.

"It is not safe," he continued, "because a snake is cold-blooded and anesthetic does not work so well or so quick with such animals, but it is better than any other thing to do. We could use ether . . . chloroform . . ." He was speaking slowly and trying to think the thing out while he talked.

"Which shall we use?"

"Chloroform," he said suddenly. "Ordinary chloroform. That is best. Now quick!" He took my arm and pulled me toward the balcony. "Drive to my house! By the time you get there I will have waked up my boy on the telephone and he will show you my poisons cupboard. Here is the key of the cupboard. Take a bottle of chloroform. It has an orange label and the name is printed on it. I stay here in case anything happens. Be quick now, hurry! No, no, you don't need your shoes!"

I drove fast and in about fifteen minutes I was back with the bottle of chloroform. Ganderbai came out of Harry's room and met me in the hall. "You got it?" he said. "Good, good. I just been telling him what we are going to do. But now we must hurry. It is not easy for him in there like that all this time. I am afraid he might move."

He went back to the bedroom and I followed, carrying the bottle carefully with both hands. Harry was lying on the bed in precisely the same position as before with the sweat pouring down his cheeks. His face was white and wet. He turned his eyes toward me and I smiled at him and nodded confidently. He continued to look at me. I raised my thumb, giving him the okay signal. He closed his eyes. Ganderbai was squatting down by the bed, and on the floor beside him was the hollow rubber tube that he had previously used as a tourniquet, and he'd got a small paper funnel fitted into one end of the tube.

He began to pull a little piece of the sheet out from under the mattress. He was working directly in line with Harry's stomach, about eighteen inches from it, and I watched his fingers as they tugged gently at the edge of the sheet. He worked so slowly it was almost impossible to discern any movement, either in his fingers or in the sheet that was being pulled.

Finally he succeeded in making an opening under the sheet and he took the rubber tube and inserted one end of it in the opening so that it would slide under the sheet along the mattress toward Harry's body. I do not know how long it took him to slide that tube in a few inches. It may have been twenty minutes, it may have been forty. I never once saw the tube move. I knew it was going in because the visible part of it grew gradually shorter, but I doubted that the krait could have felt even the faintest vibration. Ganderbai himself was sweating now, large pearls of sweat standing out all over his forehead and along his upper lip. But his hands were steady and I noticed that his eyes were watching, not the tube in his hands, but the area of crumpled sheet above Harry's stomach.

Without looking up, he held out a hand to me for the chloroform. I twisted out the ground-glass stopper and put the bottle right into his hand, not letting go till I was sure he had a good hold on it. Then he jerked his head for me to come closer and he whispered, "Tell him I'm going to soak the mattress and that it will be very cold under his body. He must be ready for that and he must not move. Tell him now."

I bent over Harry and passed on the message.

"Why doesn't he get on with it?" Harry said.

"He's going to now, Harry. But it'll feel very cold, so be ready for it."

"Oh, God Almighty, get on, get on!" For the first time he raised his voice, and Ganderbai glanced up sharply, watched him for a few seconds, then went back to his business.

Ganderbai poured a few drops of chloroform into the paper funnel and waited while it ran down the tube. Then he poured some more. Then he waited again, and the heavy sickening smell of chloroform spread out over the room bringing with it faint unpleasant memories of white-coated nurses and white surgeons standing in a white room around a long white table. Ganderbai was pouring steadily now and I could see the heavy vapor of the chloroform swirling slowly like smoke above the paper funnel. He paused, held the bottle up to the light, poured one more funnel and handed the bottle back to me. Slowly he drew out the rubber tube from under the sheet; then he stood up.

The strain of inserting the tube and pouring the chloroform must have been great, and I recollect that when Ganderbai turned and whispered to me, his voice was small and tired. "We'll give it fifteen minutes. Just to be safe."

I leaned over to tell Harry. "We're going to give it fifteen minutes, just to be safe. But it's probably done for already."

"Then why for God's sake don't you look and see!" Again he spoke loudly and Ganderbai sprang round, his small brown face suddenly very angry. He had almost pure black eyes and he stared at Harry and Harry's smiling-muscle started to twitch. I took my handkerchief and wiped his wet face, trying to stroke his forehead a little for comfort as I did so.

Then we stood and waited beside the bed, Ganderbai watching Harry's face all the time in a curious intense manner. The little Indian was concentrating all his will power on keeping Harry quiet. He never once took his eyes from the patient and although he made no sound, he seemed somehow to be shouting at him all the time, saying: Now listen, you've got to listen, you're not going to go spoiling this now, d'you hear me; and Harry lay there twitching his mouth, sweating, closing his eyes, opening them, looking at me, at the sheet, at the ceiling, at me again, but never at Ganderbai. Yet somehow Ganderbai was holding him. The smell of chloroform was oppressive and it made me feel sick, but I couldn't leave the room now. I had the feeling someone was blowing up a huge balloon and I could see it was going to burst but I couldn't look away.

At length Ganderbai turned and nodded and I knew he was ready to proceed. "You go over to the other side of the bed," he said. "We will each take one side of the sheet and draw it back together, but very slowly please, and very quietly."

"Keep still now, Harry," I said and I went around to the other side of the bed and took hold of the sheet. Ganderbai stood opposite me, and together we began to draw back the sheet, lifting it up clear of Harry's body, taking it back very slowly, both of us standing well away but at the same time bending forward, trying to peer underneath it. The smell of chloroform was awful. I remember trying to hold my breath and when I couldn't do that any longer I tried to breathe shallow so the stuff wouldn't get into my lungs.

The whole of Harry's chest was visible now, or rather the striped pyjama top which covered it, and then I saw the white cord of his pyjama trousers, neatly tied in a bow. A little farther and I saw a button, a mother-of-pearl button, and that was something I had never had on my pyjamas, a fly button, let alone a mother-of-pearl one. This Harry, I thought, he is very refined. It is odd how one sometimes has frivolous thoughts at exciting moments, and I distinctly remember thinking about Harry being very refined when I saw that button.

Apart from the button there was nothing on his stomach.

We pulled the sheet back faster then, and when we had uncovered his legs and feet we let the sheet drop over the end of the bed onto the floor.

"Don't move," Ganderbai said, "don't move, Mr. Pope"; and he began to peer around along the side of Harry's body and under his legs.

"We must be careful," he said. "It may be anywhere. It could be up the leg of his pyjamas."

When Ganderbai said this, Harry quickly raised his head from the pillow and looked down at his legs. It was the first time he had moved. Then suddenly he jumped up, stood on his bed and shook his legs one after the other violently in the air. At that moment we both thought he had been bitten and Ganderbai was already reaching down into his bag for a scalpel and a tourniquet when Harry ceased his caperings and stood still and looked at the mattress he was standing on and shouted, "It's not there!"

Ganderbai straightened up and for a moment he too looked at the mattress; then he looked up at Harry. Harry was all right. He hadn't been bitten and now he wasn't going to get bitten and he wasn't going to be killed and everything was fine. But that didn't seem to make anyone feel any better.

"Mr. Pope, you are of course *quite* sure you saw it in the first place?" There was a note of sarcasm in Ganderbai's voice that he would never have employed in ordinary circumstances. "You don't think you might possibly have been dreaming, do you, Mr. Pope?" The way Ganderbai was looking at Harry, I realized that the sarcasm was not seriously intended. He was only easing up a bit after the strain.

Harry stood on his bed in his striped pyjamas, glaring at Ganderbai, and the color began to spread out over his cheeks.

"Are you telling me I'm a liar?" he shouted.

Ganderbai remained absolutely still, watching Harry. Harry took a pace forward on the bed and there was a shining look in his eyes.

"Why, you dirty little Hindu sewer rat!"

"Shut up, Harry!" I said.

"You dirty black—"

"Harry!" I called. "Shut up, Harry!" It was terrible, the things he was saying.

Ganderbai went out of the room as though neither of us was there and I followed him and put my arm around his shoulder as he walked across the hall and out onto the balcony.

"Don't you listen to Harry," I said. "This thing's made him so he doesn't know what he's saying."

We went down the steps from the balcony to the drive and across the drive in the darkness to where his old Morris car was parked. He opened the door and got in.

"You did a wonderful job," I said. "Thank you so very much for coming."

"All he needs is a good holiday," he said quietly, without looking at me, then he started the engine and drove off. □

DISCUSSION

1. Give your own opinion, with supporting evidence, as to which of the following really happened:

(a) There *was* a krait.

(b) There was no krait and Harry Pope knew it.

(c) There was no krait but Harry Pope believed there was.

2. This story is recognized as a masterpiece of suspense. Part of the suspense is generated by the author's use of concrete details that make you feel you are on the scene, actually experiencing each tense moment. Give examples of such details.

3. (a) Was Doctor Ganderbai out of line in asking Harry Pope if he had really seen the snake?

(b) Was Harry Pope out of line in his response?

4. What would have been different about the tone and effect of the story if the author had written it in the third person?

5. Both "Poison" and "Tobermory," though containing fascinating actions, appear to develop themes. What are they?

WRITING

1. Write a different ending for the story.

2. (a) Write a stream-of-consciousness monologue describing what is going on inside Harry Pope's head during any single episode of the story.

(b) As an alternative, tell any episode of the story from Harry Pope's viewpoint.

A QUEER HEART

by Elizabeth Bowen

MRS. Cadman got out of the bus backwards. No amount of practice ever made her more agile; the trouble she had with her big bulk amused everyone, and herself. Gripping the handles each side of the bus door so tightly that the seams of her gloves cracked, she lowered herself cautiously, like a climber, while her feet, overlapping her smart shoes, uneasily scrabbled at each step. One or two people asked why the bus made, for one passenger, such a long, dead stop. But on the whole she was famous on this line, for she was constantly in and out of town. The conductor waited behind her, smiling, holding her basket, arms wide to catch her if she should slip.

Having got safe to the ground, Mrs. Cadman shook herself like a satisfied bird. She took back her shopping basket from the conductor and gave him a smile instead. The big kind scarlet bus once more ground into movement, off up the main road hill: it made a fading blur in the premature autumn dusk. Mrs. Cadman almost waved after it, for with it went the happy part of her day. She turned down the side road that led to her gate.

A wet wind of autumn, smelling of sodden gardens, blew in her face and tilted her hat. Leaves whirled along it, and one lime leaf, as though imploring shelter, lodged in her fur collar. Every gust did more to sadden the poor trees. This was one of those roads outside growing provincial cities that still keep their rural mystery. They seem to lead into something still not known. Traffic roars past one end, but the other end is in silence: you see a wood, a spire, a haughty manor gate, or your view ends with the turn of an old wall. Here some new raw-looking villas stood with spaces between them; in the spaces were orchards and market-gardens. A glasshouse roof reflected the wet grey light; there was a shut chapel farther along. And, each standing back in half an acre of ground, there were two or three stucco houses with dark windows, sombre but at the same time ornate, built years ago in this then retired spot. Dead lime leaves showered over their grass plots and evergreens. Mrs. Cadman's house, Granville, was one of these: its name was engraved in scrolls over the porch. The solid house was not large, and Mrs. Cadman's daughter, Lucille, could look after it with a daily help.

The widow and her daughter lived here in the state of cheerless meekness Lucille considered suitable for them now. *Mr.* Cadman had liked to have everything done in style. But twelve years ago he had died, travelling on business, in a hotel up in the North. Always the gentleman, he had been glad to spare them this upset at home. He had been brought back to the Midlands for his impressive funeral, whose size showed him a popular man. How unlike Mr. Cadman was Rosa proving herself. One can be most unfriendly on one's way of dying. Ah, well, one chooses one's husband; one's sister is dealt out to one by fate.

Mrs. Cadman, thumb on the latch of her own gate, looked for a minute longer up and down the road—deeply, deeply unwilling to go in. She looked back at the corner where the bus had vanished, and an immense sigh heaved up her coat lapels and made a cotton carnation, pinned to the fur, brush a fold of her chin. Laced, hooked, buttoned so tightly into her clothes, she seemed to need to deflate herself by these sudden sighs, by yawns or by those explosions of laughter that often vexed Lucille. Through her face—embedded in fat but still very lively, as exposed, as ingenuous as a little girl's—you could see some emotional fermentation always at work in her. Her smiles were frequent, hopeful and quick. Her pitching walk was due to her tight shoes.

When she did go in, she went in with a sort of rush. She let the door bang back on the hall wall, so that the chain rattled and an outraged clatter came from the letterbox. Immediately she knew she had done wrong. Lucille, appalled, looked out of the dining-room. "*Shissssh!* How can you, mother!" she said.

"Ever so sorry, dear," said Mrs. Cadman, cast down.

"She'd just dropped off," said Lucille. "After her bad night and everything. It really does seem hard."

Mrs. Cadman quite saw that it did. She glanced nervously up the stairs, then edged into the dining-room. It was not cheerful in here: a monkey puzzle,[1] too close to the window, drank the last of the light up; the room still smelt of dinner; the fire smouldered resentfully, starved for coal. The big mahogany furniture lowered, with no shine. Mrs. Cadman, putting her basket down on the table, sent an uncertain smile across at Lucille, whose glasses blankly gleamed high up on her long face. She often asked herself where Lucille could have come from. *Could* this be the baby daughter she had borne, and tied pink bows on, and christened a pretty name? In the sun in this very bow window she had gurgled into the sweet-smelling creases of Lucille's neck—one summer lost in time.

"You *have* been an age," Lucille said.

"Well, the shops were quite busy. I never *saw*," she said with irrepressible pleasure, "I never *saw* so many people in town!"

Lucille, lips tighter than ever shut, was routing about, unpacking the shopping basket, handling the packages. Chemist's and grocer's parcels. Mrs. Cadman watched her with apprehension. Then Lucille pounced; she held up a small soft parcel in frivolous wrappings. "Oho," she said. "So you've been in at Babbington's?"

"Well, I missed one bus, so I had to wait for the next. So I just popped in there a minute out of the cold. And, you see, I've been wanting a little scarf—"

"Little scarf!" said Lucille. "I don't know what to make of you, mother. I don't really. How *could* you, at such a time? How you ever could have the heart!" Lucille, standing the other side of the table, leaned across it, her thin weight on her knuckles. This brought her face near her mother's. "Can't you understand?" she said. "Can't you take *anything* in? The next little scarf *you'll* need to buy will be black!"

"What a thing to say!" exclaimed Mrs. Cadman, profoundly offended. "With that poor thing upstairs now, waiting to have her tea."

"Tea? She can't take her tea. Why, since this morning she can't keep a thing down."

Mrs. Cadman blenched and began unbuttoning her coat. Lucille seemed to feel that her own prestige and Aunt Rosa's entirely hung on Aunt Rosa's approaching death. You could feel that she and her aunt had thought up this plan together. These last days had been the climax of their complicity. And there was Mrs. Cadman—as ever, as usual—put in the wrong, frowned upon, out of things. Whenever Rosa arrived to stay Mrs. Cadman had no fun in her home, and now Rosa was leaving forever it seemed worse. A perverse kick of the heart, a flicker of naughtiness, made Mrs. Cadman say: "Oh, well, while there's life there's hope."

Lucille said: "If you won't face it, you won't. But I just say it does fall heavy on me. . . . We had the vicar round here this afternoon. He was up with Aunt for a bit, then he looked in and said he did feel I needed a prayer too. He said he thought I was wonderful. He asked where you were, and he seemed to wonder you find the heart to stay out so long. I thought from his manner he wondered a good deal."

Mrs. Cadman, with an irrepressible titter, said: "Give him something to think about! Why if I'd ha' shown up that vicar'd have popped out as fast as he popped in. Thinks I'd make a mouthful of him! Why, I've made him bolt down the street. Well, well. He's not *my* idea of a vicar. When your father and I first came here we had a rural dean. Oh, he was as pleasant as anything."

Lucille, with the air of praying for Christian patience, folded her lips. Jabbing her fingers down the inside of her waistbelt, she more tightly tucked in her tight blouse. She liked looking like Mrs. Noah—no, *Miss* Noah. "The doctor's not been again. We're to let him know of any change."

"Well, let's do the best we can," said Mrs. Cadman. "But don't keep on *talking*. You don't make things any better, keeping on going on. My opinion is one should keep bright to the last. When my time comes, oh, I would like a cheery face."

"It's well for you . . ." began Lucille. She bit the remark off and, gathering up the parcels, stalked scornfully out of the dining-room. Without comment she left exposed on the table a small carton of goodies Mrs. Cadman had bought to cheer herself up with and had concealed in the toe of the shopping bag. Soon, from the kitchen came the carefully

1. *monkey puzzle*, a South American tree with branches like candelabra, stiff sharp leaves, and edible nuts.

muffled noises of Lucille putting away provisions and tearing the wrappings off the chemist's things. Mrs. Cadman, reaching out for the carton, put a peppermint into each cheek. She, oh so badly, wanted a cup of tea but dared not follow Lucille into the kitchen in order to put the kettle on.

Though, after all, Granville *was* her house. . . .

You would not think it was her house—not when Rosa was there. While Lucille and her mother were *tête à tête* Lucille's disapproval was at least fairly tacit. But as soon as Rosa arrived on one of these yearly autumn visits—always choosing the season when Mrs. Cadman felt in her least good form, the fall of the leaf—the aunt and niece got together and found everything wrong. Their two cold natures ran together. They found Mrs. Cadman lacking; they forbade the affection she would have offered them. They censured her the whole time. Mrs. Cadman could date her real alienation from Lucille from the year when Rosa's visits began. During Mr. Cadman's lifetime Rosa had never come for more than an afternoon. Mr. Cadman had been his wife's defence from her sister—a great red kind of rumbustious fortification. He had been a man who kept every chill wind out. Rosa, during those stilted afternoon visits, had adequately succeeded in conveying that she found marriage *low*. She might just have suffered a pious marriage; she openly deprecated this high living, this state of fleshly bliss. In order not to witness it too closely she lived on in lodgings in her native town. . . . But once widowhood left her sister exposed, Rosa started flapping round Granville like a doomed bird. She instituted these yearly visits, which, she made plain at the same time, gave her not much pleasure. The journey was tedious, and by breaking her habits, leaving her lodgings, Rosa was, out of duty, putting herself about. Her joyless and intimidating visits had, therefore, only one object—to protect the interests of Lucille.

Mrs. Cadman had suspected for some time that Rosa had something the matter with her. No one looks as yellow as that for nothing. But she was not sufficiently intimate with her sister to get down to the cosy subjects of insides. This time, Rosa arrived looking worse than ever, and three days afterwards had collapsed. Lucille said now she had known her aunt was poorly. Lucille said now she had always known. "But of course you wouldn't notice, mother," she said.

Mrs. Cadman sat down by the fire and, gratefully, kicked off her tight shoes. In the warmth her plump feet uncurled, relaxed, expanded like sea-anemones. She stretched her legs out, propped her heels on the fender and wiggled her toes voluptuously. They went on wiggling of their own accord: they seemed to have an independent existence. Here, in her home, where she felt so "put wrong" and chilly, they were like ten stout confidential friends. She said, out loud: "Well, *I* don't know what I've done."

The fact was: Lucille and Rosa resented her. (She'd feel better when she had had her tea.) She should *not* have talked as she had about the vicar. But it seemed so silly, Lucille having just him. She did wish Lucille had a better time. No young man so much as paused at the gate. Lucille's aunt had wrapped her own dank virginity round her, like someone sharing a mackintosh.

Mrs. Cadman had had a good time. A real good time always lasts: you have it with all your nature and all your nature stays living with it. She had been a pretty child with long, blonde hair that her sister Rosa, who was her elder sister, used to tweak when they were alone in their room. She had grown used, in that childish attic bedroom, to Rosa's malevolent silences. Then one had grown up, full of great uppish curves. Hilda Cadman could sing. She had sung at parties and sung at charity concerts, too. She had been invited from town to town, much fêted in business society. She had sung in a dress cut low at the bosom, with a rose or carnation tucked into her hair. She had drunk port wine in great red rooms blazing with chandeliers. Mr. Cadman had whisked her away from her other gentlemen friends, and not for a moment had she regretted it. Nothing had been too good for her; she had gone on singing. She had felt warm air on her bare shoulders; she still saw the kind, flushed faces crowding round. Mr. Cadman and she belonged to the jolly set. They all thought the world of her, and she thought the world of them.

Mrs. Cadman, picking up the poker, jabbed the fire into a spurt of light. It does not do any good to sit and think in the dark.

The town was not the same now. They had all died, or lost their money, or gone. But you kept on loving the town for its dear old sake. She sometimes thought: Why not move and live at the seaside, where there would be a promenade and a band? But she knew her nature clung to the old scenes; where you had lived, you lived—your nature clung like a cat. While there was *something* to look at she was not one to repine. It kept you going to keep out and about. Things went, but then new things came in their place. You can't cure yourself of the habit of loving life. So she drank up the new pleasures—the big cafés, the barging buses, the cinemas, the shops dripping with colour, almost all built of glass. She could be perfectly happy all alone in a café, digging into a cream bun with a fork, the band playing, smiling faces all round. The old faces had not gone: they had dissolved, diluted into the ruddy blur through which she saw everything.

Meanwhile, Lucille was hard put to it, living her mother down. Mother looked ridiculous, always round town like that.

Mrs. Cadman heard Lucille come out of the kitchen and go upstairs with something rattling on a tray. She waited a minute more, then sidled into the kitchen, where she cautiously started to make tea. The gas-ring, as though it were a spy of Lucille's, popped loudly when she applied the match.

"Mother, she's asking for you."

"Oh, dear—do you mean she's—?"

"She's much more herself this evening," Lucille said implacably.

Mrs. Cadman, at the kitchen table, had been stirring sugar into her third cup. She pushed her chair back, brushed crumbs from her bosom, and followed Lucille like a big unhappy lamb. The light was on in the hall, but the stairs led up into shadow: she had one more start of reluctance at their foot. Autumn draughts ran about in the top story: up there the powers of darkness all seemed to mobilize. Mrs. Cadman put her hand on the banister knob. "Are you sure she *does* want to see me? Oughtn't she to stay quiet?"

"You should go when she's asking. You never know. . . ."

Breathless, breathing unevenly on the top landing, Mrs. Cadman pushed open the spare-room—that was the sick-room—door. In there—in here—the air was dead, and at first it seemed very dark. On the ceiling an oil-stove printed its flower-pattern; a hooded lamp, low down, was turned away from the bed. On that dark side of the lamp she could just distinguish Rosa, propped up, with the sheet drawn to her chin.

"Rosa?"

"Oh, it's you?"

"Yes; it's me, dear. Feeling better this evening?"

"Seemed funny, you not coming near me."

"They said for you to keep quiet."

"My own sister. . . . You never liked sickness, did you? Well, I'm going. I shan't trouble you long."

"Oh, don't talk like that!"

"I'm glad to be going. Keeping on lying here. . . . We all come to it. Oh, give over crying, Hilda. Doesn't do any good."

Mrs. Cadman sat down, to steady herself. She fumbled in her lap with her handkerchief, perpetually, clumsily knocking her elbows against the arms of the wicker chair. "It's such a shame," she said. "It's such a pity. You and me, after all . . ."

"Well, it's late for all that now. Each took our own ways." Rosa's voice went up in a sort of ghostly sharpness. "There were things that couldn't be otherwise. I've tried to do right by Lucille. Lucille's a good girl, Hilda. You should ask yourself if you've done right by her."

"Oh, for shame, Rosa," said Mrs. Cadman, turning her face through the dark towards that disembodied voice. "For shame, Rosa, even if you *are* going. You know best what's come between her and me. It's been you and her, you and her. I don't know where to turn sometimes—"

Rosa said: "You've got such a shallow heart."

"How should you know? Why, you've kept at a distance from me ever since we were tots. Oh, I know I'm a great silly, always after my fun, but I never took what was yours; I never did harm to you. I don't see what call we have got to judge each other. You didn't want my life that I've had."

Rosa's chin moved: she was lying looking up at her sister's big rippling shadow, splodged up there by the light of the low lamp. It is frightening, having your shadow watched. Mrs. Cadman said: "But what did I do to you?"

"I *could* have had a wicked heart," said Rosa. "A vain, silly heart like yours. I could have fretted, seeing you take everything. One thing, then another. But I was shown. God taught me to pity you. God taught me my lesson. . . . You wouldn't even remember that Christmas tree."

"What Christmas tree?"

"No, you wouldn't even remember. Oh, I thought it was lovely. I could have cried when they pulled the curtains open, and there it was, all blazing away with candles and silver and everything—"

"Well, isn't that funny. I—"

"No; you've had all that pleasure since. All of

us older children couldn't take it in, hardly, for quite a minute or two. It didn't look real. Then I looked up, and there was a fairy doll fixed on the top, right on the top spike, fixed on to a star. I set my heart on her. She had wings and long fair hair, and she was shining away. I couldn't take my eyes off her. They cut the presents down; but she wasn't for anyone. In my childish blindness I kept praying to God. If I am not to have her, I prayed, let her stay there."

"And what did God do?" Hilda said eagerly.

"Oh, He taught me and saved me. You were a little thing in a blue sash; you piped up and asked might you have the doll."

"Fancy me! Aren't children awful!" said Mrs. Cadman. "Asking like that."

"They said: 'Make her sing for it.' They were taken with you. So you piped up again, singing. You got her, all right. I went off where they kept the coats. I've thanked God ever since for what I had to go through! I turned my face from vanity that very night. I had been shown."

"Oh, what a shame!" said Hilda. "Oh, I think it was cruel; you poor little mite."

"No; I used to see that doll all draggled about the house till no one could bear the sight of it. I said to myself: that's how those things end. Why, I'd learnt more in one evening than you've ever learnt in your life. Oh, yes, I've watched you, Hilda. Yes, and I've pitied you."

"Well, you showed me no pity."

"You asked for no pity—all vain and set up."

"No wonder you've been against me. Fancy me not knowing. I didn't *mean* any harm—why, I was quite a little thing. I don't even remember."

"Well, you'll remember one day. When you lie as I'm lying you'll find that everything comes back. And you'll see what it adds up to."

"Well, if I do?" said Hilda. "I haven't been such a baby; I've seen things out in my own way; I've had my ups and downs. It hasn't been all jam." She got herself out of the arm-chair and came and stood uncertainly by the foot of the bed. She had a great wish to reach out and turn the hooded lamp round, so that its light could fall on her sister's face. She felt she should *see* her sister, perhaps for the first time. Inside the flat, still form did implacable disappointment, then, stay locked? She wished she could give Rosa some little present. Too late to give Rosa anything pretty now: she looked back—it had always, then, been too late? She thought: you poor queer heart; you queer heart, eating yourself out, thanking God for the pain. She thought: I did that to her; then what have I done to Lucille?

She said: "You're ever so like me, Rosa, really, aren't you? Setting our hearts on things. When you've got them you don't notice. No wonder you wanted Lucille. . . . You did ought to have had that fairy doll." □

DISCUSSION

1. (a) What details of Mrs. Cadman's character are made clear by the bus ride?

(b) Why does she go into town so often?

2. (a) Characterize Rosa.

(b) In what respects is Lucille like her?

3. In the last paragraph of the story, Mrs. Cadman says: "You're ever so like me, Rosa, really, aren't you? Setting our hearts on things."

(a) What does she mean?

(b) Do you agree with her statement?

4. What does the autumn setting contribute to the story?

5. The title of "Poison" is sometimes considered allegorical. How appropriate would it be for the story now titled "A Queer Heart"?

WRITING

1. Describe Mrs. Cadman and Lucille a year later.

2. Discuss the psychological undercurrents in the story.

A LITTLE COMPANION

by Angus Wilson

THEY say in the village that Miss Arkwright has never been the same since the war broke out, but she knows that it all began a long time before that—on 24th July, 1936, to be exact, the day of her forty-seventh birthday.

She was in no way a remarkable person. Her appearance was not particularly distinguished and yet she was without any feature that could actively displease. She had enough personal eccentricities to fit into the pattern of English village life, but none so absurd or anti-social that they could embarrass or even arouse gossip beyond what was pleasant to her neighbours. She accepted her position as an old maid with that cheerful good humour and occasional irony which are essential to English spinsters since the deification of Jane Austen,[1] or more sacredly Miss Austen, by the upper middle classes, and she attempted to counteract the inadequacy of the unmarried state by quiet, sensible, and tolerant social work in the local community. She was liked by nearly everyone, though she was not afraid of making enemies where she knew that her broad but deeply felt religious principles were being opposed. Any socially pretentious or undesirably extravagant conduct, too, was liable to call forth from her an unexpectedly caustic and well-aimed snub. She was invited everywhere and always accepted the invitations. You could see her at every tea or cocktail party, occasionally drinking a third gin, but never more. Quietly but well dressed, with one or two very fine old pieces of jewellery that had come down to her from her grandmother, she would pass from one group to another, laughing or serious as the occasion demanded. She smoked continuously her own, rather expensive, brand of cigarettes—"My one vice," she used to say, "the only thing that stands between me and secret drinking." She listened with patience, but with a slight twinkle in the eye, to Mr. Hodgson's endless stories of life in Dar-es-Salaam or Myra Hope's breathless accounts of her latest system of diet. John Hobday in his somewhat ostentatiously gentleman-farmer attire would describe his next novel about East Anglian life to her before even his beloved daughter had heard of it. Richard Trelawney, just down from Oxford, found that she had read and really knew Donne's sermons, yet she could swap detective stories with Colonel Wright by the hour, and was his main source for quotations when the *Times* crossword was in question.

She it was who incorporated little Mrs. Grantham into village life, when that rather underbred, suburban woman came there as Colonel Grantham's second wife, checking her vulgar remarks about "the lower classes" with kindly humour but defending her against the formidable battery of Lady Vernon's antagonism. Yet she it was also who was first at Lady Vernon's when Sir Robert had his stroke, and her unobtrusive kindliness and real services gained her a singular position behind the grim reserve of the Vernon family. She could always banter the vicar away from his hobby horse of the Greek Rite when at parish meetings the agenda seemed to have been buried forever beneath a welter of Euchologia and Menaia. She checked Sir Robert's anti-Bolshevik phobia from victimizing the county librarian for her Fabianism,[2] but was fierce in her attack on the local council when she thought that class prejudice had prevented Commander Osborne's widow from getting a council house. She led in fact an active and useful existence, yet when anyone praised her she would only laugh. "My dear," she would say, "hard work's the only excuse old maids like me have got for existing at all, and even then I don't know that they oughtn't to lethalize the lot of us." As the danger of war grew nearer in the thirties her favourite remark was, "Well, if they've got any sense this time

From *Death Dance: Twenty-Five Stories* by Angus Wilson. British title: *Such Darling Dodos and Other Stories* by Angus Wilson.

1. *Jane Austen*, famous British novelist (1775–1817) who never married.

2. *Fabianism*, a mild form of socialism.

they'll keep the young fellows at home and put us useless old maids in the trenches," and she said it with real conviction.

With her good carriage, ample figure, and large deep-blue eyes, she even began to acquire a certain beauty as middle age approached. People speculated as to why she had never married. She had in fact refused a number of quite personable suitors. The truth was that from girlhood she had always felt a certain repulsion from physical contact. Not that she was in any way prudish; she was remarkable for a rather eighteenth-century turn of coarse phrase. Indeed, verbal freedom was the easier for her in that sexual activity was the more remote. Nor would psychoanalysts have found anything of particular interest in her; she had no abnormal desires. As a child she had never felt any wish to change her sex or observed any peculiarly violent or crude incident that could have resulted in what is called a psychic trauma. She just wasn't interested, and was perhaps as a result a little overgiven to talking of "all this fuss and nonsense that's made over sex." She would, however, have liked to have had a child. She recognized this as a common phenomenon among childless women and accepted it, though she could never bring herself to admit it openly or laugh about it in the common-sensical way in which she treated her position as an old maid. As the middle years approached she found a sudden interest and even sometimes a sudden jealousy over other people's babies and children growing upon her, attacking her unexpectedly and with apparent irrelevancy to time or place. She was equally wide-awake to the dangers of the late forties and resolutely resisted such foolish fancies, though she became as a result a little snappish and overgruff with the very young. "Now, my dear," she told herself, "you *must* deal with this nonsense or you'll start getting odd." How very odd she could not guess.

The Granthams always gave a little party for her on her birthdays. "Awful nonsense at my age," she had been saying now for many years, "but I never say no to a drink." Her forty-seventh birthday party was a particular success. Mary Hatton was staying with the Granthams and, like Miss Arkwright, she was an ardent Janeite,[3] so they'd been able to talk Mr. Collins and Mrs. Elton and the Elliots to their hearts' content; then Colonel Grantham had given her some tips about growing meconopsis, and finally Mrs. Osborne had been over to see the new rector at Longhurst, so they had a good-natured but thoroughly enjoyable "cat" about the state of the rectory there. She was just paying dutiful attention to her hostess's long complaint about the grocery deliveries, preparatory to saying good-bye, when suddenly a thin, whining, but remarkably clear child's voice said loudly in her ear, "Race you home, Mummy." She looked around her in surprise, then decided that her mind must have wandered from the boring details of Mrs. Grantham's sage, but almost immediately the voice sounded again. "Come on, Mummy, you are a slowcoach. I said, 'Race you home.'" This time Miss Arkwright was seriously disturbed. She wondered if Colonel Grantham's famous high spirits had got the better of him, but it could hardly have been so, she thought, as she saw his face earnest in conversation—"The point is, Vicar, not so much whether we want to intervene as whether we've got to." She began to feel most uncomfortable, and as soon as politeness allowed she made her way home.

The village street seemed particularly hot and dusty, the sunlight on the whitewashed cottages peculiarly glaring as she walked along. "One too many on a hot day, that's your trouble, my dear," she said to herself and felt comforted by so material an explanation. The familiar trimness of her own little house and the cool shade of the walnut tree on the front lawn further calmed her nerves. She stopped for a moment to pick up a basket of lettuce that old Pyecroft had left at the door and then walked in. After the sunlight outside, the hall seemed so dark that she could hardly discern even the shape of the grandfather clock. Out of this shadowy blackness came the child's voice loudly and clearly but, if anything, more nasal than before. "Beat you to it this time," it said. Miss Arkwright's heart stopped for a moment and her lungs seemed to contract, and then almost instantaneously she had seen it—a little white-faced boy, thin, with matchstick arms and legs growing out of shrunken clothes, with red-rimmed eyes and an adenoidal open-mouthed expression. Instantaneously, because the next moment he was not there, almost like a flickering image against the eye's retina. Miss Arkwright straightened her back, took a deep breath; then she went upstairs, took off her shoes, and lay down on her bed.

It was many weeks before anything fresh occurred,

3. *Janeite*, a devotee of Jane Austen and her novels.

and she felt happily able to put the whole incident down to cocktails and the heat; indeed, she began to remember that she had woken next morning with a severe headache—"You're much too old to start suffering from hangovers," she told herself. But the next experience was really more alarming. She had been up to London to buy a wedding present at Harrods and, arriving somewhat late for the returning train, found herself sitting in a stuffy and overpacked carriage. She felt therefore particularly pleased to see the familiar slate quarries that heralded the approach of Brankston Station, when suddenly a sharp dig drove the bones of her stays into her ribs. She looked with annoyance at the woman next to her—a blowsy creature with feathers in her hat—when she saw to her surprise that the woman was quietly asleep, her arms folded in front of her. Then in her ears there sounded, "Chuff, chuff, chuff, chuff," followed by a little snort and a giggle, and then quite unmistakably the whining voice saying, "Rotten old train."

After that it seemed to her as though for a few moments pandemonium had broken loose in the carriage—shouts and cries and a monotonous thumping against the woodwork as though someone were beating an impatient rhythm with his foot—yet no other occupant seemed in the slightest degree disturbed. They were for Miss Arkwright moments of choking and agonizing fear. She dreaded that at any minute the noise would grow so loud that the others would notice, for she felt an inescapable responsibility for the incident. Yet had the whole carriage risen and flung her from the window as a witch it would in some degree have been a release from the terrible sense of personal obsession; it would have given objective reality to what now seemed an uncontrollable expansion of her own consciousness into space; it would at the least have shown that others were mad beside herself. But no slightest ripple broke the drowsy torpor of the hot carriage in the August sun. She was deeply relieved when the train at last drew into Brankston and the impatience of her invisible attendant was assuaged, but no sooner had she set foot on the platform than she heard once more the almost puling whine, the too familiar, "Race you home, Mummy." She knew then that whatever it was, it had come to stay, that her home-comings would no longer be to the familiar comfort of her house and servants, but that there would always be a childish voice, a childish face to greet her for one moment as she crossed the threshold.

And so it proved. Gradually at first, at more than weekly intervals, and then increasingly, so that even a short spell in the vegetable garden or with the rock plants would mean impatient whining, wanton scattering of precious flowers, overturning of baskets —and then that momentary vision, lengthened now sometimes to five minutes' duration, that sickly, cretinous face. The very squalor of the child's appearance was revolting to Miss Arkwright, for whom cheerful good health was the first of human qualities. Sometimes the sickliness of the features would be of the thick, flaccid, pasty appearance that suggested rich feeding and late hours, and then the creature would be dressed in a velvet suit and Fauntleroy collar that might have clothed an over-indulged French bourgeois child; at other times the appearance was more cretinous, adenoidal and emaciated, and then it would wear the shrunken uniform and thick black boots of an institution idiot. In either case it was a child quite out of keeping with the home it sought to possess—a home of quiet beauty, unostentatious comfort, and restrained good taste. Of course, Miss Arkwright argued, it was an emanation from the sick side of herself so that it was bound to be diseased, but this realization did not compensate for dribble marks on her best dresses or for sticky finger marks on her tweed skirts.

At first she tried to ignore the obsession with her deep reserve of stoic patience, but as it continued, she felt the need of the Church. She became a daily communicant and delighted the more "spikey" of her neighbours. She prayed ceaselessly for release or resignation. A lurking sense of sin was roused in her, and she wondered if small frivolities and pleasures were the cause of her visitation; she remembered that after all it had first begun when she was drinking gin. Her religion had always been of the "brisk" and "sensible" variety, but now she began to fear that she had been over-suspicious of "enthusiasm" or "pietism." She gave up all but the most frugal meals, distributed a lot of her clothes to the poor, slept on a board, and rose at one in the morning to say a special Anglican office from a little book she had once been given by a rather despised High Church cousin. The only result seemed to be to cause scandal to her comfortable, old-fashioned parlourmaid and cook. She mentioned her state of sin in general terms to the vicar, and he lent her Neale's translations of the Coptic and Nestorian rites, but they proved of little comfort. At Christmas she rather shamefacedly and secretively placed a little bed with a richly filled stocking in the corner of her bedroom, but the child was not to be blackmailed. Throughout the day she could hear faint but unsavory sounds of uncontrolled and slovenly guzzling, like the distant sound of pigs feeding, and when evening came she was pursued by ever louder retching and the disturbing smell of vomit.

On Boxing Day she visited her old and sensible friend the bishop and told him the whole story. He looked at her very steadily with the large, dramatic brown eyes that were so telling in the pulpit, and for a long time he remained silent. Miss Arkwright hoped that he would advise her quickly, for she could feel a growing tugging at her skirt. It was obvious that this quiet, spacious library was no place for a child, and she could not have borne to see these wonderful old books disturbed even if she was the sole observer of the sacrilege.

At last the bishop spoke. "You say that the child appears ill and depraved. Has this evil appearance been more marked in the last weeks?" Miss Arkwright was forced to admit that it had. "My dear old friend," said the bishop, and he put his hand on hers. "It is your sick self that you are seeing, and all this foolish abstinence, this extravagant martyrdom are making you more sick." The bishop was a great Broad Churchman of the old school. "Go out into the world and take in its beauty and its colour. Enjoy what is yours and thank God for it." And without more ado, he persuaded Miss Arkwright to go to London for a few weeks.

Established at Berners', she set out to have a good time. She was always fond of expensive meals, but her first attempt to indulge at Claridge's proved an appalling failure, for with every course the voice grew louder and louder in her ears. "Coo! what rotten stuff," it kept on repeating, "I want an ice." Henceforth her meals were taken almost exclusively on Selfridge's roof or in ice-cream parlours, an unsatisfying and indigestible diet. Visits to the theatre were at first a greater success. She saw the new adaptation of *The Mill on the Floss,* and a version of *Lear* modelled on the original Kean production. The child had clearly never seen a play before and was held entranced by the mere spectacle. But soon it began to grow restless. A performance of *Hedda Gabler* was entirely ruined by rustlings, kicks, whispers, giggles, and a severe bout of hiccoughs. For a time it was kept quiet by musical comedies and farces, but in the end Miss Arkwright found herself attending only *Where the Rainbow Ends, Mother Goose,* and *Buckie's Bears*—it was not a sophisticated child. As the run of Christmas plays drew near their end she became desperate, and one afternoon she left a particularly dusty performance at the Circus and visited her old friend Madge Cleaver—once again to tell all. "Poor Bessie," said Madge Cleaver, and she smiled so spiritually, "how real Error can seem," for Madge was a Christian Scientist. "But it's so *un*real, dear, if we can only have the courage to see the Truth. Truth denies Animal Magnetism, Spiritualism, and all other false manifestations." She lent Miss Arkwright *Science and Health* and promised that she would give her "absent treatment."

At first Miss Arkwright felt most comforted. Mrs. Eddy's denial of the reality of most common phenomena and in particular of those that are evil seemed to offer a way out. Unfortunately, the child seemed quite unconvinced of its own non-existence. One afternoon Miss Arkwright thought with horror that by adopting a theology that denied the existence of Matter and gave reality only to Spirit she might well be gradually removing herself from the scene, while leaving the child in possession. After all, her own considerable bulk was testimony enough to her material nature, while the child might well in some repulsive way be accounted spirit. Terrified by the prospect before her, she speedily renounced Christian Science.

She returned to her home and by reaction decided to treat the whole phenomenon on the most material basis possible. She submitted her body to every old-fashioned purgative; she even indulged in a little amateur blood-letting, for might not the creature be some ill humour or sickly emanation of the body itself? But this antiquarian leechcraft only produced serious physical weakness and collapse. She was forced to call in Dr. Kent, who at once terminated the purgatives and put her on to port wine and beefsteak.

Failure of material remedies forced Miss Arkwright at last to a conviction which she had feared from the start. The thing, she decided, must be a genuine psychic phenomenon. It cost her much to admit this, for she had always been very contemptuous of spiritualism and regarded it as socially undesirable where it was not consciously fraudulent. But she was by now very desperate and willing to waive the deepest prejudices to free herself from the vulgar and querulous apparition. For a month or more she attended seances in London, but though she received "happy" communications from enough small Indian or Red Indian children to have started a nursery school, no medium or clairvoyant could tell her anything that threw light on her little companion. At one of the seances, however, she met a thin, red-haired, pre-Raphaelite sort of lady in a long grey garment and sandals, who asked her to attend the Circle of the Seventh Pentacle in the Earllands Road. The people she found there did not attract Miss Arkwright; she decided that the servants of the Devil were either common frauds or of exceedingly doubtful morals, but the little group was enthusiastic when she told her story. How could she hope to fight such Black Powers, they asked, unless she was prepared to invoke the White Art? Although she resisted their arguments at first, she finally found herself agreeing to a celebration of the Satanic Mass in her own home. She sent cook and Annie away for a week and prepared to receive the Circle. Their arrival in the village caused a great stir, partly because of their retinue of goats and rabbits. It had been decided that Miss Arkwright should celebrate the Mass herself. An altar had been set up in the drawing room; she had bought an immense white maternity gown from Debenham's and had been busy all the week learning her words, but at the last minute something within her rebelled. She could not bring herself to say the Lord's Prayer backwards and the Mass had to be called off. In the morning the devotees of the Pentacle left with many recriminations. The only result seemed to be that valuable ornaments were missing from the bedrooms occupied by the less reputable, while about those rooms in which the Devil's true servants had slept there hung an odour of goat that no fumigation could remove.

Miss Arkwright had long since given up visiting her neighbours, though they had not ceased to speculate about her. A chance remark that she had "two now to provide for" had led them to think that she believed herself pregnant. After this last visitation Lady Vernon decided that the time had come to act. She visited Miss Arkwright early one morning and, seeing the maternity gown which was still lying in the sitting-room, she was confirmed in her suspicions. "Bessie dear," she said, "you've got to realize that you're seriously ill, mentally ill," and she packed Miss Arkwright off to a brain specialist in Welbeck Street. This doctor, finding nothing physically wrong, sent her to a psychoanalyst. Poor Miss Arkwright! She was so convinced of her own insanity that she could think of no argument if they should wish to shut her up. But the analyst, a smart, grey-haired Jew, laughed when she murmured "madness." "We don't talk in those terms any more, Miss Arkwright. You're a century out of date. It's true there are certain disturbing psychotic features in what you tell me, but nothing, I think, that won't yield to deep analysis," and deep analysis she underwent for eight months or more, busily writing down dreams at night and lying on a couch "freely associating" by day.

At the end of that time the analyst began to form a few conclusions. "The child itself," he said, "is unimportant; the fact that you still see it even less so. What is important is that you now surround yourself with vulgarity and whining. You have clearly a need for these things which you have inhibited too long in an atmosphere of refinement." It was decided that Miss Arkwright should sublimate this need by learning the saxophone. Solemnly each day the poor lady sat in the drawing-room—that room which had resounded with Bach and Mozart—and practised the alto sax. At last one day when she had got so far as to be able to play the opening bars of "Alligator Stomp," her sense of the ridiculous rebelled and she would play no more, though her little companion showed great restlessness at the disappearance of noises which accorded all too closely with its vulgar taste.

I shall treat myself, she decided, and after long thought she came to the conclusion that the most salient feature of the business lay in the child's constant reiteration of the challenge "Race you home, Mummy"; with this it had started and with this it had continued. If, thought Miss Arkwright, I were to leave home completely, not only this house but also England, then perhaps it would withdraw its challenge and depart.

In January 1938, then, she set out on her travels. All across Europe, in museums and cafés and opera houses, it continued to throw down the gauntlet—"Race you home, Mummy"—and there it would be in her hotel bedroom. It seemed, however, anxious to take on local colour and would appear in a diversity of national costumes, often reviving for the purpose peasant dresses seen only at folk-dance festivals or when worn by beggars in order to attract tourists. For Miss Arkwright this rather vulgar and commercial World's Fair aspect of her life was particularly distressing. The child also attempted to alter its own colour, pale brown it achieved in India, in China a faint tinge of lemon, and in America, by some misunderstanding of the term Red Indian, it emerged bright scarlet. She was especially horrified by the purple swelling with which it attempted to emulate the black of the African natives. But whatever its colour, it was always there.

At last the menace of war in September found Miss Arkwright in Morocco, and along with thousands of other British travellers she hurried home, carrying, she felt, her greatest menace with her. It was only really after Munich that she became reconciled to its continued presence, learning gradually to incorporate its noises, its appearance, its whole personality into her daily life. She went out again among her neighbours and soon everyone had forgotten that she had ever been ill. It was true that she was forced to address her companion occasionally with a word of conciliation, or to administer a slap in its direction when it was particularly provoking, but she managed to disguise these peculiarities beneath her normal gestures.

One Saturday evening in September 1939 she was returning home from the rectory, worried by the threat of approaching war and wondering how she could best use her dual personality to serve her country, when she was suddenly disturbed to hear a clattering of hoofs and a thunderous bellow behind her. She turned to see, at some yards distance, a furious bull charging down the village street. She began immediately to run for her home, the little voice whining in her ear, "Race you home, Mummy." But the bull seemed to gain upon her, and in her terror she redoubled her speed, running as she had not run since she was a girl. She heard, it is true, a faint sighing in her ears as of dying breath, but she was too frightened to stop until she was safe at her own door. In she walked and, to her amazement, indeed to her horror, look where she would, the little child was *not* there. She had taken up his challenge to a race and she had won.

She lay in bed that night depressed and lonely. She realized only too clearly that difficult as it was to get rid of him—now that the child was gone she found herself thinking of "him" rather than "it"—it would be well-nigh impossible to get him back. The sirens that declared war next morning seemed only a confirmation of her personal loss. She went into mourning and rarely emerged from the house. For a short while, it is true, her spirits were revived when the evacuee children came from the East End; some of the more cretinous and adenoidal seemed curiously like her lost one. But country air and food soon gave them rosy cheeks and sturdy legs and she rapidly lost her interest. Before the year was out she was almost entirely dissociated from the external world, and those few friends who found time amid the cares of war to visit her in her bedroom decided that there was little that could be done for one who showed so little response. The vicar, who was busy translating St. Gregory Nazianzen's prayers for victory, spoke what was felt to be the easiest and kindest verdict when he described her as "just another war casualty." □

DISCUSSION

1. (a) How do you account for Miss Arkwright's "little companion"—is he a psychic phenomenon, a figment of her imagination, or what?

(b) Does the author seem to account for it definitely in any way? Explain.

2. Are there any episodes in Miss Arkwright's background or any quirks in her character that might account for the appearance of the child? Explain.

3. Miss Arkwright tells her story at least four times. How does each of the following account for the appearance of the "little companion," what advice does each give, and how sound is that advice?

(a) The Bishop

(b) Madge Cleaver, the Christian Scientist

(c) The Circle of the Seventh Pentacle

(d) The psychoanalyst

4. At a deeper level, is there any way in which the phenomenon of the child might be related to the advent of war? Explain.

5. *Is* this a ghost story?

6. "Too much love can be as bad as not enough." Discuss the applicability of this statement to "A Queer Heart" and "A Little Companion."

WRITING

1. Write Miss Arkwright's own explanation of what happened to her.

2. A poltergeist is a mischievous spirit that tosses objects around a room, creates thumps and bumps, etc. Although Miss Arkwright's little companion has more definite attributes than a poltergeist, its activities suggest those of a poltergeist. Invent your own poltergeist and write about some of its activities around your school. Start by selecting an appropriate name for it.

A VISIT TO GRANDPA'S

by Dylan Thomas

IN the middle of the night I woke from a dream full of whips and lariats as long as serpents, and runaway coaches on mountain passes, and wide, windy gallops over cactus fields, and I heard the old man in the next room crying, "Gee-up!" and "Whoa!" and trotting his tongue on the roof of his mouth.

It was the first time I had stayed in grandpa's house. The floorboards had squeaked like mice as I climbed into bed, and the mice between the walls had creaked like wood as though another visitor was walking on them. It was a mild summer night, but curtains had flapped and branches beaten against the window. I had pulled the sheets over my head, and soon was roaring and riding in a book.

"Whoa there, my beauties!" cried grandpa. His voice sounded very young and loud, and his tongue had powerful hooves, and he made his bedroom into a great meadow. I thought I would see if he was ill, or had set his bed-clothes on fire, for my mother had said that he lit his pipe under the blankets, and had warned me to run to his help if I smelt smoke in the night. I went on tiptoe through the darkness to his bedroom door, brushing against the furniture and upsetting a candlestick with a thump. When I saw there was a light in the room I felt frightened, and as I opened the door I heard grandpa shout, "Gee-up!" as loudly as a bull with a megaphone.

He was sitting straight up in bed and rocking from side to side as though the bed were on a rough road; the knotted edges of the counterpane were his reins; his invisible horses stood in a shadow beyond the bedside candle. Over a white flannel nightshirt he was wearing a red waistcoat with walnut-sized brass buttons. The over-filled bowl of his pipe smouldered among his whiskers like a little, burning hayrick on a stick. At the sight of me, his hands dropped from the reins and lay blue and quiet, the bed stopped still on a level road, he muffled his tongue into silence, and the horses drew softly up.

"Is there anything the matter, grandpa?" I asked, though the clothes were not on fire. His face in the candlelight looked like a ragged quilt pinned upright on the black air and patched all over with goat-beards.

He stared at me mildly. Then he blew down his pipe, scattering the sparks and making a high, wet dog-whistle of the stem, and shouted: "Ask no questions."

After a pause, he said slyly: "Do you ever have nightmares, boy?"

I said: "No."

"Oh, yes, you do," he said.

I said I was woken by a voice that was shouting to horses.

"What did I tell you?" he said. "You eat too much. Who ever heard of horses in a bedroom?"

He fumbled under his pillow, brought out a small, tinkling bag, and carefully untied its strings. He put a sovereign in my hand, and said "Buy a cake." I thanked him and wished him good night.

As I closed my bedroom door, I heard his voice crying loudly and gaily, "Gee-up! gee-up!" and the rocking of the travelling bed.

In the morning I woke from a dream of fiery horses on a plain that was littered with furniture, and of large, cloudy men who rode six horses at a time and whipped them with burning bed-clothes. Grandpa was at breakfast, dressed in deep black. After breakfast he said, "There was a terrible loud wind last night," and sat in his arm-chair by the hearth to make clay balls for the fire. Later in the morning he took me for a walk, through Johnstown village and into the fields on the Llanstephan road.

A man with a whippet said, "There's a nice morning, Mr. Thomas," and when he had gone, leanly as his dog, into the short-treed green wood he should not have entered because of the notices, grandpa said: "There, do you hear what he called you? Mister!"

We passed by small cottages, and all the men who leant on the gates congratulated grandpa on the fine morning. We passed through the wood full of pigeons, and their wings broke the branches as they rushed to the tops of the trees. Among the soft, contented voices and the loud, timid flying, grandpa said, like a man calling across a field: "If you heard those old birds in the night, you'd wake me up and say there were horses in the trees."

We walked back slowly, for he was tired, and the lean man stalked out of the forbidden wood with a rabbit held as gently over his arm as a girl's arm in a warm sleeve.

On the last day but one of my visit I was taken to Llanstephan in a governess cart pulled by a short, weak pony. Grandpa might have been driving a bison, so tightly he held the reins, so ferociously cracked the long whip, so blasphemously shouted warning to boys who played in the road, so stoutly stood with his gaitered legs apart and cursed the demon strength and wilfulness of his tottering pony.

"Look out, boy!" he cried when we came to each corner, and pulled and tugged and jerked and sweated and waved his whip like a rubber sword. And when the pony had crept miserably round each corner, grandpa turned to me with a sighing smile: "We weathered that one, boy."

When we came to Llanstephan village at the top of the hill, he left the cart by the "Edwinsford Arms" and patted the pony's muzzle and gave it sugar, saying: "You're a weak little pony, Jim, to pull big men like us."

He had strong beer and I had lemonade, and he paid Mrs. Edwinsford with a sovereign out of the tinkling bag; she inquired after his health, and he said that Llangadock was better for the tubes. We went to look at the churchyard and the sea and sat in the wood called the Sticks, and stood on the concert platform in the middle of the wood where visitors sang on midsummer nights and, year by year, the innocent of the village was elected mayor. Grandpa paused at the churchyard and pointed over the iron gate at the angelic headstones and the poor wooden crosses. "There's no sense in lying there," he said.

We journeyed back furiously: Jim was a bison again.

I woke late on my last morning, out of dreams where the Llanstephan sea carried bright sailing-boats as long as liners; and heavenly choirs in the Sticks, dressed in bards' robes and brass-buttoned waistcoats, sang in a strange Welsh to the departing sailors. Grandpa was not at breakfast; he rose early. I walked in the fields with a new sling, and shot at the Towy gulls and the rooks in the parsonage trees. A warm wind blew from the summer points of the weather; a morning mist climbed from the ground and floated among the trees and hid the noisy birds; in the mist and the wind my pebbles flew lightly up like hailstones in a world on its head. The morning passed without a bird falling.

I broke my sling and returned for the midday meal through the parson's orchard. Once, grandpa told me, the parson had bought three ducks at Carmarthen Fair and made a pond for them in the centre of the garden; but they waddled to the gutter under the crumbling doorsteps of the house, and swam and quacked there. When I reached the end of the orchard path, I looked through a hole in the hedge and saw that the parson had made a tunnel through the rockery that was between the gutter and the pond and had set up a notice in plain writing: "This way to the pond."

The ducks were still swimming under the steps.

Grandpa was not in the cottage. I went into the garden, but grandpa was not staring at the fruit-trees. I called across to a man who leant on a spade in the field beyond the garden hedge: "Have you seen my grandpa this morning?"

He did not stop digging, and answered over his shoulder: "I seen him in his fancy waistcoat."

Griff, the barber, lived in the next cottage. I called to him through the open door: "Mr. Griff, have you seen my grandpa?"

The barber came out in his shirtsleeves.

He said: "He's wearing his best waistcoat." I did not know if it was important, but grandpa wore his waistcoat only in the night.

"Has grandpa been to Llanstephan?" asked Mr. Griff anxiously.

"We went there yesterday in a little trap," I said.

He hurried indoors and I heard him talking in Welsh, and he came out again with his white coat on, and he carried a striped and coloured walking-stick. He strode down the village street and I ran by his side.

When we stopped at the tailor's shop, he cried out, "Dan!" and Dan Tailor stepped from his window where he sat like an Indian priest but wearing a derby hat. "Dai Thomas has got his waistcoat on," said Mr. Griff, "and he's been to Llanstephan."

As Dan Tailor searched for his overcoat, Mr. Griff was striding on. "Will Evans," he called outside the carpenter's shop, "Dai Thomas has been to Llanstephan, and he's got his waistcoat on."

"I'll tell Morgan now," said the carpenter's wife out of the hammering, sawing darkness of the shop.

We called at the butcher's shop and Mr. Price's house, and Mr. Griff repeated his message like a town crier.

We gathered together in Johnstown square. Dan Tailor had his bicycle, Mr. Price his pony-trap. Mr. Griff, the butcher, Morgan Carpenter, and I climbed into the shaking trap, and we trotted off towards Carmarthen town. The tailor led the way, ringing his bell as though there were a fire or a robbery, and an old woman by the gate of a cottage at the end of the street ran inside like a pelted hen. Another woman waved a bright handkerchief.

"Where are we going?" I asked.

Grandpa's neighbours were as solemn as old men with black hats and jackets on the outskirts of a fair. Mr. Griff shook his head and mourned: "I didn't expect this again from Dai Thomas."

"Not after last time," said Mr. Price sadly.

We trotted on, we crept up Constitution Hill, we rattled down into Lammas Street, and the tailor still rang his bell and a dog ran, squealing, in front of his wheels. As we clip-clopped over the cobbles that led down to the Towy bridge, I remembered grandpa's nightly noisy journeys that rocked the bed and shook the walls, and I saw his gay waistcoat in a vision and his patchwork head tufted and smiling in the candlelight. The tailor before us turned round on his saddle, his bicycle wobbled and skidded. "I see Dai Thomas!" he cried.

The trap rattled on to the bridge, and I saw grandpa there; the buttons of his waistcoat shone in the sun, he wore his tight, black Sunday trousers and a tall, dusty hat I had seen in a cupboard in the attic, and he carried an ancient bag. He bowed to us. "Good morning, Mr. Price," he said, "and Mr. Griff and Mr. Morgan and Mr. Evans." To me, he said "Good morning, boy."

Mr. Griff pointed his coloured stick at him.

"And what do you think you are doing on Carmarthen bridge in the middle of the afternoon," he said sternly, "with your best waistcoat and your old hat?"

Grandpa did not answer, but inclined his face to the river wind, so that his beard was set dancing and wagging as though he talked, and watched the coracle men move, like turtles, on the shore.

Mr. Griff raised his stunted barber's pole. "And where do you think you are going," he said, "with your old black bag?"

Grandpa said: "I am going to Llangadock to be buried." And he watched the coracle shells slip into the water lightly, and the gulls complain over the fish-filled water as bitterly as Mr. Price complained:

"But you aren't dead yet, Dai Thomas."

For a moment grandpa reflected, then: "There's no sense in lying dead in Llanstephan," he said. "The ground is comfy in Llangadock; you can twitch your legs without putting them in the sea."

His neighbours moved close to him. They said: "You aren't dead, Mr. Thomas."

"How can you be buried, then?"

"Nobody's going to bury you in Llanstephan."

"Come on home, Mr. Thomas."

"There's strong beer for tea."

"And cake."

But grandpa stood firmly on the bridge, and clutched his bag to his side, and stared at the flowing river and the sky, like a prophet who has no doubt. □

DISCUSSION

1. This reminiscence evokes a world very different from the one familiar to most of us today.

(a) Comment on the author's treatment of old age and senility.

(b) Do you find anything tragic or pathetic in the story? Explain.

2. (a) What are the boy's feelings about his grandfather?

(b) What are the grandfather's feelings about the boy?

3. At one point the narrator speaks of the villagers of Llanstephan as electing the "innocent" (the town idiot) mayor every year. This is an old folk custom.

(a) In addition, what does it tell you about the people who lived in Llanstephan and the nearby area?

(b) How does it help explain the neighbors' behavior toward old Dai Thomas?

WRITING

1. Write a dialogue in which the narrator's mother or father explains to him why the grandfather behaved as he did.

2. Think back over your own childhood and write a recollection of your own. It might deal with your growing awareness of your mother or father, a grandparent, older or younger brothers and sisters, or whatever you choose. Try, however, to have it revolve around a family situation.

MY OEDIPUS COMPLEX

by Frank O'Connor

BROWN BROTHERS

FATHER was in the army all through the war—the first war, I mean—so, up to the age of five, I never saw much of him, and what I saw did not worry me. Sometimes I woke and there was a big figure in khaki peering down at me in the candlelight. Sometimes in the early morning I heard the slamming of the front door and the clatter of nailed boots down the cobbles of the lane. These were Father's entrances and exits. Like Santa Claus he came and went mysteriously.

In fact, I rather liked his visits, though it was an uncomfortable squeeze between Mother and him when I got into the big bed in the early morning. He smoked, which gave him a pleasant musty smell, and shaved, an operation of astounding interest. Each time he left a trail of souvenirs—model tanks and Gurkha knives with handles made of bullet cases, and German helmets and cap badges and button-sticks, and all sorts of military equipment—carefully stowed away in a long box on top of the wardrobe, in case they ever came in handy. There was a bit of the magpie about Father; he expected everything to come in handy. When his back was turned, Mother let me get a chair and rummage through his treasures. She didn't seem to think so highly of them as he did.

The war was the most peaceful period of my life. The window of my attic faced southeast. My mother had curtained it, but that had small effect. I always woke with the first light and, with all the responsibilities of the previous day melted, feeling myself rather like the sun, ready to illumine and rejoice. Life never seemed so simple and clear and full of possibilities as then. I put my feet out from under the clothes—I called them Mrs. Left and Mrs. Right—and invented dramatic situations for them in which they discussed the problems of the day. At least Mrs. Right did; she was very demonstrative, but I hadn't the same control of Mrs. Left, so she mostly contented herself with nodding agreement.

They discussed what Mother and I should do during the day, what Santa Claus should give a fellow for Christmas, and what steps should be taken to brighten the home. There was that little matter of the baby, for instance. Mother and I could never agree about that. Ours was the only house in the terrace without a new baby, and Mother said we couldn't afford one till Father came back from the war because they cost seventeen and six. That showed how simple she was. The Geneys up the road had a baby, and everyone knew they couldn't afford seventeen and six. It was probably a cheap baby, and Mother wanted something really good, but I felt she was too exclusive. The Geneys' baby would have done us fine.

Having settled my plans for the day, I got up, put a chair under the attic window, and lifted the frame high enough to stick out my head. The window overlooked the front gardens of the terrace behind ours, and beyond these it looked over a deep valley to the tall, red-brick houses terraced up the opposite hillside, which were all still in shadow, while those at our side of the valley were all lit up, though with long strange shadows that made them seem unfamiliar; rigid and painted.

After that I went into Mother's room and climbed into the big bed. She woke and I began to tell her of my schemes. By this time, though I never seem to have noticed it, I was petrified in my nightshirt, and I thawed as I talked until, the last frost melted, I fell asleep beside her and woke again only when I heard her below in the kitchen, making the breakfast.

After breakfast we went into town; heard Mass at

St. Augustine's and said a prayer for Father, and did the shopping. If the afternoon was fine we either went for a walk in the country or a visit to Mother's great friend in the convent, Mother St. Dominic. Mother had them all praying for Father, and every night, going to bed, I asked God to send him back safe from the war to us. Little, indeed, did I know what I was praying for!

One morning, I got into the big bed, and there, sure enough, was Father in his usual Santa Claus manner, but later, instead of uniform, he put on his best blue suit, and Mother was as pleased as anything. I saw nothing to be pleased about, because, out of uniform, Father was altogether less interesting, but she only beamed, and explained that our prayers had been answered, and off we went to Mass to thank God for having brought Father safely home.

The irony of it! That very day when he came in to dinner he took off his boots and put on his slippers, donned the dirty old cap he wore about the house to save him from colds, crossed his legs, and began to talk gravely to Mother, who looked anxious. Naturally, I disliked her looking anxious, because it destroyed her good looks, so I interrupted him.

"Just a moment, Larry!" she said gently.

This was only what she said when we had boring visitors, so I attached no importance to it and went on talking.

"Do be quiet, Larry!" she said impatiently. "Don't you hear me talking to Daddy?"

This was the first time I had heard those ominous words, "talking to Daddy," and I couldn't help feeling that if this was how God answered prayers, he couldn't listen to them very attentively.

"Why are you talking to Daddy?" I asked with as great a show of indifference as I could muster.

"Because Daddy and I have business to discuss. Now, don't interrupt again!"

In the afternoon, at Mother's request, Father took me for a walk. This time we went into town instead of out to the country, and I thought at first, in my usual optimistic way, that it might be an improvement. It was nothing of the sort. Father and I had quite different notions of a walk in town. He had no proper interest in trams, ships, and horses, and the only thing that seemed to divert him was talking to fellows as old as himself. When I wanted to stop he simply went on, dragging me behind him by the hand; when he wanted to stop I had no alternative but to do the same. I noticed that it seemed to be a sign that he wanted to stop for a long time whenever he leaned against a wall. The second time I saw him do it I got wild. He seemed to be settling himself forever. I pulled him by the coat and trousers, but, unlike Mother who, if you were too persistent, got into a wax and said: "Larry, if you don't behave yourself, I'll give you a good slap," Father had an extraordinary capacity for amiable inattention. I sized him up and wondered would I cry, but he seemed to be too remote to be annoyed even by that. Really, it was like going for a walk with a mountain! He either ignored the wrenching and pummeling entirely, or else glanced down with a grin of amusement from his peak. I had never met anyone so absorbed in himself as he seemed.

At teatime, "talking to Daddy" began again, complicated this time by the fact that he had an evening paper, and every few minutes he put it down and told Mother something new out of it. I felt this was foul play. Man for man, I was prepared to compete with him any time for Mother's attention, but when he had it all made up for him by other people it left me no chance. Several times I tried to change the subject without success.

"You must be quiet while Daddy is reading, Larry," Mother said impatiently.

It was clear that she either genuinely liked talking to Father better than talking to me, or else that he had some terrible hold on her which made her afraid to admit the truth.

"Mummy," I said that night when she was tucking me up, "do you think if I prayed hard God would send Daddy back to the war?"

She seemed to think about that for a moment.

"No, dear," she said with a smile. "I don't think he would."

"Why wouldn't he, Mummy?"

"Because there isn't a war any longer, dear."

"But, Mummy, couldn't God make another war, if he liked?"

"He wouldn't like to, dear. It's not God who makes wars, but bad people."

"Oh!" I said.

I was disappointed about that. I began to think that God wasn't quite what he was cracked up to be.

Next morning I woke at my usual hour, feeling like a bottle of champagne. I put out my feet and invented a long conversation in which Mrs. Right talked of the trouble she had with her own father till she put him in the Home. I didn't quite know what the Home was but it sounded the right place for Father. Then I got my chair and stuck my head out of the attic window. Dawn was just breaking, with a guilty air that made me feel I had caught it in the act. My head bursting with stories and schemes, I stumbled in next door, and in the half-darkness scrambled into the big bed. There was no room at Mother's side so I had to get between her and Father. For the time being I had forgotten about him, and for several minutes I sat bolt upright, racking my brains to know what I could do with him. He was taking up more than his fair share of the bed, and I couldn't get comfortable, so I gave him several kicks that made him grunt and stretch. He made room all right, though. Mother waked and felt for me. I settled back comfortably in the warmth of the bed with my thumb in my mouth.

"Mummy!" I hummed, loudly and contentedly.

"Sssh! dear," she whispered. "Don't wake Daddy!"

This was a new development, which threatened to be even more serious than "talking to Daddy." Life without my early-morning conferences was unthinkable.

"Why?" I asked severely.

"Because poor Daddy is tired."

This seemed to me a quite inadequate reason, and I was sickened by the sentimentality of her "poor Daddy." I never liked that sort of gush; it always struck me as insincere.

"Oh!" I said lightly. Then in my most winning tone: "Do you know where I want to go with you today, Mummy?"

"No, dear," she sighed.

"I want to go down the Glen and fish for thornybacks with my new net, and then I want to go out to the Fox and Hounds, and—"

"Don't-wake-Daddy!" she hissed angrily, clapping her hand across my mouth.

But it was too late. He was awake, or nearly so. He grunted and reached for the matches. Then he stared incredulously at his watch.

"Like a cup of tea, dear?" asked Mother in a meek, hushed voice I had never heard her use before. It sounded almost as though she were afraid.

"Tea?" he exclaimed indignantly. "Do you know what the time is?"

"And after that I want to go up the Rathcooney Road," I said loudly, afraid I'd forget something in all those interruptions.

"Go to sleep at once, Larry!" she said sharply.

I began to snivel. I couldn't concentrate, the way that pair went on, and smothering my early-morning schemes was like burying a family from the cradle.

Father said nothing, but lit his pipe and sucked it, looking out into the shadows without minding Mother or me. I knew he was mad. Every time I made a remark Mother hushed me irritably. I was mortified. I felt it wasn't fair; there was even something sinister in it. Every time I had pointed out to her the waste of making two beds when we could both sleep in one, she had told me it was healthier like that, and now here was this man, this stranger, sleeping with her without the least regard for her health!

He got up early and made tea, but though he brought Mother a cup he brought none for me.

"Mummy," I shouted, "I want a cup of tea, too."

"Yes, dear," she said patiently. "You can drink from Mummy's saucer."

That settled it. Either Father or I would have to leave the house. I didn't want to drink from Mother's saucer; I wanted to be treated as an equal in my own home, so, just to spite her, I drank it all and left none for her. She took that quietly, too.

But that night when she was putting me to bed she said gently: "Larry, I want you to promise me something."

"What is it?" I asked.

"Not to come in and disturb poor Daddy in the morning. Promise?"

"Poor Daddy" again! I was becoming suspicious of everything involving that quite impossible man.

"Why?" I asked.

"Because poor Daddy is worried and tired and he doesn't sleep well."

"Why doesn't he, Mummy?"

"Well, you know, don't you, that while he was at the war Mummy got the pennies from the Post Office?"

"From Miss MacCarthy?"

"That's right. But now, you see, Miss MacCarthy hasn't any more pennies, so Daddy must go out and find us some. You know what would happen if he couldn't?"

"No," I said, "tell us."

"Well, I think we might have to go out and beg for them like the poor old woman on Fridays. We wouldn't like that, would we?"

"No," I agreed. "We wouldn't."

"So you'll promise not to come in and wake him?"

"Promise."

Mind you, I meant that. I knew pennies were a serious matter, and I was all against having to go out and beg like the old woman on Fridays. Mother laid out all my toys in a complete ring round the bed so that, whatever way I got out, I was bound to fall over one of them.

When I woke I remembered my promise all right. I got up and sat on the floor and played—for hours, it seemed to me. Then I got my chair and looked out the attic window for more hours. I wished it was time for Father to wake; I wished someone would make me a cup of tea. I didn't feel in the least like the sun; instead, I was bored and so very, very cold! I simply longed for the warmth and depth of the big featherbed.

At last I could stand it no longer. I went into the next room. As there was still no room at Mother's side I climbed over her and she woke with a start.

"Larry," she whispered, gripping my arm very tightly, "what did you promise?"

"But I did, Mummy," I wailed, caught in the very act. "I was quiet for ever so long."

"Oh, dear, and you're perished!" she said sadly, feeling me all over. "Now, if I let you stay will you promise not to talk?"

"But I want to talk, Mummy," I wailed.

"That has nothing to do with it," she said with a firmness that was new to me. "Daddy wants to sleep. Now, do you understand that?"

I understood it only too well. I wanted to talk, he wanted to sleep—whose house was it, anyway?

"Mummy," I said with equal firmness, "I think it would be healthier for Daddy to sleep in his own bed."

That seemed to stagger her, because she said nothing for a while.

"Now, once for all," she went on, "you're to be perfectly quiet or go back to your own bed. Which is it to be?"

The injustice of it got me down. I had convicted her out of her own mouth of inconsistency and unreasonableness, and she hadn't even attempted to reply. Full of spite, I gave Father a kick, which she didn't notice but which made him grunt and open his eyes in alarm.

"What time is it?" he asked in a panic-stricken voice, not looking at Mother but the door, as if he saw someone there.

"It's early yet," she replied soothingly. "It's only the child. Go to sleep again. . . . Now, Larry," she added, getting out of bed, "you've wakened Daddy and you must go back."

This time, for all her quiet air, I knew she meant it, and knew that my principal rights and privileges were as good as lost unless I asserted them at once. As she lifted me, I gave a screech, enough to wake the dead, not to mind Father. He groaned.

"That damn child! Doesn't he ever sleep?"

"It's only a habit, dear," she said quietly, though I could see she was vexed.

"Well, it's time he got out of it," shouted Father, beginning to heave in the bed. He suddenly gathered all the bedclothes about him, turned to the wall, and then looked back over his shoulder with nothing showing only two small, spiteful, dark eyes. The man looked very wicked.

To open the bedroom door, Mother had to let me down, and I broke free and dashed for the farthest corner, screeching. Father sat bolt upright in bed.

"Shut up, you little puppy!" he said in a choking voice.

I was so astonished that I stopped screeching. Never, never had anyone spoken to me in that tone before. I looked at him incredulously and saw his face convulsed with rage. It was only then that I fully realized how God had codded me, listening to my prayers for the safe return of this monster.

"Shut up, you!" I bawled, beside myself.

"What's that you said?" shouted Father, making a wild leap out of bed.

"Mick, Mick!" cried Mother. "Don't you see the child isn't used to you?"

"I see he's better fed than taught," snarled Father, waving his arms wildly. "He wants his bottom smacked."

All his previous shouting was as nothing to these obscene words referring to my person. They really made my blood boil.

"Smack your own!" I screamed hysterically. "Smack your own! Shut up! Shut up!"

At this he lost his patience and let fly at me. He did it with the lack of conviction you'd expect of a man under Mother's horrified eyes, and it ended up as a mere tap, but the sheer indignity of being struck at all by a stranger, a total stranger who had cajoled his way back from the war into our big bed as a result of my innocent intercession, made me completely dotty. I shrieked and shrieked, and danced in my bare feet, and Father, looking awkward and hairy in nothing but a short grey army shirt, glared down at me like a mountain out for murder. I think it must have been then that I realized he was jealous too. And there stood Mother in her nightdress, looking as if her heart was broken between us. I hoped she felt as she looked. It seemed to me that she deserved it all.

From that morning out my life was a hell. Father and I were enemies, open and avowed. We conducted a series of skirmishes against one another, he trying to steal my time with Mother and I his. When she was sitting on my bed, telling me a story, he took to looking for some pair of old boots which he alleged he had left behind him at the beginning of the war. While he talked to Mother I played loudly with my toys to show my total lack of concern. He created a terrible scene one evening when he came in from work and found me at his box, playing with his regimental badges, Gurkha knives and button-sticks. Mother got up and took the box from me.

"You mustn't play with Daddy's toys unless he lets you, Larry," she said severely. "Daddy doesn't play with yours."

For some reason Father looked at her as if she had struck him and then turned away with a scowl.

"Those are not toys," he growled, taking down the box again to see had I lifted anything. "Some of those curios are very rare and valuable."

But as time went on I saw more and more how he managed to alienate Mother and me. What made it worse was that I couldn't grasp his method or see what attraction he had for Mother. In every possible way he was less winning than I. He had a common accent and made noises at his tea. I thought for a while that it might be the newspapers she was interested in, so I made up bits of news of my own to read to her. Then I thought it might be the smoking, which I personally thought attractive, and took his pipes and went round the house dribbling into them till he caught me. I even made noises at my tea, but Mother only told me I was disgusting. It all seemed to hinge round that unhealthy habit of sleeping together, so I made a point of dropping into their bedroom and nosing round, talking to myself, so that they wouldn't know I was watching them, but they were never up to anything that I could see. In the end it beat me. It seemed to depend on being grown-up and giving people rings, and I realized I'd have to wait.

But at the same time I wanted him to see that I was only waiting, not giving up the fight. One evening when he was being particularly obnoxious, chattering away well above my head, I let him have it.

"Mummy," I said, "do you know what I'm going to do when I grow up?"

"No, dear," she replied. "What?"

"I'm going to marry you," I said quietly.

Father gave a great guffaw out of him, but he didn't take me in. I knew it must only be pretense. And Mother, in spite of everything, was pleased. I felt she was probably relieved to know that one day Father's hold on her would be broken.

"Won't that be nice?" she said with a smile.

"It'll be very nice," I said confidently. "Because we're going to have lots and lots of babies."

"That's right, dear," she said placidly. "I think we'll have one soon, and then you'll have plenty of company."

I was no end pleased about that because it showed that in spite of the way she gave in to Father she still considered my wishes. Besides, it would put the Geneys in their place.

It didn't turn out like that, though. To begin with, she was very preoccupied—I supposed about where she would get the seventeen and six—and though Father took to staying out late in the evenings it did me no particular good. She stopped taking me for walks, became as touchy as blazes, and smacked me for nothing at all. Sometimes I wished I'd never mentioned the confounded baby—I seemed to have a genius for bringing calamity on myself.

And calamity it was! Sonny arrived in the most appalling hullabaloo—even that much he couldn't do without a fuss—and from the first moment I disliked him. He was a difficult child—so far as I was concerned he was always difficult—and demanded far too much attention. Mother was simply silly about him, and couldn't see when he was only showing off. As company he was worse than useless. He slept all day, and I had to go round the house on tiptoe to avoid waking him. It wasn't any longer a question of not waking Father. The slogan now was "Don't-wake-Sonny!" I couldn't understand why the child wouldn't sleep at the proper time, so whenever Mother's back was turned I woke him. Sometimes to keep him awake I pinched him as well. Mother caught me at it one day and gave me a most unmerciful flaking.

One evening, when Father was coming in from

work, I was playing trains in the front garden. I let on not to notice him; instead, I pretended to be talking to myself, and said in a loud voice: "If another bloody baby comes into this house, I'm going out."

Father stopped dead and looked at me over his shoulder.

"What's that you said?" he asked sternly.

"I was only talking to myself," I replied, trying to conceal my panic. "It's private."

He turned and went in without a word. Mind you, I intended it as a solemn warning, but its effect was quite different. Father started being quite nice to me. I could understand that, of course. Mother was quite sickening about Sonny. Even at mealtimes she'd get up and gawk at him in the cradle with an idiotic smile, and tell Father to do the same. He was always polite about it, but he looked so puzzled you could see he didn't know what she was talking about. He complained of the way Sonny cried at night, but she only got cross and said that Sonny never cried except when there was something up with him—which was a flaming lie, because Sonny never had anything up with him, and only cried for attention. It was really painful to see how simple-minded she was. Father wasn't attractive, but he had a fine intelligence. He saw through Sonny, and now he knew that I saw through him as well.

One night I woke with a start. There was someone beside me in the bed. For one wild moment I felt sure it must be Mother, having come to her senses and left Father for good, but then I heard Sonny in convulsions in the next room, and Mother saying: "There! There! There!" and I knew it wasn't she. It was Father. He was lying beside me, wide awake, breathing hard and apparently as mad as hell.

After a while it came to me what he was mad about. It was his turn now. After turning me out of the big bed, he had been turned out himself. Mother had no consideration now for anyone but that poisonous pup, Sonny. I couldn't help feeling sorry for Father. I had been through it all myself, and even at that age I was magnanimous. I began to stroke him down and say: "There! There!" He wasn't exactly responsive.

"Aren't you asleep either?" he snarled.

"Ah, come on and put your arm around us, can't you?" I said, and he did, in a sort of way. Gingerly, I suppose, is how you'd describe it. He was very bony but better than nothing.

At Christmas he went out of his way to buy me a really nice model railway. □

DISCUSSION

1. (a) What is the basic source of the conflict between father and son?

(b) What happens when the family triangle is squared by the arrival of Sonny?

2. Comment on the use of a first-person narrator in this story. Why is this more effective than a third-person narrative would be?

3. Much of the humor in this story depends on the narrator's innocence and the irony that stems from his naivete. Give a few examples.

4. Nowadays stories that show a healthy family relationship seem to be as rare as humorous stories. This story combines both elements.

(a) Comment on its effectiveness.

(b) How appropriate is its title?

5. Both "A Visit to Grandpa's" and "My Oedipus Complex" are narrated by a young boy. Discuss similarities and differences in the two stories.

WRITING

1. Write an imaginary conversation between Larry (the narrator) and Sonny three or four years later.

2. Write an imaginary conversation between Larry's mother and father discussing the boy's behavior.

3. Frank O'Connor has written other short stories dealing with Larry and Sonny. Read some of them and prepare a report for the class bringing them up to date on the family situation and explaining how consistent the characterization is.

THE LIMIT

by Joyce Cary

IT is a shopping street with lights at intervals. As they change, traffic is turned on and off as by a tap. First there is vacancy from pavement to pavement, then a rush from both sides—solid blocks of traffic charging like tanks and, like tanks at the charge, getting quickly out of line.

At this time in the morning young men and women are at work and the pavements are crowded with parents and grandparents doing their household shopping—serious and anxious people in serious clothes. They meet only briefly, for a few short pregnant words on grave matters, children and prices. The children are all young, below school age—they weave in and out of the slow, dark streams of shoppers. They are meeting friends on their own eye level, chasing each other, carrying out various experiments in locomotion such as hopping on one leg, swinging around a lamp-post, pacing carefully on the joints between kerbstones, or walking backwards.

The dogs, at the lowest level, are also paying attention chiefly to each other: their noses point warily about, enquiring, seeking, recording; they sidle out of doorways as if from ambush; absorbed in a lamp-post they do not even notice feet, they dodge away at the very last moment; they catch sight of a strange nose that has suddenly projected itself from behind a string bag full of potatoes, and stand with rigid tail and every muscle taut in the question, friend or enemy; they dash wildly off down side streets on some private recollection of the most urgent importance.

The relation between the three levels is one of responsible authority mixed with affection: parents hastily snatch up a child's hand to steer it in the right direction; their gestures say plainly that this is no world to wander in. Children shout peremptory advice at dogs or drag them by the collar from dangerous acquaintances.

A small boy of about four in a red and white jersey stands at the kerb holding a black mongrel puppy by a piece of string tied to its collar. The puppy has a singularly large head and feet which seem too heavy for its insignificant body. As it tosses its head and tries to bite its string, two children, girl and boy, rather smaller than its owner, desert a perambulator to play with it. Greatly flattered, it twists its neck sideways and turns up its eyes in an affected manner, then throws its front legs about and cavorts like the lion in the royal arms. The children try to tickle it; it pretends to bite them and they squeal. The boy in the striped jersey looks down with watchful but benevolent condescension.

The puppy, growing more excited and still more anxious to please, attempts a more brilliant romp, falls over its own tail and breaks the string. It wriggles upright again and runs backwards into the road, fortunately empty.

The boy with the jersey dives to catch the loose end of the string. The puppy gambols further off, the lights change and the traffic comes on with a rush—a lorry and a car hoot together. The boy tries to shoo the puppy towards the opposite pavement, but it cavorts sideways. The child makes a sharp turn to head it off and this brings him back in front of the traffic from the nearest light. A sports model, renowned in all the advertisements for its acceleration, has come away with a rush. It strikes the boy somewhere in the back, whirls him around and picks him up on the mudguard.

He makes no sound at all; it is as though a small bundle of coloured clothes has suddenly appeared in the trough of the guard. Brakes and tyres scream, the car stops, shuddering against the kerb, and the bundle slides off and collapses into itself on the roadway exactly like empty garments—limp and soft. In a moment there is a crowd, a policeman holding the ring. A young doctor, or perhaps medical student, kneels down to examine the child—he is quite dead.

The neighbourhood is poor, the car expensive—the crowd is hostile. The women are especially angry. A powerful matron at the back, her bare arms red with work, a man's felt hat balanced on her thick grey hair as if to express her mastery in life, is shouting something about bloody murderers—don't let 'em get away with it.

The motorist is well aware of his danger. At each new shout he looks round nervously; his round, plump face is shining with sweat, his hands fidget with his cap and coat, both of the gayest check. First he takes off his cap as if feeling that this is only proper in the presence of death. Then, when the policeman questions him, he puts it on again as if to show that he has no reason to humble himself before the law.

The policeman, a tall, bottle-shouldered man, also very young, with a singularly blank face, the face of authority exaggerated by a sense of the occasion, writes carefully and slowly in his notebook. He might be filling in a census form.

At last he turns to the crowd and asks for witnesses—but it appears that no one present has seen the accident. And the question seems only to make the women more angry; they are tired of these slow preliminaries, they are shouting for immediate vengeance.

The young man is terrified, his shaking fingers button and unbutton his coat—the confused idea of making it less conspicuous is followed by a fear that he may seem to be preparing for flight. He looks round the circle of muttering and screaming women and tries to make them understand that he could not have avoided the accident, but not a word can be heard, and his fear, his apologetic grimaces, his fumbling hands also enrage the crowd. It makes a surge forward at some new pressure from behind, and actually touches him. He shrinks against the policeman who stretches out his arm in a commanding and protective manner. But even as he does so he too receives a push in the back which nearly unseats his helmet.

Another wave of pressure goes through the mass and now someone at the back of the ring is shouting, "Make way there." The ring opens and a small, pale woman, perhaps forty, perhaps fifty years old, is thrust forward by the woman in the hat. Her triumphant gesture says plainly, "Here you are—this will finish the talk." The clamour falters for a moment and the young man's rapid urgent speech breaks through, "But I couldn't help it—I was just—"

The pale little woman, now also in front of the crowd, interrupts him. "That's right."

This produces a complete silence. The policeman puts his helmet straight and so recovers his dignity. He turns with his notebook at the ready. "Yes, ma'am?"

"It wasn't his fault—it wasn't anybody's fault," the little woman said in a high thin voice.

"You saw it, did you?"

She shakes her head and says, "No, I was in the shop—I couldn't see anything."

"Then how do you know it wasn't anybody's fault?"

"He was my boy."

Everybody stares at her with amazement and confusion—it is as though she has spoken in Chinese. But she is not at all disconcerted. For the first time she looks at the child's body huddled in the dust, and she says even more loudly, "No, it wasn't nobody's fault."

The policeman and the motorist gaze at her still as if she is mad. But the women are already going away. They understand why she doesn't want to blame anybody—she can't take any more bitterness. □

DISCUSSION

1. Why is the age of the mother of the dead child important?

2. What does the title of the story mean?

3. In the introductory paragraphs the author distinguishes three worlds: that of adults, that of children, that of dogs.

(a) What do these three worlds have to do with the story?

(b) How does their existence prepare the reader for the mother's statement at the end?

4. Is there any real difference in the extent of the maternal love displayed by the mothers in "My Oedipus Complex" and "The Limit"?

WRITING

1. Prepare a stream-of-consciousness monologue about what was going on in the mind of the driver of the car.

2. Assume that the following is a newspaper report of the event, and explain why Joyce Cary's story is more powerful:

BOY KILLED INSTANTLY

Jimmy Allan, the four-year-old son of Mrs. Agnes Allan, a middle-aged widow, was killed instantly on Old High Street this morning when he darted off the kerb in pursuit of his puppy and ran into the path of a sports car driven by Donald Smythe-Jones, aged twenty-five. The puppy was not injured. Mrs. Allan refused to press charges, saying that the driver was not at fault. Jimmy was her sole surviving child.

ON SATURDAY AFTERNOON

by Alan Sillitoe

I ONCE saw a bloke try to kill himself. I'll never forget the day because I was sitting in the house one Saturday afternoon, feeling black and fed-up because everybody in the family had gone to the pictures, except me who'd for some reason been left out of it. 'Course, I didn't know then that I would soon see something you can never see in the same way on the pictures, a real bloke stringing himself up. I was only a kid at the time, so you can imagine how much I enjoyed it.

I've never known a family to look as black as our family when they're fed-up. I've seen the old man with his face so dark and full of murder because he ain't got no fags or was having to use saccharine to sweeten his tea, or even for nothing at all, that I've backed out of the house in case he got up from his fireside chair and came for me. He just sits, almost on top of the fire, his oil-stained Sunday-joint maulers opened out in front of him and facing inwards to each other, his thick shoulders scrunched forward, and his dark brown eyes staring into the fire. Now and again he'd say a dirty word, for no reason at all, the worst word you can think of, and when he starts saying this you know it's time to clear out. If mam's in it gets worse than ever, because she says sharp to him: "What are yo' looking so bleddy black for?" as if it might be because of something she's done, and before you know what's happening he's tipped up a tableful of pots and mam's gone out of the house crying. Dad hunches back over the fire and goes on swearing. All because of a packet of fags.

I once saw him broodier than I'd ever seen him, so that I thought he'd gone crackers in a quiet sort of way—until a fly flew to within a yard of him. Then his hand shot out, got it, and slung it crippled into the roaring fire. After that he cheered up a bit and mashed some tea.

Well, that's where the rest of us get our black looks from. It stands to reason we'd have them with a dad who carries on like that, don't it? Black looks run in the family. Some families have them and some don't. Our family has them right enough, and that's certain, so when we're fed-up we're really fed-up. Nobody knows why we get as fed-up as we do or why it gives us these black looks when we are. Some people get fed-up and don't look bad at all: they seem happy in a funny sort of way, as if they've just been set free from clink after being in there for something they didn't do, or come out of the pictures after sitting plugged for eight hours at a bad film, or just missed a bus they ran half a mile for and seen it was the wrong one just after they'd stopped running—but in our family it's murder for the others if one of us is fed-up. I've asked myself lots of times what it is, but I can never get any sort of answer even if I sit and think for hours, which I must admit I don't do, though it looks good when I say I do. But I sit and think for long enough, until mam says to me, at seeing me scrunched up over the fire like dad: "What are yo' looking so black for?" So I've just got to stop thinking about it in case I get really black and fed-up and go the same way as dad, tipping up a tableful of pots and all.

Mostly I suppose there's nothing to look so black for: though it's nobody's fault and you can't blame anyone for looking black because I'm sure it's summat in the blood. But on this Saturday afternoon I was looking so black that when dad came in from the bookie's he said to me: "What's up wi' yo'?"

"I feel badly," I fibbed. He'd have had a fit if I'd said I was only black because I hadn't gone to the pictures.

"Well have a wash," he told me.

"I don't want a wash," I said, and that was a fact.

"Well, get outside and get some fresh air then," he shouted.

I did as I was told, double-quick, because if ever dad goes as far as to tell me to get some fresh air I know it's time to get away from him. But outside the air wasn't so fresh, what with that bloody great bike factory bashing away at the yard-end. I didn't know where to go, so I walked up the yard a bit and sat down near somebody's back gate.

Then I saw this bloke who hadn't lived long in our yard. He was tall and thin and had a face like a parson except that he wore a flat cap and had a moustache that drooped, and looked as though he hadn't had a square meal for a year. I didn't think much o' this at the time: but I remember that as he turned in by the yard-end one of the nosy gossiping women who stood there every minute of the day except when she trudged to the pawnshop with her husband's bike or best suit, shouted to him: "What's that rope for, mate?"

He called back: "It's to 'ang messen wi', missis," and she cackled at his bloody good joke so loud and long you'd think she never heard such a good 'un, though the next day she cackled on the other side of her fat face.

He walked by me puffing a fag and carrying his coil of brand-new rope, and he had to step over me to get past. His boot nearly took my shoulder off, and when I told him to watch where he was going I don't think he heard me because he didn't even look round. Hardly anybody was about. All the kids were still at the pictures, and most of their mams and dads were downtown doing the shopping.

The bloke walked down the yard to his back door, and having nothing better to do because I hadn't gone to the pictures, I followed him. You see, he left his back door open a bit, so I gave it a push and went in. I stood there, just watching him, sucking my thumb, the other hand in my pocket. I suppose he knew I was there, because his eyes were moving more natural now, but he didn't seem to mind. "What are yer going to do wi' that rope, mate?" I asked him.

"I'm going ter 'ang messen, lad," he told me, as though he'd done it a time or two already, and people had usually asked him questions like this beforehand.

"What for, mate?" He must have thought I was a nosy young bogger.

"'Cause I want to, that's what for," he said, clearing all the pots off the table and pulling it to the middle of the room. Then he stood on it to fasten the rope to the light-fitting. The table creaked and didn't look very safe, but it did him for what he wanted.

"It wain't hold up, mate," I said to him, thinking how much better it was being here than sitting in the pictures and seeing the Jungle Jim serial.

But he got nettled now and turned on me. "Mind yer own business."

I thought he was going to tell me to scram, but he didn't. He made ever such a fancy knot with that rope, as though he'd been a sailor or summat, and as he tied it he was whistling a fancy tune to himself. Then he got down from the table and pushed it back to the wall, and put a chair in its place. He wasn't looking black at all, nowhere near as black as anybody in our family when they're feeling fed-up. If ever he'd looked only half as black as our dad looked twice a week he'd have hanged himself years ago, I couldn't help thinking. But he was making a good job of that rope all right, as though he'd thought about it a lot anyway, and as though it was going to be the last thing he'd ever do. But I knew something he didn't know, because he wasn't standing where I was. I knew the rope wouldn't hold up, and I told him so, again.

"Shut yer gob," he said, but quiet like, "or I'll kick yer out."

I didn't want to miss it, so I said nothing. He took his cap off and put it on the dresser, then he took his coat off, and his scarf, and spread them out on the sofa. I wasn't a bit frightened, like I might be now at sixteen, because it was interesting. And being only ten I'd never had a chance to see a bloke hang himself before. We got pally, the two of us, before he slipped the rope around his neck.

"Shut the door," he asked me, and I did as I was told. "Ye're a good lad for your age," he said to me while I sucked my thumb, and he felt in his pockets and pulled out all that was inside, throwing the handful of bits and bobs on the table: fag-packet and peppermints, a pawn-ticket, an old comb, and a few coppers. He picked out a penny and gave it to me, saying: "Now listen ter me, young 'un. I'm going to 'ang messen, and when I'm swinging I want you to gi' this chair a bloody good kick and push it away. All right?"

I nodded.

He put the rope around his neck, and then took it off like it was a tie that didn't fit. "What are yer going to do it for, mate?" I asked again.

"Because I'm fed-up," he said, looking very unhappy. "And because I want to. My missus left me, and I'm out o' work."

I didn't want to argue, because the way he said it, I knew he couldn't do anything else except hang himself. Also there was a funny look in his face: even when he talked to me I swear he couldn't see me. It was different to the black looks my old man puts on, and I suppose that's why my old man would never hang himself, worse luck, because he never gets a look into his clock like this bloke had. My old man's look stares *at* you, so that you have to back down and fly out of the house: this bloke's look looked *through* you, so that you could face it and know it wouldn't do you any harm. So I saw now that dad would never hang himself because he could never get the right sort of look into his face, in spite of the fact that he'd been out of work often enough. Maybe mam would have to leave him first, and then he might do it; but no—I shook my head—there wasn't much chance of that even though he did lead her a dog's life.

"Yer wain't forget to kick that chair away?" he reminded me, and I swung my head to say I wouldn't. So my eyes were popping and I watched every move he made. He stood on the chair and put the rope around his neck so that it fitted this time, still whistling his fancy tune. I wanted to get a better goz at the knot, because my pal was in the scouts, and would ask to know how it was done, and if I told him later he'd let me know what happened at the pictures in the Jungle Jim serial, so's I could have my cake and eat it as well, as mam says, tit for tat. But I thought I'd better not ask the bloke to tell me, and I stayed back in my corner. The last thing he did was take the wet dirty butt-end from his lips and sling it into the empty firegrate, following it with his eyes to the black fireback where it landed—as if he was then going to mend a fault in the lighting like any electrician.

Suddenly his long legs wriggled and his feet tried to kick the chair, so I helped him as I'd promised I would and took a runner at it as if I was playing centre-forward for Notts Forest, and the chair went scooting back against the sofa, dragging his muffler to the floor as it tipped over. He swung for a bit, his arms chafing like he was a scarecrow flapping birds away, and he made a noise in his throat as if he'd just took a dose of salts and was trying to make them stay down.

Then there was another sound, and I looked up and saw a big crack come in the ceiling, like you see on the pictures when an earthquake's happening, and the bulb began circling round and round as though it was a spaceship. I was just beginning to get dizzy when, thank Christ, he fell down with such a horrible thump on the floor that I thought he'd broke every bone he'd got. He kicked around for a bit, like a dog that's got colic bad. Then he lay still.

I didn't stay to look at him. "I told him that rope wouldn't hold up," I kept saying to myself as I went out of the house, tut-tutting because he hadn't done the job right, hands stuffed deep into my pockets and nearly crying at the balls-up he'd made of everything. I slammed his gate so hard with disappointment that it nearly dropped off its hinges.

Just as I was going back up the yard to get my tea at home, hoping the others had come back from the pictures so's I wouldn't have anything to keep on being black about, a copper passed me and headed for the bloke's door. He was striding quickly with his head bent forward, and I knew that somebody had narked. They must have seen him buy the rope and then tipped-off the cop. Or happen the old hen at the yard-end had finally caught on. Or perhaps he'd even told somebody himself, because I supposed that the bloke who'd strung himself up hadn't much known what he was doing, especially with the look I'd seen in his eyes. But that's how it is, I said to myself, as I followed the copper back to the bloke's house, a poor bloke can't even hang himself these days.

When I got back the copper was slitting the rope from his neck with a pen-knife, then he gave him a drink of water, and the bloke opened his peepers. I didn't like the copper, because he'd got a couple of my mates sent to approved school for pinching lead piping from lavatories.

"What did you want to hang yourself for?" he asked the bloke, trying to make him sit up. He could hardly talk, and one of his hands was bleeding from where the light-bulb had smashed. I knew that rope wouldn't hold up, but he hadn't listened to me. I'll never hang myself anyway, but if I want to I'll make sure I do it from a tree or something like that, not a light-fitting. "Well, what did you do it for?"

"Because I wanted to," the bloke croaked.

"You'll get five years for this," the copper told him. I'd crept back into the house and was sucking my thumb in the same corner.

"That's what yo' think," the bloke said, a normal frightened look in his eyes now. "I only wanted to hang myself."

"Well," the copper said, taking out his book, "it's against the law, you know."

"Nay," the bloke said, "it can't be. It's my life, ain't it?"

"You might think so," the copper said, "but it ain't."

He began to suck the blood from his hand. It was such a little scratch though that you couldn't see it. "That's the first thing I knew," he said.

"Well I'm telling you," the copper told him.

'Course, I didn't let on to the copper that I'd helped the bloke to hang himself. I wasn't born yesterday, nor the day before yesterday either.

"It's a fine thing if a bloke can't tek his own life,"

the bloke said, seeing he was in for it.

"Well he can't," the copper said, as if reading out of his book and enjoying it. "It ain't your life. And it's a crime to take your own life. It's killing yourself. It's suicide."

The bloke looked hard, as if every one of the copper's words meant six-months cold. I felt sorry for him, and that's a fact, but if only he'd listened to what I'd said and not depended on that light-fitting. He should have done it from a tree, or something like that.

He went up the yard with the copper like a peaceful lamb, and we all thought that that was the end of that.

But a couple of days later the news was flashed through to us—even before it got to the *Post* because a woman in our yard worked at the hospital of an evening dishing grub out and tidying up. I heard her spilling it to somebody at the yard-end. "I'd never 'ave thought it. I thought he'd got that daft idea out of his head when they took him away. But no. Wonders'll never cease. Chucked 'issen from the hospital window when the copper who sat near his bed went off for a pee. Would you believe it? Dead? Not much 'e ain't."

He'd heaved himself at the glass, and fallen like a stone on to the road. In one way I was sorry he'd done it, but in another I was glad, because he'd proved to the coppers and everybody whether it was his life or not all right. It was marvellous though, the way the brainless bastards had put him in a ward six floors up, which finished him off, proper, even better than a tree.

All of which will make me think twice about how black I sometimes feel. The black coal-bag locked inside you, and the black look it puts on your face, doesn't mean you're going to string yourself up or sling yourself under a double-decker or chuck yourself out of a window or cut your throat with a sardine-tin or put your head in the gas-oven or drop your rotten sack-bag of a body on to a railway line, because when you're feeling that black you can't even move from your chair. Anyhow, I know I'll never get so black as to hang myself, because hanging don't look very nice to me, and never will, the more I remember old what's-his-name swinging from the light-fitting.

More than anything else, I'm glad now I didn't go to the pictures that Saturday afternoon when I was feeling black and ready to do myself in. Because you know, I shan't ever kill myself. Trust me. I'll stay alive half-barmy till I'm a hundred and five, and then go out screaming blue murder because I want to stay where I am. □

DISCUSSION

1. Does the first person narration, with its working-class slang expressions, add to or detract from the effect of the story? Discuss.

2. (a) Throughout the story what contrast is set up between those who are potential suicides and those who are not?

(b) Why is the narrator sure that he and his father are not?

3. (a) What does the narrator mean by "the black coal-bag locked up inside you and the black look it puts on your face"?

(b) What might be responsible for the existence of the coal-bag?

4. (a) What led up to the old man's first suicide attempt?

(b) What led to the second attempt?

(c) Do you think he was at all accountable for his actions? Explain.

5. Both "The Limit" and "On Saturday Afternoon" are based on reactions to tragic deaths.

(a) In what respects are the reactions of the boy in this story and of the mother in "The Limit" similar?

(b) In what respects are they different?

(c) Taken together, what do the two stories suggest about the conditions of working-class life in urban England?

WRITING

1. Write, either in narrative or dramatic form, one incident from the life of the elderly man several days before his attempted suicide.

2. As in the case of the narrator of this story, an early childhood experience may be recollected years later and reassessed on the basis of experience gained in the intervening years. Describe such an experience from your own background or that of someone you know. (It will probably not be as lurid as the one in the story.)

THE DESTRUCTORS

by Graham Greene

I

IT WAS on the eve of August Bank Holiday that the latest recruit became the leader of the Wormsley Common Gang. No one was surprised except Mike, but Mike at the age of nine was surprised by everything. "If you don't shut your mouth," somebody once said to him, "you'll get a frog down it." After that Mike had kept his teeth tightly clamped except when the surprise was too great.

The new recruit had been with the gang since the beginning of the summer holidays, and there were possibilities about his brooding silence that all recognized. He never wasted a word even to tell his name until that was required of him by the rules. When he said "Trevor" it was a statement of fact, not as it would have been with the others a statement of shame or defiance. Nor did anyone laugh except Mike, who finding himself without support and meeting the dark gaze of the newcomer opened his mouth and was quiet again. There was every reason why T., as he was afterwards referred to, should have been an object of mockery—there was his name (and they substituted the initial because otherwise they had no excuse not to laugh at it), the fact that his father, a former architect and present clerk, had "come down in the world" and that his mother considered herself better than the neighbours. What but an odd quality of danger, of the unpredictable, established him in the gang without any ignoble ceremony of initiation?

The gang met every morning in an impromptu car-park, the site of the last bomb of the first blitz. The leader, who was known as Blackie, claimed to have heard it fall, and no one was precise enough in his dates to point out that he would have been one year old and fast asleep on the down platform of Wormsley Common Underground Station. On one side of the car-park leant the first occupied house, number 3, of the shattered Northwood Terrace—literally leant, for it had suffered from the blast of the bomb and the side walls were supported on wooden struts. A smaller bomb and some incendiaries had fallen beyond, so that the house stuck up like a jagged tooth and carried on the further wall relics of its neighbour, a dado, the remains of a fireplace. T., whose words were almost confined to voting "Yes" or "No" to the plan of operations proposed each day by Blackie, once startled the whole gang by saying broodingly, "Wren built that house, father says."

"Who's Wren?"

"The man who built St. Paul's."

"Who cares?" Blackie said. "It's only old Misery's."

Old Misery—whose real name was Thomas—had once been a builder and decorator. He lived alone in the crippled house, doing for himself: once a week you could see him coming back across the common with bread and vegetables, and once as the boys played in the car-park he put his head over the smashed wall of his garden and looked at them.

"Been to the loo," one of the boys said, for it was common knowledge that since the bombs fell something had gone wrong with the pipes of the house and Old Misery was too mean to spend money on the property. He could do the redecorating himself at cost price, but he had never learnt plumbing. The loo was a wooden shed at the bottom of the narrow garden with a star-shaped hole in the door: it had escaped the blast which had smashed the house next door and sucked out the window-frames of No. 3.

The next time the gang became aware of Mr. Thomas was more surprising. Blackie, Mike, and a thin yellow boy, who for some reason was called by his surname Summers, met him on the common coming back from the market. Mr. Thomas stopped them. He said glumly, "You belong to the lot that play in the car-park?"

Mike was about to answer when Blackie stopped him. As the leader he had responsibilities. "Suppose we are?" he said ambiguously.

"I got some chocolates," Mr. Thomas said. "Don't like 'em myself. Here you are. Not enough to go round, I don't suppose. There never is," he added with sombre conviction. He handed over three packets of Smarties.

The gang were puzzled and perturbed by this action and tried to explain it away. "Bet someone dropped them and he picked 'em up," somebody suggested.

"Pinched 'em and then got in a bleeding funk," another thought aloud.

"It's a bribe," Summers said. "He wants us to stop bouncing balls on his wall."

"We'll show him we don't take bribes," Blackie said, and they sacrificed the whole morning to the game of bouncing that only Mike was young enough to enjoy. There was no sign from Mr. Thomas.

Next day T. astonished them all. He was late at the rendezvous, and the voting for that day's exploit took place without him. At Blackie's suggestion the gang was to disperse in pairs, take buses at random, and see how many free rides could be snatched from unwary conductors (the operation was to be carried out in pairs to avoid cheating). They were drawing lots for their companions when T. arrived.

"Where you been, T.?" Blackie asked. "You can't vote now. You know the rules."

"I've been *there,*" T. said. He looked at the ground, as though he had thoughts to hide.

"Where?"

"At Old Misery's." Mike's mouth opened and then hurriedly closed again with a click. He had remembered the frog.

"At Old Misery's?" Blackie said. There was nothing in the rules against it, but he had a sensation that T. was treading on dangerous ground. He asked hopefully, "Did you break in?"

"No. I rang the bell."

"And what did you say?"

"I said I wanted to see his house."

"What did he do?"

"He showed it me."

"Pinch anything?"

"No."

"What did you do it for then?"

The gang had gathered round: it was as though an impromptu court were about to form and to try some case of deviation. T. said, "It's a beautiful house," and still watching the ground, meeting no one's eyes, he licked his lips first one way, then the other.

"What do you mean, a beautiful house?" Blackie asked with scorn.

"It's got a staircase two hundred years old like a corkscrew. Nothing holds it up."

"What do you mean, nothing holds it up. Does it float?"

"It's to do with opposite forces, Old Misery said."

"What else?"

"There's panelling."

"Like in the Blue Boar?"

"Two hundred years old."

"Is Old Misery two hundred years old?"

Mike laughed suddenly and then was quiet again. The meeting was in a serious mood. For the first time since T. had strolled into the car-park on the first day of the holidays his position was in danger. It only needed a single use of his real name and the gang would be at his heels.

"What did you do it for?" Blackie asked. He was just, he had no jealousy, he was anxious to retain T. in the gang if he could. It was the word "beautiful" that worried him—that belonged to a class world that you could still see parodied at the Wormsley Common Empire by a man wearing a top hat and a monocle, with a haw-haw accent. He was tempted to say, "My dear Trevor, old chap," and unleash his hell hounds. "If you'd broken in," he said sadly—that indeed would have been an exploit worthy of the gang.

"This was better," T. said. "I found out things." He continued to stare at his feet, not meeting anybody's eye, as though he were absorbed in some dream he was unwilling—or ashamed—to share.

"What things?"

"Old Misery's going to be away all tomorrow and Bank Holiday."

Blackie said with relief, "You mean we could break in?"

"And pinch things?" somebody asked.

Blackie said, "Nobody's going to pinch things. Breaking in—that's good enough, isn't it? We don't want any court stuff."

"I don't want to pinch anything," T. said. "I've got a better idea."

"What is it?"

T. raised eyes, as grey and disturbed as the drab August day. "We'll pull it down," he said. "We'll destroy it."

Blackie gave a single hoot of laughter and then, like Mike, fell quiet, daunted by the serious implacable gaze. "What'd the police be doing all the time?" he said.

"They'd never know. We'd do it from inside. I've found a way in." He said with a sort of intensity, "We'd be like worms, don't you see, in an apple. When we came out again there'd be nothing there, no staircase, no panels, nothing but just walls, and then we'd make the walls fall down—somehow."

"We'd go to jug," Blackie said.

"Who's to prove? And anyway we wouldn't have

pinched anything." He added without the smallest flicker of glee, "There wouldn't be anything to pinch after we'd finished."

"I've never heard of going to prison for breaking things," Summers said.

"There wouldn't be time," Blackie said. "I've seen housebreakers at work."

"There are twelve of us," T. said. "We'd organize."

"None of us know how—"

"I know," T. said. He looked across at Blackie, "Have you got a better plan?"

"Today," Mike said tactlessly, "we're pinching free rides—"

"Free rides," T. said. "You can stand down, Blackie, if you'd rather. . . ."

"The gang's got to vote."

"Put it up then."

Blackie said uneasily, "It's proposed that tomorrow and Monday we destroy Old Misery's house."

"Here, here," said a fat boy called Joe.

"Who's in favour?"

T. said, "It's carried."

"How do we start?" Summers asked.

"He'll tell you," Blackie said. It was the end of his leadership. He went away to the back of the car-park and began to kick a stone, dribbling it this way and that. There was only one old Morris in the park, for few cars were left there except lorries: without an attendant there was no safety. He took a flying kick at the car and scraped a little paint off the rear mudguard. Beyond, paying no more attention to him than to a stranger, the gang had gathered round T.; Blackie was dimly aware of the fickleness of favour. He thought of going home, of never returning, of letting them all discover the hollowness of T.'s leadership, but suppose after all what T. proposed was possible —nothing like it had ever been done before. The fame of the Wormsley Common car-park gang would surely reach around London. There would be headlines in the papers. Even the grown-up gangs who ran the betting at the all-in wrestling and the barrow-boys would hear with respect of how Old Misery's house had been destroyed. Driven by the pure, simple, and altruistic ambition of fame for the gang, Blackie came back to where T. stood in the shadow of Misery's wall.

T. was giving his orders with decision: it was as though this plan had been with him all his life, pondered through the seasons, now in his fifteenth year crystallized with the pain of puberty. "You," he said to Mike, "bring some big nails, the biggest you can find, and a hammer. Anyone else who can better bring a hammer and a screwdriver. We'll need plenty of them. Chisels too. We can't have too many chisels. Can anybody bring a saw?"

"I can," Mike said.

"Not a child's saw," T. said. "A real saw."

Blackie realized he had raised his hand like any ordinary member of the gang.

"Right, you bring one, Blackie. But now there's a difficulty. We want a hacksaw."

"What's a hacksaw?" someone asked.

"You can get 'em at Woolworth's," Summers said.

The fat boy called Joe said gloomily, "I knew it would end in a collection."

"I'll get one myself," T. said. "I don't want your money. But I can't buy a sledge-hammer."

Blackie said, "They are working on number fifteen. I know where they'll leave their stuff for Bank Holiday."

"Then that's all," T. said. "We meet here at nine sharp."

"I've got to go to church," Mike said.

"Come over the wall and whistle. We'll let you in."

II

On Sunday morning all were punctual except Blackie, even Mike. Mike had had a stroke of luck. His mother felt ill, his father was tired after Saturday night, and he was told to go to church alone with many warnings of what would happen if he strayed. Blackie had had difficulty in smuggling out the saw, and then in finding the sledge-hammer at the back of number 15. He approached the house from a lane at the rear of the garden, for fear of the policeman's beat along the main road. The tired evergreens kept off a stormy sun: another wet Bank Holiday was being prepared over the Atlantic, beginning in swirls of dust under the trees. Blackie climbed the wall into Misery's garden.

There was no sign of anybody anywhere. The loo stood like a tomb in a neglected graveyard. The curtains were drawn. The house slept. Blackie lumbered nearer with the saw and the sledge-hammer. Perhaps after all nobody had turned up: the plan had been a wild invention: they had woken wiser. But when he came close to the back door he could hear a confusion of sound, hardly louder than a hive in swarm: a clickety-clack, a bang bang bang, a scraping, a creaking, a sudden painful crack. He thought, It's true, and whistled.

They opened the back door to him and he came in. He had at once the impression of organization, very different from the old happy-go-lucky ways under his leadership. For a while he wandered up and down stairs looking for T. Nobody addressed him: he had a sense of great urgency, and already he could begin to see the plan. The interior of the house was being carefully demolished without touching the outer walls. Summers with hammer and chisel was ripping out the skirting-boards in the ground floor dining-room: he had already smashed the panels of the door. In the same room Joe was heaving up the parquet blocks, exposing the soft wood floor-boards over the cellar. Coils of wire came out of the damaged skirting and Mike sat happily on the floor, clipping the wires.

On the curved stairs two of the gang were working hard with an inadequate child's saw on the banisters —when they saw Blackie's big saw they signalled for it wordlessly. When he next saw them a quarter of the banisters had been dropped into the hall. He found T. at last in the bathroom—he sat moodily in the least cared-for room in the house, listening to the sounds coming up from below.

"You've really done it," Blackie said with awe. "What's going to happen?"

"We've only just begun," T. said. He looked at the sledge-hammer and gave his instructions. "You stay here and break the bath and the wash-basin. Don't bother about the pipes. They come later."

Mike appeared at the door. "I've finished the wire, T.," he said.

"Good. You've just got to go wandering round now. The kitchen's in the basement. Smash all the china and glass and bottles you can lay hold of. Don't turn on the taps—we don't want a flood—yet. Then go into all the rooms and turn out drawers. If they are locked get one of the others to break them open. Tear up any papers you find and smash all the ornaments. Better take a carving-knife with you from the kitchen. The bedroom's opposite here. Open the pillows and tear up the sheets. That's enough for the moment. And you, Blackie, when you've finished in here crack the plaster in the passage up with your sledge-hammer."

"What are you going to do?" Blackie asked.

"I'm looking for something special," T. said.

It was nearly lunch-time before Blackie had finished and went in search of T. Chaos had advanced. The kitchen was a shambles of broken glass and china. The dining-room was stripped of parquet, the skirting was up, the door had been taken off its hinges, and the destroyers had moved up a floor. Streaks of light came in through the closed shutters where they worked with the seriousness of creators—and destruction after all is a form of creation. A kind of imagination had seen this house as it had now become.

Mike said, "I've got to go home for dinner."

"Who else?" T. asked, but all the others on one excuse or another had brought provisions with them.

They squatted in the ruins of the room and swapped unwanted sandwiches. Half an hour for lunch and they were at work again. By the time Mike returned, they were on the top floor, and by six the superficial damage was completed. The doors were all off, all the skirtings raised, the furniture pillaged and ripped and smashed—no one could have slept in the house except on a bed of broken plaster. T. gave his orders—eight o'clock next morning—and to escape notice they climbed singly over the garden wall, into the car-park. Only Blackie and T. were left; the light had nearly gone, and when they touched a switch, nothing worked—Mike had done his job thoroughly.

"Did you find anything special?" Blackie asked.

T. nodded. "Come over here," he said, "and look." Out of both pockets he drew bundles of pound notes. "Old Misery's savings," he said. "Mike ripped out the mattress, but he missed them."

"What are you going to do? Share them?"

"We aren't thieves," T. said. "Nobody's going to steal anything from this house. I kept these for you and me—a celebration." He knelt down on the floor and counted them out—there were seventy in all.

"We'll burn them," he said, "one by one," and taking it in turns they held a note upwards and lit the top corner, so that the flame burnt slowly towards their fingers. The grey ash floated above them and fell on their heads like age. "I'd like to see Old Misery's face when we are through," T. said.

"You hate him a lot?" Blackie asked.

"Of course I don't hate him," T. said. "There'd be no fun if I hated him." The last burning note illuminated his brooding face. "All this hate and love," he said, "it's soft, it's hooey. There's only things, Blackie," and he looked round the room crowded with the unfamiliar shadows of half things, broken things, former things. "I'll race you home, Blackie," he said.

III

Next morning the serious destruction started. Two were missing—Mike and another boy whose parents were off to Southend and Brighton in spite of the slow warm drops that had begun to fall and the rumble of thunder in the estuary like the first guns of the old blitz. "We've got to hurry," T. said.

Summers was restive. "Haven't we done enough?" he said. "I've been given a bob for slot machines. This is like work."

"We've hardly started," T. said. "Why, there's all the floors left, and the stairs. We haven't taken out a single window. You voted like the others. We are going to *destroy* this house. There won't be anything left when we've finished."

They began again on the first floor picking up the top floor-boards next the outer wall, leaving the joists exposed. Then they sawed through the joists and retreated into the hall, as what was left of the floor heeled and sank. They had learnt with practice, and the second floor collapsed more easily. By the evening an odd exhilaration seized them as they looked down the great hollow of the house. They ran risks and made mistakes: when they thought of the windows it was too late to reach them. "Cor," Joe said, and dropped a penny down into the dry rubble-filled well. It cracked and span among the broken glass.

"Why did we start this?" Summers asked with astonishment; T. was already on the ground, digging at the rubble, clearing a space along the outer wall. "Turn on the taps," he said. "It's too dark for anyone to see now, and in the morning it won't matter." The water overtook them on the stairs and fell through the floorless rooms.

It was then they heard Mike's whistle at the back. "Something's wrong," Blackie said. They could hear his urgent breathing as they unlocked the door.

"The bogies?" Summers asked.

"Old Misery," Mike said. "He's on his way." He put his head between his knees and retched. "Ran all the way," he said with pride.

"But why?" T. said. "He told me . . ." He protested with the fury of the child he had never been, "It isn't fair."

"He was down at Southend," Mike said, "and he was on the train coming back. Said it was too cold and wet." He paused and gazed at the water. "My, you've had a storm here. Is the roof leaking?"

"How long will he be?"

"Five minutes. I gave Ma the slip and ran."

"We better clear," Summers said. "We've done enough, anyway."

"Oh, no, we haven't. Anybody could do this—" "This" was the shattered hollowed house with nothing left but the walls. Yet walls could be preserved. Façades were valuable. They could build inside again more beautifully than before. This could again be a home. He said angrily, "We've got to finish. Don't move. Let me think."

"There's no time," a boy said.

"There's got to be a way," T. said. "We couldn't have got thus far . . ."

"We've done a lot," Blackie said.

"No. No, we haven't. Somebody watch the front."

"We can't do any more."

"He may come in at the back."

"Watch the back too." T. began to plead. "Just give me a minute and I'll fix it. I swear I'll fix it." But his authority had gone with his ambiguity. He was only one of the gang. "Please," he said.

"Please," Summers mimicked him, and then suddenly struck home with the fatal name. "Run along home, Trevor."

T. stood with his back to the rubble like a boxer knocked groggy against the ropes. He had no words as his dreams shook and slid. Then Blackie acted before the gang had time to laugh, pushing Summers backward. "I'll watch the front, T.," he said, and cautiously he opened the shutters of the hall. The grey wet common stretched ahead, and the lamps gleamed in the puddles. "Someone's coming, T. No, it's not him. What's your plan, T.?"

"Tell Mike to go out to the loo and hide close beside it. When he hears me whistle he's got to count ten and start to shout."

"Shout what?"

"Oh, 'Help,' anything."

"You hear, Mike," Blackie said. He was the leader again. He took a quick look between the shutters. "He's coming, T."

"Quick, Mike. The loo. Stay here, Blackie, all of you till I yell."

"Where are you going, T.?"

"Don't worry. I'll see to this. I said I would, didn't I?"

Old Misery came limping off the common. He had mud on his shoes and he stopped to scrape them on the pavement's edge. He didn't want to soil his house, which stood jagged and dark between the bomb-sites, saved so narrowly, as he believed, from destruction. Even the fan-light had been left unbroken by the bomb's blast. Somewhere somebody whistled. Old Misery looked sharply round. He didn't trust whistles. A child was shouting: it seemed to come from his own garden. Then a boy ran into the road from the car-park. "Mr. Thomas," he called, "Mr. Thomas."

"What is it?"

"I'm terribly sorry, Mr. Thomas. One of us got taken short, and we thought you wouldn't mind, and now he can't get out."

"What do you mean, boy?"

"He got stuck in your loo."

"He'd no business—Haven't I seen you before?"

"You showed me your house."

"So I did. So I did. That doesn't give you the right to—"

"Do hurry, Mr. Thomas. He'll suffocate."

"Nonsense. He can't suffocate. Wait till I put my bag in."

"I'll carry your bag."

"Oh, no, you don't. I carry my own."

"This way, Mr. Thomas."

"I can't get in the garden that way. I've got to go through the house."

"But you *can* get in the garden this way, Mr. Thomas. We often do."

"You often do?" He followed the boy with a scandalized fascination. "When? What right . . ."

"Do you see . . . ? The wall's low."

"I'm not going to climb walls into my own garden. It's absurd."

"This is how we do it. One foot here, one foot there, and over." The boy's face peered down, an arm shot out, and Mr. Thomas found his bag taken and deposited on the other side of the wall.

"Give me back my bag," Mr. Thomas said. From the loo a boy yelled and yelled. "I'll call the police."

"Your bag's all right, Mr. Thomas. Look. One foot there. On your right. Now just above. To your left." Mr. Thomas climbed over his own garden wall. "Here's your bag, Mr. Thomas."

"I'll have the wall built up," Mr. Thomas said, "I'll not have you boys coming over here, using my loo." He stumbled on the path, but the boy caught his elbow and supported him. "Thank you, thank you, my boy," he murmured automatically. Somebody shouted again through the dark. "I'm coming, I'm coming," Mr. Thomas called. He said to the boy beside him, "I'm not unreasonable. Been a boy myself. As long as things are done regular. I don't mind you playing round the place Saturday mornings. Sometimes I like company. Only it's got to be regular. One of you asks leave and I say Yes. Sometimes I'll say No. Won't feel like it. And you come in at the front door and out at the back. No garden walls."

"Do get him out, Mr. Thomas."

"He won't come to any harm in my loo," Mr. Thomas said, stumbling slowly down the garden. "Oh, my rheumatics," he said. "Always get 'em on Bank Holiday. I've got to go careful. There's loose stones here. Give me your hand. Do you know what my horoscope said yesterday? 'Abstain from any dealings in first half of week. Danger of serious crash.' That might be on this path," Mr. Thomas said. "They speak in parables and double meanings." He paused at the door of the loo. "What's the matter in there?" he called. There was no reply.

"Perhaps he's fainted," the boy said.

"Not in my loo. Here, you, come out," Mr. Thomas said, and giving a great jerk at the door he nearly fell on his back when it swung easily open. A hand first supported him and then pushed him hard. His head hit the opposite wall and he sat heavily down. His bag hit his feet. A hand whipped the key out of the lock and the door slammed. "Let me out," he called, and heard the key turn in the lock. "A serious crash," he thought, and felt dithery and confused and old.

A voice spoke to him softly through the star-shaped hole in the door. "Don't worry, Mr. Thomas," it said, "we won't hurt you, not if you stay quiet."

Mr. Thomas put his head between his hands and pondered. He had noticed that there was only one lorry in the car-park, and he felt certain that the driver would not come for it before the morning. Nobody could hear him from the road in front, and the lane at the back was seldom used. Anyone who passed there would be hurrying home and would not pause for what they would certainly take to be drunken cries. And if he did call "Help," who, on a lonely Bank Holiday evening, would have the courage to investigate? Mr. Thomas sat on the loo and pondered with the wisdom of age.

After a while it seemed to him that there were sounds in the silence—they were faint and came from the direction of his house. He stood up and peered through the ventilation-hole—between the cracks in one of the shutters he saw a light, not the light of a lamp, but the wavering light that a candle might give. Then he thought he heard the sound of hammering and scraping and chipping. He thought of burglars—perhaps they had employed the boy as a scout, but why should burglars engage in what sounded more and more like a stealthy form of carpentry? Mr. Thomas let out an experimental yell, but nobody answered. The noise could not even have reached his enemies.

IV

Mike had gone home to bed, but the rest stayed. The question of leadership no longer concerned the gang. With nails, chisels, screwdrivers, anything that was sharp and penetrating they moved around the inner walls worrying at the mortar between the bricks. They started too high, and it was Blackie who hit on the damp course and realized the work could be halved if they weakened the joints immediately above. It was a long, tiring, unamusing job, but at last it was finished. The gutted house stood there balanced on a few inches of mortar between the damp course and the bricks.

There remained the most dangerous task of all, out in the open at the edge of the bomb-site. Summers was sent to watch the road for passers-by, and Mr. Thomas, sitting on the loo, heard clearly now the sound of sawing. It no longer came from his house, and that a little reassured him. He felt less concerned. Perhaps the other noises too had no significance.

A voice spoke to him through the hole. "Mr. Thomas."

"Let me out," Mr. Thomas said sternly.

"Here's a blanket," the voice said, and a long grey sausage was worked through the hole and fell in swathes over Mr. Thomas's head.

"There's nothing personal," the voice said. "We want you to be comfortable tonight."

"Tonight," Mr. Thomas repeated incredulously.

"Catch," the voice said. "Penny buns—we've buttered them, and sausage-rolls. We don't want you to starve, Mr. Thomas."

Mr. Thomas pleaded desperately. "A joke's a joke, boy. Let me out and I won't say a thing. I've got rheumatics. I got to sleep comfortable."

"You wouldn't be comfortable, not in your house, you wouldn't. Not now."

"What do you mean, boy?" but the footsteps receded. There was only the silence of night: no sound of sawing. Mr. Thomas tried one more yell, but he was daunted and rebuked by the silence—a long way off an owl hooted and made away again on its muffled flight through the soundless world.

At seven next morning the driver came to fetch his lorry. He climbed into the seat and tried to start the engine. He was vaguely aware of a voice shouting, but it didn't concern him. At last the engine responded and he backed the lorry until it touched the great wooden shore that supported Mr. Thomas's house. That way he could drive right out and down the street without reversing. The lorry moved forward, was momentarily checked as though something were pulling it from behind, and then went on to the sound of a long rumbling crash. The driver was astonished to see bricks bouncing ahead of him, while stones hit the roof of his cab. He put on his brakes. When he climbed out the whole landscape had suddenly altered. There was no house beside the car-park, only a hill of rubble. He went round and examined the back of his car for damage, and found a rope tied there that was still twisted at the other end round part of a wooden strut.

The driver again became aware of somebody shouting. It came from the wooden erection which was the nearest thing to a house in that desolation of broken brick. The driver climbed the smashed wall and unlocked the door. Mr. Thomas came out of the loo. He was wearing a grey blanket to which flakes of pastry adhered. He gave a sobbing cry. "My house," he said. "Where's my house?"

"Search me," the driver said. His eye lit on the remains of a bath and what had once been a dresser and he began to laugh. There wasn't anything left anywhere.

"How dare you laugh," Mr. Thomas said. "It was my house. My house."

"I'm sorry," the driver said, making heroic efforts, but when he remembered the sudden check to his lorry, the crash of bricks falling, he became convulsed again. One moment the house had stood there with such dignity between the bomb-sites like a man in a top hat, and then, bang, crash, there wasn't anything left—not anything. He said, "I'm sorry. I can't help it, Mr. Thomas. There's nothing personal, but you got to admit it's funny." □

DISCUSSION

1. What in T.'s past might have caused him to decide to wreck Old Misery's house?

2. This story focuses on the destructive tendencies that lie beneath the surface in all of us. Do you think the story exaggerates? Explain.

3. Mike's parents order him to go to church (and evidently he customarily attends church); the boys give Old Misery a blanket and buy him food so he won't go hungry. How can these positive acts be reconciled with the wanton destruction of Old Misery's house?

4. (a) What might be the significance of Old Misery's name?

(b) How is his past similar to that of T.'s father?

(c) What influence might this have had on T.?

(d) Might T.'s behavior have been influenced by the fact that he originally came from a higher social class than the working-class boys of Wormsley Common? Explain.

5. (a) What parallel can be drawn between the Blitz bombings and the activities of the boys?

(b) What generalization might the author be hinting at?

6. To what extent is the "black coal-bag locked up inside you" which is mentioned in "On Saturday Afternoon" also at work on the characters in "The Destructors"?

WRITING

1. Write the explanation given by one of the boys (preferably T.) to his parents or to the police of what happened to Old Misery's house.

2. Write an ending—happy or unhappy—for Old Misery's story once his house has been destroyed.

THE PHOENIX

by Sylvia Townsend Warner

LORD Strawberry, a nobleman, collected birds. He had the finest aviary in Europe, so large that eagles did not find it uncomfortable, so well laid out that both humming-birds and snow-buntings had a climate that suited them perfectly. But for many years the finest set of apartments remained empty, with just a label saying: "PHOENIX. *Habitat: Arabia.*"

Many authorities on bird life had assured Lord Strawberry that the phoenix is a fabulous bird, or that the breed was long extinct. Lord Strawberry was unconvinced: his family had always believed in phoenixes. At intervals he received from his agents (together with statements of their expenses) birds which they declared were the phoenix but which turned out to be orioles, macaws, turkey buzzards dyed orange, etc., or stuffed cross-breeds, ingeniously assembled from various plumages. Finally Lord Strawberry went himself to Arabia, where, after some months, he found a phoenix, won its confidence, caught it, and brought it home in perfect condition.

It was a remarkably fine phoenix, with a charming character—affable to the other birds in the aviary and much attached to Lord Strawberry. On its arrival in England it made a great stir among ornithologists, journalists, poets, and milliners, and was constantly visited. But it was not puffed up by these attentions, and when it was no longer in the news, and the visits fell off, it showed no pique or rancour. It ate well, and seemed perfectly contented.

It costs a great deal of money to keep up an aviary. When Lord Strawberry died he died penniless. The aviary came on the market. In normal times the rarer birds, and certainly the phoenix, would have been bid for by the trustees of Europe's great zoological societies or by private persons in the U.S.A.; but as it happened Lord Strawberry died just after a world war, when both money and bird-seed were hard to come by (indeed the cost of bird-seed was one of the things which had ruined Lord Strawberry). The London *Times* urged in a leader that the phoenix be bought for the London Zoo, saying that a nation of bird-lovers had a moral right to own such a rarity; and a fund, called the Strawberry Phoenix Fund, was opened. Students, naturalists, and school children contributed according to their means; but their means were small, and there were no large donations. So Lord Strawberry's executors (who had the death duties to consider) closed with the higher offer of Mr. Tancred Poldero, owner and proprietor of Poldero's Wizard Wonderworld.

For quite a while Mr. Poldero considered his phoenix a bargain. It was a civil and obliging bird, and adapted itself readily to its new surroundings. It did not cost much to feed, it did not mind children; and though it had no tricks, Mr. Poldero supposed it would soon pick up some. The publicity of the Strawberry Phoenix Fund was now most helpful. Almost every contributor now saved up another half-crown in order to see the phoenix. Others who had not contributed to the fund, even paid double to look at it on the five-shilling days.

But then business slackened. The phoenix was as handsome as ever, and as amiable; but, as Mr. Poldero said, it hadn't got Udge. Even at popular prices the phoenix was not really popular. It was too quiet, too classical. So people went instead to watch the antics of the baboons, or to admire the crocodile who had eaten the woman.

One day Mr. Poldero said to his manager, Mr. Ramkin:

"How long since any fool paid to look at the phoenix?"

"Matter of three weeks," replied Mr. Ramkin.

"Eating his head off," said Mr. Poldero. "Let alone the insurance. Seven shillings a week it costs me to insure that bird, and I might as well insure the Archbishop of Canterbury."

"The public don't like him. He's too quiet for them, that's the trouble. Won't mate nor nothing. And I've tried him with no end of pretty pollies, ospreys, and Cochin-Chinas, and the Lord knows what. But he won't look at them."

"Wonder if we could swap him for a livelier one," said Mr. Poldero.

"Impossible. There's only one of him at a time."

"Go on!"

"I mean it. Haven't you ever read what it says on the label?"

They went to the phoenix's cage. It flapped its wings politely, but they paid no attention. They read:

"PANSY. *Phoenix phoenixissima formosissima arabiana.* This rare and fabulous bird is UNIQUE. The World's Old Bachelor. Has no mate and doesn't want one. When old, sets fire to itself and emerges miraculously reborn. Specially imported from the East."

"I've got an idea," said Mr. Poldero. "How old do you suppose that bird is?"

"Looks in its prime to me," said Mr. Ramkin.

"Suppose," continued Mr. Poldero, "we could somehow get him alight? We'd advertise it beforehand, of course, work up interest. Then we'd have a new bird, and a bird with some romance about it, a bird with a life-story. We could sell a bird like that."

Mr. Ramkin nodded.

"I've read about it in a book," he said. "You've got to give them scented woods and what not, and they build a nest and sit down on it and catch fire spontaneous. But they won't do it till they're old. That's the snag."

"Leave that to me," said Mr. Poldero. "You get those scented woods, and I'll do the ageing."

It was not easy to age the phoenix. Its allowance of food was halved, and halved again, but though it grew thinner its eyes were undimmed and its plumage glossy as ever. The heating was turned off; but it puffed out its feathers against the cold, and seemed none the worse. Other birds were put into its cage, birds of a peevish and quarrelsome nature. They pecked and chivied it; but the phoenix was so civil and amiable that after a day or two they lost their animosity. Then Mr. Poldero tried alley cats. These could not be won by good manners, but the phoenix darted above their heads and flapped its golden wings in their faces, and daunted them.

Mr. Poldero turned to a book on Arabia, and read that the climate was dry. "Aha!" said he. The phoenix was moved to a small cage that had a sprinkler in the ceiling. Every night the sprinkler was turned on. The phoenix began to cough. Mr. Poldero had another good idea. Daily he stationed himself in front of the cage to jeer at the bird and abuse it.

When spring was come, Mr. Poldero felt justified in beginning a publicity campaign about the ageing phoenix. The old public favourite, he said, was nearing its end. Meanwhile he tested the bird's reactions every few days by putting a few tufts of foul-smelling straw and some strands of rusty barbed wire into the cage, to see if it were interested in nesting yet. One day the phoenix began turning over the straw. Mr. Poldero signed a contract for the film rights. At last the hour seemed ripe. It was a fine Saturday evening in May. For some weeks the public interest in the ageing phoenix had been working up, and the admission charge had risen to five shillings. The enclosure was thronged. The lights and the cameras were trained on the cage, and a loud-speaker proclaimed to the audience the rarity of what was about to take place.

"The phoenix," said the loud-speaker, "is the aristocrat of bird-life. Only the rarest and most expensive specimens of oriental wood, drenched in exotic perfumes, will tempt him to construct his strange love-nest."

Now a neat assortment of twigs and shavings, strongly scented, was shoved into the cage.

"The phoenix," the loud-speaker continued, "is as capricious as Cleopatra, as luxurious as la du Barry, as heady as a strain of wild gypsy music. All the fantastic pomp and passion of the ancient East, its languorous magic, its subtle cruelties . . ."

"Lawks!" cried a woman in the crowd. "He's at it!"

A quiver stirred the dulled plumage. The phoenix turned its head from side to side. It descended, staggering, from its perch. Then wearily it began to pull about the twigs and shavings.

The cameras clicked, the lights blazed full on the cage. Rushing to the loud-speaker Mr. Poldero exclaimed:

"Ladies and gentlemen, this is the thrilling moment the world has breathlessly awaited. The legend of centuries is materializing before our modern eyes. The phoenix . . ."

The phoenix settled on its pyre and appeared to fall asleep.

The film director said:

"Well, if it doesn't evaluate more than this, mark it instructional."

At that moment the phoenix and the pyre burst into flames. The flames streamed upwards, leaped out on every side. In a minute or two everything was burned to ashes, and some thousand people, including Mr. Poldero, perished in the blaze. □

DISCUSSION

1. Contrast the two owners of the phoenix and their treatment of the bird.
2. What major mistakes did Mr. Poldero make about the phoenix?
3. (a) What is the major target of the satire in this story?
(b) Are there any minor targets? Explain.
4. Both "The Destructors" and "The Phoenix" contain allegorical elements. What are they?

WRITING

1. Write a news story describing the mysterious conflagration.
2. Bring some other mythological creature—the Sphinx, a centaur, or a dragon, for example—into the modern world and concoct a story around its activities.

SILVER CIRCUS

by A. E. Coppard

I

HANS Siebenhaar, a street porter, is basking on his stool in a fine street of Vienna, for anybody to hire for any sort of job. He is a huge man with a bulbous hairless face that somehow recalls a sponge, and this sponge is surmounted by a flat peaked hat encircled by a white band bearing these words in red: *Wiener Dienstmann.*[1] His voice, which we shall hear later on, is a vast terrifying voice that seems to tear a rent in Space itself. At fifty years of age Hans is a conspicuous man. But a street porter! Not a profitable way of life, yet it must serve, and must continue to serve. It is a hot July morn, tropical; there are many noises, but no one speaks. The fruit-stall women are silent and hidden; they have pinned newspapers around the edges of their big red umbrellas. It is stifling, languorous; one thinks of lilac, of cool sea, of white balloons; the populace tears off its hat, fans itself desperately, sips ice in the cafés, and still perspires. The very street sounds are injurious to the mind. The drivers of carts wear only their breeches, their bodies are brown as a Polynesian's and lovely to behold.

Just such a day it was as the day twelve months gone when Mitzi Siebenhaar, his second wife, had run away with that Julius Damjancsics. Yes, please very much, she had left him. Hans took off his hat. After contemplating its interior as though it was a coffer of extraordinary mystery, he sighed huskily into it. How was it possible to understand such an accident? Smoothing his brown bald skull with the other hand, he collected so much sweat upon his hairy freckled fingers that as he shook them the drops simply splashed upon the pavement. Young Mitzi! It was her youth. Ah, God bless, she had the pull of him there, a whole fifteen years, fifteen years younger; youth as well as beauty, beauty as well as youth. At thirty-five she was as lovely as a girl, fitful and furious just like a girl, so he was only able to keep her for one little year; that is to say, keep her faithful, to himself. One little year! That is not long, but for a man of fifty it is so difficult, yes; but then Julius Damjancsics was just as old. And she had gone off with him! What could she see in Julius Damjancsics? How was it possible to understand such an accident? They had all been friends together, and Julius could play the mandolin, but Hans could pound him into dust. What could she see in Julius Damjancsics? He could crush him in one fist, like a gherkin. If he had caught them—but that was difficult too. Belgrade he had gone to, for Julius Damjancsics was a Serbian, and Buda-Pesth he had gone to, for Mitzi was Hungarian, but this Julius was a wandering fellow and very deceitful. So. Well, it was pitiful to think of in such hot weather, there was nothing to be done, he had come back to Vienna. And now here he was brooding, here he was groaning; pitiful to think of. At last he said to himself: "Let us wipe our tears and forget that Christ died. *Gloria Patri et Filio et Spiritu Sancto,*" he murmured, for he was a good Catholic man, as Father Adolf of Stefans Dom could testify.

"Porter!" cried a voice.

Hans looked up quickly and put on his hat.

"Sir," said he.

A big man, with a big important foreign face and fat and flourishing appearance and shiny black boots with grey cloth tops stood as it were examining the porter. Although the boots were fastened with what appeared to be pearl buttons, they were rather uncared for, but to offset this a large gold watch-chain was lavishly displayed, with jewelled tiepin and studs. The man's fists were in his trousers pockets; he twirled a long, thin cigar between his rich red lips. Immense and significant, he might have been a Turk or a Tartar, but he was neither; he was the boss of a Rumanian Circus.

"Come with me, I want you," and the huge Hans followed the circus man to a *Biergarten,* where another man was waiting who might have been a Tartar or a Turk. He called him Peter, he was cer-

1. *Wiener Dienstmann,* Viennese porter (German).

tainly his brother, and Peter called him Franz. All three sat down and drank together.

"Tell me, Hans Siebenhaar," said Franz, "you are a strong man?"

"Yes, I am a strong man, that is so."

"You have a good voice?"

"Please—" Hans paused. "I am no singer, not much."

"Ah! No, no, no. You have a strong voice to speak, to shout, you can make great sounds with your voice?"

"Oh, ay," Hans agreed. "I have a strong voice, that is so, very strong, I can make a noise." And there and then he accorded them a succession of hearty bellows in testimony. There was only one other occupant of the *Biergarten,* a man with an Emperor Franz-Josef sort of face and white whiskers like the wings of an easy chair, who sat smoking a china pipe under an acacia tree. And he seemed to be deaf, for he did not take the slightest notice of the appalling outcry. Two waiters rushed with alarm into the garden, but Franz waved them away.

"Good," said Franz reflectively. "Listen now." And sitting there between the brothers Hans heard them propound to him a scheme that smote him with amazement and bereft him of sympathy; it filled him indeed with any and every emotion but that of satisfaction. They wanted him, in brief, to become a tiger.

"No." Hans was indignant, and he was contemptuous. "I do not understand, but I do not do this."

Not at once, they cried, not today. No, no. Plenty of time, a week's time in fact. And they would instruct him in the art of impersonating a tiger, they would rehearse him, and for a single performance, one night only, they would give him two hundred Austrian shillings. Peter the Turk declared it was far too much money. Franz the Tartar invoked his God.

There is more in this, thought Hans, than strokes my ear; I have to beware of something. Aloud he inquired: "Two hundred shillings?"

"Two hundred," said Peter.

"Shillings," echoed Franz, scratching the table with a wooden toothpick.

"And, please very much, I am to do?"

They told him what he was to do. He was to be sewn up in the skin of a tiger; he was to enact the part of a tiger in their menagerie; he was to receive two hundred shillings. Very, very simple for a strong man. Hans Siebenhaar was to be sewn up in the tiger's hide for two hundred shillings; he was to prance and fight and hideously roar in the best way he knew so that the hearts of the audience be rocked within them and fly into their throats—and the two hundred shillings was his. It was his voice, it was because of his great bellowing tigerish voice that they had come to him. Such a voice was worth some riches to them, and so they were going to pay two hundred shillings for his services.

"Two hundred shillings?" murmured Hans.

"Two hundred," said Peter, and Franz said: "Two hundred."

It is not, thought Hans, to be sneezed at, but there is more in this than strokes my hearing; I must be wary.

"Why do you not have," he asked them, "a real tiger?"

"But we had!" they both cried.

"And now he is dead," said Peter.

"A real proper tiger," Franz declared.

"But now he is dead," repeated his brother. "Ah, he had paws like a hassock."

"And the ferocity!"

"Beautiful," said Peter. "He died of grief."

"No, no, no," objected Franz. "I would not say that of this tiger."

"But yes," affirmed Peter. "Of grief. He loved me, and lately I married again."

"The heart was broken, yes, perhaps," Franz admitted.

"His voice died away like a little whistle." There was sorrow in Peter's eyes. "No fury."

"Two hundred shillings," said Franz.

"Brrr-o-o-o-owh!" Hans suddenly roared, and skipping up he began capering and pawing madly about the garden. "Ookah, pookah, boddle, oddle, moddle, miowh!" he roared.

The deaf old gentleman with the Franz-Josef whiskers gently laid his china pipe on the table before him; he neither observed nor heeded Hans, he only put his fingers into his mouth and extracted his false teeth. These he calmly examined, as though they were a foreign substance he had never noticed before and was wondering how it came to be there. Hans began crashing over the tables and chairs; waiters rushed into the garden and, flinging themselves upon the perspiring maniac, rolled him over into a corner.

"That is good," cried Franz, "very good!"

"Absolutely," Peter said, "absolutely!"

Three waiters clung to Hans Siebenhaar with the clear intention of throttling him.

"Enough!" shouted Franz. "Let him go," and with his powerful hands he dragged two of the waiters from the prostrate body of Hans as you would draw two pins from a pincushion, and likewise did Peter do with the other waiter.

"It is all right," said Franz, and Peter said it was quite all right. They gave the waiters a few coins and soothed them. In the meantime Hans had resumed his seat, and the deaf old gentleman was replacing his teeth.

To Hans the brothers said: "Listen," and Hans listened. Their circus-menagerie was now on view in the Prater, and at the festival next week they had contemplated to stage a novel performance, nothing less than a combat between a lion and a tiger—ah, good business!—but just at this critical moment what does their tiger do?

"It dies," suggested Hans.

"Dies," agreed Franz. "It dies. So now!"

"Yes, now?" Hans said, and nodded.

"You must be our tiger, that is the simple fact of the business. You have the voice of a tiger, and the character. You will get the two hundred shillings. Hooray! It is like lapping honey, yes."

"But what is this?" cried Hans. "To fight a lion!"

"Pooh," Peter said. "It is more friendly and harmless than any kitten."

"No," said Hans. "No."

"Yes," said Franz. "Yes. It is, it is but a caterpillar, I tell you."

"No!" shouted Hans.

"It has no teeth."

"Not I," cried the intended victim.

"It has been in our family for a hundred years."

"Never," declared Hans with absolute finality, and he got up as if to go. But the brothers seized each an arm and held him down in his chair.

"Have no fear, Mr. Siebenhaar; it will love you. Two hundred and fifty shillings!"

"No, I will not—ha!"

"Mr. Siebenhaar, we can guarantee you. Three hundred shillings," said Peter.

"And fifty," added Franz.

"Three hundred and fifty!" repeated Hans. "So? But what? I cannot fight a lion. No, no. I am not a woman, I have my courage, but what is three hundred and fifty shillings for my life's blood and bones?" In short, a lion was not the kind of thing Mr. Siebenhaar was in the habit of fighting.

"Ach! Your blood and bones will be as safe as they are in your trousers. You will not have to fight this lion—"

"No, I will not—ha!"

"—you have only to play with it. This lion does not fight, Mr. Siebenhaar; it will not, it cannot."

"Why so?"

"It is too meek, it is like a lamb in a meadow that cries baa. You have only to prance about before it and roar and roar, to make a noise and a fuss. It will cringe before you. Have no fear of him. A show, you understand, make a show."

"I understand a show," said Hans, "but, please very much, permit me, I will not make a spectacle of my blood and bones."

"So help me Heaven!" shouted Franz, exasperated, "do you think we want your bones?"

"Not a knuckle!" cried Hans.

Peter intervened. "You misunderstand us, Mr. Siebenhaar; we desire only entertainment, we do not want a massacre."

"You do not want a massacre!"

"A massacre is very well in its way, perhaps, in its time and place," Peter continued, "but a massacre is one thing, and this is another."

"Thank you," said Hans, "it is very clear, that is very good."

And Franz and Peter intimated that they were simple men of business whose only care it was to bring joy and jollity into the life of the Viennese populace; that the fury of the lion was a figment, its courage a mockery, its power a profanation of all men's cherished fears. If there was one animal in the world more deserving the kindness and pity of mankind, more subservient, more mercifully disposed than any other, Franz assured him, it was a lion. And if there was one lion among all lions more responsive to the symptoms of affection, added Peter, it was this identical lion. Was three hundred and fifty shillings nothing to him?

"No," Hans conceded.

"Is it a bunch of beans?"

"No, no."

"Three hundred and fifty shillings is three hundred and fifty shillings, is it not?" Peter questioned him; and Hans replied: "For what is past, yes; but for what is yet to come, no. The future—pardon, gentleman, does not lie in our behinds."

"Three hundred and fifty shillings is three hundred and fifty shillings, it is not a bunch of beans," said Franz severely. They had men in their employ who implored him on their knees to be honourably permitted to enact the part of this tiger, but they had not the physique, they had not the voice, and, if Mr. Siebenhaar would pardon him, they had not the artist's delicate touch. One thing he, Franz, was certain of: he knew an artist when he saw one, hence this three hundred and fifty shillings.

At the end of it all Hans once more determined to wipe his tears and forget that Christ died. In effect, he agreed to be sewn up on such and such a date in the tiger's hide and to make a manifestation with Messrs. Franz and Peter's ingenuous lion, on the solemnest possible undertaking that no harm should befall his own blood and bones.

"Thunder and lightning! What could harm you?"

"Good."

And after parting from Hans, and when they were well out of hearing, Mr. Franz said: "Ha, ha!" and Mr. Peter said: "Ho, ho!"

II

Hans Siebenhaar had several rehearsals before the eventful day. Submitting himself to be sewn up in the tiger's skin, he dashed his paws upon the floor, pranced, gnashed, snarled, whirled his mechanical tail, and delivered himself of a gamut of howls eminently tigerish. Perfectly satisfactory.

"Where," Hans would ask, "do you keep this old lion?"

"Yes," the brothers always replied, "he is not well, he is sleeping; you see him next time."

And thus it happened that Hans did not see his adversary until they met in the cage of battle. The morning of that day was dull and Hans too was dull, for on awakening he felt so strange, so very unwell, that he greatly feared he would have to send Franz word that he could not come to perform his tiger; but as the day wore on and brightened, Hans, sitting on his stool in the sunny street, brightened with it, and while thinking of the three hundred and fifty shillings his sickness left him. A nice sum of money that! And what would he do with it? Ah, please very much, what would he not have done if Mitzi, the shameless one, had not forsaken him! They might have gone again, as they had gone of old, on one of those excursions to the Wiener Wald. He liked excursions, they were beautiful. With their happy companions they could climb the mountains, prowl in the forest for raspberries and mushrooms, and at noon they would sit under the chestnuts in the *Biergarten* at the Hunter's Meadow and lap the rich soup and gulp lager and talk of love and wealth and food and childhood. That was life, that was wonderful! Then they would all go and loaf in the grass and Mitzi would throw off her frock and lie half naked, browning her sleek shining body, while Julius Damjancsics thrummed his mandolin and they all murmured songs. Ah, such music! She loved it. She had a dimple behind each shoulder, a rare thing, very beautiful. In the cool of the evening there would be dancing, and they would be at Dreimarkstein in time to see the fireworks go up from the Prater—he liked fireworks, lovely. Or to the trotting races, they might go and win some more money, for when luck was on you the fancy could never deceive; beautiful horses, he loved horses. Or to the baths at Gänsehaufel—the things one could do with a little money! But there was no longer any Mitzi, she had gone with Julius Damjancsics. Gone wife, gone friend; there were no more journeys now. But a man with three hundred and fifty shillings need never lack companions, there was a lot of friendship in three hundred and fifty shillings. But that Mitzi—she was very beautiful, that little Mitzi.

So the day wore on and the evening came and the Prater began to sparkle with the lights of its many booths and cafés, to throb with its much music, for youth was gallant and gay and there was love and money in the world. It was the hour at last. Hans had been sewn up in the tiger's skin. Now he crouched in a corner of a shuttered cage, alone, trembling in darkness, seeing no one and seen of none. There was a door in the side of his cage that led into a large empty lighted cage, and beyond that was another like his own in which walked a lion. At a certain moment the doors of the end cages would be opened and he would have to go into that central cage and face that other beast. But no, he could not, he was limp with fear. To the stricken man came the excited voices of the people coming in to witness his calamity, and the harsh tones of the trumpeting band playing in pandemonium outside on the platform, where there was a large poster of a combat between a tiger and a lion. Hans recalled that the lion's teeth were buried in the tiger's belly amid the gushing blood, and it seemed that his very heart violently cried: "No! No! Let me out!"

Beating upon the walls of his cage he gasped: "In Christ's name, let me out!" but nobody heeded, no one replied, and although he tore at his tiger-skin, his paws were too cumbersome for him to free himself. He was in a trap, he knew now he had been trapped. For an eternal anguishing time the clamour went on, then that dreadful side door which led into the central cage slid quietly open. Hans saw that this cage was yet empty, the lion's door was still closed, he was to be the first to enter. But he averted his eyes, he lay in the corner of his trap and would not budge from it. Almighty Heaven! was he going to sacrifice himself for a few pitiful pieces of silver that he had never seen and never would see? He was not fit to do it, he was an old man, even his wife, Mitzi, had left him for another man—did they not know that! And all day long he had been unwell, sick as a dog. As he lay in his corner, refusing to budge and sweating most intensely, a sharp iron spear came through the bars and pricked him savagely in the behind. With a yell he leaped up, trying to snatch the spear. He would use it, it would save him—but he could not grasp it with his giant paws. Then came bars of red-hot iron searing him, and more spears; he was driven screaming into the central cage. The door closed behind him and he was left alone behind those terrible bars with a vast audience gazing at him. Then, ah then, in a frenzy, an epilepsy of fear, he dashed himself so violently against the bars that the crowd was spellbound. The band played riotously on, drowning his human cries. The other side door slid open, there was silence in that other cage, but he dared not turn to meet whatever was there; he crouched half swooning, until he caught sight of a face in the audience that he knew. Wonder of God! It was Mitzi, she herself! Oh, but there was something to fight for now and he turned resolutely. As he did so, there was a titter in the audience that surged into general laughter—the lion had come into the cage. Truly, it was a cadaverous lion. Without the least display of ferocity or fear it stepped quietly into that cage and fixed its strong eyes upon the eyes of its enemy. Not a leap did it make, not a roar did it give, it padded forwards quietly, and the tiger retreated before it. Thus they circled and circled round the cage. Would that mocking laughter never stop?

God! Hans could bear it no longer, he turned and faced the lion, in appearance bold, though trembling in his soul. The lion paused too.

"*Pater noster qui es in coelis,*"[2] Hans gasped involuntarily.

To his unspeakable astonishment he heard the lion answer:

"*Et ne nos inducas in tentationem. Sed libera nos a malo.*"[3]

In an incredible flash Hans realized that the lion also was a spurious creature like himself; his fears vanished, he knew now the part he had to play, and he hurled himself upon the lion, howling:

"Brrr-o-o-owh! Ookah, pookah, boddle, oddle, moddle, miowh!"

Over they rolled, lion and tiger, together, and the onlookers shook with mirth.

"Not so rough, brother!" cried a voice from inside the lion, and the tones struck a strange echo in the mind of Hans Siebenhaar. They disengaged and stood up on all fours facing each other. From the moment's silence that ensued there issued a piercing cry of fear from a woman in the audience. Hans turned. The lion turned. It was Mitzi, shrieking: "Julius! Watch out!" Hans's throbbing mind caught at that fatal name, Julius. By all the gods, was it possible! Heaven and hell, he would tear the heart out of *that* lion! *Not so rough, brother!* Ha, ha, he knew it now, that voice! Ho, ho! and with a cruel leap he jumped with his heels savagely in the middle of the lion's back, the back of Julius Damjancsics, thief of Mitzi, the beloved of Hans, and down sank the lion with the tiger tearing at its throat as fearfully as any beast of the jungle. Ah, but how the people applauded; this was good in spite of the deception! They had paid to see a real lion and a real tiger contending, and they felt defrauded, insulted; but this was good, yes, it was very comical, good, good. When they noticed a man's hand appear outside the flapping paw of the tiger their joy was unbounded.

"Tear him!" they cried, as one cries to a hound with a fox. "Ha, ha, tear him!" And Hans's loosened hand ripped up the seam in the lion's neck, and his hand went searching within the rent for a throat to tear. At once the teeth of Julius ground themselves upon it; in a trice Hans's smallest finger was gone, severed. But Hans never uttered a cry, he gripped

---

2. The first line of the Lord's Prayer: "Our Father who art in Heaven."

3. The next two lines of the prayer: "And lead us not into temptation, but deliver us from evil."

the throat with his wounded hand and crushed everlastingly upon it, moment after moment, until he knew that Julius Damjancsics was gone, and for ever, to hell or glory, whatever destiny had devised for him. The lion moved no more, it lay on its back with its hind legs crooked preposterously, it forelegs outspread like one crucified. The people hushed their laughter as Hans slunk trembling and sweating from that droll oaf wrapped in a lion's skin. He was afraid of it now and he crawled on all fours to the bars of the cage. The thing behind him was awfully still. The onlookers were still. They were strange, as strange as death. Mitzi was there, craning forward, her face as pale as snow. Hans caught hold of the cage bars and lifted himself to his feet. The onlookers could hear wild tormenting sobs bursting from the throat of the tiger as it hung ridiculously there. The door of Hans's first cage now slid open again, it was finished, he could go. But Hans did not go. □

DISCUSSION

1. A recurring theme in modern literature is that of "assuming the mask": when a person disguises or covers his face in any way, his civilized veneer disappears and his personality becomes more primitive, more savage. Explain how this theme applies to "Silver Circus."

2. (a) Can this story be legitimately criticized for overuse of coincidence?

(b) What is the significance of the title?

3. One reader has called this "a strangely powerful story." Do you agree? Its strangeness is evident, but in what does its power lie?

4. "The Phoenix" and "Silver Circus" are similar in that the former uses a bird and a menagerie background, the latter, "animals" and a circus background to reveal various aspects of human nature. Compare the two with regard to these aspects and the way in which their backgrounds and "nonhuman" characters function.

WRITING

1. Prepare a dialogue between Hans and Mitzi, his wife, after the killing of Julius.

2. Write your own story about someone who "assumes the mask."

MISS PINKERTON'S APOCALYPSE

by Muriel Spark

ONE evening, a damp one in February, something flew in at the window. Miss Laura Pinkerton, who was doing something innocent to the fire, heard a faint throbbing noise overhead. On looking up, "George! come here! come quickly!"

George Lake came in at once, though sullenly because of their quarrel, eating a sandwich from the kitchen. He looked up at the noise then sat down immediately.

From this point onward their story comes in two versions, his and hers. But they agree as to the main facts; they agree that it was a small round flattish object, and that it flew.

"It's a flying object of some sort," whispered George eventually.

"It's a saucer," said Miss Pinkerton, keen and loud, "an antique piece. You can tell by the shape."

From the book *The Go-Away Bird and Other Stories* by Muriel Spark. Reprinted by permission of J. B. Lippincott Company and Harold Ober Associates Incorporated.

"It can't be an antique, that's absolutely certain," George said.

He ought to have been more tactful, and would have been, but for the stress of the moment. Of course it set Miss Pinkerton off, she being in the right.

"I know my facts," she stated as usual, "I should hope I know my facts. I've been in antique china for twenty-three years in the autumn," which was true, and George knew it.

The little saucer was cavorting round the lamp.

"It seems to be attracted by the light," George remarked, as one might distinguish a moth.

Promptly, it made as if to dive dangerously at George's head. He ducked, and Miss Pinkerton backed against the wall. As the dish tilted on its side, skimming George's shoulder, Miss Pinkerton could see inside it.

"The thing might be radio-active. It might be dangerous." George was breathless. The saucer had climbed, was circling high above his head, and now made for him again, but missed.

"It is not radio-active," said Miss Pinkerton, "it is Spode."

"Don't be so damn silly," George replied, under the stress of the occasion.

"All right, very well," said Miss Pinkerton, "it is not Spode. I suppose you are the expert, George, I suppose you know best. I was only judging by the pattern. After the best part of a lifetime in china—"

"It must be a forgery," George said unfortunately. For, unfortunately, something familiar and abrasive in Miss Pinkerton's speech began to grind within him. Also, he was afraid of the saucer.

It had taken a stately turn, following the picture rail in a steady career round the room.

"Forgery, ha!" said Miss Pinkerton. She was out of the room like a shot, and in again carrying a pair of steps.

"I will examine the mark," said she, pointing intensely at the saucer. "Where are my glasses?"

Obligingly, the saucer settled in a corner; it hung like a spider a few inches from the ceiling. Miss Pinkerton adjusted the steps. With her glasses on she was almost her sunny self again, she was ceremonious and expert.

"Don't touch it, don't go near it!" George pushed her aside and grabbed the steps, knocking over a blue glass bowl, a Dresden figure, a vase of flowers and a decanter of sherry; like a bull in a china shop, as Miss Pinkerton exclaimed. But she was determined, and struggled to reclaim the steps.

"Laura!" he said desperately. "I believe it is Spode. I take your word."

The saucer then flew out of the window.

They acted quickly. They telephoned to the local paper. A reporter would come right away. Meanwhile, Miss Pinkerton telephoned to her two scientific friends—at least, one was interested in psychic research and the other was an electrician. But she got no reply from either. George had leaned out of the window, scanning the rooftops and the night sky. He had leaned out of the back windows, had tried all the lights and the wireless. These things were as usual.

The news man arrived, accompanied by a photographer.

"There's nothing to photograph," said Miss Pinkerton excitably. "It went away."

"We could take a few shots of the actual spot," the man explained.

Miss Pinkerton looked anxiously at the result of George and the steps.

"The place is a wreck."

Sherry from the decanter was still dripping from the sideboard.

"I'd better clear the place up. George, help me!" She fluttered nervously, and started to pack the fire with small coals.

"No, leave everything as it is," the reporter advised her. "Did the apparition make this mess?"

George and Miss Pinkerton spoke together.

"Well, indirectly," said George.

"It wasn't an apparition," said Miss Pinkerton.

The reporter settled on the nearest chair, poising his pencil and asking, "Do you mind if I take notes?"

"Would you mind sitting over here?" said Miss Pinkerton. "I don't use the Queen Annes normally. They are very frail pieces."

The reporter rose as if stung, then perched on a table which Miss Pinkerton looked at uneasily.

"You see, I'm in antiques," she rattled on, for the affair was beginning to tell on her, as George told himself. In fact he sized up that she was done for; his irritation abated, his confidence came flooding back.

"Now, Laura, sit down and take it easy." Solicitously he pushed her into an easy chair.

"She's overwrought," he informed the pressmen in an audible undertone.

"You say this object actually flew in this window?" suggested the reporter.

"That is correct," said George.

The camera-man trained his apparatus on the window.

"And you were both here at the time?"

"No," Miss Pinkerton said. "Mr. Lake was in the kitchen and I called out, of course. But he didn't see inside the bowl, only the outside, underneath where the manufacturer's mark is. I saw the pattern so I got the steps to make sure. That's how Mr. Lake knocked my things over. I saw inside."

"I am going to say something," said George.

The men looked hopefully towards him. After a pause, George continued, "Let us begin at the beginning."

"Right," said the reporter, breezing up.

"It was like this," George said. "I came straight in when Miss Pinkerton screamed, and there was a white convex disc, you realize, floating around up there."

The reporter contemplated the spot indicated by George.

"It was making a hell of a racket like a cat purring," George told him.

"Any idea what it really was?" the reporter enquired.

George took his time to answer. "Well, yes," he said, "and no."

"Spode ware," said Miss Pinkerton.

George continued, "I'm not up in these things. I'm extremely sceptical as a rule. This was a new experience to me."

"That's just it," said Miss Pinkerton. "Personally, I've been in china for twenty-three years. I recognised the thing immediately."

The reporter scribbled and enquired, "These flying discs appear frequently in China?"

"It was a saucer. I've never seen one flying before," Miss Pinkerton explained.

"I am going to ask a question," George said.

Miss Pinkerton continued, "Mr. Lake is an art framer. He handles old canvases but next to no antiques."

"I am going to ask. Are you telling the story or am I?" George said.

"Perhaps Mr. Lake's account first and then the lady's," the reporter ventured.

Miss Pinkerton subsided crossly while he turned to George.

"Was the object attached to anything? No wires or anything? I mean, someone couldn't have been having a joke or something?"

George gave a decent moment to the possibility.

"No," he then said. "It struck me, in fact, that there was some sort of Mind behind it, operating from outer space. It tried to attack me, in fact."

"Really, how was that?"

"Mr. Lake was not attacked," Miss Pinkerton stated. "There was no danger at all. I saw the expression on the pilot's face. He was having a game with Mr. Lake, grinning all over his face."

"Pilot?" said George. "What are you talking about—pilot!"

Miss Pinkerton sighed. "A tiny man half the size of my finger," she declared. "He sat on a tiny stool. He held the little tiny steering-wheel with one hand and waved with the other. Because, there was something like a sewing-machine fixed near the rim, and he worked the tiny treadle with his foot. Mr. Lake was not attacked."

"Don't be so damn silly," said George.

"You don't mean this?" the reporter asked her with scrutiny.

"Of course I do."

"I would like to know something," George demanded.

"You only saw the under side of the saucer, George."

"You said nothing about any pilot at the time," said George. "I saw no pilot."

"Mr. Lake got a fright when the saucer came at him. If he hadn't been dodging he would have seen for himself."

"You mentioned no pilot," said George. "Be reasonable."

"I had no chance," said she. She appealed to the cameraman. "You see, I know what I'm talking about. Mr. Lake thought he knew better, however. Mr. Lake said, 'It's a forgery.' If there's one thing I do know, it's china."

"It would be most unlikely," said George to the reporter. "A steering-wheel and a treadle machine these days, can you credit it?"

"The man would have fallen out," the cameraman reflected.

"I must say," said the reporter, "that I favour Mr. Lake's long-range theory. The lady may have been subject to some hallucination, after the shock of the saucer."

"Quite," said George. He whispered something to the photographer. "Women!" Miss Pinkerton heard him breathe.

The reporter heard him also. He gave a friendly laugh. "Shall we continue with Mr. Lake's account, and then see what we can make of both stories?"

But Miss Pinkerton had come to a rapid decision. She began to display a mood hitherto unknown to George. Leaning back, she gave way to a weak and artless giggling. Her hand fluttered prettily as she spoke between gurgles of mirth. "Oh, what a mess! What an evening! We aren't accustomed to drink, you see, and now oh dear, oh dear!"

"Are you all right, Laura?" George enquired severely.

"Yes, yes, yes," said Miss Pinkerton, drowsy and amiable. "We really oughtn't have done this, George. Bringing these gentlemen out. But I can't keep it up, George. Oh dear, it's been fun though."

She was away into her giggles again. George looked bewildered. Then he looked suspicious.

"It's definitely the effect of this extraordinary phenomenon," George said firmly to the Press.

"It was my fault, all my fault," spluttered Miss Pinkerton.

The reporter looked at his watch. "I can quite definitely say you saw a flying object?" he asked. "And that you were both put out by it?"

"Put down that it was a small, round, flattish object. We both agree to that," George said.

A spurt of delight arose from Miss Pinkerton again. "Women, you know! It always comes down to women in the finish," she told them. "We had a couple of drinks."

"Mr. Lake had rather more than I did," she added triumphantly.

"I assure you," said George to the reporter.

"We might be fined for bringing the Press along, George. It might be an offence," she put in.

"I assure you," George insisted to the photographer, "that we had a flying saucer less than an hour ago in this room."

Miss Pinkerton giggled.

The reporter looked round the room with new eyes; and with the air of one to whom to understand all is to forgive all, he folded his notebook. The camera-man stared at the pool of sherry, the overturned flowers, the broken glass and china. He packed up his camera, and they went away.

George gave out the tale to his regular customers. He gave both versions, appealing to their reason to choose. Further up the road at her corner shop, Miss Pinkerton smiled tolerantly when questioned. "Flying saucer? George is very artistic," she would say, "and allowances must be made for imaginative folk." Sometimes she added that the evening had been a memorable one, "Quite a party!"

It caused a certain amount of tittering in the neighbourhood. George felt this; but otherwise, the affair made no difference between them. Personally, I believe the story, with a preference for Miss Pinkerton's original version. She is a neighbour of mine. I have reason to believe this version because, not long afterwards, I too received a flying visitation from a saucer. The little pilot, in my case, was shy and inquisitive. He pedalled with all his might. My saucer was Royal Worcester, fake or not I can't say. □

DISCUSSION

1. This story is a spoof that makes its point by interpreting "flying saucer" literally. But it also spoofs some basic human traits. What are they?

2. Why does Miss Pinkerton tell the newspapermen that she and Mr. Lake had been drinking?

3. What *is* Miss Pinkerton's apocalypse?

4. What effect does the speaker's confession in the final paragraph have on the story as a whole?

5. According to Samuel Taylor Coleridge, the enjoyment of a work of imaginative literature depends upon the reader's "willing suspension of disbelief." Both "Silver Circus" and "Miss Pinkerton's Apocalypse" require this suspension.

(a) Which of the two requires it to a greater extent? Why?

(b) How do the two stories differ in purpose?

(c) To what extent are their fantastic elements necessary to achieving that purpose?

WRITING

1. Write either (or both) of two television interviews, one with Miss Pinkerton and the other with George Lake.

2. Try writing your own flying saucer story or poem, or spoofing some other natural or man-made phenomenon, such as sunspots or remote control TV.

THE MACHINE STOPS

by E. M. Forster

EDMUND KAPP, LONDON

I. THE AIR-SHIP

IMAGINE, if you can, a small room, hexagonal in shape, like the cell of a bee. It is lighted neither by window nor by lamp, yet it is filled with a soft radiance. There are no apertures for ventilation, yet the air is fresh. There are no musical instruments, and yet, at the moment that my meditation opens, this room is throbbing with melodious sounds. An arm-chair is in the center, by its side a reading-desk—that is all the furniture. And in the arm-chair there sits a swaddled lump of flesh—a woman, about five feet high, with a face as white as a fungus. It is to her that the little room belongs.

An electric bell rang.

The woman touched a switch and the music was silent.

"I suppose I must see who it is," she thought, and set her chair in motion. The chair, like the music, was worked by machinery, and it rolled her to the other side of the room, where the bell still rang importunately.

"Who is it?" she called. Her voice was irritable, for she had been interrupted often since the music began. She knew several thousand people; in certain directions human intercourse had advanced enormously.

But when she listened into the receiver, her white face wrinkled into smiles, and she said:

"Very well. Let us talk, I will isolate myself. I do not expect anything important will happen for the next five minutes—for I can give you fully five minutes, Kuno. Then I must deliver my lecture on 'Music during the Australian Period.'"

She touched the isolation knob, so that no one else could speak to her. Then she touched the lighting apparatus, and the little room was plunged into darkness.

"Be quick!" she called, her irritation returning. "Be quick, Kuno; here I am in the dark wasting my time."

But it was fully fifteen seconds before the round plate that she held in her hands began to glow. A faint blue light shot across it, darkening to purple, and presently she could see the image of her son, who lived on the other side of the earth, and he could see her.

"Kuno, how slow you are."

He smiled gravely.

"I really believe you enjoy dawdling."

"I have called you before, mother, but you were always busy or isolated. I have something particular to say."

"What is it, dearest boy? Be quick. Why could you not send it by pneumatic post?"

"Because I prefer saying such a thing. I want—"

"Well?"

"I want you to come and see me."

Vashti watched his face in the blue plate.

"But I can see you!" she exclaimed. "What more do you want?"

"I want to see you not through the Machine," said Kuno. "I want to speak to you not through the wearisome Machine."

"Oh, hush!" said his mother, vaguely shocked. "You mustn't say anything against the Machine."

"Why not?"

"One mustn't."

"You talk as if a god had made the Machine," cried the other. "I believe that you pray to it when you are unhappy. Men made it, do not forget that. Great men, but men. The Machine is much, but it is not everything. I see something like you in this plate, but I do not see you. I hear something like you through this telephone, but I do not hear you. That is why I want you to come. Come and stop with me. Pay me a visit, so that we can meet face to face, and talk about the hopes that are in my mind."

She replied that she could scarcely spare the time for a visit.

"The air-ship barely takes two days to fly between me and you."

"I dislike air-ships."

"Why?"

"I dislike seeing the horrible brown earth, and the sea, and the stars when it is dark. I get no ideas in an air-ship."

"I do not get them anywhere else."

"What kind of ideas can the air give you?"

He paused for an instant.

"Do you not know four big stars that form an oblong, and three stars close together in the middle of the oblong, and hanging from these stars, three other stars?"

"No, I do not. I dislike the stars. But did they give you an idea? How interesting; tell me."

"I had an idea that they were like a man."

"I do not understand."

"The four big stars are the man's shoulders and his knees. The three stars in the middle are like the belts that men wore once, and the three stars hanging are like a sword."

"A sword?"

"Men carried swords about with them, to kill animals and other men."

"It does not strike me as a very good idea, but it is certainly original. When did it come to you first?"

"In the air-ship—" He broke off and she fancied that he looked sad. She could not be sure, for the Machine did not transmit nuances of expression. It only gave a general idea of people—an idea that was good enough for all practical purposes, Vashti thought. The imponderable bloom, declared by a discredited philosophy to be the actual essence of intercourse, was rightly ignored by the Machine, just as the imponderable bloom of the grape was ignored by the manufacturers of artificial fruit. Something "good enough" had long since been accepted by our race.

"The truth is," he continued, "that I want to see these stars again. They are curious stars. I want to see them not from the air-ship, but from the surface of the earth, as our ancestors did, thousands of years ago. I want to visit the surface of the earth."

She was shocked again.

"Mother, you must come, if only to explain to me what is the harm of visiting the surface of the earth."

"No harm," she replied, controlling herself. "But no advantage. The surface of the earth is only dust and mud, no life remains on it, and you would need a respirator, or the cold of the outer air would kill you. One dies immediately in the outer air."

"I know; of course I shall take all precautions."

"And besides—"

"Well?"

She considered, and chose her words with care. Her son had a queer temper, and she wished to dissuade him from the expedition.

"It is contrary to the spirit of the age," she asserted.

"Do you mean by that, contrary to the Machine?"

"In a sense, but—"

His image in the blue plate faded.

"Kuno!"

He had isolated himself.

For a moment Vashti felt lonely.

Then she generated the light, and the sight of her room, flooded with radiance and studded with electric buttons, revived her. There were buttons and switches everywhere—buttons to call for food, for music, for clothing. There was the hot-bath button, by pressure of which a basin of (imitation) marble rose out of the floor, filled to the brim with a warm deodorized liquid. There was the cold-bath button. There was the button that produced literature. And there were of course the buttons by which she communicated with her friends. The room, though it contained nothing, was in touch with all that she cared for in the world.

Vashti's next move was to turn off the isolation-switch, and all the accumulations of the last three minutes burst upon her. The room was filled with the noise of bells, and speaking-tubes. What was the new food like? Could she recommend it? Had she had any ideas lately? Might one tell her one's own ideas? Would she make an engagement to visit the public nurseries at an early date?—say this day month.

To most of these questions she replied with irritation—a growing quality in that accelerated age. She said that the new food was horrible. That she could not visit the public nurseries through press of engagements. That she had no ideas of her own but had just been told one—that four stars and three in the middle were like a man: she doubted there was much in it. Then she switched off her correspondents, for it was time to deliver her lecture on Australian music.

The clumsy system of public gatherings had been long since abandoned; neither Vashti nor her audience stirred from their rooms. Seated in her armchair she spoke, while they in their arm-chairs heard her, fairly well, and saw her, fairly well. She opened with a humorous account of music in the pre-Mongolian epoch, and went on to describe the great outburst of song that followed the Chinese conquest. Remote and primeval as were the methods of I-San-So and the Brisbane school, she yet felt (she said) that study of them might repay the musician of today: they had freshness; they had, above all, ideas.

Her lecture, which lasted ten minutes, was well received, and at its conclusion she and many of her audience listened to a lecture on the sea; there were ideas to be got from the sea; the speaker had donned a respirator and visited it lately. Then she fed, talked to many friends, had a bath, talked again, and summoned her bed.

The bed was not to her liking. It was too large, and she had a feeling for a small bed. Complaint was useless, for beds were of the same dimension all over the world, and to have had an alternative size would have involved vast alterations in the Machine. Vashti isolated herself—it was necessary, for neither day nor night existed under the ground—and reviewed all that had happened since she had summoned the bed last. Ideas? Scarcely any. Events—was Kuno's invitation an event?

By her side, on the little reading-desk, was a survival from the ages of litter—one book. This was the Book of the Machine. In it were instructions against every possible contingency. If she was hot or cold or dyspeptic or at loss for a word, she went to the book, and it told her which button to press. The Central Committee published it. In accordance with a growing habit, it was richly bound.

Sitting up in the bed, she took it reverently in her hands. She glanced round the glowing room as if someone might be watching her. Then, half ashamed, half joyful, she murmured "O Machine! O Machine!" and raised the volume to her lips. Thrice she kissed it, thrice inclined her head, thrice she felt the delirium of acquiescence. Her ritual performed, she turned to page 1367, which gave the times of the departure of the air-ships from the island in the southern hemisphere, under whose soil she lived, to the island in the northern hemisphere, whereunder lived her son.

She thought, "I have not the time."

She made the room dark and slept; she awoke and made the room light; she ate and exchanged ideas with her friends, and listened to music and attended lectures; she made the room dark and slept. Above her, beneath her, and around her, the Machine hummed eternally; she did not notice the noise, for she had been born with it in her ears. The earth, carrying her, hummed as it sped through silence, turning her now to the invisible sun, now to the invisible stars. She awoke and made the room light.

"Kuno!"

"I will not talk to you," he answered, "until you come."

"Have you been on the surface of the earth since we spoke last?"

His image faded.

Again she consulted the book. She became very nervous and lay back in her chair palpitating. Think of her as without teeth or hair. Presently she directed the chair to the wall, and pressed an unfamiliar button. The wall swung apart slowly. Through the opening she saw a tunnel that curved slightly, so that its goal was not visible. Should she go to see her son, here was the beginning of the journey.

Of course she knew all about the communication-system. There was nothing mysterious in it. She would summon a car and it would fly with her down the tunnel until it reached the lift that communicated with the air-ship station: the system had been in use for many, many years, long before the universal establishment of the Machine. And of course she had studied the civilization that had immediately preceded her own—the civilization that had mistaken the functions of the system, and had used it for bringing people to things, instead of for bringing things to people. Those funny old days, when men went for change of air instead of changing the air in their rooms! And yet—she was frightened of the tunnel: she had not seen it since her last child was born. It curved—but not quite as she remembered; it was brilliant—but not quite as brilliant as a lecturer had suggested. Vashti was seized with the terrors of direct experience. She shrank back into the room, and the wall closed up again.

"Kuno," she said, "I cannot come to see you. I am not well."

Immediately an enormous apparatus fell on to her out of the ceiling, a thermometer was automatically inserted between her lips, a stethoscope was automatically laid upon her heart. She lay powerless. Cool pads soothed her forehead. Kuno had telegraphed to her doctor.

So the human passions still blundered up and down in the Machine. Vashti drank the medicine that the doctor projected into her mouth, and the machinery retired into the ceiling. The voice of Kuno was heard asking how she felt.

"Better." Then with irritation: "But why do you not come to me instead?"

"Because I cannot leave this place."

"Why?"

"Because, any moment, something tremendous may happen."

"Have you been on the surface of the earth yet?"

"Not yet."

"Then what is it?"

"I will not tell you through the Machine."

She resumed her life.

But she thought of Kuno as a baby, his birth, his removal to the public nurseries, her one visit to him there, his visits to her—visits which stopped when the Machine had assigned him a room on the other side of the earth. "Parents, duties of," said the Book of the Machine, "cease at the moment of birth. P. 422327483." True, but there was something special about Kuno—indeed there had been something special about all her children—and, after all, she must brave the journey if he desired it. And "something tremendous might happen." What did that mean? The nonsense of a youthful man, no doubt, but she must go. Again she pressed the unfamiliar button, again the wall swung back, and she saw the tunnel that curved out of sight. Clasping the Book, she rose, tottered on to the platform, and summoned the car. Her room closed behind her: the journey to the northern hemisphere had begun.

Of course it was perfectly easy. The car approached and in it she found arm-chairs exactly like her own. When she signalled, it stopped, and she tottered into the lift. One other passenger was in the lift, the first fellow creature she had seen face to face for months. Few travelled in these days, for, thanks to the advance of science, the earth was exactly alike all over. Rapid intercourse, from which the previous civilization had hoped so much, had ended by defeating itself. What was the good of going to Pekin when it was just like Shrewsbury? Why return to Shrewsbury when it would be just like Pekin? Men seldom moved their bodies; all unrest was concentrated in the soul.

The air-ship service was a relic from the former age. It was kept up, because it was easier to keep it up than to stop it or to diminish it, but it now far exceeded the wants of the population. Vessel after vessel would rise from the vomitories of Rye or of Christchurch (I use the antique names), would sail into the crowded sky, and would draw up at the wharves of the south—empty. So nicely adjusted was the system, so independent of meteorology, that the sky, whether calm or cloudy, resembled a vast kaleidoscope whereon the same patterns periodically recurred. The ship on which Vashti sailed started now at sunset, now at dawn. But always, as it passed above Rheims, it would neighbour the ship that served between Helsingfors and the Brazils, and, every time it surmounted the Alps, the fleet of Palermo would cross its track behind. Night and day, wind and storm, tide and earthquake, impeded man no longer. He had harnessed Leviathan. All the old literature, with its praise of Nature, and its fear of Nature, rang false as the prattle of a child.

Yet as Vashti saw the vast flank of the ship, stained with exposure to the outer air, her horror of direct experience returned. It was not quite like the air-ship in the cinematophote. For one thing it smelt—not strongly or unpleasantly, but it did smell, and with her eyes shut she should have known that a new thing was close to her. Then she had to walk to it from the lift, had to submit to glances from the other passengers. The man in front dropped his Book—no great matter, but it disquieted them all. In the rooms, if the Book was dropped, the floor raised it mechanically, but the gangway to the air-ship was not so prepared, and the sacred volume lay motionless. They stopped—the thing was unforeseen—and the man, instead of picking up his property, felt the muscles of his arm to see how they had failed him. Then some one actually said with direct utterance: "We shall be late"—and they trooped on board, Vashti treading on the pages as she did so.

Inside, her anxiety increased. The arrangements were old-fashioned and rough. There was even a female attendant, to whom she would have to announce her wants during the voyage. Of course a revolving platform ran the length of the boat, but she was expected to walk from it to her cabin. Some cabins were better than others, and she did not get the best. She thought the attendant had been unfair, and spasms of rage shook her. The glass valves had closed, she could not go back. She saw, at the end of the vestibule, the lift in which she had ascended going quietly up and down, empty. Beneath those corridors of shining tiles were rooms, tier below tier, reaching far into the earth, and in each room there sat a human being, eating, or sleeping, or producing ideas. And buried deep in the hive was her own room. Vashti was afraid.

"O Machine! O Machine!" she murmured, and caressed her Book, and was comforted.

Then the sides of the vestibule seemed to melt together, as do the passages that we see in dreams, the lift vanished, the Book that had been dropped slid to the left and vanished, polished tiles rushed by like a stream of water, there was a slight jar, and the air-ship, issuing from its tunnel, soared above the waters of a tropical ocean.

It was night. For a moment she saw the coast of Sumatra edged by the phosphorescence of waves, and crowned by lighthouses, still sending forth their disregarded beams. These also vanished, and only the stars distracted her. They were not motionless, but swayed to and fro above her head, thronging out of one skylight into another, as if the universe and not the air-ship was careening. And, as often happens on clear nights, they seemed now to be in perspective, now on a plane; now piled tier beyond tier into the infinite heavens, now concealing infinity, a roof limiting forever the visions of men. In either case they seemed intolerable. "Are we to travel in the dark?" called the passengers angrily, and the attendant, who had been careless, generated the light, and pulled down the blinds of pliable metal. When the air-ships had been built, the desire to look direct at things still lingered in the world. Hence the extraordinary number of skylights and windows, and the proportionate discomfort to those who were civilized and refined. Even in Vashti's cabin one star peeped through a flaw in the blind, and after a few hours' uneasy slumber, she was disturbed by an unfamiliar glow, which was the dawn.

Quick as the ship had sped westwards, the earth had rolled eastwards quicker still, and had dragged back Vashti and her companions towards the sun. Science could prolong the night, but only for a little, and those high hopes of neutralizing the earth's diurnal revolution had passed, together with hopes that were possibly higher. To "keep pace with the sun," or even to outstrip it, had been the aim of the civilization preceding this. Racing aeroplanes had been built for the purpose, capable of enormous speed, and steered by the greatest intellects of the epoch. Round the globe they went, round and round, westward, westward, round and round, amidst humanity's applause. In vain. The Globe went eastward quicker still, horrible accidents occurred, and the Committee of the Machine, at the time rising into prominence, declared the pursuit illegal, unmechanical, and punishable by Homelessness.

Of Homelessness more will be said later.

Doubtless the Committee was right. Yet the attempt to "defeat the sun" aroused the last common interest that our race experienced about the heavenly bodies, or indeed about anything. It was the last time that men were compacted by thinking of a power outside the world. The sun had conquered, yet it was the end of his spiritual dominion. Dawn, midday, twilight, the zodiacal path, touched neither men's lives nor their hearts, and science retreated into the ground, to concentrate herself upon problems that she was certain of solving.

So when Vashti found her cabin invaded by a rosy finger of light, she was annoyed, and tried to adjust the blind. But the blind flew up altogether, and she saw through the skylight small pink clouds, swaying against a background of blue, and as the sun crept higher, its radiance entered direct, brimming down the wall, like a golden sea. It rose and fell with the air-ship's motion, just as waves rise and fall, but it advanced steadily, as a tide advances. Unless she was careful, it would strike her face. A spasm of horror shook her and she rang for the attendant. The attendant too was horrified, but she could do nothing; it was not her place to mend the blind. She could only suggest that the lady should change her cabin, which she accordingly prepared to do.

People were almost exactly alike all over the world, but the attendant of the air-ship, perhaps owing to her exceptional duties, had grown a little out of the common. She had often to address passengers with direct speech, and this had given her a certain roughness and originality of manner. When Vashti swerved away from the sunbeams with a cry, she behaved barbarically—she put out her hand to steady her.

"How dare you!" exclaimed the passenger. "You forget yourself!"

The woman was confused, and apologized for not having let her fall. People never touched one another. The custom had become obsolete, owing to the Machine.

"Where are we now?" asked Vashti haughtily.

"We are over Asia," said the attendant, anxious to be polite.

"Asia?"

"You must excuse my common way of speaking. I have got into the habit of calling places over which I pass by their unmechanical names."

"Oh, I remember Asia. The Mongols came from it."

"Beneath us, in the open air, stood a city that was once called Simla."

"Have you ever heard of the Mongols and of the Brisbane school?"

"No."

"Brisbane also stood in the open air."

"Those mountains to the right—let me show you them." She pushed back a metal blind. The main chain of the Himalayas was revealed. "They were once called the Roof of the World, those mountains."

"What a foolish name!"

"You must remember that, before the dawn of civilization, they seemed to be an impenetrable wall that touched the stars. It was supposed that no one but the gods could exist above their summits. How we have advanced, thanks to the Machine!"

"How we have advanced, thanks to the Machine!" said Vashti.

"How we have advanced, thanks to the Machine!" echoed the passenger who had dropped his Book the night before, and who was standing in the passage.

"And that white stuff in the cracks?—what is it?"

"I have forgotten its name."

"Cover the window, please. These mountains give me no ideas."

The northern aspect of the Himalayas was in deep shadow: on the Indian slope the sun had just prevailed. The forests had been destroyed during the literature epoch for the purpose of making newspaper-pulp, but the snows were awakening to their morning glory, and clouds still hung on the breasts of Kinchinjunga. In the plain were seen the ruins of cities, with diminished rivers creeping by their walls, and by the sides of these were sometimes the signs of vomitories, marking the cities of today. Over the whole prospect air-ships rushed, crossing and intercrossing with incredible aplomb, and rising nonchalantly when they desired to escape the perturbations of the lower atmosphere and to traverse the Roof of the World.

"We have indeed advanced, thanks to the Machine," repeated the attendant, and hid the Himalayas behind a metal blind.

The day dragged wearily forward. The passengers sat each in his cabin, avoiding one another with an almost physical repulsion and longing to be once more under the surface of the earth. There were eight or ten of them, mostly young males, sent out from the public nurseries to inhabit the rooms of those who had died in various parts of the earth. The man who had dropped his Book was on the homeward journey. He had been sent to Sumatra for the purpose of propagating the race. Vashti alone was travelling by her private will.

At midday she took a second glance at the earth. The air-ship was crossing another range of mountains, but she could see little, owing to clouds. Masses of black rock hovered below her, and merged indistinctly into grey. Their shapes were fantastic; one of them resembled a prostrate man.

"No ideas here," murmured Vashti, and hid the Caucasus behind a metal blind.

In the evening she looked again. They were crossing a golden sea, in which lay many small islands and one peninsula.

She repeated, "No ideas here," and hid Greece behind a metal blind.

II. THE MENDING APPARATUS

By a vestibule, by a lift, by a tubular railway, by a platform, by a sliding door—by reversing all the steps of her departure did Vashti arrive at her son's room, which exactly resembled her own. She might well declare that the visit was superfluous. The buttons, the knobs, the reading-desk with the Book, the temperature, the atmosphere, the illumination—all were exactly the same. And if Kuno himself, flesh of her flesh, stood close beside her at last, what profit was there in that? She was too well-bred to shake him by the hand.

Averting her eyes, she spoke as follows:

"Here I am. I have had the most terrible journey and greatly retarded the development of my soul. It is not worth it, Kuno, it is not worth it. My time is too precious. The sunlight almost touched me, and I have met with the rudest people. I can only stop a few minutes. Say what you want to say, and then I must return."

"I have been threatened with Homelessness," said Kuno.

She looked at him now.

"I have been threatened with Homelessness, and I could not tell you such a thing through the Machine."

Homelessness means death. The victim is exposed to the air, which kills him.

"I have been outside since I spoke to you last. The tremendous thing has happened, and they have discovered me."

"But why shouldn't you go outside!" she exclaimed. "It is perfectly legal, perfectly mechanical, to visit the surface of the earth. I have lately been to a lecture on the sea; there is no objection to that; one simply summons a respirator and gets an Egression-permit. It is not the kind of thing that spiritually-minded people do, and I begged you not to do it, but there is no legal objection to it."

"I did not get an Egression-permit."

"Then how did you get out?"

"I found out a way of my own."

The phase conveyed no meaning to her, and he had to repeat it.

"A way of your own?" she whispered. "But that would be wrong."

"Why?"

The question shocked her beyond measure.

"You are beginning to worship the Machine," he said coldly. "You think it irreligious of me to have found out a way of my own. It was just what the Committee thought, when they threatened me with Homelessness."

At this she grew angry. "I worship nothing!" she cried. "I am most advanced. I don't think you irreligious, for there is no such thing as religion left. All the fear and the superstition that existed once have been destroyed by the Machine. I only meant that to find out a way of your own was— Besides, there is no new way out."

"So it is always supposed."

"Except through the vomitories, for which one must have an Egression-permit, it is impossible to get out. The Book says so."

"Well, the Book's wrong, for I have been out on my feet."

For Kuno was possessed of a certain physical strength.

By these days it was a demerit to be muscular. Each infant was examined at birth, and all who promised undue strength were destroyed. Humanitarians may protest, but it would have been no true kindness to let an athlete live; he would never have been happy in that state of life to which the Machine had called him; he would have yearned for trees to climb, rivers to bathe in, meadows and hills against which he might measure his body. Man must be adapted to his surroundings, must he not? In the dawn of the world our weakly must be exposed on Mount Taygetus, in its twilight our strong will suffer euthanasia, that the Machine may progress, that the Machine may progress, that the Machine may progress eternally.

"You know that we have lost the sense of space. We say 'space is annihilated,' but we have annihilated not space, but the sense thereof. We have lost a part of ourselves. I determined to recover it, and I began by walking up and down the platform of the railway outside my room. Up and down, until I was tired, and so did recapture the meaning of 'Near' and 'Far.' 'Near' is a place to which I can get quickly *on my feet,* not a place to which the train or the air-ship will take me quickly. 'Far' is a place to which I cannot get quickly on my feet; the vomitory is 'far,' though I could be there in thirty-eight seconds by summoning the train. Man is the measure. That was my first lesson. Man's feet are the measure for distance, his hands are the measure for ownership, his body is the measure for all that is lovable and desirable and strong. Then I went further: it was then that I called to you for the first time, and you would not come.

"This city, as you know, is built deep beneath the surface of the earth, with only the vomitories protruding. Having paced the platform outside my own room, I took the lift to the next platform and paced that also, and so with each in turn, until I came to the topmost, above which begins the earth. All the platforms were exactly alike, and all that I gained by visiting them was to develop my sense of space and my muscles. I think I should have been content with this—it is not a little thing—but as I walked and brooded, it occurred to me that our cities had been built in the days when men still breathed the outer air, and that there had been ventilation shafts for the workmen. I could think of nothing but these ventilation shafts. Had they been destroyed by all the food-tubes and medicine-tubes and music-tubes that the Machine has evolved lately? Or did traces of them remain? One thing was certain. If I came upon them anywhere, it would be in the railway-tunnels of the topmost story. Everywhere else, all space was accounted for.

"I am telling my story quickly, but don't think that I was not a coward or that your answers never depressed me. It is not the proper thing, it is not mechanical, it is not decent to walk along a railway-tunnel. I did not fear that I might tread upon a live rail and be killed. I feared something far more intangible—doing what was not contemplated by the Machine. Then I said to myself, 'Man is the measure,' and I went, and after many visits I found an opening.

"The tunnels, of course, were lighted. Everything is light, artificial light; darkness is the exception. So when I saw a black gap in the tiles, I knew that it was an exception, and rejoiced. I put in my arm—I could put in no more at first—and waved it round and round in ecstasy. I loosened another tile, and put in my head, and shouted into the darkness: 'I am coming, I shall do it yet,' and my voice reverberated down endless passages. I seemed to hear the spirits of those dead workmen who had returned each evening to the starlight and to their wives, and all the generations who had lived in the open air called back to me, 'You will do it yet, you are coming.'"

He paused, and, absurd as he was, his last words moved her. For Kuno had lately asked to be a father, and his request had been refused by the Committee. His was not a type that the Machine desired to hand on.

"Then a train passed. It brushed by me, but I thrust my head and arms into the hole. I had done enough for one day, so I crawled back to the platform, went down in the lift, and summoned my bed. Ah, what dreams! And again I called you, and again you refused."

She shook her head and said:

"Don't. Don't talk of these terrible things. You make me miserable. You are throwing civilization away."

"But I had got back the sense of space and a man cannot rest then. I determined to get in at the hole and climb the shaft. And so I exercised my arms. Day after day I went through ridiculous movements, until my flesh ached, and I could hang by my hands and hold the pillow of my bed outstretched for many minutes. Then I summoned a respirator, and started.

"It was easy at first. The mortar had somehow rotted, and I soon pushed some more tiles in, and clambered after them into the darkness, and the spirits of the dead comforted me. I don't know what I mean by that. I just say what I felt. I felt, for the first time, that a protest had been lodged against corruption, and that even as the dead were comforting me, so I was comforting the unborn. I felt that humanity existed, and that it existed without clothes. How can I possibly explain this? It was naked, humanity seemed naked, and all these tubes and buttons and machineries neither came into the world with us, nor will they follow us out, nor do they matter supremely while we are here. Had I been strong, I would have torn off every garment I had, and gone out into the outer air unswaddled. But this is not for me, nor perhaps for my generation. I climbed with my respirator and my hygienic clothes and my dietetic tabloids! Better thus than not at all.

"There was a ladder, made of some primeval metal. The light from the railway fell upon its lowest rungs, and I saw that it led straight upwards out of the rubble at the bottom of the shaft. Perhaps our ancestors ran up and down it a dozen times daily, in their building. As I climbed, the rough edges cut through my gloves so that my hands bled. The light helped me for a little, and then came darkness and, worse still, silence which pierced my ears like a sword. The Machine hums! Did you know that? Its hum penetrates our blood, and may even guide our thoughts. Who knows! I was getting beyond its power. Then I thought: 'This silence means that I am doing wrong.' But I heard voices in the silence, and again they strengthened me." He laughed. "I had need of them. The next moment I cracked my head against something."

She sighed.

"I had reached one of those pneumatic stoppers that defend us from the outer air. You may have noticed them on the air-ship. Pitch dark, my feet on the rungs of an invisible ladder, my hands cut; I cannot explain how I lived through this part, but the voices still comforted me, and I felt for fastenings. The stopper, I suppose, was about eight feet across. I passed my hand over it as far as I could reach. It was perfectly smooth. I felt it almost to the centre. Not quite to the centre, for my arm was too short. Then the voice said: 'Jump. It is worth it. There may be a handle in the centre, and you may catch hold of it and so come to us your own way. And if there is no handle, so that you may fall and are dashed to pieces —it is still worth it: you will still come to us your own way.' So I jumped. There was a handle, and—"

He paused. Tears gathered in his mother's eyes. She knew that he was fated. If he did not die to-day he would die to-morrow. There was not room for such a person in the world. And with her pity disgust mingled. She was ashamed at having borne such a son, she who had always been so respectable and so full of ideas. Was he really the little boy to whom she had taught the use of his stops and buttons, and to whom she had given his first lessons in the Book? The very hair that disfigured his lip showed that he was reverting to some savage type. On atavism the Machine can have no mercy.

"There was a handle, and I did catch it. I hung tranced over the darkness and heard the hum of these workings as the last whisper in a dying dream. All the things I had cared about and all the people I had spoken to through tubes appeared infinitely little. Meanwhile the handle revolved. My weight had set something in motion and I span slowly, and then—

"I cannot describe it. I was lying with my face to the sunshine. Blood poured from my nose and ears and I heard a tremendous roaring. The stopper, with me clinging to it, had simply been blown out of the earth, and the air that we make down here was escaping through the vent into the air above. It burst up like a fountain. I crawled back to it—for the upper air hurts—and, as it were, I took great sips from the edge. My respirator had flown goodness knows where, my clothes were torn. I just lay with my lips close to the hole, and I sipped until the bleeding stopped. You can imagine nothing so curious. This hollow in the grass—I will speak of it in a minute,—the sun shining into it, not brilliantly but through marbled clouds,—the peace, the nonchalance, the sense of space, and, brushing my cheek, the roaring fountain of our artificial air! Soon I spied my respirator, bobbing up and down in the current high above my head, and higher still were many air-ships. But no one ever looks out of air-ships, and in any case they could not have picked me up. There I was, stranded. The sun shone a little way down the shaft, and revealed the topmost rung of the ladder, but it was hopeless trying to reach it. I should either have been tossed up again by the escape, or else have fallen in, and died. I could only lie on the grass, sipping and sipping, and from time to time glancing around me.

"I knew that I was in Wessex, for I had taken care to go to a lecture on the subject before starting. Wessex lies above the room in which we are talking now. It was once an important state. Its kings held all the southern coast from the Andredswald to Cornwall, while the Wansdyke protected them on the north, running over the high ground. The lecturer was only concerned with the rise of Wessex, so I do not know how long it remained an international power, nor would the knowledge have assisted me. To tell the truth I could do nothing but laugh, during this part. There was I, with a pneumatic stopper by my side and a respirator bobbing over my head, imprisoned, all three of us, in a grass-grown hollow that was edged with fern."

Then he grew grave again.

"Lucky for me that it was a hollow. For the air began to fall back into it and to fill it as water fills a bowl. I could crawl about. Presently I stood. I breathed a mixture, in which the air that hurts predominated whenever I tried to climb the sides. This was not so bad. I had not lost my tabloids and remained ridiculously cheerful, and as for the Machine, I forgot about it altogether. My one aim now was to get to the top, where the ferns were, and to view whatever objects lay beyond.

"I rushed to the slope. The new air was still too bitter for me and I came rolling back, after a momentary vision of something grey. The sun grew very feeble, and I remembered that he was in Scorpio—I had been to a lecture on that too. If the sun is in Scorpio[1] and you are in Wessex, it means that you must be as quick as you can, or it will get too dark. (This is the first bit of useful information I have ever got from a lecture and I expect it will be the last.) It made me try frantically to breathe the new air and to

1. *Scorpio,* the 8th sign of the zodiac. The sun is in Scorpio from October 24 to November 22.

advance as far as I dared out of my pond. The hollow filled so slowly. At times I thought that the fountain played with less vigour. My respirator seemed to dance nearer the earth; the roar was decreasing."

He broke off.

"I don't think this is interesting you. The rest will interest you even less. There are no ideas in it, and I wish that I had not troubled you to come. We are too different, mother."

She told him to continue.

"It was evening before I climbed the bank. The sun had very nearly slipped out of the sky by this time, and I could not get a good view. You, who have just crossed the Roof of the World, will not want to hear an account of the little hills that I saw—low colourless hills. But to me they were living and the turf that covered them was a skin, under which their muscles rippled, and I felt that those hills had called with incalculable force to men in the past, and that men had loved them. Now they sleep—perhaps forever. They commune with humanity in dreams. Happy the man, happy the woman, who awakes the hills of Wessex. For though they sleep, they will never die."

His voice rose passionately.

"Cannot you see, cannot all your lecturers see, that it is we who are dying, and that down here the only thing that really lives is the Machine? We created the Machine, to do our will, but we cannot make it do our will now. It has robbed us of the sense of space and of the sense of touch, it has blurred every human relation and narrowed down love to a carnal act, it has paralyzed our bodies and our wills, and now it compels us to worship it. The Machine develops—but not on our lines. The Machine proceeds—but not to our goal. We only exist as the blood corpuscles that course through its arteries, and if it could work without us, it would let us die. Oh, I have no remedy—or, at least, only one—to tell men again and again that I have seen the hills of Wessex as Ælfrid saw them when he overthrew the Danes.

"So the sun set. I forgot to mention that a belt of mist lay between my hill and other hills, and that it was the colour of pearl."

He broke off for the second time.

"Go on," said his mother wearily.

He shook his head.

"Go on. Nothing that you say can distress me now. I am hardened."

"I had meant to tell you the rest, but I cannot: I know that I cannot: good-bye."

Vashti stood irresolute. All her nerves were tingling with his blasphemies. But she was also inquisitive.

"This is unfair," she complained. "You have called me across the world to hear your story, and hear it I will. Tell me—as briefly as possible, for this is a disastrous waste of time—tell me how you returned to civilization."

"Oh—that!" he said, starting. "You would like to hear about civilization. Certainly. Had I got to where my respirator fell down?"

"No—but I understand everything now. You put on your respirator and managed to walk along the surface of the earth to a vomitory, and there your conduct was reported to the Central Committee."

"By no means."

He passed his hand over his forehead, as if dispelling some strong impression. Then, resuming his narrative, he warmed to it again.

"My respirator fell about sunset. I had mentioned that the fountain seemed feebler, had I not?"

"Yes."

"About sunset, it let the respirator fall. As I said, I had entirely forgotten about the Machine, and I paid no great attention at the time, being occupied with other things. I had my pool of air, into which I could dip when the outer keenness became intolerable, and which would possibly remain for days, provided that no wind sprang up to disperse it. Not until it was too late, did I realize what the stoppage of the escape implied. You see—the gap in the tunnel had been mended: the Mending Apparatus; the Mending Apparatus was after me.

"One other warning I had, but I neglected it. The sky at night was clearer than it had been in the day, and the moon, which was about half the sky behind the sun, shone into the dell at moments quite brightly. I was in my usual place—on the boundary between the two atmospheres—when I thought I saw something dark move across the bottom of the dell, and vanish into the shaft. In my folly, I ran down. I bent over and listened, and I thought I heard a faint scraping noise in the depths.

"At this—but it was too late—I took alarm. I determined to put on my respirator and to walk right out of the dell. But my respirator had gone. I knew exactly where it had fallen—between the stopper and the aperture—and I could even feel the mark that it had made in the turf. It had gone, and I realized that something evil was at work, and I had better escape to the other air, and, if I must die, die running towards the cloud that had been the colour of a pearl. I never started. Out of the shaft—it is too horrible. A worm, a long white worm, had crawled out of the shaft and was gliding over the moonlit grass.

"I screamed. I did everything that I should not have done. I stamped upon the creature instead of flying from it, and it at once curled round the ankle. Then we fought. The worm let me run all over the dell, but edged up my leg as I ran. 'Help!' I cried. (That part is too awful. It belongs to the part that you will never know.) 'Help!' I cried. (Why cannot we suffer in silence?) 'Help!' I cried. Then my feet were wound together, I fell, I was dragged away from the dear ferns and the living hills, and past the great metal stopper (I can tell you this part), and I thought it might save me again if I caught hold of the handle. It also was enwrapped, it also. Oh, the whole dell was full of the things. They were searching it in all directions, they were denuding it, and the white snouts of others peeped out of the hole, ready if needed. Everything that could be moved they brought—brushwood, bundles of fern, everything, and down we all went intertwined into hell. The last things that I saw, ere the stopper closed after us, were certain stars, and I felt that a man of my sort lived in the sky. For I did fight, I fought till the very end, and it was only my head hitting against the ladder that quieted me. I woke up in this room. The worms had vanished. I was surrounded by artificial air, artificial light, artificial peace, and my friends were calling to me down speaking-tubes to know whether I had come across any new ideas lately."

Here his story ended. Discussion of it was impossible, and Vashti turned to go.

"It will end in Homelessness," she said quietly.

"I wish it would," retorted Kuno.

"The Machine has been most merciful."

"I prefer the mercy of God."

"By that superstitious phrase, do you mean that you could live in the outer air?"

"Yes."

"Have you ever seen, round the vomitories, the bones of those who were extruded after the Great Rebellion?"

"Yes."

"They were left where they perished for our edification. A few crawled away, but they perished, too—who can doubt it? And so with the Homeless of our own day. The surface of the earth supports life no longer."

"Indeed."

"Ferns and a little grass may survive, but all higher forms have perished. Has any air-ship detected them?"

"No."

"Has any lecturer dealt with them?"

"No."

"Then why this obstinacy?"

"Because I have seen them," he exploded.

"Seen *what?*"

"Because I have seen her in the twilight—because she came to my help when I called—because she, too, was entangled by the worms, and, luckier than I, was killed by one of them piercing her throat."

He was mad. Vashti departed, nor, in the troubles that followed, did she ever see his face again.

III. THE HOMELESS

During the years that followed Kuno's escapade two important developments took place in the Machine. On the surface they were revolutionary, but in either case men's minds had been prepared beforehand, and they did but express tendencies that were latent already.

The first of these was the abolition of respirators.

Advanced thinkers, like Vashti, had always held it foolish to visit the surface of the earth. Air-ships might be necessary, but what was the good of going out for mere curiosity and crawling along for a mile or two in a terrestrial motor? The habit was vulgar and perhaps faintly improper: it was unproductive of ideas, and had no connection with the habits that really mattered. So respirators were abolished, and with them, of course, the terrestrial motors, and except for a few lecturers, who complained that they were debarred access to their subject-matter, the development was accepted quietly. Those who still wanted to know what the earth was like had after all only to listen to some gramophone, or to look into some cinematophote. And even the lecturers acquiesced when they found that a lecture on the sea was none the less stimulating when compiled out of other lectures that had already been delivered on the same subject. "Beware of first-hand ideas!" exclaimed one of the most advanced of them. "First-hand ideas do not really exist. They are but the physical impressions produced by love and fear, and on this gross foundation who could erect a philosophy? Let your ideas be second-hand, and if possible tenth-hand, for then they will be far removed from the disturbing element—direct observation. Do not learn anything about this subject of mine—the French Revolution. Learn instead what I think that Enicharmon thought Urizen thought Gutch thought Ho-Yung thought Chi-Bo-Sing thought Lafcadio Hearn thought Carlyle thought Mirabeau[2] said about the French Revolution. Through the medium of these eight great minds, the blood that was shed at Paris and the windows that were broken at Versailles will be clarified to an idea which you may employ most profitably in your daily lives. But be sure that the intermediates are many and varied, for in history one authority exists to counteract another. Urizen must counteract the skepticism of Ho-Yung and Enicharmon, I must myself counteract the impetuosity of Gutch. You who listen to me are in a better position to judge about the French Revolution than I am. Your descendants will be even in a better position than you, for they will learn what you think I think, and yet another intermediate will be added to the chain. And in time"—his voice rose—"there will come a generation that has got beyond facts, beyond impressions, a generation absolutely colourless, a generation

seraphically free
From taint of personality,

which will see the French Revolution not as it happened, nor as they would like it to have happened, but as it would have happened, had it taken place in the days of the Machine."

Tremendous applause greeted this lecture, which did but voice a feeling already latent in the minds of men—a feeling that terrestrial facts must be ignored, and that the abolition of respirators was a positive gain. It was even suggested that air-ships should be abolished too. This was not done, because air-ships had somehow worked themselves into the Machine's system. But year by year they were used less, and mentioned less by thoughtful men.

The second great development was the re-establishment of religion.

This, too, had been voiced in the celebrated lecture. No one could mistake the reverent tone in which the peroration had concluded, and it awakened a responsive echo in the heart of each. Those who had long worshipped silently, now began to talk. They described the strange feeling of peace that came over them when they handled the Book of the Machine, the pleasure that it was to repeat certain numerals out of it, however little meaning those numerals conveyed to the outward ear, the ecstasy of touching a button, however unimportant, or of ringing an electric bell, however superfluously.

"The Machine," they exclaimed, "feeds us and clothes us and houses us; through it we speak to one another, through it we see one another, in it we have our being. The Machine is the friend of ideas and the enemy of superstition: the Machine is omnipotent, eternal; blessed is the Machine." And before long this allocution was printed on the first page of the Book, and in subsequent editions the ritual swelled into a complicated system of praise and prayer. The word "religion" was sedulously avoided, and in theory the Machine was still the creation and the implement of man. But in practice all, save a few retrogrades, worshipped it as divine. Nor was it worshipped in unity. One believer would be chiefly impressed by the blue optic plates, through which he saw other believers; another by the mending apparatus, which sinful Kuno had compared to worms; another by the lifts, another by the Book. And each would pray to this or that, and ask it to intercede for him with the Machine as a whole. Persecution—that also was present. It did not break out, for reasons that will be set forward shortly. But it was latent, and all who did not accept the minimum known as "undenominational Mechanism" lived in danger of Homelessness, which means death, as we know.

To attribute these two great developments to the Central Committee, is to take a very narrow view of civilization. The Central Committee announced the developments, it is true, but they were no more the cause of them than were the kings of the imperialistic period the cause of war. Rather did they yield to some invincible pressure, which came no one knew whither, and which, when gratified, was succeeded by some new pressure equally invincible. To such a state of affairs it is convenient to give the name of progress. No one confessed the Machine was out of hand. Year by year it was served with increased efficiency and decreased intelligence. The better a man knew his own duties upon it, the less he understood

2. *Enicharmon . . . Mirabeau.* Only the last three men named were actual persons. The French statesman Mirabeau was a leader in the French Revolution. Thomas Carlyle wrote a history of that revolution. Hearn was an American journalist and writer famous for his exotic and fantastic tales, who spent much time in Japan. Enicharmon and Urizen are characters in William Blake's prophetic books.

the duties of his neighbour, and in all the world there was not one who understood the monster as a whole. Those master brains had perished. They had left full directions, it is true, and their successors had each of them mastered a portion of those directions. But Humanity, in its desire for comfort, had overreached itself. It had exploited the riches of nature too far. Quietly and complacently, it was sinking into decadence, and progress had come to mean the progress of the Machine.

As for Vashti, her life went peacefully forward until the final disaster. She made her room dark and slept; she awoke and made the room light. She lectured and attended lectures. She exchanged ideas with her innumerable friends and believed she was growing more spiritual. At times a friend was granted Euthanasia, and left his or her room for the homelessness that is beyond all human conception. Vashti did not much mind. After an unsuccessful lecture, she would sometimes ask for Euthanasia herself. But the death-rate was not permitted to exceed the birth-rate, and the Machine had hitherto refused it to her.

The troubles began quietly, long before she was conscious of them.

One day she was astonished at receiving a message from her son. They never communicated, having nothing in common, and she had only heard indirectly that he was still alive, and had been transferred from the northern hemisphere, where he had behaved so mischievously, to the southern—indeed, to a room not far from her own.

"Does he want me to visit him?" she thought. "Never again, never. And I have not the time."

No, it was madness of another kind.

He refused to visualize his face upon the blue plate, and speaking out of the darkness with solemnity said:

"The Machine stops."

"What do you say?"

"The Machine is stopping, I know it, I know the signs."

She burst into a peal of laughter. He heard her and was angry, and they spoke no more.

"Can you imagine anything more absurd?" she cried to a friend. "A man who was my son believes that the Machine is stopping. It would be impious if it was not mad."

"The Machine is stopping?" her friend replied. "What does that mean? The phrase conveys nothing to me."

"Nor to me."

"He does not refer, I suppose, to the trouble there has been lately with the music?"

"Oh no, of course not. Let us talk about music."

"Have you complained to the authorities?"

"Yes, and they say it wants mending, and referred me to the Committee of the Mending Apparatus. I complained of those curious gasping sighs that disfigure the symphonies of the Brisbane school. They sound like someone in pain. The Committee of the Mending Apparatus say that it shall be remedied shortly."

Obscurely worried, she resumed her life. For one thing, the defect in the music irritated her. For another thing, she could not forget Kuno's speech. If he had known that the music was out of repair—he could not know it, for he detested music—if he had known that it was wrong, "the Machine stops" was exactly the venomous sort of remark he would have made. Of course he had made it at a venture, but the coincidence annoyed her, and she spoke with some petulance to the Committee of the Mending Apparatus.

They replied, as before, that the defect would be set right shortly.

"Shortly! At once!" she retorted. "Why should I be worried by imperfect music? Things are always put right at once. If you do not mend it at once, I shall complain to the Central Committee."

"No personal complaints are received by the Central Committee," the Committee of the Mending Apparatus replied.

"Through whom am I to make my complaint, then?"

"Through us."

"I complain then."

"Your complaint shall be forwarded in its turn."

"Have others complained?"

This question was unmechanical, and the Committee of the Mending Apparatus refused to answer it.

"It is too bad!" she exclaimed to another of her friends. "There never was such an unfortunate woman as myself. I can never be sure of my music now. It gets worse and worse each time I summon it."

"I too have my troubles," the friend replied. "Sometimes my ideas are interrupted by a slight jarring noise."

"What is it?"

"I do not know whether it is inside my head, or

inside the wall."

"Complain, in either case."

"I have complained, and my complaint will be forwarded in its turn to the Central Committee."

Time passed, and they resented the defects no longer. The defects had not been remedied, but the human tissues in that latter day had become so subservient, that they readily adapted themselves to every caprice of the Machine. The sigh at the crisis of the Brisbane symphony no longer irritated Vashti; she accepted it as part of the melody. The jarring noise, whether in the head or in the wall, was no longer resented by her friend. And so with the mouldy artificial fruit, so with the bath water that began to stink, so with the defective rhymes that the poetry machine had taken to emit. All were bitterly complained of at first, and then acquiesced in and forgotten. Things went from bad to worse unchallenged.

It was otherwise with the failure of the sleeping apparatus. That was a more serious stoppage. There came a day when over the whole world—in Sumatra, in Wessex, in the innumerable cities of Courland and Brazil—the beds, when summoned by their tired owners, failed to appear. It may seem a ludicrous matter, but from it we may date the collapse of humanity. The Committee responsible for the failure was assailed by complainants, whom it referred, as usual, to the Committee of the Mending Apparatus, who in its turn assured them that their complaints would be forwarded to the Central Committee. But the discontent grew, for mankind was not yet sufficiently adaptable to do without sleeping.

"Some one is meddling with the Machine—" they began.

"Some one is trying to make himself king, to reintroduce the personal element."

"Punish that man with Homelessness."

"To the rescue! Avenge the Machine! Avenge the Machine!"

"War! Kill the man!"

But the Committee of the Mending Apparatus now came forward, and allayed the panic with well-chosen words. It confessed that the Mending Apparatus was itself in need of repair.

The effect of this frank confession was admirable.

"Of course," said a famous lecturer—he of the French Revolution, who gilded each new decay with splendour—"of course we shall not press our complaints now. The Mending Apparatus has treated us so well in the past that we all sympathize with it, and will wait patiently for its recovery. In its own good time it will resume its duties. Meanwhile let us do without our beds, our tabloids, our other little wants. Such, I feel sure, would be the wish of the Machine."

Thousands of miles away his audience applauded. The Machine still linked them. Under the seas, beneath the roots of the mountains, ran the wires through which they saw and heard, the enormous eyes and ears that were their heritage, and the hum of many workings clothed their thoughts in one garment of subserviency. Only the old and the sick remained ungrateful, for it was rumoured that Euthanasia, too, was out of order, and that pain had reappeared among men.

It became difficult to read. A blight entered the atmosphere and dulled its luminosity. At times Vashti could scarcely see across her room. The air, too, was foul. Loud were the complaints, impotent the remedies, heroic the tone of the lecturer as he cried: "Courage, courage! What matter so long as the Machine goes on? To it the darkness and the light are one." And though things improved again after a time, the old brilliancy was never recaptured, and humanity never recovered from its entrance into twilight. There was an hysterical talk of "measures," of "provisional dictatorship," and the inhabitants of Sumatra were asked to familiarize themselves with the workings of the central power station, the said power station being situated in France. But for the most part panic reigned, and men spent their strength praying to their Books, tangible proofs of the Machine's omnipotence. There were gradations of terror—at times came rumours of hope—the Mending Apparatus was almost mended—the enemies of the Machine had been got under—new "nerve-centres" were evolving which would do the work even more magnificently than before. But there came a day when, without the slightest warning, without any previous hint of feebleness, the entire communication-system broke down, all over the world, and the world, as they understood it, ended.

Vashti was lecturing at the time and her earlier remarks had been punctuated with applause. As she proceeded the audience became silent, and at the conclusion there was no sound. Somewhat displeased, she called to a friend who was a specialist in sympathy. No sound: doubtless the friend was sleeping. And so with the next friend whom she tried to summon, and so with the next, until she remembered Kuno's cryptic remark, "The Machine stops."

The phrase still conveyed nothing. If Eternity was stopping it would of course be set going shortly.

For example, there was still a little light and air—the atmosphere had improved a few hours previously. There was still the Book, and while there was the Book there was security.

Then she broke down, for with the cessation of activity came an unexpected terror—silence.

She had never known silence, and the coming of it nearly killed her—it did kill many thousands of people outright. Ever since her birth she had been surrounded by the steady hum. It was to the ear what artificial air was to the lungs, and agonizing pains shot across her head. And scarcely knowing what she did, she stumbled forward and pressed the unfamiliar button, the one that opened the door of her cell.

Now the door of the cell worked on a simple hinge of its own. It was not connected with the central power station, dying far away in France. It opened, rousing immoderate hopes in Vashti, for she thought that the Machine had been mended. It opened, and she saw the dim tunnel that curved far away towards freedom. One look, and then she shrank back. For the tunnel was full of people—she was almost the last in that city to have taken alarm.

People at any time repelled her, and these were nightmares from her worst dreams. People were crawling about, people were screaming, whimpering, gasping for breath, touching each other, vanishing in the dark, and ever and anon being pushed off the platform on to the live rail. Some were fighting round the electric bells, trying to summon trains which could not be summoned. Others were yelling for Euthanasia or for respirators, or blaspheming the Machine. Others stood at the doors of their cells fearing, like herself, either to stop in them or to leave them. And behind all the uproar was silence—the silence which is the voice of the earth and of the generations who have gone.

No—it was worse than solitude. She closed the door again and sat down to wait for the end. The disintegration went on, accompanied by horrible cracks and rumbling. The valves that restrained the Medical Apparatus must have been weakened, for it ruptured and hung hideously from the ceiling. The floor heaved and fell and flung her from her chair. A tube oozed towards her serpent fashion. And at last the final horror approached—light began to ebb, and she knew that civilization's long day was closing.

She whirled round, praying to be saved from this, at any rate, kissing the Book, pressing button after button. The uproar outside was increasing, and even penetrated the wall. Slowly the brilliancy of her cell was dimmed, the reflections faded from her metal switches. Now she could not see the reading-stand, now not the Book, though she held it in her hand. Light followed the flight of sound, air was following light, and the original void returned to the cavern from which it had been so long excluded. Vashti continued to whirl, like the devotees of an earlier religion, screaming, praying, striking at the buttons with bleeding hands.

It was thus that she opened her prison and escaped—escaped in the spirit: at least so it seems to me, ere my meditation closes. That she escaped in the body—I cannot perceive that. She struck, by chance, the switch that released the door, and the rush of foul air on her skin, the loud throbbing whispers in her ears, told her that she was facing the tunnel again, and that tremendous platform on which she had seen men fighting. They were not fighting now. Only the whispers remained, and the little whimpering groans. They were dying by hundreds out in the dark.

She burst into tears.

Tears answered her.

They wept for humanity, those two, not for themselves. They could not bear that this should be the end. Ere silence was completed their hearts were opened, and they knew what had been important on the earth. Man, the flower of all flesh, the noblest of all creatures visible, man who had once made god in his image, and had mirrored his strength on the constellations, beautiful naked man was dying, strangled in the garments that he had woven. Century after century had he toiled, and here was his reward. Truly the garment had seemed heavenly at first, shot with the colours of culture, sewn with the threads of self-denial. And heavenly it had been so long as it was a garment and no more, so long as man could shed it at will and live by the essence that is his soul, and the essence, equally divine, that is his body. The sin against the body—it was for that they wept in chief; the centuries of wrong against the muscles and the nerves, and those five portals by which we can alone apprehend—glozing it over with talk of evolution, until the body was white pap, the home of ideas as colourless, last sloshy stirrings of a spirit that had grasped the stars.

"Where are you?" she sobbed.

His voice in the darkness said, "Here."

"Is there any hope, Kuno?"

"None for us."

"Where are you?"

She crawled towards him over the bodies of the dead. His blood spurted over her hands.

"Quicker," he gasped, "I am dying—but we touch, we talk, not through the Machine."

He kissed her.

"We have come back to our own. We die, but we have recaptured life, as it was in Wessex, when Ælfrid overthrew the Danes. We know what they know outside, they who dwelt in the cloud that is the colour of a pearl."

"But Kuno, is it true? Are there still men on the surface of the earth? Is this—this tunnel, this poisoned darkness—really not the end?"

He replied:

"I have seen them, spoken to them, loved them. They are hiding in the mist and the ferns until our civilization stops. Today they are the Homeless—tomorrow—"

"Oh, tomorrow—some fool will start the Machine again, tomorrow."

"Never," said Kuno, "never. Humanity has learnt its lesson."

As he spoke, the whole city was broken like a honeycomb. An air-ship had sailed in through the vomitory into a ruined wharf. It crashed downwards, exploding as it went, rending gallery after gallery with its wings of steel. For a moment they saw the nations of the dead, and, before they joined them, scraps of the untainted sky.

DISCUSSION

1. Cite some instances of the isolation and alienation of Vashti's life.

2. What aspects of modern living are being criticized in this story?

3. At one point in the story Vashti mentions the bones of those expelled from the Machine during the Great Rebellion. Why does the author include a reference to such a rebellion?

4. To what do you attribute the breakdown of the Mending Apparatus?

5. Not long before the Machine stops, the Committee makes two changes in living conditions:

(a) It bans respirators.

(b) It revives religion.

What is the reasoning behind each of these moves?

6. (a) If you had to live in the Machine, what parts of your life would you find most difficult?

(b) What compensations might there be?

7. What, if anything, might drive modern man to make his home underground?

8. Although both "Miss Pinkerton's Apocalypse" and "The Machine Stops" could be loosely categorized as science fiction, there are certainly basic differences between the two stories. What are they?

9. "Youth" and "The Machine Stops" are longer than most short stories, and thus able to probe more deeply into the human condition.

(a) How are the characters of young Marlow and Kuno similar?

(b) In what respects do their elders show themselves concerned with abiding by the rules and preserving the status quo?

(c) It has been pointed out that the world in which Conrad placed Marlow was a young, vigorous world; that in which Forster placed Kuno was an old, decadent world. If this is so, discuss the following:

—the extent to which each story demonstrates youth's power to control or affect his world.

—each author's purpose in writing his story.

—the purpose served by placing "Youth" first in this collection of modern short stories and "The Machine Stops" last, rather than vice versa.

WRITING

1. Write several pages from Kuno's journal, covering important events in the story.

2. Describe the reactions of the people who live on the surface of the earth when they investigate the wreckage of the Machine cities.

3. Write a warning to mankind, fiction or nonfiction, concentrating on some hazard which you see as threatening human existence.

READERS' THEATER

1. Convert any of the stories in this unit into a short play and present it to the class. If you select a longer story, such as "Youth" or "The Machine Stops," you may wish to use only one or two episodes.

2. Take an extended dialogue from any of the stories and, by making necessary adjustments and supplying a musical background, present it as a sort of nonsinging pop opera. You may find it advisable to tape this and play the tape to the class.

chapter ten

POETRY

TESS JARAY, "ST. STEPHENS WAY," 1964. COLLECTION OF THE ARTS COUNCIL OF GREAT BRITAIN.

Twentieth-Century Poetry
Part One:

A POETIC REVOLUTION

A line will take us hours maybe;
Yet if it does not seem a moment's thought,
Our stitching and unstitching has been naught.
W. B. Yeats

I. William Butler Yeats 1865 / 1939

THE LAKE ISLE OF INNISFREE

I will arise and go now, and go to Innisfree,[1]
And a small cabin build there, of clay and wattles made;
Nine bean rows[2] will I have there, a hive for the honeybee,
And live alone in the bee-loud glade.

5 And I shall have some peace there, for peace comes dropping slow,
Dropping from the veils of the morning to where the cricket sings;
There midnight's all a-glimmer, and noon a purple glow,
And evening full of the linnet's wings.

I will arise and go now, for always night and day
10 I hear lake water lapping with low sounds by the shore;
While I stand on the roadway, or on the pavements gray,
I hear it in the deep heart's core.

(1893)

1. *Innisfree*, an island in Lough Gill, a lake in County Sligo, where Yeats lived as a boy.
2. *Nine bean rows.* Celtic poets liked to use the mystic numbers three, five, seven, and their multiples. The bean rows are an allusion to something Yeats had read in Thoreau's *Walden.*

THE SONG OF WANDERING AENGUS[1]

I went out to the hazel wood,
Because a fire was in my head,
And cut and peeled a hazel wand,
And hooked a berry to a thread;
5 And when white moths were on the wing,
And moth-like stars were flickering out,
I dropped the berry in a stream
And caught a little silver trout.

When I had laid it on the floor
10 I went to blow the fire aflame,
But something rustled on the floor,
And some one called me by my name:
It had become a glimmering girl
With apple blossom in her hair
15 Who called me by my name and ran
And faded through the brightening air.

Though I am old with wandering
Through hollow lands and hilly lands,
I will find out where she has gone,
20 And kiss her lips and take her hands;
And walk among long dappled grass,
And pluck till time and times are done
The silver apples of the moon,
The golden apples of the sun.[2]

(1899)

1. *Aengus* (Angus), Celtic god of love (and also of youth, beauty, and poetry). The poem is based on an ancient Irish legend.

2. *And pluck . . . sun,* i.e., take and savor the greatest and most attractive treasures that love offers, night and day, moontime and suntime.

THE OLD MEN ADMIRING THEMSELVES IN THE WATER

I heard the old, old men say,
"Everything alters,
And one by one we drop away."
They had hands like claws, and their knees
5 Were twisted like the old thorn-trees
By the waters.
I heard the old, old men say,
"All that's beautiful drifts away
Like the waters."

(1904)

THE SCHOLARS

Bald heads forgetful of their sins,
Old, learned, respectable bald heads
Edit and annotate the lines
That young men, tossing on their beds,
5 Rhymed out in love's despair
To flatter beauty's ignorant ear.

All shuffle there; all cough in ink;
All wear the carpet with their shoes;
All think what other people think;
10 All know the man their neighbour knows.
Lord, what would they say
Did their Catullus[1] walk that way?

(1919)

1. *Catullus,* lyric poet of ancient Rome, who died at age 30 (or 33?). He wrote many love lyrics, and influenced English poets from Chaucer on.

ADAM'S CURSE

We sat together at one summer's end,
That beautiful mild woman, your close friend,
And you[1] and I, and talked of poetry.
I said, "A line will take us hours maybe;
5 Yet if it does not seem a moment's thought,
Our stitching and unstitching has been naught.
Better go down upon your marrow-bones
And scrub a kitchen pavement, or break stones
Like an old pauper, in all kinds of weather;
10 For to articulate sweet sounds together
Is to work harder than all these, and yet
Be thought an idler by the noisy set
Of bankers, schoolmasters, and clergymen
The martyrs call the world."

And thereupon
15 That beautiful mild woman for whose sake
There's many a one shall find out all heartache
On finding that her voice is sweet and low
Replied, "To be born woman is to know—
Although they do not talk of it at school—
20 That we must labour to be beautiful."

I said, "It's certain there is no fine thing
Since Adam's fall but needs much labouring.
There have been lovers who thought love should be
So much compounded of high courtesy
25 That they would sigh and quote with learned looks
Precedents out of beautiful old books;
Yet now it seems an idle trade enough."

We sat grown quiet at the name of love;
We saw the last embers of daylight die,
30 And in the trembling blue-green of the sky
A moon, worn as if it had been a shell
Washed by time's waters as they rose and fell
About the stars and broke in days and years.

I had a thought for no one's but your ears:
35 That you were beautiful, and that I strove
To love you in the old high way of love;
That it had all seemed happy, and yet we'd grown
As weary-hearted as that hollow moon.

(1904)

CULVER PICTURES, INC.

1. *you,* Maude Gonne, the Irish actress, painter, and revolutionary patriot whom Yeats loved and proposed to in vain, and to whom he refers in many of his poems.

OF CRITICAL INTEREST

Yeats's revisions of "The Scholars"

The second stanza gave Yeats much trouble. In *Poetry*, February 1916, this read:

> They'll cough in the ink to the world's end;
> Wear out the carpet with their shoes;
> Earning respect, have no strange friend,
> If they have sinned nobody knows:
> Lord, what would they say
> Should their Catullus walk that way?

He was not satisfied with the revision of the poem which made the first four lines of the last stanza begin with "all," feeling perhaps that their rhetoric was too easy. In his 1928 diary he wrote down another version in which he changed from the third person to direct address:

> Shuffle there, cough in the ink,
> Wear out the carpet with your shoes,
> Think what all good people think,
> Youth could sin, but old age knows.
> Lord, what would you say
> Did your Catullus walk that way?

But he did not alter the published version, which had a better ring to it.

Yeats did not always take so frowning a view of scholarship. A poem written three and a half years later declared, "Truth flourishes where the student's lamp has shown."

THE WILD SWANS AT COOLE[1]

The trees are in their autumn beauty,
The woodland paths are dry,
Under the October twilight the water
Mirrors a still sky;
5 Upon the brimming water among the stones
Are nine-and-fifty swans.

The nineteenth autumn has come upon me
Since I first made my count;
I saw, before I had well finished,
10 All suddenly mount
And scatter wheeling in great broken rings
Upon their clamorous wings.

I have looked upon those brilliant creatures,
And now my heart is sore.
15 All's changed since I, hearing at twilight,
The first time on this shore,
The bell-beat of their wings above my head,
Trod with a lighter tread.

Unwearied still, lover by lover,
20 They paddle in the cold
Companionable streams or climb the air;
Their hearts have not grown old;
Passion or conquest, wander where they will,
Attend upon them still.

25 But now they drift on the still water,
Mysterious, beautiful;
Among what rushes will they build,
By what lake's edge or pool
Delight men's eyes when I awake some day
30 To find they have flown away?

(1919)

1. *Coole,* Coole Park, the ancestral home of Yeats's friend Lady Gregory, the Irish playwright.

subconciously a being (sphinx image)
yr. 2000 foreshadowing
man will destroy himself

THE SECOND COMING[1]

Turning and turning in the widening gyre[2]
The falcon cannot hear the falconer;
Things fall apart; the centre cannot hold;
Mere anarchy is loosed upon the world,
5 The blood-dimmed tide is loosed, and everywhere
The ceremony of innocence is drowned;
The best lack all conviction, while the worst
Are full of passionate intensity.

Surely some revelation is at hand;
10 Surely the Second Coming is at hand.
The Second Coming! Hardly are those words out
When a vast image out of *Spiritus Mundi*[3]
Troubles my sight: somewhere in sands of the desert
A shape with lion body and the head of a man,
15 A gaze blank and pitiless as the sun,
Is moving its slow thighs, while all about it
Reel shadows of the indignant desert birds.
The darkness drops again; but now I know
That twenty centuries of stony sleep
20 Were vexed to nightmare by a rocking cradle,
And what rough beast, its hour come round at last,
Slouches towards Bethlehem to be born?

(1921)

1. *Second Coming.* Yeats believed that history moves in 2000-year cycles; at the end of each cycle, a new god will reveal himself to man.

2. *gyre* (jīr), a symbol used by Yeats in much of his later poetry. He thought of the gyres as a pair of cones or spirals with touching points. They symbolized the opposing elements that make up the whole of existence.

3. *Spiritus Mundi,* also called by Yeats the Great Memory. He means something similar to what the psychologist Jung called the Collective Unconscious—a kind of storehouse of racial memories from which come universal symbols that appear spontaneously in the dreams, myths, and creative fantasies of all men.

OF CRITICAL INTEREST

"The Second Coming"

The notion that a new god comes at regular intervals to replace the old god is a familiar one in Theosophy; every cycle is said to have its special deity. . . . Yeats's poems are thick with allusions to the coming of some god, or of some change in the world's complexion, and in his early and middle periods he usually longs for the impending transformation. . . .

But "The Second Coming" differs from previous prophecies in envisaging the new god's arrival with horror. The first World War and the Black and Tan War[1] seemed foreshadowings, and, if these were not enough, Mrs. Yeats's automatic writing[2] constantly impressed the word "terror" upon him. In entitling his poem "The Second Coming," Yeats took over a device which he had used in his early story, "The Adoration of the Magi," where he gave Christian parallelism to a prediction of the return of the old pagan gods by calling the three old men who receive the new revelation "magi." The title of the poem is even more shocking, for it depends upon a fusion of Christ's prediction in Matthew 24 of his second coming, and St. John's vision of the coming of the beast of the Apocalypse, or Antichrist.

The first stanza prepares the way for the ominous event of the second stanza. Until the beginning of the thirteenth line the reader can still hope that the Second Coming will be Christ's beneficent although awesome reappearance. But with the word "troubles" and the description of the image this hope is converted to fear. Whatever the new dispensation can bring, it inspires only a sense of horrible helplessness to avert what no man can desire. That the image comes from *Spiritus Mundi,* the storehouse of images, is important because it indicates that the image is not a personal one, that he has not deliberately thought it up but has had it forced into his consciousness. He is "inspired," not by a god, but by an equally irresistible and all-knowing power.

Although he refers to the image as a "shape," and intends the indeterminate label to increase its portentousness, he makes clear that it is, or is like, the Egyptian sphinx, which is male (unlike the Greek sphinx). This beast has been in stony sleep for two thousand years, and even now it seems to be moving as if in nightmare towards birth and awakening. "The rocking cradle" of Christianity has at last made way for its opposite, for Christianity has reached its utmost bound. Movements call up their opposites . . . whether willingly or unwillingly. While Yeats is not fond of Christianity, and regards its suppression of individual personality as having led to the present anarchy, yet at the end of the poem he envisages something far worse. The final intimation that the new god will be born in Bethlehem, which Christianity associates with passive infancy and the tenderness of maternal love, makes its brutishness particularly frightful.

1. *Black and Tan War,* a conflict between the Irish Republican Army and British police, who were known as "Black and Tans" from the colors of their uniforms.

2. *Mrs. Yeats's automatic writing.* Mrs. Yeats was a spiritualist medium; see the Yeats biography.

SAILING TO BYZANTIUM[1]

I

That is no country for old men. The young
In one another's arms, birds in the trees,
—Those dying generations—at their song,
The salmon-falls, the mackerel-crowded seas,
5 Fish, flesh, or fowl, commend all summer long
Whatever is begotten, born, and dies.
Caught in that sensual music all neglect
Monuments of unaging intellect.

II

An aged man is but a paltry thing,
10 A tattered coat upon a stick, unless
Soul clap its hands and sing, and louder sing
For every tatter in its mortal dress,
Nor is there singing school but studying
Monuments of its own magnificence;
15 And therefore I have sailed the seas and come
To the holy city of Byzantium.

III

O sages standing in God's holy fire
As in the gold mosaic of a wall
Come from the holy fire, perne in a gyre,[2]
20 And be the singing-masters of my soul.
Consume my heart away; sick with desire
And fastened to a dying animal
It knows not what it is; and gather me
Into the artifice of eternity.

1. *Byzantium,* ancient name of the city that became Constantinople and then Istanbul. For Yeats, however, it was not so much a place as an ideal, a symbol for the timeless world of art and the intellect as opposed to the natural world of biological change. It was a "holy city," literally because it was the capital of Eastern Christendom, symbolically because it fostered that development of intellect and imagination which produces artistic perfection. Byzantine art was highly stylized, abandoning all naturalistic representation.

2. *perne in a gyre,* whirl or spin in a spiral motion.

IV

25 Once out of nature I shall never take
My bodily form from any natural thing,
But such a form as Grecian goldsmiths make[3]
Of hammered gold and gold enameling
To keep a drowsy Emperor awake;
30 Or set upon a golden bough to sing
To lords and ladies of Byzantium
Of what is past, or passing, or to come.

(1927)

3. *such a form . . . make.* Yeats said: "I have read somewhere that in the Emperor's palace at Byzantium was a tree of gold and silver, and artificial birds that sang."

OF CRITICAL INTEREST

"Sailing to Byzantium"

In "Sailing to Byzantium," an old man faces the problem of old age, of death, and of regeneration, and gives his decision. Old age, he tells us, excludes a man from the sensual joys of youth; the world appears to belong completely to the young, it is no place for the old; indeed, an old man is scarcely a man at all—he is an empty artifice, an effigy merely, of a man; he is a tattered coat upon a stick. This would be very bad, except that the young also are excluded from something; rapt in their sensuality, they are ignorant utterly of the world of the spirit. Hence if old age frees a man from sensual passion, he may rejoice in the liberation of the soul; he is admitted into the realm of the spirit; and his rejoicing will increase according as he realizes the magnificence of the soul. But the soul can best learn its own greatness from the great works of art; hence he turns to those great works, but in turning to them, he finds that these are by no means mere effigies, or monuments, but things that have souls also; these live in the noblest element of God's fire, free from all corruption; hence he prays for death, for release from his mortal body; and since the insouled monuments exhibit the possibility of the soul's existence in some other matter than flesh, he wishes reincarnation, not now in a mortal body, but in the immortal and changeless embodiment of art. . . .

From UNDER BEN BULBEN

VI

Under bare Ben Bulben's[1] head
In Drumcliff[2] churchyard Yeats is laid.
An ancestor was rector there
Long years ago, a church stands near,
5 By the road an ancient cross.
No marble, no conventional phrase;
On limestone quarried near the spot
By his command these words are cut:
Cast a cold eye
On life, on death.
Horseman, pass by!

(1939)

1. *Ben Bulben,* a mountain in County Sligo, Yeats's boyhood home.
2. *Drumcliff,* a village in Sligo. Yeats died in France in 1939 and was buried there, but in 1948 he was reburied, according to his wish, in Drumcliff churchyard.

DISCUSSION

1. It has been said that Yeats wrote "The Lake Isle of Innisfree" after reading Henry David Thoreau's *Walden* (1854), in which Thoreau describes his retreat to Walden Pond near Concord, Massachusetts, where he built a cabin and planted a garden (including rows of beans).

(a) After reading Thoreau or discussing *Walden* with a fellow student who has read him, explore the similarities and differences in the "escapist" impulses of Thoreau and Yeats.

(b) Discuss the feasibility today of retreating in the way Thoreau actually did retreat or the way Yeats yearns to retreat.

2. Many readers have identified with the speaker in "The Song of Wandering Aengus," even though they have never caught a fish that turned into a beautiful girl. What is in the poem that readers might identify with?

3. For a poet to write poetry, for a woman to be beautiful, for lovers to maintain their love—how are all these related to each other (and to the title) in "Adam's Curse"?

4. In "The Wild Swans at Coole," the speaker tells us that, since his first view of the swans some nineteen years before, he has compared his life and feelings to theirs. At first he identified with the swans, but now, almost two decades later, he notices deep differences.

(a) What are these differences?

(b) How do they color the entire poem?

5. (a) Describe in your own words the state of the world that Yeats has envisioned in the first stanza of "The Second Coming."

(b) Discuss the effect of the question posed in the last two lines of the poem.

6. In "Sailing to Byzantium," the first two stanzas describe a country the speaker has left, and the last two stanzas describe the country (Byzantium) to which he has gone. Both countries are in a sense symbolic only, not places to be found on a map. Discuss the symbolism of the two countries, and explain the speaker's desire to sail to Byzantium.

II. T. S. Eliot 1888 / 1965

CULVER PICTURES, INC.

PORTRAIT OF A LADY

Thou hast committed—
Fornication: but that was in another country,
And besides, the wench is dead.
The Jew of Malta.

I

AMONG the smoke and fog of a December afternoon
You have the scene arrange itself—as it will seem to do—
With "I have saved this afternoon for you";
And four wax candles in the darkened room,
5 Four rings of light upon the ceiling overhead,
An atmosphere of Juliet's tomb
Prepared for all the things to be said, or left unsaid.
We have been, let us say, to hear the latest Pole
Transmit the Preludes, through his hair and fingertips.
10 "So intimate, this Chopin, that I think his soul
Should be resurrected only among friends
Some two or three, who will not touch the bloom
That is rubbed and questioned in the concert room."
—And so the conversation slips
15 Among velleities[1] and carefully caught regrets
Through attenuated tones of violins
Mingled with remote cornets
And begins.
"You do not know how much they mean to me, my friends,
20 And how, how rare and strange it is, to find
In a life composed so much, so much of odds and ends,
[For indeed I do not love it . . . you knew? you are not blind!
How keen you are!]
To find a friend who has these qualities,
25 Who has, and gives
Those qualities upon which friendship lives.
How much it means that I say this to you—
Without these friendships—life, what *cauchemar!*"[2]

Among the windings of the violins
30 And the ariettes
Of cracked cornets
Inside my brain a dull tom-tom begins
Absurdly hammering a prelude of its own,
Capricious monotone
35 That is at least one definite "false note."
—Let us take the air, in a tobacco trance,
Admire the monuments,
Discuss the late events,
Correct our watches by the public clocks.
40 Then sit for half an hour and drink our bocks.

1. *velleity* (ve lē′ə tē), a slight wish or inclination.

2. *cauchemar* (kōsh′mär′), nightmare (French).

II

Now that lilacs are in bloom
She has a bowl of lilacs in her room
And twists one in her fingers while she talks.
"Ah, my friend, you do not know, you do not
know
45 What life is, you who hold it in your hands";
(Slowly twisting the lilac stalks)
"You let it flow from you, you let it flow,
And youth is cruel, and has no remorse
And smiles at situations which it cannot see."
50 I smile, of course,
And go on drinking tea.
"Yet with these April sunsets, that somehow recall
My buried life, and Paris in the Spring,
I feel immeasurably at peace, and find the world
55 To be wonderful and youthful, after all."

The voice returns like the insistent out-of-tune
Of a broken violin on an August afternoon:
"I am always sure that you understand
My feelings, always sure that you feel,
60 Sure that across the gulf you reach your hand.

You are invulnerable, you have no Achilles' heel.
You will go on, and when you have prevailed
You can say: at this point many a one has failed.
But what have I, but what have I, my friend,
65 To give you, what can you receive from me?
Only the friendship and the sympathy
Of one about to reach her journey's end.

I shall sit here, serving tea to friends. . . ."

I take my hat: how can I make a cowardly
amends
70 For what she has said to me?
You will see me any morning in the park
Reading the comics and the sporting page.
Particularly I remark
An English countess goes upon the stage.
75 A Greek was murdered at a Polish dance,
Another bank defaulter has confessed.
I keep my countenance,
I remain self-possessed
Except when a street piano, mechanical and tired
80 Reiterates some worn-out common song
With the smell of hyacinths across the garden
Recalling things that other people have desired.
Are these ideas right or wrong?

III

The October night comes down; returning as before
85 Except for a slight sensation of being ill at ease
I mount the stairs and turn the handle of the door
And feel as if I had mounted on my hands and
knees.
"And so you are going abroad; and when do you
return?
But that's a useless question.
90 You hardly know when you are coming back,
You will find so much to learn."
My smile falls heavily among the bric-à-brac.

"Perhaps you can write to me."
My self-possession flares up for a second;
95 *This* is as I had reckoned.
"I have been wondering frequently of late
(But our beginnings never know our ends!)
Why we have not developed into friends."
I feel like one who smiles, and turning shall remark
100 Suddenly, his expression in a glass.
My self-possession gutters; we are really in the
dark.

"For everybody said so, all our friends,
They all were sure our feelings would relate
So closely! I myself can hardly understand.
105 We must leave it now to fate.
You will write, at any rate.
Perhaps it is not too late.
I shall sit here, serving tea to friends."

And I must borrow every changing shape
110 To find expression . . . dance, dance
Like a dancing bear,
Cry like a parrot, chatter like an ape.
Let us take the air, in a tobacco trance—

Well! and what if she should die some afternoon,
115 Afternoon grey and smoky, evening yellow and
rose;
Should die and leave me sitting pen in hand

With the smoke coming down above the
housetops;
Doubtful, for a while
Not knowing what to feel or if I understand
120 Or whether wise or foolish, tardy or too soon . . .
Would she not have the advantage, after all?
This music is successful with a "dying fall"
Now that we talk of dying—
And should I have the right to smile?

(1917)

OF CRITICAL INTEREST

"Portrait of a Lady"

Under a sophisticated surface Eliot develops a conflict of feelings which weaves its sensuous imagery into patterns of changing mood and significance. Yet it is not so much the portrait of a lady as the portrait of another uncertain Prufrock,[1] adolescent rather than prematurely aged, suspended between feelings of attraction and repulsion. The epigraph from Marlowe's *Jew of Malta* (IV. i) suggests the situation, in which the dash after "committed" is important, for it indicates the moral uncertainty in the poem that parallels the uncertainty of accusation in the play . . . .

This affair runs through a year, and the seasons are important to the development of its tone and theme. First of all the time measures the attraction, within which other feelings develop. The youth passes from a feeling of superiority to a feeling of uneasiness and uncertainty, which threatens altogether to displace the earlier feeling . . . .

In imagined retrospect he [the youth] contemplates her [the lady's] death after his going away—an event which would consummate the situation of the epigraph. But the issue is by no means certain, either in the rightness of his action or the quality of his feeling. The perplexity of his feelings is not resolved by this event, which seems to give her the emotional advantage and ironically to make her music successful. His final discomfiture is to become doubtful of "the right to smile."

What has he committed? Has he been tempted but inhibited? Did he run away from a problem rather than solve it? Essentially the break between "committed" and "fornication" has developed into a theme of emotional frustration. He has been disturbed but baffled by the situation, and has been able to deal with it only by flight. *Fornication* is insufficient to characterize the action unless it includes the attraction and repulsion of sex complicated by moral feeling.

1. *Prufrock,* narrator in Eliot's poem *The Love Song of J. Alfred Prufrock.*

What did Eliot intend by the epigraph?

The epigraph from Marlowe's *The Jew of Malta* at first glance looks anomalous. It cannot be announcing a literal fact; the young man and the lady have certainly not "committed fornication." It becomes clearer if taken as Eliot's blunt but probably afterthoughted chiding of the young man's attitude. For, though exaggerative, its bravado corresponds in moral callousness to the surface tone of the poem itself. By penetrating to the depths of the lady's lonely and empty life, the young man has committed a psychological rape; this is far worse than fornication, for he has not respected her human condition. Now, one of the remarkable things about this poem is its innocence with respect to the young man's moral duty. Except for the epigraph, it could not be said to dictate judgment of his character. Indeed, one can imagine a reader willing to accept him at his own valuation, if only because of his ceremonious trust of reason. And the young man is entirely reasonable by "social" standards. It would be interesting to know, therefore, whether Eliot did want the point of view suspected . . . .

SWEENEY AMONG THE NIGHTINGALES[1]

ὤμοι, πέπληγμαι καιριαν πληγὴν ἔσω.[2]

1

Apeneck Sweeney[3] spreads his knees
Letting his arms hang down to laugh,
The zebra stripes along his jaw
Swelling to maculate[4] giraffe.

2

5 The circles of the stormy moon
Slide westward toward the River Plate,[5]
Death and the Raven[6] drift above
And Sweeney guards the hornèd gate.[7]

3

Gloomy Orion and the Dog[8]
10 Are veiled; and hushed the shrunken seas;
The person in the Spanish cape
Tries to sit on Sweeney's knees

4

Slips and pulls the table cloth
Overturns a coffee-cup,
15 Reorganized upon the floor
She yawns and draws a stocking up;

5

The silent man in mocha brown
Sprawls at the window-sill and gapes;
The waiter brings in oranges
20 Bananas figs and hothouse grapes;

6

The silent vertebrate in brown
Contracts and concentrates, withdraws;
Rachel *née* Rabinovitch
Tears at the grapes with murderous paws;

7

25 She and the lady in the cape
Are suspect, thought to be in league;
Therefore the man with heavy eyes
Declines the gambit, shows fatigue,

8

Leaves the room and reappears
30 Outside the window, leaning in,
Branches of wistaria
Circumscribe a golden grin;

9

The host with someone indistinct
Converses at the door apart,
35 The nightingales are singing near
The Convent of the Sacred Heart,

10

And sang within the bloody wood
When Agamemnon cried aloud,
And let their liquid siftings fall
40 To stain the stiff dishonoured shroud.

(1918)

1. *Nightingales.* In Greek myth, the nightingale was a symbol for the transformation of human lust into deathless art. The idea was embodied in the myth of Philomela who was raped by her brother-in-law Tereus. He had her tongue cut out so that she could not report the crime. She was turned into a nightingale that sings eternally.
2. "Alas, I am smitten with a mortal blow," the offstage cry of King Agamemnon as he is murdered by his wife Clytemnestra in the play *Agamemnon* by Aeschylus. This play is part of a trilogy, the *Oresteia,* which deals ultimately with the theme of divine justice.
3. *Sweeney,* who appears in several poems of Eliot's, represents the primitive, animal nature in man.
4. *maculate,* spotted, stained.
5. *River Plate* (Plata), on the eastern coast of South America.
6. *Raven,* a constellation; also a symbol of death.
7. *hornèd gate,* in Greek mythology, one of the two gates of the abode of Sleep. Through it, dreams that are true rise to the upper world.
8. *Orion and the Dog,* constellations. All three constellations mentioned suggest death.

OF CRITICAL INTEREST

"Sweeney Among the Nightingales"

In "Sweeney Among the Nightingales" the emphasis is upon the distinction between two atmospheres, two attitudes toward reality. On the one hand there is human life conceived in a religious and moral framework; on the other, there is the disintegrated, rootless, unstable, isolated position of the individual in the midst of the futility and anarchy of pure materialism. There is, of course, no overt reference to this. After the setting of the first two verses the drama sweeps in one long sentence of descriptive vision to the climax which links Agamemnon with the contemporary scene. That, and the epigraph from Aeschylus, lead some readers to seek a parallel in the *action* between the murder of Agamemnon and the scene in the poem. But it seems more characteristic of Eliot that the relationship should be symbolic; that it is everything that Agamemnon and his story (and myth in general) stands for, that has been killed by Sweeney and his like.

The link between the two worlds, that of myth and of the immediate actuality, is the nightingales. They are present in both, but Sweeney and his companions do not hear them. They are as deaf to their song as to the story behind the song. It is a horrible story of cruelty and revenge, just as the Agamemnon myth is, and the story of the "bloody wood." Here Eliot is using a favorite device of his, the telescoping of associations to get greater pressure and intensity. Agamemnon, after all, was not killed in a wood. The wood is that from which Frazer[1] named his great work *The Golden Bough,* and from which Eliot took the title for his first essays, *The Sacred Wood,* where he uses it as a symbol for the immortal poetic tradition, always dying and being reborn. The opening chapter of Frazer traces the story of the wood of Nemi, which was the scene of the bloody ritual by which the old priest of the grove was slain by a younger one, who succeeded as both priest and king until he in his turn was slain. Frazer shows how this ritual is the basis for all the oldest symbols of the human race. It was bound up with the concept of the Fertility God and his resurrection every spring, and extended into the larger theme of the death and resurrection of the human spirit. Eliot's purpose is to emphasize that pattern. Philomela is raped, but magical powers render her voice inviolable and immortal. It lives on in a bird, linking together man and nature, the animal and the spiritual. Agamemnon is murdered and Clytemnestra is murdered and Orestes is pursued by the Furies, but the end of the trilogy is the transcendence of revenge by reconciliation and mercy—just as the Sacred Heart too embodies the same values. All these stories create a pattern of reality which gives *meaning* to human hate and horror and sacrifice and suffering, because they are related to an order and value beyond the temporal and immediate. Agamemnon too represents another tradition, that of the heroic ideal of Greek tragedy.

The basic ironic contrasts of the poem are those between the suggestions of the significance of life seen in such terms of value and order and the complete *in*significance of the modern scene.

These people [Sweeney and his friends] have neither vitality nor order, and Eliot places them against a background which has both. The punctuation is significant here. After the introduction of Sweeney as a medley of animal shapes and markings, there are six lines of complete contrast which put him within a cosmic setting. There is no period at the end of these lines, just a semicolon, and the sentence runs on to the end of the poem and the final climax of the Convent, the nightingales, the bloody wood, and Agamemnon. The contemporary scene, that is, fades in from the background of the great ordered rhythms of the natural world, and fades out into the reminders of the great ordered patterns of myth. The permanence of the rhythmic patterns of nature, the moon and stars, the seas and the rivers are still there, just as the deathless reality of Agamemnon, and the bloody wood and the nightingales and the Sacred Heart are still there. But their clarity and brightness is lost and their relationship with humanity.

1. *Frazer,* Sir James George Frazer (1854–1941), Scottish scholar and anthropologist, whose 12-volume work on comparative religion and anthropology, *The Golden Bough,* had a significant influence on the literary world. Many of his conclusions are now discredited, but his work has been the basis of most later scholarship in the fields he dealt with.

OF CRITICAL INTEREST

"Sweeney Among the Nightingales"

Eliot once remarked that all he consciously set out to create in "Sweeney Among the Nightingales" was a sense of foreboding. Yet the very exactitude with which he has built up his impression by means of the close details of his nighttown scene, as well as by the way he underlines his effect through a reference both in the epigraph and in the final stanza to another scene of foreboding that ended in the murder of Agamemnon, inevitably causes his delineation to take on wider implications. The sharp contrast that seems at first simply to be mocking a debased present as it juxtaposes Sweeney with the hero of antiquity, ends in establishing also an undercurrent of moving drama: for a sympathetic feeling for Sweeney is set up by the realization that he is a man as well as Agamemnon, and that his plotted death is therefore likewise a human tragedy.

very negative, man no destination.
purgatory - between heaven/hell
Afraid of future

THE HOLLOW MEN

man brings self to a low

Mistah Kurtz—he dead.[1]

A penny for the Old Guy.[2]

I

We are the hollow men
We are the stuffed men
Leaning together
Headpiece filled with straw. Alas!
Our dried voices, when
We whisper together
Are quiet and meaningless
As wind in dry grass
Or rats' feet over broken glass
In our dry cellar

Shape without form, shade without color,
Paralysed force, gesture without motion;

Those who have crossed
With direct eyes,[3] to death's other Kingdom[4]
Remember us—if at all—not as lost
Violent souls, but only
As the hollow men
The stuffed men.

II

Eyes[5] I dare not meet in dreams
In death's dream kingdom
These do not appear:
There, the eyes are
Sunlight on a broken column
There, is a tree swinging
And voices are
In the wind's singing
More distant and more solemn
Than a fading star.

Let me be no nearer
In death's dream kingdom
Let me also wear
Such deliberate disguises
Rat's coat, crowskin, crossed staves
In a field
Behaving as the wind behaves
No nearer—

Not that final meeting
In the twilight kingdom.

III

This is the dead land
This is cactus land } hell (?).
Here the stone images
Are raised, here they receive
The supplication of a dead man's hand
Under the twinkle of a fading star.

Is it like this
In death's other kingdom
Waking alone
At the hour when we are
Trembling with tenderness
Lips that would kiss
Form prayers to broken stone.

IV

The eyes are not here
There are no eyes here
In this valley of dying stars } no hope
In this hollow valley
This broken jaw of our lost kingdoms

---

1. *Mistah Kurtz—he dead,* a quotation from Joseph Conrad's novel *Heart of Darkness.* Mr. Kurtz was a European trader who had gone into "the heart of darkness"—the central African jungle—with European standards of life and conduct. Because he had no moral or spiritual strength to sustain him, he was soon turned into a barbarian. He differs, however, from Eliot's "hollow men": he is not paralyzed as they are, but commits acts of overwhelming evil; and he is not blind as they are, but on his death glimpses the nature of his actions when he exclaims, "The horror! The horror!" Kurtz is thus one of the "lost / Violent souls" mentioned in lines 15–16.
2. *A penny . . . Guy,* cry of English children soliciting money for fireworks to celebrate Guy Fawkes Day, November 5, which commemorates the thwarting of the "gunpowder plot" of 1605 in which Guy Fawkes and other conspirators planned to blow up both houses of Parliament. On this day—which of course celebrates the *failure* to produce an explosion—straw-stuffed images of Fawkes (the "Old Guy") are burned.
3. *Those . . . direct eyes,* those who have represented something positive (direct), either for good or bad.
4. *death's other Kingdom,* the afterlife; eternity.
5. *Eyes,* the eyes of those in the afterworld who had confident faith; those who represent positive spiritual force as opposed to spiritual stagnation or paralysis.

Imagery → cactus/kingdom/ doesn't tie together
uses clear vocabulary

In this last of meeting places
We grope together
And avoid speech
60 Gathered on this beach of the tumid river

Sightless, unless
The eyes reappear
As the perpetual star
Multifoliate rose[6]
65 Of death's twilight kingdom
The hope only
Of empty men.

V

Here we go round the prickly pear
Prickly pear prickly pear
70 *Here we go round the prickly pear*
At five o'clock in the morning.

Between the idea
And the reality
Between the motion
75 And the act
Falls the Shadow
For Thine is the Kingdom

Between the conception
And the creation
80 Between the emotion
And the response
Falls the Shadow
Life is very long

Between the desire
85 And the spasm
Between the potency
And the existence
Between the essence
And the descent
90 Falls the Shadow
For Thine is the Kingdom

For Thine is
Life is
For Thine is the

95 *This is the way the world ends*
This is the way the world ends
This is the way the world ends
Not with a bang but a whimper.

(1925)

6. *Multifoliate rose,* in Dante's *Divine Comedy,* a symbol of Paradise, in which the saints are the many petals of the rose.

OF CRITICAL INTEREST

"The Hollow Men"

In "The Hollow Men" all the richness and complexity of culture which gives "The Waste Land" such thickness of texture disappears. The poem takes place in a twilight realm of disembodied men and forces. The complexity of relations making up the subjective realm of Eliot's ideal descriptions of it is replaced by the vagueness and impalpability of "Shape without form, shade without colour, / Paralysed force, gesture without motion." The hollow men are walking corpses ("Mistah Kurtz—he dead"), and their emptiness is the vacuity of pure mind detached from any reality. They are cut off from one another. Their voices are whispers, "quiet and meaningless." Groping together, they "avoid speech." They are detached from nature, and live in a place which is devoid of any spiritual presence, a "dead land," a "cactus land," a "valley of dying stars," hollow like the men themselves. The eyes of the hollow men are not only averted from one another, but from those other eyes, the returning look from the divine place which those who cross "with direct eyes" to "death's other Kingdom" will encounter. There are no eyes in the hollow valley, and the empty men are bereft of God. Even within their own hollowness detachment is the law. The "Shadow" which falls between idea and reality, conception and creation, emotion and response, desire and spasm, potency and existence, is the paralysis which seizes men who live in a completely subjective world. Mind had seemed the medium which binds all things together in the unity of an organic culture. Now it is revealed to be the Shadow which isolates things from one another, reduces them to abstraction, and makes movement, feeling, and creativity impossible. "The Hollow Men" is an eloquent analysis of the vacuity of subjective idealism, and the state of the hollow men appears in Eliot's later work as the "distraction, delusion, escape into dream, pretense" of the unenlightened people in his plays, each one of whom is a "fugitive from reality."

JOURNEY OF THE MAGI[1]

"A cold coming we had of it,
Just the worst time of the year
For a journey, and such a long journey:
The ways deep and the weather sharp,
5 The very dead of winter."[2]
And the camels galled, sore-footed, refractory,
Lying down in the melting snow.
There were times we regretted
The summer palaces on slopes, the terraces,
10 And the silken girls bringing sherbet.
Then the camel men cursing and grumbling
And running away, and wanting their liquor and women,
And the night-fires going out, and the lack of shelters,
And the cities hostile and the towns unfriendly
15 And the villages dirty and charging high prices:
A hard time we had of it.
At the end we preferred to travel all night,
Sleeping in snatches,
With the voices singing in our ears, saying
20 That this was all folly.

Then at dawn we came down to a temperate valley,
Wet, below the snow line, smelling of vegetation;
With a running stream and a water mill beating the darkness,
And three trees on the low sky,
25 And an old white horse galloped away in the meadow.
Then we came to a tavern with vine-leaves over the lintel,
Six hands at an open door dicing for pieces of silver,
And feet kicking the empty wineskins.[3]
But there was no information, and so we continued
30 And arrived at evening, not a moment too soon
Finding the place; it was (you may say) satisfactory.

---

1. *Magi,* the three wise men who journeyed to Bethlehem to see the infant Jesus.

2. *"A cold . . . winter,"* adapted from a Nativity sermon by the 17th-century divine Lancelot Andrewes.

3. *Then at dawn . . . wineskins.* Images in this passage suggest both renewal of life ("vegetation"; "running stream") and death, foreshadowing events in the life of Christ. The "three trees" suggest the Crucifixion; the men "dicing for pieces of silver" suggest both Judas's betrayal of Christ for thirty pieces of silver, and the soldiers who cast lots for Christ's garments at the foot of the cross. The white horse is mentioned in Revelation 6:2 and 19:11 in passages alluding to the end of the world.

All this was a long time ago, I remember,
And I would do it again, but set down
This set down
35 This: were we led all that way for
Birth or Death? There was a Birth, certainly,
We had evidence and no doubt. I had seen birth and death,
But had thought they were different; this Birth was
Hard and bitter agony for us, like Death, our death.
40 We returned to our places, these Kingdoms,
But no longer at ease here, in the old dispensation,[4]
With an alien people clutching their gods.
I should be glad of another death.

(1927)

4. *the old dispensation,* the old pagan religion.

DISCUSSION

1. Examine each of the three sections of "Portrait of a Lady" and determine what time of year it is, what kind of imagery dominates, and what happens or seems to have happened in the relationship between the speaker and the lady.

2. In Aeschylus's play *Agamemnon,* King Agamemnon, leader of the Greek forces in the Trojan War, is murdered by his wife Clytemnestra upon his return home. Explore the meaning of Eliot's references to this story in the epigraph and in the last stanza of "Sweeney Among the Nightingales."

3. The last two lines of "The Hollow Men" are among the most quoted in 20th-century poetry.

(a) What do they mean?

(b) How do they epitomize the spirit of the hollow men?

(c) Using the footnotes as a guide, explore the possible relevance of Eliot's epigraphs ("Mistah Kurtz—he dead" and "A penny for the Old Guy") to these last lines.

4. In "Journey of the Magi":

(a) Why does the speaker say: "this Birth was / Hard and bitter agony for us, like Death, our death"?

(b) What does the speaker mean when he says in the last line that he "should be glad of another death"?

III. Poets of World War I

SUICIDE IN THE TRENCHES

by Siegfried Sassoon

I knew a simple soldier boy
Who grinned at life in empty joy,
Slept soundly through the lonesome dark,
And whistled early with the lark.

5 In winter trenches, cowed and glum,
With crumps and lice and lack of rum,
He put a bullet through his brain.
No one spoke of him again.

. . .

You smug-faced crowds with kindling eye
10 Who cheer when soldier lads march by,
Sneak home and pray you'll never know
The hell where youth and laughter go.

DREAMERS

by Siegfried Sassoon

Soldiers are citizens of death's gray land,
Drawing no dividend from time's tomorrows.
In the great hour of destiny they stand,
Each with his feuds, and jealousies, and sorrows.
5 Soldiers are sworn to action; they must win
Some flaming, fatal climax with their lives.
Soldiers are dreamers; when the guns begin
They think of firelit homes, clean beds, and wives.

I see them in foul dug-outs, gnawed by rats,
10 And in the ruined trenches, lashed with rain,
Dreaming of things they did with balls and bats,
And mocked by hopeless longing to regain
Bank-holidays, and picture shows, and spats,
And going to the office in the train.

THE NEXT WAR

by Wilfred Owen

War's a joke for me and you,
While we know such dreams are true.

—SASSOON

Out there, we've walked quite friendly up to Death;
Sat down and eaten with him, cool and bland,—
Pardoned his spilling mess-tins in our hand.
We've sniffed the green thick odour of his breath,—
5 Our eyes wept, but our courage didn't writhe.
He's spat at us with bullets and he's coughed
Shrapnel. We chorused when he sang aloft;
We whistled while he shaved us with his scythe.

Oh, Death was never enemy of ours!
10 We laughed at him, we leagued with him, old chum.
No soldier's paid to kick against his powers.
We laughed, knowing that better men would come,
And greater wars; when each proud fighter brags
He wars on Death—for Life; not men—for flags.

THE SOLDIER

by Rupert Brooke

If I should die, think only this of me:
That there's some corner of a foreign field
That is forever England. There shall be
In that rich earth a richer dust concealed;

5 A dust whom England bore, shaped, made aware,
Gave, once, her flowers to love, her ways to roam,
A body of England's breathing English air,
Washed by the rivers, blest by suns of home.

And think, this heart, all evil shed away,
10 A pulse in the eternal mind, no less,
Gives somewhere back the thoughts by England given:
Her sights and sound; dreams happy as her day;
And laughter, learnt of friends; and gentleness,
In hearts at peace, under an English heaven.

THE HILL

by Rupert Brooke

Breathless, we flung us on the windy hill,
Laughed in the sun, and kissed the lovely grass.
You said, "Through glory and ecstasy we pass;
Wind, sun, and earth remain, the birds sing still,
5 When we are old, are old. . . ." "And when we die
All's over that is ours; and life burns on
Through other lovers, other lips," said I,
"Heart of my heart, our heaven is now, is won!"
"We are Earth's best, that learnt her lesson here.
10 Life is our cry. We have kept the faith!" we said;
"We shall go down with unreluctant tread
Rose-crowned into the darkness! . . ." Proud we were,
And laughed, that had such brave true things to say.
And then you suddenly cried, and turned away.

DISCUSSION

1. Explain the title of "Dreamers." Why not "Warriors" or "Fighters"?
2. In "Suicide in the Trenches," identify the "You" addressed in the last stanza, and discuss the effectiveness or ineffectiveness of this stanza.
3. Explain the sudden change of feeling in the last line of Rupert Brooke's "The Hill."
4. Rupert Brooke died in uniform in World War I shortly after "The Soldier" was published.
(a) How does knowledge of this fact affect your reaction to the poem?
(b) What elements in the poem keep it from becoming sentimental or even arrogant in its patriotic feelings about England?
5. (a) In the "greater wars" predicted in the last lines of "The Next War," what is it precisely that "each proud fighter brags"?
(b) How does the speaker in the poem differ from such proud, bragging fighters of the greater wars to come?

IV. Enduring Romantics

THE LISTENERS

by Walter de la Mare

"Is there anybody there?" said the Traveler,
Knocking on the moonlit door;
And his horse in the silence champed the grasses
Of the forest's ferny floor;
And a bird flew up out of the turret,
Above the Traveler's head;
And he smote upon the door again a second time;
"Is there anybody there?" he said.
But no one descended to the Traveler;
10 No head from the leaf-fringed sill
Leaned over and looked into his gray eyes,
Where he stood perplexed and still.
But only a host of phantom listeners
That dwelt in the lone house then
15 Stood listening in the quiet of the moonlight
To that voice from the world of men;
Stood thronging the faint moonbeams on the dark
stair,
That goes down to the empty hall,
Hearkening in an air stirred and shaken
20 By the lonely Traveler's call.
And he felt in his heart their strangeness,
Their stillness answering his cry,
While his horse moved, cropping the dark turf,
'Neath the starred and leafy sky;
25 For he suddenly smote on the door, even
Louder, and lifted his head—
"Tell them I came, and no one answered,
That I kept my word," he said.
Never the least stir made the listeners,
30 Though every word he spake
Fell echoing through the shadowiness of the still
house
From the one man left awake.
Aye, they heard his foot upon the stirrup,
And the sound of iron on stone,
35 And how the silence surged softly backward,
When the plunging hoofs were gone.

"The Listeners" from *The Complete Poems of Walter de la Mare,* 1970. Reprinted by permission of The Literary Trustees of Walter de la Mare and the Society of Authors as their representative.

THE LEGS

by Robert Graves

1
There was this road,
And it led up-hill,
And it led down-hill,
And round and in and out.
2
5 And the traffic was legs,
Legs from the knees down,
Coming and going,
Never pausing.
3
And the gutters gurgled
10 With the rain's overflow,
And the sticks on the pavement
Blindly tapped and tapped.
4
What drew the legs along
Was the never-stopping,
15 And the senseless, frightening
Fate of being legs.
5
Legs for the road,
The road for legs,

"The Legs" from *Collected Poems* by Robert Graves. Copyright © 1955 by Robert Graves. Reprinted by permission of Collins-Knowlton-Wing, Inc.

Resolutely nowhere
In both directions. 20

6

My legs at least
Were not in that rout:
On grass by the road-side
Entire I stood,

7

Watching the unstoppable 25
Legs go by
With never a stumble
Between step and step.

8

Though my smile was broad
The legs could not see, 30
Though my laugh was loud
The legs could not hear.

9

My head dizzied, then:
I wondered suddenly,
Might I too be a walker 35
From the knees down?

10

Gently I touched my shins.
The doubt unchained them:
They had run in twenty puddles
Before I regained them. 40

THE VISITATION

by Robert Graves

Drowsing in my chair of disbelief
I watch the door as it slowly opens—
A trick of the night wind?

Your slender body seems a shaft of moonlight
Against the door as it gently closes. 5
Do you cast no shadow?

Your whisper is too soft for credence,
Your tread like blossom drifting from a bough,
Your touch even softer.

You wear that sorrowful and tender mask 10
Which on high mountaintops in heather-flow
Entrances lonely shepherds;

And though a single word dispels all doubts
I quake for wonder at your choice of me:
Why, why and why? 15

TURN OF THE MOON

by Robert Graves

Never forget who brings the rain
In swarthy goatskin bags from a far sea:
It is the Moon as she turns, repairing
Damages of long drought and sunstroke.

Never count upon rain, never foretell it, 5
For no power can bring rain
Except the Moon as she turns; and who can rule her?

She is prone to delay the necessary floods,
Lest such a gift might become obligation,
A month, or two, or three; then suddenly 10
No relenting but by way of whim
Will perhaps conjure from the cloudless west
A single raindrop to surprise with hope
Each haggard, upturned face.

Were the Moon a Sun, we could count upon her 15
To bring rain seasonably as she turned;
Yet no one thinks to thank the regular Sun
For shining fierce in summer, mild in winter—
Why should the Moon so drudge?

But if one night she brings us, as she turns, 20
Soft, steady, even, copious rain
That harms no leaf nor flower, but gently falls
Hour-after-hour, sinking to the taproots,
And the sodden earth exhales at dawn
A long sigh scented with pure gratitude, 25
Such rain—the first rain of our lives, it seems,
Neither foretold, cajoled, nor counted on—
Is woman giving as she loves.

AUBADE

by Edith Sitwell

Jane, Jane,
Tall as a crane,
The morning light creaks down again.

Comb your cockscomb-ragged hair;
5 Jane, Jane, come down the stair.

Each dull blunt wooden stalactite
Of rain creaks, hardened by the light,

Sounding like an overtone
From some lonely world unknown.

10 But the creaking empty light
Will never harden into sight,

Will never penetrate your brain
With overtones like the blunt rain.

The light would show (if it could harden)
15 Eternities of kitchen-garden,

Cockscomb flowers that none will pluck,
And wooden flowers that 'gin to cluck.

OF CRITICAL INTEREST

"Aubade"

"The morning light creaks down again." The author said "creaks" because, in a very early dawn, after rain, the light has a curious uncertain quality, as though it does not run quite smoothly. Also, it falls in hard cubes, squares, and triangles, which, again, give one the impression of a creaking sound, because of the association with wood. *"Each dull, blunt wooden stalactite of rain creaks, hardened by the light."* In the early dawn, long raindrops are transformed by the light, until they have the light's own quality of hardness; also they have the dull and blunt and tasteless quality of wood; as they move in the wind, they seem to creak. *"Sounding like an overtone from some lonely world unknown."* Though it seems to us as though we heard them sensorily, yet the sound is unheard in reality; it has the quality of an overtone from some unknown and mysterious world. *"But the creaking, empty light will never harden into sight, will never penetrate your brain with overtones like the blunt rain."* The poem is about a country servant, a girl on a farm, plain and neglected and unhappy, and with a sad bucolic stupidity, coming down in the dawn to light the fire; and this phrase means that to her poor mind the light is an empty thing which conveys nothing. It cannot bring sight to her—she is not capable of seeing anything; it can never bring overtones to her mind, because she is not capable of hearing them. She scarcely knows even that she is suffering. *"The light would show, if it could harden, eternities of kitchen garden, cockscomb flowers that none will pluck, and wooden flowers that 'gin to cluck."* If she were capable of seeing anything, still she would only see the whole of eternity as the world of kitchen gardens to which

From *Poetry and Criticism,* by Edith Sitwell. Henry Holt and Company, 1926.

In the kitchen you must light
Flames as staring, red and white

20 As carrots or as turnips, shining
Where the cold dawn light lies whining.

Cockscomb hair on the cold wind
Hangs limp, turns the milk's weak mind. . . .

Jane, Jane,
25 Tall as a crane,
The morning light creaks down again!

---

she is accustomed, with flowers red and lank as cockscombs (uncared for, just as she is uncared for), and those hard flowers that dip and bend beneath the rain till they look (and seem as though they must sound) like hens clucking. "*In the kitchen you must light flames as staring red and white as carrots or as turnips—shining where the cold dawn light lies whining.*" To the author's sight, the shivering movement of a certain cold dawn light upon the floor suggests a kind of high animal whining or whimpering, a kind of half-frightened and subservient urge to something outside our consciousness. "*Cockscomb hair on the cold wind hangs limp, turns the milk's weak mind,*" is obviously a joke, and a joke may be permitted even to a poet.

DISCUSSION

1. Critic Louis Untermeyer has said of "The Listeners": "Never . . . has the symbolism of man's courage facing the cryptic riddle of life been more memorably expressed."

(a) Explain this statement with reference to the poem.

(b) Explain why you agree or disagree with Untermeyer's interpretation.

(c) "The Listeners" is widely regarded as a masterpiece in its expression of the mysterious. What might account for this?

2. (a) Characterize the activities of the legs (in "The Legs") as described in the first five stanzas of the poem.

(b) At the end of the poem, what is the significance of the speaker's discovery that his legs "had run in twenty puddles" before he "regained them"?

3. In "The Visitation," how are the first and last stanzas related?

4. Explore the effectiveness of the analogy that is made explicit at the end of "Turn of the Moon." Are the characteristics given to the moon throughout the poem also meant to suggest the characteristics of woman? Explain.

5. Read Edith Sitwell's comment on "Aubade" and discuss what she means when she says that the last (tenth) couplet of the poem "is obviously a joke, and a joke may be permitted even to a poet."

Twentieth-Century Poetry
Part Two:
THE AGE OF ANXIETY

Follow, poet, follow right
To the bottom of the night,
With your unconstraining voice
Still persuade us to rejoice. . . .
W. H. Auden

put on a monument - perfect man, "saint"
fit into society's mold.
parallel to "unknown soldier" and 1984.

I. W. H. Auden 1907 / 1973

people love him, but don't know why
*only told statistics, nothing about feelings or personality.

THE UNKNOWN CITIZEN

(To JS/07/M/378
This Marble Monument
Is Erected by the State)

He was found by the Bureau of Statistics to be
One against whom there was no official complaint,
And all the reports on his conduct agree
That, in the modern sense of an old-fashioned word, he was a saint,
5 For in everything he did he served the Greater Community.
Except for the War till the day he retired
He worked in a factory and never got fired,

But satisfied his employers, Fudge Motors Inc.
Yet he wasn't a scab or odd in his views,
10 For his Union reports that he paid his dues,
(Our report on his Union shows it was sound)
And our Social Psychology workers found
That he was popular with his mates and liked a drink.
The Press are convinced that he bought a paper every day
15 And that his reactions to advertisements were normal in every way.
Policies taken out in his name prove that he was fully insured,
And his Health-card shows he was once in hospital but left it cured.
Both Producers Research and High-Grade Living declare
He was fully sensible to the advantages of the Instalment Plan
20 And had everything necessary to the Modern Man,
A phonograph, a radio, a car and a frigidaire.
Our researchers into Public Opinion are content
That he held the proper opinions for the time of year;
When there was peace, he was for peace; when there was war, he went.
25 He was married and added five children to the population,
Which our Eugenist says was the right number for a parent of his generation,
And our teachers report that he never interfered with their education.
Was he free? Was he happy? The question is absurd:
Had anything been wrong, we should certainly have heard.

JILL KREMENTZ, N.Y.

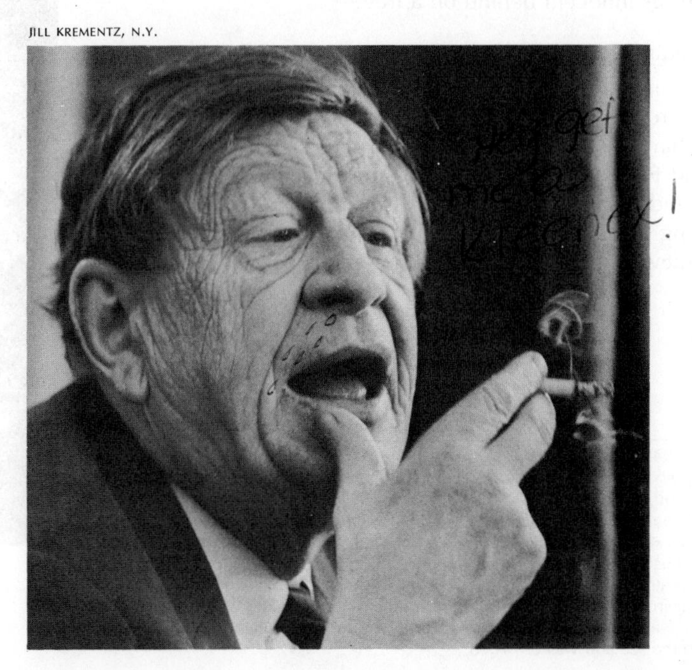

MUSÉE DES BEAUX ARTS[1]

by W. H. Auden

About suffering they were never wrong,
The Old Masters: how well they understood
Its human position; how it takes place
While someone else is eating or opening a window or just
walking dully along;
5 How, when the aged are reverently, passionately waiting
For the miraculous birth, there always must be
Children who did not specially want it to happen, skating
On a pond at the edge of the wood:
They never forgot
10 That even the dreadful martyrdom must run its course
Anyhow in a corner, some untidy spot
Where the dogs go on with their doggy life and the
torturer's horse
Scratches its innocent behind on a tree.

In Brueghel's *Icarus*,[2] for instance: how everything turns away
15 Quite leisurely from the disaster; the ploughman may
Have heard the splash, the forsaken cry,
But for him it was not an important failure; the sun shone
As it had to on the white legs disappearing into the green
Water; and the expensive delicate ship that must have seen
20 Something amazing, a boy falling out of the sky,
Had somewhere to get to and sailed calmly on.

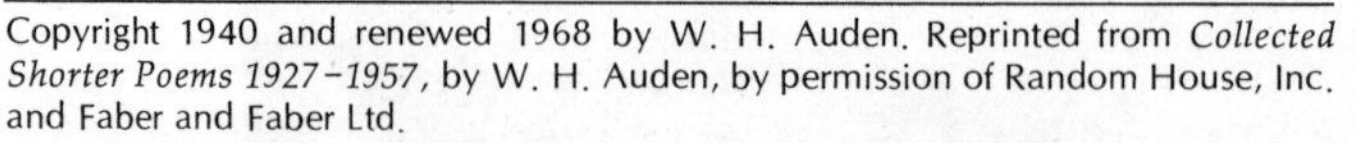

1. *Musée des Beaux Arts,* the Royal Museum of Fine Arts in Brussels.
2. *Brueghel's Icarus.* Brueghel was Pieter Brueghel the Elder (1525?–1569). His painting, "The Fall of Icarus," was inspired by the Greek myth which relates how the cunning artisan Daedalus made wings of feathers and wax for his son Icarus and himself in order to escape from imprisonment on the island of Crete. Despite his father's warnings, Icarus flew too close to the sun; his wings melted off, and he fell into the sea and was drowned.

"THE FALL OF ICARUS" BY PIETER BRUEGHEL (1525?–1569). MUSÉE ROYAUX DES BEAUX-ARTS DE BELGIQUE, BRUXELLES.

IN MEMORY OF W. B. YEATS

(d. Jan. 1939)

1

He disappeared in the dead of winter:
The brooks were frozen, the airports almost deserted,
And snow disfigured the public statues;
The mercury sank in the mouth of the dying day.
5 What instruments we have agree
The day of his death was a dark cold day.

Far from his illness
The wolves ran on through the evergreen forests,
The peasant river was untempted by the fashionable quays;
10 By mourning tongues
The death of the poet was kept from his poems.

But for him it was his last afternoon as himself,
An afternoon of nurses and rumours;
The provinces of his body revolted,
15 The squares of his mind were empty,
Silence invaded the suburbs,
The current of his feeling failed; he became his admirers.

Now he is scattered among a hundred cities
And wholly given over to unfamiliar affections;
20 To find his happiness in another kind of wood
And be punished under a foreign code of conscience.
The words of a dead man
Are modified in the guts of the living.

But in the importance and noise of to-morrow
25 When the brokers are roaring like beasts on the floor of
the Bourse,[1]
And the poor have the sufferings to which they are
fairly accustomed,
And each in the cell of himself is almost convinced of
his freedom,
A few thousand will think of this day
As one thinks of a day when one did something slightly unusual.
30 What instruments we have agree
The day of his death was a dark cold day.

---

1. *Bourse*, stock exchange.

2

You were silly like us; your gift survived it all:
The parish of rich women, physical decay,
Yourself. Mad Ireland hurt you into poetry.
35 Now Ireland has her madness and her weather still,
For poetry makes nothing happen: it survives
In the valley of its making where executives
Would never want to tamper, flows on south
From ranches of isolation and the busy griefs,
40 Raw towns that we believe and die in; it survives,
A way of happening, a mouth.

3

Earth, receive an honoured guest:
William Yeats is laid to rest:
Let the Irish vessel lie
45 Emptied of its poetry.

In the nightmare of the dark
All the dogs of Europe bark,
And the living nations wait,
Each sequestered in its hate;

50 Intellectual disgrace
Stares from every human face,
And the seas of pity lie
Locked and frozen in each eye.

Follow, poet, follow right
55 To the bottom of the night,
With your unconstraining voice
Still persuade us to rejoice;

With the farming of a verse
Make a vineyard of the curse,
60 Sing of human unsuccess
In a rapture of distress;

In the deserts of the heart
Let the healing fountain start,
In the prison of his days
65 Teach the free man how to praise.

OF CRITICAL INTEREST

"In Memory of W. B. Yeats"

"In Memory of W. B. Yeats" contains two basic, related points: that a poet's work ultimately becomes independent of him, because he has no control over the interpretation which posterity will give it; and that therefore it is conditioned by society, and its role in society can be no more than a passive one. The rather sinister dramatization of Yeats's death in the first section is thus an essential part of the mystery of a poet's destiny, and the numb elegiacs reinforce the sense that the external world, in the grip of winter, is quite irrelevant to the internal world of poetry: the external "instruments" measure the fact of the weather and the fact of Yeats's death, but the internal "guts" receive and modify his life's work.

Similarly, the metaphor of revolution represents the purely material fate of the poet's body: the city is in revolt, but the countryside (the poetry) goes on as usual. The poems, by being still read, continue to live ("By mourning tongues / The death of the poet was kept from his poems") and the poet, in ceasing to be a physical being, takes on the affective value of his *oeuvre* ("he became his admirers").

O WHERE ARE YOU GOING?

"O where are you going?" said reader to rider,
"That valley is fatal when furnaces burn,
Yonder's the midden[1] whose odours will madden,
That gap is the grave where the tall[2] return."

5 "O do you imagine," said fearer to farer,
"That dusk will delay on your path to the pass,
Your diligent looking discover the lacking
Your footsteps feel from granite to grass?"

"O what was that bird," said horror to hearer,
10 "Did you see that shape in the twisted trees?
Behind you swiftly the figure comes softly,
The spot on your skin is a shocking disease."

"Out of this house"—said rider to reader,
"Yours never will"—said farer to fearer,
15 "They're looking for you"—said hearer to horror,
As he left them there, as he left them there.

---

1. *midden*, garbage or refuse heap.
2. *tall*, used in the old sense of "brave, courageous."

DISCUSSION

1. In the next-to-last line of "The Unknown Citizen" we are asked: "Was he free? Was he happy?" Are these questions answered in the poem? How?

2. As the first two words of "Musée des Beaux Arts" indicate, it is a poem "about suffering."

(a) What is the point made "about suffering"?

(b) Relate the point to your own experience.

3. In "In Memory of W. B. Yeats":

(a) Explain: "The words of a dead man / Are modified in the guts of the living."

(b) In the second section, how is it that "poetry makes nothing happen"?

(c) In the third section, what appears to be the role of poetry in the world (since it "makes nothing happen")?

4. (a) Relate the answers given in the last stanza of "O Where Are You Going?" to the questions posed in the first three stanzas.

(b) Contrast rider, farer, hearer as a group with reader, fearer, horror.

II. Stephen Spender 1909 /

THE LANDSCAPE NEAR AN AERODROME

More beautiful and soft than any moth
With burring furred antennae feeling its huge path
Through dusk, the air liner with shut-off engines
Glides over suburbs and the sleeves set trailing tall
5 To point the wind. Gently, broadly, she falls,
Scarcely disturbing charted currents of air.

Lulled by descent, the travellers across sea
And across feminine land indulging its easy limbs
In miles of softness, now let their eyes trained by watching
10 Penetrate through dusk the outskirts of this town
Here where industry shows a fraying edge.
Here they may see what is being done.

Beyond the winking masthead light
And the landing ground, they observe the outposts
15 Of work: chimneys like lank black fingers
Or figures, frightening and mad: and squat buildings
With their strange air behind trees, like women's faces
Shattered by grief. Here where few houses
Moan with faint light behind their blinds,
20 They remark the unhomely sense of complaint, like a dog
Shut out, and shivering at the foreign moon.

In the last sweep of love, they pass over fields
Behind the aerodrome, where boys play all day
Hacking dead grass: whose cries, like wild birds,
25 Settle upon the nearest roofs
But soon are hid under the loud city.

Then, as they land, they hear the tolling bell
Reaching across the landscape of hysteria,
To where, louder than all those batteries
30 And charcoaled towers against that dying sky,
Religion stands, the Church blocking the sun.

AN ELEMENTARY SCHOOL CLASS ROOM IN A SLUM

Far far from gusty waves, these children's faces.
Like rootless weeds the torn hair round their paleness.
The tall girl with her weighed-down head. The paper-
seeming boy with rat's eyes. The stunted unlucky heir
5 Of twisted bones, reciting a father's gnarled disease,
His lesson from his desk. At back of the dim class
One unnoted, sweet and young: his eyes live in a dream
Of squirrels' game, in tree room, other than this.

On sour cream walls, donations. Shakespeare's head
10 Cloudless at dawn, civilized dome riding all cities.
Belled, flowery, Tyrolese valley. Open-handed map
Awarding the world its world. And yet, for these
Children, these windows, not this world, are world,
Where all their future's painted with a fog,
15 A narrow street sealed in with a lead sky,
Far far from rivers, capes, and stars of words.

Surely Shakespeare is wicked, the map a bad example
With ships and sun and love tempting them to steal—
For lives that slyly turn in their cramped holes
20 From fog to endless night? On their slag heap, these children
Wear skins peeped through by bones and spectacles of steel
With mended glass, like bottle bits in slag.
Tyrol is wicked; map's promising a fable:
All of their time and space are foggy slum,
25 So blot their maps with slums as big as doom.

Unless, governor, teacher, inspector, visitor,
This map becomes their window and these windows
That open on their lives like crouching tombs
Break, O break open, till they break the town
30 And show the children to the fields and all their world
Azure on their sands, to let their tongues
Run naked into books, the white and green leaves open
The history theirs whose language is the sun.

THE WAR GOD

Why cannot the one good
Benevolent feasible
Final dove descend?

And the wheat be divided?
5 And the soldiers sent home?
And the barriers torn down?
And the enemies forgiven?
And there be no retribution?

Because the conqueror
10 Is an instrument of power,
With merciless heart hammered
Out of former fear,
When to-day's vanquished
Destroyed his noble father,
15 Filling his cradle with anguish.

His irremediable victory
Chokes back sobbing anxiety
Lest children of the slain
(When the ripe ears grow high
20 To the sickles of his own
And the sun goes down)
Rise in iron morning
To stain with blood the sky
And avenge their fathers again.

25 His heart broke before
His raging splendour.
The virgins of prayer
Fumble vainly for that day
Buried under ruins,
30 Of his pride's greatest murder
When his heart which was a child
Asking and tender,
He hunted and killed.

The lost filled with lead
35 On the helpless field
May dream the pious reason
Of mercy, but also
Their eyes know what they did
In their own proud season,
40 Their dead teeth bite the earth
With semen of new hatred.

For the world is the world
And not the slain
Nor the slayer, forgive,
45 Nor do wild shores
Of passionate histories
Close on endless love;
Though hidden under seas
Of chafing despair,
50 Love's need does not cease.

DISCUSSION

1. In the last stanza of "The Landscape Near an Aerodrome," explore the meaning and effect of the loudness of the tolling church bell, and of the closing image of "the Church blocking the sun."

2. (a) In the third stanza of "An Elementary School Class Room in a Slum," what is the meaning of the words: "Shakespeare is wicked"; "Tyrol is wicked"?

(b) In the last stanza, the poet points to the possibility of the map becoming the window of the classroom and the actual windows breaking. What does he mean?

3. (a) What is the cycle described in "The War God" which seems to make wars inevitable?

(b) How does the last stanza modify or qualify the pessimistic view of the poem?

III. Dylan Thomas 1914 / 1953

BETTMANN ARCHIVE, INC.

THE FORCE THAT THROUGH THE GREEN FUSE DRIVES THE FLOWER

The force that through the green fuse drives the
  flower
Drives my green age; that blasts the roots of trees
Is my destroyer.
And I am dumb to tell the crooked rose
5 My youth is bent by the same wintry fever.

The force that drives the water through the rocks
Drives my red blood; that dries the mouthing
  streams
Turns mine to wax.
And I am dumb to mouth unto my veins
10 How at the mountain spring the same mouth sucks.

The hand that whirls the water in the pool
Stirs the quicksand; that ropes the blowing wind
Hauls my shroud sail.
And I am dumb to tell the hanging man
15 How of my clay is made the hangman's lime.

The lips of time leech to the fountain head;
Love drips and gathers, but the fallen blood
Shall calm her sores.
And I am dumb to tell a weather's wind
20 How time has ticked a heaven round the stars.

And I am dumb to tell the lover's tomb
How at my sheet goes the same crooked worm.

OF CRITICAL INTEREST

"The Force that Through the Green Fuse . . ."

The contending forces of growth and decay find their natural expression in antithetical imagery, one image posed against its opposite in imitation of the balance of forces. The gunpowder conceit of the first line (the flower seen as an explosion at the top of its stem, the fuse) supplies the "blasts" of the second line, which, however, utilizes the alternative meaning of *blasts* retained in *fever;* and *blasts* is recalled in *wintry,* a third connotation.

Antithetical form is very clear in the first stanza: the force that, on the one hand, brings the flowering of youth causes, on the other hand, destruction, which is then emphasized in the refrain. The second stanza repeats the form.

"Mouthing streams" are streams at the mouth, the estuary. The mouth sucking at the mountain spring can be thought of as the estuary, sucking down the whole course of the stream into the sea. The force that drives the water through the rocks is the same as that which sucks it in at the mouth: in short, the creating and destroying forces are identical. This same mouth, the estuary, sucks at the veins. The poet is leading up to a leech image in stanza four, but here the image is of the bloodstream, the stream of life, beginning in youth, with time slowly sucking away the vitality, pulling toward the estuary, death. The force that drives the blood also dries it; the force of youth pulls one on to age.

The same idea is represented differently in the next stanza. The force that whirls the water (positive action) stirs quicksand (betokening death). The force blows both the ship of life and the ship of death. The two forces are one.

Is this same kind of two-way cross current in the refrain? We certainly wouldn't see it unless we were looking for it. The poet's mortal clay is not only dead but is the receptor for dead flesh, doubly dead. Though the positive doesn't have much chance here, *lime* no doubt came down from *quicksand* (via quicklime) and shares the same implication of "quick." The lime pit is, in a sense, cleansing. Positive effects can, according to Thomas' way of looking at things, come out of the macabre.

This is the point of the next image. Time is a leech, which sucks at the fountain-head of Love, making a sore wound. But the loss of blood, in keeping with archaic lore, is beneficial. The refrain of this stanza makes the same assertion of unexpected good coming from evil. *Heaven* must be positive; Thomas would not use it ironically here. When Time, usually the agent of destruction, ticks a *heaven* round the stars, it is unexpected, but that is the whole point—positive comes out of the usually negative.

The real subject of the poem is the idea of contending forces in nature and the vital role of destruction. Of course, the forces do cause dismay, and regret is the dominant response to the world of flux. The refrains communicate this tone, which is summed up in the final isolated couplet. The poet is expressing his identity with the dead lover, knowing himself to be mortal, the worm already at his sheet as though it were his shroud. The pathos here seems to set at nought the *heaven* of the previous lines. At the end of his celebration of the dual processes in nature, the poet emphasizes the negative . . . .

Abridged and slightly adapted from *Entrances to Dylan Thomas' Poetry* by Ralph Maud. By permission of the University of Pittsburgh Press.

FERN HILL

Now as I was young and easy under the apple boughs
About the lilting house and happy as the grass was green,
The night above the dingle starry,
Time let me hail and climb
5 Golden in the heydays of his eyes,
And honoured among wagons I was prince of the apple towns
And once below a time I lordly had the trees and leaves
Trail with daisies and barley
Down the rivers of the windfall light.

10 And as I was green and carefree, famous among the barns
About the happy yard and singing as the farm was home,
In the sun that is young once only,
Time let me play and be
Golden in the mercy of his means,
15 And green and golden I was huntsman and herdsman, the calves
Sang to my horn, the foxes on the hills barked clear and cold,
And the sabbath rang slowly
In the pebbles of the holy streams.

All the sun long it was running, it was lovely, the hay
20 Fields high as the house, the tunes from the chimneys, it was air
And playing, lovely and watery
And fire green as grass.
And nightly under the simple stars
As I rode to sleep the owls were bearing the farm away,
25 All the moon long I heard, blessed among stables, the night-jars
Flying with the ricks, and the horses
Flashing into the dark.

And then to awake, and the farm, like a wanderer white
With the dew, come back, the cock on his shoulder: it was all
30 Shining, it was Adam and maiden,
The sky gathered again
And the sun grew round that very day.
So it must have been after the birth of the simple light
In the first, spinning place, the spellbound horses walking warm
35 Out of the whinnying green stable
On to the fields of praise.

And honoured among foxes and pheasants by the gay house
Under the new made clouds and happy as the heart was long,
In the sun born over and over,
40 I ran my heedless ways,
My wishes raced through the house high hay
And nothing I cared, at my sky blue trades, that time allows
In all his tuneful turning so few and such morning songs
Before the children green and golden
45 Follow him out of grace,

Nothing I cared, in the lamb white days, that time would take me
Up to the swallow thronged loft by the shadow of my hand,
In the moon that is always rising,
Nor that riding to sleep
50 I should hear him fly with the high fields
And wake to the farm forever fled from the childless land.
Oh as I was young and easy in the mercy of his means,
Time held me green and dying
Though I sang in my chains like the sea.

OF CRITICAL INTEREST

"Fern Hill"

If one sought to describe this poem within the compass of a single phrase, it might be called "an elegy in praise of lost youth." Lament and celebration sound throughout the work: the latter strongly at the beginning, the former gaining tone as the poem progresses.

But, as with all great threnodies in English—with Milton's *Lycidas,* Gray's *Elegy,* Shelley's *Adonais,* and Arnold's *Thyrsis*—the particularity of the cause of grief is lost in a sorrow which speaks for all men. Nostalgic recollection of a child's farm holiday is the leaping-off point for the poem; but—once launched—so intense and poignant a memory overtakes the poet, that his words convey more than a merely topographical homesickness. The farm becomes Eden before the Fall, and time the angel with a flaming sword.

But no such intrusive personification operates within the poem. The farm is invested with a light as radiant as the unforfeited Garden, and time exercises its function as irrevocably as God's excluding angel. So, though at the end we are faced with nothing worse than a farmstead which cannot be revisited, in actual poetic terms we have experienced the states of innocence and eternity, and been subjected to corruption, time, and change.

The poem is constructed from six nine-line stanzas, with only an infrequent rhyme. The absence of rhyme suffices to make the lyrically undulating lines more natural. The artifice and architectonic of the poem consists not in the usual technical devices, but in the repetition, in later stanzas, of *motifs* established in the first. These *motifs* are not worked out with any mechanical regularity; and their place and precedence in the poem are not formally observed. The *motifs* I find to be mainly three: that of the unwitting situation of childhood; that of the delight in this situation; that of time's operation, by which the situation becomes a fate.

DO NOT GO GENTLE INTO THAT GOOD NIGHT

Do not go gentle into that good night,
Old age should burn and rave at close of day;
Rage, rage against the dying of the light.

Though wise men at their end know dark is right,
5 Because their words had forked no lightning they
Do not go gentle into that good night.

Good men, the last wave by, crying how bright
Their frail deeds might have danced in a green bay,
Rage, rage against the dying of the light.

10 Wild men who caught and sang the sun in flight,
And learn, too late, they grieved it on its way,
Do not go gentle into that good night.

Grave men, near death, who see with blinding sight
Blind eyes could blaze like meteors and be gay,
15 Rage, rage against the dying of the light.

And you, my father, there on the sad height,
Curse, bless, me now with your fierce tears, I pray.
Do not go gentle into that good night.
Rage, rage against the dying of the light.

OF LITERARY INTEREST

The Villanelle

"Do Not Go Gentle" is a villanelle, an intricate poetic form consisting of five or more three-line stanzas (tercets) and a final four-line stanza (quatrain), all relying on only two rhymes. The first and third lines of the poem alternate as the last lines of the three-line stanzas, and together end the quatrain. This exacting form is chiefly used in Medieval French poetry, although a few poets writing in English have used it. One is W. H. Auden, who has written a Villanelle that is sometimes also called "If I Could Tell You."

A REFUSAL TO MOURN THE DEATH, BY FIRE, OF A CHILD IN LONDON

Never until the mankind making
Bird beast and flower
Fathering and all humbling darkness
Tells with silence the last light breaking
5 And the still hour
Is come of the sea tumbling in harness

And I must enter again the round
Zion of the water bead
And the synagogue of the ear of corn
10 Shall I let pray the shadow of a sound
Or sow my salt seed
In the least valley of sackcloth to mourn

The majesty and burning of the child's death.
I shall not murder
15 The mankind of her going with a grave truth
Nor blaspheme down the stations of the breath
With any further
Elegy of innocence and youth.

Deep with the first dead lies London's daughter,
20 Robed in the long friends,
The grains beyond age, the dark veins of her mother,
Secret by the unmourning water
Of the riding Thames.
After the first death, there is no other.

OF LITERARY INTEREST

Dylan Thomas on breeding images

A poem by Cameron needs no more than one image; it moves around one idea, from one logical point to another, making a full circle. A poem by myself needs a host of images because its center is a host of images. I make one image—though "make" is not the word, I let, perhaps, an image be "made" emotionally in me and then apply to it what intellectual and critical forces I possess—let it breed another, let that image contradict the first, make of the third image bred out of the other two together, a fourth contradictory image, and let them all, within my imposed formal limits, conflict. Each image holds within it the seeds of its own destruction, and my dialectical method, as I understand it, is a constant building up and breaking down of the images that come out of the central seed, which is itself destructive and constructive at the same time.

Reading back over that, I agree it looks preciously like nonsense. To say that I "let" my images breed and conflict is to deny my critical part in the business. But what I want to try to explain—and it's necessarily vague in me—is that the *life* in any poem of mine cannot move concentrically round a central image; the life must come out of the centre; an image must be born and die in another; and any sequence of my images must be a sequence of creations, recreations, destructions, contradictions. I cannot either . . . make a poem out of a single motivating experience. I believe in the single thread of action through a poem, but that is an intellectual thing aimed at lucidity through narrative. My object is . . . conventionally to "get things straight." Out of the inevitable conflict of images—inevitable because of the creative, recreative, destructive, and contradictory nature of the motivating centre, the womb of war—I try to make that momentary peace which is a poem. I do not want a poem of mine to be, nor can it be, a circular piece of experience placed neatly outside the living stream of time from which it came; a poem of mine is, or should be, a watertight section of the stream that is flowing all ways, all warring images within it should be reconciled for that small stop of time.

DISCUSSION

1. (a) "The Force That Through the Green Fuse Drives the Flower" opens with a juxtaposition of creative and destructive forces, or forces of life and forces of death. Trace the linking of these forces throughout the poem and discuss the effect.

(b) How does the poet relate these elements in nature to himself?

2. Explain the last two lines of "Fern Hill": "Time held me green and dying / Though I sang in my chains like the sea."

3. When Dylan Thomas wrote "Do Not Go Gentle," his father was ill and apparently had only a short time to live. The poem was not published until after the old man's death.

(a) Stanzas 2–5 mention four kinds of men. How does each type meet death, and why?

(b) Light and dark (night) are contrasted throughout the poem. What does each signify?

(c) Explore the possible implications of the often-repeated phrase "good night."

(d) It has been stated that this poem would not be half so moving without the ritualistic repetition with variation that the villanelle form demands. Discuss.

4. (a) The structure of the first sentence of "A Refusal to Mourn," extending through the first two and into the third stanza, is puzzling and might be rearranged thus:

Never until
  the mankind-making, bird-beast-and-flower Fathering,
  and all-humbling darkness
  Tells, with silence, the last light breaking;
And [never until] the still hour of the sea,
  tumbling in harness, is come;

And [never until] I must enter again
  the round Zion of the water bead
  And the synagogue of the ear of corn
Shall I let [myself] pray the shadow of a sound
Or sow my salt seed in the least valley of sackcloth
to mourn the majesty and burning of the child's death.

The poet thus asserts that he will not pray or shed tears ("sow my salt seed") or (in later stanzas) present "grave truth" in an elegy for the dead child. Yet in the last stanza, the poem turns affirmative for the first time and becomes something like a traditional elegy. What is affirmed in the closing lines?

(b) Explicate the first three lines of stanza two: "And I must enter again the round / Zion of the water bead / And the synagogue of the ear of corn."

IV. Variations on Anxiety

NEARING AGAIN THE LEGENDARY ISLE

by C. Day-Lewis

Nearing again the legendary isle
Where sirens sang and mariners were skinned,
We wonder now what was there to beguile
That such stout fellows left their bones behind.
5 Those chorus-girls are surely past their prime,
Voices grow shrill and paint is wearing thin,
Lips that sealed up the sense from gnawing time
Now beg the favor with a graveyard grin.
We have no flesh to spare and they can't bite,
10 Hunger and sweat have stripped us to the bone;
A skeleton crew we toil upon the tide
And mock the theme-song meant to lure us on:

No need to stop the ears, avert the eyes
From purple rhetoric of evening skies.

THE UNEXPLODED BOMB

by C. Day Lewis

Two householders (semi-detached) once found,
Digging their gardens, a bomb underground—
Half in one's land, half in t'other's, with the fence
between.
Neighbours they were, but for years had been
5 Hardly on speaking terms. Now X. unbends
To pass a remark across the creosoted fence:
"Look what I've got!"
"Oh, you've got it too.
Then what, may I ask, are you proposing to do
About this object of yours which menaces my wife,
10 My kiddies, my property, my whole way of life?"
"Your way of life," says Y., "is no credit to humanity.
I don't wish to quarrel; but, since you began it, I
Find your wife stuck-up, your children repel me,
And let me remind you that we too have the telly.
15 This bomb of mine—"
"I don't like your tone!
And I must point out that, since I own
More bomb than you, to create any tension
Between us won't pay you."
"What a strange mis-
apprehension!"
Says the other: "my portion of bomb is near
20 Six inches longer than yours. So there!"

"They seem," the bomb muttered in its clenched
and narrow
Sleep, "to take me for a vegetable marrow."

"It would give me," said X., "the very greatest
pleasure
To come across the fence now with my tape-
measure—"
25 "Oh no," Y. answered, "I'm not having you
Trampling my flowerbeds and peering through
My windows."
"Oho," snarled X., "if that's
Your attitude, I warn you to keep your brats
In future from trespassing upon my land,
30 Or they'll bitterly regret it."
"You misunderstand.
My family has no desire to step on
Your soil; and my bomb is a peace-lover's weapon."
Called a passing angel, "If you two shout
And fly into tantrums and keep dancing about,
35 The thing will go off. It is surely permissible
To say that your bomb, though highly fissible,
Is in another sense one and indivisible;
By which I mean—if you'll forgive the phrase,
Gentlemen—the bloody thing works both ways.
40 So let me put forward a dispassionate proposal:
Both of you, ring for a bomb-disposal
Unit, and ask them to remove post-haste
The cause of your dispute."

X. and Y. stared aghast
At the angel. "Remove my bomb?" they sang
45 In unison both: "allow a gang
To invade my garden and pull up the fence
Upon which my whole way of life depends?
Only a sentimental idealist
Could moot it. I, thank God, am a realist."

50 The angel fled. The bomb turned over
In its sleep and mumbled "I shall soon discover,
If X. and Y. are too daft to unfuse me,
How the Devil intends to use me."

OXFORD UNIVERSITY PRESS

THE ROOM

by C. Day-Lewis

For George Seferis

To this room—it was somewhere at the palace's
Heart, but no one, not even visiting royalty
Or reigning mistress, ever had been inside it—
To this room he'd retire.
5 Graciously giving himself to, guarding himself from
Courtier, suppliant, stiff ambassador,
Supple assassin, into this unviewed room
He, with the air of one urgently called from
High affairs to some yet loftier duty,
10 Dismissing them all, withdrew.

And we imagined it suitably fitted out
For communing with a God, for meditation
On the Just City; or, at the least, a bower of
Superior orgies . . . He
15 Alone could know the room as windowless
Though airy, bare yet filled with the junk you find
In any child-loved attic; and how he went there
Simply to taste himself, to be reassured
That under the royal action and abstraction
20 He lived in, he was real.

AUTOBIOGRAPHY

by Louis MacNeice

In my childhood trees were green
And there was plenty to be seen.

Come back early or never come.

My father made the walls resound,
5 He wore his collar the wrong way round.

Come back early or never come.

My mother wore a yellow dress;
Gently, gently, gentleness.

Come back early or never come.

10 When I was five the black dreams came;
Nothing after was quite the same.

Come back early or never come.

The dark was talking to the dead;
The lamp was dark beside my bed.

15 *Come back early or never come.*

When I woke they did not care;
Nobody, nobody was there.

Come back early or never come.

When my silent terror cried,
20 Nobody, nobody replied.

Come back early or never come.

I got up; the chilly sun
Saw me walk away alone.

Come back early or never come.

PRAYER BEFORE BIRTH

by Louis MacNeice

I am not yet born; O hear me.
Let not the bloodsucking bat or the rat or the stoat or the
club-footed ghoul come near me.

I am not yet born, console me.
5 I fear that the human race may with tall walls wall me.
with strong drugs dope me, with wise lies lure me,
on black racks rack me, in blood-baths roll me.

I am not yet born; provide me
With water to dandle me, grass to grow for me, trees to talk
10 to me, sky to sing to me, birds and a white light
in the back of my mind to guide me.

I am not yet born; forgive me
For the sins that in me the world shall commit, my words
when they speak me, my thoughts when they think me,
15 my treason engendered by traitors beyond me.
my life when they murder by means of my
hands, my death when they live me.

I am not yet born; rehearse me
In the parts I must play and the cues I must take when
20 old men lecture me, bureaucrats hector me, mountains
frown at me, lovers laugh at me, the white
waves call me to folly and the desert calls
me to doom and the beggar refuses
my gift and my children curse me.

25 I am not yet born; O hear me,
Let not the man who is beast or who thinks he is God
come near me.

I am not yet born; O fill me
With strength against those who would freeze my
30 humanity, would dragoon me into a lethal automaton.
would make me a cog in a machine, a thing with
one face, a thing, and against all those
who would dissipate my entirety, would
blow me like thistledown hither and
35 thither or hither and thither
like water held in the
hands would spill me.
Let them not make me a stone and let them not spill me.
Otherwise kill me.

THE TAXIS

by Louis MacNeice

In the first taxi he was alone tra-la,
No extras on the clock. He tipped ninepence
But the cabby, while he thanked him, looked
askance
As though to suggest someone had bummed a ride.

5 In the second taxi he was alone tra-la
But the clock showed sixpence extra; he tipped
according
And the cabby from out his muffler said: "Make
sure
You have left nothing behind tra-la between you."

In the third taxi he was alone tra-la
10 But the tip-up seats were down and there was an
extra
Charge of one-and-sixpence and an odd
Scent that reminded him of a trip to Cannes.

As for the fourth taxi, he was alone
Tra-la when he hailed it but the cabby looked
15 Through him and said: "I can't tra-la well take
So many people, not to speak of the dog."

FRUITLESS FABLE

by Muriel Spark

Mr. Chiddicott, being a bachelor,
Purchased from a reputable department store
(Barkers') a morning-tea machine
At the price of fifteen pounds fifteen.
5 Easy to work, all plugged and wired.
Each night, he set the time required,
And every morning when he heard
The bell, he found his tea prepared.
But being by profession something mechanic
10 Mr. Chiddicott began to perfect it,
So that before long when it woke him up
It actually handed him the cup.

Years pass. Mr. Chiddicott grows
Successful as a cabbage rose,
15 Mellow, unmated and serene,
Served by the morning-tea machine.
Alas, the transience of bliss—
There came a sudden end to his.

One morning as it rang the bell,
20 The tea-machine said, "What the hell,
I've stood this treatment long and dumb;
Mr. Chiddicott, the time has come
For you to make the tea instead.
Nip out and let me into bed."
25 And when our friend demurred, alack,
The tea-machine gave him a dreadful crack.
Mr. Chiddicott murmured as he curled
Up, "It is the end of the world."
But it wasn't, for Mr. Chiddicott came
30 To, and finally admitted blame,
And every morning now he can be seen
(From the windows across the street, I mean)
Serving tea to his perfected tea-machine.

POETRY FOR SUPPER

by R. S. Thomas

"Listen, now, verse should be as natural
As the small tuber that feeds on muck
And grows slowly from obtuse soil
To the white flower of immortal beauty."

5 "Natural, hell! What was it Chaucer
Said once about the long toil
That goes like blood to the poem's making?
Leave it to nature and the verse sprawls,
Limp as bindweed, if it break at all
10 Life's iron crust. Man, you must sweat
And rhyme your guts taut, if you'd build
Your verse a ladder."
"You speak as though
No sunlight ever surprised the mind
Groping on its cloudy path."

15 "Sunlight's a thing that needs a window
Before it enter a dark room.
Windows don't happen."
So two old poets,
Hunched at their beer in the low haze
Of an inn parlour, while the talk ran
20 Noisily by them, glib with prose.

DISCUSSION

1. In "Nearing Again the Legendary Isle," does the poet seem to think that it is an improvement or a loss that the legendary temptresses are no longer seductive? Discuss.
2. In "The Unexploded Bomb," why do X. and Y. consider themselves not "sentimental idealists" but "realists"?
3. In "The Room," what actual purpose does the isolated room serve the monarch?
4. In Louis MacNeice's "Autobiography," what are the "black dreams" that change the life of the child?
5. "Prayer Before Birth" presents a view of the contemporary world that is not very reassuring. Are the dangers envisioned in the poem real or imaginary? Discuss.
6. In "The Taxis," what or who are the invisible presences with the taxi-rider?
7. Why is Muriel Spark's poem, "Fruitless Fable," called a *fable?*
8. In R. S. Thomas's "Poetry for Supper," explain the meaning of the one poet who says: "Windows don't happen."

Twentieth-Century Poetry
Part Three:
THE SEARCH FOR VALUES

You ask a poet to sing
Why
Even the birds are hoarse.
The nightingale that long ago
Numbed Keats, is dead.
Alan Bold

ON THE MOVE

by Thom Gunn

"Man, you gotta Go."

The blue jay scuffling in the bushes follows
Some hidden purpose, and the gust of birds
That spurts across the field, the wheeling swallows,
Have nested in the trees and undergrowth.
5 Seeking their instinct, or their poise, or both,
One moves with an uncertain violence
Under the dust thrown by a baffled sense
Or the dull thunder of approximate words.

On motorcycles, up the road, they come:
10 Small, black, as flies hanging in heat, the Boys,
Until the distance throws them forth, their hum
Bulges to thunder held by calf and thigh.
In goggles, donned impersonality,
In gleaming jackets trophied with the dust,
15 They strap in doubt—by hiding it, robust—
And almost hear a meaning in their noise.

Exact conclusion of their hardiness
Has no shape yet, but from known whereabouts
They ride, direction where the tires press.
20 They scare a flight of birds across the field:
Much that is natural, to the will must yield.
Men manufacture both machine and soul,
And use what they imperfectly control
To dare a future from the taken routes.

25 It is a part solution, after all.
One is not necessarily discord
On earth; or damned because, half animal,
One lacks direct instinct, because one wakes
Afloat on movement that divides and breaks.
30 One joins the movement in a valueless world,
Choosing it, till, both hurler and the hurled,
One moves as well, always toward, toward.

A minute holds them, who have come to go:
The self-defined, astride the created will
35 They burst away: the towns they travel through
Are home for neither bird nor holiness,
For birds and saints complete their purposes.
At worst, one is in motion; and at best,
Reaching no absolute, in which to rest,
40 One is always nearer by not keeping still.

WHATEVER HAPPENED?

by Philip Larkin

At once whatever happened starts receding.
Panting, and back on board, we line the rail
With trousers ripped, light wallets, and lips bleeding.

Yes, gone, thank God! Remembering each detail
5 We toss for half the night, but find next day
All's kodak-distant. Easily, then (though pale),

"Perspective brings significance," we say,
Unhooding our photometers, and, snap!
What can't be printed can be thrown away.

10 Later, it's just a latitude: the map
Points out how unavoidable it was:
"Such coastal bedding always means mishap."

Curses? The dark? Struggling? Where's the source
Of these yarns now (except in nightmares, of
course)?

SECURITY

by Michael Hamburger

1

So he's got there at last, been received as a partner—
In a firm going bankrupt;
Found the right place (walled garden), arranged for a
mortgage—
But they're pulling the house down
5 To make room for traffic.

Worse winds are rising. He takes out new policies
For his furniture, for his life,
At a higher premium
Against more limited risks.

2

10 Who can face the winds, till the panes crack in their
frames?
And if a man faced them, what in the end could he
do
But look for shelter like all the rest?
The winds too are afraid, and blow from fear.

3

I hear my children at play
15 And recall that one branch of the elm-tree looks
dead;
Also that twenty years ago now I could have been
parchment
Cured and stretched for a lampshade,[1]
Who now have children, a lampshade
And the fear of those winds.

20 I saw off the elm-tree branch
To find that the wood was sound;
Mend the fences yet again,
Knowing they'll keep out no one,
Let alone the winds.
25 For still my children play
And shall tomorrow, if the weather holds.

1. *twenty years ago . . . lampshade.* One of the actrocities committed by the Nazis was to make the skins of their murdered prisoners into lampshades.

HAWK ROOSTING

by Ted Hughes

I sit in the top of the wood, my eyes closed.
Inaction, no falsifying dream
Between my hooked head and hooked feet:
Or in sleep rehearse perfect kills and eat.

5 The convenience of the high trees!
The air's buoyancy and the sun's ray
Are of advantage to me;
And the earth's face upward for my inspection.

My feet are locked upon the rough bark.
10 It took the whole of Creation
To produce my foot, my each feather:
Now I hold Creation in my foot

Or fly up, and revolve it all slowly—
I kill where I please because it is all mine.
15 There is no sophistry in my body:
My manners are tearing off heads—

The allotment of death.
For the one path of my flight is direct
Through the bones of the living.
20 No arguments assert my right:

The sun is behind me.
Nothing has changed since I began.
My eye has permitted no change.
I am going to keep things like this.

THE JAGUAR

by Ted Hughes

The apes yawn and adore their fleas in the sun.
The parrots shriek as if they were on fire, or strut
Like cheap tarts to attract the stroller with the nut.
Fatigued with indolence, tiger and lion

5 Lie still as the sun. The boa-constrictor's coil
Is a fossil. Cage after cage seems empty, or
Stinks of sleepers from the breathing straw.
It might be painted on a nursery wall.

But who runs like the rest past these arrives
10 At a cage where the crowd stands, stares,
mesmerized,
As a child at a dream, at a jaguar hurrying enraged
Through prison darkness after the drills of his eyes

On a short fierce fuse. Not in boredom—
The eye satisfied to be blind in fire,
15 By the bang of blood in the brain deaf the ear—
He spins from the bars, but there's no cage to him

More than to the visionary his cell:
His stride is wildernesses of freedom:
The world rolls under the long thrust of his heel.
20 Over the cage floor the horizons come.

SECOND GLANCE AT A JAGUAR

by Ted Hughes

Skinfull of bowls, he bowls them,
The hip going in and out of joint, dropping the spine
With the urgency of his hurry
Like a cat going along under thrown stones, under cover,
5 Glancing sideways, running
Under his spine. A terrible, stump-legged waddle
Like a thick Aztec disemboweller,
Club-swinging, trying to grind some square
Socket between his hind legs round,
10 Carrying his head like a brazier of spilling embers,
And the black bit of his mouth, he takes it
Between his back teeth, he has to wear his skin out,
He swipes a lap at the water-trough as he turns,
Swivelling the ball of his heel on the polished spot,
15 Showing his belly like a butterfly,
At every stride he has to turn a corner
In himself and correct it. His head
Is like the worn down stump of another whole jaguar,
His body is just the engine shoving it forward,
20 Lifting the air up and shoving on under,
The weight of his fangs hanging the mouth open,
Bottom jaw combing the ground. A gorged look,
Gangster, club-tail lumped along behind gracelessly,
He's wearing himself to heavy ovals,
25 Muttering some mantrah, some drum-song of murder
To keep his rage brightening, making his skin
Intolerable, spurred by the rosettes, the cain-brands,
Wearing the spots off from the inside,
Rounding some revenge. Going like a prayer-wheel,
30 The head dragging forward, the body keeping up,
The hind legs lagging. He coils, he flourishes
The blackjack tail as if looking for a target,
Hurrying through the underworld, soundless.

DISCUSSION

1. In Thom Gunn's "On the Move," what do the bluejays and swallows have that the motorcyclists have lost?

2. In Philip Larkin's "Whatever Happened?":

(a) What might have happened in this poem?

(b) Why is the poet vague about whatever it was that happened?

3. In Michael Hamburger's "Security":

(a) What does the wind symbolize?

(b) Why does the poem say that the winds too "blow from fear"?

4. (a) How does the jaguar differ from the other animals described in Ted Hughes' "The Jaguar"?

(b) Explain the last two lines of the poem: "The world rolls under the long thrust of his heel. / Over the cage floor the horizons come."

5. Discuss the point of view of "Hawk Roosting."

(a) How does the physical perspective of the hawk reënforce his feelings of dominance?

(b) Does the poem tend to support or undercut the hawk's view presented in the last stanza that he has prevented and will continue to prevent change?

6. Compare "Second Glance at a Jaguar" with "The Jaguar."

(a) Which strikes you as the more vivid, and why?

(b) What change can you detect in the poet's attitude toward the jaguar?

THE O-FILLER

by Alastair Reid

One noon in the library, I watched a man—
imagine!—filling in O's, a little, rumpled
nobody of a man, who licked his stub of pencil
and leaned over every O with a loving care,
5 shading it neatly, exactly to its edges,
until the open pages
were pocked and dotted with solid O's, like villages
and capitals on a map. And yet, so peppered,
somehow the book looked lived in and complete.

10 That whole afternoon, as the light outside softened,
and the library groaned woodenly,
he worked and worked, his O-so-patient shading
descending like an eyelid over each open O
for page after page. Not once did he miss one,
15 or hover even a moment over an *a*,
or an *e* or a *p* or a *g*. Only the O's—
oodles of O's, O's multitudinous, O's manifold,
O's italic and roman.
And what light on his crumpled face when he discovered—
20 as I supposed—odd words like *zoo* and *ooze*,
polo, *oolong* and *odontology!*

Think now. In that limitless library,
all round the steep-shelved walls, bulging in their bindings,
books stood, waiting. Heaven knows how many
25 he had so far filled, but no matter, there still were
uncountable volumes of O-laden prose, and odes
with inflated capital O's (in the manner of Shelley),
O-bearing Bibles and biographies,
even whole sections devoted to O alone,
30 all his for the filling. Glory, glory, glory!
How lovely and open and endless the world must have seemed
to him,
how utterly clear-cut! Think of it. A pencil
was all he needed. Life was one wide O.

Anyway, why in the end should O's not be closed
35 as eyes are? I envied him. After all,

---

sitting across from him, had I accomplished
anything as firm as he had, or as fruitful?
What could I show? A handful of scrawled lines,
an afternoon yawned and wondered away,
40 and a growing realization that in time
even my scribbled words would come
under his grubby thumb, and the blinds be drawn
on all my O's. And only this thought for comfort—
that when he comes to this poem, a proper joy
45 may amaze his wizened face, and, O, a pure pleasure
make his meticulous pencil quiver.

CURIOSITY

by Alastair Reid

may have killed the cat; more likely
the cat was just unlucky, or else curious
to see what death was like, having no cause
to go on licking paws, or fathering
5 litter on litter of kittens, predictably.

Nevertheless, to be curious
is dangerous enough. To distrust
what is always said, what seems,
to ask odd questions, interfere in dreams,
10 leave home, smell rats, have hunches
does not endear him to those doggy circles
where well-smelt baskets, suitable wives, good
lunches
are the order of things, and where prevails
much wagging of incurious heads and tails.

15 Face it. Curiosity
will not cause him to die—
only lack of it will.
Never to want to see
the other side of the hill,
20 or that improbable country
where living is an idyll
(although a probable hell)
would kill us all.
Only the curious
25 have, if they live, a tale
worth telling at all.

Dogs say he loves too much, is irresponsible,
is changeable, marries too many wives,
deserts his children, chills all dinner tables
30 with tales of his nine lives.
Well, he is lucky. Let him be
nine-lived and contradictory,
curious enough to change, prepared to pay
the cat price, which is to die
35 and die again and again,
each time with no less pain.
A cat minority of one
is all that can be counted on
to tell the truth. And what he has to tell
40 on each return from hell
is this: that dying is what the living do,
that dying is what the loving do,
and that dead dogs are those who do not know
that dying is what, to live, each has to do.

THE BASILISK[1]

by D. M. Black

Lifting a tangle of roots away from the bank I
found
a serpent hatching cocks' eggs; and already the
X-ray blackness of the small basilisks could be
seen moving in the opalescent membranes. I
5 took up
two in each hand, watched by the torpid serpent.

Back to the
glass-fronted bungalow, laid my a-
mazing discovery on the polished table. Four
10 active eggs! I
filled a tray with sand and set them on it. They
writhed and
struggled, wrestled with one another through the
rubbery obstruction. One, the
largest, was almost always on top.

15 Night
fell; I drew the Venetian blinds; called for a
lamp. Sat
avidly over the lighted arena.

Darkness
20 hung at the window; hung behind my head.

Slit
in the glossy rubber: it was the
largest: he
came out hump-necked, butting upward with com-
25 pacted spines. Small and
blood-red, but faded quickly. A
spruce dragon, 4 inches long; strolled from the
egg's wreckage. I
moved the lamp closer. Had become a
sort of khaki colour.
(History, I
30 thought, like the English army.)

He
walked confidently to the other eggs and
chopped them apart with
long jaws—in a
35 bloody scramble sucked and chomped, orderlessly
leaping from one to one and in under eighty-five
seconds
was alone with four cleaned relics. Had
grown no bigger but was
hard as stone. Stood on the
40 brink of the tray.
I fitted a bell-jar over his head and
pressured him back to the sand; but a
rap of his front foot
shivered the glass. He
45 waited impassively under the tumbling shards.

And he be-
gan to grow—was
suddenly four feet high, by a-
bout eight feet long—crouched on the
50 juddering table. A
massive shadow over the small lamp. I
backed to the door—with a

"The Basilisk" from *Scottish Poetry, Number Two,* edited by George Bruce, Maurice Lindsay, and Edwin Morgan.

1. *basilisk,* a legendary reptile whose breath and glance were supposedly fatal; said to be hatched from the egg of a seven-year-old cock.

broom ad-
vanced: whacked at the
55 solid bulk: somewhere up by the shoulder. As he
turned the
lamp crashed
to the ground and smashed. I
fled.

"Come on get out!" In-
60 sanely I
screamed at the wife, and I
hauled the
children, blankets and all, out of the back-door. Barri-
caded the
door of the study. Then from the garage I
65 dragged two drums of petrol, hacked them gaping
over the barricade, and a
brief fuse
rolled out of newspaper let me escape the conclusion.
The
back-door, left open, created the appropriate draught.

70 Ex-
plosion! and
fire like a mania. A-
ppalling smashing of glass. Later we discovered the entire house tilted, for in his flight the
75 basilisk removed the glass-wall's central pillar. E-
laborate damage by fire, and firemen's foam. And
great pits in the garden; of
soil in which we preferred not to grow vegetables.

AN ADDRESS TO THE INDIVIDUAL

by Laughton Johnston

Man, you are not an island,
you are on it!

You say you are a social animal,
but you only put up with it.
5 You are no more social than the shrew,
you are all bluff!

Man, you are even collective
in your isolation,
like a battery hen.

10 Man, you are marooned on that island
and only you can get yourself off.

Man, when are you going to learn to swim?

ECHOES OF VENUS OVER CAR RADIO

by D. M. Thomas

(the first landing on Venus, October 1967)

"must guard against the impression that we control
control
Venus having merely probed its atmosphere
fear fear
5 Listen now to our recording
of the response of Venus
simple timeless obsessive
. . . .

One risk must have concerned them to take care
10 *take care*
that alien life-forms don't come
don't come
into a world by taking root inside
inside
15 the capsule . . .
Professor Tikhov may we ask you to
you too
predict the findings of this great exploit
exploit
20 do you share Lovell's theory that primeval
evil
sea-spores might exist despite the nature
nature
of our twin-planet's atmosphere and this heat
25 *this heat*
which the probe has recorded deep down
deep down
beneath the clouds   May I say it would be madness
madness
30 to be certain at this stage   suppose
suppose
there is a sea and it breeds life what then . . ."
what then?

RECITATIVE

by Alan Bold

"Come, let's away to prison;
We two alone will sing like birds i' the cage."
SHAKESPEARE: *King Lear*

"Whereas a man may have noon audience,
Noght helpeth it to tellen his sentence."
CHAUCER: *Prologue to the Nun's Priest's Tale*

You ask a poet to sing
Why
Even the birds are hoarse.
The nightingale that long ago
5 Numbed Keats, is dead.
What of the wind whispering through the trees
When no one cares to hear?
Perhaps you think—
"Ah! the golden skinned lassies
10 Can still move a poet."

Once I sang
But that was before I knew
What went on in the world.
Yes! I was blithe,
15 Chirping away happily,
And, like Chauntecleer, closing my eyes
To do it.
I was, however, ignoring
The modern world
20 With all its blessings
And all its faults.
When I saw gestant China
Bear well—I rejoiced,
But did not sing.
25 Could I ignore the toll of the struggle?

Damn it!
Our voices are not made for singing now
But for straight-talking.
As the sea-surge turns over more filth
30 We may do some good
By exposure.
Look at the moon tonight
Or at the sea.
But before an easy praise of nature
35 Reflect on those folk
Who have not our sensitive thoughts,
For whom bread, not words, is life:
They matter.
Song implies melody; but the poet
40 Is after harmony,
Speaking for myself.
Songs have been sung
And dances have been danced
And slaves have done the singing
45 And peasants have done the dancing
To lessen their hell.
It may be that after this
When people are really allowed
To live,
50 The birds will sing afresh,
And then the poets will join them.
But for the present
We have enough songs that lie
Unsung.
55 Most of them by great singers.
Our job is to try
To change things.
After Hiroshima
You ask a poet to sing.

DISCUSSION

1. In "The O-Filler," explain the attitude of the poet toward the O-filler in the last stanza.
2. Discuss the "truth" that the cat can be counted on to tell in "Curiosity" (referred to in the last stanza).
3. What evidence can you find for reading "The Basilisk" symbolically?
4. In "Address to the Individual," what does the island represent?
5. Explore in detail the effect of the echoing words (those in italics, in alternate lines) in "Echoes of Venus over Car Radio."
6. In "Recitative," Alan Bold has written a poem about the impossibility of a poet singing in this time. How do you explain this irony?

chapter eleven DRAMA

BEN NICHOLSON, "STONE AND DARK MAUVE," 1965. MARLBOROUGH FINE ART GALLERY, LONDON.

ANDROCLES AND THE LION

A Fable Play by Bernard Shaw

PROLOGUE

OVERTURE: forest sounds, roaring of lions, Christian hymn faintly.

A jungle path. A lion's roar, a melancholy suffering roar, comes from the jungle. It is repeated nearer. The lion limps from the jungle on three legs, holding up his right forepaw, in which a huge thorn sticks. He sits down and contemplates it. He licks it. He shakes it. He tries to extract it by scraping it along the ground, and hurts himself worse. He roars piteously. He licks it again. Tears drop from his eyes. He limps painfully off the path and lies down under the trees, exhausted with pain. Heaving a long sigh, like wind in a trombone, he goes to sleep.

Androcles and his wife Megaera come along the path. He is a small, thin, ridiculous little man who might be any age from thirty to fifty-five. He has sandy hair, watery compassionate blue eyes, sensitive nostrils, and a very presentable forehead; but his good points go no further: his arms and legs and back, though wiry of their kind, look shrivelled and starved. He carries a big bundle, is very poorly clad, and seems tired and hungry.

His wife is a rather handsome pampered slattern, well fed and in the prime of life. She has nothing to carry, and has a stout stick to help her along.

MEGAERA *(suddenly throwing down her stick).* I wont go another step.

ANDROCLES *(pleading wearily).* Oh, not again, dear. Whats the good of stopping every two miles and saying you wont go another step? We must get on to the next village before night. There are wild beasts in this wood: lions, they say.

MEGAERA. I dont believe a word of it. You are always threatening me with wild beasts to make me walk the very soul out of my body when I can hardly drag one foot before another. We havnt seen a single lion yet.

ANDROCLES. Well, dear, do you want to see one?

MEGAERA *(tearing the bundle from his back).* You cruel brute, you dont care how tired I am, or what becomes of me *(she throws the bundle on the ground)* always thinking of yourself. Self! self! self! always yourself! *(She sits down on the bundle.)*

ANDROCLES *(sitting down sadly on the ground with his elbows on his knees and his head in his hands).* We all have to think of ourselves occasionally, dear.

MEGAERA. A man ought to think of his wife sometimes.

ANDROCLES. He cant always help it, dear. You make me think of you a good deal. Not that I blame you.

MEGAERA. Blame me! I should think not indeed. Is it my fault that I'm married to you?

ANDROCLES. No, dear: that is my fault.

MEGAERA. Thats a nice thing to say to me. Arnt you happy with me?

ANDROCLES. I dont complain, my love.

MEGAERA. You ought to be ashamed of yourself.

ANDROCLES. I am, my dear.

MEGAERA. Youre not: you glory in it.

ANDROCLES. In what, darling?

MEGAERA. In everything. In making me a slave, and making yourself a laughing-stock. It's not fair. You get me the name of being a shrew with your meek ways, always talking as if butter wouldnt melt in your mouth. And just because I look a big strong woman, and because I'm goodhearted and a bit hasty, and because youre always driving me to do things I'm sorry for afterwards, people say "Poor man: what a life his wife leads him!" Oh, if they only knew! And you think I dont know. But I do, I do, *(screaming)* I do.

ANDROCLES. Yes, my dear: I know you do.

MEGAERA. Then why dont you treat me properly and be a good husband to me?

ANDROCLES. What can I do, my dear?

MEGAERA. What can you do! You can return to your duty, and come back to your home and your friends, and sacrifice to the gods as all respectable people do, instead of having us hunted out of house and home for being dirty disreputable blaspheming atheists.

ANDROCLES. I'm not an atheist, dear: I am a Christian.

MEGAERA. Well, isnt that the same thing, only ten times worse? Everybody knows that the Christians are the very lowest of the low.

ANDROCLES. Just like us, dear.

MEGAERA. Speak for yourself. Dont you dare to compare me to common people. My father owned his own public-house; and sorrowful was the day for me when you first came drinking in our bar.

ANDROCLES. I confess I was addicted to it, dear. But I gave it up when I became a Christian.

MEGAERA. Youd much better have remained a drunkard. I can forgive a man being addicted to drink: it's only natural; and I dont deny I like a drop myself sometimes. What I cant stand is your being addicted to Christianity. And whats worse again, your being addicted to animals. How is any woman to keep her house clean when you bring in every stray cat and lost cur and lame duck in the whole countryside? You took the bread out of my mouth to feed them: you know you did: dont attempt to deny it.

ANDROCLES. Only when they were hungry and you were getting too stout, dearie.

MEGAERA. Yes: insult me, do. *(Rising)* Oh! I wont bear it another moment. You used to sit and talk to those dumb brute beasts for hours, when you hadnt a word for me.

ANDROCLES. They never answered back, darling. *(He rises and again shoulders the bundle.)*

MEGAERA. Well, if youre fonder of animals than of your own wife, you can live with them here in the jungle. Ive had enough of them and enough of you. I'm going back. I'm going home.

ANDROCLES *(barring the way back).* No, dearie: dont take on like that. We cant go back. Weve sold everything: we should starve; and I should be sent to Rome and thrown to the lions—

MEGAERA. Serve you right! I wish the lions joy of you. *(Screaming)* Are you going to get out of my way and let me go home?

ANDROCLES. No, dear—

MEGAERA. Then I'll make my way through the forest; and when I'm eaten by the wild beasts youll know what a wife youve lost. *(She dashes into the jungle and nearly falls over the sleeping lion.)* Oh! Oh! Andy! Andy! *(She totters back and collapses into the arms of Androcles, who, crushed by her weight, falls on his bundle.)*

ANDROCLES *(extracting himself from beneath her and slapping her hands in great anxiety).* What is it, my precious, my pet? Whats the matter? *(He raises her head. Speechless with terror, she points in the direction of the sleeping lion. He steals cautiously towards the spot indicated by Megaera. She rises with an effort and totters after him.)*

MEGAERA. No, Andy: youll be killed. Come back.

(The lion utters a long snoring sigh. Androcles sees the lion, and recoils fainting into the arms of Megaera, who falls back on the bundle. They roll apart and lie staring in terror at one another. The lion is heard groaning heavily in the jungle.)

ANDROCLES *(whispering).* Did you see? A lion.

MEGAERA *(despairing).* The gods have sent him to punish us because youre a Christian. Take me away, Andy. Save me.

ANDROCLES *(rising).* Meggy: theres one chance for you. Itll take him pretty nigh twenty minutes to eat me (I'm rather stringy and tough) and you can escape in less time than that.

MEGAERA. Oh, dont talk about eating. *(The lion rises with a great groan and limps towards them.)* Oh! *(She faints.)*

ANDROCLES *(quaking, but keeping between the lion and Megaera).* Dont you come near my wife, do you hear? *(The lion groans. Androcles can hardly stand for trembling.)* Meggy: run. Run for your life. If I take my eye off him, it's all up. *(The lion holds up his wounded paw and flaps it piteously before Androcles.)* Oh, he's lame, poor old chap! He's got a thorn in his paw. A frightfully big thorn. *(Full of sympathy)* Oh, poor old man! Did um get an awful thorn into um's tootsums wootsums? Has it made um too sick to eat a nice little Christian man for um's breakfast? Oh, a nice little Christian man will get um's thorn out for um; and then um shall eat the nice Christian man and the nice Christian man's nice big tender wifey pifey. *(The lion responds by moans of self-pity.)* Yes, yes, yes, yes, yes. Now, now *(taking the paw in his hand),* um is not to bite and not to scratch, not even if it hurts a very very little. Now make velvet paws. Thats right. *(He pulls gingerly at the thorn. The lion, with an angry yell of pain, jerks back his paw so abruptly that Androcles is thrown on his back.)* Steadeee! Oh, did the nasty cruel little Christian man hurt the sore paw? *(The lion moans assentingly but apologetically.)* Well, one more little pull and it will be all over. Just one little, little, leetle pull; and then um will live happily ever after. *(He gives the thorn another pull. The lion roars and snaps his jaws with a terrifying clash.)* Oh, mustnt frighten um's good kind doctor, um's affectionate nursey. That didnt hurt at all: not a bit. Just one more. Just to shew how the brave big lion can bear pain, not like the little crybaby Christian man. Oopsh! *(The thorn comes out. The lion yells with pain, and shakes his paw wildly.)* Thats it! *(Holding up the thorn)* Now it's out. Now lick um's paw to take away the nasty inflammation. See? *(He licks his own hand. The lion nods intelligently and licks his paw industriously.)* Clever little liony-piony! Understands um's dear old friend Andy Wandy. *(The lion licks his face.)* Yes, kissums Andy Wandy. *(The lion, wagging his tail violently, rises on his hind legs, and embraces Androcles, who makes a wry face and cries)* Velvet paws! Velvet paws! *(The lion draws in his claws.)* Thats right. *(He embraces the lion, who finally takes the end of his tail in one paw, places that tight round Androcles' waist, resting it on his hip. Androcles takes the other paw in his hand, stretches out his arm, and the two waltz rapturously round and round and finally away through the jungle.)*

MEGAERA *(who has revived during the waltz).* Oh, you coward, you havnt danced with me for years; and now you go off dancing with a great brute beast that you havnt known for ten minutes and that wants to eat your own wife. Coward! Coward! Coward! *(She rushes off after them into the jungle.)*

Act One

EVENING. The end of three converging roads to Rome. Three triumphal arches span them where they debouch on a square at the gate of the city. Looking north through the arches one can see the campagna threaded by the three long dusty tracks.

On the east and west side of the square are long stone benches. An old beggar sits on the east side, his bowl at his feet.

Through the eastern arch a squad of Roman soldiers tramps along escorting a batch of Christian prisoners of both sexes and all ages, among them one Lavinia, a good-looking resolute young woman, apparently of higher social standing than her fellow-prisoners. A centurion, carrying his vinewood cudgel, trudges alongside the squad, on its right, in command of it. All are tired and dusty; but the soldiers are dogged and indifferent, the Christians lighthearted and determined to treat their hardships as a joke and encourage one another.

A bugle is heard far behind on the road, where the rest of the cohort is following.

CENTURION *(stopping)*. Halt! Orders from the Captain. *(They halt and wait.)* Now then, you Christians, none of your larks. The Captain's coming. Mind you behave yourselves. No singing. Look respectful. Look serious, if youre capable of it. See that big building over there! Thats the Coliseum. Thats where youll be thrown to the lions or set to fight the gladiators presently. Think of that; and itll help you to behave properly before the Captain. *(The Captain arrives.)* Attention! Salute! *(The soldiers salute.)*

A CHRISTIAN *(cheerfully)*. God bless you, Captain!

THE CENTURION *(scandalized)*. Silence!

(The Captain, a patrician, handsome, about thirty-five, very cold and distinguished, very superior and authoritative, steps up on a stone seat at the west side of the square, behind the centurion, so as to dominate the others more effectually.)

THE CAPTAIN. Centurion.

THE CENTURION *(standing at attention and saluting)*. Sir?

THE CAPTAIN *(speaking stiffly and officially)*. You will remind your men, Centurion, that we are now entering Rome. You will instruct them that once inside the gates of Rome they are in the presence of the Emperor. You will make them understand that the lax discipline of the march cannot be permitted here. You will instruct them to shave every day, not every week. You will impress on them particularly that there must be an end to the profanity and blasphemy of singing Christian hymns on the march. I have to reprimand you, Centurion, for not only allowing this, but actually doing it yourself.

THE CENTURION *(apologetic)*. The men march better, Captain.

THE CAPTAIN. No doubt. For that reason an exception is made in the case of the march called Onward Christian Soldiers. This may be sung, except when marching through the forum or within hearing of the Emperor's palace; but the words must be altered to "Throw them to the Lions."

(The Christians burst into shrieks of uncontrollable laughter, to the great scandal of the Centurion.)

CENTURION. Silence! Silen-n-n-n-nce! Wheres your behavior? Is that the way to listen to an officer? *(To the Captain)* Thats what we have to put up with from these Christians every day, sir. Theyre always laughing and joking something scandalous. Theyve no religion: thats how it is.

LAVINIA. But I think the Captain meant us to laugh, Centurion. It was so funny.

CENTURION. Youll find out how funny it is when youre thrown to the lions tomorrow. *(To the Captain, who looks displeased)* Beg pardon, Sir. *(To the Christians)* Silennnnce!

THE CAPTAIN. You are to instruct your men that all intimacy with Christian prisoners must now cease. The men have fallen into habits of dependence upon the prisoners, especially the female prisoners, for cooking, repairs to uniforms, writing letters, and advice in their private affairs. In a Roman soldier such dependence is inadmissible. Let me see no more of it whilst we are in the city. Further, your orders are that in addressing Christian prisoners, the manners and tone of your men must express abhorrence and contempt. Any shortcoming in this respect will be regarded as a breach of discipline. *(He turns to the prisoners.)* Prisoners.

CENTURION *(fiercely)*. Prisonerrrrs! Tention! Silence!

THE CAPTAIN. I call your attention, prisoners, to the fact that you may be called on to appear in the Imperial Circus at any time from tomorrow onwards, according to the requirements of the managers. I may inform you that as there is a shortage of Christians just now, you may expect to be called on very soon.

LAVINIA. What will they do to us, Captain?

CENTURION. Silence!

THE CAPTAIN. The women will be conducted into the arena with the wild beasts of the Imperial Menagerie, and will suffer the consequences. The men, if of an age to bear arms, will be given weapons to defend themselves, if they choose, against the

Imperial Gladiators.

LAVINIA. Captain: is there no hope that this cruel persecution—

CENTURION *(shocked)*. Silence! Hold your tongue, there. Persecution, indeed!

THE CAPTAIN *(unmoved and somewhat sardonic)*. Persecution is not a term applicable to the acts of the Emperor. The Emperor is the Defender of the Faith. In throwing you to the lions he will be upholding the interests of religion in Rome. If you were to throw him to the lions, that would no doubt be persecution.

(The Christians again laugh heartily.)

CENTURION *(horrified)*. Silence, I tell you! Keep silence there. Did anyone ever hear the like of this?

LAVINIA. Captain: there will be nobody to appreciate your jokes when we are gone.

THE CAPTAIN *(unshaken in his official delivery)*. I call the attention of the female prisoner Lavinia to the fact that as the Emperor is a divine personage, her imputation of cruelty is not only treason, but sacrilege. I point out to her further that there is no foundation for the charge, as the Emperor does not desire that any prisoner should suffer; nor can any Christian be harmed save through his or her own obstinacy. All that is necessary is to sacrifice to the gods: a simple and convenient ceremony effected by dropping a pinch of incense on the altar, after which the prisoner is at once set free. Under such circumstances you have only your own perverse folly to blame if you suffer. I suggest to you that if you cannot burn a morsel of incense as a matter of conviction, you might at least do so as a matter of good taste, to avoid shocking the religious convictions of your fellow citizens. I am aware that these considerations do not weigh with Christians; but it is my duty to call your attention to them in order that you may have no ground for complaining of your treatment, or of accusing the Emperor of cruelty when he is shewing you the most signal clemency. Looked at from this point of view, every Christian who has perished in the arena has really committed suicide.

LAVINIA. Captain: your jokes are too grim. Do not think it is easy for us to die. Our faith makes life far stronger and more wonderful in us than when we walked in darkness and had nothing to live for. Death is harder for us than for you: the martyr's agony is as bitter as his triumph is glorious.

THE CAPTAIN *(rather troubled, addressing her personally and gravely)*. A martyr, Lavinia, is a fool. Your death will prove nothing.

LAVINIA. Then why kill me?

THE CAPTAIN. I mean that truth, if there be any truth, needs no martyrs.

LAVINIA. No; but my faith, like your sword, needs testing. Can you test your sword except by staking your life on it?

THE CAPTAIN *(suddenly resuming his offical tone)*. I call the attention of the female prisoner to the fact that Christians are not allowed to draw the Emperor's officers into arguments and put questions to them for which the military regulations provide no answer. *(The Christians titter.)*

LAVINIA. Captain: how can you?

THE CAPTAIN. I call the female prisoner's attention specially to the fact that four comfortable homes have been offered her by officers of this regiment, of which she can have her choice the moment she chooses to sacrifice as all wellbred Roman ladies do. I have no more to say to the prisoners.

CENTURION. Dismiss! But stay where you are.

THE CAPTAIN. Centurion: you will remain here with your men in charge of the prisoners until the arrival of three Christian prisoners in the custody of a cohort of the tenth legion. Among these prisoners you will particularly identify an armorer named Ferrovius, of dangerous character and great personal strength, and a Greek tailor reputed to be a sorcerer, by name Androcles. You will add the three to your charge here and march them all to the Coliseum, where you will deliver them into the custody of the master of the gladiators and take his receipt, countersigned by the keeper of the beasts and the acting manager. You understand your instructions?

CENTURION. Yes, sir.

THE CAPTAIN. Dismiss. *(He throws off his air of parade, and descends from his perch. The Centurion seats himself on it and prepares for a nap, whilst his men stand at ease. The Christians sit down on the west side of the square, glad to rest. Lavinia alone remains standing to speak to the Captain.)*

LAVINIA. Captain: is this man who is to join us the famous Ferrovius, who has made such wonderful conversions in the northern cities?

THE CAPTAIN. Yes. We are warned that he has the strength of an elephant and the temper of a mad bull. Also that he is stark mad. Not a model Christian, it would seem.

LAVINIA. You need not fear him if he is a Christian, Captain.

THE CAPTAIN *(coldly)*. I shall not fear him in any case, Lavinia.

LAVINIA *(her eyes dancing)*. How brave of you, Captain!

THE CAPTAIN. You are right: it was a silly thing to say. *(In a lower tone, humane and urgent)* Lavinia: do Christians know how to love?

LAVINIA *(composedly)*. Yes, Captain: they love even their enemies.

THE CAPTAIN. Is that easy?

LAVINIA. Very easy, Captain, when their enemies are as handsome as you.

THE CAPTAIN. Lavinia: you are laughing at me.

LAVINIA. At you, Captain! Impossible.

THE CAPTAIN. Then you are flirting with me, which is worse. Dont be foolish.

LAVINIA. But such a very handsome captain.

THE CAPTAIN. Incorrigible! *(Urgently)* Listen to me. The men in that audience tomorrow will be the vilest of voluptuaries: men in whom the only passion excited by a beautiful woman is a lust to see her tortured and torn shrieking limb from limb. It is a crime to gratify that passion. It is offering yourself for violation by the whole rabble of the streets and the riff-raff of the court at the same time. Why will you not choose rather a kindly love and an honorable alliance?

LAVINIA. They cannot violate my soul. I alone can do that by sacrificing to false gods.

THE CAPTAIN. Sacrifice then to the true God. What does his name matter? We call him Jupiter. The Greeks call him Zeus. Call him what you will as you drop the incense on the altar flame: He will understand.

LAVINIA. No. I couldnt. That is the strange thing, Captain, that a little pinch of incense should make all that difference. Religion is such a great thing that when I meet really religious people we are friends at once, no matter what name we give to the divine will that made us and moves us. Oh, do you think that I, a woman, would quarrel with you for sacrificing to a woman god like Diana, if Diana meant to you what Christ means to me? No: we should kneel side by side before her altar like two children. But when men who believe neither in my god nor in their own—men who do not know the meaning of the word religion—when these men drag me to the foot of an iron statue that has become the symbol of the terror and darkness through which they walk, of their cruelty and greed, of their hatred of God and their oppression of man—when they ask me to pledge my soul before the people that this hideous idol is God, and that all this wickedness and falsehood is divine truth, I cannot do it, not if they could put a thousand curel deaths on me. I tell you, it is physically impossible. Listen, Captain: did you ever try to catch a mouse in your hand? Once there was a dear little mouse that used to come out and play on my table as I was reading. I wanted to take him in my hand and caress him; and sometimes he got among my books so that he could not escape me when I stretched out my hand. And I did stretch out my hand; but it always came back in spite of me. I was not afraid of him in my heart; but my hand refused: it is not in the nature of my hand to touch a mouse. Well, Captain, if I took a pinch of incense in my hand and stretched it out over the altar fire, my hand would come back. My body would be true to my faith even if you could corrupt my mind. And all the time I should believe more in Diana than my persecutors have ever believed in anything. Can you understand that?

THE CAPTAIN *(simply)*. Yes: I understand that. But my hand would not come back. The hand that holds the sword has been trained not to come back from anything but victory.

LAVINIA. Not even from death?

THE CAPTAIN. Least of all from death.

LAVINIA. Then I must not come back from death either. A woman has to be braver than a soldier.

THE CAPTAIN. Prouder, you mean.

LAVINIA *(startled)*. Prouder! You call our courage pride?

THE CAPTAIN. There is no such thing as courage: there is only pride. You Christians are the proudest devils on earth.

LAVINIA *(hurt)*. Pray God then my pride may never become a false pride. *(She turns away as if she did not wish to continue the conversation, but softens and says to him with a smile)* Thank you for trying to save me.

THE CAPTAIN. I knew it was no use; but one tries in spite of one's knowledge.

LAVINIA. Something stirs, even in the iron breast of a Roman soldier?

THE CAPTAIN. It will soon be iron again. I have seen

many women die, and forgotten them in a week.

LAVINIA. Remember me for a fortnight, handsome Captain. I shall be watching you, perhaps.

THE CAPTAIN. From the skies? Do not deceive yourself, Lavinia. There is no future for you beyond the grave.

LAVINIA. What does that matter? Do you think I am only running away from the terrors of life into the comfort of heaven? If there were no future, or if the future were one of torment, I should have to go just the same. The hand of God is upon me.

THE CAPTAIN. Yes: when all is said, we are both patricians, Lavinia, and must die for our beliefs. Farewell. *(He offers her his hand. She takes it and presses it. He walks away, trim and calm. She looks after him for a moment, and cries a little as he disappears through the eastern arch. A trumpet-call is heard from the road through the western arch.)*

CENTURION *(waking up and rising)*. Cohort of the tenth with prisoners. Two file out with me to receive them. *(He goes out through the western arch, followed by four soldiers in two files.)*

(Lentulus and Metellus come into the square from the west side with a little retinue of servants. Both are young courtiers, dressed in the extremity of fashion. Lentulus is slender, fairhaired, epicene. Metellus is manly, compactly built, olive skinned, not a talker.)

LENTULUS. Christians, by Jove! Lets chaff them.

METELLUS. Awful brutes. If you knew as much about them as I do you wouldnt want to chaff them. Leave them to the lions.

LENTULUS *(indicating Lavinia, who is still looking towards the arches after the Captain)*. That woman's got a figure. *(He walks past her, staring at her invitingly; but she is preoccupied and is not conscious of him.)* Do you turn the other cheek when they kiss you?

LAVINIA *(starting)*. What?

LENTULUS. Do you turn the other cheek when they kiss you, fascinating Christian?

LAVINIA. Dont be foolish. *(To Metellus, who has remained on her right, so that she is between them)* Please dont let your friend behave like a cad before the soldiers. How are they to respect and obey patricians if they see them behaving like street boys? *(Sharply to Lentulus)* Pull yourself together, man. Hold your head up. Keep the corners of your mouth firm; and treat me respectfully. What do you take me for?

LENTULUS *(irresolutely)*. Look here, you know: I—you—I—

LAVINIA. Stuff! Go about your business. *(She turns decisively away and sits down with her comrades, leaving him disconcerted.)*

METELLUS. You didnt get much out of that. I told you they were brutes.

LENTULUS. Plucky little filly! I suppose she thinks I care.

(With an air of indifference he strolls with Metellus to the east side of the square, where they stand watching the return of the Centurion through the western arch with his men, escorting three prisoners: Ferrovius, Androcles, and Spintho. Ferrovius is a powerful, choleric man in the prime of life, with large nostrils, staring eyes, and a thick neck: a man whose sensibilities are keen and violent to the verge of madness. Spintho is a debauchee, the wreck of a good-looking man gone hopelessly to the bad. Androcles is overwhelmed with grief, and is restraining his tears with great difficulty.)

THE CENTURION *(to Lavinia)*. Here are some pals for you. This little bit is Ferrovius that you talk so much about. *(Ferrovius turns on him threateningly. The Centurion holds up his left forefinger in admonition.)* Now remember that youre a Christian, and that youve got to return good for evil. *(Ferrovius controls himself convulsively; moves away from temptation to the east side near Lentulus; clasps his hands in silent prayer; and throws himself on his knees.)* Thats the way to manage them, eh! This fine fellow *(indicating Androcles, who comes to his left, and makes Lavinia a heartbroken salutation)* is a sorcerer. A Greek tailor, he is. A real sorcerer, too: no mistake about it. The tenth marches with a leopard at the head of the column. He made a pet of the leopard; and now he's crying at being parted from it. *(Androcles sniffs lamentably.)* Aint you, old chap? Well, cheer up, we march with a Billy goat *(Androcles brightens up)* thats killed two leopards and ate a turkey-cock. You can have him for a pet if you like. *(Androcles, quite consoled, goes past the Centurion to Lavinia, and sits down contentedly on the ground on her left.)* This dirty dog *(collaring Spintho)* is a real Christian. He mobs the temples, he does *(at each accusation he gives the neck of Spintho's tunic a twist)*; he goes smashing things mad drunk, he does; he steals the gold vessels, he does; he assaults the priestesses, he does—

yah! *(He flings Spintho into the middle of the group of prisoners.)* Youre the sort that makes duty a pleasure, you are.

SPINTHO *(gasping).* Thats it: strangle me. Kick me. Beat me. Revile me. Our Lord was beaten and reviled. Thats my way to heaven. Every martyr goes to heaven, no matter what he's done. That is so, isnt it, brother?

CENTURION. Well, if youre going to heaven, *I* dont want to go there. I wouldnt be seen with you.

LENTULUS. Haw! Good! *(Indicating the kneeling Ferrovius)* Is this one of the turn-the-other-cheek gentlemen, Centurion?

CENTURION. Yes, sir. Lucky for you too, sir, if you want to take any liberties with him.

LENTULUS *(to Ferrovius).* You turn the other cheek when youre struck, I'm told.

FERROVIUS *(slowly turning his great eyes on him).* Yes, by the grace of God, I do, now.

LENTULUS. Not that youre a coward, of course; but out of pure piety.

FERROVIUS. I fear God more than man; at least I try to.

LENTULUS. Lets see. *(He strikes him on the cheek. Androcles makes a wild movement to rise and interfere; but Lavinia holds him down, watching Ferrovius intently. Ferrovius, without flinching, turns the other cheek. Lentulus, rather out of countenance, titters foolishly, and strikes him again feebly.)* You know, I should feel ashamed if I let myself be struck like that, and took it lying down. But then I'm not a Christian: I'm a man. *(Ferrovius rises impressively and towers over him. Lentulus becomes white with terror; and a shade of green flickers in his cheek for a moment.)*

FERROVIUS *(with the calm of a steam hammer).* I have not always been faithful. The first man who struck me as you have just struck me was a stronger man than you: he hit me harder than I expected. I was tempted and fell; and it was then that I first tasted bitter shame. I never had a happy moment after that until I had knelt and asked his forgiveness by his bedside in the hospital. *(Putting his hands on Lentulus's shoulders with paternal weight)* But now I have learnt to resist with a strength that is not my own. I am not ashamed now, nor angry.

LENTULUS *(uneasily).* Er—good evening. *(He tries to move away.)*

FERROVIUS *(gripping his shoulders).* Oh, do not harden your heart, young man. Come: try for yourself whether our way is not better than yours. I will now strike you on one cheek; and you will turn the other and learn how much better you will feel than if you gave way to the promptings of anger. *(He holds him with one hand and clenches the other fist.)*

LENTULUS. Centurion: I call on you to protect me.

CENTURION. You asked for it, sir. It's no business of ours. Youve had two whacks at him. Better pay him a trifle and square it that way.

LENTULUS. Yes, of course. *(To Ferrovius)* It was only a bit of fun, I assure you: I meant no harm. Here. *(He proffers a gold coin.)*

FERROVIUS *(taking it and throwing it to the old beggar, who snatches it up eagerly, and hobbles off to spend it).* Give all thou hast to the poor. Come, friend: courage! I may hurt your body for a moment; but your soul will rejoice in the victory of the spirit over the flesh. *(He prepares to strike.)*

ANDROCLES. Easy, Ferrovius, easy: you broke the last man's jaw.

(Lentulus, with a moan of terror, attempts to fly; but Ferrovius holds him ruthlessly.)

FERROVIUS. Yes; but I saved his soul. What matters a broken jaw?

LENTULUS. Dont touch me, do you hear? The law—

FERROVIUS. The law will throw me to the lions tomorrow: what worse could it do were I to slay you? Pray for strength; and it shall be given to you.

LENTULUS. Let me go. Your religion forbids you to strike me.

FERROVIUS. On the contrary, it commands me to strike you. How can you turn the other cheek, if you are not first struck on the one cheek?

LENTULUS *(almost in tears).* But I'm convinced already that what you said is quite right. I apologize for striking you.

FERROVIUS *(greatly pleased).* My son: have I softened your heart? Has the good seed fallen in a fruitful place? Are your feet turning towards a better path?

LENTULUS *(abjectly).* Yes, yes. Theres a great deal in what you say.

FERROVIUS *(radiant).* Join us. Come to the lions. Come to suffering and death.

LENTULUS *(falling on his knees and bursting into tears).* Oh, help me. Mother! mother!

FERROVIUS. These tears will water your soul and make it bring forth good fruit, my son. God has greatly blessed my efforts at conversion. Shall I tell you a miracle—yes, a miracle—wrought by me in Cappadocia? A young man—just such a one as you, with golden hair like yours—scoffed at and struck me as you scoffed at and struck me. I sat up all night with that youth wrestling for his soul; and in the morning not only was he a Christian, but his hair was as white as snow. *(Lentulus falls in a dead faint.)* There, there: take him away. The spirit has overwrought him, poor lad. Carry him gently to his house; and leave the rest to heaven.

CENTURION. Take him home. *(The servants, intimidated, hastily carry him out. Metellus is about to follow when Ferrovius lays his hand on his shoulder.)*

FERROVIUS. You are his friend, young man. You will see that he is taken safely home.

METELLUS *(with awestruck civility)*. Certainly, sir. I shall do whatever you think best. Most happy to have made your acquaintance, I'm sure. You may depend on me. Good evening, sir.

FERROVIUS *(with unction)*. The blessing of heaven upon you and him.

(Metellus follows Lentulus. The Centurion returns to his seat to resume his interrupted nap. The deepest awe has settled on the spectators. Ferrovius, with a long sigh of happiness, goes to Lavinia, and offers her his hand.)

LAVINIA *(taking it)*. So that is how you convert people, Ferrovius.

FERROVIUS. Yes: there has been a blessing on my work in spite of my unworthiness and my backslidings—all through my wicked, devilish temper. This man—

ANDROCLES *(hastily)*. Dont slap me on the back, brother. She knows you mean me.

FERROVIUS. How I wish I were weak like our brother here! for then I should perhaps be meek and gentle like him. And yet there seems to be a special providence that makes my trials less than his. I hear tales of the crowd scoffing and casting stones and reviling the brethren; but when I come, all this stops: my influence calms the passions of the mob: they listen to me in silence; and infidels are often converted by a straight heart-to-heart talk with me. Every day I feel happier, more confident. Every day lightens the load of the great terror.

LAVINIA. The great terror? What is that?

(Ferrovius shakes his head and does not answer. He sits down beside her on her left, and buries his face in his hands in gloomy meditation.)

ANDROCLES. Well, you see, sister, he's never quite sure of himself. Suppose at the last moment in the arena, with the gladiators there to fight him, one of them was to say anything to annoy him, he might forget himself and lay that gladiator out.

LAVINIA. That would be splendid.

FERROVIUS *(springing up in horror)*. What!

ANDROCLES. Oh, sister!

FERROVIUS. Splendid to betray my master, like Peter? Splendid to act like any common blackguard in the day of my proving! Woman: you are no Christian. *(He moves away from her to the middle of the square, as if her neighborhood contaminated him.)*

LAVINIA *(laughing)*. You know, Ferrovius, I am not always a Christian. I dont think anybody is. There are moments when I forget all about it, and something comes out quite naturally, as it did then.

SPINTHO. What does it matter? If you die in the arena, youll be a martyr; and all martyrs go to heaven, no matter what they have done. Thats so, isnt it, Ferrovius?

FERROVIUS. Yes: that is so, if we are faithful to the end.

LAVINIA. I'm not so sure.

SPINTHO. Dont say that. Thats blasphemy. Dont say that, I tell you. We shall be saved, no matter WHAT we do.

LAVINIA. Perhaps you men will all go into heaven bravely and in triumph, with your heads erect and golden trumpets sounding for you. But I am sure I shall only be allowed to squeeze myself in through a little crack in the gate after a great deal of begging. I am not good always: I have moments only.

SPINTHO. Youre talking nonsense, woman. I tell you, martyrdom pays all scores.

ANDROCLES. Well, let us hope so, brother, for your sake. Youve had a gay time, havnt you? with your raids on the temples. I cant help thinking that heaven will be very dull for a man of your temperament. *(Spintho snarls.)* Dont be angry: I say it only to console you in case you should die in your bed tonight in the natural way. Theres a lot of plague about.

SPINTHO *(rising and running about in abject terror)*. I never thought of that. Oh Lord, spare me to be martyred. Oh, what a thought to put into the mind of a brother! Oh, let me be martyred today, now. I shall die in the night and go to hell. Youre a sorcerer: youve put death into my mind. Oh, curse you, curse you! *(He tries to seize Androcles by the throat.)*

FERROVIUS *(holding him in a grasp of iron)*. Whats this, brother? Anger! Violence! Raising your hand to a brother Christian!

SPINTHO. It's easy for you. Youre strong. Your nerves are all right. But I'm full of disease. *(Ferrovius takes his hand from him with instinctive disgust.)* Ive drunk all my nerves away. I shall have the horrors all night.

ANDROCLES *(sympathetic)*. Oh, dont take on so, brother. We're all sinners.

SPINTHO *(snivelling, trying to feel consoled)*. Yes: I daresay if the truth were known, youre all as bad as I am.

LAVINIA *(contemptuously)*. Does that comfort you?

FERROVIUS *(sternly)*. Pray, man, pray.

SPINTHO. Whats the good of praying? If we're martyred we shall go to heaven, shant we, whether we pray or not?

FERROVIUS. Whats that? Not pray! *(Seizing him again)* Pray this instant, you dog, you rotten hound, you slimy snake, you beastly goat, or—

SPINTHO. Yes: beat me: kick me. I forgive you: mind that.

FERROVIUS *(spurning him with loathing)*. Yah! *(Spintho reels away and falls in front of Ferrovius.)*

ANDROCLES *(reaching out and catching the skirt of Ferrovius's tunic)*. Dear brother: if you wouldnt mind—just for my sake—

FERROVIUS. Well?

ANDROCLES. Dont call him by the names of the animals. Weve no right to. Ive had such friends in dogs. A pet snake is the best of company. I was nursed on goat's milk. Is it fair to them to call the like of him a dog or a snake or a goat?

FERROVIUS. I only meant that they have no souls.

ANDROCLES *(anxiously protesting)*. Oh, believe me, they have. Just the same as you and me. I really dont think I could consent to go to heaven if I thought there were to be no animals there. Think of what they suffer here.

FERROVIUS. Thats true. Yes: that is just. They will have their share in heaven.

SPINTHO *(who has picked himself up and is sneaking past Ferrovius on his left, sneers derisively)*!!

FERROVIUS *(turning on him fiercely)*. Whats that you say?

SPINTHO *(cowering)*. Nothing.

FERROVIUS *(clenching his fist)*. Do animals go to heaven or not?

SPINTHO. I never said they didnt.

FERROVIUS *(implacable)*. Do they or do they not?

SPINTHO. They do: they do. *(Scrambling out of Ferrovius's reach)* Oh, curse you for frightening me! *(A bugle call is heard.)*

CENTURION *(waking up)*. Tention! Form as before. Now then, prisoners: up with you and trot along spry. *(The soldiers fall in. The Christians rise.)*

(A man with an ox goad comes running through the central arch.)

THE OX DRIVER. Here, you soldiers! clear out of the way for the Emperor.

THE CENTURION. Emperor! Wheres the Emperor? You aint the Emperor, are you?

THE OX DRIVER. It's the menagerie service. My team of oxen is drawing the new lion to the Coliseum. You clear the road.

CENTURION. What! Go in after you in your dust, with half the town at the heels of you and your lion! Not likely. We go first.

THE OX DRIVER. The menagerie service is the Emperor's personal retinue. You clear out, I tell you.

CENTURION. You tell me, do you? Well, I'll tell you something. If the lion is menagerie service, the lion's dinner is menagerie service too. This *(pointing to the Christians)* is the lion's dinner. So back with you to your bullocks double quick; and learn your place. March. *(The soldiers start.)* Now then, you Christians: step out there.

LAVINIA *(marching)*. Come along, the rest of the dinner. I shall be the olives and anchovies.

ANOTHER CHRISTIAN *(laughing)*. I shall be the soup.

ANOTHER. I shall be the fish.

ANOTHER. Ferrovius shall be the roast boar.

FERROVIUS *(heavily)*. I see the joke. Yes, yes: I shall be the roast boar. Ha! ha! *(He laughs conscientiously and marches out with them.)*

ANDROCLES *(following)*. I shall be the mince pie. *(Each announcement is received with a louder laugh by all the rest as the joke catches on.)*

CENTURION *(scandalized)*. Silence! Have some sense of your situation. Is this the way for martyrs to behave? *(To Spintho, who is quaking and loitering)* I know what youll be at that dinner. Youll be the emetic. *(He shoves him rudely along.)*

SPINTHO. It's too dreadful: I'm not fit to die.

CENTURION. Fitter than you are to live, you swine.

(They pass from the square westward. The oxen, drawing a waggon with a great wooden cage and the lion in it, arrive through the central arch.)

Act Two

BEHIND the Emperor's box at the Coliseum, where the performers assemble before entering the arena. In the middle a wide passage leading to the arena descends from the floor level under the imperial box. On both sides of this passage steps ascend to a landing at the back entrance to the box. The landing forms a bridge across the passage. At the entrance to the passage are two bronze mirrors, one on each side.

On the west side of this passage, on the right hand of anyone coming from the box and standing on the bridge. the martyrs are sitting on the steps. Lavinia is seated halfway up, thoughtful, trying to look death in the face. On her left Androcles consoles himself by nursing a cat. Ferrovius stands behind them, his eyes blazing, his figure stiff with intense resolution. At the foot of the steps crouches Spintho, with his head clutched in his hands, full of horror at the approach of martyrdom.

On the east side of the passage the gladiators are standing and sitting at ease, waiting, like the Christians, for their turn in the arena. One (Retiarius) is a nearly naked man with a net and a trident. Another (Secutor) is in armor with a sword. He carries a helmet with a barred visor. The editor of the gladiators sits on a chair a little apart from them.

The Call Boy enters from the passage.

THE CALL BOY. Number six. Retiarius versus Secutor. *(The gladiator with the net picks it up. The gladiator with the helmet puts it on; and the two go into the arena, the net thrower taking out a little brush and arranging his hair as he goes, the other tightening his straps and shaking his shoulders loose. Both look at themselves in the mirrors before they enter the passage.)*

LAVINIA. Will they really kill one another?

SPINTHO. Yes, if the people turn down their thumbs.

THE EDITOR. You know nothing about it. The people indeed! Do you suppose we would kill a man worth perhaps fifty talents to please the riffraff? I should like to catch any of my men at it.

SPINTHO. I thought—

THE EDITOR *(contemptuously)*. You thought! Who cares what you think? Youll be killed all right enough.

SPINTHO *(groans and again hides his face)*!!!

LAVINIA. Then is nobody ever killed except us poor Christians?

THE EDITOR. If the vestal virgins turn down their thumbs, thats another matter. Theyre ladies of rank.

LAVINIA. Does the Emperor ever interfere?

THE EDITOR. Oh, yes: he turns his thumb up fast enough if the vestal virgins want to have one of his pet fighting men killed.

ANDROCLES. But dont they ever just only pretend to kill one another? Why shouldnt you pretend to die, and get dragged out as if you were dead; and then get up and go home, like an actor?

THE EDITOR. See here: you want to know too much. There will be no pretending about the new lion: let that be enough for you. He's hungry.

SPINTHO *(groaning with horror)*. Oh, Lord! cant you stop talking about it? Isnt it bad enough for us without that?

ANDROCLES. I'm glad he's hungry. Not that I want him to suffer, poor chap! but then he'll enjoy eating me so much more. Theres a cheerful side to everything.

THE EDITOR *(rising and striding over to Androcles)*. Here: dont you be obstinate. Come with me and drop the pinch of incense on the altar. Thats all you need do to be let off.

ANDROCLES. No: thank you very much indeed; but I really mustnt.

THE EDITOR. What! Not to save your life?

ANDROCLES. I'd rather not. I couldnt sacrifice to Diana: she's a huntress, you know, and kills things.

THE EDITOR. That dont matter. You can choose your own altar. Sacrifice to Jupiter: he likes animals: he turns himself into an animal when he goes off duty.

ANDROCLES. No: it's very kind of you; but I feel I cant save myself that way.

THE EDITOR. But I dont ask you to do it to save yourself: I ask you to do it to oblige me personally.

ANDROCLES *(scrambling up in the greatest agitation)*. Oh, please dont say that. This is dreadful. You mean so kindly by me that it seems quite horrible to disoblige you. If you could arrange for me to sacrifice when theres nobody looking, I shouldnt mind. But I must go into the arena with the rest. My honor, you know.

THE EDITOR. Honor! The honor of a tailor?

COMING ATTRACTION
MAXIMUS & MINIMUS
CHRISTIANS
LIONS!

ANDROCLES *(apologetically).* Well, perhaps honor is too strong an expression. Still, you know, I couldnt allow the tailors to get a bad name through me.

THE EDITOR. How much will you remember of all that when you smell the beast's breath and see his jaws opening to tear out your throat?

SPINTHO *(rising with a yell of terror).* I cant bear it. Wheres the altar? I'll sacrifice.

FERROVIUS. Dog of an apostate. Iscariot!

SPINTHO. I'll repent afterwards. I fully mean to die in the arena: I'll die a martyr and go to heaven; but not this time, not now, not until my nerves are better. Besides, I'm too young: I want to have just one more good time. *(The gladiators laugh at him.)* Oh, will no one tell me where the altar is? *(He dashes into the passage and vanishes.)*

ANDROCLES *(to the Editor, pointing after Spintho).* Brother: I cant do that, not even to oblige you. Dont ask me.

THE EDITOR. Well, if youre determined to die, I cant help you. But I wouldnt be put off by a swine like that.

FERROVIUS. Peace, peace: tempt him not. Get thee behind him, Satan.

THE EDITOR *(flushing with rage).* For two pins I'd take a turn in the arena myself today, and pay you out for daring to talk to me like that.

(Ferrovius springs forward.)

LAVINIA *(rising quickly and interposing).* Brother, brother: you forget.

FERROVIUS *(curbing himself by a mighty effort).* Oh, my temper, my wicked temper! *(To the Editor, as Lavinia sits down again, reassured)* Forgive me, brother. My heart was full of wrath: I should have been thinking of your dear precious soul.

THE EDITOR. Yah! *(He turns his back on Ferrovius contemptuously, and goes back to his seat.)*

FERROVIUS *(continuing).* And I forgot it all: I thought of nothing but offering to fight you with one hand tied behind me.

THE EDITOR *(turning pugnaciously).* What!

FERROVIUS *(on the border line between zeal and ferocity).* Oh, dont give way to pride and wrath, brother. I could do it so easily. I could—

(They are separated by the Menagerie Keeper, who rushes in from the passage, furious.)

THE KEEPER. Heres a nice business! Who let that Christian out of here down to the dens when we were changing the lion into the cage next the arena?

THE EDITOR. Nobody let him. He let himself.

THE KEEPER. Well, the lion's ate him.

(Consternation. The Christians rise, greatly agitated. The gladiators sit callously, but are highly amused. All speak or cry out or laugh at once. Tumult.)

LAVINIA. Oh, poor wretch! FERROVIUS. The apostate has perished. Praise be to God's justice! ANDROCLES. The poor beast was starving. It couldnt help itself. THE CHRISTIANS. What! Ate him! How frightful! How terrible! Without a moment to repent! God be merciful to him, a sinner! Oh, I cant bear to think of it! In the midst of his sin! Horrible, horrible! THE EDITOR. Serve the rotter right! THE GLADIATORS. Just walked into it, he did. He's martyred all right enough. Good old lion! Old Jock doesnt like that: look at his face. Devil a better! The Emperor will laugh when he hears of it. I cant help smiling. Ha ha ha!!!!!

THE KEEPER. Now his appetite's taken off, he wont as much as look at another Christian for a week.

ANDROCLES. Couldnt you have saved him, brother?

THE KEEPER. Saved him! Saved him from a lion that I'd just got mad with hunger! a wild one that came out of the forest not four weeks ago! He bolted him before you could say Balbus.

LAVINIA *(sitting down again).* Poor Spintho! And it wont even count as martyrdom!

THE KEEPER. Serve him right! What call had he to walk down the throat of one of my lions before he was asked?

ANDROCLES. Perhaps the lion wont eat me now.

THE KEEPER. Yes: thats just like a Christian: think only of yourself! What am *I* to do? What am I to say to the Emperor when he sees one of my lions coming into the arena half asleep?

THE EDITOR. Say nothing. Give your old lion some bitters and a morsel of fried fish to wake up his appetite. *(Laughter)*

THE KEEPER. Yes: it's easy for you to talk; but—

THE EDITOR *(scrambling to his feet).* Sh! Attention there! The Emperor. *(The Keeper bolts precipitately into the passage. The gladiators rise smartly and form into line.)*

(The Emperor enters on the Christians' side, conversing with Metellus, and followed by his suite.)

THE GLADIATORS. Hail, Caesar! those about to die salute thee.

CAESAR. Good morrow, friends.

(Metellus shakes hands with the Editor, who accepts his condescension with bluff respect.)

LAVINIA. Blessing, Caesar, and forgiveness!

CAESAR *(turning in some surprise at the salutation).* There is no forgiveness for Christianity.

LAVINIA. I did not mean that, Caesar. I mean that we forgive you.

METELLUS. An inconceivable liberty! Do you not know, woman, that the Emperor can do no wrong and therefore cannot be forgiven?

LAVINIA. I expect the Emperor knows better. Anyhow, we forgive him.

THE CHRISTIANS. Amen!

CAESAR. Metellus: you see now the disadvantage of too much severity. These people have no hope; therefore they have nothing to restrain them from saying what they like to me. They are almost as impertinent as the gladiators. Which is the Greek sorcerer?

ANDROCLES *(humbly touching his forelock).* Me, your Worship.

CAESAR. My Worship! Good! A new title. Well: what miracles can you perform?

ANDROCLES. I can cure warts by rubbing them with my tailor's chalk; and I can live with my wife without beating her.

CAESAR. Is that all?

ANDROCLES. You dont know her, Caesar, or you wouldnt say that.

CAESAR. Ah, well, my friend, we shall no doubt contrive a happy release for you. Which is Ferrovius?

FERROVIUS. I am he.

CAESAR. They tell me you can fight.

FERROVIUS. It is easy to fight. *I* can die, Caesar.

CAESAR. That is still easier, is it not?

FERROVIUS. Not to me, Caesar. Death comes hard to my flesh; and fighting comes very easily to my spirit *(beating his breast and lamenting)* Oh, sinner that I am! *(He throws himself down on the steps, deeply discouraged.)*

CAESAR. Metellus: I should like to have this man in the Pretorian Guard.

METELLUS. *I* should not, Caesar. He looks a spoilsport. There are men in whose presence it is impossible to have any fun: men who are a sort of walking conscience. He would make us all uncomfortable.

CAESAR. For that reason, perhaps, it might be well to have him. An Emperor can hardly have too many consciences. *(To Ferrovius)* Listen, Ferrovius. *(Ferrovius shakes his head and will not look up.)* You and your friends shall not be outnumbered today in the arena. You shall have arms; and there will be no more than one gladiator to each Christian. If you come out of the arena alive, I will consider favorably any request of yours, and give you a place in the Pretorian Guard. Even if the request be that no questions be asked about your faith I shall perhaps not refuse it.

FERROVIUS. I will not fight. I will die. Better stand with the archangels than with the Pretorian Guard.

CAESAR. I cannot believe that the archangels—whoever they may be—would not prefer to be recruited from the Pretorian Guard. However, as you please. Come: let us see the show.

(As the Court ascends the steps, Secutor and Retiarius return from the arena through the passage: Secutor covered with dust and very angry: Retiarius grinning.)

SECUTOR. Ha, the Emperor. Now we shall see. Caesar: I ask you whether it is fair for the Retiarius, instead of making a fair throw of his net at me, to swish it along the ground and throw the dust in my eyes, and then catch me when I'm blinded. If the vestals had not turned up their thumbs I should have been a dead man.

CAESAR *(halting on the stair).* There is nothing in the rules against it.

SECUTOR *(indignantly).* Caesar: is it a dirty trick or is it not?

CAESAR. It is a dusty one, my friend. *(Obsequious laughter)* Be on your guard next time.

SECUTOR. Let him be on his guard. Next time I'll throw my sword at his heels and strangle him with his own net before he can hop off. *(To the Retiarius)* You see if I dont. *(He goes out past the gladiators, sulky and furious.)*

CAESAR *(to the chuckling Retiarius).* These tricks are not wise, my friend. The audience likes to see a dead man in all his beauty and splendor. If you smudge his face and spoil his armor they will shew their displeasure by not letting you kill him. And when your turn comes, they will remember it against you and turn their thumbs down.

RETIARIUS. Perhaps that is why I did it, Caesar. He bet me ten sesterces that he would vanquish me. If I had had to kill him I should not have had the money.

CAESAR *(indulgent, laughing).* You rogues: there is no end to your tricks. I'll dismiss you all and have elephants to fight. They fight fairly. *(He goes up to his box, and knocks at it. It is opened from with-*

in by the Captain, who stands as on parade to let him pass.)

(The Call Boy comes from the passage, followed by three attendants carrying respectively a bundle of swords, some helmets, and some breastplates and pieces of armor which they throw down in a heap.)

THE CALL BOY. By your leave, Caesar. Number eleven! Gladiators and Christians!

(Ferrovius springs up, ready for martyrdom. The other Christians take the summons as best they can, some joyful and brave, some patient and dignified, some tearful and helpless, some embracing one another with emotion. The Call Boy goes back into the passage.)

CAESAR *(turning at the door of the box).* The hour has come, Ferrovius. I shall go into my box and see you killed, since you scorn the Pretorian Guard. *(He goes into the box. The Captain shuts the door, remaining inside with the Emperor. Metellus and the rest of the suite disperse to their seats. The Christians, led by Ferrovius, move towards the passage.)*

LAVINIA *(to Ferrovius).* Farewell.

THE EDITOR. Steady there. You Christians have got to fight. Here! arm yourselves.

FERROVIUS *(picking up a sword).* I'll die sword in hand to shew people that I could fight if it were my Master's will, and that I could kill the man who kills me if I chose.

THE EDITOR. Put on that armor.

FERROVIUS. No armor.

THE EDITOR *(bullying him).* Do what youre told. Put on that armor.

FERROVIUS *(gripping the sword and looking dangerous).* I said, No armor.

THE EDITOR. And what am I to say when I am accused of sending a naked man in to fight my men in armor?

FERROVIUS. Say your prayers, brother; and have no fear of the princes of this world.

THE EDITOR. Tsha! You obstinate fool! *(He bites his lips irresolutely, not knowing exactly what to do.)*

ANDROCLES *(to Ferrovius).* Farewell, brother, till we meet in the sweet by-and-by.

THE EDITOR *(to Androcles).* You are going too. Take a sword there; and put on any armor you can find to fit you.

ANDROCLES. No, really: I cant fight: I never could: I cant bring myself to dislike anyone enough. I'm to be thrown to the lions with the lady.

THE EDITOR. Then get out of the way and hold your noise! *(Androcles steps aside with cheerful docility.)* Now then! Are you all ready there?

(A trumpet is heard from the arena.)

FERROVIUS *(starting convulsively).* Heaven give me strength!

THE EDITOR. Aha! That frightens you, does it?

FERROVIUS. Man: there is no terror like the terror of that sound to me. When I hear a trumpet or a drum or a clash of steel or the hum of the catapult as the great stone flies, fire runs through my veins: I feel my blood surge up hot behind my eyes: I must charge: I must strike: I must conquer: Caesar himself will not be safe in his imperial seat if once that spirit gets loose in me. Oh, brothers, pray! exhort me! remind me that if I raise my sword my honor falls and my Master is crucified afresh.

ANDROCLES. Just keep thinking how cruelly you might hurt the poor gladiators.

FERROVIUS. It does not hurt a man to kill him.

LAVINIA. Nothing but faith can save you.

FERROVIUS. Faith! Which faith? There are two faiths. There is our faith. And there is the warrior's faith, the faith in fighting, the faith that sees God in the sword. How if that faith should overwhelm me?

LAVINIA. You will find your real faith in the hour of trial.

FERROVIUS. That is what I fear. I know that I am a fighter. How can I feel sure that I am a Christian?

ANDROCLES. Throw away the sword, brother.

FERROVIUS. I cannot. It cleaves to my hand. I could as easily throw a woman I loved from my arms. *(Starting)* Who spoke that blasphemy? Not I.

LAVINIA. I cant help you, friend. I cant tell you not to save your own life. Something wilful in me wants to see you fight your way into heaven.

FERROVIUS. Ha!

ANDROCLES. But if you are going to give up our faith, brother, why not do it without hurting anybody? Dont fight them. Burn the incense.

FERROVIUS. Burn the incense! Never.

LAVINIA. This is only pride, Ferrovius.

FERROVIUS. Only pride! What is nobler than pride? *(Conscience stricken)* Oh, I'm steeped in sin. I'm proud of my pride.

LAVINIA. They say we Christians are the proudest devils on earth—that only the weak are meek. Oh, I am worse than you. I ought to send you to death; and I am tempting you.

ANDROCLES. Brother, brother: let them rage and

kill: let us be brave and suffer. You must go as a lamb to the slaughter.

FERROVIUS. Aye, aye: that is right. Not as a lamb is slain by the butcher; but as a butcher might let himself be slain by a *(looking at the Editor)* by a silly ram whose head he could fetch off in one twist.

(Before the Editor can retort, the Call Boy rushes up through the passage, and the Captain comes from the Emperor's box and descends the steps.)

THE CALL BOY. In with you: into the arena. The stage is waiting.

THE CAPTAIN. The Emperor is waiting *(To the Editor)* What are you dreaming of, man? Send your men in at once.

THE EDITOR. Yes, sir: it's these Christians hanging back.

FERROVIUS *(in a voice of thunder)*. Liar!

THE EDITOR *(not heeding him)*. March. *(The gladiators told off to fight with the Christians march down the passage.)* Follow up there, you.

THE CHRISTIAN MEN AND WOMEN *(as they part)*. Be steadfast, brother. Farewell. Hold up the faith, brother. Farewell. Go to glory, dearest. Farewell. Remember: we are praying for you. Farewell. Be strong, brother. Farewell. Dont forget that the divine love and our love surround you. Farewell. Nothing can hurt you: remember that, brother. Farewell. Eternal glory, dearest. Farewell.

THE EDITOR *(out of patience)*. Shove them in, there.

(The remaining gladiators and the Call Boy make a movement towards them.)

FERROVIUS *(interposing)*. Touch them, dogs; and we die here, and cheat the heathen of their spectacle. *(To his fellow Christians)* Brothers: the great moment has come. That passage is your hill to Calvary. Mount it bravely, but meekly; and remember! not a word of reproach, not a blow nor a struggle. Go. *(They go out through the passage. He turns to Lavinia.)* Farewell.

LAVINIA. You forget: I must follow before you are cold.

FERROVIUS. It is true. Do not envy me because I pass before you to glory. *(He goes through the passage.)*

THE EDITOR *(to the Call Boy)*. Sickening work, this. Why cant they all be thrown to the lions? It's not a man's job. *(He throws himself moodily into his chair.)*

(The remaining gladiators go back to their former places indifferently. The Call Boy shrugs his shoulders and squats down at the entrance to the passage, near the Editor.

Lavinia and the Christian women sit down again, wrung with grief, some weeping silently, some praying, some calm and steadfast. Androcles sits down at Lavinia's feet. The Captain stands on the stairs, watching her curiously.)

ANDROCLES. I'm glad I havent to fight. That would really be an awful martyrdom. I am lucky.

LAVINIA *(looking at him with a pang of remorse)*. Androcles: burn the incense: youll be forgiven. Let my death atone for both. I feel as if I were killing you.

ANDROCLES. Dont think of me, sister. Think of yourself. That will keep your heart up.

(The Captain laughs sardonically.)

LAVINIA *(startled: she had forgotten his presence)*. Are you there, handsome Captain? Have you come to see me die?

THE CAPTAIN *(coming to her side)*. I am on duty with the Emperor, Lavinia.

LAVINIA. Is it part of your duty to laugh at us?

THE CAPTAIN. No: that is part of my private pleasure. Your friend here is a humorist. I laughed at his telling you to think of yourself to keep up your heart. *I* say, think of yourself and burn the incense.

LAVINIA. He is not a humorist: he was right. You ought to know that, Captain: you have been face to face with death.

THE CAPTAIN. Not with certain death, Lavinia. Only death in battle, which spares more men than death in bed. What you are facing is certain death. You have nothing left now but your faith in this craze of yours: this Christianity. Are your Christian fairy stories any truer than our stories about Jupiter and Diana, in which, I may tell you, I believe no more than the Emperor does, or any educated man in Rome?

LAVINIA. Captain: all that seems nothing to me now. I'll not say that death is a terrible thing; but I will say that it is so real a thing that when it comes close, all the imaginary things—all the stories, as you call them—fade into mere dreams beside that inexorable reality. I know now that I am not dying for stories or dreams. Did you hear of the dreadful thing that happened here while we were waiting?

THE CAPTAIN. I heard that one of your fellows bolted, and ran right into the jaws of the lion. I laughed. I still laugh.

LAVINIA. Then you dont understand what that meant?

THE CAPTAIN. It meant that the lion had a cur for his breakfast.

LAVINIA. It meant more than that, Captain. It meant that a man cannot die for a story and a dream. None of us believed the stories and the dreams more devoutly than poor Spintho; but he could not face the great reality. What he would have called my faith has been oozing away minute by minute whilst Ive been sitting here, with death coming nearer and nearer, with reality become realler and realler, with stories and dreams fading away into nothing.

THE CAPTAIN. Are you then going to die for nothing?

LAVINIA. Yes: that is the wonderful thing. It is since all the stories and dreams have gone that I have now no doubt at all that I must die for something greater than dreams or stories.

THE CAPTAIN. But for what?

LAVINIA. I dont know. If it were for anything small enough to know, it would be too small to die for. I think I'm going to die for God. Nothing else is real enough to die for.

THE CAPTAIN. What is God?

LAVINIA. When we know that, Captain, we shall be gods ourselves.

THE CAPTAIN. Lavinia: come down to earth. Burn the incense and marry me.

LAVINIA. Handsome Captain: would you marry me if I hauled down the flag in the day of battle and burnt the incense? Sons take after their mothers, you know. Do you want your son to be a coward?

THE CAPTAIN *(strongly moved)*. By great Diana, I think I would strangle you if you gave in now.

LAVINIA *(putting her hand on the head of Androcles)*. The hand of God is on us three, Captain.

THE CAPTAIN. What nonsense it all is! And what a monstrous thing that you should die for such nonsense, and that I should look on helplessly when my whole soul cries out against it! Die then if you must; but at least I can cut the Emperor's throat and then my own when I see your blood.

(The Emperor throws open the door of his box angrily, and appears in wrath on the threshold. The Editor, the Call Boy, and the gladiators spring to their feet.)

THE EMPEROR. The Christians will not fight; and your curs cannot get their blood up to attack them. It's all that fellow with the blazing eyes. Send for the whip. *(The Call Boy rushes out on the east side for the whip.)* If that will not move them, bring the hot irons. The man is like a mountain. *(He returns angrily into the box and slams the door.)*

(The Call Boy returns with a man in a hideous Etruscan mask, carrying a whip. They both rush down the passage into the arena.)

LAVINIA *(rising)*. Oh, that is unworthy. Can they not kill him without dishonoring him?

ANDROCLES *(scrambling to his feet and running into the middle of the space between the staircases)*. It's dreadful. Now *I* want to fight. I cant bear the sight of a whip. The only time I ever hit a man was when he lashed an old horse with a whip. It was terrible: I danced on his face when he was on the ground. He mustnt strike Ferrovius: I'll go into the arena and kill him first. *(He makes a wild dash into the passage. As he does so a great clamor is heard from the arena, ending in wild applause. The gladiators listen and look inquiringly at one another.)*

THE EDITOR. Whats up now?

LAVINIA *(to the Captain)*. What has happened, do you think?

THE CAPTAIN. What can happen? They are killing them, I suppose.

ANDROCLES *(running in through the passage, screaming with horror and hiding his eyes)!!!*

LAVINIA. Androcles, Androcles: whats the matter?

ANDROCLES. Oh dont ask me, dont ask me. Something too dreadful. Oh! *(He crouches by her and hides his face in her robe, sobbing.)*

THE CALL BOY *(rushing through from the passage as before)*. Ropes and hooks there! Ropes and hooks!

THE EDITOR. Well, need you excite yourself about it? *(Another burst of applause)*

(Two slaves in Etruscan masks, with ropes and drag hooks, hurry in.)

ONE OF THE SLAVES. How many dead?

THE CALL BOY. Six. *(The slave blows a whistle twice; and four more masked slaves rush through into the arena with the same apparatus.)* And the basket. Bring the baskets. *(The slave whistles three times, and runs through the passage with his companion.)*

THE CAPTAIN. Who are the baskets for?

THE CALL BOY. For the whip. He's in pieces. Theyre all in pieces, more or less. *(Lavinia hides her face. Two more masked slaves come in with a basket and follow the others into the arena, as the Call Boy turns to the gladiators and exclaims, exhausted)* Boys: he's killed the lot.

THE EMPEROR *(again bursting from his box, this time in an ecstasy of delight).* Where is he? Magnificent! He shall have a laurel crown.

(Ferrovius, madly waving his bloodstained sword, rushes through the passage in despair, followed by his co-religionists, and by the menagerie keeper, who goes to the gladiators. The gladiators draw their swords nervously.)

FERROVIUS. Lost! lost for ever! I have betrayed my Master. Cut off this right hand: it has offended. Ye have swords, my brethren: strike.

LAVINIA. No, no. What have you done, Ferrovius?

FERROVIUS. I know not; but there was blood behind my eyes; and theres blood on my sword. What does that mean?

THE EMPEROR *(enthusiastically, on the landing outside his box).* What does it mean? It means that you are the greatest man in Rome. It means that you shall have a laurel crown of gold. Superb fighter: I could almost yield you my throne. It is a record for my reign: I shall live in history. Once, in Domitian's time, a Gaul slew three men in the arena and gained his freedom. But when before has one naked man slain six armed men of the bravest and best? The persecution shall cease: if Christians can fight like this, I shall have none but Christians to fight for me. *(To the Gladiators)* You are ordered to become Christians, you there: do you hear?

RETIARIUS. It is all one to us, Caesar. Had I been there with my net, the story would have been different.

THE CAPTAIN *(suddenly seizing Lavinia by the wrist and dragging her up the steps to the Emperor).* Caesar: this woman is the sister of Ferrovius. If she is thrown to the lions he will fret. He will lose weight; get out of condition—

THE EMPEROR. The lions? Nonsense! *(To Lavinia)* Madam: I am proud to have the honor of making your acquaintance. Your brother is the glory of Rome.

LAVINIA. But my friends here. Must they die?

THE EMPEROR. Die! Certainly not. There has never been the slightest idea of harming them. Ladies and gentlemen: you are all free. Pray go into the front of the house and enjoy the spectacle to which your brother has so splendidly contributed. Captain: oblige me by conducting them to the seats reserved for my personal friends.

THE MENAGERIE KEEPER. Caesar: I must have one Christian for the lion. The people have been promised it; and they will tear the decorations to bits if they are disappointed.

THE EMPEROR. True, true: we must have somebody for the new lion.

FERROVIUS. Throw me to him. Let the apostate perish.

THE EMPEROR. No, no: you would tear him in pieces, my friend; and we cannot afford to throw away lions as if they were mere slaves. But we must have somebody. This is really extremely awkward.

THE MENAGERIE KEEPER. Why not that little Greek chap? He's not a Christian: he's a sorcerer.

THE EMPEROR. The very thing: he will do very well.

THE CALL BOY *(issuing from the passage).* Number twelve. The Christian for the new lion.

ANDROCLES *(rising, and pulling himself sadly together).* Well, it was to be, after all.

LAVINIA. I'll go in his place, Caesar. Ask the Captain whether they do not like best to see a woman torn to pieces. He told me so yesterday.

THE EMPEROR. There is something in that: there is certainly something in that—if only I could feel sure that your brother would not fret.

ANDROCLES. No: I should never have another happy hour. No: on the faith of a Christian and the honor of a tailor, I accept the lot that has fallen on me. If my wife turns up, give her my love and say that my wish was that she should be happy with her next, poor fellow! Caesar: go to your box and see how a tailor can die. Make way for number twelve there. *(He marches out along the passage.)*

(The vast audience in the amphitheatre now sees the Emperor re-enter his box and take his place as Androcles, desperately frightened, but still marching with piteous devotion, emerges from the other end of the passage, and finds himself at the focus of thousands of eager eyes. The lion's cage, with a heavy portcullis grating, is on his left. The Emperor gives a signal. A gong sounds. Androcles shivers at the sound; then falls on his knees and prays. The grating rises with a clash. The lion bounds into the arena. He rushes round frisking in his freedom. He sees Androcles. He stops; rises stiffly by straightening his legs; stretches out his nose forward and his tail in a horizontal line behind, like a pointer, and utters an appalling roar. Androcles crouches and hides his face in his hands. The lion gathers himself for a spring, swishing his tail to and fro through the dust in an ecstasy of anticipation. Androcles throws up his hands in supplication to heaven. The lion

checks at the sight of Androcles's face. He then steals towards him; smells him; arches his back; purrs like a motor car; finally rubs himself against Androcles, knocking him over. Androcles, supporting himself on his wrist, looks affrightedly at the lion. The lion limps on three paws, holding up the other as if it was wounded. A flash of recognition lights up the face of Androcles. He flaps his hand as if it had a thorn in it, and pretends to pull the thorn out and to hurt himself. The lion nods repeatedly. Androcles holds out his hands to the lion, who gives him both paws, which he shakes with enthusiasm. They embrace rapturously, finally waltz round the arena amid a sudden burst of deafening applause, and out through the passage, the Emperor watching them in breathless astonishment until they disappear, when he rushes from his box and descends the steps in frantic excitement.)

THE EMPEROR. My friends, an incredible! an amazing thing! has happened. I can no longer doubt the truth of Christianity. *(The Christians press to him joyfully.)* This Christian sorcerer—*(with a yell, he breaks off as he sees Androcles and the lion emerge from the passage, waltzing. He bolts wildly up the steps into his box, and slams the door. All, Christians and gladiators alike, fly for their lives, the gladiators bolting into the arena, the others in all directions. The place is emptied with magical suddenness.)*

ANDROCLES *(naïvely)*. Now I wonder why they all run away from us like that. *(The lion, combining a series of yawns, purrs, and roars, achieves something very like a laugh.)*

THE EMPEROR *(standing on a chair inside his box and looking over the wall)*. Sorcerer: I command you to put that lion to death instantly. It is guilty of high treason. Your conduct is most disgra—*(the lion charges at him up the stairs)* Help! *(He disappears. The lion rears against the box; looks over the partition at him; and roars. The Emperor darts out through the door and down to Androcles, pursued by the lion.)*

ANDROCLES. Dont run away, sir: he cant help springing if you run. *(He seizes the Emperor and gets between him and the lion, who stops at once.)* Dont be afraid of him.

THE EMPEROR. I am not afraid of him. *(The lion crouches, growling. The Emperor clutches Androcles.)* Keep between us.

ANDROCLES. Never be afraid of animals, your worship: thats the great secret. He'll be as gentle as a lamb when he knows that you are his friend. Stand quite still; and smile; and let him smell you all over just to reassure him; for, you see, he's afraid of you; and he must examine you thoroughly before he gives you his confidence. *(To the lion)* Come now, Tommy; and speak nicely to the Emperor, the great good Emperor who has power to have all our heads cut off if we dont behave very very respectfully to him.

(The lion utters a fearful roar. The Emperor dashes madly up the steps, across the landing, and down again on the other side, with the lion in hot pursuit. Androcles rushes after the lion; overtakes him as he is descending; and throws himself on his back, trying to use his toes as a brake. Before he can stop him the lion gets hold of the trailing end of the Emperor's robe.)

ANDROCLES. Oh bad wicked Tommy, to chase the Emperor like that! Let go the Emperor's robe at once, sir: wheres your manners? *(The lion growls and worries the robe.)* Dont pull it away from him, your worship. He's only playing. Now I shall be really angry with you, Tommy, if you dont let go. *(The lion growls again.)* I'll tell you what it is, sir: he thinks you and I are not friends.

THE EMPEROR *(trying to undo the clasp of his brooch)*. Friends! You infernal scoundrel *(the lion growls)* —dont let him go. Curse this brooch! I cant get it loose.

ANDROCLES. We mustnt let him lash himself into a rage. You must shew him that you are my particular friend—if you will have the condescension. *(He seizes the Emperor's hands and shakes them cordially.)* Look, Tommy: the nice Emperor is the dearest friend Andy Wandy has in the whole world: he loves him like a brother.

THE EMPEROR. You little brute, you damned filthy little dog of a Greek tailor: I'll have you burnt alive for daring to touch the divine person of the Emperor. *(The lion growls.)*

ANDROCLES. Oh dont talk like that, sir. He understands every word you say: all animals do: they take it from the tone of your voice. *(The lion growls and lashes his tail.)* I think he's going to spring at your worship. If you wouldnt mind saying something affectionate. *(The lion roars.)*

THE EMPEROR *(shaking Androcles's hands frantically)*. My dearest Mr Androcles, my sweetest friend, my long lost brother, come to my arms. *(He embraces*

Androcles.) Oh, what an abominable smell of garlic!

(The lion lets go the robe and rolls over on his back, clasping his forepaws over one another coquettishly above his nose.)

ANDROCLES. There! You see, your worship, a child might play with him now. See! *(He tickles the lion's belly. The lion wriggles ecstatically.)* Come and pet him.

THE EMPEROR. I must conquer these unkingly terrors. Mind you dont go away from him, though. *(He pats the lion's chest.)*

ANDROCLES. Oh, sir, how few men would have the courage to do that!

THE EMPEROR. Yes: it takes a bit of nerve. Let us have the Court in and frighten them. Is he safe, do you think?

ANDROCLES. Quite safe now, sir.

THE EMPEROR *(majestically)*. What ho, there! All who are within hearing, return without fear. Caesar has tamed the lion. *(All the fugitives steal cautiously in. The menagerie keeper comes from the passage with other keepers armed with iron bars and tridents.)* Take those things away. I have subdued the beast. *(He places his foot on it.)*

FERROVIUS *(timidly approaching the Emperor and looking down with awe on the lion)*. It is strange that I, who fear no man, should fear a lion.

THE CAPTAIN. Every man fears something, Ferrovius.

THE EMPEROR. How about the Pretorian Guard now?

FERROVIUS. In my youth I worshipped Mars, the God of War. I turned from him to serve the Christian god; but today the Christian god forsook me; and Mars overcame me and took back his own. The Christian god is not yet. He will come when Mars and I are dust; but meanwhile I must serve the gods that are, not the God that will be. Until then I accept service in the Guard, Caesar.

THE EMPEROR. Very wisely said. All really sensible men agree that the prudent course is to be neither bigoted in our attachment to the old nor rash and unpractical in keeping an open mind for the new, but to make the best of both dispensations.

THE CAPTAIN. What do you say, Lavinia? Will you too be prudent?

LAVINIA *(on the stairs)*. No: I'll strive for the coming of the God who is not yet.

THE CAPTAIN. May I come and argue with you occasionally?

LAVINIA. Yes, handsome Captain: you may. *(He kisses her hand.)*

THE EMPEROR. And now, my friends, though I do not, as you see, fear this lion, yet the strain of his presence is considerable; for none of us can feel quite sure what he will do next.

THE MENAGERIE KEEPER. Caesar: give us this Greek sorcerer to be a slave in the menagerie. He has a way with the beasts.

ANDROCLES *(distressed)*. Not if they are in cages. They should not be kept in cages. They must be all let out.

THE EMPEROR. I give this sorcerer to be a slave to the first man who lays hands on him. *(The menagerie keepers and the gladiators rush for Androcles. The lion starts up and faces them. They surge back.)* You see how magnanimous we Romans are, Androcles. We suffer you to go in peace.

ANDROCLES. I thank your worship. I thank you all, ladies and gentlemen. Come, Tommy. Whilst we stand together, no cage for you: no slavery for me. *(He goes out with the lion, everybody crowding away to give him as wide a berth as possible.)*

□

AUTHOR'S AFTERWORD

In this play I have presented one of the Roman persecutions of the early Christians, not as the conflict of a false theology with a true, but as what all such persecutions essentially are: an attempt to suppress a propaganda that seemed to threaten the interests involved in the established law and order, organized and maintained in the name of religion and justice by politicians who are pure opportunist Have-and-Holders. People who are shewn by their inner light the possibility of a better world based on the demand of the spirit for a nobler and more abundant life, not for themselves at the expense of others, but for everybody, are naturally dreaded and therefore hated by the Have-and-Holders, who keep always in reserve two sure weapons against them. The first is a persecution effected by the provocation, organization, and arming of that herd instinct which makes men abhor all departures from custom, and, by the most cruel punishments and the wildest calumnies, force eccentric people to behave and profess exactly as other people do. The second is by leading the herd to war, which immediately and infallibly makes them forget everything, even their most cherished and hard-won public liberties and private interests, in the irresistible surge of their pugnacity and the tense preoccupation of their terror.

There is no reason to believe that there was anything more in the Roman persecutions than this. The attitude of the Roman Emperor and the officers of his staff towards the opinions at issue were much the same as those of a modern British Home Secretary towards members of the lower middle classes when some pious policeman charges them with Bad Taste, technically called blasphemy: Bad Taste being a violation of Good Taste, which in such matters practically means Hypocrisy. The Home Secretary and the judges who try the case are usually far more sceptical and blasphemous than the poor men whom they persecute; and their professions of horror at the blunt utterance of their own opinions are revolting to those behind the scenes who have any genuine religious sensibility; but the thing is done because the governing classes, provided only the law against blasphemy is not applied to themselves, strongly approve of such persecution because it enables them to represent their own privileges as part of the religion of the country.

Therefore my martyrs are the martyrs of all time, and my persecutors the persecutors of all time. My Emperor, who has no sense of the value of common people's lives, and amuses himself with killing as carelessly as with sparing, is the sort of monster you can make of any silly-clever gentleman by idolizing him. We are still so easily imposed on by such idols that one of the leading pastors of the Free Churches in London denounced my play on the ground that my persecuting Emperor is a very fine fellow, and the persecuted Christians ridiculous. From which I conclude that a popular pulpit may be as perilous to a man's soul as an imperial throne.

All my articulate Christians, the reader will notice, have different enthusiasms, which they accept as the same religion only because it involves them in a common opposition to the official religion and consequently in a common doom. Androcles is a humanitarian naturalist, whose views surprise everybody. Lavinia, a clever and fearless freethinker, shocks the Pauline[1] Ferrovius, who is comparatively stupid and conscience ridden. Spintho, the blackguardly debauchee, is presented as one of the typical Christians of that period on the authority of St Augustine, who seems to have come to the conclusion at one period of his development that most Christians were what we call wrong uns. No doubt he was to some extent right: I have had occasion often to point out that revolutionary movements attract those who are not good enough for established institutions as well as those who are too good for them. . . .

A

In short, a Christian martyr was thrown to the lions not because he was a Christian, but because he was a crank: that is, an unusual sort of person. And multitudes of people, quite as civilized and amiable as we, crowded to see the lions eat him just as they now crowd the lion-house in the Zoo at feeding-time, not because they really cared twopence about Diana or Christ, or could have given you any intelligent or correct account of the things Diana and Christ stood against one another for, but simply because they wanted to see a curious and exciting spectacle. You, dear reader, have probably run to see a fire; and if somebody came in now and told you that a lion was chasing a man down the street you would rush to the window. And if anyone were to say that you were as cruel as the people who let the lion loose on the man, you would be justly indignant. Now that we may no longer see a man hanged, we assemble outside the jail to see the black flag run up. That is our duller method of enjoying ourselves in the old Roman spirit. And if the Government decided to throw persons of unpopular or eccentric views to the lions in the Albert Hall or the Earl's Court stadium tomorrow, can you doubt that all the seats would be crammed, mostly by people who could not give you the most superficial account of the views in question. Much less unlikely things have happened. It is true that if such a revival does take place soon, the martyrs will not be members of heretical religious sects: they will be Peculiars, Anti-Vivisectionists, Flat-Earth men, scoffers at the laboratories, or infidels who refuse to kneel down when a procession of doctors goes by. But the lions will hurt them just as much, and the spectators will enjoy themselves just as much, as the Roman lions and spectators used to do. . . . □

B

1. *Pauline,* following the doctrines of the Apostle Paul.

DISCUSSION

Prologue

1. How are the characters of Androcles and his wife Megaera established in the Prologue?

2. Megaera does not appear again in the play, but Androcles refers to her. Are these references consistent with her character as we come to know it in the Prologue?

3. How does the comedy of the Prologue set the tone for the action which follows and how does it help determine our reaction to the play as a whole?

Act One

1. In a serious religious discussion, the Roman Captain tells Lavinia that the Christians can easily free themselves by burning a little incense to the Roman gods, and he pleads: "Sacrifice to the true God. What does his name matter? We call him Jupiter. The Greeks call him Zeus. Call him what you will as you drop the incense on the altar flame: He will understand."

(a) Is the Captain's argument persuasive? Explain.

(b) What is the nature of Lavinia's reply, and how may it be related to the serious meaning of the play?

2. When the two young courtiers, Lentulus and Metellus, appear, the "slender, fair-haired" Lentulus cannot refrain from taunting the Christians. What do we learn about the character of (a) Lavinia and (b) Ferrovius from these exchanges?

3. What is revealed about Spintho's character to suggest that he might not be able to go through with his martyrdom when confronted with actual death?

Act Two

1. Spintho's death is reported by the Menagerie Keeper shortly after Spintho has rushed off to find the pagan altar and instead becomes the lion's dinner. What is the effect of his death on (a) the other characters in the play, and (b) on you as a representative of the audience? Explain.

2. (a) Explain the violent action of Ferrovius in the arena.

(b) Explain the Emperor's attitude toward him after he has murdered six of the Emperor's slaves.

3. Discuss the relationship of the Emperor and Androcles at the end of the play.

(a) The Emperor exclaims, after Androcles and the lion make peace in the arena, that he can no longer doubt the truth of Christianity. How deep is his conversion?

(b) How genuine is the friendship the Emperor expresses for Androcles?

General

1. (a) Reread the passage in the Author's Afterword marked *A* and explore the ways in which it is justified by the characters and events in the play.

(b) Explore the ways in which the passage marked *B* is or is not justified by your experience in the world.

2. The subtitle of *Androcles and the Lion* is "A Fable Play." Explore (a) the meaning of this subtitle and (b) the ways in which it might apply to the play.

PHOTOGRAPHS ON PAGES 677, 681, 685, 688, AND 695, COURTESY OF THE UNIVERSITY OF MIAMI, CORAL GABLES, FLORIDA.

"Return Journey" is a radio play first produced in England on the BBC in 1947. The reader should keep in mind that no scenes are presented visually, that the total effect of the play must be made through the language as it creates scenes through the imagination.

RETURN JOURNEY

by Dylan Thomas

NARRATOR. It was a cold white day in High Street, and nothing to stop the wind slicing up from the Docks; for where the squat and tall shops had shielded the town from the sea lay their blitzed flat graves marbled with snow and headstoned with fences. Dogs, delicate as cats on water, as though they had gloves on their paws, padded over the vanished buildings. Boys romped, calling high and clear, on top of a levelled chemist's and a shoeshop; and a little girl, wearing a man's cap, threw a snowball in a chill deserted garden that had once been the Jug and Bottle of the Prince of Wales. The wind cut up the street with a soft sea-noise hanging on its arm, like a hooter in a muffler. I could see the swathed hill stepping up out of the town, which you never could see properly before, and the powdered fields of the roofs of Milton Terrace and Watkin Street and Fullers Row. Fish-frailed, net-bagged, umbrella'd, pixie-capped, fur-shoed, blue-nosed, puce-lipped, blinkered like dray-horses, scarved, mittened, goloshed, wearing everything but the cat's blanket, crushes of shopping women crunched in the little Lapland of the once grey drab street, blew and queued and yearned for hot tea, as I began my search through Swansea town cold and early on that wicked February morning. I went into the hotel. "Good morning."

The hall-porter did not answer. I was just another snowman to him. He did not know that I was looking for someone after fourteen years, and he did not care. He stood and shuddered, staring through the glass of the hotel door at the snowflakes sailing down the sky, like Siberian confetti. The bar was just opening, but already one customer puffed and shook at the counter with a full pint of half-frozen Tawe water in his wrapped-up hand. I said "Good morning," and the barmaid, polishing the counter vigorously, as though it were a rare and valuable piece of Swansea china, said to her first customer:

BARMAID. Seen the film at the Elysium Mr. Griffiths there's snow isn't it did you come up on your bicycle our pipes burst Monday . . .

NARRATOR. A pint of bitter, please.

BARMAID. Proper little lake in the kitchen got to wear your Wellingtons when you boil a egg one and four please . . .

CUSTOMER. The cold gets me just here . . .

BARMAID. . . . and eightpence change that's your liver Mr. Griffiths you been on the cocoa again . . .

NARRATOR. I wonder whether you remember a friend of mine? He always used to come to this bar, some years ago. Every morning, about this time.

CUSTOMER. Just by here it gets me. I don't know what'd happen if I didn't wear a band . . .

BARMAID. What's his name?

NARRATOR. Young Thomas.

BARMAID. Lots of Thomases come here it's a kind of home from home for Thomases isn't it Mr. Griffiths what's he look like?

NARRATOR *(slowly)*. He'd be about seventeen or eighteen . . .

BARMAID. . . . I was seventeen once . . .

NARRATOR. . . . and above medium height. Above medium height for Wales, I mean, he's five foot six and a half. Thick blubber lips; snub nose; curly mouse-brown hair; one front tooth broken after playing a game called cats and dogs in the Mermaid. Mumbles; speaks rather fancy; truculent; plausible; a bit of a shower-off; plus fours and no breakfast, you know; used to have poems printed in the *Herald of Wales;* there was one about an open-air performance of *Electra* in Mrs. Bertie Perkins' garden in Sketty; lived up the Uplands; a bombastic adolescent provincial bohemian with a thick-knotted artist's tie made out of his sister's scarf—she never knew where it had gone—and a cricket-shirt dyed bottle-green; a gabbing, ambitious, mock-tough, pretentious young man; and mole-y, too.

BARMAID. There's words what d'you want to find *him* for I wouldn't touch him with a bargepole . . . would you, Mr. Griffiths? Mind, you can never tell. I remember a man came here with a monkey. Called for 'alf for himself and a pint for the monkey. And he wasn't Italian at all. Spoke Welsh like a preacher.

NARRATOR. The bar was filling up. Snowy business bellies pressed their watch chains against the counter; black business bowlers, damp and white now as Christmas puddings in their cloths, bobbed in front of the misty mirrors. The voice of commerce rang sternly through the lounge.

FIRST VOICE. Cold enough for you?

SECOND VOICE. How's your pipes, Mr. Lewis?

THIRD VOICE. Another winter like this'll put paid to me, Mr. Evans.

FOURTH VOICE. I got the flu . . .

FIRST VOICE. Make it a double . . .

SECOND VOICE. Similar . . .

BARMAID. Okay, baby . . .

CUSTOMER *(confidentially)*. I seem to remember a chap like you described. There couldn't be two like him let's hope. He used to work as a reporter. Down the Three Lamps I used to see him. Lifting his ikkle elbow.

NARRATOR. What's the Three Lamps like now?

CUSTOMER. It isn't like anything. It isn't there. It's nothing mun. You remember Ben Evans' stores? It's right next door to that. Ben Evans isn't there either . . .

(Fade.)

NARRATOR. I went out of the hotel into the snow and walked down High Street, past the flat white wastes where all the shops had been. Eddershaw Furnishers, Curry's Bicycles, Donegal Clothing Company, Doctor Scholl's, Burton Tailors, W. H. Smith, Boots Cash Chemists, Leslie's Stores, Upson's Shoes, Prince of Wales, Tucker's Fish, Stead and Simpson—all the shops bombed and vanished. Past the hole in space where Hodges and Clothiers had been, down Castle Street, past the remembered, invisible shops, Price's Fifty Shilling, and Crouch the Jeweller, Potter Gilmore Gowns, Evans Jeweller, Master's Outfitters, Style and Mantle, Lennard's Boots, True Form, Kardomah, R. E. Jones, Dean's Tailors, David Evans, Gregory Confectioners, Bovega, Burton's, Lloyd's Bank and nothing. And into Temple Street. There the Three Lamps had stood, old Mac magisterial in his corner. And there the Young Thomas I was searching for used to stand at the counter on Friday paynights with Freddie Farr, Half Hook, Bill Latham, Cliff Williams, Gareth Hughes, Eric Hughes, Glyn Lowry, a man among men, his hat at a rakish angle, in that snug, smug, select, Edwardian holy of best-bitter holies . . .

(Bar noises in background.)

OLD REPORTER. Remember when I took you down the mortuary for the first time, Young Thomas? He'd never seen a corpse before, boys, except old Ron on a Saturday night. "If you want to be a proper newspaperman," I said, "you got to be well known in the right circles. You got to be *persona grata*[1] in the mortuary, see." He went pale green, mun.

FIRST YOUNG REPORTER. Look he's blushing now . . .

OLD REPORTER. And when we got there, what d'you think? The decorators were in at the mortuary, giving the old home a bit of a re-do like. Up on ladders having a slap at the roof. Young Thomas didn't see 'em; he had his popeyes glued on the slab, and when one of the painters up the ladder said "Good morning, gents" in a deep voice, he

1. *persona grata,* an acceptable person (Latin).

upped in the air and out of the place like a ferret. Laugh!

BARMAID *(off)*. You've had enough, Mr. Roberts. You heard what I said.

(Noise of a gentle scuffle.)

SECOND YOUNG REPORTER *(casually)*. There goes Mr. Roberts.

OLD REPORTER. Well fair do's they throw you out very genteel in this pub . . .

FIRST YOUNG REPORTER. Ever seen Young Thomas covering a soccer match down the Vetch and working it out in tries?

SECOND YOUNG REPORTER. And up the Mannesman Hall shouting "Good footwork, sir," and a couple of punch-drunk colliers galumphing about like jumbos.

FIRST YOUNG REPORTER. What you been reporting today, Young Thomas?

SECOND YOUNG REPORTER. Two-typewriter Thomas the ace news-dick . . .

OLD REPORTER. Let's have a dekko at your notebook. "Called at British Legion. Nothing. Called at Hospital. One broken leg. Auction at the Metropole. Ring Mr. Beynon *re* Gymanfa Ganu. Lunch. Pint and pasty at the Singleton with Mrs. Giles. Bazaar at Bethesda Chapel. Chimney on fire at Tontine Street. Walters Road Sunday School Outing. Rehearsal of the *Mikado* at Skewen"—all front-page stuff . . .

[*Fade.*]

NARRATOR. The voices of fourteen years ago hung silent in the snow and ruin, and in the falling winter morning I walked on through the white havoc'd centre where once a very young man I knew had mucked about as chirpy as a sparrow after the sips and titbits and small change of the town. Near the *Evening Post* building and the fragment of the Castle, I stopped a man whose face I thought I recognised from a long time ago. I said: I wonder if you can tell me . . .

PASSER-BY. Yes?

NARRATOR. He peered out of his blanketing scarves and from under his snowballed balaclava like an Eskimo with a bad conscience. I said: If you can tell me whether you used to know a chap called Young Thomas. He worked on the *Post* and used to wear an overcoat sometimes with the check lining inside out so that you could play giant draughts on him. He wore a conscious woodbine, too . . .

PASSER-BY. What d'you mean, conscious woodbine?

NARRATOR. . . . and a perched pork-pie with a peacock feather, and he tried to slouch like a newshawk even when he was attending a meeting of the Gorseinon Buffalos . . .

PASSER-BY. Oh, *him!* He owes me half a crown. I haven't seen him since the old Kardomah days. He wasn't a reporter then; he'd just left the Grammar School. Him and Charlie Fisher—Charlie's got whiskers now—and Tom Warner and Fred Janes, drinking coffee-dashes arguing the toss.

NARRATOR. What about?

PASSER-BY. Music and poetry and painting and politics. Einstein and Epstein, Stravinsky and Greta Garbo, death and religion, Picasso and girls . . .

NARRATOR. And then?

PASSER-BY. Communism, symbolism, Bradman, Braque, the Watch Committee, free love, free beer, murder, Michelangelo, ping-pong, ambition, Sibelius and girls . . .

NARRATOR. Is that all?

PASSER-BY. How Dan Jones was going to compose the most prodigious symphony, Fred Janes paint the most miraculously meticulous picture, Charlie Fisher catch the poshest trout, Vernon Watkins and Young Thomas write the most boiling poems, how they would ring the bells of London and paint it like a tart . . .

NARRATOR. And after that?

PASSER-BY. Oh, the hissing of the butt-ends in the drains of the coffee-dashes and the tinkle and the gibble-gabble of the morning young lounge lizards as they talked about Augustus John, Emil Jannings, Carnera, Dracula, Amy Johnson, trial marriage, pocket money, the Welsh sea, the London stars, King Kong, anarchy, darts, T. S. Eliot and girls . . . Diw, it's cold!

NARRATOR. And he hurried on, into the dervish snow, without a good morning or goodbye, swaddled in his winter woollens like a man in the island of his deafness, and I felt that perhaps he had never stopped at all to tell me of one more departed stage in the progress of the boy I was pursuing. The Kardomah Café was razed to the snow, the voices of the coffee-drinkers—poets, painters, and musicians in their beginnings—lost in the willynilly flying of the years and the flakes.

Down College Street I walked then, past the remembered invisible shops, Langley's, Castle Cigar Co., T. B. Brown, Pullar's, Aubrey Jeremiah,

Goddard Jones, Richards, Hornes, Marles, Pleasance and Harper, Star Supply, Sidney Heath, Wesley Chapel and nothing. . . . My search was leading me back, through pub and job and café, to the school.

(Fade. School bell.)

SCHOOLMASTER. Oh yes, yes, I remember him well,
though I do not know if I would recognise him now:
nobody grows any younger, or better,
and boys grow into much the sort of men one would suppose
though sometimes the mustaches bewilder
and one finds it hard to reconcile one's memory of a small
none-too-clean urchin lying his way unsuccessfully out of his homework
with a fierce and many-medalled sergeant-major with three children or a divorced chartered accountant;
and it is hard to realise
that some little tousled rebellious youth whose only claim
to fame among his contemporaries was his undisputed right
to the championship of the spitting contest
is now perhaps one's own bank manager.
Oh yes, I remember him well, the boy you are searching for:
he looked like most boys, no better, brighter, or more respectful:
he cribbed, mitched, spilt ink, rattled his desk and
garbled his lessons with the worst of them;
he could smudge, hedge, smirk, wriggle, wince,
whimper, blarney, badger, blush, deceive, be
devious, stammer, improvise, assume
offended dignity or righteous indignation as though to the manner born;
sullenly and reluctantly he drilled, for some small
crime, under Sergeant Bird, so wittily nicknamed
Oiseau, on Wednesday half-holidays,
appeared regularly in detention classes,
hid in the cloakroom during algebra,
was, when a newcomer, thrown into the bushes of the
lower playground by bigger boys,
and threw newcomers into the bushes of the lower
playground when *he* was a bigger boy;
he scuffled at prayers,
he interpolated, smugly, the time-honoured wrong
irreverent words into the morning hymns,
he helped to damage the headmaster's rhubarb,
was thirty-third in trigonometry,
and, as might be expected, edited the school magazine.

(Fade.)

NARRATOR. The hall is shattered, the echoing corridors charred where he scribbled and smudged and yawned in the long green days, waiting for the bell and the scamper into the yard; the school on Mount Pleasant Hill has changed its face and its ways. Soon, they say, it may be no longer the school at all he knew and loved when he was a boy up to no good but the beat of his blood; the names are havoc'd from the hall and the carved initials burned from the broken wood. But the names remain. What names did he know of the dead? Who of the honoured dead did he know such a long time ago? The names of the dead in the living heart and head remain forever. Of all the dead whom did he know?

(Funeral Bell.)

VOICE. Evans, K. J., Haines, G. C., Roberts, I. L., Moxham, J., Thomas, H., Baines, W., Bazzard, F. H., Beer, L. J., Bucknell, R., Twford, G., Vagg, E. A., Wright, G.

(Fade.)

NARRATOR. Then I tacked down the snowblind hill, a cat-o'-nine-gales whipping from the sea, and, white and eiderdowned in the smothering flurry, people padded past me up and down like prowling featherbeds. And I plodded through the ankle-high one cloud that foamed the town, into flat Gower Street, its buildings melted, and along long Helen's Road. Now my search was leading me back to the seashore.

(Noise of sea, softly.)

NARRATOR. Only two living creatures stood on the promenade, near the cenotaph, facing the tossed crystal sea: a man in a chewed muffler and a ratting cap, and an angry dog of a mixed make. The man diddered in the cold, beat his bare blue hands together, waited for some sign from sea or snow; the dog shouted at the weather, and fixed his bloodshot eyes on Mumbles Head. But when the man and I talked together, the dog piped down and fixed his eyes on me, blaming me for the snow. The man spoke towards the sea. Year in, year out, whatever the weather, once in the daytime, once in the dark, he always came to look at the sea. He knew all the dogs and boys and old men who came to see the sea, who ran or gambolled on the sand or stooped at the edges of the waves as though over a wild, wide, rolling ashcan. He knew the lovers who went to lie in the sandhills, the striding masculine women who roared at their terriers like tiger tamers, the loafing men whose work it was in the world to observe the great employment of the sea. He said:

PROMENADE-MAN. Oh yes, yes, I remember him well, but I didn't know what was his name. I don't know the names of none of the sandboys. They don't know mine. About fourteen or fifteen years old, you said, with a little red cap. And he used to play by Vivian's Stream. He used to dawdle in the arches, you said, and lark about on the railway lines and holler at the old sea. He'd mooch about the dunes and watch the tankers and the tugs and the banana boats come out of the Docks. He was going to run away to sea, he said. *I* know. On Saturday afternoon he'd go down to the sea when it was a long way out, and hear the foghorns though he couldn't see the ships. And on Sunday nights, after chapel, he'd be swaggering with his pals along the prom, whistling after the girls.

(Titter.)

GIRL. Does your mother know you're out? Go away now. Stop following us.

(Another girl titters.)

GIRL. Don't you say nothing, Hetty, you're only encouraging. No thank *you*, Mr. Cheeky, with your cut-glass accent and your father's trilby![2] I don't want *no* walk on *no* sands. What d'you say? Ooh, listen to him, Het, he's swallowed a dictionary. No, I don't want to go with nobody up no lane in the moonlight, see, and I'm not a baby-snatcher neither. I seen you going to school along Terrace Road, Mr. Glad-Eye, with your little satchel and wearing your red cap and all. You seen me wearing my . . . no you never. Hetty, mind your glasses! Hetty Harris, you're as bad as them. Oh, go away and do your homework, you. No I'm not then. I'm nobody's homework, see. Cheek! Hetty Harris, don't you let him! Oooh, there's brazen! Well, just to the end of the prom, if you like. No further, mind . . .

2. *trilby,* a felt hat.

PROMENADE-MAN. Oh yes, I knew him well. I've known him by the thousands . . .

NARRATOR. Even now, on the frozen foreshore, a high, far cry of boys, all like the boy I sought, slid on the glass of the streams and snowballed each other and the sky. Then I went on my way from the sea, up Brynmill Terrace and into Glanbrydan Avenue where Bert Trick had kept a grocer's shop and, in the kitchen, threatened the annihilation of the ruling classes over sandwiches and jelly and blancmange. And I came to the shops and houses of the Uplands. Here and around here it was that the journey had begun of the one I was pursuing through his past.

(Old piano cinema-music in the background.)

FIRST VOICE. Here was once the flea-pit picture-house where he whooped for the scalping Indians with Jack Basset and banged for the rustler's guns.

NARRATOR. Jackie Basset, killed.

THIRD VOICE. Here once was Mrs. Ferguson's, who sold the best gob-stoppers and penny packets full of surprises and a sweet kind of glue.

FIRST VOICE. In the fields behind Cwmdonkin Drive, the Murrays chased him and all cats.

SECOND VOICE. No fires now where the outlaws' fires burned and the paradisiacal potatoes roasted in the embers.

THIRD VOICE. In the Craig beneath Town Hill he was a lonely killer hunting the wolves (or rabbits) and the red Sioux tribe (or Mitchell brothers).

(Fade cinema-music into background of children's voices reciting, in unison, the names of the counties of Wales.)

FIRST VOICE. In Mirador School he learned to read and count. Who made the worst raffia doilies? Who put water in Joyce's galoshes, every morning prompt as prompt? In the afternoons, when the children were good, they read aloud from *Struwwelpeter.* And when they were bad, they sat alone in the empty classroom, hearing, from above them, the distant, terrible, sad music of the late piano lesson.

(The children's voices fade. The piano lesson continues in background.)

NARRATOR. And I went up, through the white Grove, into Cwmdonkin Park, the snow still sailing and the childish, lonely, remembered music fingering on in the suddenly gentle wind. Dusk was folding the park around, like another, darker snow. Soon the bell would ring for the closing of the gates, though the park was empty. The park-keeper walked by the reservoir, where swans had glided, on his white rounds. I walked by his side and asked him my questions, up the swathed drives past buried beds and loaded utterly still furred and birdless trees towards the last gate. He said:

PARK-KEEPER. Oh yes, yes, I knew him well. He used to climb the reservoir railings and pelt the old swans. Run like a billygoat over the grass you should keep off of. Cut branches off the trees. Carve words on the benches. Pull up moss in the rockery, go snip through the dahlias. Fight in the bandstand. Climb the elms and moon up the top like a owl. Light fires in the bushes. Play on the green bank. Oh yes, I knew him well. I think he was happy all the time. I've known him by the thousands.

NARRATOR. We had reached the last gate. Dusk drew around us and the town. I said: What has become of him now?

PARK-KEEPER. Dead.

NARRATOR. The park-keeper said . . .

(The park bell rings.)

PARK-KEEPER. Dead . . . Dead . . . Dead . . . Dead . . . Dead . . . Dead. □

DISCUSSION

1. (a) Discuss the problems of an actual production of this radio play, with special attention to the transitions from one scene to another.

(b) It is possible that a production suitable for the stage could be designed. What are the major problems to be overcome?

2. In a radio play, of course, there is no visual impact except through the imagination. Thus the language is very important.

(a) Explore the ways in which Thomas re-creates the specific scenes in the play through its language.

(b) Discuss the use of language throughout the play, especially in passages where it seems to surge out of control. What is the effect?

3. Explain the meaning of the title, "Return Journey."

4. The Narrator is in search of his previous selves, his own past. How would you characterize the Narrator as his personality emerges gradually throughout the play—ordinary, brilliant, girl-crazy, bad, good, foolish, wise . . . ?

5. How many stages of the Narrator's past are presented in the play, and in what order?

6. Discuss the meaning of the end of the play, when the Narrator asks what has become of young Thomas, and the park-keeper answers, "Dead . . . Dead. . . ."

7. Compare the effect of this play with Dylan Thomas' poem "Fern Hill."

"ASCENDING AND DESCENDING HERO" BY BRIDGET RILEY. COURTESY OF THE ART INSTITUTE OF CHICAGO.

THE BLACK AND WHITE

by Harold Pinter

The FIRST OLD WOMAN *is sitting at a milk bar table. Small.*

A SECOND OLD WOMAN *approaches. Tall. She is carrying two bowls of soup, which are covered by two plates, on each of which is a slice of bread. She puts the bowls down on the table carefully.*

SECOND. You see that one come up and speak to me at the counter?

(She takes the bread plates off the bowls, takes two spoons from her pocket, and places the bowls, plates, and spoons.)

FIRST. You got the bread, then?

SECOND. I didn't know how I was going to carry it. In the end I put the plates on top of the soup.

FIRST. I like a bit of bread with my soup.

(They begin the soup. Pause.)

SECOND. Did you see that one come up and speak to me at the counter?

FIRST. Who?

SECOND. Comes up to me, he says, hullo, he says, what's the time by your clock? Bloody liberty. I was just standing there getting your soup.

FIRST. It's tomato soup.

SECOND. What's the time by your clock? he says.

FIRST. I bet you answered him back.

SECOND. I told him all right. Go on, I said, why don't you get back into your scraghole, I said, clear off out of it before I call a copper.

(Pause.)

FIRST. I not long got here.

SECOND. Did you get the all-night bus?

FIRST. I got the all-night bus straight here.

SECOND. Where from?

FIRST. Marble Arch.

SECOND. Which one?

FIRST. The two-nine-four, that takes me all the way to Fleet Street.

SECOND. So does the two-nine-one. *(Pause.)* I see you talking to two strangers as I come in. You want to stop talking to strangers, old piece of boot like you, you mind who you talk to.
FIRST. I wasn't talking to any strangers.
(Pause. The FIRST OLD WOMAN *follows the progress of a bus through the window.)*
That's another all-night bus gone down. *(Pause.)* Going up the other way. Fulham way. *(Pause.)* That was a two-nine-seven. *(Pause.)* I've never been up that way. *(Pause.)* I've been down to Liverpool Street.
SECOND. That's up the other way.
FIRST. I don't fancy going down there, down Fulham way, and all up there.
SECOND. Uh-uh.
FIRST. I've never fancied that direction much.
(Pause.)
SECOND. How's your bread?
(Pause.)
FIRST. Eh?
SECOND. Your bread.
FIRST. All right. How's yours?
(Pause.)
SECOND. They don't charge for the bread if you have soup.
FIRST. They do if you have tea.
SECOND. If you have tea they do. *(Pause.)* You talk to strangers they'll take you in. Mind my word. Coppers'll take you in.
FIRST. I don't talk to strangers.
SECOND. They took me away in the wagon once.
FIRST. They didn't keep you though.
SECOND. They didn't keep me, but that was only because they took a fancy to me. They took a fancy to me when they got me in the wagon.
FIRST. Do you think they'd take a fancy to me?
SECOND. I wouldn't back on it.
(The FIRST OLD WOMAN *gazes out of the window.)*
FIRST. You can see what goes on from this top table. *(Pause.)* It's better than going down to that place on the embankment, anyway.
SECOND. Yes, there's not too much noise.
FIRST. There's always a bit of noise.
SECOND. Yes, there's always a bit of life.
(Pause.)
FIRST. They'll be closing down soon to give it a scrub-round.
SECOND. There's a wind out.
(Pause.)
FIRST. I wouldn't mind staying.
SECOND. They won't let you.
FIRST. I know. *(Pause.)* Still, they only close hour and half, don't they? *(Pause.)* It's not long. *(Pause.)* You can go along, then come back.
SECOND. I'm going. I'm not coming back.
FIRST. When it's light I come back. Have my tea.
SECOND. I'm going. I'm going up to the Garden.
FIRST. I'm not going down there. *(Pause.)* I'm going up to Waterloo Bridge.
SECOND. You'll just about see the last two-nine-six come up over the river.
FIRST. I'll just catch a look of it. Time I get up there.
(Pause.)
It don't look like an all-night bus in daylight, do it? □

DISCUSSION

1. The old women express fear in talking with strangers, and fear of being taken in by "coppers." What do these discussions suggest about the kind of life they lead?
2. The old women talk aimlessly about the bread and about the buses they ride or don't ride. What does this talk reveal about them?
3. In the opening speeches of the play, although the second speech is in response to the first, it does not seem to have any relation to it. Find other instances in which the old women talk *to* but not *with* each other. What is the effect of this kind of dialogue on the audience (or reader)?
4. What are some of the possible meanings of the title, "The Black and White"?

BIOGRAPHIES

Wystan Hugh Auden 1907 / 1973

At Oxford University, Auden was the nucleus of a group of young socially concerned thinkers which included his friends Spender and MacNeice. Politically active, Auden spent 1928–1929 in Germany. He drove an ambulance for the anti-Franco Loyalists in the Spanish Civil War, but during the decade of the 1930's the orientation of his beliefs shifted from political to humanistic and Christian.

A diverse and prolific writer with a disciplined professional regard for his art, Auden wrote drama, criticism, and documentary films as well as poetry. He taught at Oxford and at various universities in the United States.

Auden became an American citizen in 1939, and for many years lived part of the year in New York City. Recently, however, he returned to England and spent his last months in Oxford.

David Macleod Black 1941 /

Though he was born in South Africa, Black was raised and educated in Scotland. He has held a variety of jobs in Europe and Japan, and earned an M. A. in philosophy from the University of Edinburgh in 1966. His first book of poems was published the following year.

Alan Bold 1943 /

Alan Bold describes himself not only as a poet but as a journalist and critic whose work expresses concern with modern technology and politics. As a youth in Edinburgh, where he was born and still lives, he was a garage hand, an apprentice baker, and (while a student at the University of Edinburgh) a jazz saxophonist. He has also served on the staff of the *Times Educational Supplement* and translated the poems of Baudelaire. He named his daughter Valentina in honor of the first woman in space.

Elizabeth Bowen 1899 / 1973

Anglo-Irish novelist and short-story writer Elizabeth Bowen was born in Dublin but spent most of her life in or near London. As a young woman she decided to devote her life to writing, and she was on her own at 21. She worked in a hospital for shell-shocked patients near Dublin, and during World War II worked in the Ministry of Information during the day and as an air-raid warden at night.

She inherited her ancestral house in Ireland, and wrote a history of it and of ten generations of the Bowen family.

Rupert Brooke 1887 / 1915

An aura of glamor surrounded Rupert Brooke. He was handsome and energetic, well educated, kept illustrious company, and died young. He was educated at Rugby, where his father was a housemaster, and at Kings College, Cambridge, where he studied early British drama and was head of the Fabian Society, a socialist group. His friends included Walter de la Mare, to whom he bequeathed part of his publishing royalties. At the outbreak of the First World War, Brooke enlisted in the army. He died during the Dardanelles campaign of an infection from an insect bite.

Joyce Cary 1888 / 1957

Cary had studied art in Edinburgh and Paris and had had a military career before his first literary work was published, when he was 44. Fame and financial success, however, did not come until he was 56, with the publication of his tenth book, *The Horse's Mouth.*

Cary was born in Ireland and attended Oxford University, where, according to his friend the critic John Middleton Murry, he did very little work. During the Balkan War in 1912 he served in the British Red Cross. During World War I he fought in the Cameroons in Africa and was wounded. Then he served as a colonial administrator in a series of remote West African posts. In 1920 he returned to England to become a writer. His first novels are about Africa and interracial problems.

In the last years of his life Cary was the victim of a progressive and incurable paralysis but he continued to write, propped up in bed, his pen tied to his hand. When he became unable to use his limbs, he dictated.

Joseph Conrad 1857 / 1924

Conrad was born Teodor Josef Konrad Korzeniowski in the Ukraine, then part of Russian Poland. His parents, wealthy and cultured Poles, were exiled as a result of his father's leadership in the Polish revolution against Russia.

A good education and a comfortable career were planned for him by an uncle, but Conrad had other dreams—he was determined to become an Englishman and a sailor. At 16 he joined the French Mercantile Marine, and after three years spent in Marseilles and the West Indies, he transferred to a British ship. In 1878 he set foot on British soil for the first time; he was 21, and spoke no English. By the time he was 27 he was a Master (a captain) in the British Marine, a naturalized British citizen, and had changed his name to Joseph Conrad.

He remained at sea for twenty years and during that time stored up memories of incidents, experiences, impressions, and people which he later used in his writing. He was almost 40 when his first book, *Almayer's Folly,* was published. Public and critical reception was so favorable that he decided to give up the sea and concentrate on writing.

Among Conrad's best-known works are the novels *Nostromo, Heart of Darkness,* and *Lord Jim,* and the short stories "Youth" and "The Secret Sharer." Much of his writing explores what happens when a man's character is tested under conditions of extreme danger and difficulty.

A(lfred) E(dgar) Coppard 1878 / 1957

Coppard, the son of working-class parents, was self-educated. At the age of 9 he was a shop-boy for a trouser maker's establishment. Reading poetry the while, he also worked as an office boy and as a professional sprinter. Eventually he became a clerk and accountant, and this led to his employment at an Oxford engineering firm. Through exposure to the life of a university town, Coppard became interested in writing, and in 1919 decided to devote himself seriously to writing. His first book, *Adam and Eve and Pinch Me,* a collection of short stories, was published two years later by the Golden Cockerel Press, a communal crafts society.

Roald Dahl 1916 /

Dahl was born in Wales of Norwegian parents. His father was a painter, shipbroker, and horticulturist. He himself worked for Shell Oil Company of East Africa from 1932–1939 and has traveled widely. He is married to actress Patricia Neal.

Cecil Day-Lewis 1904 / 1972

The poet and critic C. Day-Lewis, the recent poet laureate of England, has been an editor at the Ministry of Information and professor at various universities, including Harvard, Cambridge, and Oxford. In his student days at Oxford he was co-editor of the poetry magazine.

Day-Lewis was born in Ireland, but his father was an Anglican minister and moved his family back to England when the boy was young. Like many other intellectuals of the thirties, Day-Lewis was politically involved. His critical piece *A Hope for Poetry* (1934) was considered the manifesto of the Left Poetry Movement of that era.

He also wrote detective stories under the pseudonym Nicholas Blake.

Walter de la Mare 1873 / 1956

When he was sixteen years old, Walter de la Mare established a magazine at the St. Paul's Cathedral Choir School in London. The *Chorister's Review* ran nine issues. The following year he became a clerk with the Anglo-American branch of the Standard Oil Company, a job he held for eighteen years, until a government grant and pension permitted him to devote himself completely to writing. He published more than eighty books of poetry and fiction. Many of his poems were nominally written for children.

Thomas Stearns Eliot 1888 / 1965

St. Louis-born Eliot wrote one of his most famous poems, "The Love Song of J. Alfred Prufrock," while still a student at Harvard. A formidable scholar, he did graduate work at Harvard, the Sorbonne in France, and Oxford. He settled in London in 1915, becoming a British citizen in 1927. His writings attracted attention from the start, but because of financial pressures he taught school for a time, worked in a bank, and eventually became an editor and a director of a major British publishing house. He was awarded the Nobel Prize for literature in 1948.

As poet and critic, Eliot had an enormous influence on twentieth-century poetry. In his criticism he discussed his distaste for romanticism and the emotions it expresses. In his own poetry he made a complete break with the literary conventions of the Romantics and Victorians. Instead of using traditional "poetic diction," he turned to the idiom and rhythms of natural speech; instead of relying on abstractions and generalities, he expressed himself through sense impressions and concrete images.

In early poems such as "Prufrock," "The Hollow Men," and "The Waste Land," Eliot pictured the sterility, boredom, and spiritual emptiness of the modern world. In 1927, however, he became a convert to the Anglican Church, and in his later poetry turned to religion as the one possible hope for modern man.

In addition to poetry and criticism, Eliot wrote a number of verse dramas, of which *Murder in the Cathedral* is considered the best.

E(dward) M(organ) Forster 1879 / 1970

Although he wrote only a small number of novels, Forster is regarded as one of the major novelists of the early twentieth century.

After graduating from Kings College, Cambridge, he lived for a time in Italy, where he worked on two novels: *Where Angels Fear to Tread* and *A Room with a View*. During World War I he was a civilian worker in Egypt. Two trips to India—one in 1911 and another in 1921—provided material for his most famous novel, *A Passage to India*. In it he lays bare the difficulties of establishing ordinary social contact between Englishmen and Indians. An early novel, *Maurice*, remained unpublished until after his death.

Forster also wrote notable short stories, many of them allegorical. His *Collected Short Stories* appeared in 1948. He published no novels after 1924, but did produce a few books of literary criticism, biographies, and collections of literary and sociological essays, one of which was *Two Cheers for Democracy*. In 1951 he wrote the libretto for his friend Benjamin Britten's opera *Billy Budd*.

As a young man, Forster was a member of the Bloomsbury Group, a circle of young artists, writers, and intellectuals who opposed Victorian orthodoxy. He was a political liberal, and often critical of conventional middle-class values.

Robert Graves 1895 /

Graves was born in London into a large family headed by a poet/ballad-writer. Though he had been accepted at Oxford, he went into the trenches of the First World War, serving in the same regiment as Siegfried Sassoon. He published three books of poetry while on active duty. After the war he finished his formal education, and upon recommendation of T. E. Lawrence (Lawrence of Arabia) spent a year as a professor at Cairo's Egyptian University. Except for a period during the Spanish Civil War, Graves has lived on the island of Majorca since 1929. He has owned a jazz club, appeared in the 1968 movie "Deadfall," and writes prodigiously in a variety of genres, including historical novels like *I, Claudius* that have been described as "scholarly and mischievous."

Graham Greene 1904 /

Greene is a Roman Catholic convert, and his serious novels—for example, *The Power and the Glory* and *A Burnt-Out Case*—reflect his religious convictions and his concern with problems of good and evil. He has also written popular adventure thrillers like *The Third Man* and *Our Man in Havana* which he refers to as "entertainments." A number of his books have been made into successful movies.

Graham Greene has been a member of the staff of the London *Times* and Indo-China correspondent for the *New Republic*. As a student at Oxford, he sometimes used to travel through England disguised as a bum, or with a barrel organ.

Thom Gunn 1929 /

Thom Gunn was born in Gravesend, brought up in London, educated at Oxford, and has both studied and taught in California. He believes that his personal life should remain private.

Michael Hamburger 1924 /

Hamburger was born in Berlin and educated in London and at Oxford. He has used his bilingual talents in various ways. During the Second World War he served the British army as an interpreter, and has since taught German literature in American and British universities. He has also published translations and criticism of German literature.

Ted Hughes 1930 /

Ted Hughes has had considerable American experience. Born and educated in England, he has taught in the United States. In 1956 he married an American poet, the late Sylvia Plath. He was a Guggenheim Fellow in 1959–1960. Besides teaching and writing, he has also worked as a rose gardener, a night watchman, and a reader for Pinewood Film Studios.

James Joyce 1882 / 1941

Joyce came from the kind of background that ordinarily would not be expected to produce a revolutionary genius of literature. He was one of ten children. His father was a civil servant, continually in financial difficulties; his mother was conventionally pious. He himself was educated at Dublin's Jesuit schools, where he was a brilliant scholar, and at one time thought of entering the priesthood. At a crucial time in his life, however, he felt he had to renounce both his religion and his native land in order to develop in his own way. In 1904 he went to Trieste with Nora Barnacle, a Dublin chambermaid with whom he had fallen in love, and from then on lived on the continent. When he could, he supported his family by working as a language teacher; at other times he had to depend on the charity of relatives and friends. During the twenties, he lived in Paris and was a central figure in the artistic ferment there, but until his later years he earned almost nothing from his writings.

Joyce was extremely gifted in languages—he was fluent in French, German, and Italian and knew twelve other languages, including Lapp. As a student he had taught himself Norwegian in order to read the plays of Henrik Ibsen. His knowledge of languages is displayed in the intricate multilingual puns in *Finnegan's Wake.*

Joyce's first major work was a collection of short stories called *Dubliners,* published in 1914 but written some years earlier. In his semi-autobiographical first novel, *A Portrait of the Artist as a Young Man* (1916), he reviewed the steps that had led to his adolescent revolt. The revolutionary novel *Ulysses* followed in 1922, and the highly experimental *Finnegan's Wake* in 1939.

In form and content much of Joyce's work was controversial. During his lifetime, publication was often delayed (Irish printers refused to set *Dubliners* in type), and his works were banned, burned, pirated, and confiscated. The ruling of U.S. Federal Judge Woolsey in 1933 permitting the American publication of *Ulysses* was a landmark in the fight against literary censorship. Only in recent years has Joyce's reputation reached its present eminence.

Philip Larkin 1922 /

Larkin received B.A. and M.A. degrees from Oxford, and since 1955 has been librarian at the University of Hull. He has written novels as well as poetry, and also writes on jazz for the London *Daily Telegraph.*

D(avid) H(erbert) Lawrence 1885 / 1930

Like the hero of his early novel *Sons and Lovers,* Lawrence was born in an English coal-mining town, the son of an uneducated miner and an ambitious mother who was a teacher. He himself taught school for a time before he established himself in London literary circles and became a writer. In 1912 he eloped with an aristocratic German, Frieda von Richthofen. She was married at the time, but eventually became his wife. During World War I, he and Frieda (whose brother was the famous German flyer) lived for a time on the south coast of England where they had hoped to find a community of like-minded people striving for a freer life. Unfortunately the neighbors were not sympathetic, and indiscretions such as leaving lights burning at night and loudly singing German songs made the Lawrences suspected of pro-German sympathies. They began a life of wandering, seeking for a place undamaged by modern civilization, and at various times lived in Italy, Germany, the French Riviera, Australia, New Zealand, Ceylon, Tahiti, and Mexico. They settled finally for a number of years in Taos, New Mexico.

All his life, Lawrence revolted against puritanism, mediocrity, and the dehumanization of an industrial society. Since much of his work is an exploration of the primitive and sexual in man's nature *(The Plumed Serpent, Women in Love, Lady Chatterley's Lover),* he was often in trouble with the censors. In addition to novels, he wrote short stories, poetry, criticism, and travel books.

Louis MacNeice 1907 / 1963

A classics scholar, MacNeice was a professor at universities in England and the United States, and director of the British Institute in Athens. He was a close friend of Auden and Spender, and one of the "poets of social protest" of the 1930's. He was a prolific writer whose work included poetry, criticism, radio scripts, and translations—most notably of Goethe's *Faust.*

Katherine Mansfield 1888 / 1923

Katherine Mansfield was born in New Zealand, the daughter of a prominent banker. She published her first poem at the age of 9, and was an excellent cellist as a young woman. She went to London in 1902 to study music at Queens College. By the time she completed her studies, however, she had decided to become a writer. Depressed by the failure of a brief, unhappy marriage and by the difficulty of getting her first stories published, she joined a traveling opera troupe. The rigors of this life undermined her delicate health, and she was forced to spend much of the rest of her short life traveling in search of relief from the tuberculosis that eventually developed.

Her first published collection of stories (1911) was

written in Germany. Here she also met the literary critic and scholar John Middleton Murry with whom she collaborated on a short-lived literary magazine and whom she eventually married. The Murrys had a circle of literary friends which included the Lawrences, Aldous Huxley, and Virginia Woolf.

It has been suggested that Katherine Mansfield's consciousness of the imminence of death heightened her awareness and helps account for the sensitivity for which her writing is noted. She died in France of tuberculosis at the age of 34.

H. H. Munro (Saki) 1870 / 1916

Hector Hugh Munro was born in Burma, the son of a police inspector-general. His mother died when he was two, and he was sent home to Scotland to live with relatives. His formal education ended with grammar school, but his father tutored him on extensive travels. In 1893 his father secured him a post with the Burma police, but his delicate health forced his return to Britain. There he took up a career in writing, and it was while doing political sketches for the *Westminster Gazette* that he adopted the pen name of Saki—the name of the cup-bearer in the *Rubáiyát of Omar Khayyám.*

After serving for a time as a foreign correspondent for the *Morning Post,* he returned to London to devote himself to the writing of stories and novels. When World War I began, he enlisted as a private, declining several offers of commissions. He was killed in action in 1916.

Frank O'Connor 1903 / 1966

In his autobiography, *An Only Child,* Frank O'Connor, who was christened Michael O'Donovan, traces his life from his birth in a slum in Cork to his release in 1923 from imprisonment as a revolutionary during the Irish fight for independence. His early life was hard, unhappy, and poverty-stricken, yet he was able to look back on it with humor and compassion—qualities that are dominant in most of his stories.

He had learned Gaelic from his grandmother, and his knowledge of this language enabled him to collaborate with William Butler Yeats on translations of Gaelic poems. He began writing as a boy, but was undecided whether to become a painter or a writer. He abandoned painting, he claimed, because it was too expensive. His bicycle tours through Ireland provided him with subjects for stories and made him intimately acquainted with the Irish people and Irish speech.

In later years he lectured and taught at Harvard, Northwestern, and Stanford.

Wilfred Owen 1893 / 1918

Wilfred Owen enlisted in the British army in 1915, served ably as an officer in France, and earned the Military Cross for bravery. He was killed in action exactly a week before the Armistice was declared. He published very little during his lifetime—only four poems—but today is generally considered the best of the poets of World War I.

Harold Pinter 1930 /

Harold Pinter was born in Hackney in East London, and left school at 16. When he wrote his first play, *The Room,* in 1957, he was an actor touring with a provincial repertory company, playing all sorts of parts. Since then he has written four full-length plays *(The Birthday Party* [a flop], *The Caretaker* [a success], *The Homecoming,* and *Old Times),* twelve short plays, some of them for radio and TV, short sketches, poetry, and eight filmscripts, including *The Servant, The Pumpkin Eater, The Quiller Memorandum, Accident, The Birthday Party,* and *The Go-Between.* He occasionally acts in his own films and also directs plays, his own and those of others (he directed Robert Shaw's *The Man in the Glass Booth).* He has won critics' awards for *The Caretaker, The Homecoming,* and the film *The Servant.*

Pinter is considered one of the most important writers of the Absurdist school. The term "Pinteresque" has come to connote ambiguity, mystery, an undefinable terror of situation, and characters created out of minimal information. Many of his plays deal with the ambiguity of truth —the difficulty or impossibility of determining what is true or false, real or unreal, what has actually occurred or only seems to have occurred.

Alastair Reid 1926 /

Born and educated in Scotland, Reid has taught in the U.S. (at Sarah Lawrence College) and is a correspondent for the *New Yorker.* He has traveled extensively, and was twice the recipient of a Guggenheim Fellowship.

Siegfried Sassoon 1886 / 1967

Sassoon, who attended Cambridge University, was always more interested in poetry than in studies. He was twice wounded in World War I, received two medals for bravery, and rose to the rank of captain. However, his war experiences made him an outspoken pacifist, and as an antiwar protest he threw his Military Cross into the sea. Instead of being court-martialed as he hoped, he was judged temporarily insane and hospitalized. He met Wilfred Owen during one of his hospital stays, and encouraged him in his writing.

George Bernard Shaw 1856 / 1950

"Things have not happened to me," Shaw once said; "on the contrary, it is I who have happened to things." Shaw's public image was that of a witty and somewhat arrogant iconoclast, supporter of socialism, antivivisection, and vegetarianism. But under the mask of eccentricity was a man seriously concerned with solving mankind's problems.

Shaw was born in Dublin. He went to London in 1876, and for a number of years worked as a music and drama critic on a newspaper. He began writing for the stage in 1885, but since his caustic wit was generally directed at things traditionally considered too sacred for ridicule (marriage, parenthood, heroism), most of his early plays were banned by the censor or refused production. In hopes of winning readers, if not viewers, of his plays, he began publishing them with elaborate stage directions and long prefaces in which he presented his ideas. His sense of the comic and his skill in argumentation won him a public and eventually aroused interest in seeing his works performed. By the time of World War I, his plays were highly successful on stage.

Shaw's plays are entertaining, but he thought of them mainly as vehicles for presenting his ideas. Many of the plays argue that preconceived notions about human character may be far from true. For example, in *Widower's Houses,* his first play, he presents the paradox of a genuinely honest man who owns festering tenements.

Among his best-known plays are *Mrs. Warren's Profession, Candida, The Devil's Disciple, Caesar and Cleopatra, Man and Superman, Major Barbara, Androcles and the Lion, Pygmalian* (later made into the musical *My Fair Lady*), *St. Joan,* and *Heartbreak House.* He was awarded the Nobel Prize for Literature in 1925.

Shaw was an advocate of spelling reform, and in his own writings used such devices as omitting apostrophes in some contractions; he insisted that his publishers retain these changes. His will stipulated that the money in his estate be used to promote a more rational system of English spelling.

Alan Sillitoe 1928 /

Sillitoe began to write while stationed in Malaya during World War II. His novels and stories deal with working-class people struggling against the Establishment and conventional morality.

Sillitoe was born in Nottingham, the son of a laborer, and left school at fourteen. He has worked in a plywood mill and in a bicycle plant. He is married to the American-born poet Ruth Fainlight.

His long short story, *The Loneliness of the Long-Distance Runner,* was made into an excellent film.

Edith Sitwell 1887 / 1964

Edith Sitwell became Dame Edith—Commander of the Order of the British Empire—in 1954. A member of an aristocratic and cultured family, she was privately educated at the family estate. She was a great eccentric, affecting the manner and dress of her conception of a poet. She towered six feet tall in brocaded, medieval-style gowns, strange headgear, and elaborate jewels. *Façade,* her innovative program of poems, with music by William Walton, was considered scandalously avante-garde at the time of its presentation in 1923.

Dame Edith once sent an owl to a critic whom she thought too stuffy, and she objected to the Beat poets because of their smell.

Muriel Spark 1918 /

Muriel Spark was born in Edinburgh. She is known primarily as a novelist, though she has published several volumes of poetry, nonfiction, and short fiction. She was once on the staff of a magazine for the precious-stone trade, and worked for the Foreign Office's Department of Intelligence during World War II. From 1947 to 1949 she edited the *Poetry Review.* She was honored with the Order of the British Empire in 1967.

Stephen Spender 1909 /

At 17, Spender started his own small printing business. With a hand press he turned out chemists' labels and friends' manuscripts. The son of a novelist-journalist, he became a literary journalist and critic. He was intensely concerned with social and political reform as a young man, and was in Germany in the early 1930's and in Spain during its civil war. As he grew older, he became less critic and more poet, especially after he made a significant break with organized politics.

Spender has taught in the United States, has been co-editor of the British magazine *Encounter*, and was once a fireman in the London Auxiliary Fire Service.

Donald Michael Thomas 1935 /

Thomas, a professor, has taught in the United States and has contributed to various magazines. In addition to poetry, he is especially inclined toward science fiction, which he considers a major mythological force of this century.

Dylan Thomas 1914 / 1953

Thomas was born in the seacoast town of Swansea in Wales and left school at 16. He tried reporting for a local newspaper for a year, but poetry-writing, which he had been doing since he was a small boy, was more to his taste than journalism. He published his first volume of poetry at 19 and continued to publish well-received books of verse during the 1930's. *Portrait of the Artist as a Young Dog*, a collection of stories about his childhood and youth, appeared in 1940. Another book of boyhood reminiscences, *Quite Early One Morning*, and a verse play, *Under Milk Wood*, were published after his death.

Thomas worked for the B.B.C. during World War II as a documentary film editor and also as a radio broadcaster; his magnificent Welsh voice reading poetry or stories enchanted listeners. In the early 1950's he made several enormously successful lecture-poetry reading trips to the United States. His visits to New York were always marked by parties and drinking-bouts; he liked to hold court in a favorite seamen's bar. On his third lecture tour, he died suddenly in New York.

Ronald Stuart Thomas 1913 /

Though not related to Dylan Thomas, R. S. Thomas is also from Wales. He was educated there and has been a minister since 1937.

Sylvia Townsend Warner 1893 /

Besides being a writer, Sylvia Townsend Warner is an expert on the music of the fifteenth and sixteenth centuries. The daughter of a teacher, she was privately educated. Like many other intellectuals of the time, she supported the anti-Franco side during the Spanish Civil War. She was formerly a guest critic for the old New York *Herald-Tribune;* her stories appear frequently in the *New Yorker.*

Angus Wilson 1913 /

Angus Wilson studied medieval history at Oxford. After graduation he held a variety of jobs—as secretary, tutor, manager of a catering establishment, restaurant manager, social organizer. Except for employment in the Foreign Office during World War II, he worked as deputy superintendent of the British Museum Reading Room from 1937 to 1955. He began to write short stories as therapy after suffering a nervous breakdown near the end of the war, and after the war, continued writing on weekends. A volume of his stories was published in 1949 and attracted immediate attention. There followed a number of successful novels (*Hemlock and After, Anglo-Saxon Attitudes,* and others) and further collections of short stories.

Virginia Woolf 1882 / 1941

When Virginia Stephen was born, her godfather wrote some verses praying she would grow up to be "a sample of Heredity." This was no small wish, for she was the daughter of a distinguished writer and critic, Sir Leslie Stephen, the granddaughter of the novelist Thackeray, and was related to the Darwins, Stracheys, and other distinguished scholarly families.

A brilliant young woman, she grew up in a literary atmosphere and was educated in her father's extensive library. The famous group of intellectuals which came to be known as the Bloomsbury Group originated in gatherings of Cambridge University graduates and their friends at the house where Virginia was living with her brother and sister. She married one of the young men, Leonard Woolf. A few years later, the Woolfs started the Hogarth Press. It became a successful publishing house, and published not only Virginia Woolf's own first short stories, but the early works of Katherine Mansfield, E. M. Forster, and T. S. Eliot. It also introduced the works of Freud to English readers.

In novels like *Mrs. Dalloway* and *To the Lighthouse* Virginia Woolf experimented with new techniques, particularly new ways of capturing the flow of time. She believed that much imaginative literature is false to life because it relates episodes in a straight line, whereas our experiences actually flow together like a stream. She also wrote a great deal of literary criticism and many essays, some of which deal with women's emancipation.

Despite what must have been a rewarding life, Virginia Woolf was a troubled woman. She suffered a nervous breakdown in her thirties, and from then on worried that the illness would strike again. She was depressed by the war, and despite efforts of her husband and friends to maintain her emotional equilibrium, in her late fifties she began to feel the symptoms of another collapse. In 1941 she committed suicide by drowning.

William Butler Yeats 1865 / 1939

Yeats's father was a well-known Anglo-Irish portrait painter, and the son also studied art as a young man. This interest was soon overshadowed by his success in writing poetry and plays. He went to London with his family in 1887, and was welcomed into a literary group known as the Rhymers Club. However, he felt shy in London and probably would not have stayed there had he not met Maud Gonne, an ardent Irish nationalist. Through her influence, he became involved in Irish politics and the Irish theater. He was in love with her for many years, and she appears in much of his poetry. However, she refused to marry him.

Yeats returned to Ireland in 1896 and became the acknowledged leader of the Irish literary renaissance. He was interested in both the ancient culture and the contemporary political and social problems of his country. With the playwright Lady Gregory and others, he founded a theater society which later became the celebrated Abbey Theater, for which he wrote many plays. He was elected to the senate of the new Irish Free State in 1922. In 1923 he was awarded the Nobel Prize for Literature.

Magic and the occult were other interests of Yeats. His wife, whom he married in 1917, was a spiritualist medium, and with the help of her trances and automatic writing he composed *A Vision,* a book in which he tried to construct a system of magic, a philosophy of history, and a philosophic basis for his belief in the reality of dreams and the continuing life of the spirit through many incarnations. These ideas furnished him a system of symbols which he used in his poetry and plays, especially the later works.

GLOSSARY OF LITERARY TERMS

ABSURD, a term frequently used to describe the meaninglessness of life in today's world. (See *existentialism.*)

ADAPTATION, the redoing of a literary work to fit another genre or audience. For example, many novels, such as *War and Peace,* have been adapted for the movies.

ALEXANDRINE, twelve-syllable *iambic* line.

ALLEGORY, a narrative in which characters, action, and sometimes *setting* represent abstract concepts or moral qualities to form a consistent pattern of meaning in a one-to-one relationship.

ALLITERATION, repetition of consonant sounds at the beginnings of words or accented syllables.

ALLUSION, a brief, often indirect, reference to a person, event, or work of art.

AMBIGUITY, the expression of an idea to suggest more than one meaning. Deliberate and effective, ambiguity enriches the meaning of the passage in which it occurs; accidental or ineffective, it blurs the meaning.

ANACHRONISM, placing something at a time or place contrary to historical fact.

ANALOGY, a comparison made between two, frequently dissimilar, items or situations in order to provide insight into the nature of one or both of them.

ANAPEST, three-syllable metrical *foot,* consisting of two unaccented syllables followed by an accented syllable.

ANASTROPHE, inversion of the usual order of the parts of a sentence.

ANTAGONIST, a character who opposes the *protagonist,* often the villain.

ANTI-HERO, a kind of *protagonist* who lacks the conventional heroic qualities; he is frequently an outsider who passively observes the futile lives of those about him. See *hero, romantic hero.*

APHORISM, a short, pithy saying.

APOSTROPHE, a *figure of speech* in which an absent person, an abstract concept, or an inanimate object is addressed directly.

APOTHEGM, a brief saying, terse and pointed; a maxim.

ARCHETYPE, an image, story-pattern, or character type which recurs frequently and evokes strong, often unconscious, associations in the reader. For example: the wicked witch, the enchanted prince, the sleeping beauty, and the fairy godmother are widely dispersed throughout folk literature, and appear in slightly different forms in poetry, drama, and novels.

ASSONANCE, repetition of vowel sound.

ATMOSPHERE, the prevailing emotional aura or *tone* of a literary work.

BALLAD, a narrative song passed on in the oral tradition. The ballad *stanza* usually consists of four lines alternating iambic *tetrameter* and *trimeter* and rhyming the second and fourth lines. (See *literary ballad.*)

BILDUNGSROMAN, German term ("novel of formation") designating a story depicting the hero's maturing, or movement from childhood to manhood, in a spiritual, educational, or emotional sense.

BLANK VERSE, unrhymed iambic pentameter, ten-syllable lines with five unstressed syllables alternating with five stressed syllables. An unstressed syllable begins the line.

BROADSIDE, a large sheet of paper printed on one side (like a handbill). During earlier periods, some works of literature were distributed as broadsides.

BURDEN, a chorus or refrain (especially in medieval lyrics).

BURLESQUE, a means of ridiculing people, actions, or literary works by mimicking.

CAESURA, pause in a line of verse.

CARICATURE, exaggeration of prominent features of appearance or character.

CAROL, a dance, and also the song sung with the dance: thus, a literary song.

CARPE DIEM, "seize the day" (Latin), the name applied to a theme frequently found in *lyric* poetry: make the most of youth while you are young.

CATASTROPHE, a term sometimes applied to the ending of a *tragedy,* where the *conflict* is resolved and the actions resulting from the *climax* are completed.

CATHARSIS, a word used by Aristotle in his *Poetics* to describe the desired effect of *tragedy,* the "purgation" of the emotions of pity and fear; that is, in feeling pity and fear for the *tragic hero,* the viewer's own emotional tensions are released and temporarily resolved.

CAVALIER POETRY, poetry full of grace, elegance, and wit, emphasizing pleasure, love, and chivalry, and identified with poets connected with the court of Charles I, early seventeenth century. See Sir John Suckling and Richard Lovelace.

CHARACTERIZATION, *techniques* used by the writer in creating a character.

CHORUS, a group of actors, speaking in unison, whose purpose is to comment on the action of the play. Where a chorus is not employed, one or more of the individual characters in the play may take over this "choric function."

CLASSIC, in the special sense, the art and literature of Greece and Rome; in the general sense, art and literature of any time recognized as of the highest excellence.

CLASSICAL TRAGEDY, the tragedies of ancient Greece and Rome; those dealing with Greek and Roman subjects; and those written according to the "rules" of tragic drama derived from Aristotle. Such classically constructed plays enjoyed a great revival in the seventeenth and eighteenth centuries.

CLICHÉ, an expression or phrase that is so overused as to become trite.

CLIMAX. As a term of dramatic structure, this refers to the decisive point in a play, where the action changes course and begins to resolve itself. The word is also used to describe the point of highest emotional intensity in a play.

COMEDY, a play written to amuse the audience. In addition to arousing laughter, comic writing often appeals to the intellect. Thus the comic mode has often been used to "instruct" the audience about the follies of certain social conventions and human foibles, as in *satire.*

COMEDY OF MANNERS, a comedy in which the humor arises largely from violations of the conventions of a sophisticated society.

CONCEIT, an elaborate and surprising *figure of speech* comparing two very dissimilar things.

CONFLICT, the struggle that grows out of the interplay between two opposing forces. The four basic kinds of conflict are: (1) a person against another person; (2) a person against nature; (3) a person against society; (4) two elements within a person struggling for mastery.

CONNOTATION, the emotional associations surrounding a word, as opposed to its literal meaning. (See *denotation, diction.*)

CONSONANCE, the repetition of consonant sounds (within a line of poetry, usually).

CONVENTION, any artful *technique* widely accepted as appropriate to a given type of literature.

COUPLET, a *verse form* of two rhyming lines.

CRITICISM, the analysis of works of literature for the purpose of understanding and evaluating them. Criticism is sometimes confined to *explication.*

DACTYL, three-syllable metrical *foot,* consisting of one accented syllable followed by two unaccented syllables.

DENOTATION, the strict, literal meaning of a word. (See *connotation, diction.*)

DENOUEMENT, the final untying of the *plot.*

DEUS EX MACHINA, literally, "god from a machine"—as in ancient Greek drama, in which a god was lowered onto the stage in a machine; now, any element suddenly introduced into a literary work to resolve a situation.

DIALECT, the imitation of regional speech in writing, using altered, phonetic spelling.

DIALOGUE, the conversation between two or more people represented in a literary work. Dialogue can serve many purposes, among them: (1) *characterization* (of those speaking and spoken of); (2) *exposition;* (3) the creation of *mood;* (4) the advancement of *plot;* (5) the development of a *theme;* (6) a comment on the action.

DICTION, the particular choice of words made in a literary work. This choice considers both the *connotative* and the *denotative* meanings of a word and the level or type of usage.

DRAMA, a story told by means of characters speaking *dialogue,* usually for presentation in a theater.

DRAMATIC IRONY, a situation in which facts known to the reader and some of the characters are unknown to other characters.

DRAMATIC MONOLOGUE, poem in which the speaker addresses one or more persons who are present but whose replies are not recorded.

DRAMATIC POINT OF VIEW. See *point of view.*

ELEGY, a traditional poetic form that treats of death, or some other grave topic, in a formal, philosophic way.

END RHYME, the rhyming of words at the ends of lines of verse. (Compare *internal rhyme.*)

END-STOPPED, a term applied to a verse line or a couplet which contains a complete thought, thus necessitating the use of a semicolon or a period at the end.

EPIC, a long narrative poem—originally handed down in oral tradition, later a traditional literary form—dealing with national heroes, having a world-wide or cosmic setting, and written in a deliberately ceremonial style. By extension, *epic* may refer to any writing with similar qualities.

EPIGRAM, originally, an inscription; later, any very short, highly polished verse or saying, usually ending with a witty turn.

EPILOGUE, concluding section added to a work, serving to round out or interpret it.

EPISODE, an incident in the course of a *plot* which has a unity of its own.

ESSAY, a brief piece of nonfiction which presents a personal point of view either through informal discourse or formal analysis and argument.

EXISTENTIALISM, a system of philosophy which sees a person as morally responsible in a universe without meaning or values. Therefore, the existentialist's position as a moral being is *absurd* and his commitment is without ultimate reward.

EXPLICATION, the explanation of a literary text derived from close reading and careful internal analysis.

EXPOSITION, the beginning of a work of fiction, wherein the author sets the *atmosphere* and *tone,* and provides the reader with the information he will need in order to understand the unfolding of the *plot.*

EXTENDED METAPHOR, a comparison that is used throughout an entire work or a large portion of it.

FABLE, a brief tale, in which the characters are often animals, told to point out a *moral* truth.

FALLING ACTION, the action in a narrative which represents the working out of the decisive action of the *climax.*

FANTASY, a work which takes place in an unreal world, concerns incredible characters, or employs physical and scientific principles not yet discovered.

FARCE, a type of *comedy* which depends for its effect on outlandish situations rather than on witty *dialogue, plot,* and character.

FIGURES OF SPEECH, specific devices, such as *metaphors* and *similes,* used to gain renewed meaning through imaginative transformations.

FLASHBACK, interruption of the narrative to show an episode that happened prior to that particular point in the story.

FOIL, a character whose traits are the opposite of those of another character.

FOLKLORE, the customs, legends, songs, and tales of a people or nation.

FOOT, a metrical division consisting of one accented syllable and all unaccented syllables associated with it. (Exception: the *spondee.*)

FORESHADOWING, a hint given to the reader of what is to come.

FRAME, a narrative device presenting a story or group of stories within the frame of a larger narrative.

FREE VERSE, a type of poetry which differs from conventional verse forms in being "free" from a fixed pattern of *meter* and *rhyme,* but using *rhythm* and other poetic devices.

GENRE, a form or type of literary work. For example, the *novel,* the short story, and the poem are all genres. The term is a very loose one, however, so that subheadings under these three would themselves also be called genres, e.g., the *picaresque novel,* the tale, the *epic* poem.

GOTHIC NOVEL, type of novel which aims at evoking terror through a gloomy *setting* and sensational, supernatural action.

HAIKU, a seventeen-syllable Japanese verse form with vivid images and compressed, subtle meaning.

HERO, the chief male character in an imaginative work. Since in popular use the word also connotes a person with certain noble qualities, the more neutral term *protagonist* is often preferred.

HEROIC COUPLET, a pair of rhymed verse lines in *iambic pentameter.*

HEROIC SIMILE, a *simile* sustained for several lines and giving a *connotation* of the heroic in nature or quality.

HEROINE, the chief female character in an imaginative work, the female *protagonist.*

HEXAMETER, a verse line of six *feet.*

HOMILY, a sermon, or serious moral talk.

HUMOURS, in medieval and Renaissance literature, the body fluids that shaped temperament and behavior—blood, choler, black bile, and phlegm.

HYPERBOLE, a *figure of speech* involving great exaggeration for expressive or comic effect.

IAMB, two-syllable metrical *foot* consisting of one unaccented syllable followed by one accented syllable.

IDYL OR IDYLL, a *pastoral poem.*

IMAGERY, the sensory details which provide vividness and immediacy and tend to evoke in the reader a complex of emotional suggestions which abstract language does not.

IMPERFECT RHYME, *slant rhyme* in which the vowel sounds are not quite identical.

IN MEDIAS RES, "in the middle of things"; for example, in a traditional epic the opening scene may begin in the middle of the action.

INTERNAL RHYME, rhyming words within, rather than at the end of, lines.

INVOCATION, the call on the muse for help and inspiration found at the beginning of traditional *epic* poems.

IRONY, a term used to describe any situation where two meanings or interpretations are at odds. In verbal irony the actual meaning of a statement is different, often opposite, from what the statement literally says. Irony of situation refers to an occurrence which is contrary to what is expected or appropriate.

KENNING, metaphorical compound word used as a poetic *convention.*

LAY, a short narrative song; also, a *ballad.*

LEGEND, a traditional story about a particular person, place, or deity, often popularly accepted as history.

LITERARY BALLAD, a *ballad* composed in the traditional form in order to achieve the feeling of folk art.

LOCAL COLOR, detailed representation in fiction of *setting,* speech, and customs of a particular region.

LYRIC, a short poem intended mainly to express feelings, thoughts, or a state of mind.

MADRIGAL, a short poem written to be sung by several voices without accompaniment. The subject is usually love.

MASQUE, an elaborate entertainment combining fine costumes, scenery, music, and dancing.

MAXIM, a brief saying embodying a *moral.* (Compare *aphorism* and *proverb.*)

MELODRAMA, a type of *tragedy* with an exaggerated *plot* and *stereotyped* characters, whose credibility are sacrificed for emotional response.

METAPHOR, a *figure of speech* involving an implied comparison. (Compare *simile.*)

METAPHYSICAL POETRY, poetry exhibiting a highly intellectual style which is witty, subtle, and sometimes fantastic, particularly in spinning out *conceits.* See especially John Donne and other seventeenth-century poets.

METER, the patterns of stressed and unstressed syllables used in poetry.

MICROCOSM, literally, "little world," an object or a situation which reflects in miniature a pattern implicit in the world as a whole.

MIRACLE PLAY, medieval verse drama dealing with a subject from the Bible or the life of a saint.

MOCK EPIC, a *satire* using the form of an *epic* poem to develop a trivial incident.

MONOLOGUE, an extended speech given by one speaker.

MOOD, the prevailing emotional aura of a literary work.

MORAL, the lesson taught in a work such as a *fable.* A moral suggests that the reader act in a certain way.

MORALITY PLAY, medieval drama in which the characters are *personifications* of virtues and vices.

MOTIF, a character, incident, or idea that recurs frequently in various works or in various parts of the same work.

MOTIVATION, the portrayal of circumstances and aspects of personality which make a character's actions and reactions appear believable or inevitable to the reader.

MYSTERY PLAY, another term for *miracle play.*

MYTH, a traditional tale of unknown authorship involving gods or other supernatural beings; often attempts to express some interpretation of an aspect or phenomenon of the natural world.

NARRATOR, the teller of a story, usually either an anonymous voice used by the author, or a character in the story itself.

NATURALISM, writing that depicts events as rigidly determined by the forces of heredity and environment. The world described tends to be a bleak and hopeless place.

NEOCLASSICISM, writing that shows the influence of Greek and Roman *classics,* as, for example, eighteenth-century British literature.

NOVEL, a long work of prose fiction dealing with characters, situations, and *settings* that imitate those of real life.

NOVELLA, a brief tale, especially the early tales of French and Italian writers which are considered to be the form which engendered the later *novel. Novella* is also used as a synonym for novelette, or short novel.

OBJECTIVE CORRELATIVE, a set of objects or *images* which, in a work of literature, carry or arouse the emotion the author wishes to convey.

OCTAVE, first eight lines of a *sonnet,* particularly the Italian sonnet.

ODE, a long *lyric* poem, formal in style and complex in form, often written for a special occasion.

OMNISCIENT POINT OF VIEW. See *point of view.*

ONOMATOPOEIA, words used in such a way that the sound of the words imitates the sound of the thing spoken about.

PARABLE, a brief fictional work which concretely illustrates an abstract idea. It differs from a *fable* in that the characters in it are generally people rather than animals; and it differs from an *allegory* in that its characters do not necessarily represent abstract qualities.

PARADOX, a statement that seems to be self-contradictory but which turns out to have valid meaning.

PARALLEL, a likeness, usually in pattern or structure (of a sentence, character, situation, etc.).

PARODY, a kind of *burlesque* aimed particularly at making the style of an author ridiculous.

PASTORAL POETRY, a conventional form of *lyric* poetry using an idealized picture of rural life.

PATHOS, the quality of literature which evokes pity.

PENTAMETER, metrical line of five *feet.*

PERSONA, the mask or voice which a writer assumes in a particular work.

PERSONIFICATION, the representation of ideas, animals, or objects as human beings, by endowing them with human qualities.

PICARESQUE NOVEL, an episodic narrative, generally comic or satiric, portraying a "picaro" (Spanish for "rogue"), or rascal, who lives by his wits and who undergoes little or no change through his adventures.

PLOT, in the simplest sense, a series of happenings in a literary work; but often used to refer to the action as it is organized around a *conflict* and builds through complication to a *climax* followed by a *denouement* or resolution.

POINT OF VIEW, the relation assumed between the teller of a story and the characters in it. The teller, or *narrator,* may himself be a character; or he may be a remote and anonymous voice to be identified, more or less, with the author. A writer who describes, in the third person, both the thoughts and the actions of his characters is said to use the *omniscient point of view;* one who describes only what can be seen, like a newspaper reporter, is said to use the *dramatic point of view.* A narrator's attitude toward his subject is also capable of much variation: it can range from one of apparent indifference to one of extreme conviction and feeling. When a narrator appears to have some bias regarding his subject, it becomes especially important to determine whether he and the author are to be regarded as the same person.

PROLOGUE, section of a work preceding the main part, serving as an introduction.

PROP, short for property, any kind of movable piece used in staging a play.

PROPAGANDA, writing which directly advocates a certain doctrine as the solution to some social or political problem.

PROTAGONIST, the leading character in a literary work.

PROTOTYPE, the original or the pattern from which subsequent works of literature (or elements in literature) derive. Sometimes called a model or archetype.

PROVERB, a brief, traditional saying. (Compare *aphorism* and *maxim.*)

PUN, simultaneous use of two or more different senses of the same word or different words with the same sound (homonyms) for expressive or humorous effect.

QUATRAIN, verse *stanza* of four lines.

QUIBBLE (rare), a play on words.

REALISM, a way of representing life as it seems to the common reader. Material selected tends to deal with ordinary people in everyday experiences.

REFRAIN, the repetition of one or more lines in each *stanza* of a poem.

RHETORIC, conventional *techniques* used in prose to heighten an effect. The term is sometimes used to disparage overblown language.

RHYME, exact repetition of sounds in at least the final accented syllables of two or more words.

RHYME SCHEME, any pattern of *rhymes* in a *stanza* which is a conventional pattern or which is repeated in another stanza.

RHYTHM, usually refers to sound patterns in poetry, but also often to patterns found in both poetry and prose, produced by a recurrence of sounds, *images, themes,* types of sentence structure, and feelings.

RISING ACTION, the building of tension between opposing characters or forces toward a *climax.*

ROMANCE, a long narrative in *verse* or prose that originated in the Middle Ages. Its main elements are adventure, love, and magic.

ROMANTIC HERO, the traditional hero figure who possesses great courage, a strong sense of dedication, and other admirable qualities.

ROMANTICISM, unlike *realism,* stresses man's glory and freedom rather than his limitations. Generally speaking, romantic writers take an optimistic view of individuals; they prefer to stress the past over the present, and to dwell on the exciting, the exotic, and the beautiful.

SARCASM, the use of exaggerated praise to imply dispraise. Similar to *irony,* but more specific in intent, and heavier, less subtle in tone.

SATIRE, the *technique* which employs wit to ridicule a subject, usually some social institution or human foible, with the intention to inspire reform.

SCOP, professional reciter of poems in Anglo-Saxon times.

SESTET, the concluding six lines of a *sonnet,* particularly the Italian sonnet.

SETTING, the literal place and time in which the action of a work of fiction occurs, as opposed to the emotional aura evoked by the work.

SIMILE, a *figure of speech* involving a comparison made explicit by the use of the word *like* or *as.* (Compare *metaphor.*)

SLANT RHYME, *imperfect rhyme* in which the vowel sounds are not quite identical.

SOLILOQUY, a dramatic *convention* which allows a character to speak his thoughts aloud, apparently unheard by others who may be on stage.

SONNET, a *lyric* poem with a traditional form of fourteen *iambic pentameter* lines and one of several fixed *rhyme schemes.*

SPENSERIAN STANZA, a *stanza* of nine *iambic* lines, eight of which have five *feet,* the ninth line, six feet, rhyming ababbcbcc.

SPONDEE, metrical *foot* of two accented syllables.

SPRUNG RHYTHM, metrical form which prescribes only the number of accented syllables in a line.

STAGE DIRECTION, a dramatist's direction as to how scenes are to be set, how lines are to be spoken, and how his play is to be produced.

STANZA, a group of lines which are set off and form a division in a poem, sometimes interconnected by *rhyme scheme.*

STEREOTYPE, an expression, character, or plot that embodies only the conventional and expected, and thus possessing no individuality or particularity.

STREAM OF CONSCIOUSNESS, the recording of a character's flow of thought without any apparent attempt at clarification.

STRUCTURE, the pattern, outline, or "blueprint" which underlies a finished work of literature. An analysis of structure is an important aspect of *explicating* and understanding a literary work.

STYLE, the distinctive handling of language by a given author, involving the specific choices he makes with regard to *diction, syntax, figurative language,* etc.

SUBPLOT, a *plot* of secondary importance carried on in partial or complete independence of the main plot.

SURREALISM, a term used in both painting and literature to apply to incongruous and dreamlike *images* and sequences which are associated with the unconscious.

SYMBOLISM, the use in literature of objects or events to represent something other than themselves, frequently abstract ideas or concepts.

SYNTAX, sentence structure.

TECHNIQUE, the craftsmanship used by an author to give his work form and meaning. Also, a specific literary device, such as *symbolism* or *satire,* may be referred to as a technique.

TEMPO, rate of movement, speed.

TERZA RIMA, verse form with a three-line *stanza* rhyming aba, bcb, cdc, etc.

TETRAMETER, metrical line of four *feet.*

THEATER OF THE ABSURD, a movement in twentieth-century *drama* which seeks to depict the unsettled state of modern man through the use of various experimental, especially nonrealistic, *techniques.* These include eccentric *settings* evoking a sense of madness, distorted language, and seemingly aimless *plot* structure. The roots of the Theater of the Absurd have often been traced back to such plays as William Shakespeare's *King Lear.* (See *existentialism.*)

THEME, a central idea developed in a literary work.

TONE, the attitude and feelings of an author expressed in a given work, by such things as word choice and arrangement.

TRAGEDY, dramatic or narrative writing in which the *protagonist* suffers disaster after a serious and significant struggle, but faces his downfall in such a way as to attain heroic stature. According to Aristotle, tragedy evokes—and thus purges—the emotions of pity and fear.

TRAGIC FLAW, flaw of character in a tragic *hero* which precipitates his downfall.

TRIMETER, metrical line of three *feet.*

TROCHEE, metrical *foot* made up of one accented syllable followed by an unaccented syllable.

UNITIES. Classical dramatic criticism insisted that a good play must have (a) a unified action, taking place during (b) a single continuous time, in (c) one place. These criteria are known as the three *unities.*

UNITY, the quality achieved by an artistic work when all its elements are so interrelated as to form a complete whole.

VERSE. In its most general sense *verse* is a synonym of *poetry. Verse* also may be used to refer to poetry carefully composed as to *rhythm* and *rhyme* scheme, but of inferior literary value. Finally, *verse* may mean a single line of poetry.

GLOSSARY

PRONUNCIATION KEY

a	hat, cap	j	jam, enjoy	u	cup, butter
ā	age, face	k	kind, seek	u̇	full, put
ä	father, far	l	land, coal	ü	rule, move
		m	me, am		
b	bad, rob	n	no, in	v	very, save
ch	child, much	ng	long, bring	w	will, woman
d	did, red			y	young, yet
		o	hot, rock	z	zero, breeze
e	let, best	ō	open, go	zh	measure, seizure
ē	equal, be	ô	order, all		
ėr	term, learn	oi	oil, voice		
		ou	house, out		
f	fat, if				
g	go, bag	p	paper, cup		
h	he, how	r	run, try	ə represents:	
		s	say, yes		a in about
i	it, pin	sh	she, rush		e in taken
ī	ice, five	t	tell, it		i in pencil
		th	thin, both		o in lemon
		ŦH	then, smooth		u in circus

ETYMOLOGY KEY

<	from, derived from, taken from
?	possibly
accus.	accusative
cf.	compare
dim.	diminutive
gen.	genitive
neut.	neuter
pp.	past participle
ppr.	present participle
pt.	past tense
ult.	ultimately
var.	variant
AF	Anglo-French (=Anglo-Norman, the dialect of French spoken by the Normans in England, esp. 1066–c. 1164)
E	English
F	French
G	German
Gk.	Greek (from Homer to A.D.300)
Gmc.	Germanic (parent language of Gothic, Scandinavian, English, Dutch, German)
Ital.	Italian
L	Latin (Classical Latin 200 B.C.–A.D. 300)
LGk.	Late Greek (300–700)
LL	Late Latin (300–700)
ME	Middle English (1100–1500)
Med.Gk.	Medieval Greek (700–1500)
Med.L	Medieval Latin (700–1500)
MF	Middle French (1400–1600)
MHG	Middle High German (1100–1450)
MLG	Middle Low German (1100–1450)
NL	New Latin (after 1500)
OE	Old English (before 1100)
OF	Old French (before 1400)
Pg.	Portuguese
Scand.	Scandinavian (one of the languages of Northern Europe before Middle English times; Old Norse unless otherwise specified)
Sp.	Spanish
VL	Vulgar Latin (a popular form of Latin, the main source of French, Spanish, Italian, Portuguese, and Rumanian)

a baft (ə baft′), *prep.* back of; behind. —*adv.* at the stern; toward the stern. [< *a-* on + ME *baft,* OE *beæftan* < *be* by + *æftan* behind]

a bash (ə bash′), *v.* embarrass and confuse; make uneasy and somewhat ashamed: *The shy girl was abashed when she saw the room filled with strangers.* [< OF *esbaïss-,* stem of *esbaïr* be astonished < VL *batare* gape] **—a bash′ment,** *n.* **—Syn.** disconcert, chagrin.

ab ject (ab′jekt), *adj.* 1. wretched; miserable: *abject poverty.* 2. deserving contempt; degraded: *an abject flatterer.* 3. slavish: *abject submission.* [< L *abjectus,* pp. of *abjicere* < *ab-* down + *jacere* throw] **—ab ject′ly,** *adv.* **—Syn.** 2. contemptible, despicable.

a blu tion (a blü′shən), *n.* 1. a washing of one's person. 2. washing or cleansing as a religious ceremony of purification. 3. the water or other liquid used. [< L *ablutio, -onis* < *abluere* < *ab-* away + *lavere* wash]

ab ste mi ous (ab stē′mē əs), *adj.* sparing in eating and drinking; moderate; temperate. [< L *abstemius* < *ab-* off + unrecorded *temum* intoxicating drink] **—ab ste′mi ous ly,** *adv.* **—ab ste′mi ous ness,** *n.*

ab struse (ab strüs′), *adj.* hard to understand. [< L *abstrusus,* pp. of *abstrudere* < *ab-* away + *trudere* thrust] **—ab struse′ly,** *adv.* **—ab struse′ness,** *n.* **—Syn.** profound, recondite. **—Ant.** obvious.

ac qui esce (ak′wē es′), *v.,* **-esced, -esc ing.** give consent by keeping silent; submit quietly: *We acquiesced in their plan because we could not suggest a better one.* **—Syn.** accede, assent.

ad duce (ə düs′ or ə dyüs′), *v.,* **-duced, -duc ing.** offer as a reason; give as proof or evidence; bring up as an example. [< L *adducere* < *ad-* to + *ducere* lead]

af fec tive (ə fek′tiv), *adj.* of the feelings; emotional.

a lac ri ty (ə lak′rə tē), *n.* 1. brisk and eager action; liveliness: *Although the man was very old, he still moved with alacrity.* 2. cheerful willingness.

al lo cu tion (al′ə kyü′shən), *n.* an address, especially one that is encouraging or authoritative.

al tru is tic (al′trü is′tik), *adj.* thoughtful of the welfare of others; unselfish. **—al′tru is′ti cal ly,** *adv.*

a man u en sis (ə man′yü en′sis), *n., pl.* **-ses** (-sēz). person who writes down what another says; person who copies what another has written. [< L *amanuensis* < *(servus) a manu* secretary]

am bi gu i ty (am′bə gyü′ə tē), *n., pl.* **-ties.** 1. possibility of two or more meanings. 2. word or expression that can have more than one meaning.

am big u ous (am big′yü əs), *adj.* 1. having more than one possible meaning: *"After John hit Dick he ran away," is ambiguous because one cannot tell which boy ran away.* 2. doubtful; not clear; uncertain: *He was left in an ambiguous position by his friend's failure to appear and help him.* [< L *ambiguus* < *ambigere* < *ambi-* in two ways + *agere* drive] **—am big′u ous ly,** *adv.* **—am big′u ous ness,** *n.* **—Syn.** 1. equivocal. 2. vague.

a mi a ble (ā′mē ə bəl), *adj.* good-natured and friendly; pleasant and agreeable. [< OF *amiable* < LL *amicabilis* < L *amicus* friend. Doublet of AMICABLE.] **—a′mi a bly,** *adv.*

a nal o gous (ə nal′ə gəs), *adj.* 1. alike in some way; similar; comparable. 2. in biology, corresponding in function, but not in structure and origin. **—a nal′o gous ly,** *adv.*

an a logue (an′ə lôg or an′ə log), *n.* something analogous.

an i mad ver sion (an′ə mad vėr′zhən), *n.* criticism; blame; unfavorable comment. [< L *animadversio, -onis* < *animadvertere.*]

an nals (an′lz), *n.pl.* 1. a written account of events year by year. 2. historical records; history. [< L *annales (libri)* annual (books) < *annus* year]

a nom a lous (ə nom′ə ləs), *adj.* departing from the common rule; irregular; abnormal: *A position as head of a department, but with no real authority, is anomalous.* [< LL < Gk. *anomalos* < *an-* not + *homalos* even]

a nom a ly (ə nom′ə lē), *n., pl.* **-lies.** 1. departure from a general rule; irregularity. 2. something abnormal: *A dog with six legs is an anomaly.*

an ti quat ed (an′tə kwā′tid), *adj.* 1. old-fashioned; out-of-date. 2. too old for work, service, etc.

an tith e sis (an tith′ə sis), *n., pl.* **-ses** (-sēz). 1. the direct opposite: *Hate is the antithesis of love.* 2. contrast of ideas. *Example:* "To err is human; to forgive, divine." 3. opposition; contrast (*of* or *between*): *antithesis of theory and fact.* [< L < Gk. *antithesis* < *anti-* against + *tithenai* set]

an ti thet ic (an′tə thet′ik), *adj.* 1. of or using antithesis. 2. contrasted; opposite.

an ti thet i cal (an′tə thet′ə kl), *adj.* antithetic.

a plomb (ə plom′), *n.* self-possession; assurance; poise. [< F *aplomb* < *à plomb* according to the plummet]

a poc a lypse (ə pok′ə lips), *n.* 1. revelation. 2. **the Apocalypse,** last book of the New Testament; book of Revelation. [< L *apocalypsis* < Gk. *apokalypsis* < *apo-* off, un- + *kalyptein* cover]

a poc a lyp tic (ə pok′ə lip′tik), *adj.* 1. of the Apocalypse. 2. like a revelation; giving a revelation.

ap o gee (ap′ə jē), *n.* 1. point farthest from the earth in the orbit of the moon or an earth satellite. 2. furthermost point; highest point. [< F *apogée* < Gk. *apogaion* < *apo-* away from + *ge* or *gaia* earth]

a pos tle (ə pos′əl), *n.* 1. **Apostle,** one of the twelve disciples, **the Apostles,** chosen by Christ to go forth and preach the gospel to all the world. 2. any early Christian leader or missionary. Paul was frequently called the "Apostle to the Gentiles." 3. the first Christian missionary to any country or region. 4. leader of any reform movement or belief. 5. one of the council of twelve officials of the Mormon Church who help administer the affairs of the church. [< L < Gk. *apostolos* messenger < *apo-* off + *stellein* send]

ap os tol ic (ap′ə stol′ik), *adj.* 1. of the Apostles; having to do with the Apostles. 2. according to the beliefs and teachings of the Apostles. 3. of the Pope; papal.

ap os tol i cal (ap′ə stol′ə kəl), *adj.* apostolic.

ap pre hend (ap′ri hend′), *v.* 1. look forward to with fear; fear; dread: *A guilty man apprehends danger in every sound.* 2. arrest: *The thief was apprehended and put in jail.* 3. understand; grasp with the mind. [< L *apprehendere* < *ad-* upon + *prehendere* seize]

ar cha ic (är kā′ik), *adj.* 1. no longer in general use. 2. old-fashioned; out-of-date. 3. ancient. [< Gk. *archaikos,* ult. < *arche* beginning]

ar chi tec ton ic (är′kə tek ton′ik), *adj.* 1. having to do with architecture, construction, or design. 2. showing skill in construction or design. 3. directive; controlling.

ar gent (är′jənt), *n.* *Archaic* or *Poetic.* silver. —*adj.* silvery. [< F < L *argentum*]

ar i ette (ar′ē et or er′ē et), *n.* a short aria (operatic melody).

ar ti fice (är′tə fis), *n.* 1. a clever device; trick. 2. trickery; craft. 3. *obs.* the production or making of something, especially in arts or crafts. 4. *Archaic.* artistic skill or style. [< F < L *artificium* < *ars, artis* art + *facere* make]

as cer tain (as′ər tān′), *v.* find out; determine.

a skance (ə skans′), *adv.* 1. with suspicion or disapproval: *The students looked askance at the suggestion for having classes on Saturday.* 2. sideways; to one side.

as say (ə sā′), *v.* 1. analyze (an ore, alloy, etc.) to find out the quantity of gold, silver, or other metal in it. 2. try; test; examine. 3. *U.S.* (of ore) contain, as shown by analysis, a certain proportion of metal. 4. *Archaic.* attempt. —*n.* 1. analysis of an ore, alloy, etc., to find out the amount of metal in it. 2. trial; test; examination. 3. the substance analyzed or tested. 4. a list of the results of assaying an ore, drug, etc. [< OF *a(s)sayer,* ult. < LL < VL *exagere* weigh] **—as say′er,** *n.*

as sid u ous (ə sij′ü əs), *adj.* careful and attentive; diligent. [< L *assiduus* < *assidere* sit at] **—as sid′u ous ly,** *adv.*

as suage (ə swāj′), *v.,* **-suaged, -suag ing.** 1. make easier or milder: *assuage pain.* 2. satisfy; appease; quench: *assuage thirst.* [< OF *assuagier,* ult. < L *ad-* + *suavis* sweet] **—as suag′er,** *n.*

at a vism (at′ə viz əm), *n.* 1. resemblance to a remote ancestor. If a child of very quiet, home-loving parents and grandparents should display the love of travel and adventure that had characterized a sea-captain ancestor, it would be called a case of atavism. 2. reversion to a primitive type. [< L *atavus* ancestor]

a thwart (ə thwôrt′), *adv.* crosswise;

across from side to side. *—prep.* 1. across. 2. across the line or course of. 3. in opposition to; against.

at ten u ate (ə ten′yü āt), *v.*, **-at ed, -at ing.** 1. make or become thin or slender. 2. weaken; reduce. 3. make less dense; dilute. [< L *attenuare* < *ad-* + *tenuis* thin]

au re ate (ô′rē it or ô′rē āt), *adj.* golden; gilded. [< L *aureatus* < *aurum* gold]

bal dric (bôl′drik), *n.* belt for a sword, horn, etc., hung from one shoulder to the opposite side of the body. [akin to MHG *balderich* girdle]

balk (bôk), *v.* 1. stop short and stubbornly refuse to go on. 2. thwart; hinder; check: *The police balked the robber's plans.* 3. fail to use; let slip; miss. 4. in baseball, make a balk. [< n.] *—n.* 1. hindrance; check; defeat. 2. blunder; mistake. 3. ridge between furrows; strip left unplowed. 4. a large beam or timber. 5. failure of a baseball pitcher to complete a pitch he has started. Also, **baulk.** [OE *balca* ridge]

bal last (bal′əst), *n.* 1. something heavy carried in a ship to steady it. 2. weight carried in a balloon or dirigible to control it. 3. anything which steadies a person or thing. 4. gravel or crushed rock used in making the bed for a road or railroad track. *—v.* 1. put ballast in (ships, balloons, etc.). 2. put gravel or crushed rock on. [apparently < Scand. (ODanish) *barlast* < *bar* bare + *last* load]

balm y (bä′mē or bäl′mē), *adj.*, **balm i er, balm i est.** 1. mild; gentle; soothing: *a balmy breeze.* 2. fragrant. [< *balm*] **—balm′i ly,** *adv.* **—balm′i ness,** *n.*

ban (ban), *v.*, **banned, ban ning,** *n.* *—v.* 1. prohibit; forbid: *Swimming is banned in this lake.* 2. place a ban on; pronounce a curse on. *—n.* 1. the forbidding of an act or speech by authority of the law, the church, or public opinion. 2. a solemn curse by the church. 3. sentence of outlawry. [< Scand. *banna* forbid] **—Syn.** *v.* 2. curse. *—n.* 1. prohibition, taboo. 2. excommunication.

ban dy (ban′de), *v.*, **-died, -dy ing,** *adj.* *—v.* 1. throw back and forth; toss about. 2. give and take; exchange: *To bandy words with a foolish person is a waste of time.* *—adj.* having a bend or curve outward: *bandy legs.* [cf. F *bander* bandy, *se bander* band together < Gmc.]

bar row (bar′ō), *n.* mound of earth or stones over an ancient grave. [OE *beorg*]

baulk (bôk), *v.* 1. *Archaic.* to pass over or by. 2. to check or stop by, or as if by, an obstacle; block.

bea dle (bē′dəl), *n.* a minor officer in the Church of England. In former times if a person went to sleep in church, the beadle woke him up. [OE *bydel*]

beet ling (bēt′ling), *adj.* projecting; overhanging.

be guile (bi gīl′), *v.*, **-guiled, -guil ing.** 1. deceive; cheat: *His pleasant ways beguiled me into thinking that he was my friend.* 2. take away from deceitfully or cunningly. 3. entertain; amuse. 4. while away (time) pleasantly. **—be guil′er,** *n.* **—Syn.** 1. delude.

be guil ing (bi gīl′ing), *adj.* 1. deceiving. 2. entertaining; amusing. **—be guil′ing ly,** *adv.*

be night ed (bi nī′tid), *adj.* 1. not knowing right and wrong; ignorant. 2. overtaken by night; being in darkness. [< obsolete verb *benight* < *be-* + *night*]

be nign (bi nīn′), *adj.* 1. gentle; kindly: *a benign old lady.* 2. favorable; mild: *a benign climate.* 3. doing no harm: *A benign swelling or tumor can usually be cured.* [< OF < L *benignus* < *bene* well + *gnus* born] **—be nign′ly,** *adv.* **—Syn.** 1. gracious. 2. salutary. **—Ant.** 3. malignant.

be reft (bi reft′), *adj.* 1. bereaved; deprived. 2. left desolate. *—v.* a pt. and a pp. of **bereave.**

bil let (bil′it), *n.*, *v.*, **-let ed, -let ing.** *—n.* 1. a written order to provide board and lodging for a soldier. 2. place where a soldier is lodged. 3. job; position. *—v.* assign to quarters by billet: *Soldiers were billeted in all the houses of the village.* [< OF *billette,* dim. of *bille* bill]

bit tern (bit′ərn), *n.* a small kind of heron that lives in marshes and has a peculiar booming cry. [< OF *butor*]

blanc mange (blə mänzh′), *n.* a sweet dessert made of milk thickened with gelatin, cornstarch, etc. [< OF *blancmanger* white food]

blench (blench), *v.* 1. turn pale. 2. make white. [var. of *blanch*]

bom bast (bom′bast), *n.* fine-sounding language that is unsuitable. [earlier *bombace* < OF *bombace, bambace* < Med.L < Med.Gk. *bambax* cotton < Gk. *bombyx* silk]

bra va do (brə vä′dō), *n.* a great show of boldness without much real courage; boastful defiance without much real desire to fight. [< Sp. *bravada* < *bravo.*]

buck ler (buk′lər), *n.* 1. a small, round shield. 2. protection; defense. [< OF *boucler* shield, originally, one with a boss < *boucle* boss < L *buccula.*]

bu col ic (byü kol′ik), *adj.* 1. of shepherds; pastoral. Bucolic poetry is seldom written by shepherds themselves. 2. rustic; rural. *—n.* poem about shepherds. [< L *bucolicus* < Gk. *boukolikos* rustic < *boukolos* shepherd]

bul wark (bu̇l′wərk), *n.* 1. defense; protection. 2. earthwork or other wall for defense against an enemy. 3. breakwater for protection against the force of the waves. 4. Usually, **bulwarks,** *pl.* a ship's side above the deck. *—v.* 1. defend; protect. 2. provide with a bulwark or bulwarks. [ME *bulwerk,* apparently < *bole* + *work,* a work made of tree trunks. Akin to *boulevard.*]

bum ble (bum′bəl), *v.* buzz, drone.

ca dav er ous (kə dav′ər əs), *adj.* 1. of or like a cadaver. 2. pale and ghastly. 3. thin and worn.

hat, āge, fär; let, ēqual, tėrm;
it, īce; hot, ōpen, ôrder;
oil, out; cup, pu̇t, rüle; ch, child;
ng, long; sh, she; th, thin;
ᴛʜ, then; zh, measure;

ə represents *a* in about,
e in taken, *i* in pencil,
o in lemon, *u* in circus.

ca jole (kə jōl′), *v.*, **-joled, -jol ing.** persuade by pleasant words, flattery, or false promises; coax. [< F *cajoler*] **—ca jol′er,** *n.* **—Syn.** beguile, wheedle.

ca jol er y (kə jō′lər ē), *n.*, *pl.* **-er ies.** persuasion by smooth, deceitful words; flattery; coaxing.

cal i bra tion (kal′ə brā′shən), *n.* 1. a set of graduations or marks to indicate quantity or values.

ca lum ni ous (kə lum′nē əs), *adj.* slanderous. **—ca lum′ni ous ly,** *adv.*

ca price (kə prēs′), *n.* 1. a sudden change of mind without reason; unreasonable notion or desire. 2. tendency to change suddenly and without reason. 3. capriccio. [< F < Ital. *capriccio.* Doublet of CAPRICCIO.] **—Syn.** 1. whimsy, whim, humor, fancy.

ca pri cious (kə prish′əs), *adj.* guided by one's fancy; full of unreasonable notions; changeable; fickle: *A spoiled child is often capricious.* **—ca pri′cious ly,** *adv.* **—ca pri′cious ness,** *n.*

car bun cle (kär′bung kəl), *n.* 1. a very painful, inflamed swelling under the skin. 2. pimple. 3. a smooth, round garnet or other deep-red jewel. [< L *carbunculus* < *carbo* coal]

cas ti gate (kas′tə gāt), *v.*, **-gat ed, -gat ing.** criticize severely; punish. [< L *castigare,* ult. < *castus* pure] **—cas′ti ga′tor,** *n.*

cate (kāt), *n.* *Archaic.* a delicacy; dainty.

caulk (kôk), *v.* fill up (a seam, crack, or joint) so that it will not leak; make watertight. Sailors caulk boats with oakum and tar. Plumbers caulk joints with lead. Also, **calk.** [< OF *cauquer* < L *calcare* tread, press in]

cav il (kav′əl), *v.*, **-iled, -il ing** or *esp. Brit.* **-illed, -il ling,** *n.* *—v.* find fault unnecessarily; raise trivial objections. *—n.* a petty objection; trivial criticism. [< F < L *cavillari* jeer] **—cav′il er,** *esp. Brit.* **cav′il ler,** *n.* **—Syn.** *v.* carp, criticize.

chi mer i cal (kə mer′ə kəl or kī mer′ə kl), *adj.* 1. unreal; imaginary. 2. absurd; impossible: *chimerical schemes for getting rich.* 3. wildly fanciful; visionary.

cinc ture (singk′chər), *n.*, *v.*, **-tured, -tur ing.** *—n.* 1. belt; girdle. 2. border; enclosure. *—v.* encircle; surround. [< L *cinctura* < *cingere* bind, gird]

cloy (kloi), *v.* 1. weary by too much, too sweet, or too rich food. 2. weary by too much of anything pleasant. [ME *acloy, ancloy* drive a nail into, stop up, fill full < OF *encloyer* < *en-* in (< L *in-*) + *clou* nail (< L *clavus*)] **—Syn.** 2. surfeit, pall.

cocks comb (koks′kōm′), *n.* 1. the fleshy, red part on the head of a rooster. 2. a pointed cap somewhat like this, worn by a jester or clown. 3. plant with crested or feathery clusters of red or yellow flowers.

cof fer (kô′fər), *n.* 1. box, chest, or trunk, especially one used to hold money or other valuable things. 2. an ornamental panel in a ceiling, etc. 3. cofferdam. 4. **coffers,** *pl.* treasury; funds. [< OF *cofre* < L *cophinus* basket]

col lier y (kol′yər ē), *n., pl.* **-lier ies.** a coal mine and its buildings and equipment.

com mis er a tion (kə miz′ə rā′shən), *n.* pity; sympathy.

com ple ment (*n.* kom′plə mənt; *v.* kom′plə mənt), *n.* 1. something that completes or makes perfect. 2. number required to fill: *The ship now had its full complement of men, and no more could be taken on.*

con strained (kən strānd′), *adj.* 1. forced. 2. restrained; stiff; unnatural: *a constrained smile.*

con vey anc er (kən vā′ən sər), *n.* lawyer who investigates the ownership of property and prepares contracts, deeds, etc., for its transfer from one person to another.

co pi ous (kō′pē əs), *adj.* 1. plentiful; abundant. 2. containing much matter. 3. containing many words. **—co′pi ous ly,** *adv.* **—co′pi ous ness,** *n.* **—Syn.** ample.

cop pice (kop′is), *n.* a thicket of small trees, bushes, shrubs, etc. [< OF *coupeiz* a cut-over forest < *couper* cut, ult. < L < Gk. *kolaphos* a blow]

Copt (kopt), *n.* 1. native of Egypt descended from the ancient Egyptians. 2. member of the Coptic Church.

co ra cle (kôr′ə kəl), *n.* a small, light boat made by covering a wooden frame with waterproof material. [< Welsh *corwgl* < *corwg* round body or vessel, torso, carcass]

cor rob o rate (kə rob′ə rāt), *v.,* **-rat ed, -rat ing.** make more certain; conform: *Witnesses corroborated the policeman's statement.* [< L *corroborare* strengthen < *com-* + *robur* oak] **—cor rob′o ra′tor,** *n.*

cov ert (kuv′ərt or kō′vərt), *adj.* secret; hidden; disguised: *covert glances.* —*n.* 1. shelter; hiding place. 2. thicket in which animals hide. [< OF *covert,* pp. of *covrir*] **—cov′ert ly,** *adv.* **—cov′ert ness,** *n.*

cre ance (krē′əns), *n.* leash for a hawk.

cre dence (krēd′ns), *n.* belief: *Never give credence to gossip.* [< Med.L *credentia* < L *credere* believe]

cre ta ceous (kri tā′shəs), *adj.* 1. like chalk; containing chalk. 2. **Cretaceous,** of or having to do with the geological period when most of the chalk deposits were made or with rocks formed in this period.

cre tin ism (krē′tən iz əm), *n.* inborn deformity, usually accompanied with idiocy, caused by a deficiency in the thyroid gland.

crump (krump), *n.* 1. *Brit.* thump. 2. the explosion of a bomb or shell. 3. bomb, shell.

cur ate (kyůr′it), *n.* *Esp. Brit.* clergyman who is an assistant to a pastor, rector, or vicar. [< Med.L *curatus* < *cura* cure < L *cura* care. Doublet of CURÉ.]

cur sor y (kėr′sər ē), *adj.* hasty; superficial; without attention to details: *Even a cursory reading of the letter showed many errors.* [< LL *cursorius* of a race < *currere* run] **—cur′so ri ly,** *adv.* **—Syn.** rapid, hurried.

da do (dā′dō), *n., pl.* **-does** or **-dos.** the lower part of an interior wall when decorated with moldings or facings; also, the molding, facing, or other decoration.

dal li ance (dal′ē əns), *n.* 1. flirtation. 2. a playing; trifling.

dam a scene (dam′ə sēn or dam′ə sēn′), *v.,* **-scened, -scen ing.** ornament (metal) with inlaid gold or silver or with a wavy design. [< L *Damascenus* < Gk. *Damaskenos* of Damascus]

daunt (dônt), *v.* 1. frighten. 2. discourage. [< OF *danter* < L *domitare* < *domare* tame] **—Syn.** 1. intimidate. 2. dismay, dishearten.

dec a dence (dek′ə dəns or di kād′ns), *n.* a falling off; decline; decay: *The decadence of morals was one of the causes of the fall of Rome.* [< F < Med.L *decadentia* < L *de-* + *cadere* fall]

de cus sat ed (dek′ə sāt′id or dē′kə-sāt′id), *adj.* in the form of an x.

de i fi ca tion (dē′ə fə kā′shən), *n.* 1. a deifying. 2. being deified.

de i fy (dē′ə fī), *v.,* **-fied, -fy ing.** 1. make a god of. 2. worship or regard as a god. [< OF *deifier* < LL *deificare* < *deus* god + *facere* make] **—de′i fi′er,** *n.*

de lin e a tion (di lin′ē ā′shən), *n.* 1. drawing; sketch. 2. description.

de mur (di mėr′), *v.,* **-murred, -mur ring,** *n.* —*v.* object: *The clerk demurred at working overtime without extra pay.* —*n.* an objection. [< OF *demurer* < L *demorari* < *de-* + *morari* delay]

dep re ca to ry (dep′rə kə tô′rē or dep′-rə kə tō′rē), *adj.* 1. deprecating. 2. *Informal.* apologetic.

des cant (*v.* des kant′ or dis kant′; *n.* des′kant), *v.* 1. talk at great length; discourse: *She descanted upon the wonders of her trip to Europe.* 2. sing or play a melody with another melody. —*n.* 1. part music. 2. melody to be played or sung with another melody. [< OF *deschanter* < Med.L *discantare* < L *dis-* + *cantus* song < *canere* sing]

de spoil (di spoil′), *v.* rob; plunder. [< OF *despoillier* < L *despoliare* < *de-* + *spolium* armor, booty]

des ul to ry (des′əl tô′rē), *adj.* jumping from one thing to another; unconnected: without aim or method: *The careful study of a few books is better than the desultory reading of many.* [< L *desultorius* of a leaper, ult. < *de-* down + *salire* leap] **—des′ul to′ri ly,** *adv.* **—des′ul to′ri ness,** *n.*

det ri ment (det′rə mənt), *n.* 1. damage; injury; harm: *No one can tell lies without detriment to his character.* 2. something that causes damage or harm. [< L *detrimentum* < *deterere* < *de-* away + *terere* wear]

de vi a tion (dē′vē ā′shən), *n.* a turning aside from a way, course, rule, truth, etc.; divergence: *The iron in the ship caused a deviation of the magnetic needle of the compass.*

di a lec tic (dī′ə lek′tik), *n.* 1. art or practice of logical discussion employed in finding out the truth of a theory or opinion. 2. logical argumentation; discussion of the logical truth of an opinion or theory. —*adj.* 1. having to do with logical discussion: *dialectic criticism.* 2. dialectal.

di a pa son (dī′ə pā′zn or dī′ə pā′sn), *n.* 1. harmony. 2. melody; strain. 3. a swelling musical sound. 4. the whole range of a voice or instrument. 5. a fixed standard of musical pitch. 6. either of two principal stops in an organ: **a. open diapason,** a stop giving full, majestic tones. **b. stopped diapason,** a stop giving powerful flutelike tones. [< L < Gk. *diapason* < *dia pason (chordon)* across all (the notes of the scale)]

di dac tic (dī dak′tik), *adj.* 1. intended to instruct: *Aesop's "Fables" are didactic stories; each one has an instructive moral.* 2. inclined to instruct others; teacherlike: *The older brother was called "Professor" because of his didactic manner.* [< Gk. *didaktikos* < *didaskein* teach] **—di dac′ti cal ly,** *adv.*

din gle (ding′gəl), *n.* a small deep, shady valley. [origin uncertain]

dis a buse (dis′ə byüz′), *v.,* **-bused, -bus ing.** free from deception or error: *Education should disabuse people of foolish prejudices.*

dis man tle (dis man′tl), *v.,* **-tled, -tling.** 1. strip of covering, equipment, furniture, guns, rigging, etc.: *The warship was dismantled before the hull was sold for scrap metal.* 2. pull down; take apart: *We had to dismantle the bookcases in order to move them.* [< OF *desmanteler* < *des-* (< L *dis-*) + *mantel* mantle < L *mantellum*]

dis pen sa tion (dis′pən sā′shən), *n.* 1. act of giving out; act of distributing: *the dispensation of charity to the poor.* 2. thing given out or distributed: *They gave thanks for the dispensations of Providence.* 3. rule; management: *England under the dispensation of Elizabeth I.* 4. management or ordering of the affairs of the world by Providence or Nature. 5. a religious system: *the Christian dispensation.* 6. official permission to disregard a rule.

di ur nal (dī ėr′nl), *adj.* 1. occurring every day; daily. 2. of or belonging to the daytime. 3. lasting a day. [< LL *diurnalis* < L *dies* day. Doublet of JOURNAL.]

dom i cile (dom′ə sīl), *n., v.,* **-ciled, -cil ing.** —*n.* 1. house; home; residence.

2. in law, place of permanent residence. One may have several residences, but only one legal domicile at a time. *—v.* 1. settle in a domicile. 2. dwell; reside. [< F < L *domicilium* < *domus* house + *colere* dwell]

dot ard (dō′tərd), *n.* person who is weak-minded and childish because of old age.

dra goon (drə gün′), *n.* soldier who fights on horseback. Dragoons formerly rode horses to the battlefield, but sometimes fought on foot. *—v.* 1. oppress or persecute by dragoons. 2. compel by oppression or persecution: *He was dragooned into signing a false statement.* [< F *dragon* dragon, pistol, (later) soldier]

dul ci mer (dul′sə mər), *n.* a musical instrument with metal strings, played by striking the strings with two hammers. [< OF *doulcemer,* var. of *doulcemele* < L *dulcis* sweet < *melos* song (< Gk.)]

dun (dun), *n., adj.* dull, grayish brown. [OE *dunn,* ? < Celtic]

dys pep si a (dis pep′sē ə), *n.* poor digestion; indigestion. [< L < Gk. *dyspepsia* < *dys-* bad + *pep-* cook, digest]

dys pep tic (dis pep′tik), *adj.* 1. having to do with dyspepsia. 2. suffering from dyspepsia. 3. gloomy; pessimistic. *—n.* person who has dyspepsia.

ed i fi ca tion (ed′ə fə kā′shən), *n.* moral improvement; spiritual benefit; instruction.

ef fi gy (ef′ə jē), *n., pl.* **-gies.** 1. statue, etc., of a person; image: *The dead man's monument bore his effigy.* 2. **burn** or **hang in effigy,** burn or hang a stuffed image of a person to show hatred or contempt.

ef flu vi a (i flü′vē ə), *n.* pl. of **effluvium.**

ef flu vi um (i flü′vē əm), *n., pl.* **-vi a** or **-vi ums.** 1. an unpleasant vapor or odor. 2. vapor; odor.

ef fron ter y (ə frun′tər ē), *n., pl.* **-ter ies.** shameless boldness; impudence: *The politician had the effrontery to ask the people he had insulted to vote for him.* [< F *effronterie* < OF *esfront* shameless < L *effrons* < *ex-* out + *frons* brow] **—Syn.** presumption, insolence.

ef ful gence (i ful′jəns), *n.* brightness; radiance.

e gre gious (i grē′jəs), *adj.* 1. remarkably or extraordinarily bad; outrageous; flagrant: *an egregious lie.* 2. remarkable; extraordinary. [< L *egregius* < *ex-* out + *grex* herd, flock] **—e gre′gious ly,** *adv.*

e lu ci date (i lü′sə dāt), *v.,* **-dat ed, -dat ing.** make clear; explain: *The scientist elucidated his theory by a few simple experiments.* [< LL *elucidare* < L *ex-* out + *lucidus* bright]

em a na tion (em′ə nā′shən), *n.* 1. a coming forth. 2. anything that comes forth from a source: *Light and heat are emanations from the sun.* 3. a gas given off by a disintegrating, radioactive substance.

em u late (em′yə lāt), *v.,* **-lat ed, -lat ing.** try to equal or excel: *The proverb tells us to emulate the industry of the ant.*

en gen der (en jen′dər), *v.* bring into existence; produce; cause: *Filth engenders disease.*

e nig ma (i nig′mə), *n.* 1. a puzzling statement; riddle: *To most of the audience the philosopher seemed to speak in enigmas.* 2. a baffling or puzzling problem, situation, person, etc.: *The queer behavior of the child was an enigma even to her parents.* [< L *aenigma* < Gk. *ainigma* < *ainissesthai* speak darkly < *ainos* fable]

en ig mat ic (en′ig mat′ik or ē′nig-mat′ik), *adj.* like a riddle; baffling; puzzling; mysterious.

en join (en join′), *v.* 1. order; direct; urge: *Parents enjoin good behavior on their children.* 2. in law, issue an authoritative command. Through an injunction a judge may enjoin a person to do (or not do) some act. **—Syn.** 1. prescribe, command, charge, bid.

en sconce (en skons′), *v.,* **-sconced, -sconc ing.** 1. shelter safely; hide: *The soldiers were ensconced in strongly fortified trenches.* 2. settle comfortably and firmly: *The cat ensconced itself in the armchair.* [< *en-* + *sconce* fortification, probably < Dutch *schans*]

en toil (en toil′), *v.* trap, entwine.

e pit o me (i pit′ə mē′), *n.* 1. a condensed account; summary. An epitome contains only the most important points of a literary work, subject, etc. 2. some thing or part that is typical or representative of the whole: *Solomon is often spoken of as the epitome of wisdom.* [< L < Gk. *epitome* < *epitemnein* cut short < *epi-* into + *temnein* cut]

e pit o mize (i pit′ə mīz), *v.,* **-mized, -miz ing.** make an epitome of; summarize. **—Syn.** abridge, condense.

es tu ar y (es′chü er′ē), *n., pl.* **-ar ies.** 1. a broad mouth of a river into which the tide flows. 2. inlet of the sea. [< L *aestuarium* < *aestus* tide]

e the re al (i thir′ē əl), *adj.* 1. light; airy; delicate: *Her ethereal beauty made her seem more like a spirit than a human being.* 2. not of the earth; heavenly. 3. of or having to do with the upper regions of space. 4. of or having to do with the ether diffused through space. **—e the′re al ly,** *adv.* **—Syn.** 1. intangible.

eu cho lo gion (yü′kə lō′jən), *n.* a collection of prayers; a prayer book; a book of ritual, primarily of the Greek Church.

eu lo gis tic (yü′lə jis′tik), *adj.* praising highly. **—eu′lo gis′ti cal ly,** *adv.*

eu phe mism (yü′fə miz′əm), *n.* 1. use of a mild or indirect expression instead of one that is harsh or unpleasantly direct. 2. a mild or indirect expression used in this way. "Pass away" is a common euphemism for "die." The name *Eumenides* for the Furies was a euphemism. [< Gk. *euphemismos* < *euphemizein* speak with fair words < *eu-* good + *pheme* speaking]

➤ **euphemism, euphuism.** *Euphemism* is a world-wide trait, the effect of superstition, squeamishness, tact, or kindness. *Euphuism,* in its exact sense, was a passing fad; in a broader sense it includes tendencies to artificiality which may be shown by individuals. *Euphuism* relates to a sustained style; *euphemism* to a particular expression.

hat, āge, fär; let, ēqual, tėrm;
it, īce; hot, ōpen, ôrder;
oil, out; cup, pu̇t, rüle; ch, child;
ng, long; sh, she; th, thin;
ᴛʜ, then; zh, measure;

ə represents *a* in about,
e in taken, *i* in pencil,
o in lemon, *u* in circus.

eu phe mis tic (yü′fə mis′tik), *adj.* of or showing euphemism; containing a euphemism.

eu tha na sia (yü′thə nā′zhə), *n.* 1. an easy, painless death. 2. a painless killing, especially to end a painful and incurable disease. [< Gk. *euthanasia* < *eu-* easy + *thanatos* death]

ex e cra tion (ek′sə krā′shən), *n.* 1. abhorrence; loathing; detestation. 2. a cursing. 3. a curse: *The mob shouted angry execrations.* 4. person or thing execrated.

ex i gen cy (ek′sə jən sē), *n., pl.* **-cies.** 1. Usually, **exigencies,** *pl.* an urgent need; demand for immediate action or attention: *The exigencies of business kept him from leaving town.* 2. situation demanding immediate action or attention; urgent case.

ex or cise (ek′sôr sīz), *v.,* **-cised, -cis ing.** 1. drive out (an evil spirit) by prayers, ceremonies, etc. 2. free (a person or place) from an evil spirit. **—ex′or cis′er,** *n.*

ex pan sive (ek span′siv), *adj.* 1. capable of expanding; tending to expand. 2. wide; spreading. 3. taking in much or many things; broad; extensive. 4. showing one's feelings freely and openly; unrestrained; effusive. **—ex pan′sive ly,** *adv.* **—ex-pan′sive ness,** *n.*

ex pos tu la tion (ek spos′chə lā′shən), *n.* earnest protest; remonstrance: *The teacher's expostulations failed, and he resorted to threats.*

ex tem po rize (ek stem′pə rīz′), *v.,* **-rized, -riz ing.** 1. speak, play, sing, or dance, composing as one proceeds: *The pianist was extemporizing.* 2. compose off-hand; make for the occasion: *The campers extemporized a shelter for the night.* **—ex-tem′po ri za′tion,** *n.*

fain (fān), *Archaic* and *Poetic.* *—adv.* by choice; gladly. *—adj.* 1. willing but not eager; forced by circumstances. 2. glad; willing. 3. eager; desirous.

fal low (fal′ō), *adj.* plowed and left unseeded for a season or more; uncultivated; inactive. *—n.* 1. land plowed and left unseeded for a season or more. 2. the plowing of land without seeding it for a season in order to destroy weeds, improve the soil, etc.

fath om (faTH′əm), *n., pl.* **fath oms** or *(esp. collectively)* **fath om,** *v.* —*n.* a unit of measure equal to 6 feet, used mostly in measuring the depth of water and the length of ships' ropes, cables, etc. —*v.* 1. measure the depth of. 2. get to the bottom of; understand fully. [OE *fæthm* width of the outstretched arms]

fe al ty (fē′əl tē), *n., pl.* **-ties.** 1. loyalty and duty owed by a vassal to his feudal lord: *The nobles swore fealty to the king.* 2. loyalty; faithfulness; allegiance. [< OF *feauté* < L *fidelitas.* Doublet of FIDELITY.]

fea si ble (fē′zə bəl), *adj.* 1. capable of being done or carried out easily; practicable: *The committee selected the plan that seemed most feasible.* 2. likely; probably: *The witness's explanation of the accident sounded feasible.* 3. suitable; convenient: *The road was too rough to be feasible for travel by automobile.* [< OF *faisable,* ult. < L *facere* do] **—fea′si ble ness,** *n.* **—fea′si bly,** *adv.*

fea si bil i ty (fē′zə bil′ə tē), *n.* quality of being easily done or carried out.

fen (fen), *n. Brit.* marsh; swamp; bog. [OE *fenn*]

fe ral (fir′el), *adj.* 1. wild; untamed. 2. brutal; savage. [< L *fera* beast]

fig ment (fig′mənt), *n.* something imagined; made-up story. [< L *figmentum* < *fingere* to form, fashion]

fir ma ment (fėr′mə mənt), *n.* arch of the heavens; sky. [< L *firmamentum,* ult. < *firmus* firm]

flac cid (flak′sid), *adj.* limp; weak; *flaccid muscles, a flaccid will.* [< L *flaccidus* < *flaccus* flabby]

flout (flout), *v.,* 1. treat with contempt or scorn; mock; scoff at: *The foolish boy flouted his mother's advice.* 2. show contempt or scorn; scoff. —*n.* a contemptuous speech or act; insult; mockery; scoffing. [var. of *flute,* v.] **—flout′er,** *n.* **—flout′ing ly,** *adv.* **—Syn.** *v.* 1. jeer, taunt.

flum mer y (flum′ər ē), *n., pl.* **-mer ies.** 1. pudding made of milk, eggs, flour, sugar, etc. 2. an empty compliment; nonsense. [Welsh *llymru*]

fore peak scut tle, *n.* the forward lower compartment of a ship, used for storage.

fraught (frôt), *adj.* loaded; filled: *A battlefield is fraught with horror.* [pp. of obsolete *fraught* load, v. use of n., < MDutch or MLG *vracht* freight]

fru gal (frü′gəl), *adj.* 1. avoiding waste; saving; tending to avoid unnecessary spending. 2. costing little; barely sufficient: *He ate a frugal supper of bread and milk.* [< L *frugalis* < *frugi* temperate] **—fru′gal ly,** *adv.* **—Syn.** 1. sparing, thrifty.

fus tian (fus′chən), *n.* 1. a coarse, heavy cloth made of cotton and flax. Fustian was used for clothing in Europe throughout the Middle Ages. 2. a thick cotton cloth like corduroy. 3. pompous, high-sounding language; would-be eloquence. —*adj.* 1. made of fustian. 2. pompous and high-sounding, but cheap. [< OF *fustaigne* < LL *fustaneum* < L *fustis* stick of wood]

gall (gôl), *v.* 1. make or become sore by rubbing: *The rough strap galled the horse's skin.* 2. annoy; irritate. —*n.* 1. a sore spot on the skin caused by rubbing. 2. cause of annoyance or irritation.

gam bit (gam′bit), *n.* way of opening a game of chess by purposely sacrificing a pawn or a piece to gain some advantage. [< F < Provençal *cambi* an exchange]

gan grene (gang′grēn or gang grēn′), *n., v.,* **-grened, -gren ing.** —*n.* decay of a part of a living person or animal when the blood supply is interfered with by injury, infection, freezing, etc.

gar ner (gär′nər), *v.* gather and store away: *Wheat is cut and garnered at harvest time.* —*n.* 1. storehouse for grain. 2. a store of anything.

gar ru lous (gar′ə ləs), *adj.* 1. talking too much about trifles. 2. using too many words. [< L *garrulus* < *garrire* chatter] **—gar′ru lous ly,** *adv.* **—gar′ru lous ness,** *n.* **—Syn.** 1. talkative, loquacious.

gaunt (gônt), *adj.* 1. very thin and bony; with hollow eyes and a starved look: *Hunger and suffering make people gaunt.* 2. looking bare and gloomy; desolate; forbidding; grim. [origin uncertain] **—gaunt′ly,** *adv.* **—gaunt′ness,** *n.* **—Syn.** 1. lean, spare, lank.

geld (geld), *v.,* **geld ed** or **gelt, geld ing.** remove the male glands of (a horse or other animal); castrate. [< Scand. *gelda castrate* < *geldr* barren]

geld ing (gel′ding), *n.* a gelded horse or other animal.

ge ne al o gy (jē′nē al′ə jē, jē′nē ol′ə jē, jen′ē al′ə jē, or jen′ē ol′ə jē), *n., pl.* **—gies.** 1. account of the descent of a person or family from an ancestor or ancestors. 2. descent of a person or family from an ancestor; pedigree; lineage. 3. the making or investigation of accounts of descent; study of pedigrees. [< L < Gk. *genealogia,* ult. < *genea* generation + *-logos* treating of]

ge ner ic (jə ner′ik), *adj.* 1. having to do with or characteristic of a genus of plants or animals: *Cats and lions show generic differences.* 2. having to do with a class or group of similar things; inclusive; not specific: *Liquid is a generic term.* 3. referring to a group or class; general; not special. [<L *genus, generis* kind] **—ge ner′i cal ly,** *adv.*

ges tant (jes′tənt), *adj.* pregnant.

glean (glēn), *v.* 1. gather (grain) left on a field by reapers. 2. gather little by little or slowly. [< OF *glener* < LL *glennare* < Celtic] **—glean′er,** *n.*

gloze (glōz), *v.,* **glozed, gloz ing.** 1. smooth over; explain away: *His friends glozed over his faults.* 2. talk speciously or flatteringly.

gob stop per, *n. Brit. slang.* spherical, hard sucking candy: "jawbreaker."

gorge (gôrj), *n.* 1. a deep, narrow valley, usually steep and rocky. 2. a gorging; gluttonous meal. 3. contents of a stomach. 4. feeling of disgust, indignation, resentment, or the like. 5. a narrow rear entrance from a fort into an outwork or outer part. 6. mass stopping up a narrow passage: *An ice gorge blocked the river.* 7. *Archaic.* throat; gullet. [< OF *gorge* throat, ult. < LL *gurges* throat, jaws < L *gurges* abyss, whirlpool] **—gorg′er,** *n.*

graf fi to (grə fē′tō), *n., pl.* **graf fi ti.** inscription or drawing found on walls.

gra tu i tous (grə tü′ə təs or grə tyü′ə təs), *adj.* 1. freely given or obtained; free. 2. without reason or cause; unnecessary; uncalled-for. **—gra tu′i tous ly,** *adv.* **—gra tu′i tous ness,** *n.* **—Syn.** 2. unwarranted.

gripes, *n.* canvas strips which secure a ship's lifeboat to its cradle.

gu los i ty (gü los′ə tē), *n.* greediness.

gut ter (gut′ər), *v.* 1. form gutters in. 2. flow or melt in streams: *A candle gutters when the melted wax runs down its sides.* 3. become channeled. [< OF *goutiere,* ult. < L *gutta* drop]

har mo ni um (här mō′nē əm), *n.* a small organ with metal reeds.

hec tor (hek′tər), *n.* a bragging, bullying fellow. —*v.* 1. bluster; bully. 2. tease.

her e tic (her′ə tik), *n.* person who holds a belief that is different from the accepted belief of his church, school, profession, etc. —*adj.* holding such a belief. [< F *hérétique* < LL *haereticus* < Gk. *hairetikos* able to choose] **—Syn.** *n.* dissenter.

het er o ge ne ous (het′ər ə jē′nē əs), *adj.* 1. different in kind; unlike; not at all similar; varied. 2. made up of unlike elements or parts; miscellaneous. [< Med.L *heterogeneus,* ult. < Gk. *heteros* other + *genos* kind] **—het′er o ge′ne ous ly,** *adv.*

his tri on ic (his′trē on′ik), *adj.* 1. having to do with actors or acting. 2. theatrical; insincere. [< L *histrionicus* < *histrio* actor]

ham string (ham′string′), *n., v.,* **-strung** or *(Rare)* **-stringed, -string ing.** —*n.* 1. one of the tendons at the back of the knee in man. 2. the great tendon at the back of the hock of a four-footed animal. —*v.* 1. cripple by cutting the hamstring. 2. cripple; disable; destroy the activity, efficiency, etc., of.

i de al ism (ī dē′ə liz′əm), *n.* 1. an acting according to one's ideals of what ought to be, regardless of circumstances or of the approval or disapproval of others. 2. a cherishing of fine ideals. 3. in art or literature, representing imagined types rather than an exact copy of any one person, instance, or situation. Idealism is opposed to realism. 4. in philosophy, belief that all our knowledge is a knowledge of ideas and that it is impossible to know whether there really is a world of objects on which our ideas are based. Idealism is opposed to materialism, which holds that objects really exist apart from our ideas.

im pal pa ble (im pal′pə bəl), *adj.* **1.** that cannot be perceived by the sense of touch: *Sunbeams are impalpable. A thread of a spider's web is so thin as to be almost impalpable.* **2.** very hard for the mind to grasp: *impalpable distinctions.* **—im pal′pa bly,** *adv.*

im per i ous (im pir′ē əs), *adj.* **1.** haughty; arrogant; domineering; overbearing. **2.** imperative; necessary; urgent. [< L *imperiosus* commanding] **—im pe′ri ous ly,** *adv.* **—im per′i ous ness,** *n.* **—Syn. 1.** dictatorial.

im per turb a ble (im′pər tėr′bə bəl), *adj.* **1.** not capable of being excited or disturbed. **2.** not easily excited; calm. **—im′per turb′a bly,** *adv.*

im pla ca ble (im plā′kə bəl), *adj.* that cannot be placated, pacified, or appeased; relentless. **—im pla′ca bly,** *adv.* **—Syn.** unforgiving, inexorable.

im pon der a ble (im pon′dər ə bəl), *adj.* without weight that can be felt or measured: *Faith and love are imponderable forces.* *—n.* something imponderable. **—im pon′der a bly,** *adv.*

im por tu nate (im pôr′chə nit), *adj.* asking repeatedly; annoyingly persistent; urgent. **—im por′tu nate ly,** *adv.*

im por tune (im′pôr tün′ or im′pôr tyün′), *v.,* **-tuned, -tun ing.** ask urgently or repeatedly; trouble with demands. [< MF < L *importunus* inconvenient]

im por tu ni ty (im′pôr tü′nə tē or im′pôr tyü′nə tē), *n., pl.* **-ties.** persistence in asking; act of demanding again and again.

im pute (im pyüt′), *v.,* **-put ed, -put ing.** consider as belonging; attribute; charge (a fault, etc.) to a person; blame: *I impute his failure to laziness.* **—im put′a ble,** *adj.*

in dig e nous (in dij′ə nəs), *adj.* **1.** originating in the region or country where found; native: *Lions are indigenous to Africa.* **2.** innate; inherent. [< L *indigena* a native] **—in dig′e nous ly,** *adv.*

in gen u ous (in jen′yü əs), *adj.* **1.** frank; open; sincere. **2.** simple; natural; innocent. [< L *ingenuus,* originally, native, free born] **—in gen′u ous ly,** *adv.* **—in gen′u ous ness,** *n.* **—Syn. 1.** candid. **2.** naïve.

in im i cal (in im′ə kəl), *adj.* **1.** unfriendly; hostile. **2.** adverse; unfavorable; harmful: *Lack of ambition is inimical to success.* [< LL *inimicalis* < L *inimicus* < *in-* not + *amicus* friendly] **—in im′i cal ly,** *adv.* **—Syn. 1.** antagonistic.

in sid i ous (in sid′ē əs), *adj.* **1.** wily; sly; crafty; tricky; treacherous. **2.** working secretly or subtly: *an insidious disease.* [< L *insidiosus* < *insidiae* ambush < *insidere* < *in-* in + *sedere* sit] **—in sid′i ous ly,** *adv.* **—in sid′i ous ness,** *n.* **—Syn. 1.** cunning.

in ter ces sion (in′tər sesh′ən), *n.* act or fact of interceding or pleading for another.

in ter mi na ble (in tėr′mə nə bəl), *adj.* endless; so long as to seem endless.

in tes tate (in tes′tāt), *adj.* **1.** having made no will. **2.** not disposed of by a will. *—n.* person who has died without making a will. [< L *intestatus* < *in-* not + *testari* make a will < *testis* witness]

in ure (i nyůr′), *v.,* **-ured, -ur ing.** **1.** toughen or harden; accustom; habituate: *Poverty had inured the beggar to hardships.* **2.** have effect; be useful: *The agreement inures to the benefit of the employees.*

in vec tive (in vek′tiv), *n.* violent attack in words; abusive language.

in vid i ous (in vid′ē əs), *adj.* likely to arouse ill will or resentment; giving offense because unfair or unjust. [< L *invidiosus* < *invidia* envy. Related to *envy.*] **—in vid′i ous ly,** *adv.* **—in vid′i ous ness,** *n.* **—Syn.** hateful.

ir i des cence (ir′ə des′ns), *n.* changing or play of colors, as in mother-of-pearl, opals, a peacock's feathers.

ir rev o ca ble (i rev′ə kə bəl), *adj.* not to be recalled, withdrawn, or annulled: *an irrevocable decision.* **—ir rev′o ca bly,** *adv.*

jin go (jing′gō), *n., pl.* **-goes,** *adj.* *—n.* person who favors an aggressive foreign policy that might lead to war with other nations. *—adj.* of jingoes; like that of jingoes. [origin uncertain]

jin go is tic (jing′gō is′tik), *adj.* of jingoes; like that of jingoes.

joc und (jok′ənd), *adj.* cheerful; merry; gay. [< L *jocundus,* var. (influenced by *jocus* a jest) of *jucundus* pleasant < *juvare* please] **—joc′und ly,** *adv.*

jud der (jud′ər), *v.* to vibrate intensely; jar forcefully.

jux ta pose (juk′stə pōz′), *v.,* **-posed, -pos ing.** put close together; place side by side. [< F *juxtaposer* < L *juxta* beside + F *poser* place]

ka lei do scope (kə lī′də skōp), *n.* **1.** tube containing bits of colored glass and two mirrors. As it is turned, it reflects continually changing patterns. **2.** anything that changes continually; a continually changing pattern. [< Gk. *kalos* pretty + *eidos* shape + E *-scope*]

keen[2] (kēn), *Irish.* *—n.* a wailing lament for the dead. *—v.* wail; lament. [< Irish *caoine*] **—keen′er,** *n.*

kettle-hat, *n.* kind of helmet used in the fourteenth and fifteenth centuries.

kir tle (kėr′tl), *n.* *Archaic.* **1.** skirt or dress. **2.** a man's short coat. [OE *cyrtel,* probably < L *curtus* short]

krait (krīt), *n.* a highly poisonous snake found in Eastern Asia.

las si tude (las′ə tüd or las′ə tyüd), *n.* lack of energy; weakness; weariness. [< L *lassitudo* < *lassus* tired]

hat, āge, fär; let, ēqual, tėrm;
it, īce; hot, ōpen, ôrder;
oil, out; cup, pu̇t, rüle; ch, child;
ng, long; sh, she; th, thin;
ᴛʜ, then; zh, measure,

ə represents *a* in about,
e in taken, *i* in pencil,
o in lemon, *u* in circus.

la tent (lāt′nt), *adj.* present but not active; hidden; concealed: *latent germs of disease, latent powers, latent ability.* [< L *latens, -entis,* ppr. of *latere* lie hidden] **—la′tent ly,** *adv.*

Syn. Latent, potential mean existing as a possibility or fact, but not now showing itself plainly. **Latent** means actually existing as a fact, but lying hidden, not active or plainly to be seen at the present time: *The power of a grain of wheat to grow into a plant remains latent if it is not planted.* **Potential** means existing as a possibility and capable of coming into actual existence or activity if nothing happens to stop development: *That boy has great potential ability in science.*

laz a ret or **laz a rette** (laz′ə ret′), *n.* lazaretto.

laz a ret to (laz′ə ret′ō), *n., pl.* **-tos.** **1.** hospital for people having contagious or loathsome diseases; pesthouse. **2.** building or ship used for quarantine purposes. **3.** place in some merchant ships, near the stern, in which supplies are kept. [< Ital. *lazzaretto,* blend of *lazzaro* lazar, and name of hospital, Santa Maria di *Nazaret*]

leech (lēch), *n.* **1.** worm living in ponds and streams that sucks the blood of animals. Doctors formerly used leeches to suck blood from sick people. **2.** person who tries persistently to get what he can out of others. **3.** *Archaic.* doctor. *—v. Archaic.* cure; heal. [OE *lǣce*]

lees (lēz), *n.pl.* dregs; sediment. [< F *lie* < Celtic]

le vi a than (lə vī′ə thən), *n.* **1.** in the Bible, a huge sea animal. **2.** a huge ship. **3.** any great and powerful person or thing. [< LL < Hebrew *liwyāthān* dragon, crocodile, probably < *lavāh* twist, wind]

lin tel (lin′tl), *n.* a horizontal beam or stone over a door, window, etc., to support the structure above it.

lis some or **lis som** (lis′əm), *adj.* **1.** lithe; limber; supple. **2.** nimble; active. [var. of *lithesome* < *lithe*]

lit a ny (lit′n ē), *n., pl.* **-nies.** **1.** series of prayers by the minister with responses by the congregation. **2.** a repeated series.

lu gu bri ous (lü gü′brē əs or lü gyü′brē əs), *adj.* sad; mournful. [< L *lugubris* < *lugere* mourn] **—lu gu′bri ous ly,** *adv.* **—Syn.** dismal, doleful, melancholy.

ma caw (mə kô′), *n.* any of several large parrots of South and Central America, characterized by long tails, brilliant feathers, and harsh voices. [< Pg. *macao* < Brazilian]

mag pie (mag′pī), *n.* **1.** a noisy bird, black and white with a long tail and short wings, related to the jays. **2.** person who chatters.

man a cle (man′ə kəl), *n., v.,* **-cled, -cling.** —*n.* **1.** Usually, **manacles,** *pl.* handcuff; fetter for the hands. **2.** restraint. —*v.* **1.** put manacles on: *The pirates manacled their prisoners.* **2.** restrain. [< OF < L *manicula,* dim. of *manicae* sleeves, manacles < *manus* hand]

man i fes ta tion (man′ə fə stā′shən), *n.* **1.** a manifesting. **2.** being manifested. **3.** thing that manifests: *A brave deed is a manifestation of courage.* **4.** a public demonstration.

man na (man′ə), *n.* **1.** in the Bible, the food miraculously supplied to the Israelites in the wilderness. Exod. 16:14-36. **2.** food for the soul. **3.** a much needed thing that is unexpectedly supplied.

man tra (män′trə), *n.* a mystical incantation in Hinduism and Buddhism.

mat tock (mat′ək), *n.* tool like a pickax, but having a flat blade on one side or flat blades on both sides, used for loosening soil and cutting roots. [OE *mattuc*]

maul er (môl′ər), *n. slang.* fist.

mec o nop sis (mek ə nop′sis), *n.* type of annual or perennial flowering plant.

meet (mēt), *adj.* suitable; proper; fitting: *It is meet that you should help your friends.* [OE *(ge)mǣte*]

mete (mēt), *v.,* **met ed, met ing. 1.** give to each a share of; distribute; allot. **2.** *Poetic.* measure. [OE *metan*]

me tic u lous (mə tik′yə ləs), *adj.* extremely or excessively careful about small details. [< L *meticulosus* < *metus* fear] **—me tic′u lous ly,** *adv.*

met tle (met′l), *n.* **1.** disposition; spirit; courage. **2. on one's mettle,** ready to do one's best. [var. of *metal*]

mil len ni um (mə len′ē əm), *n., pl.* **mil len ni ums, mil len ni a** (mə len′ē ə). **1.** period of a thousand years: *The world is many millenniums old.* **2.** the period of a thousand years during which, according to the Bible, Christ is expected to reign on earth. Rev. 20:1-7. **3.** a period of righteousness and happiness. [< NL < L *mille* thousand + *annus* year]

mit ti mus (mid′ə məs), *n.* a warrant which commits one to prison.

miz zen (miz′n), *n.* **1.** a fore-and-aft sail on the mizzenmast. **2.** mizzenmast. [< F < Ital. *mezzana* < L *medianus* in the middle < *medius* middle]

miz zen mast (miz′n mast′ or miz′nməst), *n.* mast nearest the stern in a two-masted or three-masted ship.

moot (müt), *adj.* debatable; doubtful: *a moot point.* —*v.* **1.** argue. **2.** bring forward (a point, subject, case, etc.) for discussion. [OE *mōtian* < *(ge)mōt* meeting] —*n.* assembly.

moun te bank (moun′tə bangk), *n.* **1.** person who sells quack medicines in public, appealing to his audience by tricks, stories, jokes, etc. **2.** anybody who tries to deceive people by tricks, stories, and jokes. [< Ital. *montambanco* for *monta in banco* mount-on-bench]

mul ti fo li ate (mul′tə fō′lē it), *adj.* having many leaves.

mu ta bil i ty (myü′tə bil′ə tē), *n.* **1.** tendency to change. **2.** fickleness.

ne gus (nē′gəs), *n.* a drink made of wine, hot water, sugar, lemon, and nutmeg. [named after Colonel Francis *Negus* (died 1732), its inventor]

Nes tor i an (nes tôr′ē ən), *adj.* of or relating to Nestorianism, an Eastern branch of Christianity whose conception of the nature of Jesus Christ and objections to calling Mary the Mother of God have been considered heretical by other Christian sects.

nig gard ly (nig′ərd lē), *adj.* **1.** stingy. **2.** meanly small or scanty: *a niggardly gift.* —*adv.* stingily. **—nig′gard li ness,** *n.* **—Syn.** *adj.* **1.** miserly, illiberal, stinting. **—Ant.** *adj.* **1.** generous, liberal, munificent.

nu ance (nü äns′, nyü äns′, nü′äns, or nyü′äns), *n.* **1.** shade of expression, meaning, feeling, etc. **2.** shade of color or tone. [< F]

oa kum (ō′kəm), *n.* a loose fiber obtained by untwisting and picking apart old ropes, used for stopping up the seams or cracks in ships. [OE *ācumba* offcombings]

ob se qui ous (əb sē′kwē əs), *adj.* polite or obedient from hope of gain or from fear; servile; fawning: *Obsequious courtiers greeted the king.* [< L *obsequiosus,* ult. < *ob-* after + *sequi* follow] **—ob se′qui ous ly,** *adv.* **—ob se′qui ous ness,** *n.* **—Syn.** slavish.

ob tuse (əb tüs′ or əb tyüs′), *adj.* **1.** not sharp or acute; blunt. **2.** having more than 90° of angle but less than 180°. **3.** slow in understanding; stupid: *He was too obtuse to take the hint.* **4.** not sensitive; dull: *One's hearing often becomes obtuse in old age.* **—ob tuse′ly,** *adv.*

oeu vre (oe′vrə), *n.* body of work of a writer, an artist, or a composer.

of fi cious (ə fish′es), *adj.* too ready to offer services or advice; minding other people's business; fond of meddling. [< L *officiosus* dutiful < *officium* service] **—of fi′cious ly,** *adv.* **—of fi′cious ness,** *n.* **—Syn.** meddlesome, intrusive.

o pal es cent (ō′pə les′nt), *adj.* having a play of colors like an opal's.

or ni thol o gist (ôr′nə thol′ə jist), *n.* person who studies birds or who knows much about birds.

os prey (os′prē), *n., pl.* **-preys.** a large hawk that feeds on fish.

pad dock (pad′ək), *n.* **1.** a small field near a stable or house, used as a pasture. **2.** pen for horses at a race track. [var. of *parrock,* OE *pearroc* enclosed space, fence < Med.L *parricus* enclosure. Doublet of PARK.]

pal at a ble (pal′ə tə bəl), *adj.* agreeable to the taste; pleasing. **—pal′at a bly,** *adv.*

pal frey (pôl′frē), *n., pl.* **-freys.** a gentle riding horse, especially one used by ladies.

pal pi tate (pal′pə tāt), *v.,* **-tat ed, -tat ing. 1.** beat very rapidly: *Your heart palpitates when you are excited.* **2.** quiver; tremble: *His body palpitated with terror.*

pal pi ta tion (pal′pə tā′shən), *n.* **1.** very rapid beating of the heart. **2.** a quivering; trembling.

pal try (pôl′trē), *adj.,* **-tri er, -tri est.** almost worthless; trifling; petty; mean. **—pal′tri ly,** *adv.* **—pal′tri ness,** *n.* **—Syn.** insignificant.

pan de mo ni um (pan′də mō′nē əm), *n.* **1.** abode of all the demons. **2.** place of wild disorder or lawless confusion. **3.** wild uproar or lawlessness. **4. Pandemonium,** hell's capital. [< NL < Gk. *pan-* all + *daimon* demon]

pa rab o la (pə rab′ə lə), *n., pl.* **-las.** a plane curve formed by the intersection of a cone with a plane parallel to a side of the cone.

par si mo ny (pär′sə mō′nē), *n.* extreme economy; stinginess. [< L *parsimonia* < *parcere* to spare]

pat er nos ter (pat′ər nos′tər or pā′tərnos′tər), *n.* **1.** the Lord's Prayer, especially in Latin. **2.** one of the beads of a rosary on which the Lord's Prayer is said. [< L *pater noster* our father]

pa tri ar chal (pā′trē är′kəl), *adj.* **1.** suitable to a patriarch; having to do with a patriarch. **2.** under the rule of a patriarch: *patriarchal life, a patriarchal church.*

pa tron ize (pā′trə nīz or pat′rə nīz), *v.,* **-ized, -iz ing. 1.** be a regular customer of; give regular business to. **2.** act as a patron toward; support or protect. **3.** treat in a condescending way. **—pa′tron iz′ing ly,** *adv.*

pe dan tic (pi dan′tik), *adj.* **1.** displaying one's knowledge more than is necessary. **2.** tediously learned; scholarly in a dull and narrow way. **—pe dan′ti cal ly,** *adv.*

pelf (pelf), *n.* money or riches, thought of as bad or degrading. [< OF *pelfre* spoils]

pel lu cid (pə lü′sid), *adj.* **1.** transparent; clear: *a pellucid stream.* **2.** clearly expressed; easy to understand: *pellucid language.* [< L *pellucidus,* ult. < *per-* through + *lucere* to shine]

pen ur y (pen′yər ē), *n.* great poverty.

per am bu late (pə ram′byə lāt), *v.,* **-lat ed, -lat ing. 1.** walk through. **2.** walk about. **3.** walk through and examine. [< L *perambulare* < *per-* through + *ambulare* to walk] **—per am′bu la′tion,** *n.*

per am bu la tor (pə ram′byə lā′tər), *n.* **1.** a small carriage in which a baby is pushed about. **2.** person who perambulates.

per e grine (per′ə grən), *n.* a large falcon, formerly much used in Europe for hawking. —*adj.* foreign; strange. [< L *per-*

egrinus from foreign parts, ult. < *per-* outside + *ager (Romanus)* the (Roman) territory. Doublet of PILGRIM.]

pe remp tor y (pə remp′tər ē), *adj.* 1. imperious; positive: *a peremptory teacher.* 2. allowing no denial or refusal: *a peremptory command.* 3. leaving no choice; decisive; final; absolute: *a peremptory decree.* [< L *peremptorius* deadly, that puts an end to, ult. < *per-* to destruction + *emere,* originally, take] **—per emp′tor i ly,** *adv.* **—per emp′tor i ness,** *n.* **—Syn.** 1. arbitrary, dogmatic.

per i gee (per′ə jē), *n.* point closest to the earth in the orbit of the moon or an earth satellite. [< F < NL < Gk. *perigeion* < *peri-* near + *ge* earth]

per ni cious (pər nish′əs), *adj.* 1. that will destroy or ruin; causing great harm or damage: *Gambling is a pernicious habit.* 2. fatal. [< L *perniciosus,* ult. < *per-* + *nex* death] **—per ni′cious ly,** *adv.* **—Syn.** 1. injurious, noxious.

per o ra tion (per′ə rā′shən), *n.* last part of an oration or discussion. It sums up what has been said.

per se ver ance (pėr′sə vir′əns), *n.* a sticking to a purpose or an aim; never giving up what one has set out to do. **—Syn.** tenacity, diligence.

per tur ba tion (pėr′tər bā′shən), *n.* 1. a perturbing. 2. perturbed condition. 3. thing, act, or event that causes it.

pet u lance (pech′ə ləns), *n.* peevishness; bad humor; being irritated by trifles.

pil chard (pil′chərd), *n.* 1. sardine. 2. a small sea fish like it.

pin ion (pin′yən), *n.* 1. the last joint of a bird's wing. 2. wing. 3. any one of the stiff flying feathers of the wing. *—v.* 1. cut off or tie the pinions of (a bird) to prevent flying. 2. bind; bind the arms of; bind (to something): *pinion a man's arms.*

pique (pēk), *n., v.,* **piqued, pi quing.** *—n.* a feeling of anger at being slighted; wounded pride: *In a pique, she left the party.* *—v.* 1. cause a feeling of anger in; wound the pride of: *It piqued her that they should have a secret she did not share.* 2. arouse; stir up: *The curiosity of the boys was piqued by the locked trunk.* 3. **pique oneself on** or **upon,** feel proud about. [< F *piquer* prick, sting < *pic* a pick (< Gmc.)]

pir ou ette (pir′ü et′), *n., v.,* **-et ted, -et ting.** *—n.* a whirling about on one foot or on the toes, as in dancing. *—v.* whirl in this way. [< F *pirouette* spinning top]

plait (plāt or plat *for 1;* plāt or plēt *for 2*), *n., v.* 1. braid. 2. pleat.

ply (plī), *v.,* **plied, ply ing.** 1. work with; use: *The dressmaker plies her needle.* 2. keep up work on; work away at or on: *We plied the water with our oars.* 3. work busily or steadily. 4. urge again and again: *The enemy plied our messenger with questions to make him tell his errand.* 5. supply with in a pressing manner: *ply a person with food or drink.* 6. go back and forth regularly between certain places: *A bus plies between the station and the hotel.* 7. go back and forth regularly on: *Boats ply the river.* 8. travel; go; move.

pneu mat ic (nü mat′ik or nyü mat′ik), *adj.* 1. filled with air; containing air: *a pneumatic tire.* 2. worked by air: *a pneumatic drill.* 3. having to do with air and other gases. **—pneu mat′i cal ly,** *adv.*

poign ant (poi′nənt or poi′nyənt), *adj.* 1. very painful; piercing: *poignant suffering.* 2. keen; intense: *a subject of poignant interest.* 3. sharp to the taste or smell: *poignant sauces.* **—poign′ant ly,** *adv.* **—Syn.** 1. severe.

poop (püp), *n.* 1. deck at the stern above the ordinary deck, often forming the roof of a cabin. 2. stern of a ship. *—v.* of a wave, break over the stern of (a ship).

por ten tous (pôr ten′təs), *adj.* 1. indicating evil to come; ominous; threatening. 2. amazing; extraordinary. **—por ten′tous ly,** *adv.* **—por ten′tous ness,** *n.* **—Syn.** 1. foreboding. 2. wonderful, marvelous.

pos tu late (pos′chə lāt), *v.,* **-lat ed, -lat ing.** 1. take for granted; assume without proof as a basis of reasoning; require as a fundamental principle or necessary condition. 2. require; demand; claim. **—pos′tu la′tion,** *n.*

pre cur sor (pri kėr′sər), *n.* forerunner: *A severe cold may be the precursor of pneumonia.* [< L *praecursor,* ult. < *prae-* before + *currere* run] **—Syn.** predecessor, herald.

pre di lec tion (prē′də lek′shən or pred′ə lek′shən), *n.* a liking; preference. [< F *prédilection,* ult. < L *prae-* before + *diligere* choose] **—Syn.** partiality, predisposition.

pre pos sess ing (prē′pə zes′ing), *adj.* making a favorable first impression; attractive; pleasing.

priv y (priv′ē), *adj., n., pl.* **priv ies.** *—adj.* 1. private. 2. *Archaic.* secret; hidden. 3. **privy to,** having secret or private knowledge of. *—n.* a small outhouse used as a toilet. [< OF *privé* < L *privatus.* Doublet of PRIVATE.]

pro pi tious (prə pish′əs), *adj.* 1. favorable: *propitious weather for our trip.* 2. favorably inclined; gracious. **—pro pi′tious ly,** *adv.* **—pro pi′tious ness,** *n.* **—Syn.** 1. auspicious, promising.

pro to type (prō′tə tīp), *n.* the first or primary type of anything; the original or model: *A modern ship has its prototype in the hollowed log used by savages.* [< NL < Gk. *prototypon,* originally neut. of *prototypos* original, primitive < *protos* first + *typos* type, model]

psal ter y (sôl′tər ē), *n., pl.* **-ter ies.** an ancient musical instrument played by plucking the strings.

punt (punt), *n.* 1. a shallow, flat-bottomed boat having square ends, usually moved by pushing with a pole against the bottom of a river, etc. 2. kick given to a football before it touches the ground after dropping it from the hands.

pur blind (pėr′blīnd′), *adj.* 1. nearly blind. 2. slow to discern or understand. [earlier *pur blind* pure blind] **—pur′blind′ness,** *n.*

pur ga tive (pėr′gə tiv), *n.* medicine that empties the bowels. Castor oil is a purgative. *—adj.* purging.

hat, āge, fär; let, ēqual, tėrm;
it, īce; hot, ōpen, ôrder;
oil, out; cup, pu̇t, rüle; ch, child;
ng, long; sh, she; th, thin;
TH, then; zh, measure;

ə represents *a* in about,
e in taken, *i* in pencil,
o in lemon, *u* in circus.

qua drille (kwo dril′), *n.* 1. a square dance for four couples that has five parts or movements. 2. music for it. [< F < Sp. *cuadrilla* troop < *cuadro* battle square < L *quadrus* square]

quer u lous (kwer′ə ləs or kwer′yə ləs), *adj.* 1. complaining; faultfinding. 2. fretful; peevish. **—quer′u lous ly,** *adv.* **—quer′ u lous ness,** *n.* **—Syn.** 2. petulant.

qui es cent (kwī es′nt), *adj.* inactive; quiet; still; motionless. [< L *quiescens, -entis,* ppr. of *quiescere* to rest < *quies,* n., rest] **—qui es′cent ly,** *adv.*

quoit (kwoit), *n.* 1. a heavy, flattish iron or rope ring thrown to encircle a peg stuck in the ground or to come as close to it as possible. 2. **quoits,** *pl.* game so played. [< OF *coite* cushion]

rail ler y (rā′lər ē), *n., pl.* **-ler ies.** 1. good-humored ridicule; joking; teasing. 2. a bantering remark.

rai ment (rā′mənt), *n.* clothing; garments. [short for *arraiment* < *array*]

rak ish (rā′kish), *adj.* like a rake; immoral; dissolute. **—Syn.** licentious.

ram i fi ca tion (ram′ə fə kā′shən), *n.* 1. dividing or spreading out into branches or parts. 2. branch; part.

rap ture (rap′chər), *n.* 1. a strong feeling that absorbs the mind; very great joy. 2. Often, **raptures,** *pl.* expression of great joy. [< *rapt*]

rap tur ous (rap′chər əs), *adj.* full of rapture; expressing or feeling rapture. **—rap′tur ous ly,** *adv.*

ra tion al ism (rash′ə nə liz′əm), *n.* principle or habit of accepting reason as the supreme authority in matters of opinion, belief, or conduct.

rav en ous (rav′ə nəs), *adj.* 1. very hungry. 2. greedy. 3. rapacious. **—rav′en ous ly,** *adv.* **—rav′en ous ness,** *n.*

re buke (ri byük′), *v.,* **-buked, -buk ing,** *n.* *—v.* express disapproval of; reprove. *—n.* expression of disapproval; scolding. [< AF *rebuker.* Cf. OF *rebuchier* < *re-* back + *buchier* to strike] **—re buk′er,** *n.* **—re buk′ing ly,** *adv.* **—Syn.** *v.* reprimand, censure.

re cip ro cate (ri sip′rə kāt), *v.*, **-cat ed, -cat ing.** 1. give, do, feel, or show in return: *She likes me, and I reciprocate her liking.* 2. move or cause to move with an alternating backward and forward motion. **—re cip′ro ca′tion,** *n.*

rec on cile (rek′ən sīl), *v.*, **-ciled, -cil ing.** 1. make friends again. 2. settle (a quarrel, disagreement, etc.). 3. make agree; bring into harmony: *It is impossible to reconcile his story with the facts.* 4. make satisfied; make no longer opposed: *It is hard to reconcile oneself to being sick a long time.* **—rec′on cil′a ble,** *adj.* **—rec′on cil′er,** *n.*

re it e rate (rē it′ə rāt′), *v.*, **-at ed, -at ing.** say or do several times; repeat (an action, demand, etc.) again and again: *The boy did not move though the teacher reiterated her command.* [< L *reiterare,* ult. < *re-* again + *iterum* again] **—re it′er a′tion,** *n.*

re lent less (ri lent′lis), *adj.* without pity; unyielding; harsh: *The storm raged with relentless fury.* **—re lent′less ly,** *adv.* **—Syn.** ruthless, implacable.

rend (rend), *v.*, **rent, rend ing.** 1. pull apart violently; tear: *Wolves will rend a lamb.* 2. split: *Lightning rent the tree.* 3. disturb violently: *His mind was rent by doubt.* 4. remove with force or violence. [OE *rendan*] **—Syn.** 1. rip.

re proach (ri prōch′), *n.* 1. blame. 2. disgrace. 3. object of blame, censure, or disapproval. 4. expression of blame, censure, or disapproval. —*v.* 1. blame. 2. disgrace.

re proach ful (ri prōch′fəl), *adj.* full of reproach; expressing reproach. **—re proach′ful ly,** *adv.*

Req ui em or **req ui em** (rek′wē əm), *n.* 1. Mass for the dead; musical church service for the dead. 2. music for it. [< L *requiem,* accus. of *requies* rest; the first word of the Mass for the dead]

res o lute (rez′ə lüt), *adj.* determined; firm; bold: *He was resolute in his attempt to climb to the top of the mountain. A soldier must be resolute in battle.* **—res′o lute ly,** *adv.*

re splend ent (ri splen′dənt), *adj.* very bright; shining; splendid: *The queen was resplendent with jewels.* **—re splend′ent ly,** *adv.*

res ur rect (rez′ə rekt′), *v.* 1. raise from the dead; bring back to life. 2. bring back to sight, use, etc.: *resurrect an old custom.*

re tain er (ri tā′nər), *n.* person who serves a person of rank; vassal; attendant; follower.

ret i nue (ret′n ü or ret′n yü), *n.* group of attendants or retainers; following: *The king's retinue accompanied him on the journey.*

ret ri bu tion (ret′rə byü′shən), *n.* a deserved punishment; return for evil done, or sometimes for good done. [< L *retributio, -onis,* ult. < *re-* back + *tribuere* assign]

ret ro grade (ret′rə grād), *adj.*, *v.*, **-grad ed, -grad ing.** —*adj.* 1. moving backward; retreating. 2. becoming worse. —*v.* 1. move or go backward. 2. fall back toward a worse condition; grow worse; decline. [< L *retrogradus* < *retrogradi,* ult. < *retro-* backward + *gradi* go]

rheu mat ic (rü mat′ik), *adj.* 1. of rheumatism. 2. having rheumatism; liable to have rheumatism. 3. causing rheumatism. 4. caused by rheumatism. **Rheumatic fever** is a fever that accompanies inflamed and painful joints. —*n.* 1. person who has rheumatism. 2. **rheumatics,** *pl. Informal.* rheumatism.

rheu ma tism (rü′mə tiz′əm), *n.* disease with inflammation, swelling, and stiffness of the joints.

rime (rīm), *n.*, *v.*, **rimed, rim ing.** —*n.* white frost; hoarfrost. —*v.* cover with rime. [OE *hrīm*]

rout (rout), *n. Archaic.* a large evening party.

ruck (ruk), *n.* crowd; the great mass of common or inferior people or things. [< Scand. (Norwegian dial.) *ruka*]

rud dy (rud′ē), *adj.*, **-di er, -di est.** 1. red. 2. healthy red: *ruddy cheeks.* [OE *rudig*] **—rud′di ly,** *adv.* **—rud′di ness,** *n.* **—Syn.** 1. reddish, rubicund, florid. 2. rosy.

rue[1] (rü), *v.*, **rued, ru ing.** 1. be sorry for; regret. 2. *Archaic.* feel sorrow. [OE *hrēowan*]

rue[2] (rü), *n.* plant with yellow flowers and leaves that have a strong smell and a bitter taste.

rune (rün), *n.* 1. any letter of an ancient Teutonic alphabet. 2. mark that looks like a rune and has some mysterious, magic meaning. [< Scand. *rūn*]

ru nic (rü′nik), *adj.* consisting of runes; written in runes; marked with runes.

sa ga cious (sə gā′shəs), *adj.* 1. wise in a keen, practical way; shrewd. 2. intelligent. **—sa ga′cious ly,** *adv.* **—sa ga′cious ness,** *n.* **—Syn.** 1. astute, perspicacious.

sa li ent (sā′lē ənt), *adj.* 1. standing out; easily seen or noticed; prominent; striking: *the salient features in a landscape, the salient points in a speech.* 2. pointing outward; projecting: *a salient angle.* 3. leaping; jumping. A lion salient on a coat of arms is standing with forepaws raised as if jumping. **—sa′li ent ly,** *adv.* **—Syn.** *adj.* 1. noticeable, conspicuous.

sal ver (sal′vər), *n.* tray. [< F < Sp. *salva,* originally, foretasting, ult. < L *salvus* safe]

san guine (sang′gwən), *adj.* 1. naturally cheerful and hopeful: *a sanguine disposition.* 2. confident; hopeful: *sanguine of success.* 3. having a healthy red color; ruddy: *a sanguine complexion.* 4. in the old physiology, having an active circulation, a ruddy color, and a cheerful and ardent disposition. 5. sanguinary. [< L *sanguineus* < *sanguis* blood] **—san′guine ly,** *adv.* **—Syn.** 1. optimistic.

sar don ic (sär don′ik), *adj.* bitter; sarcastic; scornful; mocking: *a fiend's sardonic laugh.* [< F < L < Gk. *Sardonios,* a supposed Sardinian plant that produced hysterical convulsions] **—sar don′i cal ly,** *adv.*

screed (skrēd), *n.* 1. a long speech or writing. 2. strip of plaster (or wood) of the proper thickness, applied to the wall as a guide in plastering.

scru pu los i ty (skrü′pyə los′ə tē), *n.*, *pl.* **-ties.** 1. a being scrupulous; strict regard for what is right; scrupulous care. 2. an instance of this.

scru pu lous (skrü′pyə ləs), *adj.* 1. having or showing a strict regard for what is right. 2. attending thoroughly to details; very careful: *A soldier must pay scrupulous attention to orders.* **—scru′pu lous ly,** *adv.* **—scru′pu lous ness,** *n.*

scut tle (skut′l), *n.*, *v.*, **-tled, -tling.** —*n.* 1. an opening in the deck or side of a ship, with a lid or cover. 2. opening in a wall or roof, with a lid or cover. 3. the lid or cover for any such opening. —*v.* 1. cut a hole or holes through the bottom or sides of (a ship) to sink it. 2. cut a hole or holes in the deck of (a ship) to salvage the cargo. [? < F < Sp. *escotilla* hatchway]

sé ance (sā′äns), *n.* 1. a sitting; session. 2. a meeting of people trying to communicate with spirits of the dead by the help of a medium. [< F *séance* < *seoir* sit < L *sedere*]

sed u lous (sej′ə ləs), *adj.* hard-working; diligent; painstaking. **—sed′u lous ly,** *adv.* **—sed′u lous ness,** *n.* **—Syn.** industrious, assiduous, persevering, untiring.

sep ul cher (sep′əl kər), *n.* place of burial; tomb; grave. —*v.* bury (a dead body) in a sepulcher. [< OF < L *sepulcrum* < *sepelire* bury]

se pul chral (sə pul′krəl), *adj.* 1. of sepulchers or tombs. 2. of burial: *sepulchral ceremonies.* 3. deep and gloomy; dismal; suggesting a tomb.

se ques ter (si kwes′tər), *v.* 1. remove or withdraw from public use or from public view: *The shy old lady sequestered herself from all strangers.* 2. take away (property) for a time from an owner until a debt is paid or some claim is satisfied. 3. seize by authority; take and keep: *The soldiers sequestered food from the people they conquered.*

se raph ic (sə raf′ik), *adj.* 1. of seraphs. 2. like a seraph; angelic. **—se raph′i cal ly,** *adv.*

sev er (sev′ər), *v.* 1. cut apart; cut off: *sever a rope. The ax severed his head from his body.* 2. break off: *The two countries severed friendly relations.* 3. part; divide; separate: *a church severed into two factions. The rope severed and the swing fell down.* [< OF *sevrer,* ult. < L *separare* separate] **—sev′er a ble,** *adj.*

shard (shärd), *n.* 1. a broken piece; fragment. 2. piece of broken earthenware or pottery. 3. the hard case that covers a beetle's wing. Also, **sherd.** [OE *sceard*]

shrive (shrīv), *v.*, **shrove** or **shrived, shriv en** or **shrived, shriv ing.** *Archaic.*

1. hear the confession of, impose penance on, and grant absolution to. 2. make confession. 3. hear confessions. 4. **shrive oneself,** confess to a priest and do penance. [OE *scrīfan* < L *scribere* write]

shroud (shroud), *n.* 1. cloth or garment in which a dead person is wrapped for burial. 2. something that covers, conceals, or veils: *The fog was a shroud over the city.* 3. Usually, **shrouds,** *pl.* rope from a mast to the side of a ship. Shrouds help support the mast. —*v.* 1. wrap for burial. 2. cover; conceal; veil: *The earth is shrouded in darkness.* [OE *scrūd*]

sil lion (sil′yən), *n.* a narrow ridge or strip of land between two furrows. (Obsolete form of *selion*)

sim per (sim′pər), *v.* 1. smile in a silly, affected way. 2. express by a simper; say with a simper. —*n.* a silly, affected smile. [cf. G *zimper* affected, coy]

som nam bu lism (som nam′byə liz′əm), *n.* sleepwalking. [< L *somnus* sleep + *ambulare* walk]

soph ist ry (sof′ə strē), *n., pl.* **-ries.** 1. unsound reasoning. 2. a clever but misleading argument. 3. art, practice, or learning of the ancient Greek sophists, especially of their type of argument.

spec u la tion (spek′yə lā′shən), *n.* 1. thought; reflection; conjecture: *Former speculations about electricity were often mere guesses.* 2. a buying or selling when there is a large risk, with the hope of making a profit from future price changes: *His speculations in stocks made him poor.*

spleen (splēn), *n.* 1. a ductless gland at the left of the stomach in man, and near the stomach or intestine in other vertebrates. People used to think that the spleen caused low spirits, bad temper, and spite. 2. bad temper; spite; anger. 3. low spirits.

stee ple chase (stē′pl chās′), *n.* a horse race over a course having ditches, hedges, and other obstacles.

stip ple (stip′əl), *v.,* **-pled, -pling,** *n.* —*v.* 1. paint, draw, or engrave by dots. 2. produce a stippled effect on. —*n.* 1. the method of painting, drawing, or engraving by stippling. 2. effect produced by this method. 3. stippled work. [< Dutch *stippelen*] **—stip′pler,** *n.*

strait en (strāt′n), *v.* 1. limit by the lack of something; restrict. 2. make narrow. 3. *Archaic.* confine; confine within narrow limits. 4. **in straitened circumstances,** needing money badly.

sub jec tive (səb jek′tiv), *adj.* 1. existing in the mind; belonging to the person thinking rather than to the object thought of: *Base your subjective opinions on objective facts.* 2. about the thoughts and feelings of the speaker, writer, painter, etc.; personal: *a subjective poem.* **—sub jec′tive ly,** *adv.* **—sub jec′tive ness,** *n.*

sub li mate (*v.* sub′lə māt; *adj., n.* sub′lə mit or sub′lə māt), *v.,* **-mat ed, -mat ing,** *adj., n.* —*v.* 1. purify; refine. 2. change (an undesirable impulse or trait) into a desirable activity. [< L *sublimare,* originally, raise < *sublimis* lofty]

su pine (*adj.* sü pīn′; *n.* sü′pīn), *adj.* 1. lying flat on the back. 2. lazily inactive; listless. **—su pine′ly,** *adv.* **—Syn.** *adj.* 2. languid, indolent, inert.

sur feit (sėr′fit), *n.* too much; excess: *A surfeit of food makes one sick. A surfeit of advice annoys me.* —*v.* overfeed. [< OF *surfait,* originally pp., overdone < *sur-* over (< L *super-*) + *faire* do < L *facere*] **—Syn.** *v.* glut, gorge.

ta bu (tə bü′), *adj., v.,* **-bued, -bu ing,** *n., pl.* **-bus.** —*adj.* 1. forbidden; prohibited; banned. 2. set apart as sacred or cursed. Among the Polynesians certain things, places, and persons are tabu. —*v.* forbid; prohibit; ban. —*n.* 1. a prohibition; ban. 2. system or act of setting things apart as sacred or cursed. [< Tongan (lang. of the Tonga Islands in the S Pacific) *tabu*]
➤ **taboo, tabu.** *Taboo* is more generally used than *tabu,* except in anthropology.

tac it ly (tas′it lē), *adv.* 1. without sound. 2. without words; by implication from action or circumstances.

tac i turn (tas′ə tėrn), *adj.* speaking very little; not fond of talking. **—Syn.** reserved.

tac i tur ni ty (tas′ə tėr′nə tē), *n.* habit of keeping silent; disinclination to talk much.

taw dry (tô′drē), *adj.,* **-dri er, -dri est.** showy and cheap; gaudy. [ult. alteration of *St. Audrey,* from cheap laces sold at St. Audrey's fair in Ely, England] **—taw′dri ly,** *adj.* **—taw′dri ness,** *n.*

ten u i ty (ten yü′ə tē or ti nü′ə tē), *n.* rarefied condition; thinness; slightness.

tes sel late (*v.* tes′l āt; *adj.* tes′l it or tes′l āt), *v.,* **-lat ed, -lat ing,** *adj.* —*v.* make of small squares or blocks, or in a checkered pattern. —*adj.* made in small squares or blocks or in a checkered pattern.

the os o phy (thē os′ə fē), *n.* philosophy or religion that claims to have a special insight into the divine nature through spiritual self-development. Modern theosophy includes many of the teachings of Buddhism and Brahmanism. [< Med.L < LGk. *theosophia,* ult. < Gk. *theos* god + *sophos* wise]

thrall (thrôl), *n.* 1. person in bondage; slave. 2. thralldom; bondage; slavery. [< Scand. *thræll*]

thwart (thwôrt), *v.* oppose and defeat; keep from doing something. —*n.* 1. seat across a boat, on which a rower sits. 2. brace in a canoe.

tim or ous (tim′ər əs), *adj.* easily frightened; timid. [< Med.L *timorosus* < L *timor* fear] **—tim′or ous ly,** *adv.* **—tim′or ous ness,** *n.*

tip pet (tip′it), *n.* 1. scarf for the neck and shoulders with ends hanging down in front. 2. a long, narrow, hanging part of a hood, sleeve, or scarf.

tor pid (tôr′pid), *adj.* 1. dull; inactive; sluggish. 2. not moving or feeling. Animals that hibernate become torpid in winter. 3. numb. **—tor′pid ly,** *adv.* **—tor′pid ness,** *n.* **—Syn.** 1. lethargic, apathetic.

torque (tôrk), *n.* 1. force causing rotation. 2. necklace of twisted metal. The ancient

hat, āge, fär; let, ēqual, tėrm;
it, īce; hot, ōpen, ôrder;
oil, out; cup, pu̇t, rüle; ch, child;
ng, long; sh, she; th, thin;
ᴛʜ, then; zh, measure;

ə represents *a* in about,
e in taken, *i* in pencil,
o in lemon, *u* in circus.

Gauls and Britons wore torques. [< L *torques* twisted neck chain < *torquere* twist]

tran sient (tran′shənt), *adj.* 1. passing soon; fleeting; not lasting. 2. passing through and not staying long: *a transient guest in a hotel.* —*n.* visitor or boarder who stays for a short time. [< L *transiens, -entis,* ppr. of *transire* pass through < *trans-* through + *ire* go] **—tran′sient ly,** *adv.*

trep i da tion (trep′ə dā′shən), *n.* 1. nervous dread; fear; fright. 2. a trembling.

tripe (trīp), *n.* 1. the walls of the first and second stomachs of an ox, etc., used as food. 2. *Slang.* something foolish, worthless, offensive, etc. [< OF *tripe* entrails < Arabic *tharb*]

truc u lent (truk′yə lənt or trü′kyə lənt), *adj.* savagely threatening or bullying; fierce and cruel. **—truc′u lent ly,** *adv.*

tu mid (tü′mid or tyü′mid), *adj.* 1. swollen. 2. swollen with big words; pompous.

tur bid (tėr′bid), *adj.* 1. muddy; thick; not clear: *a turbid river.* 2. confused; disordered: *a turbid imagination.* **—tur′bid ly,** *adv.* **—tur′bid ness,** *n.*

un con scion a ble (un kon′shə nə bəl), *adj.* 1. not influenced or guided by conscience: *an unconscionable liar.* 2. unreasonable; very great: *wait an unconscionable time for someone.* **—un con′scion a bly,** *adv.*

un couth (un küth′), *adj.* 1. awkward; clumsy; crude: *uncouth manners.* 2. unusual and unpleasant; strange: *The poor idiot made uncouth noises.* **—un couth′ness,** *n.*

un prec e dent ed (un pres′ə den′tid), *adj.* having no precedent; never done before; never known before. **—Syn.** unexampled, new.

up braid ing (up brād′ing), *n.* a severe reproof; scolding. —*adj.* full of reproach.

u su ri ous (yü zhu̇r′ē əs), *adj.* 1. taking extremely high or unlawful interest for the use of money. 2. of or having to do with usury: *Fifty per cent is a usurious rate of interest.*

u surp (yü zėrp′), *v.* seize and hold (power, position, authority, etc.) by force or without right: *The king's brother tried to usurp the throne.* **—u surp′er,** *n.*

va cu i ty (va kyü′ə tē), *n., pl.* **-ties.** 1. emptiness. 2. an empty space; vacuum. 3. lack of thought or intelligence. 4. something foolish or stupid. 5. absence or lack (of something specified).

vamp (vamp), *n.* 1. the upper front part of a shoe or foot. 2. piece or patch added to an old thing to make it look new. [< OF *avanpié* < *avant* before (< L *ab* from + *ante* before) + *pié* foot < L *pes*]

vel lum (vel′əm), *n.* 1. the finest kind of parchment, used for writing, binding books, etc. 2. paper or cloth imitating such parchment. *—adj.* of vellum. [< OF *velin* < *veel* calf]

ver dur ous (vėr′jər əs), *adj.* green and fresh.

ver meil (vėr′ml), *n., adj.* 1. *Poetic.* vermilion. 2. silver or bronze coated with gilt.

ver mil ion (vər mil′yən), *n.* 1. a bright red. 2. a bright-red coloring matter. *—adj.* bright-red.

ver nal (vėr′nl), *adj.* 1. of spring; having to do with spring: *vernal green, vernal flowers, vernal months.* 2. like spring; suggesting spring. 3. youthful: *Everyone admired the young girl's vernal freshness.*

vi car i ous (vī ker′ē əs), *adj.* 1. done or suffered for others: *vicarious work.* 2. felt by sharing in others' experience: *The invalid received vicarious pleasure from reading travel stories.* 3. taking the place of another; doing the work of another: *a vicarious agent.* 4. delegated: *vicarious authority.* **—vi car′i ous ly,** *adv.* **—vi-car′i ous ness,** *n.*

vi cis si tude (və sis′ə tüd or və sis′ə-tyüd), *n.* 1. change in circumstances, fortune, etc.: *The vicissitudes of life may suddenly make a rich man very poor.* 2. change; variation. 3. regular change: *the vicissitude of day and night.* [< L *vicissitudo* < *vicis* (gen.) change]

vict ual (vit′l), *n., v.,* **-ualed, -ual ing** or *esp. Brit.* **-ualled, -ual ling.** *—n.* Usually, **victuals,** *pl. Informal* or *Dialect.* food. *—v.* 1. supply with food. 2. take on a supply of food: *The ship will victual before sailing.*

vouch safe (vouch sāf′), *v.,* **-safed, -saf ing.** be willing to grant or give; deign (to do or give): *The proud man vouchsafed no reply when we spoke to him.* [original meaning "guarantee," to *vouch* for as *safe*]

wain scot (wān′skōt or wān′skət), *n., v.,* **-scot ed, -scot ing,** *esp. Brit.* **-scot ted, -scot ting.** *—n.* 1. a lining of wood, usually in panels, on the walls of a room. 2. the lower part of the wall of a room when it is decorated differently from the upper part. *—v.* line with wood: *a room wainscoted in oak.* [< MLG *wagenschot* < *wagen* wagon + *schot* partition]

wan (won), *adj.,* **wan ner, wan nest.** 1. pale; lacking natural color: *Her face looked wan after her long illness.* 2. looking worn or tired; faint; weak: *The sick boy gave the doctor a wan smile.* [OE *wann* dark] **—wan′ly,** *adv.* **—wan′ness,** *n.*

wan ton (won′tən), *adj.* 1. reckless; heartless: *That bad boy hurts animals from wanton cruelty.* 2. without reason or excuse: *a wanton attack, wanton mischief.* 3. not moral; not chaste: *a wanton woman.* 4. *Poetic.* frolicsome; playful: *a wanton breeze, a wanton child.* 5. *Poetic.* not restrained: *a wanton mood.* *—n.* a wanton person. **—wan′ton ly,** *adv.* **—wan′ton-ness,** *n.*

wat tled (wot′ld), *adj.* 1. having wattles. 2. formed by interwoven twigs; interlaced.

ween (wēn), *v. Archaic.* think; suppose; believe; expect. [OE *wēnan*]

weft (weft), *n.* the threads running from side to side across a fabric; the woof. [OE *weft* < *wefan* weave]

whip pet (hwip′it), *n.* 1. very swift dog that looks somewhat like a small greyhound, often used in racing. 2. a small, fast, armored tank that was used in the first World War. [< *whip* in sense of "move quickly"]

wim ple (wim′pəl), *n., v.,* **-pled, -pling.** *—n.* cloth for the head arranged in folds about the head, cheeks, chin, and neck, worn by nuns and formerly by other women. *—v.* 1. cover or muffle with a wimple. 2. ripple or cause to ripple. 3. *Archaic.* lie or lay in folds, as a veil. [OE *wimpel*]

wiz ened (wiz′nd), *adj.* dried up; withered; shriveled: *a wizened apple, a wizened face.* [pp. of dialectal *wizen,* OE *wisnian* shrivel]

woof (wüf), *n.* 1. the threads running from side to side across a woven fabric. The woof crosses the warp. 2. fabric; cloth; texture. [OE *ōwef*]

wright (rīt), *n.* (now usually in combinations) a maker of something. A wheelwright makes wheels. A playwright makes plays for the theater. [OE *wryhta,* var. of *wyrhta* < *weorc* work]

wry (rī), *adj.,* **wri er, wri est.** turned to one side; twisted: *She made a wry face to show her disgust.* [ult. < OE *wrīgian* turn] **—wry′ly,** *adv.*

ze nith (zē′nith), *n.* 1. the point in the heavens directly overhead. 2. the highest point: *At the zenith of its power Rome ruled all of civilized Europe.*

SPECIAL FEATURES AND SHORT ARTICLES

OF LITERARY INTEREST

OF CRITICAL INTEREST

(cont.)

OF HUMAN INTEREST

OF HISTORICAL INTEREST

GENERAL INDEX

Names of authors represented in the text appear in capital letters. Page numbers immediately following an author's name refer to biographical information. Titles of selections or articles which appear in the text are printed in italic type. Special features and brief articles not included in the general index are listed separately on pages 733–734.

A

B

C

D

E

F

G

H

I

J

K

L

M

N

O

P

Q

R

S

T

U

V

W

Y